MICROECONOMICS

Irwin/McGraw-Hill Advanced Series in Economics

Consulting Editor
N. Gregory Mankiw

Economic Growth
Robert J. Barro and Xavier Sala-i-Martin

Advanced Macroeconomics
David Romer

Money, Credit, and Capital
James Tobin, with Stephen S. Golub

THIRD EDITION

MICROECONOMICS

Michael L. Katz
University of California at Berkeley

Harvey S. Rosen
Princeton University

Boston, Massachusetts Burr Ridge, Illinois Dubuque, Iowa
Madison, Wisconsin New York, New York San Francisco, California St. Louis, Missouri

Irwin/McGraw-Hill

A Division of The ***McGraw-Hill*** *Companies*

MICROECONOMICS

This book is printed on acid-free paper.

2 3 4 5 6 7 8 9 0 VH VH 9 0 9 8 7

IBSN 0-256-17176-9

Editorial director: *Michael W. Junior*
Publisher: *Gary Burke*
Developmental editor: *Amy K. Winston*
Marketing manager: *Nelson Black*
Senior project supervisor: *Jean Lou Hess*
Production supervisor: *Pat Frederickson/Lori Koetters*
Designer: *Michael Warrell*
Compositor: *Shepard Poorman Communications*
Typeface: *10.5/12 Galliard*
Printer: *Von Hoffmann Press, Inc*

Library of Congress Cataloging-in-Publication Data

Katz, Michael L.
Microeconomics/Michael L. Katz, Harvey S. Rosen—3rd ed.
p. cm.
Includes index.
ISBN 0-256-17176-9
1. Microeconomics. I. Rosen, Harvey S. II. Title.
HB172.K37 1998
338.5—dc21 96-40004

About the cover: The cover image is a reproduction of the painting entitled "Jupiter Fruit and Grain Merchant," created by an unknown artist in the Middle Ages.

When ordering the title, use ISBN 0-07-115354-3.

http://www.mhhe.com

To Our Students

About the Authors

MICHAEL L. KATZ

Michael L. Katz is the Edward J. and Mollie Arnold Professor of Business Administration at the University of California at Berkeley. In 1989 and 1993, he received the Earl F. Cheit Outstanding Teaching Award. In 1994 and 1995 he served as the Chief Economist of the U.S. Federal Communications Commission. His articles on standardization, cooperative R&D, technology licensing, and agency theory have been published in leading economics journals, including the *American Economic Review, Journal of Political Economy*, and *Rand Journal of Economics*. He is currently on the editorial board of the *Journal of Economics & Management Strategy*.

HARVEY S. ROSEN

Harvey S. Rosen is the John L. Weinberg Professor of Economics and Business Policy at Princeton University. Professor Rosen, a Fellow of the Econometric Society and a Research Associate of the National Bureau of Economic Research, is well known for his contributions to the fields of Public Finance, Labor Economics, and Applied Microeconomics. From 1989 to 1991, he served as Deputy Assistant Secretary (Tax Analysis) at the U.S. Treasury. His articles have appeared in such journals as *Econometrica, American Economic Review*, and *Journal of Political Economy*. He is currently on the editorial boards of the *Journal of Economic Literature, Journal of Public Economics*, and *Public Finance Quarterly*.

Preface

WHY WE WROTE THIS BOOK

This book is about microeconomic theory and how it is used to analyze and evaluate contemporary market systems. Understanding markets is important for every well-educated citizen. Throughout the world, societies are debating, sometimes violently, the merits of market-oriented approaches to dealing with social problems. Some nations with long histories of central planning are turning to markets. At the same time, within several market-oriented economies, critics are arguing that the government should take over more functions from private markets. Understanding these controversies requires a firm grounding in microeconomics.

Modern Topics

Economists have studied markets for over 200 years, but several innovations in recent decades have contributed important new insights. For example, traditionally it was assumed that all market participants had perfect certainty about the consequences of their actions. In contrast, modern economics recognizes that the world is pervaded by uncertainty, and this has important consequences for individual behavior and market outcomes. A cursory examination of the leading professional journals indicates that among today's researchers attention to uncertainty is now essentially routine. In textbooks, however, it is still either ignored or regarded as an "advanced" topic. We believe that this material is part of the "core" of economics, and it should be presented as such to students. In this book, uncertainty and other central modern topics, such as game theory and asymmetric information, are given the same careful treatment as traditional issues.

A natural question is whether such subjects are intrinsically too hard for most students. True, in the professional journals these topics are often presented in articles of formidable technical difficulty. But the reason that these theories have taken such a firm hold on the profession is that, fundamentally, they are very intuitive. We believe that with careful and patient exposition, they can be made accessible to all students using only simple algebra and graphs. Many users of earlier editions of *Microeconomics* commented that they initially had reservations about their students' ability to deal with the "advanced" topics, but these fears proved to be groundless. Indeed, one instructor told us that his students were able to cope with the material on asymmetric information better than the traditional subjects, because the former seemed more realistic to them!

Applications

On the subject of realism—one of our goals is to make clear the links between microeconomics and the real world. Readers of previous editions reported that they liked our examples and wanted more. As believers in consumer sovereignty, we were happy to oblige. Readers of the current edition will see the theory of the consumer used to analyze actual price and income data from contemporary Russia; the value of information illustrated by Hollywood executives' efforts at market research; the theory of externalities applied to the issue of cigarette taxation; and many other examples of microeconomics in action. Generally we do not box off the applications and case studies from the rest of the text. Rather, they are integrated into discussions of the theory, a pedagogical approach that we have found works well.

Modern Organization

In addition to including new subjects, this book has a somewhat novel organizational scheme. Conventionally, a section called something like "Factor Markets" appears near the end of microeconomics books. Input markets are treated there, long after the basic theories of consumer and firm behavior have been covered. In contrast, modern economic theory integrates the treatment of commodity and factor markets. Households' input supplies and commodity demands both derive from the maximization of utility subject to a budget constraint. To drive this point home, we discuss both phenomena in the part of the book devoted to household behavior. Similarly, we present business output and input decisions together as joint implications of profit maximization, not as unrelated choices. This treatment provides students with a more coherent view of how the various pieces of a market economy fit together. At the same time, it exhibits the power and versatility of economic tools. Users of previous editions told us they agree.

A second organizational distinction is the placement of the chapter on welfare economics. Economists rely heavily on welfare economics for assessing the consequences of market imperfections. It would therefore seem sensible to present welfare economics prior to discussing market imperfections. Nevertheless, this topic appears near, or at, the end of most texts. This book covers welfare economics as soon as the competitive model is completely developed. The discussion of welfare economics sets the stage for subsequent chapters that explain how various market failures arise, what the consequences are, and the implications for public policy.

A third organizational innovation is that we begin our discussion of the firm by laying out the theory in a quite general form. In particular, we derive two rules for finding the profit-maximizing output level that are valid for any profit-maximizing firm. We take this approach for two reasons. One, by first deriving these rules in their general form, students are able to see the power of the economic theory of the firm: it provides a coherent set of basic principles that can be applied in a wide variety of market settings. The unified approach also has the advantage of presenting the student with less to remember—he or she has to learn these concepts only once. The later chapters then serve to reinforce and amplify the basic themes laid out at the beginning.

The other reason for covering the implications of profit maximization at the start of the theory of the firm is that the basic rules derived in that discussion show the importance of the concepts of marginal cost and average cost for economic decision making. This means that when we study production and cost functions in the following chapters, students know the reason why these concepts receive so much attention. In the traditional arrangement of chapters, where the cost chapter comes before any discussion of profit maximization, the study of marginal and average cost curves is a sterile exercise in curve manipulation. In fact, unless we have already made some assumption about the firm's interest in profit maximization, how do we know that the firm is even interested in minimizing its production costs?

A final innovation is that, in response to requests from several instructors, we have included a separate chapter on game theory. While closely tied to the chapter on oligopoly, the game theory chapter discusses the much broader applicability of game theory to a variety of real world problems. Because we are aware of the time constraints that many instructors face, we have written this chapter so that it can easily be skipped without loss of continuity.

Treatment of Costs

The subject of costs is another area in which we have departed from tradition. The standard treatment of cost is to begin by defining economic costs as opportunity costs. So far, so good. But then, the typical book goes on to define the expenditures on factors of production that are fixed in the short run as "fixed costs"—despite the fact that these expenditures are not *economic costs*. All is not lost, of course, because the next step in the standard treatment is to tell students that what they really should care about is short-run variable costs, not short-run total cost. This approach is needlessly confusing and complicated. Here, we consistently apply the definition of economic cost as opportunity cost. In addition to having the virtue of logical consistency, this approach is simpler than the traditional one. The firm is concerned with its short-run economic cost in the short run, and its long-run economic cost in the long run. It is thus a simple matter to state the rules by which a firm finds its profit-maximizing output level, whether we are talking about the short run, or the long run.

Comments from users of the first two editions confirm what we have experienced in our own classrooms: students have a much easier time with the approach taken here than with the traditional one. However, several instructors suggested to us that it would be useful to present our approach in a way that seamlessly blends with the one that students may have learned in earlier courses. In response, we have made numerous modifications throughout the chapters on the theory of the firm to achieve this consistency. Our aim is to achieve backward compatibility as we introduce a new (and, we believe, improved) development of cost theory.

PEDAGOGICAL FEATURES

The chapters are broken up into several numbered sections, each of which develops a major theme. Each of these sections ends with a short "Section Recap," which summarizes its main points. Breaking up the chapters in this way gives students a "breather" before they move ahead. In addition, it provides instructors an easy way to pick and choose topics for assigning. However, it has long been understood that no matter how clear a book's exposition and organization, passive reading of new material does not lead to its mastery. As Jean-Jacques Rousseau noted, "To read little and meditate a great deal upon our reading . . . that is the way to thoroughly digest it." To facilitate this digestive process, interspersed throughout the chapters are "Progress Check" questions. These are straightforward exercises whose answers appear at the end of the book. A student who is unable to answer a Progress Check question correctly should go back and reread the preceding pages before moving forward. More challenging exercises appear at the end of every chapter. These problems encourage students to apply and extend the principles that they have learned.

As stressed above, the only mathematics in the text is high school algebra and geometry. However, for instructors who would like to use this book in a calculus-based course, we have included two appendices (after Chapters 3 and 9) that reinterpret certain key results from the theories of the household and the firm using calculus.

Supplements

Study Guide to accompany Microeconomics
Robert Rosenman, Washington State University

Each chapter of this completely revised supplement offers a discussion of chapter goals, a case study application project, multiple-choice questions, and problems of varying levels of difficulty for your students. The integration of mathematical, graphical, and verbal explanations is emphasized throughout.

Instructor's Manual to accompany Microeconomics
Robert Rosenman, Washington State University

The Instructor's Manual has been extensively revised for this edition of *Microeconomics.* It includes lecture outlines and discussion suggestions for each chapter, as well as alternative examples and exercises. Also, where appropriate, suggestions for interactive classroom activities are provided. Finally, the answers to the end-of-chapter questions can be found in this supplement.

Test Bank to accompany Microeconomics
Christopher Stevens, Washington State University

The Test Bank, which has also been extensively revised, offers approximately 40 multiple-choice questions for each chapter. The level of difficulty is indicated for each question, and page references are provided to direct you to the related text coverage.

Computerized test banks are now available in Windows and Macintosh versions. The test generator allows instructors to select questions randomly, add and edit questions and equations, save and reload tests, create different versions of each test, attach graphics to questions and answers, select questions by level of difficulty, and write to word-processing files.

Overhead Transparency Acetates to accompany Microeconomics
This supplement offers selected illustrations from the text in an acetate format, allowing for easy integration into your classroom presentation.

Applied Price Theory Courseware
Howard Marvel (Macintosh format); David Boyd (Windows format)

This interactive program, available in both Macintosh and Windows formats, allows students to experiment with various economic models. Students can enter values and immediately see the impact of their choice on an economic model, thus reinforcing the graphical techniques used in microeconomic analysis.

The Development of *Microeconomics*, Third Edition: Your Story

The development of this new edition of *Microeconomics* was truly a collaborative effort—an active process in which you, microeconomics instructors from across the country, participated. Before we touched a word of the second edition, we distributed over 1,000 market surveys asking for your input and guidance in this revision process. You responded in great numbers, providing us with insight into the focus and direction of your courses, your teaching methods, and the skills and preferences of your students. This input, combined with that gleaned from a second e-mail survey, provided us with the base that we needed to create this edition of *Microeconomics*.

Before you is the fruit of your labors, tailored by the masterful hands of Michael Katz and Harvey Rosen. At your direction, the authors have made several significant changes to this edition of *Microeconomics*. Most notably, the coverage of game theory has been expanded, reflecting the increased emphasis that modern topics are receiving in your classrooms. This material is now presented as Chapter 16. Also in response to your feedback, Professors Katz and Rosen have modified the treatment of cost to provide a presentation that is more compatible with the approach that your students may have learned in their introductory courses. The authors have made numerous modifications to the theory of the firm material in order to create a consistent, logical approach to this topic

Finally, at your request, the ancillary materials for *Microeconomics* have been significantly revised. Because you indicated that your students needed better support materials, we completely overhauled the Study Guide, beginning from scratch to create a more comprehensive, interesting, and useful learning tool for your students. Also, for your use, we have a new Test Bank and an extensively revised Instructor's Manual.

The revisions mentioned here are only a few among many, but they are illustrative of your impact on our work in the creation of the third edition of *Microeconomics*. Thank you for the time and effort that you expended in this development process. Your active involvement is clearly a reflection of the level of dedication and enthusiasm that you have for your profession and for your students. We hope that you are pleased with this—your—final product.

Acknowledgments

We wish to thank the reviewers and other readers, who contributed greatly to the content, organization, and focus of the current and earlier editions of this book and its supplements.

Robert M. Aduddel
Loyola University, Chicago

Peter von Allmen
Moravian College

Neil Alper
Northeastern University

Lann Arvan
University of Illinois

Robert A. Becker
Indiana University

David E. Black
University of Delaware

John Boschen
College of William and Mary

Vic Brajer
California State University, Fullerton

Calcum Carmichael
Carleton College

Myong-Hun Chang
Cleveland State University

Karen Conway
University of New Hampshire

Gregg Davis
Marshall University

LuAnn M. Duffus
California State University, Hayward (retired)

Maxim Engers
University of Virginia

Fred Floss
Buffalo State College

A. Myrick Freeman III
Bowdoin College

Dan A. Fuller
Weber State College

Paul Gabriel
Loyola University

James D. Gaisford
The University of Calgary

Joseph C. Gallo
University of Cincinnati

Zvi Griliches
Harvard University

Eila Hanni
University of South Florida

John Helmuth
Rochester Institute of Technology

L. Dean Hiebert
Illinois State University

Peter Huang
Tulane University

Emily P. Hoffman
Western Michigan University

Sherry L. Jarrell
Southern Methodist University

Hyman Joseph
University of Iowa

Mohammed Kasraian
University of Wisconsin, Milwaukee

Sharon Levin
University of Missouri, St. Louis

William Kolberg
Ithaca College

Melvin Krauss
New York University

Robert Kuenne
Princeton University

Anthony Marino
University of Southern California

Larry Martin
Michigan State University

Chuck Mason
University of Wyoming

Tom McGuckin
New Mexico State University

Michael McKee
University of New Mexico/ Albuquerque

Francisco Merlero
Russell Sage College

Gilbert Metcalf
Tufts University

Margaret J. Morgan-Davie
Ithaca College

John Nye
Washington University

Carlo Perroni
Wilfred Laurier University

Carol Rankin
Xavier University

David Reitman
The Ohio State University

Janet Rives
University of Northern Iowa

Joshua Rosenbloom
University of Kansas

Bee Yan Roberts
Pennsylvania State University

Roj Rox
University of Toledo

William Sanders
DePaul University

Nindy Sandhu
California State University, Fullerton

Stephen C. Sheppard
Virginia Polytechnic Institute and State University

Allan G. Sleeman
Western Washington University

Bill Smith
University of Memphis

Lars Stole
University of Chicago

Rafael Tenorio
University of Notre Dame

Greg Trandel
University of Georgia

Daniel Vincent
Northwestern University

Michael Wasylenko
Syracuse University

Andrew Weiss
Boston University

John Whitehead
East Carolina University

George Zodrow
Rice University

Habib Z. Zuberi
Central Michigan State University

Mark Zupan
University of Southern California, Los Angeles

The students of Business Administration 201A
University of California at Berkeley

We suspect that coping with a pair of compulsive authors is not part of the standard job description for a textbook editor. Hence, special appreciation goes to the people at Irwin/McGraw-Hill, who treated us with patience and aplomb. They contributed greatly to improving the quality of the final product. Finally, we are grateful to Jennifer Hobart and Marsha Novick, who provided financial and emotional support during the entire writing of this book (well, at least most of the time).

M.L.K.
H.S.R.

Brief Contents

Contents

MICROECONOMICS

CHAPTER 1

The Market Economy

> ***What is to be done?***
> —Lenin

When future historians look back on the close of the 20th century, one of the most sweeping changes they will note is the collapse of centrally planned economies in Eastern Europe. It is not far off to say that the Cold War between the United States and the Soviet Union was won not by the armies of the United States and its allies, but by the productive power of Western market economies. Mikhail Gorbachev, then leader of the Soviet Union, concluded that his country's economy could not afford to continue its global military competition with the United States. The Soviet economy was simply too inefficient. He set his country on a new, more market-oriented course, in the process touching off political and economic upheavals.

Why did centrally planned economies fail while market systems survived? Gorbachev's own words provide some insight. In a 1987 speech, four years before the Soviet Union's abandonment of communism, he noted that "One can see children using a loaf of bread as a ball in football." Presumably, Gorbachev was irked by the wastefulness of using bread for child's play. But even if Gorbachev was irritated by seeing the bread squandered, one still wonders why he bothered to bring it up in a major speech. To think about this issue, one must ask why the Soviet youngsters were playing with the bread in the first place. The answer is that Soviet consumers did not put much value on bread because the price they paid for it was very low. Provided that they could buy all the bread they wanted at this low price, why would consumers bother to economize on its use? If a loaf of bread cost only the equivalent of a few pennies, *why not* let the children have a little fun by playing football with it!

We think that Gorbachev may have related this anecdote because he viewed it as symptomatic of the problems facing the Soviet economy. In 1987, the prices of all goods were set by central planners in Moscow. In many cases, commodities were priced so low that consumers felt no compunction about being wasteful. Moreover, many prices were set below production costs. In such cases, producers had little incentive to bring their wares to market: "[M]uch food rots long before it gets to the grocery store . . . Supplies are sporadic—butter one day, none the next—so most shoppers cruise the stores daily and hoard whatever looks interesting, just in case" (Keller 1988, A6). Other economies based on the Soviet model experienced similar problems. Polish Prime Minister Zbigniew Messner, for example, complained "There are . . . erroneous motivational systems, shortcomings in the organization of labor, lack of respect for social property" (Tagliabue 1987, 11). These difficulties were an important reason for the political upheavals that swept Eastern Europe, beginning in 1989 and ending with the overthrow of communism. Thinking about why centrally planned economies had such difficulties will help us define the subject matter of economics and the purpose of this book.

1.1 SCARCITY AND ECONOMICS

The difficulties of the centrally planned societies were a consequence of the way in which they dealt with the phenomenon of scarcity. Virtually all resources are scarce, meaning that there are not enough of them to satisfy all the desires of all people. By "resources" we refer not only to natural resources (oil, trees, land, and water) but also to human resources (labor) and capital resources (machines and factories). An important implication of the presence of scarcity is that people and societies must make choices among a limited set of possibilities. The choice to have more of one thing, like bread, necessarily means having less of other things. In the Soviet Union, these decisions were made by central planners; in effect, Gorbachev was complaining that this approach to dealing with scarcity was leading to undesirable results. Indeed, in a subsequent speech, he was more explicit: "The tendency to encompass every nook of life with detailed centralized planning and control literally straitjackets society."

The problem of scarcity is not confined to centrally planned economies. All societies must make choices about how to use their scarce resources; the way that societies differ is in *how* these decisions are made. **Economics** is the study of how people and societies deal with scarcity. The subject of this book is **microeconomics,** which focuses on the economic behavior of individual decision-making units. The prefix *micro,* which means "small," is somewhat misleading. To be sure, microeconomists spend a lot of time analyzing the behavior of relatively small decision makers, such as individual households and firms. But microeconomists are equally concerned with the big picture—how these individual decisions fit together and what kind of results they produce for society. However, we exclude a systematic treatment of how the economywide inflation and unemployment rates move over time (the business cycle). These topics belong in the realm of **macroeconomics,** which focuses on the behavior of the economy as a whole, with relatively less attention devoted to the activities of individual units.

economics
The study of how people and societies deal with scarcity.

microeconomics
The branch of economics focusing on the economic behavior of individual decision-making units, such as households and firms, and how these individual decisions fit together.

macroeconomics
The branch of economics focusing on the behavior of the economy as a whole, especially inflation, unemployment, and business cycles.

THE THREE QUESTIONS

Because of scarcity, every society *inescapably* has to answer three questions:

1. What Is to Be Produced?

As already stressed, in the presence of scarcity, producing more of one thing means producing less of another. A society therefore has to choose how many compact disc players, ballpoint pens, missiles, and every other commodity it is going to produce. This leads us to an important concept in economics: opportunity cost. When more of commodity X is produced, resources are used up. These resources could have been used to produce alternative commodities. The most highly valued of these forgone alternatives is the **opportunity cost** of X. Essentially, the opportunity cost of something is *what you give up* by having it.

opportunity cost
The value of the most highly valued forgone alternative.

President Dwight Eisenhower showed a keen grasp of the concept of opportunity cost in this discussion of the true cost of defense:

> Every gun that is made, every warship launched, every rocket fired signifies, in the final sense, a theft from those who hunger and are not fed, those who are cold and are not clothed. This world in arms is not spending money alone. It is spending the sinew of its laborers, the genius of its scientists, the hopes of its children (Ambrose 1984, 95).

The notion of opportunity cost is as applicable at the individual level as at the societal. Consider, for example, a peasant from China named Xiong Qiangyun, who proudly told a reporter that his son was in college: "It's been expensive, so I haven't been able to build a very nice house or buy a television. But my boy's in college" (Kristof 1991, 15). The opportunity cost of the education of Mr. Qiangyun's son was the consumer durables forgone by the rest of the family.

2. How Is It to Be Produced?

In the children's story of "The Three Little Pigs," we are told that a house may be constructed out of straw, sticks, or brick. This illustrates the important point that even after deciding what we want to produce, we have to decide how to produce it. Should houses be constructed of wood or should brick be used instead, so that the wood can be used for fuel? Perhaps straw should be used for housing, but then less would be available for fodder for livestock. Given that all resources are scarce, society must decide which resources to allocate to the production of various commodities.

3. Who Gets the Output?

Because of scarcity, no one can have all of everything that he or she wants. Every society must develop some kind of mechanism for dividing up the output among its members. And in every society, the question of whether this mechanism leads to a "fair" distribution of the output is likely to be the subject of intense debate.

The way that our three questions are answered is referred to as the **allocation of resources**—how society's resources are divided up among the various outputs, among the different organizations that produce these outputs, and among the members of society. Although every society has to decide how to allocate its resources, societies differ greatly in how these decisions are made. As noted earlier, in centrally planned economies these decisions are made by government bureaus. In contrast, the societies like the United States, Canada, the United Kingdom, and Australia rely more heavily on a **market system,** in which resource allocation decisions are determined by the independent decisions of individual consumers and producers, without any central direction. Because the market system is the most important mechanism for resource allocation in Western societies, it is the main focus of this book. Our goal is to understand how markets work, and to develop criteria for evaluating market outcomes. (PC 1.1)

allocation of resources
How society's resources are divided among the various outputs, among the different organizations that produce these outputs, and among the members of society.

market system
A mode of organization in which resource allocation is determined by the independent decisions and actions of individual consumers and producers.

1.1 PROGRESS CHECK

Evaluate this statement: "Saudi Arabia can pump all the oil that it needs. Therefore, consumption of oil is free in Saudi Arabia."

SECTION RECAP

All societies face the problem of scarcity—there are not enough resources to satisfy all people's desires for all things. Economics studies how individuals and societies deal with scarcity. Due to scarcity, every society needs some mechanism for deciding what to produce, how to produce it, and who gets the output. The focus of this book is on how a market system answers these questions. (See Progress Check 1.1.)

1.2 MODELS

model
A simplified description of some aspect of the economy, often containing equations and graphs.

The task that we have set ourselves appears daunting indeed. In any large economy there are millions of products, consumers, and firms. In a market system, consumers and firms all make their own decisions; we have to understand how these decisions are made and how they fit together. How can we possibly hope to encompass all of this complexity? The answer is that we won't even try. Instead, we study how economies work using **models,** which are descriptions of phenomena that abstract from the details of reality. By "abstracting" from details we mean ignoring those details that are not directly essential to understanding the phenomenon at hand. That way we can concentrate on the really important factors. A classic example of a model is a road map. If you are trying to drive from Chicago to Detroit, you do *not* want a perfectly "realistic" description of the terrain that shows the location of every road, every house, and every hill. Such a map would be so complicated that it would be useless. Instead, you want a map that abstracts from most details of the terrain and shows only the main highways and where they intersect.

A MODEL OF SCHOOL ATTENDANCE

You might never have thought about it this way, but like the Chinese peasant mentioned previously, your decision to attend college implicitly involved a choice in the presence of scarce resources. After all, you and your family only have so much money; spending it on tuition means having less available for other things. Even if tuition were zero, college would still be costly because your time has an opportunity cost—the time that you spend in school could be spent working, for example. Let's construct a model of the decision to attend college. Such an exercise will not only give you a good idea of what an economic model really is, but it will also introduce you to the way that economists typically approach problems.

Our simple model is based on the assumption that people make schooling decisions on the basis of monetary costs and benefits. What are these monetary costs and benefits? As already suggested, some of the opportunity costs are explicit or direct (such as tuition and books); in addition we must take into account the opportunity costs of the student's time. On the benefits side, each year of education leads to some increase in the person's earning capacity—better-educated people get higher-paying jobs. Our model posits that, before deciding to enroll in school each year, an individual considers the monetary costs and benefits of doing so. If the additional monetary benefits exceed the costs, he enrolls, and otherwise not. For example, if attending the first year of college costs \$10,000 but this will enhance your lifetime earnings by \$15,000, then you go to college. On the other hand, if it enhances your earnings by only $8,000, you do not. Why pay $10,000 to obtain a benefit of only $8,000?

Now, this model may strike you as being absurdly simple. It does not allow for the possibility that someone is in school just because his or her parents insisted on it. Neither does the model take into account that some people simply enjoy learning and are happy to pay tuition even if their future earnings aren't enhanced at all. However, the whole point of model building is to simplify as much as possible so that a problem is reduced to its essentials. Literary critic Lytton Strachey said that "Omission is the beginning of all art" (Lipton 1977, 93). Omission is also the beginning of all good economic analysis. A model should not be judged on the basis of whether or not it is "true," but on whether the model is plausible and informative. If a model founded on the assumption that educational decisions are based on monetary returns gives us good predictions, then it is useful, even if it does not encompass every possible explanation or predict the behavior of every single individual.

Sometimes, however, a model can be *too* simple for one's purposes. For instance, suppose that it is harder for students from poor families to borrow money than it is for those from rich families. Then students from poor families may not be able to borrow enough money for tuition, even though attending college would greatly enhance their earnings. If such borrowing constraints are really important, then a model that ignored them would not produce very good predictions about educational decisions. A model must be as simple as possible, but not simpler! How do you know if a particular model is too simple? Unfortunately, there is no easy answer. If the model appears to be doing a good job of explaining the problem at hand, then there is no reason to complicate it further. Economists have found that models that explain educational decisions on the basis of financial returns do a pretty good job of predicting people's actual decisions. (See, for example, Blackburn et al. 1991.)

So far, our model of educational decisions has used only words to describe the phenomenon; it is a verbal model. Verbal models are just fine, but sometimes our understanding is enhanced when models are represented graphically. In Panel A of Figure 1.1, years of education are measured on the horizontal axis, and dollars are measured on the vertical. The schedule labeled *MC* shows the cost of each ***additional*** year of school for a student whom we'll call Bert. In economics, the word ***marginal*** is used to mean "additional," so the additional cost is called the ***marginal cost.*** The marginal cost is drawn sloping upward, reflecting the assumption that the additional cost of each year of education increases over time, perhaps because tuition rises or because forgone wages become higher as the student becomes more educated. The schedule *MB* shows the marginal monetary benefit of each year of schooling for Bert. It is drawn sloping downward, which reflects the assumption that as more education is purchased, the amount by which it increases future earnings gets successively smaller. For example, the eighth year of schooling increases Bert's lifetime earnings by $20,000. His 17th year increases lifetime earnings by $4,500, a smaller increase, but an increase nonetheless.

How much education does Bert consume? Note that at any level of education to the left of 12 years, the marginal benefit exceeds the marginal cost. Hence, from a monetary point of view, taking another year of education makes sense. On the other hand, at any level of education to the right of 12 years, the marginal benefit is less than the marginal cost. Our model therefore predicts that Bert will enroll in school for just 12 years, the point at which the marginal benefit of a year

Figure 1.1
A Model of Educational Choice

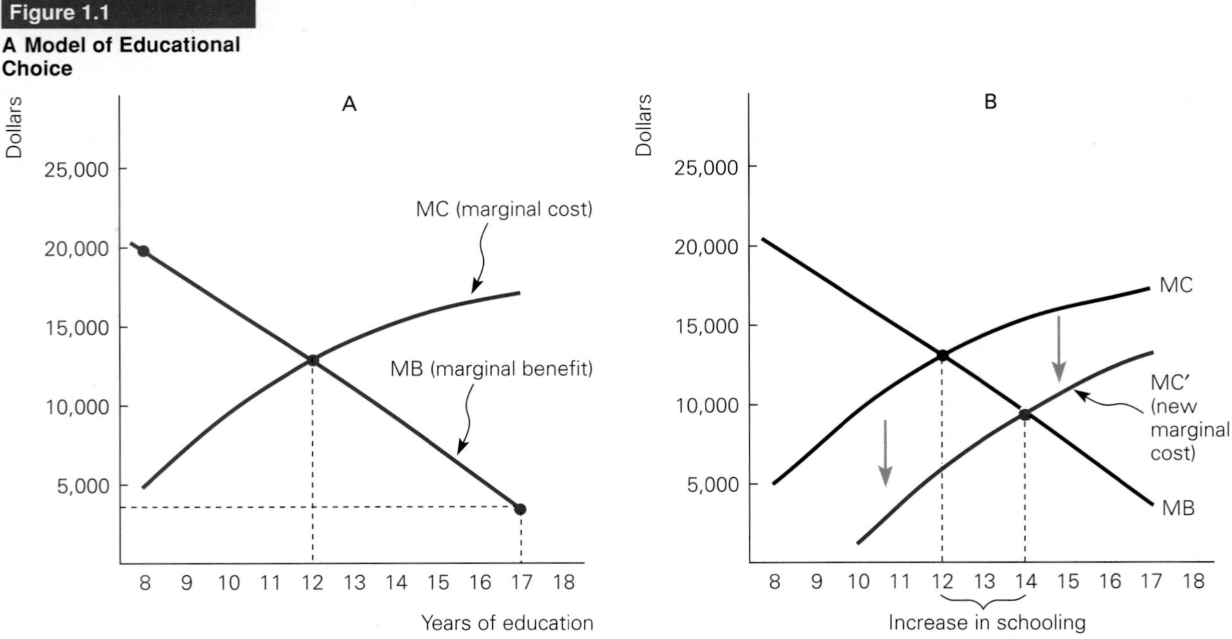

Assuming that schooling decisions are based on monetary motives only, an individual attends only as long as the marginal benefit exceeds the marginal cost. In Panel A, to the right of 12 years the marginal cost exceeds the marginal benefit, so the student does not attend more than 12 years. Panel B embodies a prediction—if the marginal costs of school attendance fall, a person will spend more time in school.

of education just equals its marginal cost. The notion that sensible decision making requires an individual to set marginal benefit equal to marginal cost is sometimes called the ***equimarginal rule***, and it will be encountered in various guises throughout this book.

Now suppose that Bert's circumstances change. The marginal cost of each year of Bert's education goes down, perhaps because of a decrease in current wage rates. (Remember, forgone wages are part of the cost of education.) Assuming that the marginal benefits stay the same, the new situation is depicted in Panel B. Similar logic to that of Panel A indicates that with lower costs Bert chooses to go to school for 14 years. (He would attend two years of college.) A comparison of Panels A and B reveals an important function of models—they allow us to make predictions of how behavior will change when circumstances change. This is crucial, because it permits us to *test* whether the model is doing a good job. As stressed above, if the model provides us with good predictions, it is fine. On the other hand, if the model is not consistent with real-world observations, it must either be modified or discarded altogether. As the Chinese leader Deng Ziaoping said, "Seek truth from facts."

Models can be mathematical as well as verbal or graphical. Let MB be the marginal benefit of each year of schooling, and MC the marginal cost. Then our main result is that people purchase schooling up to the point that the marginal benefit equals the marginal cost. This notion is expressed mathematically as

$$MB = MC.$$

The nice thing about mathematical equations is that they allow us to summarize a model very succinctly. In this book, we will rely on all three types of models: verbal, graphical, and mathematical. (PC 1.2)

1.2 PROGRESS CHECK

Suppose that there is a reduction in the marginal monetary benefits to attending school. Use Panel A of Figure 1.1 to predict how this would affect schooling decisions.

Interestingly, a methodology based on model building is by no means limited to economics. It is employed in "hard sciences" as well. The great theoretical physicist Stephen Hawking (1988, 11) observed, "A theory is a good theory if it satisfies two requirements: It must accurately describe a large class of observations on the basis of a *model* that contains only a few arbitrary elements, and it must make definite predictions about the results of future observation" (emphasis added). Like the economy, the physical world is too complicated to be studied without recourse to models.

POSITIVE AND NORMATIVE ANALYSIS

positive analysis Descriptive statements of cause and effect.

We will use models for both positive and normative analysis. **Positive analysis** deals with statements of cause and effect. For example, a positive statement is "If the U.S. government cuts tuition subsidies to students from middle-income households, then the number of such students attending college will decrease." Note that a positive statement can in principle be confirmed or refuted by appeal to real world observations. In this case, what you would have to do is determine whether enrollment of middle-income students actually fell after the subsidies were decreased.[1]

normative analysis Statements that embody value judgments.

Positive statements do not indicate whether the phenomenon under consideration is "good" or "bad"—they merely attempt to describe the world. In contrast, **normative analysis** deals with statements that embody value judgments. The assertion "All individuals who want to attend college ought to have free tuition," is a normative statement. One cannot confirm this statement by appealing to data; its validity depends upon one's ethical views. Keeping positive and normative views separated is sometimes difficult, but it is worth trying very hard to do so. One's views about how the world *is* should not be clouded by opinions on how it *ought* to be.

There are important links between normative and positive analysis. First, our normative views heavily influence the topics to which we apply positive analysis. Economists spend a lot more time studying the market for labor than the market for eggplant. This is due to an implicit ethical view that people are important, so that one should understand the forces determining their incomes. Second, the results of positive analysis can indicate how best to achieve one's normative goals. For example, by itself the normative view that society ought to help the poor does not indicate what steps would be most effective in attaining that goal. Would a minimum wage, a food subsidy, or a progressive income tax be most effective? Only hard-headed positive analysis of the various alternatives can produce an answer. If your interest in economics is based on a desire to improve the

[1]This can be a tricky exercise, because you also have to account for other factors that may have changed at the same time that the subsidies were changed. For details on the subsidies, see Congressional Budget Office (1991).

current system in some fashion, that's great. Just understand that a necessary first step is to understand how the system works.

SECTION RECAP

The real world is too complicated to study in all its detail. Therefore, economists rely on models, which are descriptions of reality that abstract from the details of reality. No model can be "true" in the sense of reflecting every aspect of reality. A good model is plausible and informative. Economists use models to make both positive (descriptive) as well as normative (judgmental) statements.

1.3 THE WORKINGS OF A PRICE SYSTEM: A PREVIEW

Now that you have been introduced to the methodology of model building, we are ready to return to our main task—seeing how the pieces of a market economy fit together.

THE CIRCULAR FLOW MODEL

It is useful to think of the economy as consisting of two sectors: households and businesses. Households[2] own various productive resources—labor, capital, and land. Businesses use these resources as inputs to the production of goods and services. (Inputs are sometimes referred to as *factors.*) Households purchase goods and services from businesses. Where do households get the money to buy the goods and services? Households receive their incomes by supplying inputs to businesses. In effect, then, economic activity is circular. The money that households spend on goods and services comes back around to them in the form of income from the sales of inputs.

circular flow model
A representation of how the business and household sectors are linked: the physical flows of commodities and inputs between businesses and households, and the expenditures for commodities and inputs going in the opposite direction.

This concept is summarized in the **circular flow model** in Figure 1.2. The model consists of two circles. The inner circle shows physical flows—flows of goods and services, and of inputs. The outer circle shows monetary flows—expenditures that households make for goods and services, and that businesses make for inputs. Note that the physical and monetary flows go in opposite directions. When households supply their labor to businesses, this represents a flow of labor to the business sector, but a flow of wage income to the household sector. Similarly, when businesses supply goods and services to households, this represents a flow of physical goods from businesses to households, but a flow of expenditures from households to businesses.

The circular flow model indicates that markets somehow regulate the flows between the two sectors. Households and businesses "meet" in the goods market; the outcome determines what goods are produced. They "meet" again in the factor market; the outcome determines how things are produced (that is, what inputs are used). In addition, the factor market determines how much income households get for supplying their inputs; hence, it also determines who gets the goods and services that are produced. Thus, the circular flow model shows how a market economy answers the three fundamental questions posed by the existence of scarcity.

[2]For convenience, we use the terms *household* and *individual* interchangeably, implicitly assuming that a household consisting of more than one person can be treated as a single decision-making unit.

Figure 1.2

The Circular Flow Model

The circular-flow-of-income model illustrates that economic activity is circular. The inner circle shows the flows of physical goods and services and of inputs through the system. Firms supply goods and services that are demanded by households; households supply inputs that are demanded by businesses. The outer circle shows the flows of money. Households spend money on goods and services that flow to businesses as revenues; these revenues flow to households as payments for supplying their inputs.

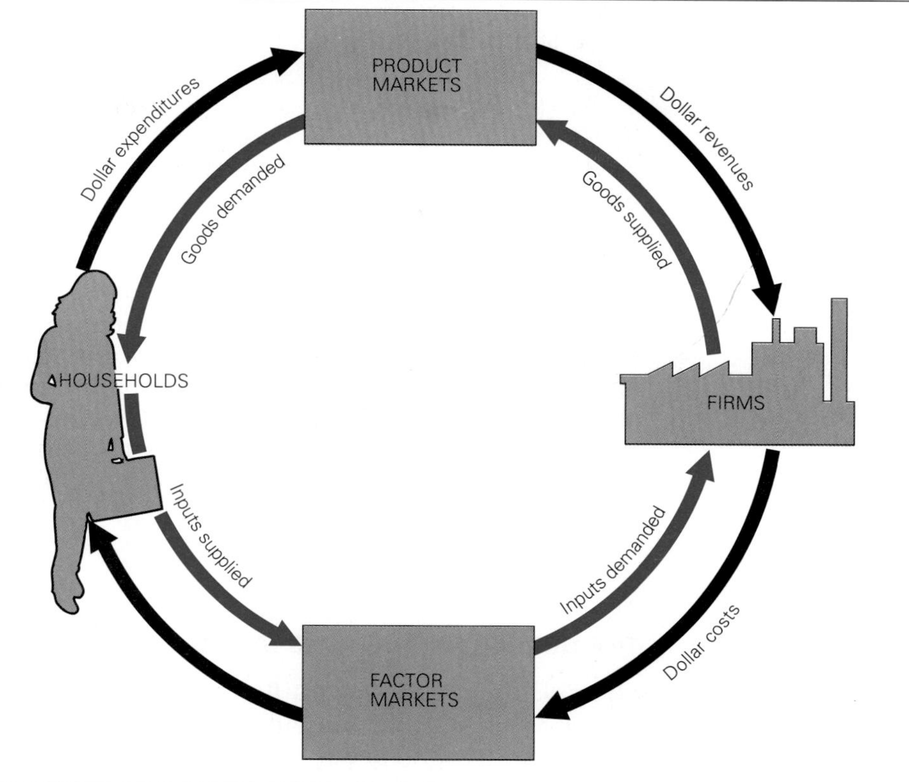

Does the circular flow model summarize everything that goes on in a market economy? The answer is certainly not, for at least three reasons:

1. The model amalgamates all firms into a single sector. Hence, it ignores transactions that take place among firms—dairy farms sell cream to ice cream manufacturers, aluminum manufacturers sell aluminum to bicycle producers, and so on.

2. The model assumes that all production takes place within businesses. In fact, important forms of production occur within households. For example, households produce "cleaning services," using as inputs their own labor and capital in the form of machines such as vacuum cleaners.

3. Perhaps most significantly, the circular flow model presented here ignores one of the most important forces in the economy—the government. Even in market-oriented economies, the government plays an enormous role. In the United States, the ratio of tax revenues to total output is 30 percent; in Canada the figure is 35 percent; in the United Kingdom, 38 percent; and in Sweden, 57 percent. Indeed, a sophisticated market system could not even exist without government. Why? Fundamentally, market transactions are trades—you give a person something you own (perhaps your labor) in return for something the other party owns. Such a system cannot function unless some agency is empowered to define and defend individuals' property rights. Otherwise, after the other person agreed to trade something to you, he could just steal it back. Thus,

government provision of "law and order" is a necessary condition for the emergence of a market system.

We have shown that the circular flow model omits important aspects of reality. Does this mean that it is a bad model? Our earlier remarks suggest that if the model sheds light on the phenomenon in which we are interested, then there is no problem if it abstracts from other issues. In this sense, the circular flow model is successful. It is a simplification of the real world, but it is a useful one because it illuminates the relationships in which we are interested.

The circular flow model is this book's organizing device. Chapters 2 through 6 deal with the household sector. We examine how households make their decisions both as demanders of goods and services, and as suppliers of inputs to firms. Chapters 7 through 10 look at businesses, both in their roles as suppliers of goods and services, and demanders of inputs. Chapters 11 through 17 then look at markets, the institutions that mediate between households and firms. We study different types of markets, see how they operate, and evaluate the outcomes they produce.

THE SUPPLY AND DEMAND MODEL

Our discussion of the circular flow model did not say much about how the activities of the household and business sectors are coordinated. Given that people make their decisions about what to buy and what to sell in isolation, what prevents business firms from producing purple scarves when households would rather have red shirts? What guarantees that the number of computer programmers employed by businesses will equal the number of people who want to be in that occupation? As our previous discussion of centrally planned economies indicated, *we cannot take it for granted that economic activity will end up being properly coordinated.*

In a market system, coordination is accomplished in a decentralized fashion by prices. How does this happen? Let's return to the commodity discussed at the beginning of this chapter—bread. Suppose that the current price of bread is $1.25 per loaf. Suppose further that at this price, bakers are producing more bread than households want to consume. In a market system, the bakers become aware of the fact that they are producing too much bread because it piles up on their shelves. In effect, there is a bread glut. As a consequence, the price of bread falls, perhaps to $1.10 per loaf. This price decrease has two effects. First, because it has become cheaper, households are willing to purchase more bread than before. Second, with a lower price, bakers are not willing to produce as much bread as they did before. Both effects tend to reduce the magnitude of the "glut." Eventually, the price falls enough so that the number of loaves that people are willing to buy equals the number of loaves that firms are willing to produce. The price of bread has coordinated the activities of producers and consumers.

More generally, if "too much" of a commodity is being produced in a market system, its price falls; if "too little" is being produced, its price increases. The price remains stable only when a balance has been achieved between what producers are willing to produce and what consumers are willing to consume.

This model of how prices guide the behavior of both producers and consumers is called the *supply and demand model.* Let us examine this model more carefully, using graphical techniques. We look first at the demand side of the market, next at supply, and then put them together.

Demand

What factors influence households' decisions to consume a certain good? Continuing with the specific case of bread, our model-building methodology suggests that we should assemble the shortest possible list of factors that might affect the amount of bread that people want to consume during a given period of time.

Price We expect that as the price goes up, the quantity demanded goes down. As bread becomes more expensive, households turn to other goods, perhaps buying more muffins or sweet rolls instead. The notion that price and quantity demanded normally are inversely related is called the *Law of Demand.*

Income Changes in income modify people's consumption opportunities. It is hard to say in advance, however, what effect such changes have upon consumption of a given good. One possibility is that as incomes go up, people use some of their additional income to purchase more bread. On the other hand, as incomes increase, people may consume less bread, perhaps spending their money on cake instead. If an increase in income increases demand (other things being the same), the good is called a *normal good.* If an increase in income decreases demand (other things being the same) the good is called an *inferior good.*

Prices of Related Goods Suppose the price of crackers goes up. If people can substitute bread for crackers, this increase in the price of crackers increases the amount of bread people wish to consume. Now suppose the price of butter goes up. If people tend to consume bread and butter together, this tends to decrease the amount of bread consumed. Goods like bread and crackers are called *substitutes;* goods like bread and butter are called *complements.*

Tastes The extent to which people "like" a good also affects the amount they demand. Presumably, less bread is demanded by people concerned with weight problems than by those who are skinny.

demand schedule
The relation between the market price of a good and the quantity demanded of that good during a given time period, other things (such as income, tastes, and other prices) being the same.

ceteris paribus
Latin for "other things being the same"; an economic assumption holding all other variables constant in order to focus on the specified ones.

We have just completed a verbal model that suggests that a wide variety of things can affect demand. For purposes of constructing a graphical version of the model, it is useful to focus on the relationship between the quantity of a commodity demanded and its price. Suppose that we hold constant income, the prices of related goods, and tastes. We can imagine varying the price of bread and seeing how the quantity demanded changes under the assumption that the other relevant variables stay at their fixed values. A **demand schedule** (or **demand curve**) is the relation between the market price of a good and the quantity demanded of that good during a given time period, other things being the same. (Economists often use the Latin **ceteris paribus** for "other things being the same.") In particular applications, one must always specify just what period of time is being considered, because generally different quantities of a commodity are demanded over a day, a month, a year, and so on.

A hypothetical demand schedule for bread is represented graphically by curve *D* in Figure 1.3. The horizontal axis measures the number of loaves of bread, and the price per loaf is measured on the vertical axis. Thus, for example, if the price

Figure 1.3
A Demand Curve

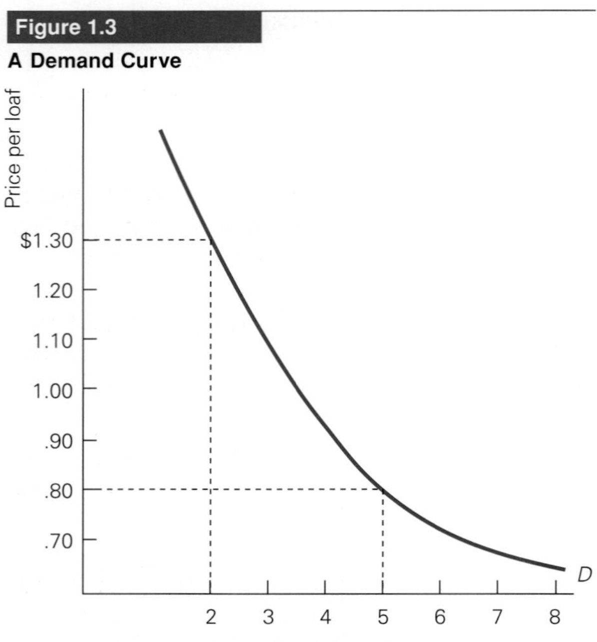

Schedule *D* shows the quantity of bread that people are willing to buy at each price, other things being the same. It is called the *demand curve* for bread.

Figure 1.4
Shifting a Demand Curve

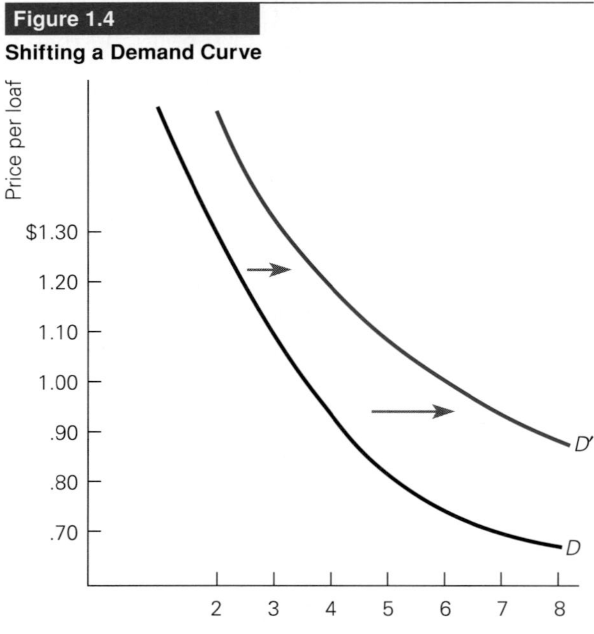

When the price of muffins increases, there will be a tendency to purchase more bread. This is reflected in an outward shift of the demand curve for bread.

is $1.30 per loaf, households are willing to consume 2 million loaves; when the price is only $0.80, they are willing to consume 5 million loaves. The downward slope of the demand schedule reflects the reasonable assumption that when the price goes up, the quantity demanded goes down, and vice versa.

As stressed above, the demand curve is drawn on the assumption that all other variables that might affect quantity demanded do not change. What happens if one of them does? Suppose, for example, that the price of muffins increases and, as a consequence, people want to buy more bread. In Figure 1.4, schedule *D* from Figure 1.3 (before the increase) is reproduced. Because of the increase in the price of muffins, at each price of bread people are willing to purchase more bread than they did previously. In effect, an increase in the price of muffins shifts each point on *D* to the right. The collection of new points is *D*′. Because *D*′ shows how much people are willing to consume at each price, *ceteris paribus*, it is by definition the new demand curve.

More generally, a change in any variable that influences the demand for a good—except its own price—*shifts* the demand curve. A change in a good's own price, however, induces a *movement along* the demand curve, causing a change in quantity demanded. Economists have developed some terminology to help clarify this distinction. A *change in demand* refers to a shift of the entire demand schedule, as in Figure 1.4. A *change in quantity demanded* refers to a movement along a given demand curve, as occurs in Figure 1.3 when the price of bread increases from $0.80 to $1.30.

Supply

Now let's consider the business part of the circular flow. What factors determine the quantity of a commodity that firms supply to the market during a given time period?

Price Typically, it is reasonable to assume that the higher the price per loaf of bread, the greater the quantity that firms are willing to supply. Higher prices make it profitable for firms to produce more output.

Price of Inputs Bread producers have to use inputs to produce bread—labor, flour, mixing bowls, and so on. If their input costs go up, the amount of bread that they can profitably supply at any given price goes down.

Conditions of Production The most important factor here is the state of technology. If there is a technological improvement in bread production, the supply increases.

As with the demand curve, it is useful to focus attention on the relationship between the quantity of a commodity supplied and the price, holding the other variables at fixed levels. The **supply schedule** is the relation between the market price and the amount of a good that producers are willing to supply during a given period of time, *ceteris paribus.*

supply schedule
The relation between the market price and the amount of a good that producers are willing to supply during a given period of time, *ceteris paribus.*

A supply schedule for bread is depicted as S in Figure 1.5. Its upward slope reflects the assumption that the higher the price, the greater the quantity supplied, *ceteris paribus.*

When any variable that influences supply (other than the commodity's own price) changes, the supply schedule shifts. Suppose, for example, that the price of flour increases. This increase reduces the amount of bread that firms are willing to supply at any given price. The supply curve therefore shifts to the left. As depicted in Figure 1.6, the new supply curve is S'. In contrast, a change in the commodity's price induces a movement *along* the supply curve. Analogous to the terminology we introduced for demand curves, a *change in supply* refers to a shift of the entire supply curve, and a *change in quantity supplied* refers to a movement along a given supply curve.

Equilibrium

The demand and supply curves provide answers to a set of hypothetical questions: *If* the price of bread were $2 per loaf, how much would households be willing to purchase? *If* the price were $1.75 per loaf, how much would firms be willing to supply? Neither schedule by itself tells us the actual price and quantity. But taken together, the schedules do determine price and quantity.

equilibrium
A state of affairs that will persist because no one has any incentive to change his or her behavior. In the supply and demand model, equilibrium is characterized by the equality of quantity supplied and quantity demanded at a particular price.

In Figure 1.7 we superimpose demand schedule D from Figure 1.3 on supply schedule S from Figure 1.5. We want to find the price and output at which there is an **equilibrium**—a situation that will continue to persist because no one has any incentive to change his or her behavior. Suppose the price is $1.30 per loaf. At this price, businesses are willing to supply 8 million loaves, but consumers are willing to purchase only 2 million. A price of $1.30 cannot be maintained, because firms want to supply more bread than consumers are willing to purchase. This excess supply tends to push the price down, as suggested by the arrows.

Figure 1.5

A Supply Curve

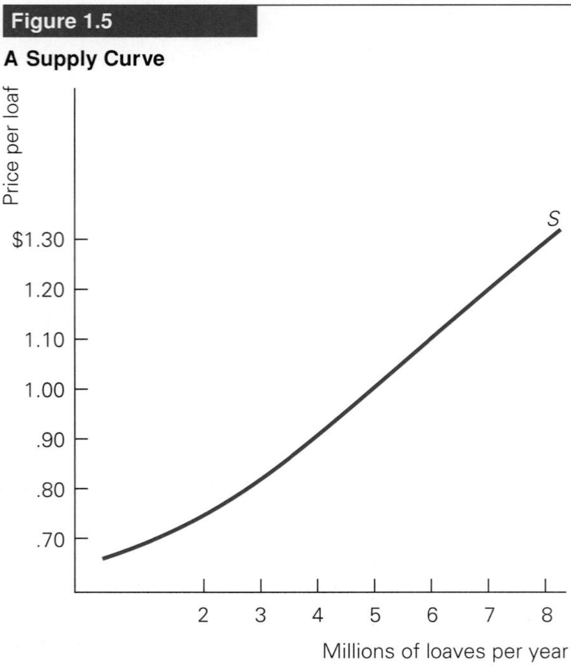

Schedule *S* is the supply curve of bread. It shows the quantity that producers are willing to sell at each price.

Figure 1.6

Shifting a Supply Curve

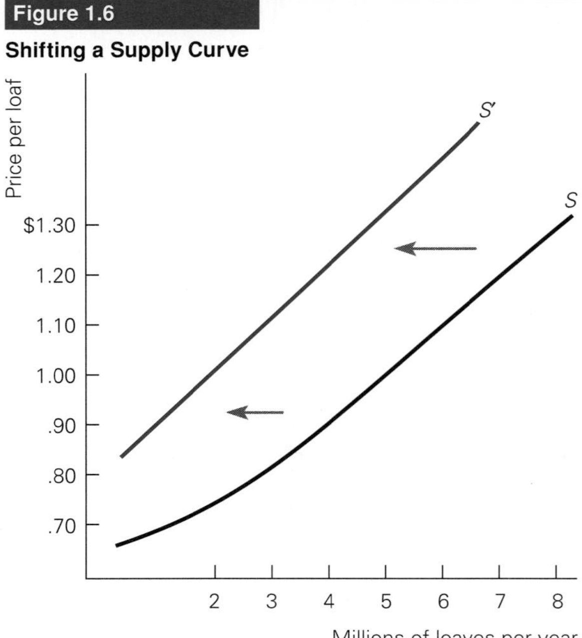

When the price of flour, an input to the production of bread, increases, producers are willing to sell less at any given price. As a consequence, the supply curve shifts inward, from *S* to *S'*.

Will a price of $0.80 per loaf successfully coordinate buyers and sellers? At this price, the quantity of bread demanded, 5 million loaves, exceeds the quantity supplied, 3 million. At a price of 80 cents, then, there isn't enough bread to go around. Because there is excess demand for bread, we expect the price to rise.

Similar reasoning suggests that any price at which the quantity supplied and quantity demanded are unequal cannot be an equilibrium. In Figure 1.7, quantity demanded equals quantity supplied at a price of $0.90. The associated output level is 4 million loaves. Unless something else in the system changes, this price and output combination will continue year after year. It is an equilibrium. Thus, Figure 1.7 demonstrates how price coordinates the activities of producers and households.

Suppose now that something else does change. For example, suppose that the price of flour increases. In Figure 1.8, *D* and *S* are reproduced from Figure 1.7, and the original equilibrium price and output are illustrated. Now, as a consequence of the increase in flour prices, the supply curve shifts to the left, say to *S'*. Given the new supply curve, $0.90 is no longer the equilibrium price. Rather, equilibrium is found at the intersection of *D* and *S'*, where the price is $1.10 and output 3 million loaves. Note that, as one might expect, the increase in flour prices leads to a higher price and smaller output. More generally, our model predicts that a change in any variable that affects supply or demand creates a new equilibrium combination of price and quantity. (PC 1.3)

1.3 PROGRESS CHECK

Suppose the market for bread at a given time is correctly depicted by Figure 1.7. Suddenly, the price of butter increases substantially. Use the supply and demand model to predict what happens to the price of bread, and the number of loaves consumed.

Figure 1.7

Price Determination by Supply and Demand

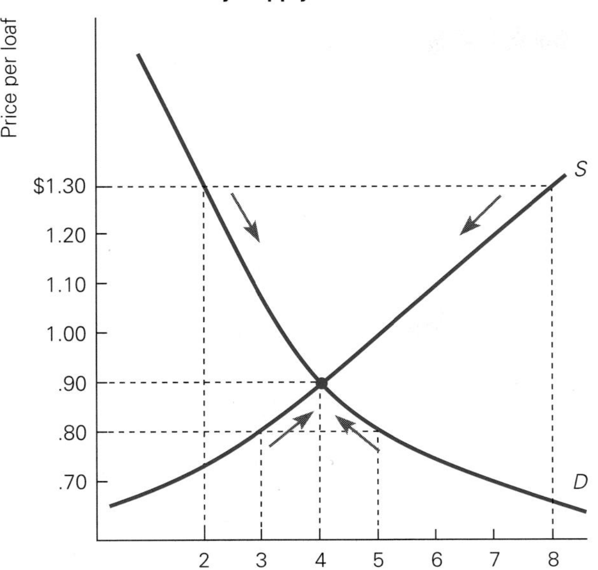

At any price above 90 cents, firms want to produce more than consumers are willing to purchase, so the price falls. At any price below 90 cents, consumers want to purchase more than firms are willing to produce, so the price increases. An equilibrium is obtained at a price of 90 cents, where quantity demanded equals quantity supplied.

Figure 1.8

Effect of a Supply Shift on Price and Quantity

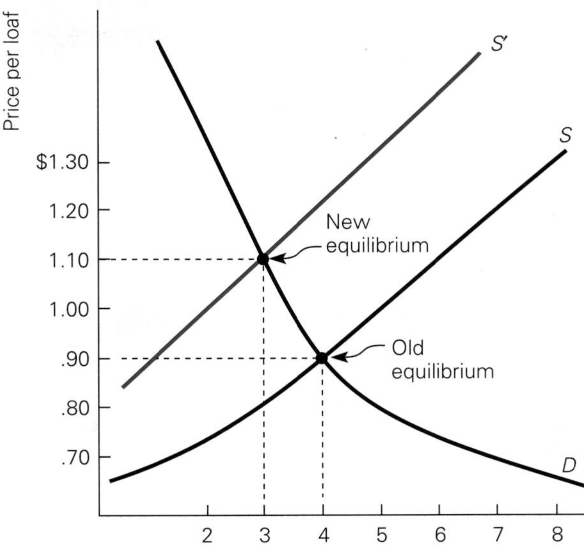

When flour becomes more expensive, the supply curve shifts to S', and 90 cents is no longer the equilibrium price. The new equilibrium price is $1.10, where the new quantities demanded and supplied are equal.

Supply and Demand for Inputs

So far we have been examining how supply and demand regulate the top part of the circular flow—the flow of goods from firms to households. The supply and demand model applies just as well to the bottom part, which focuses on the flow of inputs from households to firms. The main difference is that now the households are suppliers of inputs, and firms are demanders.

In Figure 1.9, for example, we measure the number of bakers on the horizontal axis. The price of bakers—their wage rate in dollars per hour—is on the vertical. The supply curve of bakers, *S*, is drawn upward sloping, based on the assumption that as the rewards to being a baker increase, more people enter that profession, *ceteris paribus.* The demand for bakers, *D*, is drawn downward sloping, reflecting the assumption that as bakers become more expensive, firms hire fewer bakers, perhaps substituting machines for them. Using exactly the same sort of arguments as above, our model predicts that 6,200 people choose to be bakers, and each makes a wage of $11.50 per hour. In this way, the wage rate coordinates economic activity in the labor market.

The Roles of Prices

Our simple supply and demand model illustrates nicely several related roles that prices serve in a market economy:

Figure 1.9

Supply and Demand for an Input

The supply and demand model also applies to productive inputs such as labor. The wage rate for bakers and the number of bakers are determined by the intersection of the demand and supply curves for bakers.

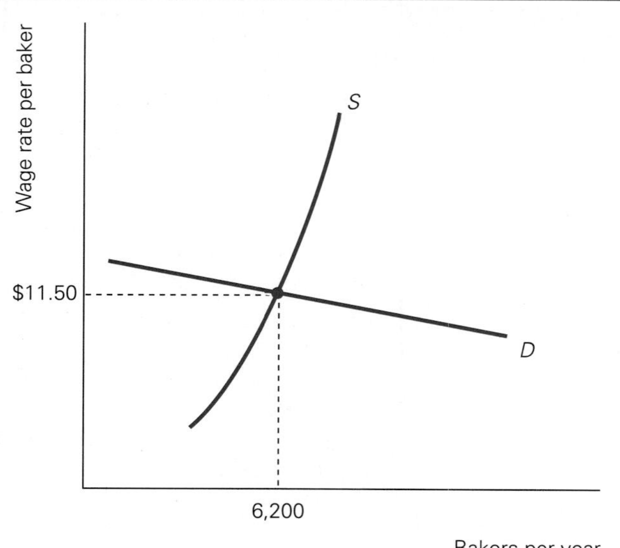

1. *Prices convey information.* Households do not have to know how bread is produced, and firms do not have to know why households use bread. Prices are signals that contain all the information needed to ensure consistency in the decisions of households and firms. For example, if flour becomes more expensive, no central directive is needed to ensure that people consume less bread. Rather, as illustrated in Figure 1.8, the price rises, which signals that bread is more costly and provides incentives for households to reduce their consumption. By signaling what is relatively scarce and what is relatively abundant, prices can efficiently channel production and consumption.

2. *Prices ration scarce resources.* If bread were free, a huge quantity of it would be demanded. Because the resources used to produce bread are scarce, the actual amount of bread has to be rationed among its potential users. Not everyone can have all the bread that they could possibly want. The bread must be rationed somehow; the price system accomplishes this in the following simple way: Everyone who is willing to pay the equilibrium price gets the good, and everyone who is not, does not. In this connection, it is informative to ponder this headline from 1990: "Soviet Legislators Back Market Economy, but Balk at Bread Price Increase" (Keller 1990, A18). One can sympathize with the reluctance to raise bread prices, which had stayed constant for 30 years. Nevertheless, saying that you want to have markets without allowing prices to ration commodities is like saying you want to have a bath without using any water. Both belie a fundamental misunderstanding of how the process works.

3. *Prices determine incomes.* As noted above, a society somehow has to decide who gets what is produced. In a market system, your money income depends on the prices of the inputs that you supply to the market. As illustrated in Figure 1.9, this is determined both by the supplies and demands of the various inputs.

Is This All There Is to It?

Now that you've seen how a supply and demand model deals with the problems associated with scarcity, you might be wondering if there is anything left to do. The answer is "quite a bit," for several reasons.

First, we haven't said much about where the supply and demand curves come from. We know that the demand for goods and the supply of inputs are the outcomes of household decision making, but how do households make their choices? Similarly, how do firms make their input and output decisions? What determines the shapes of demand and supply curves? Do demand curves *have* to slope down, and supply curves up?

Second, like *any* model, supply and demand does not explain every aspect of the real world. We have to spell out precisely the conditions under which supply and demand are likely to operate as in Figures 1.7 and 1.9. Equally important, for situations in which markets are not well characterized by supply and demand, we must formulate alternative models of resource allocation.

So, you're off to a good start, but there is a lot more to do!

SECTION RECAP

The circular flow model shows how firms and households are linked together. Households supply inputs to firms; the firms pay households for these inputs; and households use the income to purchase the outputs produced by the firms. Households and firms "meet" in both output and input markets. The supply and demand model provides an explanation of how these markets work. The price and quantity of each output (and input) are determined by the intersection of its demand and supply curves.

SUMMARY

Scarcity is part of the basic human condition. Scarcity forces societies to decide what will be produced, how it will be produced, and who gets the output. Economics studies how people and societies deal with the problem of scarcity. The focus of microeconomics is on how individual households and firms make their decisions, and how these decisions get translated into social outcomes.

- Every society has to decide what is to be produced, how to produce it, and who gets the output.
- Because of the complexity of the real world, when economists want to understand some phenomenon, they construct a model—a description of reality that abstracts from all the details of reality.
- Models are used for positive analysis, that is, to make statements relating to cause and effect. They also deal with normative issues—issues that concern value judgments.
- The circular flow model shows how the business and household sectors are linked. Households supply inputs to firms; firms supply commodities to households.
- In a market economy, prices for inputs and commodities coordinate the activities of firms and households. Also, prices ration scarce resources and determine incomes.
- An important model of price determination is supply and demand. The demand curve shows how the quantity demanded varies with price, *ceteris paribus*. The supply curve shows how the quantity supplied varies with price, *ceteris paribus*. The intersection of the two curves determines the market price and the quantity exchanged.

DISCUSSION QUESTIONS

1.1 Evaluate each of the following statements:

a. A society can always produce more automobiles if it chooses to do so. Hence, there can never be any real scarcity of automobiles.

b. Governments have the power to raise all the money they want by taxation. Hence, scarcity is not a problem for governments.

c. Citizens of Sweden are lucky because they have free health care, while citizens of the United States have to pay for it.

1.2 What is the opportunity cost of each of the following items?

a. Enrollment in an economics course.

b. Clean air.

c. Waiting in line to get into a free concert.

1.3 Suppose that the government introduced the following system of compulsory public service: Each college student would be required to withdraw from school for one year and participate in various projects such as forest reclamation. Participants would receive food and shelter, but no pay. How would you estimate the cost of this program?

1.4 After the fall of communism in East Germany, earnings opportunities for both men and women increased substantially. At the same time, the birth rate fell precipitously. When asked about her decision not to have a second child, a German woman named Karla Hofmann said, "A second child would mean we couldn't go on vacation" (Benjamin 1994, A1). Relate Hofmann's statement to the concept of opportunity cost. On the basis of Hofmann's statement, develop an equimarginal rule for the number of children to have.

1.5 The Nobel prize winning economist Kenneth Arrow "graduated from City College in 1940. Employment opportunities for young graduates were rare at the time, so he decided to pursue graduate work in statistics" (Tregarthen 1992, 82). Was Arrow's behavior consistent with the model of educational choice presented in Figure 1.1?

1.6 In preparation for the 1996 Olympic Games, the city of Atlanta, Georgia, embarked upon a $500 million construction program. Brick masons who had earned $13 to $14 an hour in 1993 were commanding $17 to $18 in 1995 (Thomas 1995, A1). Use a supply and demand model to represent this situation.

1.7 In the United States, delays at airports are a common experience. Many observers attribute part of the problem to congestion on runways during peak hours. Explain how a market solution to this problem could be obtained.

1.8 An article about the market for marijuana made the following three observations: (a) In 1991, the price was $80 an ounce; several years earlier the price was $30 an ounce. (b) By 1991, marijuana smoking was no longer in vogue—"the great marijuana cloud has grown wispy . . . as health concerns . . . have risen above the desire to get giddy." (c) "Relentless police pressure" had turned marijuana into a "scarce commodity" (Treaster 1991, A.1). Draw a set of supply and demand curves that are capable of reconciling these observations.

1.9 Federal law prohibits the buying and selling of body parts. "Every year 10,000 to 12,000 people die in a manner that makes them potential organ donors, mostly from head injuries, but organs are collected from only about one-third. By contrast, the number of people on the national waiting list for organ transplants exceeds 35,000 . . ." (Young 1994, B7). How are body parts rationed under the status quo? How would a market ration body parts? Do you think that it would be desirable to allow individuals to sell their internal organs?

1.10 Suppose that the market demand curve for haircuts in some town is

$$D = 80 - 2P + 5I,$$

where D is quantity demanded per month, P is price per haircut, and I is consumer income (in tens of thousands of dollars). The supply curve is

$$S = 4P,$$

where S is the quantity supplied per month.

a. According to this model, are haircuts a normal or inferior good?

b. Suppose $I = 3$. Find the equilibrium price and quantity of haircuts.

c. Because of a recession, I falls to 2. What happens in the haircut market?

PART one

The Household

A primary goal of microeconomics is to understand individual behavior and how this behavior affects societal outcomes. Individuals are at center stage. Even when analyzing institutions such as firms or governments, economists keep their eyes on individuals and their interactions.

We introduce the basic model of individual behavior in Chapter 2. It discusses how people make sensible decisions in the presence of scarcity. In particular, it shows how people decide what to buy and in what quantities, given their incomes and the prices of various goods and services.

Chapter 1 stressed that a good model should help us make predictions about how people's behavior will change when their circumstances change. Chapter 3 takes the basic model of behavior from Chapter 2 and uses it to generate such predictions. A major focus of this chapter is how people modify their behavior when market prices change. This is of central importance, because in a market economy, a commodity's price is a signal of its relative scarcity. We need to find out how people react to these market signals.

Chapter 4 looks at how price changes affect people's welfare. One important use of the powerful tools presented in this chapter is to assess the consequences of various government interventions in a market system.

So far we have been thinking about people as demanders of commodities. But our circular flow model makes it clear that they are also suppliers of inputs. Chapter 5 looks at households in this role, emphasizing their decisions concerning how much labor and capital to provide to firms. Although this is a new topic, it does not require any new analytical tools. Like commodity-demand decisions, factor-supply decisions involve rational choice in the presence of scarcity. Hence, the framework developed in Chapters 2 through 4 can be used. Incidentally, this illustrates a nice aspect of microeconomics: Once an analytical technique is mastered, it can be applied to a variety of problems.

Our discussion of household behavior concludes with Chapter 6, which discusses decision making in the presence of uncertainty. You are well aware that it is not always possible to know for sure what the consequences of your actions will be. A theory of behavior that could not deal with situations involving uncertainty would be of limited relevance to the real world. Chapter 6 modifies the conventional models to accommodate uncertainty.

CHAPTER 2

Consumer Choice

You can't always get what you want.
—Mick Jagger and Keith Richards

In a survey of its readers' finances several years ago, *Consumer Reports* magazine discussed the situation of young, two-earner couples:

> This group fits the Yuppie stereotype in that it's young . . . and professional . . . Household income is high: One-quarter of the families in this group have an income of over $59,000.
>
> These readers eat out a lot. They spend more than any other group on vacations and recreation (nearly $2,500 a year) . . . Although readers in this group spend a lot of money, they save a lot, too. This group had one of the highest savings rates . . .
>
> With all that, you'd expect people in this group to be delighted with their financial position. They weren't. (*Consumer Reports* 1986, 585)

The article went on to explain that despite their high incomes, the Yuppies complained about high housing costs, taxes, and so forth.

Unlike *Consumer Reports*, most economists would not be surprised that such families were not "delighted with their financial position." Economics posits that people's desires are virtually unlimited, while their resources are finite. Even $59,000 a year is not enough to buy everything one wants. Whether you are a Yuppie deciding between taking a European vacation and buying a new Volvo, or impoverished parents choosing between food and clothing for their children, one thing is certain: Choices have to be made.

In this chapter, we develop a theory of how households make choices. Such a theory is important for several reasons:

- We saw in Chapter 1 that households' demand curves in product markets and supply curves in factor markets play a crucial role in allocating resources in a market economy. The theory of choice allows us to "go behind" the household demand and supply curves—to derive these curves using a model of how individuals adjust to changes in prices.

- The theory of choice also is interesting in its own right. It provides a general framework for understanding important aspects of human behavior and yields insights into a wide range of activities, from occupational choice to tax evasion.
- The theory embodies an approach to thinking about normative issues that allows us to discuss whether various interventions in markets are likely to be desirable.

This chapter focuses on the roles of households as demanders of commodities in product markets. In later chapters, we will use the same framework to understand households' supply decisions in factor markets.

2.1 BASIC SETUP

We begin our discussion by looking at the problem facing a typical consumer. Like everyone else, her resources are limited relative to her desires; that is, she does not have enough income or time to consume every commodity that she could possibly want. The theory of consumer choice examines how a person makes sensible decisions in the presence of such scarcity.

Stating the problem this way suggests that three steps are involved in understanding consumer behavior:

1. We must know what the consumer *wants* to do. Without knowing her preferences for various commodities, we cannot know what a "good" solution to the problem of scarcity is from her point of view. Thus, we need a representation of consumer tastes.
2. We also need to know what the individual *can* do, given her income and the prices she faces. Hence, we must model the constraints imposed on the decision maker by her limited budget.
3. The third step is simply putting the consumer's preferences (which show what she wants to do) together with her constraints (which show what she can do). This allows us to determine which feasible choice maximizes her well-being. These three steps are summarized in Figure 2.1.

An important implication of this framework is that the theory of choice shows how an individual makes a decision, *given her particular tastes.* The theory indicates how many Wagnerian operas an individual should attend, given preferences for Wagnerian operas and other commodities; it does not say whether it is "rational" to like Wagnerian operas in the first place. *Economists cannot judge whether an individual's goals are sensible; they can only say whether or not an individual is attempting to attain his or her goals in a rational fashion.*

This point relates to another issue, the definition of an "economic good." It is natural to think of a good as something that is tangible—a steak, a necktie, a Walkman, or a tennis racket. However, economists have something much broader in mind when they use the term. A good is anything that, when consumed, positively affects the individual's level of satisfaction. If you like to breathe clean (as opposed to polluted) air, then clean air is a good. If you like to relax, then leisure is a good.

Occasionally, one hears complaints that economists view people as caring only about buying as many things as possible: "Economists, . . . if pressed, admit and even insist that economic agents are greedy" (Brockway 1988, 15). This assertion

Figure 2.1
A Model of Individual Decision Making

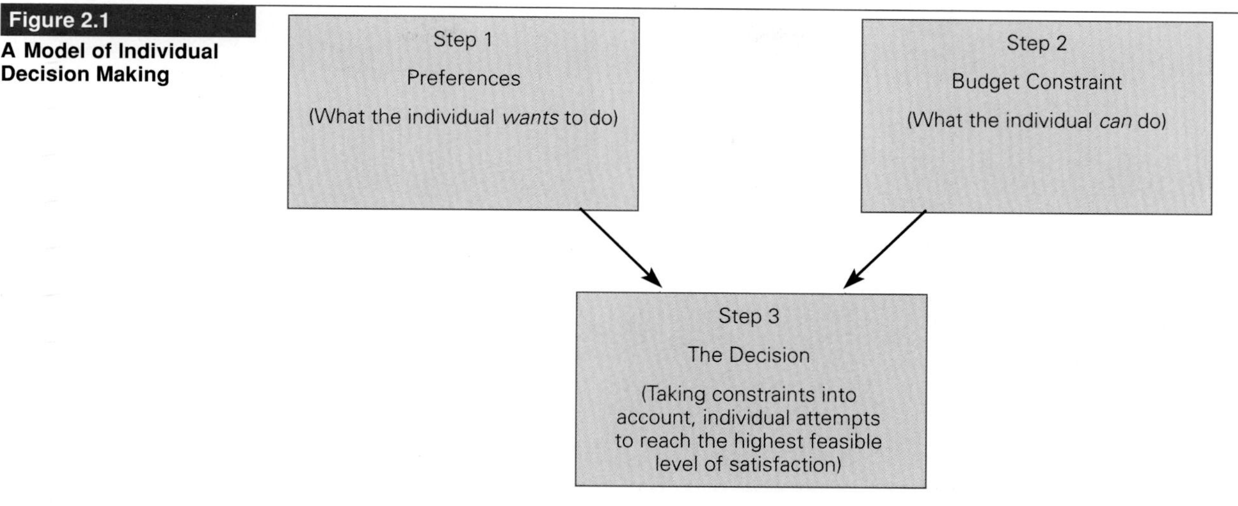

is wrong. Economic theory says only that people act sensibly in attaining their goals, not that these goals are materialistic in a narrow sense. If you enjoy giving money to the poor, then charity is an economic good! In fact, we will see that economic theory provides valuable predictions about how charitable giving responds to changes in economic variables such as tax rates.

2.2 TASTES

The first step in Figure 2.1 is representing the consumer's tastes for all goods. Given that literally thousands of commodities are available, this is a tall order. To keep things simple, assume that only two commodities are available. Clearly this assumption is unrealistic. However, we will see later that the theory for the choice between two commodities is applicable to choices involving any number of commodities. Virtually all of the important insights of the theory can be obtained from the two-commodity case.

This typifies the approach to modeling discussed in Chapter 1: Make the problem as simple as possible without losing its essential aspects. If we can understand the important aspects of decision making by studying a two-good problem, then, despite its unrealistic nature, it suits our purposes just fine. An *unrealistic* assumption is not necessarily a *bad* assumption.

Let us examine the preferences of a single consumer, Elizabeth, who is choosing between hamburgers and tacos. To represent her tastes, we need some data on her likes and dislikes. Suppose we can ask Elizabeth questions about her preferences among various *bundles* of hamburgers and tacos, where a bundle is just a particular combination of the two commodities. For example, in Figure 2.2, weekly consumption of hamburgers is measured on the horizontal axis, and consumption of tacos on the vertical. Bundle a consists of 3 hamburgers and 2 tacos, and bundle b consists of 4 hamburgers and 1 taco. We might, then, ask Elizabeth whether she prefers a to b, b to a, or regards the two bundles as equivalent.

To begin, we specify that consumer tastes satisfy three assumptions.

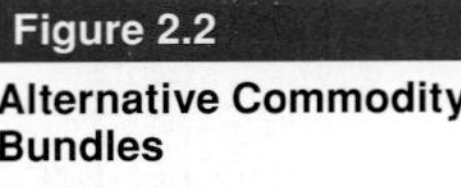

Figure 2.2

Alternative Commodity Bundles

Each point represents a bundle of the commodities. Bundle *a* has 3 hamburgers and 2 tacos; bundle *b* has 4 hamburgers and 1 taco; bundle *f* has 4 hamburgers and 3½ tacos.

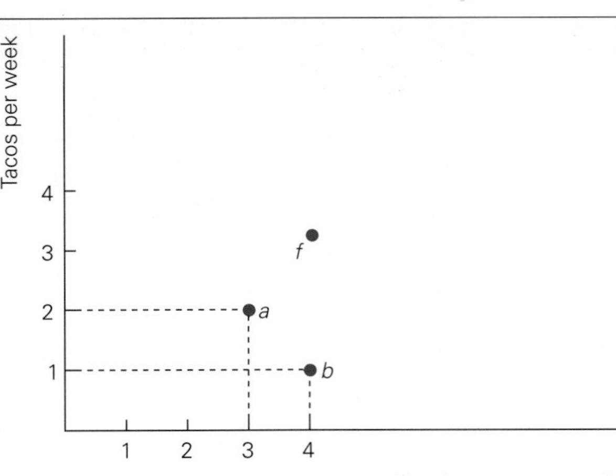

Assumption 1 (Completeness)

When confronted with any two bundles, the consumer can tell us which one she prefers, or whether she is indifferent between them. This is called the **completeness assumption.**

completeness assumption
A consumer, when confronted with any two bundles, can tell us which one she prefers, or whether she is indifferent between them.

If a consumer cannot tell us whether one bundle is preferred to another, then we can hardly be expected to predict which bundle she will choose under varying circumstances. Hence, if consumer preferences are not "complete," we have no hope of constructing a theory of consumer choice.

Suppose Elizabeth's preferences are complete, so we can imagine asking her to rank all conceivable combinations of the various goods. While any set of rankings is possible, some are inconsistent with what is conventionally thought of as rationality. The following assumption rules out a certain type of inconsistency.

Assumption 2 (Transitivity)

Preferences among various bundles are consistent in the sense that if bundle *x* is preferred to bundle *y*, and bundle *y* is preferred to bundle *z*, then *x* is preferred to *z*. This is the **transitivity assumption.** For example, if spending the afternoon water skiing is preferred to watching soap operas, and watching soap operas is preferred to bowling, then water skiing is also preferred to bowling. Transitivity guarantees that consumer preferences will be consistent.

transitivity assumption
Preferences are such that if bundle *x* is preferred to bundle *y*, and bundle *y* is preferred to bundle *z*, then *x* is preferred to *z*.

Our third assumption is often sensible to impose on consumer preferences although, as we shall see, there are important exceptions.

Assumption 3 (Nonsatiation)

For all feasible quantities of the commodities, the consumer is never satiated. A bundle with more of either commodity is always preferred to a bundle with less. This property is referred to as **nonsatiation.**

nonsatiation assumption
More is better.

An irreverent description of the nonsatiation assumption is the "pig principle"—if some is good, more is better. The assumption has a neat graphical interpretation. Consider Figure 2.3. According to the nonsatiation assumption, bundle *c* is preferred to bundle *d*, because *c* has more of both hamburgers and

Figure 2.3

Ranking Commodity Bundles

According to the assumption of nonsatiation, bundles *c* and *f* are preferred to *d*; while *d* is preferred to *g* and *h*.

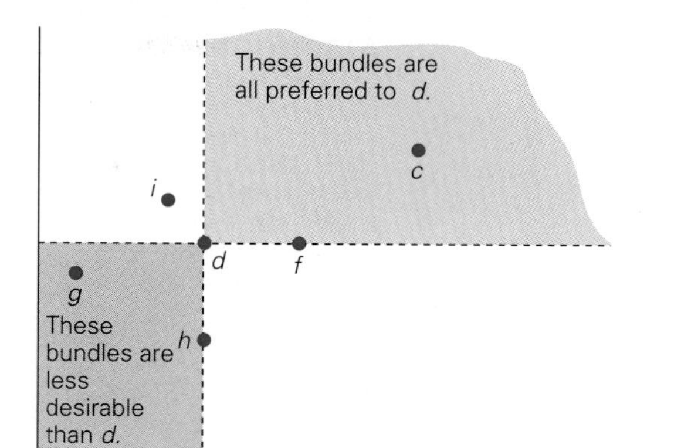

tacos. Bundle *f* has more hamburgers than bundle *d* and no fewer tacos; therefore, *f* is also preferred to *d*. Indeed, any point to the northeast of bundle *d* is preferred to *d*.

The same reasoning suggests that bundle *d* is preferred to bundle *g*, because *g* has fewer hamburgers and fewer tacos than *d*. Bundle *h* is also less desirable than *d*, because although it has the same number of hamburgers as *d*, it has fewer tacos. Point *d* is preferred to any point southwest of it.

Nonsatiation is less "fundamental" than completeness and transitivity because rational consumers may become satiated with some goods after a point. While you might prefer 3 rock concerts a month to 2 rock concerts, 50 concerts might not be better. There is nothing "irrational" about getting tired of rock concerts after some point, but if you do, then your preferences for them do not satisfy the nonsatiation assumption. Nevertheless, it is often convenient to assume that preferences for all commodities satisfy nonsatiation; we will explore later what happens when this is not the case. (PC 2.1)

2.1 PROGRESS CHECK

A computer "hacker" is offered a choice between 10 floppy disks and 5 software manuals, or 9 floppy disks and 20 software manuals. All you know about the hacker is that her preferences satisfy our three assumptions. On the basis of this information alone, can you predict which bundle she will choose?

DERIVING AN INDIFFERENCE CURVE

Let's assume Elizabeth's tastes for hamburgers and tacos satisfy completeness, transitivity, and nonsatiation. We can imagine asking her a series of questions concerning her preferences among consumption bundles and then summarizing this information in a table. But such a table would be very, very long, and quite inconvenient to use. Fortunately, there is a simple graphical way to depict a consumer's preferences.

Recall from Figure 2.3 that the assumption of nonsatiation *by itself* allows us to identify some bundles that Elizabeth ranks above and below any arbitrarily

Figure 2.4

An Indifference Curve

The indifference curve U_1 is generated by connecting bundles of the commodities among which the consumer is indifferent. Bundle *n*, which lies above indifference curve U_1, is preferred to any bundle on U_1.

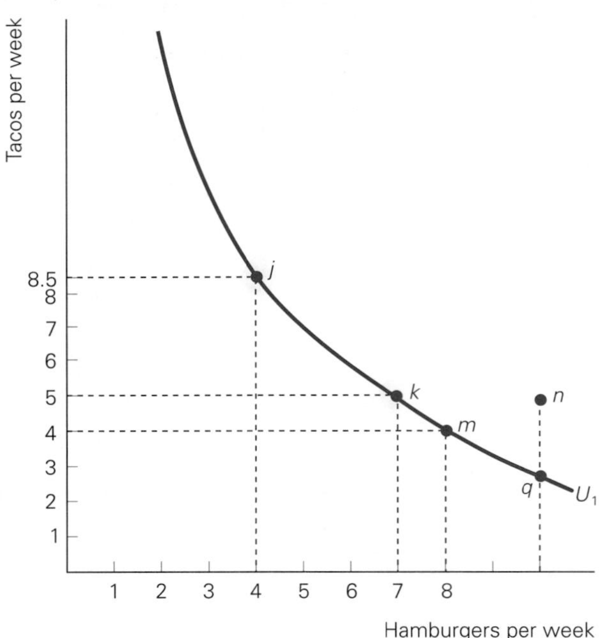

selected bundle. Can we find some bundles that she views as being exactly equivalent to some arbitrarily selected bundle? To do so, we need to ask Elizabeth more questions. Consider bundle *k* in Figure 2.4, which consists of 7 hamburgers and 5 tacos per week. Imagine posing the following question to Elizabeth: "If you were consuming bundle *k*, and I took away three hamburgers, how many tacos would I need to give you to make you *just* as satisfied as you were initially?" Suppose Elizabeth (honestly) answers that she would require 3½ more tacos. Then by definition, she is indifferent between the bundle consisting of 4 hamburgers and 8½ tacos and the original bundle *k*. This bundle is denoted *j* in Figure 2.4.

We could find another such bundle by asking: "Starting again at point *k*, suppose we take away 1 taco. How many hamburgers would we have to give you to keep you as well off as you were originally?" If the answer is 1 hamburger, then Elizabeth is also indifferent between the bundle with 8 hamburgers and 4 tacos (denoted *m* in Figure 2.4) and the initial bundle, *k*.

We could go on like this indefinitely—start at point *k*, take away various amounts of one commodity, find out the amount of the other commodity required for compensation, and record the results on Figure 2.4. Assuming that fractions of units of the commodities can be consumed, the outcome is the curve U_1, which shows all bundles among which the consumer is indifferent. Hence, U_1 is referred to as an **indifference curve.** Note that the indifference curve divides all the bundles into three categories: those that are equivalent to point *k* (on U_1); those that are better than point *k* (above U_1); and those that are inferior to point *k* (below U_1). How do we know that any point above U_1 is preferred to *k*? Consider bundle *n*, which is above U_1. The assumption of nonsatiation tells us that *n* is preferred to bundle *q*, because *n* has more tacos and no fewer hamburg-

indifference curve
The set of all bundles among which a consumer is indifferent.

Figure 2.5

With Nonsatiation, an Indifference Curve Cannot Slope Upward

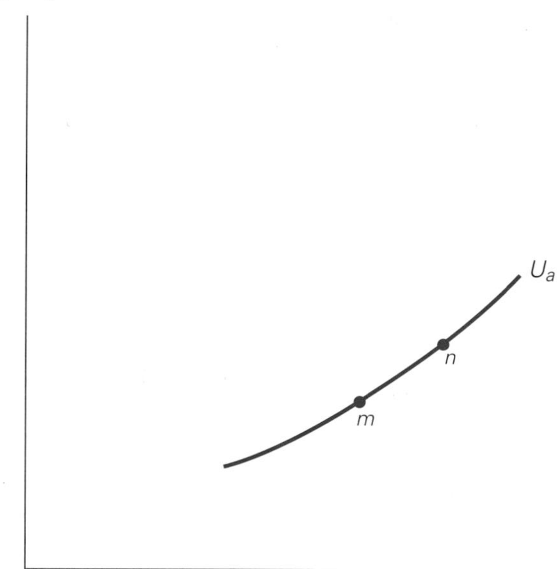

The upward-sloping indifference curve U_a violates the assumption of nonsatiation.

Figure 2.6

Diminishing Marginal Rate of Substitution

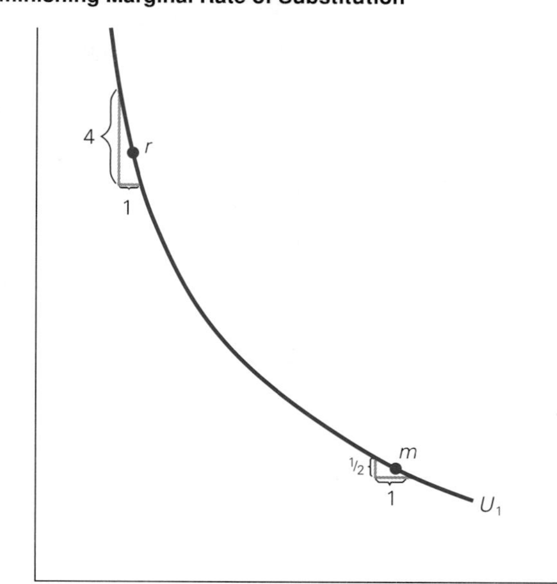

The negative of the slope of the indifference curve is the marginal rate of substitution. Indifference curve U_1 exhibits a diminishing marginal rate of substitution: the negative of the slope around bundle *m* (½) is less than the negative of the slope around *r* (4).

ers than *q*. But by transitivity, if *n* is preferred to *q*, it must also be preferred to any other bundle on U_1, because Elizabeth views all bundles on U_1 as equivalent. Using similar arguments, it is easy to show that any bundle below U_1 is inferior to any bundle that is on U_1.

Now let's examine the shape of the indifference curve more carefully. The *slope* of any curve is the change in the value of the variable measured on the vertical axis divided by the change in the variable measured on the horizontal—the "rise over the run." The slope of U_1 is negative. That is, whenever the number of hamburgers increases, the number of tacos decreases. The fact that the indifference curve slopes downward is no accident—it must if nonsatiation holds. To see why, consider Figure 2.5, which shows an upward-sloping indifference curve. Two points on the curve are marked *m* and *n*. According to the definition of indifference curve, the consumer must be indifferent between *m* and *n*. But by the assumption of nonsatiation, *n* must be preferred to *m*. A person cannot simultaneously be indifferent between two bundles *and* prefer one to the other. Thus, as long as nonsatiation holds, an indifference curve must slope downward.

marginal rate of substitution
(*MRS*) The negative of the slope of an indifference curve; it measures the rate at which the consumer is willing to trade one good for the other.

The slope of an indifference curve has an important economic interpretation. It shows the rate at which the consumer is willing to trade one good for another. For example, around bundle *r* in Figure 2.6, the slope of the indifference curve is −4. But by the definition of an indifference curve, 4 is just the number of tacos

2.2 PROGRESS CHECK

At point g in the accompanying diagram, Louise is purchasing 150 Russian novels and 30 comic books. She would be willing to reduce her consumption of Russian novels by 3 if she were given 2 more comic books. Around point g on Louise's indifference curve U_l, what is her marginal rate of substitution of Russian novels for comic books?

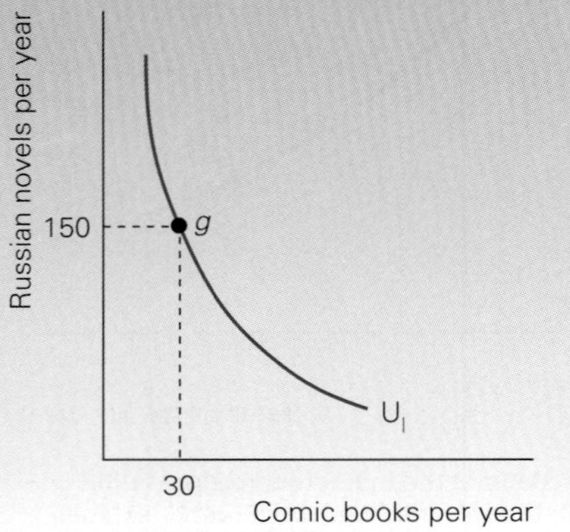

that Elizabeth is willing to substitute for one hamburger. For this reason, the negative of the slope of the indifference curve, at any particular point, is referred to as the **marginal rate of substitution** of tacos for hamburgers, abbreviated MRS_{th}. What is the word *marginal* doing there? In economics, marginal generally means "additional" or "incremental." The indifference curve's slope is the marginal rate of substitution because it indicates the rate at which the consumer would be willing to substitute tacos for *one additional* hamburger, and still be as happy as she was before.

We now add to the three assumptions at the beginning of this chapter a fourth assumption relating to the shape of indifference curves:

Assumption 4 (Diminishing Marginal Rate of Substitution)

As drawn in Figure 2.6, the marginal rate of substitution declines as we move down the indifference curve. Around point m, for example, MRS_{th} is ½, which is smaller than its value of 4 around point r. Introspection suggests that this is reasonable. Around bundle r, Elizabeth has a lot of tacos relative to hamburgers, and is therefore willing to give up quite a few tacos in return for an additional hamburger—hence a high MRS_{th}. On the other hand, around point m, Elizabeth has a lot of hamburgers relative to tacos, so she is not willing to sacrifice many tacos in return for yet another hamburger. The decline of MRS_{th} as we move down along an indifference curve, which we will generally assume, is called a **diminishing marginal rate of substitution.** Note that an indifference curve with a diminishing marginal rate of substitution is bowed inward. In mathematical terms, this shape is called *convex to the origin*. (PC 2.2)

diminishing marginal rate of substitution
When the marginal rate of substitution falls as we move down along an indifference curve.

DERIVING AN INDIFFERENCE MAP

Recall that our construction of indifference curve U_1 in Figure 2.4 was based upon bundle k as a starting point. But bundle k was chosen arbitrarily and we could just as well have started at any other point. If we start with point c in Figure 2.7 and proceed in the same way, we generate indifference curve U_2. Or starting at point d, we generate indifference curve U_0. In short, an indifference curve can be drawn through each point in the quadrant. The entire collection of indifference curves is referred to as the **indifference map.** The indifference map tell us everything there is to know about the individual's preferences. Figure 2.7 indicates that Elizabeth prefers any bundle on U_2 to any point on U_1. Why? Recall that, given nonsatiation, any bundle that lies above indifference curve U_1 is preferred to any point on U_1. Thus, point c is preferred to any point on U_1. But by the definition of an indifference curve, all bundles on U_2 are equivalent to c. Hence, all bundles on U_2 are superior to all bundles on U_1. Exactly the same logic suggests that Elizabeth prefers any bundle on U_1 to any bundle on U_0. We conclude that if Elizabeth wants to make herself as well off as possible, she will seek to consume a bundle on the highest indifference curve that she can.

indifference map
The entire collection of indifference curves.

Figure 2.7

An Indifference Map

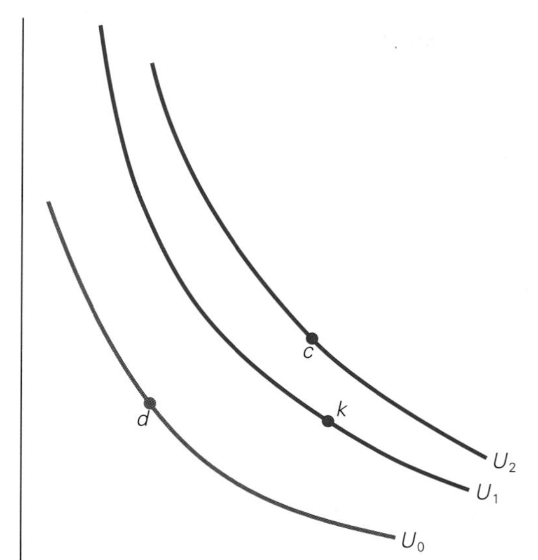

An indifference curve can be drawn through any point. The collection of indifference curves is referred to as the indifference map.

Figure 2.8

Indifference Curves Cannot Cross

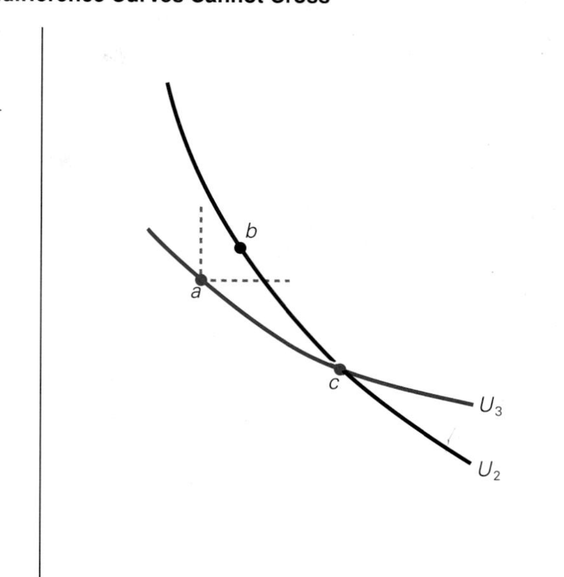

Indifference curves cannot intersect. Intersecting indifference curves would lead to the outcome that *b* is equivalent to *a* and simultaneously *b* is preferred to *a*. This violates the assumption of transitivity.

Figure 2.7 raises an interesting question. Given that many indifference curves inhabit the same quadrant, can they intersect? As long as our assumptions about preferences hold, the answer is a definite no. To demonstrate this, consider Figure 2.8, which shows an indifference curve U_3 intersecting with indifference curve U_2 at bundle *c*. Because bundles *a* and *c* are on the indifference curve U_3, by definition the consumer is indifferent between *a* and *c*. Similarly, because *b* and *c* both lie on indifference curve U_2, bundle *b* is regarded as equivalent to bundle *c*. Since Elizabeth's preferences are transitive, it follows that she is indifferent between *a* and *b*. But note that *a* contains less of both hamburgers and tacos than *b*. According to the assumption of nonsatiation, *b* is preferred to *a*. Thus, a contradiction emerges—*a* cannot simultaneously be worse than *b* and equivalent to *b*. Hence, we conclude that ***intersecting indifference curves are inconsistent with our model of consumer preferences.***

Because a person's indifference curves cannot intersect, you might conclude that they have to be "parallel." However, this need not be the case. The indifference curves in Figure 2.9 are perfectly legitimate, even though they are not parallel. Remember from geometry that in theory lines have no width. Hence, indifference curves can get closer and closer to each other, yet still never intersect.

Figure 2.9

Indifference Curves Don't Have to Be "Parallel"

Although indifference curves cannot intersect, they need not be "parallel." They can get closer and closer to each other.

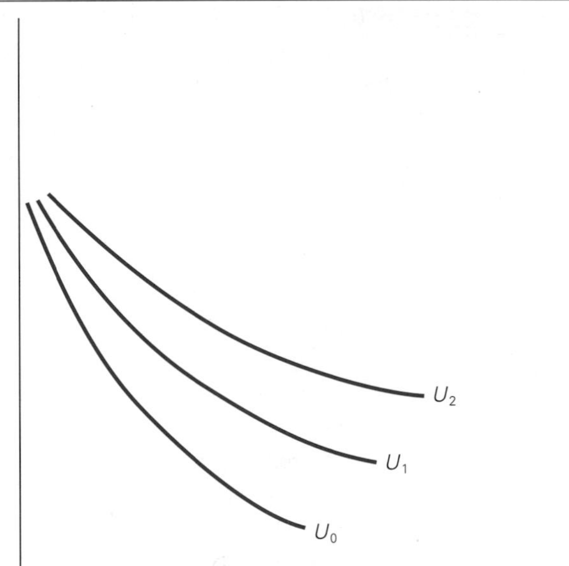

Figure 2.10

Properties of "Typical" Convex Indifference Curves

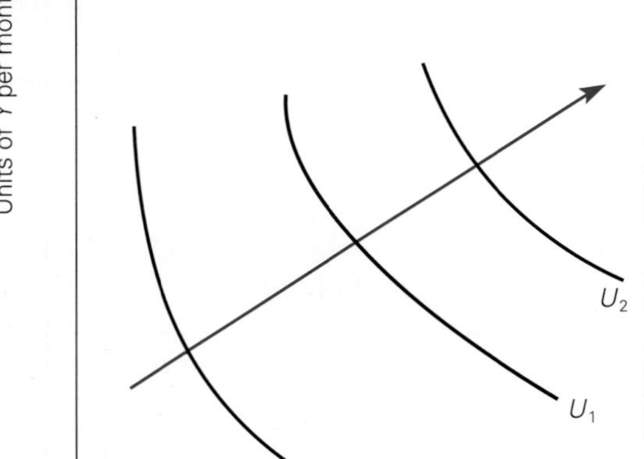

1. Negative Slope
2. Marginal Rate of Substitution (MRS_{YX}) = negative of slope
3. Diminishing MRS_{YX}
4. Indifference curves lying to the northeast represent higher levels of satisfaction
5. Indifference curves cannot cross

Summary of Properties of Indifference Curves

Convex indifference curves such as those exhibited in Figure 2.7 play a key role in analyzing consumer choice. For purposes of easy reference, Figure 2.10 summarizes the essential properties of such indifference curves.

OTHER TYPES OF INDIFFERENCE CURVES

The indifference curves in Figure 2.7 were based on the assumptions of nonsatiation and diminishing marginal rate of substitution. In some situations these assumptions are inappropriate. But when you change the assumptions, you may change the shapes of the indifference curves. This section provides a few examples.

Perfect Substitutes

Philip is choosing between two commodities, Alcoa aluminum foil and a generic brand of aluminum foil produced by his local grocery store. As far as Philip is concerned, 1 square foot of Alcoa foil is exactly equivalent to 2 square feet of the generic brand—any wrapping job that can be done with 1 square foot of Alcoa requires 2 square feet of the generic brand if the job is to be done as well. Thus, Philip is always willing to trade Alcoa for the generic brand at a rate of 2 square feet of generic for each square foot of Alcoa. In terms of our jargon, the marginal rate of substitution of generic for Alcoa foil is an unchanging 2 to 1. What do the indifference curves between Alcoa and generic foil look like? Recall that the negative of the slope of the indifference curve is the marginal rate of substitution. Since the marginal rate of substitution is always 2 to 1, the slope must always be -2. But a "curve" with an unchanging slope is a straight line. Hence, the indifference map consists of a set of straight lines with slopes of -2 (see Figure 2.11). Goods that can be substituted for each other at a constant rate are called **perfect substitutes.** In short, perfect substitutes have a constant marginal rate of substitution, so their indifference curves are straight lines.

perfect substitutes
Goods that can be substituted for each other at a constant rate, that is, that have a constant marginal rate of substitution.

Perfect Complements

Charles eats vanilla ice cream and Oreo cookies only together, and then only if they are mixed in a fixed ratio of 1 pint of ice cream to 3 crushed Oreos. Suppose that Charles is currently consuming bundle *a* in Figure 2.12, which consists of 2 pints of ice cream and 6 cookies. You now offer him a third pint of ice cream, bundle *b*. Charles is likely to respond along these lines: "Thanks very much, but without 3 Oreos to go with it, an additional pint of ice cream really doesn't do me any good. Given my tastes, I can derive benefit from an additional pint of ice cream only if it is accompanied by 3 more Oreos."

Charles's preferences violate the assumption of nonsatiation. In effect, given that he has ice cream and Oreos in a ratio of 1 to 3, Charles is "satiated" with ice cream, unless he receives just the right quantity of Oreos to accompany the ice cream. Because bundle *b* makes Charles no better off, by definition it lies on the same indifference curve as *a*. Similarly, points that are 2, 3, and more units to the right of *a* are on the same indifference curve. In the same way, Charles views bundles that are directly above point *a* (which represent more Oreos without more ice cream) as equivalent to *a*. Connecting up all of these points yields the right angle indifference curve labeled U_1. The only way to get to a higher indifference curve is to receive more ice cream *and* more Oreos. For example, the move from *a* to *c* raises Charles to a higher indifference curve, U_2.

Figure 2.11

Perfect Substitutes

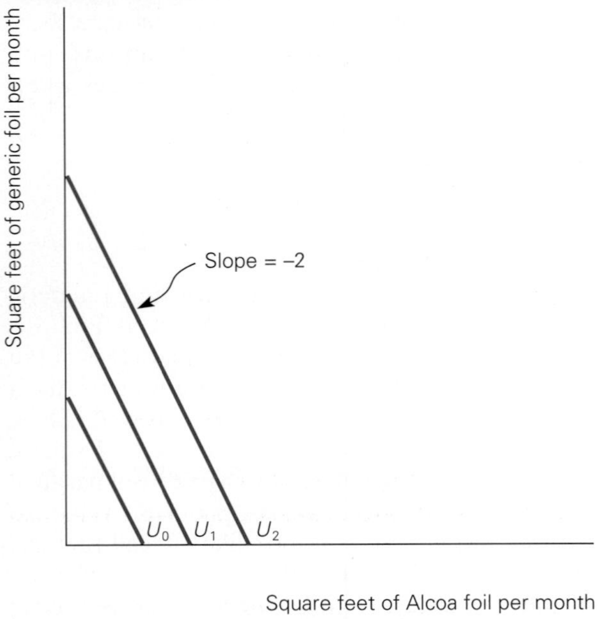

Square feet of generic foil per month

Slope = −2

U_0 U_1 U_2

Square feet of Alcoa foil per month

The indifference map for perfect substitutes consists of a series of parallel straight lines, because the marginal rate of substitution is constant as we move along the indifference curve. In this particular case, the marginal rate of substitution is 2, because the consumer is always willing to substitute 2 square feet of generic foil for 1 square foot of Alcoa foil.

Figure 2.12

Perfect Complements

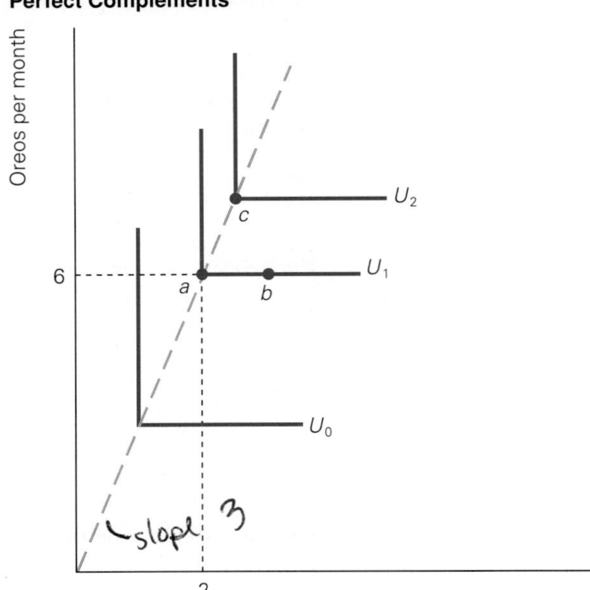

Perfect complements have to be consumed in a fixed proportion. The indifference curves for perfect complements are right angles. Because Oreos and pints of ice cream must be consumed in a ratio of 3 to 1, the right angles lie along a ray from the origin whose slope is 3.

perfect complements Goods that have to be consumed in fixed proportions.

Goods that have to be consumed in fixed proportions are referred to as **perfect complements.** The indifference map for a pair of perfect complements is a series of right angles. The right angles are placed on a ray from the origin whose slope is the ratio in which the goods are consumed. (PC 2.3)

"Bads"

Our examples so far have concerned commodities that are economic "goods": When more of the commodity is given to an individual, it either makes him better off or no worse off. But we also consume many things that we don't like very much at all, even though we might not think of these things as "commodities." Polluted air is a prominent example of such a "bad." How do we model preferences when one of the commodities is a "bad"?

Think about the dilemma that faced the town of Tacoma, Washington, several years ago. The U.S. Environmental Protection Agency asked the town to decide whether it would prefer to close a copper smelter that provided 800 jobs or accept some risk of cancer from arsenic in the air that the smelter generated. We can think of the mayor of Tacoma as having to choose amounts of two com-

2.3 PROGRESS CHECK

Consider a diagram with the quantity of nickels measured on the horizontal axis, and the quantity of dimes on the vertical. Assuming that the weight of the coins is of no importance to the individual, sketch an indifference map for these two "commodities."

Figure 2.13

Indifference Curves with a "Bad"

When one of the commodities is a "bad," such as pollution, the assumption of nonsatiation is violated, and the indifference curves slope upward. The curvature of the indifference curves suggests that, incrementally, the more pollution that this individual consumes, the more he dislikes it.

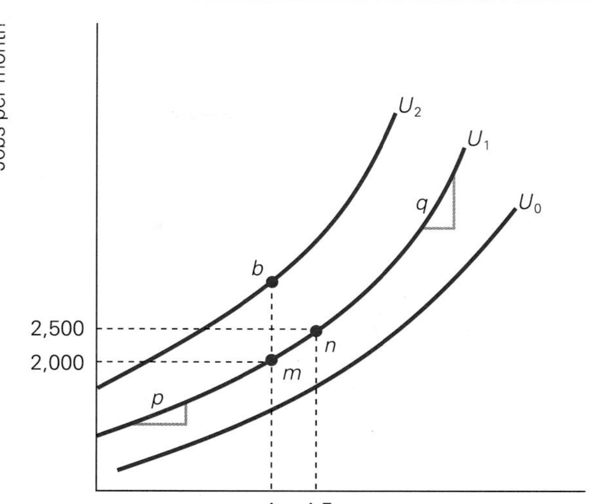

modities, one that makes him feel better off (*jobs*) and one that decreases his welfare (*pollution*).

To draw the indifference map between jobs and pollution, the first thing to realize is that tastes for pollution do *not* satisfy the assumption of nonsatiation. Other things being the same, more pollution is always worse, not better. Hence, unlike the indifference curves between two goods, the indifference curves between jobs and pollution slope upward. To see why, consider Figure 2.13, which has units of air pollution (measured in terms of the concentration of arsenic) on the horizontal axis and number of jobs on the vertical. Suppose that the current bundle is *n*, which consists of breathing air with 4.5 parts per million of arsenic and 2,500 jobs. Now pose the following question: "We are thinking of closing down your smelter. As a consequence, the concentration of arsenic will fall to 4 parts per million. How many jobs would you be willing to give up in return for the cleaner air?" The mayor replies that he would be willing to accept a loss of 500 jobs. Hence, by definition, the bundle consisting of 2,000 jobs and 4 parts per million of arsenic, denoted by *m*, lies on the same indifference curve as bundle *n*. As before, one could ask a series of questions to determine how many jobs the mayor would require to compensate him for enduring various quantities of pollution. Connecting all of the bundles generated in this way yields the upward sloping indifference curve U_1.

As usual, the slope of U_1 measures the rate at which the individual is willing to trade one commodity for the other. In Figure 2.13, as we move up along U_1, its slope increases. To understand the significance of this, observe that around bundle *p*, where there is a relatively low amount of pollution, the mayor does not require many jobs to compensate him for accepting more pollution. But at point *q*, where the concentration of arsenic is relatively high, he requires quite a few jobs to compensate him for accepting yet more pollution. In short, the shape of U_1 in Figure 2.13 suggests that incrementally, the more pollution that the mayor consumes, the more he dislikes it.

Just as before, we can draw an entire indifference map to represent preferences between jobs and pollution. In Figure 2.13, U_0 and U_2 are two other indifference curves in the mayor's indifference map. Which curve would the mayor prefer, U_0 or U_2? Bundle b on U_2 has more jobs than bundle m, and no more pollution. Hence, b is preferred to m. But using the definition of indifference curve and appealing to the assumption of transitivity, this means that every point on U_2 is preferred to every point on U_1. A similar argument indicates that the mayor would rather be on U_1 than U_0.

Another important example of upward-sloping indifference curves occurs in the theory of finance. When people are selecting a stock in which to invest, they generally like the rate of return to be as high as possible. On the other hand, people generally prefer less risky to more risky investments. In effect, return is a "good" and risk is a "bad." Hence, in a graph with return on the vertical axis and risk on the horizontal axis, an individual's indifference map would look like the one in Figure 2.13. To help a client select a stock, the stockbroker needs to find out how much the client is willing to trade off risk for return; that is, the broker needs to know the client's marginal rate of substitution between risk and return.

UTILITY THEORY: ASSIGNING NUMBERS TO INDIFFERENCE CURVES

An important feature of our theory of consumer preferences is that it never requires us to attach to various commodity bundles numerical measures of how much satisfaction they give. All we need is information of the type, "bundle a is preferred to bundle b"; *not* "bundle a is three times as good as bundle b."

Nevertheless, the ability to attach numerical "scores" to each bundle can be very convenient, particularly when dealing with problems in which the consumer makes choices involving a lot of goods. In a two-good case, keeping track of the rankings among all possible bundles in a diagram is relatively easy. For 50, 100, or 1,000 goods, however, it is cumbersome to keep track of the rankings of the various bundles this way. A more convenient way to summarize this information is to assign each commodity bundle a number that indicates how much satisfaction it creates. If bundle a has a higher score than bundle b, this means that the consumer prefers a to b. If a has the same score as c, the consumer is indifferent between a and c. The numerical score associated with each commodity bundle is called its **total utility.** A **utility function** is a formula that shows the total utility associated with each bundle. Algebraically, suppose that the individual consumes n goods, in quantities $x_1, x_2, x_3, \ldots, x_n$. The utility function, $U(x_1, x_2, x_3, \ldots, x_n)$, tells us the amounts of total utility associated with various quantities of each of the goods. Sometimes a bundle's utility score is called its number of *utils.*

total utility
The total satisfaction, sometimes given by a numerical score, of consuming a particular commodity bundle.

utility function
A formula showing the total utility associated with each commodity bundle.

Suppose, for example, that Elizabeth's utility function for hamburgers (x) and tacos (y) is $2x + \sqrt{y}$. This means that a bundle consisting of 4 hamburgers and 9 tacos is associated with a utility of 11 utils ($= 2 \times 4 + \sqrt{9}$). A bundle consisting of 3.5 hamburgers and 16 tacos also has 11 utils ($= 2 \times 3.5 + \sqrt{16}$), and hence, Elizabeth is indifferent between it and a bundle with $x = 4$ and $y = 9$. On the other hand, a bundle with $x = 5$ and $y = 8$ is preferred to either of these bundles, because its utility is 12.8 ($= 2 \times 5 + \sqrt{8}$).

How does utility relate to indifference curves? Consider points m and n in Figure 2.14, which lie on the same indifference curve, U_1. Suppose that the utility associated with bundle m is 80. Then, by definition of indifference curve, every bundle on U_1 produces a utility of 80. It is therefore natural to associate

Figure 2.14

Ordinal Utility Numbers

A utility function allows us to associate a certain amount of utility with each indifference curve. Indifference curves farther to the northeast have higher levels of utility.

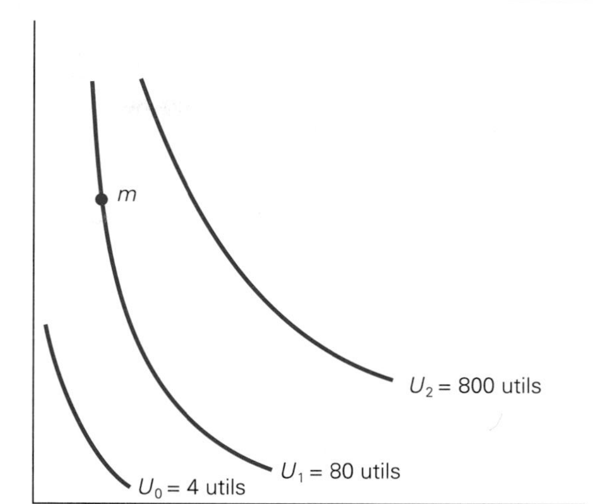

indifference curve U_1 with the number 80. Indifference curves to the northeast of U_1 are preferred to U_1; hence, they must have higher utility levels than 80. For example, indifference curve U_2 might have a utility index of 800. Bundles on indifference curves below U_1 are associated with lower levels of utility, such as U_0, which has a utility of 4.

The interpretation of utility numbers requires extreme care. The fact that U_2 has a score of 800 utils and U_1 has a score of 80 utils does not mean that bundles on U_2 are 10 times as good as bundles on U_1. These numbers tell us that U_2 is better than U_1, but not by how much. Think of it this way: When you know that Runner I was first in a marathon race and Runner II was second, all this tells you is that II was slower than I. It does not tell you that II took twice as long. In the same way, utility numbers only indicate the ranks of various bundles, not precisely how they are valued relative to each other. Numbers such as "first," "second," and "third," which provide only information on orderings, are referred to as *ordinal numbers.* Therefore, the utility function that gives rise to the indifference curves in Figure 2.14 is referred to as an **ordinal utility function.** Just because an ordinal utility function allows us to associate a certain number of utils with each bundle does *not* mean that we can objectively measure "happiness." Such an interpretation is ruled out because the utils are only ordinal numbers.

ordinal utility function
A utility function allowing the ranking of bundles by their amount of utility, but not precise comparisons of how various bundles are valued relative to each other.

Ordinal versus Cardinal Utility

Can ordinal utility numbers be used to compare the welfares of two different individuals? Superficially, the answer might appear to be yes. All you need to do is compare their utility levels. If, for example, Elizabeth has more utils than Philip, then she is happier than he is.

Unfortunately, this reasoning is totally incorrect, because it ignores the essential arbitrariness of ordinal utility numbers. Because Elizabeth's utility numbers are ordinal, we can transform them in any fashion we choose, as long as we keep the ordering of the indifference curves intact. For example, we could say that utility at U_0 is 5 utils; at U_1 931 utils; and at U_2 4,028 utils. But if we can arbitrarily characterize Elizabeth's utility level as 13.2 utils, or 38 trillion utils, what sense does it make to compare this number to the (equally arbitrary) level of utility attained by Philip?

Lurking behind this technical discussion is a simple intuitive proposition—there is no scientific way to compare the amounts of happiness that different people derive from consuming various commodities. As the British economist Lionel Robbins noted:

> Suppose that A and B fall into conversation about their respective enjoyments and A says to B, "Of course, I get more satisfaction than you out of music," and B vigorously asserts the contrary. Needless to say, you and I as outsiders can form our own judgments. But these are essentially subjective, not objectively ascertainable fact. There is no available way in which we can measure and compare the satisfactions which A and B derive from music. Intelligent talk? But that may be misleading. Facial expression? That too may be deceptive . . . We are left with the ultimate difficulty of interpersonal comparisons. (quoted in Rappoport 1988, 86)

In short, our theory of consumer choice does *not* allow us to make interpersonal comparisons of utility.

If, however, we are willing to make different assumptions on the nature of the utility function, then such comparisons are possible. In particular, assume that a bundle that creates 40 utils is not merely "better" than a bundle with 10 utils, it is precisely four times as good. More generally, assume that the utility numbers assigned to bundles tell you exactly how much happier one bundle makes the consumer than another bundle. Now, numbers like "one," "two," and "three" (as opposed to "first," "second," and "third"), tell us that "three" is exactly three times the size of "one," and the absolute difference between them is two. Such numbers are referred to as *cardinal numbers.* Therefore, utility functions whose values tell us exactly how much better some bundles are than other bundles are called **cardinal utility functions.** Unlike an ordinal utility function, you cannot arbitrarily double or triple the values of a cardinal utility function. Therefore, *if* utility functions are cardinal and *if* people have the same utility functions, then people's utilities can be compared.

cardinal utility function The values of the utility function tell us exactly how much better some commodity bundles are than other bundles.

We have just noted, however, that there is no way to establish whether individuals derive the same amount of satisfaction from consuming the same commodity bundle. In effect, the assumption of identical cardinal utility functions is fundamentally untestable. The remainder of our discussion of consumer theory will therefore assume that utility functions are ordinal.

SECTION RECAP

Understanding individual decision making requires a model of consumer tastes. This section has provided such a model. The model assumes that people can rank all sets of bundles and that these rankings are consistent. Where the choice is between two commodities, consumer preferences can be represented graphically by indifference curves. Indifference curves are a versatile tool. They can be used to represent many different types of preferences. Commodities can be complements or substitutes, subject to an increasing or decreasing marginal rate of substitution, and they may be "goods" or "bads." Ordinal utility functions allow us to assign numerical scores to each commodity bundle. These scores do not measure the amount of happiness associated with each bundle; they only rank the bundles relative to each other.

2.3 BUDGET CONSTRAINTS

We have now completed the first step in Figure 2.1—modeling tastes. The indifference map or utility function represents what the consumer *wants* to do in the sense of telling us which bundles are preferred to others. In this section, we proceed to the second step, the budget constraint, which shows what the individual *can* do.

PRICE-TAKING CONSUMERS

Let's return to Elizabeth, a consumer of hamburgers and tacos. Suppose Elizabeth has a weekly food budget of $60, all of which she spends on hamburgers and tacos. (Later we will discuss what happens when she can save some of her income.) Suppose further that each taco costs $3, each hamburger costs $6, and Elizabeth's purchases of hamburgers and tacos will not cause their price to change. A consumer in this situation is said to be a **price taker**—the consumer has no control over the prices she faces, in the sense that the price of each unit is not affected by the number of units she purchases.

price taker
A consumer whose price per unit of a commodity is not affected by the number of units purchased.

What are Elizabeth's options? Given our assumptions, Elizabeth's hamburger expenditure and taco expenditure must sum to exactly $60. Her expenditure on hamburgers is the price of hamburger ($6) times the number of hamburgers she buys. Letting x denote the number of hamburgers Elizabeth consumes, her hamburger expenditure is $\$6x$. Similarly, if y denotes the number of tacos, her taco expenditure is $\$3y$. Since Elizabeth's total expenditure is $60, this means that if she spends her entire income, Elizabeth's purchases must satisfy the equation

$$6x + 3y = 60. \tag{2.1}$$

Thus, for example, if Elizabeth buys 10 tacos, Equation (2.1) tells us that she can only buy 5 hamburgers: $(6 \times 5) + (3 \times 10) = 60$. Alternatively, if her hamburger consumption is 6, then her taco consumption can only be 8: $(6 \times 6) + (3 \times 8) = 60$.

To represent Elizabeth's choices diagrammatically, we must plot several points that satisfy Equation (2.1). This is easy once we recall from basic algebra that this is simply the equation of a straight line. Given two points on the line, the rest of the line is determined by connecting them. In Figure 2.15, point r represents 5 hamburgers and 10 tacos, and point s represents 6 hamburgers and 8 tacos. Therefore, the line associated with Equation (2.1) is B_1, which passes through these points. By construction, any combination of hamburgers and tacos that lies along B_1 satisfies Equation (2.1). Line B_1 is known as the **budget constraint** because it shows how the consumer's income and the prices she faces constrain her choices. Any bundle on or below B_1 (the shaded area) can be purchased because it involves an expenditure less than or equal to income. The collection of bundles that can be purchased is referred to as the **feasible set.** Any point above B_1 is not in the feasible set because it involves an expenditure greater than income.

budget constraint
The representation of the bundles among which a consumer may choose, given her income and the prices she faces.

feasible set
The collection of bundles satisfying the budget constraint.

Two aspects of the budget constraint B_1 are worth noting.

Figure 2.15

Linear Budget Constraint

The budget constraint identifies those bundles that are feasible and those that are infeasible. The slope of the budget constraint shows the rate at which the market permits the individual to trade one commodity for the other. The slope of −2 indicates that the price of the commodity on the horizontal axis is twice the price of the commodity on the vertical axis.

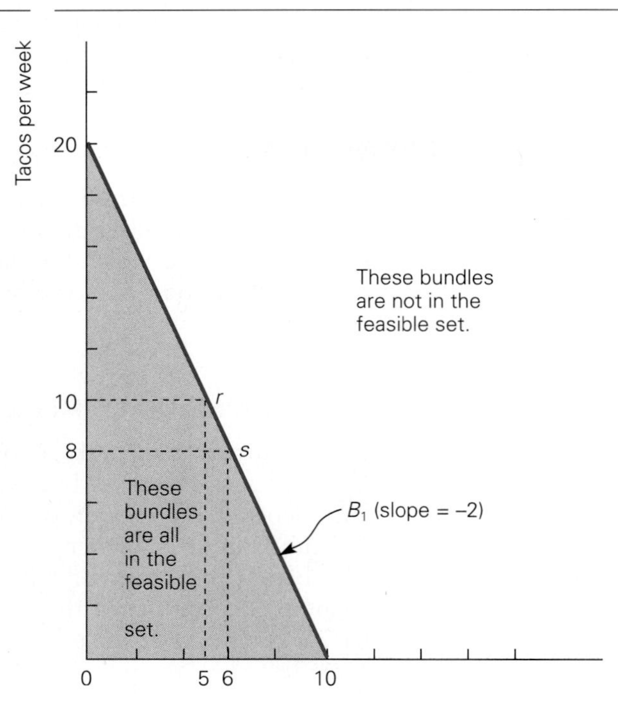

First: The vertical and horizontal intercepts represent bundles in which only one of the commodities is consumed. By definition, the vertical intercept is the point associated with $x = 0$. At this point, Elizabeth spends her entire income of \$60 on tacos, buying 20 of them. (This is just total income of \$60 divided by the price of \$3 per taco.) Similarly, at the horizontal intercept, Elizabeth has no tacos, but can afford 10 hamburgers (= 60/6).

Second: The slope of the budget line has an economic interpretation. To calculate the slope, note that the "rise" is 20 and the "run" is 10, so the slope is −2. Note also that 2 is the ratio of the price per hamburger (\$6) to the price per taco (\$3). This is no accident. The negative of the slope of the budget constraint indicates the rate at which the market permits an individual to substitute one commodity for the other. Because the price of a hamburger is twice the price of a taco, the consumer can trade two tacos for each hamburger. In other words, the slope of the budget constraint shows the opportunity cost of one good in terms of the other—the amount of one good that the consumer gives up when she consumes an additional unit of another good. The fact that the negative of the slope of the budget constraint is 2 indicates that the opportunity cost of 1 hamburger is 2 tacos.

To generalize this discussion, suppose that the price per unit of x is p_x, the price per unit of y is p_y, and income is I. Then, by analogy to Equation (2.1), the budget constraint is

$$p_x \times x + p_y \times y = I. \tag{2.2}$$

If x is measured on the horizontal axis and y on the vertical, then the vertical intercept is total income divided by the price of y, or I/p_y. Similarly, the horizontal intercept is I/p_x. Dividing the rise (I/p_y) by the run (I/p_x), the slope of the budget constraint is $-p_x/p_y$. A common mistake is to assume that because y is measured on the vertical axis, the negative of the slope of the budget constraint is p_y/p_x. However, p_x/p_y is the price of x in terms of y. If p_x goes up, the price of x in terms of y must go up, but only if p_x is in the numerator.

CHANGES IN PRICES AND INCOME

The budget constraint shows the feasible consumption bundles, given current income and the prevailing prices. What if any of these change? Consider again the case where $p_x = 6$, $p_y = 3$, and $I = 60$. The associated budget line, $6x + 3y = 60$, is drawn as B_1 in Figure 2.16. Now suppose that income falls to 30. Substituting into Equation (2.2), the new budget line is described by $6x + 3y = 30$. The vertical intercept of this line is 10 and the horizontal intercept is 5. Connecting these two points, we find that the new budget constraint is line B_0. The slope of B_0 is -2, just like that of B_1, because an income change does not affect p_x/p_y, the opportunity cost of hamburgers in terms of tacos. Because B_1 and B_0 have the same slope, by definition they are parallel.

In summary, *when income changes but relative prices do not, a parallel shift in the budget constraint is induced. If income decreases, the constraint shifts in toward the origin; if income increases, it shifts out from the origin.*

> **2.4 PROGRESS CHECK**
>
> The trustees of a university have allocated \$500,000 for spending on new faculty positions and undergraduate scholarships. Each faculty position costs \$50,000; each scholarship costs \$10,000. The president of the university is trying to decide how to spend the money. (*a*) Write a formula for the president's budget constraint. (*b*) What is the opportunity cost of a faculty position? (*c*) Sketch the constraint and show the feasible set. (*d*) Show what happens to the constraint if the trustees reduce funding to \$300,000. (*e*) Show what happens to the constraint if funding is returned to \$500,000, but the price of a faculty position decreases to \$25,000.

Return again to the original constraint, $6x + 3y = 60$, which is reproduced in Figure 2.17 as B_1. Suppose that the price of a hamburger increases to \$12, but everything else stays the same. By Equation (2.2), the relevant budget constraint is then $12x + 3y = 60$. This new budget constraint has a vertical intercept of 20, which is the same as that of B_1. Because the price of tacos has stayed the same, if Elizabeth spends *all* of her money on tacos, she can buy just as many as she did before. The horizontal intercept, however, is now located at 5 hamburgers (= 60/12). Connecting the two intercepts, we find the new budget constraint is B_3, whose slope is -4. This value reflects the fact that the market now allows people to trade 4 tacos for each hamburger.

More generally, *when the price of one commodity changes and other things stay the same, the budget line moves along the axis of the good whose price changes. If the price goes up, the line pivots in; if the price goes down, the line pivots out.* (PC 2.4)

Summary of Properties of Linear Budget Constraints

Whenever people are price takers, their budget constraints are straight lines. For easy reference, the properties of linear budget constraints are listed in Figure 2.18.

Figure 2.16

Effect of a Change in Income on the Budget Constraint

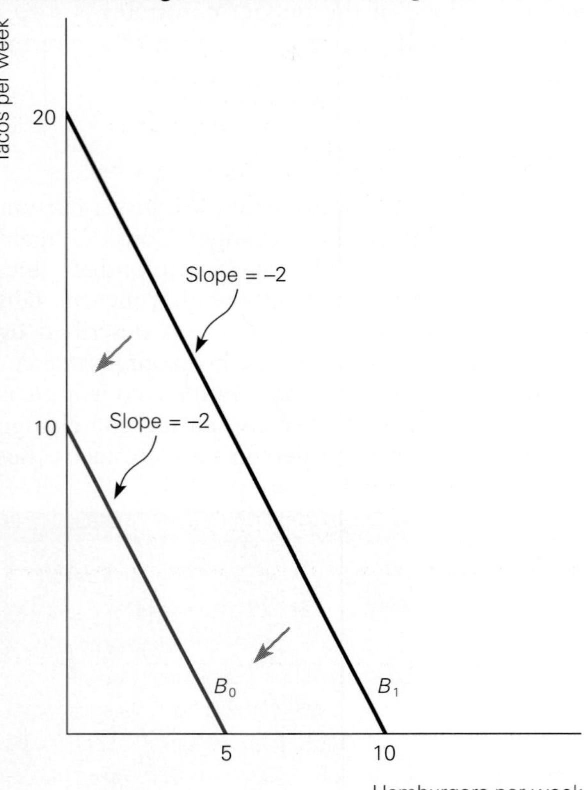

A decrease in income, other things being the same, induces a parallel shift of the budget constraint toward the origin.

Figure 2.17

Effect of a Change in Relative Prices on the Budget Constraint

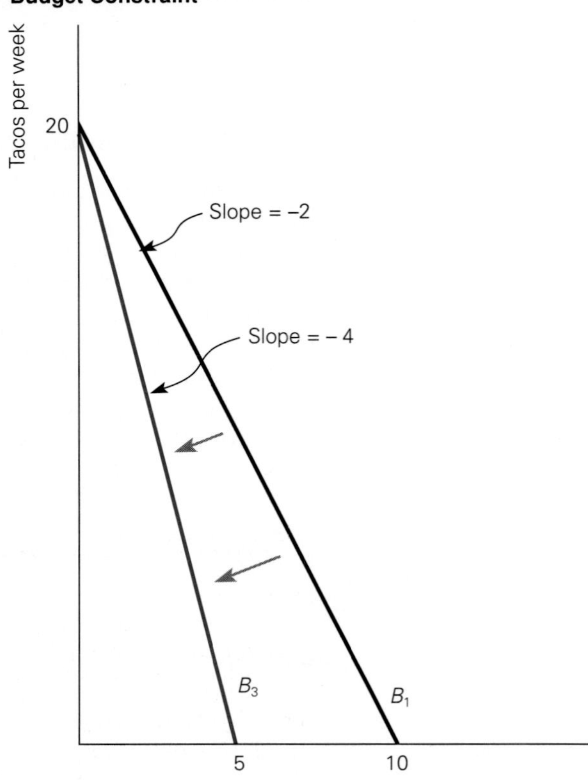

An increase in the price of a commodity moves the budget line in along the axis of the good whose price has increased.

NONLINEAR BUDGET CONSTRAINTS

In the previous section, all of the budget constraints could be represented as straight lines. Linear budget constraints arise from the assumption that the consumer is a price taker—he can purchase all he wants of a commodity at the going price. Although budget constraints often are linear, sometimes they are not. This section provides several examples of nonlinear budget constraints.

Quantity Rationing

In the early 1990s, Moscow's city council instituted cigarette rationing. This scheme allowed each individual to purchase at most 15 packs of cigarettes per month at the official price of about one-third of a ruble per pack.

To analyze the budget constraint associated with quantity rationing, consider Ivan, who has a monthly income of 100 rubles and consumes two commodities: cigarettes and cabbage. The price of cigarettes is 0.33 rubles per pack; the price

Figure 2.18

Properties of Linear Budget Constraints

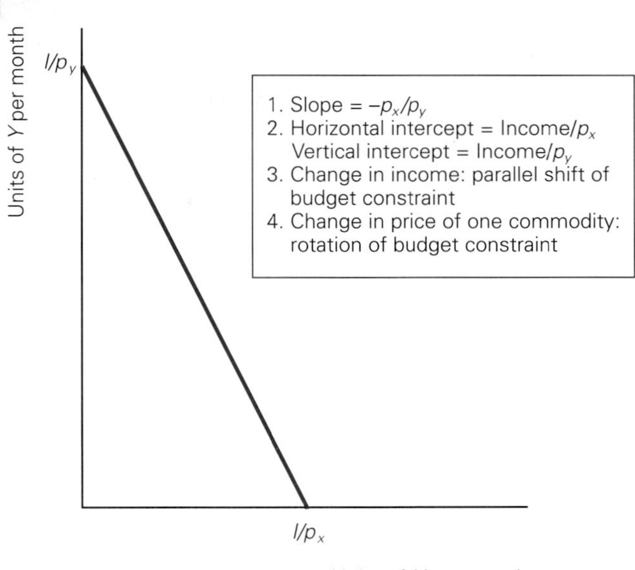

Figure 2.19

A Budget Constraint with Quantity Rationing

Without rationing, areas G and H represent the set of feasible bundles. With rationing, only those bundles in G are feasible.

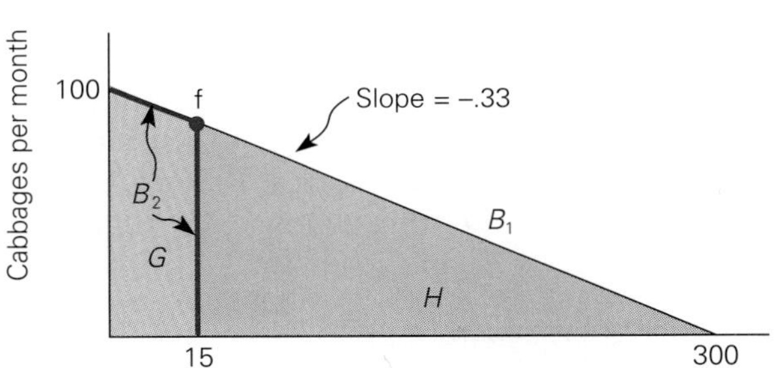

of each cabbage is 1 ruble. Under these assumptions, if Ivan can purchase as much of each commodity as he wants at the going price, his budget constraint is straight line B_1 in Figure 2.19. The horizontal intercept is 300 packs (= 100/0.33), the maximal number of packs that Ivan could purchase if he spent his entire income on cigarettes.

Suppose now that the government institutes cigarette rationing. Under the rationing scheme, each citizen is issued 15 nontradable coupons per month. For each pack of cigarettes an individual wishes to purchase, he must not only pay 0.33 rubles, but also submit a ration coupon. Thus, the maximal number of cigarettes that Ivan can purchase is 15 packs per month. What does his budget constraint look like now? For quantities of cigarettes less than 15 packs, Ivan can trade off cigarettes and cabbage at a rate of one-third cabbage per pack of cigarettes. Hence, for quantities of cigarettes less than 15, his budget constraint coincides with B_1. But to the right of point *f*, points on B_1 simply are not available to Ivan. Because he has only 15 ration coupons, he cannot purchase any bundles to the right of *f*. Hence, his budget constraint is kinked line B_2.

Like the straight-line budget constraints in the previous section, budget constraint B_2 divides consumption bundles into those that are obtainable (on or below B_2) and those that are not obtainable (above B_2). And just like a linear budget constraint, the slope of B_2 shows the relative price of one good in terms of another. To the left of bundle *f*, the slope is -0.33, indicating that the opportunity cost of a pack of cigarettes is one-third of a cabbage. Along the vertical segment of B_2, the slope is infinite. This is no surprise—under this rationing scheme, more than 15 packs of cigarettes cannot be obtained at any price; in effect, then, the price of cigarettes is infinite.

Finally, we note that quantity rationing is not exclusively an Eastern European phenomenon. For example, in the United States during World War II, numerous commodities were subject to quantity rationing. During the energy crisis of the 1970s, several public figures suggested that gasoline be rationed in this way. Gasoline rationing was never implemented, although ration coupons were actually printed just in case. And when California experienced a severe drought in the early 1990s, several communities instituted water rationing.

Quantity Discounts

As already noted, a budget constraint is linear only if the price per unit of each good is the same regardless of the number of units purchased. In some important cases, households are not price takers. In the United States, for example, about 40 percent of public utilities sell water according to a "declining block schedule," which means that the charge per unit of water declines with increasing water use (Congressional Budget Office 1987, 6–7). Consider Anne, who spends her monthly income of I dollars on two commodities, bread and water. Bread costs \$1 per loaf. Anne's local water works charges p_1 per gallon for each of the first 500 gallons consumed in a month, p_2 per gallon for each of the next 250 gallons consumed during the month, and p_3 per gallon in excess of 750. Declining block pricing means that $p_1 > p_2 > p_3$. What does her budget constraint look like?

> **2.5 PROGRESS CHECK**
>
> In response to the drought mentioned above, many California water companies switched to *increasing* block pricing. The idea was to allow people to meet their needs at a low price, but to discourage "wasteful" uses of water. Sketch the budget constraint for a consumer facing an increasing block pricing scheme.

In Figure 2.20, gallons of water are measured on the horizontal axis and loaves of bread on the vertical. One option for Anne is bundle a, where she spends all of her income on bread and none on water. As Anne begins spending money on water, the price per gallon is p_1. Thus, initially the slope of the budget constraint is $-p_1$. (Remember, the price of bread is \$1, and $-p_1/1 = -p_1$.) However, when water consumption reaches 500 gallons (at point *b*), the price of additional water goes down to p_2. Since $p_2 < p_1$, this price change is reflected in a budget constraint that is flatter to the right of *b*. And when consumption of water hits 750 gallons (at point *c*), the slope in absolute value becomes p_3, which is flatter yet. Thus, the budget constraint is a kinked line that is bowed inward toward the origin. More generally, *when the price per unit of a commodity varies with the number of units purchased, the changes in its price are reflected in the slope of the budget constraint.* (PC 2.5)

Figure 2.20

Budget Constraint with Declining Prices

When the price per unit of a commodity depends on the number of units purchased, the budget constraint is nonlinear. In this figure, the price of water falls as more units are consumed. Because the negative of the slope of the budget constraint equals the price of water, the constraint becomes flatter as more gallons are consumed.

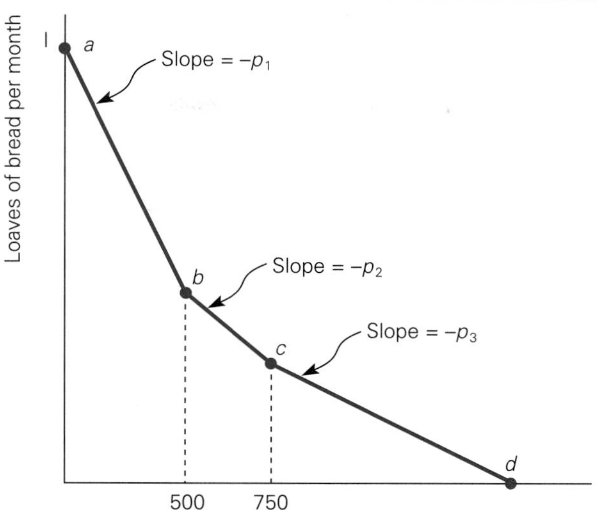

SECTION RECAP

The consumer's budget constraint shows the opportunities that are available to him. It indicates which bundles of commodities are feasible and which are not, given the prices of the commodities and the individual's income. When consumers are price takers—their purchases of commodities do not affect the going prices—the budget constraint is a straight line (see Figure 2.18). However, in many important real-world situations the budget constraint is not a straight line. Do not always assume that a straight line is the right way to characterize a consumer's opportunities. Rather, when attempting to sketch the budget constraint associated with a situation, "go back to basics"—first ask yourself which opportunities are available to the individual, and then translate them into geometric form.

2.4 THE CONSUMER'S EQUILIBRIUM

We have now completed the first two steps depicted in Figure 2.1. The indifference map shows us what a consumer *wants* to do; the budget constraint shows us what she *can* do. To find out what the consumer actually does, the two steps must be put together.

INTERIOR SOLUTIONS

Let's return to Elizabeth's choice between hamburgers and tacos one more time. Recall that her indifference curves have the "conventional" shape depicted in Figure 2.7, and her budget constraint is the straight line B_1 from Figure 2.15.

Figure 2.21

Consumer Equilibrium

Which bundle will the consumer select? Bundle *a* is impossible, bundle *b* involves throwing away income, and bundle *c* is on a lower indifference curve than is possible. Only at bundle *e*, where the indifference curve is tangent to the budget constraint, is the consumer doing as well for herself as possible.

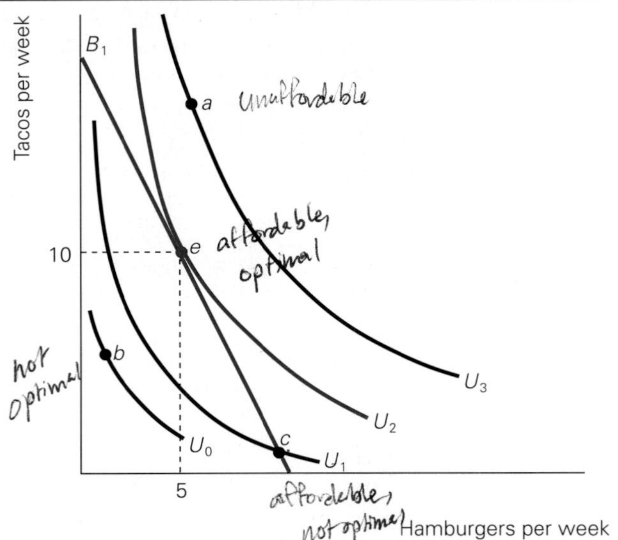

In Figure 2.21, we superimpose Elizabeth's indifference map upon her budget constraint. The problem is to find Elizabeth's most preferred combination of hamburgers and tacos subject to the constraint that her expenditures cannot exceed her income. That is the bundle we expect her to consume.

Consider first the bundle *a* on indifference curve U_3. This point is ruled out, because it lies above line B_1. Elizabeth might like to be on indifference curve U_3, but she simply cannot afford it.

Now consider point *b*. That bundle is certainly feasible, because it lies below the budget constraint. But it cannot be optimal, because Elizabeth is not spending her whole income. In effect, at bundle *b*, she is just throwing away money that could have been spent on hamburgers and/or tacos. (Remember that in this chapter we are assuming that income cannot be saved.)

What about point *c*? Because it lies on the budget constraint, this bundle is feasible, and Elizabeth is not throwing away any income. Yet she can still do better in the sense of putting herself on a higher indifference curve. Finally, consider bundle *e*, where she consumes 5 hamburgers and 10 tacos. Because this bundle lies on B_1, it is feasible. Moreover, it is more desirable than bundle *c*, because *e* lies on U_2, which is above U_1. Indeed, no point on B_1 touches an indifference curve that is higher than U_2. Therefore, bundle *e* maximizes Elizabeth's well-being, subject to budget constraint B_1. In other words, there is no way that Elizabeth could reallocate her income between hamburgers and tacos that would make her better off than she is at bundle *e*. Elizabeth's consumption of bundle *e* is referred to as an ***equilibrium***—a situation that will persist because the individual has no incentive to change his or her behavior. Observe that bundle *e* contains at least some amount of each commodity—it is interior to the quadrant. Such an equilibrium is called an **interior solution.** (In the next section, we will discuss equilibria that are *not* in the interior.)

interior solution
An equilibrium bundle that contains some amount of each good.

Note too that at the equilibrium, indifference curve U_2 just "barely touches" the budget constraint. This occurs because the consumer is trying to attain the very highest indifference curve she can while still keeping on B_1. Technically, line B_1 is *tangent* to curve U_2 at point e. This means that at point e, the slope of the indifference curve U_2 is equal to the slope of the budget constraint B_1.

This observation suggests an equation for characterizing the equilibrium bundle. Recall that, by definition, the negative of the slope of the indifference curve is the marginal rate of substitution of tacos for hamburgers, MRS_{yx}. Moreover, as demonstrated in the previous section, the negative of the slope of the budget line is p_x/p_y. But we just showed that at equilibrium, the two slopes are equal, or

$$MRS_{yx} = \frac{p_x}{p_y}. \tag{2.3}$$

If a particular bundle makes a consumer as well off as possible, then it must satisfy Equation (2.3).[1] That is, if the consumer's marginal rate of substitution is not equal to the price ratio, then she could do better by reallocating her income between the two commodities.

To firm up your intuition behind Equation (2.3), consider Figure 2.22, which magnifies the region around point c from Figure 2.21. At point c, Elizabeth would be willing to give up 1 hamburger if she received 1 taco in return (because g and c both lie on indifference curve U_1). But given that hamburgers are twice as expensive as tacos, if she gives up 1 hamburger she can get 2 tacos. It is certainly worthwhile for Elizabeth to make this trade, which moves her to bundle h, which is on a higher indifference curve than bundle c. Similar arguments can be used to show that at any point on B_1, Elizabeth can make herself better off by trading in the direction of e.

In short, *the marginal rate of substitution shows the rate at which the consumer is willing to trade one good for the other; the slope of the budget constraint is the rate at which she is able to trade one good for the other. In equilibrium, these must be equal.*

We cannot assess whether an individual is behaving sensibly merely by looking at the amount of each commodity he consumes. Consider Philip, who has the same income as Elizabeth and faces the same prices for hamburgers and tacos. Philip therefore has the same budget constraint, which is drawn in Figure 2.23. This figure also shows Philip's indifference curves, which are labeled with a superscript letter P. Given Philip's indifference map, the best bundle is e_1. Clearly, this is very different from Elizabeth's optimal bundle e from Figure 2.21. That the bundles are different does not mean that one consumer is "right" and the other is "wrong." As emphasized at the beginning of this chapter, an individual's rationality can only be judged relative to his or her goals, and by this criterion Elizabeth and Philip are both rational. *According to Equation (2.3), it is the relationship between the marginal rate of substitution and the price ratio that is crucial to determining whether individuals are rational. Different people can satisfy this equality even if their equilibrium bundles are not the same.*

[1]This statement is correct only for an interior solution. As shown below, if the consumption of some commodity is zero, then Equation (2.3) may not hold. In addition, if indifference curves have kinks (as in Figure 2.12), or if the budget constraint has a kink, then the *MRS* may not equal the price ratio even when there is an interior solution.

Figure 2.22

A Disequilibrium Bundle

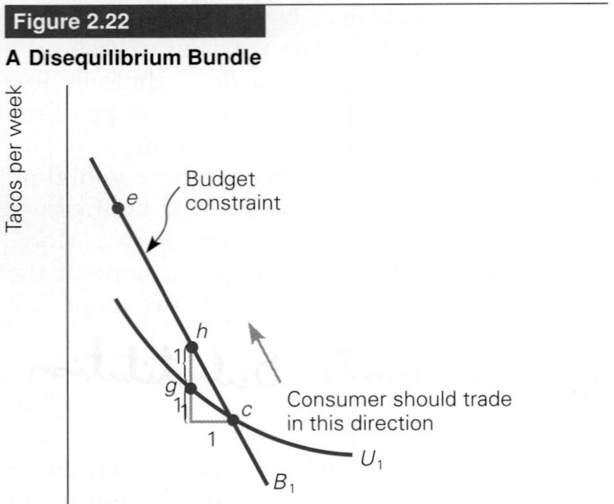

At bundle *c* the *MRS* is unequal to the price ratio. The market is willing to let the consumer trade 2 tacos for 1 hamburger, while she requires only 1 taco to give up 1 hamburger. Hence, *c* cannot be an equilibrium, because she would be better off by moving away from that bundle.

Figure 2.23

Equilibrium with Another Set of Preferences

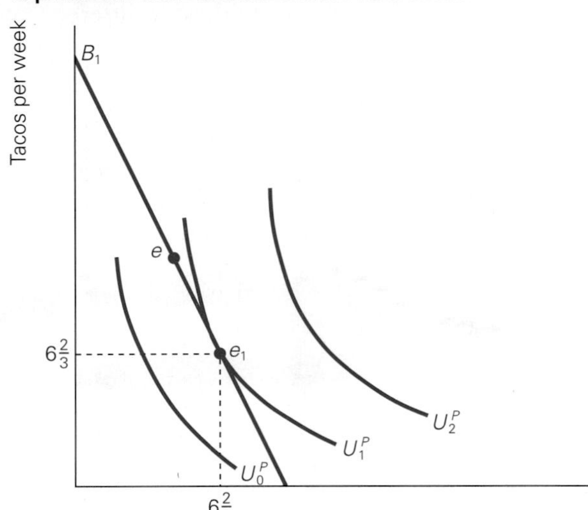

The equilibrium bundle depends on an individual's preferences as embodied in his indifference curves. Compare bundle e_1 in this figure to bundle *e* in Figure 2.21. The people in both diagrams are behaving rationally, despite the fact that their decisions are very different.

CORNER SOLUTIONS

The equilibria described so far were interior solutions—they involved at least some amount of each commodity. However, because thousands of commodities are available, one cannot expect a consumer to purchase some of everything. Moreover, the fact that you do not purchase a particular commodity does not necessarily imply that you dislike it. You may "like" the commodity in the sense that if someone gave you some of it free, it would increase your welfare. But given your income and the prices you face, it isn't worthwhile for you to purchase any of it.

corner solution
An equilibrium bundle in which the consumption of some commodity is zero.

How can the equilibrium bundle in such a situation be characterized? Figure 2.24 depicts the situation of Mary, who faces the same prices for hamburgers and tacos as Elizabeth. Mary's indifference curves are marked with a superscript *M*. According to the figure, point e_2 is on the highest indifference curve that can be reached subject to the budget constraint. She devotes all of her income to tacos and none to hamburgers. Because the equilibrium occurs at the corner formed by the budget constraint and the axis, it is referred to as a **corner solution.** Look closely at the equilibrium and you will notice that contrary to Equation (2.3), MRS_{yx} is not equal to p_x/p_y. Rather, the indifference curve is flatter than the budget constraint, that is, p_x/p_y exceeds MRS_{yx}. The fact that MRS_{yx} is not equal to the price ratio tells us that Mary would like to trade some of one good for the other at the prevailing prices. In particular, the marginal rate of substitution of tacos for hamburgers is less than the price ratio. Thus, Mary

Figure 2.24

Corner Solution

A corner solution to the consumer's choice problem is characterized by an inequality between the marginal rate of substitution and the price ratio. At point e_2, $MRS_{yx} \leq p_x/p_y$.

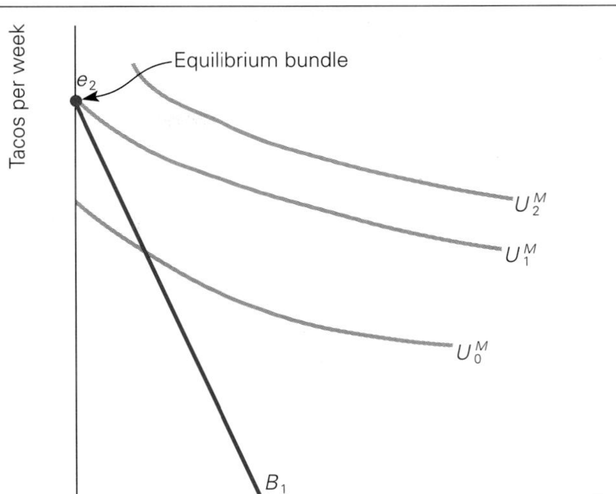

would like to purchase fewer hamburgers and use the money to purchase additional tacos. Why do we conclude that she is in equilibrium? Because Mary is already consuming as few hamburgers as possible: none at all. Consequently, no reallocation of Mary's income can increase her well-being. Hence, e_2 is her equilibrium consumption bundle.

In summary, for a corner solution involving zero hamburgers, the condition for an equilibrium is characterized not by an equality, but by the inequality

$$MRS_{yx} \leq \frac{p_x}{p_y}. \tag{2.4}$$

The *MRS* is "less than or equal to" p_x/p_y rather than "strictly less than" p_x/p_y to allow for the possibility that at the corner, the slope of the budget constraint just happens to equal the slope of the indifference curve. (At the other corner—where taco consumption is zero—the inequality goes the other way.) (PC 2.6)

2.6 PROGRESS CHECK

Records cost $10 apiece; tapes cost $2 apiece. In equilibrium, Victoria consumes both records and tapes; Albert consumes only tapes. What can you infer about Victoria's marginal rate of substitution of records for tapes? What about Albert's? Draw diagrams depicting their situations.

EQUILIBRIUM WITH COMPOSITE COMMODITIES

Indifference curves allow us to examine only two commodities at a time. Sometimes, however, we want to recognize explicitly that an individual consumes more than two goods. Suppose, for example, that we want to focus on George's consumption of videotapes while keeping in mind that he purchases many other goods as well. The trick is to think of him as dividing his budget between two commodities: The first is *videotapes* and the second is *a composite of all goods other than videotapes.* How do we measure units of *all*

Figure 2.25

Equilibrium with a Composite Commodity

When we define units of a composite commodity such that the price per unit is $1, then the quantity consumed also represents expenditures on the composite. In this figure, the individual spends $51 on all goods other than videotapes.

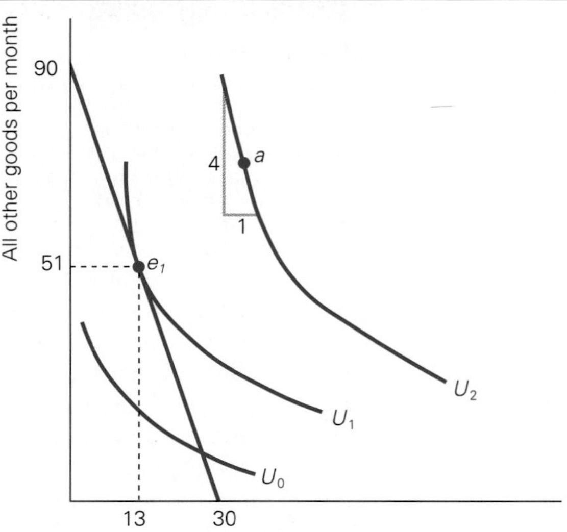

other goods? For convenience, define a unit of *all other goods* as the amount that you could purchase by spending $1.

In Figure 2.25, the quantity of videotapes is measured on the horizontal axis, and the quantity of *all other goods* is measured on the vertical. Assuming that George's income is $90, the price per videotape is $3, and the price per unit of the composite commodity is $1, then sketching the budget constraint is routine. It is a straight line with slope of -3 and vertical intercept of 90 units of *all other goods*. As usual, any point on the budget constraint shows combinations of the two commodities that just exhaust the individual's income.

The next step is to depict the individual's preferences between videotapes and *all other goods*. It is natural to draw a set of "typical" indifference curves, which is also done in Figure 2.25. However, the interpretation of the slopes of these indifference curves requires a bit of care. Consider point *a*, where the marginal rate of substitution between *all other goods* and videotapes is 4. This means that around point *a*, in return for one more videotape George is willing to give up whatever bundle of *all other goods* that he would purchase with an additional $4 of income.

Given the budget constraint and indifference curves, we can use the usual methods to find the equilibrium bundle: 13 videotapes and 51 units of *all other goods*. Because *all other goods* are measured in units such that the price per unit is $1, the number of units purchased also is the expenditure. Thus, in equilibrium, George spends $51 on *all other goods* and the remainder of his budget on videotapes.

Thus, the two-good assumption is really less restrictive than it might seem. By suitably defining composites of various commodities, we can use two-dimensional diagrams to analyze decisions that involve a consumer's entire budget.[2]

[2]More rigorously, it is permissible to treat a group of commodities as a single composite only if their prices always change in the same proportion (see Hicks 1946, 312–13).

USING UTILITY TO CHARACTERIZE THE CONSUMER'S EQUILIBRIUM

Toward the end of the previous section we introduced ordinal utility functions, which allow us to rank bundles according to their numerical scores. The notion of a utility function permits a restatement of the consumer's objective. Before, we stated that the consumer's goal was to reach the highest indifference curve that was possible, given her budget constraint. But the highest possible indifference curve has the highest possible level of utility. Hence, *the consumer's objective is to maximize the value of her utility function subject to her budget constraint.*

marginal utility
The change in total utility associated with consumption of one additional unit of a good.

The notion of utility also allows us to reinterpret the necessary condition for utility maximization. To do so, we begin by defining the **marginal utility** of a taco, denoted MU_y, as the change in total utility associated with the consumption of an additional taco. The marginal utility of a hamburger, MU_x, is defined analogously. Now think about a small movement down and along an indifference curve between tacos and hamburgers. This movement involves a loss of Δy tacos and Δx hamburgers. (The Greek letter Δ, "delta," is used to represent "the change in" a variable. Hence, Δy means "the change in y.") The loss of Δy tacos decreases the individual's utility by $\Delta y \times MU_y$. At the same time, the gain of Δx hamburgers increases the individual's utility by $\Delta x \times MU_x$.

Now, all points on an indifference curve are associated with the same amount of utility. Hence, the loss in utility associated with Δy tacos must equal the gain in utility from Δx hamburgers. Using algebra,

$$MU_x \times \Delta x + MU_y \times \Delta y = 0.$$

Rearranging this equation gives us

$$-\frac{\Delta y}{\Delta x} = \frac{MU_x}{MU_y}.$$

But $-\Delta y/\Delta x$ is the negative of the slope of the indifference curve, that is, it is the marginal rate of substitution of tacos for hamburgers. Hence, we have shown that

$$MRS_{yx} = \frac{MU_x}{MU_y}. \tag{2.5}$$

Equation (2.5) tells us that the marginal rate of substitution equals the ratio of marginal utilities *everywhere* along an indifference curve.

Now, as long as there is an interior solution, recall from Equation (2.3) that *in equilibrium*

$$MRS_{yx} = \frac{p_x}{p_y}.$$

Substituting (2.3) into (2.5) therefore tells us that *in equilibrium*

$$\frac{MU_x}{MU_y} = \frac{p_x}{p_y}. \tag{2.6}$$

Thus, we can characterize consumer equilibrium either in terms of the marginal rate of substitution between two goods, Equation (2.3), or in terms of the ratio of their marginal utilities, Equation (2.6).

Two points must be made in connection with Equation (2.6). The first is technical. Recall from our earlier discussion that because utility functions are ordinal, the particular value of utility associated with a given indifference curve is irrelevant. This reasoning carries over to Equation (2.6), in the sense that all that matters is the *ratio* of the marginal utilities of the two goods. If $p_x/p_y = 2$, we could just as well have $MU_x = 20$ and $MU_y = 10$ or $MU_x = 720$ and $MU_y = 360$. Thus, our theory requires only that individuals can rank goods ordinally, not cardinally.

The second point surrounds the question: Why did we get involved with marginal utilities in the first place? One reason is that a slight rearrangement of Equation (2.6) leads to some very nice intuition behind the necessary condition for utility maximization. Specifically, divide each side of (2.6) by p_x, and multiply each side by MU_y. Then at equilibrium:

$$\frac{MU_x}{p_x} = \frac{MU_y}{p_x}. \tag{2.7}$$

Now, the marginal utility of a commodity divided by its price is just the marginal utility per dollar spent on the good. Hence, (2.7) says that a bundle maximizes *total* utility only if the *marginal* utility of the last dollar spent on each good is the same.

To understand condition (2.7), begin by recalling the consumer's basic goal—to get the most utility for his money that he can. Now consider Charles, who has one more dollar to spend on hamburgers (x) and tacos (y). If he spent the dollar on tacos, he could buy $1/p_y$ tacos. [For example, if each taco cost 25 cents, he could purchase 4 ($= 1/.25$).] Since by definition each taco would contribute MU_y more utility, his total utility would rise by $(1/p_y) \times MU_y$, or MU_y/p_y. Similarly, if Charles spent the additional dollar on hamburgers, he could buy $1/p_x$ more hamburgers, and his total utility would rise by MU_x/p_x.

These facts imply that for Charles to consume both commodities in equilibrium, MU_x/p_x must equal MU_y/p_y. To see why, suppose that Charles had chosen a commodity bundle in which MU_y/p_y is less than MU_x/p_x. By spending a dollar less on tacos and a dollar more on hamburgers, utility would rise, even though Charles's total expenditures would stay the same. Therefore, the original bundle could not have been an equilibrium. Similarly, if Charles were at a point where MU_y/p_y is greater than MU_x/p_x, he could increase his utility without spending more money simply by switching a dollar from hamburgers to tacos. Stated positively, we have just shown that for the consumer to maximize utility, he must choose a commodity bundle such that

$$\frac{MU_x}{p_x} = \frac{MU_y}{p_y},$$

which is exactly condition (2.7). In short, *when the marginal utility of the last dollar is the same for each commodity, there is no way that income can be reallocated between commodities so as to increase total utility*. This is another example of the equimarginal principle that was introduced in Chapter 1. (PC 2.7)

2.7 PROGRESS CHECK

The price of car transportation is 30 cents per mile; the price of public bus transportation is 60 cents per mile. Currently, the marginal utility of Willy's last mile of car transportation is 80 utils, and the marginal utility of his last mile of bus transportation is 150 utils. Is Willy maximizing his utility?

PRELIMINARY EVALUATION OF THE THEORY OF CHOICE

The goals that we set for this chapter have now been met. We developed models of individual preferences and budget constraints, and put them together to show how decisions are made. Therefore, now is a good time to step back and ask ourselves whether our theory of consumer choice is any good.

A number of objections to the theory can indeed be raised. A common one is that the whole structure is unrealistic. Most people have never heard of indifference curves, utility functions, or budget constraints. How can we then assume that they go around setting their marginal rates of substitution equal to price ratios? The response is that the model's purpose is to help us to obtain good predictions of how people will behave under alternative circumstances. As long as people behave *as if* they are trying to maximize utility, then the model is serving its purpose well. One can think of the theory of consumer choice as a metaphor that helps us make predictions. Such metaphors are also common in the natural and physical sciences. When you learned in physics that "nature abhors a vacuum" it didn't mean that Mother Nature starts shrieking whenever she sees a vacuum. Rather, it means that the behavior of a physical system in the presence of a vacuum can be well predicted by assuming that the system *acts as if* it "abhors" the vacuum and hence "wants" to fill it.

Even if one accepts this "as if" approach to model building, one can still believe that a theory based on rational self-interest doesn't lead to very good predictions. After all, you probably know someone who spent an entire month's earnings on a frivolous purchase that he or she later regretted. One response to this challenge is to deny that the observed behavior really is irrational: "If the individual made the decision, given all the information available to him, then the decision must have raised the individual to his highest feasible indifference curve. Otherwise, he wouldn't have made the decision in the first place."

The problem with this defense is that it reduces the theory of consumer behavior to a *tautology*—a proposition that has to be true by definition. Since a tautology cannot be rejected by *any* evidence, how is one to know whether it is correct? Our view is that it is more sensible to admit that there may be individual departures from rationality, and then ask whether this is fatal to the theory. The answer depends on what we want the theory to do. If we require the theory to describe the behavior of every person at every instant in time, then it probably is a failure. Fortunately, our goals are generally much more modest—we want to use the model to predict how groups of people will behave. Even if some individuals' behavior is "irrational," if they are in a minority, then we still may be able to obtain good predictions. One objective of the next chapter is to show how the theory of choice is used to generate such predictions. Hence, if you are feeling skeptical about the theory of choice, try to reserve judgment for at least one more chapter.

SECTION RECAP

We have described the outcome when an individual maximizes his welfare subject to a budget constraint. Assuming that (*a*) the individual is a price taker and (*b*) some of each commodity is consumed, the equilibrium bundle is characterized by a very simple relationship: The price ratio of any two goods equals the individual's marginal rate of substitution between the two goods. When either of these two assumptions fails to hold, it may not be possible to characterize the equilibrium so simply. But in any case, the procedure for isolating the equilibrium is the same—find the bundle where the highest possible indifference curve touches the budget constraint.

SUMMARY

Households' demands for products play a crucial role in allocating resources in a market economy. This chapter has developed a theory of how these decisions are made. According to this theory, the choices are the ones that make individuals as well off as possible, given their incomes and the prices they face.

- The theory assumes that individuals can rank all bundles (completeness) and that their decision making is consistent (transitivity).
- In many cases, we can represent the individual's preferences by a set of indifference curves—curves that show bundles that the consumer views as equivalent. The marginal rate of substitution measures the willingness of the consumer to substitute one good for another, and equals the negative of the slope of an indifference curve.
- One can associate with each bundle of commodities a number that indicates the amount of satisfaction or utility associated with that bundle. These utility numbers are ordinal—they indicate only the rankings of bundles, not precisely how much more one bundle is valued than another.
- The consumer's budget constraint shows his opportunities, given his income and the prices he faces. The negative of the slope of the budget constraint is the ratio of the prices of the two goods—it shows the opportunity cost of one good in terms of the other.
- The consumer chooses the bundle that places him on the highest indifference curve that is also on his budget constraint. Consumption of this bundle is an equilibrium—a situation that will persist because the individual has no incentive to change his behavior.
- In the case of an interior equilibrium solution (both goods are consumed), the marginal rate of substitution equals the price ratio.
- The marginal utility of a good is the change in utility associated with the consumption of one more unit. For an interior solution, the marginal utility per dollar must be the same for each good.

DISCUSSION QUESTIONS

2.1 Which of the following statements are not consistent with the assumptions of completeness and transitivity? Explain why.

a. I just can't decide whether I would rather take a vacation in California or purchase a pair of skis.

b. After I've played two games of billiards, I don't want to play any more.

c. If you give me a ticket to the baseball game, I'll give you my new pair of socks.

2.2 A newspaper article discussing the buying patterns of young health-conscious professionals noted that such "people spend their calorie allowance very carefully *to get maximum pleasure out of it*" (Rose 1991, 100; emphasis added).

a. In terms of the jargon developed in this chapter, what does the italicized phrase mean?

b. Consider the case of Ken, who enjoys premium ice cream (70 calories per ounce) and brownies (140 calories per ounce). Ken's nutritional adviser has indicated that he can safely consume 980 calories worth of ice cream and brownies each week. Assume that Ken has enough money to buy all the ice cream and brownies that he could possibly want—income is not a constraint on his junk food decisions. Sketch Ken's budget constraint. What is the opportunity cost of an ounce of brownies?

c. Show how Ken's equilibrium bundle of ice cream and brownies is determined. What is the marginal rate of substitution between brownies and ice cream?

2.3 "The more Whoopi Goldberg movies I see, the more I like them."

a. According to this statement, how does the marginal rate of substitution between *all other goods* and Whoopi Goldberg movies change as the consumption of Whoopi Goldberg movies increases?

b. Sketch the indifference map between Whoopi Goldberg movies and *all other goods.*

c. Suppose that the price of admission to each Whoopi Goldberg movie is $5. Assuming that weekly income is $150, sketch the budget constraint.

d. Find the equilibrium bundle.

2.4 "I always require 1,000 milligrams of Tylenol® to obtain the same amount of pain relief provided by 500 milligrams of aspirin."

a. Sketch the indifference map between aspirin and Tylenol.

b. Characterize the equilibrium bundle of aspirin and Tylenol under the following circumstances:

i. The price per milligram of each is the same.

ii. The price per milligram of Tylenol is three times the price per milligram of aspirin.

iii. The price per milligram of Tylenol is one-third the price per milligram of aspirin.

2.5 Trans-Continental Airlines (TCA) offers the following frequent flyer program to its customers: For the first 30,000 miles flown each year, customers pay full fare. For the next 20,000 miles flown during the year, the fare is reduced by 20 percent; for all flights beyond that, the fare is reduced by 50 percent. Sketch the budget constraint that faces a typical TCA passenger.

2.6 Assume that

a. Andrew, a sports fan, derives utility from attending football and basketball games.

b. The price of each football ticket is \$5; the price of a basketball game is \$10.

c. Each football game takes three hours; each basketball game takes two hours.

i. Assume that Andrew has \$50 per month to spend on game tickets, and that he has more than enough time to attend all the games he wants. Sketch Andrew's budget constraint.

ii. Now assume that Andrew can only spend 18 hours per month at sporting events, but he has more than enough money to attend all the games that he wants. Sketch the budget constraint.

iii. Now assume that Andrew has only \$50 per month to spend *and* only 18 hours per month available. Sketch the budget constraint, and explain why it can be characterized as having a kink.

iv. Suppose that Andrew's point of maximum utility occurs at the kink. What can you say about the value of the marginal rate of substitution in equilibrium? What is the *MRS* if the equilibrium is not at the kink?

2.7 The rationing example of Figure 2.19 is based on the assumption that it is impossible for Ivan to obtain more than his allocation of 15 packs of cigarettes per month. Suppose that, instead, he can obtain additional cigarettes on the black market for five rubles per pack. Show how the existence of the black market affects Ivan's budget constraint. Will Ivan change the number of cigarettes he purchases?

2.8 A dense Amazonian rain forest covers over 80 percent of the area of Suriname. Several huge Asian companies are seeking the right to "cut the ancient trees to make plywood, ornamental moldings, and furniture" (de Palma 1995, L1). This has led to a contentious debate within Suriname. Some people do not care very much about losing the trees if it will lead to economic development, while others argue that the trees are a very important part of the nation's heritage. Sketch a set of indifference curves between "trees" and "income" that might represent the preferences for each of the two groups.

2.9 Abe and Mary both purchase cigarettes and beer at their friendly neighborhood convenience store. The two friends have different tastes for cigarettes and beer, different incomes, and they end up purchasing very different quantities of the two commodities. Nevertheless, they have the same marginal rate of substitution of beer for cigarettes. Explain how this is possible.

2.10 For couples who practice birth control, choosing to have a child is associated with a price in terms of the consumption and time that must be sacrificed for the child. Assume that for any particular couple, the price per child is constant. (For example, each additional child costs \$8,000 per year.)

a. What are the "commodities" in this problem?

b. Sketch the budget constraint.

c. The Smiths choose to have one child, while the Joneses choose to have no children. For each family, sketch an indifference map that is consistent with the observed behavior.

d. Do you think that this is an adequate model of child-bearing decisions? Why or why not? What kind of data would you need to judge its adequacy?

2.11 Joe College has 25 hours available to study for examinations in economics, calculus, and psychology. Suppose that Joe's goal is to maximize the sum of his grades on the three exams. Use Equation (2.7) to develop a strategy for how much time to devote to each course. Does your pattern of studying conform to such a strategy?

2.12 Suppose a country has drastic inflation, and over a period of one year all prices and incomes exactly triple. According to our model of consumer behavior, how would this phenomenon affect individuals' consumption bundles and their levels of utility?

2.13 A student spends eight hours per day listening to music. M hours are devoted to Mozart and B hours to Beethoven. The student's utility function is $U = M^{1/4} B^{3/4}$, where U measures utility.

A calculator may prove useful in answering the following questions:

a. Sketch an indifference curve corresponding to a utility level of 4.

b. On the same diagram, sketch an indifference curve corresponding to a utility level of 5.

c. Write an equation for the student's budget constraint. Sketch the budget constraint on the same diagram.

d. On the basis of your diagram, what are the approximate utility-maximizing quantities of M and B?

e. In equilibrium, what is the value of the ratio of the marginal utility of Beethoven to the marginal utility of Mozart?

CHAPTER 3

Comparative Statics and Demand

> ***Other Things Being Equal—One of the old-time greats in economics; you can generally tell whether a man is an economist by the number of times he uses this particular phrase.***
>
> —William Davis

When American magnate Donald Trump's real estate and gambling empire was on the verge of collapse several years ago, his creditors demanded that Trump cut his personal expenditures. Specifically, the bankers insisted that Trump reduce his *monthly* spending from $583,000 to $450,000. Journalists speculated on how Trump would adjust to his reduced circumstances. Would he sell his private helicopter, give up his 50-room penthouse in Manhattan, or perhaps lay off some of his personal servants?

It may be hard to empathize with Trump, but all of us face situations that are similar in a generic way. Our economic environments—our incomes and the relative prices we face—often change, and when they do we have to adjust our behavior. An important goal of microeconomics is to predict how people will respond to such changes. Last chapter's theory of decision making provides a natural, three-step strategy for doing so.

1. Determine the equilibrium bundle *before* the particular change under consideration.
2. Find the equilibrium *after* the change.
3. Compare the two bundles.

comparative statics The process of comparing two equilibria.

This process of comparing two equilibria is called **comparative statics.** (The word *statics* emphasizes that the procedure compares two static equilibria, without analyzing the dynamics of how the consumer moves from the first equilibrium to the second.)

The analysis of comparative statics is important because it leads to testable predictions of how people will behave under new circumstances. Indeed, one of the main reasons for building a model is to use it for comparative statics. Constructing a model has been likened to building a violin. Analyzing the comparative statics is using that violin to produce music. In this chapter, we will conduct comparative statics analysis with our model of household decision making. In the process, we will attain one of our primary goals—to show where consumers' demand curves for commodities come from. Finally, toward the end of the chapter we will introduce the notion of an *elasticity*, a convenient way to summarize the outcome of a comparative statics exercise.

3.1 PRICE AND INCOME CHANGES

In this section, we examine how an individual's consumption of a commodity is affected when the price of that commodity changes, when the price of a related commodity changes, and when her income changes.

OWN-PRICE CHANGES

Figure 3.1 reproduces Elizabeth's budget constraint and indifference map for hamburgers and tacos from Figure 2.21. When the price per hamburger (p_x) is \$6, the price per taco (p_y) is \$3, and her income is \$60, Elizabeth has budget line B_1, and her most preferred bundle is e_1, where she consumes x_1 hamburgers and y_1 tacos. Now suppose that the price per hamburger falls to \$4. The constraint B_1 pivots around its vertical intercept to a point that is farther out on the horizontal axis. The new budget constraint is B_2. With constraint B_2, e_1 is no longer an equilibrium. The fall in the price of hamburgers creates new opportunities for Elizabeth, and we expect her to take advantage of them. Specifically, subject to budget constraint B_2, Elizabeth's most preferred bundle is e_2, where she consumes x_2 hamburgers and y_2 tacos. This is a typical example of comparative statics analysis. The model tells us how the individual modifies her behavior in response to a change in her environment. However, the analysis does *not* tell us the particular path that Elizabeth takes to get from e_1 to e_2, or just how long the adjustment takes. In most cases, however, knowing where the individual ends up is sufficient to address the problem at hand.

Interestingly, at the new equilibrium, the amounts of both hamburgers *and* tacos have increased relative to the old equilibrium ($x_2 > x_1$ and $y_2 > y_1$). The decrease in the price of hamburgers allows Elizabeth to purchase more hamburgers and still have money left over to purchase more tacos. Although this is common, it need not always be the case. The impact of a price change upon an individual's equilibrium bundle depends upon his or her tastes. Suppose that Philip has the same income as Elizabeth and also faces the same prices. Figure 3.2 shows Philip's indifference map and his budget constraints before and after the decrease in the price of hamburgers. According to Figure 3.2, Philip's consumption of hamburgers is unchanged when their price falls. His bundles e_1 and e_2 have exactly the same quantity of hamburgers; only taco consumption increases.

To summarize: A change in the price of a commodity changes the position of the budget constraint, which changes the consumer's opportunities. The consumer therefore "reoptimizes." That is, she finds the most preferred bundle,

Figure 3.1

Effect of a Price Decrease on the Equilibrium

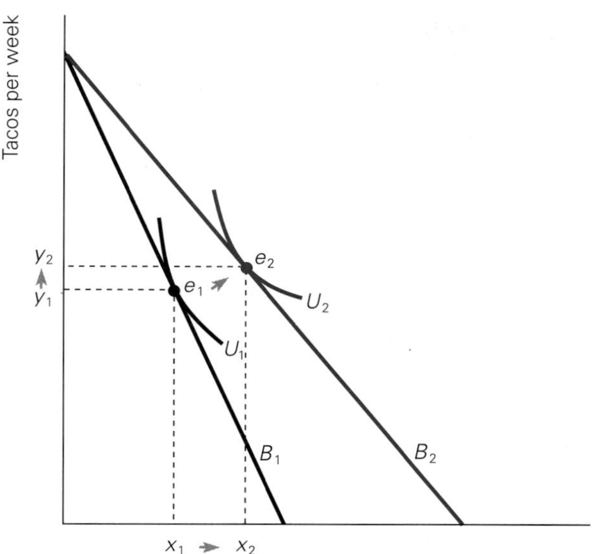

A decrease in the price of hamburgers changes the budget constraint from B_1 to B_2. Consequently, the equilibrium shifts from e_1 to e_2: the quantities consumed of both hamburgers and tacos increase.

Figure 3.2

A Case Where a Decrease in a Commodity's Price Does Not Affect Its Quantity Demanded

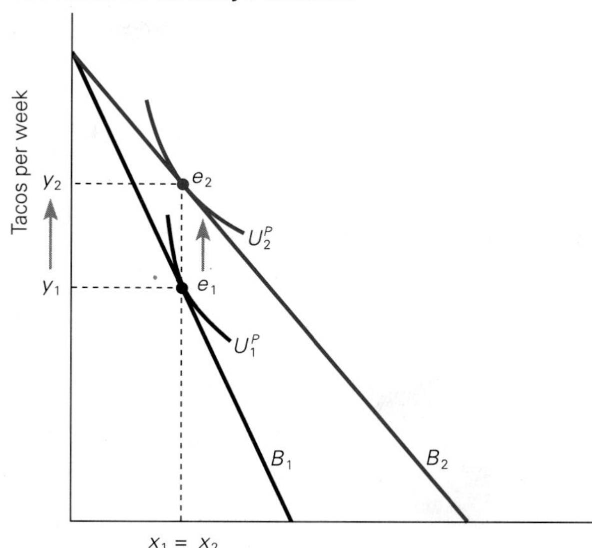

For Philip, a decrease in the price of hamburgers leads to no change in the consumption of hamburgers. However, taco consumption does increase, from y_1 to y_2.

given the new budget constraint. However, as Figures 3.1 and 3.2 indicate, without information on the individual's tastes, we cannot know for sure how the new equilibrium bundle compares with the old one. But whatever the outcome, we *do* know that as long as the new bundle is an interior solution, it is characterized by a tangency between the new budget line and an indifference curve—the marginal rate of substitution equals the new price ratio.

Even though the individual ends up with a new commodity bundle when her budget constraint changes, it is not correct to say that her tastes have changed. True, the consumer is on a new indifference curve, but this indifference curve is part of the original indifference map, which is not affected by a change in price (or any other variable that determines the budget constraint). Put another way, the individual's "tastes" are how she ranks various bundles, independent of her income and any particular set of prices. When prices and/or income change, the utility maximizing bundle changes, but the underlying set of tastes (the utility function) does not. (PC 3.1)

3.1 PROGRESS CHECK

Margaret has the same income and faces the same prices as Elizabeth and Philip. When the price of hamburgers falls, Margaret's hamburger consumption increases, and her taco consumption is unchanged. Sketch some budget constraints and indifference curves that are consistent with this behavior.

Derivation of the Individual's Demand Curve

Recall that the individual's demand curve for a commodity shows the maximum quantity that she is willing to consume at any given price of the commodity, other things being the same. The "other things" are the individual's tastes (as embodied in the indifference map), income, and the prices of other goods. In effect, the demand curve provides answers to a set of hypothetical questions such as "*If* the price of commodity x takes some value, what quantity of x will the consumer purchase, other things being the same?" Instead of repeating the phrase "other things being the same" over and over, economists use the more compact Latin equivalent *ceteris paribus.*

Chapter 1 stressed the crucial role played by demand curves in allocating resources in a market economy. It is therefore important to know exactly where they come from. We now demonstrate that deriving the consumer's demand curve is simply a matter of doing a series of comparative statics exercises. Panel A of Figure 3.3 reproduces Elizabeth's situation from Figure 3.1, and indicates that she desires to purchase x_1 hamburgers per week when the price per hamburger is \$6, the price per taco is \$3, and her income is \$60. Now look at Panel B, which also measures the number of hamburgers on the horizontal axis, but on the vertical measures the price per hamburger. Point e_1' in the lower panel records that when the price per hamburger is \$6, the quantity demanded is x_1. Note that Panel B contains no new information. It is just a reinterpretation of information that is already contained in Panel A. The only difference is that in the upper panel the price per hamburger is *implicit* in the slope of the budget constraint while in the lower panel, it is *explicitly* expressed on the vertical axis.

We can now employ our comparative statics techniques to show how the quantity of hamburgers demanded varies as the price of hamburgers changes, holding other things fixed. When the price of hamburgers falls to p_2, *ceteris paribus*, Elizabeth's quantity demanded increases to x_2. This fact is recorded at point e_2' in Panel B. Similarly, when the price of hamburgers decreases to p_3, the quantity demanded increases to x_3 (point e_3' in Panel B); and when the price increases to p_4, the quantity demanded decreases to x_4 (point e_4' in Panel B). Each new price leads to a new equilibrium bundle. In Panel A, the set of bundles traced out as the price of hamburgers varies is called the **price consumption curve** for hamburgers. What would be a good label for the corresponding curve traced out in the bottom panel? It shows how the quantity of hamburgers demanded varies with the price of hamburgers, holding fixed the price of tacos (at \$3 per taco), income (at \$60), and tastes (because the indifference map is fixed). It is nothing other than Elizabeth's demand curve for hamburgers, denoted d. Thus, *we have shown that, by using the method of comparative statics, an individual's demand curve for a commodity can be derived from her indifference map.* The demand curve neatly summarizes all the information on how the behavior of a price-taking consumer changes when prices vary, *ceteris paribus.*

price consumption curve
The set of commodity bundles traced out as the price of a commodity varies, *ceteris paribus.*

CROSS-PRICE CHANGES

The government of Hong Kong provides the synthetic narcotic *methadone* at a price of only 13 cents per dose. The policy's purpose is to wean heroin addicts away from that drug. Many addicts, however, appear to drift back and forth between methadone and heroin. In particular, when the price of heroin increases, regular heroin users show up at the methadone clinics. A social worker at one of

Figure 3.3

Deriving a Demand Curve

Panel A shows how the equilibrium bundle changes as the price of hamburgers changes, *ceteris paribus*. In Panel B this information is recorded in a diagram with quantity of hamburgers on the horizontal axis, and price on the vertical. Hence, the curve traced in Panel B is the demand curve for hamburgers.

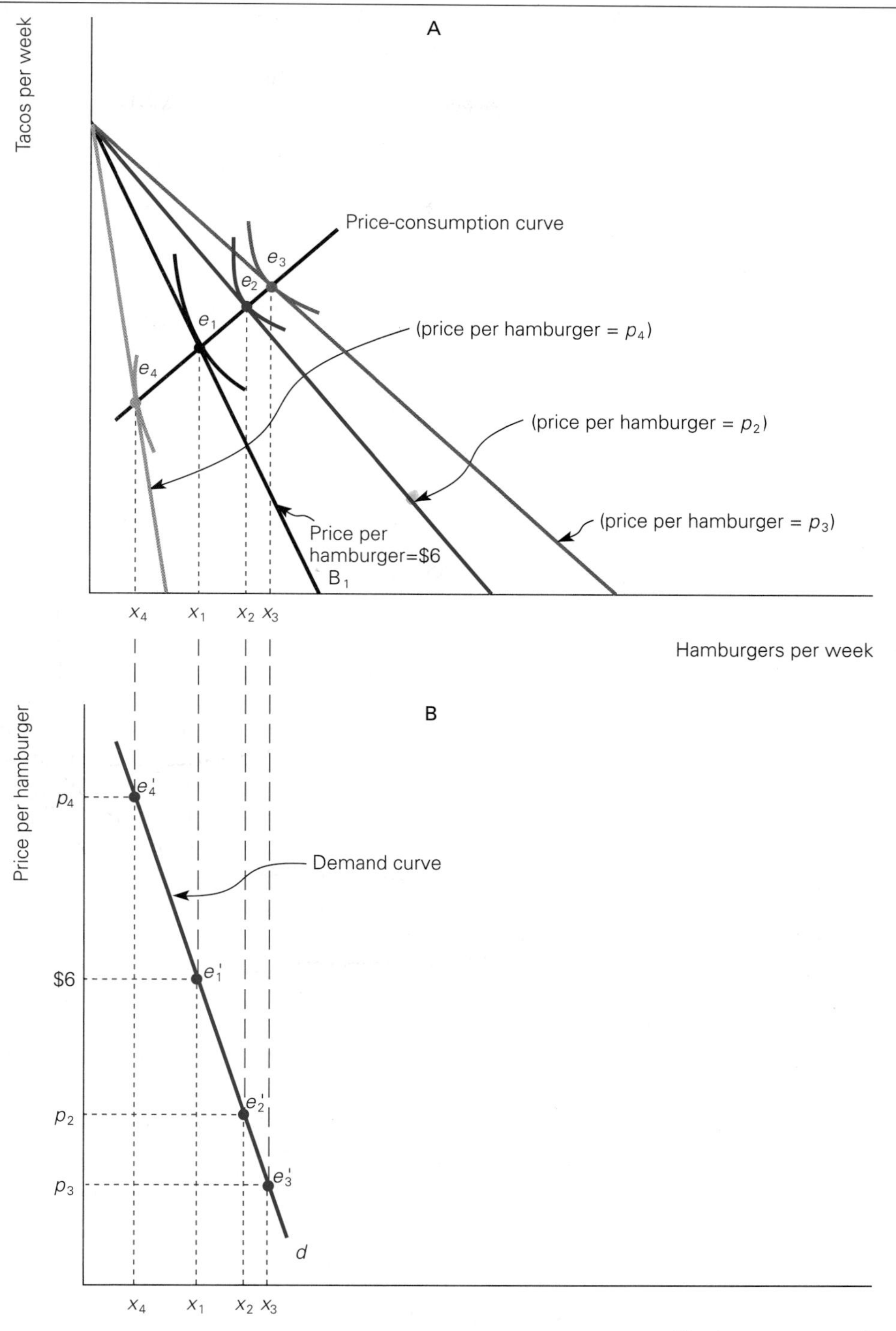

the largest methadone clinics explained it this way: "Maybe the price of heroin will go up and people will come in for just a few days to get methadone" (*New York Times*, June 17, 1987, B9).

cross-price effect
The impact of a change in the price of one good on the quantity demanded of another good.

This behavior is an example of a **cross-price effect**—the change in the price of one good affects the quantity demanded of *another* good. Just as was true for own-price effects, comparative statics methods can be used to analyze cross-price effects. In both cases, we compare the equilibrium bundle before a price change with the equilibrium bundle after. For own-price effects, we focus on the consumption of the commodity whose own price has changed; for cross-price effects, we focus on some other commodity that the household consumes.

substitutes
Two goods that satisfy similar wants. An increase in the price of one good leads to an increase in the quantity demanded of a substitute, *ceteris paribus*.

Figure 3.4 illustrates the anecdote above. An increase in the price of heroin induces an increase in the quantity demanded of methadone from y_1 to y_2. Goods such as heroin and methadone, where an increase in the price of one leads to an increase in the quantity demanded of the other, are referred to as **substitutes.** More prosaic examples of substitutes are coffee and tea, Toyotas and Hondas, and air conditioners and fans. Intuitively, substitutes are goods that satisfy about the same want, so that if one becomes more expensive, the consumer turns to the other. In the case of *perfect* substitutes discussed in the last chapter (see Figure 2.11), when the price of one good decreases, the consumer may abandon the other good altogether.

complements
Two goods that tend to be used together. An increase in the price of one good leads to a decrease in the quantity demanded of a complement, *ceteris paribus*.

unrelated goods
An increase in the price of one good has no impact on the quantity demanded of the other, *ceteris paribus*.

A different type of cross-price effect is illustrated in Figure 3.5, which depicts a gardener's choice between weed killer and fertilizer. Here, an increase in the price of weed killer induces a decrease in the quantity demanded of fertilizer from y_1 to y_2. Such goods are referred to as **complements.** Complements are goods that people consume jointly, so that when the price of one of the goods goes up, the consumer desires less of each of them. Coffee and cream are complements; so are cars and gasoline, and baseball gloves and baseballs.

Some goods are neither complements nor substitutes. When an increase in the price of one good has no impact on the quantity demanded of the other, the goods are said to be **unrelated goods** in consumption. Turn back to Progress Check 3.1 for an example. For that consumer, consumption of tacos is unaffected by a change in the price of hamburgers, so hamburgers and tacos are unrelated goods.

Theory alone cannot tell us whether two goods are substitutes, complements, or unrelated. We need to analyze data on how consumption patterns react to various price changes. Indeed, two commodities that are substitutes for one consumer might be complements for another. For example, if you view Oreos and vanilla ice cream as two different possibilities for a bedtime snack, then they are substitutes. If you like to mix Oreos into your ice cream, then they are complements. If you insist on mixing them together in fixed proportions, they are *perfect* complements. (See the discussion surrounding Figure 2.12.)

Demand Curves and Cross-Price Effects

We next consider how a commodity's demand curve changes when the price of a related good changes. Figure 3.6 exhibits William's demand curve for weed killer, *d*. As suggested by Figure 3.5, we could derive this demand curve by varying the price of weed killer while holding the price of fertilizer constant. Suppose that the price of fertilizer used for these purposes was \$3 per pound, but that now the price of fertilizer increases to \$4. When this happens, *d* (in effect) becomes obsolete. Recall that *d* shows the quantity of weed killer demanded at each price of

Figure 3.4

Substitutes in Consumption

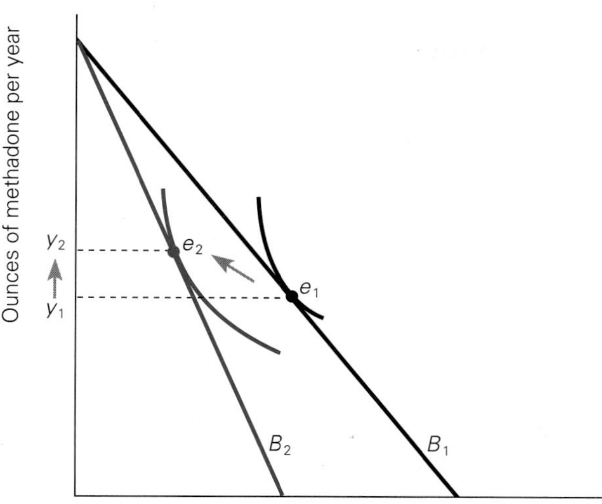

An increase in the price of heroin, represented by the budget constraint pivoting from B_1 to B_2, leads to an increase in the consumption of methadone. Hence, heroin and methadone are substitutes.

Figure 3.5

Complements in Consumption

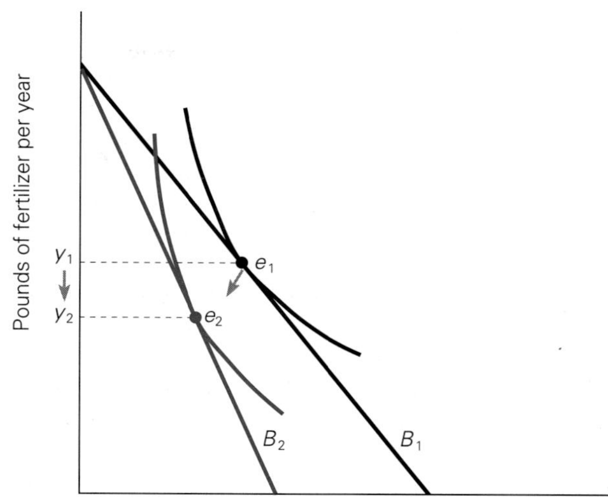

An increase in the price of weed killer, represented by the budget constraint pivoting from B_1 to B_2, decreases consumption of fertilizer. Hence, weed killer and fertilizer are complements.

weed killer, assuming the price of fertilizer is \$3. Therefore, when the price of fertilizer increases to \$4, *d* is no longer the demand curve because it does not correctly answer the question, How much weed killer is William willing to purchase at each price per gallon?

When the price of fertilizer goes up, we have to derive the demand curve for weed killer all over again. First, we find a new price-consumption curve for weed killer by varying its price while holding the price of fertilizer constant at its new level. We then record the new quantity demanded of weed killer at each price per gallon.

How does this new demand curve compare with the original? Consider point *a* on the demand curve, which shows that, given the initial price of fertilizer, William consumes 12 gallons per year when the price of weed killer is \$1. Because fertilizer and weed killer are complements, when the price of fertilizer increases to \$4, William is no longer willing to purchase 12 gallons of weed killer at \$1 per gallon—instead, his quantity demanded is 5 gallons. This point, denoted *b* in Figure 3.6, is on the new demand curve for weed killer.

But recall that point *a* was chosen arbitrarily. Because weed killer and fertilizer are complements, when the price of fertilizer increases, William demands less weed killer at every price of weed killer. For example, starting at point *f*, we move to point *g*; starting at point *h*, we move to *i*. Connecting these new points gives us the schedule *d*′, which is the demand curve for weed killer when the price of fertilizer is \$4. In summary, because fertilizer and weed killer are complements, an increase in the price of fertilizer shifts the demand curve for weed killer to the left. Similar reasoning suggests that for substitutes such as heroin and methadone

change in demand
A shift of the entire demand schedule.

change in quantity demanded
A movement along a given demand schedule.

Figure 3.6

Increase in the Price of a Complement Shifts Demand Curve Inward

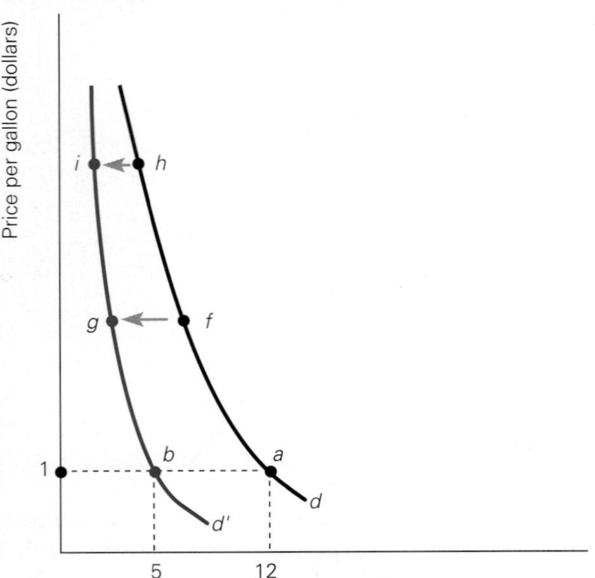

If weed killer and fertilizer are complements, then an increase in the price of fertilizer shifts the demand curve for weed killer inward, from *d* to *d'*.

Figure 3.7

Increase in the Price of a Substitute Shifts Demand Curve Outward

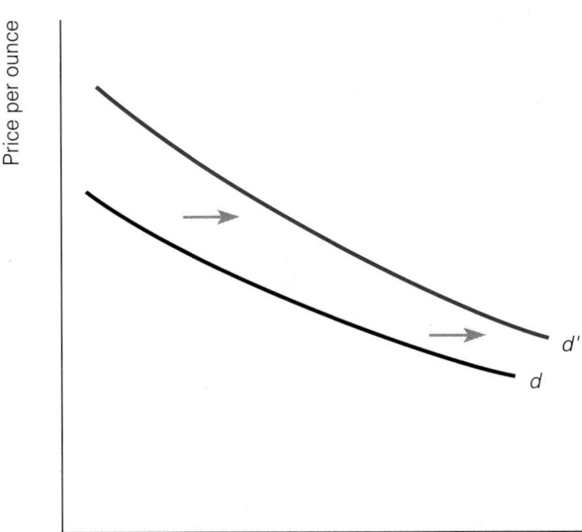

If heroin and methadone are substitutes, then an increase in the price of methadone shifts the demand curve for heroin outward, from *d* to *d'*.

(see Figure 3.4), if the price of methadone increases, the demand curve for heroin shifts to the right. Such a shift is illustrated in Figure 3.7.

To clarify the discussion of own-price and cross-price effects, it helps to distinguish between a **change in demand** and a **change in quantity demanded.** A change in demand refers to a shift of the entire demand schedule, as in Figures 3.6 and 3.7. A change in quantity demanded refers to a movement along a given demand schedule. Thus, we have shown that a change in the price of a substitute or complement generates a *change in demand.*[1] On the other hand, a movement along a demand curve induced by a change in its own price is a *change in quantity demanded.* For example, in Figure 3.6, the movement from point *a* to point *f* is a change in quantity demanded along demand curve *d.* (PC 3.2)

3.2 PROGRESS CHECK

Suppose the price of polyester shirts increases. What happens to an individual's demand curve for cotton shirts? Is this a change in demand or a change in quantity demanded?

INCOME CHANGES

The novelist John Steinbeck once noted, "When people are broke, the first thing they give up are books." In effect, Steinbeck's observation describes the outcome

[1]The notion that the change in the price of a related good can shift the demand curve was introduced intuitively in Chapter 1. We have now put that discussion on a rigorous basis by showing that such shifts are the result of optimizing behavior by individuals.

of a comparative statics exercise in which income (rather than price) is the variable that changes. To see how changes in income affect the consumer's equilibrium, consider Roth, who consumes books and grapes. In Figure 3.8, the grapes of Roth are measured on the vertical axis, and his books on the horizontal. Roth's initial budget constraint is B_1, and the equilibrium bundle is e_1. To analyze the effect of a decrease in income, we apply the method of comparative statics: Draw the budget constraint associated with the lower income level, find the new equilibrium, and compare it with the original bundle. We already know from Chapter 2 that a decrease in income is represented by a parallel shift inward of the original budget constraint, say from B_1 to B_2. Given the opportunities now available to him, Roth is best off with bundle e_2. Hence, the effect of the decrease in income is to change his consumption of books from x_1 to x_2, and of grapes from y_1 to y_2.

normal good
A good for which an increase in income increases consumption, *ceteris paribus*.

inferior good
A good for which an increase in income decreases consumption, *ceteris paribus*.

As a result of the decrease in income, Roth decreases his consumption of both books and grapes. A commodity for which consumption decreases when income decreases, or, equivalently, whose consumption increases when income increases, *ceteris paribus*, is referred to as a **normal good.** Now consider Figure 3.9, which depicts some consumer's preferences for macaroni and cheese versus steaks. According to the figure, when income increases, consumption of macaroni and cheese *decreases*, from y_1 to y_2. A commodity for which consumption decreases when income increases, *ceteris paribus*, is referred to as an **inferior good.** Housing and restaurant meals are examples of normal goods. Intercity railway transportation, on the other hand, is an example of an inferior good. When their incomes rise, people use automobiles and airplanes rather than trains for intercity travel. [See Houthakker and Taylor (1970, 118).]

3.3 PROGRESS CHECK

According to one statistical analysis of spending behavior, a change in personal income induces little or no change in wine consumption (Ruhm 1994). Sketch an indifference map that is consistent with this behavior. Verify your answer by drawing the budget constraints and equilibrium bundles for two different income levels.

Note that in Figure 3.8 each commodity is normal, while in Figure 3.9 one commodity (steak) is normal and one commodity (macaroni and cheese) is inferior. Can we draw a diagram in which *every* commodity is inferior? Absolutely not. Remember that, by assumption, all income is spent. Therefore, it is a simple matter of arithmetic that when income goes up, the consumption of *something* has to increase. If a consumer purchases 1,000 goods, 999 of them (*at most*) can be inferior. (PC 3.3)

Income Consumption Curve

income consumption curve
The set of equilibrium commodity bundles traced out as the consumer's income varies, *ceteris paribus*.

Given a particular set of prices, we can determine the set of equilibrium bundles traced as income changes, *ceteris paribus*. Mechanically, this involves finding the equilibrium bundles that correspond to a series of parallel shifts of the original budget constraint. The set of equilibrium commodity bundles traced as the consumer's income varies, *ceteris paribus*, is called the **income consumption curve.** It is illustrated in Figure 3.10. Just as we used the price-consumption curve to find the relationship between quantity demanded and price (see Figure 3.3), we can use the income-consumption curve to find the relationship between quantity

Figure 3.8

Normal Goods

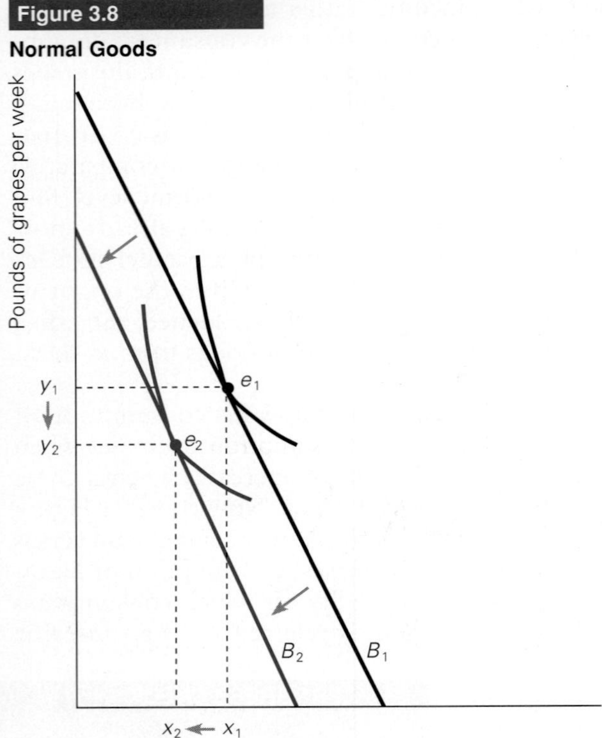

A decrease in income, represented by a parallel shift of the budget constraint from B_1 to B_2, decreases consumption of both books and grapes. Hence, books and grapes are both normal goods.

Figure 3.9

A Normal Good and an Inferior Good

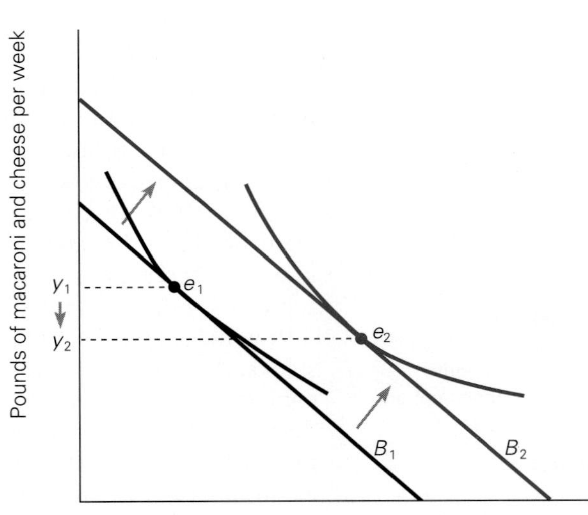

An increase in income represented by a parallel shift outward of the budget constraint, decreases the consumption of macaroni and cheese. Hence, macaroni and cheese is an inferior good.

Engel curve
A representation of the relationship between income and the consumption of a commodity, *ceteris paribus*.

demanded and income. This relationship is called the **Engel curve,**[2] and its derivation is left as an exercise for the reader.

Demand Curves and Income Changes

Our earlier discussion of cross-price effects showed that, when the price of a substitute or a complement changes, the demand curve for a commodity shifts. Likewise, a change in income shifts the demand curve. If a good is normal and income increases, the consumer wants to consume more at any given price. Hence, if books are normal goods, then an increase in income shifts the demand curve for books to the right, like the move from *d* to *d′* in Figure 3.11. On the other hand, if a commodity is inferior, its demand curve shifts to the left if income increases.

INTERPRETING DATA ON CONSUMER DEMAND

Ultimately, our information about how consumers behave has to come from real-world data on their expenditure patterns. Nevertheless, unless such data are

[2]Named after the 19th-century Prussian statistician, Ernst Engel.

Figure 3.10

The Income Consumption Curve

The income consumption curve shows the quantities of the two commodities consumed at each level of income.

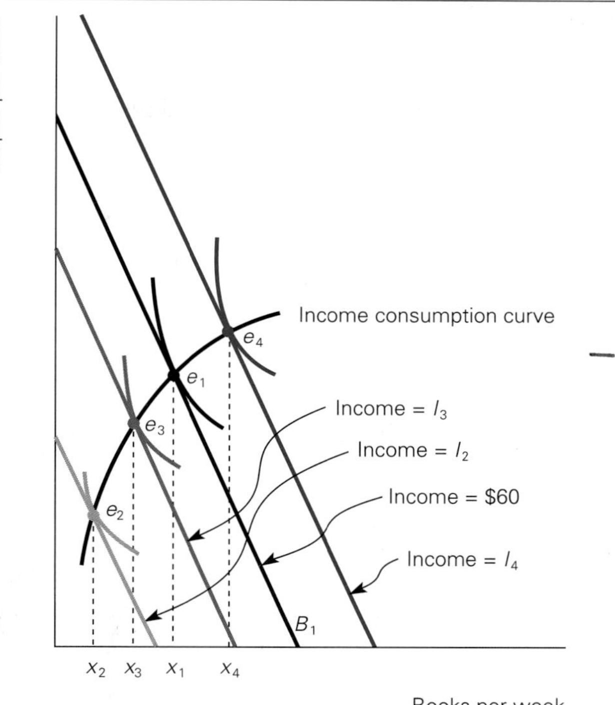

interpreted using the insights from economic theory, quite misleading conclusions can be drawn.

Suppose that in 1997 the price of gasoline is $1.25 per gallon, and in 1998 the price is $1.75 per gallon. We observe that Smith consumes 150 gallons of gasoline in 1997, and 200 gallons in 1998. Looking at these numbers, one might argue that Smith's demand curve for gasoline slopes upward!

The implicit assumption behind this conclusion is that in Figure 3.12, point *a* (price = $1.25, quantity = 150) and point *b* (price = $1.75, quantity = 200) lie on the same demand curve, *d*. However, our theory stipulates that to be "legitimate," a demand curve must show the quantities demanded at each price, *ceteris paribus.* There is no guarantee that between 1997 and 1998 other things *did* stay the same. For example:

1. Smith's income might have increased. If gasoline is a normal good, this would shift his demand curve for gasoline to the right. Thus, points *a* and *b* might lie on *two* downward-sloping demand curves (marked *d′* and *d″* in Figure 3.12), rather than a single upward-sloping demand curve.

2. As a consequence of a fall in the relative price of gas-guzzling cars, Smith might have purchased one in 1998. This fall in the price of a complement would also shift Smith's demand curve for gasoline to the right.

3. The relative price of public transportation in Smith's town may have increased. An increase in the price of a substitute could also be responsible for an outward shift in the demand curve.

Figure 3.11

Effect of an Income Change on Demand

If a commodity is a normal good, an increase in income shifts the demand curve to the right.

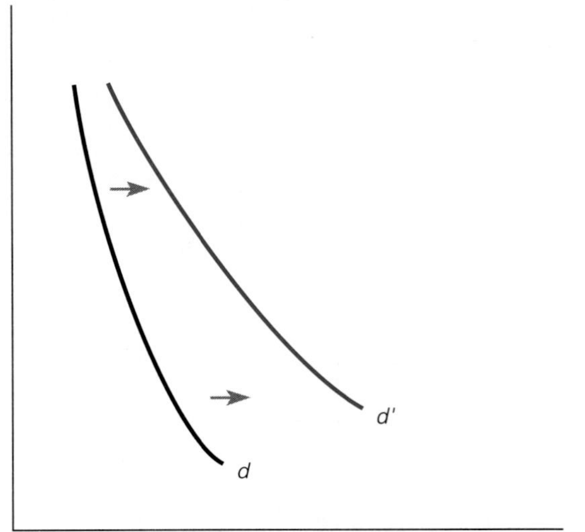

Figure 3.12

Analyzing Price and Quantity Changes over Time

Points *a* and *b* represent two different price-quantity pairs for gasoline. Because they are from two different time periods, there is no reason to assume that they lie on the same demand curve *d*. Instead, they might lie on two different demand curves, *d′* and *d″*.

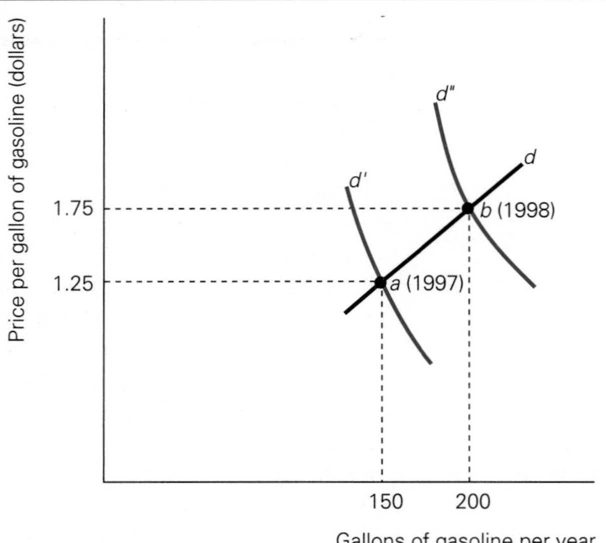

These explanations are not mutually exclusive, and you can doubtless think of many more. The moral is that considerable care must be exercised in deciding whether various observations on price and quantity actually lie on the same demand curve. This does ***not*** mean that it is impossible to use real-world data to estimate the shapes of demand curves. Statisticians have developed an arsenal of powerful tools for doing so. But it *does* mean that one must be very careful not to forget about *ceteris paribus* when trying to interpret consumption data.

Figure 3.13

Horizontal Summation of Demand Curves

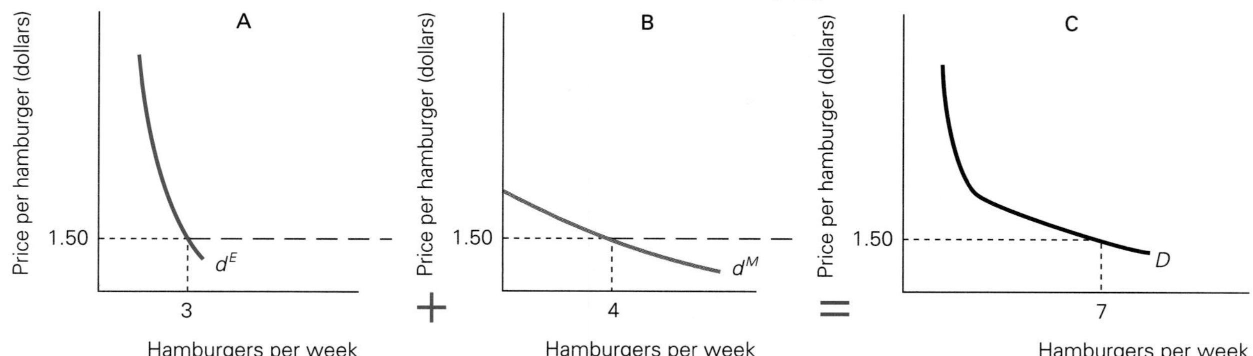

The market demand curve, *D* in Panel C, is found by horizontal summation of the individuals' demand curves.

MARKET DEMAND

market demand curve The relationship between a commodity's price and the quantity demanded by all market participants, *ceteris paribus.*

Our focus so far has been on the individual's demand for a commodity. However, the supply and demand model of Chapter 1 emphasized the role of the **market demand curve,** which shows at each price the quantity demanded by *all participants* in the market, *ceteris paribus.* Luckily, once we have each individual's demand curve, it is straightforward to derive the market demand curve.

Assume for simplicity that there are only two people in the market for hamburgers, Elizabeth and Margaret. Elizabeth's demand curve for hamburgers, d^E, is shown in Panel A of Figure 3.13. (The superscript *E* reminds you that it is Elizabeth's demand curve.) Margaret's demand curve, d^M, is shown in Panel B. We want to add these individual demand curves to find the market demand curve. That is, we want to construct a schedule stating the aggregate quantity of hamburgers that the two consumers demand at any given price.

horizontal summation The process of adding together individual demand curves to derive the market demand curve.

For a given price, we find the quantities demanded by each person and add these quantities together. For instance, Panel A shows that when the price is \$1.50, Elizabeth demands 3 hamburgers per week. Panel B indicates that at the same price, Margaret demands 4 hamburgers. The total quantity demanded when the price is \$1.50 is therefore 7. We have found one point on the market demand curve for hamburgers, which is labeled *D* in Panel C. Notice that we use *D* for market demand and *d* for individual demand. Also notice that finding the total quantity demanded at any price involves summing the horizontal distances between individuals' demand curves and the vertical axis at that price. This process of adding together individual demand curves to find the market demand curve is referred to as **horizontal summation** of the individual demand curves.

Individual versus Market Demand Curves

Demand curves are based on the theory of rational decision making but, as we noted in the last chapter, there are a number of objections to this theory. One of them is that it doesn't seem to be a good description of some people's behavior. You might know a "conspicuous consumer," for example, who likes to buy more of a certain kind of wine when its price goes up. Clearly, some individuals' consumption patterns are erratic, so our theory has no hope of explaining the behavior of every person at every instant of time. However, as also stressed in the last chapter, this really isn't too important. One of the main goals of the theory of choice is to derive *market* demand curves, as in Figure 3.13. Even if some individuals' demand curves exhibit peculiar properties, if these individuals are few, market demand curves will still slope downward.

A related use of demand theory is to make predictions about how people, or certain groups of people, will react in various circumstances. (If we subsidize flu shots, how many more people will take them?) Again, the fact that *some* individuals' behavior is inconsistent need not prevent us from making good predictions about the group. Some people may purchase "too much" of a commodity and others "too little." As long as these errors roughly cancel out, it may be possible to obtain good predictions about market behavior. And that is what we are really trying to do.

SECTION RECAP

One goal of microeconomics is to predict how people's behavior will change when their circumstances change. The method of comparative statics allows us to do just that. All we have to do is to convert the "change in circumstances" to a change in the budget constraint, and then find the individual's utility-maximizing decision subject to the new budget constraint. Of particular interest is how the consumption of a commodity changes when its price changes, *ceteris paribus*. Finding the answer to this question allows us to derive the individual's demand curve for the commodity.

3.2 COMPARATIVE STATICS APPLIED

In this section, we examine two examples that show how the analysis of comparative statics can yield important insights to real-world policy problems.

IN-KIND TRANSFERS

in-kind transfer
A payment made to an individual in the form of a commodity or service.

In 1982, headlines were made when the U.S. Department of Agriculture offered 224 million pounds of surplus cheese, butter, and dried milk to low-income Americans. Since then, the program has distributed over 5.5 billion pounds of food. This program is a minor example of an **in-kind transfer**—a payment to an individual in terms of a commodity or service as opposed to cash. We often think of government in-kind transfers as being directed toward lower-income individuals; food stamps, Medicaid, and public housing come to mind. However, middle- and upper-income people are also the beneficiaries of in-kind transfers. A prominent example is public education. An important public policy question is how in-kind transfers affect recipients' consumption bundles and whether direct cash transfers might be preferred. The method of comparative statics provides a framework for thinking carefully about these questions.

The first step is to determine how an in-kind transfer affects an individual's budget constraint. Figure 3.14 represents the situation of Edward, who divides an income of \$300 per month between cheese and housing. (The quantity of housing is measured in square feet of space.) The price of cheese is \$2 per pound;

Figure 3.14

Analysis of an In-Kind Transfer

With an in-kind transfer of 60 pounds of cheese, the budget constraint is *AFD* and the utility-maximizing bundle is e_2. With an equivalent cash transfer, the budget constraint is *HD* and utility is maximized at e_3. This individual prefers the cash transfer.

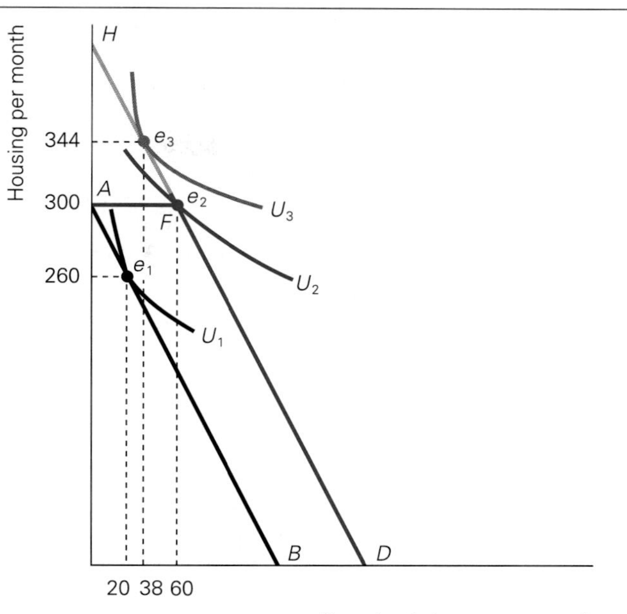

the price of housing is \$1 per square foot. Cheese consumption is measured on the horizontal axis and housing on the vertical. In the absence of any in-kind transfer program, Edward's budget constraint is line *AB*, whose slope is −2.

Now suppose the government provides Edward with 60 pounds of cheese per month, *which he is prohibited from reselling on the market.* How does the cheese program change his situation? At any level of housing consumption, Edward can now consume 60 more pounds of cheese than previously. Thus, his new budget constraint is found by taking each bundle on *AB* and adding to it 60 pounds of cheese. Geometrically, this amounts to moving *AB* to the right by an amount equal to 60 pounds of cheese. Hence, the new budget constraint is the kinked line *AFD*.

Next we introduce the individual's indifference curves. In Figure 3.14, in the absence of the program, Edward's utility-maximizing choice is bundle e_1, which consists of 20 pounds of cheese and 260 square feet of housing. With the program, the highest indifference curve that can be reached subject to constraint AFD is U_2. The utility-maximizing bundle is e_2—at the corner, where Edward's consumption of cheese is 60 pounds and his consumption of housing is 300 square feet. Interestingly, compared with his original bundle, Edward consumes more of both cheese and housing. Because the government provides him with free cheese, Edward can devote to housing money that otherwise would have been spent on cheese.

Now suppose that instead of giving Edward 60 pounds of cheese, the government gave him cash equal to its market value, \$120. An increase in income of \$120 leads to a budget line that is exactly 120 units above *AB* at every point, line *HD* in Figure 3.14. Note that the cash transfer allows Edward to consume along segment *HF*. This opportunity was not available under the cheese program because Edward was not allowed to trade government cheese for any other goods.

Figure 3.15

A Consumer Who Is Indifferent between an In-Kind Transfer and a Cash Grant

Sarah's utility is maximized at e_5 regardless of whether the transfer is in-kind or cash. She is indifferent between the two schemes.

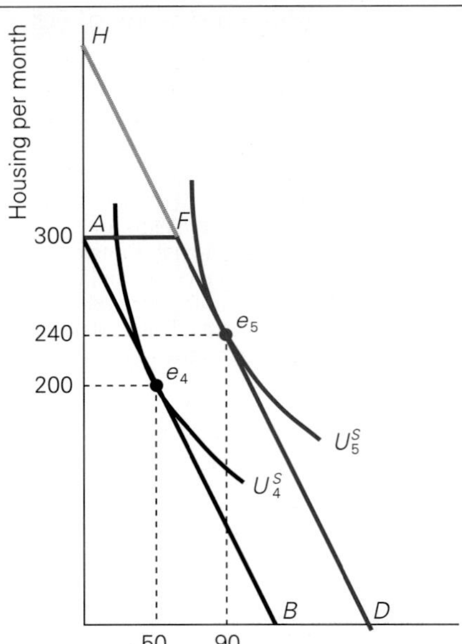

Facing budget line *HD*, Edward maximizes utility at e_3, where he consumes 38 pounds of cheese and 344 units of housing. Comparing points e_3 and e_2, we can conclude that (1) under the cash transfer program, Edward consumes less cheese and more housing than under the cheese giveaway program, and (2) $120 worth of cheese does not make Edward as well off as $120 of income. Because e_3 is on a higher indifference curve than point e_2, the cash transfer makes him better off. Intuitively, the problem with the cheese program is that it "forces" Edward to consume the full 60 pounds of cheese. He would prefer to sell some of the cheese and spend the proceeds on housing.

Is an in-kind transfer always worse than the cash equivalent? Not necessarily. Figure 3.15 depicts the situation of Sarah, whose income is identical to Edward's, and who therefore faces exactly the same budget constraints (*AB* before the cheese program, and *AFD* afterwards). However, Sarah has a different indifference map. Before the subsidy, she maximizes utility at point e_4, consuming 50 pounds of cheese and 200 square feet of housing. After the subsidy, she consumes 90 pounds of cheese and 240 square feet of housing. Sarah would not be better off with a cash transfer because her most-preferred point along *HD* is available under the cheese program anyway. Because Sarah is happy to consume more than 60 pounds of cheese, the restriction that she consume at least 60 pounds does her no harm.

In summary, from the recipient's point of view, an in-kind transfer can be as good as cash, but it can never be better and may be worse. Several studies have indicated that a dollar's worth of an in-kind transfer is indeed worth less than a dollar of cash. For example, Smeeding (1982) estimated that a dollar received in public housing is worth only 80 cents received in cash.

The importance of fungibility. Our analysis of the cheese program has emphasized the stipulation that recipients of the cheese could not sell it. What is the budget constraint if a black market for cheese develops? Because the price of cheese is $2 per pound, Edward can get $120 for his 60 pounds of cheese. The cheese program is equivalent to an increase in Edward's income of $120, which shifts his budget line outward from *AB* to *HD*.

This discussion illustrates a very general and very important proposition—*as long as all goods can be bought and sold freely on the market, the fact that a transfer comes in an in-kind form is pretty much irrelevant.* The commodity involved in the transfer can be converted to cash, which can then be used to purchase any other commodity. A commodity is said to be **fungible** when it is freely exchangeable into another commodity. In our example of an in-kind transfer, fungibility holds only to the extent that the black market functions smoothly. For example, if some people do not participate because they are afraid of getting caught, the commodity is not fully fungible. (PC 3.4)

3.4 PROGRESS CHECK

Recently a neighborhood group on the West Side of Manhattan instituted a program to reduce panhandling. Under the plan, residents can give 25-cent vouchers to panhandlers instead of cash. The vouchers are redeemable at local stores for food but not alcohol. The idea is to make sure that money given to help the panhandlers will not end up being used for alcohol or drugs. Use the concept of fungibility to discuss whether or not this program is likely to be successful.

fungible
The quality of being freely exchangeable into another commodity.

CHARITABLE GIVING

People all over the world contribute to charity. In the United States, about three-quarters of all households contribute an average of $978 annually, about 2 percent of personal income.[3] In Britain, voluntary personal contributions are about 0.2 percent of personal income; in Canada, 0.5 percent; and in Germany, 1.7 percent. Is such behavior consistent with individual utility maximization? It certainly is. As we noted in the last chapter, if donating money to others gives you satisfaction, then charitable giving can be regarded as a commodity, and the standard tools can be used to analyze individuals' decisions about how much to give.

Consider William, who divides his income of $25,000 between two commodities, *donations to charity* (x), and his own consumption of a composite of *all other goods* (y). William's preferences between the two goods are represented by a set of convex indifference curves in Figure 3.16.

To find out how much William donates, we have to draw in his budget constraint. This requires that we know the price of each commodity. As usual, we assume that the price per unit of the composite y is $1. What is the price of a unit of charitable contributions? For each dollar William donates, he forgoes $1 of his own consumption. Therefore, the "price" of each dollar of charity is simply $1. Putting this information together with the fact that William's after-tax income is $25,000, his budget constraint is

$$1x + 1y = 25{,}000.$$

[3]See Barringer (1992) and Clotfelter (1985, 97–98).

Figure 3.16
Charitable Giving

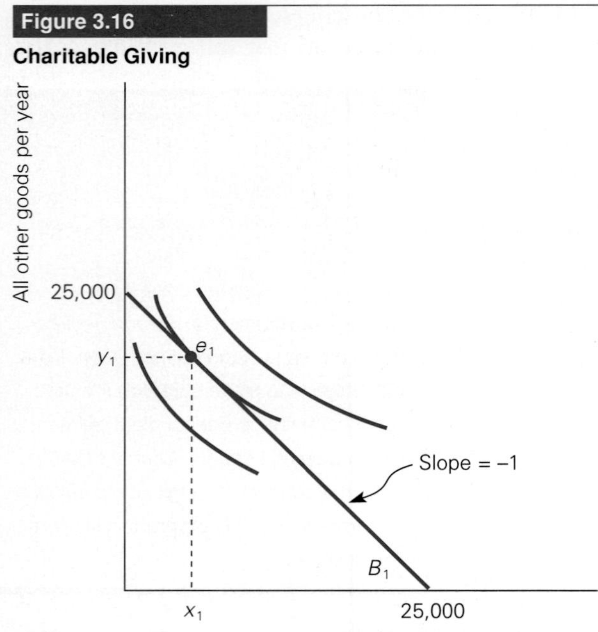

The "price" of each dollar of charitable donations is $1. Hence, the budget constraint for charitable donations and own consumption is a straight line, the slope of which is −1.

Figure 3.17
Charitable Giving with a Tax Deduction

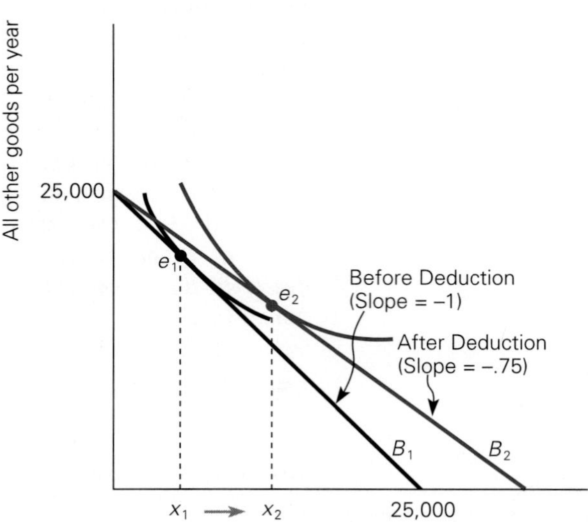

A charitable deduction lowers the opportunity cost of giving, pivoting the budget constraint from B_1 to B_2. The slope of B_2 is the negative of one minus the tax rate.

In Figure 3.16, this budget constraint is straight line B_1, whose slope is -1. William's most preferred bundle is e_1, where he donates x_1 to charity and spends the rest of his income on y_1 units of *all other goods.*

Canada, Germany, Japan, and the United States, among other countries, allow individuals to deduct contributions from their taxable incomes. We can use our comparative statics methods to analyze the effects of such provisions. The key to the analysis is that tax deductibility changes a person's effective price of making a contribution and shifts the budget constraint. To see why, suppose that William was paying 25 percent of his taxable income to the government. Without deductibility, if William gave $1 to charity, he had $1 less to spend on *all other goods.* But with deductibility, if William gives $1 to charity, his tax bill is reduced by $.25. Hence, the amount of money to spend on *all other goods* falls by only $.75. The opportunity cost of charitable giving (in terms of forgone consumption of *all other goods*) is now only $.75. With deductibility, William's budget constraint is

$$0.75x + 1y = 25{,}000.$$

In Figure 3.17, this constraint is represented by line B_2, the slope of which is -0.75. More generally, if the tax rate on each dollar of taxable income is t, then a charitable deduction reduces the opportunity cost of each dollar of giving from $1 to $\$(1 - t)$.

Finding out the effect of the tax deduction is now only a standard comparative statics exercise. With budget constraint B_2, the most preferred bundle is e_2, where charitable donations are x_2. William's donations increase from x_1 to x_2 because of the deduction. Of course, by now you have had enough experience doing comparative statics to realize that, depending on the shapes of the individual's indifference curves, he or she might increase donations by more or less than this amount, or not at all. In fact, statistical studies for Britain, Germany, and the United States have all indicated that when the effective price of charity falls by 10 percent, on average charitable donations increase by 10 percent or more (Clotfelter 1985, 98–99). Thus, the amount of charitable giving depends quite heavily on the existence of the deduction.

Does this mean that charitable giving is a cynical tax dodge? The answer is no. After all, even with a tax deduction, a donation reduces a person's level of personal consumption. However, it would be equally incorrect to believe that even very generous people ignore the cost of "doing good." As with most other commodities, the demand for charitable giving slopes downward.

SECTION RECAP

The method of comparative statics allows us to determine how a consumer's behavior changes when his or her economic environment changes. As our charitable-giving example illustrates, this procedure has wide applicability, particularly if we are flexible in defining what a commodity is. In the process of doing comparative statics, we also find out whether any particular change makes an individual better or worse off—all we have to do is see whether he or she ends up on a higher or lower indifference curve. The example of in-kind transfers shows how we can use this fact to examine the effects of alternative policies on individuals' welfare.

3.3 ELASTICITY

The demand curve embodies huge amounts of information on how consumers' behavior responds to price changes. It would be convenient to have a compact way to summarize the information generated by various comparative statics exercises. In this section, we describe a simple numerical measure that accomplishes this goal.

PRICE ELASTICITY OF DEMAND

We often need to measure the responsiveness of quantity demanded to changes in price; that is, to describe the "shape" of the market demand curve. For instance, if a city transit authority is considering a subway fare hike, such information is needed to predict the fall in subway ridership.

Because slopes have come up so often in this and previous chapters, you might think that the slope of the demand curve is a natural measure of responsiveness. Unfortunately, it is not. To see why, consider the two panels in Figure 3.18, each of which illustrates a hypothetical demand curve for beef. Using slope as our measure of responsiveness, we would have to conclude that demand in Panel B is much more responsive than demand in Panel A—the demand curve in Panel B is much flatter so that any given price change seems to lead to a bigger quantity change.

So what's the problem? The graph drawn in Panel A is exactly the *same* demand curve graphed in Panel B. The only reason that they appear different is that

Figure 3.18

Price Elasticity Does Not Depend on Units

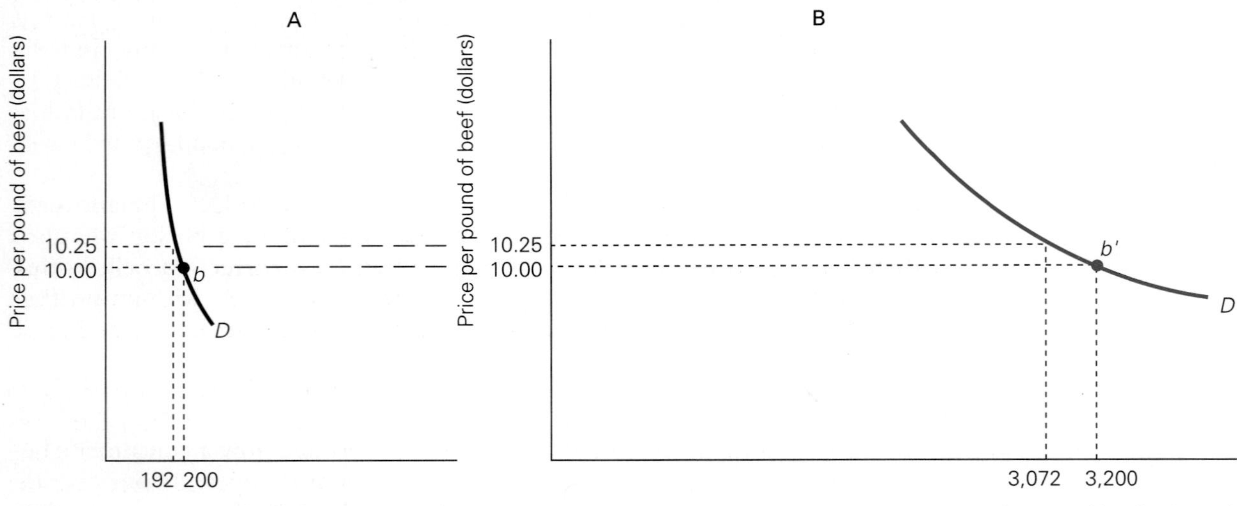

The demand curves in Panels A and B contain identical information about how the quantity of beef demanded responds to changes in its price. Yet, if this responsiveness is measured by the ratio of the change in quantity demanded to change in price, very different answers are obtained because the units of measurement are different in the two panels. The elasticity measure, which is based on *percentage* changes, avoids this flaw.

the units on the two horizontal axes are different. In Panel A, the units are pounds of beef per week; in Panel B, the units are ounces of beef per week. Because these two graphs are alternative representations of exactly the same demand curve, we certainly do not want to claim that the curve graphed in one panel is more responsive than the demand curve graphed in the other panel. We conclude that for purposes of summarizing the shape of a demand curve, the slope by itself is virtually useless because it depends on the units in which quantities and prices are measured.

price elasticity of demand
The negative of the percentage change in quantity demanded divided by the percentage change in price.

To be useful, a measure must not depend arbitrarily on the units in which quantity and price are measured. A measure that fits the bill is the **price elasticity of demand,** defined as the negative of the percentage change in quantity demanded divided by the percentage change in price. Algebraically, if we denote the price elasticity of demand by ϵ (lower-case Greek epsilon), then

$$\epsilon = -\frac{\%\Delta X}{\%\Delta p}, \tag{3.1}$$

where "%Δ" means *percentage change.* Because demand curves slope downward, the percentage change in price and the percentage change in quantity have opposite signs, and their ratio is negative. However, it is tedious and sometimes confusing for price elasticities to be negative. The reason for the minus sign is to avoid this problem—as long as the demand curve slopes downward, ϵ is positive. With this convention, a larger value of ϵ means that demand is *more* responsive to price.

Computing Elasticities

The easiest way to show that elasticity does not depend upon units is to do some actual calculations. In practice, elasticity can be computed in several ways. The starting point for all approaches is to note that for a price p and an associated quantity demanded X, the expression for ϵ can be written as

$$-\frac{\Delta X}{X} \div \frac{\Delta p}{p}, \tag{3.2}$$

where Δp is an increase in p, and ΔX is the induced change in the quantity demanded of X. The reason that Expression (3.2) is an elasticity is that when any number Z changes by some amount ΔZ, the *percentage* change is $\Delta Z/Z$. For example, if Z increases from 100 to 101, $\Delta Z = 1$ and $\Delta Z/Z = 1/100$, or 1 percent. Hence, $\Delta X/X$ and $\Delta p/p$ are percentage changes in quantity demanded and price, respectively.

Let us use this expression to compute the elasticity of demand at point b on the hypothetical beef demand curve in Panel A of Figure 3.18. At this point, $p =$ \$10 and $X = 200$ pounds per week. Now consider a small increase in p to \$10.25 per pound, so that $\Delta p =$ \$0.25. Then $\Delta p/p$ is $0.25/10 = 0.025$. Because the quantity falls to 192 pounds per week, $-\Delta X$ is 8 and $-\Delta X/X$ is 0.04 ($= 8/200$). Substituting these values into Expression (3.2) gives us an elasticity of $0.04/0.025 = 1.6$. This means that around point b, a 1 percent increase in the price of beef would lead to a 1.6 percent decrease in the quantity demanded.

Next, we calculate the elasticity at the comparable point in Panel B, point b'. As in Panel A, $\Delta p/p$ is 0.025. Now $-\Delta X = 128$, but $X = 3{,}200$, so $-\Delta X/X$ equals 0.04, just as before. The elasticity at point b' is therefore $0.04/0.025 = 1.6$, which is identical to the value we obtained for point b in Panel A.

Thus, as we hoped, elasticity does not depend on choice of units. Intuitively, percentage changes do not depend on units of measurement because the units cancel out in the numerator and denominator. If you state that your weight has increased by 15 percent, the same information is conveyed whether your weight is measured in pounds, ounces, kilograms, or metric tons. Another advantage of using percentages is that it facilitates comparisons across commodities. A \$1 increase in the price of a stick of bubble gum means something very different than a \$1 increase in the price of a Mercedes Benz. If we want to compare how responsive the demands of these two commodities are, it makes more sense to ask how the quantity demanded of each changes when its price increases by 1 percent, not by 1 dollar. This is precisely what the elasticity does. (PC 3.5)

> **3.5 PROGRESS CHECK**
>
> In the African nation of Côte d'Ivoire, the price elasticity of demand for beef is 1.91 (Deaton 1988, 429). Suppose that the price of beef goes up by 10 percent. How much will the quantity demanded fall?
>
> Do you know the name of the currency used in Côte d'Ivoire, and its value in dollars? Do you know the unit of weight in Côte d'Ivoire? Probably not. Then how were you able to find the change in quantity demanded?

A practical issue in computing elasticities relates to the calculation of percentage changes. When calculating the percentage change from one point on the demand curve to another, how do we know which point is the original (initial) point? Should the percentage difference between 10 and 10.25 be calculated as

0.25/10 or 0.25/10.25? The answer is that the choice of the initial point is arbitrary. However, as long as the two points are relatively close to each other on the demand curve, the particular selection of an original point has little effect on ϵ. For instance, when we recalculate the elasticity of demand for beef by substituting $p = \$10.25$ per pound and $X = 192$ pounds into Expression (3.2), the answer is 1.7, not very different from the 1.6 we found above.[4]

For small price changes, there is a convenient way to express price elasticity. If we invert the fraction in the denominator of (3.2) and rearrange, we obtain

$$-\frac{\Delta X}{\Delta p}\,\frac{p}{X}. \tag{3.3}$$

Notice that $\Delta X/\Delta p$ is just the inverse of the slope of the demand curve.[5] Hence, the elasticity at a point on a demand curve—known as the *point elasticity of demand*—is formed by multiplying the inverse of the slope at that point by the ratio of p to X. Algebraically, if we denote the slope by s, then we can write

$$\textit{Point elasticity of demand} = -\frac{1}{s}\,\frac{p}{X}. \tag{3.4}$$

In general, as we move along a demand curve, the value of the slope changes as well as the ratio of p to X. Hence, in general, the value of the elasticity differs at different points on the demand curve. Therefore, when we say that "the" price elasticity of demand for beer in the United States is 0.3, we mean that if the *going price* were to be raised by 1 percent, the quantity demanded would fall by 0.3 percent.[6] At a much higher or much lower price, however, the value of ϵ could be quite different.

As noted above, point elasticity is useful when considering small price changes. However, sometimes one must compute elasticities that are associated with relatively large changes in price. For example, within a two-week period several years ago, the price of broccoli almost doubled after some scientists claimed that eating it might reduce the risk of cancer. In such cases, the choice of an original point can make a substantial difference. For example, if a price goes from \$10 to \$15, is this a 50 percent change (5/10) or a 33 percent change (5/15)? As already suggested, there is no "correct" answer. The important thing is to make some choice and then follow it consistently. The conventional choice is to compromise; rather than use \$10 or \$15 as the base point, take their average, \$12.50. Using this convention, we would define the percentage difference between 10 and 15 to be $5/12.5 = 0.40$. Similarly, the percentage change in quantity demanded is found by dividing the change in quantity demanded by the average of the first and second quantities. An elasticity computed this way is called an *arc elasticity of demand.*

We can describe this procedure algebraically. Define $\overline{X}$ to be the average value of the first and second quantities, and $\overline{p}$ to be the average of the first and second

[4]As Δp becomes infinitesimally small, there is no ambiguity at all. See the Appendix to this chapter for details.

[5]If we wrote the demand function algebraically, $X = f(p)$, then $\Delta X/\Delta p$ would be the slope of the demand *function*, not its inverse. However, $\Delta X/\Delta p$ is the inverse of the slope of the demand *curve* because demand curves are conventionally drawn with the quantity on the horizontal axis. There is no real reason for this convention except tradition—economists have been doing it this way since the time of the British economist Alfred Marshall (1842–1924).

[6]See Grossman, Sindelar, Mullahy, and Anderson (1993).

Table 3.1

Price Elasticity of Demands for Selected Commodities in the United States

Commodity	Elasticity
Restaurant meals	2.27
Tobacco products	0.46
Shoes and other footwear	0.73
Jewelry and watches	0.41
Electricity	0.13
Water	0.20
Rental housing	0.18
Kitchen appliances	0.67
Telephone	0.26
Legal services	0.37

Source: Houthakker and Taylor (1970)

prices. The percentage change in quantity demanded is $\Delta X/\overline{X}$, and the percentage change in price is $\Delta p/\overline{p}$. Then

$$\textit{Arc elasticity of demand} = -\frac{\Delta X}{\overline{X}} \div \frac{\Delta p}{\overline{p}}. \tag{3.5}$$

To summarize: The price elasticity of demand is the negative of the percentage change in quantity demanded divided by the percentage change in price. For small changes in price, the easiest way to calculate an elasticity is to substitute into Equation (3.4); for large changes, it is necessary to use the arc elasticity of demand, Equation (3.5). In either case, the price elasticity does not depend on the units in which prices or quantities are measured.

3.6 PROGRESS CHECK

When the price of Winesap Personal Computers falls from $3,000 to $2,500, the quantity demanded increases from 4 million to 5 million per year. Compute the arc elasticity of demand for Winesap Personal Computers.

Table 3.1 provides a sampling of elasticities that economists have estimated by analyzing data on U.S. consumer expenditure patterns. Such information can be important for policy purposes. Suppose, for example, that the government wishes to raise the price of tobacco products to reduce smoking by 10 percent. The fact that the price elasticity for tobacco products is 0.46 tells policymakers they would have to raise prices by 21.7 percent to bring about this reduction in quantity demanded (because $0.46 \times 21.7 = 10$). (PC 3.6)

PRICE ELASTICITY AND TOTAL EXPENDITURE

total expenditure The amount of money consumers spend on a commodity, computed as the number of units purchased times the price per unit.

With the price elasticity of demand, we can predict how the amount spent on a commodity changes when its price changes. To be more specific, define **total expenditure** as the amount of money consumers spend on a commodity. By definition, total expenditure is the number of units purchased (X) times the price per unit (p), that is,

$$\textit{Total expenditure} = p \times X.$$

For example, in 1995 people rented about 3 billion video cassettes at an average price of $2.67 per rental. Hence, total expenditures during that period were $10 billion (= 3 billion × $2.67).

Figure 3.19

Price Changes and Total Expenditure

When the price is p_1, total expenditure is $A + B$. When the price increases to p_2, total expenditure is $A + C$. Which total expenditure is larger depends on the relative sizes of areas B and C. For this particular situation, total expenditure falls when price increases, so the elasticity exceeds one.

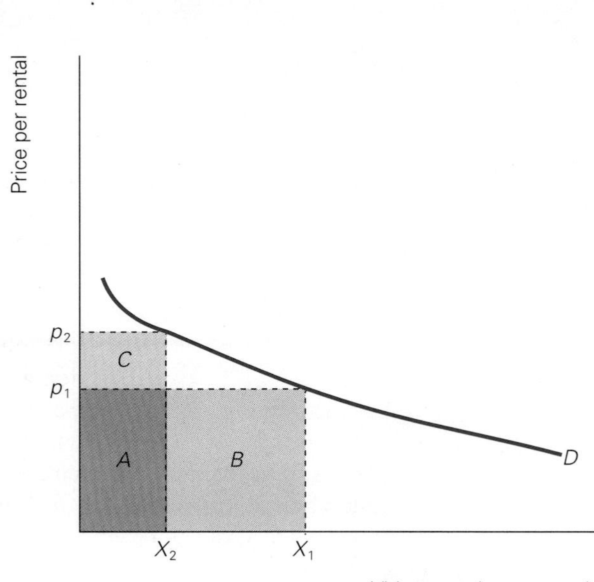

Now, suppose that p increases. Because the market demand curve slopes downward, X decreases. Thus, *in general, we do not know what happens to total expenditure when price increases.* To illustrate this point, consider Figure 3.19, which shows the market demand curve for video rentals. According to the diagram, when the price per rental is p_1, the quantity demanded is X_1. Now, p_1 is the height of the rectangle whose area is $A + B$, and X_1 is its width. Hence, the product of p_1 and X_1 is just the rectangular area $A + B$. Because $p_1 \times X_1$ is total expenditure when the price is p_1, rectangle $A + B$ shows total expenditure when the price is p_1.

Assume that the price per rental rises to p_2. The quantity demanded falls to X_2 and, using the same logic as before, total expenditure is area $A + C$. Has total expenditure gone up or down? Comparing the two rectangles, we see that when the price increases, total expenditure increases by area C because people are spending more for each rental. But total expenditure falls by area B because people rent fewer videos when their price goes up. Which area is bigger, C or B? In this particular case, B is bigger, but in general it can go either way—the effect on total expenditure of a price change depends on the shape of the demand curve under consideration.

Now suppose we are given an additional piece of information—the price elasticity of demand is less than one ($\epsilon < 1$). By definition, this means that when the price goes up by a given percentage, the quantity demanded falls by a smaller percentage. (This has to be true because their quotient, the elasticity, is less than one.) Because X falls by a smaller percentage than p rises, their product must increase. Therefore, when $\epsilon < 1$, total expenditure increases when price increases. A demand curve for which $\epsilon < 1$ at some price is said to be **inelastic** at that price. Intuitively, when the demand for a commodity is inelastic, quantity demanded is not very responsive to changes in price. Because the quantity demanded does not

inelastic
Price elasticity of demand is less than one.

Table 3.2

Price Elasticity of Demand and Total Expenditure

Price Elasticity	Effect on Total Expenditure When Price Increases	Effect on Total Expenditure When Price Decreases
Inelastic ($\epsilon < 1$)	Increase	Decrease
Unitary ($\epsilon = 1$)	Same	Same
Elastic ($\epsilon > 1$)	Decrease	Increase

go down very much when price increases, consumers end up spending more money on the commodity.

elastic
Price elasticity of demand is greater than one.

Next, let us consider a commodity whose price elasticity of demand is greater than one ($\epsilon > 1$). Such a demand curve is said to be **elastic** at that price. In this case, the percentage decrease in quantity demanded is greater than the percentage increase in price. Because the percentage reduction in quantity demanded more than offsets the percentage increase in price, total expenditure decreases. For commodities with $\epsilon > 1$, the quantity demanded is so responsive to price that total expenditure actually falls when the price rises. (This is the situation depicted in Figure 3.19.)

unit elastic
The price elasticity of demand equals one.

This leaves us only with the middle case of $\epsilon = 1$. When demand is **unit elastic,** the percentage increase in price exactly equals the percentage decrease in quantity demanded. Because the percentage increase in one number exactly offsets the percentage decrease in the other, their product does not change. When price goes up and demand is unit elastic, expenditures on the commodity stay the same.

The relationship between changes in total expenditure and the price elasticity of demand is summarized in Table 3.2. If you know the price elasticity of demand, you can predict how total expenditure will change when price changes, *ceteris paribus.* At the same time, if you observe how total expenditure changes in response to a change in price, you can infer the price elasticity of demand.

Determinants of the Price Elasticity of Demand

What determines the price elasticity of a market demand curve? Several factors are involved.

1. *The presence of close substitutes for a commodity tends to make its demand more elastic.* If people consider Hondas to be close substitutes for Toyotas, then if the price of Toyotas increases, *ceteris paribus,* many consumers will defect to Hondas. Hence, the elasticity of demand for Toyotas is quite elastic. Insulin, on the other hand, has no close substitutes, and we would expect it to have a very inelastic demand. In this context, note that the precise way in which a commodity is defined can have a major impact on its price elasticity. The demand for *shoes* is inelastic because it is difficult to go outside without them. However, the demand for *Reeboks* (or any other particular brand) is quite elastic, because consumers can substitute one company's product for another fairly easily. In general, the demand for a narrowly defined commodity (such as *denim jeans*) is more elastic than the demand for a more broadly defined commodity (such as *clothing*).

2. *The elasticity depends on the commodity's share in the consumer's budget.* In general (although not always), the smaller the fraction of income absorbed by a commodity, the less elastic the demand, *ceteris paribus.* We don't expect people

to cut back their safety pin purchases when safety pins become more expensive. In contrast, if auto prices go up, many families will purchase fewer cars.

3. *The elasticity depends upon the time frame of the analysis.* As noted earlier, the comparative statics exercises that lie behind the demand curve compare various equilibria, but they do not say how long it takes to get from one equilibrium to another. Sometimes it may take quite a while for consumers to respond fully to changes in price. Thus, the elasticity of demand for a commodity may be greater in the long run than in the short run. Unfortunately, this fact is often ignored by decision makers.

Consider, for example, the problem of commuter rail transportation. When public transit authorities need to increase revenues, a typical tactic is to increase fares. The implicit assumption behind this strategy is that, although some travelers may defect from public transit if its price goes up, their numbers will be small enough that the price increase will outweigh any fall in quantity. In terms of our jargon, the transit authorities are assuming that the demand for commuter rail transportation is inelastic.

This assumption of inelastic demand is quite plausible for the short run. If the price of a ticket goes up on June 3, on June 4 the typical commuter has little choice but to take the same trip he or she took the day before. Indeed, in a careful statistical study, Voith (1991) analyzed the demand for commuter rail ridership in the Philadelphia area and found that the short-run elasticity of demand is 0.54. In the short run, a fare increase leads to higher transit authority revenues.

What about the long run? Given time, a consumer can respond to an increase in price by buying an automobile (or a second automobile), joining a car pool, moving to a new residence that is closer to work, or finding a job that is closer to home. Thus, given a longer time horizon, the elasticity of demand for public transportation may be considerably greater than the short-run elasticity. Voith found that the long-run elasticity for Philadelphia commuter ridership was 1.84. Because short-run demand is inelastic, an increase in fares initially raises revenues, so that transit authorities believe the strategy is "successful." However, the policy is a failure in the long run. Because the elasticity is greater than one after one year, total expenditure falls when price is increased. This is just one example of how public policy can go awry when decisions are made without properly accounting for the reactions of consumers to changes in prices.

Another important example of the impact of the time horizon on elasticities is provided by gasoline. In a one-year time frame, the price elasticity of demand is 0.11. For a 5-year horizon, however, it rises to 0.49, and over a 10-year period it is 0.82 (see Poterba 1991, 16). Thus, price increases are a powerful way to encourage conservation of gasoline use, but the full impact may take several years to be felt.

PRICE ELASTICITY FOR SOME SPECIAL CASES

The elasticities of certain special types of demand curves are worth noting.

Vertical Demand Curve

Let's return to the case of insulin. We expect that over some range of prices, quantity demanded may not respond at all to changes in price. This situation is illustrated in Figure 3.20, where the demand curve is a vertical line. Because the

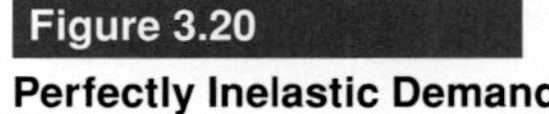

Figure 3.20

Perfectly Inelastic Demand

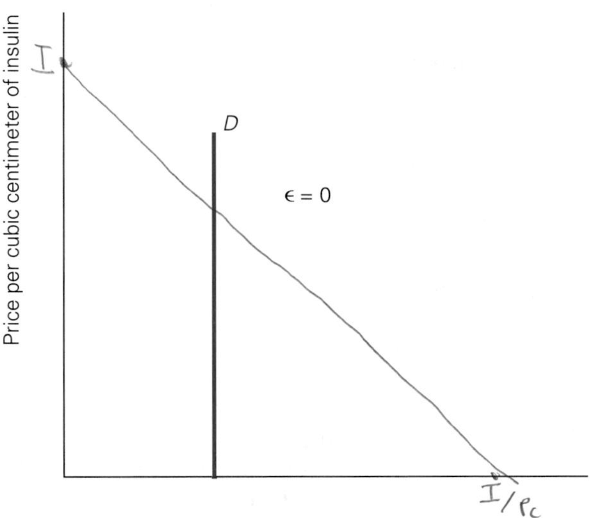

When the demand curve is vertical, quantity demanded does not change when price changes. Hence, the price elasticity of demand is zero.

Figure 3.21

Perfectly Elastic Demand

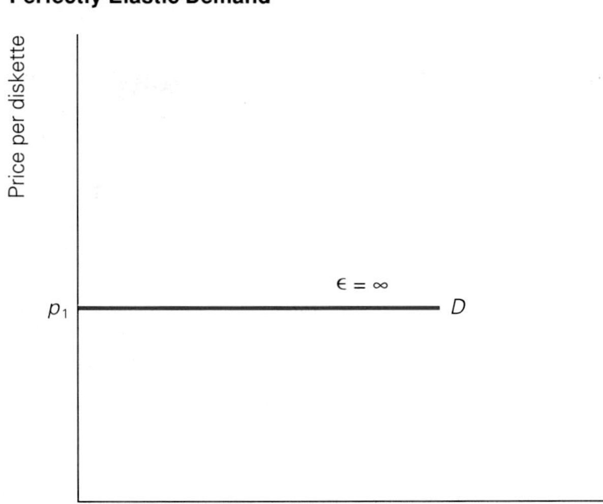

When the demand curve is horizontal, consumers are willing to purchase as much of the commodity as they can at the going price. But if the price increases even by a bit, quantity demanded falls to zero. The price elasticity of demand is infinite.

quantity demanded does not change at all when price increases, by definition, $\epsilon = 0$. A vertical demand curve is called **perfectly inelastic.** It is hard to think of a commodity that is literally perfectly inelastic at all prices. After all, if $\epsilon = 0$ for a commodity and the price is high enough, then total expenditure on the commodity could exhaust people's entire budgets. Nevertheless, over some price ranges, the demand for certain commodities might be perfectly inelastic. Think about the demand for an appendectomy by a person in the midst of an appendicitis attack.

perfectly inelastic
The price elasticity of demand equals zero; quantity demanded does not change at all when price changes.

Horizontal Demand Curve

Suppose that the computer diskettes produced by the Acme Company are regarded by consumers as indistinguishable from all other diskettes. Then if Acme raises its price above the market price p_1, it will sell no diskettes at all. In this case, the demand curve for Acme's diskettes is horizontal at p_1 (see Figure 3.21). A horizontal demand curve indicates that consumers are willing to purchase as much as they can at the going price. But if the price goes even a penny above p_1, the quantity demanded falls to zero. Because of the huge drop in quantity demanded when price increases, this is referred to as a **perfectly elastic** or **infinitely elastic** demand curve. The demand curve for a commodity is infinitely elastic if it is a perfect substitute for some other commodity.

perfectly elastic or infinitely elastic
The price elasticity of demand equals infinity; the demand curve is horizontal.

Unit Elastic Demand Curve

Suppose that the market demand curve for sunglasses has $\epsilon = 1$ at *every* price. What does the demand curve look like? Recall that if $\epsilon = 1$ *everywhere* on the demand curve, then total expenditure is always the same regardless of price. For example, suppose that the total expenditure for sunglasses is \$16 million. Then for *all* points on the demand curve, $p \times X = \$16$ million. Thus, if $p = \$8$, then $X = 2$ million; if $p = \$4$, then $X = 4$ million; and so on. Graphing all such points leads to the demand curve depicted in Figure 3.22.[7]

A common mistake is to think that when the elasticity is a constant at 1, then the demand curve must be a straight line. This mistake results from confusing slopes and elasticities. If the *slope* is constant, then the demand curve *is* a straight line. But, as Figure 3.22 demonstrates, a constant elasticity does not in general imply a constant slope.

Linear Demand Curve

What is the elasticity of a downward-sloping demand curve that is a straight line? This is a trick question, because as we move along a linear demand curve, the elasticity changes from point to point. To see why, suppose that the demand function for dental services is linear: $X = a - bp$, where X is the number of visits to the dentist, p is the price per visit, and a and b are positive numbers. This demand curve is plotted in Figure 3.23. At *every* point on the line $\Delta X/\Delta p = -b$. Substituting this fact into Expression (3.3) yields

$$\epsilon_L = b\frac{p}{X}, \tag{3.6}$$

where ϵ_L is the elasticity at a point on a linear demand curve.

This expression tells us that at the horizontal intercept, where $p = 0$, ϵ_L must also be zero. Moreover, as we move upward from this point, ϵ_L steadily increases because b is a constant and p/X increases as we move upward along the demand curve. Indeed, at the vertical intercept, where $X = 0$, the elasticity is infinite. (Just evaluate the expression for ϵ_L as X approaches zero.)

If ϵ_L steadily increases from zero to infinity as we move upward, then at some point ϵ_L must be exactly one. It turns out that at the midpoint on a linear demand curve, the elasticity is just equal to one. (See Discussion Question 3.12.) Thus, on a linear demand curve, points below the midpoint are price inelastic, and points above the midpoint are price elastic.

CROSS-PRICE ELASTICITY OF DEMAND

cross-price elasticity of demand for good *X* with respect to the price of good *Y*
The percentage change in the quantity of X demanded that is induced by a percentage change in the price of Y; a measure of the degree to which two goods are substitutes or complements.

So far our focus has been on summarizing how the quantity demanded of a commodity changes when its own price changes. However, our earlier analysis of cross-price effects indicated that the change in the price of one commodity can affect the quantity demanded of another. The **cross-price elasticity of demand for good *X* with respect to the price of good *Y***, ϵ_{xy}, is the percentage change in the quantity demanded of X induced by a percentage change in the price of Y. Algebraically,

$$\epsilon_{xy} = \frac{\%\Delta X}{\%\Delta p_y}. \tag{3.7}$$

[7]You may remember from algebra that such a curve is referred to as a *rectangular hyperbola*.

Figure 3.22

Demand Curve with Constant Elasticity of One

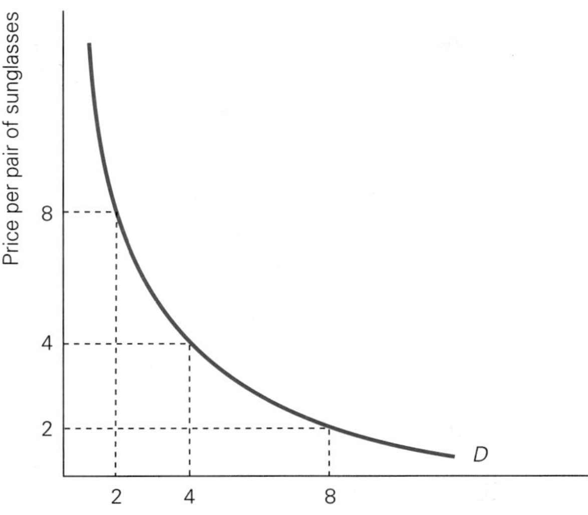

When the price elasticity of demand is unity at every price, then total expenditure is the same at every price. The demand curve for such a commodity is a rectangular hyperbola.

Figure 3.23

Elasticity along a Linear Demand Curve

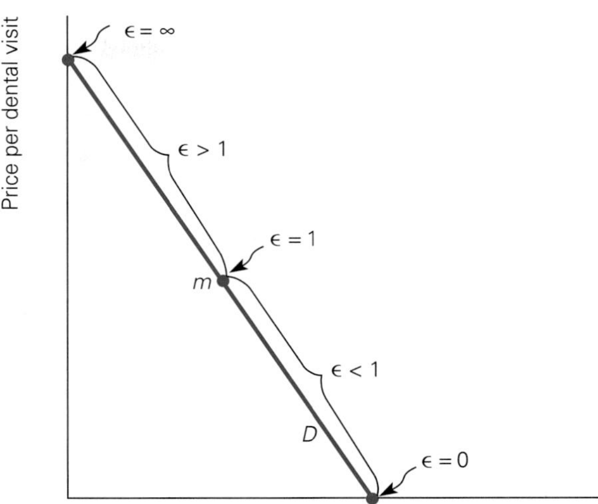

Along a linear demand curve, the price elasticity of demand is less than one below the midpoint *m*, greater than one above the midpoint, and equal to one at the midpoint.

Note that unlike the own-price elasticity of demand, Equation (3.1), there is no minus sign for ϵ_{xy}. The cross-price elasticity can be either positive or negative, and we want to keep track of the sign because it tells us how X and Y are related to each other. If X and Y are substitutes, when the price of Y goes up, the consumption of X increases; so ϵ_{xy} is positive. For complements, ϵ_{xy} is negative. For unrelated goods, an increase in the price of Y has no impact on the demand for X; therefore, $\%\Delta X$ is zero, and so is ϵ_{xy}. Thus, for example, the fact that the cross elasticity of demand for General Motors autos with respect to the price of Ford autos is 7.01 tells us that the two types of cars are substitutes—when the price of Fords increases by 1 percent, people increase their purchases of GMs by 7 percent, *ceteris paribus*. [See Berndt, Friedlaender, and Chiang (1990).]

3.7 PROGRESS CHECK

Consider the following quotation from a young Bosnian lawyer: "Smoking is a Bosnian tradition. If you had coffee, you had cigarettes; if you had cigarettes, you had coffee" (Sudetic 1993, L3). If this information is correct, what is the sign of the cross-price elasticity of demand for coffee with respect to the price of cigarettes in Bosnia?

The value of ϵ_{xy} for two commodities can be an important issue in legal battles. In the 1950s, the Department of Justice charged that Du Pont had monopolized the market for cellophane. Du Pont argued that although it did sell 75 percent of the cellophane in the United States, consumers were not at its mercy because if Du Pont raised cellophane prices, consumers would switch to other flexible wrappers (such as waxed paper). Hence, the question turned on whether the cross-price elasticity of demand for cellophane with respect to the price of other flexible wrappers was high. The Supreme Court's 1956 decision included these remarks:

> If a slight decrease in the price of cellophane causes a considerable number of customers of other flexible wrappings to switch to cellophane, it would be an indication that a high cross elasticity of demand exists between them; that the products compete in the same market. The court below held that the "great sensitivity of customers in the flexible packaging markets to price or quality changes" prevented Du Pont from possessing monopoly control over price. The record sustains these findings. (*U.S. Reports* 1956, 400).

Thus, Du Pont was found not guilty, in part because of a high value of the cross elasticity of demand. (PC 3.7)

INCOME ELASTICITY OF DEMAND

income elasticity of demand
The percentage change in quantity demanded with respect to a percentage change in income.

Elasticities can be used to summarize relationships between any pair of variables. An important example is the **income elasticity of demand,** the percentage change in quantity demanded with respect to a percentage change in income. If we let $\%\Delta I$ equal the percentage change in income, then the income elasticity, ϵ_I, is

$$\epsilon_I = \frac{\%\Delta X}{\%\Delta I}. \tag{3.8}$$

luxury good
A commodity whose income elasticity of demand is greater than one.

Like the cross price elasticity of demand, ϵ_I can be positive or negative. If a commodity is normal, ϵ_I is positive; if it is inferior, ϵ_I is negative. When $\epsilon_I > 1$, consumption of a commodity is quite responsive to income in the sense that a percentage increase in income leads to a greater percentage increase in consumption. Such commodities are sometimes referred to as **luxury goods.** The word *luxuries* usually brings to mind things such as furs and caviar, but more mundane items are also luxuries by this definition. This fact is illustrated in Table 3.3, which presents estimated income elasticities of demand for selected commodities. According to these estimates, furniture is a luxury good—a 10 percent increase in income would lead to a 26 percent increase in the amount of furniture demanded. Alcoholic beverage consumption, on the other hand, is much less responsive to income. A 10 percent increase in income would increase the quantity demanded by only 2.9 percent.

The concept of income elasticity can help explain some important trends in an economy. For example, much has been made of the United States becoming a "service economy"—in 1959, 40 percent of consumption expenditures were devoted to services, but by the mid 1990s this figure was about 57 percent (*Economic Report of the President 1996*, 294). Some view this trend as symptomatic of the country's losing its competitive edge in manufacturing. A less depressing interpretation of the same data is simply that the income elasticity of demand for services is greater than one. From this point of view, because ϵ_I for services exceeds one, as income has increased over time, the demand for services has increased by a greater proportion. But if the consumption of services increases at a faster rate than income then, *ceteris paribus*, the proportion of income devoted to services must increase. This is not to say that the value of ϵ_I for services is necessarily the sole or even the dominant factor in determining the share of na-

Table 3.3

Income Elasticity of Demand for Selected Commodities in the United States

Commodity	Income elasticity
Alcoholic beverages	0.29
Restaurant meals	1.61
Motion pictures	0.81
Books and maps	1.67
Dentists	0.38
Furniture	2.60
Funeral expenses	0.48
Automobile repair	1.03
Taxicabs	1.14
Toys	0.59

Source: Houthakker and Taylor (1970). To be more precise, these are short-run elasticities with respect to total expenditure rather than income. That is, saving is omitted from the analysis.

tional income going to services. Nevertheless, any analysis of this phenomenon that ignores the income elasticity is likely to be seriously deficient.

SECTION RECAP

We began this section looking for a simple numerical way to summarize comparative statics outcomes. Slopes are generally not useful for this purpose, because they depend on the units in which the variables are measured. Elasticities, on the other hand, depend on percentage changes, and hence are independent of units. Elasticities provide a great deal of information about consumer behavior. The value of the price elasticity of demand, for example, tells us how total expenditure for a commodity changes when its price changes. The cross-price elasticity of demand indicates whether two goods are complements or substitutes, and the income elasticity tells us whether a commodity is inferior or normal.

SUMMARY

This chapter used the theory of choice to show how people respond to changes in prices and incomes. All that needs to be done is to modify the budget constraint appropriately, and compare the new equilibrium with the old one. This process of comparing equilibria is called comparative statics.

- Using comparative statics methods, we can determine how the quantity demanded of a commodity varies with its price, holding constant the prices of other goods, income, and tastes. This is the information embodied in a demand curve.
- A change in the price of the commodity induces a *change in quantity demanded*—a movement along the demand curve. A change in the price of a related good, income, or tastes induces a *change in demand*—a shift of the entire demand schedule.
- The price elasticity of demand is the negative of the percentage change in quantity demanded divided by the percentage change in price. It measures the sensitivity of quantity demanded to changes in price. Because the elasticity depends on percentage changes, its value is not affected by the units in which quantity and price are measured.
- When a commodity's price elasticity of demand is less than one, an increase in its price leads to an increase in total expenditure. If the elasticity is greater than one, an increase in price leads to a decrease in total expenditure.
- An elasticity measure can be used whenever we want to summarize how one variable changes in response to another. The cross price elasticity of demand is the percentage change in the quantity demanded of one good divided by the percentage change in the price of another, and the income elasticity of demand is the percentage change in quantity demanded divided by the percentage change in income.

DISCUSSION QUESTIONS

3.1 "The worst economic slump since the Depression has created an audience for the argument that pollution restrictions are luxuries that Southern California cannot afford . . . " (Reinhold 1993, A1).

a. According to this quotation, is *clean air* a normal or inferior good?

b. Consider an individual who consumes *clean air* and a composite of *all other goods.* Show how this individual's budget constraint and equilibrium bundle are affected by a decrease in income.

3.2 Consider Figure 3.20, which depicts a demand curve with zero elasticity. Sketch an indifference map and budget constraints that would give rise to such a demand curve.

3.3 Otis consumes two commodities, health care and all other goods.

a. Assuming that Otis can consume all the health care he wants at a price of p_H per unit, sketch his budget constraint.

b. Suppose that the government announces that it will provide H^* units of health care to Otis at no charge to him. However, enrollment in the government program precludes the purchase of health care from private practitioners. Sketch the budget constraint associated with this program.

c. Suppose that Otis has a choice between purchasing health care in the market or participating in the government program. Using your answers to parts *a* and *b*, show how it is possible that "free" provision of health care by the government may lead to a *decrease* in the consumption of health care.

3.4 For Jones, X and Y are perfect substitutes. Specifically, he is always willing to substitute 3 units of X for 2 units of Y. The price per unit of X is \$5, the price per unit of Y is \$8, and Jones's income is \$40.

a. Sketch Jones's indifference map and budget constraint.

b. How much X does Jones consume?

c. Suppose that the price of X increases to \$6, and everything else stays the same. How much X does Jones consume?

d. Sketch the demand curve for X.

3.5 The diagram below provides information on Marie's consumption of cake before and after an increase in the price of cake. According to the diagram, is Marie's price elasticity of demand for cake greater, less than, or equal to one?

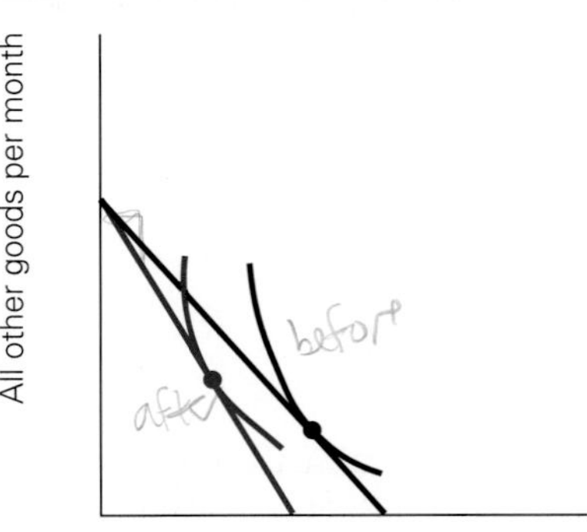

3.6 Discuss: "In 1990, consumption of water per capita in Nevada was 1,690 gallons. In Florida it was 3,130 gallons. In that year, per capita income was \$20,248 in Nevada and \$18,785 in Florida (U.S. Bureau of the Census 1994, 229, 457). On the basis of these data, one can conclude that water is an inferior good."

3.7 In Canada, a taxpayer can deduct charitable contributions from his taxable income, but the deduction cannot exceed 20 percent of his income. Consider a Canadian with an income of \$40,000. Show how the tax law affects his budget constraint for charitable donations and "all other goods." Will this law stimulate giving?

3.8 According to Pommerehne and Kirchgassner (1987), the price elasticity of demand for theater tickets in Germany is 1.73. Suppose that the price of theater tickets falls by 10 percent. What happens to the quantity demanded? What happens to total expenditure on theater tickets?

3.9 A number of states have debated whether to institute lotteries. One argument used to great effect by lottery proponents is that lottery revenues will be devoted to education.

Sketch a state's budget constraint between "education" and "expenditures on all other commodities." Show how the introduction of revenues from a lottery affects the budget constraint. Draw an indifference map, and show how education expenditures compare before and after the lottery. According to your diagram, do education expenditures increase by the full amount of the lottery revenues? Why would it be difficult to determine whether the government was keeping its promise to spend all the lottery revenues on education? Use the concept of fungibility in your answer.

3.10 According to van Ours (1995), the elasticity of demand for opium is 0.7 in the short run and 1.0 in the long run.

a. Explain why the elasticity of demand for opium should be greater in the long run than in the short run.

b. What happens to total expenditure on opium when its price increases, both in the short and long runs? What do you think happens to the amount of opium-related crime?

3.11 Figure 3.23 shows how the elasticity of demand varies along a linear demand curve. Use the relationship between elasticity and total expenditure to confirm graphically the results in that figure. (Hint: Use the techniques applied in Figure 3.19.)

3.12 Suppose the demand curve for X is linear: $X = a - bp$, where a and b are constants.

a. Sketch the demand curve. What is its slope, and what are its intercepts?

b. Show that at the midpoint of the demand curve, the price is (½) × (a/b). What is the quantity demanded at this price?

c. Use Expression (3.4) to show that at the midpoint of a linear demand curve, the price elasticity of demand is one.

***3.13** Abe consumes guns (x) and butter (y). His utility function is $U(x,y) = x - 3/y$.

a. Suppose $p_x = 9$, $p_y = 16$, and $I = 900$. Find the utility maximizing quantities of x and y.

b. Find the demand functions for x and y.

c. What are the price elasticities of demand for x and y? What are the income elasticities of demand for x and y?

d. What happens to Abe's utility-maximizing bundle if all prices and his income increase by the same percentage?

e. Jeff's utility function for x and y is $15 + 10(x - 3/y)$. Find Jeff's demand functions for x and y, and compare them to Abe's. What role does the ordinality of utility functions play in explaining your findings?

*Requires use of mathematical techniques presented in the Appendix to this chapter.

APPENDIX

3A An Algebraic Approach to Consumer Choice

Our approach to the theory of consumer choice has been primarily graphical. This Appendix employs mathematical tools. The use of these tools allows some interesting reinterpretations of many of the basic results from Chapters 2 and 3. In addition, we can derive some new results that would be difficult or impossible to obtain using only graphical models.

3A.1 UTILITY AND MARGINAL UTILITY

We saw in Chapter 2 that for each consumer we can define a *utility function*—a formula that attaches a *total utility* score to each bundle. For example, suppose that Henry's utility function for hamburgers (x) and tacos (y) is $U(x,y) = x^{3/4}y^{1/4}$. If Henry consumes 16 hamburgers and 81 tacos, then his total utility is $(16)^{3/4} \times (81)^{1/4} = 8 \times 3 = 24$.

Using calculus, the *marginal utility* of a commodity given some bundle is defined as the partial derivative of the utility function with respect to the amount of that good. It reflects how the consumer's total utility changes as the amount of the commodity is increased by an infinitesimally small amount, holding constant the amounts consumed of other goods. For Henry, the marginal utility of hamburgers is $\partial U(x,y)/\partial x = 3/4\ x^{-1/4}y^{1/4}$. (PC 3A.1)

3A.1 PROGRESS CHECK

What happens to Henry's marginal utility of a hamburger as the number of hamburgers increases? Explain your answer intuitively.

Chapter 2 also defined the marginal rate of substitution (MRS)—the negative of the slope of the indifference curve. We can use calculus to relate the MRS to the ratio of marginal utilities. To begin, note that if $U = U(x,y)$, then the change in total utility induced by a small change in x and y is

$$dU = MU_x\, dx + MU_y\, dy. \tag{3A.1}$$

As we move along an indifference curve, $dU = 0$, because utility is constant. Setting $dU = 0$ in 3A.1 and rearranging gives us

$$-\frac{dy}{dx} = \frac{MU_x}{MU_y}$$

Since $-\frac{dy}{dx}$ is the negative of the slope of the indifference curve, we have shown that

$$MRS_{yx} = \frac{MU_x}{MU_y}. \tag{3A.2}$$

3A.2 THE LAGRANGE METHOD FOR FINDING THE CONSUMER'S EQUILIBRIUM

The equilibrium bundle is the bundle that maximizes the value of the individual's utility function subject to his or her budget constraint. Formally, the consumer's problem is to maximize $U(x,y)$ subject to the constraint that $p_x x + p_y y = I$, where p_x and p_y are the prices of x and y, respectively, and I is income. A number of techniques can be used to solve this problem. The most popular approach is the *Lagrange Method*, which involves the following steps:

Step 1. Write down the *Lagrangean expression*

$$\mathcal{L} = U(x,y) + \lambda(I - p_x x - p_y y).$$

That is, write the function to be maximized (here, utility) plus λ times the constraint (here, the budget constraint). The interpretation of the variable λ (the Greek letter "lambda") will be discussed below.

Step 2. Differentiate the Langrangean expression with respect to x, y, and λ and set the derivatives equal to zero:

$$\frac{\partial \mathcal{L}}{\partial x} = MU_x - \lambda p_x = 0$$

$$\frac{\partial \mathcal{L}}{\partial y} = MU_y - \lambda p_y = 0$$

$$\frac{\partial \mathcal{L}}{\partial \lambda} = I - p_x x - p_y y = 0$$

These three equations can be rewritten as

$$\begin{aligned} MU_x &= \lambda p_x \\ MU_y &= \lambda p_y \\ p_x x + p_y y &= I. \end{aligned} \tag{3A.3}$$

Step 3. Note that the system (3A.3) can be regarded as 3 equations in 3 unknowns (x, y, and λ). Solve these equations for x, y, and λ. The values of x and y that emerge give you the utility-maximizing bundle.[1]

Let's use the Lagrange method to find Henry's utility-maximizing bundle when $p_x = 6$, $p_y = 3$, and $I = 120$.

Step 1. The Lagrangean expression is

$$\mathcal{L} = x^{3/4}y^{1/4} + \lambda(120 - 6x - 3y).$$

Step 2. Differentiating the Lagrangean gives us

$$\frac{\partial \mathcal{L}}{\partial x} = \frac{3}{4}x^{-1/4}y^{1/4} - 6\lambda = 0 \tag{3A.4}$$

[1]More precisely, this claim holds assuming certain second order conditions are satisfied.

$$\frac{\partial \mathcal{L}}{\partial y} = \frac{1}{4} x^{3/4} y^{-3/4} - 3\lambda = 0 \tag{3A.5}$$

$$\frac{\partial \mathcal{L}}{\partial \lambda} = 120 - 6x - 3y = 0 \tag{3A.6}$$

Step 3. Solve the three equations for x, y, and λ. Dividing equation (3A.4) by Equation (3A.5) gives us $3y/x = 2$ or $x = 3y/2$. Substituting this into (3A.6) gives us $9y + 3y = 120$, or $y = 10$. Substituting $y = 10$ into (3A.6) gives us $x = 15$. The utility maximizing bundle consists of 15 hamburgers and 10 tacos.

What about λ? Substituting $x = 15$ and $y = 10$ into either (3A.4) or (3A.5), yields $\lambda = 0.113$. What does this tell us? It turns out that λ is the *marginal utility of income*—the additional utility that is generated by an extra dollar of income, dU/dI. To prove this, totally differentiate the utility function with respect to income, I:

$$\frac{dU}{dI} = MU_x \frac{dx}{dI} + MU_y \frac{dy}{dI}. \tag{3A.7}$$

Substituting the expressions for MU_x and MU_y from (3A.3) gives us

$$\frac{dU}{dI} = \lambda p_x \frac{dx}{dI} + \lambda p_y \frac{dy}{dI} = \lambda(p_x dx + p_y dy)/dI. \tag{3A.8}$$

Next totally differentiate the budget constraint:

$$dI = p_x\, dx + p_y\, dy. \tag{3A.9}$$

Substituting (3A.9) into (3A.8) gives us

$$\frac{dU}{dI} = \lambda(p_x\, dx + p_y\, dy)/(p_x\, dx + p_y\, dy) = \lambda. \tag{3A.10}$$

This fact allows us to recharacterize the conditions for utility maximization, 3A.3. Rewriting the first of these equations gives us $MU_x/p_x = \lambda$; the second is $MU_y/p_y = \lambda$. Hence, the marginal utility of the last dollar spent on each good must equal a common value, and this value is the marginal utility of income.

DERIVING DEMAND CURVES

In the example above, we showed how to find the utility maximizing values of x and y for specific numerical values of p_x, p_y, and I. However, one could just as well leave p_x, p_y, and I as variables; solve for x as a function of p_x, p_y, and I; and then do the same for y. These functions are the respective demand functions for x and y because they show how the quantity of each commodity varies with its price. Let's compute Henry's demand functions for x and y using the Lagrange Method. First write the Lagrangean expression:

$$\mathcal{L} = x^{3/4} y^{1/4} + \lambda(I - p_x x - p_{xy})$$

Next differentiate the expression:

$$\frac{\partial \mathcal{L}}{\partial x} = \frac{3}{4} x^{-1/4} y^{1/4} - \lambda p_x = 0$$

$$\frac{\partial \mathcal{L}}{\partial y} = \frac{1}{4} x^{3/4} y^{-3/4} - \lambda p_y = 0$$

$$\frac{\partial \mathcal{L}}{\partial \lambda} = I - p_x x - p_y y = 0.$$

Solving for x and y yields

$$x = \frac{3}{4} I/p_x$$

$$y = \frac{1}{4} I/p_y ,$$

which are the demand functions for x and y, respectively. (PC 3A.2)

3A.2 PROGRESS CHECK

Do Henry's demand curves for x and y slope downward? Are hamburgers a normal good or an inferior good? How about tacos? For Henry, are hamburgers and tacos complements, substitutes, or unrelated goods?

3A.3 ELASTICITY

In Chapter 3 we defined the point elasticity of demand as

$$\epsilon = -\frac{\Delta X}{\Delta p} \times \frac{P}{X}.$$

Using calculus, we replace the ratio of discrete changes, $\Delta X/\Delta p$, with the derivative, dX/dp. Thus, the price elasticity of demand is

$$\epsilon = -\frac{dX}{dp} \times \frac{p}{X}. \tag{3A.11}$$

For example, if the demand curve is $X = 10 - 2p$, then $dX/dp = -2$, and the elasticity is $2p/X$. Note that the elasticity is not constant; it depends on the values of p and X. Thus, if the price is 2, then the quantity demanded is 6, and the point elasticity is ⅔.

For another example, consider Henry's demand function for hamburgers, which we saw above is $X = \frac{3}{4} I/p_x$. Then dX/dp_x is $-\frac{3}{4} I/p_x^2$, and substituting into (3A.11) gives us

$$\epsilon = -3/4 \frac{I}{p_x^2} \frac{p_x}{\left[\frac{3}{4} I/p_x\right]} = 1.$$

Thus, Henry has a constant elasticity of demand for hamburgers—it is always one.

In the text, we defined *total expenditure*, *TE*, as the amount of money consumers spend on a commodity: $TE = p \times X$. It is often interesting to know how total expenditure changes as the price changes. Using the multiplication rule for differentiation to calculate the derivative of total expenditure with respect to price gives us

$$\frac{dTE}{dp} = X + p \times \frac{dX}{dp}.$$

By factoring out X on the right-hand side of the above equation, we obtain this relation between total expenditure and the price elasticity of demand:

$$\frac{dTE}{dp} = X\left(1 + \frac{dX}{dp} \times \frac{p}{X}\right) = X(1 - \epsilon). \tag{3A.12}$$

The sign of dTE/dp tells us whether total expenditure rises or falls as the price increases. Because X is positive, total expenditure rises as the price increases if $\epsilon < 1$ (that is, demand is inelastic). Similarly, total expenditure falls as the price increases if $\epsilon > 1$ (that is, demand is elastic). Moreover, if $\epsilon = 1$, then total expenditure remains the same if the price increases. These are precisely the results derived intuitively in the text and summarized in Table 3.2.

SUMMARY

This Appendix uses calculus to reinterpret the results from the theory of consumer choice.

- To derive demand functions, use the Lagrange Method to maximize the individual's utility function subject to his budget constraint.
- The multiplier used to solve the Lagrange problem, λ, is the marginal utility of income.
- The price elasticity of demand can be written in terms of derivatives of the demand function. This allows us to write a formula for total expenditure in terms of the price elasticity of demand.

DISCUSSION QUESTIONS

3A.1 Suppose that the demand curve for commodity X is $X = 25p_x^{-1/2}p_y^{1/3}I^{3/4}$, where p_x = price of X, p_y = price of Y, and I = income. Find the own-price elasticity of demand for X, the cross-price elasticity of demand for X with respect to the price of Y, and the income elasticity of demand for X.

3A.2 Suppose that the market demand function for sunblock is $X = 100 - 5p$. At what price is total expenditure on sunblock maximized? What is the price elasticity of demand at this price?

CHAPTER

4

Price Changes and Consumer Welfare

What costs little is valued less.
—Cervantes, *Don Quixote*

If you have a sweet tooth, the following facts might interest you: The price of sugar produced in the Third World is generally below 10 cents per pound. However, consumers in the United States and the European Union have to pay about twice that.[1] The difference is so large that U.S. customs officials have had to stop people from importing jam and kosher pizza because importers of these commodities could make money extracting and then selling the sugar in them! U.S. and European consumers are forced to pay these high prices because their governments protect domestic sugar producers from foreign competition by restricting imports of Third World sugar.

How much are consumers hurt by this more than doubling of the price of sugar? One way to measure the damage would be to find out how much extra they ended up paying for sugar—about $1.1 billion for the United States. But there is more to the story. Suppose that the price of sugar is seven cents per pound, and Jones consumes 3 pounds per week. An import restriction is then imposed, which raises the price to 23 cents. In response, Jones reduces his sugar consumption to zero. Obviously, because Jones consumes no sugar, he does not pay the 16 cents per pound premium on the price of sugar. Do we want to say that Jones is unaffected by the import restriction? Prior to the restriction, Jones had the option of consuming no sugar, but he chose to buy 3 pounds weekly, so he must have preferred spending the money on sugar rather than on other items. Thus, despite the fact that Jones consumes no sugar after the restriction, it makes him worse off.

This example is a bit extreme. From our theory of consumer choice, we expect an increase in price to diminish the quantity demanded, but not to drive it

[1]Of course, the precise prices vary from year to year.

all the way to zero. Nevertheless, the basic result holds—the price increase induced by the import restriction distorts economic decisions, and this reduces consumer welfare. Moreover, merely counting the change in expenditures can be misleading. We must account for consumer reactions to the price change.

Having made this point, we are still left with the practical problem of actually measuring the change in consumers' welfare associated with a price change. This chapter builds upon the theory of demand to develop a framework for analyzing the welfare consequences of price movements. To do so, we require a deeper understanding of the forces set in motion when prices change, and a greater appreciation for the amount of useful information embodied in demand curves.

4.1 INCOME AND SUBSTITUTION EFFECTS

In Chapters 2 and 3 we argued that if the price of a commodity goes up, then, *ceteris paribus*, the quantity demanded goes down. In other words, demand curves slope downward. This notion is called the **"Law of Demand."** The reason for the quotes is that, although this "law" seems to be a good description of reality, its validity is not a theoretical necessity. To understand fully the consequences of price changes, an important first step is to set forth precisely the conditions that are required for the Law of Demand to hold.

"Law of Demand"
The notion that demand curves slope downward—when the price of a commodity goes up, the quantity demanded goes down, *ceteris paribus.*

Consider the situation of Samson, who uses his income of I dollars to consume sugar and a composite of all other goods. Initially, the price of sugar is p_1 per pound, the price of *all other goods* is \$1 per unit, and Samson's budget constraint is line B_1 in Figure 4.1. Suppose that the price of sugar rises from p_1 to p_2. As shown in Figure 4.1, Samson's budget constraint pivots from B_1 to B_2. This price increase has two consequences. First, it makes sugar more expensive relative to the other commodities. This effect is reflected in the increased steepness of B_2; after the price increase, Samson has to give up more units of *all other goods* in order to get an additional pound of sugar. Second, for any given amount of sugar that Samson chooses to buy, he now has less money to spend on *all other goods.* This effect is shown by the fact that Samson's feasible set after the price increase lies inside of his feasible set prior to the price increase. In effect, the price increase reduces Samson's "real income"—it makes him poorer by reducing his budget set.

Of course, when the price of sugar increases, both effects occur simultaneously. Nevertheless, it is very useful to separate the two effects and discuss them one at a time. First, the **substitution effect** of a price increase is the effect on quantity demanded due *exclusively* to the fact that its relative price has changed. Second, the **income effect** of a price increase is the effect on quantity demanded due *exclusively* to the fact that the consumer's real income has fallen. As we show below, the net effect of a price change depends on the sum of the substitution and income effects.

substitution effect
The effect of a price change on the quantity demanded due exclusively to the fact that its relative price has changed.

income effect
The effect of a price change on the quantity demanded due exclusively to the fact that the consumer's real income has changed.

GRAPHICAL REPRESENTATION

To understand how income and substitution effects work, it is useful to analyze them graphically. Lift the transparency on Figure 4.2. You will see (reproduced from Figure 4.1) Samson's original budget line B_1, whose slope is $-p_1$. Subject to budget constraint B_1, Samson maximizes utility at bundle e_1 on indifference

Figure 4.1

A Price Increase Changes the Feasible Set

When the price of sugar increases, the budget line pivots from B_1 to B_2. As a consequence, the opportunity cost of sugar increases (B_2 is steeper than B_1). In addition, the consumer is poorer in the sense that bundles in the shaded area are no longer available.

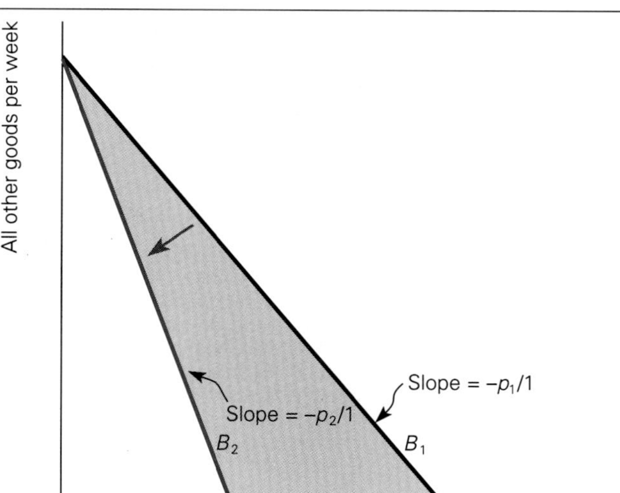

curve U_1, where he consumes x_1 pounds of sugar and y_1 units of all other goods. Now suppose that the price of sugar increases to p_2. Samson's budget constraint becomes B_2, and he maximizes utility at bundle e_2 on indifference curve U_2, which consists of x_2 pounds of sugar and y_2 units of all other goods. Thus, when the price of sugar increases from p_1 to p_2, the response we observe is a decrease in quantity demanded from x_1 to x_2.

So far, this is all review. Our new problem is to decompose the movement from x_1 to x_2 into an income effect and a substitution effect. To do so, recall that the substitution effect shows the impact of the change in relative prices *alone*. The change in "real income" associated with the income effect must not be taken into account. That is, to isolate the substitution effect, we must examine the effect of the price change holding the initial level of "real income" constant.

The notion of "real income" is a bit tricky in this context. One possibility is to say that a consumer has the same real income in two situations if he can consume exactly the same set of commodities in the two situations—the consumer's budget constraint is the same. Then to maintain Samson's real income after the price of sugar increases, we must give him enough money so that he has exactly the same opportunity set as before. But it is *impossible* to give Samson enough money to obtain exactly the same budget constraint as before. Look again at Figure 4.2. Budget constraints B_1 and B_2 have different slopes because they embody different prices of sugar. After the price of sugar increases, we can raise Samson's real income by giving him money, but this results in a parallel movement outward of B_2. The new budget line will be steeper than the initial budget line B_1, and hence can never coincide with it. We conclude that some other notion of "real income" is needed to isolate the substitution effect.

A more useful definition of a person's real income is his level of utility. How can Samson attain the same level of utility after the increase in sugar prices lowers him to indifference curve U_2? He must be given just enough income so that he

Figure 4.2

Substitution and Income Effect: Normal Good

A price increase leads to both a substitution effect and an income effect. The substitution effect is the change in quantity demanded induced by the higher price while keeping the individual at his initial utility level. It is represented by the movement from e_1 to e_c. The income effect is the change in quantity demanded induced by the change in income, and is represented by the movement from e_c to e_2. Distance C on the vertical axis is known as the compensating variation of the price change.

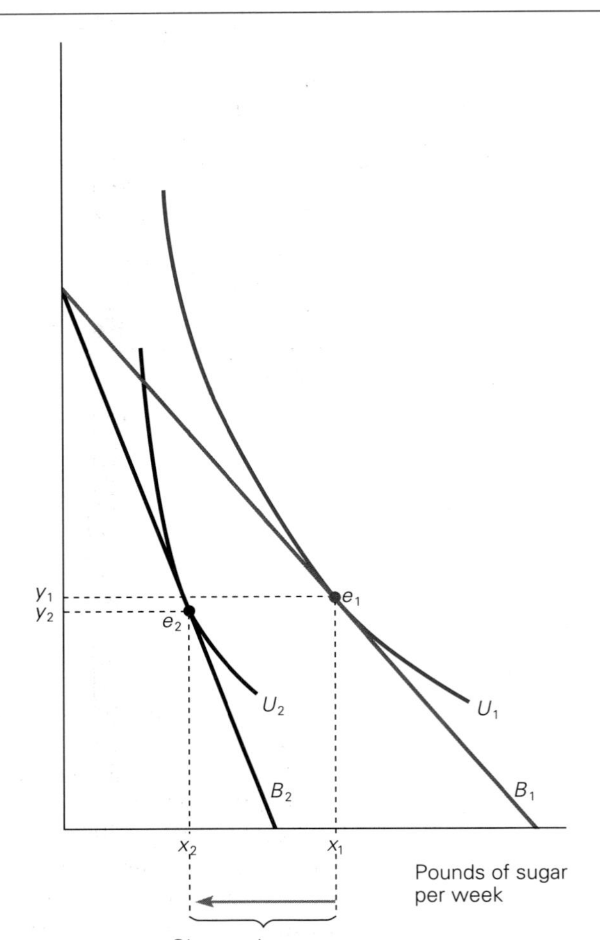

can get from indifference curve U_2 back to indifference curve U_1. How much income is that? To find the amount of income required to move Samson back to his original utility level, we make a parallel shift in B_2 until it just touches indifference curve U_1. The vertical distance by which the budget constraint must be moved measures the amount of *all other goods* required to compensate Samson. But because the price per unit of *all other goods* is \$1, this distance is also the amount of income required. Now lower the transparency on Figure 4.2, and note that if budget constraint B_2 is shifted up by distance C, it is tangent to the indifference curve U_1 at point e_c. Hence, in order to compensate Samson for the increased price of sugar, he needs to receive C dollars.

We are now ready to read off the substitution and income effects from Figure 4.2. The movement from bundle e_1 to e_c shows how the quantity demanded changes when the price goes up and simultaneously income is adjusted so that the level of utility is the same. By definition, then, the movement from e_1 to e_c is the substitution effect of the change. Notice that we have just pivoted around the U_1-indifference curve. Therefore, the quantity demanded *must* fall—the substitution effect of a price increase is *always* negative. The movement from e_c to e_2

shows how the quantity demanded changes when income falls, but relative prices stay the same. (We know that relative prices stay the same because B_c is parallel to B_2.) Hence, the movement from e_c to e_2 is the income effect of the change.

In short, when the price of sugar increases, the quantity demanded falls from x_1 to x_2. This observed response can be decomposed into the substitution effect (from x_1 to x_c) and the income effect (from x_c to x_2). Because the substitution effect is generated by changing the price and (hypothetically) simultaneously *compensating* the individual with income, it is referred to as the **compensated response** to a price change. Not surprisingly, the change in quantity that we actually observe (that is, from x_1 to x_2) is sometimes called the **uncompensated response.**

compensated response
The change in quantity demanded resulting from changing the price while simultaneously compensating the individual with income; the substitution effect.

uncompensated response
The observed change in quantity demanded in response to a change in price.

Note that in Figure 4.2, the income effect of the price increase lowers the quantity demanded—x_c is greater than x_2. Thus, for Samson, sugar is a normal good, and the income and substitution effects reinforce each other. Both effects indicate that when price goes up, quantity demanded goes down, and vice versa. Hence, normal goods *necessarily* satisfy the Law of Demand.

In contrast, Figure 4.3 depicts the situation of Delilah, who has the same budget constraint as Samson, but has different tastes as reflected in her indifference map. For Delilah, the observed (or uncompensated) response of the price change is from bundle e'_1 to e'_2; using the same logic as before, this can be decomposed into a substitution effect (e'_1 to e'_c) and an income effect (e'_c to e'_2). Note that for Delilah, sugar is an inferior good—the income effect by itself tends to *increase* the quantity demanded of sugar, from x'_c to x'_2. Nevertheless, Delilah's behavior satisfies the Law of Demand because the substitution effect (from x'_1 to x'_c) is more powerful than the income effect. Just because a good is inferior does not mean that it fails to obey the Law of Demand.

However, *if* the income effect of an inferior good dominates the substitution effect, then the quantity demanded increases when price increases—the demand curve slopes upward. A good whose demand curve slopes upward is referred to as a **Giffen good,** named after the 19th-century researcher Robert Giffen, who discussed this possibility. This phenomenon is illustrated in Figure 4.4, which shows Dagon's indifference curves for sugar and all other goods. The increase in the price of sugar induces a movement from e''_1 to e''_2; the substitution effect is from e''_1 to e''_c. As always, the substitution effect of a price increase tends to decrease the quantity demanded—x''_c is less than x''_1. But this decrease is overwhelmed by the increase induced by the large income effect, which increases quantity demanded from x''_c *to* x''_2. Thus, Figure 4.4 provides an example of the theoretically possible case of a Giffen good.

Giffen good
A commodity (which is always inferior) whose demand curve slopes upward.

It is important to recognize that although a Giffen good is always inferior, a commodity may be inferior and still *not* be a Giffen good. As long as the substitution effect dominates, the demand curve still slopes down. There are many examples of inferior goods that obey the Law of Demand. For example, intercity railroad transportation in the United States is an inferior good (the *income* elasticity of demand is −1.35); nevertheless, it has a downward-sloping demand curve (the *price* elasticity of demand is 1.1).[2] On the other hand, every Giffen good *must* be an inferior good. Since the substitution effect *always* leads to a decrease in quantity demanded when price increases, the only way the demand curve for a commodity can slope upward is for the substitution effect to be dominated by a positive income effect of a price increase. When a fall in income

[2]See Houthakker and Taylor (1970).

Figure 4.3

Substitution and Income Effect: Inferior Good

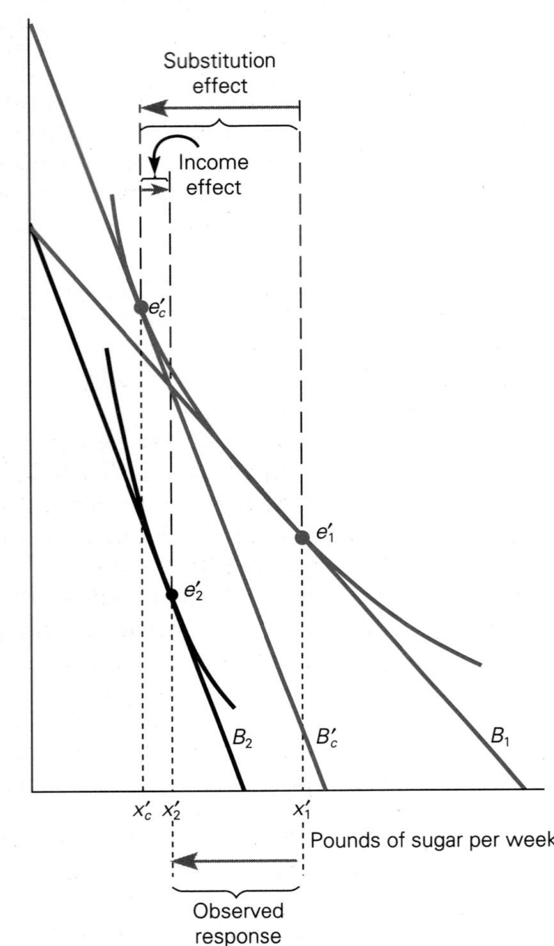

For Delilah, when income increases, *ceteris paribus*, the quantity demanded of sugar goes down. Hence, the income effect of a price increase increases quantity demanded, from x_c' to x_2'. Nevertheless, quantity demanded falls when price increases, because the substitution effect (from x_1' to x_c') outweighs the income effect.

Figure 4.4

Substitution and Income Effect: Giffen Good

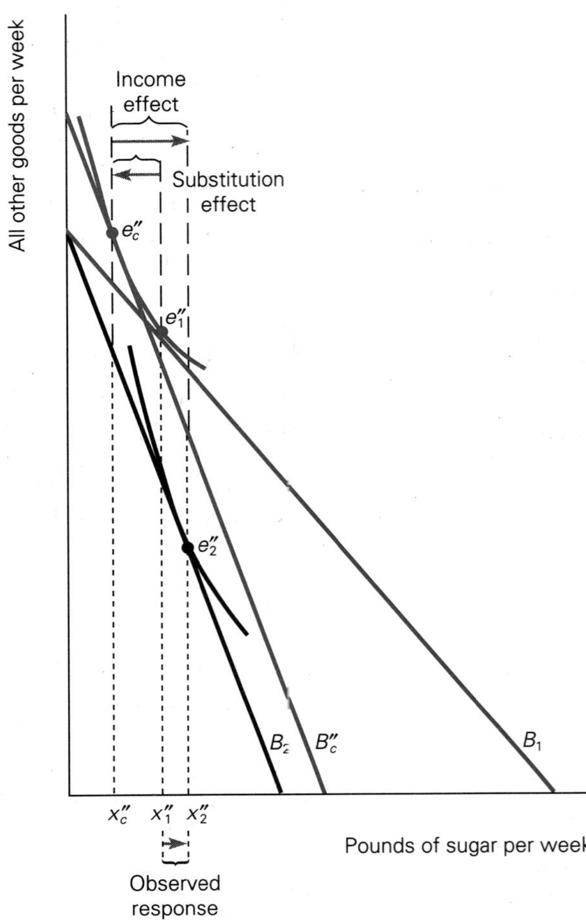

For Dagon, quantity demanded increases from x_1'' to x_2'' in response to an increase in price. Hence, sugar is not only inferior, it is a Giffen good. The huge income effect, which increases quantity demanded from x_c'' to x_2'', outweighs the substitution effect, which decreases quantity demanded from x_1'' to x_c''.

raises consumption, the good is inferior by definition. All of this is summarized in Table 4.1.

Although the Giffen good is a theoretical possibility, its empirical significance is extremely limited. The classic example is associated with the increase in potato prices during the Irish potato famine of the 19th century. Giffen argued that the rise in potato prices was such a large drain on the resources of poor Irish families that they were forced to reduce their consumption of meat and other more expensive foods. Since potatoes were still the cheapest food, however, they were demanded in larger quantities as consumers attempted to meet their dietary

Table 4.1

Impact of an Increase in the Price of a Good

Type of Good	Substitution Effect	Income Effect	Total Effect
Normal	Quantity decreases	Quantity decreases	Quantity decreases
Inferior (but not Giffen)	Quantity decreases	Quantity increases	Quantity decreases
Giffen	Quantity decreases	Quantity increases	Quantity increases

needs. Hence, according to Giffen, when the price of potatoes went up, the quantity demanded increased.

Giffen's analysis of the Irish data has been disputed, however, and many economists now believe that the demand for potatoes during the famine did in fact slope downward. Indeed, statisticians have studied the demand curves for hundreds of commodities, and no one has ever found convincing evidence for a Giffen good. As Nobel Laureate George Stigler (1966) noted, anyone who successfully isolated an exception to the Law of Demand "would be assured of immortality (professionally speaking) and rapid promotion. Since most economists would not dislike either reward, we may assume that the total absence of exceptions is not from lack of trying to find them." (PC 4.1)

4.1 PROGRESS CHECK

Starting with the initial budget constraint B_1 in Figure 4.1, suppose that the price of sugar decreases. Assuming that sugar is a normal good, represent graphically the income and substitution effects of the price decrease. Repeat, assuming that sugar is an inferior good. Show that the substitution effect increases quantity demanded in both cases.

ALGEBRAIC REPRESENTATION

The decomposition of the observed response into a substitution and income effect can be compactly represented in a single equation. To begin, let's summarize the discussion surrounding Figure 4.2 as follows:

$$\text{Observed response} = \text{Substitution effect} + \text{Income effect.} \tag{4.1}$$

Algebraically, denote the *observed* quantity change, Δx, in response to the price change, Δp, as $\Delta x/\Delta p$. Similarly, denote the associated substitution effect by $(\Delta x/\Delta p)_{\text{comp}}$. The subscript "comp" stands for "compensated," because the "substitution effect" is also called the "compensated response." Recall that $(\Delta x/\Delta p)_{\text{comp}}$ *must* be negative as long as the indifference curves exhibit a diminishing marginal rate of substitution. Using this notation, we can rewrite Equation (4.1) as

$$\frac{\Delta x}{\Delta p} = \left(\frac{\Delta x}{\Delta p}\right)_{\text{comp}} + \text{Income effect.} \tag{4.2}$$

Our only problem now is to represent the income effect algebraically. The income effect is the product of two terms. The first is the number of dollars by which money income decreases as a consequence of the Δp increase in price, the second is the change in quantity demanded per dollar decrease in income. To obtain the first term of the product, suppose that Samson is consuming 3 pounds of sugar and its price goes up by \$1 per pound. Then in the absence of any substitution effect, he is \$3 worse off. (We ignore substitution possibilities because, by definition, these are excluded from the income effect.) More generally, if sugar consumption is x_1 pounds, then the change in income induced by a dollar increase in its price is simply $-x_1$. (The minus is there because the effect of an increase in price is to *reduce* income.) Turning now to the second term in the income effect, we denote the change in quantity demanded per dollar increase in income as $\Delta x/\Delta I$. Hence, the income effect of a price change is $-x_1$ times $\Delta x/\Delta I$. Substituting our expression for the income effect into Equation (4.2) gives us

$$\frac{\Delta x}{\Delta p} = \left(\frac{\Delta x}{\Delta p}\right)_{\text{comp}} - x_1 \times \frac{\Delta x}{\Delta I} \tag{4.3}$$

Slutsky Equation
A decomposition of the effect of a price change on quantity demanded into a substitution effect and an income effect.

Equation (4.3) is called the **Slutsky Equation,** after Russian economist Eugene Slutsky, who suggested this decomposition just before the Bolshevik Revolution.

The Slutsky equation suggests a number of interesting observations about income and substitution effects. First, if the commodity is normal, then $\Delta x/\Delta I$ is positive by definition. It follows that $-x_1 \times (\Delta x/\Delta I)$ is negative. Coupled with the fact that $(\Delta x/\Delta p)_{\text{comp}}$ is always negative, the Slutsky equation tells us that when x is normal, $(\Delta x/\Delta p)$ is necessarily negative. But stating that $(\Delta x/\Delta p)$ is negative is just another way of saying that when price goes up, quantity demanded goes down. Hence, as Table 4.1 indicated, *when a good is normal, it necessarily obeys the Law of Demand.*

A second implication of the Slutsky equation is that as x_1 becomes smaller and smaller, *ceteris paribus*, the income effect becomes smaller and smaller. Thus, if the amount of the good being consumed is small, then the income effect is not very important, and there is not much difference between the compensated and observed responses. Intuitively, if you don't consume very much of a good, then if its price goes up, you do not become significantly "poorer." For example, if the price of pencils were to double, you probably would not feel much poorer as a result. If the price of housing doubled, you probably would feel poorer. This insight, incidentally, helps explain why Giffen goods are such a remote possibility. Most goods that occupy a large portion of people's budgets (such as housing) are normal goods. An inferior good that forms a small part of a consumer's budget has a very small income effect, rendering the actual occurrence of a Giffen good unlikely. Moreover, even if a few exceptional people in a market do exhibit a Giffen response, this is unlikely to lead to an upward-sloping *market* demand curve—in the process of adding individual demand curves to obtain the market curve, the Giffen responses got swamped by the much more numerous "ordinary" responses.

SECTION RECAP

A change in the price of a good sets two forces in motion. First is an income effect—the consumer is richer if the price goes down and poorer if the price goes up. Second is a substitution effect—the consumer tends to consume more of the good whose relative price falls. We have shown how the observed response to a price change can be decomposed into its income and substitution effects. This decomposition, which is summarized by the Slutsky equation, is important for understanding why demand curves are likely to slope downward.

4.2 COMPENSATING AND EQUIVALENT VARIATIONS

The discussion surrounding Figure 4.2 shows clearly that when the price of sugar increases, Samson is made worse off (it lowers him from indifference curve U_1 to U_2). The purpose of this section is to develop a measure of just how much worse off he is. A first stab at solving this problem would be to compare the amounts of utility associated with indifference curves U_1 and U_2, and then declare the difference between them to be the amount by which his welfare has fallen. But such an approach is useless. Recall from Chapter 2 that utility numbers are merely ordinal, and taking their difference is totally uninformative.

Because a *util* measure of the change in welfare is useless, we must try to obtain a *dollar* measure. In monetary terms, how much worse off is Samson because the price of sugar has increased? Stated this way, the question is ambiguous, because it can mean two distinct things:

1. *After* the price of sugar increases, how much money does Samson need to bring him back to his initial level of utility? Because the idea is to find the amount of money that the individual would need to compensate him for the increase in the price of sugar, this measure of the welfare loss is called the **compensating variation** of the price change.
2. Given his bundle *before* the price increase, how much money would you have to take away from the individual to reduce his welfare as much as the price increase does? Here the idea is to find an income reduction that is equivalent to the price increase, so this measure is called the **equivalent variation** of the price increase.

compensating variation The amount of money by which an individual would need to be compensated for a price change to remain at his initial level of utility.

equivalent variation A change in income that is equivalent in its effect on utility to a change in the price of a commodity.

The best way to understand the difference between the compensating and equivalent variations is to compute each of them.

Compensating Variation (CV)

Recall from Figure 4.2 that to isolate the substitution effect of a price increase, we have to give Samson just enough money to restore him to his initial utility level. In Figure 4.2, this amount of money is exactly $\$C$. By definition, then, $\$C$ is the compensating variation of the price change. Thus, finding the compensating variation is just a by-product of our computation of the substitution effect! Note that the fact that utilities are ordinal has absolutely no effect on the amount of the compensating variation. Regardless of the utility numbers assigned to indifference curves U_1 and U_2, the compensating variation is still $\$C$.

Equivalent Variation (EV)

The equivalent variation is the amount of money that we have to take away from the individual to lower his utility as much as the price increase does. The EV is found by moving the original budget line toward the origin in a parallel fashion, until it is just tangent to indifference curve U_2. In Figure 4.5, the amount by which the budget line B_1 has to be shifted down until it is tangent to indifference curve U_2—distance E—is the equivalent variation of the price change.

Figure 4.5

Equivalent Variation

To find the equivalent variation, take the budget constraint associated with the *initial* prices (B_1), and shift it in a parallel fashion until it is tangent to the new indifference curve. This gives us E as the equivalent variation.

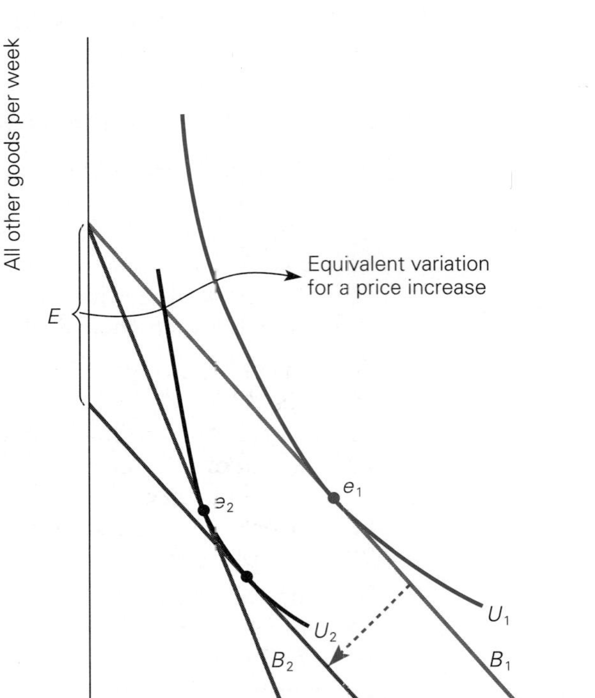

Comparing the CV and EV

Observe that distances C in Figure 4.2 and E in Figure 4.5 are not equal—the compensating and equivalent variations provide different estimates of the dollar value between the two indifference curves. As noted at the outset, we should not expect them always to be equal, because they are answering two somewhat different questions. Specifically, the two measures are different because they evaluate the welfare change in terms of different sets of relative prices. The compensating variation determines how much income, given the *new* prices, is required to compensate for the price increase. This is reflected by the fact that computation of the compensating variation involves shifting B_2, whose slope is determined by the *new* price ratio. On the other hand, the equivalent variation determines how much income we would have to take away at the *original* prices to do equivalent damage to the consumer's welfare as does the price change. Thus, finding the equivalent variation involves shifting B_1, whose slope is the initial price ratio.

4.2 PROGRESS CHECK

Several years ago, the price on Moscow subways increased from 10 to 30 rubles per ride. Consider a typical Muscovite who rides the subway and who purchases a composite of *all other goods*. Draw an indifference map and use it to illustrate the compensating and equivalent variations of this price change.

SECTION RECAP

An important purpose of microeconomics is to analyze how changes in prices affect consumer welfare. There is no single, unambiguous dollar measure. However, there are two appealing measures: the compensating variation (which is based on the new set of prices) and the equivalent variation (which is based on the old set of prices). How should you decide whether to use the compensating or equivalent variation? As we will see in the next section, the answer depends on the particular problem being considered. (PC 4.2)

4.3 APPLYING COMPENSATING AND EQUIVALENT VARIATIONS

As the following examples illustrate, compensating and equivalent variations are extremely useful for thinking about numerous important economic problems.

EVALUATING PRICE SUBSIDIES

Governments throughout the world subsidize the consumption of various commodities. Housing, for example, is subsidized in the United States, the United Kingdom, Israel, and many other countries. Such subsidies can take several forms. For low-income individuals, apartments in public housing may be rented at below-market prices. In British Council Housing, for example, rents can be 45 percent below the market price; in Hong Kong, the subsidy to public housing is 70 to 80 percent (Minford, et al. 1987 and Wong and Liu 1988). For middle- and upper-income individuals, housing subsidies often take the form of tax breaks that reduce the cost of owning a house. In the United States, it is estimated that such subsidies cost the Treasury over \$70 billion annually.[3] For our purposes, the essential characteristic of all such programs is that they reduce the relative price of housing consumption. In this section, we use the equivalent variation and other tools of demand theory to evaluate the subsidy.

Consider Peter, who has a fixed income of I dollars, which he spends on housing and a composite of all other goods. For simplicity, we will assume that the amount of housing consumed is measured solely by the square feet of the dwelling. A more detailed analysis would take into account that the quantity of housing services produced by a particular dwelling depends on attributes other than its size, such as the quality of its plumbing, whether or not it is air conditioned, and how well it is maintained. However, this would complicate the analysis without changing its important aspects. The price per square foot of housing is p, and the price per unit of *all other goods* is \$1. In Figure 4.6, Peter's consumption of housing is measured on the horizontal axis and the consumption of *all other goods* on the vertical. His budget constraint is line B_1, which has a slope of $-p$, and a horizontal intercept of I/p. Assuming that Peter is a utility maximizer, he chooses point e_1, where he consumes x_1 square feet of housing and y_1 units of *all other goods.*

Suppose that the government provides a subsidy on housing at a percentage rate of s, so that Peter now faces a housing price of $(1 - s)p$. The subsidy changes Peter's budget constraint to line B_2 in Figure 4.6, which has a slope of $-(1 - s)p$, and a horizontal intercept of $I/[(1 - s)p]$. Because the price of *all other goods* is still \$1, the before- and after-subsidy budget constraints have the same vertical intercept.

Note that for any given level of housing consumption, the vertical distance between B_1 and B_2 shows the amount of Peter's subsidy. To see why, consider an arbitrary quantity of x_a square feet of housing on the horizontal axis. Before the subsidy was implemented, Peter could have both x_a square feet of housing and y_a

[3]U.S. Bureau of the Census (1994, 336).

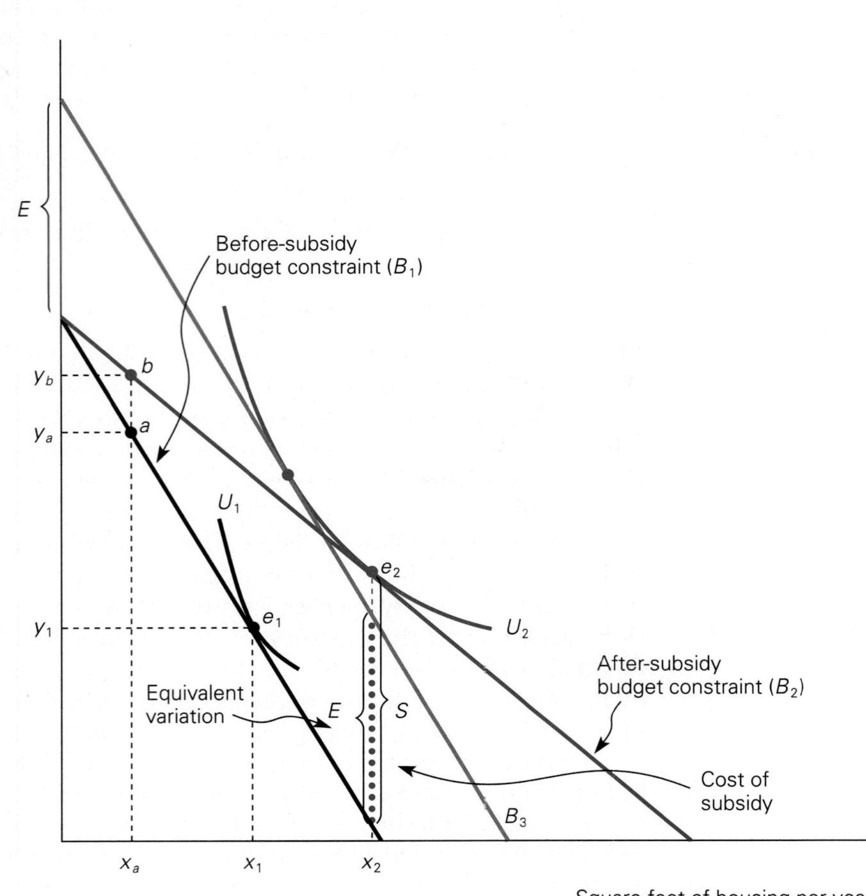

Figure 4.6

Analysis of a Price Subsidy

A subsidy on housing consumption changes the individual's budget constraint from B_1 to B_2. After the subsidy, x_2 units of housing are consumed, and the subsidy costs the government S dollars. This exceeds the benefit of the subsidy program, which is measured by the equivalent variation associated with the reduction in the price of housing, E.

units of *all other goods*: Point *a* lies on the before-subsidy budget constraint. After the subsidy, while consuming the same x_a square feet of housing, he could afford y_b units of *all other goods.* The difference in *y*, distance $y_b - y_a$, must therefore represent the subsidy that Peter receives, measured in terms of *all other goods.* Because units of *all other goods* are defined so that the price per unit is \$1, distance $y_b - y_a$ also represents the dollar amount of the subsidy.

So far we have not indicated which point Peter chooses on his new budget constraint, B_2. Figure 4.6 shows that his most preferred bundle is e_2. The associated distance between budget constraints B_1 and B_2 is *S*, which means that the actual outlay of government funds is \$*S*. Clearly, Peter is better off at e_2 than he was at e_1.[4] A more subtle issue is whether the subsidy on housing is an efficient way to raise Peter from indifference curve U_1 to indifference curve U_2. That is, could an alternative scheme have raised Peter to indifference curve U_2 at a cost less than \$*S*?

[4]This ignores the effects of taxes that might have been levied to finance the subsidy.

To answer this question, we need a way to put a dollar value on Peter's gain in welfare from this subsidy. Since we are trying to find the amount of income we would have to give Peter to produce an equivalent welfare gain, the equivalent variation seems a sensible measure. Remember that finding the equivalent variation involves shifting the original budget constraint. Hence, we shift B_1 outward in a parallel fashion until it is tangent to indifference curve U_2. In Figure 4.6, the equivalent variation so computed is marked E on the vertical axis. Now, because lines B_3 and B_1 are parallel, the vertical distance between these two lines is always equal to E. In particular, the length of the dotted line is also equal to E. Therefore, E is less than S.

This suggests a rather remarkable result: The value of the subsidy to the recipient (measured by the dollars of equivalent variation, E) is less than the cost of the subsidy (measured by the dollars spent by the government, S). In other words, if the subsidy program had been replaced with a direct income transfer of E dollars, the recipient would have been no worse off and the government would have saved the difference between S and E. Alternatively, if the government had spent the same amount of money (S) on a direct income transfer program instead of a subsidy, the recipient would have been better off because he could have attained a higher indifference curve. Hence, we conclude that the housing subsidy program is inefficient in the sense just described.

You might be suspicious that this result is an artifact of the particular way the indifference curves are drawn in Figure 4.6. This is not the case. As *long as indifference curves have the usual shape, any subsidy that changes relative prices is inefficient in the sense that the value to the recipient is less than the cost to the government.*[5]

Intuitively, a direct income transfer lets recipients spend the money in the way that they see fit. In contrast, a commodity subsidy "distorts" the recipients' choice by changing the relative prices of the commodities—it induces the recipients to purchase "too much" of the subsidized commodity relative to what they would have purchased given the presubsidy prices. Hence, although the commodity subsidy does make Peter better off, his welfare would have been enhanced even further if he had received the same amount of money as a lump sum. Because of the inefficiency of subsidies, many economists, representing a broad range of political thought, believe that it would be preferable to replace commodity subsidies with direct cash grants.

If all of this is true, then why are commodity subsidies so popular? Several factors are probably at work. At least for those subsidies that are targeted at the poor, paternalism may be present. Donors may believe that the poor are not capable of making sensible spending decisions, so that they must be induced to make purchases that are "good" for them. The U.S. food stamp program is a good example. A recipient cannot (legally) use food stamps to purchase alcoholic beverages and tobacco.

Political considerations are also important. Commodity subsidies are attractive politically because they help not only the beneficiary, but also the producers of the favored commodity. For example, housing subsidies increase the demand for housing, which benefits construction firms, construction workers, and the savings and loan industry. These "special interests" are therefore happy to lend their support to a political coalition in favor of such programs.

[5]This assumes that there are no market "imperfections" such as externalities. See Chapter 12.

PRESIDENT CARTER'S GASOLINE TAX

In the late 1970s, the U.S. government was considering policies to reduce gasoline consumption. A tax on gasoline was one alternative. However, many people believed that it would be unfair to punish certain individuals just because they happened to consume a lot of gasoline. Therefore, the Carter administration proposed the following scheme: Levy a tax on gasoline and rebate the proceeds back to gasoline consumers. This proposal encountered severe criticism, particularly from then-presidential-candidate, Ronald Reagan, who argued that it would not work because the rebate would cancel the tax.

Who was right, Carter or Reagan? Let's use the tools developed in this chapter to find out. Figure 4.7 depicts the situation of Jimmy, a typical consumer who allocates his income of I dollars between gasoline (measured on the horizontal axis) and *all other goods* (measured on the vertical axis). Initially, the price per gallon of gasoline is p, and the price per unit of all other goods is $1. Subject to the resulting budget constraint (line B_1 in the diagram), Jimmy's most preferred bundle consists of x_1 gallons of gasoline and y_1 units of *all other goods.*

Suppose the government levies a tax of u dollars per gallon that raises the price of gasoline from p to $p + u$.[6] Jimmy's budget constraint now has a slope of $-(p + u)$, and a horizontal intercept of $I/(p + u)$—budget constraint B_2 in Figure 4.7.

Now, recall from our earlier discussion of the housing subsidy that the vertical distance between the before- and after-subsidy budget constraints measured the amount of subsidy paid at any given level of housing consumption. Using the same logic, the vertical distance between the before- and after-tax budget constraints in Figure 4.7 shows the amount of tax paid for each quantity of gasoline consumed. Hence, if Jimmy's most preferred bundle after the gasoline tax is e_2, then his tax bill is the associated vertical distance between B_1 and B_2, T.

If the Carter scheme had consisted solely of the tax, our analysis would be complete. But we still have to analyze what happens when the tax proceeds are rebated. Let us assume that the full $\$T$ of tax revenues are rebated to Jimmy. Given that his budget constraint after the tax is B_2, Jimmy's new budget constraint must be parallel to B_2 and exactly T above it when he receives $\$T$ as a lump sum—line B_3 in Figure 4.7. And given budget constraint B_3, Jimmy's most preferred bundle is e_3, where his gasoline consumption is x_3 gallons and his consumption of all other goods is y_3.

Figure 4.7 yields the following insights:

1. The Carter plan reduces gasoline consumption by less than would a gasoline tax alone—x_3 is greater than x_2.
2. Nevertheless, the Carter plan does induce conservation of gasoline relative to no action at all—x_3 is less than x_1.
3. Although the rebate contributes to an increase in the consumer's level of welfare (indifference curve U_R is higher than indifference curve U_2), he is still worse off than he was initially (indifference curve U_1 is higher than indifference curve U_R).

[6]As shown in Chapter 11, the actual extent to which the price paid by the consumer rises because of a tax depends upon the shapes of the market demand and supply curves. However, the analysis that follows is applicable to whatever price rise is engendered by the tax.

Figure 4.7

Gasoline Tax with Rebate

x_1 is gasoline consumption before the tax; x_2 is gasoline consumption after the tax; and x_3 is gasoline consumption when the tax proceeds are rebated. The tax increases the opportunity cost of gasoline in terms of all other goods, which is why B_2 is steeper than B_1. Hence, even though the tax is rebated, gasoline consumption after the rebate (x_3) is less than the original level.

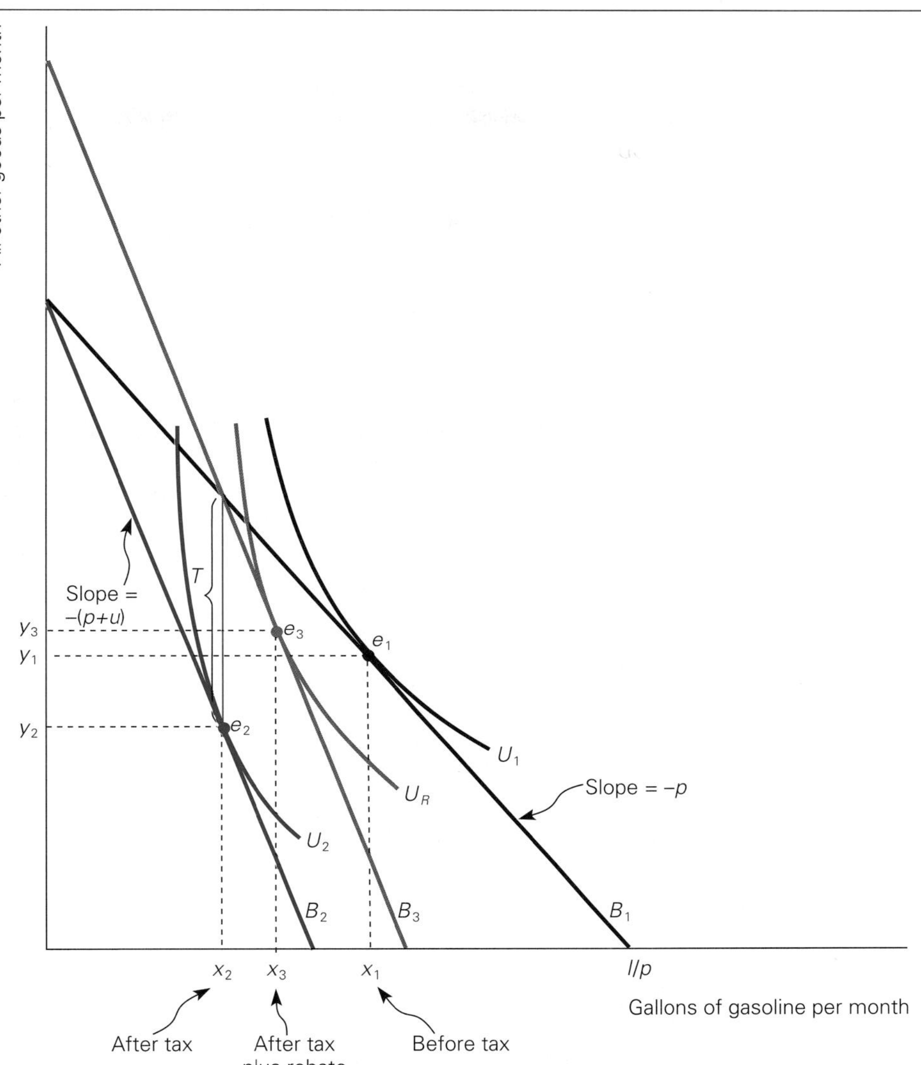

Intuitively, x_3 is greater than x_2 because the increase in Jimmy's income from the rebate induces him to consume more gasoline. In other words, Figure 4.7 assumes that gasoline is a normal good, a reasonable assumption. Nevertheless, *because the tax on gasoline raises its opportunity cost in terms of all other goods, it is in the consumer's interest to consume less gasoline than he did initially—even after the rebate.* That is why x_3 is less than x_1.

Note that the movement from x_1 to x_3 is approximately the substitution effect associated with the increase in the price of gasoline. The reason for the "approximately" is that the exact substitution effect is found by giving the consumer just enough money to attain his initial *real* income, the compensating variation. In contrast, the Carter plan would have given consumers only enough money

($\$T$) to attain their initial *money* income. This accounts for the fact that even after receiving the rebate, consumers are worse off than they were initially.

So who was right, Carter or Reagan? The analysis seems to favor Carter. It is likely that if the tax/rebate scheme had been administratively feasible, it would have indeed induced some decrease in gasoline consumption. This is just the (approximate) substitution effect in action. However, if the goal of the rebate was to assure that gasoline consumers would be no worse off because of the tax, then our analysis suggests that it would not quite have succeeded—the rebate was less than the compensating variation of the price increase.

SECTION RECAP

The examples in this section have shown how compensating and equivalent variations can be used to illuminate a wide variety of important policy problems. We have used these tools to demonstrate that a price subsidy is generally worth less to an individual than an equivalent lump-sum transfer, and that a tax on a commodity accompanied by a rebate of the tax can reduce demand for the commodity.

4.4 CONSUMER SURPLUS

We have seen that the compensating variation is a powerful tool for measuring changes in people's welfare. As shown in Figure 4.2, its calculation uses the individual's indifference map. However, it is often convenient to represent welfare changes in terms of a demand curve. In this section, we describe how this is done and use the results to obtain a practical method for approximating changes in consumer welfare.

THE DEMAND CURVE AS A MARGINAL VALUATION SCHEDULE

To demonstrate that demand curves are useful for measuring welfare changes, we must first show that each point on the demand curve reveals the approximate monetary value that the individual places on consuming the associated unit of the commodity. Consider Alexander, who consumes telephone services (measured in minutes of calling) and a composite of *all other goods*. Alexander's demand curve for telephone calls, d, is shown in Figure 4.8. Unlike our typical demand curves, d is drawn as a series of steps rather than declining continuously. As you will see shortly, this is just for convenience, and has no effect on the basic argument.

According to Figure 4.8, when the price of telephone calls is 50 cents per minute, Alexander's quantity demanded is 1 minute per day. How much does he value that minute of time spent on the telephone? Because the price is 50 cents, Alexander is willing to give up 50 cents for the minute, but no more. Hence, the value that Alexander places on his first minute of telephone time is 50 cents. In short, the price on the demand curve associated with the first minute represents Alexander's willingness to pay for that minute. Graphically, this is represented in Figure 4.8 by the area of rectangle A, whose height is 50 cents, and whose width is one minute of telephone time.

What about the second minute? According to Figure 4.8, the price associated with the second minute per day is 34 cents. Using exactly the same reasoning as above, the amount of money that Alexander would be willing to give up for the

Figure 4.8

The Demand Curve as a Marginal Willingness to Pay Schedule

The marginal value of consuming a unit of a commodity is the price on the associated point of the demand curve. In this case, the marginal value of the first unit is 50 cents, of the second unit, 34 cents, and the third unit, 26 cents. These amounts correspond to areas under the demand curve *A*, *B*, and *C*, respectively.

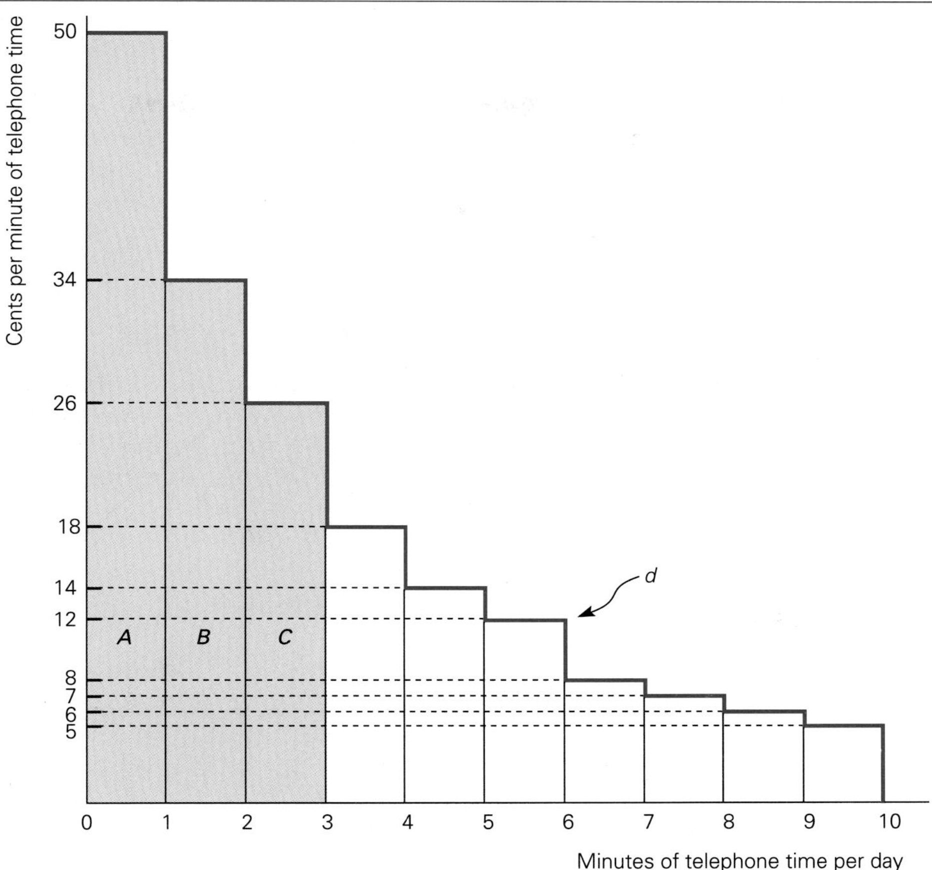

second minute must be 34 cents, represented by rectangle B. More generally, the value that a consumer places on consuming an additional unit of a commodity is simply the associated price on his demand curve. For this reason, the demand curve can be thought of as a *marginal valuation schedule*—for each unit of consumption, it shows the value that the consumer attaches to that additional (i.e., marginal) unit.

Suppose that we want to know how much Alexander values his first three minutes of telephone time each day, taken together. The answer is found by adding the marginal valuations associated with the first, second, and third minutes. In Figure 4.8, this is the sum of rectangles A, B, and C, or \$1.10 (= \$.50 + \$.34 + \$.26). More generally, the value placed on consuming a given number of units of a commodity is the sum of the marginal valuations of each of the units, and is represented graphically as the area underneath the demand curve between the first and last units under consideration.

Now consider the demand schedule for sugar in Figure 4.9, which is a smooth curve rather than a step function. Using the same logic as in Figure 4.8, the height of the curve at any given consumption level is the value to the individual of consuming that unit. For example, p_1 is the marginal value of consuming

Figure 4.9

Measuring Total Willingness to Pay

When the demand curve is smooth, we can still interpret the vertical distance from the horizontal axis to the curve as the marginal value placed on the corresponding unit. Hence, in analogy to Figure 4.8, the area under the curve between two levels of consumption represents the total value placed on those units of consumption.

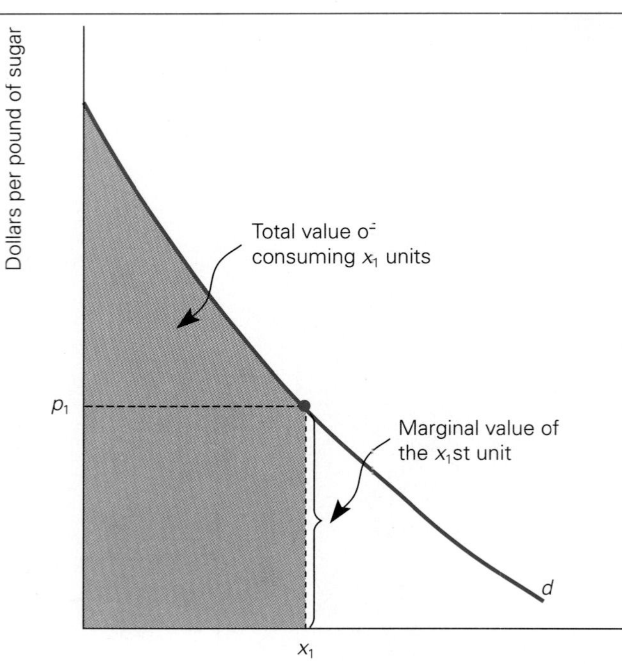

unit x_1. In analogy to Figure 4.8, the total value of units 1 through x_1 is the corresponding shaded area under the demand curve.

PRICES AND CONSUMER SURPLUS

Armed with the knowledge that the demand curve is in effect a marginal valuation schedule, we are very close to being able to obtain a neat graphical representation of the compensating variation. To take the next step, consider Figure 4.10, which reproduces Alexander's demand curve for telephone calls. When the market price of telephone time is 8 cents per minute, Alexander demands seven minutes per day, and pays a total of 56 cents.

Consider the first minute of telephone time. Alexander would be willing to pay 50 cents for that minute, but he only has to pay the going price of 8 cents per minute. Alexander comes out "ahead" on the purchase by the difference between 50 cents and 8 cents, or 42 cents. The difference between what a consumer is willing to pay and what he has to pay is called the **consumer surplus,** also sometimes referred to as **Marshallian consumer surplus**, after British economist Alfred Marshall, who popularized this approach. In Figure 4.10, the consumer surplus associated with the first minute of telephone time is area *M*.

consumer surplus
The difference between what a consumer is willing to pay and what she has to pay. Also referred to as **Marshallian consumer surplus.**

Alexander also enjoys a surplus on the purchase of the second minute of telephone time. He would be willing to pay 34 cents for his second minute; given a price per minute of 8 cents, his consumer surplus is 26 cents, area *N*. Despite the fact that the surplus on the second minute is less than that on the first, it still *is* surplus, and therefore it is worthwhile for Alexander to purchase the second minute. Alexander continues to enjoy a surplus on every minute purchased until

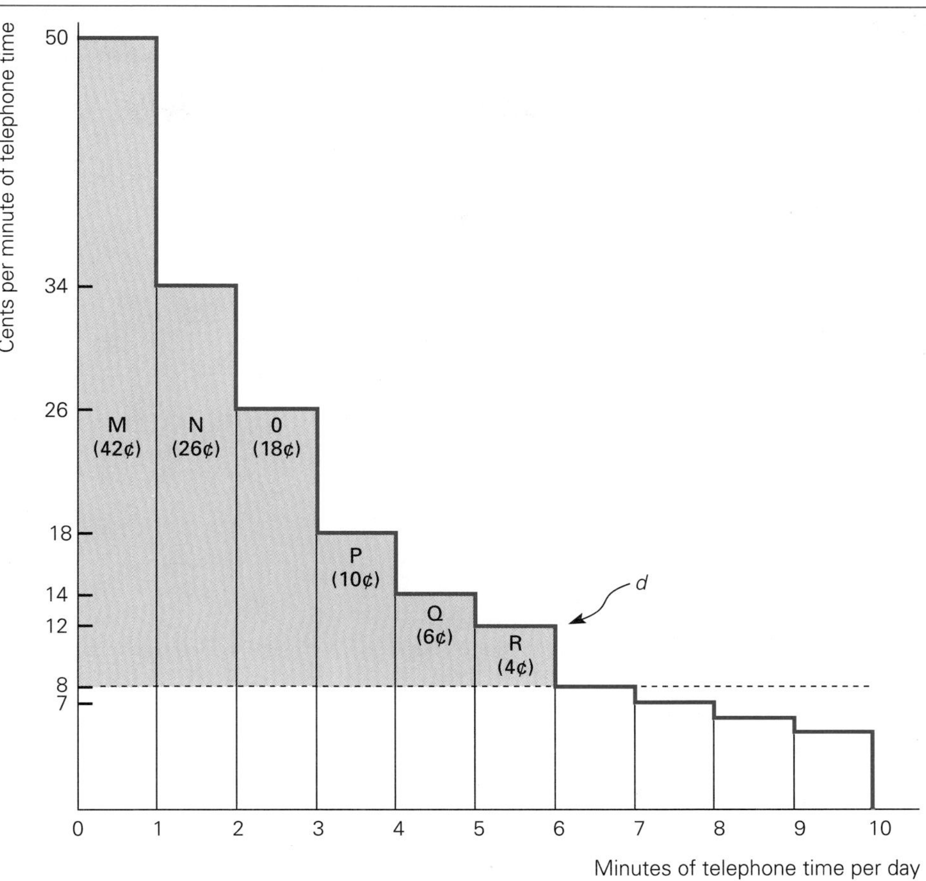

Figure 4.10

Consumer Surplus

The surplus on each unit purchased is the marginal valuation of that unit minus the price. Hence, if the market price is 8 cents, the consumer surplus for the first unit is area *M*; for the second unit, area *N*; and so on. The consumer surplus associated with the ability to buy as many units as demanded at the going price is the area beneath the demand curve and above the going price.

the seventh one, for which his surplus is exactly zero. That is, Alexander comes out neither behind nor ahead on his purchase of the seventh unit. Note that if Alexander purchased an eighth minute, the associated surplus would be negative—the price (8 cents) would exceed the marginal value (7 cents). This is another way of stating what we knew already—it is not in Alexander's interest to purchase more than seven minutes of telephone time when the price is 8 cents per minute.

What is the total amount of surplus that Alexander obtains by being able to purchase seven minutes of telephone time at a price of 8 cents per minute? The total surplus is just the sum of the surplus obtained on each minute purchased, or the sum of shaded areas M + N + O + P + Q + R, which is $1.06. More generally, ***the consumer surplus associated with the ability to purchase as many units of a commodity as you want at the going price is the area under the demand curve and above the going price.*** The shaded area in Figure 4.11, for example, is the consumer surplus when the price of sugar is p_2.

To firm up your intuition about consumer surplus, consider the following situation. To gain access to the telephone system, you have to pay a monthly fee. Once you have paid this fee, you can buy as many minutes of phone service as you want at the going price. What is the largest access fee you would pay, rather

Figure 4.11

Consumer Surplus with a Smooth Demand Curve

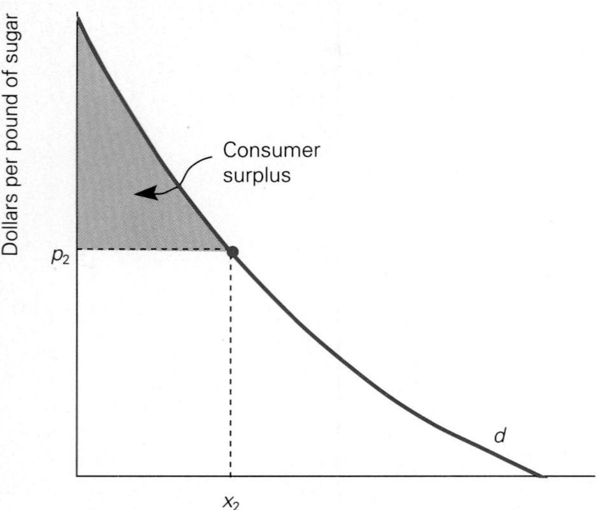

When the individual consumes x_2 units of sugar at the going price of p_2, the consumer surplus is the area underneath the demand curve and above the price.

Figure 4.12

Effect of a Price Change on Consumer Surplus

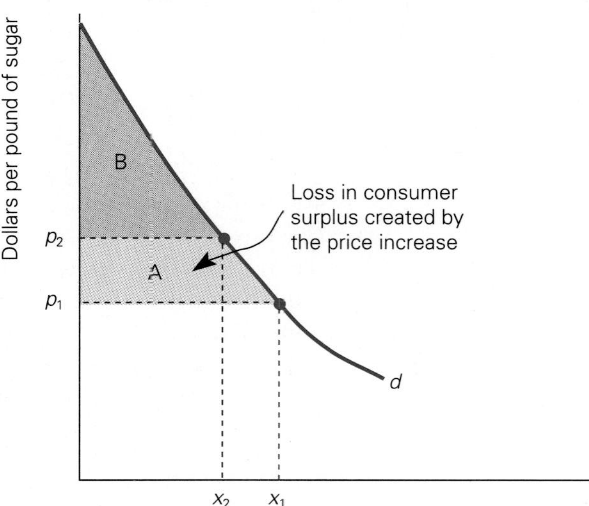

When the price is p_1, consumer surplus is area $A + B$. At price p_2, surplus is area B. Hence, when the price increases from p_1 to p_2, the consumer's welfare decreases by the difference between these two areas, A.

than do without telephone service at all? The answer you provide is your consumer surplus from telephone service. The levying of an access fee is a practice common to many telephone companies. The observation that most people are willing to pay such fees indicates that the consumer surplus from telephone service exceeds the fee. Other examples of access fees are cover charges at bars, and entry charges at amusement parks at which patrons must also pay for rides once they are inside. Such a pricing scheme is referred to as a **two-part tariff**—the consumer first pays a lump sum for the right to purchase a good, and then pays some price for each unit of the good actually purchased.

two-part tariff
A pricing system under which a consumer first pays a lump sum for the right to purchase a good, and then pays a price for each unit of the good actually purchased.

Effect of Price Changes on Consumer Surplus

We are now in a good position to measure the welfare effects of a price change. Figure 4.12 represents Samson's demand curve for sugar. When the price is p_1 per pound, Samson demands x_1 pounds, and his consumer surplus is the sum of areas A and B. Now suppose that the price increases to p_2 per pound. At this price, the quantity demanded falls to x_2. How much is the consumer surplus now? The basic principle still holds—consumer surplus is the area underneath the demand curve and above the price. Since the price is now p_2, the surplus is area B. As a consequence of the price increase, then, consumer surplus decreases from area $(A + B)$ to area B, a loss of area A. Hence, area A is a dollar measure of the loss in welfare associated with the increase in the price of sugar.

More generally, *when the price of a commodity changes from p_1 to p_2, the area behind the demand curve and between the two prices is a dollar measure of the resulting change in welfare.* (PC 4.3)

4.3 PROGRESS CHECK

Here you see Mickey's demand curve for baseball games. Compute how much his welfare improves when the price per game falls from $8 to $6.

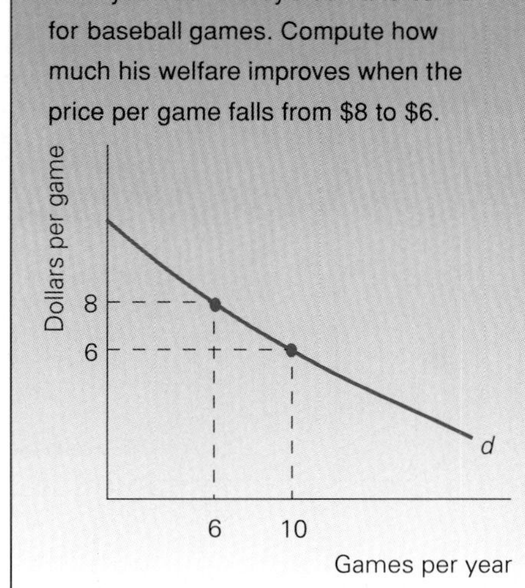

APPLICATION OF CONSUMER SURPLUS: ANALYSIS OF A TRADE QUOTA

trade quota
A restriction on the quantity of some commodity that can be imported into the country.

Starting in 1981, the number of Japanese automobiles imported into the United States was limited by the U.S. Government.[7] A **trade quota** is a restriction on the quantity of some commodity that can be imported into the country. Technically, the quota was "voluntary" in the sense that Japan imposed the quota on itself. However, it was clear that if Japan had not agreed to restrain its exports to the United States voluntarily, then a quota would have been imposed by the United States itself. Quotas play an important role in the trade policies of the United States and of many other countries as well. In the United States there are quotas on a wide array of products—including beef, steel, color televisions, textiles, and as mentioned at the beginning of this chapter, sugar. By restricting the supply of a commodity, a quota raises its price. In this section, we use consumer surplus to analyze some of the consequences of the quota on Japanese automobiles.

In Figure 4.13, D is the U.S. demand for Japanese cars. According to Tarr and Morkre (1984), in 1981, in the absence of any quota, the average price per Japanese car would have been $4,573, and at this price 2.69 million cars would have been imported. As a consequence of the quota, however, imports were restricted to 1.91 million cars. To find the price associated with this fixed supply, one needs to find the price on the demand curve associated with a quantity of 1.91 million cars; Tarr and Morkre estimated this was $4,967. The quota raised the price of Japanese cars by $394.

How did this affect the welfare of American consumers? As we demonstrated in the last section, the loss of consumer surplus associated with a price increase is the area behind the demand curve between the two prices. In Figure 4.13, this is the sum of areas F and G. Using the formula for the area of a trapezoid, this area is $908 million. Thus, as a consequence of the "voluntary" restraints, U.S. consumers were worse off by $908 million (in 1981 dollars).

Where did the lost consumer surplus go? Part of it was transferred to Japanese producers in the form of higher prices for the cars they sold under the quota. The benefits of these higher prices to the foreign producer are sometimes referred to as *quota rents.* Specifically, for each of the 1.91 million cars they sold under the quota, Japanese producers received an extra $394, or a total of $753 million

[7]The analysis here is a simplified version of the one presented by Tarr and Morkre (1984, chap. 3).

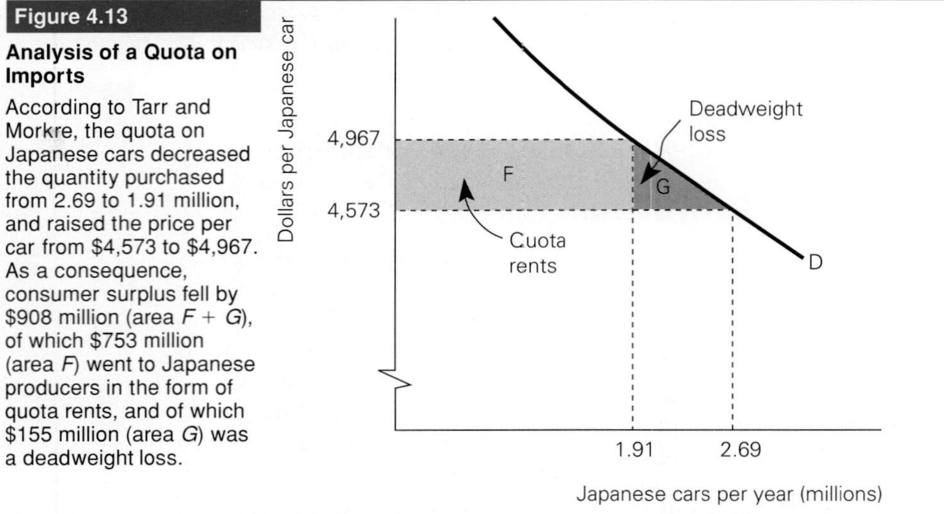

Figure 4.13

Analysis of a Quota on Imports

According to Tarr and Morkre, the quota on Japanese cars decreased the quantity purchased from 2.69 to 1.91 million, and raised the price per car from $4,573 to $4,967. As a consequence, consumer surplus fell by $908 million (area *F* + *G*), of which $753 million (area *F*) went to Japanese producers in the form of quota rents, and of which $155 million (area *G*) was a deadweight loss.

dollars in quota rents. In Figure 4.13, $394 dollars is the height of rectangle *F* and 1.91 million is its width, so this $753 million transfer is represented by area *F*. This still leaves triangle *G*, whose area is $155 million, unaccounted for. Who received this portion of the surplus lost by American consumers? Nobody. It is a pure loss induced by the fact that the increase in Japanese car prices distorted Americans' choices between Japanese autos and other goods. The quota prevented Americans from buying 780,000 cars that they valued at more than the market price of $4,573. By foreclosing Americans' opportunities to make these purchases, the quota reduced their welfare without an offsetting gain to anyone else. This pure waste induced by an increase in price above the competitive level is called a **deadweight loss.** In short, the quota on Japanese automobiles inflicted a loss in consumer surplus of $908 million per year; part of the loss was a transfer to foreign producers, and part was a deadweight loss that benefited no one.

deadweight loss
The pure waste induced by an increase in price above the efficient level.

So far we have ignored the impact of the quota on the market for domestic autos. We will have to wait until we develop a theory of supply in product markets to analyze fully such effects. Nevertheless, we can summarize the main results. As a consequence of the quota on Japanese autos, prices in the domestic car market increased, and consumer surplus was transferred to domestic automobile firms and their employees rather than to foreign producers. Tarr and Morkre (1984) estimated the transfer of consumer surplus to domestic producers to be $105 million in 1981 dollars.

As noted earlier, there are many industries that receive protection from international competition. According to Hufbauer and Elliott (1994), for the 21 U.S. industries that have the heaviest protection, there is a transfer of surplus from consumers to producers of $15.8 billion, which is associated with a deadweight loss of $10.7 billion.[8] This observation leads one to ponder why the protection comes into existence in the first place. Why do the interests of the producers and

[8]This figure includes the effects of tariffs as well as quotas.

their employees dominate those of the consumers in the political arena? Issues of this kind are discussed in Chapter 14.

"EXACT" CONSUMER SURPLUS AND THE COMPENSATED DEMAND CURVE

We noted at the outset of this section that Marshallian consumer surplus is only an approximate measure of consumer welfare. To see why, recall that the demand curve shows the relationship between price and quantity demanded, holding fixed other things, including money income. However, with a fixed money income, the value that an individual puts on an additional unit of a good may depend on the amount that he has already spent on previous units of the good. Hence, the vertical distance up to the demand curve may not exactly measure the consumer's marginal valuation of the associated unit of output. In more technical terms, an exact marginal valuation schedule must eliminate the "income effects" that are embodied in the demand curve. We next show how to find such a marginal valuation schedule, and then discuss the conditions under which the exact measure and the Marshallian counterpart are likely to differ substantially.

Compensated Demand Curve

compensated demand curve
A schedule that shows how the quantity demanded varies with price, assuming that, as price changes, consumers are compensated with enough income to keep them at their initial utility level.

We begin by defining the **compensated demand curve** for a commodity: a schedule that shows how the quantity demanded varies with price, assuming that as price changes, consumers are compensated with enough income to keep them on their initial indifference curve, that is, at the initial utility level. Note the distinction between the *compensated* demand curve and the *ordinary* demand curve that was derived in Chapter 3. The ordinary demand curve shows the relationship between price and quantity demanded, holding *money income* constant. The compensated demand curve, on the other hand, shows the relationship between price and quantity demanded, holding the level of *real income* (utility) constant. The compensated demand curve shows only the substitution effect of a price change, while the ordinary demand curve shows the observed response to a price change—the substitution effect *and* the income effect.

Once we understand income and substitution effects, the derivation of the compensated demand curve from an indifference map is straightforward. Panel A of Figure 4.14 reproduces the information from Figure 4.2. When the price of sugar is p_1 per pound, the price of each unit of *all other goods* is \$1, and Samson's money income is I, then his budget constraint is B_1. Samson's utility maximizing bundle is e_1, which includes x_1 pounds of sugar. As usual, the fact that the price of sugar is p_1 is not explicit; it is implicit in the slope of the budget constraint. Point e'_1 in Panel B of Figure 4.14 records explicitly that when the price is p_1, quantity demanded is x_1.

Now suppose that the price of sugar increases to p_2. This pivots the budget constraint to B_2. If the price increase were the only change, then Samson would consume bundle e_2, with the quantity of sugar demanded falling to x_2. But the definition of compensated demand curve requires that we examine the change in quantity demanded, holding fixed the level of utility. Clearly, e_2 represents a lower level of utility than e_1. Hence, if we want to show how quantity demanded changes while holding the level of utility fixed, we must compensate Samson with enough income to return him to indifference curve U_1. This is done by moving B_2 up in a parallel fashion until it is tangent to the original indifference curve.

Figure 4.14

Deriving a Compensated Demand Curve

The compensated demand curve shows how the quantity demanded varies with price, holding the level of utility constant. In Panel A, when the price increases from p_1 to p_2 and utility is held constant, the quantity demanded falls from x_1 to x_c. Therefore, these two combinations of price and quantity fall on the compensated demand curve. This is recorded in Panel B.

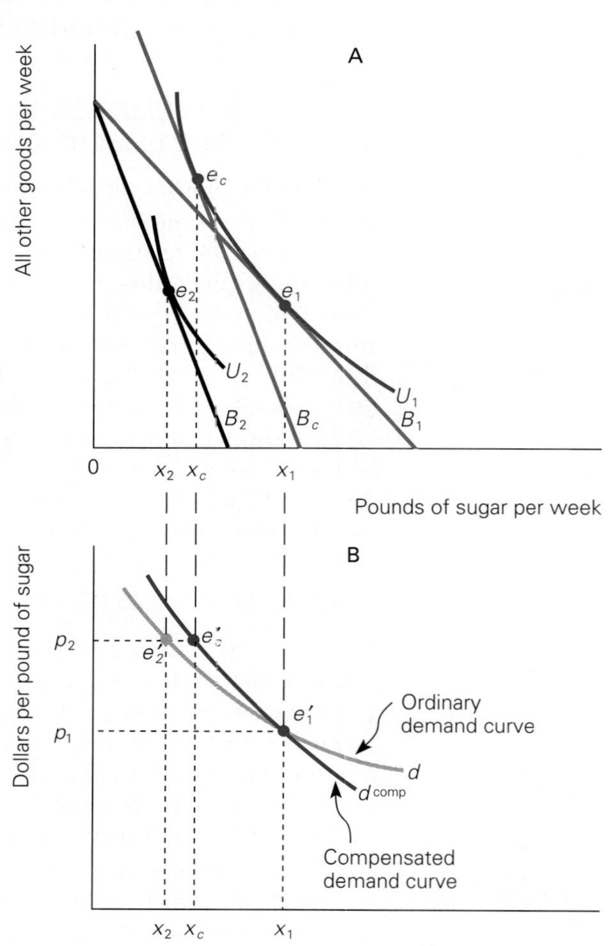

The tangency occurs at point e_c, where the quantity of sugar is x_c. Point e'_c in Panel B records the fact that when the price goes up to p_2 *and* utility is held constant, the quantity demanded falls to x_c. Hence, by definition, point e'_c must lie on the compensated demand curve for sugar.

Now, imagine repeating this process over and over for various price changes:

1. Pivot the budget line in (for price increases) or out (for price decreases).
2. Shift the new budget line away from the origin (for price increases), or toward the origin (for price decreases) in a parallel fashion until it is just tangent to the original indifference curve.
3. Record the new point of tangency in Panel B of Figure 4.14.

The collection of points generated by following this three-step process is Samson's compensated demand curve for sugar, labeled d^{comp}.

In the process of deriving the compensated demand curve, you simultaneously uncover the information required to draw the ordinary demand curve, which shows the *observed* responses to price changes. For example, when the price goes from p_1 to p_2 and there is no compensation, the quantity demanded falls from x_1 to x_2. Hence, the point at which the price is p_2 and quantity is x_2 (point e'_2) lies on the ordinary demand curve. For purposes of reference, the ordinary demand curve, d, is superimposed on the compensated demand curve in Panel B.

Note that the ordinary demand curve is flatter than the compensated demand curve. Is this always true? The answer is to be found in our earlier discussion of income and substitution effects. When sugar is a normal good, as in Figure 4.14, the income and substitution effects reinforce each other. Hence, the observed response to a price change (for example, $x_1 - x_2$) exceeds the corresponding compensated response, $(x_1 - x_c)$. But if the uncompensated quantity demanded falls faster than the compensated quantity demanded when price goes up, then the ordinary demand curve must be *flatter* than the compensated demand curve. On the other hand, when sugar is an inferior good, the income and substitution effects work in opposite directions. Hence, the observed response is less than the compensated response to a price change, and the ordinary demand curve is steeper than the compensated demand curve. In short, the compensated demand curve for a commodity is not *necessarily* steeper than the ordinary demand curve.

We can apply to the compensated demand curve the same process for finding consumer surplus that we applied to the ordinary demand curve in Figure 4.11—find the marginal valuation associated with each level of output, and interpret the difference between the marginal valuation and price as a measure of surplus. However, unlike the marginal valuation measure obtained by using the ordinary demand curve, the measure using the compensated demand curve is not contaminated by income effects. This is simply because, by definition, income effects are excluded from the compensated demand curve.

Marshallian consumer surplus is only an approximation to the exact value that can be computed using the compensated demand curve. If so, why should we ever use the Marshallian approach? To see why, think about the practical steps necessary to implement the exact approach. The first step is to use statistical data on individuals' consumption patterns to estimate the shape of the compensated demand curve for the commodity under consideration. On the basis of consumer demand data, compute how quantity demanded varies with price, *ceteris paribus*, $(\Delta x/\Delta p)$ and how quantity demanded varies with money income, *ceteris paribus*, $(\Delta x/\Delta I)$. Substitute these estimates into the Slutsky Equation (4.3) to compute the compensated demand response. Once the compensated demand curve is known, it is straightforward to compute the relevant areas under the curve.

4.4 PROGRESS CHECK

Indicate whether each statement is true or false for a rational individual.

a. The ordinary demand curve must slope down.

b. The compensated demand curve must slope down.

c. The compensated demand curve must be steeper than the ordinary demand curve.

There is a potential problem, however. In some cases, we may not have sufficient data to estimate how the quantity demanded changes with money income, *ceteris paribus*. In these cases, the best we can do is estimate the *ordinary* demand curve, despite the fact that the *compensated* demand curve is what we need to compute exact consumer surplus. In most situations economists regard Marshallian consumer surplus as a good approximation to the exact measure. (PC 4.4)

SECTION RECAP

Information about consumer behavior generally comes to us via demand curves. Therefore, it is useful to have a way to use demand curves for measuring changes in consumer welfare. The key insight required for this is that each point on the demand curve represents the approximate incremental value that the consumer places on the associated unit of consumption. This result allows us to measure consumer surplus—the difference between what a consumer is willing to pay for a good and what he or she has to pay for the good. Geometrically, consumer surplus can be approximated by the area under the demand curve and above the commodity's price. By measuring how consumer surplus changes in response to a price increase or decrease, we can estimate how the change affects consumer welfare.

SUMMARY

This chapter develops methods for measuring how changes in the prices of the commodities people consume affect consumer welfare.

- Whenever the price of a commodity changes, there is an income effect and a substitution effect. When the price increases, the income effect is the impact on quantity demanded that is due exclusively to the fact that the price increase lowers the individual's real income. The substitution effect is the change in quantity demanded due exclusively to the change in relative prices.
- The observed response to a price change, the income effect, and the substitution effect are linked by a relationship called the Slutsky equation.
- To isolate the substitution effect of a price increase, one must give the individual enough income to attain his or her initial level of utility. This amount of money is called the compensating variation, and is one way to measure (in dollar terms) the effect of the price change on consumer welfare.
- An alternative measure is the equivalent variation, which is the amount of money you would have to take away from the individual to reduce his or her welfare as much as the price increase does.
- Consumer surplus is the difference between what the consumer is willing to pay and what he or she has to pay. Consumer surplus is measured by the area under the ordinary demand curve and above the price.
- A compensated demand curve shows how the quantity demanded of a commodity varies with price, holding the level of utility constant. The area under the compensated demand curve provides an exact measure of how much the individual is willing to pay for each unit of consumption.

DISCUSSION QUESTIONS

4.1 In Japan, restrictions on the import of rice keep the price of rice at about 10 times the world level. Suppose that these restrictions were relaxed. Show how this change would affect the equilibrium bundle of a Japanese consumer. Decompose the change into income and substitution effects. Show the compensating and equivalent variations of the reduction in the price of rice.

4.2 The local swimming pool charges nonmembers \$10 per visit. If you join the pool, you can swim for \$5 per visit, but you have to pay an annual fee of \$$F$. Use an indifference curve diagram to find the value of F that would make it just worthwhile for you to join the pool. Suppose that the pool charged you exactly that value. Would you swim more or less than you did before joining? Use income and substitution effects to explain your answer.

4.3 Discuss: "Because utilities are ordinal, the utility numbers assigned to indifference curves are arbitrary. This is why it is impossible to find an unambiguous dollar measure of the welfare difference between two indifference curves."

4.4 Consider the following data: In 1990, the average monthly wage in Russia was 303 rubles; the price of sugar was 0.4 rubles per pound, and the price of bread was 0.11 rubles per pound. In 1994, the average monthly wage was 181,483 rubles per month; sugar was 552 rubles per pound and bread was 264 rubles per pound (Barringer 1994, E5).

Sketch the 1990 budget constraint, draw an indifference map, and show the utility maximizing bundle. Now sketch the 1994 budget constraint. Which would cost more: to give the individual enough money in 1994 so that he could afford the 1990 commodity bundle, or to give the individual enough money in 1994 so that he could attain his 1990 utility level? Illustrate with your diagram and explain your answer.

4.5 Explain: "In order to make the Cervantes quote at the beginning of this chapter correct, one should add the words 'at the margin'."

4.6 Boris's demand curve for tennis games, *d*, is shown below. At the local tennis club, the cost per tennis game for members is p_t dollars. In order to be a member, one must pay an annual fee. Show on the diagram the largest fee that Boris would be willing to pay.

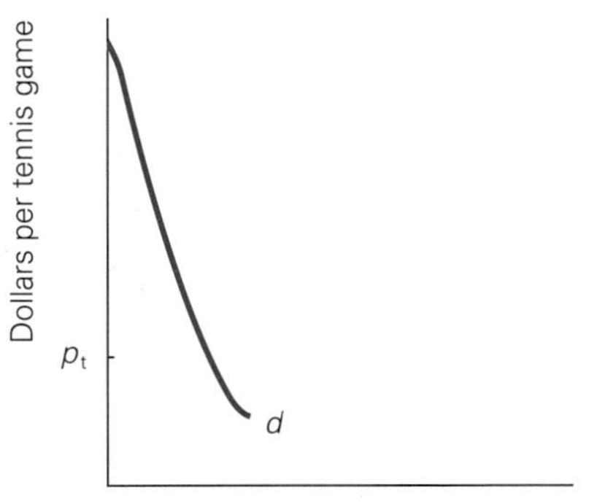

4.7 Below you see Marsha's demand curve for housing, *d*. She can purchase all the housing she desires at the market price of p_1 per square foot. Marsha is also eligible for housing in a government project. If she chooses this option, she only needs to pay p_2 per square foot, but she must consume an apartment of x_2 square feet. Which option does she choose?

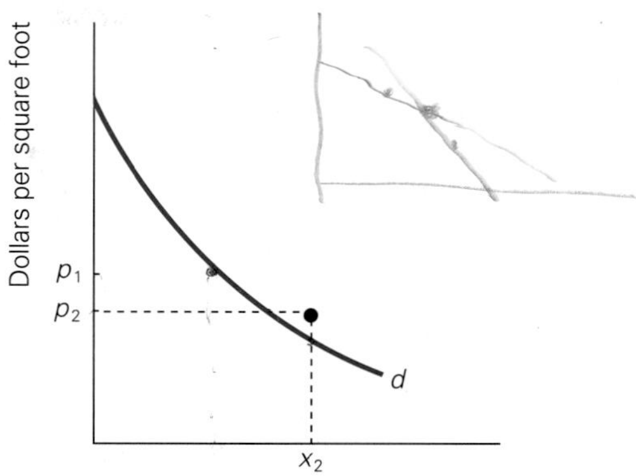

4.8 At his local grocery store, Tim can purchase potatoes at $2 per pound, and he buys 20 pounds per year. A "price club" opens near Tim's home. At the price club, potatoes cost $1 per pound, but Tim has to pay an annual membership fee of $20. Assume that potatoes are the only commodity carried by the price club that Tim would purchase if he were a member. Do you expect that Tim would join the price club? Use the concept of consumer surplus in your answer.

4.9 Imelda consumes shoes and a composite of *all other goods*. For Imelda, the income effect of a change in the price of shoes is always zero.

a. Sketch Imelda's indifference map.

b. Compare the compensating and equivalent variations of a price change.

c. Sketch Imelda's compensated and uncompensated demand curves for shoes.

d. Explain the following assertion: "For Imelda, the use of Marshallian consumer surplus to measure the effect of a change in shoe prices gives just the same answer as the use of the exact measure."

4.10 Consider again the discussion of automobile quotas that surrounded Figure 4.13. Suppose that instead of convincing the Japanese to adopt quotas, the United States had levied a tax of $394 per Japanese car imported to the United States. Such a tax on imports is referred to as a *tariff.* In a move from a tariff to a quota, who gains and who loses? (Include the government in your calculations.)

4.11 Bundle *A* is said to be *revealed preferred* to bundle *B* if both *A* and *B* are affordable, and the consumer chooses *A* over *B*. Use the notion of revealed preference to analyze the following situation: Each week, Jon divides $200 between renting video games and purchasing *all other goods.* When the price per game is \$4, Jon rents 10 games per week, and spends \$160 on *all other goods.* The local video store then institutes a new, two-part tariff pricing policy: Jon has to pay a weekly membership fee of \$30, but he can then rent games at a price of \$1 each. Does the new policy make Jon better off, worse off, or have no effect on him?

4.12 Suppose that the demand curve for plums is given by $Z = 10 - 2p$, where Z is the number of pounds demanded per year and p is the price per pound. Suppose that the price is \$1 per pound. Find the quantity demanded, total expenditure, and consumer surplus. Now suppose that the government initiates a program to limit the supply of plums. (There really is such a program!) Suppose further that, as a consequence of the plan, the price per pound goes up to \$2. What is consumer surplus after the price increase? What is the maximum amount that plum consumers would be willing to bribe legislators to repeal the supply limitation program?

*4.13 Gideon's utility function for doughnuts (x) and popcorn (y) is $U = x^{1/2} y^{1/2}$. The price per doughnut is 9, and the price per package of popcorn is 16.

a. Consider some arbitrary level of utility, U_0. Find the minimum level of expenditure on doughnuts and popcorn that can attain U_0. [Hint: Use the Lagrangean method to minimize total expenditure subject to the constraint $U_0 = x^{1/2} y^{1/2}$. Your answer will be a function of U_0.]

b. How much x and y are in the bundle in part *a*? (Again, your answer will depend on U_0.)

c. Suppose the price of x increases from 9 to 25. Calculate the compensating variation.

d. Now generalize your answer to part *b* by letting the price of x be p_x and the price of y be p_y. That is, write x as a function of p_x, p_y, and U_0, and similarly for y.

e. You have just derived the compensated demand curves for x and y. Explain why.

*This questions is for students who have studied the material in the Appendix to Chapter 3.

CHAPTER 5

The Household as Supplier

> *There are two cardinal sins from which all the others spring: impatience and laziness.*
>
> —Franz Kafka

In the 1980s and early 1990s, governments throughout the world slashed income tax rates. The United States cut its maximum marginal tax rate from 70 percent to 33 percent; the United Kingdom, from 83 percent to 60 percent; and Sweden, from 50 percent to 20 percent. [See Pechman (1988) and Steuerle (1992).] An important reason for these reductions was the belief that they would stimulate economic activity—with lower tax rates, people would work and save more. While these claims are debatable, they do focus our attention on an important truth: People's incomes depend at least in part on their *decisions*, and these decisions are influenced by the rewards to working and saving. In contrast, the models employed in the previous three chapters assumed that people's incomes were *fixed*. While this is a very useful assumption if one's goal is to study the allocation of income among various goods, it leaves unanswered the important question, Where does income come from?

The circular flow model of the first chapter provides an answer: In factor markets, people receive income by supplying inputs to the production sector of the economy. In return for supplying its labor, a household receives wage income; in return for supplying its capital, the household receives dividends and interest. This chapter analyzes the household in its role as a supplier.

Although this may sound like a new topic, it really isn't. The problem of supplying inputs is just a problem in rational choice—given the costs and benefits of supplying inputs, what decision maximizes the individual's utility? The same analytical apparatus that we developed to analyze the household's role as a demander of commodities can be used to study its role as a supplier of inputs. This is one of the beauties of microeconomic theory. Often, a technique used to solve one problem can be applied fruitfully to other problems that, at least on the surface, seem to be quite different.

The two most important inputs supplied by households are their labor and their capital. We discuss each of these in turn.

5.1 LABOR SUPPLY

For most households, the single most important source of income is labor. In the United States, for example, families headed by nonelderly married couples receive on average about 89 percent of their income from wages and salaries (Blank 1988). This section discusses labor supply choices.

BUDGET CONSTRAINT AND INDIFFERENCE CURVES

Othello has only a certain amount of time at his disposal each week. He devotes some of it to work in the market. The remaining hours are spent on nonmarket activities, which include housework, child care, and leisure. However, for simplicity and following tradition, we use the label *leisure* to characterize *all* nonmarket activity. Othello derives satisfaction ("utility") from the consumption of leisure and the consumption of *all other goods.* To buy these goods, he must earn money income. But to earn income he must work, and thereby surrender leisure time. Othello's problem is to find the combination of leisure and consumption that maximizes his utility.

To solve this problem, we need to illustrate the various combinations of leisure and consumption that are available to Othello—that is, to sketch his budget constraint. In Figure 5.1, the horizontal axis measures the number of hours devoted to leisure, n. (This notation reminds us that "leisure" is really "all *n*onmarket activity.") Even if Othello does not work at all, there is an upper limit to the amount of leisure that he can consume because there are only so many hours in a week. This number of hours, referred to as the **time endowment,** is T hours in Figure 5.1. Given our definition of leisure, time not spent on leisure is devoted to work in the market. If, for example, an individual's time endowment is 112 hours per week and he or she consumes 70 hours of leisure, then this individual works 42 hours. Geometrically, any point on the horizontal axis simultaneously indicates hours of leisure and hours of work. For example, at point a, n_a hours are devoted to leisure, and the difference between that and the time endowment, T, represents time spent at work, l_a. Algebraically, $l_a = T - n_a$.

time endowment
The upper limit of time that can be dedicated to labor or leisure by an individual in a specified period.

Our first problem is to illustrate how Othello's consumption of a composite of all market goods and services, c, which is measured on the vertical axis, varies with his hours of work. He earns a wage of $\$w_1$ per hour, so his earnings for any number of hours worked are just $\$w_1$ multiplied by the number of hours. Suppose, for example, Othello does not work at all. If labor is his only source of income, his income is simply zero. This option of zero work and zero income is represented by point T.

If Othello works one hour each week, by definition he consumes leisure equal to his time endowment minus one hour. This point is one hour to the left of T on the horizontal axis. Working one hour gives him a total $\$w_1$ for consumption. The combination of one hour of work with consumption of w_1 is labeled point b. If Othello works two hours—moves two hours to the left of T—his total consumption is $2 \times \$w_1$ which is labeled point f. Continuing in this way, we can trace out all the leisure/consumption combinations available to Othello—the straight line B_1, whose slope is minus the wage rate. Note that B_1 is the analog of the budget constraint in the usual analysis of the choice between two commodities. Here, however, the commodities are *consumption and leisure.* As always, the slope of the budget constraint reflects the opportunity cost of one commodity in

Figure 5.1

Budget Constraint between Leisure and Consumption

If an individual can work as many hours as he or she wants at a wage rate of w_1, then the individual's budget constraint between leisure and consumption is a straight line whose slope is $-w_1$. At point a, leisure is n_a hours, and number of hours of work is $l_a = T - n_a$.

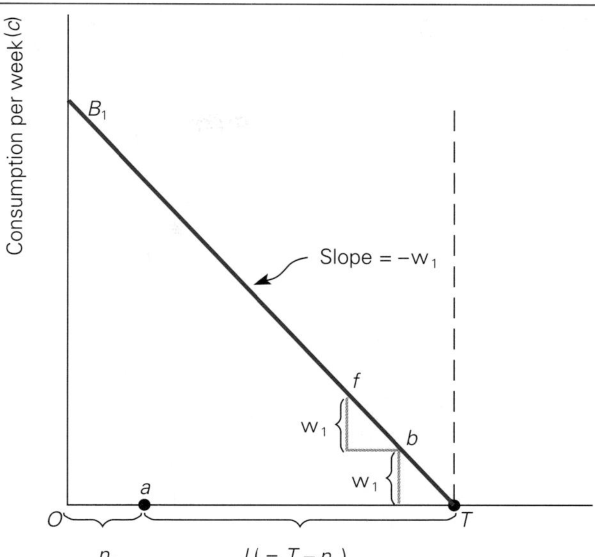

terms of another. The opportunity cost of an hour of leisure is the consumption forgone by not working that hour, which is just the wage rate. In this model, then, time is literally money.

To represent the budget constraint algebraically, note that since the price of c is \$1 per unit, c represents expenditures on market consumption. This must equal earnings, the product of the number of hours worked $(T - n)$ times the wage rate per hour (w). Hence, the budget constraint is

$$c = w \times (T - n).$$

We can rewrite this equation as

$$c + w \times n = w \times T. \tag{5.1}$$

For example, if Othello's wage rate is \$10 per hour and his time endowment is 112 hours per week, then his budget constraint is

$$c + 5n = 560.$$

Equation (5.1) highlights the essential similarity to the standard budget constraint in Chapter 2. As before, on the left-hand side, the commodities (c and n) are multiplied by their respective prices. However, there is a slight difference from the standard case, in which a fixed amount of income appears on the right-hand side. In (5.1), the right-hand side, $w \times T$, is the **value of the time endowment**—the amount of money the individual would have if he worked every available hour. The value of the time endowment is the individual's income in the sense that it shows the total amount of money he has to "spend" on leisure and consumption. In fact, the value of the time endowment is sometimes referred to as *full income*. When the wage rate changes, it not only affects the opportunity cost

value of the time endowment
The amount of money an individual would have if he worked every available hour.

Figure 5.2

Equilibrium Bundle of Leisure and Consumption

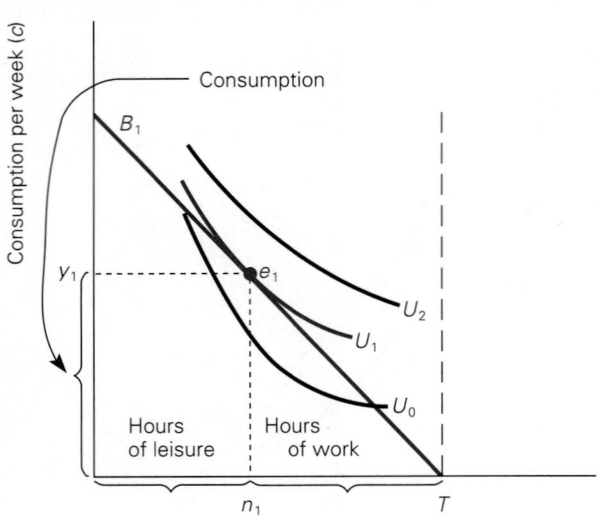

The optimal amount of labor to supply is defined by a tangency between the budget constraint and an indifference curve. Utility is maximized at point e_1, where $(T - n_1)$ hours of work are supplied to the market.

Figure 5.3

A Wage Decrease Reducing Hours of Labor Supplied

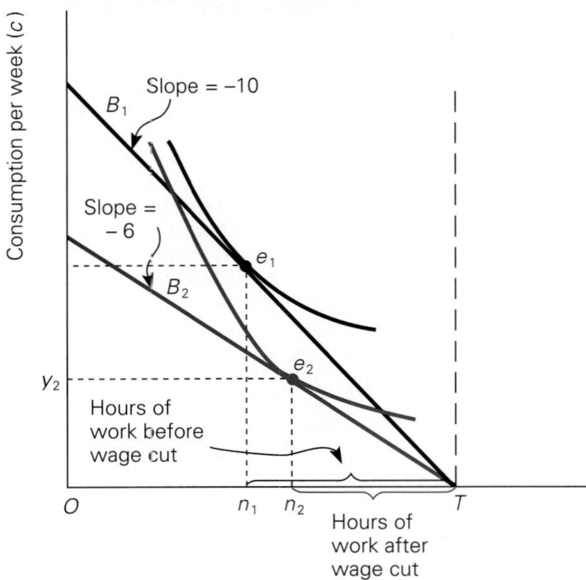

A decrease in the wage rate from \$10 to \$6 changes the budget constraint from B_1 to B_2. At the new equilibrium, labor supply is $(T - n_2)$ hours, which is less than the original supply of $(T - n_1)$ hours.

of leisure (on the left-hand side); it also affects full income (on the right-hand side).

To determine which point on B_1 Othello chooses, we need information on his tastes as well as his budget. A natural way to characterize his tastes is a set of convex indifference curves between leisure and *consumption*. In Figure 5.2, such an indifference map is superimposed on Othello's budget constraint. As usual, an interior solution is located at the tangency of the budget constraint to an indifference curve, bundle e_1, which consists of n_1 hours of leisure and y_1 units of *consumption*. Given a fixed time endowment of T hours, consumption of n_1 hours of leisure implies that Othello supplies $(T - n_1)$ hours of labor to the market.

COMPARATIVE STATICS WITH THE CONSUMPTION-LEISURE MODEL

Suppose that Othello's wage rate falls from \$10 to \$6. When Othello consumes an hour of leisure, he now gives up only \$6, not \$10. In effect, the wage reduction reduces the opportunity cost of an hour of leisure. This observation is represented in Figure 5.3. The budget constraint facing Othello is now the flatter line, B_2, whose slope is -6. Because of the wage cut, the original consumption/leisure choice, e_1, is no longer attainable. Othello must choose a point somewhere along the new budget constraint B_2. In Figure 5.3, this is e_2, where he consumes n_2 hours of leisure, works $T - n_2$ hours, and has a *consumption* level of y_2 units. The wage cut has lowered Othello's labor supply by $n_2 - n_1$ hours.

Figure 5.4

A Wage Decrease Increasing Hours of Labor Supplied

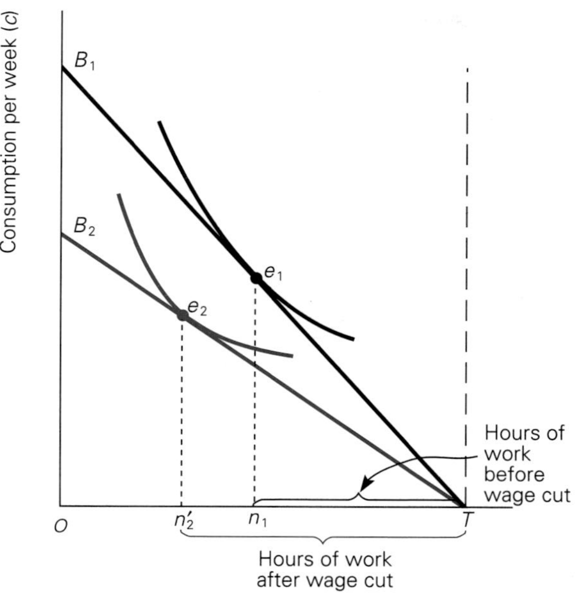

For Desdemona, a decrease in the wage rate (represented by the budget constraint moving from B_1 to B_2) increases hours of work from $(T - n_1)$ to $(T - n_2')$.

Figure 5.5

Substitution Effect of a Wage Change That Dominates the Income Effect

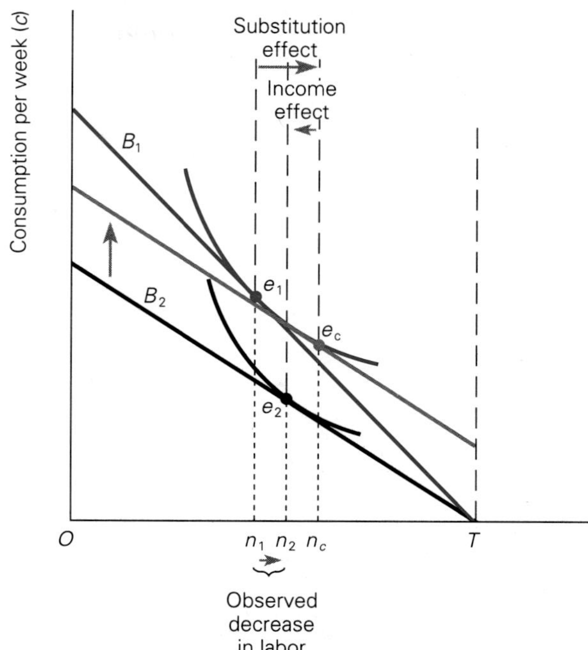

To find the substitution effect of a wage decrease, shift up budget constraint B_2 until it is tangent to the original indifference curve, at point e_c. The substitution effect is the movement from e_1 to e_c. The income effect is from e_c to e_2. The substitution effect dominates the income effect; hence, the cut in the wage rate decreases the supply of labor.

Will a "rational" individual always reduce labor supply in response to a cut in his or her wage rate? To answer this question, consider Desdemona, who faces exactly the same before- and after-tax budget constraints as Othello, and who chose to work the same number of hours as Othello prior to the wage cut. As indicated in Figure 5.4, when Desdemona's wage falls, she ***increases*** her work effort by $n_1 - n_2'$ hours. There is nothing "irrational" about this. Depending upon a person's tastes, it is possible to want to work more, less, or the same amount in response to a decrease in the wage rate.

The source of this ambiguity can be found by decomposing the impact of the wage change into substitution and income effects. Figure 5.5 reproduces Othello's situation from Figure 5.3. As explained in the last chapter, the substitution effect of the wage decrease is found by giving Othello enough income so that he can attain his original level of utility. This corresponds to a shift upward in budget constraint B_2 until it is just tangent to the original indifference curve, at point e_c. Thus, the substitution effect is the movement from e_1 to e_c. On the other hand, the income effect, due exclusively to the reduction in income associated with the wage decrease, is the move from e_c to e_2.

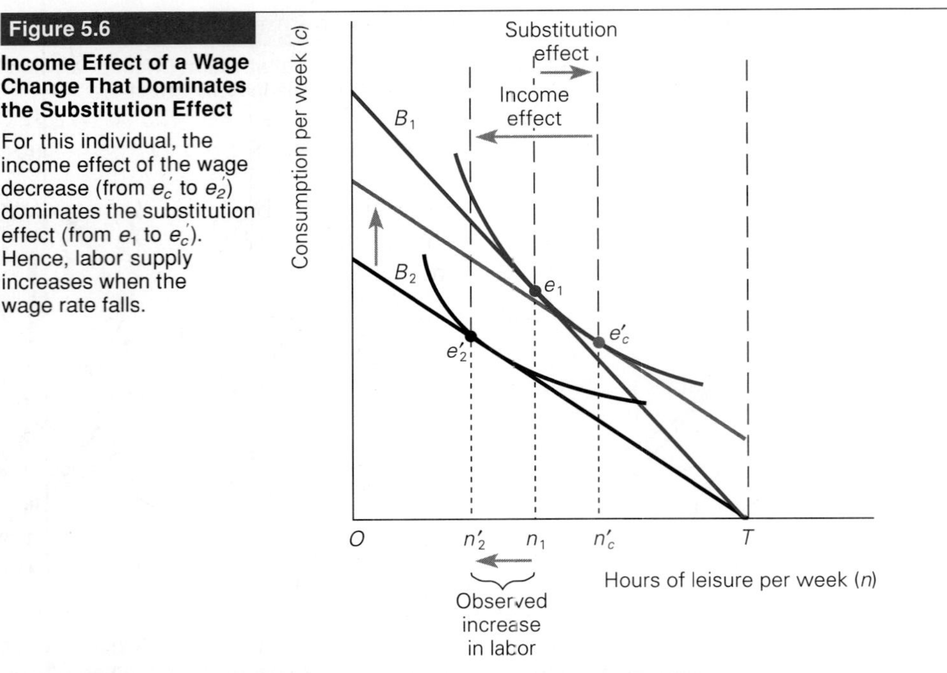

Figure 5.6

Income Effect of a Wage Change That Dominates the Substitution Effect

For this individual, the income effect of the wage decrease (from e_c' to e_2') dominates the substitution effect (from e_1 to e_c'). Hence, labor supply increases when the wage rate falls.

Note that in Figure 5.5, the substitution effect of the wage cut increases hours of leisure (from n_1 to n_c), while the income effect decreases hours of leisure (from n_c to n_2). On balance, Othello's hours of work decrease by $n_2 - n_1$ because the substitution effect dominates the income effect. In contrast, in Figure 5.6, Desdemona's hours of work increase by $n_1 - n_2'$ when the wage falls, because the income effect (from e_c' to e_2') is more powerful than the substitution effect (from e_1 to e_c'). When the income and substitution effects work in opposite directions, theory alone cannot predict how labor supply will change, since we cannot know a priori which effect is more powerful.

Intuitively, when the wage goes down, the consumption of goods and services becomes more expensive in the sense that the worker has to give up more leisure for each unit of *consumption*. Hence, there is a tendency to substitute leisure for *consumption*, that is, to decrease labor supply. This is the substitution effect of a wage decrease and, as shown in Figures 5.5 and 5.6, it *always* tends to decrease labor supply. To think about the income effect of a wage decrease, consider the fact that for any number of hours worked, less income is earned after the wage reduction. In essence, the individual is poorer, and this induces an income effect. As usual, the direction of the income effect depends on whether the good is normal or inferior. The typical assumption, which is borne out by numerous statistical studies of labor supply behavior, is that leisure is a normal good. Hence, when income goes down, the demand for leisure goes down, *ceteris paribus.* Again, this is reflected in both Figures 5.5 and 5.6. (In Figure 5.5, $n_c > n_2$, and in Figure 5.6, $n_c' > n_2'$.) Hence, as long as leisure is a normal good, the income and substitution effects work in opposite directions, and the outcome is logically ambiguous.

Note the contrast with the case of conventional goods discussed in Chapter 4. A price reduction in something you are *selling* (labor) *reduces* your real income, whereas a price reduction in something you are *buying* (commodities) *increases* your real income. This is why income and substitution effects go together for normal goods that are bought and go against each other for normal goods that are sold.

To strengthen your intuition about income and substitution effects, consider the following two statements:

1. "Now that my wage rate has fallen, it's really not worth it for me to work as much as I used to."
2. "Now that my wage rate has fallen, I have to work more to maintain my standard of living."

5.1 PROGRESS CHECK

When taxes were raised in 1994, a financial planner advised some of his clients to work less: "The motivation to work hard and make money is gone. Spend time with your family" (*The Wall Street Journal*, 1994, A5). Evaluate this advice using the consumption-leisure model, taking into account income and substitution effects.

For the person making statement (1), the substitution effect dominates while in statement (2) the income effect dominates. Both statements can reflect perfectly rational behavior for the individuals involved. Thus, only by observing how people actually behave when their wages change can we find out how labor force behavior is affected. This example demonstrates that one of the major purposes of microeconomic theory is to make us aware of the areas of our ignorance. (PC 5.1)

LABOR SUPPLY CURVE

In Chapter 3, we defined the demand curve for a commodity as the relationship between quantity demanded and price, *ceteris paribus.* We also showed how it could be derived from the individual's underlying preferences by noting how the quantity demanded varied as the budget constraint was pivoted appropriately. Exactly the same strategy can be used to derive the individual's demand for leisure, which shows how the quantity of leisure demanded varies with the wage rate. Moreover, given a fixed time endowment, once we know the quantity of leisure demanded at any wage rate, we also know the quantity of labor supplied. Hence, by finding the leisure demand curve, we also find the **labor supply curve,** which shows how the quantity of labor supplied varies with the wage rate, *ceteris paribus.*

labor supply curve
A schedule showing the relationship between the quantity of labor supplied and the wage rate, *ceteris paribus.*

Consider Panel A of Figure 5.7. It indicates that when Othello's wage rate is \$10, his demand for leisure is n_1 hours, and his optimal labor supply is $(T - n_1)$ hours. In Panel B, the wage rate is measured on the vertical axis and hours of *work* on the horizontal. The fact that labor supply is $(T - n_1)$ hours when the wage rate is \$10 is recorded in Panel B at point e_1'. Similarly, when the wage rate is \$6 he supplies $(T - n_2)$ hours, which is recorded in Panel B at point e_2'; and when the wage rate is \$3.50, he supplies $(T - n_3)$ hours, which is recorded in Panel B at point e_3'. By definition, the curve traced out in Panel B is Othello's supply curve of labor, denoted s. The fact that the supply curve slopes upward—labor supply increases with the wage rate—indicates that, for Othello, the substitution effect dominates the income effect.

Figure 5.7

Deriving an Upward-Sloping Supply Curve of Labor

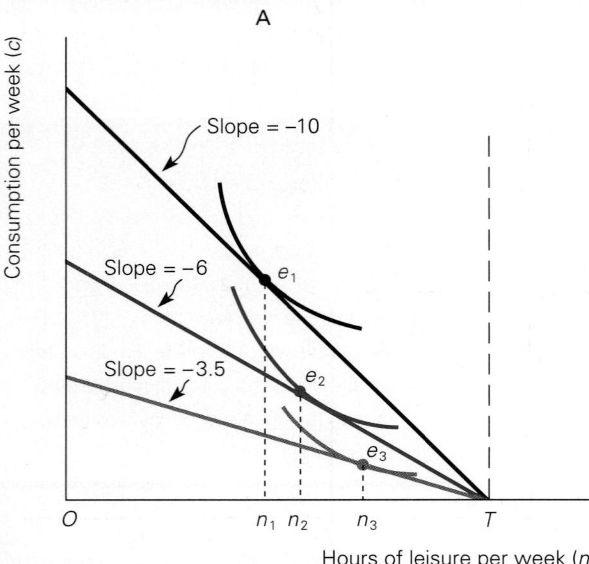

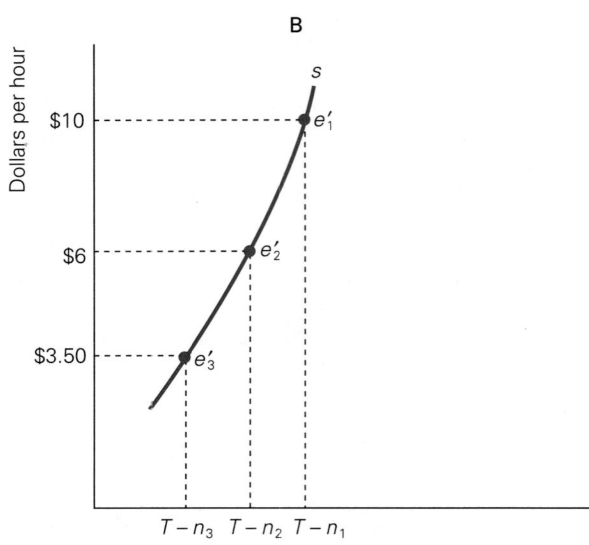

The supply of labor curve (s in Panel B) is found by determining the utility-maximizing number of hours associated with each wage rate (from the indifference curve diagram is Panel A). Curve s slopes upward because the substitution effect dominates the income effect.

What does the supply of labor curve look like when the income effect dominates the substitution effect? This case is analyzed in Figure 5.8. Panel A shows that for Desdemona, when the wage decreases, the quantity of labor supplied increases. When the various combinations of the wage rate and quantity of labor supplied are recorded in Panel B, we obtain schedule s', which shows an inverse relationship between the wage rate and the quantity of labor supplied.

Note that in Figure 5.7 the substitution effect dominates at *every* wage rate, while in Figure 5.8 the income effect dominates at *every* wage rate. Theoretically, it is quite possible that, for a particular individual, the substitution effect dominates at some wage rates and the income effect at others. Consider the case of Iago in Figure 5.9. When the wage rate is low, an increase in the wage leads to more hours of work for him—the substitution effect dominates. But as the wage continues to increase, he starts to work fewer hours—the income effect dominates. As shown in Panel B of Figure 5.9, his labor supply curve first slopes upward, and then bends back on itself. Such a schedule is called a *backward-bending labor supply curve.* This type of supply curve might be a good characterization of the behavior of some highly paid physicians and lawyers who work only four days a week.

PRELIMINARY EVALUATION

Our exposition of labor supply theory has emphasized the similarities to the general theory of choice among various commodities. Exactly the same techniques are used; one simply has to reinterpret what the "commodities" are. While this

Figure 5.8

Deriving a Downward-Sloping Supply Curve of Labor

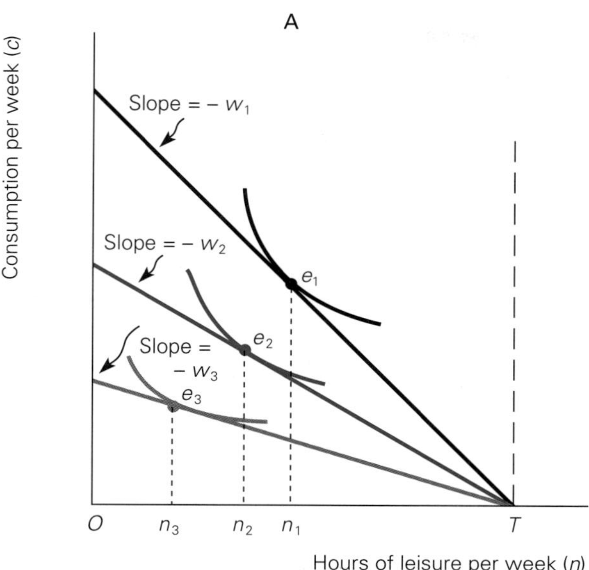

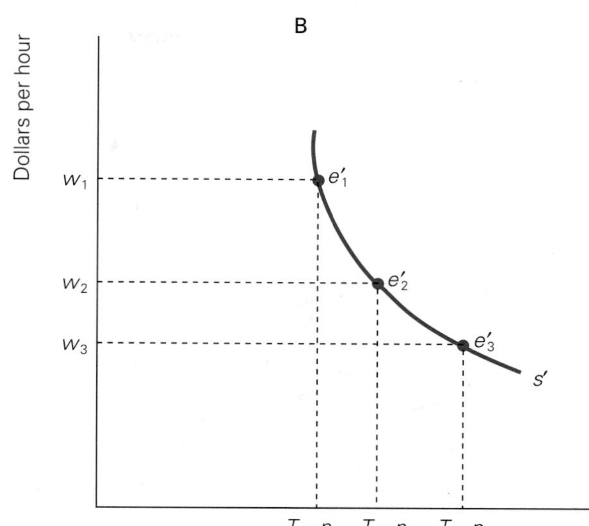

In Panel A, the income effect of a wage change dominates the substitution effect. Hence, the labor supply curve in Panel B slopes downward.

Figure 5.9

Deriving a Supply Curve That Bends Back on Itself

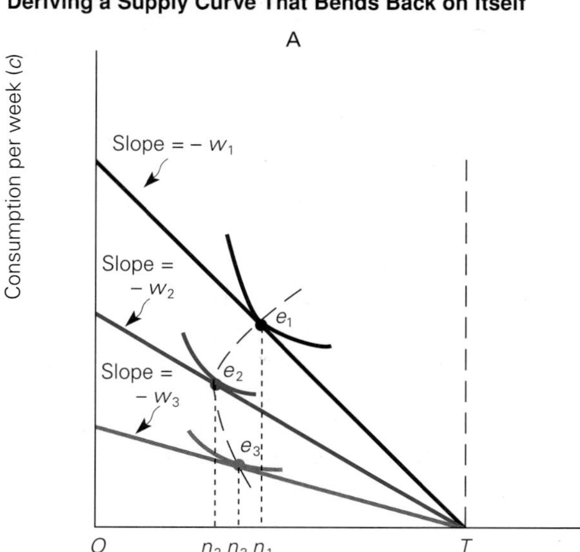

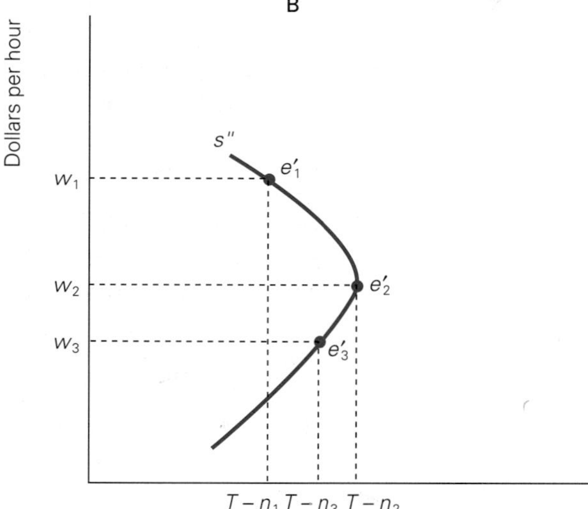

For this individual, the substitution effect dominates at low wage rates and the income effect dominates at high wage rates. Hence, the labor supply schedule bends back on itself.

is all very elegant, does our theory of rational choice help us understand people's actual labor supply decisions?

One possible objection to the theory is that it presumes an unrealistic amount of flexibility—often your boss tells you how many hours you will work on a job; it's not your decision. But while workers do not have total flexibility in selecting their hours of work, this does not imply that they have no flexibility at all. One way a worker can affect her hours of work is by the choice of a job itself. Some jobs require many hours of work; others are part time. Young lawyers in high-powered New York law firms work 2,500 to 3,000 hours per year; in other firms, the figure is more like 1,700 hours. By moving from one type of job to another, a worker in effect is controlling her labor supply. Even in a given job, there may be flexibility in deciding whether to work overtime or how long a vacation to take. From a lifetime perspective, the individual has some control over her date of retirement. In short, people have more control over their labor supply decisions than you might guess, so the theory should not be dismissed out of hand on the basis of the argument that workers really don't have a choice.

Indeed, the theory of leisure-consumption choice has served as a useful framework for a good deal of research on people's labor supply behavior. One goal of this research has been to use data on individuals' work decisions to estimate the elasticity of hours of work with respect to the wage rate. Although not all studies have obtained exactly the same results, it would be fair to say that the following two important general tendencies have been observed:[1]

1. For males between roughly the ages of 20 and 60, the effect of changes in the wage rate upon hours of work is quite small. Most elasticity estimates fall in the range between −0.2 and zero. Interestingly, then, there is evidence of a downward-sloping supply curve for this group, implying that the income effect dominates the substitution effect.
2. The hours of work and labor-force participation decisions of married women are quite sensitive to changes in the wage rate. A number of investigators have found elasticities of hours worked with respect to the wage between 0.2 and 1.0. Hence, for this group, the substitution effect dominates the income effect.

Of course, the purpose of the theory is not simply to facilitate conducting research for its own sake. As we will now see, it helps us understand important policy issues.

THE WORK INCENTIVES OF AFDC

Prior to 1997, one of the most important income-maintenance programs in the United States was Aid to Families with Dependent Children (AFDC). This program provided cash to families with dependent children and an absent or incapacitated parent.[2] The great majority of AFDC families were headed by women. In 1992 about 14 million people received a total of $22.1 billion under this program (U.S. Bureau of the Census 1994, p. 384).

The rules governing the relationship between an individual's earnings and his or her AFDC grant were complicated. For our purposes, it is safe to characterize the system as reducing the grant by one dollar for each dollar of earnings. That welfare benefits react sharply to earnings suggests that incentives to work may

[1]See Hansson and Stuart (1985, 340–41).

[2]In some states, aid was given if both parents were present but one of them was unemployed.

Figure 5.10

Labor Supply Decision under AFDC

When the welfare authorities reduce an individual's grant by the full amount of his or her earnings, the budget constraint is the kinked line, *zrn*. Subject to that budget constraint, the bundle with maximum utility may be *z*, where zero hours of work are supplied to the market.

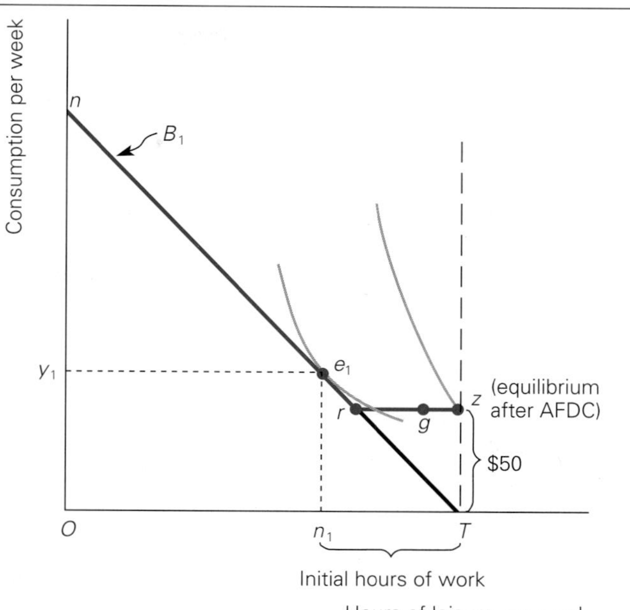

be reduced. The question of whether welfare adversely affects participation in the labor market and increases dependence on the government has dominated discussions of income-maintenance policy for years, and was particularly important in the debate over AFDC. Our model of leisure-consumption choice provides an excellent framework for analyzing AFDC's work incentives.

Figure 5.10 depicts the situation of Gertrude. Prior to the introduction of the welfare system, she faces a typical linear budget constraint, B_1, and chooses to work $(T - n_1)$ hours, giving her a consumption level of y_1. Suppose now that the welfare authorities announce that Gertrude is eligible to receive a grant of $50 per week, but the grant will be reduced by $1 for each dollar she earns. How does introduction of the program modify her budget constraint?

To answer this question, recall that the budget constraint is supposed to reflect all the combinations of leisure and consumption that are available to the individual. Clearly, one option available is point *z*, which is associated with zero hours of work and an income of $50 from welfare. Now suppose that Gertrude works one hour. Graphically, this is represented by a one-hour movement to the left from *z*. When Gertrude works one hour, she receives a wage of $$w$ from her employer, but simultaneously her AFDC payment is reduced by the same amount. The hour of work has netted her nothing—her total income is still $50. In effect, the AFDC system taxed these earnings at a rate of 100 percent. This is shown by point *g*, where there is one hour of work and total consumption is still $50. Additional hours of work continue to produce no net gain in income, so the budget constraint is flat. This continues until point *r*, at which point Gertrude's earnings exceed $50, so that she is out of the AFDC system altogether. Beyond that point, each hour of work raises her consumption by $$w$. Thus, the budget constraint is the kinked line *zrn*, whose segment *zr* has zero slope, and whose segment *rn* has a slope of $-w$.

How will Gertrude respond to such incentives? Figure 5.10 shows that one distinct possibility is a corner solution: She maximizes utility at point *z*, at which no labor is supplied. On the other hand, if her indifference curves are flat enough, she may select a point along segment *rn*. But in no case will a rational person work more than zero hours along segment *rz*, because at any such point it is always possible to attain a higher indifference curve by moving to the right. This is no surprise. Why should individuals work if they can receive the same income by not working? In terms of income and substitution effects, AFDC hit work incentives with a double whammy. Because leisure is a normal good, provision of the grant tended to promote consumption of leisure, that is, reduce labor supply. At the same time, the implicit tax rate of 100 percent reduced the opportunity cost of leisure over the relevant range to zero. Since leisure was so "cheap," the substitution effect tended to promote consumption of leisure as well.

Thus, our model of the consumption-leisure choice provides a strong prediction that AFDC, with an implicit tax of 100 percent, would diminish the labor supply of recipients. There is considerable evidence that this prediction was valid. (See Moffitt, 1992.) This is one of the reasons why, in 1996, Congress abolished the program, helping President Clinton to "end welfare as we know it." (PC 5.2)

5.2 PROGRESS CHECK

A newspaper article described the situation of an elderly woman who worked in a dress factory. After learning that she was eligible for a federal welfare program called Supplemental Security Income, she "applied and soon began receiving $280 a month, far more than she made in the factory at $40 a week. She has not worked since" (Dunn 1995, 1). Use a consumption-leisure diagram to illustrate the woman's situation both before and after the receipt of the welfare payments.

PRODUCER SURPLUS

In Chapter 4 we showed how the demand curve for a commodity can be used to measure the welfare effects of a price change. The main tool for doing this was consumer surplus—the benefit that consumers receive from consumption of a commodity in excess of what they have to pay. In the same way, we can define **producer surplus** as the amount of income individuals receive in excess of what they would require to supply a given number of units of a factor. To measure producer surplus, consider Lear's labor supply curve, which is reproduced in Figure 5.11. Each point on the labor supply curve shows the wage rate required to coax Lear into supplying the associated number of hours of work. However, the wage rate equals the marginal rate of substitution between leisure and *consumption*—the amount of consumption that Lear requires in order to give up each hour of leisure. Hence, the distance between any point on the labor supply curve and the wage rate is the difference between the minimum payment that Lear needs to receive for that hour of work (the marginal rate of substitution) and the amount he actually receives (the wage rate). Thus, *the area above the supply curve and below the wage rate is the producer surplus.*

producer surplus
The amount of income an individual receives in excess of what she would require in order to supply a given number of units of a factor.

To strengthen your understanding of producer surplus, imagine that initially Lear works 2,000 hours per year at a wage of $20 per hour, but then his wage falls to $15 per hour. How much worse off is he as a consequence of this fall in wages? One possible answer is: "He was working 2,000 hours and is now earning $5 less per hour, so he is worse off by $10,000." This corresponds to area $(A + C)$ in Figure 5.11. However, producer surplus analysis tells us that this answer is incorrect. Before the wage cut, Lear's surplus is area $(A + B)$. When the wage rate falls to $15, his surplus falls to B. Hence, Lear's welfare loss from the wage cut is area A. This is less than the naive answer of $(A + C)$. Intuitively,

Figure 5.11

Producer Surplus

Producer surplus is the area below the wage rate and above the supply curve. When the wage rate is \$20, producer surplus is area ($A + B$); when the wage is \$15, producer surplus is B. As a consequence of the wage cut, then, the worker is worse off by area A. If the wage rate is \$20 and the individual becomes unemployed, he or she is worse off by area ($A + B$).

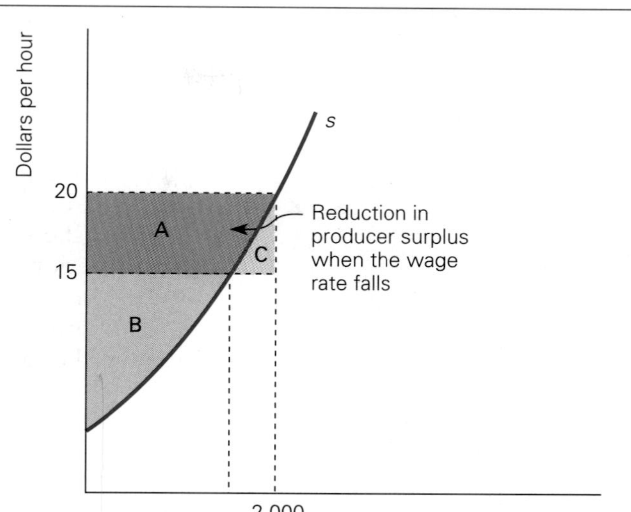

the naive answer overstates the loss in welfare because it ignores the fact that when a person's wage falls, he can substitute leisure for consumption. While the increased consumption of leisure certainly does not fully compensate for the wage decrease, it does have some value.

Unemployment Insurance

Every developed country has some kind of public unemployment insurance (UI) system, which provides benefits to people who lose their jobs. An important issue in the design of UI is how much money people require to compensate them for the loss of their job. Producer surplus provides a framework for analyzing this issue. Consider again the situation of Lear, who initially works 2,000 hours per year at a wage rate of \$20 per hour, giving him an income of \$40,000. (See Figure 5.11.) If Lear is thrown out of his job, he does not need to receive \$40,000 to compensate him for his job loss. The correct measure of his decrease in welfare is his loss of surplus, area ($A + B$) in the figure, a sum that is less than \$40,000. Although unemployment forces Lear to consume more leisure than he would prefer, he does place some value on that leisure, and this must be taken into account in determining the net cost to him of becoming unemployed.

THE SUPPLY OF LABOR TO OCCUPATIONS

So far our theory has focused on the individual's choice regarding hours of work. However, we are often interested in knowing how the *total* number of hours supplied to a particular *occupation* is determined. For example, in the United States, there is perennial concern over whether public policies should be undertaken to increase the supply of nurses. Similarly, some observers believe that the supply of people into the legal profession is "too high" and into engineering

Figure 5.12

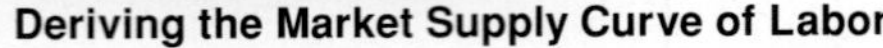
Deriving the Market Supply Curve of Labor

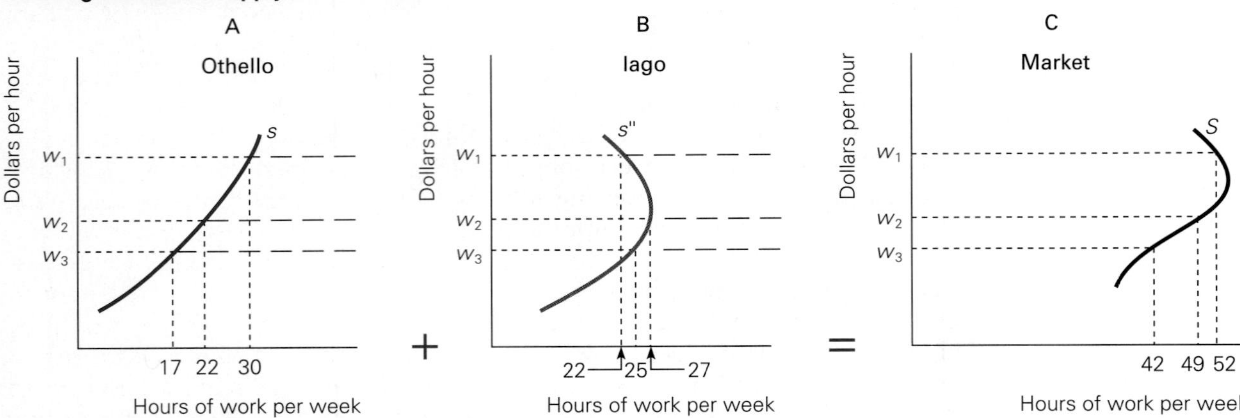

At wage rate w_1, Othello supplies 30 hours (Panel A), and Iago supplies 22 hours (Panel B). Hence, 52 hours are supplied on the market when the wage is w_1, which is recorded in Panel C. Similarly, the market supply of hours at each wage rate is found by horizontally summing the individuals' supply curves.

"too low." This section builds on the theory of the *individual's* labor supply decision to understand the *market* supply of labor to various occupations.

Simple arithmetic tells us that the total number of hours supplied to a given occupation is the total number of hours in the economy times the proportion of hours devoted to that profession. This identity suggests a natural framework for our discussion. First, we discuss the derivation of the total supply of hours, and then we turn to the determinants of an individual's choice of where to supply his or her hours.

Market Supply Curve of Labor

In Chapter 3, we saw that to go from individuals' demand curves for a commodity to the market demand curve, all that was necessary was to add the quantities demanded at each price. Similarly, to find the market supply of labor at each wage rate, we add the quantities supplied at each price. Thus, if we assume that Othello (Figure 5.7) and Iago (Figure 5.9) are the only two workers in the society, the market supply curve of labor is the horizontal sum of their supply curves. In Figure 5.12, Panels A and B show Othello's and Iago's supply curves, respectively, and Panel C shows their horizontal summation. Curve S in Panel C is the **market supply curve of labor**—a schedule showing the aggregate quantity that the households in the market are willing to supply at each wage rate, *ceteris paribus.*

market supply curve of labor
A schedule showing the aggregate quantity of labor that all individuals in the market are willing to supply at each wage rate, *ceteris paribus.*

Occupational Choice

The composer Wolfgang Amadeus Mozart once wrote, "Believe me, my sole purpose is to make as much money as possible . . . " (Baumol and Baumol 1991). If all people behaved this way, then it would be simple to model occupational choice—just assume that each person takes the job that pays the highest salary.

But this is a bad model, because people are also concerned about the nonmonetary aspects of their jobs. *Ceteris paribus*, most people prefer clean and safe jobs to those that are dirty and dangerous. Similarly, jobs with power and prestige are generally preferred to those without these attributes. A better model is that a person supplies his or her labor to that job in which the *package* of monetary and nonmonetary characteristics gives the highest possible level of *utility*.

To see the implications of this model, imagine a group of people with identical abilities choosing between jobs as college professors or as investment bankers. Suppose that college teaching has more desirable characteristics—less stress, more flexible hours, opportunities to interact with the leaders of tomorrow, and so on. If this is true, what would happen if the monetary rewards for college teaching and investment banking were the same? Hardly anyone would want to go into investment banking, because the *utility* of college teaching would be higher. As a consequence, wages in investment banking would have to rise in order to attract workers. Indeed, the wage in investment banking would have to rise just enough so that the *utility* from each job received by the marginal worker was the same. In short, jobs with "undesirable" characteristics have to pay higher salaries. The additional amount paid is referred to as a **compensating differential.** Intuitively, if a college professor earns $60,000 less than an investment banker, he must be valuing the nonmonetary characteristics of his job by at least $60,000. Otherwise, he would quit his job and become an investment banker. (In the 1980s, when there was a large increase in the relative wages of investment bankers, a number of professors did just that!)

compensating differential
The wage premium paid to compensate workers for taking jobs with undesirable characteristics.

Several empirical studies have estimated the compensating differentials associated with various job attributes. Garen (1988) studied the effect of the probability of death in an occupation on the wages in that occupation. Suppose we compare two workers who have identical job qualifications (education, experience, and so on), but one is in a riskier job than the other. The theory of compensating differentials suggests that the individual in the riskier job will have a higher wage to compensate for the higher probability of death. Garen's analysis of wage data suggested that increasing by one the number of fatalities per 100,000 workers in an occupation, leads to an annual compensating differential of about 0.55 percent. Thus, if one occupation has 10 more fatalities per 100,000 workers than another, its wages will be about 5.5 percent higher, *ceteris paribus.*

It is crucial to observe that the theory of compensating differentials is meant to account for wage differences among jobs that require about the same type of skills. Garbage collectors earn less than physicians, despite the fact that garbage collecting is much less pleasant. This observation does *not* contradict the theory of compensating differentials, because the two jobs require different types of skills, and these skills are valued differently by the market. The theory *does* predict that garbage collecting will pay a higher wage than a job with similar skill requirements but more pleasant working conditions; for example, janitorial work.

To illustrate this observation, assume for simplicity that every job can be characterized by its amount of a single attribute, *safety*, measured by the proportion of workers who escape serious injury each year. The theory of compensating differentials indicates that for an individual with given skills, the safer the job, the lower the wage rate. In Figure 5.13, curve B_1 represents the various combinations of wage rates and safety available to Antony. Its curvature reflects the assumption that the safer a job becomes, the greater the additional cost of an additional unit of safety in terms of forgone wages. Given the preferences embodied in his indif-

Figure 5.13

Compensating Differentials

For a low-skilled individual, the available set of combinations of safety and wage rates (B_1) lies below that for a high-skilled individual (B_2). The fact that the high-skilled individual has both a higher-paying and safer job does not contradict the theory of compensating differentials.

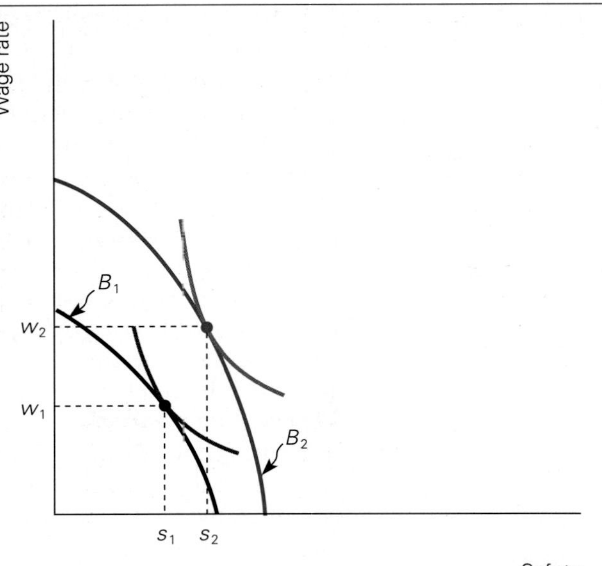

ference curves, he chooses a job with a wage rate of w_1 and s_1 units of safety. In the same diagram, curve B_2 represents the choices available to Octavian, whose skill level is higher than Antony's. The fact that Octavian's skills are higher is reflected by the fact that at any given level of safety, he can command a higher wage than Antony (B_2 lies above B_1). As shown in the diagram, Octavian's optimal job has a wage rate of w_2 and s_2 units of safety.

Note that although we observe one individual with *both* a higher wage and a safer job than the other, this does *not* contradict the theory of compensating differentials. Because B_1 and B_2 both slope downward, each individual faces a trade-off between safety and wage rates.

Finally, it is important to note that compensating differentials are not necessarily the only source of wage differentials between people of equal ability. Sex or race discrimination by employers could also lead to wage differentials. More generally, looking at the supply side of the market alone cannot tell us everything about the equilibrium pattern of wages across jobs. The demand side of the market must also be considered. This is done in Chapter 11.

SECTION RECAP

Economic theory views labor supply as a problem involving choice in the face of scarcity. Hence, the usual tools for analyzing individual decision making can be used to study labor supply. The theory of individual choice adds substantially to our understanding of real world labor supply issues. The theory explains, for example, why rational people may choose to work less when their wages increase; why income-maintenance programs often reduce labor supply; and why unpleasant jobs pay more than pleasant ones, *ceteris paribus.* In addition, the concept of producer surplus provides us with a powerful tool for analyzing how changes in wages affect workers' welfare.

5.2 CAPITAL SUPPLY

real capital
Physical aids to production, for example, computers or factory buildings.

financial capital
Money that is lent to firms to purchase or rent real capital.

In the circular flow, firms use real capital as well as labor to produce output. By **real capital** we mean those things made to aid future production, such as drill presses, factory buildings, office desks, and computers. Just like labor, capital is supplied to the business sector by households. Of course, individuals do not literally drag drill presses into their local business firms. Rather, they lend some portion of their income to firms; the firms then use this money (referred to as **financial capital**) to buy or rent the drill presses. More specifically, people supply to firms the portion of their income that exceeds their consumption—that is, their saving. Thus, the theory of capital supply is really the theory of saving.

LIFE-CYCLE MODEL

life-cycle model
A model that says people's consumption and saving decisions during a given year are the outcome of a decision-making process that takes into account their lifetime economic circumstances.

The analysis of saving decisions rests on the **life-cycle model.** This model says people's consumption and saving decisions during a *given year* are the result of a planning process that takes into account their *lifetime* economic circumstances. That is, the amount you save each year depends not only on your income that year, but also on the income that you expect in the future and the income you have had in the past.

To understand the structure of the life-cycle model, recall that in the problems we have explored so far, a person's utility during a particular period of time depends on the quantities of various commodities that he consumes during that period of time. The life-cycle model takes a broader perspective. It assumes that the amount of utility that an individual obtains over the course of his entire lifetime depends on the amount he consumes in each period of his lifetime. As an example, consider Hamlet, who expects to live two periods: "now" (period 0) and the "future" (period 1). Hamlet has an income of I_0 dollars in the present period, and knows that his income will be I_1 dollars in the future. (Think of "now" as "working years," when I_0 is labor earnings; and the "future" as "retirement years," when I_1 is a fixed pension income.) If Hamlet consumes more now, then, *ceteris paribus*, he will have less in the future. His problem is to take this trade-off into account and then choose amounts of consumption each period that maximize his lifetime utility. Importantly, when Hamlet decides how much to consume in period 0, he simultaneously decides how much to save or borrow. If his consumption this period exceeds his current income, he must borrow. If his consumption is less than current income, he saves.

As was the case with labor supply, we can use budget constraints and indifference curves to analyze the choice of how much capital to supply (that is, how much to save). We first discuss the budget constraint and then turn to the indifference map.

Intertemporal Budget Constraint

intertemporal budget constraint
The budget constraint in a life-cycle model, showing the trade-off between consumption levels in different time periods.

As always, the budget constraint depicts the various options available to an individual. In this particular case, the options are the possible combinations of *present consumption* and *future consumption* available to Hamlet. Because the budget constraint in a life-cycle model shows the trade-off between consumption levels in different time periods, it is referred to as an **intertemporal budget constraint.**

To sketch this constraint, consider Figure 5.14, in which the amount of *current consumption* (c_0) is measured on the horizontal axis, and the amount of

Figure 5.14

Intertemporal Budget Constraint

If the individual's endowment point is (I_0, I_1), and he can borrow and lend at an interest rate of i, then his intertemporal budget constraint is line B_1, which passes through the endowment point and has a slope equal to $-(1 + i)$.

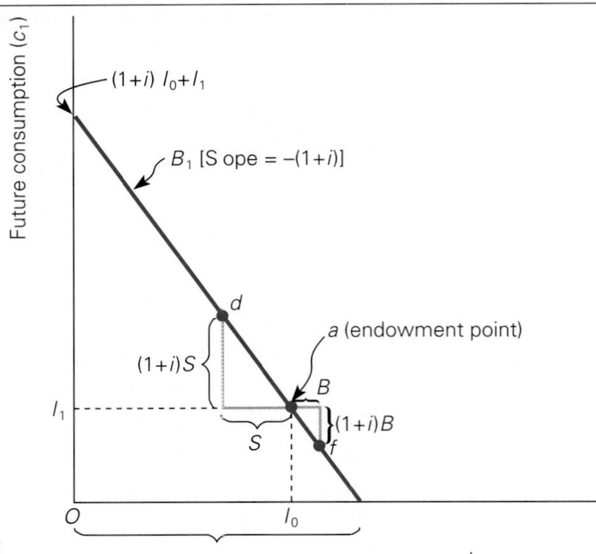

endowment point
The feasible consumption bundle if the individual makes no trades with the market; in a life-cycle model, the bundle an individual can consume if he or she neither saves nor borrows.

future consumption (c_1) is measured on the vertical axis. One option available to Hamlet is to consume all his income just as it comes in—to consume I_0 in the present and I_1 in the future. This bundle, which is called the **endowment point,** is denoted by a in Figure 5.14. At the endowment point, Hamlet neither saves nor borrows, because consumption in each period is exactly equal to income.

Another option is to save out of current income to be able to consume more in the future. Suppose that Hamlet decides to save S dollars this period by consuming only $I_0 - S$ today. If he invests his savings in an asset with a rate of return of i, he increases his *future consumption* by $(1 + i)S$—the principal S plus the interest $i \times S$. In other words, if Hamlet decreases *present consumption* by S, he increases his *future consumption* by $(1 + i)S$. Graphically, this possibility is represented by moving S dollars to the left of the endowment point a, and $(1 + i)S$ dollars above it—point d in Figure 5.14.

Alternatively, Hamlet can consume more than I_0 in the present if he borrows against his future income. Assume that Hamlet can borrow money at the same rate of interest, i, at which he can lend. If he borrows B dollars to add to his *present consumption*, by how much must he reduce his *future consumption*? When the future arrives, Hamlet must pay back B plus interest of $i \times B$. Hence, Hamlet can increase *present consumption* by B only if he is willing to reduce future consumption by $B + i \times B = (1 + i)B$. Graphically, this involves moving B dollars to the right of the endowment point, and then $(1 + i)B$ dollars below it—point f in Figure 5.14.

By repeating this process for various values of S and B, we can determine how much *future consumption* is feasible, given any amount of *current consumption.* In the process of doing so, we trace out the intertemporal budget constraint B_1, which passes through the endowment point a, and has a slope of $-(1 + i)$. As always, the negative of the slope of the budget constraint represents the opportunity cost of one good in terms of the other. Its value of $1 + i$ indicates that the cost of \$1 of consumption in the present is $1 + i$ dollars of forgone consumption in the future.

The vertical intercept of the intertemporal budget constraint shows the amount that could be consumed in the future if *present consumption* were zero. If I_0 were entirely saved, then in the future it would be worth $(1 + i)I_0$. Adding this to the I_1 dollars received in period 1 tells us that the vertical intercept is $(1 + i)I_0 + I_1$.

present value of the endowment
The maximal level of present consumption that can be obtained, given the endowment.

On the other hand, the horizontal intercept indicates the maximal amount that Hamlet could consume in the present. This is equal to his present income, I_0, plus the amount that he can borrow against his future income. Given that Hamlet's future income is I_1, what is the greatest amount, $\hat{B}$, that he can borrow? We know that next period, Hamlet (or his heirs) must be able to pay back the loan ($\hat{B}$) plus the interest ($i \times \hat{B}$), or $(1 + i)\hat{B}$. Hence, $(1 + i)\hat{B}$ must exactly equal I_1—no one will make a loan that can't be fully paid back out of future income. Since $(1 + i)\hat{B} = I_1$, it follows that $\hat{B} = I_1/(1 + i)$. Thus, the horizontal intercept is $I_0 + I_1/(1 + i)$. Because the horizontal intercept shows the maximal level of *present consumption* that can be obtained given the endowment, it is referred to as the **present value of the endowment.**

The existence of an intertemporal budget constraint like B_1 implies that an individual need not tie his consumption during a given year too closely to his income in that year. Even if your income is very high one year and low the next does not mean that your consumption has to be high in the first year and low the second. Rather, by borrowing in years of low income and saving in years of high income, you can smooth out your consumption over time. This explains, for example, why people just out of school often borrow to finance purchases of items such as cars and furniture. Their anticipated future earnings are higher than their current earnings, so they borrow against their future earnings to raise their current consumption standard. The extent to which people actually choose to smooth their consumption depends on their preferences for consumption in different periods, which we now discuss. (PC 5.3)

5.3 PROGRESS CHECK

Brutus has an income of \$50,000 during period 0, and \$20,000 during period 1. He can save and borrow at an interest rate of 10 percent. Sketch his intertemporal budget constraint.

Intertemporal Indifference Map

To determine which point along B_1 is chosen, we need to model Hamlet's preferences for future as opposed to present consumption. If we think of c_0 and c_1 as two composite commodities, it is natural to assume a diminishing marginal rate of substitution between them. A set of indifference curves that reflects this assumption is depicted in Figure 5.15. Because more consumption in either period is preferred to less, *ceteris paribus*, indifference curves further to the northeast represent higher levels of utility.

marginal rate of time preference
The marginal rate of substitution between consumption in different time periods.

The marginal rate of substitution between c_0 and c_1 reveals the intensity of the individual's preferences for consumption in different periods of time, and hence is called the **marginal rate of time preference.** A conventional assumption relating to the marginal rate of time preference is that people are "impatient"—other things being the same, they have a tendency to prefer consumption now to

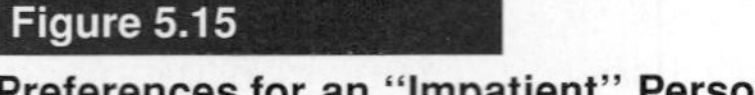

Figure 5.15

Preferences for an "Impatient" Person

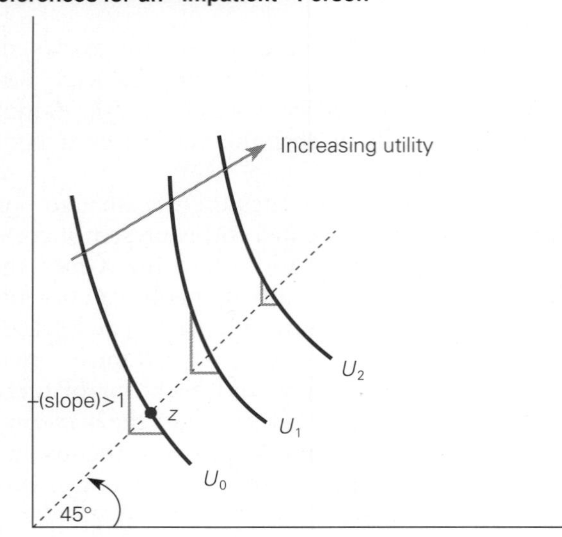

The slope of an indifference curve between current and future consumption is the marginal rate of time preference. For an "impatient" individual, the marginal rate of time preference exceeds one when future consumption equals present consumption; that is, the negative of the slope is greater than 1 around the 45° line.

Figure 5.16

Equilibrium for a Saver

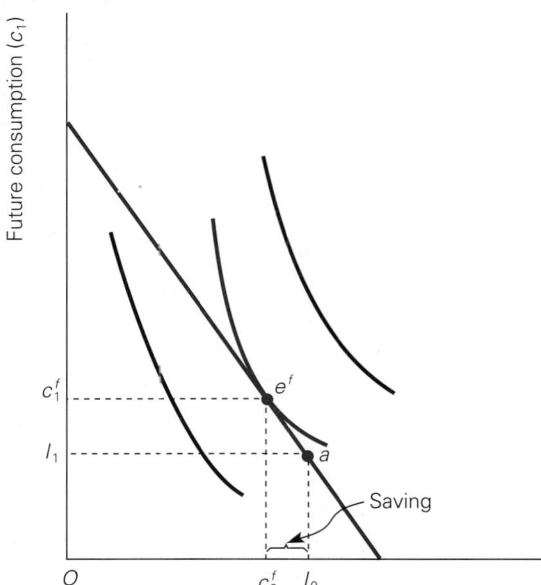

Utility is maximized at e^f where the marginal rate of time preference equals $1 + i$. For this individual, present consumption is c_0^f; hence, $I_0 - c_0^f$ is saved.

consumption in the future. This assumption is embodied in the indifference map in Figure 5.15. To see why, consider point z on indifference curve U_0. Point z lies on a 45° ray from the origin. Hence, at point z, Hamlet's consumption in the present exactly equals his consumption in the future. Now, if Hamlet were *not* impatient, we would expect that at point z he would require a bribe of only one dollar of future consumption in order to give up one dollar of present consumption. But the marginal rate of time preference around point z is greater than one. When consumption levels in each period are equal, Hamlet requires more than a dollar's worth of future consumption in order to give up a dollar of present consumption.

Hence, Hamlet's "impatience" is reflected in the fact that along a 45° ray from the origin, his marginal rate of time preference is greater than one. In contrast, for an individual who is not "impatient," the intertemporal indifference curves are symmetric around a 45° ray from the origin.

Equilibrium in the Life-Cycle Model

As usual, the equilibrium bundle maximizes utility subject to the budget constraint. In Figure 5.16, we superimpose Hamlet's indifference map from Figure 5.15 upon his budget constraint from Figure 5.14. Hamlet maximizes utility at bundle e^f, where minus the slope of the indifference curve (the marginal rate of

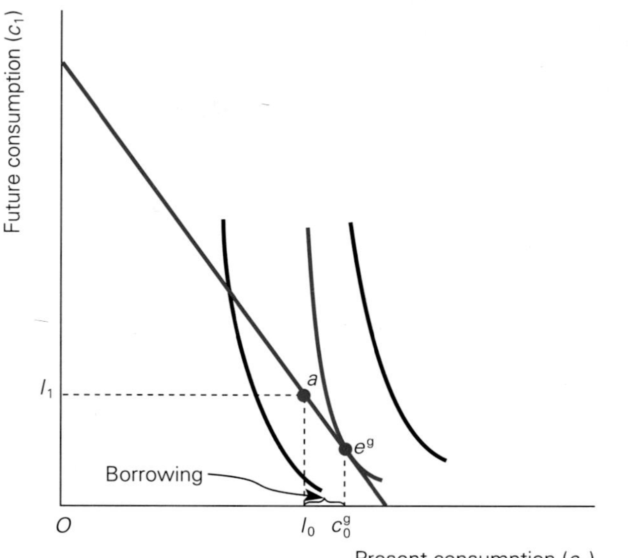

Figure 5.17

Equilibrium for a Borrower

For this individual, present consumption c_0^g exceeds present income (I_0). Hence, the individual borrows $c_0^g - I_0$.

time preference) equals one plus the interest rate (the negative of the slope of the budget constraint). At this point, he consumes c_0^f in the present and c_1^f in the future. With this information, it is easy to find how much Hamlet saves. Because present income, I_0, exceeds present consumption, c_0^f, by definition the difference, $I_0 - c_0^f$, is saving. (We have shifted from subscripts to superscripts for identifying various bundles, because we are already using subscripts to indicate time periods.)

Of course, this does not prove that it is always rational to save. For Ophelia, whose situation is depicted in Figure 5.17, the highest feasible indifference curve is tangent to her budget constraint below point *a*. Ophelia's present consumption exceeds her income, that is, she is a borrower. And Polonius, whose indifference map is shown in Figure 5.18, is neither a borrow nor a lender—his utility-maximizing bundle happens to coincide with his endowment point, so that $c_0^a = I_0$.

COMPARATIVE STATICS WITH THE LIFE-CYCLE MODEL

The life-cycle model can help us analyze the effects of changes in the economic environment on saving decisions. The response of saving to changes in the interest rate is particularly important.

Saving and Interest Rates

Consider again Hamlet's situation, which is reproduced in Figure 5.19. Suppose that the interest rate at which he can borrow and lend falls from i to i_b. How does his budget constraint change? The first thing to note is that the new constraint must also pass through the endowment point because whatever the interest rate, Hamlet always has the option of neither borrowing nor lending. But the

Figure 5.18

Equilibrium for a Person Who neither Saves nor Borrows

If the point of utility maximization coincides with the endowment point, the individual neither borrows nor lends.

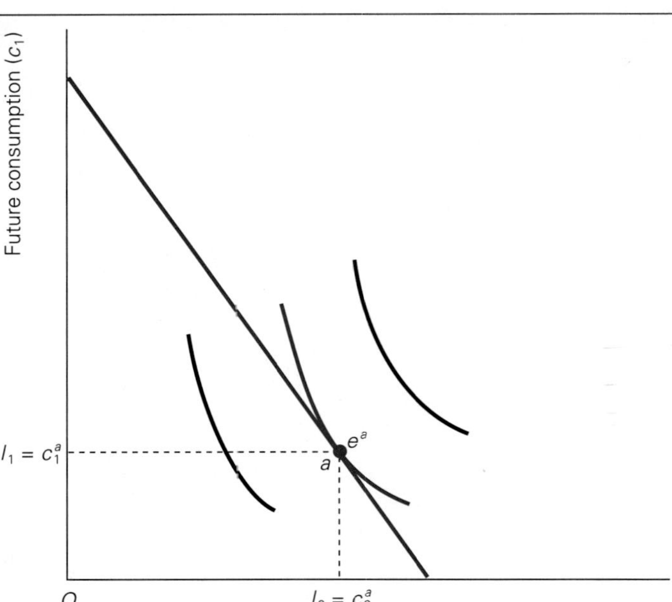

fall in the interest rate does change the slope of the budget constraint. The opportunity cost of one dollar of *present consumption* is now only $1 + i_b$ dollars of future consumption. Hence, the slope of the new budget constraint must be flatter than that of the original budget constraint. In Figure 5.19 the constraint that passes through point *a* with a slope of $-(1 + i_b)$ is B_2.

Subject to constraint B_2, Hamlet maximizes utility at point e^b, where he consumes c_0^b in the present and c_1^b in the future. Because of the decline in interest rates, Hamlet's saving falls from $I_0 - c_0^f$ to $I_0 - c_0^b$.

However, this result does not follow as a general rule. For a counterexample, consider the situation of Horatio in Figure 5.20. His budget constraints are identical to Hamlet's, as is his original equilibrium at point e^f. But in Figure 5.20, the new equilibrium occurs at point e^b, to the left of e^f. After the interest rate decline, Horatio's consumption in the present is c_0^b, and in the future, c_1^b. In this example, a fall in the interest rate actually increases saving, from $I_0 - c_0^f$ to $I_0 - c_0^b$. Thus, depending upon the individual's preferences, a decrease in the interest rate can either increase or decrease saving.

After studying the labor supply model, you may suspect that this theoretical ambiguity is a consequence of conflicting income and substitution effects. You're right! Make the reasonable assumption that c_0 and c_1 are both normal goods—when lifetime income increases, *ceteris paribus*, the individual chooses to increase consumption levels in each period of his life. Then *for an individual who is initially a saver*, when the interest rate decreases, the following effects occur:

1. *Substitution Effect.* The opportunity cost of *present consumption* decreases due to the reduction in the amount of *future consumption* that is

Figure 5.19

A Decrease in the Interest Rate Lowers Saving

A fall in the interest rate shifts the intertemporal budget constraint from B_1 to B_2. As a consequence, this individual decreases saving from $I_0 - c_0^f$ to $I_0 - c_0^b$.

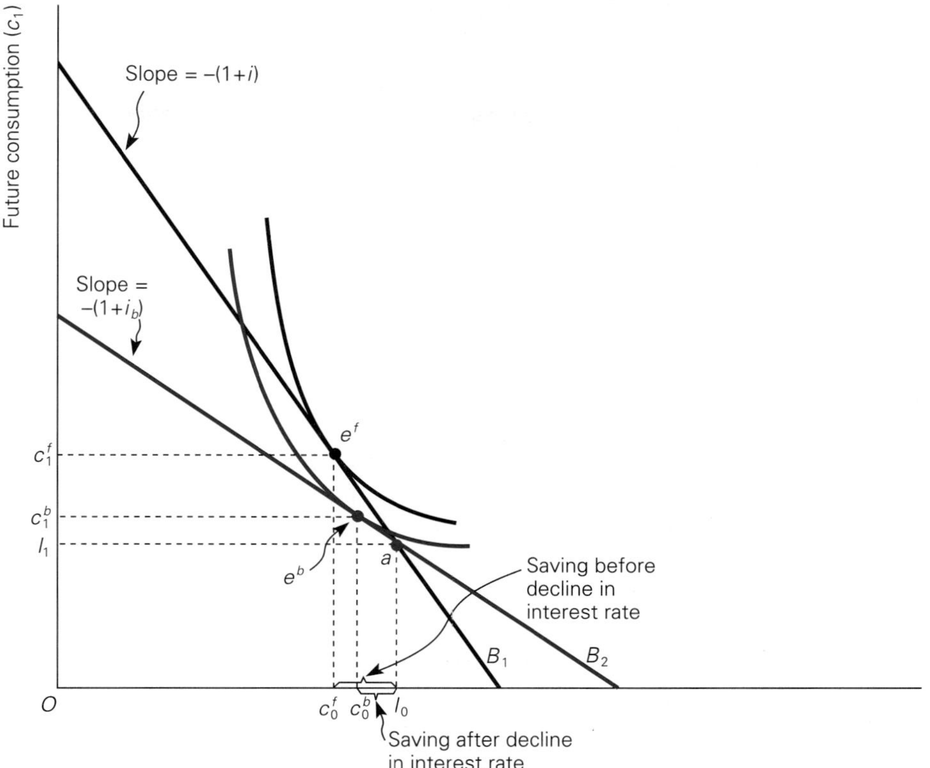

Figure 5.20

A Decrease in the Interest Rate Increases Saving

For this individual, a decrease in the interest rate increases saving from $I_0 - c_0^f$ to $I_0 - c_0^h$.

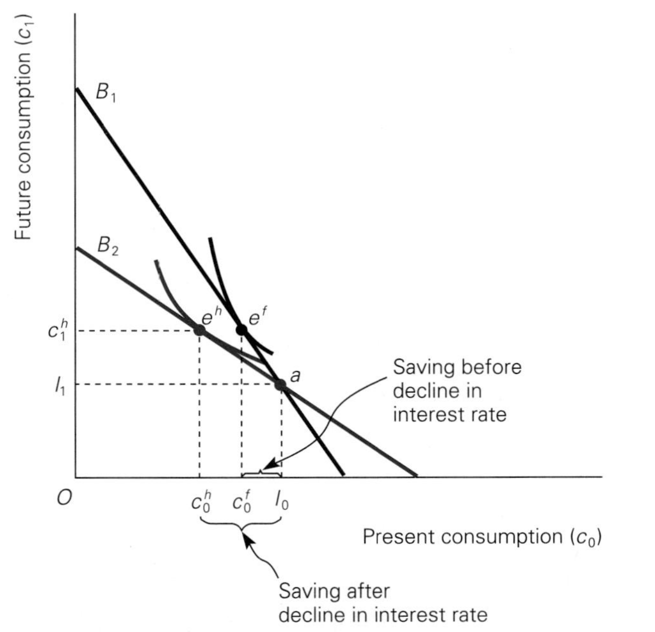

sacrificed for each dollar of *present consumption*. This tends to increase *present consumption*, and therefore *reduce* saving.

2. *Income Effect.* If you are a saver, when the interest rate decreases, you become poorer because the people to whom you lend pay you less money. Because *present consumption* is a normal good, this decrease in your income tends to lower *present consumption*, and therefore *increase* saving.

Because the income and substitution effects for a saver work in opposite directions, the outcome is logically ambiguous. If the notion that a rational person might actually increase his saving in response to a decrease in the interest rate seems bizarre to you, consider the extreme case of a "target saver," whose only goal is to have a given amount of consumption in the future—no more and no less. (Perhaps the "target saver" wants to save just enough to pay the children's future college tuition.) If the interest rate goes down, then the only way for the individual to reach his target is to increase saving. Similarly, if the interest rate goes up, the individual's target can be met with less saving. Thus, for the target saver, saving and the interest rate always move in opposite directions. Figure 5.20 demonstrates that an inverse relationship between saving and interest rates is plausible under even less extreme assumptions.

Thus far our discussion of income and substitution effects has focused on the case of an individual who is initially a saver. What happens if the person is instead a *borrower*? Just as for a saver, the substitution effect of a decrease in the interest rate is to increase *current consumption* (decrease saving). Unlike a saver, the income effect of a decline in the interest rate also tends to increase *current consumption*. Why? If you are a borrower and the interest rate goes down, you have to pay less money to your creditors, which in effect makes you richer. Because *current consumption* is a normal good, you therefore consume more of it. In short, for a person who is initially a borrower, the substitution and income effects of a decrease in the interest rate reinforce each other—saving unambiguously goes down, that is, borrowing goes up.

For purposes of easy reference, the relation between the individual's status as a saver or borrower on the one hand and income and substitution effects on the other is summarized in Figure 5.21. (PC 5.4)

5.4 PROGRESS CHECK

Many homeowners in the United States have variable-rate mortgages—the interest payments that they owe in a given year depend upon the interest rate prevailing in that year. When interest rates rose in 1988, one person with a variable-rate mortgage "stopped ogling a $600 sport coat and delayed buying parts for his steam-powered model boats," while another "cut back on dining out and theater-going" (Schwadel and Johnson 1988). Rationalize this behavior in terms of income and substitution effects.

Supply of Saving

Once you have mastered the life-cycle model, it is straightforward to derive the supply-of-saving schedule. Just find the equilibrium amount of saving associated with each interest rate, and record this information on a diagram, with saving on the horizontal axis and the interest rate on the vertical. The **market supply curve of saving,** which shows the aggregate amount of saving that all individuals are willing to supply at each interest rate (*ceteris paribus*), is then found by horizontal summation of the individuals' supply curves. In the same way, the compensated supply curve of saving is found by examining how saving varies with the interest rate, and assuming that the individuals are compensated with enough income to keep them on their initial indifference curve. The derivation of the ordinary and compensated supply-of-saving schedules is left as an exercise.

market supply curve of saving
The aggregate amount of saving that all individuals are willing to supply at each interest rate, *ceteris paribus.*

Figure 5.21

Substitution and Income Effects of a Decrease in the Interest Rate (Assuming Consumption Is a Normal Good)

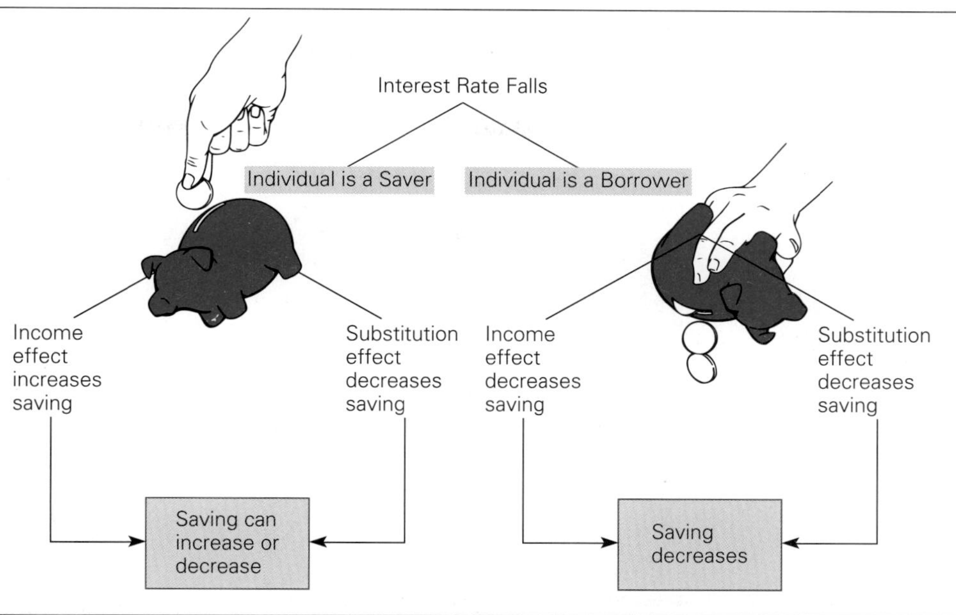

IS THE LIFE-CYCLE MODEL RELEVANT?

Some critics of the life-cycle model have suggested that its assumptions are too unrealistic to be useful abstractions. However, a good deal of observed behavior is consistent with the main thrust of the life-cycle model—people do look into the *future* to make their consumption and saving decisions *today*. For example, a newspaper article reported the following anecdote on the increase in Japanese savings rates during the mid-1990s: "Yumiko Sakurai violates a cardinal principle of Japanese cooking by refrigerating unused rice from one meal and then reheating it in the microwave. Compared with keeping rice warm in a rice-cooker, this saves about eight cents a meal . . . And when a sale comes, she buys a year's worth of clothing for [her children]. It's not that Mrs. Sakurai has suddenly become poor, but that she worries she could" (WuDunn 1995, A4). The key aspect of the quotation is that the consumer is making her current consumption decisions on the basis of expectations of future income. This is just the behavior predicted by the life-cycle model.

Such anecdotal evidence is supported by a number of statistical studies. For example, several analyses of households near retirement have found that they save enough so that their consumption during retirement is consistent with their lifetime level of income (Modigliani 1986, 305). Households appear to smooth out their consumption streams over time in a way that is consistent with the life-cycle model.

Of course, one should not expect the life-cycle hypothesis to describe the behavior of every single family. Some people may be myopic in their spending behavior; others may not have access to borrowing. Nevertheless, most economists accept the life-cycle model as a pretty good approximation to reality.

Figure 5.22

A Tax on Interest Income

When interest income is taxed at rate t, the *effective interest rate* is $(1 - t)i$. Hence, the opportunity cost of reducing current consumption by a dollar is $[1 + (1 - t)i]$ of future consumption. This is minus the slope of the after-tax budget constraint to the left of point a. To the right of a, the slope is still $-(1 + i)$. Hence, the budget constraint is the kinked line zan.

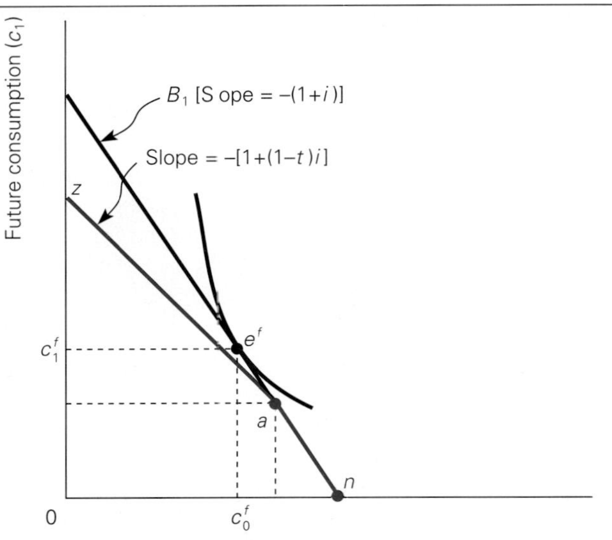

THE TAXATION OF INTEREST INCOME

As noted in the introduction, during the 1980s countries throughout the world slashed their income tax rates. In each of these countries, one of the most contentious issues was the impact of a lower tax burden on interest income. Some policymakers argued that reducing tax rates on interest would induce a great surge in saving. Others argued that taxes on interest don't have much effect one way or the other. The debate continues to rage; in 1996, several contenders for the Republican presidential nomination in the United States promised that they would abolish the taxation of interest income in order to stimulate the savings rate. This section uses the life-cycle model to examine this important question.

Figure 5.22 reproduces Hamlet's before-tax constraint B_1 from Figure 5.16. Suppose that interest is subjected to a proportional tax at the rate of 25 percent. How does this affect the budget constraint? The first thing to note is that the after-tax budget constraint must also pass through the endowment point, because interest tax or no interest tax, Hamlet always has the option of neither borrowing nor lending.

Now, starting at the endowment point a, suppose that Hamlet decides to save \$1. By how much does his consumption increase next period? The person to whom Hamlet is lending will pay him i in interest, but the government then takes an amount equal to 0.25 times i, leaving Hamlet with only 0.75 times i. Hence, saving a dollar allows Hamlet to increase his *future consumption* by $(1 + .75i)$ rather than $(1 + i)$. More generally, when interest income is taxed at rate t, a dollar decrease in *present consumption* allows him to increase his consumption next period by $[1 + (1 - t)i]$ dollars. To the left of point a, then, the opportunity cost of increasing *present consumption* by \$1 is $[1 + (1 - t)i]$ dollars of *future consumption*. Therefore, the slope of the budget constraint to the left of point a is $-[1 + (1 - t)i]$. This is represented in Figure 5.22 by segment za.

Now suppose that starting at the endowment point, Hamlet decides to borrow \$1, that is, move \$1 to the right of point a. Under the current tax law in a number of countries, including the United States, the United Kingdom, and Japan, taxpayers generally are not allowed to deduct payments of interest from their taxable income.[3] Hence, to the right of point a the opportunity cost of increasing present consumption by a dollar is still $(1 + i)$ dollars of future consumption. This coincides with segment an of the before-tax budget constraint B_1.

Putting all of this together, we see that when interest receipts are taxable but interest payments are nondeductible, the intertemporal budget constraint has a kink at the endowment point. To the left of the endowment point, the slope is $-[1 + (1 - t)i]$; to the right, it is $-(1 + i)$. What is the impact on saving? For individuals who were borrowers before the tax was imposed, the system has no effect at all. That is, if individuals maximized utility along segment an before the tax was imposed, it remains optimal for them to do so after. On the other hand, if people were savers before the tax, their choice between present and future consumption must change, because points on B_1 above point a are no longer available to them. However, just as in the discussion surrounding Figure 5.21, we cannot predict a priori whether they will save more or less. It depends on the relative strengths of the income and substitution effects.

5.5 PROGRESS CHECK

In 1994 the tax rate on high-income Americans increased from 31.0 percent to 39.6 percent. Consider an individual who was a saver prior to the tax increase. Use intertemporal budget constraints and indifference curves to analyze the effects of this tax increase.

Thus, economic theory tells us that the effect of interest taxes on the supply of saving is ambiguous. For a given individual, the outcome depends on whether he or she is a borrower or a saver and, if the person is a saver, whether the income effect or substitution effect dominates. Only empirical work can answer the question of how the tax system affects saving. A number of studies suggest that for the population as a whole, the income and substitution effects more or less cancel each other out. (PC 5.5)

SECTION RECAP

The process of saving involves trading off consumption in the present in return for even more consumption in the future. Thus, the saving decision is just another example of choice in the face of scarcity, and the standard tools can be used to analyze it. An important insight from this framework is the role of the interest rate in determining the "price" of *present consumption* in terms of forgone *future consumption*. Once we recognize that an interest rate change is "like" a price change, we realize that increasing interest rates induces both income and substitution effects, rendering the ultimate response of saving ambiguous.

5.3 MORE ON PRESENT VALUE

In our discussion of the intertemporal budget constraint in Figure 5.14, we observed that the horizontal intercept is the *present value of the individual's endowment*—the most he could consume today, given his present and future incomes.

[3]Prior to the Tax Reform Act of 1986 in the United States, interest payments generally were deductible. Currently, interest on consumer loans is not deductible, but mortgage interest is deductible.

The notion of present value turns out to be an indispensable tool for thinking about any problem that involves flows of income or expenditures that occur in different time periods. For example, attending business school may require substantial expenditures in the present and then yield returns many years in the future. How can you decide whether the future benefits are worth the present costs? In this section, we develop the concept of present value and show how it can be applied to this and other problems.

FUNDAMENTAL FORMULAS

Suppose you take \$100 to the bank and deposit it in an account that yields 5 percent annual interest. At the end of one year, you will have $(1 + .05) \times \$100 = \$105$ in the account—the \$100 principal, or initial deposit, plus \$5 in interest. Suppose further that you let the money sit in the account for another year. At the end of the second year, you will have $(1 + .05) \times \$105 = \$110.25$. This can also be written as $(1 + .05) \times (1 + .05) \times \$100 = (1 + .05)^2 \times \$100$. Similarly, if the money is put in an account for three years, it will be worth $(1 + .05)^3 \times \$100$ by the end of the third year. More generally, if you invest \$$M$ for T years at an annual interest rate of i, then at the end of T years, it will be worth $\$M \times (1 + i)^T$. This formula shows the *future value* of money invested in the present. This kind of arithmetic is familiar to anyone who has ever had a bank account.

Now suppose that someone offers a contract that promises to pay you \$100 one year from now. The person is entirely trustworthy, so you do not have to worry about default.[4] Assuming that no inflation is expected to occur over the next year, what is the maximal amount that you should be willing to pay *today* for this promise? It is tempting to say that a promise to pay \$100 is worth \$100. But this neglects the fact that the promised \$100 is not payable for a year, and that in the meantime you are forgoing the interest that could be earned on the money. Why should you pay \$100 today to receive \$100 a year from now, if you can receive \$105 a year from now simply by putting the \$100 in the bank today? Thus, the value today of \$100 payable one year from now is less than the value of \$100 today. The **present value** of an amount of money in the future is the maximal amount you would be willing to pay today for the right to receive the money in the future.

present value
The maximal amount of money you would be willing to pay today for the right to receive a given amount of money at a specified date in the future.

To find the very most you would be willing to give up *now* in exchange for \$100 payable one year in the future, you must find the number that, when multiplied by $(1 + .05)$, just equals \$100. Algebraically, if PV is the present value, then $PV \times (1 + .05) = \$100$. Therefore, PV is $\$100/(1 + .05)$, or approximately \$95.24. Note the symmetry with the familiar problem of projecting money into the future that was discussed above. To find the value of money today one year in the future, you *multiply* by 1 plus the interest rate; to find the value of money one year in the future today, you *divide* by 1 plus the interest rate.

Next, consider a promise to pay \$100 two years from now. In this case, the calculation has to account for the fact that if you deposited \$100 for two years, at the end it would be worth $\$100 \times (1 + .05)^2$. The most you would be willing to pay today for \$100 in two years is the amount that, when multiplied by $(1 + .05)^2$, yields exactly \$100, which is $\$100/(1 + .05)^2$ or about \$90.70.

[4]Additional issues that arise when you are uncertain about how much you will be paid back are discussed in subsequent chapters.

Table 5.1
Computing Present Value

Dollars Payable	Years in Future	Present Value
M_0	0	M_0
M_1	1	$M_1/(1 + i)$
M_2	2	$M_2/(1 + i)^2$
.	.	.
.	.	.
.	.	.
M_T	T	$M_T/(1 + i)^T$

In general, when the annual interest rate is i, the present value of a promise to pay $\$M$ in T years is simply $\$M/(1 + i)^T$. Thus, even in the absence of inflation, a dollar in the future is worth less than a dollar today, and must be "discounted" by an amount that depends upon the interest rate and when the money is receivable. For this reason, i is often referred to as the **discount rate.** Note that the further into the future the promised money is payable (the larger is T), the smaller is the present value. Intuitively, the longer you have to wait for a sum to be paid, the less it is worth today, *ceteris paribus.*

discount rate
The interest rate used in the computation of present value.

Finally, consider a promise to pay $\$M_0$ today, $\$M_1$ one year from now, $\$M_2$ two years from now, and so on for T years. How much is this deal worth? By now, it is clear that the naive answer ($\$M_0 + \$M_1 + \$M_2 + \ldots + \$M_T$) is incorrect because it assumes that a dollar in the future is exactly equivalent to a dollar in the present. Without taking present values, adding up dollars from different points in time is like adding up apples and oranges. The correct approach is to convert each year's amount to its present value and then add them up.

Table 5.1 shows the present value of each year's payment. To find the present value (PV) of the income stream $\$M_0$, $\$M_1$, $\$M_2$, . . . , $\$M_T$, we simply add the figures in the last column:

$$PV = M_0 + \frac{M_1}{(1 + i)} + \frac{M_2}{(1 + i)^2} + \ldots + \frac{M_T}{(1 + i)^T}. \tag{5.2}$$

PRESENT VALUE IN ACTION

We have shown that present value calculations are required to sensibly evaluate streams of income that occur in different points in time. Here are two real-world examples.

Michael Wittkowski's Lottery Prize

In 1984 a Chicago printer named Michael Wittkowski became famous (for a weekend) when national headlines announced that he had won $40 million in the Illinois State Lottery. Forty million dollars is a huge amount of money. However, if we look carefully at how the money was paid out and use present-value analysis, it turns out that the prize was worth substantially less.

Under the terms of the Illinois lottery, prizes are distributed in 20 equal installments; Wittkowski received $2 million in 1984; another $2 million in 1985, and will continue to receive $2 million per year until 2003. How much was this stream worth in 1984? Put another way, in 1984, what is the most money you would have been willing to pay Wittkowski for his winning lottery ticket?

The $2 million he received in 1984 had a present value of $2 million in that year. The long-term market interest rate at that time was about 12 percent. Hence, the present value of the 1985 payment was $1,785,714 (= $2,000,000/1.12); the 1986 payment $1,594,387 (= $2,000,000/$1.12^2$), and so on. The present value of the last check, payable in 2003, was $232,214 (= $2,000,000/$1.12^{19}$). Adding together the present values of each year's payment yields a sum of $16,731,553. Thus, the "$40 million" prize was really worth only $16,731,553. Of course, that's still enough money to induce a definite improvement in Michael Wittkowski's standard of living. But do you think that advertising the lottery award as $40 million was honest?[5] In this context, consider the case of another Michael, this one surnamed Ondrish, who won a "million dollars" in the Arizona lottery. When he discovered that the money was to be paid out over 20 years, he sued "the Arizona lottery for breach of contract, charging fraud and deception, because they never mentioned the drawn-out payment scheme. Ondrish lost his case; the court agreed with the lottery that if he didn't like the deal, he should have returned his ticket and asked for his dollar back" (Gould 1995, 40).

"Truth-in-Lending" Laws

When people obtain a mortgage to purchase a home, the agreement commits them to making a series of payments in future years to pay off the mortgage. Under U.S. law, lenders must provide borrowers with information on how much the loan will cost them. This information must include the sum of all the payments that will have to be made over the life of the loan. The idea is to provide people with good information about what the loan will really cost them, and to allow them to compare different deals.

Is this a good way to convey the truth to consumers? To make the problem more concrete, suppose that the Macbeths are trying to obtain a $75,000 loan to purchase a new house. Their friendly neighborhood banker tells them that the bank would be happy to lend them the money, and that they have two repayment options. Option A requires payments of $7,300 per year over a 30-year period, while Option B is $9,860 per year over a 15-year period.[6] The banker then shows them their truth-in-lending statement, which indicates that the cost of option A is $219,000 (= 30 × $7,300), and the cost of option B is $147,900 (= 15 × $9,860).

The Macbeths are outraged. Why should they have to pay such large sums of money for a mere $75,000 loan? Even the cheaper option costs $147,900. They stalk out of the bank, thanking their lucky stars that the truth-in-lending laws have saved them from being ripped off.

Have the Macbeths been well served by the truth-in-lending laws? The theory of present value tells us that there is a good chance that the answer is no. Because the mortgage payments are being made at different points in time, simply adding them up conveys a false sense of their true cost. If the opportunity cost of the Macbeths' funds is 7.5 percent, the present value of the 30-year mort-

[5]The fact that the prize payments are subject to the federal income tax reduces their value to the recipient even further.

[6]Option A corresponds to a 9 percent fixed-rate mortgage; option B to a 10 percent fixed-rate mortgage.

gage is $86,218; and the present value of the 15-year mortgage is $87,040. If the Macbeths had seen and understood the significance of these numbers, they might have decided to borrow the money after all. Note, by the way, that the shorter loan is not the better deal. To be sure, the longer loan involves more payments, but because many of these payments come far in the future, their present value is not very high. Of course, if the Macbeths' discount rate were lower, the shorter loan might be preferable to the longer. In any case, because they ignore present values, the figures presented in truth-in-lending documents can be highly misleading. This example reinforces the point we have been making throughout: The importance of computing present values is hard to overestimate. Major errors can be made if it is ignored.

Perpetuities

perpetuity
A stream of income that lasts forever.

To "consolidate" the debts incurred to battle Napoleon, the British government issued bonds called *consols*, which paid a fixed amount of money per period *forever*. The consol is an example of a **perpetuity**—a stream of income that lasts forever. How does one compute the present value of a perpetuity? To be more concrete, assume that the perpetuity pays $\$M$ annually. To find the present value of this stream, we need only determine how much money would have to be invested now at an annual rate of i percent to obtain $\$M$ each year. Hence, we know that $i \times PV = M$, which implies that the present value of a perpetuity is

$$PV = \frac{M}{i}. \tag{5.3}$$

Thus, for example, when the interest rate is 5 percent, the present value of a perpetuity of $250 is $5,000 (= $250/.05).

Despite the fact that consols are no longer issued, Equation (5.3) is extremely important and relevant for two reasons. First, some assets, like land, do produce returns forever, and this formula helps value them.

Second, Equation (5.3) is a handy approximation to the present value of a stream of income that comes in over a finite number of years. Suppose that you are evaluating an income stream of $2 million per year over the next 20 years, and that the interest rate is 12 percent. The computation of the present value using Equation (5.2) is straightforward but tedious. As noted in the lottery example above, the answer is $16,731,553. Suppose that instead of lasting 20 years, the stream of $2 million payments lasts forever. Then you can simply substitute the appropriate values for i and M into Equation (5.3), and find a present value of $16,666,667. Thus, the "quick and dirty" calculation using the perpetuity formula provides a fairly close approximation to the exact answer. Intuitively, the present value of sums received in the very distant future is very small, so that including them does not create a serious error.

5.6 PROGRESS CHECK

Suppose the interest rate is 5 percent. Calculate the present value of each of the following: (*a*) $1,000,000 payable 20 years from now; (*b*) $25 payable immediately *and* $50 payable one year from now; and (*c*) a perpetuity of $625.

The accuracy of the approximation depends on the size of the interest rate and the number of years involved. We stress that using the perpetuity formula is not a perfect substitute for using Equation (5.2). Still, in many cases it is an excellent way to make a quick guess about orders of magnitude. (PC 5.6)

SECTION RECAP

Many transactions involve flows of money at different points in time. To evaluate such transactions, one must explicitly take into account that dollars received (or paid) at different points in time are not directly comparable. Specifically, a dollar received in the future is worth less than a dollar received in the present because a dollar received in the present can be invested at the market rate of interest. To make future and present dollars comparable, one must compute the present value of the future dollars—the most that a person would be willing to pay *today* for the future income stream.

5.4 HUMAN CAPITAL

human capital
The investments that individuals make in education, training, and health care that raise their productive capacity.

The models of labor supply developed earlier in this chapter assume that an individual's wage rate is fixed. However, people can and do affect their wage rates by investing in **human capital**—skills and abilities that enhance their productivity. By engaging in various forms of human capital investment such as formal education and worker training, people can raise their future earnings. In the United States, for example, each year of schooling raises wages by about 8 percent (Krueger 1993). Human capital is a very important form of investment in modern economies. Kroch and Sjoblom (1986) estimated that the amount of human capital investment in the United States is more than twice the quantity of physical capital.

Drawing by W. Miller; © 1986.
The New Yorker Magazine, Inc.

Of course, human capital investment has a cost. Some of these costs are explicit. As the cartoon suggests, college tuition is a type of explicit cost that can be very high. Explicit costs for all levels of education in the United States exceed $400 billion. In addition, one must consider the opportunity cost of the time spent acquiring the human capital—if you are sitting in class, then you can't be working simultaneously at a job, and the forgone wages represent a cost as well. Whether its costs are explicit or implicit, human capital investment requires trading off lower consumption levels in the present in return for higher earnings in the future. Stating the problem in this way indicates that human capital investment is another type of intertemporal decision. Indeed, the same general approach that we used to analyze people's decisions about how much financial capital (saving) to supply to the market can be used to analyze their human capital decisions.

At the outset, to keep things simple we will analyze the situation of an individual whose *only* investment opportunity is in human capital. That is, he has no access at all to financial capital markets. After analyzing this simple model, we will analyze the more interesting case in which an individual can invest in both human and physical capital.

HUMAN CAPITAL AS THE ONLY ASSET

In Figure 5.23, the horizontal axis measures Julius's level of consumption during his youth (c_0), and the vertical axis his consumption during adulthood (c_1). In the absence of any investment in human capital, Julius can earn I_0 in youth, and I_1 in adulthood. Hence, this combination represents his endowment point.

Now suppose that Julius has the option of attending computer programming classes. Participation in each class has a cost to him in terms of forgone *present consumption*. By attending these classes, Julius can enhance his earning capacity next period. Indeed, the more classes that he attends this period, the higher his earnings will be next period. However, this process is subject to diminishing marginal returns—each hour of class raises his earnings ability by successively smaller increments. Under these assumptions, Julius's opportunities are embodied in the curved line *ba*. Curve *ba* is referred to as the **human capital production function.** It shows how an individual can transform investments in human capital (measured in terms of forgone consumption) into future gains in income.

human capital production function
The relationship between investments in human capital and future gains in income.

To determine Julius's amount of human capital investment, we must introduce his preferences between present and future consumption. In Figure 5.23, we superimpose his indifference curves upon the human capital production function. His optimal point is e^f, where he consumes c_0^f during his youth and c_1^f during adulthood. Because his endowment in youth is I_0 dollars, Julius's human capital investment (measured in dollars) is ($I_0 - c_0^f$). A consequence of making this investment is that Julius can raise his adulthood consumption from I_1 to c_1^f.

HUMAN AND PHYSICAL CAPITAL

A crucial assumption behind Figure 5.23 is that Julius has no access to financial capital markets. Now let us assume that, to the contrary, he can borrow and lend at the going rate of interest, *i*. How does this change the situation? Figure 5.24 reproduces Julius's human capital production function from Figure 5.23. Now, recall the discussion surrounding Figure 5.14, which demonstrated that when the interest rate is *i*, the intertemporal budget constraint is a straight line through the

Figure 5.23

Human Capital Decision with No Financial Markets

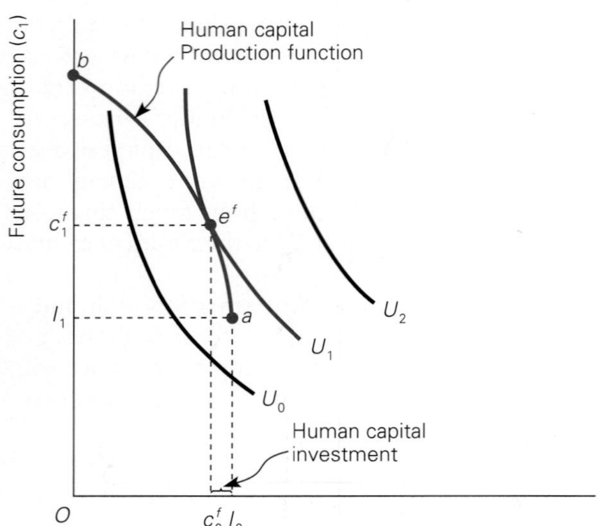

When the individual does not have access to financial capital markets, optimal human capital investment is determined at the tangency of an indifference curve and the human capital production function.

Figure 5.24

Human Capital Decision with a Financial Market

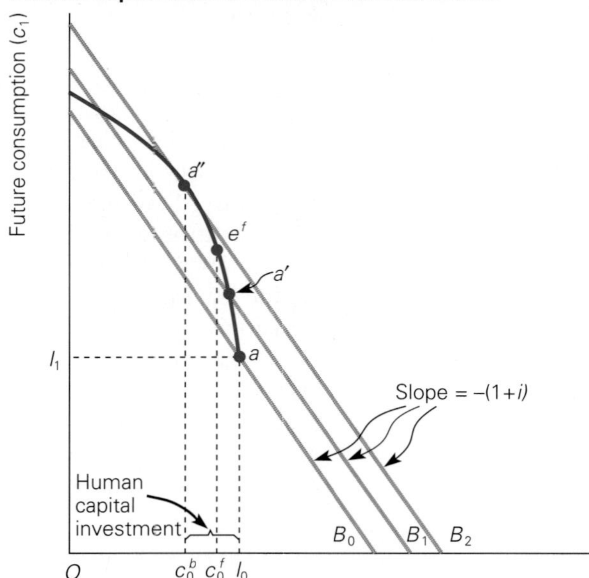

Given opportunities to borrow and lend at the market interest rate, the optimal amount of human capital investment is defined by a tangency between the human capital production function and a straight line whose slope is $-(1 + i)$. This occurs at point a''.

endowment point whose slope is $-(1 + i)$. This is represented in Figure 5.24 as line B_0. With access to the capital market, Julius can borrow by moving from a along B_0 if he chooses to do so.

However, in the presence of a human capital production function, there is more to the story. For example, by attending a few computer classes, Julius can attain point a'. Once he is at point a', the options available to him by borrowing and lending in the financial capital market are given by line B_1, which passes through a' and is parallel to B_0. Importantly, even without knowing Julius's indifference map, we know that he must prefer point a' on the human capital production function to a. Why? Because constraint B_1 makes available more consumption opportunities than were available with B_0. Therefore, as long as more consumption is preferred to less, constraint B_1 is more desirable than B_0.

The same logic suggests that the optimal amount of human capital investment is where a line with a slope of $-(1 + i)$ is as far out as possible from the origin yet still touching the human capital production function. In Figure 5.24 this tangency is point a'', where Julius engages in $I_0 - c_0^b$ dollars of human capital investment. Once he is at point a'', he can choose any consumption bundle along line B_2. Thus, investing in human capital up to point a'' gives Julius the greatest feasible set of consumption opportunities.

To complete the analysis, we need only show which option on line B_2 he selects. Figure 5.25 brings Julius's preferences into play, and shows that he max-

Figure 5.25

Separation of Human Capital and Consumption Decisions

Regardless of preferences between present and future consumption, the present value of the endowment is maximized at point a'' on the human capital production function. Preferences determine which point on the budget constraint B_2 is chosen.

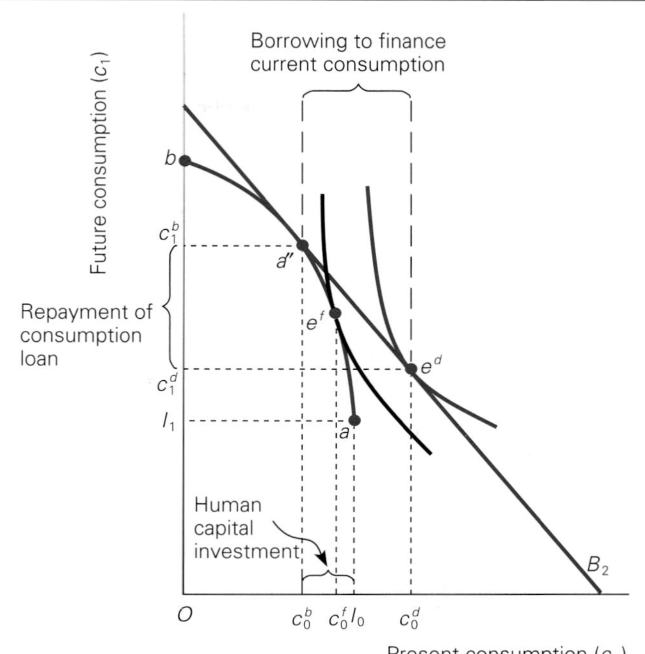

imizes utility at point e^d where he consumes c_0^d in his youth and c_1^d in the future. Let's think a little bit harder about what is really going on in Figure 5.25. Julius first decides to invest in human capital up to point a'' because this level of human capital investment maximizes his lifetime opportunities. However, given his intertemporal preferences, point a'' represents too little present consumption and too much consumption in the future. No problem. Julius goes to his bank and borrows $(c_0^d - c_0^b)$ dollars in order to increase his *present consumption*. This is represented by the movement along line B_2 from a'' to e^d. Next period, Julius repays the bank $c_1^b - c_1^d$ dollars (principal plus interest); this repayment comes out of his future income of c_1^b dollars.

If this scenario seems implausible to you, just think about all the people who borrow from their universities, their families, or the government to pay for their educations. A newspaper article titled "Study Now, Pay Later" noted, "From the Ivy League to state universities, college students are studying now and paying later, often incurring loans the size of mortgages by the time they finish graduate school" (Graham 1995, B1). One purpose of these loans is to finance a reasonable level of consumption during the period that education is taking place. Why endure a subsistence level of consumption while at school when you can borrow on your future earnings?

Figures 5.23 and 5.25 illustrate an important lesson regarding the role of financial capital markets. In Figure 5.23, in which there is no financial capital market, the individual's human capital investment decision depends on his tastes. That is, if for some reason Julius's indifference curves shifted, then his human capital investment decision would change. In contrast, in Figure 5.25, where there is a financial capital market, Julius's human capital decisions are totally *separate* from his preferences. Even with an alternate set of indifference curves, he would still choose point *a″* on his human capital production function. Whatever his preferences, Julius invests in human capital to maximize his consumption opportunities. His preferences determine which of these opportunities Julius selects, but not the human capital investment decision itself.

Thus, the capital market allows an individual to separate his human capital investment decision and his consumption decisions, and by doing so, permits him to obtain a higher level of utility. This result is sometimes called a **separation theorem** because it shows how the existence of markets allows a person to separate production from consumption decisions.

separation theorem The existence of markets allows a person to separate his production decision from his consumption decision.

To gain additional insight into the nature of the separation theorem, recall that the horizontal intercept of the intertemporal budget constraint is the present value of the individual's endowment. Hence, finding the farthest budget constraint from the origin in Figure 5.24 is equivalent to maximizing the present value of the endowment. The separation theorem tells us that *if the individual can borrow and lend at the going interest rate, he should make whatever human capital investment maximizes the present value of his endowment.* Once the present value is maximized, particular preferences determine how much to consume in the present and how much in the future.

SECTION RECAP

By investing income in the present, one can enjoy more consumption in the future. Typically, when we think of investment, we think of buying financial capital such as stocks and bonds. However, people also invest in human capital—skills, education, and so on. Human capital theory nicely ties together the labor supply and intertemporal choice models. In simple models of labor supply, the individual's wage rate is predetermined. In simple intertemporal models, the only choice is how much physical investment to make. In the human capital model, the intertemporal decision involves a choice between financial and human capital investment; the outcome of this decision determines the individual's earnings capacity. An important insight is that the presence of a market in financial capital allows individuals to separate their human capital investment decision from their consumption decision.

SUMMARY

Households play a dual role in a market economy—they are demanders of commodities and suppliers of inputs. This chapter has analyzed households in the latter role. From a formal point of view, households' supply and demand decisions are very similar, because both involve maximizing utility subject to a budget constraint.

- In the case of labor supply, the commodities between which the individual chooses are *leisure* and *consumption*. In equilibrium, the wage rate is equal to the marginal rate of substitution between consumption and leisure.
- When the wage rate changes, both income and substitution effects arise. As long as leisure is a normal good, the two effects work in opposite directions, so on the basis of theory alone, one cannot predict the impact of a wage change on labor supply.
- In the case of capital supply (saving), the commodities between which the individual chooses are *present consumption* and *future consumption*. The cost of \$1 of *present consumption* is \$$(1 + i)$ of *future consumption*, where i is the interest rate.
- When the interest rate changes, the budget constraint pivots through the endowment point; whether saving increases or decreases depends on the relative strengths of the income and substitution effects.

- To make dollar amounts received at different points in time comparable, one must compute their present values—the maximal amount that a person would pay today for the right to receive a certain amount of money in the future. The present value of a dollar received T years in the future is $1/(1 + i)^T$, where i is the interest rate.
- Individuals can enhance their future earning capacity by investing in human capital. If the individual is free to borrow and lend at the market interest rate, the human capital decision is independent of the individual's particular preferences.

DISCUSSION QUESTIONS

5.1 Teddy can work as many hours each year as he wants to at a wage rate of \$12 per hour.

a. Sketch Teddy's budget constraint in a leisure-consumption diagram.

b. Suppose that Teddy has a rich uncle who always gives him \$1,000 per year, regardless of how much Teddy earns. Sketch the associated budget constraint.

c. Use an indifference curve diagram to show how the income from his uncle affects Teddy's hours of work.

5.2 One proposal for reforming the welfare system is a *negative income tax.* Under a negative income tax, each person is entitled to a grant of G dollars per month. For every dollar the person earns, the grant is reduced by t dollars.

a. Suppose $G = 100$ and $t = 0.25$. Consider an individual whose hourly wage is \$8. Sketch the budget constraint before and after the introduction of a negative income tax.

b. How would a negative income tax affect labor supply? Compare a negative income tax to the former Aid to Families with Dependent Children (AFDC) program.

5.3 According to a certified public accountant named Leonard W. Williams (1993, A17), "One is better off to work . . . so as to pay 40 percent in taxes on \$1.1 million of income, than to slack off and pay 31 percent on \$130,000 of income." Use the theory of consumption-leisure choice to evaluate Williams's claim.

5.4 "Some people think Germans have forgotten what hard work is. Even when they are working, they work fewer hours—1,639 a year, compared with 1,904 for Americans and 1,888 for Japanese. And German workers make more money than Americans—an average of \$14.93 per hour . . . compared with \$12.39 for Americans" (Whitney 1995, E5). This quotation clearly implies that Germans are lazy compared with Americans. In the consumption-leisure model, how can the word "lazy" be interpreted? Do the data in the quotation prove that Germans are lazier than Americans?

5.5 The government levies a 30 percent wage tax on Cleopatra. It uses the money to finance a parade. The parade's value to Cleopatra is just sufficient to make her as well off as she was before the tax was levied. What is the effect of the government tax and expenditure package on Cleopatra's labor supply? (Hint: Use the theory of substitution and income effects.)

5.6 Jennifer lives two periods. In the first period her income is fixed at \$10,000; in the second, it is \$20,000. She can borrow and lend at the market interest rate of 7 percent.

a. Sketch her intertemporal budget constraint.

b. The interest rate increases to 9 percent. Sketch the new budget constraint. What effect do you expect this change to have on her saving?

c. Suppose that Jennifer is unable to borrow at any rate of interest, although she can still lend at 9 percent. Sketch her intertemporal budget constraint.

5.7 According to an analysis of international data by Campbell and Mankiw (1991), the life-cycle model does a very good job of explaining consumption patterns in Canada. However, the model does a less satisfactory job of explaining behavior in France, where spending decisions appear to depend more on current income than on lifetime income. Suppose that policymakers in each country announce a temporary tax cut this year to spur this year's consumption. Do you expect the policy to be more successful in Canada or France?

5.8 A student entering college has been given \$15,000 by his parents. This is to be the student's pocket money during all four years of college. No other gifts will be forthcoming from his parents or any other source. Suppose further that he can borrow and lend freely at a market interest rate of 5 percent.

a. Write down a formula for the student's budget constraint.

b. If the interest rate were higher than 5 percent, would the student be better or worse off? (Use your answer to part *a* to explain.)

5.9 When Hollywood stars Burt Reynolds and Loni Anderson were getting divorced, Ms. Anderson reportedly asked Mr. Reynolds for a settlement of either an immediate cash payment of $15 million or $75,000 per month for the rest of her life. Assume that you were Mr. Reynolds's financial advisor and outline how you would determine which scheme was best from the actor's point of view.

5.10 The injury rate in nursing care facilities is 17.3 injuries per 100 workers while the rate for department store workers is 10.8 (Zachary 1995, B1). Why would anyone who has the option of working in a department store choose instead to work in a nursing home?

5.11 Many universities encourage students and their families to borrow as a form of financial aid. An irate Princeton alumnus once wrote: "I would stop asking parents to go back in hock for 14 years . . . to send a child to Princeton . . . Parents should stay out of debt for education" (Huber 1987). Do you agree? Explain.

5.12 Consider Brown, who has conventional, convex to the origin indifference curves between leisure and consumption.

a. On a diagram, show how Brown's equilibrium bundle of consumption and leisure is determined. Call the initial level of leisure n_1.

b. Now assume that Brown's wage rate increases and simultaneously enough income is taken away to keep Brown at her initial utility level. Call the level of leisure associated with this wage rate n_2.

c. Repeat part *b* for a decrease in the wage rate. Call the associated level of leisure n_3.

d. Record your results in a diagram with "hours of work per week" on the horizontal axis, and "wage rate" on the vertical axis. You have now derived the compensated supply curve of labor. Why?

e. Discuss the following statement: "Even if an individual's supply curve of labor is backward bending, her compensated supply curve of labor must slope upward."

5.13 When the interest rate is i, what is the present value of a perpetuity that pays M per year? Now consider a perpetuity of M per year whose payments do not begin until T years from the present have elapsed. What is its present value? An *annuity* is a contract that pays a constant annual stream of money over a finite number of years. Use your answers to the preceding questions to write a formula for the present value of an annuity that pays M per year for a period of T years.

*5.14 Henry's yearly time endowment is T hours. He can work as many hours as he chooses at a wage rate of w.

a. Write down the budget constraint that links Henry's hours of leisure (n) and his units of consumption (c).

b. Suppose Henry's utility function is $U = 96n + nc - n^2$. What is Henry's labor supply function? [Hint: Maximize utility subject to the budget constraint, and note that labor supply is $(T - n)$.]

c. Suppose that Henry's earnings in the labor market are subject to a tax rate of 25 percent. Will his hours of work increase or decrease?

*This question is for individuals who have studied the material in the Appendix to Chapter 3.

Choice under Uncertainty

It's a crazy world. Anything can happen.
—Ilsa, in *Casablanca*

In 1965, a Frenchman named André-François Raffray thought that he had found a great deal: "He would pay a 90-year-old woman $500 a month until she died, then move into her grand apartment in a town Vincent van Gogh once roamed. But [on December 25, 1995] Raffray died at age 77, having forked over $184,000 for an apartment he never got to live in. On the same day, Jeanne Calment, now the world's oldest person at 120, dined on foie gras, duck thighs, cheese, and chocolate cake at her nursing home near the sought-after apartment" (*Trenton Times*, 1995).

Raffray's story reminds us of the truism that life is full of uncertainty. You face uncertainty both as a demander of commodities and as a supplier of inputs. The car you buy may turn out to be a lemon; when you supply your labor, you may suffer a serious accident while on the job. Of course, unexpected outcomes are not necessarily bad. You may invest in training to become a dentist, and then find that dentistry pays more than you guessed at the time you entered school. Or you might purchase a bottle of champagne and find that its quality is higher than you had supposed. Whether the eventual outcome is good or bad, the basic point remains: People often have to make decisions without knowing for certain what the consequences will be.

In this chapter, we examine how rational decision makers cope with uncertainty. Although earlier chapters ignored uncertainty, there is no need for us to start from scratch with a whole new set of analytical techniques. The basic tools that you have now mastered are flexible enough so that, with a bit of modification, they can be employed to study decision making under uncertainty.

6.1 GAMBLES AND CONTINGENT COMMODITIES

It is estimated that in the United States, people legally gamble over $500 billion per year (Simon, 1995). Clearly, gambling is an important phenomenon. The essence of a gamble, of course, is that from the gambler's point of view, the outcome is uncertain. We begin our analysis of choice under uncertainty by looking at an individual's decision whether or not to accept a gamble.

Consider Rhett, whose income is $100, and who is offered the opportunity to bet as much as he wants on the following gamble: For each dollar that Rhett bets, he loses $1 if a heart is drawn from a deck of cards, but he receives $.40 if a club, spade, or diamond appears. How many dollars will Rhett bet? In the past four chapters, we established a general procedure for modeling choice among various commodities. It would be nice to be able to apply this general framework here, but there seems to be a problem. Among what "commodities" is Rhett choosing when he decides how much to bet on the draw of a card?

To answer this question, let's make the familiar assumption that Rhett consumes a single composite commodity (denoted c) that represents all goods and services and has a price of $1. Given that his income is $100, how much of this composite commodity can Rhett consume? We cannot answer this question until we know how large a bet Rhett places, and the outcome of the card draw. If Rhett bets nothing, then he consumes 100 units of the composite commodity regardless of what card is drawn. But if Rhett does make a bet, we do not know what his consumption will be until we see what card appears. Suppose that Rhett bets $10. *If* a heart appears, Rhett loses $10, and he can only consume 90 units of the composite commodity. If a card of some other suit is drawn, however, Rhett wins $4, and he can consume 104 units. Similarly, if Rhett bets $25, his consumption of the composite commodity is either 75 ($= 100 - 25$) units if a heart is drawn, or 110 ($= 100 + .4 \times 25$) units, if some other suit is drawn. The point here is that there are really *two* commodities in the model—the level of *consumption if a heart appears* (denoted c_h), and the level of *consumption if some other suit appears* (denoted c_a; the *a* stands for "*a*ll other"). In effect, the decision of how much to bet is a choice between amounts of the commodities c_h and c_a.

6.1 PROGRESS CHECK

"A professional tennis player who happens to sprain her ankle cannot participate in a major tournament, and her income therefore is lowered." In this example, identify the states of the world and the contingent commodities.

The outcome in an uncertain situation is referred to as a **state of the world.** In the present example, there are two possible states of the world: "heart is drawn" and "some other suit is drawn." Clearly, the levels of the two commodities c_h and c_a depend on (are contingent on) which state of the world occurs. Hence, c_h and c_a are referred to as **contingent commodities.**

state of the world
The outcome of an uncertain situation.

contingent commodities
A commodity whose level depends on which state of the world occurs.

Although this notion of a commodity may seem artificial to you, it serves an extremely useful purpose. It converts the decision over a gamble into an equivalent decision about how much of each contingent commodity to consume, which allows us to study the gamble with our standard techniques for analyzing choices among commodities. We find the consumers' equilibrium by specifying their budget constraint for contingent commodities, as well as their preferences for them. We discuss each of these in turn. (PC 6.1)

BUDGET CONSTRAINT

In Figure 6.1, the horizontal axis shows the amount of *consumption if a heart appears* (c_h), and the vertical shows *consumption if some other suit appears* (c_a). Given his $100 income, what are Rhett's options? Surely, one opportunity

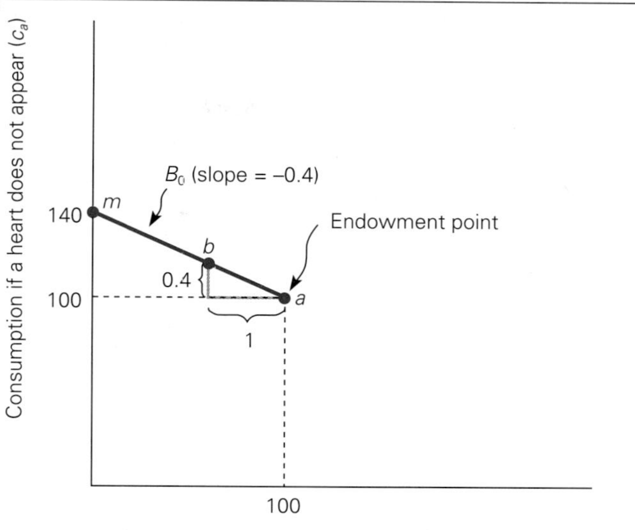

Figure 6.1

Budget Constraint for Contingent Commodities

If no bet is placed, the individual consumes 100 units in either state of the world. Hence, the point at which $c_h = c_a = 100$ is the endowment point. For each dollar that the individual bets, c_h is reduced by a dollar, and c_a increases by 40 cents. Hence, the slope of B_0 is −0.4.

is not to play the game at all. In this case, Rhett has \$100 to spend, whatever the card's suit: $c_h = 100$ and $c_a = 100$. This point is labeled a in Figure 6.1, and is called the *endowment point*. As always, the endowment point refers to the consumption bundle that the consumer can enjoy if he or she makes no trades with the market.

Now suppose that Rhett decides to bet \$1. If a heart comes up, his consumption is \$99; if some other suit, it is \$100.40. Hence, another possibility open to Rhett is $c_h = \$99$ and $c_a = \$100.40$. Geometrically, this is found by moving one unit to the left of point a in Figure 6.1, and then up by 0.4 of a unit, to point b. Hence, point b also is on Rhett's budget constraint. Similarly, for each additional dollar he bets, Rhett can lower c_h by a dollar and simultaneously raise c_a by 0.4 dollar. The most extreme possibility is to bet everything he has on the draw of the card. Because he must be able to pay off the gamble if he loses, Rhett cannot bet more than his income of \$100. If Rhett bets \$100, his *consumption if a heart appears* is zero, but if some other suit comes up his consumption is \$140, which is denoted as point m in Figure 6.1. Putting all of this together, we see that Rhett's budget constraint is line B_0, whose slope is −0.4.

Compared to the "typical" linear budget constraints that we have seen in earlier chapters, B_0 seems incomplete. Why doesn't the budget constraint extend all the way to the horizontal axis? The reason is that so far we have not allowed Rhett to select the other side of the original bet. That is, we have not allowed him to make a bet in which he wins \$1 if a heart comes up, and loses \$.40 if some other suit appears. In effect, making this option available just allows Rhett to offer to other people the same bet that has been offered to him. Suppose now that this option becomes available to Rhett. How does this change his opportunities? By taking \$1 of the other side of the bet, Rhett can increase his *consumption if a heart appears* from 100 to 101, at the cost of decreasing his *consumption*

Figure 6.2

Budget Constraint When Both Sides of the Bet Can Be Taken

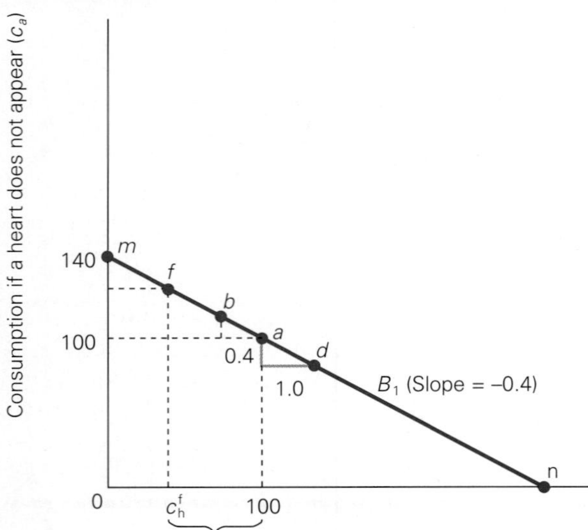

If the individual can take both sides of the bet, the budget constraint is B_1, a line which runs through the endowment point. Any point on the horizontal axis corresponds to a bet of some size. Just find the difference between that point and the endowment point. Thus, point *f* represents a bet of $100 - c_h^f$, the bracketed distance.

Figure 6.3

Slope of a Budget Constraint between Contingent Commodities

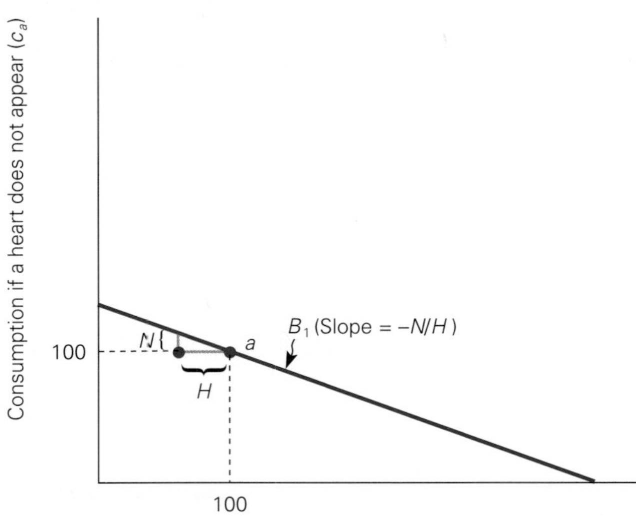

In general, the slope of the budget constraint is $-N/H$, where H is the change in consumption if the contingency on the horizontal axis occurs, and N is the change in consumption if the contingency on the vertical axis occurs.

if a heart does not appear to 99.60. Hence, the bundle at which $c_h = 101$ and $c_a = 99.60$ becomes available—point *d* in Figure 6.2. Similar logic shows that various amounts of this bet allow Rhett to consume the quantities of c_h and c_a that lie along the segment that connects points *a* and *n*, whose slope is also -0.4. We conclude that if Rhett is allowed to engage in both sides of the gamble, his budget constraint is the straight line B_1, which passes through the endowment point *a* with a slope of -0.4.

Note that every point on the horizontal axis corresponds to a bet of some size. For example, at point *f* Rhett consumes c_h^f if a heart appears. Because he would consume 100 if he did not bet at all, then the difference between the two quantities, $100 - c_h^f$, represents the amount of his bet.

Let us generalize this discussion. Suppose that the terms of the gamble are that Rhett loses $\$H$ if a heart appears, and receives $\$N$ dollars if some other suit appears. Suppose further that he can take either side of this bet. To find the associated budget constraint, we reproduce Rhett's endowment point *a* in Figure 6.3. For each dollar bet against a heart appearing, Rhett reduces c_h by H units (moves H units to the left) and simultaneously increases c_a by N units (moves up N units). Hence, the budget constraint is a straight line through the endowment point whose slope is $-N/H$. As usual, the slope of the budget constraint shows the opportunity cost of one commodity in terms of the other—the cost of increasing consumption by $\$H$ if a heart appears is a loss of $\$N$ if a heart does not appear.

Probability and Expected Value

probability
The likelihood that a given state of the world will occur.

So far we have focused on the amounts of consumption associated with each state of the world, and we have said nothing about the likelihood that different states of the world actually occur. The **probability** of a given state of the world is a measure of the likelihood that it occurs. If the event cannot happen, its probability is zero; if the event is certain to occur, its probability is one. If it might happen, but not for sure, its probability is somewhere between zero and one. For example, the probability that a heart will be drawn from a fair deck of cards is $13/52 = 1/4$ (or 0.25), the fraction of hearts in the deck. This means that there are 25 chances in 100 that this event will occur, and 75 chances in 100 that it will not. For a given random process, the probabilities of all the states of the world must sum to 1, because it is certain that one or the other of the states of the world will occur. Hence, if there are only two states of the world and the probability of the first occurring is ρ, then the probability of the second is $(1 - \rho)$. Because the probability of a heart appearing is ¼, the probability of "any other suit" is ¾.

Return now to Rhett's situation and suppose that he bets \$1 that a heart will not appear. What are his net winnings going to be on average? The answer depends on what he earns in each state of the world (whether the card drawn is a heart or not) weighted by the probabilities of the different states occurring. There is a ¾ possibility that the card is not a heart, in which case Rhett wins 40 cents. There is a ¼ chance that the card is a heart, in which case he loses \$1. Taking the sum, weighting by the probability of each outcome actually occurring, we have

$$\tfrac{3}{4} \times \$.40 + \tfrac{1}{4} \times (-\$1) = \$.30 - \$.25 = \$.05.$$

Thus, on average, Rhett can expect to have net winnings of 5 cents from each dollar that he bets. The average amount of these net winnings is also known as the expected value of the gamble.

6.2 PROGRESS CHECK

According to the National Institute for Occupational Safety and Health, the probability of a job-related injury or illness for a full-time worker in the meatpacking industry during the year is 0.33. Suppose that a meatpacker's income is \$42,000 if she remains healthy, and \$12,000 otherwise. What is her expected income?

expected value
The value of some variable, which depends on the state of the world, that occurs on average.

The notion of expected value is a general one that arises whenever we are evaluating random outcomes. Suppose that the value of some variable X depends upon the state of the world that occurs. The **expected value** of X is the value of X that occurs "on average." To find the expected value of X, you weight the value of X in each state of the world by the probability of that state of the world occurring. Suppose that there are two possible states of the world, that the value of X in state of the world 1 is X_1, and that in state of the world 2 it is X_2. If the probability of state of the world 1 is ρ, then the

$$\textit{expected value of } X = \rho \times X_1 + (1 - \rho) \times X_2. \quad \text{(PC 6.2)}$$

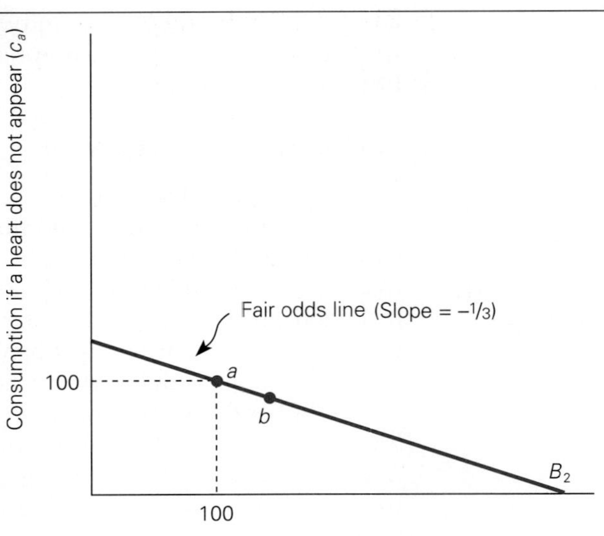

Figure 6.4

Fair Odds Line

When the contingency of the event on the horizontal axis has a probability of ¼, and the contingency of the event on the vertical axis has a probability of ¾, the slope of the fair odds line is −¼ ÷ ¾, or −⅓.

The Fair Odds Line

Now suppose that Rhett's bet had been structured so that for each dollar Rhett bet, if a heart appeared he won \$1, and if some other suit appeared he lost \$0.33⅓. For this bet, there is a ¼ chance of winning \$1 and ¾ chance of losing \$0.33⅓. Hence, the expected value is ¼ × \$1 − ¾ × \$0.33⅓ = \$0.25 − \$0.25 = 0. A gamble like this one, for which the expected monetary gain equals zero, is said to be **actuarially fair,** because on average there is neither a gain nor a loss in monetary terms. What does the budget constraint associated with this bet look like? From the discussion above, we know that in absolute value its slope must be the gain if a heart does not appear (\$0.33⅓) divided by the loss if a heart does appear (\$1), or ⅓. In Figure 6.4, the line with this slope that passes through the endowment point is B_2. A budget constraint like B_2, which reflects the opportunities presented by an actuarially fair gamble, is called the **fair odds line.** Along the fair odds line, an individual breaks even on an expected value basis. (That is, the average monetary gain equals zero.)

actuarially fair
A gamble for which the expected monetary gain equals zero.

fair odds line
A budget constraint that reflects the opportunities presented by an actuarially fair gamble.

odds
The ratio of the probabilities of two events occurring.

It is clear why this particular line is said to be "fair," but where do the "odds" come into the picture? The **odds** of two events occurring is the ratio of their probabilities. If the probability of rain today is ⅕ and the probability of no rain is ⅘, then the odds of rain are 1 to 4. The odds are a way of expressing how likely one event is in relationship to another. When the odds of rain are 1 to 4, we know that it is only one-fourth as likely that there will be rain as it is that there will be no rain. More generally, if the probability of one event is ρ and the probability of a second event is $(1 - \rho)$, the odds of the first event are $\rho/(1 - \rho)$. (PC 6.3)

Returning to the fair odds line for Rhett's gamble, you should note that minus the slope, ⅓, is equal to the probability of the contingency on the horizontal axis, ¼, divided by the probability of the contingency on the vertical axis, ¾. This is no coincidence. The negative of the slope of a fair odds line is always the ratio of the probabilities, "the odds."

Figure 6.5

Slope of the Fair Odds Line

In general, the slope of the fair odds line is minus the probability of the contingency on the horizontal axis divided by the probability of the contingency on the vertical axis.

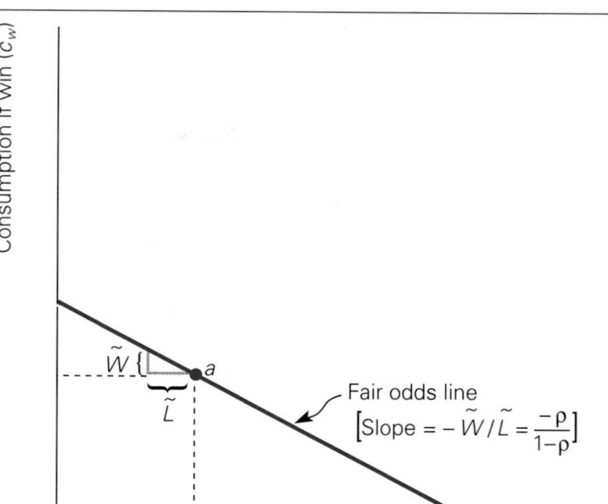

> **6.3 PROGRESS CHECK**
>
> Your income is $25. A die is to be thrown. If a one appears, you win a dollar; if any other number appears, you lose a dollar. What are the odds of winning? What is your endowment point? Sketch the fair odds line associated with this gamble. Why does it pass through the endowment point?

To prove this point in general, suppose that an individual is faced with the following actuarially fair gamble: for each bet placed, he loses L with a probability of ρ, and he wins W with a probability of $(1 - \rho)$. Given that the gamble is actuarially fair, what must the values of L and W be? Denote the actuarially fair value of W as $\tilde{W}$, and the actuarially fair value of L as $\tilde{L}$. By the definition of "actuarially fair," the expected value of the bet must be zero:

$$(1 - \rho) \times \tilde{W} - \rho \times \tilde{L} = 0, \text{ or} \qquad (6.1)$$
$$\tilde{W}/\tilde{L} = \rho/(1 - \rho).^1$$

Now that we know this ratio, we can graph the budget constraint. The relevant contingent commodities are *consumption if lose* (c_L) and *consumption if win* (c_W). In Figure 6.5, c_L is measured on the horizontal axis, c_W on the vertical, and the endowment point is *a*. But recall from the discussion surrounding Figure 6.3 that $-\tilde{W}/\tilde{L}$ is the slope of the budget constraint. Hence, as we asserted above, the slope of the fair odds line is the negative of the probability ratio, $-\rho/(1 - \rho)$.

To understand the intuition behind this result, imagine that you were facing an actuarially fair bet, and suddenly the probability of a loss increased. To keep breaking even, either the amount that you win, W, would have to increase or else the amount you stand to lose, L, would have to decrease. Either of these changes results in a line that is steeper than the original fair odds line. Thus, when ρ goes

[1]Note that *any* values of $\tilde{W}$ and $\tilde{L}$ that satisfy Equation (6.1) are actuarially fair. All that we know for sure is their *ratio*, not their particular values.

up, the fair odds line becomes steeper, which is exactly what Equation (6.1) tells us.

To explore the attributes of the fair odds line further, let's determine the expected value of Rhett's consumption at various points on his fair odds line. Consult Figure 6.4 again. At point a on the fair odds line, it is simple to compute the expected value of consumption. At this point, Rhett receives \$100 in every state of the world, so the expected value of consumption is exactly \$100. Now consider point b, where Rhett bets \$10 that a heart will appear. With fair odds, if a heart appears, Rhett wins \$10, and if some other suit appears, he loses \$3.33. Thus, at point b, $c_h = 110$ $(= 100 + 10)$, and $c_a = 96.67$ $(= 100 - 3.33)$. Because the probability of a heart appearing is ¼, Rhett's expected consumption at b is $\frac{1}{4}\ c_h + \frac{3}{4}\ c_a = \frac{1}{4} \times 110 + \frac{3}{4} \times 96.67 = \$100$. This is exactly the same as the expected value of consumption at bundle a. This is no coincidence: *the expected value of consumption is equal at every bundle on a fair odds line.*[2] Intuitively, because a bet with fair odds has a zero expected value, then the expected value of a person's consumption is the same regardless of how much of the bet he takes.

6.4 PROGRESS CHECK

You have \$50 and are given the opportunity to bet as much as you want on the following gamble: For each dollar you bet, you receive \$1.00 if a head comes up, and lose \$1.20 if a tail comes up. When the probability of heads is ½—a so-called "fair" coin—what is the expected value of a \$1.00 bet? Is the *bet* "fair"? A "weighted" coin is one that does not have a 50-50 chance of heads. What would the odds have to be on a weighted coin to make the above bet fair? Sketch the fair odds line associated with betting on this coin toss when you can take either side of it.

We conclude this discussion of budget constraints for contingent commodities by emphasizing that although the fair odds line is an important concept for reference purposes, there is no reason to assume that real-world gambles necessarily are actuarially fair. Some bets, such as those offered at casinos and horse racing tracks, offer worse than fair odds. (Of course, from the point of view of the casino and horse track owners, the odds are better than fair.) Thus, budget constraints for contingent commodities may be either steeper or flatter than the associated fair odds lines. (PC 6.4)

PREFERENCES

Let's return now to the simple card gamble of Figure 6.2. The budget constraint (B_1) shows the combinations of the two contingent commodities (c_h and c_a) that are available to Rhett. How these various alternatives are ranked depends on Rhett's preferences. In this context, we must be very clear about what Rhett cares about—the amount of consumption available to him in each state of the world. We are not asking Rhett, "Would you rather have a heart drawn than a club, diamond, or spade?" Rather, we are asking, "Which bundle of contingent commodities would you prefer?"

As in the case of typical commodities, we need to make assumptions about the individual's preferences for these commodities. We assume, as usual, that nonsatiation applies—more consumption of a contingent commodity is preferred to less. We also assume that the state of the world does not by itself affect how Rhett values additional units of consumption (the marginal utility of consumption). This assumption is quite reasonable in Rhett's case—it's silly to think that

[2]Proof: Let x be the value of consumption at the endowment point. If the individual wins his bet, his consumption is $x + \tilde{W}$; if he loses, his consumption is $x - \tilde{L}$. His expected consumption is therefore $(1 - \rho)(x + \tilde{W}) + \rho(x - \tilde{L}) = x + (1 - \rho)\tilde{W} - \rho\tilde{L}$. But from Equation (6.1), along the fair odds line, $(1 - \rho)\tilde{W} - \rho\tilde{L} = 0$. Hence the expected value along the fair odds line is always x for any bundle that satisfies (6.1), that is, for any bundle along the fair odds line.

Figure 6.6

Indifference Curves for Contingent Commodities

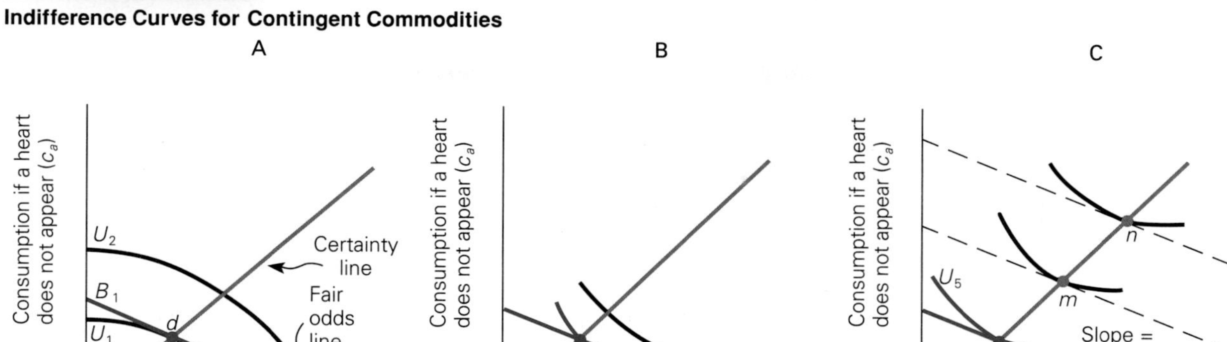

What do indifference curves for risk-averse people look like? They are *not* bowed outward like those in Panel A, because these imply that an uncertain outcome (f) is preferred to a certain outcome with the same expected value (d). They *cannot* cut through the intersection of the certainty line and the fair odds line as in Panel B, because this implies that a certain outcome is equivalent to an uncertain outcome with the same expected value. Risk aversion is correctly represented in Panel C—whenever an indifference curve intersects the certainty line, its slope is minus the odds.

the appearance of a heart per se affects the value that he places on additional units of consumption.[3]

To say anything more about an individual's indifference curves between contingent commodities, we have to know about his attitude toward risk. Three types of attitudes can be distinguished:

risk averse
An individual who will not accept an actuarially fair gamble.

1. *Risk averse.* A person is said to be **risk averse** if he will not bet when offered an actuarially fair gamble. Even though *on average* a fair bet has no effect on consumption, a risk-averse person will reject a fair bet because of the uncertainty it creates. Recall from the previous section that all bundles of contingent commodities associated with a fair gamble have the same expected value. Among all bundles that have the same expected value, a risk-averse person prefers the sure thing.

To sketch a risk-averse person's indifference curves, it helps to draw a couple of lines for reference. In Panel A of Figure 6.6, we first sketch in a 45° ray from the origin. Any point on the 45° line involves equal consumption in both states of the world. Because this consumption level is available no matter what happens, by definition it can be consumed with certainty. Therefore, the 45° line traces out the locus of all possible certain consumption levels and is referred to as the **certainty line.** Now pick an arbitrary point d on the certainty line and sketch through it the fair odds line associated with the bet. This line, labeled B_1 in the figure, has a slope of $-\rho/(1 - \rho)$, which in Rhett's case is $-1/3$.

certainty line
The locus of all possible certain consumption levels.

[3]However, this assumption does not always hold. For example, the value that you put on additional consumption in the state of the world "healthy" might differ from that in the state "unhealthy."

Next, consider the indifference curves U_1 and U_2 in Panel A. Can they represent the preferences of a risk-averse person? No. Because *f* is on a higher indifference curve than *d*, *f* is preferred to *d*. But bundle *d* offers the same expected value with certainty that *f* offers with risk. By definition, a risk-averse person would never choose *f* over *d*. We conclude that a risk-averse person's indifference curves are not bowed outward from the origin.

Next, consider indifference curves U_3 and U_4 in Panel B of Figure 6.6. Because they are bowed inward to the origin, they do not have the problem we found in Panel A. Still, they cannot be part of the indifference map of a risk-averse person. Why? Because, according to the diagram, the individual is indifferent between bundles *d* and *g*. But a risk-averse person must prefer *d* to *g*—*d* has the same expected value without any uncertainty. In short, the indifference curve of a risk-averse person cannot cut through a point where the certainty line and the fair odds line intersect.

6.5 PROGRESS CHECK

Option A consists of a gift of $1,000 for sure. Option B consists of a gift of $500 with a probability of ½, and $2,000 with a probability of ½. Bart is risk averse, Lisa is risk loving, and Maggie is risk neutral. For each individual, indicate which option he or she will choose. If you need more information to make a prediction for a particular person, explain why.

Finally, consider the indifference curve U_5 in Panel C. It is tangent to the fair odds line at *d*, so the slope of the indifference curve at *d* is $-\rho/(1-\rho)$. Because *d* is at a tangency between the fair odds line and the indifference curve, *d* is strictly preferred to every other point on the fair odds line. This is precisely in accord with the definition of risk aversion. Thus, a risk-averse person's indifference curve must look like U_5; that is, its slope when it intersects the 45° line must be $-\rho/(1-\rho)$. Moreover, recall that point *d* was chosen arbitrarily. We could choose any other points on the certainty line (such as *m* and *n*), draw the fair odds lines through them, and obtain the same result: *For a risk-averse individual, the slope of each indifference curve as it intersects the certainty line is minus the odds in favor of the event on the horizontal axis.*

It follows that if two risk-averse individuals are facing the same gamble, then their indifference curves have the same slope along the certainty line. It does *not* follow that their indifference curves are identical everywhere. Risk-averse people can and do differ in their preferences for spreading consumption across different states of the world. (See Discussion Question 6.3.)

risk loving
An individual who prefers an uncertain prospect with a particular expected value to a certainty with the same expected value.

2. *Risk loving.* A person is said to be **risk loving** if he prefers an uncertain prospect with a particular expected value to a certainty with the same expected value. Risk-lovers prefer a gamble to a sure thing. Arguments similar to those surrounding Panels B and C in Figure 6.6 suggest that the curves in Panel A of Figure 6.6 satisfy the definition of risk loving because in addition to being bowed outward from the origin, they are tangent to the fair odds line whenever the certainty line and a fair odds line intersect. For reference, these indifference curves are reproduced in Figure 6.7. Interestingly, for both risk-loving and risk-averse people, the indifference curves have a slope equal to the negative of the odds whenever they cross the certainty line. The distinction is in the curvature—risk-lovers' curves are bowed outward from the origin while risk-averters' curves are bowed inward to the origin.

risk neutral
An individual who is indifferent among alternatives with the same expected value.

3. *Risk neutral.* A person is said to be **risk neutral if he is indifferent among** all alternatives with the same expected value. As long as two outcomes have the same expected value, the person doesn't care which one he receives, regardless of whether one outcome is more uncertain than another.

Figure 6.7

Indifference Curves for a Risk Lover

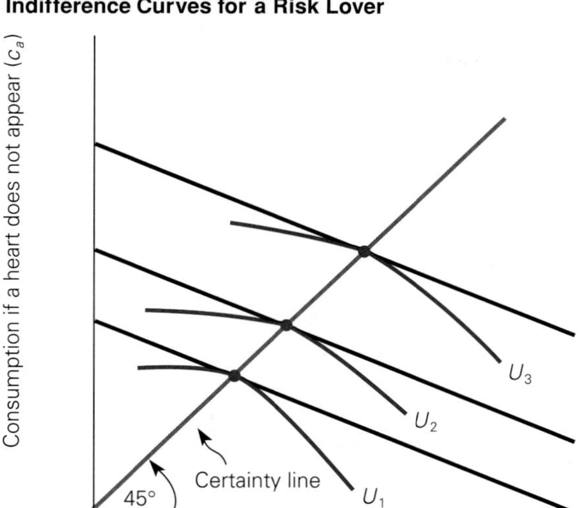

Indifference curves for a risk lover are bowed outward from the origin, and have a slope equal to minus the odds where they intersect the certainty line.

Figure 6.8

Indifference Curves for a Risk-Neutral Person

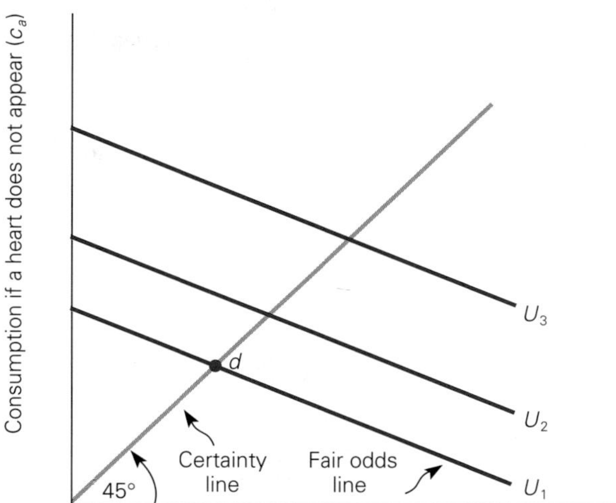

The indifference curve for a risk-neutral person coincides with the fair odds line. The indifference map consists of parallel lines; the slope of each is minus the odds.

In Figure 6.8, we once again sketch the fair odds line through an arbitrary point d on the certainty line. Recall that every point on the fair odds line has the same expected value. It follows that a risk-neutral person is indifferent among all points on the fair odds line. Therefore, the indifference curve for a risk-neutral person coincides with the fair odds line. The indifference map consists of a set of parallel straight lines; the slope of each one is the negative of the odds. (PC 6.5)

EQUILIBRIUM

Now that we have modeled both the budget constraint and preferences, we are in a position to analyze the consumer's decision. We will assume Rhett is risk averse, and that his preferences are those from Panel C of Figure 6.6. In Figure 6.9, Rhett's indifference map is superimposed upon his budget constraint from Figure 6.2. The equilibrium is at point e^a. How much of his endowment of 100 does Rhett bet? In equilibrium, his *consumption in the event of a heart* is c_h^a. As we already showed, however, the distance between a given bundle and the endowment point measures the size of the bet. Rhett bets $100 - c_h^a$. Intuitively, the fact that Rhett chooses to risk some money makes perfect sense. Recall that given the terms of the gamble embodied in budget constraint B_1, on average, taking the bet leads to a monetary gain. Hence, Rhett is willing to gamble some of his money on the bet. Importantly, however, he does not bet *all* of his money. Even though the odds are in his favor, Rhett doesn't "bet the ranch" because he is risk averse.

Now let us imagine that instead of being confronted with the bet embodied in budget constraint B_1, Rhett is faced with an actuarially fair gamble. That is, his

Figure 6.9

Equilibrium Choice of Contingent Commodities

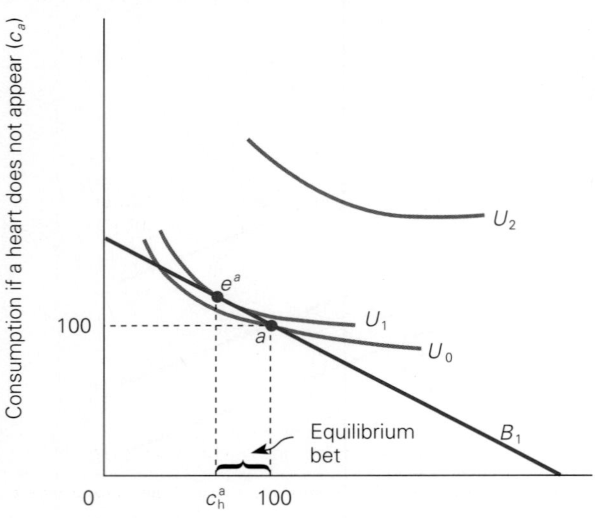

Given budget constraint B_1, the most preferred bundle is e^a. At this bundle, consumption if a heart appears, c_h^a, is less than the endowment quantity of 100. Hence, the equilibrium bet is $100 - c_h^a$.

Figure 6.10

Equilibrium with a Fair Odds Line

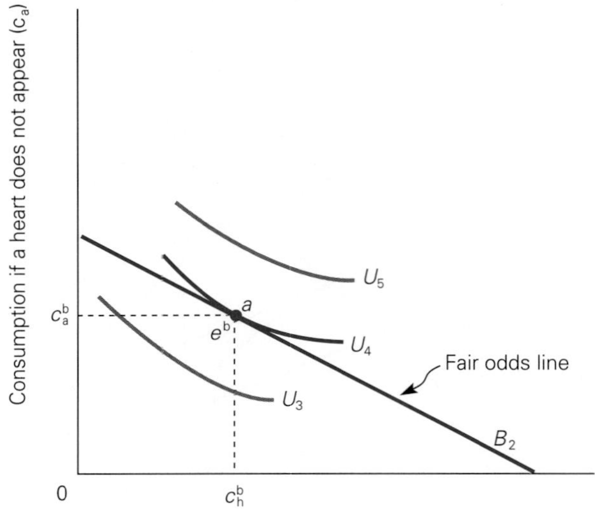

When confronted with an actuarially fair bet, a risk-averse individual maximizes utility at point e^b, which corresponds to the endowment point *a*. That is, the bet is not accepted.

budget constraint is the fair odds line B_2 from Figure 6.4. How does Rhett change the size of his bet? This is a typical comparative statics problem—we just have to find the equilibrium associated with the new budget constraint. Figure 6.10 superimposes the indifference map from Figure 6.9 upon the fair odds line. The most-preferred attainable point is e^b, at which *consumption if a heart appears* is c_h^b and *consumption if any other suit appears* is c_a^b. Note that $c_h^b = c_a^b$; consumption in both states of the world is equal. This result is no surprise. Because the budget constraint has a slope in absolute value of ⅓, the *MRS* must equal ⅓ at an equilibrium, but we already know from Panel C in Figure 6.6 in that all of the *MRS*s are ⅓ along the certainty line.

How much does Rhett bet? Because the equilibrium bundle e_b is identical to the endowment point, *a*, he has not bet at all. This merely reinforces what we already know—a risk-averse person will not accept an actuarially fair gamble.

At this point, you might be thinking that you or people you know *do* accept actuarially fair gambles. Indeed, it is not hard to find cases in which individuals are willing to accept actuarially *unfair* gambles. For example, every year some people bet on the outcome of the coin toss that determines the initial possession of the ball in the Super Bowl. Bookies generally offer 5-to-6 odds, that is, if you predict correctly you win \$5, but if you are wrong you lose \$6. This bet is actuarially unfair, because its expected value is negative: $\frac{1}{2} \times \$5 - \frac{1}{2} \times \$6 = -\$0.50$. The people who take this bet are willing to pay (in terms of forgone expected monetary value) for increased risk.

Can such behavior be rational? It can be if people are risk lovers. Assume that Hamilton is a risk lover, so that his indifference curves are bowed outward from

Figure 6.11

Equilibrium for a Risk Lover

A risk-loving individual has indifference curves that are bowed outward from the origin. For this person, equilibrium is at point *e*, where the individual places all of his money on an actuarially unfair bet.

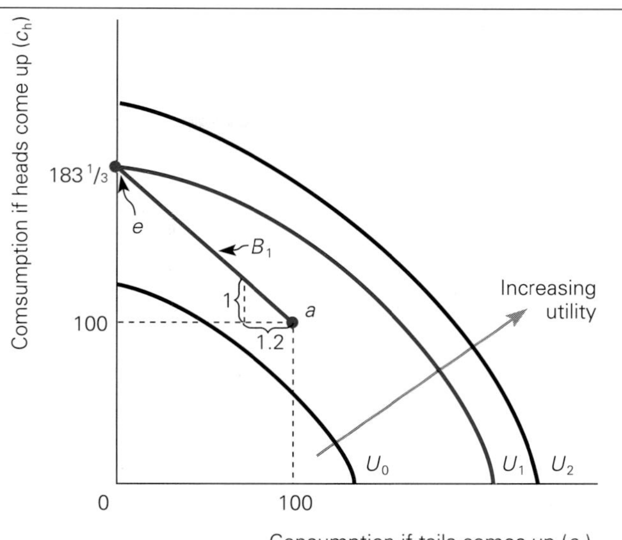

the origin as in Figure 6.7. Assume also that Hamilton's initial income is \$100, and he is offered the following actuarially unfair gamble: for each dollar he bets, if heads come up, he wins \$1.00; if tails come up, he loses \$1.20. Moreover, he does not have the opportunity to take the other side of the bet. (Only bookies can get away with those odds!) In Figure 6.11, *consumption if a tail occurs* is measured on the horizontal axis and *consumption if a head occurs* is on the vertical. Under the terms of the bet, the budget constraint is straight line B_1, whose slope is $-0.83\frac{1}{3}$ ($= -1/1.2$), and whose vertical intercept is $183\frac{1}{3}$. Given this budget constraint, the highest indifference curve that can be attained is U_1. The equilibrium (point *e*) is a corner solution. At this point, if heads come up, his consumption is $183\frac{1}{3}$, but if tails come up, his consumption is zero! This, of course, is a rather extreme case, but it does illustrate how the acceptance of a gamble with an expected monetary loss can be "rational." Remember, economics defines rationality in terms of whether an individual acts sensibly *given* his or her preferences, not whether the preferences themselves are sensible.

Which type of preference is more relevant for understanding behavior, risk averse (as in Figure 6.6, Panel C), or risk loving (as in Figure 6.11)? As we have just suggested, risk-loving behavior can be observed, and for some individuals it is not inconsequential. A Florida man named Anthony Giardino and his father once purchased 10,000 \$1 lottery tickets to bet on the state's \$115 million jackpot—and lost. More generally, the prosperity of the casinos in Las Vegas and Atlantic City suggests that many people are risk lovers. On the other hand, many casino-goers and lottery players place only relatively small bets; these people are out for a little fun and are not serious risk lovers.[4] Indeed, there is strong evidence that for the important decisions in their lives, most people are risk averse. One important piece of evidence is that most people are willing to pay substantial

[4]See Friedman and Savage (1948) for a theory explaining why rational individuals may take small gambles but still be risk averse for important decisions.

amounts of money to reduce the risks they face—they buy insurance. In a subsequent section we will more closely examine the demand for insurance.

SECTION RECAP

Any theory that claims to explain people's behavior must be able to accommodate uncertainty. This section has shown how our theory of rational decision making can be extended to allow for uncertainty. The key insight is that a person making a choice in the presence of uncertainty is really choosing among *contingent commodities.* Once this is recognized, the standard apparatus for analyzing choice among commodities can be employed. The shapes of an individual's indifference curves between contingent commodities depend on his attitude toward risk. Different results are obtained depending on whether the individual is risk averse, risk loving, or risk neutral.

6.2 SOME APPLICATIONS OF CONTINGENT COMMODITIES

The two examples of this section demonstrate the usefulness of our theory of choice under uncertainty.

RISK PREMIA

We have argued that, in general, people are more likely to be risk averse than risk loving. An important piece of evidence for this proposition is the fact that riskier assets tend to pay higher rates of return than safe assets. For example, bonds issued by the U.S. government are virtually riskless, because the chance of a default by the federal government is nil. On the other hand, even very stable corporations have some probability of going bankrupt. Hence, when you lend money to a corporation (via purchase of a bond), there is some chance that you will lose your principal. Even if you get back your principal, you may not receive all of the interest that you expected. If most people did not care about risk, then government and corporate bonds with the same expected payoff would have the same rate of return. However, if people are risk averse, they need to receive an extra rate of return to compensate them for the uncertainty associated with the corporate investment. An extreme example is provided by the Transamerican Refining Corporation. In 1995 the company was able to raise $300 million by selling bonds, even though it had gone bankrupt twice before and it was facing a suit for fraud brought against the man running the company by his own son (Norris 1995, F1). The bonds carried a yield of 18.5 percent, while government bonds were paying about 6.0 percent. This extra return to compensate for risk is called a **risk premium.**

risk premium
The extra return on an investment to compensate for risk.

How is an asset's risk premium determined? Contingent commodity analysis provides a neat and informative answer. Consider Gerald, a risk-averse individual who has $10,000 and only two choices for investing it. The first is a safe asset that will pay $5,000 interest for certain on a $10,000 investment, giving him a *sure wealth* of $15,000. The second is stock in a peanut plantation that will pay $10,000 of interest with a probability of ½, and no interest with a probability of ½. (In either case, the principal of $10,000 will be returned.) Thus, with the plantation stock, Gerald's wealth is $10,000 with a probability of ½ and $20,000 with a probability of ½, giving an *expected wealth* of $15,000. You already know that Gerald will prefer the safe asset because, when choosing between two options

Figure 6.12

Analysis of Risk Premia

Bundles *a* and *b* both have the same *expected value*, $15,000. Because the outcome with bundle *a* is certain, it is preferred to *b*, where consumption depends on the state of the world. This is reflected by the fact that the indifference curve through *a*, U_s, is above the indifference curve through *b*, U_r.

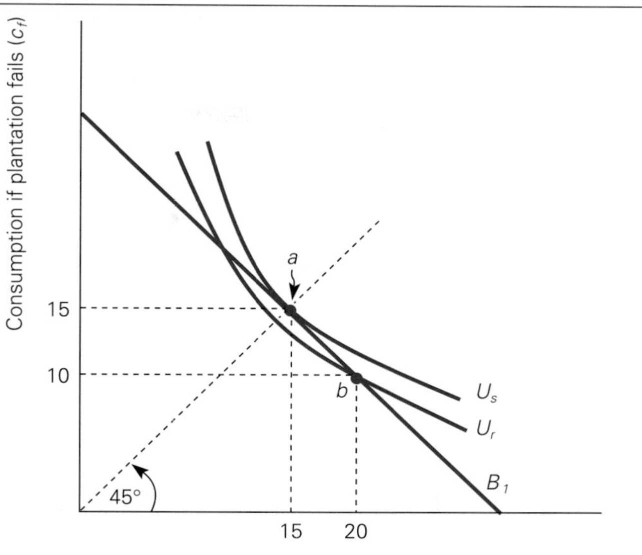

with the same expected value, a risk-averse person selects the sure thing. The question here is, how much of a premium would the plantation stock have to pay to induce Gerald to purchase it?

In Figure 6.12, the horizontal axis measures Gerald's *consumption if the plantation is successful* (c_s), and the vertical is his *consumption if the plantation fails* (c_f). (The units are thousands of dollars.) Point *a* is Gerald's bundle if he invests in the safe asset—his consumption is $15,000 regardless of what happens to the plantation. Point *b* is his consumption if he invests in the plantation—$20,000 if the plantation is successful and $10,000 if it fails. For purposes of reference, draw in line B_1, which connects points *a* and *b*. Because *b* is 5,000 units to the right of *a* and 5,000 below it, the slope of B_1 must be -1.

Suppose now that we want to draw Gerald's indifference curve that passes through point *a*. What do we know about its slope at point *a*? Recall that along the certainty line, the marginal rate of substitution of each indifference curve is the odds of the event on the horizontal axis. In this particular case, the probabilities of both events are ½, so the odds are 1. Hence, at point *a* the slope of the indifference curve is -1, the same as the slope of B_1. Thus, the indifference curve, which is labeled U_s ("s" is for safe), must be tangent to B_1 at point *a*.

Next, we draw an indifference curve through point *b* and label it U_r. All we know about the slope of this indifference curve as it passes through *b* is that the absolute value is less than one; however, the precise value is not needed for our analysis. The key thing is that the indifference curve for the risky option, U_r, is below the indifference curve for the safe option, U_s. This is because a risk averse individual prefers a sure thing to a risky venture with the same expected value.

We are now ready to find the risk premium associated with the plantation stock—how much more it would have to pay to induce Gerald to purchase it. To answer this question, let's magnify the area around bundle *b* (see Figure 6.13). Suppose that the plantation stock were to pay one more dollar in each state of the world. Geometrically, this is represented by a move from *b* to point *c*, which

Figure 6.13

Determining the Risk Premium

Starting at bundle b, the individual can attain the "safe" indifference curve U_s if he receives an extra $\$R$ for certain. Hence, $\$R$ is the risk premium associated with the uncertain outcome b.

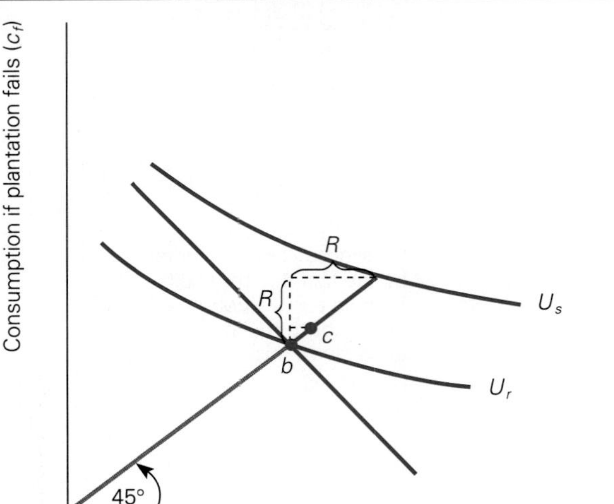

is one unit to the right of b and one unit above it. Would this \$1 premium be enough to induce Gerald to buy the stock? The answer is no, because point c is still below indifference curve U_s. To induce Gerald to buy the stock, its return must be increased just enough so that he can attain a point on the "safe" indifference curve, U_s. In Figure 6.13, Gerald must receive an additional R units of consumption in each state of the world in order to attain the "safe" level of utility. Because R is added in each state of the world, it is equivalent to the *certain* increase in the return that is necessary to make Gerald indifferent between the plantation investment and the safe asset. By definition, then, R is the risk premium. If all people are like Gerald, we would predict the expected dollar yield of shares in the cotton plantation to exceed that of the safe asset by $\$R$. Thus, the analysis of contingent commodities helps explain why assets with different risks pay different rates of return.

The Role of Diversification

So far we have assumed there is only one risky asset. Consider now the problem of choosing between two risky financial assets, shares of common stock in the Alpha Sun Screen Company and shares in the Beta Umbrella Company. Weather forecasters indicate that next summer will be either completely sunny or completely rainy, but no one knows which. If the state of the world is "sunny," Alpha pays a 7 percent return; that is, for every \$1.00 invested, the company pays back \$1.07. If the state of the world is "rainy," however, Alpha pays nothing. Beta has just the opposite pattern of returns: If the state of the world is "sunny," Beta pays nothing; but if the state of the world is "rainy," Beta pays a 7 percent return.

Consider Sue Ellen, who has \$100 to invest in a portfolio of these two stocks. Suppose that she placed all of her money in Alpha. In this case, her expected percentage return, assuming a 50–50 chance of rain, would be

$$3.5 = \tfrac{1}{2} \times 7 + \tfrac{1}{2} \times 0.$$

"Your mother called to remind you to diversify."
Drawing by M. Twohy; © 1987, The New Yorker Magazine, Inc.

Similarly, if she placed all of her money in Beta, her expected percentage return would be

$$3.5 = \tfrac{1}{2} \times 0 + \tfrac{1}{2} \times 7.$$

What would happen if Sue Ellen were to invest in both companies, say putting \$50 into Alpha and \$50 into Beta? In that case, if it rained she would earn \$0 from the \$50 invested in Alpha, but \$3.50 from the 7 percent return on the \$50 invested in Beta. If it were sunny, Sue Ellen would earn \$3.50 from the \$50 invested in Alpha, but \$0 from Beta. Hence, her expected percentage return would be equal to

$$3.5 = \tfrac{1}{2} \times 3.5 + \tfrac{1}{2} \times 3.5.$$

It does not look like purchasing both stocks has done much good; Sue Ellen earns an expected return of 3.5 percent whether she puts all of her money in Alpha, all of it in Beta, or splits it 50–50 between the two. But there is a crucial difference—by purchasing equal amounts of Alpha *and* Beta, she receives a 3.5 percent return in *every* state of the world. That is, she can obtain a perfectly safe return of 3.5 percent, and not have to worry about whether it will be sunny or rainy. This process of buying several assets to reduce risk is called **diversification.** Diversification is simply a fancy way of saying "Don't put all your eggs in one basket." As the cartoon suggests, this is a common piece of advice.

diversification
The process of buying several assets in order to reduce risk.

In our example, diversification allows the investor to get rid of risk completely because whenever one asset goes up, the other goes down by an exactly offsetting amount. In the jargon of statistics, the returns on Alpha and Beta are *perfectly negatively correlated*. In the real world, such assets are hard to find. Most asset values tend to move together. When the price of stock in IBM is high, the prices of other stocks are generally high as well. However, as long as the price movements are not completely synchronized (that is, are not perfectly positively correlated), it is possible to reduce risk by diversification. But you can't always reduce it all the way to zero.

Because diversification helps reduce risk, our theory predicts that risk-averse individuals will diversify their holdings of financial assets. There is ample evidence that this prediction is correct. Consider, for example, the existence of mutual funds, which maintain a diversified group of securities and sell shares to the public. When people purchase a share in a mutual fund, they are simply buying a proportional piece of all of its securities. Thus, a mutual fund allows individuals to hold highly diversified portfolios without having to pay large fees to stock brokers. Households hold over a trillion dollars in mutual funds (U.S. Bureau of the Census 1994, 512). Their popularity is persuasive evidence that people are risk averse and want diversified portfolios.

TAX EVASION

In 1990, baseball's career hit leader, Pete Rose, was convicted of evading federal income tax on earnings of $345,967.60. As punishment, Rose was sentenced to five months in prison and ordered to pay a $50,000 fine. Rose's case is just one particularly dramatic example of **tax evasion,** the failure to pay taxes that are legally due.

tax evasion
The failure to pay taxes that are legally due.

By its very nature, tax cheating is extremely difficult to measure. It appears, though, that tax evasion is a major problem in virtually all economies. In the United States, an estimated 6 to 8 percent of gross national product is hidden from the tax authorities. In the United Kingdom, a figure of 3.5 percent has been suggested, and in Norway, 6.3 percent (Joint Committee on Taxation 1996, 71).

What does tax evasion have to do with the theory of choice under uncertainty? Tax evasion *is* a choice under uncertainty. If you evade taxes and are not caught, you win. But as Pete Rose's experience clearly illustrates, you can also lose. Let's use our theory of decision making under uncertainty to think about the decision to evade taxes and the formulation of public policies to deal with evasion.

Consider the case of Leona, a risk-averse and amoral citizen, whose before-tax income is $1,500. She faces a tax system with the following three attributes:

1. The tax rate on every dollar that Leona reports is t. Thus, if $t = \frac{1}{3}$, then for each dollar of income that Leona reports to the tax collector, she pays $.33⅓. Put the other way, she saves $\$t$ for every dollar of taxable income that she conceals.

2. Leona's tax return will be audited with a probability of ρ; this fact is known to her. If she is audited and she has evaded taxes, the cheating will definitely be discovered.

3. If she is caught evading, Leona pays a fine of $\$f$ for each dollar of income that she has not reported. For example, if $f = 0.8$, then for each dollar of income concealed from the tax collector, Leona must pay a penalty of $.80. The penalty is in addition to the tax that should have been paid.

The two contingent commodities in this situation are *consumption if audited* (c_a), and *consumption if not audited* (c_n). In Figure 6.14, c_a is measured on the horizontal axis and c_n on the vertical. To sketch Leona's preferences, recall our

Figure 6.14

Tax Evasion

Along the 45° ray from the origin the *MRS* of each indifference curve is $\rho/(1 - \rho)$, where ρ is the probability of an audit. On the other hand, the slope of the budget constraint is minus the marginal tax rate (t) divided by the penalty rate (f). At equilibrium, taxes are understated by (c_n^g – 1,000).

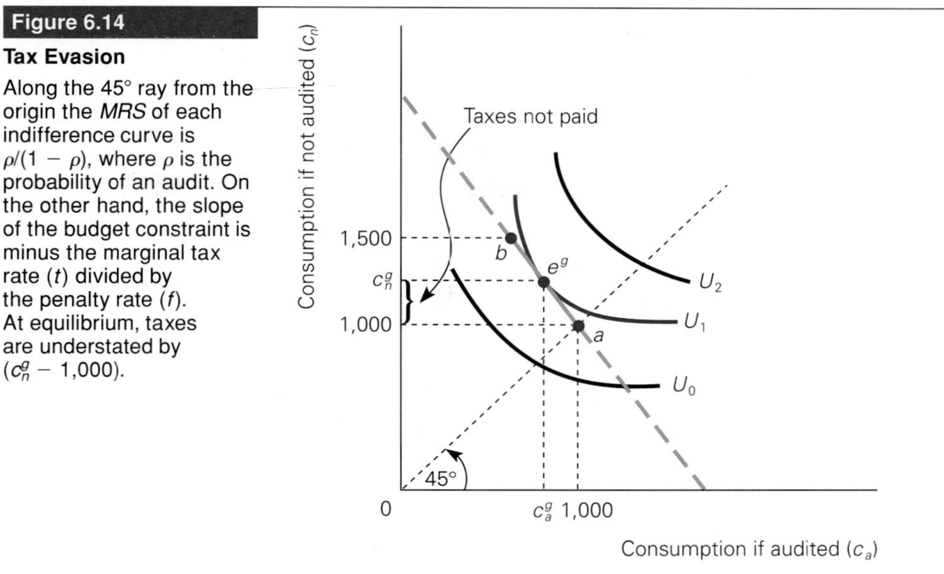

assumption that she is risk averse. Therefore, her indifference curves are convex to the origin. Moreover, because the probability of an audit is ρ, we also know that at bundles along the 45° line, the marginal rate of substitution between c_n and c_a is $\rho/(1 - \rho)$, the odds of being audited. A set of indifference curves exhibiting these properties is depicted in Figure 6.14.

We turn now to Leona's budget constraint. One option available to her is not to cheat. With a tax rate of ⅓ and before-tax income of \$1,500, Leona pays \$500 if she is honest. In this case, her after-tax income is \$1,000, regardless of whether she is audited. This bundle, marked a in Figure 6.14, is Leona's endowment point.

Now, suppose that she does cheat. For each dollar that Leona evades, her consumption is t dollars higher if she is not audited, because she pays less tax. But her consumption is f dollars lower if she is audited, because she has to pay the fine. Using our result from the last section, this means that Leona's budget constraint is a straight line connecting points b and a, whose slope is $-t/f$.[5] Note that in this context, it does not make sense to extend the line all the way through to the horizontal axis. If you decide to pay taxes on more income than you really have, the Internal Revenue Service does not give you a reward! Similarly, the budget line does not extend all the way to the vertical axis because the government does not give you a refund if your reported income is negative.

In Figure 6.14, Leona maximizes utility at point e^g, where her consumption in the event of no audit is c_n^g, distance $c_n^g - 1{,}000$ above the endowment point. This means that Leona underpays her *taxes* by $(c_n^g - 1{,}000)$ dollars. Equivalently, she understates her *income* by $(c_n^g - 1{,}000)/t$ dollars. For example, when the tax rate is ⅓, an underpayment of \$200 means that income was underreported by \$600.

[5]Because the endowment point a already embodies a tax payment, a movement of f units to the left of a implies that a tax is paid plus the penalty.

Designing Policy toward Evasion

Suppose that the tax authority wants to reduce the amount of tax evasion by people like Leona. What policies might it consider? The key result required to answer this question is that a risk-averse individual will not take an actuarially fair bet. Thus, if the penalty rate (f) and the probability of an audit (ρ) are set so that the expected gain from getting away with underreporting a dollar of income equals the expected loss from getting caught, then Leona will not underreport any income. Let $\overline{f}$ be the value of the penalty rate that would make tax evasion an actuarially fair gamble, given the values of t and ρ. Then by definition, $\rho \times \overline{f}$ (the expected loss if Leona is audited) must equal $(1 - \rho) \times t$ (the expected gain if Leona is not audited); or

$$\rho \times \overline{f} = (1 - \rho) \times t.$$

Dividing through by ρ gives us

$$\overline{f} = \frac{(1 - \rho)}{\rho} \times t. \tag{6.2}$$

Equation (6.2) tells us that in order to eliminate tax evasion, the penalty rate should be set so that it at least equals the odds of not being audited, times the tax rate. For example, if the probability of being audited is 10 percent, the odds of not being audited are 9 to 1, so a high penalty is needed. Specifically, if the tax rate is ⅓, then the penalty rate should be set at 300 percent [= (.9/.1) × ⅓]. For each dollar of income that is not reported, the evader must pay a fine of $3.00.

An interesting implication of Equation (6.2) is that, for a given probability of an audit, when t increases, so must $\overline{f}$. That is, when the tax rate is higher, higher penalties are required to discourage tax evasion. Why? The higher the tax rate, the greater the expected incremental benefit to hiding each dollar of income. As the reward to cheating grows, so must the penalty to discourage it. Indeed, in recent discussions of tax policy in both North America and Europe, proponents of reducing tax rates have argued that one of the benefits would be to reduce evasion.

Evaluating the Tax Evasion Model

Our simple tax evasion model ignores some potentially important considerations. For example, the model assumes that only consumption of contingent commodities matters. In contrast, evasion behavior may be influenced by feelings of guilt (or, for people who hate the government, by pride). Another simplification is that the probability of an audit is independent of both the amount evaded and the size of income reported. However, in most countries audit probabilities depend upon occupation, the size of reported income, and whether or not there has been a prior audit. We could extend the model to incorporate these and other features, but the basic insights would remain—higher tax rates tend to encourage cheating while higher fines and probabilities of audit tend to decrease cheating, *ceteris paribus*. As we have emphasized before, an "unrealistic" model can be a good model if it helps us understand the phenomenon under consideration. By this criterion, the tax evasion model is successful.

SECTION RECAP

The contingent commodity model generates predictions that are consistent with real world phenomena. It explains, for example, why risky securities pay higher rates of return than safe securities, and why investors seek to diversify their portfolios. It also provides a useful framework for thinking about important public policy issues such as tax evasion. In particular, it suggests how penalty rates might be set to discourage evasion.

6.3 INSURANCE

Earlier in this chapter we asked a consumer whether he wanted to take on some risk in the form of gambling. For the case of a risk-averse person facing actuarially fair odds, the answer was "No, thanks." The individual simply refused to take the risk. However, in many situations people are not asked whether they want to take on a risk; they have no choice. For example, there always is some risk that you will become sick and thus unable to work. Therefore, whether you like it or not, your consumption level is uncertain. Or, if you own a home, you may be sued by one of your guests who falls down the porch stairs.

If risk-averse people do not voluntarily take on additional risk, it stands to reason that they would also like to get rid of the risks that they have to face. The role of insurance markets is to do just that. To see how this process works, we will analyze the case of Scarlet, an obstetrician. Whenever Scarlet delivers a baby, she faces a probability ρ of being sued and losing. In response, she is contemplating the purchase of some malpractice insurance.

FAIR INSURANCE

premium
The price of obtaining insurance coverage.

To begin, we have to know the terms of the policy available to Scarlet. The price of one dollar's worth of coverage is the **premium** of the insurance policy, denoted r. (We use r to remind us that it expresses the premium as the *r*ate per dollar of coverage.)

Scarlet pays the premium of r per dollar of coverage whether she is sued or not. In the event that she is sued, she also receives one dollar from the insurance company for each dollar of coverage. Hence, in the event of a suit the *net* amount that she receives from the company per unit of insurance is $(1 - r)$ dollars—the insurance benefit minus the premium. This, incidentally, is the actual structure of most real-world insurance policies. You continue to pay your health insurance, auto insurance, and home insurance premia even if the company concurrently pays you a benefit.

actuarially fair insurance
The premium equals the expected payout by the insurance provider.

Given this structure, what is the value of r? At the outset, we will assume that the policy provides for **actuarially fair insurance,** meaning that the premium is equal to the expected payout by the insurance provider. Each unit of insurance pays \$1 in the event of a suit, and zero otherwise. Since the probability of a suit is ρ, it follows that the expected payment is $\rho \times \$1$, or simply $\$\rho$. Setting the premium and the expected payment equal, we have

$$r = \rho. \tag{6.3}$$

Figure 6.15

Budget Constraint with Actuarially Fair Insurance

If a lawsuit will result in the loss of the entire income, the endowment point is a, where c_s is zero. With an actuarially fair insurance policy, the slope of the budget constraint is $-\rho/(1-\rho)$.

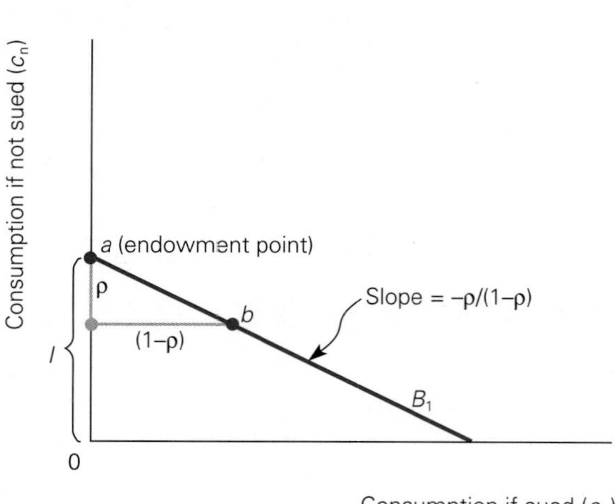

Equation (6.3) tells us that for an actuarially fair insurance policy, the premium for \$1 worth of insurance is simply the probability of the "bad" state of the world occurring. For example, if the probability of a suit is ⅕, then Scarlet can buy \$1.00 of actuarially fair insurance for \$.20.

Budget Constraint with Fair Insurance

We can now sketch Scarlet's budget constraint. First note that in this situation the contingent commodities are *consumption if sued* (c_s) and *consumption if not sued* (c_n). In Figure 6.15, c_s is measured on the horizontal axis and c_n on the vertical. Suppose that Scarlet's income is I. We assume that in the event of a lawsuit she will lose her entire income. Otherwise, she gets to consume her entire income. Under these assumptions, Scarlet's endowment point is a, which is I units above the origin on the vertical axis. The fact that a is on the vertical axis indicates that if she is sued, Scarlet will have nothing ($c_s = 0$).

Suppose that Scarlet wants to purchase a dollar's worth of insurance. How many units of c_n must she give up? By definition, the answer to this question is simply the price of obtaining \$1 worth of insurance; that is, the premium of the policy. Because the premium is ρ, when Scarlet purchases \$1 worth of insurance, it reduces her consumption in the event of no suit by ρ units. In Figure 6.15, this is depicted as a downward movement of ρ units from the endowment point a. At the same time, by virtue of buying the policy, Scarlet increases her consumption in the event of a suit by \$$(1 - \rho)$—the payoff in the event of a lawsuit (\$1) minus the premium (ρ). This is represented by a movement of $(1 - \rho)$ units to the right of a. In short, purchase of \$1 worth of coverage moves Scarlet from point a to point b, which is ρ units below point a and $(1 - \rho)$ units to the right of it. Each successive purchase of \$1 worth of coverage similarly moves Scarlet down by ρ units and to the right by $(1 - \rho)$ units. Hence, the budget constraint associated with actuarially fair insurance is straight line B_1, which passes through the endowment point a, and whose slope is $-\rho/(1 - \rho)$. For instance, if the probability of a suit is ⅕, the slope of the budget constraint is $-¼ = -(⅕)/(⅘)$.

Figure 6.16

Equilibrium with Actuarially Fair Insurance

When insurance is actuarially fair, the equilibrium occurs where $c_s = c_n$. The individual is fully insured in the sense that consumption is the same in every state of the world.

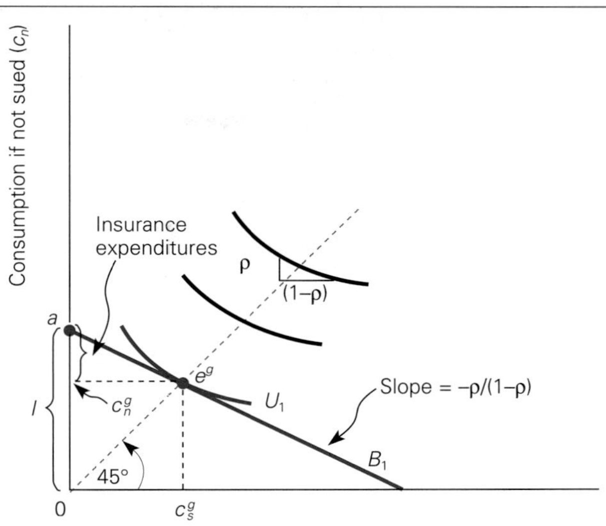

Preferences

As usual, our problem is to draw indifference curves that represent tastes for various commodity bundles. In this context, the issue is *not* whether Scarlet would prefer being sued to being left alone. Rather, the key question is how she evaluates various pairs of contingent consumption levels.

What can we say about Scarlet's indifference curves? As we showed earlier, if she is averse to risk and the outcome of the "gamble" as such does not affect the marginal utility of income, then: (*a*) the indifference curves exhibit a diminishing marginal rate of substitution; and (*b*) on points along a 45° ray from the origin, the marginal rate of substitution is $\rho/(1 - \rho)$. An indifference map with these properties is depicted in Figure 6.16.

Equilibrium Amount of Fair Insurance

The most preferred point is at e^g, where *consumption in the event of a suit* is c_s^g, *and consumption in the absence of a suit* is c_n^g. Note that $c_s^g = c_n^g$. Consumption is equal in both states of the world. This is not a coincidence. The budget constraint has a slope in absolute value equal to $\rho/(1 - \rho)$. Therefore, at equilibrium, the *MRS* must equal $\rho/(1 - \rho)$. But we know that the $MRS = \rho/(1 - \rho)$ only at points where $c_s = c_n$.

To find Scarlet's insurance coverage, all we have to do is compare the endowment point *a* with the equilibrium e^g. By moving from *a* to e^g, Scarlet reduces her *consumption in the event of no lawsuit* from *a* to c_n^g; hence $a - c_n^g$ measures the amount she spends on insurance. By making this expenditure on insurance, Scarlet totally eliminates any risk. Lawsuit or no lawsuit, her consumption is the same—she is fully insured. This result is a general one: *A risk-averse individual purchases full insurance when it is offered at actuarially fair odds.*

Figure 6.16 demonstrates how insurance markets allow an individual to smooth consumption over various states of the world. Without an insurance market, Scarlet would have been stuck at point *a*, where her consumption levels in the two states of the world were very different. Insurance allows her to obtain a higher level of welfare by evening out the amounts of consumption in each state of the world. Note the analogy to the analysis of intertemporal choice presented in the last chapter. *Just as a capital market allows an individual to spread consumption over different periods of time, an insurance market allows an individual to spread consumption over different states of the world.*

THE DEMAND FOR "UNFAIR" INSURANCE

So far we have assumed that the premium of an insurance policy equals the expected monetary benefit. Although this is a useful assumption for conceptual purposes, real-world insurance policies are "unfair" in the sense that the premium exceeds the expected monetary benefit—on average, you pay more than you receive. There are two reasons for this:

1. Fair insurance leaves no margin for insurance firms to cover their operating costs. If a firm is paying claims exactly equal to its premia (on average), where will it get money to pay salaries, rent on the building, and so on?
2. Insurance rates are only imperfectly adjusted to individuals' characteristics. If Scarlet and Frank are two physicians who have different probabilities of malpractice suits, then in principle, an insurance company would want to charge them different premia. Insurance companies do indeed charge different premia to people in various "risk classes." These risk classes are determined by observable characteristics of people. Teenage males, for example, have higher auto insurance rates than most other categories of people. Nevertheless, even within any given risk class, the probability of an accident differs across people. (Some teenage males are wilder than others.) Clearly, if people with different accident probabilities can buy insurance with the same premia, someone is buying insurance that is unfair (in the technical sense) for them.

Changing the Premium

Consider again the case of Scarlet, for whom the probability of a suit is ⅕, so that the premium for a dollar's worth of fair insurance is $.20 (see Equation 6.3). Will she purchase any insurance if her premium is $.40 per dollar of coverage?

This comparative statics problem is analyzed in Figure 6.17. First, consider the budget constraint associated with the new policy. For each dollar of insurance that Scarlet purchases, her consumption in the event of no lawsuit decreases by 0.40 units and her consumption in the event of a suit increases by 0.60 units—the benefit ($1) minus the premium ($.40). The same logic as before implies that the budget constraint associated with this policy is straight line B_2, which passes through the endowment point a and whose slope is $-0.4/0.6$, or $-2/3$. Note that it is steeper than the fair odds line B_1.

Next, consider the indifference map. Scarlet's marginal rate of substitution between the two contingent commodities is based on *her* assessment of the probability of an accident. Since her probability of an accident has not changed, her indifference map is exactly the same as it was in Figure 6.16, and it is reproduced in Figure 6.17.

The best attainable bundle is e^b, where consumption in the event of a suit is c_s^b and consumption if there is no suit, c_n^b. Observe that $c_n^b > c_s^b$. Consumption in the event of a lawsuit is *less* than consumption without a lawsuit. We have demonstrated the following important result:

Figure 6.17

Equilibrium with Actuarially Unfair Insurance

When the premium is greater than the expected payout, the budget constraint B_2 is steeper than the fair odds line B_1. The individual purchases less than full insurance.

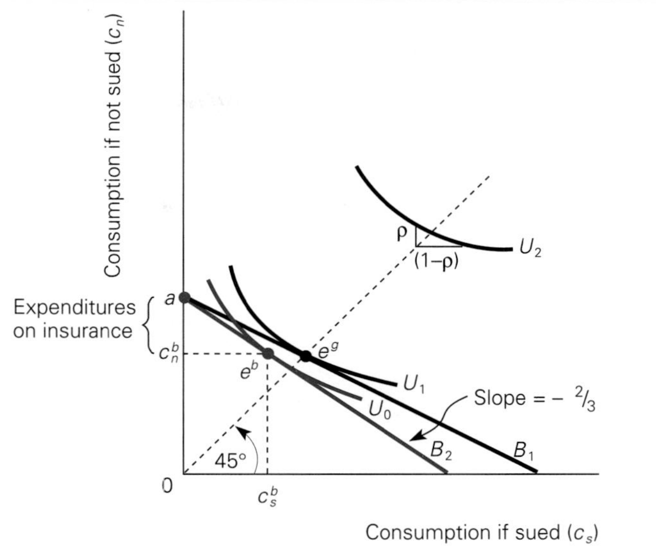

When the insurance policy is actuarially unfair, even a risk-averse individual purchases less than full insurance. Intuitively, when the premium is higher than the expected payoff, it is rational for an individual to assume some risk in return for reducing payments to the insurance provider.[6]

Changing the Probability of a Lawsuit

To make sure you understand the demand for insurance, consider the following comparative statics problem: Because of overwork and stress, the probability that Scarlet faces a lawsuit increases from ⅕ to ⅓. However, this is not observed by Scarlet's insurance company, which continues to charge her $.40 per dollar of coverage. What happens to her demand for malpractice insurance?

The first thing to realize is that this change shifts Scarlet's indifference curves, because the rate at which she is willing to trade c_s for c_n depends on ρ, the probability of an accident. To determine just how they shift, it is useful to begin by sketching in her old indifference curves from Figure 6.16. These appear in Figure 6.18 as the curves U_0, U_1, and U_2. Recall the key result that helped us sketch the old curves—along the certainty line, the marginal rate of substitution is $\rho/(1 - \rho)$. Hence, for the old indifference curves, because $\rho = ⅕$, the *MRS* at every point on the certainty line is ¼.

The rule that the $MRS = \rho/(1 - \rho)$ along the 45° ray must hold regardless of the value of ρ. Hence, when ρ becomes ⅓, then the *MRS* at all points on the 45° ray must be ½ = (⅓)/(⅔). We conclude that, given her new situation, Scarlet's indifference curves each have a slope of ½ as they pass through the certainty line. These are the indifference curves labeled U_0', U_1', and U_2' in Figure 6.18. Note that they are steeper than the original indifference curves. Intuitively, the more likely she is to be the victim of a lawsuit, the greater the amount of

[6]An exception is the special case when the individual is infinitely risk averse—he has L-shaped indifference curves. See Discussion Question 6.9.

Figure 6.18

Effect of Changing Probabilities on Preferences

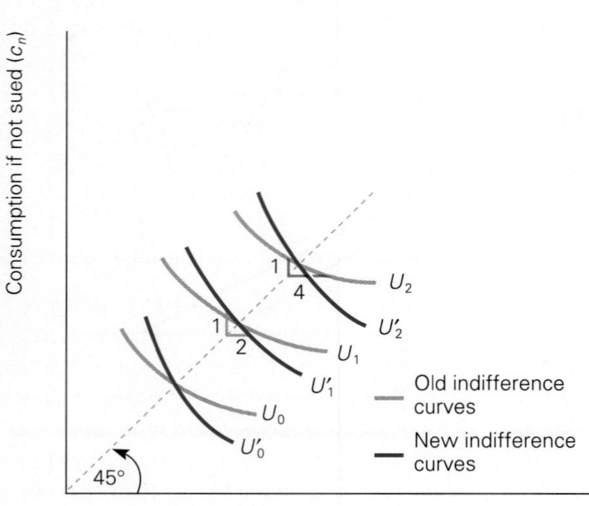

When the probability of a lawsuit increases, tastes for the contingent commodities change. The individual is willing to trade off more c_n for a unit of c_s. That is, the indifference curves become steeper.

Figure 6.19

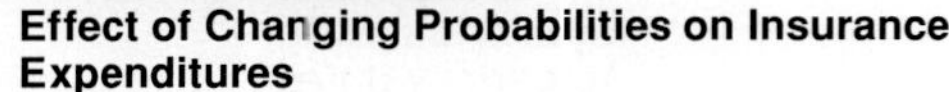

Effect of Changing Probabilities on Insurance Expenditures

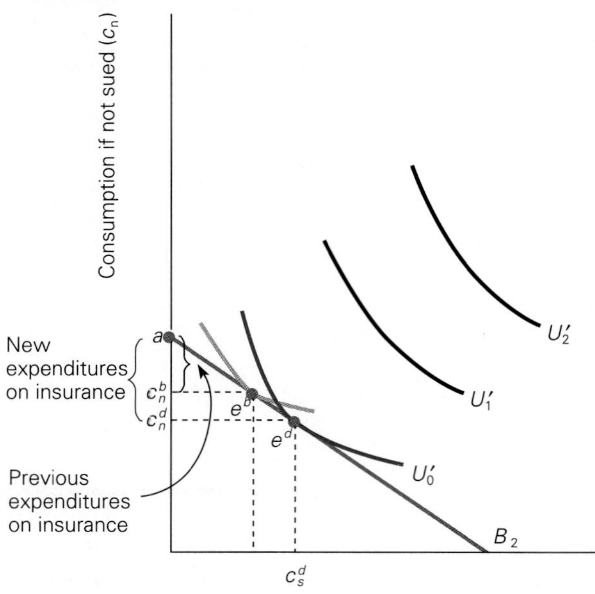

With the new indifference map reflecting a higher probability of an accident, the equilibrium bundle is e^d, where insurance expenditures are $a - c_n^d$. When the probability of an accident was lower, only $a - c_n^b$ was spent on insurance.

consumption if not sued that Scarlet is willing to give up in order to obtain a unit of *consumption if sued.*

We next consider how the change in the probability of an accident changes Scarlet's budget constraint. This part is easy—there is no effect at all. Its slope depends on the price charged by the insurance company and, by assumption, this is the same as it was before. In Figure 6.19, we therefore reproduce the old budget constraint B_2 from Figure 6.17. When we superimpose the new set of indifference curves from Figure 6.18 upon this budget constraint, we find that the optimal bundle is e^d, where consumption in the event of a lawsuit is c_s^d, and consumption in the absence of a lawsuit is c_n^d. Comparing this result to the previous equilibrium bundle (e^b), we see that insurance coverage is greater with the new indifference curves. This is an important result that will be used in later chapters:

People with a greater risk of accident purchase more insurance, ceteris paribus.

THE IMPORTANCE OF INSURANCE

Our discussion of the demand for insurance has focused on an obstetrician's decision about how much malpractice insurance to buy. As suggested earlier, there are many other examples of insurance that is purchased through formal contracts. People buy policies to insure their homes, their cars, their health, and their lives.

Understanding the demand for such policies is clearly important, yet it must be stressed that the theory of insurance demand helps us understand a much wider class of phenomena. Specifically, whenever you are contemplating whether to give up something you value in return for some reduction in risk, in effect you are deciding whether to purchase insurance. For example, a heavy car like a Mercedes reduces the risk of your being seriously injured in an accident, but it costs more than a light car like a Geo Metro. Part of the higher price for the Mercedes is like a premium on a "policy" that reduces the consequences of an accident. Or think about the choice between a safe career, such as being a civil servant, and a risky career as an entrepreneur. On average, you might make more money as an entrepreneur, but there is also a chance that you will end up broke. The lower salary you receive as a civil servant is the cost of a "policy" to guarantee a steady stream of income.

You can think of many more examples. The important point is that our theory can be utilized to analyze all such decisions, not merely those that involve formal insurance contracts. (PC 6.6)

6.6 PROGRESS CHECK

There is a 1/10 probability that Mike's house will burn down. If it burns down, his consumption level will be \$30,000; otherwise, it will be \$50,000. Mike can purchase insurance at a price of 20 cents per dollar of coverage. Is this policy fair? Assuming that Mike is risk averse, sketch his budget constraint and indifference curves. Will he purchase insurance?

SECTION RECAP

If people don't like uncertainty, they should be willing to pay something to reduce the amount of it in their lives. This insight is the basis for the theory of insurance. We have shown that a risk-averse person who can buy "fair" insurance insures fully—his consumption is the same in every state of the world. When the premium is "unfair," some insurance may be purchased, but the individual ends up bearing some risk. Like any other commodity, the demand for insurance varies across individuals if their tastes differ. In this case, tastes are importantly influenced by the individual's probability that the insurable event will occur. *Ceteris paribus*, the higher the probability of the insurable event, the more insurance a rational person purchases.

6.4 DECISION MAKING WITH MANY UNCERTAIN OUTCOMES: VON NEUMANN-MORGENSTERN UTILITY

So far our analysis has focused on situations in which there are only two possible outcomes and, hence, two contingent commodities. This assumption allowed us to use indifference curves to analyze decision making under uncertainty. In the process, we derived a number of important results. Nevertheless, in many realistic situations more than two outcomes are possible. In this section, we develop techniques for analyzing these more complicated decisions.

DECISION TREES

Consider Melanie, a college senior who is making a human capital investment decision. She can either go to law school in preparation for joining a law firm as a junior associate, or to business school to train for a career in investment banking. Melanie knows that with either choice her income will be uncertain. As a

Figure 6.20

Growing a Decision Tree

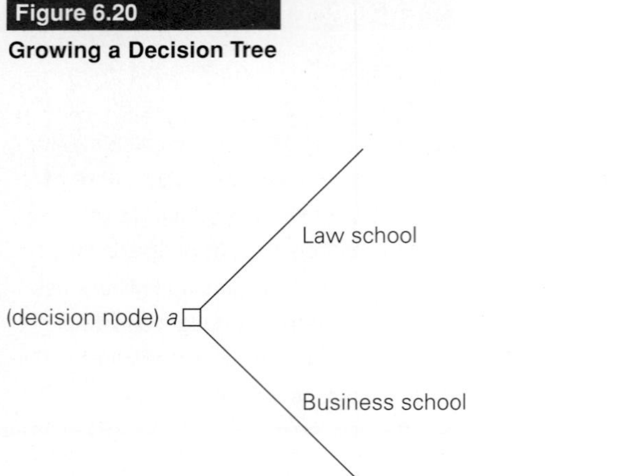

At the decision node, the individual must make a choice.

Figure 6.21

Decision Tree with Payoffs

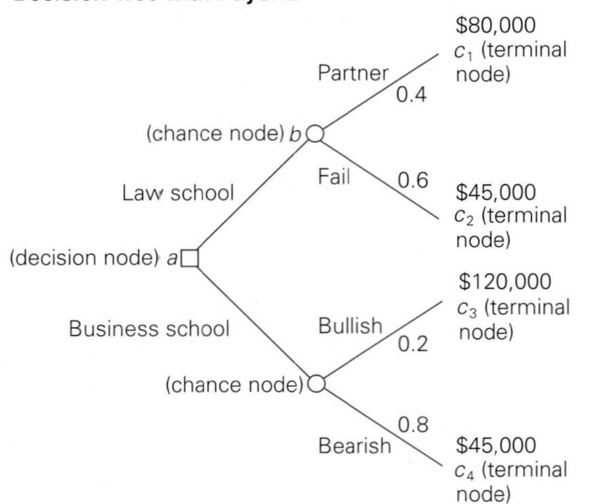

At chance nodes, the outcome is a random variable. Terminal nodes show the values of the final outcomes.

lawyer, her earnings will depend on whether she becomes a partner. As an investment banker, her income will depend on the behavior of the stock market. (She remembers that in the mid-1990s, many highly paid Wall Street professionals lost their jobs.) After some research, Melanie determines the following:

If she goes to law school, she will have 0.4 probability of becoming a partner and having annual earnings of $80,000; and she will have a 0.6 probability of not making partner and having an annual income of $45,000.

If the stock market is bullish, which will occur with a probability of 0.2, her annual earnings as an investment banker will be $120,000; with a probability of 0.8, however, the market will be bearish, and her earnings will be only $45,000. Should Melanie go to law or business school?[7]

decision tree
A schematic representation of a choice problem that shows the possible outcomes and how they are related to current actions.

decision node
A point in a decision tree where an individual faces a decision, with branches coming out of it representing the available choices.

To analyze this rather complex problem, it is useful to have a schematic representation of the possible outcomes and how they are related to current actions. Such a representation is referred to as a **decision tree.** In a decision tree, each point of branching represents a choice that has to be made. To "grow" a decision tree for Melanie, note that initially she can go in either of two directions, law school or business school. Hence, Melanie's decision tree starts out with two branches, one labeled *law school* and the other labeled *business school*, as shown in Figure 6.20. The branch along which Melanie moves depends on her decision. For this reason, point *a* in the diagram is referred to as a **decision node.** Whenever a person faces a decision, we put a small square with branches coming out of it to represent the available choices.

Suppose that Melanie moves out along the law school branch. As noted above, there are then two possibilities: She makes partner or she fails to make partner. Because there are two possible outcomes, we draw two more branches coming off the law school branch in Figure 6.21. This new pair of branches looks

[7]Of course, the incomes and probabilities of success for both law and investment banking depend in part on the level of effort. We assume that this is held constant.

a lot like the one for the choice of school. But notice a very important difference. Here, Melanie does not make an explicit choice. She would rather be a partner than not, but whether she makes partner depends on many factors that are beyond her control. By our assumptions, which of these branches Melanie moves along is the outcome of a random process; with a probability of 0.4 she makes partner and with a probability of 0.6 she does not. Because this choice of branch is random from Melanie's perspective, point b in 6.21 is referred to as a **chance node.** It often is useful to think of "Nature" making the choice at a chance node. Chance nodes are indicated by small circles.

chance node
A point in a decision tree where a random process determines which branch will be followed.

Once we have drawn all of the decision nodes and chance nodes, there are no more decisions to be reached and we have to represent the ultimate outcome; this is, after all, why Melanie is making these decisions in the first place. Points c_1 and c_2 are at the ends of branches, and show the ultimate outcome associated with the respective branches. These points are referred to as **terminal nodes** since they represent the ends of the tree.

terminal node
A point representing the ultimate outcome associated with a particular branch of a decision tree.

So far, we have drawn only one-half of Melanie's decision tree. There is another chance node off of the business school branch; from this chance node emerges a branch that has a bull market with a probability of 0.2 and a bear market with a probability of 0.8. At the end of these branches are terminal nodes c_3 and c_4, with the associated income levels \$120,000 and \$45,000, respectively.

UTILITY FUNCTIONS FOR UNCERTAIN SITUATIONS

The decision tree in Figure 6.21 lays out the various options neatly and also depicts the link between actions and consequences. However, the decision tree does *not* evaluate these consequences. Some method is needed to indicate which combinations are better than others. In effect, Melanie has to choose between two lotteries. The first offers \$80,000 with a probability of 0.4 and \$45,000 with a probability of 0.6. The second lottery offers \$120,000 with a probability of 0.2 and \$45,000 with a probability of 0.8. As already noted, because there are more than two possible outcomes, two-dimensional indifference curves cannot be used to represent preferences.

Recall that we confronted a similar situation in Chapter 2. There, the problem was representing choices among bundles with many commodities in the standard certainty case. The solution was to write down a utility function whose value depended on the quantities of each of the commodities consumed. Various bundles could be ranked by the associated value of the utility function. Exactly the same procedure can be used here, only now the variables in the utility function are quantities of the contingent commodities. Suppose there are n possible states of the world. Let c_1 be consumption contingent on the first state of the world occurring, with a probability of ρ_1. Contingent commodities c_2 through c_n are defined in the same way, as are the associated probabilities ρ_2 through ρ_n. Using this notation, the utility function that ranks all of the possible outcomes is

$$U(c_1, c_2, \ldots, c_n; \rho_1, \rho_2, \ldots, \rho_n). \tag{6.4}$$

What are the probabilities doing after the semicolon in Expression (6.4)? They are there to remind us that the probabilities affect the consumer's relative valuation of the contingent commodities. This is merely an algebraic representation of what you saw in Figure 6.18. A change in probabilities alters the rate at which an individual is willing to trade off one contingent commodity for another. In short, Expression (6.4) indicates that what the individual really cares about is the quantities of the contingent commodities, but the probabilities affect the valuation of these commodities.

From a purely theoretical point of view, the probabilities of the various states of nature can enter into the utility function in quite complex ways. Fortunately, there is a particularly simple case that is of great empirical relevance and practical importance. In this special case, the relative importance that an individual attaches to a given contingency is exactly proportional to the probability of that contingency occurring.[8] The utility of consumption in each state of the world is found and then weighted by the probability of that state of the world occurring to come up with an overall utility level:

$$U(c_1, c_2, \ldots, c_n; \rho_1, \rho_2, \ldots, \rho_n) = \rho_1 \times u(c_1) + \rho_2 \times u(c_2) + \ldots + \rho_n \times u(c_n). \tag{6.5}$$

von Neumann–Morgenstern utility function
A utility function where the utility associated with some uncertain event is the expected value of the utilities of each of the possible outcomes.

A utility function that takes this form is called a **von Neumann–Morgenstern (vN–M) utility function,** named after its originators, John von Neumann and Oskar Morgenstern. With a vN–M utility function, the utility associated with a gamble is just the expected value of the utilities of each of the outcomes. Suppose, for example, that you are offered the following gamble: A die is thrown. If a three comes up, you receive \$10; otherwise, you receive \$1. Suppose your preferences are represented by $u(10) = 18$ and $u(1) = 6$. What is the value (utility) of this *gamble* to you? Since the probability of winning \$10 is ⅙, and the probability of winning \$1 is ⅚, the value of the bet is simply the utility that it produces "on average," or

$$\tfrac{1}{6} \times u(\$10) + \tfrac{5}{6} \times u(\$1) = \tfrac{1}{6} \times 18 + \tfrac{5}{6} \times 6 = 8.$$

Suppose that someone with a vN–M utility function is confronted with several options, each of which involves some uncertainty. Which option does she choose? The value of each uncertain option is its expected utility. Hence, the option chosen will be the one with the highest expected utility. In short, the goal of an individual with a vN–M utility function is to maximize her expected utility.

It is crucial to understand that with a vN–M utility function, rational behavior calls for maximizing the expected value of utility, not the utility of the expected monetary value. To firm up your understanding of this distinction, let us assume that Melanie, whose problem is represented in Figure 6.21, has a vN–M utility function $u = \sqrt{c}$. Hence, to find the utility of each outcome, all we have to do is take the square root of the associated amount of consumption. What is her expected utility of going to law school? With a probability of 0.4, her income will be \$80,000, and hence her utility 282.8 ($= \sqrt{80{,}000}$). The fact that the utility associated with this particular terminal node is 282.8 is noted in Figure 6.22. Similarly, with probability of 0.6, her income is \$45,000 and her utility therefore 212.1. The expected utility of law school, U_{LAW}, is just $0.4 \times 282.8 + 0.6 \times 212.1 = 240.4$. Similar calculations for business school (also recorded in Figure 6.22) indicate that her utility is 346.4 with a probability of 0.2 and 212.1 with a probability of 0.8; hence, the expected utility of business school, U_{BUS}, is $0.2 \times 346.4 + 0.8 \times 212.1 = 239.0$. We conclude that Melanie will go to law school, because its expected utility is higher than that of business school. By the way, expected *income* with business school is higher by \$1,000. (You should verify this.) However, by assumption, Melanie cares about expected *utility*, not ex-

[8]The precise conditions under which preferences can be characterized this way are detailed in Kreps (1990, 72–81).

Figure 6.22

Comparing Expected Utilities

This individual chooses law school, because its expected utility exceeds that of business school.

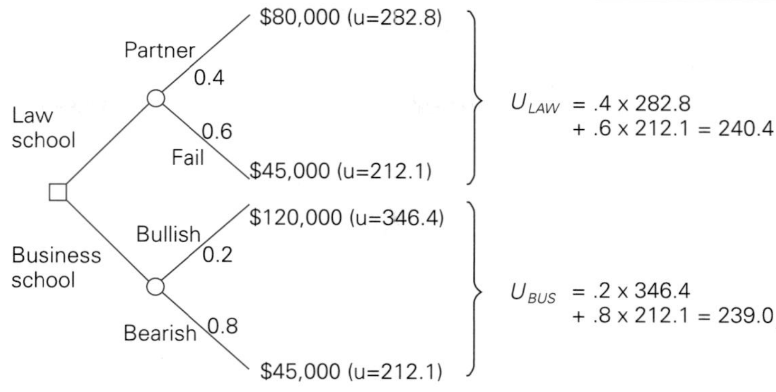

pected *income*, and hence chooses law school. Intuitively, Melanie perceives the business career to be so risky that she chooses law, even though on average business leads to a higher income.

More generally, this example shows how decision trees in conjunction with von Neumann–Morgenstern utility functions can be used to break up complex problems into simple components. Just follow these steps:

1. Sketch a decision tree to keep track of all of the outcomes. Each time a choice has to be made, draw a decision node with one branch for each alternative. Uncertainty is captured by having "Nature make the choice" at a chance node.
2. Evaluate the utility function to find the utility of the outcome at each terminal node.
3. Find the expected utility associated with each option.
4. Compare the expected utilities of the various options. Choose the one that has the highest expected utility. (PC 6.7)

6.7 PROGRESS CHECK

Sherman faces exactly the same choice between law school and business school as Melanie (see Figure 6.21). However, Sherman's utility function is $u = 1000\,c - c^2$, where c is consumption measured in ten thousands of dollars. (Thus, for example, if he goes into law, with probability of 0.4, his consumption is 8 and his utility is 7,936 = 8,000 − 64.) What option does Sherman choose?

Sequential Decisions

Our discussion of decision trees has assumed that the individual has only one choice to make—in the case of Melanie in Figure 6.22, whether to go to law school or business school. However, the real power and usefulness of decision trees come into play when we analyze situations in which multiple decisions must be made sequentially. Suppose, for example, that once Melanie is offered the partnership, she has to decide whether or not to accept it. (If Melanie turns down the partnership, she continues to earn $45,000.) The corresponding tree, drawn in Figure 6.23, merely adds to Figure 6.22 a choice node (at point *b*), with two branches, "accept" or "reject."

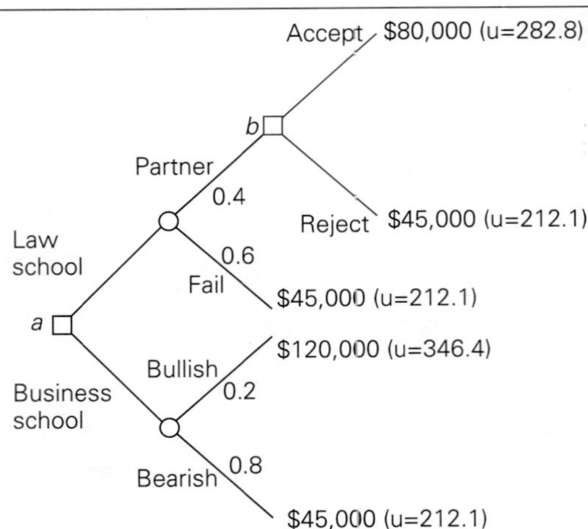

Figure 6.23

Decision Tree for a Sequential Decision

At choice node *b*, the individual has to decide whether to accept or reject a partnership if it is offered. To solve the problem, she uses backward induction—go to the end of the decision tree and work backward, choosing the optimal action at each step of the way.

How does this later decision affect Melanie's earlier choice of whether to go to law or business school? If she is going to turn down the partnership, then her income as a lawyer would be $45,000, and we know already that she would choose to go to business school. If she is always going to accept the partnership—conditional on it being offered—then, as we saw in our earlier analysis, her expected income as a lawyer would be $80,000. Moreover, we know that she would choose to go to law school. In short, Melanie's career choice depends on how she will act at decision node *b*. Now it is clear that if she ever gets to node *b*, the only decision that makes sense is for Melanie to accept the partnership. Therefore, she should go to law school.

This exercise might seem silly to you, because it's obvious that, given the assumption that all she cares about is her consumption level, Melanie will accept the partnership if it is offered. However, our discussion of Figure 6.23 illustrates an important point—to solve a problem with sequential decisions, start at the terminal nodes and work backward. At each step along the way, choose the optimal action for continuing. In the present example, to know what Melanie will do at node *a*, we first need to calculate what she will do at node *b*. This process is known as *backward induction.*

The power of backward induction is that it allows us to take a complicated sequential decision-making problem and break it down into little pieces that are easy to deal with. (For an application, see Discussion Question 6.13.)

Applying von Neumann–Morgenstern Utility Functions: The Value of Information

A recurrent theme in this chapter is that people generally prefer less uncertainty to more, and will therefore consider taking actions to reduce uncertainty. One way to reduce uncertainty is to acquire information. Before purchasing a Toyota, you may buy and read *Consumer Reports* magazine to find out about that auto's repair record. However, like any other good, information is costly. For example, anxious movie executives pay thousands of dollars to firms that provide information "on everything from which films moviegoers plan to see to which movie ads are most effective" (Turner and Emshwiller 1993, A1). In this section we use

Figure 6.24

The Value of Information

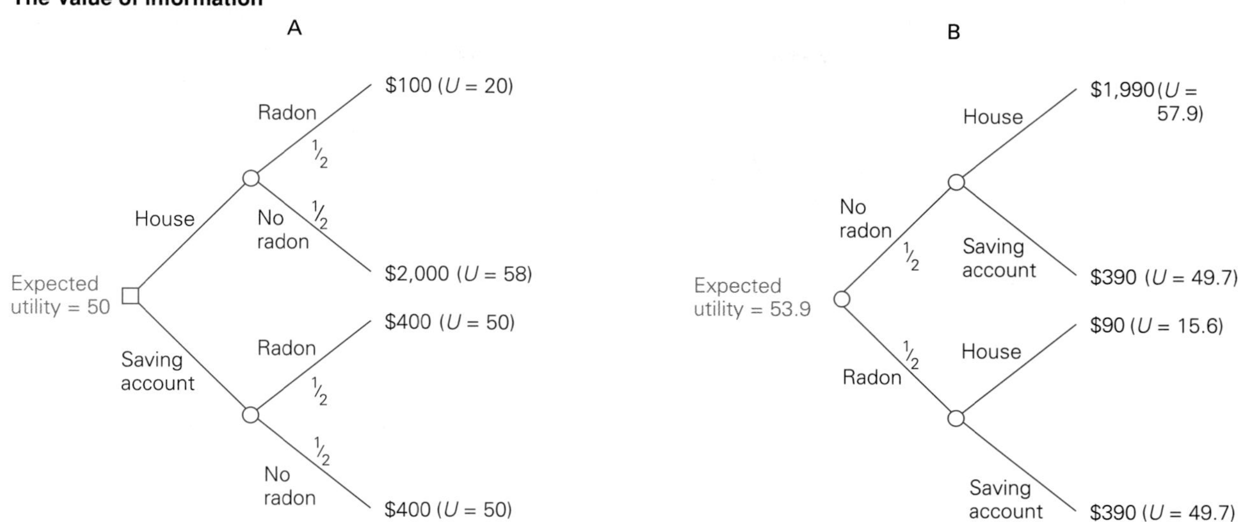

Panel A shows that expected utility without the radon test is 50. However, a $10 radon test raises expected utility to 53.9. Hence, the individual purchases the radon test.

vN–M utility functions to think about how much people are willing to pay for information.

Consider Ashley, who has some money to invest. One option is to set up a savings account; the other is to buy a house and rent it out to tenants. The savings account pays $400 per month for sure. The return on the house is uncertain because there is a 50 percent chance that it is contaminated by radon gas. If the house is free of radon, Ashley can rent it for $2,000 per month. But if radon is present, all he can get is $100 per month.

Ashley's situation is summarized in the decision tree in Panel A of Figure 6.24. At the decision node, he can either buy the house or deposit the money into a savings account. If he follows the housing path, the branches from the chance node show the payoffs depending on whether or not radon is found. If he goes down the savings account path, the payoff is $400 whether or not radon is present.

To predict Ashley's choice, we must know his utility function. Let us assume that $u = 60 - 4{,}000/c$. To find the utility of each outcome, divide the associated amount of consumption into 4,000 and subtract the result from 60. The utility figures are also noted at the terminal nodes. The expected utility of purchasing the house is $\frac{1}{2} \times 20 + \frac{1}{2} \times 58 = 39$; the expected utility of the savings account is 50, because it produces that value in every state of the world. Hence, if he seeks to maximize expected utility, Ashley chooses the savings account and he has an expected utility of 50.

Now suppose that a radon testing firm opens up, and the firm can tell him with certainty whether or not radon is present. The fee for the radon test is $10. Would Ashley be willing to pay this amount? Panel B in Figure 6.24 shows Ashley's situation *prior* to the radon inspection. As the decision tree indicates, with a probability of 0.5, the inspector will tell Ashley that he has no radon. In this event, Ashley will buy the house and have a consumption level of \$1,990 (\$2,000 minus the \$10 fee). His utility is therefore 57.9 (= 60 −4,000/1,990). On the other hand, with a probability of 0.5, the inspector will report a radon problem. In this case, Ashley will put his money in the savings account, receiving \$390 after the test fee and having a utility of 49.7. In short, if he buys the radon inspection, he will have 57.9 utils with a probability of ½, and 49.7 utils with a probability of ½, so his expected utility is 53.9 utils.

6.8 PROGRESS CHECK

Suppose that the house rents for \$450 per month in the event that radon is present. Assuming that everything else in the problem stays the same, predict Ashley's course of action if he purchases the radon test.

Now recall from Panel A that without the inspection Ashley's expected utility is 50 utils. Because Ashley's expected utility is higher if he purchases the radon test for \$10, we predict that he will do so. (PC 6.8)

If you answered the Progress Check correctly, you found that if the house rents for \$450 per month when radon is present, then Ashley should purchase the house no matter what the report says. How much should Ashley be willing to pay for the radon test? The answer is nothing. Knowing whether radon is present has no effect on Ashley's expected utility—Ashley buys the house no matter what the test says, and his expected utility is the same with or without the information. This conclusion always holds: *When a particular piece of information has no effect on an individual's actions, it has no economic value to that individual.*

More generally, our theory suggests that people will be willing to pay for information when the possession of that information raises their expected utility. The amount that they are willing to pay depends on: (*a*) the particular payoffs and the associated probabilities, and (*b*) the individual's utility function. It is sometimes claimed that we are living in an "age of information." Economic theory helps us understand why information is valuable.

SECTION RECAP

A person's utility depends on commodities available in various states of the world and the probabilities of each state of the world. In general, the various probabilities can enter into the utility function in a very complicated fashion. This section has discussed a simple and important special case—the von Neumann–Morgenstern utility function—in which the probability of each state of the world is multiplied by the utility associated with that state of the world. A person with this utility function chooses whatever option maximizes her expected utility. When used in conjunction with decision trees, this is a powerful tool for analyzing problems with many options. Sketching a decision tree allows one to see the payoffs associated with each choice. By comparing the expected utility of each option, the individual can determine her optimal strategy.

SUMMARY

If people have to make decisions in the presence of uncertainty, does rational decision making go out the window? The answer provided in this chapter is an emphatic no. The standard tools for analyzing rational choice can be modified to accommodate uncertainty.

- A person in an uncertain environment is choosing among contingent commodities—commodities whose value depends on the eventual outcome (state of the world). As with ordinary commodities, people have preferences for contingent commodities that can be represented by an indifference map.
- The slope of the budget constraint between two contingent commodities depends on the payoff associated with each state of the world. The curvature of the indifference curves depends on

whether the individual is risk averse, risk loving, or risk neutral.

- A risk-averse person will not accept an actuarially fair bet.
- Risk-averse people purchase insurance in order to spread consumption more evenly across states of the world. When risk-averse people are allowed to purchase fair insurance, they will insure themselves fully in the sense that their consumption is the same in every state of the world.
- The amount of insurance demanded depends on the premium and on the probability that the insurable event will occur.
- People with von Neumann–Morgenstern utility functions seek to maximize the expected value of their utility. The assumption of expected utility maximization, together with decision trees, can be used to break up complicated decisions into simple components that can be readily solved.

DISCUSSION QUESTIONS

6.1 Jonathan has an income of $60. He is offered the following bet: A die is thrown. If a one comes up, Jonathan loses $1. If a two, three, four, five, or six comes up, he wins $3. Jonathan can take either side of the bet and he is risk averse.

a. What are the contingent commodities in this problem?
b. Sketch the budget constraint.
c. Sketch the indifference curves.
d. Show on a diagram the amount that Jonathan bets.
e. Sketch the fair odds line associated with this bet. How much does he bet if the odds are fair?

6.2 The *certainty equivalent* of a random outcome is the amount of income received for certain that an individual considers equivalent to the random outcome. Consider Matthew, a risk-averse individual, who is considering entering a job-training program. After the program, Matthew's earnings will be $20,000 with a probability of ½ or $10,000 with a probability of ½. Sketch Matthew's indifference map. On your diagram, show the certainty equivalent of the job-training program. Prove that the certainty equivalent of the program is less than its expected monetary value. (Hint: Sketch the fair odds line through the bundle associated with the program.)

6.3 Jack and Jill, who are risk averse, have the same endowment point and both face a lawsuit with the same probability.

a. Show that both individuals purchase the same amount of fair insurance.
b. Show that both need not purchase the same amount of unfair insurance.

6.4 A risk-averse white-collar employee is considering whether to embezzle. The probability of being caught is ρ. If caught embezzling, the employee has to pay a fine of ψ for each dollar he has stolen.

a. Show graphically how the equilibrium amount of embezzlement depends upon the values of ρ and ψ.
b. Suppose ψ is $3.00. What is the lowest value of ρ that will guarantee that the employee will not embezzle?

6.5 In recent years, so-called "viatical settlements" have been growing among AIDS patients. Under a viatical settlement, an individual names some company the sole beneficiary of his or her life-insurance policy. In return, the company provides the individual with a lump-sum payment of cash. For example, a 43-year-old AIDS patient named a company the sole beneficiary of his $140,000 life insurance policy; in exchange, the company paid him $98,000 cash (Miller 1994, 54).

Assume that the owners of the company in question are risk neutral. Write an equation that indicates whether or not the company is willing to enter into a viatical settlement with a particular individual. (Hint: You will need to take advantage of present value analysis from the previous chapter.)

6.6 Samuel Johnson said, "He is no wise man that will quit a certainty for an uncertainty." Use the jargon developed in this chapter to restate this maxim more precisely.

6.7 When Hurricane Andrew hit Florida in 1992, it cost insurance companies a record $16.5 billion. In the aftermath of the storm, several insurance companies stopped selling homeowners' insurance to new customers with homes on beachfront property along the East Coast. Use contingent commodity analysis to show how the inability to purchase insurance affects the welfare of an individual with beachfront property.

6.8 Lynne's income is $2,000 and she is risk averse. The probability of someone slipping on her stairs is ⅛. If this happens, she will be sued for $1,000 and will have to pay that amount. She can purchase insurance at a price of \$.30 per dollar of coverage. Show how the equilibrium amount of insurance coverage is determined. Show how it changes if the probability of someone slipping increases to ¼, but the premium is unchanged.

6.9 If Ben's house burns down, he loses everything (his consumption is zero). Below you see Ben's indifference map between consumption if there is no fire and consumption if there is a fire.

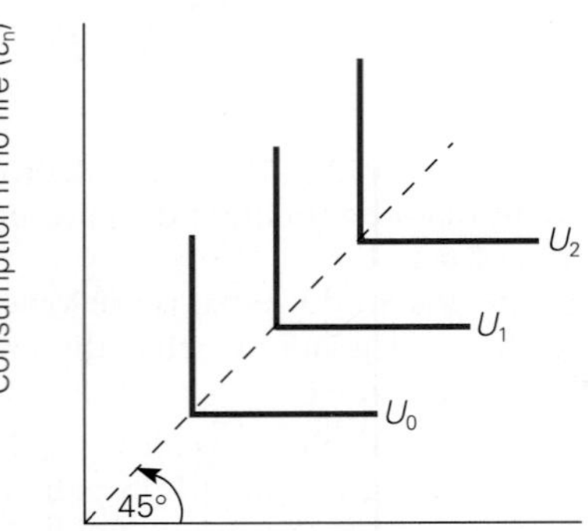

Prove that Ben will fully insure even if the premium for fire insurance is "unfair." How would you characterize Ben's preferences for risk taking?

6.10 Jen has narrowed her employment decision down to two choices. One job is very safe (there is no chance of getting hurt on the job), while the other job is rather dangerous (there is a 20 percent chance of being seriously injured). The safe job pays \$10,000. The risky job pays \$*R*.

a. Set up a decision tree illustrating Jen's problem.

b. Suppose that Jen's preferences can be represented by a von Neumann–Morgenstern utility function of the form $u = 20 - 20{,}000/c - \delta$, where c is her consumption in dollars and $\delta = 1$ if she is injured and 0 if she is not injured. (1) What is the expected utility of the safe job? (2) What is the expected utility of the dangerous job? (Write a formula that depends on R.) (3) What is the minimum value of R that would induce Jen to take the dangerous job? What is the interpretation of the difference between this value of R and \$10,000?

c. Suppose now that the safe job pays \$20,000. What is the minimum level of R that will attract Jen to the dangerous job? What is the interpretation of the difference between this value of R and \$20,000?

d. Interpret the differences between your answers to the last questions in parts *b* and *c*.

6.11 Sarah has a von Neumann–Morgenstern utility function $u = 500 - 100/c$, where c is her consumption in thousands of dollars. If Sarah becomes a clerk, she will make \$30 thousand per year for certain. If she becomes a pediatrician, she will make \$60 thousand if there is a baby boom and \$20 thousand if there is a baby bust. The probability of a baby boom is ¾; of a baby bust, ¼. A consulting firm has prepared demographic projections that indicate which event will occur. What is the most that she should be willing to pay for this information?

6.12 Alexander has a von Neumann–Morgenstern utility function $u(c)$. He is confronted with a lottery that pays X with probability ρ, and Y with probability $(1 - \rho)$. He is indifferent between this lottery and receiving Z for certain.

a. Write an equation that relates $u(X)$, $u(Y)$, and $u(Z)$.

b. Now suppose that Darius's utility function is $a + b \times u(c)$, where a is any number, b is any positive number, and $u(c)$ is the same function as Alexander's. Prove that Darius will rank the alternatives X, Y, and Z in exactly the same way as Alexander. [You have just demonstrated that a vN–M utility function can be "transformed affinely" without affecting the outcome. That is, maximizing the expected value of $u(c)$ and of $a + b \times u(c)$ produces exactly the same result.]

6.13 In recent years, several law and accounting firms have lost large lawsuits and the partners have been liable for paying the damages. The fear of such large income losses has actually deterred some individuals from accepting partnership offers. Consider again the situation of Melanie, depicted in Figure 6.23. Suppose that she believes that if she becomes a partner, there is a 10 percent chance that she will be sued and have to pay damages of \$30,000, leaving her with an income of \$50,000. Under these circumstances, will she go to law school or business school?

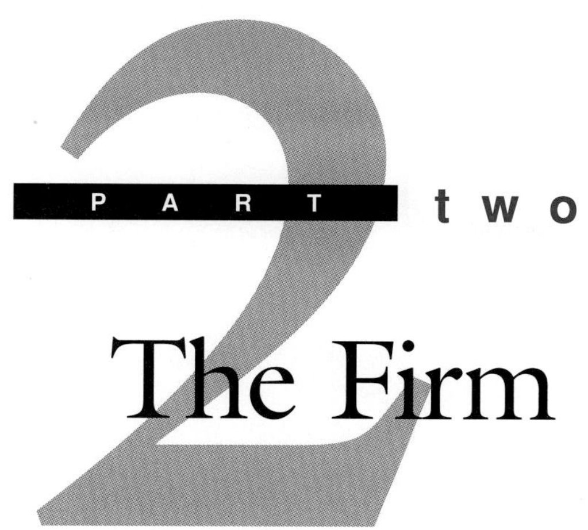

PART two

The Firm

In Chapters 2 through 6, we developed a theory of household behavior. This theory allows us to summarize the behavior of price-taking households in terms of demand curves in product markets, and supply curves in factor markets. These curves tell us what trades households will wish to make for a *given* set of prices. But what prices will prevail? We cannot answer this question until we have a complete story of how markets work. The economic theory of the household tells only half of the story in any given market; to complete the story, we must begin by asking from whom consumers buy goods and to whom do they sell their services? When we look at the circular flow diagram, we see that the answer is firms. Firms are suppliers in product markets and demanders in factor markets.

To tell the whole story of how markets work, we need to develop a theory of the firm. Just as the theory of the household is based on the assumption that households seek to maximize their utility, the theory of the firm is based on the assumption that firms seek to maximize their profits. Chapter 7 presents a careful discussion of the economic notion of profit, and it lays out some of the basic rules of behavior that are valid for *any* profit-maximizing firm.

Among other things, these rules for profit maximization show that a firm must know about certain properties of its production costs. Just as we used indifference curve analysis to go behind household demand and supply curves, we will use a similar type of analysis to go behind the firm's cost curves. Chapter 8 shows how to represent a firm's production technology and discusses important properties of this technology. Chapter 9 then shows how a firm's costs are related to its underlying production technology. As part of calculating a firm's cost level, we will see how a profit-maximizing firm chooses its production technique.

CHAPTER 7

The Firm and Its Goals

> ***The smell of profit is clean and sweet, whatever the source.***
>
> —Juvenal

In 1928, William Dreyer and Joseph Edy decided to start their own company. Since Dreyer was Professor of Advanced Ice Cream Manufacturing at the University of California at Davis, it is not surprising that the two entrepreneurs chose to sell ice cream. But they also faced many other decisions, including what kind of ice cream to make, how much to produce, where to sell it, and how to let the public know about their new ice cream. Dreyer and Edy made these decisions, and their company, Dreyer's Grand Ice Cream, went on to achieve such successes as inventing Rocky Road ice cream. But even with current revenues exceeding half a billion dollars, the company still has to confront the same issues.

In this chapter, we lay the foundation for the *theory of the firm*. This theory allows us to predict how Dreyer's Grand Ice Cream, or any other company, will make the myriad of choices that it faces every day.

The theory of the household taught us that in order to predict an individual's behavior, one must know his or her objectives. Similarly, we cannot develop predictions of firm behavior unless we know the goals of the firm's decision makers. The theory of the firm is based on the assumption that businesses seek to maximize profit. An important goal of this chapter is to define carefully what the term *profit* means and to argue that the profit maximization assumption is a reasonable one.

Knowing the firm's objective allows us to develop specific predictions for firm behavior. This chapter develops some very general rules for how a firm will choose its output level. You might recall from other courses in economics that there are various types of firms, such as "competitive" firms and "monopolistic" firms. We will have more to say about specific types of industries in subsequent chapters. In this chapter, we present results about firm behavior that are completely general, in the sense that *they apply to any firm regardless of the type of market in which it operates.* By developing these general rules here, we will be ready to apply them to a variety of market settings later.

7.1 WHAT DO FIRMS DO?

Our first task is to specify the behavior we are trying to explain—What do firms do? Consider the choices confronting the current management of Dreyer's Grand Ice Cream. There are several decisions that they, like the managers at any other firm, have to make.

1. *What should the firm produce?* The managers have to choose what type of product to sell. Should Dreyer's Grand Ice Cream sell high-fat, premium ice cream, or low-fat ice milk? Or maybe they should forget about ice cream and instead bake gourmet chocolate chip cookies.
2. *How should the firm produce its output?* A given commodity often can be produced in many different ways. Should Dreyer's ice cream be mixed and packed by people, or by machines? The managers must choose the "right" combination of inputs to make their product.
3. *How much should the firm sell, and at what price?* Should Dreyer's sell 10,000 gallons of ice cream each month, or 10 million? And should the price be $1 per pint, or $5?
4. *How should the firm promote its product?* Consumers sometimes have to be told about a product before they will buy it. The seller can take actions such as advertising to tell consumers about its product. If Dreyer's can increase its sales by advertising, how much should it do? In 1994, the firm spent $40 million promoting its products to consumers.

The answers to these four questions tell us how the firm acts, both as a supplier in product markets and as a demander in input markets. Hence, the goal of the theory of the firm is to predict how a firm answers these questions.

WHY DO FIRMS EXIST?

Before we predict firm behavior, it is worth giving some thought to why firms do anything at all. That is, why do firms exist? To answer this question, we first need to answer a more basic one: What is a firm? This question turns out to be surprisingly difficult to answer, and gives us some insight into the purpose of firms. One definition is that a firm is any organization that buys and sells goods and services. By that definition, any one of us might be considered to be a firm. We usually think of a firm as a more complex entity, with at least three types of members: (1) there are workers, people who are largely paid fixed wages and are told what to do; (2) there are managers who are responsible for making the decisions we have been talking about and who also monitor the workers to make sure that they are contributing to the welfare of the firm; (3) there are owners who fund the firm's investments and bear the financial risks associated with the business.

Why do firms exist in this form? In principle, all production could instead be organized in a series of single-person units who deal with each other solely through market transactions. The theory of **transaction costs** predicts that economic exchange will tend to be organized in ways that minimize the costs of those exchanges (Coase 1937). Economists have identified several advantages that firms have over market-based transactions.

transaction costs
The costs of conducting an economic exchange between two parties.

These benefits revolve around the fact that any contract will be incomplete. That is, there will be some chance of something happening that the contract does not cover. This happens both because it is impossible to foresee everything that can happen and because—even if everything were foreseeable—it would be prohibitively costly to have a contract that covered all possible bases.

Now, consider what happens when an uncovered contingency arises. Under a market-based relationship, the parties will bargain with each other, with each side seeking to gain advantage in the new situation. The bargaining process itself may be costly and waste time, or even lead to a breakdown in cooperation. Moreover, as Williamson (1985) has emphasized, a party may be unwilling to invest in a relationship today (say, by buying specialized machinery or going through specialized training), knowing that it may be taken advantage of in bargaining in the future. When a transaction takes place within a firm, one party has residual control rights. That is, there is one party who gets to decide what happens when an unforeseen contingency arises. Having this party make decisions can avoid costly and inefficient bargaining and thus economize on transaction costs. Moreover, this party can create an economic environment in which the other parties feel that they can make investments without worrying about later being taken advantage of. For these reasons, we expect to see large-scale production that requires extensive cooperation among, and the coordination of, many people to take place within a firm, rather than through a market.

It is important to recognize that there are also costs associated with firms. One major source of costs is that firms' employees may not have incentives to do what the owners would like, and thus the employees either act wastefully or the owners have to spend resources to realign the employees' incentives.[1] These costs explain why many transactions take place in markets.

ECONOMIC PROFIT

When we looked at household decision making, we assumed that the household's goal was to maximize its utility. Similarly, we assume that *the firm's goal is to maximize its "economic profit."*

We can get a preliminary idea of the meaning of economic profit by considering the circular flow again. Loosely speaking, profit is the difference between the amount of money that the firm takes in and the amount of money that it pays out. As shown in Figure 7.1, money flows into the firm in the product market as consumers pay for their purchases of the firm's output. The sum of the payments that the firm receives from the sale of its output is known as the firm's **total revenue.** Of course, money also flows out of the firm because it has to pay for the inputs used to produce output. These inputs (also referred to as *factors*) are purchased in factor markets. The firm's total expenditures on inputs are called the firm's **total economic cost.** The firm's **economic profit** is simply the difference between the revenues that it takes in and the costs that it pays out:

total revenue
The sum of the payments that the firm receives from the sale of its output.

total economic cost
The firm's total expenditures on the inputs used to produce output, where expenditures are measured in terms of opportunity cost.

economic profit
Total revenue minus total economic cost.

$$\textit{Economic profit} = \textit{Total revenue} - \textit{Total economic cost}. \qquad (7.1)$$

Economic profit is the income that is left over for the owners of the firm after they pay for the factors of production that they utilize.

[1]Some of these issues are discussed later in the present chapter and in Chapter 17.

Figure 7.1

The Circular Flow

The circular flow diagram illustrates the fact that firms are suppliers in product markets and demanders in factor markets.

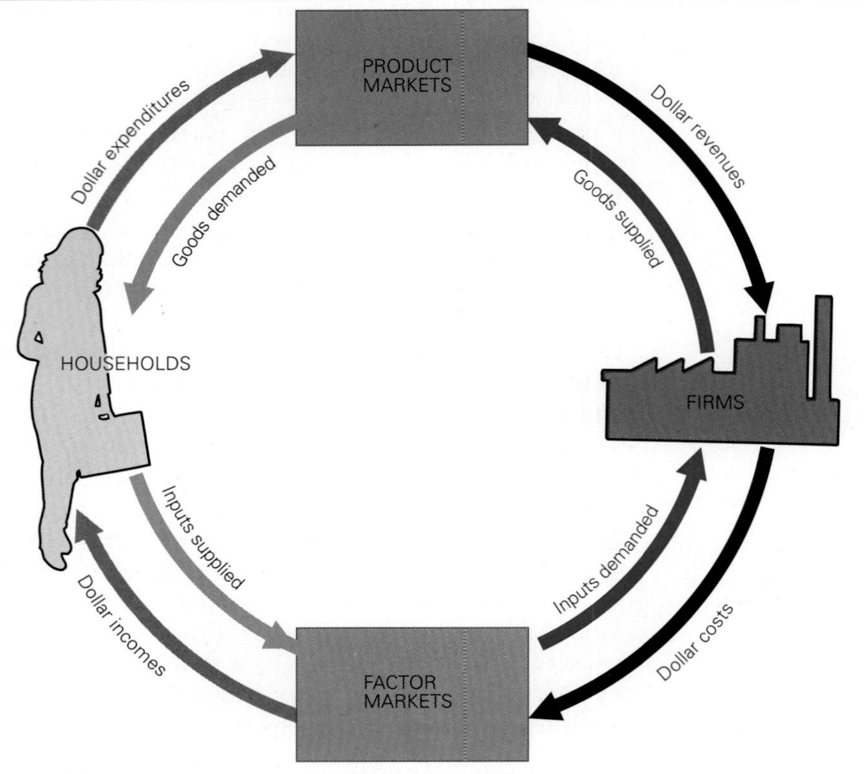

While the notion of economic profit is fairly intuitive, we have to be very careful about measuring it. In particular, when economists talk about total economic cost, they often are not referring to what an accountant (or any other noneconomist, for that matter) would call total cost. To see some of the differences between the economic and accounting definitions, let's look at the books of a hypothetical competitor of Dreyer's, the Whetter's Ice Cream Company. Jim owns Whetter's, and last year he spent 2,000 hours running his business. As shown in Table 7.1, he also hired an assistant, purchased ingredients such as milk and sugar, and rented an office. What are the firm's total economic costs for the past year? An economist and an accountant would agree that the $73,000 wages paid to the factory workers, the $24,000 rent for the factory space, and the $47,000 expense for ingredients all are costs. These expenditures add up to $144,000. Are the firm's total costs $144,000? While an accountant might answer yes, an economist would answer with an emphatic no.

The economist would object to this calculation because it fails to account for the cost of Jim's time. In effect, Jim hires himself to work for his company, and the implicit payments to him for this labor should be counted as costs to the firm. But what wage should be used to calculate this cost? The proper measure of the cost of Jim's labor is its *opportunity cost*—the value of this labor in its best alternative use. Suppose that if he were not an ice-cream magnate, Jim would earn an annual salary of $30,000 working as a pastry chef at a local restaurant. When he works for himself, Jim is implicitly buying $30,000 of his own labor. Because Jim

Table 7.1

Expenses Incurred by Whetter's for One Year of Operation

Factory workers' wages		$ 73,000
Factory rent		24,000
Cost of ingredients		
Milk	$36,000	
Sugar	10,000	
Flavors	1,000	47,000
Total		$144,000

imputed cost
The opportunity cost incurred when the owner of a factor employs the factor in one use rather than in its best alternative use.

does not literally pay himself $30,000 for his services, these implicit expenditures are said to be an **imputed cost.** Taking this imputed cost into account, Whetter's total economic cost is $144,000 + $30,000 = $174,000, not merely the $144,000 accounting cost.

The economic treatment of cost can be summarized as follows: *in order to measure economic profit, total economic cost must be calculated as the sum of the opportunity cost of all of the inputs.* For inputs such as the assistant's salary and the ingredients, the opportunity cost is simply the firm's expenditures for those inputs. For implicit expenditures such as the owner's time, the opportunity cost must be imputed by determining the input's value in its best alternative use.

To firm up your understanding of imputed costs, suppose that instead of renting factory space, Jim is considering moving into a building that he already owns. Would Whetter's total economic cost fall by $24,000 if Jim made this move? The answer depends on the opportunity cost of the space. If Jim could have rented the space to someone else for $24,000 per year, then he forgoes this rent when he uses the factory space for his ice-cream company. Therefore, the opportunity cost of using the space himself, the imputed rent, is $24,000. On the other hand, if Jim could have gotten only $10,000 per year renting the space to someone else, then the imputed rent "charged" the ice cream company would be $10,000.

The two examples that we have looked at so far suggest that accounting cost always understates economic cost. Unfortunately, life is not so simple. Sometimes, accounting cost exceeds economic cost. Suppose, for example, that four years ago Jim signed a five-year lease on a custom-made ice-cream blending machine, so that the lease has one more year to run. Moreover, suppose that this lease specifies that Jim must pay $1,000 per year for the machine. What is the cost of using this machine for one more year? An accountant would answer that the cost of the machine for the next year is $1,000. As economists, however, we cannot say what the cost is by looking at the lease agreement alone. Why not? Because the firm is committed to paying the $1,000, *whether or not it uses the machine.* Therefore, $1,000 is not a measure of the opportunity cost to the firm of having the machine in use, *given that it already has signed the lease.* Does this mean that the opportunity cost of the machine is $0? We cannot say until we determine the best alternative use of the machine. Suppose that if Jim did not use the machine in his

7.1 PROGRESS CHECK

What would the opportunity cost of the blending machine be if Jim could not sublet it? How much of the lease payment would be a sunk expenditure? What would the opportunity cost of the machine be if Jim could sublet it for $1,200?

business, he could sublease it to another company for $600. Then the opportunity cost of using the machine in his ice-cream company is the $600 in forgone sublease income, not the $1,000 lease payment. The $400 difference between the lease price and the opportunity cost is a **sunk expenditure,** so-called because once it has been spent, there is no way to get it back. Sunk expenditures are sometimes referred to as *sunk costs.* We will avoid this terminology because, while a sunk expenditure is a cost in the everyday sense of the word "cost," *a sunk expenditure is not an economic cost.* The $600 the firm could receive by putting the machine into an alternative use is an opportunity cost. The $400 sunk expenditure is not an economic cost because the firm pays that amount no matter what it does. (PC 7.1)

sunk expenditure
A factor expenditure that, once made, cannot be recovered.

USER COST OF CAPITAL

Now, let's suppose that Jim *purchases* the ice-cream packing machine. Assume that the purchase price is $8,000 and the machine lasts for exactly one year, at the end of which it can be sold for scrap at a price of $1,500. No other ice-cream company has any interest in buying the machine; during the course of the year, the machine can be sold only for scrap if Whetter decides to get rid of it. What is the cost of using the packing machine during the year? The answer depends on the exact decision that the manager is facing.

Begin by supposing that Jim is looking ahead and has not yet bought the machine. If he goes ahead and purchases the machine, he will have only $1,500 dollars at the end of the year. So the opportunity cost of the machine is at least $6,500 (= $8,000 − $1,500). This difference between the purchase price and the resale price is the **depreciation** of the machine. But the cost of the machine involves more than just depreciation. By purchasing the machine, Jim loses the use of the $8,000. Suppose that best alternative use of the money is a one-year Treasury bill paying 7 percent interest. Then Jim forgoes $560 (= .07 × $8,000) in interest by purchasing the machine. The total economic cost of purchasing the packing machine, also known as the **user cost of capital,** is the sum of the economic depreciation and forgone interest: $7,060 (= $6,500 + $560).[2]

depreciation
The fall in the value of an asset over a defined period of time.

user cost of capital
The opportunity cost that an owner incurs as a consequence of owning and using an asset.

Now, let's consider a slightly different situation. Suppose Jim has already purchased the packing machine and is deciding whether he should use it to produce ice cream. What is the user cost of the machine in this instance? Whether Jim sells the machine now or at the end of the year, he will receive $1,500 for its scrap value; so there is no depreciation. Does this mean use of the machine is free? No, we still have to account for the forgone interest. If Jim could have earned 7 percent interest, then the user cost of the machine is the $105 (= .07 × $1,500) forgone interest.

Once the packing machine has been purchased, the opportunity cost of using it to produce ice cream falls from $7,030 to $105. The reason is that the $6,500 difference between the purchase price and the resale price is not an opportunity

[2]To define the user cost of capital algebraically, consider a machine whose value is p_n now. If the price of the machine falls to p_o after one year of use, the amount of depreciation is $(p_n - p_o)$. Letting i denote the annual interest rate at which the firm can borrow and lend, the forgone interest is $i \times p_n$. Summing these two effects, the user cost of capital is: $(p_n - p_o) + i \times p_n$. The user cost of capital often is expressed as a *rate.* To do this, we divide by the original price of the machine, p_n, which yields a user cost of capital of $r = (p_n - p_o)/p_n + i = \delta + i$, where δ is the depreciation rate.

cost because Jim has purchased the machine. Rather, it is a sunk expenditure—once this expenditure has been made, there is no way that Jim can get the money back. Hence, the \$6,500 is not depreciation in this setting, and neither is there any forgone interest on the \$6,500. That is why $\$7{,}030 - \$105 = \$6{,}925 = \$6{,}500 + .07 \times \$6{,}500$.

This is just another example of the logic that has governed our entire discussion of economic cost—the opportunity cost of an input at a given time is equal to what the firm can get for this input in its best alternative use. (PC 7.2)

> **7.2 PROGRESS CHECK**
>
> What would the economic cost of the machine be if it were worthless to anyone but Jim? How does your answer depend on whether or not Jim has already purchased the machine? Would the economic cost of the machine be \$0 if the machine could be sold for \$8,000 after one year?

APPLE COMPUTER FORGETS HOW TO PRICE MEMORY

While the economic definition of costs may at first seem strange to you, the failure to use economic measures of cost can lead to problems. Apple Computer found this out the hard way. Dynamic random access memory chips (DRAMs) are an important component of personal computers, and their price fluctuates substantially. In August 1988, Apple ordered millions of 1 megabit DRAMs at a price of \$38 per chip (Schlender 1989, A6). Before Apple could use up its inventory of chips, the price fell substantially—to \$23 per chip by January 1989.

The cost of chips was an important component of the cost of the overall personal computer—there were 8 such chips in a Macintosh with one megabyte of memory, and 32 chips in a machine with four megabytes. Apple wanted to base the price of its machines on the cost of the chips. But which cost should they have used: The price they paid? Or the current market price? The notion of opportunity cost gives a clear answer. The economic cost of the chips was \$23 per chip—if Apple did not use the chips for its own machines, the price at which the chips could be sold to other computer companies (the best alternative use) was the then-current market price. Viewed another way, every time Apple used some of its chips in inventory, they would have to buy that many more new ones—at the new price—once the inventory was depleted. Either way you look at it, the economic cost was the current market price, not the price that Apple had paid in the past.

The executives at Apple did not use the economic measure of cost. Instead, they based their pricing decisions on the *historical cost*—the original purchase price of \$38 per chip. As a result of this pricing decision, Apple memory was very expensive. Consumers responded by purchasing stripped-down models of the Macintosh with little memory on them. They then bought add-on memory cards from other manufacturers who were using the correct, lower cost to determine their prices. As a result of its failure to use economic cost, Apple's profit plummeted and they were stuck with millions of unsold chips.

We close this example with an observation that should motivate you to study harder. After the memory debacle, the person primarily responsible for the pricing decision was reassigned to a job with less responsibility. Apple denied that her failure to apply economic reasoning was the reason for the reassignment, but the circumstantial evidence suggests otherwise.

SECTION RECAP

The theory of the firm is based on the assumption that firms act to maximize *economic* profit. Economic profit is the difference between revenue and economic cost. Economic cost is measured as opportunity cost—the value of an input in its best alternative use. This notion of cost may at first seem unintuitive, but consistent use of opportunity cost ensures that the firm earns the greatest return possible on its assets.

7.2 THE FIRM AS SUPPLIER: THE PROFIT-MAXIMIZING LEVEL OF OUTPUT

Now that we know how to measure profit, we can explore how the firm maximizes it. In reality, a firm may make its decisions about advertising, input levels, and output levels simultaneously, and the choices clearly are interrelated. It is useful, however, to simplify our analysis by initially examining the decisions separately. We begin with the choice of output level.

Suppose the Whetter's Ice Cream Company has decided to produce high-fat ice cream, and must choose how many gallons to sell. The firm wants to find the output level at which profit is greatest. Recall from Equation (7.1) that profit is the difference between total revenue and total economic cost. Hence, profit depends on revenue and cost at each output level. Let's look at each of these two components of profit in more detail.

TOTAL REVENUE CURVE

As noted above, the firm's total revenue is the amount of money that it receives from the sale of its output. For a firm that sells all of its output at the same price, the firm's total revenue is equal to the number of units of output sold times the price per unit. For example, if Whetter's sells 1 thousand gallons of ice cream at a price of $6 per gallon, then its total revenue is $6,000.

The fact that the firm's total revenue is equal to the number of units of output sold times the price per unit tells us that revenue depends on the output level both directly and indirectly—directly because the more output the firm sells at a given price, the higher are its revenues; indirectly through its effect on price, because the highest price at which the firm can sell its output may depend on the amount of output the firm is selling.

How does the price at which a firm can sell its output depend on the quantity being sold? From the theory of household choice, we already know that the market demand curve summarizes the relationship between the quantity of a good that consumers are willing to buy and the price of the good. The *market* demand curve, however, is not what we need for figuring the price that *this firm* can get for its output. The market demand curve tells us how much output can be sold in total by *all* of the firms in the industry at a given price. For our purposes here, we need a **firm-specific demand curve,** which is a schedule showing the quantity of this single firm's output that is demanded at any price that this firm charges.

firm-specific demand curve
A schedule showing the quantity of a single firm's output demanded for any price charged by that particular firm.

Suppose that the marketing department at Whetter's has observed the relationship between price and output depicted in Table 7.2. This table indicates that if the firm wants to sell a lot of output, then it has to set a low price. Figure 7.2 graphs this firm-specific demand curve, where it is labeled *D*. This graph holds many things constant in the background, some chosen by the firm (e.g., the product's quality and the amount of advertising) and some not (e.g., consumer

Table 7.2

The Demand Curve Faced by Whetter's

The marketing department at Whetter's has found that the relationship between price and quantity is as given here. These data summarize the firm-specific demand curve that Whetter's faces.

Quantity (000 gallons per month)	Price (per gallon)
1	$6.00
2	5.67
3	5.33
4	5.00
5	4.67
6	4.33
7	4.00
8	3.67
9	3.33

Figure 7.2

From Demand to Total Revenue

If the firm wishes to sell 4,000 gallons of ice cream per month, then the highest price it can charge is $5 per gallon. Total revenue is equal to the quantity times the price. When the firm sells 4,000 gallons per month, its total revenue is 4,000 gallons per month times $5 per gallon, or $20,000 per month (the shaded area of Figure 7.2).

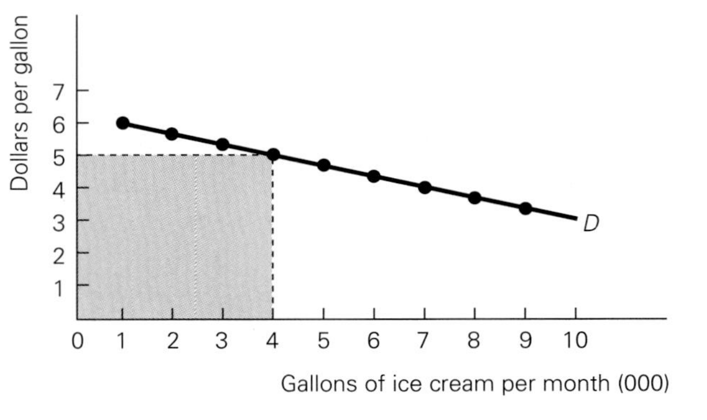

income and the prices of other goods). Because the firm is trying to find the profit-maximizing output level, our interest here is on how the price the firm receives for its output changes as the firm changes its output level, *ceteris paribus.*

Now that we know the demand curve facing Whetter's Ice Cream Company, how does it help us find total revenue? Usually, we use a demand curve to tell us the quantity demanded at a given price. Here, we want to ask the question in the other direction: What is the highest price that the firm can charge and still be able to sell 4 thousand gallons of ice cream per month? As we saw in Chapter 3, we can use the demand curve to answer this question. The demand curve in Figure 7.2, tells us that at any price higher than $5, fewer than 4 thousand gallons of ice cream per month would be demanded, and the firm would be unable to sell all of its output. At a price of $5, however, exactly 4 thousand gallons of ice cream per month would be demanded. Hence, $5 per gallon is the highest price at which the firm can sell 4 thousand gallons of ice cream.

We can use the same procedure for any other quantity in which we are interested. Given any particular quantity, we find the highest price at which it can be sold by going up to the demand curve and then reading across to the vertical axis to find the price.

total revenue curve
A schedule showing the relationship between a firm's output level and the resulting amount of revenue.

Repeating this procedure for each level of output gives us the firm's **total revenue curve,** a schedule showing the relationship between the firm's output level and the resulting amount of revenue. Start by picking an output level, say 4 thousand gallons per month. Proceeding as outlined above, find the highest price at which the firm can sell this quantity of ice cream, which is $5 per gallon. Then multiply the price times the quantity to find total revenue. When Whetter's sells 4 thousand gallons of ice cream per month, it earns total revenues of $20,000 (= 4,000 × $5) per month. To summarize what we have just shown: *the firm-specific demand curve contains all of the information the firm needs to calculate its total revenue function.* (PC 7.3)

7.3 PROGRESS CHECK

Use Figure 7.2 to find the price that the firm receives when it sells 7 thousand gallons of ice cream per month. What is the corresponding total revenue?

Of course, we can also find the firm's total revenue from numerical demand data. The first two columns of Table 7.3 reproduce the demand information from Table 7.2. Multiplying the quantity in column 1 times the price in column 2, we obtain the total revenue given in column 3.

Graphing output on the horizontal axis and total revenue on the vertical axis gives us the firm's total revenue curve, R, in Figure 7.3. At each output level, the height of the total revenue curve shows the *highest* level of total revenue the firm can obtain when it sells that amount of output. For instance, Figure 7.3 shows that when the firm sells 7 thousand gallons of ice cream per month, it can earn total revenue of $28,000 per month.

TOTAL ECONOMIC COST CURVE

We now turn to the second component of economic profit: total economic cost. The total economic cost of producing output level x is the *minimal* expenditure—measured in terms of opportunity cost—that the firm must incur to produce x units of output. (To simplify, we sometimes drop "total" from the name and talk about the "cost of producing x.") The **total economic cost curve** is the schedule that relates the firm's total cost to the amount of output produced.

total economic cost curve
A schedule showing the relationship between a firm's output level and the resulting level of total economic cost.

Suppose that the production department at Whetter's has observed the relationship between the amount of output and the total cost incurred to produce it depicted in Table 7.4. We can use these data to sketch Whetter's total cost curve, labeled C in Figure 7.4. Reading up from a given output level, the height of the C curve tells us the firm's total cost of producing that amount. Thus, for example, it would cost the firm $14,500 per month to produce 6 thousand gallons of ice cream per month.

When we specify that cost depends solely on the level of total output, we are holding several things constant:

1. *Factor prices.* For any given combination of inputs, a change in the price of one or more of the inputs changes the expenditure necessary to pay for the inputs. If the price of sugar rises, for example, then so does the cost of producing any given amount of ice cream. Of course, the firm may respond to a change in factor prices by altering the combination of inputs that it uses. In response to higher wage rates, for example, Whetter's might choose to rely more heavily on machines, and less on workers, to package its ice cream.

2. *Technological possibilities.* The expenditure necessary to produce a given output level depends on how much of the different inputs the firm needs. Thus,

Table 7.3

Whetter's Total Revenue

Multiplying the quantity times the price tells us the firm's total revenue for any given level of output.

(1) Quantity (000 gallons per month)	(2) Price (per gallon)	(3) Total Revenue (per month)
0	—	$ 0
1	$6.00	6,000
2	5.67	11,340
3	5.33	15,990
4	5.00	20,000
5	4.67	23.350
6	4.33	25,980
7	4.00	28,000
8	3.67	29,360
9	3.33	29,970

Figure 7.3

The Total Revenue Curve

The total revenue curve, *R*, relates the total revenue earned by the firm to the quantity of output produced and sold.

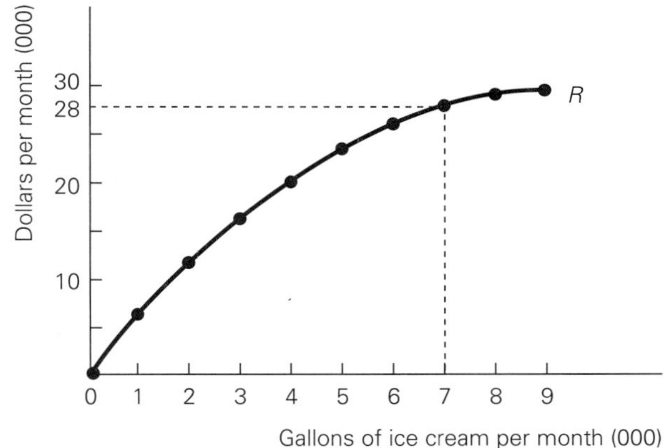

the technological relationship between inputs and output is a key determinant of the total cost curve. For example, if Whetter's devises a way to alter the packing machine so that less ice cream ends up outside the carton, its costs will fall.

3. *Product characteristics.* The input requirements for a given output level depend on the nature of the product. Boutique ice cream requires much more dairy fat than ice milk. Since dairy fat has a positive price, the cost of producing a quart of boutique ice cream is much higher than the cost of producing ice milk.

For now, we hold all of these things in the background because we are focusing on the firm's choice of output level, and the total cost curve summarizes all of the cost information we need to find this output level.

MAXIMIZING PROFIT

Now that we have looked at the two components of profit, revenue and cost, we are ready to return to the firm's choice of its profit-maximizing output level.

Table 7.4

Whetter's Total Economic Cost

The production department at Whetter's has found this relationship between total economic cost and the quantity produced.

Quantity (000 gallons per month)	Total Cost (per month)
0	$ 0
1	5,000
2	8,000
3	10,000
4	11,000
5	12,500
6	14,500
7	17,500
8	22,500
9	30,000

Figure 7.4

The Total Economic Cost Curve

The total economic cost curve, *C*, relates the total cost incurred by the firm to the quantity of output produced.

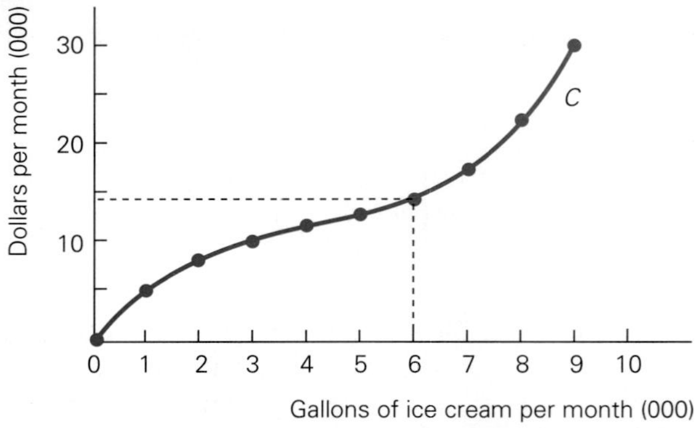

Profit is equal to the difference between total revenue and total cost. Hence, the firm must compare the total revenue curve with the total cost curve at different levels of output. Panel A of Figure 7.5 graphs Whetter's total revenue and total cost curves together. Profit is the vertical distance between the two curves. This distance is graphed explicitly in Panel B of the figure. The curve drawn in Panel B is known as the **profit function**—the relationship between the firm's profits and output level. It is denoted by the Greek letter π (pronounced "pie"). Whetter's wants to produce at the peak of its profit curve. It follows that *to maximize its profit, a firm should produce at the output level where the total revenue curve is the greatest distance above the total economic cost curve.* In Figure 7.5, the profit-maximizing output level is 6 thousand gallons of ice cream per month.

profit function
The algebraic or graphical relationship between a firm's output level and its resulting profit level.

This analysis demonstrates the key roles played by the total revenue and total economic cost curves, but it is somewhat cumbersome—to make a decision, the firm has to look at its entire cost and revenue curves all at once. It often is more convenient to divide the decision into two parts:

1. If the firm is in business, how much output should it produce?
2. Should the firm be in business at all, or should it shut down?

Figure 7.5

Total Revenue, Total Cost, and Profit Maximization

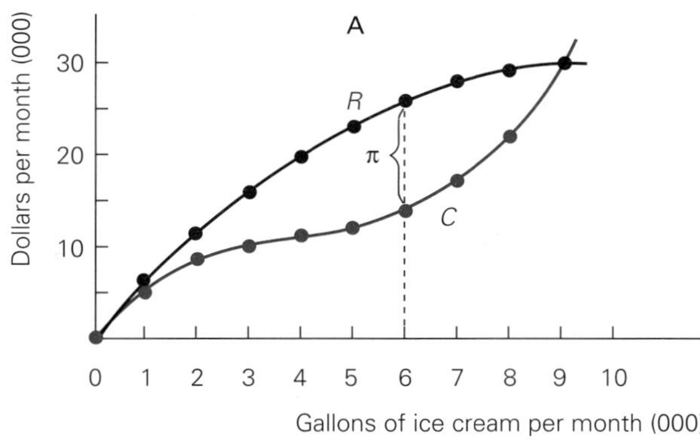

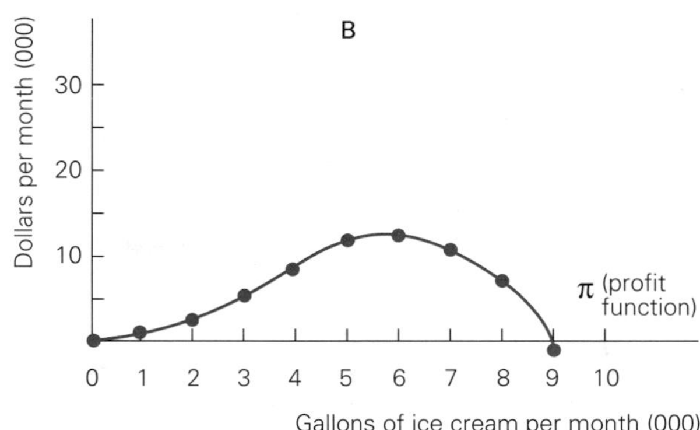

In Panel A, profit is equal to the vertical distance between the total revenue curve, *R*, and the total cost curve, *C*. This distance is graphed in Panel B. Profit is maximized at 6 thousand gallons per month, where the distance is greatest.

The Optimal Output Level for an Active Firm

Suppose Whetter's has decided to produce ice cream. How many gallons should it sell? One way to approach the problem is to look for the highest point on the entire profit curve as we did with Figure 7.5. Further insights are gained by approaching the problem another way, one which focuses specifically on how profit changes as output changes. This approach makes use of the fact that the firm cannot be maximizing profits if increasing output by one unit would raise profits. This simple idea leads to a powerful insight.

Marginal revenue and marginal cost. Since profit is equal to the difference between revenue and cost, the change in profit is equal to the change in total revenue minus the change in total cost. These changes in total revenue and total cost are sufficiently important to the theory of the firm to merit names. The change in revenue due to the sale of one more unit of output is known as the **marginal revenue** (*MR*). The first two columns of Table 7.5 present the data on the firm's total revenue schedule summarized earlier in Table 7.3. From this table, we can find the firm's marginal revenue by looking at the change in total revenue as output increases by one unit. Suppose that the firm is producing 3 thousand gallons of ice cream per month. What is its marginal revenue? If the firm increases its output from 3 thousand to 4 thousand gallons per month, then its total revenue rises from $15,990 per month to $20,000, a gain of $4,010. This fact is recorded in column 3 of Table 7.5. Similarly, if the firm increases output from 7 thousand to 8 thousand gallons per month, then total revenue rises by $1,360 (= $29,360 − $28,000) per month, and marginal revenue is $1,360 per month per thousand gallons, as shown in column 3 of Table 7.5.

marginal revenue
The change in revenue due to the sale of one more unit of output.

Notice that just as we can use data on total revenue to calculate marginal revenue, we also can use data on marginal revenue to calculate total revenue. By comparing column 2 with column 3 in Table 7.5, we see that total revenue is the

Table 7.5

Whetter's Marginal Revenue

Marginal revenue is equal to the change in total revenue that results when output is increased by one unit.

(1) Quantity (000 gallons per month)	(2) Total Revenue (per month)	(3) Marginal Revenue (per 000 gallons)
0	$ 0	
		$6,000
1	6,000	
		5,340
2	11,340	
		4,650
3	15,990	
		4,010
4	20,000	
		3,350
5	23,350	
		2,630
6	25,980	
		2,020
7	28,000	
		1,360
8	29,360	
		610
9	29,970	

sum of the marginal revenues of all of the units produced. When the firm produces 1 unit of output, its total revenue is equal to $6,000, which is equal to marginal revenue starting from 0 units of output and going up to 1 unit. The total revenue from producing 2 thousand gallons per month is equal to the marginal revenue earned by going from 0 to 1 thousand gallons plus the marginal revenue earned by going from 1 thousand to 2 thousand gallons, or $11,340 (= $6,000 + $5,340) per month. Similarly, the total revenue from selling 7 thousand gallons per month is equal to the sum of the marginal revenues for output levels 0 through 7 thousand gallons per month.

marginal cost
The change in total cost due to the production of one more unit of output.

Turning to the cost side, the concept of marginal cost is completely analogous to that of marginal revenue. **Marginal cost** (*MC*) is the change in total cost due to the production of one more unit of output. Table 7.6 presents Whetter's total cost levels in column 2. Calculating the increase in total cost as output is increased by one unit, we obtain the results given in column 3. (PC 7.4)

The marginal output rule. Using our new terminology, the change in profit when the firm produces one more unit of output equals marginal revenue minus marginal cost. It follows that an increase in output will raise profit if *MR* is greater than *MC*. For example, Table 7.7 shows that raising output from 1 thousand to 2 thousand gallons per month increases profits by $2,340 = $5,340 − $3,000.

7.4 PROGRESS CHECK

What is the marginal cost of raising production from 5 thousand gallons per month to 6 thousand?

The firm should produce more ice cream whenever the amount of money that the sale of the additional ice cream will bring into the firm (*MR*) exceeds the additional costs that the firm incurs to produce it (*MC*). This logic implies that the firm should raise its output level at least up to 6 thousand gallons per month. Should the firm go further and raise its output to a point where *MR* is less than *MC*? No, because the additional revenues would be less than the additional costs, so that profits would fall. For example, Table 7.7 shows that when the firm pushes output from 7 thousand to 8 thousand gallons per month, the change in profits is −$3,640 = $1,360 − $5,000.

Putting together what we have just shown, if it is going to be in business Whetter's should produce 6 thousand gallons of ice cream per month. At any

Table 7.6

Whetter's Marginal Cost

Marginal cost is equal to the change in total cost that results when output is increased by one unit.

Quantity (000 gallons per month)	Total Cost (per month)	Marginal Cost (per 000 gallons)
0	$ 0	
1	5,000	$5,000
2	8,000	3,000
3	10,000	2,000
4	11,000	1,000
5	12,500	1,500
6	14,500	*(fill in)*
7	17,500	3,000
8	22,500	5,000
9	30,000	7,500

Table 7.7

Finding Whetter's Profit-Maximizing Output Level

Quantity (000 gallons per month)	Total Revenue (per month)	Marginal Revenue (per 000 gallons)	Total Cost (per month)	Marginal Cost (per 000 gallons)	Profit (per month)
0	$ 0		$ 0		$ 0
1	6,000	$6,000	5,000	$5,000	1,000
2	11,340	5,340	8,000	3,000	3,340
3	15,990	4,650	10,000	2,000	5,990
4	20,000	4,010	11,000	1,000	9,000
5	23,350	3,350	12,500	1,500	10,850
6	**25,980**	2,630	**14,500**	2,000	**11,480**
7	28,000	**2,020**	17,500	**3,000**	10,500
8	29,360	1,360	22,500	5,000	6,860
9	29,970	610	30,000	7,500	−30

Profit is equal to total revenue minus total cost. Profit is maximized by expanding output as long as marginal revenue is greater than marginal cost and then stopping. Hence, Whetter's profit is maximized by expanding up to 6,000 gallons per month. Since the marginal revenue of $2,020 is less than the marginal cost of $3,000, expanding further would reduce profit.

lower output level, Whetter's could raise its profit by producing more ice cream. And at any higher output level, Whetter's could raise its profit by producing less ice cream. We have come a long way in finding what output level the firm will choose: If it decides to produce output, Whetter's maximizes profit by operating at the level where marginal revenue and marginal cost cross.

It often is convenient to draw smooth marginal cost and marginal revenue curves to represent the firm's decision. Doing so yields simple diagrams and, more important, lets us derive a compact algebraic statement of the firm's rule for profit maximization. Figure 7.6 shows the marginal cost and marginal revenue curves for Jen and Mary's Ice Cream Corporation. The logic that we have just developed tells us that Jen and Mary's profit is maximized at the point where the

Figure 7.6

The Profit-Maximizing Output Level Conditional on Being in Business

The marginal revenue curve, *MR*, relates the additional revenue earned from the sale of one more unit of output to the current quantity of output being sold. The marginal cost curve, *MC*, relates the additional cost incurred by the firm to produce one more unit of output to the current quantity of output being sold. If the firm does not shut down, then its profits are maximized at the output level where $MR = MC$: here, output x_1.

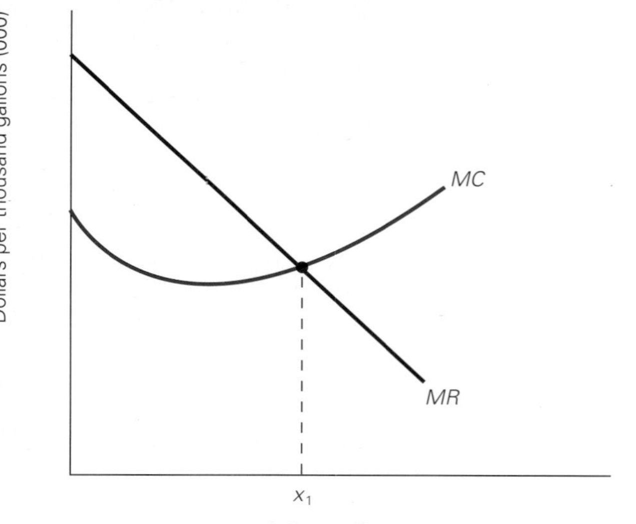

marginal cost and marginal revenue curves cross: quantity x_1. Algebraically, we have shown that the firm should produce where $MR = MC$.[3] We state this conclusion as our first rule for the profit-maximizing level of output.

> **Marginal Output Rule:** If the firm does not shut down, then it should produce output at a level where marginal revenue is equal to marginal cost.

It is important to emphasize that this rule is extremely general. *Although the precise shapes of the marginal revenue and marginal cost curves depend on the particulars of the market in which the firm operates, the rule that the firm should produce at a point where marginal revenue is equal to marginal cost is valid for any profit-maximizing firm.* This is an example of an even more general rule we already have seen: An activity should be carried out to the point where its marginal benefit (here, marginal revenue) is equal to its marginal cost (here, the marginal cost of production). In Chapter 1, we saw this principle applied to the choice of school attendance.

The Shut-Down Decision

The marginal output rule by itself is not quite enough to determine the firm's output choice, because we still have to check whether the firm could do better if it just shut down altogether. The firm must compare its profit when it does produce with the profit that it would earn if it were to shut down. We know how to calculate the firm's profit when it produces output. What profit does the firm earn

[3]We have to be a little more careful with firms whose marginal revenue and marginal cost curves cross more than once (see Discussion Question 7.5). Fortunately, our basic logic remains valid for these firms. If marginal revenue is greater than marginal cost, then the firm can raise its profit by producing more output. If the marginal revenue generated by the last unit produced is less than the marginal cost incurred, then the firm can raise its profit by cutting back its output. From these two facts, we conclude that the firm can be maximizing its profit only if it is operating at a point at which marginal revenue is equal to marginal cost.

if it shuts down? Recall that economic profit is the difference between total revenue and total economic cost. If the firm shuts down and sells no output, total revenue is zero. What about total cost? Economic cost is opportunity cost, the value of the factors in their best alternative uses. If the firm shuts down, all of the factors of production will be put to their best alternative uses. When a restaurant closes, for instance, the dishes, silverware, stoves, and other pieces of capital are all sold to other restaurants through restaurant supply houses that specialize in selling used equipment. Even if it has a long-term lease on its space, the restaurant may be able to sublet it to another tenant. The waiters and cooks seek employment with other firms. Since all of the inputs are put to their best alternative use when the firm ceases production, the firm's total economic cost is zero when its output level is zero.

When the firm shuts down, both revenues and economic costs are equal to zero, so its economic profit is zero. Given that a shut-down leads to zero profit, shutting down is preferable to staying in business if staying in business results in less than zero profit. That is, the firm should shut down if it would suffer *economic losses* by being in business. In terms of our earlier graph, the firm should shut down if for *every* choice of output level the area under the firm's marginal revenue curve (which is equal to total revenue) is less than the area under the marginal cost curve (which is equal to total cost).

Notice that a firm earning exactly zero profit will choose to stay in business. This may seem a little strange. But remember, we are talking about *economic* profit. Economic profit measures the difference between what the factors can earn in this market compared with what they can earn in their best alternative uses. When the level of economic profit is zero, the factors would not yield greater monetary returns to the owners in their best alternative uses. So, the firm might as well stay open.

That a firm earning zero economic profit will stay in business highlights the fact that the shut-down rule is not based on *accounting* profit. As we already have seen, there are important differences between economic profit and accounting profit. Sometimes economic profit is less than accounting profit and sometimes it is greater. A firm earning positive accounting profit thus might find that its economic profit is maximized by shutting down. Suppose, for example, that Washer's Ice Cream Company, a hypothetical competitor of Dreyer's and Whetter's, is deciding whether to stay in business next year. This firm has calculated that at its profit-maximizing level of output it will earn $13,000 in revenue per month, pay its factory workers $6,000 per month, pay $1,500 per month in rent, and spend $4,000 per month on ingredients (for total expenditures of $11,500). In addition, Jules, the owner of Washer's, devotes his full time to the firm. If Jules did not work for Washer's, he could earn an annual salary of $36,000 working as an auto mechanic at a local garage. The accounting profit for the Washer's Ice Cream Company will be $1,500 (= $13,000 − $11,500) per month, suggesting that the firm should remain in business. The economic profit, however, is negative; taking the opportunity cost of Jules's time into account ($3,000 per month in forgone salary), we see that the firm loses $1,500 (= $13,000 − $11,500 − $3,000) per month by remaining in operation. Profit maximization requires Washer's to shut down, even though it could earn accounting profit by continuing to produce.

In other situations, a firm earning accounting losses might find it profitable to stay in business. To see why, consider yet another hypothetical competitor of Dreyer's Ice Cream, Olde Thyme Ice Cream Company (the only company to make herb-flavored ice cream). Old Thyme has a year remaining on an unbreakable lease for a factory that has no other use. The lease calls for a $20,000 payment for the final year. The management calculates that if the firm stayed in business, the most profitable output choice (that is, the one at which $MR = MC$) would generate total revenue of $150,000 and the firm would incur expenditures on wages and ingredients totaling $140,000. The resulting accounting profit would be −$10,000 (=$150,000 − $140,000 − $20,000); the firm would suffer accounting losses.

Should the firm shut down? According to the criterion of economic profit maximization, the answer is no! If the firm were to shut down, it would not have to pay its workers, so the expenditure on wages is an economic cost. The expenditure on the factory lease, however, is *not* an economic cost. If the firm were to shut down, it still would have to make the lease payment—the lease payment is a sunk expenditure. Since the firm in this example has nothing else that it can do with the factory (that is, its best alternative use yields no benefit), the factory has an opportunity cost of $0. Using economic cost to calculate the firm's profit, we find that staying in business yields a positive profit of $10,000 (=$150,000 − $140,000). Hence, the economic measure of profit tells us that the firm should continue to produce output for another year.

To verify that the economic measure of profit gives the right answer, compare the accounting profit the firm would earn by shutting down with the accounting profit it earns by remaining in business. If the firm were to shut down, revenue would fall to $0, as would the labor costs. But the firm still would have to pay $20,000 for the factory. So now, measured in accounting terms, the firm would be losing $20,000, instead of only $10,000. Thus, even though the firm is not doing very well by staying open, it would do even worse if it were to shut down. Our economic measures of cost and profit have led us to the proper conclusion—the firm should remain in business. Indeed, the firm would earn $10,000 more in profit by staying in business for one more year rather than shutting down.

It is often useful to express the firm's shut-down criterion in terms of average amounts rather than total amounts. Specifically, define *average profit* (also referred to as *profit per unit*) as the total profit at some level of output divided by the number of units of output. For example, if total profit is $9,000 when 3 units of output are sold, then average profit is $3,000 per unit. Or, if the firm loses $5,000 when it produces 10 units, then its average profit is −$500. As a matter of arithmetic, if total profit is negative at some level of output, then average profit at that output level must also be negative. Now recall that our criterion for a firm to shut down is that total profits be negative at every level of output. It follows that we can also express the shut-down criterion as: The firm should shut down if average profit is negative, no matter what amount of output the firm produces.

To develop this idea further, we introduce the notions of average cost and average revenue. The firm's **average revenue** is equal to the firm's total revenue divided by the number of units produced. If the firm earns revenues of $60,000 per month when it sells 2 thousand gallons per month, then its average revenue is $3 per gallon. Algebraically, if the firm has total revenue of R and is producing x units of output, then its average revenue is equal to R/x.

average revenue The firm's total revenue divided by the number of units produced.

average economic cost The firm's total economic cost divided by the number of units produced.

The firm's **average economic cost** per unit of output is total cost divided by the number of units produced. We use AEC to denote the firm's average cost curve. Algebraically, if the firm's total economic cost is C and it is producing x units of output, then its average economic cost is equal to C/x. For instance, if

Whetter's can produce 2 thousand gallons per month at a total cost of $8,000 per month, its average cost is $4 per gallon.

Now, let's express the firm's shut-down criterion in terms of average revenue and cost. Since the firm's total profit or loss is equal to total revenue minus total economic cost, it follows that average profit or loss is equal to average revenue minus average economic cost. Hence, the shut-down rule tells us that the firm should not produce if doing so would lead to an average revenue that is lower than average economic cost:

> **Shut-Down Rule:** If for every choice of output level the firm's average revenue is less than its average economic cost, the firm should shut down.[4]

We can restate this rule for a firm that sells all units of its output at the same price. If the firm is charging price p per unit sold, then p is its average revenue per unit.[5] Hence, for this type of firm, we can express the shut-down rule as: If for every choice of output level the price that the firm receives for its output is less than its average economic cost, then the firm maximizes profit by shutting down.

Figure 7.7 illustrates a firm that should shut down—no matter what level of output it chooses, the firm's average economic costs are greater than the price it receives. If the firm produced 4 thousand gallons of ice cream per month, for example, it would earn total revenues equal to shaded area *H*, because this rectangle's length is the number of units and its height is the price per unit. However, the firm would incur total economic costs equal to the sum of shaded areas *H* and *I*. Hence, the firm would suffer losses equal to area *I* if it were to produce this amount of output.

Figure 7.8 illustrates a firm that should not shut down. Consider output level x_a, at which the firm would earn a profit of $p_a - c_a$ on each unit. Multiplying this quantity by the number of units sold, the firm would earn a total profit equal to the shaded area in the figure. Of course, x_a may not be the profit-maximizing output level. To find that, we would have to apply the marginal output rule. (PC 7.5)

> **7.5 PROGRESS CHECK**
>
> Using Figure 7.8, illustrate the firm's profit or loss if it sold x_b units of output.

Refractories: Staying in Business to Lose Money

At this point, you probably are wondering whether the idea that a firm should stay in business while continuing to earn accounting losses is just something that university economists have made up. It is not. Consider the refractories industry. Refractories are special bricks that are used to line furnaces for making steel. As a result of ongoing technological innovation, refractories began lasting four times as long. Because they had to be replaced much less often, the demand for new bricks plummeted. Producers of refractories found that the revenues from

[4]If we already have calculated the best output level conditional on being in business, we only have to check profit at that point: If profit is negative at the best output level, then the firm should shut down. The rule stated in the text allows us to check for shutdown without actually having to find the best point conditional on being in business.

[5]We are not saying that the firm can sell as many units of output as it wants at some fixed price; the value of p may depend on the size of x. Rather, by "a single price" we mean the firm does not sell some units of output at one price while *simultaneously* selling other units at a different price.

Figure 7.7

When the Average Cost Curve Lies above the Demand Curve, the Firm Should Shut Down

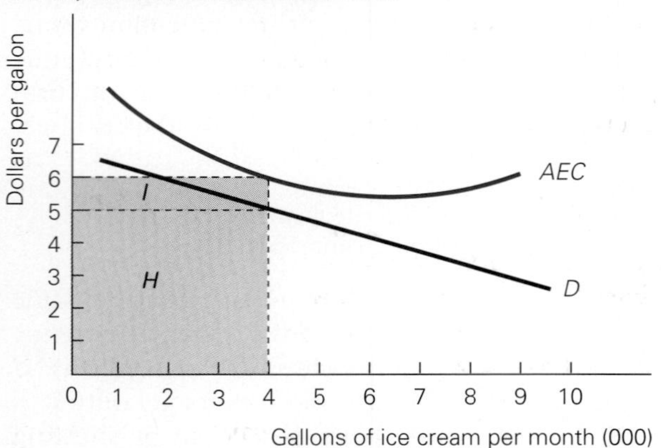

A firm with these demand and average economic cost curves should shut down. It cannot earn positive economic profit by producing output—there is no output level at which price (= average revenue) is greater than average economic cost. At 4 thousand gallons per month, for example, the firm would suffer losses equal to shaded area, *I*.

Figure 7.8

When the Average Cost Curve Crosses the Demand Curve, the Firm Should Produce Output

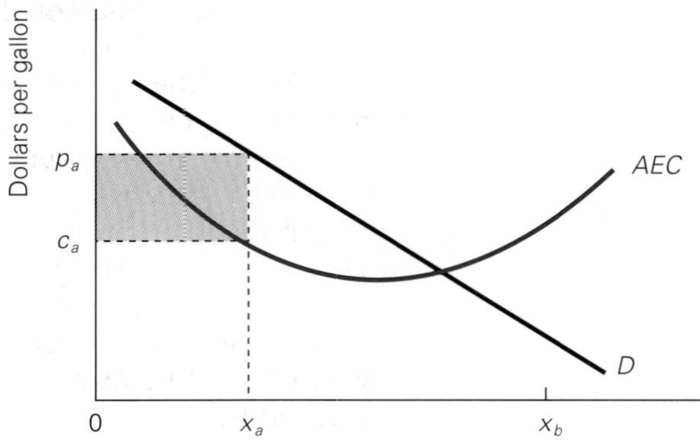

A firm with these demand and average economic cost curves can earn positive economic profit by producing output. There are output levels at which price (= average revenue) is greater than average economic cost. Producing x_a, for example, the firm would earn profit equal to the shaded area.

producing bricks failed to cover the costs of the special clay formed into bricks, the gas and oil used to fire the kilns, and the large capital costs of the plants used to produce bricks.

Faced with these accounting losses, the managers decided to keep their plants operating. The managers were being economically rational. The large expenditures on the specialized plants were sunk because the plants had no alternative uses. (Indeed, because of environmental cleanup costs the salvage values might actually be negative!) The managers correctly recognized that the costs of the plants were sunk and thus should not influence the shut-down decision. And the average *economic* costs—the materials and fuels—were below the price of bricks.

East Germany: Shutting Down an Economy

After a four-decade division, East and West Germany reunited in 1990. A key element of unification was the conversion of the East German economy from a highly subsidized system of state-owned firms to a system of private firms operating in a free-market economy. The German government created an agency called the Treuhandanstalt to oversee the sale of thousands of state firms—ranging from steel mills to restaurants to travel agencies—to private parties.

Perhaps the most vexing question facing the Treuhandanstalt was which firms to continue in operation and which to shut down. There are several reasons why these decisions were so tough. First, most of the firms had never before calculated profits. Second, the prices of the inputs and outputs used and sold by the firms were set by the East German government at levels that were often far from their free-market values. For output prices and revenues, the Treuhandanstalt looked at what similar goods sold for in free markets in other nations. What input prices should the Treuhandanstalt use to calculate costs? The short answer is, of course, opportunity costs. For many commodities like oil, there are well-functioning world markets and it is straightforward to find the appropriate prices. But what price should be put on East German labor, which is the single largest input expenditure?

To find the opportunity cost of this labor, one must calculate its best alternative use. For most of the workers, unemployment was their only alternative to employment in their current firms—approximately one-third of the eastern German labor force was either unemployed or underemployed in 1992. Thus, the opportunity cost of most workers' labor was the value of their forgone leisure. As a consequence of the government's reunification policy and aggressive union bargaining, wages in the former East Germany were set at levels far higher than opportunity cost. Consequently, many firms suffering losses at artificially high wages would be profitable if labor expenses were measured in true opportunity cost terms.

It follows that, from the perspective of maximizing Germany's profit from these firms, they should be kept in operation. The German government was aware of this fact, in part because three economists at the University of California at Berkeley pointed it out to them.[6] In response, the German government chose to keep some "unprofitable" firms in operation. Indeed, it sold some firms at negative prices (that is, subsidized the purchases) in return for commitments from the new buyers to maintain employment.

SECTION RECAP

We have come a long way toward answering the question: How much output should a firm produce? Regardless of the type of market in which the firm operates, as long as it seeks to maximize profit, the firm should produce according to the marginal output rule and the shut-down rule. To implement these rules, the firm needs to know both its firm-specific demand curve and its total cost curve. Once the firm has these data, it can calculate its marginal and average, cost and revenue curves, and it can then implement these two rules.

7.3 DO FIRMS REALLY MAXIMIZE PROFITS?

We have derived a set of rules regarding the input and output choices that apply to any *profit-maximizing* firm. A natural and important question to ask is: Do firms really maximize profits? Many people have suggested that the answer may be no. These doubts about profit maximization take several forms. First, you might question the validity of this assumption on the grounds that the executives of a paint company really do not worry whether they should produce one more gallon of paint (the "marginal" gallon). Similarly, the management of IBM does not sit down and ponder whether they should produce 103,119 units of some personal computer per year or 103,120. While it is true that firms do not fine-tune their output choices to this extent, they do not have to do so for economic theory to give valid insights into their behavior. Our objective in modeling firm behavior is to capture general tendencies, not to make predictions precise to the penny or to the machine. Moreover, this objection really comes down to an issue of what the proper size of the margin is. For Whetter's Ice Cream, the margin

[6]See Akerlof et al. (1991).

was 1,000 gallons of ice cream per month—*thousands of gallons per month* were the units used in the analysis. Clearly, that makes a lot more sense than thinking of the firm as choosing its output in terms of individual gallons per year. In any particular case, choosing the right units for analysis just requires a little common sense.

A closely related objection is that firms do not really think in terms of the marginal choice rule or the shut-down rule for *any* choice of units. For instance, in many retailing markets (e.g., grocery and department stores), the firms are said to follow *markup rules*, whereby the price of a good is set equal to its average cost plus some percentage for profit. On the face of it, this sort of rule of thumb does not look much like either of our two rules for profit maximization. But where does the markup percentage come from? Different goods have different markups, and if we look at the data we often find that the pattern is consistent with profit maximization. Like the theory of the household, the validity of the theory of the firm does not require that firms think of themselves as acting in the terms described by the theory. What is essential is that their actual behavior fits the pattern predicted by the theory. Of course, many firms do think explicitly in terms of the rules derived above. And still more firms apply these concepts, but give them somewhat different names. For example, when an airline worries whether its "cost per seat mile" is higher than the average fare that it receives on some route, the firm is simply applying the shut-down rule under a different name.

A third potential objection to the hypothesis of profit maximization is that even if firms do *try* to maximize profits, "perfect" profit maximization is impossible. The management of General Motors must choose the prices and quantities of thousands of different cars (different models with various options) that are sold in many different markets around the world. How can they possibly calculate the resulting profits from all the different possible output choices? It surely is correct to argue that managers do not know everything, but this point is no reason to abandon economic models based on the assumption of profit maximization. Even if firms are not all-knowing and sometimes do make mistakes, models based on the assumption of profit maximization still give us an idea of the general tendencies in the firms' behavior. As always, we must judge models not by their "realism," but by the usefulness of their results. Moreover, just as we extended our model of household behavior to allow for uncertainty (Chapter 6), we will extend our model of the profit-maximizing firm to situations where the firm must make decisions without knowing what the exact consequences will be.

The most serious attack on the theory of the firm comes from those who question whether firms even try to maximize their profits. In reality, a "firm" is a collection of people, not a single decision maker. This observation suggests that if we want to understand firm decision making, we must analyze the behavior of people who run the firm. Thus, we must answer two questions: First, who controls the firm? Second, what do these people want the firm to do to maximize their utility? In particular, is it in the interest of the firm's managers to maximize the firm's profit?

THE DIVORCE OF OWNERSHIP AND CONTROL

An outstanding fact of modern capitalism is that most large companies are not run by the people who own them. A large corporation typically is owned by thousands of stockholders, most of whom have nothing to do with making business decisions. Those decisions are made by a professional management team. Of course, some managers may own stock, but many do not. For the moment, let's assume that the owners and managers are two completely separate groups. These two groups may have strongly differing goals. Because ownership gives a person a claim on the profit of the firm, the greater the firm's profit, the higher the owners' income. Hence, *the owners of the firm want the firm to maximize its profit.*

Now, let's consider the goals of the managers. Presumably, managers are like any other people—they want to maximize their own well-being. A manager's utility may depend on several elements. His or her income is one of them. But, as we saw in the theory of household labor supply (Chapter 5), people care about more than money. A manager's utility may also depend on how hard she has to work, the working conditions, and the prestige attached to her job, for example. These observations suggest that if managers were left to their own devices, their pursuit of utility maximization might conflict with profit maximization for several reasons:

1. *Consumption of leisure.* A manager may value on-the-job leisure. The number of hours that a manager is at her workplace may not be a good measure of how hard she is working. A manager may be able to take it easy when no one is looking or go out for a three-martini "business" lunch; consequently, profits may suffer.

2. *Amenity maximization.* Oliver Williamson (1964) suggested that managers derive utility from perquisites such as big offices, many subordinate workers, and expensive meals. Hence, left free to pursue their own goals, managers might have the firm spend heavily on these items, at the expense of profits. When WPP Group PLC took over the J. Walter Thompson Company, they found that the firm was spending \$80,000 per year to have a butler deliver a peeled orange each day to one of the executives—that's roughly \$300 per orange (Fanning 1990, 29). This example notwithstanding, it can sometimes be difficult to separate amenity maximization from profit maximization. Is a corporate jet a profit-maximizing response to the fact that a top executive's time has a high opportunity cost, or is it an expensive executive toy?

3. *Sales maximization.* William Baumol (1967) hypothesized that a manager's prestige is attached to the size of his company's revenue, or sales. A prestige-maximizing manager thus would attempt to maximize the firm's total revenue. Figure 7.9 indicates how a revenue-maximizing manager's output choice differs from that of a profit-maximizing manager. The figure graphs the marginal revenue and marginal cost curves. Total revenue reaches its peak at x_r, the quantity at which the marginal revenue curve crosses the horizontal axis. At any quantity lower than x_r, marginal revenue is positive and the total revenue curve rises as output goes up. At any quantity greater than x_r, marginal revenue is negative and the total revenue curve falls as output rises. Thus, a revenue-maximizing manager would continue to produce additional output as long as that output contributed to the firm's revenue, regardless of its effect on cost.

In contrast, a profit-maximizing manager takes costs into account. He will choose output level x_π, where marginal revenue is equal to marginal cost. Since the revenue maximizer ignores the cost of additional output, he or she produces more output (x_r is greater than x_π). Over the range from x_π to x_r, marginal cost

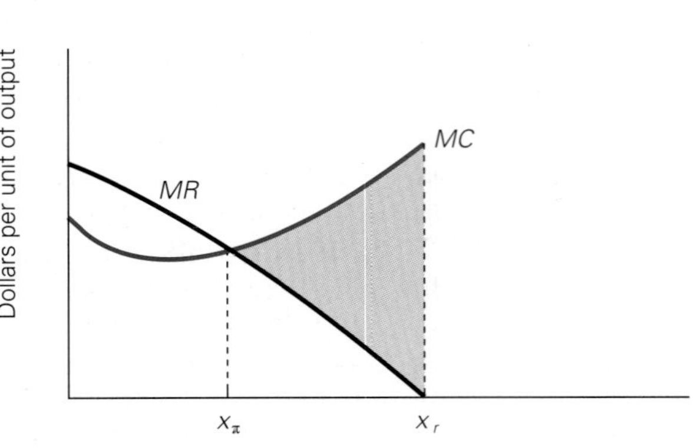

Figure 7.9

Total Revenue Maximization

A revenue-maximizing manager will choose x_r, the output level at which marginal revenue is equal to 0. In contrast, the firm's profit is maximized at x_π, the output level at which marginal revenue is equal to marginal cost. The loss in profit from the pursuit of revenue maximization is given by the shaded area.

is greater than marginal revenue, so profit falls as output rises. In other words, a revenue-maximizing manager sacrifices profit by producing too much output and setting price below the profit-maximizing level.

We see, then, that managers may have different interests and objectives than their "bosses," the stockholders. Stockholders and managers are just one example of a **principal-agent relationship.** A principal-agent relationship exists whenever one party, the *principal,* hires a second party, the *agent,* to perform some task on the first party's behalf. What makes a principal-agent relationship interesting is that the agent may not behave in the manner desired by the principal. Consequently, the principal must be concerned with ways to keep the agent in line.

principal-agent relationship
An economic relationship in which one party, the principal, hires a second party, the agent, to perform some task on the first party's behalf.

CONTROL MECHANISMS

If there were no way for the owners of the firm to control the managers, then the assumption of profit maximization would be on shaky ground indeed. However, the divergence of owners' and managers' interests has not gone unnoticed by owners. There is a variety of mechanisms through which owners try to make management pursue the owners' goal of profit maximization. We will examine several such mechanisms and see that, while no mechanism works perfectly, each one at least helps to align managerial incentives with owner interests.

Broadly speaking, we can divide these control mechanisms into those that are internal to the firm and those that are external. **Internal control mechanisms** are means of controlling the managers that involve solely the owners and managers of the firm itself. **External control mechanisms** involve people outside of the firm. We will examine the workings of each type.

internal control mechanisms
Means of controlling a firm's managers involving solely the owners and managers of the firm itself.

external control mechanisms
Control mechanisms that involve people outside of the firm.

Internal Control Mechanisms

The institutions and rules that comprise the **corporate governance scheme** constitute an important internal control mechanism. These rules specify the responsibilities of the managers and set up a body of people to monitor the managers and to replace them if necessary. The body responsible for watching over the managers is known as the *board of directors.* If members of the board feel that the

corporate governance scheme
The rules and institutions that specify the responsibilities of the managers and set up means for the shareholders to monitor the managers and to replace them if necessary.

current management team is not serving stockholder interests, then the members may fire the managers and replace them. This threat of replacement gives managers incentives to serve stockholder interests. But boards of directors do not work perfectly. It may, for example, be difficult for a board member to evaluate the complex decisions made by the management. Does the fact that Polaroid's management introduced instant home movies (with no sound and a length under three minutes) just before videocassette recorders took over the market indicate that the managers were doing a bad job? Or was this a decision that anyone in their position would have made, given the information available to them at the time? The effectiveness of boards of directors also is limited by the fact that key members of the management team often serve on the board. Moreover, the top management may have an important role in selecting the other board members. A self-interested manager will choose her friends rather than someone who is likely to look out for the stockholders' interests.

proxy fight
An election in which shareholders vote on key corporate decisions or, in some cases, choose to fire the incumbent managers.

Under the rules of corporate governance, stockholders do not have to rely solely on the board of directors to protect owner interests. Stockholders can take matters into their own hands by having an election, known as a **proxy fight,** in which they vote whether to override key decisions or in some cases to fire the managers. Proxy fights provide both a direct control of managerial actions and, through the threat of replacement, an indirect incentive mechanism. The usefulness of proxy fights as a means of controlling management is limited, however. Under Rule 14a-8 of the Securities and Exchange Act of 1934, boards of directors are able to deny votes on any issues "relating to the conduct of ordinary business operations" of the corporation (Labaton 1992, C1). An even more important limitation of this method of control is that most stockholders are apathetic when it comes to voting in corporate elections. Such apathy may be rational. It is costly for a stockholder to stay informed about the workings of every company in which he or she has stock. Rather than be an informed voter, a stockholder may say, "How I vote won't make a noticeable difference, so why should I worry about it?" When a stockholder fails to return a marked ballot, the "vote" often is automatically counted in the management's favor. This is one reason that management seldom loses a proxy fight.

There are ways in which one shareholder could make a difference. If a shareholder were to spend a lot of money running a campaign against the management, she might be able to influence enough other shareholders so that the management would lose the proxy fight. But here, a different problem arises. It is very costly to campaign actively against an incumbent management team. Rather than spend her money campaigning, a stockholder may say, "Why should I do all of the work? If someone else succeeds in making the management serve us better, I'll still get the benefits, even if I don't help. So I'll let someone else worry about it." Such stockholder apathy is just one example of a general phenomenon known as **free riding.** Free riding is said to take place when a person refrains from taking a costly action because he or she believes that someone else will undertake it (which allows the free rider to reap the benefits without bearing the costs).

free riding
Free riding is said to take place when a person refrains from taking a costly action because he or she knows that someone else will undertake it (which allows the free rider to reap the benefits without bearing the costs).

Corporate governance relies on having someone (either the board of directors or the stockholders themselves) monitor the managers to see that they serve the stockholders' interests. An alternative approach is to try to harmonize the interests of managers and owners. As noted earlier, managers are interested in their incomes, among other things. Stockholders are interested in the profit of the firm. One way to bring these two goals together is to tie the managers'

performance-based compensation
A system for compensating a firm's manager under which the amount paid to the manager depends on how well the firm does.

income to the firm's profits. Schemes under which the amount paid to its managers depends on how well the firm does are known as **performance-based compensation** schemes. IBM's then-chairman John Akers saw his salary fall 40 percent in 1991 when IBM suffered its first-ever annual loss (*The New York Times*, February 25, 1991, C1). Likewise, 1993 was a bad year for Walt Disney Company and its chairman, Michael Eisner. Because of the firm's financial performance that year, Eisner received no annual bonus and was paid only his $750,000 base salary. By 1995, Disney was doing well again and the value of Eisner's annual bonus exceeded $13 million (Walt Disney Co. 1995). Perhaps the most well-known example of a performance-based compensation scheme is the one that the investment bank Drexel Burnham Lambert used for the head of its junk bond division. In 1988, Drexel paid one of its employees, Michael Milken, $550 million based on the performance of his division!

The firm's profit is not the only measure of performance on which to base the manager's compensation. Many firms tie the manager's compensation to stock performance. They do this by giving the managers stock, or options to buy stock at a set price, as part of their compensation. Part of Michael Eisner's annual bonus comes in the form of Disney stock. When his current long-term compensation package began, he received options for 8 million shares. (Indeed, one way he got by without a bonus in 1993 was to exercise options that yielded profits of approximately $202 million (*The New York Times*, January 4, 1994, D6)). To the extent that the value of the stock reflects current profits, stock schemes work the same way as profit sharing. Stock schemes have the added advantage of taking long-run profits into account. As we will discuss shortly, the stock price depends not only on current profits, but also on expectations about the firm's future performance.

Despite several stunning examples of performance-based compensation schemes, their overall importance is limited. If these contracts have such good incentive properties, why aren't all contracts in this form? The presence of managerial risk aversion provides one answer. Uncertainty is a pervasive feature of the real world, and a firm's profits may be affected by forces beyond the managers' control. Suppose that you were hired to manage a genetic engineering company that was working on a new "miracle" drug. The company's attempt to discover the new drug might fail even if everything were properly managed. If your compensation were strongly tied to firm performance, you would bear much of the risk associated with the business. In Chapter 6, we saw that risk bearing is a bad thing from the manager's point of view when she is risk averse. And this pattern of risk bearing is inefficient if the owners are risk neutral; risk-neutral owners should bear all of the risk because it does not reduce their utility. Even if the owners are risk averse as well, the economically efficient arrangement is to have the owners share much of the risk. Indeed, the main role of the stock market is to let many people share in the risk of a company and at the same time allow investors to diversify their holdings of risky assets.

Why not offer a risk-averse manager full insurance against bad outcomes? Because this will eliminate managerial incentives to avoid low profits. In short, tying a manager's compensation to the firm's profit strengthens his or her incentives to maximize profit, but at the same time it can expose the manager to a great deal of risk. Our theory predicts that the structure of managerial compensation must make a trade-off between incentives and insurance. Thus, we expect executive earnings to be tied to performance, but not too closely. This prediction is borne out by statistical studies which suggest that the elasticity of compensation with respect to the rate of return of the company's stock is about 0.10 (Rosen 1990, 3).

External Control Mechanisms

Having looked at several internal control mechanisms, now let's consider some external control mechanisms. Recall that these control mechanisms involve people outside of the firm. One such mechanism is provided by the *market for corporate control.* If the current management does not maximize profit, someone else may be able to get control of the firm through a hostile takeover. A hostile takeover occurs when a group of investors purchases a controlling interest in a company against the management's wishes and advice to the current stockholders. Typically, the new owners use their control to oust the incumbent management.

To see why raiders might take over a badly run firm and replace its management, suppose that the current management of General Sloth is not doing a good job of maximizing the firm's profits. Let V_L (L for "low") denote the value of a share of the firm when it is run by the incumbent management. Suppose that under a good management, the firm's profit could be increased and the resulting stock price would be V_H (H for "high") per share, where $V_H > V_L$. If the corporate raiders (the good management) can purchase the company at a price less than V_H per share, then they can make money by taking over the company.

An actual takeover may replace a bad management with a good one. Moreover, the threat of a hostile takeover may itself induce the incumbent management to maximize profit rather than risk being overthrown. Despite these benefits, there are many critics of hostile takeovers. These critics have argued that hostile takeovers amount to corporate blackmail and should be outlawed. Because hostile takeovers can play a valuable role in disciplining managers, many economists believe that government policy should not limit them.

Even without a legislative prohibition of hostile takeovers, however, there are limits on the effectiveness of the market for corporate control. Managers today may take a variety of anti-takeover measures with such colorful names as "shark repellents" and "poison pills." While these measures work in different ways, all are designed to make takeovers more costly and difficult, thus giving the managers more room to pursue their own interests rather than those of the stockholders. Indeed, statistical analyses of takeover bids suggest that "existing managers can squander one-third of the firm's value before the threat of displacement becomes truly serious" (Rosen 1990, 16).

The market for corporate control also is limited by a variant of the free-rider problem that we discussed earlier. Under the old management, the stock would be selling for V_L per share, while under the new management it would be worth V_H per share. It would appear that the good management could make $V_H - V_L$ per share by buying control of the company. But suppose you were a stockholder and you heard that the good management wanted to take over the company. How much would you think your stock is worth? If the good management is going to take over, the value is V_H. Thus, if you think they are going to succeed, you would be unwilling to sell your stock for less than V_H. But if all of the existing stockholders hold out for a price of V_H, the potential corporate raiders have no incentive to mount a costly takeover attempt. There are ways around this problem, but it does limit the effectiveness of takeovers as a discipline device. Evidence shows that the acquirer seldom does well after taking over a firm.

There are other market forces that may serve to discipline managers. One is *product market competition.* A firm facing strong competition in its output markets may be forced to maximize profits just to keep from going bankrupt. Of course, if the firm does not face strong competition, management may be free to pursue other goals without risking financial distress. Some believe this is why government-owned airlines, which often are insulated from competition in their home countries, are sometimes very inefficient. Similarly, if all competing managers also fail to maximize profit, then the pressure of competition may be weak.

The firm also may be subject to *discipline from capital suppliers.* Lenders may refuse to supply capital to a firm unless it follows certain policies. The effectiveness of this external control mechanism may be limited by the difficulties lenders can have determining exactly what management is up to. A banker lending money to a compact disk manufacturer simply does not know as much as the management about how the company is operating or should operate. Moreover, once they are established, some firms can avoid the capital markets by relying entirely on internal funds (that is, profits from existing operations) to finance their investment needs.

SECTION RECAP

The assumption of profit-maximizing behavior is the cornerstone of the theory of the firm. While owners generally want their firms to maximize profit, managers may have conflicting objectives. To the extent that managers are free to pursue these other goals, the profit-maximization assumption will be rendered invalid. In this section, we have discussed a number of control mechanisms that can induce managers to maximize profit. But we have also shown that each of these mechanisms is limited in its effectiveness.

Where does all of this leave us? The net result is that managers are controlled, but only imperfectly. In the light of these doubts about the profit-maximization hypothesis, is it legitimate to base models of the firm on it? Most economists answer yes, for three reasons:

1. Because profit maximization is a fairly simple goal, it leads to models that are relatively easy to work with.
2. The widespread use of various control mechanisms suggests that the scope for non–profit-maximizing behavior is severely limited.
3. Most important, the assumption that firms maximize profits appears to work well for predicting much of the behavior that we observe in the world.

7.4 PROFIT MAXIMIZATION OVER TIME AND UNDER UNCERTAINTY

Like households, firms often have to make decisions with uncertain consequences or consequences that are felt only after some period of time. The development of a new microprocessor or a new airplane, for example, exhibits both characteristics. To begin selling the Pentium chip, Intel invested more than $4 billion over four years to design the chip and construct production capacity. There was no guarantee that computer manufacturers and their customers would use the chips in sufficient quantities to justify this investment. Similarly, when Boeing decided to move ahead with the development of the 777 aircraft in the early 1990s, that company faced $4 billion in costs prior to rollout and a great deal of uncertainty about demand (Petroski 1995). It would be five years before the plane would actually be produced by Boeing and flown by its customers. In this section, we will examine whether the profit-maximization assumption is valid when these considerations come into play.

INTERTEMPORAL CHOICE

How should management take into account the fact that the expenditures and receipts (costs and revenues) occur at different dates? If a firm simply maximized profit for the current year, it would never make investments in new equipment or in research and development—since their costs occur up front, these investments entail a sacrifice of current profits in order to reap higher future profits. But neither should management ignore the fact that a dollar today is worth more than a dollar next year (see Chapter 5). When costs and revenues occur at different dates, the firm should make its investment decisions to maximize the *present value* of its profit.

Stockholder Myopia?

It often is said that U.S. firms do not maximize the present value of their profits. In particular, critics argue that U.S. firms are too myopic, especially in comparison with Japanese firms. *The New York Times*, for example, opined that "American managers, unlike their Japanese counterparts, rarely invest when the payoff is distant" (*The New York Times*, September 10, 1989, A22). The blame for this shortsightedness typically is laid at the feet of stockholders, who are said to be concerned only with short-run performance. One "explanation" for this alleged stockholder myopia is that stockholders tend to hold stock in a given firm for only a short while and therefore do not care about the firm's long-term prospects. According to this view, shareholders want big profits and they want them quickly. Managers respond accordingly, taking actions that are profitable in the short term (such as slashing investment in research and development), but possibly detrimental to the long-term profitability of the company. "Hot money chases short-term yields, often playing havoc with long-term planning and growth" (Pennar 1986, 82–83).

Let's look more closely at this account of myopia. The argument is based on the claim that someone who holds the stock for only a short period of time cares only about the company's short-term performance. To analyze this claim, we examine a relatively simple hypothetical example, which demonstrates that the basis for this argument is fundamentally flawed.

Shareholders want to maximize the income that they receive from their stock. A share of stock in a firm is a claim to ownership of a fraction of that firm. As such, the share entitles its owner to receive a fraction of any profit that is distributed to the firm's owners. These distributions are known as **dividend payments.** A share of stock thus represents a claim to the future dividend payments made by that firm. It follows that the value of a firm's stock at a given time is the present value of its dividend stream from that time onward.

dividend payments Distributions of a firm's profit that are paid to owners of the firm's stock.

Suppose that the Hexxon Corporation is going to be in business for only two years, 1997 and 1998. At the beginning of 1997, Carl buys one share of stock at a price of p_{1997}. He plans to hold the stock for only one year. At the end of the year, he will collect the 1997 dividend of d_{1997} dollars per share and will then sell his shares at a price of p_{1998} each. His total income from this investment has two components. The first is the dividend that he receives at the end of the year that he holds the stock. The second component is the gain (or loss) that he earns as a result of a difference between the price at which he buys the stock and the price at which he sells it. The difference between the buy and sell prices is known as the **capital gain** or **capital loss,** depending on whether the selling price is higher or lower than the buying price. We will see that the myopia argument is incorrect because it ignores the fact that shareholders care about capital gains.

capital gain or **capital loss**
The difference between the buying and selling prices, depending on whether the selling price is higher or lower than the buying price.

Because Carl's income is spread out over time, we must apply our present value formula to the various components. The present value of the dividends that Carl receives over the one year that he owns the stock is $d_{1997}/(1 + i)$, where i is the one-year rate of interest. Carl's capital gain is the difference between the *discounted* selling price minus the buying price. Since Carl sells his stock at the beginning of 1998, his capital gain is $p_{1998}/(1 + i) - p_{1997}$. Notice that this is the *economic* capital gain, not the *accounting* capital gain. To see the difference, suppose that our investor both bought and sold the share of stock at a price of \$50. Most people would say that there was no capital gain or loss. But, in fact, the investor would have suffered an opportunity loss because the present value of \$50 one year from now is less than the present value of \$50 today.

Adding the dividends and capital gain together, we find that the per-share income that Carl earns by holding the stock for one year is

$$d_{1997}/(1 + i) + p_{1998}/(1 + i) - p_{1997} \qquad (7.2)$$

To figure out his income, Carl must know p_{1998}, the share price when he sells. The people buying the stock will value it for the dividends that they will receive in the coming year (after that, Hexxon will be out business). The present value of the remaining dividend, *calculated at the start of 1998, is* $d_{1998}/(1 + i)$. Therefore, this will be the price of a share at the end of the first year, $p_{1998} = d_{1998}/(1 + i)$. Substituting this expression for p_{1998} in the expression for Carl's income, Equation (7.2), we find that Carl's income is given by

$$d_{1997}/(1 + i) + d_{1998}/(1 + i)^2 - p_{1997} \qquad (7.3)$$

Assuming that Carl would like his income to be as high as possible, how would he like the firm to act? Expression (7.3) provides the answer. Since p_{1997} has already been paid, there is nothing that the firm's actions can do to change it retroactively. The interest rate, i, also is something that is beyond the firm's control. The only thing that the management can affect is the dividend payments, d_{1997} and d_{1998}. From Expression (7.3), we see that, *ceteris paribus*, Carl would like d_{1997} to be as large as possible. Moreover, other things equal, Carl would like d_{1998} to be as large as possible. This is a striking result. Despite the fact that Carl sells the stock after only one year, he cares about the dividend paid in the second year. More precisely, notice that $d_{1997}/(1 + i) + d_{1998}/(1 + i)^2$ in Expression (7.3) is the present value of the *entire future* stream of dividend payments. Regardless of when he sells his stock, Carl's income is highest when the firm maximizes the present value of its *entire future* dividend flow. It is in even a short-term stockholder's interest to have the firm's managers maximize the present value of the long-term dividend stream.

Then why not have the firm pay unlimited dividends? The answer is of course that the funds for dividends have to come out of the firm's profits. Just as a household faces an intertemporal budget constraint under which the present value of consumption expenditures must be no more than the present value of the household's income stream, the firm faces a constraint that the present value of the dividends paid out must be no greater than the present value of its profit stream. Hence, if the firm wants to maximize the present value of its dividends, it must maximize the present value of its profits. Therefore, Carl wants the managers to maximize the present value of the entire future profit stream.

Of course, our example is a special case. Most companies plan at least to be in business for more than two years. And not all stockholders know that they want to hold their shares for only one year. Nevertheless, exactly the same logic applies to a person planning to hold stock for any length of time in a company that plans to be in business for many years. The general finding is this: *A stockholder wants the firm to maximize the present value of all future profits even if he or she plans to sell the stock soon.* It is not in stockholders' interest for management to be myopic. The reason is that the price at which you can sell your stock to future investors will depend on these future profits. Once we recognize the nature of the market for corporate ownership, we see that the argument that stockholders necessarily are shortsighted is highly suspect. If American firms are myopic, the explanation must lie elsewhere.

DECISIONS UNDER UNCERTAINTY

All firms face uncertainty. The movie industry is one prominent example. *Cutthroat Island* cost roughly $115 million and brought in box office revenues of only $10 million (Sterngold 1996, 22). While *Cutthroat Island* was a particularly spectacular flop, it is not alone. On average, a major Hollywood movie in 1995 cost $54 million to produce and promote (Sterngold 1996, 22). Even including all of the revenues from home video and television, more movies suffer accounting losses than earn accounting profits.

Managers in other industries, from steel production to furniture manufacturing, all face uncertainty. How should they react to it, and what would the stockholders like them to do? Since the firm's actions influence the owners' income, it might seem to follow that if the owners are risk averse, then the firm should behave in a risk-averse manner as well. After all, in Chapter 6 we showed that a risk-averse person is willing to give up some expected income in order to have a less risky outcome. Carrying this argument through to the firm, it might seem that the owners would not want the managers simply to seek the highest level of expected profit; rather, the owners would prefer actions that reduced risk, even though they also reduced expected profit.

Let's return to the example of Boeing deciding whether to introduce a new aircraft. In the late 1970s, Boeing had to decide whether to develop the 767. One of the key features of the design was the fuel efficiency of the plane—it was planned to be 25 percent cheaper to operate than the planes it would replace. But that fuel efficiency made it necessary to develop an advanced new wing design as well as to use more expensive materials in production. Would demand for the plane justify these higher costs? The up-front research, development, and engineering costs to build a new airplane were expected to run between $1 and $2 billion in 1978 dollars. It would be three years at the earliest before the plane would actually be produced by Boeing and flown by its customers (Moriarty and Shapiro 1981, 1). If oil prices remained high and the demand for air travel strong, the airlines would have a strong demand for a fuel-efficient plane. But if oil prices fell or the demand for air travel were reduced, the demand for the 767 might be quite low, leading to large losses by Boeing. When they started the project, it was impossible to predict with certainty what would happen. The project was a risky one.

Boeing did have an alternative. Instead of designing an entirely new airframe, the company had the option of modifying an existing airframe such as the 737. This course of action might have development costs of only $100 or $200 million 1978 dollars, and thus the chance of losing huge amounts of money was greatly limited (Moriarty and Shapiro 1981, 1). On the other hand, the resulting aircraft would be a derivative one, so the potential for tremendous sales and profit also was lacking. Overall, the project was less risky, and the argument for corporate risk aversion suggests that owner interest might have best been served by modifying an existing airframe.

This argument misses a vital point, however. The existence of a stock market has an important influence on the owners' attitude toward the goal of the firm. As we saw in Chapter 6, stockholders can reduce the risk associated with the fluctuations in any one firm's profits by holding a diversified portfolio. This ability to diversify (and, hence, to share risk) is one of the great economic virtues of the stock market and is one reason for its existence. While it typically is impossible for stockholders to eliminate risk entirely, diversification works sufficiently well so that it is reasonable to assume that a well-diversified stockholder will indeed want managers to maximize expected profits. In the case of Boeing, that might have meant building a completely new airframe.

Before concluding that firms maximize expected profits, we must remember the separation of ownership and control. Will managers follow the owners' wishes? Like stockholders, most managers probably are risk averse. Unlike a stockholder, however, a manager may not be able to diversify away the risk associated with the performance of his or her company. For example, a manager's reputation (and, hence, his future income) may depend on the performance of the one firm that he is currently managing, and it is hard to imagine one person managing several different companies simultaneously in order to diversify this "reputation risk." Moreover, the incentive distortion arising from managerial risk aversion may be made even worse by the use of various performance-based compensation plans. To induce their manager to work hard, owners may want to tie managerial compensation heavily to company performance, but then riskiness of the firm's investment translates into riskiness in the manager's income.

A manager with an undiversified human capital portfolio will take the riskiness of his choices into account while well-diversified stockholders are concerned with only the expected returns. From the owner's point of view, managers will be biased against risky projects. Fortunately, there are control mechanisms that can work to correct for this bias and induce managers to try to maximize expected profit. For instance, if a manager refuses to invest in risky projects, she may find her company taken over by someone who will. At Boeing, the managers chose an even riskier strategy than the either–or choice we just analyzed—they decided to go ahead with both the new airframe and the derivative project simultaneously.

Policy Implications of Expected Profit Maximization

In 1991, Congressman Henry Waxman of California proposed a "consumer protection law" that would force firms that made "excessive profits" from anti-AIDS drugs to lower their prices. One might have expected AIDS activists to support this measure, but many, like James Driscoll (a founder of an organization that promotes development of new AIDS treatments), did not. In an article titled "Consumer Protection Could Kill AIDS Patients," Driscoll argued that Waxman's proposal would ultimately harm AIDS victims. Because "orphan drugs [i.e., drugs aimed at relatively small populations] usually produce low profits, drug companies will simply avoid them altogether if they are penalized whenever they develop a profitable orphan" (Driscoll 1991, A8). In the jargon of the present chapter, firms make their investment and production decisions on the basis of expected profits. Even if a speculative venture has some chance of incurring losses, it will be pursued if its expected profit is positive. But if the government penalizes the firm whenever the state of the world is *high profits*, then expected profits will be negative and the firm will not undertake the project. In short, if the government offers the firm a game in which the rules are "heads I win and tails you lose," then the firm won't play. Among the losers are the firm's potential customers.

Gold Mines, Shutdown, and Option Value

In the face of uncertainty, firms often have to make decisions that they may later want to change but find costly to do so. Shutting down a gold mine is one such decision. When a mine is closed, it may fill with water and the internal supports may weaken from lack of proper maintenance, making it costly to reopen. To decide whether to shut down the mine today, its managers need to predict whether they are later going to want to reopen it.

Consider a simplified example in which only two years are under consideration. There is a basic setup cost of $100,000 per year to keep the mine open and safe. In addition, it costs $380 per ounce to dig out the ore and extract the gold. In full operation, the mine can extract 1,000 ounces per year.

Suppose that in the first year the price of gold is $400 per ounce. If the firm closed the mine entirely, both its revenues and costs would be equal to $0. If the firm kept the mine open, it would have to incur the setup cost and should produce as much gold as possible; given that the mine is open, the marginal revenue of each ounce is $400 while the marginal cost is only $380 for quantities less than 1,000 ounces. Hence, if the firm decided to keep the mine open during the first year, it would earn revenues of $400,000 (= 1,000 × 400) but would incur costs of $480,000 (= 100,000 + 1,000 × 380). Looking solely at the first year, the firm would suffer losses of $80,000 by keeping the mine open.

Does this mean that the firm should shut down the mine in the first year? Suppose that it would cost the firm $500,000 to reopen the mine once it had been shut down. Then it might be worth losing $80,000 this year to avoid incurring this cost next year. When making the first-period shut-down decision, the mine managers cannot be sure what the price of gold will be next year and whether they will want to open the mine then. Suppose there is a 50-50 chance that the price of gold will rise to $920 per ounce next year and a 50-50 chance that the price will remain at $400 per ounce. What should the managers do?

Figure 7.10 shows the decision tree for their problem. In the first year, they must decide to *keep open* the mine or to *shut down* the mine. In the second year, the firm again confronts the decision whether to have the mine open or closed, but now it knows the second-year price. As always, we solve the decision problem by working backwards. If the mine were shut down in the first year, then it would cost $600,000 to make it safe to operate (the $500,000 reopening cost and the

Figure 7.10

The Mine Managers' Decision Tree

In the first year, the firm must decide whether to keep the mine open or to close it. In the second year, the firm again confronts the decision of whether to have the mine open or closed, but now it knows the second-year price.

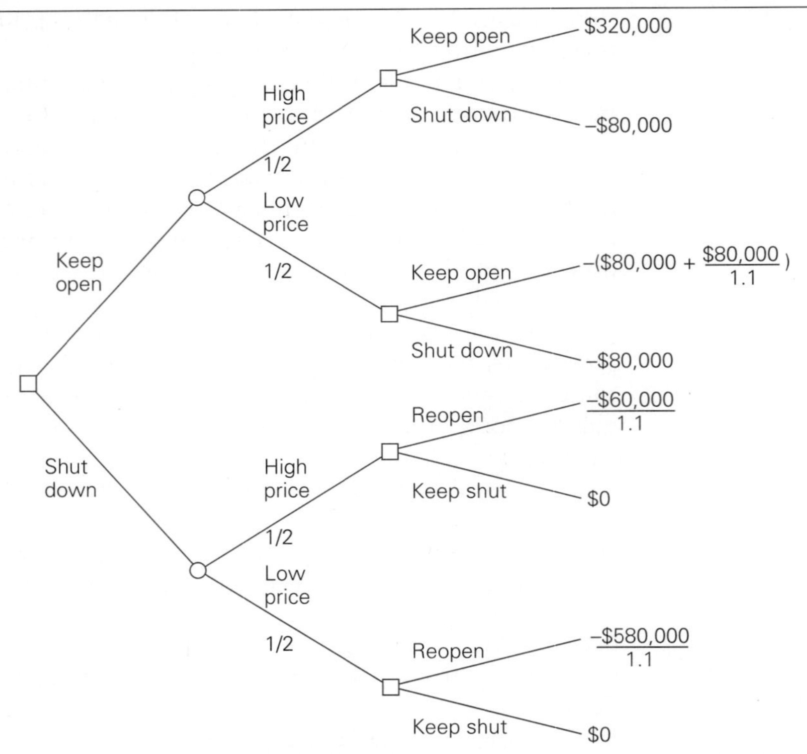

$100,000 maintenance cost). Including the cost of extraction, producing 1,000 ounces of gold in the second year would cost $980,000 (= $600,000 + 1,000 × $380). Hence, the average cost of the gold would be $980 per ounce. Even if the cost of gold rises to $920 per ounce, average revenue would be less than average cost, so the firm would not reopen the mine. Hence, the expected present value of the firm's second-year profit is $0 if the mine shuts down in the first year.

Now, consider what would happen in the second year if the firm had kept the mine open in the first year. In this case, it would cost the firm only $100,000 to keep the mine in operating condition for the second year. Hence, the firm's cost of producing 1,000 ounces of gold in the second year would be $480,000 (= $100,000 + 1,000 × $380), and its average cost would be $480 per ounce. If the price of gold were $400 an ounce, the firm would be better off shutting the mine down in the second period than keeping it open, and the present value of the mine's profit for the two years would be −$80,000, the losses suffered in the first year. There is also a 50-50 chance that the price of gold will rise to $920 per ounce. In this case, the firm would keep the mine open in the second year, during which time it would earn a profit of $440,000 (= ($920 − $480) × 1,000). Discounting this future profit by the interest rate of 10 percent and subtracting out the first-year loss, the present value of the firm's profit would be $320,000 (= $440,000/1.1 − $80,000). Of course, we have to remember that the firm does not choose the price of gold. Hence, if it keeps the mine open, there is a 50-50 chance of losing $80,000 and a 50-50 chance of making $320,000. Taking the average of these two profit levels, the firm's expected profit if it keeps the mine open is $120,000.

We have now found that by keeping the mine open for the first year, the firm earns expected profits of $120,000; by closing the mine in the first year, it earns no profit. Therefore, the firm should keep the mine open in the first year even though first-year revenue is less than first-year cost. By keeping the mine open, the firm is keeping its options open. The *option value* of an open mine is greater than the $80,000 loss suffered during the first year to keep it open.

SECTION RECAP

Firms often must make decisions whose consequences are uncertain or will be felt over a long period of time. In this section we have seen that, with some slight elaboration, the assumption of profit maximization continues to be useful. A firm facing uncertainty acts to maximize the expected value of its profits. A firm that is taking actions with long-term consequences acts to maximize the present value of its future profit stream. In each case, the stock market plays a key role in inducing firms' owners to desire profit maximization. Through the use of various control mechanisms, managers have incentives to respect the owners' interests.

SUMMARY

In this chapter, we turned from the study of households to the study of firms and we introduced some general principles that apply to the firm's behavior regardless of the type of market in which the firm operates.

- The economic theory of the firm is based on the assumption that the firm acts to maximize its profit.
- Economic profit is equal to total revenue minus total economic cost.
- Economic cost is measured by opportunity cost (the value of an input in its best alternative use). Sunk expenditures are not part of economic cost.
- Two rules determine the optimal level of output. First, there is the *marginal output rule*: If the firm does not shut down, then it should produce output at a level where marginal revenue is equal to marginal cost.
- The second general rule is the *shut-down rule*: The firm should shut down if, at every level of output, the average revenue that the firm receives for its output is less than the average economic cost of production.
- Although there are reasons to doubt the view that the firm is a single, profit-maximizing decision maker, this assumption works well in the sense of giving us good predictions about a firm's behavior. While a firm's managers might well wish to pursue individual utility maximization at the expense of profits, a variety of economic forces gives managers incentives to maximize profits.
- The theory of the firm applies to firms that must take actions having consequences spread out over time. Such firms act to maximize the present value of their profits.
- The theory of the firm applies to firms that face uncertainty about their profits. Such firms act to maximize the expected value of their profits.

DISCUSSION QUESTIONS

7.1 Suppose that a young chef opened his own restaurant. To do so, he quit his job, which was paying $28,000 per year; cashed in a $5,000 certificate of deposit that was yielding 5 percent (to purchase equipment); and took over a building owned by his wife which had been rented out for $1,000 per month. His expenses for the first year amounted to $50,000 for food, $40,000 for extra help, and $4,000 for utilities.

The chef is trying to figure out whether he would have been better off not being in business last year. He knows how to calculate his revenues, but he needs help with the cost side of the picture. What were the chef's total economic costs?

7.2 Suppose that you have opened your own word processing service. You bought an IBM-compatible machine based on the Intel Pentium chip. You paid $5,000 for the machine. As a result of increased competition in the personal computer market, the price of new Pentium machines has fallen to $2,500 and the price at which you could sell your used machine has fallen to $1,000. If you were not word processing, you could earn $20,000 per year. You have the opportunity to hire one assistant (he can do everything that you can do and could replace you) for $20,000 per year. It turns out that one person using one computer can produce 11,000 pages per year of typing services (it is impossible for two people to share one machine). Typing services can be sold for $2 per page.

Should you expand your business, shrink it but keep it running, or shut it down entirely?

7.3 The father of a family that owned a small restaurant made the following announcement: "We are going out of business because our children have grown up and will not work here. If they would work in our family business, we could make a profit, but they all are working elsewhere for higher wages." Discuss this statement.

7.4 Given below are some data on total revenue and total cost for a firm.

Total Output	Total Revenue	Total Cost
1	$15	$ 7
2	29	14
3	41	22
4	51	31
5	60	42
6	66	55
7	70	70

Calculate the firm's marginal and average cost curves and graph them. Calculate the firm's marginal and average revenue curves and graph them. How much output, if any, should this firm produce? Answer this question both numerically and graphically. How much profit does the firm earn?

7.5 Many firms must incur a one-time setup cost to begin production. For instance, whether to sell one copy of a word-processing program or a thousand, a company needs to write the basic computer code one time. Similarly, no matter how many planes it builds, an aircraft manufacturer has to incur the engineering and design costs once. As a result of setup costs, the marginal cost of the first unit may be extremely high—going from 0 to 1 unit of output triggers the need to bear the entire setup cost. More generally, costs may be such that marginal cost initially is greater than marginal revenue. The figure below illustrates a firm whose marginal cost curve crosses its marginal revenue curve at two different points. How much output, if any, should this firm plan to produce? How is your answer affected by the relative sizes of areas A and B?

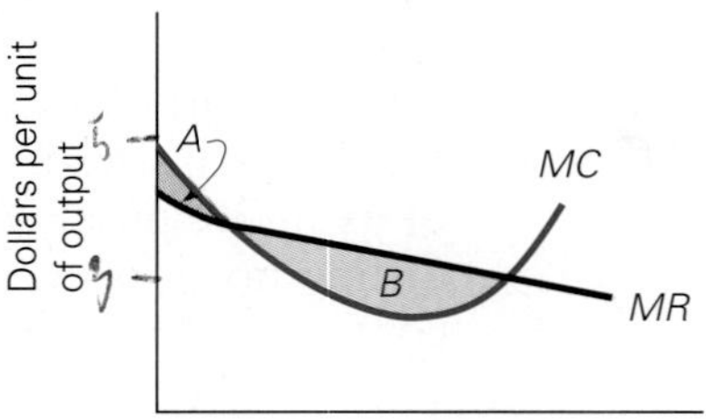

7.6 Explain what is wrong with the following argument. "Average cost tells me how much I am paying overall to produce my output. This is what I should compare the price to. Therefore, to maximize my profit, I should increase output up to the point at which my average revenue (the price of output) is equal to average cost."

7.7 In this chapter, we examined how a firm could find its profit-maximizing output level. Yet many real world firms appear to choose prices, rather than outputs. Suppose that American Certainty is sure that its demand, marginal revenue, and marginal cost curves are those graphed below. Explain why, for this firm, choosing the profit-maximizing output level is the same as choosing the profit-maximizing price level. Do you think the equivalence would still hold if the firm were uncertain about the demand curve that it faced?

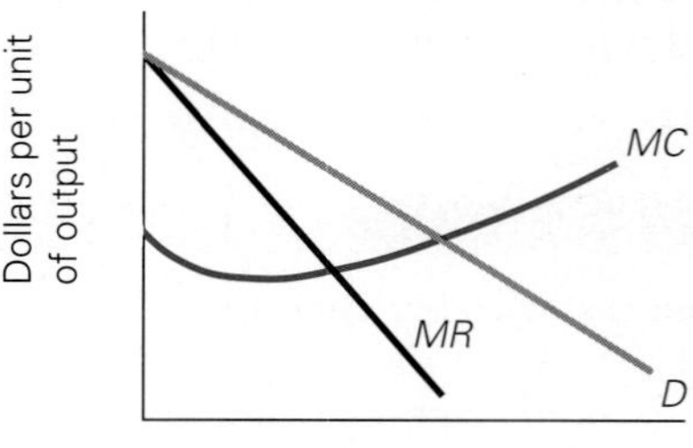

7.8 Some people have argued that hostile takeovers are more a symptom of managerial disregard for shareholder interests than a mechanism for keeping managers in line. Could a revenue-maximizing manager have incentives to make takeover bids that might be against the best interests of the firm's shareholders? Do you agree with the claim that shareholders would be better off if hostile takeovers were outlawed?

7.9 The CEO at American Trends, Inc., is examining the performance of the manager of the farm products division. The division manager is a "consumer" of only two goods, *R&D* and *executive offices*, and the division manager is given a fixed budget to spend on these two goods.

a. Suppose that the farm products division's initial budget is $\$B$ per year. Using indifference curves that exhibit diminishing marginal rate of substitution, illustrate the equilibrium amounts of R&D and executive offices.

The CEO notices that the manager seems to be allocating far too little money to R&D. The CEO responds by allocating an additional $\$I$ per year to the division with the restriction that the additional money *must be spent on R&D.*

b. Graphically illustrate the equilibrium amounts of R&D and executive offices to show that, as a result of the additional funds, the amount of R&D may rise or fall. What happens to the consumption of executive offices? Do you agree with the following claim: "Since the additional funds are targeted, they are a good way to control what the division manager is doing."

7.10 Many firms include stock options as part of their executive compensation packages. Often these options come with the requirement that the executive hold them for a minimum amount of time before he or she can exercise them. For example, when Michael Eisner of Disney receives part of his annual bonus in the form of stock, it comes with the restriction that he wait three years before selling it. Discuss how this practice may serve the interests of the firm's owners.

7.11 The Hurts Rental Car Company is deciding whether to buy a fleet of new cars to rent out. After two years, Hurts will have to sell the cars because their rental customers do not like old cars. The management at Hurts has made the following calculations: Hurts can buy the new cars for \$15,000 each. In each of the two years that a car will be rented out, it will bring in \$8,000 in revenues and cost \$2,000 to maintain. At the end of two years, Hurts will be able to sell the used cars for \$8,000 each. The firm can borrow or lend money at an annual interest rate of 10 percent. Should Hurts buy the fleet of new cars?

7.12 Consider the Hurts Rental Car Company again, under the more realistic assumption that the firm is not sure about the price at which it will be able to sell its used cars two years hence. In particular, suppose that the firm believes there is a ¼ chance that it will be able to sell the cars for \$5,000 each, and a ¾ chance that it will be able to sell the cars for \$10,000 each. Should the firm buy the fleet of cars?

7.13 In the early 1990s, there was an outcry at what were perceived to be unfairly high levels of executive compensation. Then-candidate Bill Clinton was particularly concerned that performance-based compensation was a special benefit for executives only. He called for several government actions to remedy this perceived problem, including: "Eliminate *tax deductions for excessive executive pay* . . . Companies will be allowed to deduct bonuses tied to profits for top executives only if other employees also receive bonuses . . . Restore the link between pay and performance by encouraging companies to provide for *employee ownership and profit sharing for all employees,* not just executives" (Clinton and Gore 1992, 68, emphasis in the original). What are the economic arguments for treating executives and other employees similarly or differently when designing compensation packages?

7.14 In the text, we focused on the goals of large corporations with vast numbers of owners (shareholders). There are many firms with only one or a few owners each. Suppose that Felix manages a hardware store and is the sole owner. Would you expect Felix to maximize profit? When faced with uncertainty, do you think that Felix would act to maximize expected profit? What other goals might Felix pursue? Be sure to think carefully about the economic cost of Felix's labor when you think about the firm's economic profit and whether Felix will act to maximize it.

7.15 Kaiser Health Foundation, the largest health care provider in the United States, has to build hospitals before knowing exactly what the demand for them will be. They can choose to build "small" hospitals or "large" hospitals. Large hospitals cost more to build than small ones and are unprofitable if demand turns out to be weak. Small hospitals are inadequate to meet Kaiser's needs if demand is strong.

Once built, it is very costly to expand a small hospital into a large one. However, "flexible" hospitals can be built. A flexible hospital has the same initial size as a small hospital, but can be more easily expanded. The initial cost of a flexible hospital is greater than that of a small hospital. Moreover, the total cost of a flexible hospital that has been expanded to the large size is greater than the cost of a large hospital. Why might it still make sense for Kaiser to construct flexible hospitals?

7.16 Suppose that, before choosing whether to open the mine in the first year, the owners of the gold mine discussed at the end of the chapter could purchase a perfect forecast of the second-year price. How much would this information be worth to them? (*Hint:* Recall from Chapter 6 what we did when we examined the value of information to households.)

Technology and Production

> *There is more than one way to skin a cat.*
>
> —Proverb

As 1989 drew to a close, the Japanese automotive giants Toyota and Nissan each launched a new line of cars in the American market. Nissan created its Infiniti division while Toyota set up Lexus. When these two divisions brought out their first models, each firm faced a tremendous number of choices about how to manufacture its cars. The body of a car can be made from steel, fiberglass, aluminum, or even plastic. A car can be built entirely by hand or it can be built almost entirely by robots on an automated assembly line. Like these car makers, every firm must decide what combination of inputs to use to produce output.

A firm cares about its input combinations for two reasons. First, some are better than others. Because inputs are costly to the firm, it wants to use the cheapest possible combination that can produce its chosen amount of output. Second, finding the least-cost combination of inputs enables the firm to calculate its marginal and average cost curves. As we saw in the last chapter, these curves play a major role in the firm's choice of output level. Hence, to understand firm decision making, we must understand the production choices available to it.

8.1 TECHNOLOGY

We characterize the firm's options for combining inputs to obtain output as its *technology*. This section develops an approach to modeling the firm's technological opportunities.

THE PRODUCTION FUNCTION

Consider National Motors, which uses a variety of inputs, including labor, steel, copper wire, vinyl, robots, and electricity, to produce automobiles. Let's focus on the choice between just two of these inputs: labor (which we denote L) and

Table 8.1

National Motors' Production Function

National Motors' production function summarizes the engineering data on manufacturing by giving the highest level of output the firm can produce with each different input combination.

Inputs per Day		
Laborers	Robots	Output per day
500	300	160
1,000	200	160
1,300	170	160
500	350	180
1,000	220	180
1,300	190	180

robots (which we denote K).[1] In this example and elsewhere, we use the term *capital* to refer to inputs such as factory buildings and machinery that last over time. Suppose that the managers at National Motors are trying to decide how much to automate its assembly line. To keep things simple, suppose that the other input requirements are not affected by the labor/robot decision. The managers at National Motors have asked the engineering department to determine the relationship among the various combinations of laborers and robots and the levels of output that they can produce. The engineering report is shown in Table 8.1, in which we see, for example, that the firm can assemble 160 cars per day when using 1,000 laborers and 200 robots.

production function A schedule that shows the *highest* level of output the firm can produce from given combination of inputs.

total product of L and K The highest total amount of output the firm can produce given the amounts of its inputs.

This representation of the technological choices available to the firm is known as a **production function:** a schedule that shows the *highest* level of output the firm can produce from a given combination of inputs. The highest total amount of output the firm can produce given the amounts of its inputs is also referred to as the **total product of L and K.**

We represent the production function algebraically by using $F(L,K)$ to denote the highest level of output that can be produced by using L workers and K robots.[2] For National Motors, we can use $F(L,K)$ as a shorthand way of expressing the information in Table 8.1. Referring back to that table, we see that $F(1{,}000, 200) = 160$, for example. Sometimes, we can express the production function as a specific algebraic function rather than describing it in tabular form. For instance, a firm that has 4 units of labor and 16 units of capital, and whose production function is $F(L,K) = 3L + 2\sqrt{K}$, can produce $3 \times 4 + 2\sqrt{16} = 20$ units of output.

Using the production function $F(L,K)$ to denote the total product that can be produced using L units of labor and K units of capital is quite similar to our earlier use of the utility function $U(X,Y)$ to denote the total utility that could be derived from the consumption of X units of one good and Y units of another. But there is one important difference. As noted in Chapter 2, the utility function is ordinal, not cardinal. Consequently, statements such as "Susan doubled her utility level" are meaningless. On the other hand, it makes perfect sense to say "Exxon doubled its gasoline production level."

[1]If you don't like using a K to stand for capital, you should blame noted economist Karl Marx for writing *Das Kapital.*

[2]We use F for the production function instead of P so we won't confuse it with price.

Isoquants

It also is useful to represent the production function graphically. The problem we face is graphing three variables (the two inputs and the output) on only two axes. Think about what we are going to do with the information. We want to represent the different input combinations available to the firm to produce a given amount of output. So, the axes of our graph correspond to the two inputs. This is the same trick we used to graph utility functions, where the axes were the two goods involved. Consider Figure 8.1, in which the quantity of labor, L, is measured on the horizontal axis and the quantity of robots, K, on the vertical. Each point in the quadrant represents some combination of robots and labor, and therefore is associated with some amount of output. Suppose now that we want to graph the different combinations of inputs that give us some fixed level of production, say 180 cars per day. Which combinations of inputs can the firm use? From Table 8.1, we see that 500 laborers and 350 robots will do the job; this is represented by point a in Figure 8.1. Table 8.1 tells us that the firm can also use 1,000 workers and 220 robots (point b in the figure). Although not shown in Table 8.1, many other combinations will work as well. Connecting all of these combinations together gives us an **isoquant,** a curve that shows the set for all pairs of inputs that yield the same level of output (*iso* denotes constant, and *quant* means quantity). In Figure 8.1, the curve labeled x_{180} is National Motors' isoquant for 180 automobiles per day. Note the similarity between a firm's isoquants and a household's indifference curves, which we examined in Chapter 2. A producer's isoquant indicates the various combinations of inputs that produce a fixed level of output, just as a consumer's indifference curve indicates the various combinations of commodities that produce a fixed level of utility.

isoquant
A curve showing all of the input combinations that yield the same level of output.

Of course, we selected the initial output level of 180 cars per day arbitrarily. We can draw an isoquant for any output rate. Consider an output level of 200 cars per day. We know that the isoquant for 200 cars lies above and to the right of the isoquant for 180 cars because more capital and labor are required to produce more output. Similarly, the isoquant for 160 cars lies below and to the left of the isoquant for 180 cars. These three isoquants are illustrated in Figure 8.2. The collection of all isoquants corresponding to a given production function is called the **isoquant map.** (PC 8.1)

isoquant map
The collection of all isoquants corresponding to a given production function.

How Many Inputs?

It clearly is unrealistic to assume that a firm uses only two inputs to produce its output. Even a company that makes candy bars with only two ingredients has to use many other factors, such as workers and machines to make the candy bars, and paper and foil in which to wrap them. It has to purchase trucking services to ship the candy to supermarkets and convenience stores. We examine the case of two factors not because it is realistic but because it is a useful simplification. All of the key insights that we gain from the two-factor case hold generally. Indeed, the Appendix to Chapter 9 shows how the theory developed here can be applied to any number of inputs.

8.1 PROGRESS CHECK

Suppose that National Motors has 200 robots in its plant. How many workers does the firm have to hire to produce 200 cars per day? How many workers would the firm have to hire to produce 200 cars per day if it had 300 robots?

Figure 8.1

Using an Isoquant to Graph the Production Function

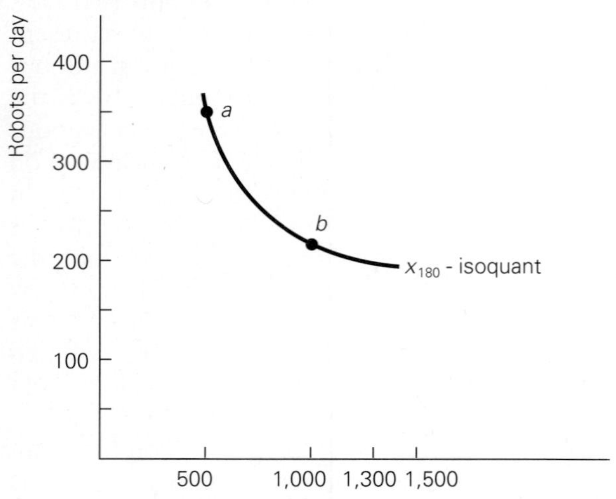

An isoquant shows the set of all input combinations that yield the same level of output.

Figure 8.2

National Motors' Isoquant Map

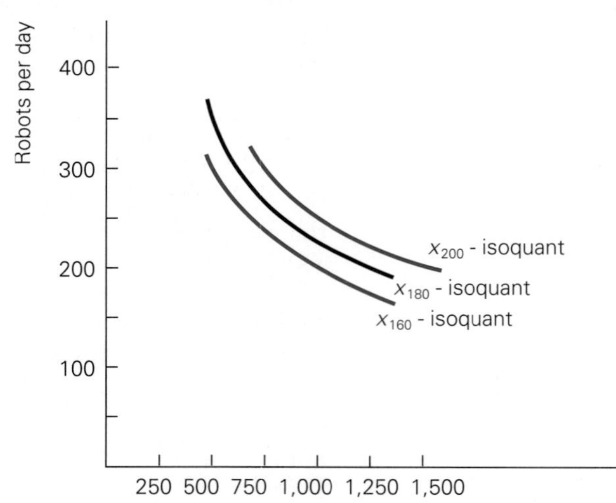

The collection of all isoquants corresponding to a given production function is called the *isoquant map*. The isoquant for 200 cars lies above the isoquant for 180 cars, because more capital and labor are required to produce more output.

What Is Output?

It is worth taking a minute to think about what a production function really measures. In the example we have been using, the output of the production process is cars. This example is typical in the sense that we tend to think of output as the end result of a process that produces something tangible—bicycles, houses, carrots, and so on. While there is nothing wrong in thinking about output this way, we should note that the notion of a production function applies to services just as well as to tangible goods. For example, hospitals combine labor (physicians and nurses) with capital (hypodermic needles and MRI machines) to produce health services. Similarly, schools use labor (teachers) and capital (desks and books) to produce education or teaching services.

We stress this point because there is a common view that producing services is not as valuable as producing tangible goods. One writer has noted disapprovingly that "in recent years the [U.S.] GNP—has increasingly consisted of the wealth-consuming service industries and much less of the wealth-producing industries" (Bingham 1988, A26). Economists view this distinction between "wealth-consuming" and "wealth-producing" industries as nonsense. Although the output levels of industries supplying services may be more difficult to measure than those of industries producing tangible goods, they are every bit as real and economically valuable. As Samuelson (1988, 50) notes, it is silly to say that making a car is useful, but "that delivering the car to the dealer (a service), selling it (a service), financing it (a service), insuring it (a service) or repairing it (a service) are all inessential jobs."

THE DECISION-MAKING HORIZON

The production function tells us whether a given input combination is capable of producing a particular amount of output. By itself, the production function does not tell us whether the firm can actually obtain the input combination under consideration. In order to know what input combinations are available to the firm, we also need to consider the time horizon over which the firm makes its input choices. Time matters because the firm's ability to vary its inputs depends on how much time it has to change them. The quantities of some inputs can be varied rather quickly. For instance, a local moving company employing unskilled workers to load its trucks may be able to hire additional employees in just a day or two. Other firms need a long time to adjust their usage of certain inputs. If Chrysler decides to use additional robots on its assembly line, there may be a lag of many months between the time the machines are ordered and the time they are installed. And the construction of a new factory can take years. Over seven years elapsed between the day that General Motors decided to construct a new factory as part of its Saturn project and the day the factory first produced automobiles.

Clearly, the firm must consider whether it can vary an input level or not. When Chrysler is setting next week's production plan, it is a waste of time to estimate how many cars could be produced if it had another 30 robots; the firm cannot order and install a new set of robots in one week. In making its choices, the firm has to concern itself with those inputs whose levels it can alter. A factor whose level can be varied is known as a **variable factor.** In contrast, a factor whose level cannot be varied is known as a **fixed factor.**

variable factor
A factor whose level can be varied over the relevant planning horizon.

fixed factor
A factor whose level cannot be varied over the relevant planning horizon.

short run
A time period over which only one of the firm's inputs is variable, while all others are fixed.

long run
A period of time long enough that all of the factors are variable and none is fixed.

Whether a given factor is variable or fixed depends on the firm's time horizon. In terms of production for the next week, robots are a fixed factor, but for a firm planning its production for next year, robots are a variable factor. In general, the more time a firm has to make its input decisions, the more options it has—the more factors will be variable rather than fixed. In other words, fewer options are available in the *short run* than in the *long run.*

To make this distinction more precise, we define the **short run** as a time period over which only one of the firm's inputs is a variable factor while all of the others are fixed factors. In other words, the short run is a time period over which the quantity of one input can be varied, but the quantities of all of the firm's other production factors cannot be adjusted. In contrast, the **long run** is a time period long enough that all of the factors are variable and none is fixed. Notice that the answer to the question, "How short is the short run?" depends on the particular technology and the markets in which the firm buys its inputs. A firm that purchases bicycles and hires people to ride on them to hand-deliver messages between businesses in a large city can buy additional bicycles in a few minutes. It may take the firm a day or two to locate and hire additional riders. One day is the short run because, in the course of a day, bicycles are a variable factor, but riders are a fixed factor. Given two days, however, the firm can vary the levels of both inputs and is making long-run decisions. For this firm, a two-day period is the long run! On the other hand, an aircraft-manufacturing firm that relies on complex machine tools that are part of a large integrated assembly process might have to wait years before it can fully adjust all of its inputs; in the aircraft industry, the short run may be several years.

If you think about aircraft manufacturing, which requires a huge number of different inputs, you may notice that talking solely about the short run and the long run is a simplification. When a firm uses just two inputs, the short run and the long run are the whole story; when only one factor is variable, the firm is in the short run, and when both factors are variable, the firm is in the long run. When a firm employs more than two factors in production, however, there may be more to the story. It is possible to have "medium runs" in which several factors are variable while several others are fixed. Fortunately, the important insights of the theory of the firm can all be seen from consideration of just the short and long runs, and we will stick to this dichotomy. The critical point to keep in mind is that the longer the firm's decision-making horizon, the greater are its opportunities to adjust its input levels.

Now, let's see how the firm can use the isoquant map to identify feasible input choices. Let's first consider a short-run decision. Assume that labor is a variable factor for National Motors (the firm can hire and fire workers in a few days) and robots are fixed (there is a 10-month lead time for ordering new ones or finding a buyer for existing ones). For this firm, 10 months is a short-run time horizon. Now, suppose that National Motors has 200 robots installed and wants to produce 160 automobiles per day beginning next week. If National Motors tried to use an input combination like point *c* in Figure 8.3 that is below the x_{160}-isoquant, it would be unable to produce 160 cars per day. Hence, input combinations under the isoquant are not feasible. The firm could use an input combination above the isoquant, point *d* for example, but the firm would be using more inputs than necessary. Because inputs are costly and the firm wants to keep costs as low as possible, it would never choose an input combination like *d* to produce 160 cars per day. Consequently, we do not need to consider such points further.

To produce 160 cars per day, the firm chooses among the input combinations lying exactly on the x_{160}-isoquant in Figure 8.3. But the firm is making a short-run decision and the number of robots is fixed at 200. Consequently, the only available input combination on the x_{160}-isoquant is (1,000, 200); if the firm wants to produce 160 automobiles per day, its only choice is to use the 200 robots it has in place and hire 1,000 laborers. Put another way, since the firm's level of capital is fixed in the short run, its input decision consists of making sure it hires just enough labor to produce the desired output—it finds the level of L that satisfies $F(L, 200) = 160$.

Now consider National Motors' long-run decision. Suppose the firm wants to produce 160 cars per day. In the long run, both labor and robots are variable, so the firm can choose from among any combination of the two that can produce 160 cars per day. The set of feasible input combinations is now given by the *entire* x_{160}-isoquant in Figure 8.3. Using our algebraic notation, the firm is free to choose any combination of L and K such that $F(L,K) = 160$. As in the short run, it would be wasteful to use an input combination above the isoquant like point *d*. Notice an important difference between the short and long runs. In the long run, the firm has more options available to produce a given level of output; it can vary the levels of all inputs. Hence, any choice the firm can make it the short run, it can also make in the long run. But the reverse is not true. Thus, we would expect the firm to spend less on the long-run combination of inputs than on the short-run combination. We will make this intuition more precise in the next chapter.

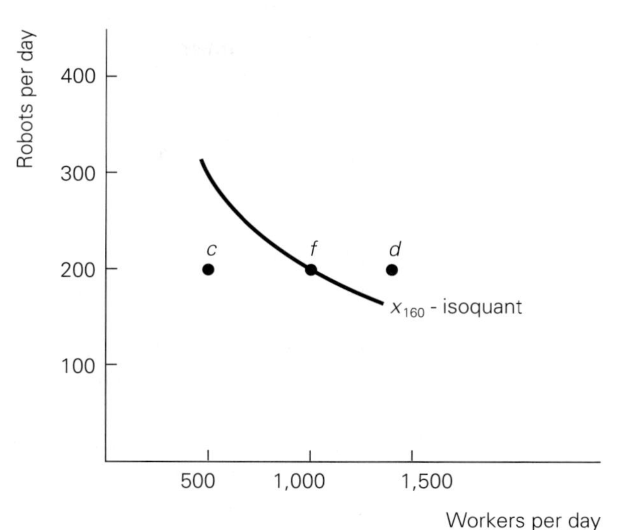

Figure 8.3

Representing the Available Input Choices

To produce 160 cars per day, the firm will choose among the input combinations lying on the x_{160}-isoquant. In the short run, the number of robots is fixed at 200, and the only available input combination on the x_{160}-isoquant is (1,000, 200). In the long run, both factors are variable, so the firm can choose any combination on the x_{160}-isoquant.

SECTION RECAP

To choose the cost-minimizing input combination, the firm must know what input choices are available to it. The production function tells the firm how much output it can obtain from each combination of inputs. With this information, the firm can identify the set of input combinations that can be used to produce any given amount of output. In the short run, only one of the firm's inputs is variable, and the firm's only choice is to make sure it uses enough of this input to produce the desired output. In the long run, the firm can vary all of its inputs, and it can pick any input combination on the appropriate isoquant.

8.2 PROPERTIES OF THE PRODUCTION FUNCTION

Before using the production function to analyze firm behavior, it is helpful to examine a few of its properties. We start by considering how production responds to a change in a single input level. This property plays an important role in short-run input choice since, in the short run, the firm has to make production decisions involving a single input level: the variable input. We then consider properties that involve changes in several inputs at once and thus are relevant to long-run decision making.

MARGINAL PHYSICAL PRODUCT

marginal physical product
The extra amount of output that can be produced when the firm uses one additional unit of an input.

When a firm is choosing how much of an input to purchase, it has to evaluate the benefit of purchasing the input. One way to measure the benefit is to calculate how much output would be contributed by one more unit of the input, holding fixed the levels of any other inputs. The extra amount of output that can be produced when the firm uses more of one input, holding the levels of other inputs constant, is known as that input's **marginal physical product** (*MPP*). Hence, if using an additional ΔL units of labor raises output by ΔX, the marginal physical product of labor:

$$MPP_L = \Delta X/\Delta L. \quad (8.1)$$

MPP is measured in terms of actual units of output per unit of input (such as cars per hour of labor).

Let's examine the relationship between the marginal physical product and the production function. Suppose that National Motors has 200 robots in place and we want to find the marginal physical product of labor when the firm has hired 1,000 workers and is considering hiring one more. This calculation requires comparing the output produced by 1,000 workers with the output produced by 1,001 workers, holding the capital stock fixed at 200 robots. According to Table 8.1, output with 1,000 workers and 200 robots is 160 cars per day. Suppose that the output with 1,001 workers and 200 robots is 160.1 cars per day. The marginal physical product of labor is 0.1. It may seem odd to you that the marginal physical product is less than 1—who would buy one-tenth of a car? What this number really tells us is that either the firm would have to hire 10 new workers to get one more car per day, or it would have to wait 10 days before it had an additional car to sell if it hired only one more worker per day. (PC 8.2)

In many situations, we want to know what happens to the marginal product of a factor as the firm increases the usage of that factor, *ceteris paribus.* As National Motors adds successively more laborers, how does the *incremental* contribution of each laborer compare with that of earlier laborers? The answer depends on the nature of the firm's technology. The marginal physical product of a factor may increase, be constant, or diminish as more of the factor is employed, *ceteris paribus.*

8.2 PROGRESS CHECK

Write an algebraic expression for the marginal physical product of capital MPP_K. What does MPP_K measure?

Increasing Marginal Returns

At least initially, the marginal productivity of an input often increases with the quantity of that input used, *ceteris paribus.* A modern chemical plant is highly automated and requires very few people to operate it. But only one worker may be incapable of running the plant alone; there simply may be too many flows to monitor and control at once. Consequently, a single plant operator may be unable to produce any output at all. Two workers may be able to run the plant, although at an extremely low rate of output. Adding a third may really help to get things going. Table 8.2 shows the total product corresponding to different numbers of laborers working in a plant of fixed size and design (the 60 units of capital may be thought of as $60 million of buildings and equipment).

From this table, we can calculate the marginal physical product of labor at various points on the production function. A single worker can produce no output alone. Hence, if the firm has no workers at the moment, then the marginal physical product of the first worker is zero. Output does rise when a second worker is hired. Taking the difference between total output with one and two workers in Table 8.2, we find that the marginal physical product of the second laborer is 8. The marginal physical product of the third worker is 24, which is even greater. (PC 8.3)

8.3 PROGRESS CHECK

What is the marginal physical product of labor when the firm has 60 units of capital and increases its labor from four workers to five?

Table 8.2

Finding the Marginal Physical Product of Labor from the Production Function

The extra amount of output that can be produced when the firm hires one additional unit of labor is called the marginal physical product of labor. The production function for this chemical plant exhibits increasing marginal returns.

Total Number of Laborers	Total Amount of Capital	Total Output	Marginal Product of Labor
0	60	0	
			0
1	60	0	
			8
2	60	8	
			24
3	60	32	
			38
4	60	70	
			(fill in)
5	60	147	
			91
6	60	238	
			192
7	60	430	

Figure 8.4

Total Product and Marginal Product with Increasing Marginal Returns to Labor

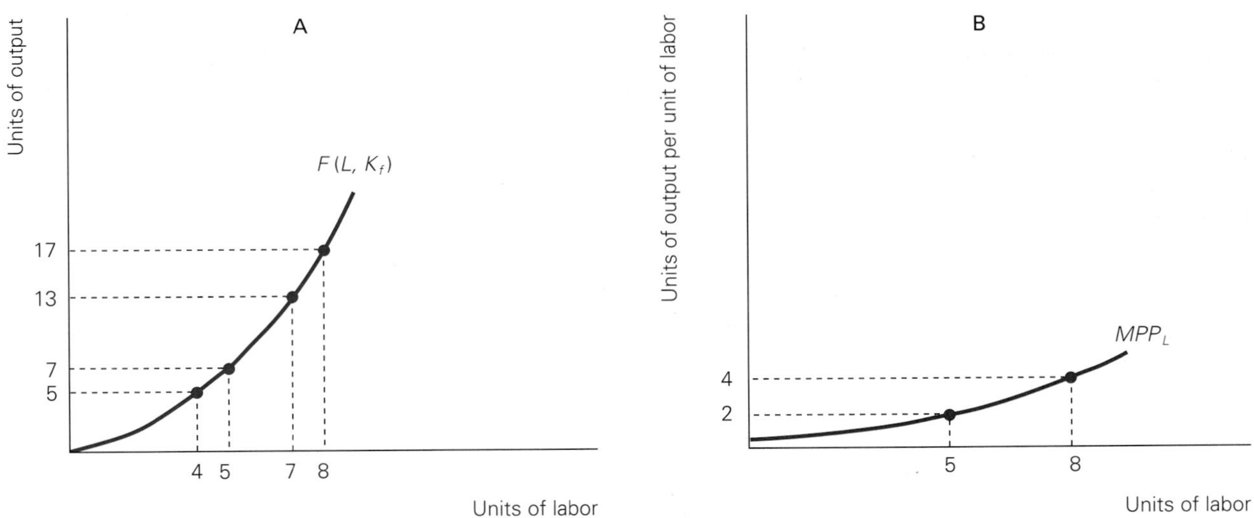

The slope of the total product curve is the marginal physical product of labor. When the firm's technology exhibits increasing marginal returns to labor, the total product curve gets steeper as we increase the quantity of labor, and the marginal physical product curve is upward sloping.

increasing marginal returns
A technology exhibits increasing marginal returns when the marginal physical product of an input rises as the amount of the input used increases.

Whenever, as in this example, the marginal physical product of labor rises as more workers are hired, we say that the associated technology is subject to **increasing marginal returns.** Stated in terms of the total product, a technology is subject to increasing marginal returns when the total product rises faster and faster as set increments of a factor are added.

Figure 8.4 illustrates the relationship between the total product curve and the marginal product curve. Panel A shows the total product curve for a firm whose capital level is fixed at K_f. Units of output are measured on the vertical axis while the amount of labor hired is on the horizontal axis. The graph of

Figure 8.5

Constant Marginal Returns to Labor

When the technology exhibits constant marginal returns, the marginal physical product of labor is unaffected by changes in the amount of labor employed, and the marginal physical product curve is flat.

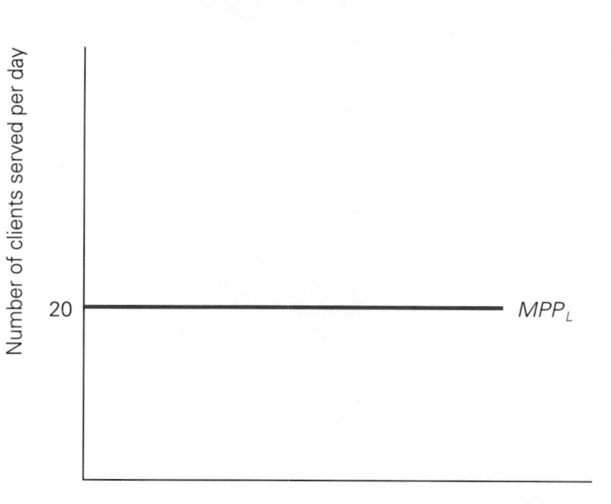

$F(L,K_f)$ illustrates how the amount of output rises as the amount of labor hired, L, is increased while holding the amount of capital hired fixed at K_f.

To see this curve's relationship to the marginal physical product of labor, suppose that the firm were hiring 4 units of labor. Reading up from 4 on the horizontal axis to the total product curve and over to the vertical axis, we see that the firm would produce 5 units of output. If the firm employs one more unit of labor, the graph indicates that output rises to 7 units. A one-unit increase in the amount of labor used in production leads to a two-unit increase in output. Hence, the slope of the total product curve is $(7 - 5)/1 = 2$. Because 2 is also the marginal physical product of labor, we have just shown that *the slope of the total product curve (as we change the amount of labor while holding the amount of capital fixed) is equal to the marginal physical product of labor*. The marginal physical product curve for labor is graphed in Panel B of Figure 8.4.

When the firm's technology exhibits increasing marginal returns to labor, the total product increases more quickly as additional units of that input are employed. The total product curve gets steeper as we increase the amount of labor hired. Because the height of the MPP_L curve is equal to the slope of the total product curve, the marginal physical product curve for labor is upward sloping in Figure 8.4.

constant marginal returns
A technology exhibits constant marginal returns when there is a range of input levels over which the marginal product of a factor remains unchanged as the amount of the factor used increases.

Constant Marginal Returns

Now consider a firm that provides walk-in legal consultations. Each lawyer hired can talk to 20 clients a day regardless of the number of other lawyers hired by the firm. Hence, the marginal physical product of labor is 20 consultations per day no matter how many lawyers the firm employs. When the marginal physical product of a factor remains unchanged as the amount of the factor used increases, the technology is said to exhibit **constant marginal returns.** With con-

8.4 PROGRESS CHECK

Draw a graph of the total product curve for the law firm described above.

Figure 8.6

Decreasing Marginal Returns to Labor

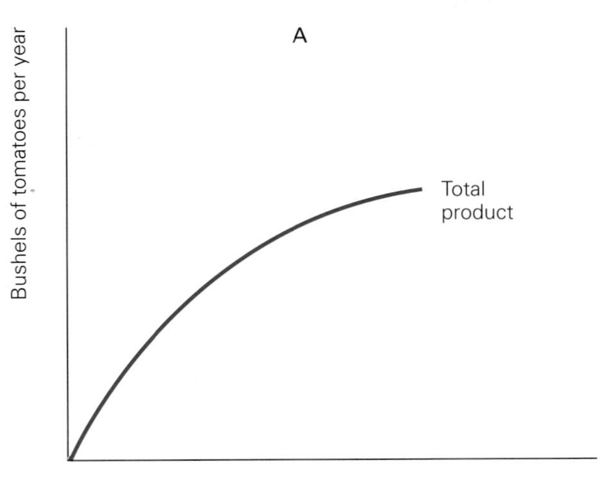

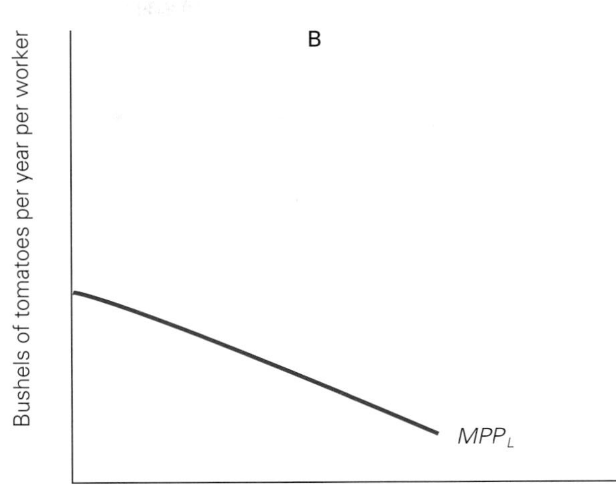

When a technology exhibits diminishing marginal returns, the marginal physical product curve falls as the quantity of the input rises, but the curve remains positive. Since the height of the marginal product curve is the slope of the total product curve, the total product increases as the number of workers rises, but at a decreasing rate (the curve becomes flatter as the amount of labor rises).

stant marginal returns, the height of the marginal physical product curve is constant and the curve is flat as illustrated in Figure 8.5. (PC 8.4)

Diminishing Marginal Returns

As a third example of how marginal returns may vary, consider a tomato farmer making a short-run production decision: She has a fixed amount of land and is considering how much labor to hire. As she hires more and more labor, the workers are better able to fertilize, water, weed, and harvest the plants. Consequently, the total harvest of tomatoes rises. Figure 8.6, Panel A, illustrates this situation. While total output increases as additional labor is hired, it does so at a decreasing rate—at some point, the plants are so well watered and weeded that there is little room for improvement. In other words, the marginal physical product of labor falls as the quantity employed rises, holding the levels of all other factors constant. A technology for which the marginal physical product falls as the input level rises is said to exhibit **diminshing marginal returns.** The corresponding MPP_L schedule is depicted in Panel B of Figure 8.6. Since the height of this curve measures the contribution from hiring one more worker, and this contribution diminishes as the number of workers increases, the MPP_L curve slopes downward. Again, we see the relationship between the slope of the total product curve and the height of the marginal product curve: As the total product curve becomes flatter, the marginal product curve falls.

diminishing marginal returns
A technology exhibits diminishing marginal returns when the marginal physical product of an input falls as the amount of the input used increases.

Note again that although *marginal* returns are diminishing, *total* returns are increasing (as shown in Panel A). As more labor is added, more tomatoes are

Figure 8.7

National Motors' Total Product and Marginal Product of Labor Curves

This figure illustrates what is perhaps the most common situation: initially there are increasing marginal returns, then a range of constant marginal returns, followed by a range of diminishing marginal returns.

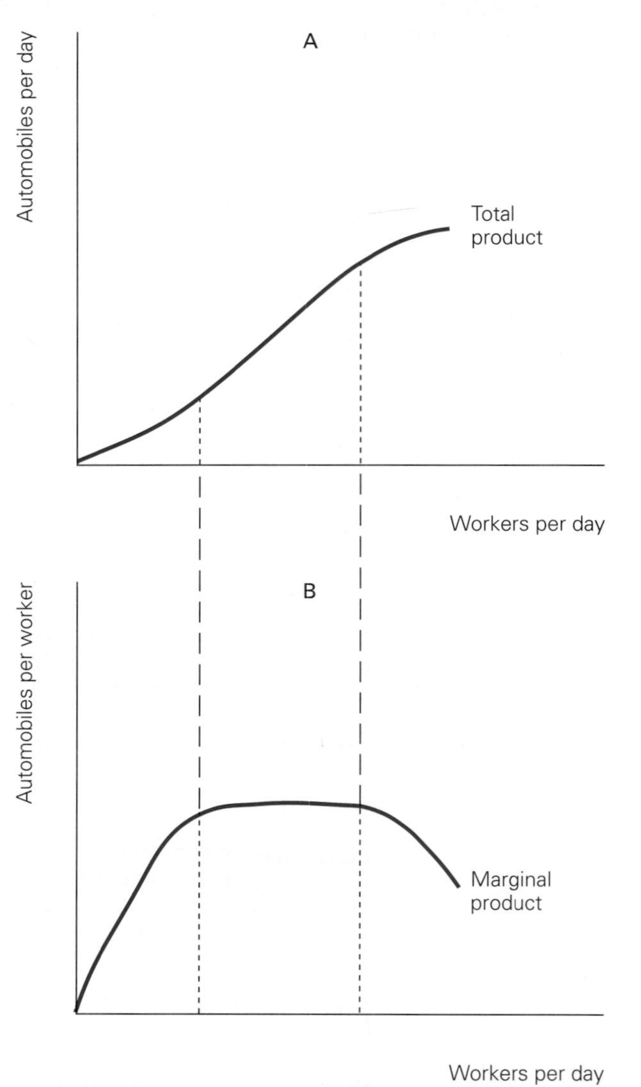

produced *overall*, although the *rate* of increase falls as the number of workers rises. The increase in total returns is reflected in a positive MPP_L curve; the increase of total returns at a diminishing rate is reflected in the downward slope of the MPP_L curve in Panel B.

A Changing Pattern of Marginal Returns

While we have examined each case separately, a single production function may exhibit all three patterns of marginal returns at different input levels. Consider National Motors' technology depicted in Figure 8.7. Initially, there are increasing marginal returns, then a brief range of constant marginal returns followed by a range of diminishing marginal returns. Panel A of Figure 8.7 illustrates the total product associated with this pattern of marginal returns, and Panel B shows the marginal returns directly.

Many other examples fit this pattern. For instance, we would expect this pattern for labor employed in a factory. At low levels of labor, the workers would have difficulty operating the machines and ensuring a smooth flow of work through the assembly process. Starting with just a few workers, added numbers can have a larger and larger incremental effect on total product—marginal returns to labor increase. At some point, however, the usefulness of more workers starts to decline. The plant eventually has more workers than can be used on the production line, because only so many people can work with a given piece of machinery. Once that point is reached, additional workers do not make much of an incremental contribution to total output. In other words, diminishing marginal returns to labor set in.

8.5 PROGRESS CHECK

In a briefing during the Persian Gulf War of 1991, U.S. Defense Secretary Cheney stated, "There is a point of diminishing returns, when you've struck all of the targets that you can strike from the air" (Pasztor and Mossberg 1991, A30). What kind of production function was Secretary Cheney characterizing? What was the variable input? What were the other inputs?

Studying for exams is another example of this pattern—one with which you probably are well familiar. A single night of studying can be a big help in reminding you about the terms and concepts that were covered earlier in the year. A second night of studying may improve your score even more than the first evening did, as you become comfortable solving problems on your own. In other words, initially, there are increasing marginal returns to studying. But at some point, you become so tired of looking at your notes and you have crammed so many ideas into your brain that spending additional time studying has little effect on your test performance—marginal returns diminish. Because diminishing marginal returns eventually appear in so many activities, people often speak of the "law" of diminishing marginal returns. (PC 8.5)

MARGINAL RATE OF TECHNICAL SUBSTITUTION

In the long run, the firm confronts choices involving changes in several input levels simultaneously. As already noted, the basic question we are trying to answer is how a firm chooses the right combination of inputs to produce a given level of output. In order to choose its long-run input mix, the firm has to be aware of the possibilities of factor substitution. For instance, if National Motors purchases more robots, by how many units can the firm reduce its labor force without reducing its total output level? This information is already implicit in the production function in Table 8.1. It indicates, for example, that when the firm is employing 1,300 laborers and 170 robots, it can lay off 300 workers and still maintain its output of 160 automobiles per day if it buys 30 more robots.

Isoquants help bring the issue of factor substitution into sharper focus. Consider Figure 8.8, in which the curve labeled x_{180} is National Motors' isoquant for 180 automobiles per day. We have already noted the similarity between a firm's isoquants and a household's indifference curves. The analogy to indifference curves is useful in understanding the economic significance of the shape of an isoquant. The slope of an indifference curve tells us the rate at which the household can trade one good for the other while maintaining the same level of utility.

Figure 8.8

Factor Substitution

If National Motors increases its labor force by ΔL from L_g to L_h, then the firm can reduce its use of robots by ΔK, from K_g to K_h, and still produce 180 cars per day. Around point g, the firm can substitute robots for workers at a rate of $K_g - K_h$ robots per $L_h - L_g$ workers.

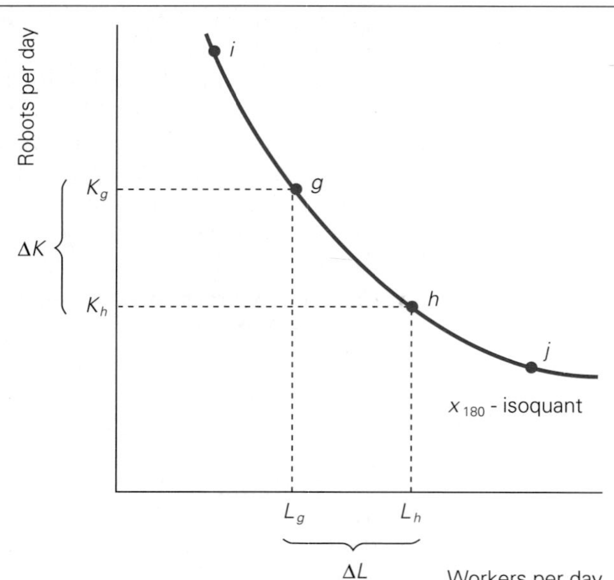

The slope of the isoquant tells us the rate at which the firm can substitute one factor for another while still producing the same level of output.

Specifically, consider point g on the x_{180}-isoquant in Figure 8.8, where National Motors employs L_g laborers and K_g robots. Suppose that National Motors decides to increase its employment of laborers by Δ_L up to L_h and wants to use them to replace some of the robots. How many fewer robots can the firm use and still produce 180 cars per day? We can find the answer graphically by moving from L_h on the horizontal axis up to point h on the isoquant and then reading over to K_h on the vertical axis. The graph indicates that the number of robots needed to produce 180 cars per day falls by $\Delta K = K_h - K_g$. Notice that because the firm is now using fewer robots, ΔK is a negative number. We have just shown that the firm can replace ΔK robots with ΔL workers without affecting its output level. In other words, around point g, the firm can substitute one input for another at a rate of $-\Delta K/\Delta L$. By definition, $\Delta K/\Delta L$ is the slope of the isoquant at point g. We conclude that the slope of the isoquant times -1 shows the rate at which the available technology allows the substitution of one factor for another. This rate is known as the **marginal rate of technical substitution** (*MRTS*). The marginal rate of technical substitution is completely analogous to the marginal rate of substitution for the household. We add *technical* to the name to distinguish the two concepts.

marginal rate of technical substitution The rate at which the available technology allows the substitution of one factor for another. It is -1 times the slope of the isoquant.

Two Polar Cases of Factor Substitution

The marginal rate of technical substitution is a very important property of a production technology. To firm up your understanding of how production functions and isoquants represent factor substitution, let's consider two polar cases.

Case I: Perfect Substitutes. Suppose a delivery company's trucks get 10 miles to the gallon using regular gasoline, G, and 8 miles to the gallon running on

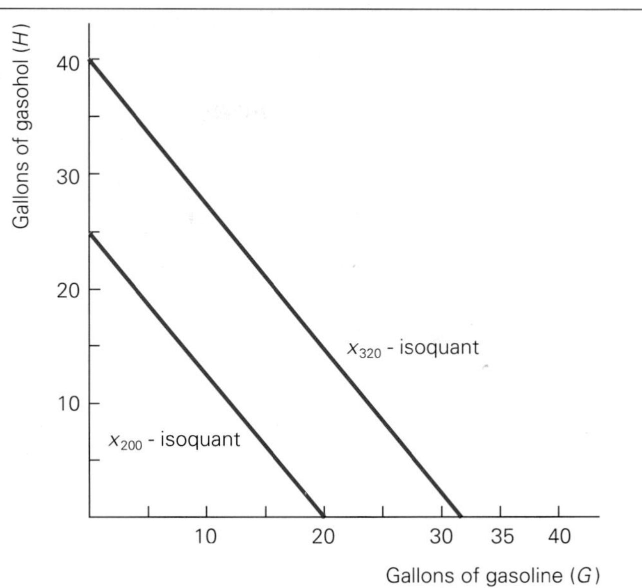

Figure 8.9

Perfect Substitutes

Whenever a technology has a constant marginal rate of technical substitution between two inputs, the resulting isoquants are straight lines. Since gasoline and gasohol can always be substituted for each other at the same rate, they are said to be perfect substitutes in this use.

gasohol, H, and that the required maintenance on the engines is the same no matter which fuel is used. This firm's production function can be summarized by the formula $F(G,H) = 10G + 8H$. What do the associated isoquants look like? To think about this question, select an arbitrary level of output, say 200 miles of deliveries, and ask what combinations of gasoline and gasohol could produce this output level. According to the production function, the combinations that can produce 200 miles of deliveries are represented by the equation $10G + 8H = 200$. This locus of combinations is a straight line. In Figure 8.9, gallons of gasoline are measured on the horizontal axis and gallons of gasohol on the vertical. Plugging in a value of 0 for H, we find that the horizontal intercept satisfies the condition that $10G = 200$. Hence, the horizontal intercept is 20 ($= 200/10$) gallons of gasoline. Similarly, the vertical intercept is 25 ($= 200/8$) gallons of gasohol. It follows that the slope of this x_{200}-isoquant is $-5/4$.

Now let's pick another arbitrary output level, say 320 miles of deliveries. This isoquant is labeled in Figure 8.9 as x_{320}. Since the firm must choose among combinations of gasoline and gasohol so that the total mileage adds up to 320, this isoquant is represented by the equation $10G + 8H = 320$. As before, the isoquant is a straight line with a slope of $-5/4$. In fact, when the production function is $F(G,H) = 10G + 8H$, every isoquant is a straight line whose slope is $-5/4$.

Now recall that -1 times the slope of an isoquant is equal to the marginal rate of technical substitution. Hence, when the production function is $F(G,H) = 10G + 8H$, the marginal rate of technical substitution always is $5/4$, regardless of the level of output and regardless of which factor combination the firm is using. This fact tells us that as inputs to the production of delivery services, 1 gallon of gasoline can be used to replace 1.25 gallons of gasohol, no matter how many total gallons of fuel the firm is using. Because gasoline and gasohol can always be substituted for each other at the same rate, for this technology gasoline and

perfect substitutes
Two inputs that have a constant marginal rate of technical substitution of one for the other.

gasohol are said to be **perfect substitutes.** More generally, whenever the isoquants for two inputs exhibit a constant marginal rate of technical substitution, the inputs are said to be perfect substitutes for one another.

It might seem to you that two inputs should be called perfect substitutes for one another only if they can be substituted on a one-for-one basis. Remember, however, that our initial choice of units of measurement was an arbitrary one. We could, for example, have declared that a "guylon" of gasohol contains five quarts (recall that a gallon holds four). Then one guylon of gasohol would be a perfect substitute for one gallon of gasoline.

Case II: No Factor Substitution. Now let's look at the opposite extreme from perfect factor substitution. Consider a candy company that produces its specialty, Almond Yummies, with two inputs, chocolate and almonds. The recipe requires that exactly 4 almonds and 1 ounce of chocolate be used for each Almond Yummy—no more, and no less. What do the isoquants associated with the Almond Yummies production function look like? In Figure 8.10, the number of almonds is measured on the horizontal axis, and the number of ounces of chocolate is on the vertical. According to the figure, the isoquants are right angles that are placed along a ray from the origin whose slope is ¼. Why? Suppose the firm is operating at point *m*, where it is using 12 almonds and 3 ounces of chocolate to produce three candy bars. If the firm were to purchase another ounce of chocolate and hold the number of almonds fixed (point *n* in the figure), how would its output change? Not at all. The almonds and chocolate have to be used in a fixed proportion of 4 to 1. The extra chocolate is useless because the firm will run out of almonds after producing three Almond Yummies. Hence, output remains constant and, by definition, points *m* and *n* are on the same isoquant as one another. Similarly, all points directly above *m* lie on the same isoquant as *m*. In the same way, starting at point *m*, if the firm purchases more almonds and holds the amount of chocolate fixed, output will not increase; therefore, all points directly to the right of point *m* are on the same isoquant as *m*. Because it is impossible to substitute chocolate for almonds, the marginal rate of technical substitution is zero along this range. From Figure 8.10, we see that the isoquants are right angles when it is impossible to substitute one input for the other. Only by increasing almonds and chocolate together can output be increased. In Figure 8.10, such an increase is represented by the movement from point *m* to point *o*. The resulting isoquant map probably looks familiar to you. Back in Chapter 2, we saw that a household has an indifference map with this pattern when the two goods are *perfect complements.* This similarity is due to the fact that, in either situation, there are two goods that have to be used together in a fixed proportion to produce what is valued (utility for the household, output for the firm).

The Relationship between *MPP* and *MRTS*

We can gain a better understanding of the marginal rate of technical substitution by examining its relationship to marginal physical product. The marginal rate of technical substitution describes a firm's ability to increase one input while decreasing the other in such a way that total output is held constant. The marginal physical product tells us what happens to output as the firm increases its use of one factor while holding the other factor level constant. These are two differ-

Figure 8.10

No Factor Substitution

When two inputs must be used together in a constant proportion, no factor substitution is possible, and the isoquants are right angles that are placed along a ray from the origin whose slope is equal to the proportion.

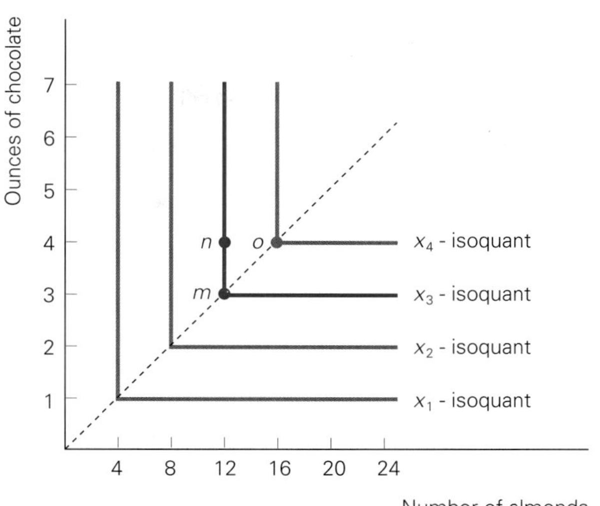

ent concepts, but they are related. We can express the marginal rate of technical substitution in terms of the marginal physical products of the factors.

To see the relationship between these two concepts, consider National Motors again. If the firm increases the number of workers employed, then it can use fewer robots and still produce the same number of cars. Figure 8.8 showed the rate of trade-off graphically by the slope of the isoquant. We also can express the rate at which the firm can substitute one factor for another algebraically. To do this, first note that when each additional worker raises output by MPP_L and the firm hires ΔL additional workers, total output rises by $MPP_L \times \Delta L$. For example, if the marginal physical product of labor is ½ and the firm hires 2 additional laborers, then the firm can produce 1 more car per day as a result of this hiring. The firm can reduce the number of robots until the amount of output lost from this reduction offsets the gain from the extra labor. If the firm employs ΔK fewer robots, the reduction in total output is $MPP_K \times \Delta K$. (Because the number of robots is being *reduced*, ΔK is a *negative* number.) Hence, to hold its total output level constant, the firm must choose ΔL and ΔK so that $MPP_L \times \Delta L$ just offsets $MPP_K \times \Delta K$, or

$$MPP_L \times \Delta L + MPP_K \times \Delta K = 0. \quad (8.2)$$

Equation (8.2) can be rewritten as

$$-\Delta K/\Delta L = MPP_L/MPP_K. \quad (8.3)$$

Recall that $-\Delta K/\Delta L$ is the marginal rate of technical substitution. Hence, Equation (8.3) tells us that

$$MRTS = MPP_L/MPP_K. \quad (8.4)$$

8.6 PROGRESS CHECK

Consider a firm with the production function $F(L,K) = L \times K$ that is using 10 units of labor and 5 units of capital. Find the marginal physical product of labor, the marginal physical product of capital, and the marginal rate of technical substitution. How would your answers change if the firm were using 20 units of capital instead of 5?

In words: *The marginal rate of technical substitution between two inputs is equal to the ratio of the marginal physical products of the inputs.* This formula will be useful to us when we examine the firm's equilibrium input choice. (PC 8.6)

We can use the relationship between *MPP* and *MRTS* to understand a common shape for isoquants. The isoquant back in Figure 8.8 is bowed inward toward the origin. In Chapter 2, we showed that an indifference curve with such a shape exhibits a diminishing marginal rate of substitution. Similarly, the isoquant in Figure 8.8 exhibits a **diminishing marginal rate of technical substitution:** Moving along the isoquant we see that as the amount of labor rises and the amount of capital falls, the *MRTS* also falls. For example, at point *i*, *MRTS* = 4, while at point *j*, *MRTS* = ⅙. Most technologies exhibit a diminishing marginal rate of technical substitution. This pattern is intuitively reasonable given the pervasiveness of diminishing marginal physical products. At point *i*, the firm is using a large amount of capital relative to the amount of labor. Since capital is relatively plentiful, its marginal physical product is low relative to that of labor. Thus, the firm could give up a lot of capital in return for a little more of the scarcer input, labor, and the isoquant is steeply sloped. At point *j*, the situation is the reverse. Here, the firm is employing a large amount of labor relative to the amount of capital. Now, capital has a high marginal physical product compared with labor. Hence, the firm can reduce its use of capital by only a small amount in return for more labor. Consequently, the isoquant is relatively flat. (PC 8.7)

diminishing marginal rate of technical substitution
A technology exhibits a diminishing rate of technical substitution when the rate at which one factor can be substituted for the other falls as the amount of the first factor rises.

8.7 PROGRESS CHECK

Draw an isoquant map that illustrates an increasing marginal rate of technical substitution.

RETURNS TO SCALE

The marginal rate of technical substitution tells us what happens as the firm substitutes one factor for another in such a way as to keep output constant. This is an important property for choosing the best way to produce a given amount of output in the long run. The firm also needs to consider what it would have to do to produce more output. Clearly, one way to get more output is for the firm to increase *all* of its inputs *proportionately*. Suppose that National Motors initially uses 1,000 laborers and 200 robots to produce 160 cars per day. How many cars per day could the firm produce if it doubled all of its inputs (that is, if it used 2,000 laborers and 400 robots)? We know that the total output would increase. But would it double, less than double, or even more than double? When a firm adjusts the levels of all of its inputs by the same proportion (here, each has been doubled), the firm is said to be changing its *scale* of operation. More generally, given an initial set of input levels, we can ask what happens if the firm changes its scale of operations by adjusting the levels of both inputs by the same proportion. The rate at which the amount of output increases as the firm increases all of its inputs proportionately is known as the **degree of returns to scale.** There are three different cases to consider: constant, increasing, and decreasing returns to scale.

degree of returns to scale
The rate at which the amount of output increases as the firm increases all of its inputs proportionately.

Constant Returns to Scale

When there are **constant returns to scale,** the amount of total output increases exactly in proportion to the increase in all of the factors. If the firm doubles its use of all factors, then total output doubles. If the firm cuts all input levels by one-third, then total output falls by one-third. We already have seen one example of a production function that exhibits constant returns to scale. The Almond Yummies production function indicates that chocolate and almonds have to be

constant returns to scale
A technology such that a proportional increase in all input levels leads to output growth in the same proportion.

used in the exact proportion of 4 to 1. Suppose that the firm initially is using 15 ounces of chocolate and 60 almonds. Since each Almond Yummy requires 1 ounce of chocolate and 4 almonds, the company can produce 15 Almond Yummies with this input combination. If the firm doubles its usage of both inputs, it also doubles its output; with 30 ounces of chocolate and 120 almonds, the firm can produce 30 Almond Yummies.

Increasing Returns to Scale

increasing returns to scale
A technology such that a proportional increase in all input levels leads to greater than proportionate output growth.

For many firms, the amount of total output rises more than proportionately with an increase in the factor levels. For example, a doubling of all inputs might triple or quadruple output. Such a technology is said to exhibit **increasing returns to scale.** For example, the production functions of railroads exhibit increasing returns to scale (Friedlander et al. 1991). The degree of returns to scale is an estimated 2.73 for the Illinois Central Gulf Railroad, which means that doubling all of the railroad's inputs would increase output by a factor of 5.46. Comparable figures for the Union Pacific Railway and the Atchison, Topeka & Santa Fe are 3.33 and 2.39, respectively.

Increasing returns to scale may arise from a variety of sources. One of the main sources is that a firm operating on a large scale can engage in extensive specialization. For example, if National Motors used only two workers and one robot, they would have to be able to perform all of the tasks necessary to manufacture an automobile. Given the tremendous number of tasks they would be called upon to perform, the workers would not be particularly effective producers. The story changes when the firm employs 600 workers and 300 robots. Now, each worker can be assigned a narrowly defined task at which he or she can excel. In the same way, it pays to develop specialized machinery. As a result, we would expect National Motors' output per worker and per robot to rise with the scale of production. Put another way, as the firm increases its scale, the amount of output rises faster than the input quantities.

There is another advantage of large-scale, high-volume production. Many studies have found that workers' productivity rises dramatically as they gain more experience producing a given product. Kaiser Permanente is the largest health maintenance organization in the United States. Because it is so large, its surgeons are able to specialize—each one concentrating on a particular type of operation. This allows a surgeon to gain tremendous experience with a given operation, resulting in higher quality operations and ultimately lower costs of providing health care (Kramon 1989, 9). Boeing finds that because workers learn through experience, the amount of labor needed to manufacture an aircraft falls dramatically as the number of planes produced rises. For instance, its 1,050th 727 aircraft required two-thirds less labor to produce than the 400th 727 (Moriarty and Shapiro 1981, 5). Similar sorts of learning take place with machinery; as managers gain experience with production, they become better able to employ the equipment effectively, and output per machine rises. A third type of economy of scale arises in industries that involve flows of liquids, such as chemicals and molten steel. The volume of a tank that holds a liquid increases with the cube of size, whereas the surface area (which determines the amount of material needed to produce the tank) rises with the square. Thus, building a tank that holds eight times as much volume requires only four times as much material. Similar effects arise in the construction of factory buildings; consequently, large factories are cheaper per square foot to build than small ones.

Decreasing Returns to Scale

decreasing returns to scale
A technology such that a proportional increase in all input levels leads to less than proportionate output growth.

When a firm increases all of its inputs by some proportion and the amount of total output rises by a smaller proportion, the technology is characterized by **decreasing returns to scale.** Some economists argue that there should be no such thing as decreasing returns to scale. To see why, suppose a firm doubles its use of all inputs. Then it would seem that, if nothing else, the firm could operate like two firms, each of which was the size of the original firm. In this way, the amount of output would simply be double what it was before. In short, provided that a firm can replicate itself, there is no reason ever to observe decreasing returns to scale.

It is difficult to reconcile this very persuasive argument with two important observations. First, several empirical studies show that some technologies exhibit decreasing returns to scale. For example, Berndt, Friedlander, and Chiang (1990) found in their analysis of General Motors' production function that the degree of returns to scale was 0.633—a doubling of all inputs would increase output by a factor of only 1.2. They also found decreasing returns for Ford (0.758) and Chrysler (0.753). Second, casual observation suggests that big firms may suffer from inefficiencies associated with having large, unwieldy organizations. In this context, one thinks of the recent downsizing of such industrial giants as General Motors and IBM.[3]

One potential explanation is that large firms could have costs just as low as those of small firms *if the managers chose to do so.* This explanation relies on the fact that managers may prefer to have a large, centralized organization that they can control rather than several autonomous divisions. In this view, the observed inefficiency of large-scale operations has nothing to do with the underlying technology as measured by the production function; rather, this inefficiency stems from the problems of managerial control discussed in the last chapter.

Another possible explanation of the finding of decreasing returns to scale is that the empirical studies fail to take into account some of the inputs used in production. Empirical studies can only take into account inputs that are readily measurable—number of workers, tons of steel, and so on. However, there are other inputs that are not so easy to quantify, such as entrepreneurial ability. Why do these omitted inputs distort the findings of these studies? Because small firms may be using more of these unmeasured inputs than large firms. Thus, the advantages of small scale may be illusory. The argument is that if truly *all* factors were taken into account, including the ones that are hard to measure, empirical studies would never find decreasing returns to scale.

Taking our pragmatic approach, we will go with the empirical literature and common observation, and we will include consideration of decreasing returns to scale technologies in the remainder of the book.

Graphing Returns to Scale

We can represent the degree of returns to scale graphically through the use of isoquants. Consider input combination *a* in Figure 8.11, with 16 units of capital and 12 of labor. A ray drawn from the origin through this point has a slope of 4/3 (= 16/12), and it shows all of those input combinations that involve the use of capital and labor in the same proportion as combination *a*. For instance, point *b* represents the combination of 8 units of capital and 6 units of labor,

[3]In some ways, IBM also tried to avoid this inefficiency by acting like a series of small firms, as suggested earlier.

Figure 8.11

Increasing Returns to Scale

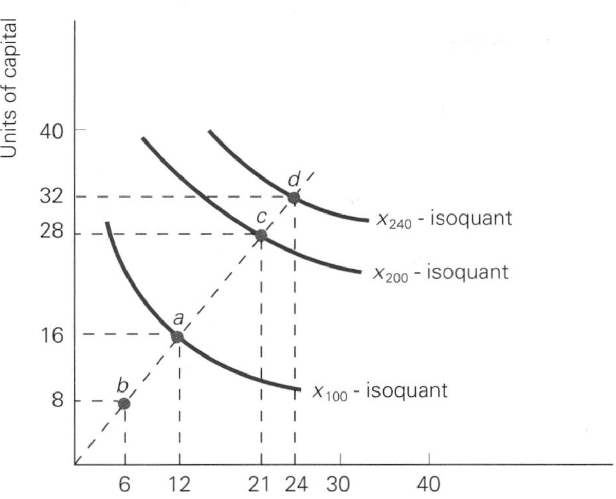

When the firm doubles its scale from using 12 units of labor and 16 units of capital to using 24 units of labor and 32 units of capital, output *more* than doubles. It rises from 100 units of output to 240 units. This technology exhibits increasing returns to scale.

Figure 8.12

Constant Returns to Scale

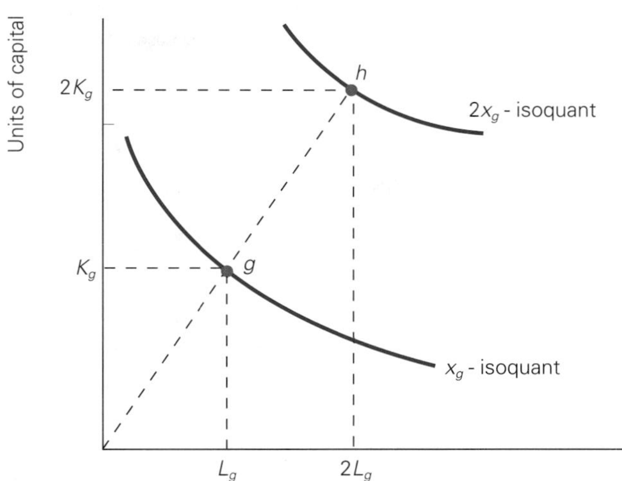

Starting at point *g* on the x_g-isoquant, the firm needs exactly to double its input levels from L_g and K_g to double its output and get to point *h* on the $2x_g$-isoquant. This technology is subject to constant returns to scale.

which again uses capital and labor in a 4-to-3 ratio. Because they all use the two inputs in the same proportion, the points on this line differ only in terms of the firm's scale of production.

Combination *a* lies on the x_{100}-isoquant, where with 12 units of labor and 16 of capital the firm can produce 100 units of output. How far along this ray does the firm have to go before doubling its output to 200 units? The answer is found by drawing the x_{200}-isoquant, which also is illustrated in the figure. Taking the intersection of the x_{200}-isoquant with the ray through point *a*, we see that the firm would have to use input combination *c* in the figure to produce 200 units of output by using capital and labor in a 4-to-3 ratio. This input combination consists of 28 units of capital and 21 units of labor, which is less than double the input combination needed to produce 100 units of output. It follows that Figure 8.11 illustrates the isoquants for a technology that is subject to increasing returns to scale. When the firm can double its output by increasing its inputs by a factor of only 7/4, we know that output would more than double if the firm doubled its inputs. In fact, from the diagram we see that the firm's output would rise to 240 units if the firm were to double its scale to using 24 units of labor and 32 units of capital.

In contrast, Figure 8.12 illustrates the isoquants for a technology that is subject to constant returns to scale: To double its output, the firm has to exactly double its use of the two inputs. Starting at point *g* on the x_g-isoquant, the firm needs exactly to double its input levels from L_g and K_g to get to point *h* which lies on the $2x_g$-isoquant. (PC 8.8)

8.8 PROGRESS CHECK

Draw an isoquant map for a production function that exhibits decreasing returns to scale.

Marginal Returns and Returns to Scale

The shapes of the marginal physical product curves (the pattern of marginal returns) and the degree of returns to scale both say something about what happens to total output as input levels are changed. But it is important to realize that the degree of returns to scale is largely independent of the shapes of the marginal physical product curves. The shape of a marginal physical product curve reflects the impact of a change in the amount of a *single* factor, while the degree of returns to scale concerns the impact of a simultaneous change in *all* of the factors *in proportion.*

A particularly dramatic example of this distinction is provided by a production function that allows no substitution. Let's consider the production function for Almond Yummies one more time. The recipe requires that exactly 4 almonds, A, and 1 ounce of chocolate, C, be used for each Almond Yummy. Suppose that the firm currently has 20 almonds. The marginal physical product of chocolate is equal to 1 if C is less than 5 ($= 20/4$); by adding another ounce of chocolate, the firm will have enough of the two inputs to produce one more Almond Yummy. But if C is greater than or equal to 5, an additional ounce of chocolate has no effect on what the firm can produce—it does not have enough almonds to produce any more Almond Yummies. Hence, when C is greater than or equal to 5, the marginal physical product of chocolate is zero. Similarly, suppose that the firm has 8 ounces of chocolate. Then the marginal physical product of almonds is equal to $1/4$ if $A/4$ is less than 8, and 0 if $A/4$ is greater than or equal to 8. For both almonds and chocolate, then, the marginal product of a factor diminishes in an especially abrupt way—it drops to zero! Although it may seem surprising, this fact does *not* imply that there are decreasing returns to scale. Indeed, as we have already seen, this technology exhibits constant returns to scale. (PC 8.9)

8.9 PROGRESS CHECK

In Progress Check 8.7, we saw that the production function $F(L,K) = L \times K$ exhibits constant marginal returns. Are the returns to scale for this technology increasing, constant, or decreasing?

SECTION RECAP

In this section, we examined three key properties of production functions. The first, marginal physical product, tells us by how much output increases when one more unit of an input is added, holding fixed all of the other input levels. The second property, the marginal rate of technical substitution, tells us the rate at which the firm can substitute one input for another while holding constant the amount of output produced. The marginal rate of technical substitution between two factors can be expressed as a ratio of the marginal physical products of those two factors. The third property, known as the degree of returns to scale, concerns what happens to the firm's output as it expands or contracts all inputs at once in the same proportion. All of these properties will be useful to consider when we turn to the derivation of the firm's optimal input choice and the calculation of its cost function.

SUMMARY

In Chapter 7, we saw that knowing a firm's cost structure is crucial to understanding the firm's behavior. Chapter 8 analyzes the firm's production technology, which is a necessary first step in showing where cost curves come from.

- The production function summarizes the firm's technological opportunities. It tells us the maximal amount of output that the firm can produce with any given combination of inputs.

- The production function can be represented graphically with isoquants. An isoquant is a curve showing all of the input combinations that yield the same level of output. There is a different isoquant for each output level.
- In the short run, only one input is variable. The production function guides short-run production decisions by showing the firm how much of the variable input is needed to produce the desired amount of output.
- In the long run, all inputs are variable. The production function guides long-run production decisions by showing the firm which combinations of inputs can produce the desired amount of output. Thus, the production function indicates what substitution possibilities are available.
- There are several important properties of the production function. The marginal physical product measures the increase in output when one more unit of a factor is hired, holding fixed all of the other input levels.
- The marginal rate of technical substitution tells us the rate at which the firm can substitute one input for another while holding constant the amount of output produced. The marginal rate of technical substitution between two factors can be expressed as a ratio of the marginal physical products of the two factors.
- The degree of returns to scale measures the impact on output when the firm expands or contracts all of its inputs at once in the same proportion.

DISCUSSION QUESTIONS

8.1 For over a decade, there has been a "shortage" of trained nurses. According to some health economists, the shortage is caused by the dependence of hospitals on relatively cheap nursing staffs to perform many nonnursing roles. In 1987 one expert said, "Since nursing salaries have gone up only 14 percent since 1983 while other hospital employees' salaries are up 20 percent, I can only conclude that hospitals are cutting costs by using nurses as substitutes for respiratory therapists, pharmacists, secretaries, and maintenance people" (Lewin 1987, A19). What sort of health care production function is implied by this statement?

8.2 Prior to the Industrial Revolution, wire was largely made by hand, and a blacksmith could produce relatively little output. However, "give a blacksmith a cheap and simple five-horsepower steam engine hooked up to a wire drawing device. With that new power source, the blacksmith would be able to produce roughly 100 times more wire than an unassisted man. One or two pounds sterling invested in an engine could thus easily produce 10 to 100 times that amount in usable goods the year after (Cowans 1991, A6)." Use the concept of diminishing marginal physical product to explain what was happening.

8.3 Explain why a firm could not have two isoquants that cut across one another. Could a firm's isoquants ever slope upward?

8.4 Assume that tomatoes are produced with two inputs: labor and land.

a. Sketch a possible isoquant map for tomatoes.

b. Recently, scientists announced that they had developed a method to alter tomatoes genetically so that they (the tomatoes, not the scientists) could stay on the vine for longer than normal, but not ripen or age. The scientists argued that these tomatoes could be shipped with less spoilage than the current type of tomatoes. Show how this genetic engineering technique would affect the isoquant map that you drew in part *a*.

8.5 Consider a company that assembles electric toasters using labor and robots. Suppose that in 1950, robots were so crude that they were useless in the assembly of toasters, so that toasters had to be assembled entirely by hand. Draw an isoquant map illustrating this situation. Now suppose that as a result of progress in robot design and manufacture, robots can be used as a substitute for labor. Draw an illustrative isoquant map. How would the isoquant map you have drawn change if further improvements were made in robots so that one new robot could do the work of two old robots?

8.6 Suppose that a firm is producing exam-taking services using only labor and capital (disguises). The firm's capital stock is fixed for the next year, and it pays $100 per month for the disguises. The following table shows the total amount of labor needed to produce various quantities of output (measured in examinations per month):

Output	1	2	3	4	5	6	7	8	9
Labor	90	125	150	170	210	300	450	690	990

Is the marginal physical product of labor increasing, constant, or diminishing? Is this firm making a short-run or a long-run decision when it is considering how many exams to take two months from now?

8.7 Fill in the missing values in the table below.

Total Number of Laborers	Total Amount of Capital	Total Output	Marginal Product of Labor
0	38	0	
1	38	—	10
2	38	25	15
3	38	—	—
4	38	65	20
5	38	—	20
6	38	95	—

8.8 Consider the production function $F(L,K) = 3L \times K$.

a. What pattern of returns does this production exhibit for labor? For capital?

b. What happens to the marginal physical product of labor when the amount of capital varies?

8.9 Consider a company whose production function is $F(L,K) = \sqrt{L} \times \sqrt{K}$. What is the firm's output when it uses 9 units of labor and 4 units of capital? What happens to the firm's output when it doubles its input levels? What if the initial levels are L_0 and K_0? Does this technology exhibit increasing, decreasing, or constant returns to scale?

CHAPTER 9

Cost

> ***Which of you, intending to build a tower, sitteth not down first, and counteth the cost, whether he have sufficient to finish it?***
>
> —Luke 14:28

In the last chapter, we saw that the Japanese automotive giants Toyota and Nissan each launched a new line of cars for the American market in 1989. Nissan created its Infiniti division and Toyota set up Lexus. Each company had to make a huge number of choices about how to manufacture its cars. For example, each company had to pick a material for the car body. Both chose steel. Each company also had to select how much capital and labor to use. Here, the companies made radically different choices. Infiniti chose to make the Q45 and M30 models largely by hand. In contrast, Lexus chose a highly automated factory for producing the ES 250 and the LS 400.

On what basis did these firms make their choices? If Toyota wants to produce 3,000 Lexus 400s during some month, the firm has to ensure that it has enough labor, steel, and other inputs to do that. But there are several input combinations sufficient to produce the desired output, and these combinations do not all have the same cost. For example, using labor on the assembly line may be much more expensive than using robots. Because a higher cost means a lower profit for the firm, a profit-maximizing firm wants to find the least expensive of the feasible input combinations.

In this chapter, we will learn how the firm chooses its optimal input combination for a *given* level of output. That is, we will develop a way for the firm to choose the cheapest way to produce its chosen amount of output.

Knowing how a firm chooses its inputs is important to understanding how the firm makes its overall choice of how much output to produce. Specifically, from the firm's input decision we will be able to *derive* the firm's total cost function and corresponding marginal and average cost curves. As we saw in Chapter 7, these cost curves play a central role in the firm's choice of output level.

Figure 9.1

Choosing the Input Mix in the Short Run

When National Motors' capital stock is fixed at 220 robots in the short run, the firm must employ 1,000 workers per day to produce 180 automobiles per day. If its capital stock were fixed at 250 robots, National Motors would need only 800 workers to produce 180 autos per day.

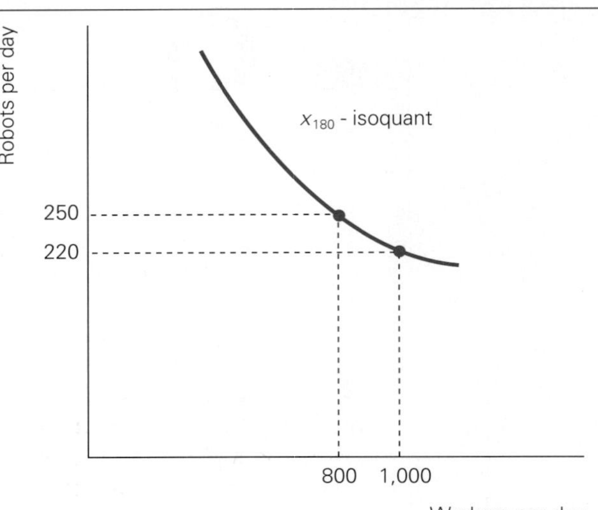

9.1 COST IN THE SHORT RUN

To find the optimal combinations of inputs and the resulting cost, a firm must follow a two-step process. First, it needs to identify its options. In the last chapter, we saw how the production function indicates which combinations of factors can be used to produce any desired amount of output. Our problem now is to determine which of those input combinations that can produce the desired output level has the lowest (opportunity) cost.

As we saw in the last chapter, the more time a firm has to make its input decisions, the more options it is likely to have. Consequently, the firm's factor choices depend on the time that it has to make them. If the set of input choices varies over time, so does the total cost of production. Thus, we need to develop cost concepts that take the time of adjustment into account. Just as we distinguished between short-run and long-run price elasticities of demand in Chapter 3, we will distinguish between short-run and long-run costs of production here.

Let's return to our example of National Motors, which uses labor and robots to produce automobiles. Recall that National Motors can hire and fire workers in a matter of a few days, so that labor is the variable factor in the short run. Robots, on the other hand, are a fixed factor in the short run; there is a 10-month lead time for ordering and installing additional robots. Suppose that the firm has 220 robots, and it wants to produce 180 automobiles per day. To produce this output, National Motors must use a factor combination that is on the x_{180}-isoquant, which is graphed in Figure 9.1. When the number of robots is fixed at 220, the only available input combination on the x_{180}-isoquant is (1,000, 220); that is, if the firm wants to produce 180 automobiles per day, in the short run its only choice is to hire 1,000 workers. Because all but one factor is fixed in the short run, the company's input decision is simple.

Once we have found the combination of inputs that the firm uses to produce the 180 cars, we need to determine what these inputs cost the firm. In doing this, we need to remember why we are calculating costs in the first place: As we saw in Chapter 7, the firm's cost curves provide information that is critical to its choice of output level. For this decision, we must use the firm's *economic* costs. It is straightforward to calculate the economic cost of producing 180 automobiles as long as we remember one critical point: *we must use opportunity cost as our measure of cost.* Specifically, suppose that the user cost of capital for robots is \$200 per robot per day and the wage rate is \$100 per day per worker. Then when the firm hires 1,000 workers and 220 robots, its expenditure on labor is \$100,000 (= \$100 × 1,000), and its expenditure on capital is \$44,000 (= \$200 × 220). Hence, the firm's total factor expenditure is \$144,000. But is \$144,000 the firm's *economic* cost of producing 180 automobiles? No. Because capital is a fixed factor in the short run, there is by definition no alternative use for it. Hence, the short-run opportunity cost (the true short-run economic cost) of using the 220 robots to produce automobiles is \$0.[1] Only the \$100,000 spent on labor is an opportunity cost. It follows that the total economic cost of producing 180 automobiles is \$100,000 when the firm's capital level is fixed at 220 robots in the short run.

The treatment of expenditures on capital may seem a little drastic—they are not counted as short-run economic costs at all. This fact is a consequence of the assumption that capital is a perfectly fixed factor in the short run. Since it is assumed to have absolutely no alternative use in the short run, the short-run opportunity cost of capital is zero. Put another way, under this assumption the expenditures on capital are *sunk expenditures* for purposes of short-run decision making.

This assumption is only an approximation in many cases. Often, firms have something else that they can do with their capital even over very short time horizons. If all else fails, they may be able to sell their machinery for scrap metal. However, even if the opportunity cost of capital is not zero, the lack of alternatives in the short run still means that the opportunity cost is lower in the short term than in the long term. These intermediate cases pose no problem for the theory of the firm. The key insight is that the alternative uses of factors typically are more limited over the short term than the long term, and the cost that the firm attaches to using these inputs should reflect their opportunity costs. Since it brings out all of the important points, we will stick to the simple case of zero short-run opportunity cost.

short-run economic cost
The minimal level of total expenditures (measured in opportunity-cost terms) needed to produce a given amount of output in the short run.

short-run variable cost
An abbreviated name for short-run total economic cost.

Because we are considering the firm's short-run decision, the resulting cost level is known as the **short-run economic cost** of producing x. The word *economic* in the definition reminds us that we are interested only in those factor expenditures that are true economic, or opportunity, costs. That is why we do not include expenditures on capital in the short run, even though the firm may well have to make payments to the capital suppliers.

Because this cost is associated with the expenditures on the variable factors of production, another name for short-run economic cost is **short-run variable cost.** Economic cost and variable cost are synonyms because if the firm cannot vary the level expenditure, then it is sunk and is not an economic cost. We denote the short-run variable cost of producing x units of output by VC_{SR}. The SR subscript reminds us that these are short-run costs.

The procedure just described allows us to find the short-run variable cost of producing any output level, say x_0, in which we are interested. This procedure is summarized as follows:

[1]We also are assuming, for simplicity, that using the robots has no effect on their maintenance costs.

Figure 9.2

Finding Short-Run Variable Cost

When the amount of capital is fixed at K_f, the firm must employ L_a units of labor to produce x_0 units of output. Hence, the short-run variable cost of producing x_0 units of output is $w \times L_a$ when w is the wage per unit of labor.

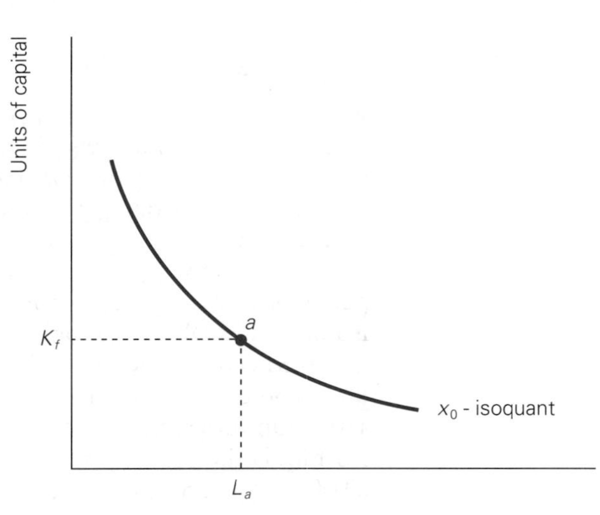

1. Draw the isoquant associated with the output level whose short-run variable cost we are trying to find (the x_0-isoquant in Figure 9.2).
2. Label the level at which capital is fixed in the short run, say K_f.
3. Read across from this fixed level of capital to find the point on the x_0-isoquant associated with K_f robots (point *a* in the figure).
4. Multiply the quantity of labor found in step (3), L_a, by the wage rate to get the short-run variable cost, $VC_{SR}(x_0)$.

To find the entire short-run variable cost schedule, we just repeat these four steps for each level of output.

Although it is not an economic cost, it is sometimes useful to keep track of the expenditure on fixed factors. As we have just discussed and as we saw in Chapter 7, this expenditure is *not* relevant for the short-run choice of how much to produce or how to produce it; because the firm's actions have no effect on this expenditure, it should have no effect on the firm's economic decisions. Why keep track of this so-called **short-run fixed cost** if it is not actually an economic cost? Because there are two ways in which the firm can use this information. First, in the long run all factors are variable, so for planning purposes the firm needs to keep track of the expenditures on all of its inputs. Second, in addition to being useful for planning future actions, fixed costs are useful for evaluating past actions. Although fixed in the present short run, the levels of the fixed factors were chosen at some point in the past. By looking at whether the sum of variable cost and fixed cost, also known as **short-run total cost,** is above or below average revenue, the firm can evaluate whether the management made good decisions in the past. This evaluation is an important part of deciding whether to keep the managers in their jobs and to reward them for past performance. In summary, while our focus will be on short-run variable cost, from time to time we will also keep track of short-run total cost.

short-run fixed cost
Expenditures on factors that are fixed in the short run.

short-run total cost
The sum of short-run variable cost and fixed cost.

PROPERTIES OF SHORT-RUN COSTS

Variable Cost

What does the firm's short-run variable cost curve look like? One thing we know is that *the short-run variable cost curve must slope upward.* Why? Because a firm operating on its production function can never get something for nothing—the firm must hire more inputs in order to produce more output, and more inputs cost more money.

Another property of the short-run variable cost curve is that its position depends on the amount of capital that is fixed in the short run. Consider again the isoquant for 180 automobiles per day in Figure 9.1. According to the figure, if the fixed capital stock were 250 robots instead of 220, the firm would need only 800 workers instead of 1,000 to produce 180 automobiles per day. Since the short-run variable cost is simply equal to the wage rate times the number of workers hired, the short-run variable cost of producing 180 automobiles falls from \$100,000 to \$80,000 (= \$100 × 800). The relationship between the fixed level of capital and short-run variable cost holds for any other output level as well. With a higher capital stock, the firm hires less labor to produce any given amount of output; hence, an increase in capital leads to a downward shift in the firm's short-run variable cost curve.

It may seem paradoxical that hiring more capital leads to lower economic cost. The key to understanding this result is to remember we are talking about short-run economic cost and that the proper measure of economic cost is *opportunity cost.* Since capital is fixed in the short run, it has no opportunity cost. This does not mean that the firm should rush out and buy unlimited amounts of capital. First, in the short run it cannot; capital is fixed. Moreover, in the long run, when the firm can adjust its capital level, capital has a positive opportunity cost: If the firm does not spend money on robots, then it has the money to spend on something else. Thus, when making long-run decisions, the firm would include expenditures on capital in its costs.

Marginal Cost

short-run marginal cost The change in short-run variable cost due to the production of one more unit of output.

Once we know the short-run variable cost function, other types of economic cost functions can easily be derived. In Chapter 7, we saw that the firm's marginal cost curve plays a central role in the determination of the profit-maximizing output level. We thus begin by defining **short-run marginal cost** (MC_{SR}) as the change in short-run variable cost due to the production of one more unit of output.[2]

By definition, marginal cost is derived from variable cost, and we have seen that variable cost is in turn derived from the production function. It therefore follows that marginal cost depends on the characteristics of the underlying technology, as summarized by the production function. To be more explicit, let's examine the relationship between marginal cost and marginal physical product (which measures the slope of the production function). If the firm wants to produce more output, in the short run it must purchase more of the variable input. Hence, in the short run the marginal cost of output is equal to the additional amount of the variable input that the firm must hire to produce the extra output

[2]Notice that an equivalent definition of short-run marginal cost is the change in short-run *total* cost due to the production of one more unit of output; short-run variable cost is the only component of short-run total cost that changes as the level of output changes.

marginal factor cost
The additional amount that the firm has to pay for a factor when it hires one more unit of the factor.

times the amount of money that the firm has to pay for each additional unit of the variable input. The additional amount that the firm has to pay when it hires one additional unit of the variable input is known as the **marginal factor cost** (*MFC*) of that input. For instance, if the firm can hire 600 workers per day for a total of $60,000, and 601 workers for a total of $60,150, the marginal factor cost of the 601st laborer (MFC_L) is $60,150 − $60,000 = $150. Expressed in terms of this new concept, *short-run marginal cost = (additional amount of the variable input needed to produce one more unit of output) × (marginal factor cost of the variable input).*

We can say more about short-run marginal cost by calculating how much more of the variable input the firm has to hire. Consider first a specific numerical example. If the marginal physical product of labor, MPP_L, at National Motors is 0.1 car per worker, how many workers does the firm need to hire to produce one more car? Since 1 worker can produce one-tenth of a car, 10 additional workers are needed. To generalize, we find the additional amount of labor needed to produce one more unit of output by dividing 1 (the additional amount of output) by MPP_L—that is, the additional labor required is $1/MPP_L$.

How much does it cost the firm has to hire $1/MPP_L$ additional units of labor required to produce 1 more unit of output? Since, by definition, each additional unit of labor costs the firm MFC_L, the total dollar cost of the additional workers is

$$MFC_L \times 1/MPP_L = MFC_L/MPP_L. \tag{9.1}$$

Since in the short run the wages paid to labor are the only economic cost of producing the additional unit of output, this is the short-run marginal cost:

$$MC_{SR} = MFC_L/MPP_L. \tag{9.2}$$

For example, if $MPP_L = .1$ and $MFC_L = \$150$, then the firm needs to hire 10 additional workers, and its wage bill rises by $1,500. The short-run marginal cost is $1,500. Of course, if some other input were the sole variable input in the short run, then we would use the marginal factor cost and marginal physical product for that factor in our calculation of short-run marginal cost. Equation (9.2) clearly demonstrates the direct linkage between the technology (as represented by the marginal physical product curve) and marginal cost.

We can say even more about the relationship between technology and marginal cost if we make the often realistic assumption that the firm is a price taker in the input market. This means that the firm makes its input choice under the belief that it cannot influence the prices of the inputs it buys and that it can purchase at a constant prevailing price as much of a factor as it wants.

Marginal Factor Cost for a Price Taker The price-taking assumption allows us to say more about the nature of marginal cost because this assumption simplifies the calculation of marginal factor cost. Suppose the going wage rate is $120 per day. If a price-taking firm hires one more worker for a day, its total wage bill rises by $120, no matter how many workers it initially has. Hence, the marginal factor cost of labor—the additional amount that the firm has to pay to hire one more unit of labor—is $120, the daily wage. This logic demonstrates that *whenever a firm is a price taker in an input market, the marginal factor cost is equal to the price of the factor.*

Short-Run Marginal Cost for a Price Taker We are now ready to find the price-taking firm's short-run marginal cost of output. Suppose that the going wage rate is w. By substituting

$$MFC_L = w \tag{9.3}$$

into our expression for marginal cost, Equation (9.2), we find that a price-taking firm's short-run marginal cost of producing an additional unit of output is

$$MC_{SR} = w/MPP_L. \tag{9.4}$$

This formula tells us that, *ceteris paribus, the higher the marginal product of labor, the lower the marginal cost of output.* This result makes sense. If a single new worker can produce a lot of output, then not many new workers are needed to produce a given amount of additional output, and the extra output does not cost very much to make.

We can use Equation (9.4) to see how the shape of the short-run marginal cost curve depends on the shape of the marginal physical product of labor curve. Since the firm may have increasing, constant, or diminishing marginal returns to labor, there are three cases to consider. Suppose first that National Motors's technology exhibits diminishing marginal returns to labor; that is, as the quantity of labor employed rises, the marginal physical product of labor falls. This means that MPP_L falls as more labor is hired to produce output. But according to Equation (9.4), when MPP_L falls, MC_{SR} rises. Hence, *when the production function exhibits a diminishing marginal product of labor, the short-run marginal cost curve is upward sloping.* With diminishing marginal returns, as the level of total output rises, the production of an additional unit of output requires increasingly large increments of labor, and thus it requires increasingly large incremental expenditures on labor. Figure 9.3 illustrates this result.

A numerical example can clarify this result. Suppose that the wage rate is \$100 per day and National Motors is producing 200 cars per day with an input combination for which the marginal physical product of labor is 0.1. At an output of 200 cars per day, short-run marginal cost is \$1,000 (= \$100/.1). Now, suppose that when National Motors hires enough additional labor to produce 250 cars per day, the marginal physical product of labor falls to .05. Then at an output of 250 cars per day, short-run marginal cost is \$2,000 (= \$100/.05). As a result of the fall in the marginal product of labor, the short-run marginal cost of output rises from \$1,000 to \$2,000.

Not all firms have production functions with diminishing marginal returns. If the firm's technology has a constant marginal product of labor, then MPP_L and hence w/MPP_L do not vary as the output level and the amount of labor used to produce it vary. In this case, the short-run marginal cost curve is flat, as illustrated in Figure 9.4. (PC 9.1)

> **9.1 PROGRESS CHECK**
>
> Draw the short-run marginal cost curve for a price-taking firm whose production function is characterized by increasing marginal returns to labor.

Before leaving the relationship between marginal productivity and marginal cost, we examine an important special case. As noted earlier in the discussion of production functions, a common situation is one in which initially there are increasing marginal returns, but eventually diminishing marginal returns set in (the so-called law of diminishing returns). Panel A of Figure 9.5 illustrates the marginal physical product schedule for such

Figure 9.3

Diminishing Marginal Returns to the Variable Factor and Short-Run Marginal Cost

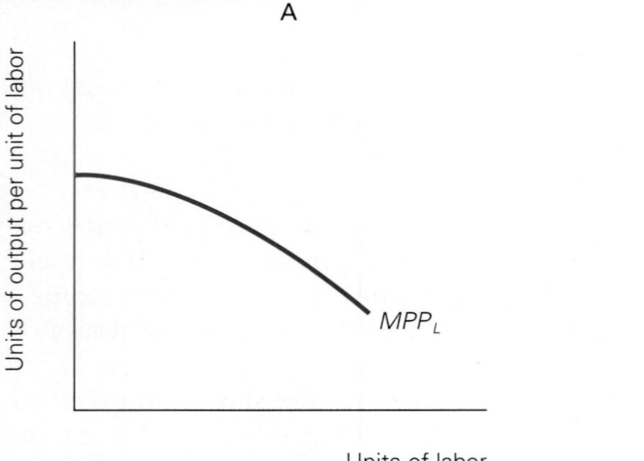

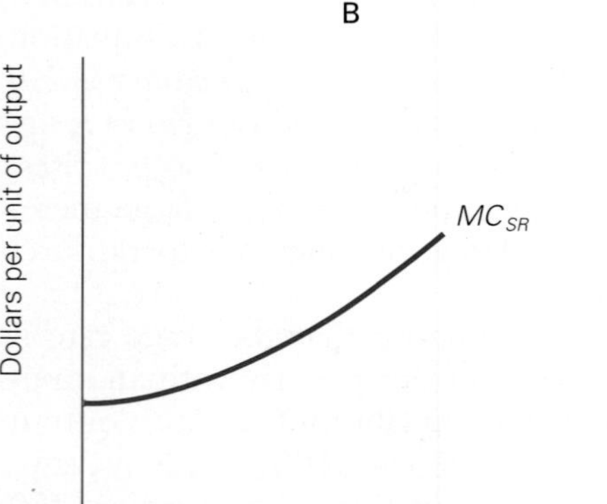

When there are diminishing marginal returns to labor, increasingly large increments of labor are needed to produce additional output. Consequently, when the MPP_L curve slopes downward, the MC_{SR} curve slopes upward.

Figure 9.4

Constant Marginal Returns to the Variable Input and Short-Run Marginal Cost

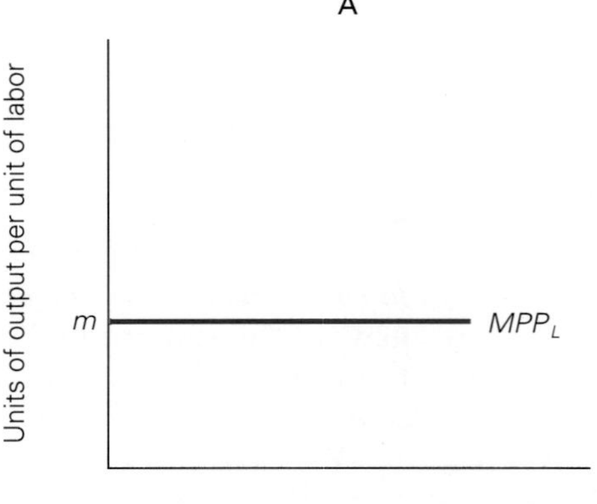

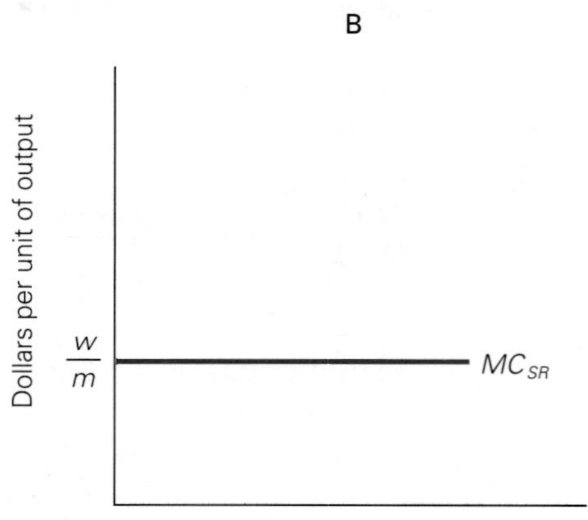

When the marginal physical product of labor is constant at m, each additional unit of output requires $1/m$ additional units of labor. Because each laborer receives a wage of w, short-run total cost rises by w/m. Hence, the short-run marginal cost is w/m at every output level.

a technology, and Panel B shows the corresponding short-run marginal cost curve. As Equation (9.4) tells us it must, short-run marginal cost falls over the initial range of increasing marginal returns. Once diminishing marginal returns set in, however, the short-run marginal curve rises.

Average Cost

We saw in Chapter 7 that average economic cost also plays an important role in the firm's output choice. When making a shut-down decision, the firm compares

Figure 9.5

Marginal Physical Product and Short-Run Marginal Cost

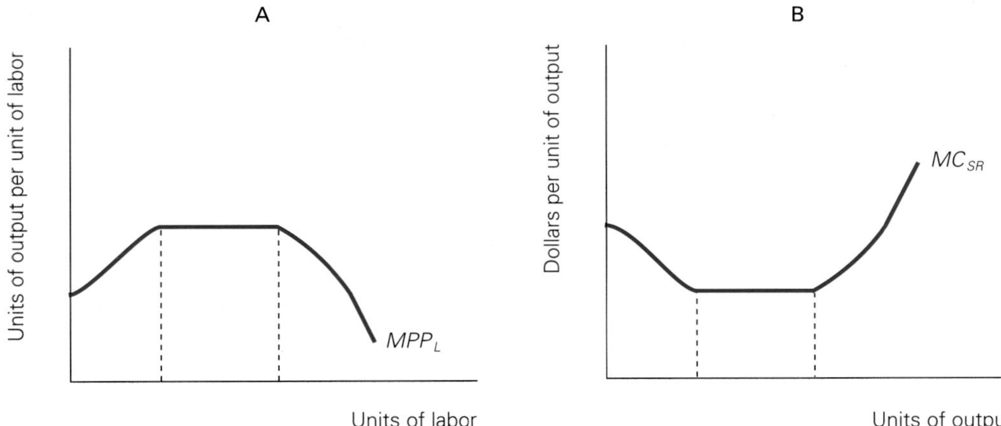

When marginal returns initially increase, then hold constant, and then diminish, short-run marginal cost follows the opposite pattern.

Table 9.1

Garyman Landscape Company's Production Function

When the Garyman Landscape Company's production function exhibits increasing marginal returns to labor, the average amount of labor used per unit of output produced falls as the level of output rises.

(1) Number of Workers	(2) Number of Tractors	(3) Number of Landscapes per Month	(4) Output per Additional Worker	(5) Average Number of Workers per Landscape
0	2	0		—
			1	
1	2	1		1.0
			2	
2	2	3		0.67
			3	
3	2	6		0.5
			4	
4	2	10		0.4
			5	
5	2	15		0.33

short-run average variable cost
Short-run variable cost divided by the number of units being produced.

its average revenue with average economic costs. In the short run, the expenditures on fixed factors are not economic costs. Thus, when making a short-run shutdown decision, the relevant measure of average cost is **short-run average variable cost,** defined as the short-run variable cost divided by the number of units being produced. Using AVC_{SR} to denote short-run average total cost of producing x units, $AVC_{SR} = VC_{SR}/x$.

Just like short-run marginal cost, short-run average variable cost can be related to the underlying technology when the firm is a price taker in factor markets. Consider the production function shown in the first three columns of Table 9.1. This production function shows how the Garyman Landscape Company can combine labor (measured in workers per month) and tractors to provide landscaping services to homeowners. As shown in column 4, this production function exhibits increasing marginal returns to labor for all input levels—total output rises at an increasing rate as more labor is hired. Dividing column 1 by column 3 gives us the average amount of labor used per unit of output, which is reported in column 5.

Table 9.2

Garyman Landscape Company's Short-Run Costs

In the short run, the expenditure on labor is the only element of variable and average variable costs. Therefore, if MPP_L increases with output, short-run average variable cost falls.

(1) Number of Landscapes per Month	(2) Total Number of Workers	(3) Monthly Wage	(4) Short-Run Total Cost	(5) Short-Run Average Cost
0	0.0	$1,000	$ 0	—
1	1.0	1,000	1,000	$1,000
2	1.6	1,000	1,600	800
3	2.0	1,000	2,000	667
6	3.0	1,000	3,000	500
10	4.0	1,000	4,000	400

The results in column 5 indicate that the average amount of labor per unit of output falls as the firm increases its output level. Intuitively, because the marginal physical product of labor is increasing, as the firm produces more output it needs fewer and fewer units of labor per additional unit of output. Since each additional unit of output requires less labor than the earlier units of output, the average amount of labor per unit of output falls as the output level rises.

The fact that the expenditure on labor is the only element of short-run economic cost used in Table 9.2 to calculate both short-run variable and average variable costs. Since the firm is a price taker in the labor market and the expenditure on labor is the only element of short-run variable cost, it follows that short-run variable cost is found by multiplying the total number of workers (column 2) by the wage rate (column 3). For example, the short-run variable cost of 3 landscapes is $2 \times \$1{,}000 = \$2{,}000$, as recorded in column 4. Short-run average variable cost can be calculated in two ways. First, we can compute it simply by dividing the short-run variable cost figures in column 4 of Table 9.2, by the corresponding output figures in column 1. For example, when the output level is 3 landscapes, $AVC_{SR} = \$2{,}000/3$, or \$667, as indicated in column 5 of Table 9.2. Alternatively, we can calculate short-run average cost by multiplying the entries in column 5 of Table 9.1 by the wage. When the firm produces 3 landscapes per month, Table 9.1 indicates that the firm uses an average of .667 workers per landscape, and the average variable cost is \$667 ($= .667 \times \$1{,}000$) per landscape. This is, of course, the same average variable cost level that we find in column 5 of Table 9.2. The reason for considering this alternative way of finding short-run average variable cost is that it helps us understand the shape of the average variable cost curve. Recall that, as a result of the increasing marginal returns to labor, the average amount of labor per landscape falls as the number of landscapes rises. Therefore, our second method of calculating the short-run average variable cost tells us that when there are increasing marginal returns, average cost should fall as output rises. This result is verified in column 5 of Table 9.2. The corresponding short-run average variable cost curve is graphed in Panel A of Figure 9.6.

9.2 PROGRESS CHECK

Draw the short-run average variable cost curve for a price-taking firm whose production function is characterized by constant marginal returns to labor at all levels.

Things are much different when the firm's technology is characterized by diminishing marginal product at all levels. In this case, the firm needs more and more units of labor per unit of output as total output rises. Therefore, short-run average variable cost rises as output rises, as indicated in Panel B of Figure 9.6. (PC 9.2)

Figure 9.6

Marginal Product and Short-Run Average Variable Cost

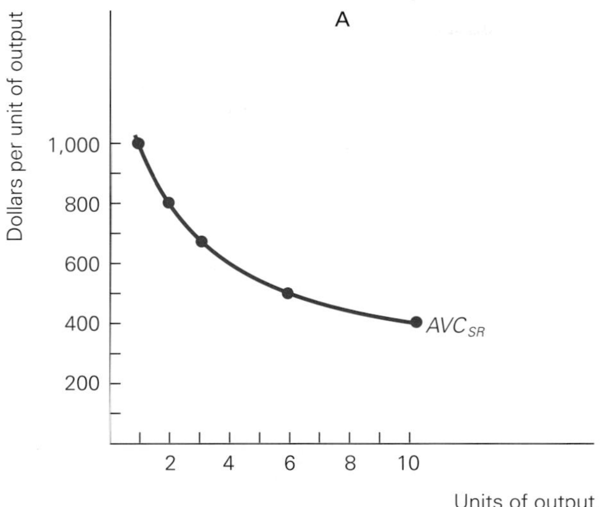

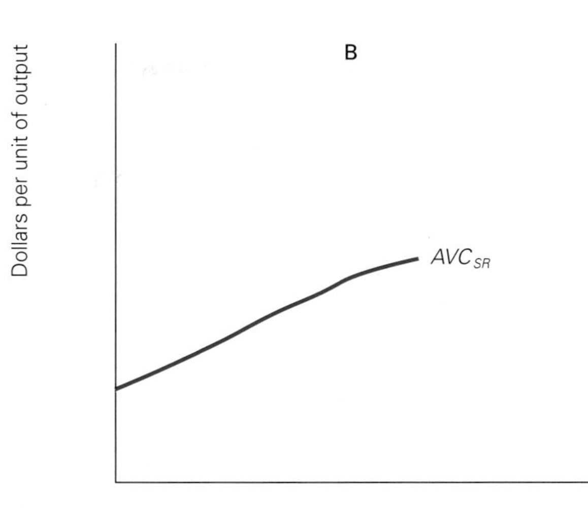

Short-run average variable cost is equal to the average amount of labor used per unit of output times the wage rate. Therefore, if a firm's technology is characterized by increasing marginal product at all levels, short-run average variable cost falls as the output level rises (Panel A). If the firm's technology is characterized by diminishing marginal product at all levels, then average variable cost rises as output rises (Panel B).

short-run average total cost
Short-run total cost divided by the number of units being produced.

short-run average fixed cost
Short-run fixed cost divided by the number of units being produced.

It is sometimes useful to graph **short-run average total cost** (ATC_{SR}), defined as short-run total cost divided by the number of units of output. As drawn in Figure 9.7, short-run average total cost and short-run average cost converge as the level of output gets large. This is not a coincidence. The difference between them is equal to **short-run average fixed cost** (AFC_{SR}), defined as short-run fixed cost divided by the number of units of output. Since short-run fixed cost is constant, short-run average fixed cost falls as output increases.

The Relationship between Short-Run Marginal Cost and Short-Run Average Variable Cost

Given that the marginal and average variable cost curves are derived from the same variable cost curve, you might guess that the two curves must somehow be related. That this guess is correct is verified in Table 9.3, which shows the short-run costs for the Off-the-Deep-End Pool Company. Notice the following relations between marginal cost and average variable cost in the table:

a. *Whenever marginal cost is below average variable cost, average variable cost falls.* For example, when output rises from 2 to 3 units, the marginal cost of \$600 is less than the average cost of \$900 at 2 units, and the average variable cost falls to \$800 at 3 units.

b. *Whenever marginal cost is above average variable cost, average variable cost rises.* When output rises from 5 to 6 units, the marginal cost of \$1,000 is greater than the average variable cost of \$700, and the average variable cost rises to \$750 at 6 units.

These phenomena are not coincidences; they hold for any marginal and average variable cost curves that are derived from the same variable cost curve. In

Figure 9.7

The Relationship between the Short-Run Variable and Total Cost Curves

The difference between short-run total cost and short-run average variable cost equals short-run average fixed cost. Because short-run average fixed cost falls as the output level rises, short-run total cost and short-run average variable cost get closer together as the output level rises.

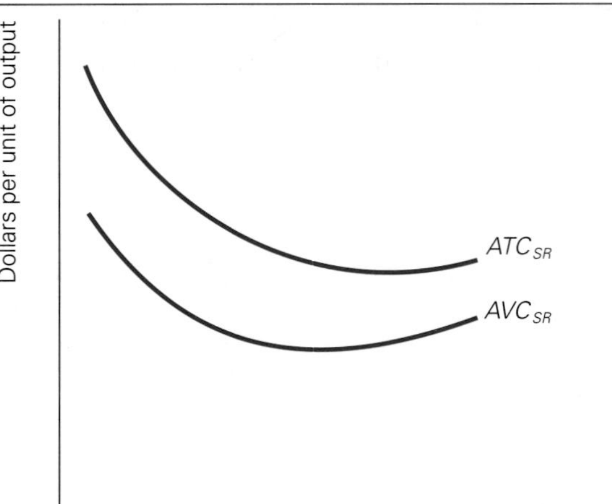

Table 9.3

Off-the-Deep-End Pool Company's Short-Run Costs

Short-run average cost is equal to short-run total cost divided by the number of pools produced. Short-run marginal cost is equal to the additional short-run cost that must be incurred to produce one more pool.

(1) Number of Pools	(2) Short-Run Total Cost	(3) Short-Run Average Cost	(4) Short-Run Marginal Cost
0	$ 0	—	
1	1,000	$1,000	$1,000
2	1,800	900	800
3	2,400	800	600
4	2,800	700	400
5	3,500	700	700
6	4,500	750	1,000
7	5,600	800	1,100

fact, they hold for any marginal and average curves at all as long as they are derived from the same total curve. For instance, they hold for marginal and average revenue curves that are derived from the same total revenue curve. To see why this relationship between marginal and average curves must hold, consider the heights of the members of the Hellenic Hoopsters basketball team: Athena, Aphrodite, Hera, Iris, Persephone, and Venus. Columns 1 and 2 of Table 9.4 list the names and heights of the different players. A running calculation of the average heights of team members is given in column 3. Notice that whenever the person who is added to the team is taller than the earlier average, the new average is higher. On the other hand, whenever the latest person to be added is shorter, the average height falls. Thinking of the last person added to the team as the "marginal" player, we see that whenever the marginal player's height is less than the average height, the average falls. Whenever the marginal player's height is greater than the average height, the average rises with the addition of this new player.

Returning to problems closer to home, think about what happens when the cost of last unit, the marginal unit, is below the average variable cost of the earlier

Table 9.4

Hellenic Hoopsters' Heights

Column (3) keeps a running average of the heights of the players. Whenever the person who is added to the team is taller than the earlier average, the average height increases. Whenever the latest person to be added is shorter than the average of the existing players, the average height falls.

(1) Player	(2) Height	(3) Average Height of Players on Team
Athena	5′10″	5′10″
Aphrodite	5′ 8″	5′ 9″
Hera	5′ 6″	5′ 8″
Iris	5′ 8″	5′ 8″
Persephone	5′ 3″	5′ 7″
Venus	6′ 1″	5′ 8″

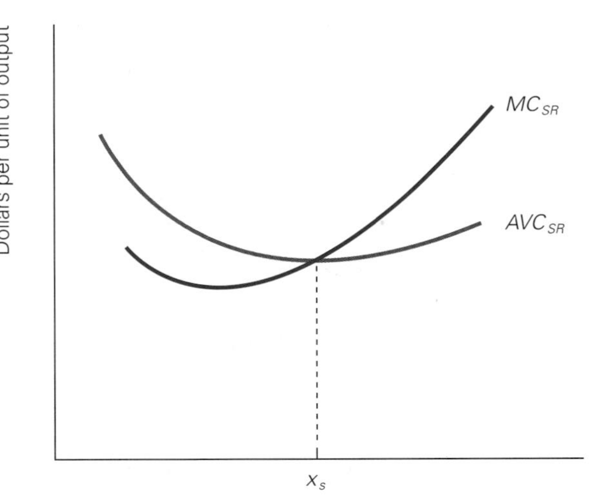

Figure 9.8

The Relationship between the Short-Run Marginal and Average Variable Cost Curves

Whenever marginal cost is below average variable cost, average variable cost falls. Whenever marginal cost is above average variable cost, average variable cost rises. The short-run marginal cost curve crosses the short-run average variable cost curve at the point where average variable cost is at a minimum.

units. When this marginal unit is included in the average, it pulls the average down from its old level—the average variable cost curve is downward sloping. On the other hand, if the cost of the marginal unit is greater than the average variable cost of the earlier units, its inclusion in the average variable cost of production pulls the average up, and the average cost curve is upward sloping. Figure 9.8 illustrates this relationship graphically. At all output levels less than x_s, the marginal cost curve lies below the average variable cost curve, and the average variable cost curve is falling. On the other hand, at all output levels greater than x_s, the marginal cost curve lies above the average variable cost curve, and the average variable cost curve is rising.

There is another important fact that will prove useful when we examine the firm's supply decision in the next two chapters. From Figure 9.8, we see that the average variable cost curve is falling before it intersects with the marginal cost

9.3 PROGRESS CHECK

Use this logic to show that the short-run marginal cost curve intersects the short-run average total cost curve at its minimum.

curve and rising afterward. It follows that the intersection of these two curves occurs at the lowest point on the average variable cost curve:

c. *The short-run marginal cost curve crosses the short-run average variable cost curve at the point where average variable cost is at a minimum.*

Although we have looked at the specific case of short-run marginal and average variable cost curves, it is worth noting that these properties are equally valid for long-run cost curves as well as for any other marginal and average curves that are derived from the same total curve. (PC 9.3)

SECTION RECAP

In the short run, there is only one variable factor, and the firm's input decision consists of making sure that it hires just enough of the variable factor to produce the desired output, given the amount of the fixed input it has on hand. The resulting expenditure on the variable input is the short-run variable cost. This amount is also the short-run economic cost. By definition, fixed factors cannot be put to any alternative uses in the short run, and they have zero opportunity cost. The short-run marginal and average variable cost schedules can both be derived from the short-run variable cost schedule. Although it is not an economic cost, it is sometimes useful to keep track of short-run fixed cost, the expenditure on fixed factors. The sum of short-run variable and fixed costs is known as short-run total cost.

9.2 COST IN THE LONG RUN

Given a long enough planning horizon, a firm can adjust the levels of all of its inputs. When the firm's time frame for a decision is sufficiently long that all of the inputs are variable and none is fixed, we say that the firm is making a long-run decision. Two important implications of all factors being variable in the long run are the following:

1. Since all factors are variable in the long run, the (explicit and imputed) expenditures on all factors are economic costs in the long run.
2. Since the levels of more than one factor can be varied, it may be possible for the firm to substitute quantities of one factor for another.

The possibility of factor substitution means that in the long run the firm has real choices to make when picking a factor mix. How does a profit-maximizing firm make these choices?

GRAPHICAL ANALYSIS

economically efficient
An input combination is economically efficient when it has the lowest opportunity cost of those input combinations that can be used to produce the desired output.

To maximize its profit, the firm must choose the cheapest combination of inputs that can produce the desired level of output. That is, the firm must make an **economically efficient** input choice. The first step in solving the firm's problem graphically, is to represent the set of factor combinations that can be used to produce the desired output. This is exactly what an isoquant curve does. The second step is to rank the costs of the alternative factor combinations that can produce the required level of output. At this point, we are missing a way to compare the costs of the different input combinations.

Isocost Lines

To compare the costs of different input combinations, imagine that we wanted to graph all the combinations of robots and labor that cost the firm \$300,000 per day. Continue to assume that the firm is a price taker in factor markets at a daily wage for labor of \$100 and a daily user cost per robot of \$200. If the firm then hires L units of labor and K robots, its total factor expenditures are $\$100 \times L + \$200 \times K$. Therefore, the combinations of L and K that cost the firm \$300,000 (given the prices of labor and robots) must satisfy the equation $\$100 \times L + \$200 \times K = \$300,000$. As we saw in our look at household budget constraints (Chapter 2), this equation defines a line. This line is drawn in Figure 9.9, where it is labeled $IC_{300,000}$. It has a vertical intercept of 1,500 and a slope of $-\frac{1}{2}$. Because this line represents all combinations of capital and labor that cost the firm the same amount (in this case, \$300,000), it is referred to as an **isocost line.**

isocost line
A line representing all input combinations that cost the firm the same amount.

Note that, *in absolute value, the slope of the isocost line is equal to the ratio of the input prices*, here ½. More generally, if the price of labor is w and the price of capital is r, then the absolute value of the slope of the isocost line is w/r. This result should seem familiar to you; it is just like the one for a household's budget constraint. A household's budget constraint and a firm's isocost line do the same thing; each one tells us the combinations of goods (final goods for a consumer, inputs for a firm) that can be purchased with a given total amount of money. In each case, the slope of the line tells us the rate at which the consumer or firm can substitute purchases of one good for the other without changing the sum of the expenditures on the two goods.

Of course, the firm does not have to limit itself to spending exactly \$300,000 on inputs. The equation for the \$200,000 isocost line is $\$100 \times L + \$200 \times K = \$200,000$, which is graphed in Figure 9.9 as $IC_{200,000}$. Notice the following characteristics of this new isocost line. First, like $IC_{300,000}$, it has a slope of $-\frac{1}{2}$. This is no surprise—the slope of the isocost line reflects the rate at which the market permits the firm to trade one input for the other, and this has not changed. Second, the new isocost line is closer to the origin than the old one is. Intuitively, the firm can purchase fewer inputs with \$200,000 than with \$300,000. (PC 9.4)

9.4 PROGRESS CHECK

Draw the isocost line corresponding to an expenditure of \$400,000 on inputs.

We can now make these generalizations: (1) for any set of input prices, there is a whole *family* of isocost lines, the **isocost map**; (2) the farther an isocost line is from the origin, the greater the expenditure it represents; and (3) for a price-taking firm, all of the isocost lines have the same slope (which, in absolute value, is the ratio of the factor prices).

isocost map
The whole family of isocost lines that exists for a given set of factor prices.

We next examine what happens to a firm's isocost curves when the price of an input changes. Suppose that initially the daily wage rate is \$100 and the daily cost of a robot is \$200. The corresponding \$300,000 isocost line is drawn again in Figure 9.10, where it is labeled $IC_{300,000}$. What happens to this isocost line when the price of labor rises to \$150 per day? The slope of each isocost line (in absolute value) is the wage rate divided by the price of capital. When the wage rate rises, this ratio increases from ½ to ¾. Thus, the isocost line becomes steeper. At the same time, we know that the vertical intercept of the new isocost line is unchanged—because the price of robots has not changed, the firm can still purchase 1,500 robots if it spends the entire \$300,000 on them. Putting these results

Figure 9.9

An Isocost Line

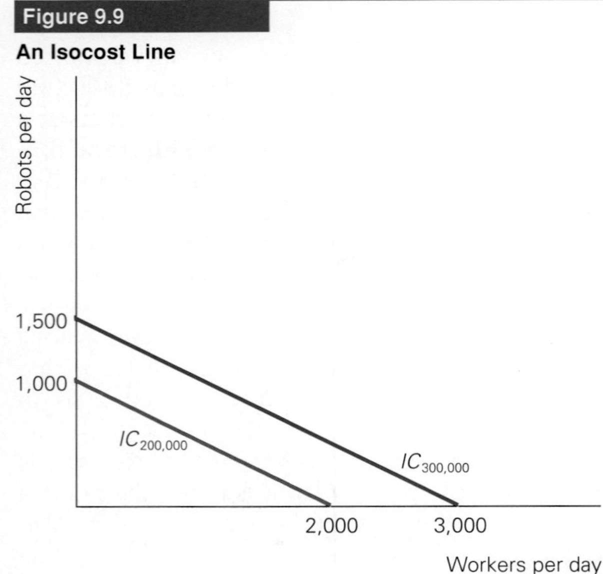

An isocost line represents all combinations of capital and labor that cost the firm the same amount. In absolute value, the slope of the isocost line is equal to the ratio of the input prices.

Figure 9.10

A Factor Price Increase Pivots the Isocost Lines Inward

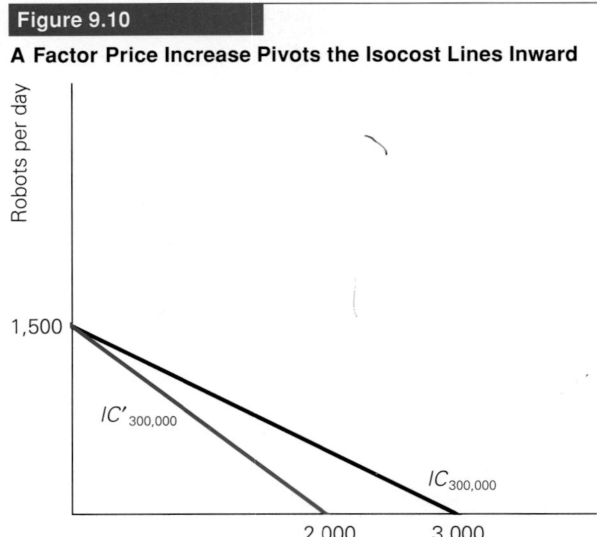

When the price of labor rises, the isocost line pivots around the intercept for robots, the factor whose price stayed constant.

together gives us the new \$300,000 isocost, $IC'_{300,000}$ in Figure 9.10. Comparing the old and new isocost lines, we see that *when the price of labor rises, the isocost line pivots around the intercept for robots, the factor whose price stayed constant.*[3] (PC 9.5)

9.5 PROGRESS CHECK

Suppose that the daily wage rate is \$100 and the initial cost of a robot is \$200 per day. Show what would happen to the isocost map if the price of robots rose to \$250 per day.

Finding the Economically Efficient Input Mix

We are now ready to use isocost lines to find the long-run, least-cost combination of inputs to produce a given level of output. Suppose that National Motors wishes to produce 200 cars per day. In Figure 9.11, the isoquant labeled x_{200} represents all the combinations of capital and labor that can produce cars at this rate in the long run. Next, we superimpose the family of isocost lines over the isoquant. Now suppose that the managers at National Motors are considering whether to use the input combination represented by point *a* on the diagram. Combination *a* can produce 200 cars per day—it is on the x_{200}-isoquant—but is *a* the least expensive way to do it? To answer this question, consider input combination *b*. It also lies on the x_{200}-isoquant, so it also can produce 200 cars per day. But *b* is cheaper than *a*. How do we know? Because *b* lies on an isocost line that is closer

[3]Another way to remember that the isocost line must pivot is this: Although an increase in the price of labor has no effect on how much the firm can buy when it spends all of its money on robots, it does affect how much the firm can buy when it spends all of its money on labor—it can buy less. Thus, when the price of labor rises, the vertical intercept is unchanged but the horizontal intercept moves inward.

Figure 9.11

Choosing the Input Mix in the Long Run

The firm minimizes the total cost of producing 200 cars by using the input bundle that is on the x_{200}-isoquant *and* on the lowest possible isocost line. This combination is e_1, which is at a tangency between the x_{200}-isoquant and the $IC_{130,000}$-isocost line.

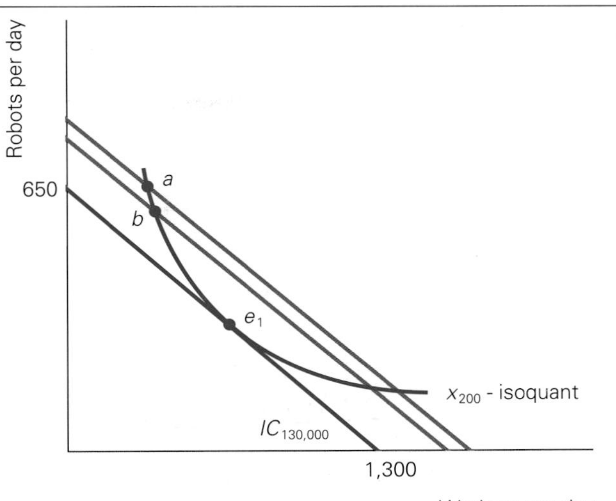

to the origin. We conclude that *a* is definitely not the cost-minimizing way to produce 200 cars.

The same logic suggests that even though input combination *b* is cheaper than *a*, the firm can do still better than *b*. Specifically, the firm minimizes the total cost of producing 200 cars by using the input bundle that is on the x_{200}-isoquant and on the lowest possible isocost line. This is input combination e_1 in Figure 9.11, which is at a tangency between the x_{200}-isoquant and the $IC_{130,000}$-isocost line. Because input combination e_1 minimizes the firm's cost of producing that output, it is the equilibrium input combination. Since factor combination e_1 is on the isocost line associated with an expenditure of $130,000, the figure tells us that the least-cost means of producing 200 automobiles per day entails factor expenditures of $130,000 per day. Hence, the long-run total cost of producing 200 automobiles per day is $130,000 per day.

Before going on, you may save yourself confusion later if you now think carefully about the similarities and differences between consumer theory and production theory. The isocost curve looks a lot like the consumer's budget constraint; both graph the various amounts of two goods (inputs in one case and products in the other) that can be purchased for a given amount of money. In the same way, isoquants look a lot like indifference curves. In each case, they say how much you can get (either output or utility) from a given combination of goods. Given these parallels, it would seem natural to do for the firm what you did for the consumer: Find the firm's equilibrium by drawing an isocost curve and then finding the highest isoquant curve that touches it. But this is not what we do, and it is instructive to see why.

The consumer starts out knowing how much he or she has to spend; what the consumer does not know initially is how much utility can be attained given this budget. The firm, in contrast, starts out knowing how much output is to be produced; what it does not know is how much it will have to spend to achieve this goal. With the consumer, we start with a given budget line and use different indifference curves to evaluate the feasible alternatives. To do so, we draw a whole family of indifference curves to find the household's equilibrium point. With the firm, we start with a single isoquant curve—the one corresponding to the desired level of output. We then evaluate the alternative factor combinations on the isoquant by drawing a whole family of isocost lines.

ALGEBRAIC INTERPRETATION

We can also characterize the firm's equilibrium input choice algebraically. At the point of tangency, e_1 in Figure 9.11, the isocost line and the isoquant line have the same slope. We showed that the slope of the isocost line is equal to the factor price ratio, w/r, in absolute value. Moreover, by definition, the negative of the slope of the isoquant is the marginal rate of technical substitution between capital and labor. Hence, at the point of tangency,

$$MRTS = w/r. \tag{9.5}$$

But now recall from Equation (8.4) that along an isoquant, $MRTS = MPP_L/MPP_K$. Using this fact, we can rewrite Equation (9.3) as

$$MPP_L/\mathrm{MPP}_K = w/r. \tag{9.6}$$

This important condition for cost minimization tells us that *a firm that takes factor prices as given should operate at a point where,* ***at the margin,*** *the inputs' marginal physical products are proportional to their prices.* We have emphasized the words *at the margin* to remind ourselves that the marginal physical products of the inputs may change as the quantities of the inputs used vary, and Equation (9.6) has to hold only for values calculated for the last units purchased.

There is an intuitive way to understand Equation (9.6). In choosing its inputs, the firm wants to get the highest possible output for its money. Suppose that the firm has one more dollar to spend on inputs. What is the most additional output it can get by spending this dollar on workers and robots? If the firm spent the dollar on capital, it could buy the services of $1/r$ more robots. Since each robot contributes MPP_K more output, total output would rise by MPP_K/r. If the firm spent the additional dollar on labor, it could hire $1/w$ more workers. Since each worker contributes MPP_L more output, total output would rise by MPP_L/w.

These facts tell us that, for the firm to use both inputs in equilibrium, MPP_K/r must equal MPP_L/w. To see why, suppose that the firm has chosen an input combination for which MPP_K/r is less than MPP_L/w. In this case, the firm gets more additional output per dollar—more bang for the buck—by hiring additional workers. By spending a dollar less on capital and a dollar more on labor, output would rise, but the total amount spent on inputs would stay the same. The firm would be getting something for nothing! Therefore, the original input combination could not have been an equilibrium. Similarly, if the firm is at a point where MPP_K/r is greater than MPP_L/w, the firm could increase output by spending a dollar more on capital and a dollar less on labor. Again, such an input combination cannot be an equilibrium. Stated positively, we have just shown that for the firm to achieve economic efficiency, it must choose an input combination for which

$$MPP_K/r = MPP_L/w. \tag{9.7}$$

Notice that Equation (9.7) is equivalent to Equation (9.6). Our two approaches to deriving an algebraic condition for the firm's equilibrium input choice yield the same answer. (PC 9.6)

This progress check shows the usefulness of the rule embodied in Equation (9.7). The rule allows a manager to determine whether the firm is choosing the profit-maximizing input combination without having to know the entire production function. The manager needs only information about the effect of small changes in the use of inputs to determine whether the firm is minimizing its costs.

9.6 PROGRESS CHECK

Suppose that the firm can hire as many workers as it wants at the going wage of $100 per day and can employ robots at a constant daily cost of $200 each. At present, the firm is producing 200 cars per day with an input combination for which $MPP_K = .3$ and $MPP_L = .1$. Is this firm using an economically efficient input combination?

COMPARATIVE STATICS

Our theory tells us how to find the firm's cost-minimizing input combination assuming that four things are held constant in the background: (1) the factor prices; (2) the production technology; (3) the characteristics of the output being produced; and (4) the amount of output being produced. For an actual firm, all of these things can change. The model of the firm that we have just developed predicts how such changes affect the economically efficient input combination.

Factor Prices

Let's continue to assume that National Motors is a price taker in factor markets. Suppose the price of labor rises from $100 per day to $115. How does this price change affect the firm's long-run input choices? To answer this question, we begin by reproducing the firm's initial situation (Figure 9.11) in Figure 9.12. The original equilibrium choice is at point e_1, where the x_{200}-isoquant is tangent to isocost line $IC_{300,000}$. The firm hires L_1 workers and uses K_1 robots. For the wage increase to change the equilibrium, it must change either the isoquant curve or the isocost line. The isoquant curve is defined entirely by the production technology and the amount of output that is produced; it has nothing to do with factor prices. Consequently, the isoquant curve is unaffected by the factor price change.

The isocost line, however, is affected by a factor price change. Each isocost line pivots around the point where it intersects the axis representing the factor whose price has *not* changed, and the new slope is the ratio of the new price of labor to the price of capital. When the wage rate increases, this ratio increases and each isocost line becomes steeper. The new isocost lines are the blue lines in Figure 9.12.

With this new family of isocost lines, the minimal-cost combination is at e_2, where isocost line $IC'_{140,000}$ is tangent to the x_{200}-isoquant. The firm now hires L_2 workers and uses K_2 robots. Comparing the new equilibrium point, e_2, with the original equilibrium, e_1, we see that the quantity of labor hired falls while the quantity of capital used rises. This makes perfect sense: *To produce a given level of output, the firm substitutes away from the factor whose price has risen.*

In this example, the increase in the price of labor has raised the firm's total cost of producing 200 cars per day from $130,000 to $140,000. With a little

Figure 9.12

The Effects of a Factor Price Increase

When the price of labor rises, the isocost lines pivot inward. The new equilibrium occurs at point e_2, the tangency between the x_{200}-isoquant and the isocost line corresponding to a $140,000 factor expenditure, $IC'_{140,000}$.

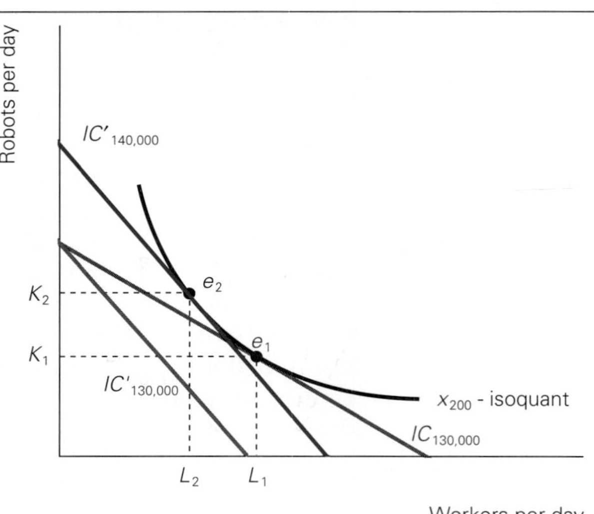

effort, we can see that *total cost must always rise in response to an increase in the price of one of the factors that the firm uses in production.* The new isocost line for the old cost level (that is, $IC'_{130,000}$) is pivoted downward from the old isocost line ($IC_{130,000}$). Since the old isocost line was just tangent to the x_{200}-isoquant, the new isocost line must lie completely below this isoquant. Thus, only higher-cost isocost lines touch the x_{200}-isoquant once the factor price has risen.

Factor substitution along the lines suggested by our theory is an important real-world phenomenon. One particularly dramatic change in factor prices came during the 1970s, when the price of oil shot up tremendously. By substituting machinery and personnel for energy, many industrial companies cut their energy usage substantially in the years following. At its Freeport, Texas, magnesium production plant, for instance, Dow Chemical Company used a variety of means (including greater use of computers to run the production process more efficiently) to reduce energy consumption by more than 40 percent from the late 1970s through 1980s (Savage 1987, 34).

More recently, telephone companies have been taking advantage of the declining cost of computers to substitute them for telephone operators. In 1995, Bell Atlantic began having computers answer when people dialed directory assistance. The computer "asks the customer first for the city and then for the listing and records the information. The computer then automatically deletes any pauses the caller makes, including 'Uhhs' and 'Umms,' before forwarding a condensed version to an operator who listens to the information and then looks up the listing" (*The New York Times* May 7, 1995, L30). This compression reduces the amount of the operator's time by roughly two seconds per call.

Technology

Suppose that someone has invented a more efficient way for workers and robots to fit dashboards into automobiles. Consequently, National Motors can now produce the same output as before while using less of both inputs. How does this change affect the firm's equilibrium? Again, we must begin by asking whether the

Figure 9.13

The Effects of a Technological Improvement

As a result of the technological improvement, the firm can continue to produce 200 cars per day while using fewer workers and robots. The isoquant shifts inward from the x_{200}-isoquant to the x'_{200}-isoquant. The new equilibrium point is e_3, and the total cost of producing 200 cars per day falls by $10,000 per day.

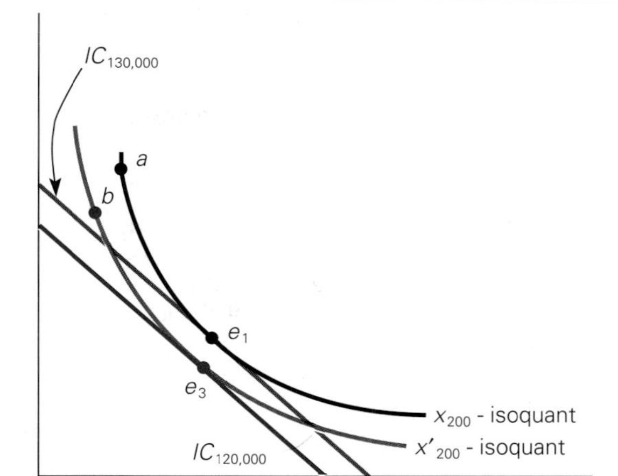

change affects the isocost map or the isoquant. This technological improvement has no effect whatsoever on factor prices; hence, the isocost map is unaffected. The isoquant curve, however, does shift. To see why, consider Figure 9.13, which reproduces the original x'_{200}-isoquant from Figure 9.11. Point *a* denotes one input combination that, before the technological change, can produce 200 cars per day. After the technological change, a point like *b*, which is below *a*, is associated with the output of 200 cars. The same considerations hold for any point on the original x_{200}-isoquant. Thus, the improvement in technology leads to a downward shift in the isoquant curve to the new x'_{200}-isoquant. Given this new isoquant, there is a new cost-minimizing method to produce 200 units, point e_3 in Figure 9.13. Although the isocost map has not changed, the new equilibrium is on a different isocost line than the old one. In fact, it is on a lower isocost line; as we would expect, the technological improvement has lowered the firm's total cost.

Isoquant shifts of the sort depicted in Figure 9.13 have been perhaps the major force behind long-term economic growth. Historical examples abound. For instance, "using the Bessemer process, Andrew Carnegie reduced the cost of making steel rails from close to $100 per ton in the early 1870s to $12 by the late 1890s. The Hall process for refining aluminum reduced the price of aluminum from 87.5 francs per kilogram in 1888 to 3.75 francs in 1895" (Rosenberg and Birdzell 1986, 213).

Technological improvements continue to change many industries dramatically. Just a few years ago, it would have cost tens of thousands of dollars to construct a basic personal computer that today can be put together for a few hundred dollars. If you went into a bank in 1970, all you saw were people; there was not an automatic teller machine in sight. Why did banks install automatic teller machines? Primarily to reduce their costs. For instance, Manufacturers Hanover Trust, a large New York bank, installed automatic teller machines at three of its branches where costs were so high that the branches were unprofitable (Zimmerman 1988). One branch saved approximately $450,000 in rent and $300,000 in operating costs such as wage payments. This technological improvement gave the firm new opportunities to get more output from capital and labor. This case also serves as another example of factor substitution in action—the installation of automatic tellers was started when the rent at one of the branches increased to five times the previous rate. In response to the increase in the price of office space, Manufacturers Hanover moved the branch to a smaller location and invested in four automatic teller machines that could serve a lot of customers from a small space. The bank substituted capital, in the form of automatic tellers, for office space.

The Nature of Output

In addition to changing the way a given product is manufactured, the firm may choose to change the nature of the product itself. Suppose that in response to foreign competition, National Motors decides to improve the quality of its cars by conducting more screening for defects along the assembly line. To produce the same number of cars, the firm has to hire more labor and machines to carry out these inspections. Using the same logic as above, this change shifts the x_{200}-isoquant outward—it takes more inputs to produce 200 of the improved cars per day. This outward shift in the isoquant curve is shown in Figure 9.14, where it is labeled the x''_{200}-isoquant.

Unlike the isoquant curve, the isocost *map* is unaffected by the firm's decision to produce higher-quality automobiles. Of course, since the isoquant curve has shifted, the firm's new equilibrium input combination, point e_4 in Figure 9.14, lies on a different isocost line than the old equilibrium combination. In fact, the new equilibrium is on a higher isocost line, which tells us that the extra quality is costly to the firm—the cheapest input combination for producing 200 high-quality cars is more expensive than the cheapest input combination for producing 200 low-quality cars.

Output Level

Suppose that National Motors decides to increase car production from 200 to 201 cars per day. Figure 9.15 shows two isoquants, the x_{200}-isoquant (the original one) and the x_{201}-isoquant (the new one for 201 cars). As was true in Figure 9.11, the minimum-cost input combination for 200 cars is e_1. Moreover, by our now-familiar analysis, if the firm produces 201 cars, it minimizes its costs by choosing the input combination where the x_{201}-isoquant is tangent to an isocost line, point e_5. Since e_5 is on the \$132,000-isocost line and e_1 is on the \$130,000-isocost line, the cost of the 201st car is \$2,000.[4]

Of course, our choice of output levels was arbitrary. We could repeat this exercise for any output levels we choose. Mechanically, this involves drawing a series of isoquants for the different output levels and then finding the corresponding tangencies. We can then draw a curve through this series of equilibrium points to trace out how the least-cost input levels vary as the level of output changes, *ceteris paribus.* The resulting curve, known as the firm's **expansion path,** is illustrated in Figure 9.16. The derivation of the expansion path is a comparative statics exercise in which we vary the level of output but hold constant the nature of technology, the nature of the product, and the prices of inputs.

expansion path
The long-run set of least-cost input levels traced out as the level of output changes, *ceteris paribus.*

[4]Although this number may seem low to you, remember that for purposes of this example we are calculating the marginal cost of *assembling* the car. We have not taken into account the cost of materials, such as steel and leather. As discussed in the appendix to this chapter, it would be straightforward to extend our analysis to the more realistic case of many inputs.

Figure 9.14

The Effects of an Increase in the Quality of Output

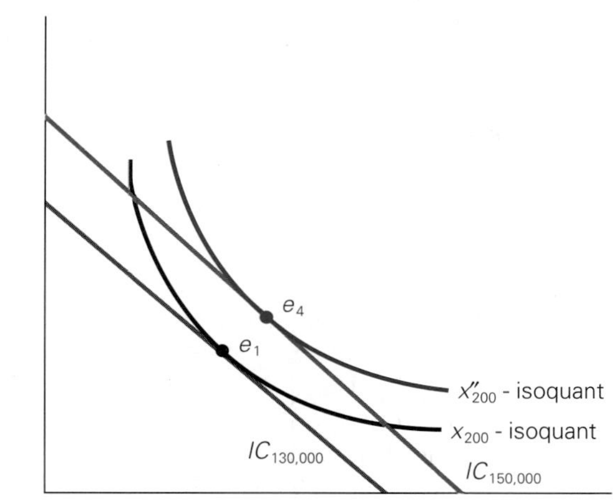

To ensure a higher quality level for its cars, National Motors has to devote more resources to the production of any given number of cars per day. The isoquant shifts outward from the x_{200}-isoquant to the x''_{200}-isoquant. The new equilibrium point is e_4, and the total cost of producing 200 cars per day rises by $20,000 per day.

Figure 9.15

The Effects of an Increase in Output

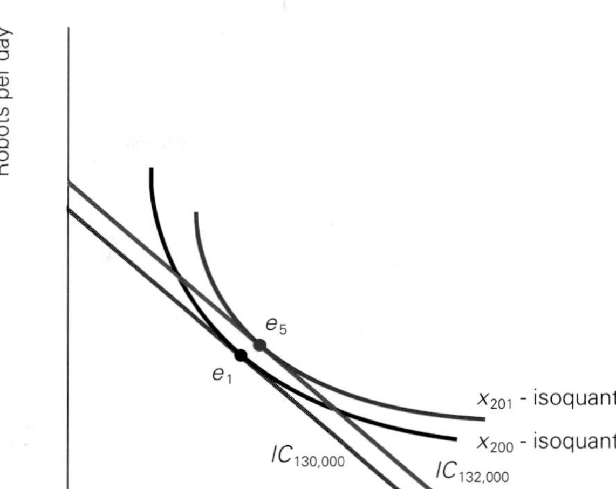

To produce more cars, the firm has to choose a factor combination on a higher isoquant curve. The least-cost way to produce 201 cars per day is combination e_5. The firm's total costs rise from $130,000 to $132,000 when it produces 201 cars per day rather than 200.

Summary of Comparative Statics Analysis

We have shown how changes in underlying conditions affect the firm's choice of inputs and the resulting cost of producing output. It is useful to summarize this comparative statics process.

1. Sketch the equilibrium that holds before there are any changes in the underlying market conditions.
2. Given a change in underlying market conditions (such as a factor price change or a shift in technology), determine whether the isoquant map or the isocost map is affected.
3. Ascertain the direction of the shift in the affected set of curves.
4. Find the new equilibrium by locating the tangency between the relevant isoquant curve and the relevant isocost line.

DERIVING THE LONG-RUN TOTAL COST CURVE

long-run total cost
The minimal level of total expenditures (measured in opportunity-cost terms) needed to produce a given amount of output in the long run.

We are ready to find the firm's long-run costs. We first derive the **long-run total cost** of producing x, denoted C_{LR}. As it turns out, we already have found part of National Motors's long-run total cost curve. The comparative statics exercise in Figure 9.15 showed us the total costs of producing both 200 and 201 automobiles. Using this diagram, we found two points on the long-run cost curve—the long-run total cost of producing 200 automobiles is $130,000, and the long-run total cost of producing 201 automobiles is $132,000. We can repeat this

Figure 9.16

The Expansion Path

The expansion path traces out how the long-run set of least-cost input levels varies as the level of output changes, *ceteris paribus*.

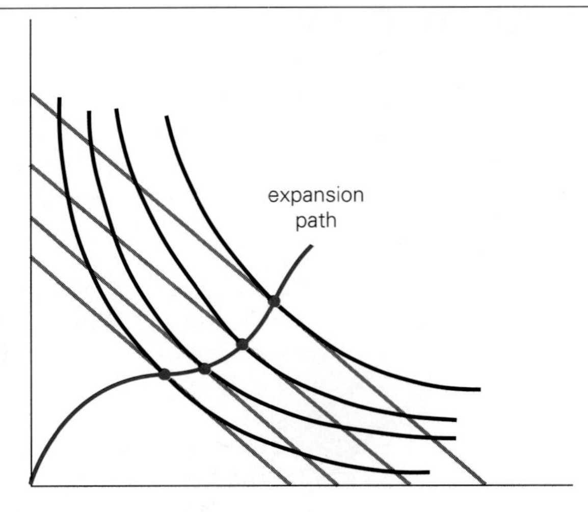

comparative statics exercise to trace out the entire long-run cost curve. Specifically, to find the entire long-run total cost schedule, just follow these steps:

1. Choose an output level.
2. Find the optimal input combination by taking the tangency of the isoquant and isocost lines.
3. Compute the cost of this input combination by multiplying the price of each input times the quantity used and then adding up the dollar total.
4. Graph this point.
5. Repeat steps (1) through (4) for each output level.

PROPERTIES OF LONG-RUN COSTS

Once we have derived the firm's long-run total cost curve, we can characterize several of its properties.

Long-Run Marginal Cost

We know from Chapter 7 that the marginal cost of output is crucial in determining how much output to produce. When the firm is making a long-run output decision, long-run marginal cost is the appropriate cost measure to use. The **long-run marginal cost** of output is equal to the change in long-run total cost due to the production of one more unit of output.

long-run marginal cost The change in long-run total cost due to the production of one more unit of output.

Thanks to the comparative statics exercise just completed, we already know how to find the marginal cost—simply look at the difference between the old and new isocost lines when the firm increases its output by one unit. For example, Figure 9.15 indicates that long-run total cost increases from $130,000 to $132,000 when the firm increases production from 200 cars to 201. Hence, the long-run marginal cost of the 201st auto is $2,000. This figure neatly demonstrates how the firm's marginal cost depends on its technology (via the isoquants) and on the factor prices it faces (via the isocost lines).

Long-Run Average Cost

long-run average cost Long-run total cost divided by the number of units being produced.

The average economic cost of production plays an important role in the firm's shut-down rule. For a long-run decision, the firm must base its choice on long-run average economic cost. Since all factor expenditures are economic costs in the long run, the long-run average economic cost of producing x units is just the long-run total cost divided by the number of units produced. Because all costs are economic costs in the long run, it is convenient to drop the word economic from long-run average economic cost and simply refer to it as **long-run average cost.** Using AC_{LR} to denote long-run average costs, we write $AC_{LR} = C_{LR}/x$. When National Motors assembles 200 cars per day, for instance, the long-run average cost is $\$650 = \$130{,}000/200$.

economies of scale When long-run average costs fall as output rises, costs are said to exhibit economies of scale.

diseconomies of scale When long-run average costs rise with the output level, costs are said to exhibit diseconomies of scale.

Economies of Scale Our analysis of short-run costs considered what happened when the firm increased the quantity of a single factor, holding the quantities of the other factors fixed. If it wanted to do so, a firm could do the same thing in the long run. But in the long run, the firm has more flexibility than this because it can also vary all of its inputs simultaneously. In other words, the firm can change the *scale* of its operations. An important question is whether there are cost advantages to being a large firm. That is, do average costs rise or fall as the firm increases its output level? When long-run average costs fall as output rises, we say that costs exhibit **economies of scale.** When long-run average costs rise with the output level, costs exhibit **diseconomies of scale.**

Economies of scale in the cost function are closely related to returns to scale of the production function. Suppose that a firm decides to double its output. If the firm's technology exhibits constant returns to scale, then the firm has to double all of its inputs to do so. Assuming that input prices do not change as the firm buys more inputs, the effect of this doubling is to double factor expenditures. Recall that average cost is the ratio of total cost to units of output. If a doubling of output leads to a doubling of input costs, then the ratio of total cost to total output is unchanged. In short, *when the production function exhibits constant returns to scale, long-run average cost remains constant as the level of output changes.* This fact is illustrated in Panel A of Figure 9.17.

If the production function is characterized by decreasing returns to scale, then an increase in output has to be accompanied by a more than proportionate increase in inputs. Hence, the factor expenditures (the total cost) rise more rapidly than the level of output, and average cost rises.[5] In other words, *when the production function exhibits decreasing returns to scale, the long-run total cost function exhibits diseconomies of scale*—the average cost curve is upward sloping, as in panel B of Figure 9.17. When the underlying technology is subject to increasing returns to scale, the average cost curve is downward sloping, like the one in Panel C. This relationship follows from the fact that to double its output, the firm has to less than double its inputs; hence, total cost rises more slowly than the output level. Therefore, *when the production function exhibits increasing returns to scale, the long-run total cost function exhibits economies of scale.*

Increasing returns to scale are not the only source of economies of scale. Economies of scale also arise from the existence of certain *set-up costs*, that is, from costs that have to be incurred once no matter how much output is

[5]Algebraically, because C_{LR} rises faster than x as the output level increases, $AC_{LR} = C_{LR}/x$ also rises with the output level.

Figure 9.17

Economies of Scale

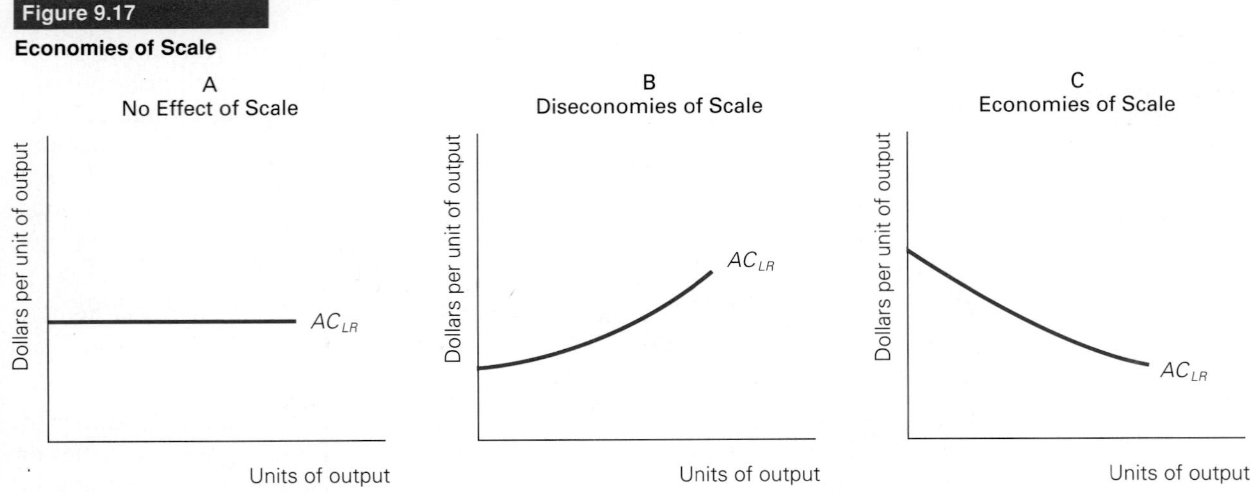

The degree of economies of scale tells us what happens to long-run average cost as output increases.

9.7 PROGRESS CHECK

In the last chapter, we noted that the Union Pacific Railway's technology exhibits increasing returns to scale, whereas General Motors' technology exhibits decreasing returns to scale. Match these two technologies to the appropriate panels in Figure 9.17.

produced.[6] Consider a software company that is planning to sell a word processing program that will compete against programs such as Word and WordPerfect. Before it can sell a single copy, the firm has to write the program—a task that may take thousands of hours of programmer time and cost hundreds of thousands of dollars. Once the program is complete, however, producing additional copies is extremely cheap. What does all of this imply about the average cost curve? It tells us that the first unit has a very high average cost—the average cost of the first unit includes the full development cost. As the firm produces more copies of the program, these set-up costs are spread over more units and the average cost falls. Average cost continues to fall as long as the marginal cost of making additional copies remains below the average cost. Thus, the more copies the firm produces, the lower its average cost—the firm's costs exhibit economies of scale.

This software company is not an isolated example. Economics textbook writing has the same pattern of costs. Many high-tech industries are similar because the amounts of inputs needed for research and development typically do not depend on the volume of output produced. A firm producing only a few units of output may have to devote as many resources to innovative activities as it would to produce thousands of units of output. Because the firm does not have to keep reproducing this research, its total costs rise less than proportionately to its output level, and it enjoys economies of scale. (PC 9.7)

Economies of Scope When it is cheaper to produce two products together in one firm rather than separately in two specialized firms, costs are said to exhibit

[6]Because the level of these costs is "fixed" once the firm begins production, they are sometimes known as *fixed costs.* We will avoid this term in order to avoid confusion with expenditures on factors that are fixed in the short run.

economies of scope When it is cheaper to produce two products together in one firm instead of separately in two specialized firms, costs are said to exhibit economies of scope.

economies of scope. Pet food is a multibillion dollar business. A company producing both cat and dog food can rely on the same plants, warehouses, and sales force to make and distribute its products. This sharing gives rise to cost savings that a firm specializing in only one type of pet food would not enjoy. Hence, the trend in the 1980s was for pet food companies that had been specializing in one type of pet food to move into both (Stuart and Collis 1991). Similarly, Boeing makes a variety of different aircraft, which enables the company divisions to share its design and manufacturing know-how and its skilled labor force. And local telephone companies share facilities to provide a variety of voice and data services to business and residential customers. As these examples illustrate, economies of scope are often closely related to economies of scale. Intuitively, economies of scale and scope both arise when a fixed facility can be "shared" to produce a large number of units of output, either of a single product or a mix of products. Economies of scope are important in many industries, which helps explain why most firms are multiproduct firms.

Long-Run Costs Compared to Short-Run Costs

We have seen that a firm's input choice depends on whether the firm is faced with a short- or long-run decision. It is not surprising, then, that the short- and long-run costs of producing a given level of output may differ. How do the short- and long-run costs compare?

There are two key differences between short-run and long-run costs, both of which stem from the two differences between the short- and long-run input decisions that we identified earlier:

1. In the short run, fixed factors are fixed. Since these fixed factors have no alternative uses, any expenditures made by the firm on these factors are sunk expenditures and thus are not economic (opportunity) costs. In the long run, however, all input levels are variable and there are no sunk expenditures; hence, everything counts as an economic cost. Because more things get counted as costs, this effect raises long-run economic cost relative to short-run economic cost.

2. Since the levels of more than one factor can be varied in the long run, it may be possible for the firm to substitute quantities of one factor for another. For example, in the long run but not in the short run, National Motors can adjust the number of robots that it uses on its assembly line. This increased flexibility tends to lower the cost of producing a given amount of output.

In terms of their effects on the relation between the short- and long-run *economic* cost curves, these two forces run in opposite directions. Consequently, in some instances the short-run variable cost of producing a given level of output may be greater than the long-run total cost, while in other cases the relationship will be the reverse. In terms of the total expenditures on inputs, only the second force comes into play. Thus, short-run total cost is always at least as large as long-run total cost.

SECTION RECAP

In the long run, more than one factor is variable, so the firm's input decision entails real choices. In making these choices, the firm wants to attain economic efficiency—it wants to choose the least costly combination of inputs that can produce the desired output. Graphically, the firm should choose the input combination that lies on the lowest isocost line that intersects (is tangent to) the isoquant curve corresponding to the desired level of output. Algebraically, the firm's long-run input combination is economically efficient only when the marginal physical product per dollar of expenditure on each input is the same across all inputs.

SUMMARY

Chapter 7 showed that knowing a firm's cost structure is crucial to understanding the firm's behavior. The present chapter shows that once we know the factor prices and technological opportunities available to the firm, we can derive all of the firm's cost curves.

- The firm's input choice depends on whether it is making a short-run or long-run decision.
- In the short run, only one factor is variable. The firm must purchase enough of the variable input to produce the required output with the fixed factors on hand. Short-run variable cost is equal to the resulting expenditure on the variable input. Expenditures on fixed factors, also known as short-run fixed costs, are not short-run *economic* costs because they are not short-run opportunity costs. For purposes of managerial performance evaluation, it is sometimes useful to keep track of short-run total cost, defined as the sum of short-run variable cost and short-run fixed cost.
- Short-run marginal cost is equal to the marginal factor cost of the variable factor divided by the marginal physical product of that factor. For a price-taking firm, the marginal factor cost is equal to the price of the variable factor, and hence short-run marginal cost is equal to the price of the variable factor divided by its marginal physical product.
- For *any* marginal cost curve and average cost curve derived from the same total cost curve, the marginal cost curve intersects the average cost curve at the point where average cost is lowest.
- In the long run, more than one factor is variable, so the firm has real input choices to make. The firm seeks the economically efficient input mix—the least costly combination of inputs that can produce the desired output. Because all factors are variable in the long run, the expenditures on all factors enter into the computation of long-run economic cost.
- To attain economic efficiency, a price-taking firm chooses an input combination such that the marginal physical products of the inputs are proportional to their input prices.
- Changes in factor prices, technology, and the nature of output can affect the total cost of producing a given output level.

DISCUSSION QUESTIONS

9.1 Question 1 refers to the following table.

Input Levels	Marginal Product of Labor	Marginal Product of Capital	Price of Labor	Price of Capital
L_1,K_1	21	10	3	1
L_2,K_2	100	50	50	10
L_3,K_3	4	20	2	10

The table above gives you information about various combinations of capital and labor, with prices for each input. The different combinations may be associated with *different* levels of output. Which of these combinations will result in minimum cost to a firm producing the output level associated with that combination of inputs at the stated input prices?

9.2 The chemical X-2000 is produced using two inputs, *benzene* and *labor* (apologies to those of you who are chemists), according to the production function: X = (minimum of B and L), where X is the number of gallons of X-2000, B is the number of gallons of benzene, and L is the number of hours of labor. Consider a firm that is a price taker in both input markets. Benzene is available at a price of \$2 per gallon and labor at \$10 per hour.

The production of this chemical generates fumes within the plant that greatly increase the incidence of cancer among the workers. All of the current employees are aware of the ill effects that the fumes have on their health. The workers would suffer no ill health effects if they were provided with masks containing a filtering system. The masks cost the firm an additional $2 for each hour that an employee works. In its present equilibrium position, the firm does *not* provide workers with these masks.

a. Illustrate the firm's current long-run equilibrium input choice in terms of an isoquant diagram.

b. Derive the firm's current long-run cost function.

c. Suppose that in response to this health hazard, the government enacts a regulation that requires the industry to provide each worker with a mask that contains a filtering system. How will this regulation affect the firm's choice of input levels for a given level of output?

d. Derive the firm's long-run cost function once the regulation is in place.

e. What does the fact that the firm does not find it profitable to provide its workers with masks says about the value that the workers themselves place on the prevention of the ill health effects? (*Hint:* Think back to the theory of compensating differentials in Chapter 5.)

9.3 Bob's Fun Fill is an independent gasoline station. Bob's has a 10,000 gallon tank that holds gasoline. Prior to a recent increase in wholesale gas prices, the station bought gasoline wholesale to fill its tank at a price of $.80 per gallon. Shortly thereafter, the wholesale price rose to $1.00 a gallon. Roberta, the owner of Bob's, is trying to figure out how to price gasoline. She knows that she has 5,000 gallons left in the tank.

a. Assuming the gas station is self-serve, what is the marginal cost of a gallon of gasoline? Would your answer change if Roberta had 6,000 gallons left in the tank?

A new local ordinance is passed that prohibits self-serve gasoline, and henceforth all gasoline must be pumped by an employee. Each gallon of gas pumped requires 1 minute of employee time. Roberta pays $6 per hour. Employee time not spent pumping gas is spent doing auto repair work for which Roberta receives $18 per employee-hour (Roberta only bills for time actually spent doing the repair work). Roberta has enough repair business to keep two workers busy full time.

b. Suppose that Roberta has one worker (she herself does not work). What is the marginal cost of a gallon of gasoline, assuming Roberta *cannot* fire the worker, change the number of hours he works, or hire new workers over the relevant decision-making horizon?

c. What would the marginal cost of a gallon of gasoline be if Roberta could fire her present worker, change the number of hours he works, or hire new workers over the relevant decision-making horizon?

9.4 In the text, we considered a firm that is a price taker in factor markets. But our analysis holds more generally. Consider Jane's Lube Joint. Jane's uses two inputs, labor and motor oil, to change the oil in automobiles. Jane's is a price-taking buyer in the labor market—it can hire as many laborers as it wants at a price of $50 per day. Jane's is not a price taker in the oil market—the supplier from which Jane's buys its oil offers quantity discounts. The first 1,000 quarts per month are available at a price of $1 per quart. Any quantity greater than 1,000 quarts per month is available at a price of $.50 per quart. Draw an isocost map for Jane's Lube Joint.

9.5 Solid Sweet is a new candy that can be made from any combination of beet sugar and high fructose corn syrup that adds up to one pound. The manufacturer of Solid Sweet is a price taker in both the sugar beet and corn syrup markets. Draw the isoquants for this firm. Is the *MRTS* increasing, constant, or decreasing? Show that for most prices, the firm will choose to make Solid Sweet either entirely from beet sugar or entirely from corn syrup.

9.6 Consider a software company that is planning to develop a new computer spreadsheet program. The development costs are projected to be $300,000. Once the program is written, it can be put onto diskettes for $1.00 per copy. Draw the long-run marginal and average cost curves for this product. Write down a formula for average cost.

9.7 Suppose that you were an airline executive and you came to work one morning to find a memorandum on your desk indicating that the Boeing 747 that your company leased to fly between New York and London was bringing in revenues of $200,000 per day. You also knew that the direct operating expenses (wages for the flight crew, aviation fuel, and food) were $180,000 per day. Finally, suppose you had calculated that the interest cost of the loan to pay for the airplane was $40,000 per day. Should you continue to fly the plane? Why might your answer depend on the decision time frame, and what additional information would you need?

9.8 The following table shows some of the long-run costs for the American Production Company:

Output	Total Cost	Average Cost	Marginal Cost
50	—	$1,000	
51	$52,000	—	—
52	—	$1,038	—
53	—	—	$5,000

a. Fill in the values wherever there is a —.

b. Over this range of output levels, does the firm's production function have increasing, decreasing, or constant returns to scale?

9.9 Vending machines are much more common in Japan than in other countries. Among other things, they are used to dispense "jewelry, fresh flowers, frozen beef, rice, whiskey, hamburgers, pornographic magazines, videocassettes and batteries." Why? "With rents sky high and labor in short supply, vending machines create more shelf space and run 24 hours a day, needing only to be refilled from time to time" (Sterngold 1992, A12).

Write down a production function for *retailing services.* Use isoquant/isocost analysis to show increases in the cost of labor would lead to greater use of vending machines (capital). Suppose that technological change enables more commodities to be sold out of vending machines than was previously possible. Analyze the impact on total costs of retailing services, using isoquants and isocost lines.

9.10 Many public utilities (gas, electricity, and water, for instance) are subject to *rate of return regulation*, under which a firm is allowed to choose its price, subject to its proving that it is not earning too much money. Typically, the firm is allowed to cover its expenditures for labor and materials exactly and to earn a "fair" rate of return on its capital investment. Can you think of any problems with this sort of regulatory scheme? In particular, what do you think that this plan does to the firm's incentives to substitute capital for labor?

9.11 Draw long-run total, marginal, and average cost curves for a firm whose production function exhibits economies of scale everywhere. Is the average cost curve upward- or downward-sloping? What is the relationship between the marginal cost curve and the average cost curve? What can you say about the shape of the long-run total cost curve?

9.12 Most of the costs incurred to provide telephone service relate to plant and equipment. Telephone companies have to put enough capacity (switches and lines connecting switches) to be able to meet peak demands, which occur during the day. Recently, a telephone company executive said "any calls at night are gravy." Explain how this statement could be correct even though the nighttime rates charged for calls are lower than the daytime rates.

APPENDIX

9A An Algebraic Approach to Technology and Cost

This appendix uses calculus to analyze production functions and cost minimization. We do this by examining New Age Vehicles, a firm that produces automobiles in competition with National Motors.

9A.1 PROPERTIES OF THE PRODUCTION FUNCTION

Suppose that the production function of New Age Vehicles is $F(L,K) = L^{\frac{1}{2}}K^{\frac{1}{2}}$. This is an example of what is known as a *Cobb-Douglas production function*.[1] Chapter 8 introduced several properties of production functions. We can express all of these concepts using calculus.

The *marginal physical product* (*MPP*) of a factor is the additional output obtained by employing one more unit of that factor. In other words, it is the rate at which output changes with use of the factor. In terms of calculus, a rate of change is a derivative, so the *MPP* of a factor is the partial derivative of the production function with respect to that factor. For example, the marginal physical product of labor for New Age Vehicles is

$$MPP_L = \partial F/\partial L = \tfrac{1}{2}L^{-\frac{1}{2}}K^{\frac{1}{2}}.$$

We sometimes are interested in how the marginal physical product for a factor behaves as we increase the amount of that factor while holding the amounts of the other factors constant. In other words, we take the derivative of marginal physical product. The production function exhibits *increasing marginal returns* to labor if the marginal physical product of labor increases as the amount of labor employed increases: $\partial MPP_L/\partial L > 0$. Likewise, it exhibits *constant marginal returns* if $\partial MPP_L/\partial L = 0$, and *diminishing marginal returns if* $\partial MPP_L/\partial L < 0$. For New Age Vehicles, $\partial MPP_L/\partial L = -\tfrac{1}{4}L^{-\frac{3}{2}}K^{\frac{1}{2}} < 0$. Hence, this technology exhibits diminishing marginal returns from labor. (PC 9A.1)

The *marginal rate of technical substitution* (*MRTS*) tells us how much more of one factor the firm needs if it is to produce a *constant* quantity of output as it reduces its use of another factor. In Equation (8.4), we showed that $MRTS = MPP_L/MPP_K$.[2] Hence for New Age Vehicles,

[1]In general, a production function having the form L^aK^b, where a and b are positive constants, is a Cobb-Douglas production function.

[2]Although the derivation in the text relies on discrete changes, one can simply replace ΔL and ΔK with dL and dK to obtain this result.

$$MRTS = \frac{MPP_L}{MPP_K} = \frac{\frac{1}{2}L^{-\frac{1}{2}}K^{\frac{1}{2}}}{\frac{1}{2}L^{\frac{1}{2}}K^{-\frac{1}{2}}} = \frac{K}{L} \tag{9A.1}$$

9A.1 PROGRESS CHECK

Find the marginal physical product of capital for New Age Vehicles' production function. Does this technology exhibit diminishing, constant, or increasing marginal returns with respect to capital?

Finally, the *degree of returns to scale* is the rate at which the amount of output increases as the firm increases all factors proportionately. We determine the returns to scale by seeing what happens to output when the firm increases all inputs in the same proportion. Let β be a constant greater than 1. Then returns to scale are increasing, constant, or decreasing, depending on whether $F(\beta L,\beta K)$ is greater than, less than, or equal to $\beta F(L,K)$. In the particular case of New Age Vehicles, we have

$$F(\beta L,\beta K) = (\beta L)^{\frac{1}{2}}(\beta K)^{\frac{1}{2}} = \beta L^{\frac{1}{2}}K^{\frac{1}{2}} = \beta F(L,K).$$

This technology exhibits constant returns to scale.

9A.2 COST MINIMIZATION IN THE LONG RUN

In this section, we examine how New Age Vehicles makes its long-run input decisions. Suppose the firm wants to produce x units of output. The firm's task is to find the combination of factors that will produce x as inexpensively as possible. Let w denote the hourly wage and r the price per unit of capital. The firm minimizes its factor expenditures, $wL + rK$, subject to the requirement that it produce x units of output, or

$$x = L^{\frac{1}{2}}K^{\frac{1}{2}} \tag{9A.2}$$

From Equation (9.5), we know the firm minimizes cost by producing where $MRTS$ equals the ratio of the factor prices

$$MRTS = \frac{w}{r}. \tag{9A.3}$$

Equation (9A.1) indicates that New Age Vehicles' $MRTS = K/L$. Substituting this expression into Equation (9A.3), we have $K/L = w/r$. Rearranging terms, $K = wL/r$.

We can now substitute this expression for K into the production constraint to find the relationship between the amount of labor and the output level

$$x = L^{\frac{1}{2}} \times \left(\frac{Lw}{r}\right)^{\frac{1}{2}}.$$

Solving this equation for L yields

$$L = w^{-\frac{1}{2}}r^{\frac{1}{2}}x. \tag{9A.4}$$

This is the cost-minimizing quantity of labor to employ. As we would expect, the cost-minimizing quantity of labor decreases as the wage rate rises and increases as the cost of capital or the amount of output rises.

Turning to the cost-minimizing quantity of capital, we earlier found that $K = wL/r$. Substituting Equation (9A.4) into this expression, we obtain

$$K = w^{\frac{1}{2}}r^{-\frac{1}{2}}x. \tag{9A.5}$$

The long-run cost of production is the factor expenditure on the cost-minimizing combination of labor and capital. The long-run cost function in this example is

$$C(x) = w \times (w^{-\frac{1}{2}}r^{\frac{1}{2}}x) + r \times (w^{\frac{1}{2}}r^{-\frac{1}{2}}x) \qquad (9A.6)$$
$$= 2w^{\frac{1}{2}}r^{\frac{1}{2}}x.$$

Notice from the last expression that an increase in either of the factor prices raises total cost. For example, if we differentiate the cost function with respect to w, we have

$$\frac{\partial C}{\partial w} = w^{-\frac{1}{2}}r^{\frac{1}{2}}x > 0. \qquad (9A.7)$$

Since the derivative is positive, cost increases with the wage.

By comparing Equation (9A.7) with (9A.4), you may have noticed that $\partial C/\partial w$ equals the cost-minimizing quantity of labor. This is no coincidence: In general, *the derivative of the cost function with respect to a factor price is the cost-minimizing quantity of that factor.*

9A.3 MORE THAN TWO FACTORS OF PRODUCTION

We have focused on New Age Vehicles' use of labor and robots (capital) to produce automobiles, but clearly other inputs are needed as well. For instance, electricity is needed to light the factory and to power the robots. It is difficult to deal with more than two inputs using the graphical approach taken in the text. Fortunately, the use of algebra shows that all of the key insights gained from the two-factor case hold more generally.

PROPERTIES OF THE PRODUCTION FUNCTION

Let's suppose that New Age Vehicles uses electricity, E, in addition to labor and capital. The fact that there are three inputs provides no problem for our definition of the total product, which we now write as $F(L,K,E)$.

As before, the marginal physical product of a factor is equal to the additional output that is obtained when one more unit of the factor is employed in production, holding all other input levels fixed. The marginal physical product of electricity, for example, is

$$MPP_E = \partial F/\partial E.$$

We can also examine the marginal rate of technical substitution for a production function that uses more than two inputs. The only new point we have to remember is that we are keeping the levels of the other inputs constant when we calculate the rate at which one input can be substituted for another. Hence, we speak of the marginal rate of substitution of labor for capital, *given a fixed amount of electricity.* As in the two-input case, we can express the marginal rate of technical substitution between two inputs as the ratio of their marginal physical products. For instance, the marginal rate of technical substitution between capital and electricity is given by

$$MRTS = MPP_K/MPP_E.$$

Lastly, we can examine the returns to scale of a technology that uses more than two inputs. Suppose that the firm simultaneously increases the quantities of L, K, and E by proportion β. Then returns to scale are increasing, constant, or decreasing, depending on whether $F(\beta L,\beta K,\beta E)$ is greater than, less than, or equal to $\beta F(L,K,E)$.

COST MINIMIZATION IN THE LONG RUN: THE LAGRANGE METHOD

Now, consider New Age's long-run factor choice when it uses three inputs. Let t denote the price per kilowatt of electricity. The firm's objective is to find the cost-minimizing method of producing x units of output. That is, the firm wants to minimize $wL + rK + tE$, subject to the constraint that the input combination produces the desired output level, $F(L,K,E) = x$.

We can solve this problem by using the Lagrange Method introduced in the Appendix to Chapter 3:

Step 1 *Form the Lagrangean as the sum of the firm's objective function and the Lagrange multiplier times the constraint that it faces:*

$$\mathcal{L} = wL + rK + tE + \mu(x - L^{\frac{1}{3}}K^{\frac{1}{3}}E^{\frac{1}{3}}).$$

The variable μ—the Greek letter *mu*—is the Language multiplier for this problem.[3]

Step 2 *Differentiate the Lagrangean with respect to L, K, E, and μ.* Then set the derivatives equal to 0:

$$\partial\mathcal{L}/\partial L = w - \mu \times MPP_L = w - \tfrac{1}{3}\mu L^{-\frac{2}{3}}K^{\frac{1}{3}}E^{\frac{1}{3}} = 0,$$

$$\partial\mathcal{L}/\partial K = r - \mu \times MPP_K = r - \tfrac{1}{3}\mu L^{\frac{1}{3}}K^{-\frac{2}{3}}E^{\frac{1}{3}} = 0,$$

$$\partial\mathcal{L}/\partial E = t - \mu \times MPP_E = t - \tfrac{1}{3}\mu L^{\frac{1}{3}}K^{\frac{1}{3}}E^{-\frac{2}{3}} = 0,$$

and

$$\partial\mathcal{L}/\partial \mu = x - F(L,K) = x - L^{\frac{1}{3}}K^{\frac{1}{3}}E^{\frac{1}{3}} = 0.$$

Note that this last equation is the production constraint.

Step 3 *Solve these equations for L, K, E, and μ.* Solving, we obtain,

$$L = w^{-\frac{2}{3}}r^{\frac{1}{3}}t^{\frac{1}{3}}x,$$

$$K = w^{\frac{1}{3}}r^{-\frac{2}{3}}t^{\frac{1}{3}}x,$$

$$E = w^{\frac{1}{3}}r^{\frac{1}{3}}t^{-\frac{2}{3}}x,$$

and

$$\mu = 3w^{\frac{1}{3}}r^{\frac{1}{3}}t^{\frac{1}{3}}.$$

The resulting total cost is $wL + rK + tE = 3w^{\frac{1}{3}}r^{\frac{1}{3}}t^{\frac{1}{3}}x$.

[3]Notice that here, the firm's objective is to minimize its expenditures on the inputs, whereas earlier the household's objective was to maximize utility. Fortunately, the same techniques are valid in both cases.

Although we have looked at the case of a three-factor production decision, you should convince yourself that the same technique could be applied to any number of factors.

9A.4 ESTIMATING PRODUCTION FUNCTIONS

The last two chapters have shown the centrality of production functions to firm decision making; the production function determines how much output the firm can expect to produce given its inputs, how easy or difficult it is to substitute one input for another, and how much output expands when the firm increases all of its inputs proportionately (returns to scale). Because production functions are so important, economists have engaged in a great deal of research aimed at estimating their shapes. This section describes the issues involved in estimating production functions.

ALTERNATIVE STRATEGIES

Suppose that we are interested in determining the production function for automobiles. One way to proceed is to collect data on the amounts of labor, capital, research and development, steel, plastic, and other inputs employed in automobile manufacturing during each of several years, say from 1955 to 1998. By looking at how total automobile output varies from year to year as the annual inputs vary, we can make inferences about the shape of the production function. Because such a study relies on a series of observations from different points in time, it is referred to as a *time series study.*

Another way to proceed is to collect the same sorts of data from a group of different firms during a particular year, say 1996. By seeing how the output levels at Ford, Toyota, GM, and so forth vary with their use of various inputs, we can similarly make inferences about the shape of the production function. This is referred to as a *cross-sectional study.* We can combine the time series and cross-sectional approaches by observing a group of different firms over a series of years. This is a *panel-data study.*

A quite different approach is to use *engineering data.* Here we imagine the technicians who work within the firm varying the amounts of the different inputs on an experimental basis and reporting how output changes as a consequence. The engineering approach has not been very popular among economists because engineering data generally concern only some component of a firm's activities while the important issue is the production of total output.

ESTIMATION PROBLEMS

Several problems arise in any attempt to use real-world data to estimate production functions. One of them is *aggregation.* The notion that there is an input called "labor" is in some sense a fiction. It is an aggregate of factory workers, janitors, mail clerks, executives, and so on. Assuming that all of these different inputs can be lumped together into a single input may lead to incorrect inferences about the contributions of labor to output. In exactly the same way, "capital" refers to a variety of inputs, including robots, drill presses, computers, factory buildings, and so on. Again, incorrect inferences may result.

A second problem arises because, at any particular point in time, a firm may not be operating fully efficiently. Because of errors or constraints about which the investigator is unaware, the firm may not be optimally combining inputs to get output, so that the observation is not really on the firm's production function.

These difficulties do not mean that it is hopeless to try to learn about the shapes of production functions from real-world data. It merely means that we should be cautious in interpreting the results that emerge from any given study.

USING THE COBB-DOUGLAS PRODUCTION FUNCTION

The Cobb-Douglas production function introduced at the beginning of this appendix provides a useful framework for estimating production functions. In its general form, the Cobb-Douglas production function relates output (x) to labor and capital by the formula

$$x = L^a K^b,$$

where a and b are parameters. If we assume that production is Cobb-Douglas, then "all" the investigator has to do is estimate the values of a and b. Once a and b are known, we know everything about the firm's technology. The sum of a and b is particularly important, because if $(a + b) > 1$ there are increasing returns to scale; if $(a + b) < 1$ there are decreasing returns to scale; and if $(a + b) = 1$ there are constant returns to scale. To see why, let's see what happens when we double both L and K, so that L becomes $2L$ and K becomes $2K$. The new level of output is

$$F(2L, 2K) = (2L)^a(2K)^b = 2^{(a+b)}L^aK^b$$
$$= 2^{(a+b)}x.$$

Thus, if $(a + b) = 1$, then a doubling of all the inputs exactly doubles output. If $(a + b) > 1$, output more than doubles, and if $(a + b) < 1$, output less than doubles.

A Cobb-Douglas example is provided by Griliches' (1986) study of production functions in U.S. manufacturing. Using a 1977 cross-sectional sample of 491 large firms, he estimated a Cobb-Douglas production function with three inputs, labor, capital, and research and development (R). According to his estimates, the production function is

$$x = AL^{0.61}K^{0.29}R^{0.09},$$

where A is a constant. According to this production function, manufacturing is approximately characterized by constant returns to scale, because the three relevant parameters sum to 0.99.

It can be demonstrated that each of the parameters of the Cobb-Douglas function shows the elasticity of output with respect to the associated input. (Use the calculus definition of elasticity from Appendix 3A.) Hence, an implication of this production function is that a 10 percent increase in R&D increases output by 0.9 percent, while a 10 percent increase in labor increases output by 6.1 percent.

SUMMARY

Calculus and other mathematical techniques help us further analyze a firm's production decisions and costs.

- We can express marginal physical production, the pattern of marginal returns, and marginal rate of technical substitution in terms of derivatives of the production function.
- There is a concise mathematical statement of the degree of returns to scale.
- The technique of Lagrange multipliers can be used to find the cost-minimizing input combination for a firm using any number of inputs.
- The derivative of total cost with respect to the price of a factor is equal to the quantity of the input used by the firm.
- Statistical analysis can be used to estimate actual production functions from time series or cross-sectional data.

DISCUSSION QUESTIONS

9A.1 Consider New Age Vehicles' rival, Overseas Energetic. Overseas Energetic's production function is $L^{\frac{3}{4}}K^{\frac{1}{4}}$, where L and K denote the amounts of labor and capital, respectively. Let w denote the price per unit of labor and r denote the price per unit of capital.

a. Find the MPP_L and MPP_K for this production function.

b. Calculate Overseas Energetic's long-run cost function.

9A.2 Ski 'n' Sweat makes home exercise ski machines with labor (L) and steel (S). The production function for ski machines is $x = L^{2/3} + S^{2/3}$.

a. Find the marginal physical products of labor and steel. What is the marginal rate of technical substitution?

b. Does this production technology exhibit increasing, decreasing, or constant returns to scale?

c. Ski 'n' Sweat wishes to produce 2,600 ski machines. What is the cost-minimizing combination of labor and steel when the wage is \$25 and the price of capital is \$5? What is the total cost of producing 2,600 ski machines?

PART three

The Competitive Model

In Part Two, we developed general rules for profit-maximizing input and output decisions. The application of these rules depends in part on the nature of the supply and demand curves that the firm faces. In Chapter 10, we parallel the theory of the household by assuming that the firm is a price taker, both as a seller of output and a buyer of inputs. While not all firms are price takers, many are, and this model provides important insights into firm behavior.

When both firms and households are price takers, market prices serve as important guides to economic behavior. Prices give signals that influence the quantities of commodities that households consume and the amounts of inputs that they supply. These same prices influence the output and input decisions of firms. But where do these prices come from? The supply and demand model presented in Chapter 1 provides the answer: Prices arise from the interaction of households and firms in the market. Now that we have developed a detailed understanding of individual household and firm behavior, we can analyze the workings of supply and demand in much greater detail. The centerpiece of this analysis is the model known as *perfect competition,* which is presented in Chapter 11.

The basic competitive model is extended in two important ways in Chapter 12. First, we see how the various markets in a competitive system interact with each other, a subject known as *general equilibrium analysis.* Second, we introduce the subject of *welfare economics,* which develops criteria that can be used to assess the social desirability of market outcomes. Thus, as promised in Chapter 1, we continue to follow an agenda that stresses both positive and normative issues. We want to know not only how markets work, but also whether they produce good outcomes.

CHAPTER

10

The Price-Taking Firm

I took one Draught of life—
I'll tell you what I paid—
Precisely an existence—
The market price, they said.
—Emily Dickinson

In 1987, life was anything but a bowl of cherries for America's two thousand sour cherry farmers. The price of sour cherries had tumbled to $300 per ton from $460 the previous year. Growers such as Lee D. Brown of Hudson, New York, had to decide whether to bother harvesting any cherries at all. At such a low price, he reasoned, it might not be worth picking the cherries off the tree. Some farmers actually considered bulldozing their cherry trees and replanting with a more profitable crop (Faber 1987, 16).

Mr. Brown and other farmers had to decide how many cherries to sell and how many workers to hire to pick, wash, and box the cherries. They had to decide whether to stay in the cherry business or to replant their orchards with apple trees. Chapters 7 and 9 developed the basic economic theory of the firm to explain how firms make these decisions. Although this theory provides general rules for analyzing firms' input and output choices, it is not yet in a form that can be used to make detailed predictions.

To see what is missing, consider a sour cherry grower's supply decision. In Chapter 7, we showed that at the profit-maximizing level of output, marginal revenue equals marginal cost, and average revenue is no less than average economic cost. To maximize profits, the firm must know the shapes of its marginal and average economic cost curves as well as the shapes of the average and marginal revenue curves that it faces. The last chapter showed how to derive the firm's marginal and average cost functions. But what do its marginal and average revenue curves look like? This chapter will provide an answer for the particular case of a price-taking firm. It will then examine a price-taking firm's behavior both as a supplier of output and a demander of inputs.

We need to be clear about what we mean by a price-taking firm. Since a firm is both a supplier and a demander, this characterization has two parts. First, in its role as a product-market supplier, the firm believes that it can sell as much output as it wants at a fixed prevailing price. Second, in its role as a factor-market demander, the firm believes that it can purchase as much of a factor as it wants at a fixed prevailing price. In summary, a **price-taking firm** chooses its actions under the assumption that it cannot influence the prices of the output that it sells or the inputs that it buys.

price-taking firm
A price-taking firm chooses its actions under the assumption that it cannot influence the prices of the output that it sells or the inputs that it buys.

There are several reasons for examining the behavior of price-taking firms:

1. Most important, many firms are price takers. For example, no single sour cherry farmer is large enough to influence the price of cherries. Even if one farmer were to shut down entirely, he would barely make a dent in the total market quantity supplied. Also, a single farmer simply does not buy enough fertilizer or farm machinery to have an impact on the prices of these inputs. The producers in most other agricultural markets (such as corn, wheat, and soybeans) also are price takers, both as sellers of their crops and as buyers of inputs. Many manufacturing firms are price takers as well.
2. We can summarize a price-taking firm's behavior entirely in terms of its supply curves in product markets and its input demand curves in factor markets. In Chapter 11, we will combine these curves with household demand curves in product markets and supply curves in factor markets to derive predictions about the equilibrium prices that individual market participants take as given.
3. It is particularly easy to analyze a price-taking firm's input and output choices. Thus, this is a good starting point for applying our theory of the firm.

Our first task in this chapter is to derive the marginal and average revenue curves for a price-taking firm so that we can apply our general rules for profit maximization to analyze such a firm's output decisions. Our goal is to be able to predict how much output a price-taking firm will supply at any given price. In other words, we will derive a price-taking firm's supply curve in a product market.

After considering output decisions, we will turn to input demand. Some of the consequences of price taking for input choices were investigated in Chapter 9. In that chapter, however, we took the level of output to be a fixed quantity and asked only how the firm would go about producing it. We did not say how the output level was determined. In the present chapter, we will look at how a price taker simultaneously chooses its input and output levels. Thus, we will also derive a firm's demand curve in a factor market.

10.1 SUPPLY IN PRODUCT MARKETS

Let's begin by considering the output choice of a single firm, Pitts Cherry Orchard. Our goal is to construct Pitts Orchard's supply function. That is, we want to use our model of firm behavior to answer the question: For any given price, how many tons of cherries is Pitts Cherry Orchard willing to supply?

TWO RULES FOR PROFIT MAXIMIZATION

Like any profit-maximizing firm, Pitts Orchard answers this question by following the two rules for the profit-maximizing output level developed in Chapter 7:

1. *Marginal Output Rule:* If the firm does not shut down, then it should produce output at a level where marginal revenue is equal to marginal cost.

Figure 10.1

A Price-Taking Firm's Demand Curve Coincides with Its Marginal Revenue Curve

A price-taking firm faces a demand curve that is infinitely elastic at the prevailing price, here $300 per ton. When the firm increases its output by one unit from 2 to 3, total revenue rises by shaded area *B*, which is equal to $300. For a price taker, the marginal revenue curve, average revenue curve, and demand curve coincide.

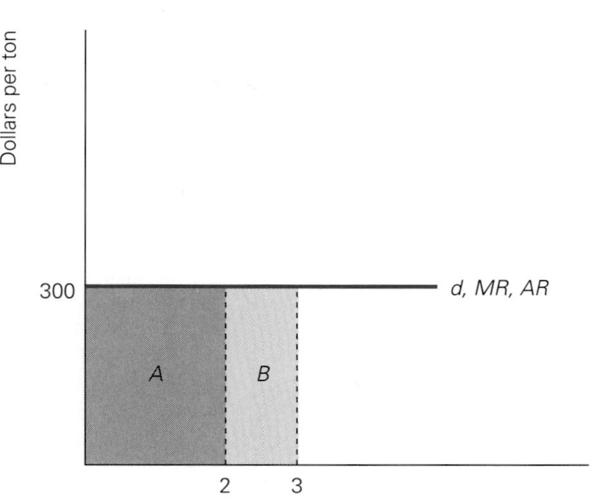

2. *Shut-Down Rule:* If for every choice of output level the firm's average revenue is less than its average economic cost, then the firm should shut down.

To implement these two rules, the firm must calculate its average and marginal cost and revenue functions. Suppose that the manager at Pitts Cherry Orchard has followed the last chapter's procedures for deriving the firm's marginal and average cost curves. The firm still needs to know its revenue curves. Suppose that the orchard is a price taker in its output market—it can sell as many cherries as it would like at a constant price of $300 per ton. Pitts's firm-specific demand curve is therefore the horizontal line labeled *d* in Figure 10.1. Using the terminology developed in Chapter 3, this demand curve is *perfectly elastic* at a price of $300 per ton.

Since Chapter 7 showed that the firm-specific demand curve is simultaneously the firm's average revenue curve, Pitts's average revenue is always equal to $300 per ton. All we are missing is a way to find Pitts's marginal revenue curve.

By definition, the firm's marginal revenue equals the change in total revenue as the firm increases its output by one unit. When a price-taking firm such as Pitts Cherry Orchard sells one more unit of output, it does so at the going price, here $300 per ton. The revenue earned from the other units is unaffected, so the only change in total revenue is the additional revenue earned from the sale of the marginal unit itself. But this marginal revenue is just equal to the price. Thus, we conclude that *a price-taking firm's marginal revenue is always equal to the price that it takes as given.* At every output level Pitts's marginal revenue is $300 per ton, the price that it takes as given. Figure 10.1 illustrates the relationship between the firm-specific

10.1 PROGRESS CHECK

Suppose that Pitts Cherry Orchard faced a price of $200 per ton. Graph the firm's demand curve, average revenue curve, and marginal revenue curve.

demand curve and the associated marginal revenue curve. As the figure shows, the two curves coincide. (PC 10.1)

Marginal Output Rule

With the relevant revenue and cost curves in hand, we can apply the general rules for the profit-maximizing choice of output level to the case of a price-taking firm. The first rule states that a firm's marginal revenue must be equal to marginal cost in equilibrium. We have just seen that for a price taker, marginal revenue is equal to the price of its output. Hence, for a price-taking firm the marginal output rule can be stated as follows:

> ***Marginal Output Rule for a Price Taker:*** If a firm takes the price of its output as given, then unless the firm shuts down entirely, it should produce output at a level where the price is equal to marginal cost.

10.2 PROGRESS CHECK

Suppose that the firm produced 60 tons of cherries per year in Figure 10.2. Find the area that represents the loss in profit in comparison with producing 50 tons.

Figure 10.2 illustrates this rule in action. The firm takes a price of $325 per ton as given. Hence, the firm's marginal revenue is constant at $325. The marginal output rule tells us that (if it produces at all) the firm's profits are maximized where marginal cost is equal to $325, which is 50 tons of cherries in Figure 10.2. (PC 10.2)

Shut-Down Rule

We can also tailor the second general rule to the specific case of a price-taking firm. Under the shut-down rule, the firm compares the average revenue received from the sale of output with the average economic cost of producing it. As already shown, a price taker's average revenue always is equal to the price that the firm takes as given. Hence, applied to a price-taking firm, the shut-down rule is as follows:

> ***Shut-Down Rule for a Price Taker:*** If the firm takes the price of its output as given and this price is less than average economic cost for every output level, then the firm should shut down.

10.3 PROGRESS CHECK

Suppose that the price facing the orchard in Figure 10.3 is $460 per ton. Should the firm shut down? Can you answer this question without knowing the marginal revenue curve?

Figure 10.3 illustrates the firm-specific demand curve and the average cost curve for a cherry orchard that would be better off shutting down than producing. At every output level, the average cost of production is greater than average revenue of $300 per ton. Even if the firm were to produce 100 tons of output, the level at which average cost is lowest, the firm still would suffer losses (equal to the shaded area) since the average revenue taken in would be less than the average cost paid out. (PC 10.3)

THE LONG AND THE SHORT OF THE MATTER

We are almost ready to construct the firm's supply curve. However, we first have to consider the firm's decision horizon. How much time does the firm have to make its supply choice? We need to answer this question because the firm's supply decision depends on the firm's marginal and average economic costs of produc-

Figure 10.2

The Marginal Output Rule for a Price-Taking Firm

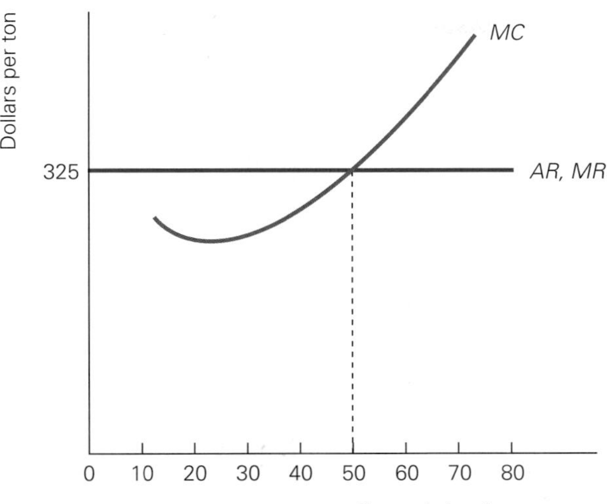

This firm's marginal revenue is constant at $325. The marginal output rule tells us that (if it produces at all) the firm's profit is maximized at the output level at which marginal cost is equal to this marginal revenue. That output level is 50 tons of cherries.

Figure 10.3

The Shut-Down Rule for a Price-Taking Firm

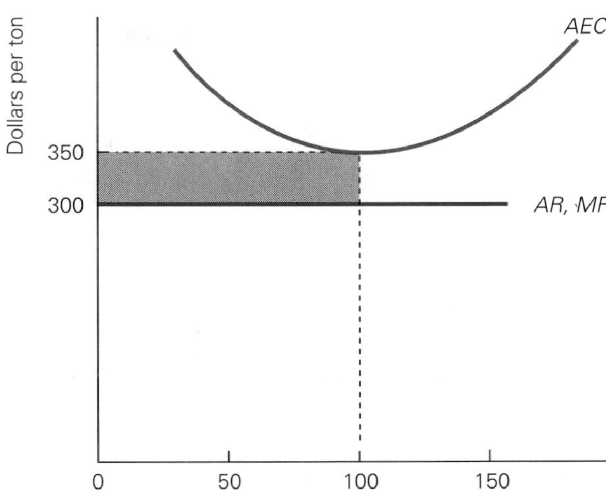

This figure illustrates the firm-specific demand curve and the average economic cost curve for a cherry orchard that would be better off shutting down than producing. At every output level, the average economic cost of production is greater than average revenue of $300 per ton. For example, if the firm produces 100 tons, it incurs losses equal to the shaded area.

tion, and—as we saw in the last chapter—these costs depend, in turn, on the time frame.

Consider a farmer who uses trees and labor to produce sour cherries. How will he respond to a rise in the price of sour cherries from $350 per ton to $400 per ton? Over a period of a few days, the only way to get more cherries would be to hire more labor in order to get every last cherry off the trees. There is not enough time to add more trees—only labor can be varied. In Chapter 8, we defined the *short run* as a decision period over which only one factor is variable. Hence, in this case the farmer is making a short-run production decision, and his supply decision is based on his short-run marginal and average economic cost curves. Recall from Chapter 9 that, in the short run, only the expenditure on the variable factor is an economic cost. Therefore, short-run average economic cost is given by the short-run average variable cost curve.

Given enough time, the farmer can respond by adjusting *all* of his inputs—purchasing additional orchard land and planting cherry trees on it. Recall from Chapter 8 that the period of time over which the firm can adjust all of its factors is said to be the *long run*. When determining how many trees to plant, the farmer is making a long-run supply decision, which is based on long-run marginal and average cost curves.

Since they are based on different cost curves, a firm's short- and long-run supply curves generally will be different. Given this difference, it is worth looking at the two separately when deriving them.

SHORT-RUN SUPPLY CURVES

Let's begin by considering a firm's short-run supply decision. In particular, suppose that the firms in the sour cherry industry have chosen the levels of their fixed factors (such as the number of cherry trees), and we want to know how much output each firm in the industry is willing to supply at some particular price.

The Firm's Short-Run Supply Curve

To construct a short-run supply curve for a price-taking firm such as Pitts Cherry Orchard, we simply apply the two rules for the profit-maximizing output level. To begin, we draw the short-run marginal and average variable cost curves in Figure 10.4. Suppose that the firm can sell its output at a price of \$350 per ton. How much output would the firm supply? The marginal output rule tells us that if it's going to produce at all, the firm should grow 60 tons of cherries because this is the quantity at which marginal cost equals \$350 per ton, the marginal revenue. The shut-down rule tells us that the firm is better off producing than shutting down because the average revenue earned selling 60 tons of cherries, \$350 per ton, exceeds the average variable cost, \$300 per ton. By selling 60 tons of cherries at a price of \$350 per ton, Pitts earns a positive *economic* profit of $60 \times (\$350 - \$300) = \$3{,}000$, the shaded area in Figure 10.4. We have found one point on Pitts Cherry Orchard's short-run curve. Pitts supplies 60 tons of cherries per year when their price is \$350 per ton. Similar reasoning tells us that Pitts Cherry Orchard would want to supply 70 tons of cherries at a price of \$400.

In fact, for any price greater than p^*, the firm's profit is maximized by producing at the point where price is equal to marginal cost. The relevant feature of p^* is that it is the price equal to the minimal value of the firm's short-run average variable cost. At any price higher than p^*, the firm can find some output level at which average revenue is greater than average variable cost, and it will prefer producing output to shutting down. Notice that it is no coincidence that marginal cost is equal to average cost at p^*. We know from Chapter 9 that the marginal and average variable cost curves must intersect at the minimum of the average variable cost curve.

What should the firm do if the price at which it can sell its output is lower than p^*, such as \$170 per ton in Figure 10.5? By the first rule for profit maximization, if the firm is going to produce output, then it should produce 25 tons. But at this price, the firm's average variable cost, distance A, is greater than its average revenue, \$170 per ton. Consequently, if it were to produce 25 tons of cherries, Pitts Orchard would suffer losses equal to the shaded area in Figure 10.5. The firm is better off shutting down. Similar reasoning tells us that the firm will shut down at any price that is less than p^*.

What if the price is equal to p^*? The marginal output rule tells us that the firm should produce x^* tons of cherries, *if* it is going to produce anything at all. Should the firm produce anything? At this price and output combination, the price is just equal to the firm's average variable cost. Hence, the firm earns zero economic profit whether it stays in business or chooses to shut down. Thus, the profit-maximizing firm is indifferent between selling x^* tons of cherries at a price of p^* and shutting down. It may seem strange to you that a firm earning zero profit should stay in business. But remember, we are talking about *economic* profit. By definition, a firm earning zero economic profit has no superior alternative use for the inputs it employs, so it may as well stay in business.

Figure 10.4

Pitts's Short-Run Supply Decision When Price Exceeds the Minimum of Short-Run Average Cost

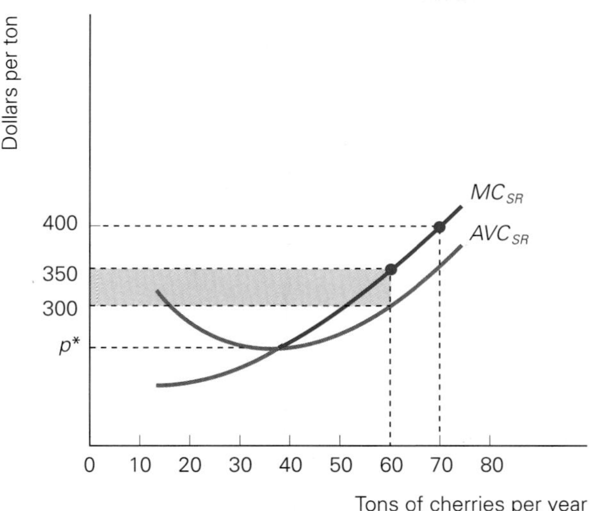

When price is $350 per ton, if it's going to produce at all, the firm should grow 60 tons of cherries; at this quantity, $MR = MC_{SR}$. The shut-down rule tells us that the firm is better off producing 60 tons of cherries than shutting down; at this quantity, $AR > AVC_{SR}$. Pitts Cherry Orchard's resulting profit is the shaded area. Whenever price exceeds p^*, the firm will produce at the associated point on its marginal cost curve.

Figure 10.5

Pitts's Short-Run Supply Decision When Price Is Less Than the Minimum of Short-Run Average Cost

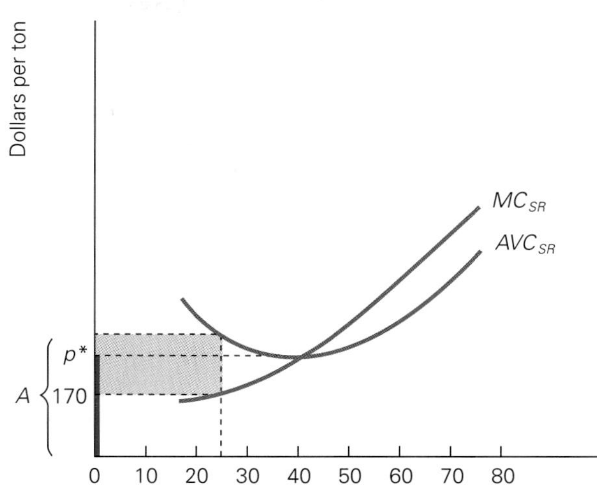

The first rule for profit maximization tells us that if the firm is going to produce output at a price of $170, it should produce 25 tons. But at this price, the firm's average variable cost, distance *A*, is greater than its average revenue, $170, so the firm would suffer losses equal to the shaded area. The firm is better off by shutting down. Similar reasoning tells us that the firm will shut down at any price that is less than p^*.

Now, let's put together the discussion surrounding Figures 10.4 and 10.5. Figure 10.5 shows that whenever price is above the minimum of average variable cost, the quantity supplied is found by reading over to the firm's marginal cost curve. Figure 10.5 shows that, for any price below the lowest point on the short-run average variable cost curve, the firm will supply no output. Hence, *a price-taking firm's short-run supply curve coincides with the vertical axis at prices less than the minimum of its short-run average variable cost. The short-run supply curve coincides with the firm's short-run marginal cost curve where it is above the firm's short-run average variable cost curve.* The dark lines in Figure 10.6 illustrate Pitts Cherry Orchard's short-run supply decision.

Before concluding this discussion of the price-taker's short-run supply curve, it is worth noting that the firm may supply cherries even when it is suffering short-run *accounting* losses. That is, the firm may continue to operate even when its revenues are less than its short-run total costs, the sum of the expenditures on both *fixed* and variable inputs. In terms of *average* magnitudes, this means that the firm may operate when the price of output is less than the average total cost (*ATC*). Figure 10.7 illustrates this possibility. Why does this firm continue to produce in the short run? Because it would have to pay for the fixed factors even if it were to cease producing cherries. As long as price is greater than the average expenditures on the variable factor—short-run average variable cost—the firm would suffer even greater accounting losses if it were to shut down. Thus, this

Figure 10.6

A Price-Taking Firm's Short-Run Supply Curve

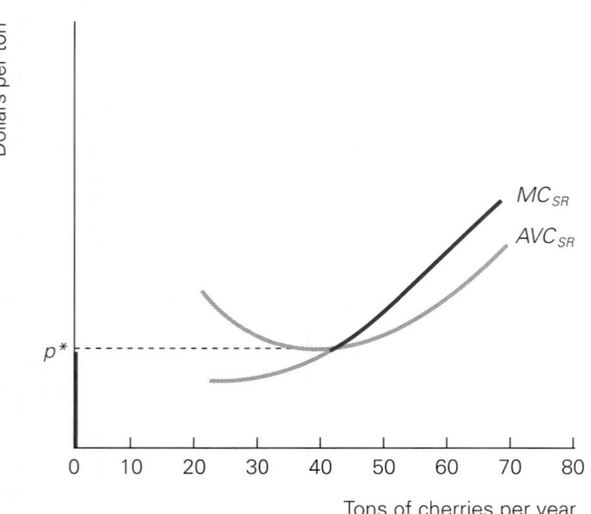

A price-taking firm's short-run supply curve coincides with its short-run marginal cost curve above its short-run average variable cost curve. For any price below the lowest point on the short-run average variable cost curve, the firm will supply no output.

Figure 10.7

A Firm Suffering Accounting Losses That Does Not Shut Down in the Short Run

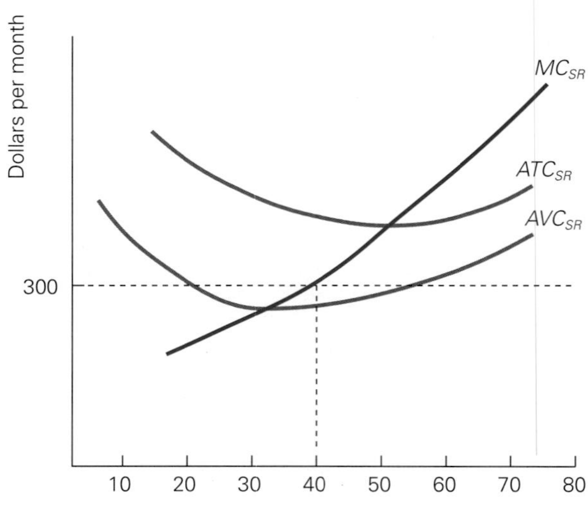

At a price of $300 per ton, the firm will supply 40 tons of cherries in the short run, even though short-run average total cost is greater than the price. In the short run, only expenditures on the variable factor are relevant for economic decision making, and expenditures on fixed factors do not affect the firm's short-run supply choice.

figure reinforces one of our basic themes: Sensible decision making depends only on *economic* costs. The firm in Figure 10.7 is making a profit with respect to economic costs. That is all that one needs to know to predict that the firm is willing to stay open. The *ATC* curve adds no useful information for short-run production decisions. (PC 10.4)

10.4 PROGRESS CHECK

A newspaper report on the turkey industry stated that "the price paid to growers has fallen to about 60 cents a pound, slightly below what it costs to raise a turkey." However, an expert in the industry "was not aware of any growers driven out of business by depressed prices." (*The New York Times,* November 11, 1991, D2). Why might a turkey farmer stay in business if he or she were losing money?

LONG-RUN SUPPLY CURVES

When the firm faces a price change that results in a new, long-lasting price level, it has enough time to adjust all of its factors of production in response. Hence, its long-run supply decisions are based on the firm's long-run marginal and average cost curves.

Deriving a Firm's Long-Run Supply Curve

Suppose that farmers expect the price of cherries to stay at $400 per ton for a long enough time that they can adjust all of their factors of production in response to this price. In this case, firms are by definition making long-run supply decisions.

Although they are based on different cost curves, the procedures for deriving short- and long-run supply curves are very similar. As was true for the short-run supply curve, to find a firm's long-run supply curve we simply apply our two rules for the profit-maximizing choice of output level. The only difference is that now we use the *long-run* marginal and average economic cost curves, rather than their short-run counterparts. In the long run, all factors are variable, so all factor expenditures are economic costs. Hence, average economic costs are simply given the long-run average cost curve.

Figure 10.8 illustrates the long-run marginal and average cost curves for Pitts Cherry Orchard. Suppose that the price of cherries is $400 per ton. The marginal output rule tells us that the firm should produce 70 tons of cherries if it is going to be in business—at this point marginal revenue equals marginal cost. Moreover, the shut-down rule tells us that the firm should not exit the market—the price is above the firm's average cost level, so it is earning economic profit. At a price below $300 per ton, however, the firm would shut down.

Carrying out this procedure repeatedly, we can trace out the firm's long-run supply curve. Thus, *a price-taking firm's long-run supply curve coincides with the vertical axis at prices less than the minimum of its long-run average cost. The long-run supply curve coincides with the firm's long-run marginal cost curve where it is above the firm's long-run average cost curve.* The resulting long-run supply curve is made up of the two dark lines in Figure 10.8.

Comparison of the Firm's Short- and Long-Run Supply Curves

It is instructive to compare the firm's short- and long-run supply curves. Can we say whether, at a given price, the firm will produce more in the short run or in the long run? It turns out that we cannot. The firm's supply curve depends on its marginal and average economic cost curves, and we saw in Chapter 9 that there are two important differences between short- and long-run cost curves:

1. In the short run, some factors are fixed and expenditures on these fixed factors are not short-run economic costs. In the long run, all factors are variable and expenditures on them are economic costs.

2. In the long run, the firm has opportunities to substitute one factor for another. In the short run, it does not.

Figure 10.9 illustrates how these differences among cost curves translate into differences between the short- and long-run supply curves. As shown by the figure, long-run supply is more responsive to price changes (that is, is more elastic). This makes sense intuitively because over the long run the firm has greater opportunities to make adjustments.

Let's think about this adjustment process a little further. Suppose that the farmer had been selling 70 tons of cherries per year at a price of $400 per ton, and consider how the farmer responds when price increases to $450 per ton. In the short run, the firm has only one way to expand production—hire more of the variable factor, labor. This factor may be subject to strongly diminishing marginal returns, which, as we saw in Chapter 9, give rise to sharply increasing short-run marginal costs. Since the short-run supply curve coincides with the short-run marginal cost curve above the short-run average variable cost curve, S_{SR} also rises with the output level. In the long run, however, a firm can vary the levels of all of its inputs—the farmer can plant more trees and increase output further. Consequently, the firm's long-run supply curve remains relatively flat and, at a price of $450 per ton, this firm will supply more output in the long run than in the short run.

Figure 10.8

A Price-Taking Firm's Long-Run Supply Curve

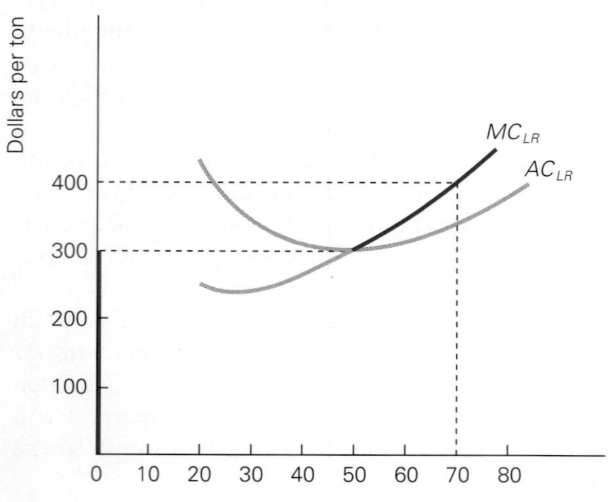

A price-taking firm's long-run supply curve coincides with its long-run marginal cost curve above its long-run average cost curve. For any price below the lowest point on the long-run average cost curve, the firm will supply no output.

Figure 10.9

Comparison of Short-Run and Long-Run Supply Curves

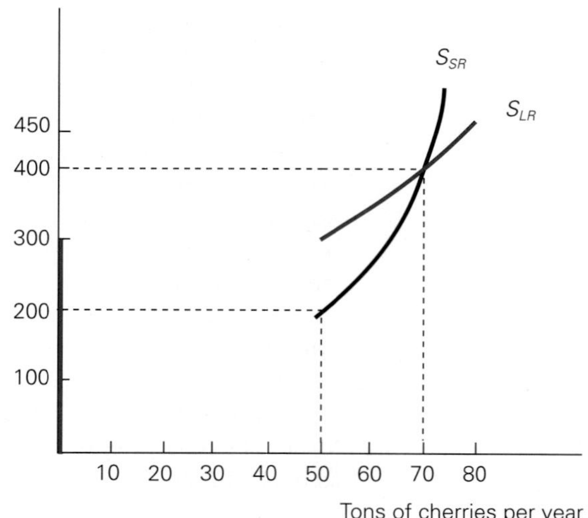

Because the firm has more opportunities to make adjustments, the long-run supply curve is more price elastic than is the short-run supply curve.

At prices below $400 per ton, the relationship between the short-run quantity supplied and the long-run quantity supplied is reversed. At a price of $200 per ton, the firm produces 50 tons of cherries in the short run, but goes out of business entirely in the long run! To understand what is going on here, we need to think carefully about the shutdown and exit decisions. At one level of abstraction, the firm's short- and long-run decisions are the same: The firm should stop producing if its average revenue is less than its average economic cost. But there is an important difference. When a firm with fixed inputs shuts down in the short run, the firm continues to own those inputs even though it does not produce any output. Since the firm continues to own them and they have no alternative use, the opportunity cost of these inputs is 0. Hence, if the firm can earn revenues that are greater than the costs of the variable inputs, it should continue to produce output in the short run. In contrast, when a firm shuts down in the long run, not only does it cease production, but it ceases to own any fixed factors that are dedicated to production in that market. That's why we compare average revenue with average variable cost in the short run and average total cost in the long run. Viewed another way, factors that are fixed in the short run are variable in the long run and thus have positive opportunity costs in the long run. If the firm's revenues cannot cover these costs, as well as the costs of the other factors, then long-run exit is the most profitable course of action. In summary, when the price of output falls, a firm that continues to produce in the short run may cease producing in the long run.

Which Run Is Which? (Optional Section) At this point, you may think that the firm faces a dilemma when making supply decisions: Should it use short-run costs or long-run costs? Consider a firm that is thinking about whether to build a factory. In order to know whether the factory will be profitable, the firm needs to know how much output it will produce. When thinking about building the plant, the firm is making a long-run decision. Hence, the firm must use *long-run* marginal and average costs to find the profit-maximizing output level and evaluate whether the plant would be profitable.

Suppose that the firm has gone ahead and built the plant. How much output should it sell? Since the plant is now a fixed input, the firm is making a short-run decision and the sunk expenditures made on the plant are not economic costs. Now, the profit-maximizing output level and the resulting profit level are calculated based on *short-run* marginal and average variable costs.

It looks as if the firm is being irrational. It appears that before the plant is built, the firm plans to produce one amount of output; after the plant is built, it produces a different amount: One decision is based on long-run cost and the other based on short-run cost. Fortunately, this irrationality is more apparent than real. To see why, we need to understand two important facts about the relationship between short- and long-run marginal costs.

The first fact is that long-run marginal cost is equal to short-run marginal cost when the level of capital is fixed at its long-run equilibrium value. Consider a firm that is producing x_0 units of output and faces factor prices w and r. In the short run, capital is fixed and the firm can expand its output level only by increasing its use of labor. To produce one more unit of output, the firm must hire $1/MPP_L$ additional workers at a daily wage of w per worker, where MPP_L is the marginal physical product of labor. As we saw in Chapter 9, short-run marginal cost is w/MPP_L. In the long run, the firm has more options available to it. If the firm chooses to adjust only its use of labor, it must hire $1/MPP_L$ additional workers at a wage of w per worker. Hence, the marginal cost would be w/MPP_L, just as in the short run. If the firm increases only capital, it must hire $1/MPP_K$ additional units at a price of r per unit, and the additional cost would be r/MPP_K. Of course, the firm could decide to adjust both factors at once. Given all of these choices, what is the firm's marginal cost? To pin down the answer, we have to use an important result we derived earlier—a firm that is a price taker in factor markets should operate at a point where the price of each input is proportional to its marginal physical product. Hence, when the firm has made its long-run equilibrium input choices, $w/MPP_L = r/MPP_K$ (see Equation 9.7). It follows that no matter what combination of adjustments the firm makes, its long-run marginal cost is equal to w/MPP_L.

We now are ready to compare short- and long-run marginal costs. It looks as if they are always the same—in each case, the formula is w/MPP_L. But as your mother (or some other relative given to platitudes) should have told you, looks can be deceiving. The value of the marginal physical product of labor depends on the input combination that the firm is using—the capital level helps determine the value of the marginal physical product of labor. In general, the firm may use different input combinations in the short and long runs, and thus short- and long-run marginal costs may differ. They are equal, however, when the firm uses the same input combination in both the short and long runs. We thus can conclude that *long-run marginal cost is equal to short-run marginal cost when the level of capital is fixed at its long-run equilibrium value.*

Figure 10.10

Consistency of the Firm's Plans

Suppose the firm constructs the plant size that is optimal given the expectation that the price of output will be $70 per unit. As long as the price after construction is indeed $70 per unit, the firm will choose to produce 1,400 units whether it uses its short- or long-run supply curve. If the output price rises to $90 per unit *after the factory has been built,* then the firm will choose to product 1,700 units of output per day based on its *short-run* supply curve.

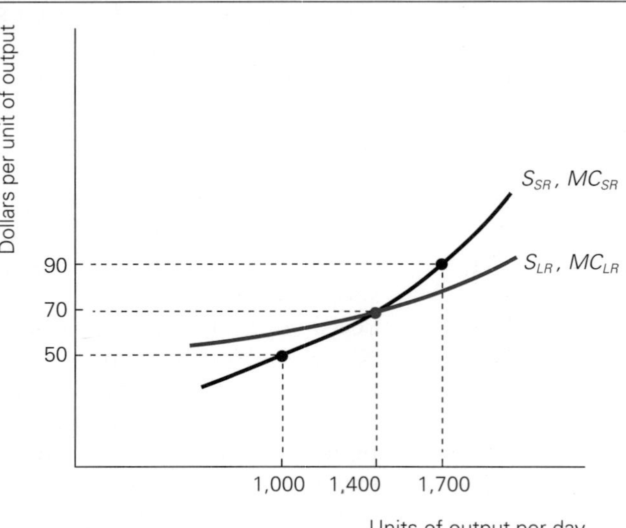

Since the firm's short- and long-run supply curves coincide with its short- and long-run marginal cost curves (where each is above the associated average economic cost curve), the relationship between marginal cost curves tells us that when the firm chooses to build a plant that is the profit-maximizing size, it selects the same output level whether it uses the short- or long-run supply curve. As illustrated in Figure 10.10, at a price of $70 per unit, the firm supplies 1,400 units of output per day according to either curve. The firm does not face a dilemma or run any risk of being inconsistent. Underlying all of this is the fact that long-run marginal cost is equal to $70 when output is 1,400 units per day, as is short-run marginal cost given that this particular plant is in place.

Like the marginal choice rule, the shutdown rule differs depending on whether the firm is using short- or long-run cost (here, average economic cost). The second important fact about the relationship between short- and long-run costs is that, when the amount of the fixed factor is at its long-run equilibrium value, short-run average variable cost is less than long-run average cost. Why? Since the short-run capital level is fixed at its long-run value anyway, the lack of flexibility does not raise short-run costs relative to long-run costs. However, the expenditures on the fixed factor are not short-run economic or variable costs, but are long-run economic costs. Thus, when the fixed factor quantity is at its long-run equilibrium value, short-run average variable cost is less than long-run average cost.

This implies that (provided the price is what the firm expected when making its long-run plans) the firm will not shut down in the short run once the plant has been built. Again, there is no inconsistency in the firm's plans. Of course, if the output price subsequently *changes,* then the firm will have to adjust its output level, holding the plant size fixed. At the new price, the short- and long-run supply curves will diverge. Since this new output decision is for a fixed plant size, the short-run supply curve is the relevant one. For example, suppose that the output price rises to $90 per unit *after the factory has been built.* As shown in

Figure 10.10, the firm's *short-run* supply curve indicates that the profit-maximizing response is to produce 1,700 units of output per day.

Similarly, since the expenditures on the plant are sunk, to induce the firm to leave the market once it has entered, the price must fall to a lower level than the one needed to keep the firm from coming into the market in the first place. For example, if the firm had foreseen a price of $50 per unit, it would not have built the factory—the long-run quantity supplied is 0 at this price. But once the plant is built, the firm continues to produce at this price—the firm is making a short-run decision and the short-run supply curve in Figure 10.10 shows that the firm will supply 1,000 units of output per day at a price of $50 per unit. This difference makes perfect sense. Once the firm has built the factory, it is a sunk expenditure and the firm cannot get its money back by leaving. The firm should make use of the plant as long as the revenues generated are greater than the costs of the variable inputs. But prior to building the plant, the firm can save the entire expenditure on the plant by not going ahead with the project.

SECTION RECAP

For a price-taking firm, the two general rules for finding the profit-maximizing output level take special forms: (1) If it is going to produce at all, the firm should choose an output level at which marginal cost is equal to the price of output; (2) The firm should shut down if the price is less than the lowest value of its average economic cost. We can apply these rules for a variety of different hypothetical prices to trace out the firm's short-run supply curve. The short-run supply curve coincides with the portion of the firm's short-run marginal cost curve that is above the short-run average variable cost curve. Similarly, the long-run supply curve coincides with the firm's long-run marginal cost curve where it is above the long-run average cost curve.

10.2 FACTOR DEMAND

Now that we have analyzed a price-taking firm's role as a supplier in product markets, let's examine its demand decisions in factor markets. A firm demands commodities for different reasons than a household. A household purchases goods and services for the satisfaction, or utility, that consumption of these goods and services generates. In contrast, a firm does not value inputs for their own sake—the acquisition of a machine that stamps metal into forks and spoons does not in itself create pleasure for its owner. Rather, the input is valued for the output that it can produce, which in turn can be sold to generate revenue. Thus, the demand for an input depends on, or is derived from, the demand for the final product. Therefore, the demand for an input is said to be a **derived demand**.

derived demand
A firm's demand for an input is known as derived demand because it depends on, or is derived from, the demand for the firm's output.

Just as we distinguish between a firm's short- and long-run *supply* decisions, in the next two sections we distinguish between its short- and long-run *demand* decisions.

SHORT-RUN FACTOR DEMAND

Suppose that Pitts Cherry Orchard uses two factors of production: capital (cherry trees) and labor (farm workers). In the short run, the amount of labor, L, is variable, but the amount of capital is fixed at K_f. Since the amount of capital is fixed in the short run, the firm's only input demand decision is how much labor to employ. We already looked at the firm's short-run choice of inputs in Chapter 9. There we assumed that the firm knew how much output it wanted to produce, and the firm calculated how much labor to hire by finding the point on the relevant isoquant curve. The problem faced by the firm here is a bit more complicated—the firm does not yet know how much output it is going to produce. The firm must consider its input and output choices simultaneously.

Fortunately, the marginalist logic used to calculate the optimal output level can also be applied to find the profit-maximizing input level. First, the firm calculates the marginal cost and benefit of hiring an additional unit of the input. Then the firm compares the benefit with the cost. If the marginal benefit is greater than the marginal cost, the firm hires more of the factor: Since benefits rise faster than costs, profit rises as well. The firm hires each unit of input whose marginal benefit exceeds its marginal cost, and it continues until the marginal benefit is equal to the marginal cost. What happens if the firm increases its input level still further to a point at which the marginal benefit is less than the marginal cost? In this instance, hiring an additional unit lowers the firm's profit; benefits rise by less than costs. Hence, *the firm should hire an input just up to the amount at which the marginal benefit to the firm is equal to the marginal cost.*

Of course, to apply this rule we need to know how to find the marginal benefit and cost of hiring an additional unit of an input. Let's look at each one in turn.

The Marginal Benefit of an Input

When a firm employs more of a factor, the firm's output rises. In Chapter 8, we defined the additional amount of output that can be produced when the firm hires one additional unit of an input as that input's marginal physical product (*MPP*). Recall that *MPP* is measured in physical units of output per unit of input (such as tons of cherries per acre of land or quarts of ice cream per gallon of milk). Marginal physical product is not itself a measure of the benefit to the firm. The reason for producing output is to earn money from its sale. What the firm really cares about is how its *revenue* changes when it uses one additional unit of a factor. The change in revenue due to the sale of the additional output contributed by the hiring of one more unit of the factor is known as the factor's **marginal revenue product** (*MRP*). *MRP* is measured as dollars of revenue per unit of input (such as dollars of revenue per hour of labor). We call the increase in revenue the marginal *revenue* product to distinguish it from the marginal *physical* product.

marginal revenue product
The change in revenue due to the sale of the additional output contributed by the hiring of one more unit of a factor.

Although marginal revenue product and marginal physical product are distinct concepts, they are closely related. Suppose, for instance, that the marginal physical product of labor for the third worker at a cherry orchard is 7 tons of cherries. If each ton of cherries brings an additional $300 to the firm, then the marginal revenue product of labor is $2,100. More generally, *to find the marginal revenue product of an input, simply multiply its marginal physical product by the marginal revenue associated with each unit of output.* We can express this relationship algebraically. For labor, it is

$$MRP_L = MPP_L \times MR. \qquad (10.1)$$

Marginal Revenue Product for a Price Taker The formula for marginal revenue product is simpler for a price-taking firm. Let's find the marginal revenue product

Table 10.1

Calculating Marginal Revenue Product from Price and Production Data

From the production function, we find MPP_L. For a price-taking firm, we multiply MPP_L times the price of output to obtain MRP_L.

(1) Labor (workers)	(2) Output (tons)	(3) MPP_L (tons/worker)	(4) MR (= p) ($/ton)	(5) MRP_L ($/worker)
0	0			
		16.0	$300	$4,800
1	16			
		11.0	300	3,300
2	27			
		7.0	300	2,100
3	34			
		4.0	300	1,200
4	38			
		1.2	300	360
5	39.2			
		0.8	300	240
6	40			
		0.7	300	210
7	40.7			

for labor hired by Pitts Cherry Orchard. A price taker's marginal revenue curve is constant at the price at which the firm can sell its output. *Hence, for a price-taking firm, a factor's marginal revenue product is equal to its marginal physical product multiplied by the price of output.* Algebraically, if the price of output is p, then substituting p for MR in Equation (10.1) gives us

$$MRP_L = MPP_L \times p. \tag{10.2}$$

This fact is used in Table 10.1 to calculate the values in column 5 from the data in columns 3 and 4.

The Marginal Cost of an Input

Now that we have a measure of the marginal benefit that the firm derives from using an additional unit of an input, the next step is to compute the marginal cost. In Chapter 9, we defined the increase in the firm's total expenditures on inputs when it hires one more unit of a factor to be the *marginal factor cost.*

Marginal Factor Cost for a Price Taker We also saw in Chapter 9 that whenever a firm is a price taker in an input market, the marginal factor cost is equal to the price of the factor. If the firm can hire as many workers as it wants to at the going wage of $210 per week, then its marginal factor cost of labor is $210 for any level of employment.

The Profit-Maximizing Input Level

After the breakup of the Soviet Union, thousands of Russian scientists lost their jobs. Western companies soon learned that they could hire virtually unlimited numbers of such scientists to do research for them in the new states at a wage of about $40 to $50 per *month.* AT&T, for example, hired 100 scientists, and Corning Inc. hired 115 (Passell 1992, D1). How does a price-taking firm decide how many scientists—or any other factor—to hire?

Once we know both the costs and benefits of hiring additional units of the factor, we can answer this question by applying the general principle that the firm should operate at the point where the marginal benefit is equal to the marginal cost:

> **Factor Hiring Rule:** A profit-maximizing firm should hire a factor up to the point at which its marginal revenue product is equal to its marginal factor cost ($MRP = MFC$).

Figure 10.11

The Factor Hiring Rule

At any input level less than L_1, $MRP_L > MFC_L$, and the firm's profit rises if it hires more labor. At any input level greater than L_1, $MRP_L < MFC_L$, and the firm's profit rises if it cuts back employment. The firm's profit is maximized by hiring L_1 hours of labor.

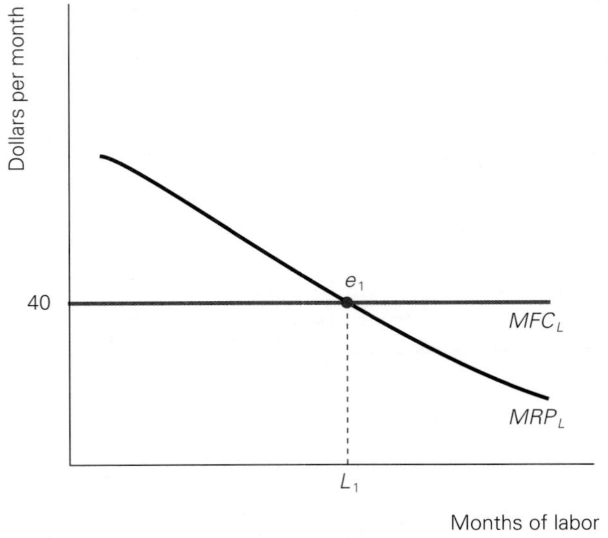

Figure 10.11 depicts the factor hiring rule graphically for the scientific publishing company Tomes "R" Us. For this firm, the marginal physical product of Russian scientists diminishes as the firm hires more of them. Consequently, the marginal revenue product curve is downward sloping. Because this firm is a price taker in the labor market, the marginal factor cost curve is constant at the prevailing wage of \$40 per month. At any input level less than L_1, the marginal benefit of hiring an additional scientist exceeds the marginal cost; $MRP_L > MFC_L$, and the firm's profit rises if it increases employment. At any input level greater than L_1, the marginal benefit of hiring one more scientist is less than the marginal cost; $MRP_L < MFC_L$, and the firm's profit rises if it cuts back its use of labor. The firm maximizes profit by hiring L_1 Russian scientists. Note the similarity between this rule and our earlier one for the profit-maximizing level of output, $MR = MC$. The logic behind the two rules is the same—equate the benefits and costs at the margin.

Are These Rules Consistent? The mention of the marginal output choice rule raises a new consideration. The marginal output rule provides one way of calculating the profit-maximizing output level. But the factor hiring rule provides another—the firm's capital level is fixed in the short run, so the amount of labor hired determines the amount of output produced. Since the factor hiring rule is implicitly determining the level of output, it had better give us the same answer as the marginal output rule.

The two rules do indeed agree, which we can see by expressing each rule in terms of basic concepts. The factor hiring rule states that the firm should hire an input up to the level at which $MRP = MFC$. Since $MRP = MPP \times MR$, the factor hiring rule also can be written as

$$MPP \times MR = MFC. \tag{10.3}$$

The marginal output rule states that the firm should choose an output level at which $MR = MC$. Using Equation (9.2) from the last chapter, we know that $MC = MFC/MPP$. Using this fact, we can write the marginal output rule as

$$MR = MFC/MPP. \tag{10.4}$$

Looking at Equations (10.3) and (10.4), we see that they are simply two ways of expressing the same algebraic relationship between marginal revenue, marginal physical product, and marginal factor cost. In other words, the factor hiring rule and the marginal output rule give the same answer to the question of how much output the firm should produce.

The Factor Hiring Rule for a Price Taker For a price-taking firm, marginal revenue product is equal to the marginal physical product times the output price (p), and marginal factor cost is equal to the input price (w). Using these facts, we can rewrite Equation (10.3) to simplify the factor hiring rule:

> ***Factor Hiring Rule for a Price Taker:*** A firm that is a price taker in both the factor market and the output market maximizes its profit by hiring a factor up to the point at which marginal physical product times the output price is equal to the input price, or $MPP \times p = w$.

To apply this rule, let's develop further our cherry orchard example in Table 10.1. If the wage rate initially is \$210 per week, then the factor hiring rule tells us that the firm hires labor up to the point at which its marginal revenue product is \$210. Column 5 of Table 10.1 tells us that this occurs when the firm hires 6 workers and harvests 40 tons of cherries. Thus the firm demands 6 workers when the price of labor is \$210 per week.[1] In other words, we have found the point on the firm's demand curve for labor that corresponds to a wage of \$210 per week. This point on the demand curve is labeled a in Figure 10.12. (PC 10.5)

Suppose that the wage rate rises to \$240 per week. In this case, the firm stops hiring labor at the point where its marginal revenue product is equal to \$240 since \$240 is now the marginal factor cost. Table 10.1 tells us that this occurs when the firm hires only 5 workers and harvests 39.2 tons of cherries. We now have a second point on the firm's labor demand curve, point b, in Figure 10.12.

Notice that to find the profit-maximizing level of labor usage at each wage rate, all we have to do is read the answer off of the marginal revenue product curve. In other words, *the short-run derived demand curve for a firm that is a price taker in the market for the variable input coincides with the firm's marginal revenue product curve for that factor.* The curve in Figure 10.12 illustrates the

10.5 PROGRESS CHECK

Between July 1991 and February 1992, U.S. wheat prices increased by about 50 percent. Shortly thereafter, the Northern Plains Equipment Company of Mandan, North Dakota, found that its tractor business increased by about 33 percent (*The Wall Street Journal*, February 20, 1992). Explain carefully why the increase in the price of wheat leads to an increase in the demand for tractors.

[1]More precisely, the firm is indifferent between stopping with six workers and hiring the seventh worker—because $MRP_L = MFC_L$, the seventh worker would generate additional revenue just equal to the cost of hiring him.

Figure 10.12

A Price-Taking Firm's Derived Demand Curve

When a firm is a price taker in the market for the variable input, the firm's short-run derived demand curve for the variable input, d_L, coincides with the firm's marginal revenue product curve for that input.

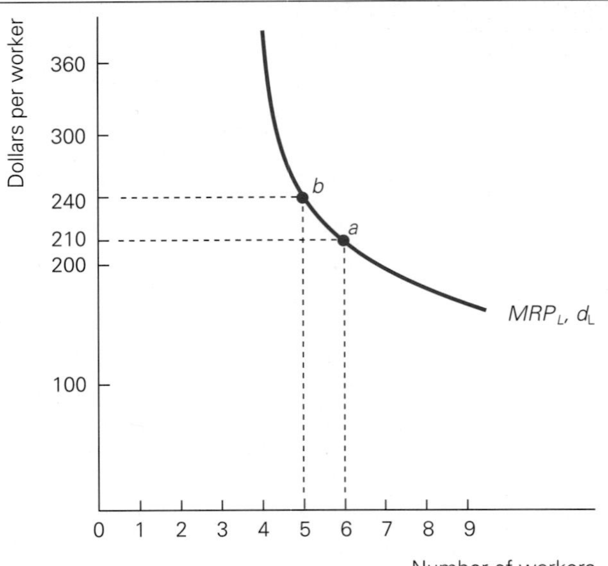

labor demand curve for Pitts Cherry Orchard found by applying this rule to the data in Table 10.1.

The labor demand curve in Figure 10.12 slopes downward—when the wage rate goes up, the quantity of labor goes down. Intuitively, when the price of a variable factor increases, so does the firm's short-run marginal cost of producing output. This upward shift in the firm's marginal cost curve leads it to cut back the amount of *output* that it supplies, as shown in Panel A of Figure 10.13. Because the firm's output level declines, it can cut back its usage of the variable input, as illustrated in the isoquant diagram in Panel B. The short-run derived demand for an input is downward sloping due to this **output effect**—a higher input price leads to a lower output and therefore to less of the input being demanded.

output effect
The change in the quantity demanded of an input due to the change in the firm's output level that results from an increase in the input's price.

LONG-RUN FACTOR DEMAND

In the long run, a firm can adjust the quantities of both capital and labor. In such a situation, when the price of labor rises there are two effects on the long-run quantity of labor demanded. First, there is an *output effect,* just as there was in the short run. As labor becomes more expensive, the marginal cost of producing output may rise, reducing the equilibrium output level and the firm's overall input usage. When total output falls, the quantity of at least one input must fall. The second effect of the price increase on long-run factor demand is absent in the short run. In the long run, the firm can substitute one factor for another factor whose price has risen. In this particular instance, the firm substitutes capital for labor in response to an increase in the price of labor. When examining long-run input demand, we must consider this **factor substitution effect** in addition to the output effect.

factor substitution effect
The reduction in the quantity demanded of an input that results from the firm's substituting away from that factor when its price rises.

In reality, when an input price changes, the factor substitution effect and the output effect come into play simultaneously. It is useful, however, to start by

Figure 10.13

The Output Effect

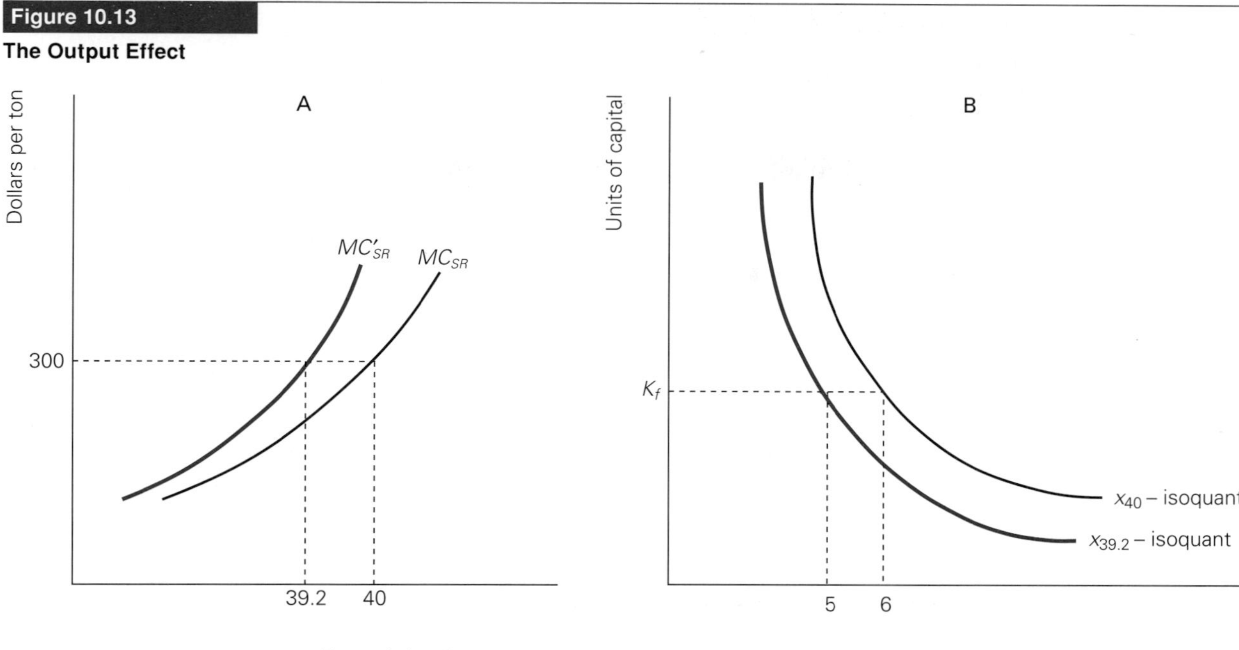

When the price of labor rises, so does the firm's short-run marginal cost of producing cherries, from MC_{SR} to MC'_{SR} in Panel A. This upward shift in the firm's marginal cost curve leads it to cut back the amount of *output* it supplies. Because the firm is producing less output, it chooses an input combination on a lower isoquant curve, as shown in Panel B. Because the level of capital is fixed in the short run at K_f, the firm adjusts its input use by reducing the amount of labor.

examining each of these effects in isolation. We already have examined the output effect in our short-run analysis, so we begin our long-run analysis by looking at the factor substitution effect.

Factor Substitution Effect

To isolate the factor substitution effect, we take advantage of the isoquant-isocost analysis developed in Chapter 9. This framework allows us to find the optimal input mix for producing a given level of output at a given set of input prices. The solid lines in Figure 10.14 illustrate the isoquant curve and isocost lines for Pitts Cherry Orchard. The initial prices of labor and capital are w_a and r_a, respectively. At these prices, the firm's equilibrium input levels are L_a and K_a, and its output level is x_m.

Suppose the price of labor rises to w_b. This price increase has both an output effect and a factor substitution effect. We can separate the factor substitution effect from the output effect in much the same way that we separated the substitution effect from the income effect when studying household demand in Chapter 4. There, to isolate the substitution effect, we showed how equilibrium along a single indifference curve changed as market prices changed. Here, by analogy, we look at what happens to input usage when the firm adjusts to a change in a factor price but stays on the same isoquant (that is, maintains the original output level).

Figure 10.14

The Effects of an Increase in the Price of Labor

To isolate the factor substitution effect, we examine how the equilibrium along a single isoquant (here, the x_m-isoquant) changes as the factor price changes. The solid lines are the isocost lines when the prices of labor and capital are w_a and r_a, respectively. At these prices, the firm's input levels are L_a and K_a. When the price of labor rises to w_b, the new isocost lines are the steeper dashed lines. The new equilibrium occurs at point b. The fall in labor from L_a to L_b is the factor substitution effect.

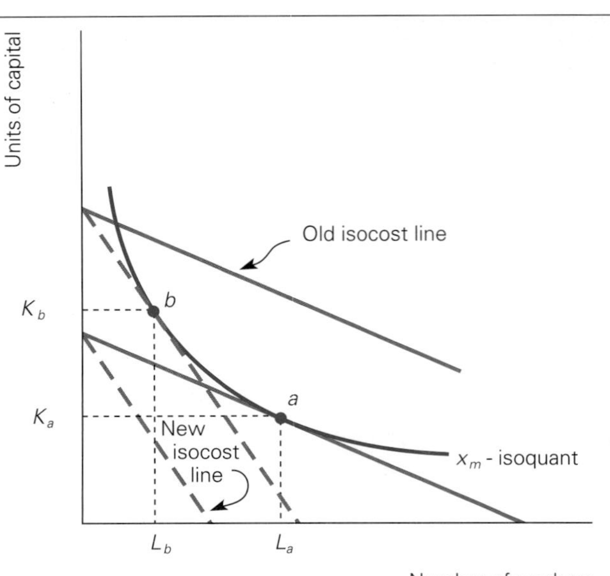

While the isoquant stays the same, the increased price of labor leads to a new family of isocost lines. Each new isocost line (the dashed lines in Figure 10.14) is an old one pivoted downward around its intercept with the vertical axis. The new equilibrium occurs at the tangency between the x_m-isoquant curve and the relevant member of the new family of isocost lines, factor combination (L_b, K_b). Because the new isocost line is steeper than the old one, the new tangency, point b, must occur to the left of the original one, point a. As the diagram indicates, the firm uses less labor and more capital to produce the given amount of output. This fall in the quantity of labor demanded from L_a to L_b is the factor substitution effect. (PC 10.6)

10.6 PROGRESS CHECK

Draw an isoquant diagram to show that an increase in the price of capital leads to a fall in the quantity of capital demanded by the firm when it holds its output level constant.

To summarize our discussion of the factor substitution effect, *when the price of one factor rises relative to the other, the firm substitutes away from the factor whose price has risen and replaces it with the factor whose relative price has fallen (as long as it is possible for the firm to substitute one input for the other in production)*. Notice that the factor substitution effect of an input price increase always is negative. Hence, the factor substitution effect is one reason that long-run derived demand curves are downward sloping.

Output Effect

Of course, in the long run as in the short run, a firm may respond to a factor price change by adjusting the amount of output. Let's look at the long-run output effect more closely. Suppose we know that total output falls from x_m to x_n when the price of labor rises from w_a to w_b. We can use isoquant analysis to tell us how this fall in output affects input levels—we find a tangency between the new x_n-isoquant and the relevant isocost line from the new isocost map (drawn for the new factor prices). At a wage of w_b, the new equilibrium input combination is (L_c, K_c), point c in Figure 10.15. The change from point a to point c is

Figure 10.15

Separating the Output Effect and the Factor Substitution Effect

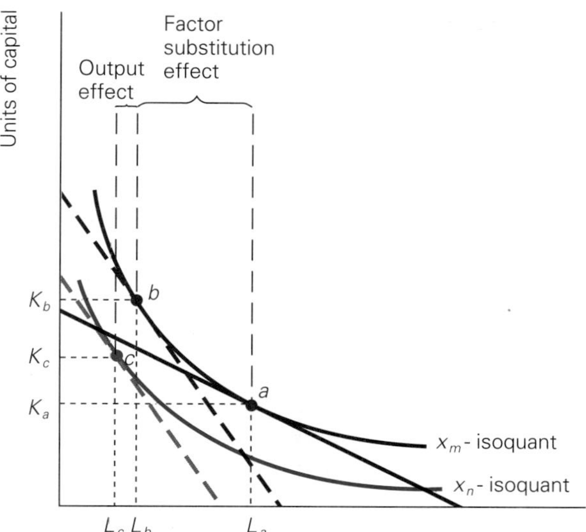

The change from point *a* to point *b* is due to *both* the output effect and the factor substitution effect. $L_a - L_b$ is the decline in the quantity of labor demanded due to the factor substitution effect. The remaining change in the firm's input level, $L_b - L_c$, is due to the output effect.

Figure 10.16

The Output Effect May Be Positive

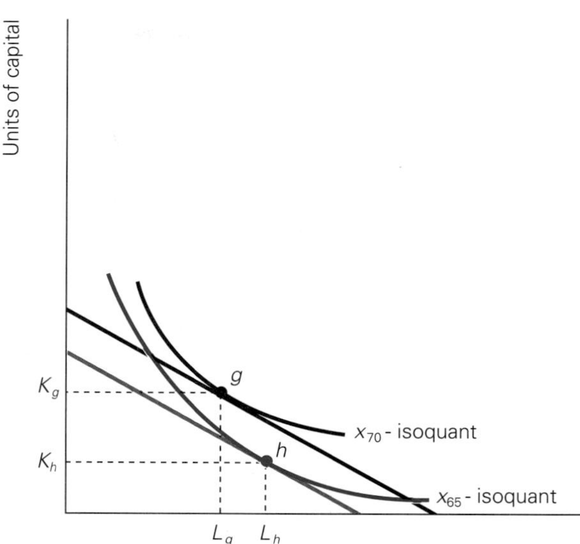

When total output *falls* from 70 tons per year to 65, this firm's equilibrium use of labor *rises* from L_g to L_h.

due to both the output effect and the factor substitution effect. Because the movement from *a* to *b* is the factor substitution effect, the remaining change in the firm's input level, from *b* to *c* in Figure 10.15, is due to the output effect. (Note the analogy to finding the income effect for the household in Chapter 4.)

In Figure 10.15, the output effect leads the firm to use less labor. In most cases, this is what we would expect to happen. In fact, when we examined the firm's short-run demand for labor, we saw that the output effect must be negative when only one factor is variable. But in the long run, when the firm can adjust both capital and labor, it is possible for a firm to demand more labor when its total output falls. Figure 10.16 illustrates one such case. When the firm's output falls from 70 tons per year to 65, its equilibrium bundle of inputs changes from *g* to *h*. Although the quantity of capital demanded falls from K_g to K_h, the quantity of labor demanded actually rises from L_g to L_h. In this case, the output effect of a price increase is positive.

How can a decrease in total output lead to an increase in the quantity of a factor demanded? Think about a manufacturer that is planning to scrap its current factory and build a new factory in order to increase its production level. If the increase in output is substantial, then the firm may choose to build a highly automated factory requiring almost no workers. Thus, even though output has increased, the quantity of labor hired will go down.

Of course, in other cases the firm may increase both the amount of capital and the number of workers when it increases its output. We conclude that *in the long run, the output effect may be positive or negative.* In fact, we cannot even be sure that total output falls as the price of a factor rises: A factor price increase may actually lower marginal cost over some ranges of output, raising the firm's profit-maximizing output level. The only thing of which we can be sure *a priori* is that if the level of total output falls, the usage of at least one factor must fall with it.

Factor Substitution and Output Effect Simultaneously

We know that the factor substitution effect of an input price increase is negative, while the output effect may be positive or negative. What can we say about the combined effect? You might suspect that the answer is *nothing*. When we looked at a household's demand for a good, it was theoretically possible for a positive income effect to swamp the negative substitution effect—a so-called *Giffen good*. For a firm, however, *when the price of a factor rises, the quantity of that input demanded falls—the sum of the factor substitution effect and the output effect always is negative.* In other words, derived demand curves always slope downward.

The intuition behind this result is the following. Suppose that the price of a factor, say capital, rises, Could this price increase lead the firm to purchase more capital? Even at the old price of capital, the firm had the option to purchase more capital. The fact that the firm did not do so tells us that the increase in the expenditure on additional capital outweighed any benefits in terms of additional revenue or reduced expenditures on other factors. Once the price of capital rises, the option of purchasing more capital is even less profitable than it was before. Hence, a profit-maximizing firm never would increase its use of an input in response to an increase in that input's price.[2]

You still might be wondering why the answer differs from the one we got for the household; why aren't there Giffen factors? The key observation in this context is that the household starts with a budget constraint and then makes its choice to maximize utility. When the price of a good rises, the household's feasible set shrinks. The household cannot afford the original commodity bundle after a price increase. A firm, on the other hand, can keep doing the same thing after a price increase—the original input levels are no longer the profit-maximizing ones, but they still are feasible. Any new choices must be superior to the original input combination, and that implies using less of the input that has become more expensive.

[2]Formally, suppose that the cost of capital rises from r_a to r_b. Denote the original levels of capital, labor, and output as K_a, L_a, and x_a, respectively, and denote the new levels of capital, labor, and output K_b, L_b, and x_b, respectively. Let p denote the price of output and w the wage rate, both of which remain constant.

At the original cost of capital and levels of capital, labor, and output, profit was $p \times x_a - w \times L_a - r_a \times K_a$. Similarly, if the firm were to choose option b at the *original* price of capital, its profit would be $p \times x_b - w \times L_b - r_a \times K_b$. Because the firm chose combination a over b, b must yield *lower* profit at the *original* factor prices:

$$p \times (x_b - x_a) - r_a \times (K_b - K_a) - w \times (L_b - L_a) \leq 0. \qquad (*)$$

Because the firm chose combination b over a at the new factor prices, b must yield *higher* profit at the *new* factor prices:

$$p \times (x_b - x_a) - r_b \times (K_b - K_a) - w \times (L_b - L_a) \geq 0. \qquad (**)$$

Subtracting expression (**) from expression (*), we have $(r_b - r_a) \times (K_b - K_a) \leq 0$. When the price of capital rises, we have $r_b - r_a > 0$, and therefore $K_b - K_a$ must be less than or equal to 0.

Algebraic Approach

To analyze long-run factor demand algebraically, we apply the *factor hiring rule for a price taker:* The firm should hire a factor up to the point at which the output price times the marginal physical product of the factor is equal to the factor's price. While we derived this rule for a short-run input choice (when there is only one variable factor), the rule is equally valid for long-run decisions. The only difference from the short-run algebraic analysis is that now more than one factor is variable, so we must apply the rule to every factor.

Let's return to our orchard, which uses labor, L, and capital, K, to produce sour cherries. Suppose that the price of cherries is p per ton, while labor costs w per unit and capital r. Applying the factor hiring rule to each input, the firm's quantities of labor and capital satisfy

$$p \times MPP_L = w \tag{10.5}$$

and

$$p \times MPP_K = r. \tag{10.6}$$

Only a combination of capital and labor that satisfies both of these conditions at once will maximize profits.

We can relate this algebraic approach to our earlier analysis of the cost-minimizing input choice in Chapter 9. Dividing Equation (10.5) by (10.6), we obtain

$$MPP_L/MPP_K = w/r \tag{10.7}$$

Equation (10.7) is our familiar condition for cost-minimization, Equation (9.6). It tells us that the marginal physical product of each input should be proportional to its marginal factor cost at the margin. Thus, whether we think of the problem of input choice as one of maximizing profits or minimizing costs, we obtain the same answer.

Investment and the Demand for Capital

Firms often make input decisions that have consequences over time. Suppose a firm is deciding whether to buy a customized machine tool with no salvage value. The machine is purchased today, but generates output and, hence, revenue for two years: MRP_0 in the first year and MRP_1 in the second. As we saw in Chapter 7, when the firm's costs and revenues accrue over time, application of the factor hiring rule requires the firm to equate the *present value* of the marginal revenue product with the present value of marginal factor cost.

Suppose that the firm is considering how many machines to purchase at a prevailing price of p_M. Since the full cost of purchasing the machine is borne today, the present value of the marginal factor cost is simply the price of the machine;

$$MFC_M = p_M. \tag{10.8}$$

The present value of the stream of revenues generated by the machine is equal to $MRP_0 + MRP_1/(1 + i)$.

Since this firm is a price taker as a seller of output, each period's marginal revenue product is equal to the output price in that period times the marginal

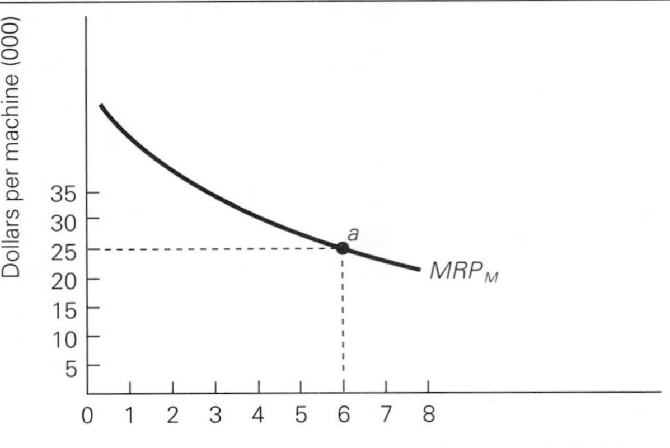

Figure 10.17

The Present Value of the Marginal Revenue Product of Machines

The firm should hire machines up to the point at which $MRP_M = MFC_M$. Because the firm is a price taker, the marginal factor cost is equal to the price of machines. As always, for a price taker, the factor demand curve coincides with the *MRP* curve.

physical product of the machine. Hence, the present value of marginal revenue product is

$$MRP = p_0 \times MPP_0 + p_1 \times MPP_1/(1 + i) \tag{10.9}$$

where p_0 and p_1 are the first- and second-year output prices, respectively.

Now that we have expressed marginal revenue product and marginal factor cost in present value terms, we can apply our factor hiring rule: The firm should purchase additional machines up to the point at which

$$p_0 \times MPP_0 + p_1 \times MPP_1/(1 + i) = p_M. \tag{10.10}$$

The present value of the marginal revenue product of machines is graphed in Figure 10.17, where it is labeled MRP_M. As drawn, the MRP_M curve falls as the level of output rises. (This shape reflects the underlying diminishing marginal returns to capital in each of the two periods.) Suppose that the price of machines is $25,000. Applying the factor hiring rule, the firm purchases six machines, point *a* in Figure 10.17. (PC 10.7)

10.7 PROGRESS CHECK

How many machines will the firm demand when the price of machines is $30,000?

We can rewrite Equation (10.10) to express the factor hiring rule in another useful form. Subtracting p_M from both sides of Equation (10.10), we find that the firm should purchase machines up to the point at which

$$\{p_0 \times MPP_0 - p_M\} + p_1 \times MPP_1/(1 + i) = 0. \tag{10.11}$$

We can understand Equation (10.11) as follows: $p_0 \times MPP_0 - p_M$ is the firm's net cash flow in the first period—the revenue generated by the machine in the first period minus the money paid for it. $p_1 \times MPP_1/(1 + i)$ is the firm's discounted cash flow from the second period. Hence, the left-hand side of Equation (10.11) is the formula for the net present value of the machine. As long as the net present value of investing in one more machine is positive, the firm should purchase an additional machine. We conclude that *the firm should invest in a project if and only if it has a nonnegative net present value.*

Notice that it is the *marginal* machine or piece of capital that exactly satisfies Equation (10.11) (i.e., that just breaks even). Other projects in which the firm invests may well earn strictly positive profits. The point is that the firm keeps purchasing capital up to the point that there are no profitable investment opportunities left untaken.

Figure 10.18

The Number of Machines Demanded as a Function of the Interest Rate

The higher the interest rate, the lower the present value of any given machine, and the fewer the number of machines that will have a positive net present value. Hence, as the interest rate rises, the number of machines demanded falls, *ceteris paribus.*

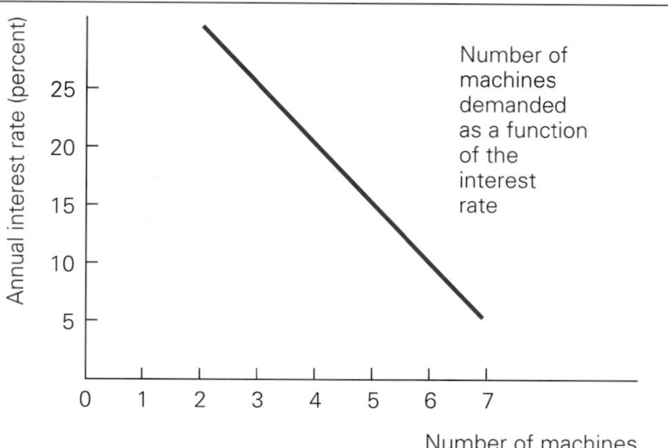

The Demand Curve for Capital As usual, the marginal revenue product curve coincides with the factor demand curve when the firm is a price taker in the factor market. The downward slope tells us that as the price of machines rises, the quantity demanded falls.

Because of the importance of the interest rate in the user cost of capital (see Chapter 7), it can be useful to think of the interest rate as serving the role of a price. To see how a change in the interest rate affects the number of machines demanded, suppose that the interest rate, i, rises. Since, by assumption, all purchase costs are incurred this year,[3] the interest rate change does not affect the present value of the marginal factor cost. Similarly, the present value of the marginal revenue product today is unaffected. But the present value of the marginal product one year from now, $MRP_1/(1 + i)$, falls. Consequently, so does the present value of the total marginal revenue product over the life of the machine.

Expressed in terms of our net-present-value investment criterion, these facts tell us that the higher the interest rate, the lower the present value of any given machine, and the fewer the number of machines that will have a positive net present value. Hence, as the interest rate rises, the amount of capital (that is, the number of machines) demanded falls. Figure 10.18 graphs this downward sloping demand function, with the number of machines demanded measured on the horizontal axis and the interest rate on vertical axis.

SECTION RECAP

In the short run, the firm has only one variable input. The firm's choice of how much of this input to use thus determines how much output the firm produces and what revenue it earns—the firm makes its input and output choices simultaneously. Any profit-maximizing firm hires a factor until the input's marginal revenue product is equal to its marginal factor cost. For a firm that is a price taker in both the factor and output markets, we can express this rule as follows: Hire a factor up to the point at which marginal physical product times the output price is equal to the input price. When the price of the input rises, producing output becomes more expensive and the firm sells less of it. Since it produces less output, the firm does not need as much of the input. In the short run, the demand curve for the variable input is downward sloping solely because of this output effect.

[3]Because the machine has no salvage value, it fully depreciates in the first year.

In the long run, all inputs are variable. The firm should hire each input up to the point at which its marginal revenue product is equal to its price. An input price increase has two effects on the quantity of that input demanded. First, there is the factor substitution effect: At any given quantity of output, the firm substitutes away from the factor whose price has risen. Second, there is the output effect: As a result of the price increase, the firm may change its output level and adjust its input usage accordingly. The long-run output effect on a firm's derived demand may be either positive or negative. The net result of the factor substitution effect and the output effect is, however, always negative. Like short-run derived demand curves, long-run derived demand curves are always downward sloping.

SUMMARY

Chapters 7 and 9 developed general rules governing the behavior of profit-maximizing firms. In the present chapter, we have applied these rules to the specific case of a firm that is a price taker in both input and output markets.

- A price-taking firm chooses its actions under the assumption that it cannot influence the prices of the output that it sells or the inputs that it buys.
- Like any firm, a price taker follows two rules to determine its optimal level of output: the marginal output rule and the shut-down rule.
- For a price-taking firm, the marginal output rule can be expressed as follows: If a firm takes the price of its output as given, then unless the firm shuts down entirely, it should produce output at a level where price is equal to marginal cost.
- For a price-taking firm, the shut-down rule can be expressed as follows: If the firm takes the price of its output as given and this price is less than average economic cost for every output level, then the firm maximizes profit by shutting down.
- *Any* profit-maximizing firm follows the factor hiring rule: Hire a factor up to the point at which its marginal revenue product is equal to its marginal factor cost. For a price-taking firm, this rule can be expressed as follows: Hire a factor up to the point at which the price of output times the marginal physical product of the factor is equal to the price of the factor.
- A firm's short-run derived demand curve for a variable input is downward sloping because of the output effect. When the price of the factor rises, so does the firm's marginal cost of producing output. In response, the firm cuts back its production of output and uses less of the variable input.
- In the long run, a factor price increase has two effects on the quantity demanded of an input. First is the factor substitution effect: At any given quantity of output, the firm substitutes away from the factor whose price has risen. Second is the output effect: As a result of the price increase, the firm may produce less output and adjust its input usage accordingly. While the output effect may be either positive or negative, the combined result of the factor substitution effect and the output effect always is negative; derived demand curves are downward sloping.

DISCUSSION QUESTIONS

10.1 The American Binder Company (ABC) makes binders, using plastic and a special forming machine. Suppose that the company already has bought 10 machines. What does its short-run supply curve look like? In answering this question, draw what you consider to be plausible shapes for the relevant cost curves. Now suppose the machines have worn out and ABC is deciding whether to replace them. What does ABC's supply curve look like now, and how does it compare with the one that you found above? Identify whether each of the supply curves is a short-run or a long-run supply curve.

10.2 Consider a new growth hormone that dairy farmers can inject into a cow every 14 days. Each injection costs \$7.00. A price-taking farmer announces that he will use the drug if it increases the average daily production of his cows from 80 pounds (yes, pounds) of milk a day to at least 90 pounds. At what price per pound must the farmer be selling his milk?

10.3 Consider a firm that is a price taker in both the input and output markets. The output price is $10 per unit and the wage rate per worker is $40 per day. The firm's total product schedule is as follows:

Worker days	0	1	2	3	4	5
Units of total product	0	7	13	18	22	25

a. Derive the firm's demand curve for labor and graph it.

b. On the same graph, draw the labor supply curve facing the firm. How many workers will the firm hire?

10.4 In Chapter 8, we considered Almond Yummies, which require exactly 1 ounce of chocolate and 4 almonds per Almond Yummy to produce. Suppose that the firm already has signed a contract for 10,000 ounces of chocolate. Chocolate sells for 50 cents per ounce. The firm can buy almonds at a price of $.30 each (they are special almonds). How many Almond Yummies will the firm supply in the short run at a price of $1.50 per Almond Yummy, and how many will it supply in the long run?

10.5 Resolve the following paradox:

> Because of the increased opportunities for factor substitution in the long run, the average total cost of producing a given level of output should be lower in the long run than in the short run. However, a price-taking firm that decides not to shut down in the short run may shut down in the long run.

In resolving this paradox, you should assume that input and output prices do *not* change over time.

10.6 Consider a competitor of Pitts Cherry Orchard. Suppose that the price of cherries is $400 per ton, and that the firm can hire as many workers as it would like at a wage of $270 per week. Taking as given the number of trees, amount of land, and number of tractors that it has, the firm finds the following relationship between total product and the amount of labor hired:

Worker weeks	0	1	2	3	4	5	6	7
Tons of cherries	0	12	19	23	24	24.9	25.6	26

Suppose that one of the employees of this orchard figures out a more effective way for workers to get cherries out of the trees. As a result of this suggestion, the relationship between total product and the amount of labor hired is as follows:

Worker weeks	0	1	2	3	4	5	6	7
Tons of cherries	0	14	22	27	28.2	29.2	30.1	30.5

By how much does this suggestion raise the firm's profit in the short run? Would your answer be different if we were considering a long-run situation in which the firm could change the levels of the other inputs as well?

10.7 In California, the single biggest consumer of water is "irrigated pasture: grass grown in the near desert climate for cows." The main reason for this is that the Bureau of Reclamation sells the water to cattle farmers "at astonishingly subsidized rates often as little as a quarter of a cent per ton" (Reisner 1988, E4). Suppose that the price of water for cattle farmers increased. What would happen on a typical California cattle farm to the marginal product of water, the marginal revenue product of water, and the amount of water used in cattle production? Illustrate your answer with a graph.

10.8 A manufacturer is choosing between two equivalent light bulbs to provide illumination in his factory over a 6-year period. A 100-watt incandescent bulb costs $1.25 and lasts 6 months. A 25-watt compact fluorescent bulb lasts 6 years, but costs $15. If the annual interest rate is 5 percent, which bulb will the manufacturer choose? What if the interest rate is 15 percent? (In answering this question, ignore the costs of electricity and the labor costs of replacing the bulbs.)

10.9* The price-taking Marvelous Marshmallow Company produces output according to the production function $x = L^{1/2}K^{1/2}$, where x is output, L is labor, and K is capital. The prices of units of x, L, and K are $25, $16, and $9, respectively.

a. In the short run, the capital stock is fixed at 36 units. How much labor does the firm hire, and how many marshmallows does it produce?
Hint: Calculate the short-run marginal cost of marshmallows.

b. What are the profit-maximizing levels of output, labor, and capital in the long run? (*Hint:* Form a Lagrangean.)

*This problem is for students who have studied the Appendix to Chapter 9.

CHAPTER 11

Equilibrium in Competitive Markets

> ***Economics is a subject that does not greatly respect one's wishes.***
>
> —Nikita S. Khrushchev

After decades of communist rule, Poles had become accustomed to stores with largely empty shelves. Whenever word got out that a store had something in stock, long lines would form as people waited for a chance to buy whatever was available. Then, as 1989 drew to a close, something startling happened. As one observer at the time noted,

> In one stroke, a miracle . . . vanquished the empty shelves and endless lines of communism. Now, cheesecakes gorge the bakeries, sausages festoon the butcher shops, groceries bust with bananas. The lines are gone. Just like that. . . .
>
> Poles don't sneak out from work anymore to jam the shops in pursuit of a coat or hair dryer. They know the shops have coats and hair dryers and everything else everyone hunted for last year.
>
> The catch is that this year, it is all too expensive to buy (Newman 1990, A1).

The miracle that the Poles witnessed was the power of the price system. Suddenly, prices, instead of long lines, were used to allocate scarce goods. This miracle arose because prices were no longer decreed by government workers. But if central planners were no longer setting prices, who was?

On a smaller scale, we saw in the last chapter that the price of sour cherries fell by roughly 30 percent in 1987, creating great dismay among sour cherry farmers. Why did prices fall so dramatically? As it turns out, we are not quite ready to answer either this question or our question about Polish prices. To see why, think about the sour cherry market. Our theory of the price-taking firm gives us the answers to a set of hypothetical questions: How many tons of cherries would the firms supply at each price? The theory also gives the answer to another set of hypothetical questions: How much would buyers of sour cherries (firms that make pies and jams) demand at each price? While we know how the market participants will respond to any hypothetical price, we do not know what the *actual* price will be. Consequently, in its present form, the theory does not tell us why sour cherry prices fell, nor does it allow us to predict the directions of any future price changes in response to changing market conditions.

To understand how the price of cherries (or any other good) is determined, we need to bring the two sides of the market together to study their interaction. That's exactly what we did in Chapter 1 when we studied the supply and demand model. If we are simply back to the material of Chapter 1, what has been the good of the intervening chapters? In the words of poet T. S. Eliot, we have arrived "where we started and know the place for the first time." In Chapter 1, we took the market supply and demand curves as basic pieces of information, and we contented ourselves with finding the market quantity supplied and demanded. In contrast, our theories of the household and the firm tell us how these curves are derived from the underlying tastes and technologies. Moreover, once we have found the market price, we can use it to find the equilibrium quantities supplied and demanded by *individual* firms and households. This more detailed approach allows us to say much more about both positive and normative aspects of markets.

This full-blown model of equilibrium at both the market and individual level is known as *perfect competition*. We will begin by describing the basic setup of the perfectly competitive model. Once we have described the model and identified the type of situation in which it is appropriate, we will turn to finding the equilibrium of a competitive market.

11.1 THE BASIC MODEL OF PERFECT COMPETITION

We first lay out the basic assumptions that underlie our model of price determination. We will then spend some time looking at what sorts of real world markets fit these assumptions.

FUNDAMENTAL ASSUMPTIONS

The competitive model relies on four fundamental assumptions. These assumptions are maintained regardless of whether the market under consideration is a product market or a factor market. The first three assumptions deal with the supply side of the market, while the fourth assumption concerns the demand side.

The first assumption is that sellers are price takers. That is, in a competitive market, each seller acts as if it can sell as much or as little output as it wants to without affecting the prevailing market price.

1. *Sellers are price takers.* There are two aspects of this assumption. First, each individual supplier believes that its output choice has a negligible direct effect on the market price; a change in its output level has little effect on the price when all other suppliers hold their output levels constant. Second, each supplier believes it has no effect on the collective actions of other suppliers. This condition is needed because, if it were not satisfied, a single firm's actions might trigger responses by other suppliers that would collectively affect the market price. This

Table 11.1
Fundamental Assumptions of the Perfect Competition Model

1. Seller influence on price	Sellers are price takers.
2. Extent of strategic behavior	Sellers do not behave strategically.
3. Conditions of entry	Entry into the market is free.
4. Buyer influence on price	Buyers are price takers.

second aspect of assumption 1 is sufficiently important that we break it out as a separate assumption.

2. *Sellers do not behave strategically.* Saying that a supplier does not behave strategically means that the supplier does not anticipate any reaction by rival suppliers when it chooses its own actions. In choosing how many tons of cherries to sell, for instance, a farmer does not worry that other farmers will change their sales in response to what he or she has chosen to do. In contrast to a nonstrategic supplier, a strategic supplier would expect rivals to react and would take these reactions into account when determining its course of action. For example, when the Coca-Cola Company considers changing the price of Coke, it must take into account the likely reaction by the makers of Pepsi.

3. *Entry into the market is free.* Our third assumption about the suppliers in a competitive market concerns how difficult or costly it is for a new supplier to begin producing output. When the supplier can enter a market without incurring any special costs, that market is said to be characterized by **free entry.** By special costs of entry we mean costs that an entrant would have to bear that the incumbents did not. Of course, any supplier will have to incur some costs to produce output. Free entry means that there are no restrictions on the *process of entry;* it does not mean that a supplier can enter the market and produce output for free.

free entry
A market is said to be characterized by free entry when new suppliers can enter the market without any restrictions on the process of entry.

blocked entry
A market is said to be characterized by blocked entry when it is impossible for new suppliers to enter the market at any reasonable cost.

At the opposite extreme, a market might have **blocked entry**; that is, it might be impossible for new firms to enter the market at any reasonable cost. Entry can be blocked by either legal barriers or technological barriers. A firm trying to start an airline flying from New York to Paris, for instance, would face a severe legal barrier—its entry would almost certainly be blocked by the French government. In other markets, entry by new suppliers is limited by their inability to obtain the technical knowledge necessary to produce the good, or by an inability to obtain some other needed input. You would be hard-pressed to start an aluminum firm given that the good supplies of bauxite—an ore essential to production—are already tied up.

Clearly, whether entry is blocked or free has an important effect on the nature of market equilibrium. The perfectly competitive model is based on the assumption that there are no impediments to entry.

4. *Buyers are price takers.* The remaining fundamental assumption of the competitive model concerns decision makers on the demand side of the market. We assume that buyers, like sellers, take price as given.

In a competitive market, each buyer (whether a firm or a household) believes that it can purchase as much as it wishes to at the going price without having any effect on that price.

Table 11.1 summarizes the fundamental assumptions of the perfectly competitive model.

THE APPROPRIATE MARKET STRUCTURE

On a purely formal level, a market is perfectly competitive if it meets the four assumptions in Table 11.1. But when are these assumptions likely to be satisfied in practice? In other words, how do we know a competitive market when we see one? The answer depends on the environment in which the buyers and sellers operate. This environment is known as the **market structure.**

market structure
The economic environment in which buyers and sellers in an industry operate.

There are several important dimensions to market structure. For each dimension, we will examine which conditions are consistent with the assumptions of perfect competition.

1. The size and number of buyers.
This dimension of market structure is important because it affects whether individual buyers have the power to influence prices. When there are just a few buyers, each of whom makes huge purchases, these buyers may be able to affect the price of the good by changing the amount they buy. General Motors, for instance, purchases about 7 percent of all of the steel sold in the United States, a sufficiently large share that its purchases can affect the market price. Similarly, Northern Foods has to consider its influence on the price when it buys about 17 percent of all the milk produced by farmers in England and Wales (Hargreaves and Urry 1993, 19). On the other hand, when there are many buyers, each one may be so small that it cannot influence the price. When you go to a supermarket to buy milk for your breakfast cereal, you purchase such a small part of the total that you have no discernible effect on the market price, thus, *the assumption of buyer price taking is most appropriate when there are many buyers.*

2. The size and number of suppliers.
The size and number of suppliers in the industry have important effects on (1) whether suppliers are price takers and on (2) the degree of strategic behavior. When there are many suppliers, each of whom is small relative to the market, any particular supplier's output decision has little direct effect on the total market supply. Even a large percentage change in one supplier's output is a small percentage change in the market quantity and hence leads to a small percentage change in the market price. Using the jargon we developed earlier, the elasticity of firm-specific demand is very high. If you were a farmer accounting for 1/10,000 of the total crop, then even doubling your output would raise the market total by only .01 percent. With a *market* price elasticity of 2, the price would fall by only .005 percent in response to your doubling your output,[1] and your *firm-specific* elasticity would be 20,000 = −(100 percent quantity increase)/(.005 percent price decrease). With this firm-specific elasticity, you would have to produce over 200 times as much output as before in order to lower the market price by 1 percent.

In this example, the firm-specific elasticity is equal to the market elasticity divided by the firm's market share: 20,000 = 2/0.0001. This relationship is a general one. If we use m to denote the firm's market share, $m = x/X$, then

[1]This price change can be calculated as follows. By definition of the price elasticity, ϵ_{mkt} = − *(percentage change in quantity)/(percentage change in price)*. Rearranging these terms, *percentage change in price* = − *(percentage change in quantity)*/ϵ_{mkt}. If the other firms were to decrease their output levels in response to a fall in the market price, their actions would tend to dampen the price change, which would make the firm-specific price elasticity of demand even higher.

$\epsilon_{\text{firm}} = \epsilon_{\text{mkt}}/m.$[2]

This expression tells us that the smaller the firm's share of the industry total, the greater the firm-specific elasticity of demand, *ceteris paribus.* The greater the firm-specific elasticity, the closer the supplier is to being a price taker, because the firm can change its output without an appreciable impact on its price.

In addition to affecting the degree to which suppliers are price takers, the size and number of suppliers also is an important determinant of whether suppliers behave strategically. If there are just a few suppliers in the industry, each one is likely to take note of the others. There are three major carriers in the American market for long-distance residential telephone services—AT&T, MCI, and Sprint. When any one carrier considers lowering its rates, it knows that the other two may respond: These firms behave strategically. On the other hand, when there are many suppliers, each of whom has a small impact on the price, suppliers are unlikely to react to one another's actions. Hence, *the assumptions both of price taking and of nonstrategic behavior by suppliers are most likely to be satisfied when there are many suppliers in the market.*

3. The degree of substitutability of different sellers' products.

homogeneous goods Perfect substitutes with a marginal rate of substitution of one. Homogeneous goods are considered identical by buyers.

Two products are said to be **homogeneous goods** if consumers consider them to be identical (i.e, the marginal rate of substitution between them is a constant at 1). When all buyers view the products of different sellers to be identical, the buyers will make all of their purchases from the supplier charging the lowest price that the buyers know about. Hence, when the suppliers provide homogeneous commodities, any one supplier that tries to raise its price above the common level will find that it can make no sales. For instance, all teenagers look alike to some large fast-food chains. Any one teenager's attempt to get more than the going wage for his or her labor will be met with unemployment. Each teenager faces a perfectly elastic demand curve for his or her labor and is a price-taking supplier.

In contrast, when the products of different suppliers are not homogeneous, a supplier may be able to raise its price without losing all of its sales. Consider the nightclub market in New York City. There are hundreds of clubs, no one of which has a significant market share. But each club offers a product (entertainment) that is different from the products of other clubs. The clubs are at different locations, play different types of music, have differing dress codes, and offer differing varieties of food to go with the music. If the owners of a club decide to raise the cover charge, they will not lose all of their patrons. To some consumers, that particular club is sufficiently better than others so that it is worth the higher price. In other words, this nightclub faces a downward sloping demand curve and is not a price taker.

Since perfect competition is a model of price-taking sellers, the most appropriate market structure is one in which the outputs of different suppliers are homogeneous products.

[2]By definition, the firm-specific elasticity of demand is $\epsilon_{\text{firm}} = -(\Delta x/x) \div (\Delta p/p)$, where x is the firm's output level. Rearranging terms, we find $\epsilon_{\text{firm}} = -(p/x) \div (\Delta p/\Delta x)$. The term $\Delta p/\Delta x$ tells us how the market price changes with the firm's output level. Because, by assumption, other firms are not changing their output levels, when the firm produces one more unit of output, the market output level rises by one unit as well. Consequently, the price change is given by the slope of the market demand curve, s, and $\Delta p/\Delta x = s$. Hence, $\epsilon_{\text{firm}} = -(p/x)(1/s)$. By Equation (3.4), however, $\epsilon_{\text{mkt}} = -(p/X)(1/s)$. Comparing these expressions for the firm-specific and market elasticities, we obtain the formula in the text.

Table 11.2

A Perfectly Competitive Market Structure

a. The size and number of buyers	Many buyers, no one of which is large relative to the overall market.
b. The size and number of sellers	Many sellers, no one of which is large relative to the overall market.
c. The degree of substitutability among different sellers' products	The outputs of different sellers are homogeneous.
d. The extent to which buyers are informed about prices and available alternatives	Buyers are well informed about the offerings of competing suppliers.
e. The conditions of entry	Neither technological nor legal barriers to entry exist.

4. The extent to which buyers are informed about prices and available alternatives.
We noted above that, with homogeneous goods, buyers will seek the very lowest price, which tends to keep sellers from raising their prices above the going rate. This logic rests on the assumption that buyers are well-informed about alternatives available in the market. In contrast, seller-specific demand may be much less sensitive to price when buyers are imperfectly informed about prices and available alternatives. If a supplier wants to sell more output, can it attract new customers by lowering its price? Not if no one knows that the price has fallen. Similarly, when a supplier raises its price and consumers are not aware of the available alternatives, the supplier may retain some of its sales simply because its customers do not know that better deals are available.

Price taking by sellers is one of the fundamental assumptions of the competitive model. *For the assumption that sellers are price takers to be a sensible one, buyers must be well informed about the available alternatives.*

5. The conditions of entry.
For the free entry assumption of perfect competition to be valid, new firms must not face barriers to their entering the market. As noted above, barriers may be technological or legal. *None of these barriers to entry is present in a perfectly competitive market.*

Identifying a Competitive Market Structure

Table 11.2 summarizes the conditions for which the competitive model is most appropriate. Armed with this list, we can look at a market and determine whether the competitive model is likely to be a good fit. For instance, does the competitive model apply to the sour cherry market? Sour cherries are sold to companies that make pies and jam. There are many buyers, no one of which is large enough to influence the price. It is reasonable to assume that these buyers are price takers. There are many suppliers in the market as well, with over 1,700 sour cherry orchards in Michigan alone. Moreover, cherries from different orchards are close substitutes, and the buyers are well informed because it is their job to be. These structural conditions all make seller price taking and nonstrategic behavior reasonable assumptions. Finally, we must consider the conditions of entry. The government allows cherry growing, orchard land can readily be purchased,

11.1 PROGRESS CHECK

From what you know of the automobile industry, does it fit the conditions of the perfectly competitive model?

and the knowledge needed to raise cherries is widely available. There are neither technological barriers nor legal barriers to cherry production. In summary, this industry has a perfectly competitive market structure.

As we shall see, the competitive model also captures the behavior of many other product and factor markets. This does not mean that these markets fit all of the assumptions of perfect competition exactly. The perfectly competitive model is based on strong assumptions. As we have stressed before, the key to judging a model is not necessarily how realistic it is. Rather, the key is how well it helps us understand market behavior. The perfectly competitive model has proven to be an extremely powerful and useful means of understanding a variety of markets, ranging from labor markets to agricultural markets to the housing market. (PC 11.1)

FINDING A COMPETITIVE EQUILIBRIUM

Now that we have carefully stated the conditions required for perfect competition, we are almost ready to find the equilibrium of a competitive market. Because both suppliers and demanders in a competitive market are price takers, we can summarize the behavior of each side of the market by either a supply curve or demand curve. We can then use the supply and demand analysis of Chapter 1 to find the equilibrium market price and quantity.

We have one slight problem, however. The equilibrium market price and quantity are found by using *market* demand and supply curves. Our analyses of households' demand and supply choices in Chapters 3 and 5 showed how to find their market demand and supply curves. But our study of price-taking firms in Chapter 10 focused exclusively on the demand and supply curves of *individual* firms. We still need to find out how to construct the market demand and market supply curves of firms.

Our study of firms indicates that there are important differences between short- and long-run behavior. In the short run, new firms cannot enter the market because they cannot obtain the needed fixed inputs. Hence, in the short run finding market curves simply requires adding up the supply or demand curves of the individual firms that already are in the market. Over the long run, however, new firms can enter the market and existing firms can exit. As a result, the number of firms in the industry in the long run is not something that we can take for granted—the number is itself determined as part of the equilibrium. Because of this important distinction, we will consider the short and long runs separately.

THE SHORT RUN

To examine the short-run competitive equilibrium, our first task is to construct a market supply curve from the individual supply curves of firms.

Market Supply by Firms

To see how to construct the market supply curve, suppose for the moment that there are only two firms in the sour cherry market, Bowles Orchard and Redding Farm. The theory developed in Chapter 10 tells us how to construct each firm's individual supply curve. Bowles' is labeled s^B in Figure 11.1, while Redding's is labeled s^R. We want to add up these firm-specific supply curves to find the market supply curve for cherries. We do this just the way we found households' market

FIGURE 11.1

Horizontally Summing Individual Supply Curves to Find the Short-Run Market Supply Curve

When the price is $400 per ton, Bowles Orchard is willing to supply 50 tons of cherries and Redding Farm is willing to supply 100 tons. (Adding these two quantities (summing horizontally), we find that the market quantity supplied at this price is 150 tons.

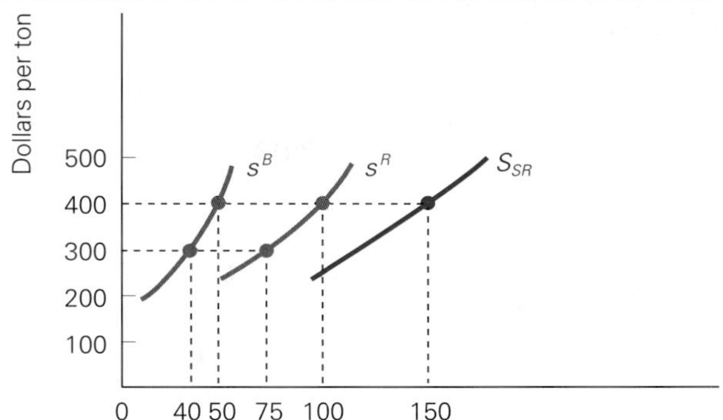

supply curve in Chapter 5—for a given price, we find the individual quantities at that price and we add these quantities together. For instance, Figure 11.1 indicates that when the price of cherries is $400 per ton, Bowles Orchard is willing to supply 50 tons of cherries and Redding Farm is willing to supply 100 tons. Adding these two quantities, the market quantity supplied at this price is 150 tons. We have found one point on the market supply curve: At a price of $400 per ton, the market quantity supplied is 150 tons. As always, we have found the market quantity by adding sideways. We do this because we are asking: At a given price, what total *quantity* of the goods are the firms in the industry willing to supply? Since quantity is measured on the horizontal axis, we add the curves horizontally to answer this question.

11.2 PROGRESS CHECK

Suppose that the price of cherries were $300 per ton. How much would each firm supply, and what would the market quantity supplied be?

When it comes to constructing market supply curves, if you have seen one price (and know what to do with it), you have seen them all. For any price, we can horizontally sum the firms' individual quantities supplied to find the associated market quantity supplied. Following this process repeatedly allows us to construct the entire market supply curve, S_{SR}, in Figure 11.1. (PC 11.2)

Perfectly competitive markets have many suppliers. When there are more than two firms in the industry, we simply have to add up more individual output levels to find the market total at each price. But how many producers are there? During the short run, firms not already producing in that market do not have enough time to obtain the inputs necessary for production during that period. For example, instead of writing a textbook, Katz and Rosen could decide to call themselves K&R Motors and produce automobiles. Given that these two have no training, no factory, and no machines, there is no need to draw in their supply curve when looking at the automobile industry—their quantity supplied is zero at any reasonable price. For all practical purposes, Katz and Rosen are not in the industry in the short run. Only those firms with the needed levels of fixed inputs are in the industry in the short run. All other firms are out of the industry and thus irrelevant. Since the number of firms in the industry is fixed in the short run, adding up individual supply curves presents no special difficulties.

Figure 11.2

Short-Run Equilibrium in the Sour Cherry Market

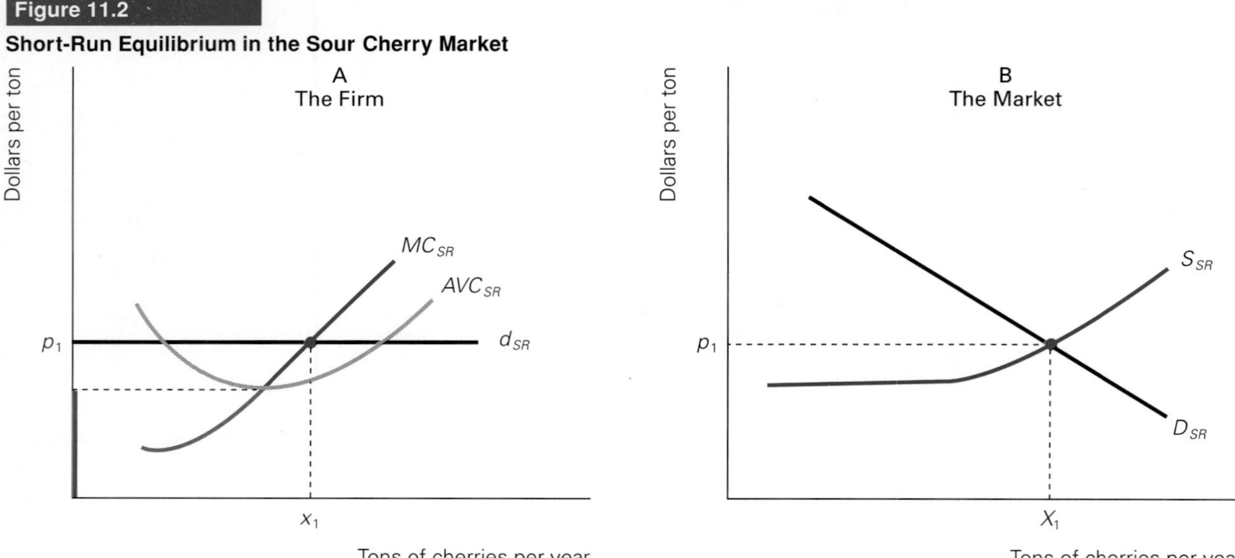

Equilibrium occurs at the price and output combination where the supply curve intersects the demand curve. At this price, p_1, the market quantity demanded is equal to the market quantity supplied—both are equal to X_1. Each supplier faces a firm-specific demand curve that is perfectly elastic at the price p_1, curve d_{SR} in Panel A.

The market supply curve for sour cherries, S_{SR}, is shown in Panel B of Figure 11.2.

Market Demand

The assumption that buyers are price-takers allows us to summarize buyer behavior in terms of a market demand curve. When the product being sold is consumed by households, we simply follow the process outlined in Chapter 3 to find each consumer's demand curve. When the good is a factor (such as sour cherries used to make pies and jam), the buyers are firms and we find their derived demand curves as discussed in Chapter 10. In either case, finding the market demand curve involves nothing new; we horizontally sum the individual demand curves. The market demand curve for sour cherries, D_{SR}, is illustrated in Panel B of Figure 11.2.

Market Equilibrium

With the market supply and demand curves in hand, we are ready to see how the market price brings the two sides of the market together into equilibrium. Since all market participants are price takers, a competitive market is in equilibrium when: (1) buyers are choosing their optimal purchase levels, given the prevailing market price; (2) sellers are choosing their optimal output levels, given the prevailing price; and (3) suppliers are willing to produce as much as buyers wish to purchase and buyers are willing to purchase as much as suppliers choose to produce.

As shown in Chapter 1, the equilibrium price is p_1 in Panel B of Figure 11.2: the price at which the supply and demand curves intersect. At this price, the

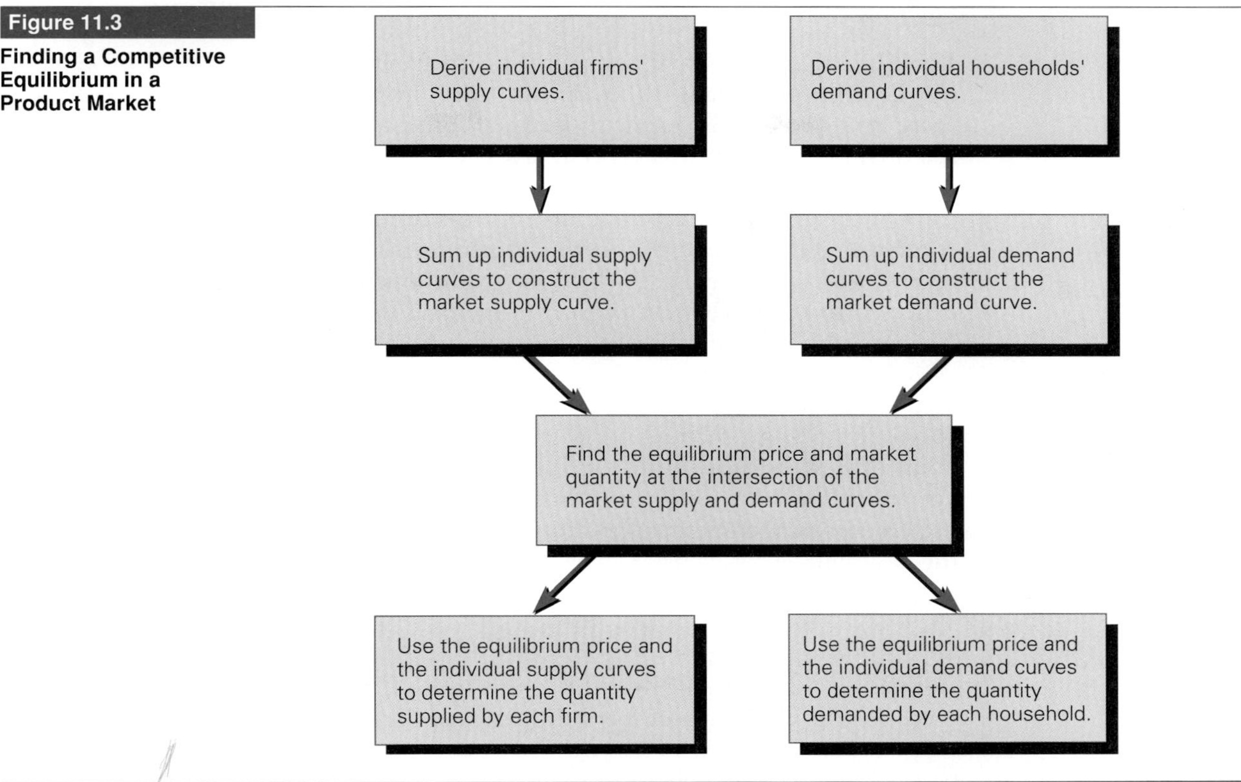

Figure 11.3

Finding a Competitive Equilibrium in a Product Market

quantity demanded is equal to the quantity supplied; both are equal to X_1. Any buyer who wishes to make a purchase at this price can do so, and any producer who wishes to sell output at this price can do so as well. Consequently, there is no tendency for the price either to increase or decrease.

The Individual Supplier's Perspective

We have been looking at the competitive equilibrium in terms of market supply and market demand. It is also worth looking at the behavior of individual suppliers. An individual supplier bases its decisions on its firm-specific demand curve. Given the assumption that each firm is a price taker, the firm-specific curve is d_{SR} in Panel A of Figure 11.2. As we saw in Chapter 10, this is also the firm's marginal revenue curve. We know that if the firm sells any output, it does so at the market price—charging a lower price would be foolish, and charging a higher price is impossible. The firm's equilibrium quantity is where the firm-specific supply curve intersects the firm-specific demand curve—x_1 in Panel A. (PC 11.3)

> **11.3 PROGRESS CHECK**
>
> Verify that x_1 satisfies the two rules for the profit-maximizing choice of output level.

Figure 11.3 depicts how we go from modeling the behavior of individual decision makers (households and firms) to modeling market behavior and then back again.

The Role of Price

Equilibrium requires that suppliers and demanders have consistent production and consumption plans. Who or what guarantees this? In a competitive market, there is no person who explicitly works to bring the quantity supplied in line with the quantity demanded. This vital task is undertaken by the impersonal forces of the market.

On the face of it, reaching an equilibrium could be extremely difficult and complex—the choices available to any one decision maker depend on the actions taken by all market participants. How could one cherry farmer, for instance, be expected to know what every other farmer and what every pie company is doing? The amazing fact we have just demonstrated is that there is no need for an individual decision maker to gather such information in a perfectly competitive market. In deciding how much to purchase, a buyer does not have to know anything about technology, factor prices, or the number of suppliers. From the buyer's point of view, market conditions can be summarized entirely in terms of the market price. Similarly, a supplier does not have to know anything about consumer preferences or incomes; as for a buyer, market conditions can be summarized by the prevailing market price. This economizing on information is an important virtue of the market system. We will explore it further in the next chapter.

THE LONG RUN

Over a long enough time period, new suppliers can enter the market and old suppliers can exit. As a result, the short- and long-run equilbria of a market may be very different. In this section, we will examine the long-run equilibrium of a competitive market. We start by finding the market supply curve.

Market Supply

As usual, to find the market supply curve, we add up the supply curves of all of the suppliers in the market. If entry into the market were blocked, this would be a simple matter because the number of suppliers would be fixed. When entry is free, as it is in a perfectly competitive market, the long-run market supply curve is not as simple to find. The number of firms in the industry is determined by decisions that the firms themselves make in response to the price. Specifically, in the long run a firm can assemble all of the inputs (plants, machinery, and workers) needed to enter the market. Similarly, unprofitable firms can liquidate their positions in the industry entirely. In summary, each firm makes a long-run decision whether to be or not to be in the market. To know the market quantity supplied at a given price, we need to find both the quantities supplied by each firm in the market and the number of suppliers who choose to be in the market at that price.

Suppose that there is a virtually unlimited number of potential suppliers, all of whom have access to the same technology. Moreover, suppose that no matter how many firms come into this industry, the input prices remain unchanged. In other words, there is a tremendous number of potential suppliers, all of whom have the long-run cost curves drawn in Figure 11.4. For later use, notice that the lowest level of long-run average cost is equal to p* in the figure. As always, marginal cost is equal to average cost at this output level.

Suppose that the market price is p_a in Panel A of Figure 11.4. The positive part of a price-taking firm's supply curve is the portion of its marginal cost curve

Figure 11.4

Long-Run Equilibrium in the Sour Cherry Market

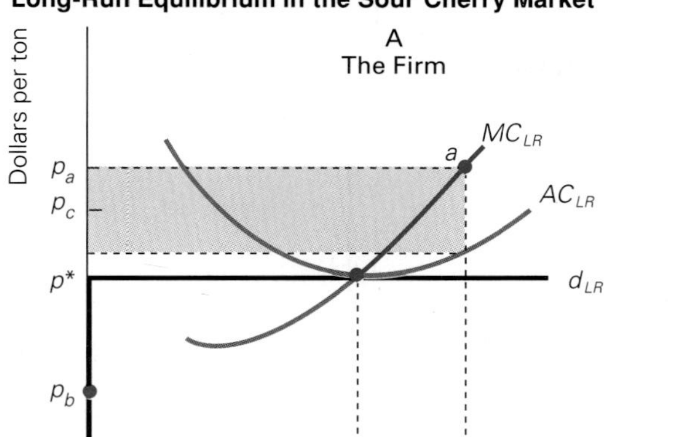

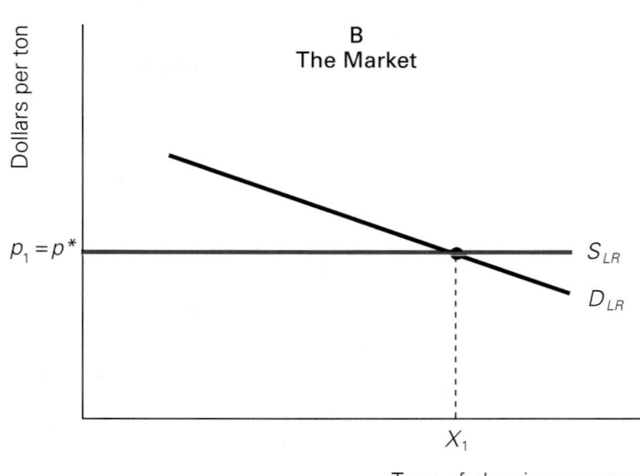

When the level of industry input demand has no effect on the prices of these inputs, the long-run supply curve for a perfectly competitive industry is flat at a price equal to the minimum of long-run average cost. The equilibrium price is found by looking for the price at which long-run supply and demand are equal. The long-run equilibrium price is p_1 and the equilibrium quantity bought and sold in the market is X_1. Each firm produces x^* tons.

above its average cost curve, the dark blue curve in Panel A. At a price of p_a, a firm in the market would produce x_a tons of cherries. From the figure, we see that price is greater than average cost when the firm produces this amount of output, and the firm earns a positive profit equal to shaded area *A*.

Seeing a price of p_a, new firms will be attracted to the industry by the prospect of earning this positive economic profit. Each time a new firm enters the market, the total quantity supplied rises by x_a. Since new firms will continue to enter the industry as long as the price stays at p_a, the market quantity supplied is unlimited at this price. Of course, the quantity cannot literally be unlimited, if for no other reason than that the world has limited resources. We will soon see that saying "supply would be unlimited" is a shorthand way of saying that firms would be willing to supply more than consumers would demand at this price.

The same argument applies for any other price that exceeds p^*. When entry is free and the price is greater than minimum average cost, a firm can earn positive profit by entering the market. The possibility of earning positive profit attracts new firms to enter the industry, increasing the market quantity supplied ever more. We conclude that *when entry is free, the long-run market quantity supplied is infinite for any price greater than the minimum of long-run average cost.*

What does the long-run market supply curve look like for prices below p^*? Suppose that the price is p_b in Panel A of Figure 11.4. Since p_b is less than p^*, no matter what the firm does, the price it receives for its output is less than its average cost. Hence, a firm already in the market is better off exiting than producing, and a firm not in the market is better off staying out than entering. When every firm's long-run quantity supplied is 0 (point *b*), the market quantity clearly is 0 as well. The same would hold true at any other price below p^*. We conclude that *the market quantity supplied is 0 at any price less than the minimum of long-run average cost.*

Finally, suppose that the market price is exactly equal to p^*. At this price, a firm that is in the market maximizes its profit by producing x^* tons of cherries in Figure 11.4, because that is the quantity at which marginal cost is equal to marginal revenue. At this price and output combination, average revenue equals average cost, and the firm earns zero economic profit. Such a firm would be indifferent between being in and out of the market. Thus, any number of firms are willing to enter the market and supply x^* tons of cherries each. It follows that *the firms collectively are willing to supply any quantity at a price of* p^**, the minimum of long-run average cost.*

Putting all of this discussion together, we see that the long-run market supply curve is a horizontal line at a price equal to the minimum level of long-run average cost. This curve is graphed as S_{LR} in Panel B of Figure 11.4. It is extremely important to remember how the quantity adjustment in response to a price change embodied in S_{LR} takes place. It is not the case that each firm produces more output in order to expand industry output. Each firm in the market produces x^* tons of cherries (as indicated in Panel A) no matter what the market total. Rather, the adjustment takes place entirely through the entry and exit of firms. Notice that the average cost of production is p^* no matter what the long-run quantity supplied is. For this reason, this type of market is said to be a **constant-cost industry.** (PC 11.4)

11.4 PROGRESS CHECK

Suppose that the price of output were p_c in Panel A of Figure 11.4. How much output would a single firm supply? How much would the market supply?

constant-cost industry An industry in which long-run average costs remain unchanged as industry output rises.

Market Demand

Now that we have examined the long-run supply curve, we turn to the demand side of the market. When the product is being sold to households, the only difference between the short and long runs arises because in the long run buyers have greater opportunities for substitution. Consequently, as we discussed in Chapter 3, market demand is likely to be more elastic in the long run.

Increased long-run substitution possibilities also come into play in factor markets. In the particular example of cherry farming, the long-run demand curve is likely to be more elastic because pie and jam producers can switch to other fruits. Moreover, because the demand for an input is derived from the demand for the buyers' output, we have to consider the effects of time on the demand for this output. We would expect the demand for the buyers' output (cherry pies) to be more elastic over time, which would make the demand for the input (sour cherries) more elastic over time as well.

There is one final complication. Since buyers in factor markets are firms, the number of buyers is determined as part of the market equilibrium. In the long run, we would expect an increase in the price of sour cherries to induce some firms selling cherry pies to exit the market, further reducing the demand for sour cherries. We will have more to say about these interactions across markets in the next chapter.

In summary, for both households and firms we expect long-run demand to be more elastic than short-run demand. The long-run market demand curve for sour cherries is labeled D_{LR} in Panel B of Figure 11.4.

Market Equilibrium

With the long-run supply and demand curves in hand, we are ready to find the long-run equilibrium price and quantity. As in the short-run case, the equilibrium price is at the intersection of the market supply and demand curves. In

Figure 11.4, the long-run equilibrium occurs at point e_1, where the price is p_1 and the market quantity exchange is X_1.

The Individual Supplier's Perspective

Having found that the long-run equilibrium price is p^*, we know that each supplier faces a firm-specific demand curve, d_{LR} in Panel A of Figure 11.4, that is horizontal at a price of p^*. Faced with a price of p^*, the firm maximizes its profit by producing x^* units of output if it produces at all. We have already seen that the firm earns zero profit at this price and output combination, and it is indifferent between producing or not.

How many firms will choose to be in the industry and produce x^*? In the long-run equilibrium, enough firms choose to be in the industry (producing x^* each) that market supply is equal to market demand, X_1. Since we know the total amount produced and how much is produced by each firm, it is a simple matter to calculate the equilibrium number of firms in the long run. Using N_1 to denote the equilibrium number of firms, we know that the number of firms adjusts until $N_1 \times x^* = X_1$. Solving for the equilibrium number of firms, $N_1 = X_1/x^*$.

THE LONG RUN IS A SHORT RUN TOO

While we have analyzed short- and long-run equilibria separately, it is important to note their relationship. A long-run equilibrium is also a short-run equilibrium: Each firm in the industry is producing at a point where price is equal to marginal cost and no firm that is operating could increase its profit by shutting down. However, it is not the case that every short-run equilibrium is a long-run equilibrium. To find a long-run equilibrium, there must be the right number of firms in the industry. Specifically, a short-run equilibrium cannot persist in the long run if the firms are earning positive economic profits or are suffering economic losses. When all suppliers have the same cost curves, the long-run equilibrium number of firms must be such that each earns zero economic profit. Here we see an important role of prices. A high price will lead to high profits for producers, and new suppliers will be attracted to the market. The profitability of the personal computer industry in the 1980s, for example, induced many firms to invest millions of dollars to enter this relatively new and growing market. Similarly, low prices lead to low profits and even losses. These losses will help to shift resources away from markets where they are no longer needed, such as the typewriter market. It is crucial to realize that losses play just as central a role as profits. Frank Borman, a former astronaut and president of Eastern Airlines, once remarked that "Capitalism without bankruptcy is like Christianity without hell."

INPUT PRICE TAKING BY THE FIRM BUT NOT BY THE INDUSTRY

Having looked at the basic case of a perfectly competitive market, we can now consider two more complicated situations. First, we consider what happens when the industry as a whole does not take input prices as given. We follow by examining the consequences of the producers having different costs of supply.

In a perfectly competitive market, each individual supplier is a price taker in the output market, but collectively suppliers are price makers; the firm-specific demand curve is horizontal, but the industry demand curve is downward sloping. A similar situation can arise in the factor markets from which the suppliers

Figure 11.5

Long-Run Supply Decisions When Input Prices Rise with the Market Output Level

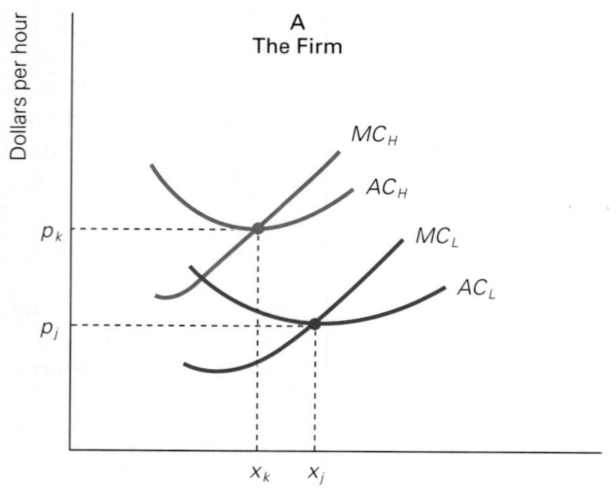

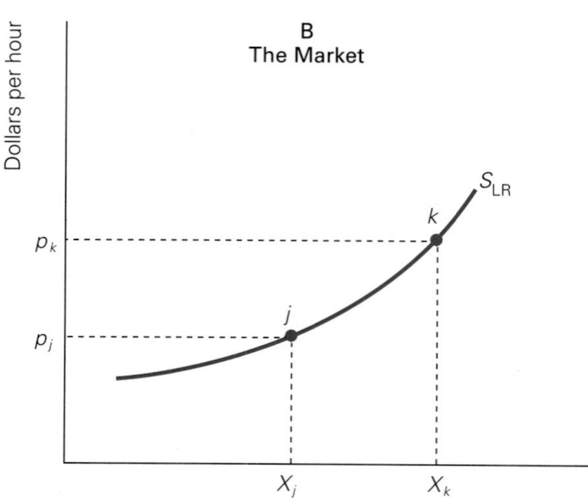

As the level of market output rises, so does the industry's use of inputs. When this increase raises the prices of the inputs, individual firms find their cost curves shifted upward. In order to induce firms to supply additional output, the price of output must rise. As a result, the long-run market supply curve is upward sloping.

purchase their inputs. Even though any one firm's *individual* input choices have no discernible effect on input prices, an *industrywide* increase in the quantities of inputs demanded may drive up their prices.

For example, the city of Seattle, Washington, experienced a residential construction boom in 1990. This led to increased demand for the output of firms that supplied electrical contracting services to construction companies erecting new buildings. While any individual electrical contracting firm could hire more workers at the going wage, when *all* of the firms decided to hire more workers, the market wage of electricians was driven upward.

To see what effect this phenomenon had on supply, consider Figure 11.5. Panel A depicts the situation of a typical firm that provides electrical contracting services, and Panel B shows what is happening in the Seattle market as whole. To begin, we ask what price the electrical contractors would have to receive to be willing to supply a total of X_j hours of service per year in Panel B. At this level of output, the number of workers demanded by the industry is relatively low, and so is the wage rate paid by the firms to their employees. Given the low wage level, an individual contractor has the marginal and average cost curves, MC_L and AC_L, respectively, in Panel A. Electrical contractors with these costs are willing to supply a total of X_j hours of service per year at a price equal to p_j which is the minimum of average cost when the wage rate is low. We have just shown that the point labeled j in Panel B is on the industry's long-run supply curve; when the price is p_j, the market quantity supplied is X_j.

Let's ask what price the firms in the industry would have to receive to be willing to supply a total of X_k hours of service per year in Panel B. Since X_k is greater than X_j, a greater number of workers is needed to produce this output,

Figure 11.6

Long-Run Equilibrium When Firms are Price Takers but the Industry is Not

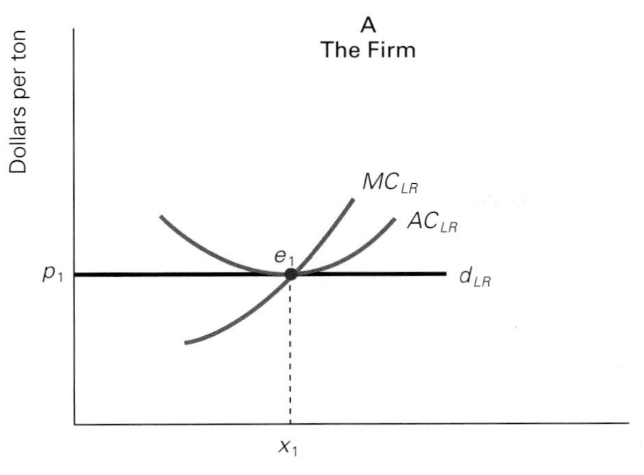

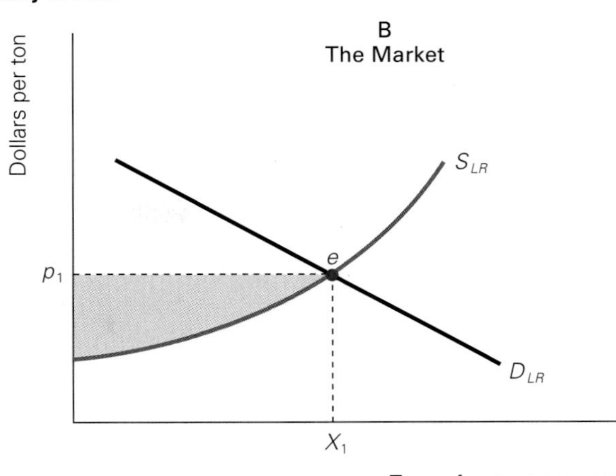

When the long-run supply curve is upward sloping due to input price effects, all firms in the market earn zero profits in long-run equilibrium. The producer surplus shown by the shaded area accrues to input suppliers.

and the wage rate is greater as well. At the higher wage, an individual contracting company's marginal and average cost curves rise to MC_H and AC_H, respectively, in Panel A. Hence, the firms are willing to supply a total of X_k hours of service per year at a price equal to p_k—the minimum of the average cost curve that arises when the wage rate is high. We have shown that point k in Panel B also lies on the industry's long-run supply curve. The important thing to note is that the firms must receive a higher price to supply more output; p_k is higher than p_j.

Repeating this procedure for all prices gives us the entire long-run market supply curve, which is labeled S_{LR} in Panel B. This curve is upward sloping. It is tempting to think that this curve slopes upward for the same reason as a short-run supply curve. It does not. A short-run supply curve slopes upward when each firm faces increasing marginal costs due to the diminishing marginal physical product of its variable factor; *a short-run supply curve may be upward sloping even when input prices paid by the firms are constant.* In contrast, the long-run supply curve is flat when input prices paid by the firms are constant and all firms are the same. *When all suppliers are the same, any upward slope in the long-run supply curve is due to an industrywide price effect*— as the industry increases the quantities of inputs demanded, the input prices faced by all firms rise. Because the long-run average costs of producing output rise with the industry output level, such a market is said to be an **increasing-cost industry.**

increasing-cost industry An industry in which long-run average costs rise with the industry output level.

The long-run market supply curve is reproduced in Panel B of Figure 11.6 where the long-run industry demand curve, D_{LR}, is also drawn. Finding the intersection of the market supply and demand curves, we see that the long-run equilibrium price and quantity are p_1 and X_1, respectively.

Since the long-run market supply curve is upward sloping, the price that suppliers receive for their output is greater than the height of the supply curve for all but the last of the units that they supply. Recall from our examination of labor supply by households in Chapter 5 that the area under the price line and above the supply curve (the shaded area in Panel B) is defined as *producer surplus.* As discussed when we looked at labor supply, producer surplus represents the difference between what a supplier actually is paid and the minimum payment that it needs to be willing to supply the good. When the supplier is a firm, that firm's producer surplus is equal to its profit.

In Panel B of Figure 11.6, it looks like the firms in this industry are earning positive profits equal to the producer surplus shown for this market. But, as they often are, looks are deceiving. Appearance aside, the firms in this industry still earn zero profits. To see why, we need to remember why the long-run supply curve is upward sloping—as the industry output rises, so do the input prices. At the equilibrium output level of X_1, the input prices are sufficiently high that the minimum of long-run average cost is just equal to the equilibrium average revenue of p_1. Panel A of Figure 11.6 illustrates this situation. Since average revenue is equal to average cost, each firm earns zero economic profit in the long-run equilibrium.

If the firms in the industry are making zero profits, who gets the producer surplus shown in Panel B? The answer is the input suppliers. Since the price of the input rises with the quantity purchased by this industry, it must be that the *input* market itself has an upward sloping supply curve. There are two reasons why that supply curve might be upward sloping. First, the producers of the input might themselves collectively not be price takers. If this is so, then the question is pushed back to consideration of the firms that supply the inputs to the inputs! Of course, the process could continue backward even more. But at some point we have to stop moving backward. We must eventually come to the second reason that the long-run supply curve may be upward sloping: Different producers have different costs of production. We will examine this situation in the next section.

Before doing so, it is worth noting that the long-run supply curve can also slope downward, as drawn in Figure 11.7. This situation could arise when *production of the inputs* to this industry is subject to such strong economies of scale that the input prices fall as total quantities of the inputs used by the industry rise. Some electronics industries fit this pattern. As more and more electronic keyboards are sold, the producers of the integrated circuits that go into them are able to use large-scale production techniques that lower the costs, and prices, of this input. Disk drives for personal computers have followed a similar course. As more disk drives are sold, the prices of the components for making them fall. Since the average costs of production fall as industry output rises, such markets are said to be **decreasing-cost industries.**

decreasing-cost industry
An industry in which long-run average costs fall as industry output rises.

HETEROGENEOUS SUPPLIERS

In the basic model of perfect competition, all firms have the same technologies and, hence, the same costs. However, in real markets the situation may be more complicated; different producers may have different costs. Because they are not all the same, such producers are said to be **heterogeneous suppliers.** In this subsection, we return to the assumption that factor prices are constant even as the market quantities demanded vary, but we drop the assumption that all suppliers are alike.

heterogeneous suppliers
Producers of a single good who have different costs of production from one another.

Gold mining is one example of a market in which different producers have markedly different production costs. Some mines have very low-grade ore, from which it is extremely costly to extract the gold. Others have high-grade ore.

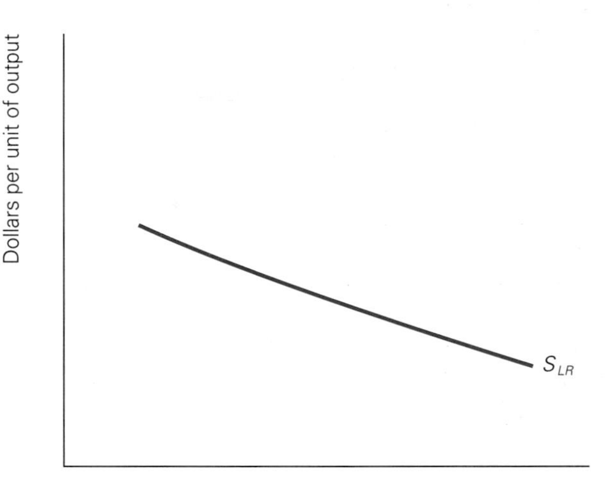

Figure 11.7

The Long-Run Market Supply Curve in a Decreasing-Cost Industry

When input prices fall as industry production and input levels rise, individual firms will find their cost curves shifting downward as the industry expands. As a result, the long-run market supply curve is downward sloping.

Mines also differ in how hard it is to extract the ore itself. Some ore is near the surface; other veins are deep underground. In light of the considerable variations in costs, we should expect different mines to have very different individual supply curves, and they do.

To see what implications this has for the market equilibrium, let's begin by supposing that there are only two types of gold mines, "good" and "bad." Four of the mines are good ones with high-grade deposits that give them lower costs than the other mines. While there is a limited number of good mines, there is an unlimited number of entrepreneurs who could enter the market and set up mines with the higher cost curves. In other words, there is free entry by bad mines.

Short-Run Analysis

As always, our rule for finding the short-run market equilibrium is as follows: Find the intersection of the short-run market supply curve with the short-run market demand curve. The marginal and average variable cost curves for the good mines are labeled MC^G_{SR} and AVC^G_{SR}, respectively, in Panel A of Figure 11.8. The marginal and average variable cost curves for the other firms, the bad mines, are labeled MC^B_{SR} and AVC^B_{SR}, respectively. The dark blue lines in Panel A of Figure 11.8 graph the positive portions of the short-run supply curves for individual firms of each type. As always in the short run, the number of mines in operation is fixed. Each firm has an upward sloping supply curve due to the diminishing marginal returns to labor in mining and smelting. That firms have differing short-run supply curves poses no additional difficulties. To obtain the short-run market supply curve, we simply take the horizontal sum of the supply curves of the mines that are active in the short run.

The market supply curve is graphed in Panel B along with the industry demand curve. From Panel B we see that the equilibrium market price is p_1. This tells us that the individual firm faces a firm-specific demand curve that is

Figure 11.8

Short-Run Equilibrium When Suppliers Are Heterogeneous

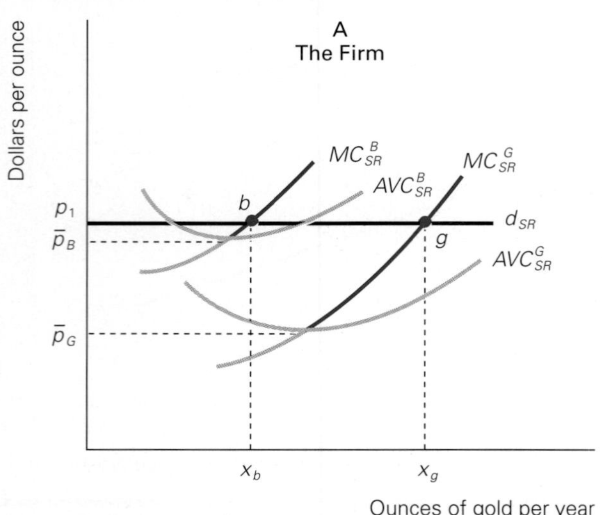

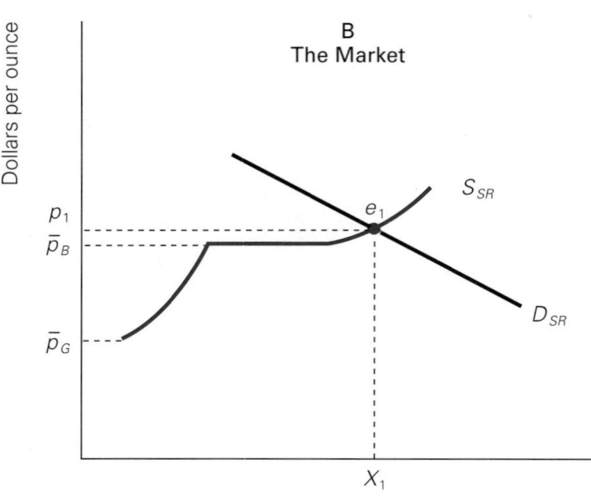

Taking the horizontal sum of the individual supply curves, we find the market supply curve, S_{SR}, in Panel B. The equilibrium price is given by the intersection of the industry supply and demand curves in Panel B. Once we have found that price, we can use it to construct the firm-specific demand curve, d_{SR}, faced by each supplier. Panel A shows the equilibrium position of each type of supplier.

horizontal at a price of p_1. From Panel A, we see that at this price good mines each produce x_g ounces of gold, while bad mines each produce x_b ounces.

Long-Run Analysis

What does the long-run industry equilibrium look like for this market? To answer this question, we begin by finding the long-run market supply curve. Let's consider the market quantity supplied at a few different prices. First, suppose that the price is p_h, which is below p_G^* in Figure 11.9. At this price, no firm is willing to supply output, and the market quantity supplied is zero. Supply is likewise zero at any other price below the good mines' minimal average cost.

Now, consider price p_i, which is above p_G^* but below p_B^*. At this price, no bad mine finds it profitable to produce output, but each good mine maximizes its profit by operating on its supply curve and producing x_i ounces. Hence, the market quantity supplied is $4x_i$, as shown in Panel B of Figure 11.9. For any price between p_G^* and p_B^*, the market quantity supplied is simply four times the quantity supplied by a single good mine.

Finally, suppose that the price is exactly equal to p_B^*. In this case, each good mine is willing to supply x_j ounces. Each bad mine is indifferent between staying out of the market entirely and coming in to produce x_B^* ounces. Hence, the market quantity supplied at this price ranges anywhere from $4x_j$ ounces to an unlimited quantity. Of course, if the price were any higher than p_B^*, the market would be flooded with entrants, and the market quantity supplied would be infinite as all firms tried to supply output.

Figure 11.9

Long-Run Supply Decisions in a Market with Heterogeneous Suppliers

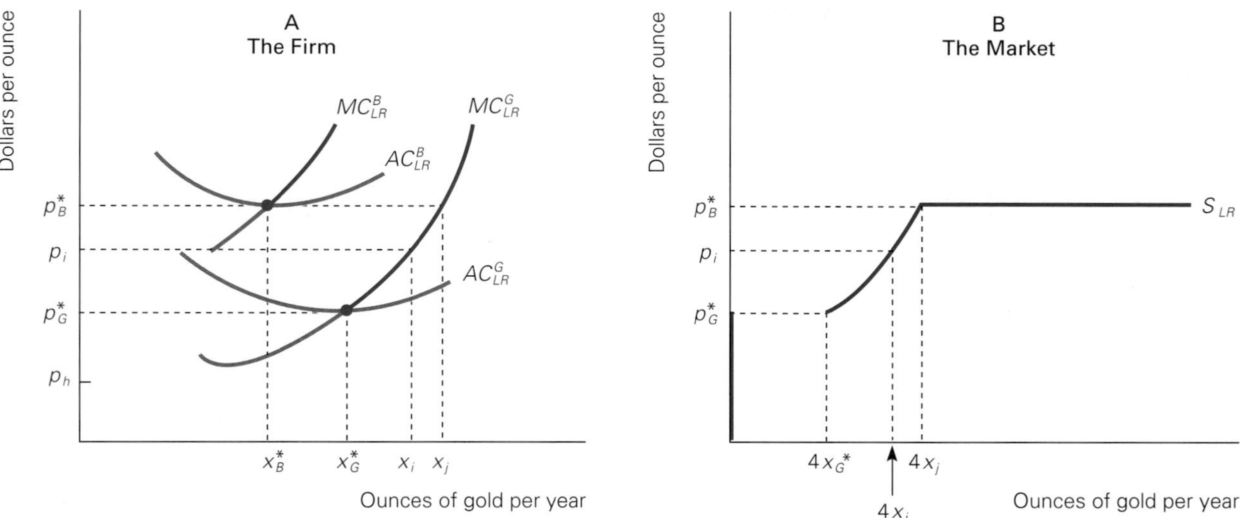

When there are only four good mines and entry by bad mines is free, the long-run industry supply curve initially is upward sloping and then becomes flat at the price equal to the minimal long-run average cost of a bad mine.

The resulting market supply curve is S_{LR} in Panel B of Figure 11.9. We can understand the shape of this curve as follows. A price increase leads firms already in the market to expand along their long-run marginal cost curves, and it leads new, higher-cost suppliers to enter the market. New suppliers continue to enter the market until the marginal supplier (the one with the highest cost of those in the market) just earns zero economic profits at the prevailing price. The other suppliers, with lower costs, earn positive economic profits.

Taking the intersection of the market supply and demand curves, S_{LR} and D_{LR}, in Panel B of Figure 11.10, we find that the equilibrium price is $p_B{}^*$. At this price, each high-cost mine operates at the output where average cost is lowest and produces $x_B{}^*$ ounces of gold. The high-cost mines receive a price that is equal to their average cost; they earn zero economic profit. That is what we would expect, given the free entry by this type of mine. The low-cost mines, on the other hand, do not operate at the minimum of their average cost curves. Each good mine produces x_j ounces of gold, and earns a positive economic profit equal to shaded area *H* in Panel A. How is it that these firms earn positive economic profits even in the long run? The reason that these positive economic profits do not attract additional entry is that there are no other firms with costs as low as these four. There is no potential entrant out there who could come into the market and earn positive economic profit at the equilibrium price of $p_B{}^*$.

Of course, in reality, there are many different qualities of ore deposits, not just two. We can handle this additional complication simply by drawing more sets of cost curves. Our theory tells us that as the price of gold rises, it becomes profitable to open mines to extract ore of poorer and poorer quality. This is just what happens. There are high-cost mines that operate in periods when the price of

Figure 11.10

Long-Run Equilibrium When Suppliers are Heterogeneous

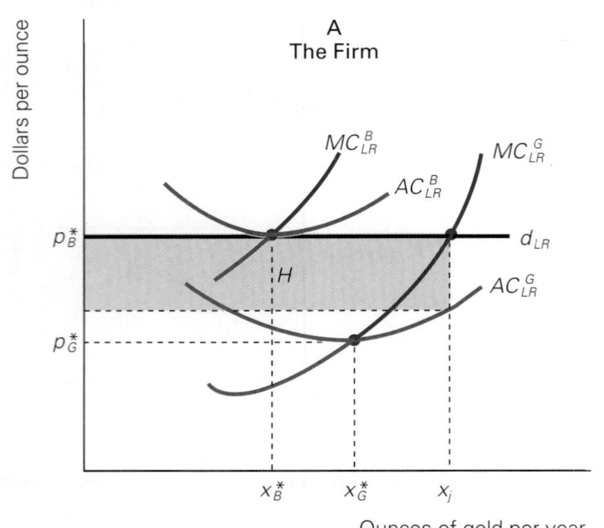

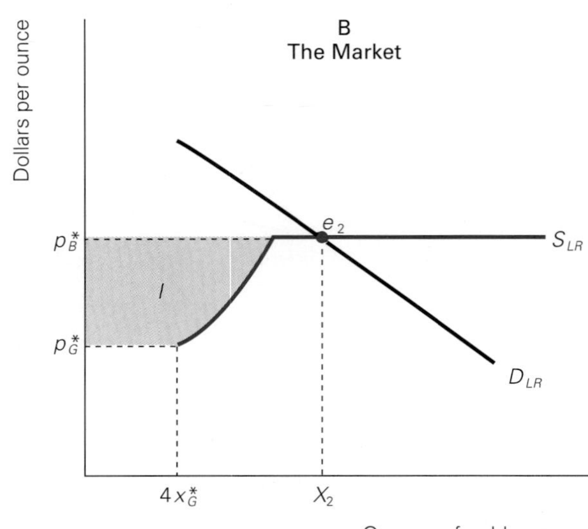

Here, the long-run equilibrium price is equal to the minimal value of the long-run average cost of a bad mine, $p_B{}^*$. At this price, bad mines earn zero economic profits, but good mines earn positive economic profits equal to shaded area *H* in Panel A.

gold is high, and shut down when the price of gold is low (Seabrook 1989, 45). The resulting long-run market supply curve, S_{LR} in Figure 11.11, is a series of scallops, one for each new mine that comes in as the price rises. At p_s, a level well above the current price of gold, it would be profitable to extract gold from sea water. The amount of gold that could be recovered this way is essentially unlimited, which is why S_{LR} is a horizontal line at p_s.

Equilibrium can now be found by drawing a market demand curve and going to its intersection with the market supply curve. When there are more than two different types of firms, the analysis becomes more complicated, but the general principle is the same: Entry occurs as long as the entering firms can earn positive economic profits. Those firms with relatively low costs find entry the most profitable and come in first. As more firms enter the market, the market supply curve shifts outward and the equilibrium price falls. Entry continues as higher-cost firms come into the market and the price falls further. Entry stops when the last firm coming into the market just breaks even at the prevailing market price. The lower-cost firms already in the market all earn positive profits in equilibrium, while all of the firms that choose to stay out of the market have sufficiently high costs that they would suffer economic losses were they to produce in this industry and sell their output at the prevailing market price.

Economic Rent

In our look at gold mining, we have made no distinction between the operator of the mine and the owner of the land itself. The analysis just completed implicitly assumes that the land owners and the mine operators are one and the same. For a market such as this where the land is an important input that varies in quality,

Figure 11.11

The Long-Run Supply of Gold

When there are ore deposits of many different qualities and there are just a few deposits of each quality, the long-run supply curve is upward sloping over a wide range. At price p_S, the price of gold is so high that it is profitable to extract gold from sea water. Since the amount of gold that can be recovered this way is essentially unlimited, this segment of the market supply curve is a horizontal line.

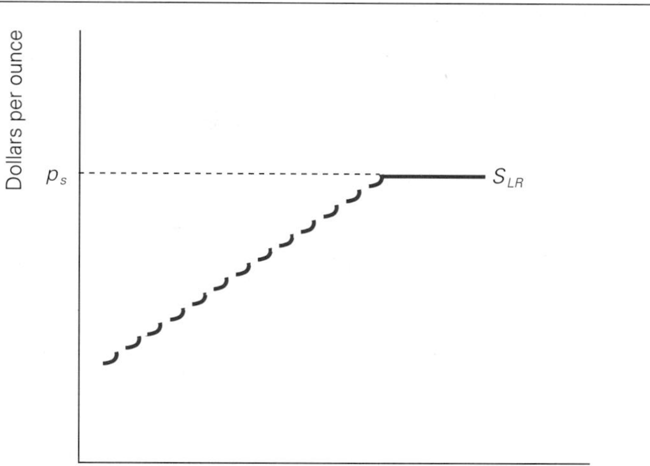

it often is important to distinguish between the owners of an input and the firms that use it.

To see why, suppose that the set of people who own the mineral rights to land containing gold ore is completely different from the set of people who own mining companies. Which group would we expect to earn the producer surplus given by shaded area I in Figure 11.10, Panel B? When there is free entry into the business of being a mine operator and the same technology is available to everyone, we expect mine operators to earn zero economic profits as the result of long-run entry. Because the owners of the mineral rights control the scarce resource, we would expect them to capture the producer surplus. In particular, a land owner with high-grade ore should be able to sell the mineral rights to his or her land for more than the owner of a low-grade ore deposit.

How big will this price differential be? Figure 11.10 provides the answer. For the sake of argument, suppose that the land for all mines sold at the same price. In this event, operators with good mines would each be able to earn positive economic profits equal to shaded area H in Panel A of Figure 11.10. But then all operators would try to buy the mineral rights to the good ore. Consequently, mine operators will drive up the price of the rights to good ore until *the mineral rights for a good mine sell for more than the mineral rights to a bad ore deposit by an amount equal to shaded area H.*

If we think harder about this market, we can say more about what area H represents. Suppose that all of the land is equally productive in uses other than gold mining. In that case the equilibrium price of land with bad ore will be equal to the opportunity cost of land. The premium earned by owners of land with good ore will represent a payment in excess of the opportunity cost of that land. In other words, this premium is producer surplus accruing to the owners of land with good ore.

There are many other examples in which different pieces of land have different values in certain uses. For example, some land is fertile and easily plowed, while other soil has few nutrients and is on steep hillsides. Clearly, the former is

economic rent
What the supplier of a good or service gets paid above and beyond what is needed to induce it to supply the output.

better suited to farming and should command a higher price if used in agriculture. Because differences in land values are such a common source of producer surplus, another name for producer surplus is **economic rent,** whether or not the good being supplied is land. Economic rent, economic profit, and producer surplus are all ways of expressing the same idea—a supplier enjoys surplus when the amount that it is paid to provide a good exceeds the economic cost of providing the good.

We close our discussion of rent and producer surplus with one word of caution. We must remember to be careful about the interpretation of producer surplus in market supply and demand diagrams. When input prices are fixed and the supply curve is upward sloping, either because we are in a short-run situation or because different firms have different costs, the area below the price line and above the supply curve does indeed represent surplus enjoyed by suppliers *in that market.* But when the supply curve is upward sloping because the firms in the industry collectively are price makers in the factor markets, the surplus accrues to the producers *supplying factors to the market under consideration*, not to the output producers in the market itself. In either case, it is surplus accruing to some supplier, so we will call it all producer surplus.

SECTION RECAP: FOUR STEPS TO FINDING AN EQUILIBRIUM

This section examined the equilibrium of a perfectly competitive market both at the marketwide level and from the perspective of an individual supplier. To do so, we followed the four steps outlined in Figure 11.3:

1. *Derive individual supply and demand curves.* From the underlying data on tastes, incomes, and costs, we construct individual decision makers' supply and demand curves. For firms, we use the procedures discussed in Chapter 10. For households, we use an indifference curve diagram to derive an individual's demand or supply curve.
2. *Sum up individual curves to obtain market curves.* To determine equilibrium behavior, we need to find the price, and this can only be done by looking at the *market* supply and demand curves. Having found the individual curves, we sum horizontally to obtain the market curves. In the short run, the number of suppliers is fixed. In finding the long-run curves, we have to keep track of how many firms choose to enter the market.
3. *Find the equilibrium price and market output levels.* Given the market supply and demand curves, we go to their intersection to find the equilibrium price and market quantity.
4. *Find the individual production and consumption levels.* Having found the equilibrium price, we go back to the individual supply curves to find the individual quantities supplied at the prevailing market price, and we go back to individual demand curves to find the individual quantities demanded at the prevailing market price.

Table 11.3 lists the conditions that characterized the short- and long-run equilibria of a perfectly competitive market. The short-run market supply curve is upward sloping due to the diminishing marginal returns of the variable factor. The shape of the long-run market supply curve depends on how factor prices vary

Table 11.3

Conditions for Short- and Long-Run Equilibria

	Short Run	Long Run*
Marginal Output Rule: As long as they do not shut down, firms operate at the point where this condition is satisfied.	$p = MC_{SR}$	$p = MC_{LR}$
Shut-Down Rule: Firms shut down unless this condition is satisfied.	$p \geq AVC_{SR}$	$p \geq AC_{LR}$
Free Entry Condition: Entry occurs until this condition is satisfied.	—	$p \leq$ minimum AC_{LR}

*The three conditions for long-run equilibrium imply that $MC_{LR} = p = AC_{LR}$.

with the level of industry output and the extent to which cost structures of firms differ.

11.2 USING THE COMPETITIVE MODEL

The competitive model can help us understand how markets respond to changes in underlying economic conditions. In this section, we use it to derive several comparative statics results.

THE EFFECTS OF TAXES

ad valorem tax
A tax whose amount depends on the value of the transaction being taxed.

unit tax
A tax that is levied as a fixed amount per unit of the item subject to taxation.

statutory incidence of a tax
The economic agent who is legally responsible for payment of the tax.

economic incidence of a tax
The change in the distribution of income brought about by the imposition of the tax.

Sales taxes, which raise over \$200 billion annually in the United States, are typically levied on a percentage basis. In Alameda County, California, for example, there is a 8.25 percent sales tax on clothing, magazines, automobiles, restaurant food, and many other goods and services. Such a tax is called an **ad valorem tax** because the tax depends on the value of the commodity being taxed. In other cases, such as the state and federal taxes on gasoline and cigarettes, the taxes are levied as fixed amounts *per unit*. In 1992, for example, state excise taxes on gasoline ranged from 4 cents per gallon in Florida to 29 cents per gallon in Connecticut (U.S. Bureau of the Census 1996, Table 479). Such tax is said to be a **unit tax**. Let's look carefully at the impact of one particular unit tax, the federal tax on wine.

One question of interest (to wine producers and consumers at least) is who pays the wine tax? The tax laws provide one answer. The **statutory incidence of a tax** indicates who is legally responsible for paying it. In the case of the tax on wine, the statutory incidence of the tax is on the seller.

The statutory incidence does not, however, tell the whole story (or even the most interesting part) of who pays the tax. To determine who really pays the tax, we must calculate its **economic incidence**—the change in the distribution of income brought about by the imposition of the tax. As we will see, the economic incidence of a tax may differ dramatically from its statutory incidence. The difference between the two is due to what is known as *tax shifting*.

Suppose that in the absence of any taxation, the wine market is competitive and has the market supply and demand curves graphed in Figure 11.12. Prior to

Figure 11.12

The Before-Tax Equilibrium in the Wine Market

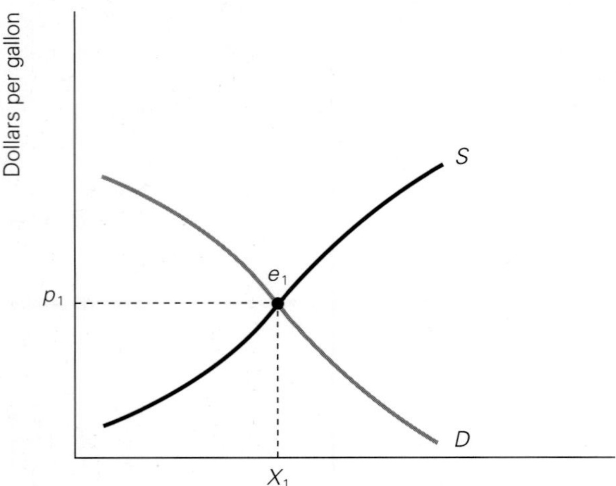

Prior to the imposition of the tax, the equilibrium price and quantity of wine are p_1 and X_1, respectively.

Figure 11.13

The Effects of the Wine Tax on the Supply Curve as Perceived by Consumers

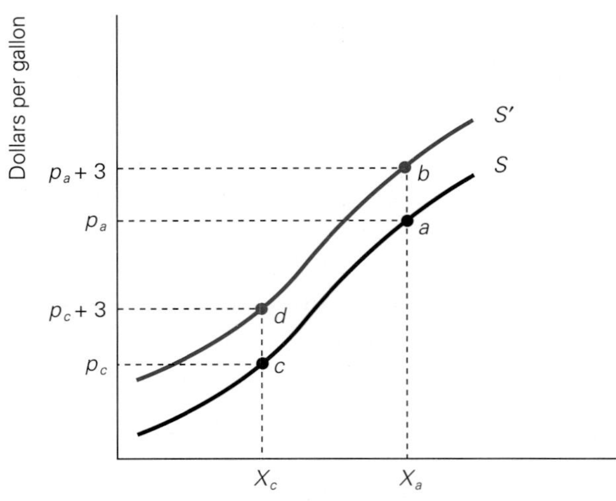

The imposition of a unit tax paid by suppliers raises the supply schedule as perceived by consumers by exactly the amount of the tax, in this case by \$3 per gallon. The supply schedule as perceived by consumers is labeled S'.

the imposition of the tax, the equilibrium price and quantity of wine are p_1 and X_1, respectively.

Suppose that a unit tax of \$3 per gallon of wine is imposed on each purchase, and the statutory incidence is on the seller. How does the tax on wine affect the supply schedule? Consider an arbitrary point a on the supply curve in Figure 11.13. That this point is on the supply curve tells us that firms must receive a price of at least p_a to induce them to supply X_a gallons of wine. After the imposition of the unit tax, suppliers *still* must receive a net price of p_a to be induced to supply this amount. For firms to receive this net price, however, consumers must pay a price of $p_a + 3$ per gallon of wine. This point is labeled b in Figure 11.13.

Point a was chosen arbitrarily, and the story is the same at any other point on the supply curve. Thus, for example, after the tax is imposed, suppliers must receive a net price of p_c to be induced to supply X_c gallons of wine, which means that consumers must pay a price of $p_c + 3$ per gallon of wine. This point is labeled d in Figure 11.13. Continuing in this fashion for each output level, we see that *the imposition of a unit tax paid by suppliers raises the supply schedule as perceived by consumers by exactly the amount of the tax*, in this case \$3 per gallon. The supply schedule as perceived by consumers is labeled S' in Figure 11.13. Of course, from the sellers' perspective, the supply curve remains S, because all a supplier cares about is what it actually receives from each transaction.

Once we have found the supply curve that prevails after the tax is imposed, we are ready to find the equilibrium quantity of wine when it is subject to the

Figure 11.14

The After-Tax Equilibrium in the Wine Market When the Statutory Incidence of the Tax Falls on Suppliers

The after-tax equilibrium quantity is at the point where the demand and effective supply curves cross, point e_2. The after-tax equilibrium quantity is X_2. The equilibrium price paid by the buyers is at the intersection of the demand and effective supply curves, p_2. Comparing p_1 and p_2, we see that the price paid by consumers rises. While the *gross* price that suppliers receive from consumers rises to p_2, the price *net* of the tax falls to $p_2 - 3$.

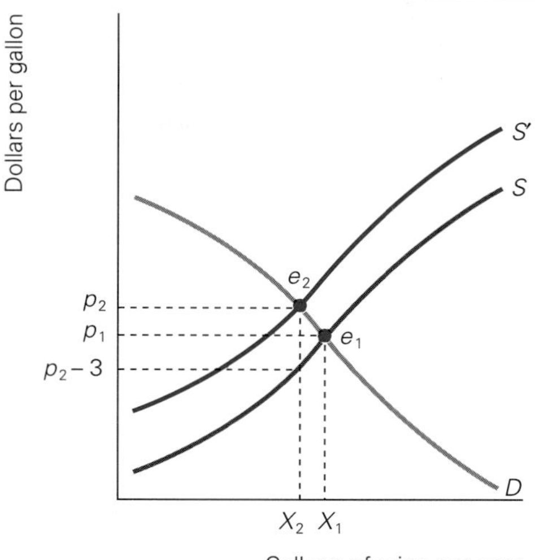

unit tax. The after-tax equilibrium quantity is X_2, the output level at point e_2 where the demand and supply curves cross in Figure 11.14.

The next step is to find the equilibrium price. It is important to note that while previously we had only to keep track of a single price for a commodity, in the presence of a tax there really are two prices at the new equilibrium: the price paid by the buyers and the price received by the sellers. The price paid by the buyers is at the intersection of the demand and effective supply curves, which is p_2 in Figure 11.14. Comparing p_1 and p_2, we see that the price paid by consumers rises—consumers bear some of the burden of the tax even though producers are legally responsible for actually paying it. Does this mean that producers are unaffected by the tax? No, some of the tax burden also falls on wine producers. While the gross price that suppliers receive from consumers rises, the price *net* of the tax falls from p_1 to $p_2 - 3$. From this analysis, we reach our first major insight into the effects of taxation: *The economic incidence of a tax may be very different from the statutory incidence.*

In the example just considered, the statutory incidence was on the shoulders of the suppliers. Suppose that the tax law were changed so that buyers were responsible for physically paying the tax to the government. How would this change in the statutory incidence of the wine tax affect its economic incidence? To answer this question, consider the original demand curve for wine, which is redrawn in Figure 11.15. Taking point g as an example, the demand curve tells us that p_g is the highest price that consumers are willing to pay to consume X_g gallons of wine. This is true whether or not there is a tax. Once consumers take into account that they have to pay \$3 on top of the producers' price, the most that they are willing to pay to the sellers to consume X_g gallons of wine falls to $p_g - 3$ per gallon. Hence, D is no longer the demand curve as perceived by sellers. *From the perspective of the sellers, the after-tax demand curve, D', is*

Figure 11.15

The Effects of the Wine Tax on the Demand Curve as Perceived by Suppliers

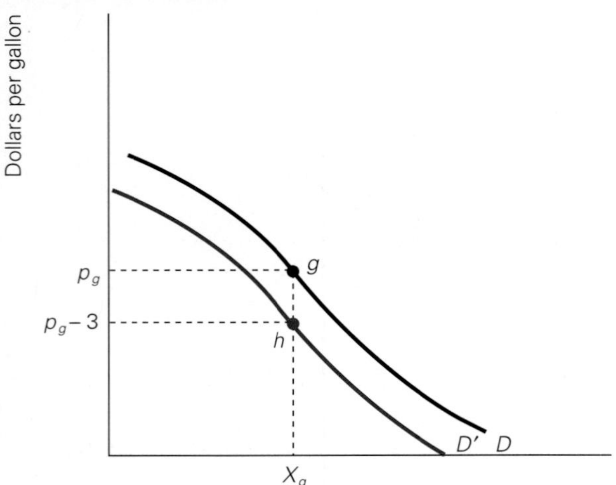

From the perspective of the sellers, the after-tax demand curve, D', is equivalent to the before-tax demand curve, D, shifted downward by exactly the amount of the tax.

Figure 11.16

The After-Tax Equilibrium in the Wine Market When the Statutory Incidence of the Tax Falls on Consumers

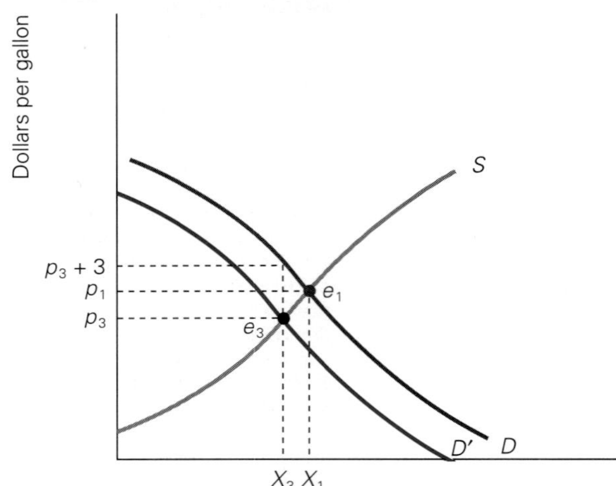

Equilibrium occurs at the intersection of the supply curve and the after-tax demand curve as perceived by suppliers, point e_3. The equilibrium output level is X_3. The price that suppliers receive from consumers is at the intersection of the supply and effective demand curves, p_3. While the price paid to producers falls, the total price paid by consumers (including the tax) rises to $p_3 + 3$.

equivalent to the before-tax demand curve shifted downward by exactly the amount of the tax.

Expressed in terms of the price that the sellers receive, the supply curve is unaffected by the tax when it is levied on consumers. Drawing the supply curve and after-tax demand curve as perceived by suppliers on the same graph in Figure 11.16, we see that the equilibrium output level is X_3. The next step is to find the equilibrium prices. The price that suppliers receive from consumers is at the intersection of the supply and effective demand curves, p_3. Comparing p_1 and p_3, we see that the price received by suppliers has fallen even though the tax is "paid" by consumers. Not all of the burden of the tax falls on producers, however. While the price paid to producers falls, the total price paid by consumers (including the tax) rises from p_1 to $p_3 + 3$.

Notice that the after-tax equilibrium quantity in Figure 11.16 occurs at the point where the vertical distance between the *original* (before-tax) supply and demand curves is equal to the amount of the tax. This is exactly the quantity that was found in Figure 11.14 when the tax was levied on suppliers. Hence, $X_2 = X_3$. Similarly, the increase in the price paid by consumers and the decrease in the price received by sellers are identical in Figures 11.14 and 11.16. From our analysis, we reach the following startling conclusion: *In a competitive market, the economic incidence of a unit tax is independent of whether it is levied on consumers or producers.*

Figure 11.17

The Effects of a Unit Tax When Demand Is Perfectly Elastic

D is the demand curve for handguns produced in Cook County and *S* is the supply curve. A $30 per gun tax charged to buyers shifts the effective demand curve as perceived by sellers downward to *D*′, which is the *D* curve shifted downward by $30 per gun. As a result of the tax, the equilibrium price received by Cook County gun manufacturers falls from $350 to $320 per gun.

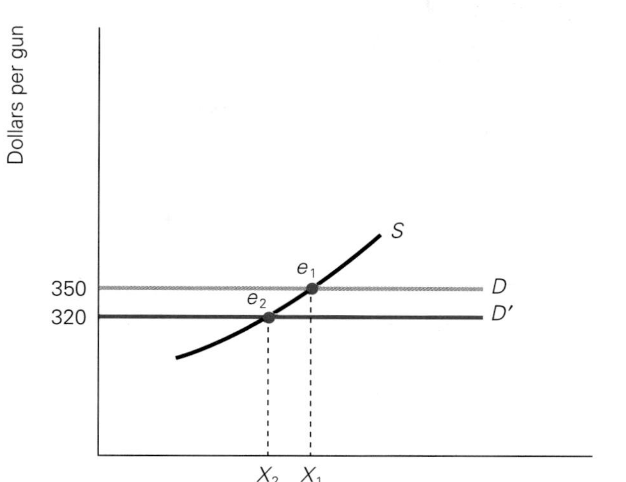

This result reinforces our earlier statement that the statutory incidence of a tax tells us nothing of the economic incidence of the tax. It is irrelevant whether the tax collector (figuratively) stands next to the consumer and takes $3 every time he or she buys a gallon of wine, or stands next to the seller and collects $3 every time he or she sells a gallon. Looking at Figures 11.14 and 11.16, we see that what matters is the size of the wedge that the tax introduces between the price paid by consumers and the price received by producers. It does not matter from which side the wedge is introduced.

Elasticities and Incidence

If the statutory incidence does not determine how much of the tax burden falls on each side of the market, what does? The following examples suggest an answer. Suppose that Cook County, Illinois, decided to levy a $30 unit tax on all handguns produced in its jurisdiction. Who would bear this tax? To answer this question, we need to draw supply and demand diagrams. In Figure 11.17, *D* is the demand curve for handguns produced in Cook County and *S* is the supply curve. Notice that the demand curve for *guns produced by Cook County manufacturers* has been drawn so that it is *perfectly elastic* at a price of $350 per gun; $350 represents the equilibrium price for the entire U.S. market in the absence of the tax. The demand curve is flat at this point because, collectively, the Cook County gun manufacturers are price takers. If they were to raise the price of their guns, customers would simply buy from producers located elsewhere.

Consider the effects of the unit tax. Suppose that after lobbying by gun producers, the government assigns the statutory incidence of the gun tax to the buyers. The tax shifts the effective demand curve as perceived by sellers downward to *D*′. The distance between *D* and *D*′ reflects the difference between what the suppliers receive per gun and what the buyers pay for it. Hence, the *D*′ curve is simply the D curve shifted downward by \$30. After the tax is imposed, the equilibrium price received by Cook County producers falls to \$320. Notice the effect of the tax on the price that buyers pay. Before the tax, the buyers paid \$350. After the tax, buyers pay only \$320 to the producers, but the buyers also have to pay \$30 to the county government. Hence, the full price paid by buyers (including the tax) stays constant at \$350. Suppliers, on the other hand, see the price they receive net of the tax fall by the full amount of the tax—from \$350 to \$320. In other words, suppliers bear the entire burden of the tax. Their lobbying effort is defeated by market forces!

Consider the opposite extreme. Suppose that the demand for insulin is perfectly inelastic at a quantity of X_a over a broad range of prices, while the supply curve is neither perfectly inelastic nor perfectly elastic. As shown in Figure 11.18, the equilibrium price and quantity in the absence of a tax are p_a and X_a, respectively. Suppose that a unit tax is levied on consumers. Once the tax is imposed, the demand curve shifts downward by the full amount of the tax. But because the demand curve is vertical, this shift has no effect on the equilibrium price paid by consumers to suppliers or on the equilibrium quantity. The consumers continue to pay p_a per ounce of insulin and they now have to pay the unit tax on top of that. With this combination of supply and demand curves, the economic incidence is the opposite of the handgun case in Figure 11.17—now the entire burden of the tax falls on consumers.

elasticity of supply
The percentage change in the quantity supplied divided by the percentage change in price.

These two examples illustrate the following general point: *The greater the elasticity of demand, the less the tax burden is borne by buyers, ceteris paribus.*

11.5 PROGRESS CHECK

The supply of land in Toronto, Ontario, is perfectly inelastic because the total amount is fixed. Assuming that the demand curve for land in Toronto is neither perfectly elastic nor perfectly inelastic, who would bear the burden of a unit tax on land?

The incidence of the tax also depends on the **elasticity of supply**—the percentage change in the quantity supplied divided by the percentage change in the price. Suppose, for example, that the town of Newport, Rhode Island, decides to levy a tax on purchases of yachts by its citizens. Since Newport is small relative to the world yacht market, the supply of yachts to Newport is perfectly elastic at the going price, p_b. Assuming that the demand curve slopes downward, the Newport yacht market is illustrated in Figure 11.19. Our model of tax incidence suggests that because the supply elasticity is infinite, the entire burden of the tax will be borne by Newport residents. (PC 11.5)

This second pair of examples illustrates the fact that *the greater the elasticity of supply, the less the tax burden is borne by suppliers, ceteris paribus.*[3]

Our findings indicate that nothing about the incidence of a tax can be known without information on the relevant elasticities of supply and demand. Intuitively, elasticity provides a rough measure of an economic agent's ability to avoid the tax. The more elastic the demand for a good, for instance, the easier it is for buyers to substitute other goods for the one that is taxed. Hence, consumers will turn to other goods unless producers bear most of the tax burden and keep the price paid by consumers close to its pretax level. Similarly, when supply is elastic, producers will shut down rather than bear the tax, leaving consumers to shoulder the burden. This shifting is not the result of any explicit bargaining. Rather, it is a consequence of the impersonal workings of the competitive model.

[3]Using algebra, we can express the general relationship between tax incidence and the elasticities of supply and demand as follows. Denote the price elasticities of supply and demand by ϵ_S and ϵ_D, respectively. Then in response to a \$1-per-unit tax, the price paid by buyers (including their share of the tax burden) rises by $\epsilon_S/(\epsilon_S + \epsilon_D)$ and the price received by sellers (subtracting their share of the tax) falls by $\epsilon_D/(\epsilon_S + \epsilon_D)$.

Figure 11.18

The Effects of a Unit Tax When Demand Is Perfectly Inelastic

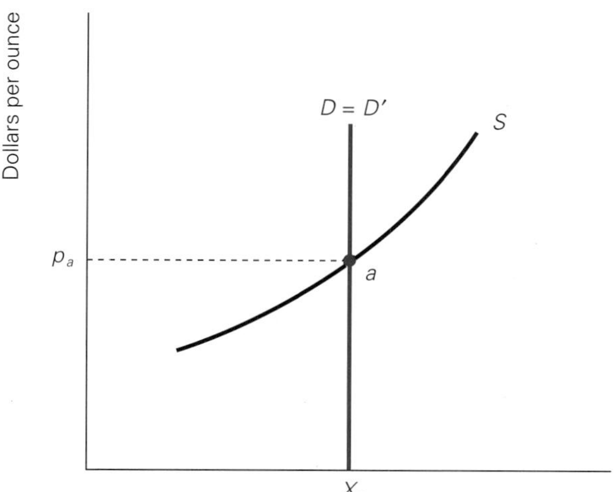

When the market demand for insulin is perfectly inelastic and the market supply is less than perfectly inelastic, the full burden of the tax falls on consumers. The price received by the producers remains unchanged.

Figure 11.19

The Effects of a Unit Tax When Supply Is Perfectly Elastic

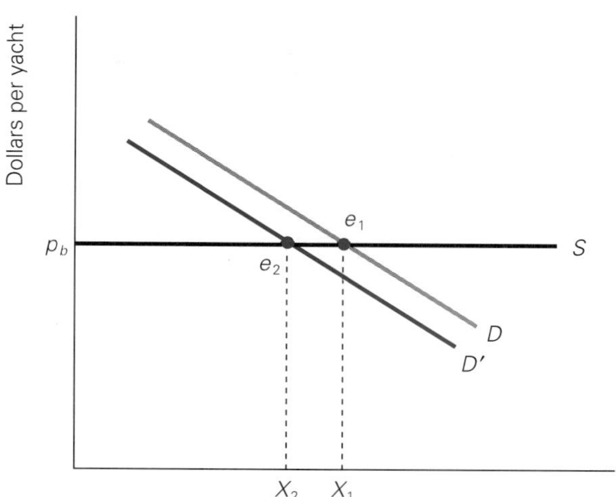

When the market supply of a commodity is perfectly elastic and the market demand is less than perfectly elastic, the full burden of the tax falls on consumers. The price received by the producers remains unchanged.

WHO PAYS FOR SOCIAL SECURITY?

Social Security—officially Old Age, Survivors, and Disability Insurance—is the largest single domestic spending program of the U.S. government. It is also one of the largest sources of government "revenue" ("taxes" to the rest of us). In the 1994 fiscal year alone, the government collected over $335 billion in Social Security taxes and contributions (U.S. Bureau of the Census, 1995, Table 518).

In brief, the system works as follows. During their working lives, members of the system and their employers make contributions to the system by means of a tax on payrolls. Upon retirement, members are eligible for payments based in part upon their contributions. Social Security also provides benefits for disabled workers and for the dependents and survivors of disabled and retired workers. Today, virtually every worker in the United States is covered either by Social Security or some other government retirement program.

The payroll tax used to fund Social Security is a flat percentage of the employee's gross wages (15.3 percent in 1995) up to some fixed amount ($61,200 in 1995). Half of the tax is paid by employers and half by employees. Apparently, the legislative intent behind splitting the statutory burden of this tax was to share the cost of the program equally between workers and firms. But as we know, the economic incidence of the Social Security payroll tax (or any other tax) may be very different from the statutory incidence. In fact, it is extremely unlikely that the actual division of the burden of this tax is 50-50.

This point is illustrated in Figure 11.20, where *D* is the pretax demand curve for labor and *S* is the pretax supply curve. For purposes of illustration, this

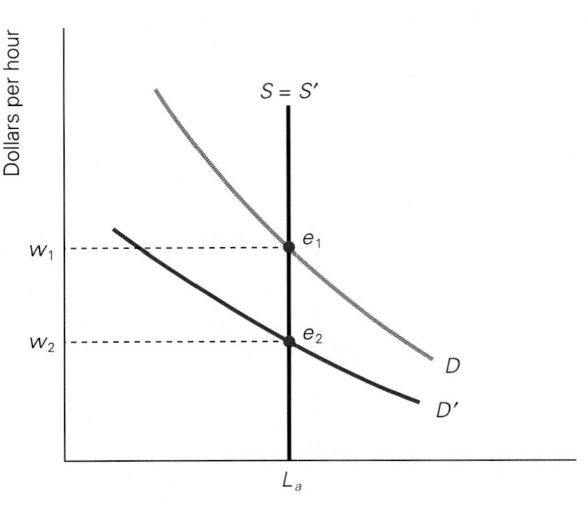

Figure 11.20

The Effects of the Social Security Tax When Labor Supply Is Perfectly Inelastic

D is the pretax demand curve for labor, *S* is the pretax supply curve, and w_1 is the pretax equilibrium wage rate. The employer tax shifts the effective demand curve downward to *D*′. The employee tax shifts the effective supply curve upward by the amount of the tax to *S*′, which coincides with *S*. After the imposition of the tax, the wage paid by employers to workers falls to w_2, while the full price for labor paid by employers (including the tax payments) stays constant at w_1.

diagram is drawn so that the supply of labor is perfectly inelastic at a quantity of L_a. Prior to the imposition of the Social Security tax, the equilibrium wage rate is w_1.

The payroll tax paid by employers shifts the effective demand curve downward to *D*′. As usual, the distance between *D* and *D*′ reflects the difference between what is paid for an item and what is received by those who supply it. Notice that the distance between the pre- and post-tax effective demand curves is not constant—at higher wages, the vertical distance between the two curves is greater. This is a consequence of the fact that Social Security is financed by an ad valorem tax—it is levied as a *percentage* of the wage. The higher the wage, the greater the tax wedge between the two demand curves. Turning to the supply side of the market, the part of the payroll tax paid by employees shifts the effective supply curve upward by the amount of the tax to *S*′. In this figure, the labor supply curve is perfectly inelastic; hence *S* and *S*′ coincide.

The post-tax equilibrium is determined by the intersection of *D*′ and *S*′, at point e_2 in Figure 11.20. Comparing points e_1 and e_2, we can see that after the tax is imposed, the wage paid by employers to workers falls to w_2. Importantly, the full price for labor paid by employers (including the tax payments) stays constant at w_1. In other words, none of the tax is borne by employers. Workers, on the other hand, pay their half of the tax directly to the government and pay for the employers' share of the tax in the form of lower wages. In this example, despite the statutory division of the tax, workers bear the entire burden—the after-tax wage rate received by the workers falls by exactly the amount of the tax. Of course, we could have gotten the opposite result by drawing a perfectly elastic supply of labor curve. (You might try doing it yourself.) The key point is that nothing about the incidence of the Social Security payroll tax can be known without information on the relevant elasticities of supply and demand.

Actual estimates of supply elasticities place the elasticity of the total supply of hours of labor near zero for men (Pencavel, 1986) and slightly higher for women

(Killingsworth and Heckman, 1986). The elasticity of demand is about −1.0 (Hamermesh, 1986). These estimates suggest that the model in Figure 11.20 is not far from the actual situation. That is, workers bear most of the Social Security tax burden, Congressional intent notwithstanding. This analysis of taxation shows how the goals of government policymakers can be defeated by the operation of the market. It is an example of the dictum by Khrushchev quoted at the beginning of this chapter.

THE ELASTICITY OF DERIVED DEMAND

In the examples above, we have seen that the elasticities of supply and demand play key roles in determining the impact of a government policy such as a tax. Given the importance of the price elasticity of demand, it is worth taking some time to consider the determinants of the elasticity of the derived demand for a factor. The perfectly competitive model and the theory of derived demand developed in Chapter 10 help us find features of a market that affect the price elasticity of demand for a factor. Specifically, the theory tells us that we need to identify characteristics of the market that influence the magnitude of either the output effect or the factor substitution effect.

The Elasticity of Demand for the Final Product The demand for inputs by firms is derived from the demand for their output. In the light of this, it is not surprising that the nature of the demand for factors by firms is influenced by the nature of the demand that households or firms in other industries have for the output of input buyers. Indeed, we can see that the total output effect on *factor* demand increases as the price elasticity of demand for the *final* product increases. Tobacco is an input into the production of cigarettes. If the demand for cigarettes were perfectly inelastic, there would be no effect on the quantity of final output demanded when cigarette suppliers raise their prices in response to the higher costs of the tobacco they are using as an input. In this case, there is no output effect on the derived demand for tobacco.

At the other extreme, suppose that the *market* demand curve for cigarettes were perfectly elastic. Then all of the adjustment in response to the higher marginal cost brought about by a factor price increase would have to take the form of a cutback in the level of output; the tobacco suppliers cannot respond to the cost increase by raising the price of their output because to do so would cut off all of their sales. Hence, when the price of tobacco rises, cigarette producers respond to the higher marginal costs of tobacco production by cutting back on the number of cigarettes produced. This fall in the level of output then leads to a fall in the quantity of tobacco demanded.

The Closeness of Substitutes The size of the factor substitution effect clearly depends on the extent to which substitute factors are available. Consider a commercial airline's elasticity of demand for pilots and compare this with its elasticity of demand for frozen lasagna. Both factors are inputs to the production of airline services, but there are many more substitutes for lasagna than there are for airline pilots. If the price of lasagna rises, airlines serve less lasagna and more boiled chicken bits. When airline pilots' wages rise, however, the amount of factor substitution is severely limited. Some factor substitution is possible—airlines have increased the automation of their aircraft in order to reduce the size of the flight crews from three members to two. But these substitution possibilities clearly are limited. Would you want to fly on a plane with no pilot, or even half of one? Consequently, an airline's demand for pilots is much less elastic than its demand for frozen lasagna.

The price of elasticity of supply of substitutes is a closely related market characteristic. If the industry faces a relatively inelastic supply curve for a substitute input, then it is expensive for all firms in the industry to switch to this substitute. Consequently, the factor substitution effect is small and the derived demand for the original factor comparatively inelastic.

The Time Frame Considered Substitution in production and consumption both affect the demand for an input. Both types of substitution take time. The greater the amount of time that consumers and producers have to make adjustments, the greater the adjustments they will find it economical to make. For reasons discussed in Chapter 3, the long-run price elasticity of market demand for the *final* product is likely to be greater than the short-run price elasticity. Hence, the longer the time frame, the more powerful the output effect on derived demand.

A long period of adjustment also increases the scope for factor substitution, as we already have discussed and the following example further illustrates. In the 1970s, the price of jet fuel increased dramatically. In the short run, airlines responded by doing things like washing their aircraft more frequently in order to reduce wind resistance and improve the mileage of their planes (in a sense, the airlines substituted soapy water for jet fuel). In the medium run, some airlines stopped painting their planes, since the paint added several hundred pounds of weight to the aircraft. In the long run (in this case a period of almost 10 years) airlines turned to planes with expensive but lightweight materials, such as carbon-fiber wing panels. This increasing factor substitution led to a steady decline in the number of gallons of jet fuel used to produce a seat-mile of airline service.

In summary, when the output effect (induced by the substitution made by buyers of the *output*) and the factor substitution effect work in the same direction, the longer the time frame, the more elastic is the input demand.

The Importance of the Factor in Total Costs of Production When a factor accounts for only a tiny fraction of the total cost of the output, a firm is unlikely to make a large adjustment in its level of output solely because the price of that factor has risen.[4] Consider airline services again. Many factors are used in the production of airline services. Measured in terms of the amount spent on them, aviation fuel is one of the most important inputs. Fuel expenditures can be as much as 20 percent of an airline's costs. When the price of jet fuel rises, the airlines' costs rise significantly, which leads to an increase in air fares and a reduction in the number of passenger-miles flown. In early 1990, American, United, and several other major carriers announced fare increases of 10 percent in response to higher fuel prices. In contrast to the cost of aviation fuel, an airline spends only pennies per passenger on plastic forks to accompany in-flight meals.[5] Even if the cost of plastic forks doubled, it would have little effect on airline ticket prices or the amount of flying. Consequently, the output effect is significant in

[4]Theoretically, a change in a relatively insignificant factor could lead to a large total output effect if the industry demand for the output of the firms demanding the input were extremely elastic.

[5]A typical major airline spent a total of $4.45 per passenger on food in 1995 (McDowell 1996, F7).

Figure 11.21

Total Surplus in the Wine Market

Consumer surplus is the area below the demand curve and above the price line, shaded area *A*. Producer surplus is the area above the supply curve and below the price line, shaded area *B*. Total surplus is the sum of areas *A* and *B*.

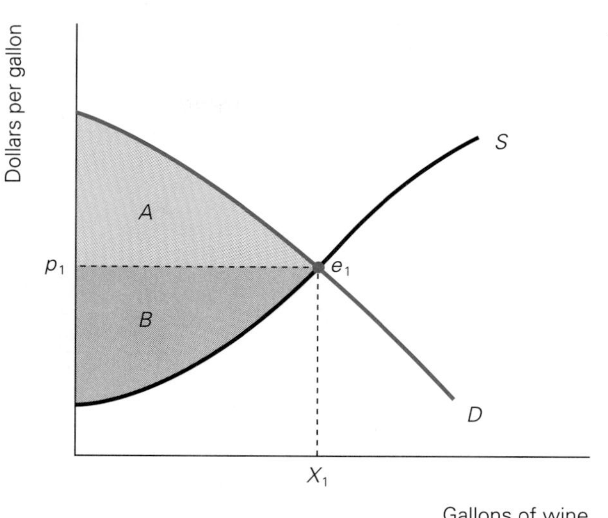

the airlines' derived demand for aviation fuel, but not in their derived demand for plastic forks.

SECTION RECAP

The following steps summarize how to do comparative statics with the competitive market model:

1. Sketch the original equilibrium that holds before there are any changes in the underlying market conditions.
2. Given a change in underlying market conditions, such as the imposition of a tax, figure out whether the supply curve or the demand curve is affected.
3. Determine the direction of the shift in the affected curve.
4. Find the new equilibrium at the intersection of the new supply and demand curves.

By applying this procedure, we have seen that the price elasticities of supply and demand are important determinants of the effects of many government policies.

11.3 NORMATIVE ANALYSIS OF PERFECT COMPETITION

Until now, this chapter has examined how a competitive market operates. In many situations, however, we want to know not only how a competitive market works, but also whether the results are in some sense "good." In this section, we consider one measure of how well a market performs.

TOTAL SURPLUS AS A MEASURE OF PERFORMANCE

Our measure of market performance is based on conventional supply and demand diagrams. Figure 11.21 depicts the supply and demand curves for wine, *S* and *D*,

Figure 11.22

Total Surplus Is Equal to Total Willingness to Pay Minus Total Cost

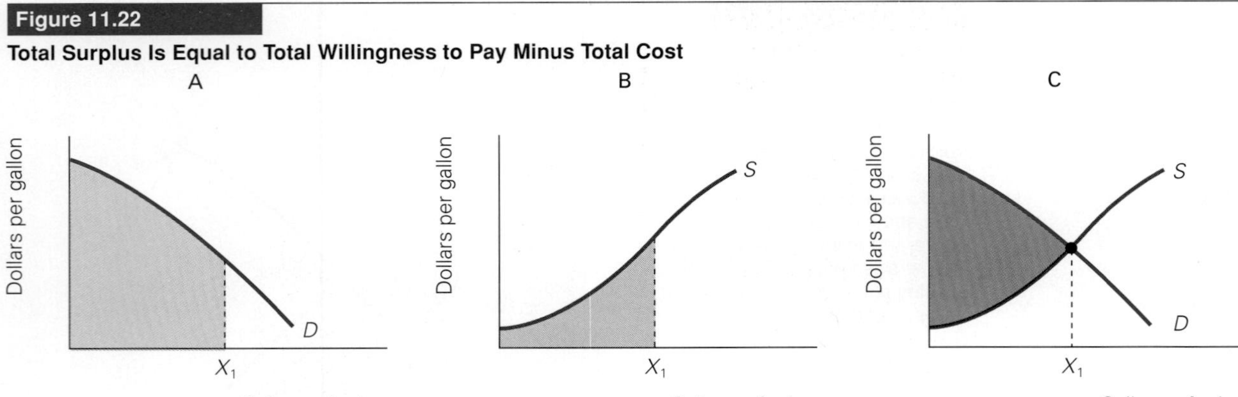

The total benefit derived from consuming X_1 gallons of wine is the shaded area in Panel A. The total cost of producing X_1 gallons of wine is the shaded area in Panel B. Taking the difference, total surplus is the shaded area in Panel C.

respectively. As shown earlier, if the wine market is competitive, then in equilibrium X_1 gallons of wine are exchanged at a price of p_1 per gallon. What is the gain to consumers from being able to purchase that amount of wine at this price? Chapter 4 showed that the gain is equal to their consumer surplus, depicted graphically as the area below the demand curve and above the price for each unit that is purchased, shaded area A in Figure 11.21.[6] In the same way, the gain to producers from being able to sell quantity X_1 at a price per gallon of p_1 is their producer surplus, area B. From society's point of view, the total gain is the sum of the consumer and the producer surplus, or areas A plus B. This sum of consumer and producer surplus is known as **total surplus.**

total surplus
The sum of consumer and producer surplus.

Total surplus can also be viewed as the total benefits derived from consumption of the good minus the total costs of producing it. The total benefit derived from consuming X_1 gallons of wine is the area under the willingness-to-pay schedule (the demand curve) up to the quantity consumed, the shaded area in Panel A of Figure 11.22. The total cost of producing X_1 gallons of wine is equal to the area under the marginal cost curve up to the quantity produced, the shaded area in Panel B. Taking the difference, total surplus is the shaded area in Panel C. Notice that this area equals the sum of areas A and B in Figure 11.21, as it should, since the areas in the two diagrams are measuring the same thing.

The same procedure can be used to compute the total surplus associated with any quantity of wine. It is the area under the demand curve and above the marginal cost curve up to the particular quantity consumed. Hence, we can associate with any level of output the amount of total surplus it generates.

Now that we have total surplus as a measure of market performance, a key question is whether total surplus is maximized at the competitive equilibrium. If some other allocation had a higher total surplus, then output level X_1 would not

[6]As noted in Chapter 4, consumer surplus is only an approximation to the welfare gain as long as income effects are not zero. We shall assume that income effects are sufficiently small so that the approximation is adequate.

Figure 11.23

Total Surplus in the Wine Market Is Greatest When Total Output Is at the Competitive Level

Total surplus in the wine market is greatest when total output is equal to the perfectly competitive equilibrium level X_1. Lowering output from X_1 to X_a would lower total surplus by area G. Raising output from X_1 to X_h would lower total surplus by area J.

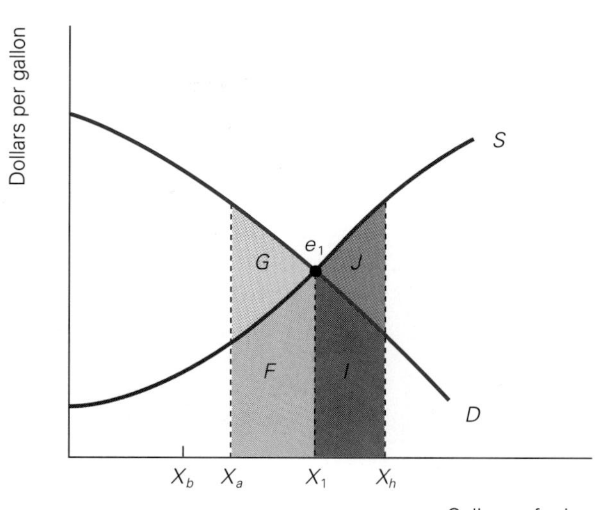

be efficient because it would be possible to make consumers and producers collectively better off. If, on the other hand, there is no alternative that leads to a higher level of total surplus, then the competitive equilibrium is efficient in this sense.

To see whether the competitive equilibrium maximizes total surplus, let's begin by considering output level X_a in Figure 11.23. X_a is less than the competitive level. How do the corresponding levels of total surplus compare? That is, as we move from X_a to X_1, does total surplus increase or decrease? We must consider both the incremental benefits and costs of the move. To consumers, the benefit of consuming the additional $X_1 - X_a$ gallons (ignoring, for the moment, the cost) is the area under the demand curve between X_a and X_1. This area is equal to the sum of shaded areas F and G in the figure. Graphically, the cost of supplying the additional output is given by the area under the supply curve from X_a to X_1, area F. The figure indicates that the gain in consumption benefits exceeds the additional cost by area G. Hence, total surplus is greater when the quantity of the good exchanged in the market is at the competitive equilibrium level rather than at X_a. (PC 11.6)

11.6 PROGRESS CHECK

Compare the level of total surplus under the competitive equilibrium with the level of total surplus when total output is X_b.

The same approach can be used to show that any other level of output below X_1 is also too small in the sense that total surplus would be higher at the competitive output level. In moving from a lower output level to X_1, the value of the additional output, as measured by consumers' willingness to pay, exceeds its cost.

Let's consider an output level exceeding the competitive level, such as X_h in Figure 11.23. To determine whether increasing output from X_1 to X_h is desirable from society's point of view, we must again consider its incremental benefits and costs. The benefit to consumers of the additional $X_b - X_1$ gallons is the area under the demand curve between X_1 and X_b, shaded in area I. The cost of supplying this additional quantity is the area under the supply curve from X_1 to X_b, the sum of areas I and J. Hence, the cost to suppliers exceeds the gain to consumers by area J. That is, the net result of exchanging more than the equilibrium quantity is to lower total surplus. While allowing individuals to consume more wine does indeed increase their gross consumption benefits, this increase is not enough to offset the cost of producing the additional wine. The same argument can be used to show that any other output level greater than X_1 yields less total surplus.

We have seen that total surplus is lower whenever industry output is either less than or greater than the competitive equilibrium level. We conclude that *in a competitive market, total surplus is maximized at the equilibrium output level.* This is an important finding. It tells us that under the conditions of perfect competition, markets do a good job (as measured by total surplus) of allocating society's resources. Of course, this result does not guarantee that the conditions of perfect competition always hold. As we will see in the following chapters, they often do not. Even in those situations, however, this result is useful because it provides a benchmark against which to compare market performance under other conditions.

Are Value Judgments Being Made?

In addition to questioning whether the conditions of perfect competition really hold, you might also wonder about the validity of total surplus as a measure of market performance. Implicit in our use of total surplus is the claim that society is best off when the total surplus is maximized. But you might be worried that there is some kind of value judgment behind that claim. If you are, you are correct; there is. The value judgment is that a dollar to each person is given the same weight, whether that person is a consumer or producer, rich or poor. When the price of a good rises, consumers lose surplus and the producers gain. Our total surplus measure is based on the *net* change in dollar benefits. Suppose that consumers lose \$100 of surplus and producers gain \$100 of profit. Total surplus is unchanged—the gains and losses exactly cancel one another, so "society" is neither better nor worse off. However, if consumers tend to be low-income households and the producers are relatively wealthy individuals, you may well consider this transfer of income to be socially undesirable. The total surplus measure does not capture such distributional concerns.

Thus, maximizing total surplus leads to an outcome that is efficient, but not necessarily "fair." In the light of this fact, is total surplus a useful measure of social well-being? The justification for this approach is that once total surplus is maximized, it can be redistributed later in accord with the community's notions of fairness—make the pie as big as possible and then worry about dividing it. Maximizing total surplus is a first step, with redistributing income a second. This procedure is reasonable as long as we believe that there would not be much of a shift in the supply and demand curves if income were redistributed fairly. When this condition is satisfied (as economists assume it is in most practical situations), the appropriate first step does not depend on the particular second step chosen. Hence, evaluating alternative allocations on the basis of the total amount of surplus they provide often is a sensible procedure.

Prices versus Quantities and Their Roles in Attaining Efficiency

We have been comparing the level of total surplus under competitive equilibrium with the surplus levels that would arise at different market *quantities*, but we have said nothing about *prices* because if we know what the quantity is, then we have all the information needed to calculate total surplus.

Does this mean that prices are unimportant? No, it does not. Prices play important roles in a competitive market where consumers and producers make their consumption and production choices taking the market price as given. Prices convey information to suppliers and demanders, and they generate incentives guiding production and consumption. Thus, in competitive markets, prices affect quantity decisions and thus (indirectly) affect total surplus.

Another role for prices is to transfer income from consumers to producers. Unlike the other roles, this one does not really matter for efficiency—*for a given quantity*, a change in the price merely results in a transfer of surplus, not net creation or loss of surplus. Of course, consumers and producers are interested not just in the total amount of surplus, but also in their shares of the total. These shares depend on prices.

The roles of prices and their differing effects on total surplus (and its components, producer surplus and consumer surplus), can be seen by considering two examples. In the first example, government policy influences price directly. In the second, government policy has an indirect influence on price.

EVALUATING RENT CONTROL

What do New York, Paris, and Berkeley have in common? All have rent control laws. In practice, rent control laws can be very complicated, but their main feature is that they stipulate maximum rents that landlords can collect from tenants. Supporters of rent control argue that the imposition of price ceilings helps tenants by ensuring that they can rent housing at low prices. Detractors, however, argue that rent control makes it impossible for any but a lucky few to obtain rental housing, and that in the end it actually reduces the amount of housing available. We can use the competitive model to get a handle on the effects of rent control.

To model the market for rental housing, think of each apartment as generating a certain amount of *housing services.* The quantity of housing services depends on such factors as the size of the apartment, the quality of the plumbing, and how well it is maintained. In Figure 11.24, D is the demand for housing services in a particular city and S is the supply. The demand curve for housing slopes downward because as the price per unit of housing services goes up, people want smaller, lower-quality apartments. The supply curve slopes upward because when the price of housing services goes up, landlords are induced to build more housing as well as to maintain better existing structures. From Figure 11.24 we see that in the absence of rent control, the competitive equilibrium quantity of housing services is X_1 and the market rental rate is p_1. What about surplus? Graphically, consumer surplus is the area below the demand curve and above the price line up to the market quantity. Hence, in the absence of rent control, consumer surplus is the sum of areas A and B. Producer surplus is the area below the price line and above the supply curve up to the market quantity, the sum of areas C, D, and E in Figure 11.24.

Figure 11.24

The Effects of Rent Control on Consumer and Producer Surplus

In the absence of rent control, the competitive equilibrium is at point e_1. Imposition of a rent ceiling equal to $\bar{p}$ lowers the quantity of housing supplied from X_1 to X_a. Total surplus falls by the sum of areas B and D as a result.

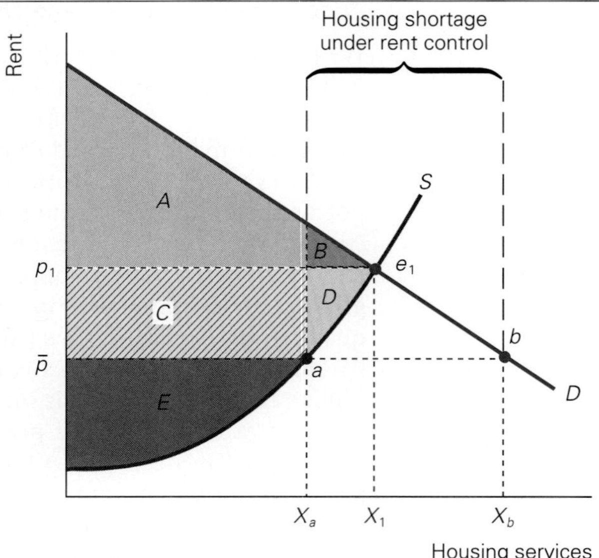

Now suppose that a rent ceiling of $\bar{p}$ is imposed, and that it is effectively enforced so that no one can cheat.[7] Figure 11.24 indicates that when the price is $\bar{p}$, the quantity demanded is X_b. But at price $\bar{p}$, the most that suppliers will provide is X_a. Since X_b is greater than X_a, there is a shortage of $X_b - X_a$ units of housing services.

How large is this gap? The answer depends on how responsive supply and demand are to price changes. That is, on the elasticities of demand and supply. In the short run, the supply of housing may be quite inelastic—there is little else that landlords can do with their apartment buildings because rent control laws usually restrict owners' ability to sell their buildings as condominiums. As long as the rental ceiling is greater than short-run average variable cost, landlords will continue to rent in the short run. In the long run, however, the quantity supplied is much more responsive to price. As existing buildings wear down, owners may be unwilling to undertake the needed maintenance. As old buildings are torn down, the land may be used for office buildings rather than for replacement apartments. Poterba (1984) has estimated the long-run price elasticity of supply for housing to be about 2.0. If this estimate is correct, it tells us that a rent control policy that keeps the price 10 percent below the free-market level would lead to a 20 percent fall in the total amount of rental housing supplied. Because the elasticity of demand is positive—so that a fall in the price will increase the quantity demanded—the gap can be very substantial indeed.

[7]Cheating can come in many forms. Shortly before Berkeley's rent control law went into effect, one landlord founded the First National German American Sebastian Kneipp and Mineral Water Church. To become a tenant, you must become a member of the church—for a $1,200 fee that you pay to the landlord—and you must promise not to engage in " 'loud solo or choir singing' before 8:00 A.M. or after 10:00 P.M." (Rauber 1990, 2).

We are now in a position to use this model to find out who benefits and who loses from rent control. In the absence of rent control, the price is p_1 and the market quantity is X_1. Under the rent control regime, the price falls to $\overline{p}$ and the quantity falls to X_a. These price and quantity changes lead to changes in producer, consumer, and total surplus.

- *Producers are worse off with rent control.* Producer surplus is the area below the new price line and above the supply curve up to the new market quantity, shaded area E in Figure 11.24. In the absence of rent control, producer surplus was the sum of areas C, D, and E. Producer surplus has fallen, and the fall has two components. Shaded rectangle C represents the loss to producers from having to rent X_a apartments at a lower price under rent control. Area D represents the loss from the fact that at the lower rent, it is not worth supplying as many apartments as before.
- *Some households are better off because of rent control.* Those consumers who are lucky enough to obtain apartments under rent control are better off by an amount equal to the reduction in rent times the number of units rented. The price falls from p_1 to $\overline{p}$ on X_a units, so this gain to consumers is shaded rectangle C in Figure 11.24.
- *Some households lose from rent control.* There are people who would have been willing to pay the competitive price, p_1, and who would have gotten an apartment in a free market, but who do not get apartments when rent control is imposed and the quantity of housing supplied falls. The only effect of rent control on these people is to shut them out of the housing market. Their lost surplus is area B in Figure 11.24.

While those people who get an apartment under the controlled price gain from rent control, landlords and people who are unable to obtain apartments lose. This contrast opens the obvious question: On balance, do the gains outweigh the losses? Is rent control a "good" policy?

Supporters of rent control in the city government of Berkeley tried to answer this question by conducting a survey of people living in rent-controlled apartments. Not surprisingly, these people favored rent control. As our surplus analysis tells us, these are exactly the people who gain from rent control. To measure the effects of rent control correctly, we have to compare the gains of these renters with the losses suffered by the landlords and those households who get frozen out of the rental market.

A total surplus measure provides a valuable framework for making this comparison. In terms of surplus analysis, our central question can be rephrased: Does rent control raise or lower total surplus? To answer this question, we need to add up the effects on consumers and suppliers. As just discussed, those consumers who obtain apartments under rent control are better off by an amount equal to the reduction in rent times the number of units rented, area C. But this area does not represent a net gain to society because area C is equal to the loss suffered by landlords from having to rent out X_a apartments at the lower price. In other words, area C is merely a *transfer* of income from landlords to this group of tenants—it does not represent any net change in total surplus. The only net effects of rent control are the losses suffered by those renters who are unable to obtain apartments as a result (area B) and the additional losses suffered by landlords from the reduction in the quantity of housing that they rent (area D). *As a*

Figure 11.25

Excess Burden of a Wine Tax

From the buyers' perspective, the tax on wine shifts the supply curve upward by \$3. The equilibrium shifts from e_1 to e_2. As a result of the tax, total surplus falls by area *E*, which is referred to as the excess burden of the tax.

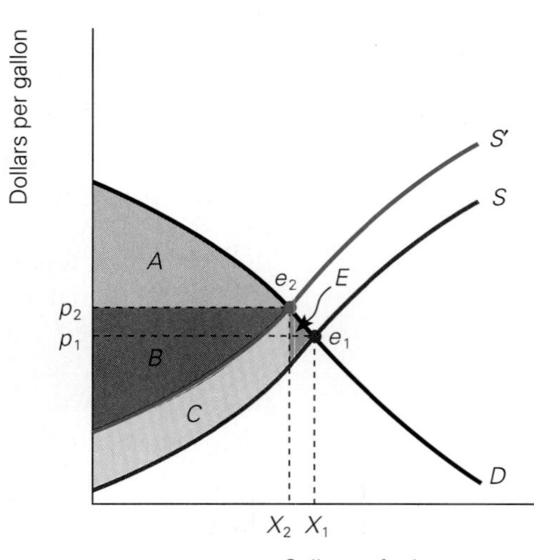

result of rent control, total surplus falls by the sum of areas B and D.[8] Intuitively, we see that people would have been willing to purchase the $X_1 - X_a$ units of housing services eliminated by rent control at a price that producers would have been willing to accept. By eliminating these opportunities for mutually beneficial trade, rent control lowers total welfare.

NORMATIVE ANALYSIS OF A SALES TAX

Earlier, we saw that the relative price elasticities of supply and demand determine how the burden of a tax is split between buyers and sellers. Here, we will use our surplus analysis to say more about the overall burden of a tax.

Let's look at the effects of the federal tax on wine. In the absence of any taxation, the equilibrium is at the intersection of the market supply and demand curves graphed in Figure 11.25. Prior to the imposition of the tax, the equilibrium price and quantity of wine are p_1 and X_1, respectively. The resulting total surplus is the sum of the shaded areas *A, B, C,* and *E.*

Suppose that a unit tax of \$3 per gallon of wine is imposed on each purchase. As shown in Figure 11.14, from the buyers' perspective, this tax shifts the supply curve upward by \$3, and the new equilibrium quantity is where the demand curve and the new supply curve cross, point e_2 in Figure 11.25. The after-tax equilibrium quantity is X_2.

What is the resulting level of total surplus? It is tempting to say "the sum of shaded areas *A* and *B.*" If this answer were correct, then we would say that total surplus had fallen by the sum of areas *C* and *E.* But this approach misses an important point—the tax revenues collected are not a true cost to society. The revenues are simply a transfer from wine producers and consumers to the

[8]The loss of total surplus from rent control could be even higher. In the figure, we have assumed that those who most desire apartments are the ones who get them. But with rent control, there is no guarantee that the consumers who value rental units the most are the ones who rent them.

government. Put another way, when the government is involved in the market, even if only indirectly, we have to be sure to include government surplus in our calculation of total surplus for the market. The government's surplus is the tax revenue that it collects. Here, the tax revenue collected is equal to \$3 times the number of gallons sold after the tax has been imposed, which is shaded area *C* in Figure 11.25. Since it is a pure transfer, area *C* represents neither a gain nor a loss in total surplus.

Where does all of this leave us? Since the total surplus is the area under the demand curve and above the marginal cost curve up to the market quantity, we see that after-tax total surplus is the sum of areas *A*, *B*, and *C*. Total surplus has fallen by area *E*. Intuitively, by distorting prices, the unit tax on wine induces consumers to buy, and producers to sell, less than the competitive equilibrium level of output. Consequently, even though producers would be willing to supply an additional $X_1 - X_2$ gallons of wine for less than the amount that consumers would be willing to pay for them, these gallons are not produced and consumed. By blocking these mutually beneficial trades, the tax lowers total surplus by area *E*. This loss above what is collected in tax revenue is known as the **excess burden** of the tax. This loss is also known as a *deadweight loss* because it is a loss to firms and households that is not offset by a gain to the government collecting the tax.[9] (PC 11.7)

excess burden
The amount by which the loss of surplus suffered by consumers and producers exceeds the tax revenue collected.

11.7 PROGRESS CHECK

Draw a graph on which you show the change in consumer surplus that results from the imposition of the tax. Draw a second graph on which you show the change in producer surplus that results from the imposition of the tax.

SECTION RECAP

Total surplus is an important measure of market performance. It is equal to the net difference between total consumption benefits (as measured by the area under the demand curve) and total production costs (as measured by the area under the supply curve). Total surplus is greatest when the quantity traded in the market is equal to the competitive equilibrium level. Any policy that distorts total output away from the competitive level will lower total surplus.

SUMMARY

This chapter examines the perfect competition model, which provides a useful framework for analyzing the behavior of many important markets.

- The competitive model relies on four fundamental assumptions: (1) sellers are price takers; (2) sellers do not behave strategically; (3) entry into the market is free; and (4) buyers are price takers.
- The fundamental assumptions underlying the competitive model are most likely to be valid when: (a) there are many buyers; (b) there are many sellers; (c) the outputs of different suppliers are close substitutes; (d) buyers are well-informed about the available alternatives; and (e) new firms face neither technological nor legal barriers to their entering the market.
- In the short run, the number of firms in the industry is fixed. Market supply and demand curves are determined by horizontally summing individual curves. The market equilibrium is determined by the intersection of the market supply and market demand curves.

[9]We also used the term *deadweight loss* in Chapter 4 to refer to the pure waste associated with a trade quota. In each case, it represents a loss for which there is no offsetting gain.

- In the long run, the number of firms in a market varies in response to market conditions. In a product market where the industry as a whole takes input prices as given and all firms have the same cost curves, the long-run supply curve is flat at a price equal to the minimal value of average cost.
- The long-run supply curve is upward sloping in a product market in which increased demand for inputs by the entire industry drives up the prices of these inputs. The equilibrium price and output level still are found by taking the intersection of the market supply and demand curves.
- The long-run supply curve is upward sloping in a market in which suppliers have heterogeneous costs. In equilibrium, the marginal firm active in the market earns zero economic profit.
- The perfectly competitive equilibrium results in the level of output that maximizes total surplus.
- The perfectly competitive model indicates that the effects of a tax or a price ceiling may be very different from the effects intended by policymakers.

DISCUSSION QUESTIONS

11.1 Consider the market for snails in China. There are many buyers, no one of which accounts for a large part of the market. There are many suppliers in the market as well—you can raise them right in your apartment. Moreover, the snails of different farmers are close substitutes, and the buyers are well informed (they are professionals who export the snails that they purchase to France). The government allows snail growing, little skill is needed, you can build a snail corral yourself, and there are people who are happy to show you everything you need to know to raise snails. Is this market one for which the competitive model is appropriate? Explain whether each of the fundamental assumptions underlying the perfectly competitive model holds.

11.2 Consider a market in which the short-run market supply curve is upward sloping, but the long-run supply curve is flat. Why do the two curves look so different from one another?

11.3 Consider a competitive industry consisting of 100 identical firms, each of which has the following cost schedule:

Output:	0	1	2	3	4	5
Total cost:	300	400	450	510	590	700

Output:	6	7	8	9
Total cost:	840	1020	1250	1540

Market demand is given by the following schedule:

Price:	360	290	230	180	140	110	80
Quantity:	400	500	600	700	800	900	1000

a. Draw the supply curve for an individual firm. On a separate graph, draw the supply and demand curves for the industry as a whole. Indicate the equilibrium price and output. Now draw the individual firm's demand curve on the first graph and show the firm's equilibrium price and output.

b. Explain why the equilibrium found in (*a*) is a short-run equilibrium only. What will happen in the long run? Describe the long-run equilibrium in as much detail as possible.

11.4 A friend was once looking for an apartment in New York City and found one under rent control that was, for New York at least, very cheap. The apartment came with furniture: a broken bed, an old table, and two chairs. To rent the apartment you had to buy the furniture. Its selling price was $10,000. Someone did indeed rent the apartment and buy the furniture at this price. Explain what is going on here.

Draw supply and demand curves for rental housing that have the usual shapes. On this figure, illustrate what the going price for furniture rental would be.

11.5 *The Florida Chainsaw Massacre.* When hurricane Andrew struck the East Coast of the United States in 1992, it did tremendous damage. Florida was particularly hard hit, and trees fell across many roads and onto people's houses. As a result, the demand for chainsaws increased tremendously. Moreover, it was difficult for companies to ship additional chainsaws to their retail outlets to add to their inventories. What effects would you expect these occurrences to have on the price of chainsaws and the quantity sold?

In response to all of this, the attorney general of Florida prosecuted firms for price gouging if they charged more than the prehurricane price for a chainsaw. What effect would you expect this policy to have on the market for chainsaws in Florida? Can you see any problems with this policy?

11.6 Since the Fair Labor Standards Act was passed in 1938, the U.S. government has set a lower limit on the wages that many employers can pay their workers. Since 1997, that limit has been $5.15 per hour. Proponents of the minimum wage argue that it is vital for protecting low-income workers and ensuring that they receive a decent wage for their labor. Opponents argue that it unfairly drives firms' costs above the free-market level and hurts workers by reducing the number of jobs. Use a supply and demand model of the labor market to analyze the effects of the minimum wage and assess the validity of these competing claims. (*Hint:* A minimum wage price floor can be analyzed along the lines used in the chapter to examine a rent control price ceiling.)

11.7 In problem 11.6 you should have found that a minimum wage harms employers, helps some workers, and hurts others. How do these effects add up? In other words, what effect does the minimum wage have on the level of total surplus? Does imposition of a minimum wage law lead to an efficient outcome?

11.8 Suppose that you owned a firm that makes the cases for clones of IBM personal computers. Would you expect the demand for your output to be elastic or inelastic? What about the market demand curve faced collectively by all the manufacturers of computer cases?

11.9 From time to time, the United States government has considered taxing gasoline in an effort to stimulate conservation. Use supply and demand analysis to illustrate the effects of such a tax on consumers and producers.

11.10 In the United States, 6,000 different companies offer credit cards; The single largest issuer has only 4 percent of the market. (Despite the fact that your card may say "MasterCard" or "Visa," they are essentially clearing houses.) In late 1991, the U.S. Senate voted to cap the interest rate on credit cards at 14 percent. Eventually, the Bush administration and the banking industry managed to kill the idea (Rosenbaum 1991, E2). Suppose the Senate bill had become law. What would have been the effect on consumer surplus, producer surplus, and total surplus in the market for credit borrowing?

11.11 In 1992, the Russian government under President Boris Yeltsin allowed the prices of most commodities to be determined by the market, but continued to set ceilings on some basic goods such as certain foods and fuels. A journalist noted that "*Even at* the controlled prices, basic goods have been scarce. . ." (Schmemann 1992, A1, italics added). Explain why, as it stands, the journalist's statement betrays a lack of understanding of how competitive markets operate. What replacements to the italicized words would make the statement sensible?

11.12 Israeli immigrant Shy Oogav thought he was living the American dream on South Padre Island, Texas, back in 1993. Within a year of buying a T-shirt printing shop, he had been able to use the initial profits to buy out his partner and repay the bank. What he didn't foresee was that the number of T-shirt stores in South Padre would jump from roughly 10 to 40 within two years. Now he laments, "Every day you have to compete with other shops," and it is difficult to earn a profit (Pawlosky 1995, B1). Explain why Mr. Oogav should have seen his problems coming.

CHAPTER 12

General Equilibrium and Welfare Economics

> *The highest and best form of efficiency is the spontaneous cooperation of a free people.*
>
> —Bernard Baruch

The U.S. government began a serious battle against the cigarette industry in the 1990s. One might think that the only affected businesses would be in tobacco-growing states like Virginia and North Carolina, but the effects were felt throughout the economy. The trucking industry was hurt because of reductions in cigarette shipments. Corner grocery stores that depended on cigarette sales found their existence jeopardized. "Everyone you know is once-removed from the tobacco industry," said one analyst, perhaps with some exaggeration (Ono 1995, A1). Firms that pasted up billboard ads were worse off because of restrictions on cigarette advertising, but other advertisers were made better off by the lower rates. Reductions in cigarette consumption changed the demands for various kinds of health care personnel, and the fortunes of firms that sold substitutes for cigarettes improved.

The distinctive aspect of this episode is that the effects of the anticigarette crusade spilled over from one market into others. Hence, to understand the crusade's consequences, we must analyze different markets together. The last chapter was devoted to looking at equilibrium in one market in isolation, known as **partial equilibrium analysis.** In this chapter, we study the equilibrium of all markets simultaneously, referred to as **general equilibrium analysis.**

partial equilibrium analysis
The study of equilibrium in one market in isolation.

general equilibrium analysis
The study of the equilibrium of all markets simultaneously.

General equilibrium analysis gives us a sense of how the various pieces of an economy fit together to work *as a whole*. In addition to knowing how the system operates, we also want to find out if it produces "good" results. The second part of the chapter therefore discusses *welfare economics*, the branch of economics concerned with the social desirability of alternative economic states. Welfare economics provides a set of criteria for evaluating an economic system.

Figure 12.1

General Equilibrium with Supply and Demand Curves

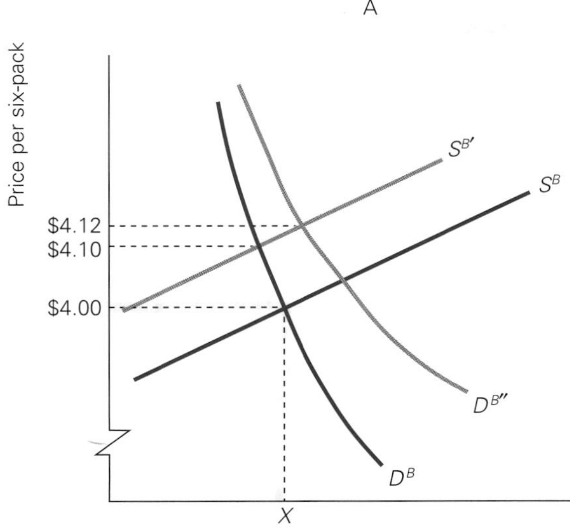

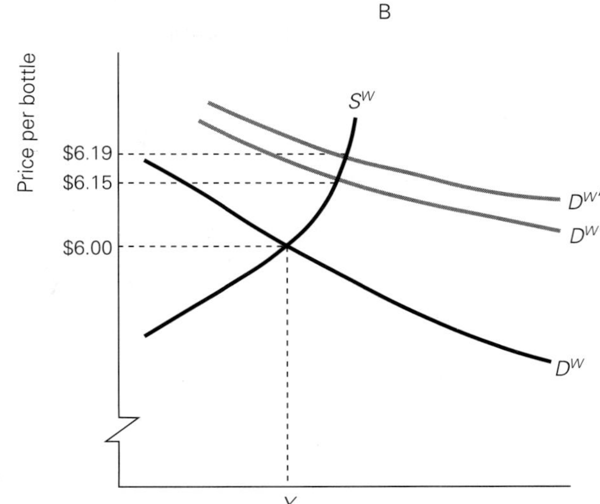

Initially, the economy is in equilibrium when the price of beer is $4.00 per six-pack and the price of wine is $6.00 per bottle. The tax initially raises the price of beer from $4.00 to $4.10. This shifts the demand for wine from D^W to $D^{W'}$; increasing the price of wine to $6.15, which in turn shifts the demand for beer to $D^{B''}$. Ultimately, the economy settles down to a new general equilibrium.

12.1 GENERAL EQUILIBRIUM ANALYSIS

SUPPLY AND DEMAND CURVES

General equilibrium spillovers can occur with any market structures. In this chapter, however, our focus is on competitive markets that can be analyzed using the familiar supply and demand model.

A nice application is provided by the 16¢ increase in the tax per six-pack of beer that was levied by the federal government in 1991. In Panel A of Figure 12.1, D^B and S^B are the demand and supply curves, respectively, for beer before the tax. The equilibrium price is $4 per six-pack, and the associated output is X. Panel B depicts the market for wine, a substitute for beer. Prior to the beer tax, D^W is the demand curve for wine, S^W is the supply curve, the equilibrium price is $6 per bottle, and output is Y. Assuming that all the other markets in the economy were also in equilibrium before the tax increase, then $4 per six-pack of beer and $6 per bottle of wine were a set of general equilibrium prices, meaning that they were consistent with equilibrium in every market.

Now comes the beer tax. As shown in Chapter 11, the imposition of a unit tax raises the supply schedule as perceived by consumers by exactly the amount of the tax, in this case 16¢. The new supply schedule is $S^{B'}$, and we find the new price facing consumers at the intersection of $S^{B'}$ and D^B—$4.10 per six-pack.

If this were a partial equilibrium analysis, we would be done. But in a general equilibrium model, we must take into account linkages to other markets. Specifically, because beer is a substitute for wine, an increase in the price of beer increases the demand for wine. In Panel B, the demand curve shifts from D^W to $D^{W'}$, and the new price per bottle is \$6.15.

Are the new general equilibrium prices \$4.10 per six-pack of beer and \$6.15 per bottle of wine? No. Remember that the original demand curve for beer is found by varying the price of beer and holding everything else constant, including the prices of related goods (see Chapter 3). This means that D^B is drawn on the assumption that the price of wine, a substitute, is at its original value of \$6.00. When the price of wine increases from \$6.00 to \$6.15, the demand for beer shifts outward, from D^B to $D^{B''}$. The new equilibrium price of beer is determined by the intersection of $S^{B'}$ and $D^{B''}$ at \$4.12. But the change in the price of beer from \$4.10 to \$4.12 induces another shift in the demand for wine, from $D^{W'}$ to $D^{W''}$, which affects the price of wine, which in turn affects the price of beer, and so on. In each round of adjustments, the feedback effects become smaller and smaller. Ultimately, a new set of prices for beer and wine is found so that the quantity supplied for each equals its quantity demanded.

The general equilibrium analysis of Figure 12.1 ignores other possible linkages. Changes in wine prices could affect the demand for grapes, which could affect the demand for agricultural workers, which could affect flows of immigration, and so on. Conceivably, every market in the economy might be affected, not only the two depicted in the figure. Nevertheless, our simple model well illustrates two important insights of general equilibrium theory:

1. The markets for two goods are linked if the two items are "related" (substitutes or complements) or if one of them is an input into the production of the other. When markets are linked, a shift in the supply or demand curve in one market has consequences for price and output in the second market. Thus, when policymakers consider intervention in one market (e.g., a tax or regulation), they should try to think about the effects in other markets as well.
2. Suppose that the commodities *X* and *Y* are related, and there is a shift in either the supply or demand curve of commodity *X*. A partial equilibrium analysis of the effect of the shift may be in error because of feedback effects from the market for *Y*. For example, in Figure 12.1, Panel A, the ultimate price of beer is somewhat higher than the value of \$4.10 that would have been predicted when ignoring feedbacks.

12.1 PROGRESS CHECK

In 1995, insects devastated cotton crops in China, the world's biggest cotton grower. As a consequence, prices paid to U.S. cotton farmers increased by 40 percent. Trace the possible general equilibrium implications of this event.

This discussion of feedback effects might be somewhat distressing—it substantially complicates what was basically a very simple supply and demand exercise. Do you really have to consider what happens to every market in the whole world every time the supply or demand in one market changes? General equilibrium analysis tells us that feedbacks may occur, *not* that they are necessarily important. If the failure to take into account some feedback leads to a prediction that is off by a small percentage, then it doesn't matter very much and it is safe to use partial equilibrium analysis.

Having said this, we should also point out that in cases where there are large shifts in supply or demand in important sectors of the economy, ignoring linkages might lead to erroneous predictions. A good example is the Arab oil boycott of the early 1970s, which led to a drastic increase in crude oil prices and had important consequences in the markets for gasoline,

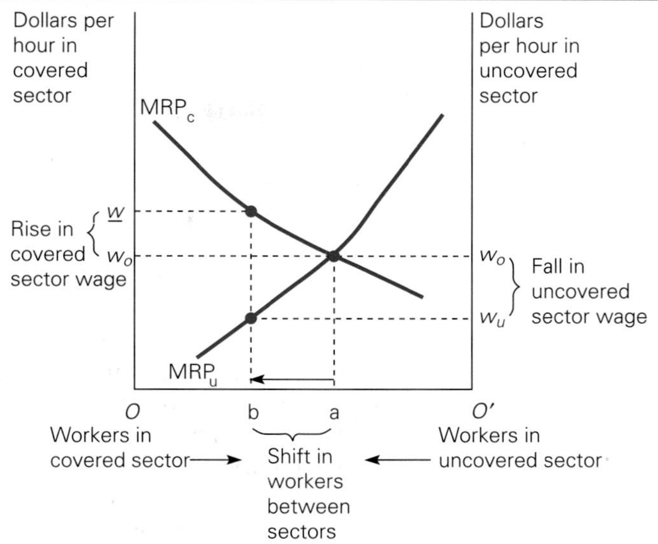

Figure 12.2

General Equilibrium Analysis of the Minimum Wage

In the absence of a minimum wage, the wage rate is w_0 in both sectors. When a minimum wage of $\underline{w}$ is imposed, employment in the covered sector decreases by *ab* workers. When these workers seek employment in the uncovered sector, the wage rate there falls from w_0 to w_u.

automobiles, home insulation material, and many other commodities. In deciding whether to apply partial or general equilibrium analysis to a particular problem, one must first think about whether the feedbacks are likely to be important. If they are, then a general equilibrium approach is required. (PC 12.1)

GENERAL EQUILIBRIUM AND THE MINIMUM WAGE

A *minimum wage law* sets a wage rate below which employers cannot pay their employees. The partial equilibrium analysis of minimum wage laws is straightforward using the supply and demand model of the labor market that was introduced in Chapter 1. Provided that the minimum wage exceeds the equilibrium wage, then at the minimum wage, the quantity demanded of labor is less than the quantity supplied. That is, all the workers who seek jobs at the minimum wage cannot find them, and unemployment results. The workers who are able to obtain employment at the minimum wage come out ahead, because they receive a higher wage. But those who lose their jobs altogether come out behind.

Behind this analysis is the assumption that all firms are covered by the minimum wage law, so that if an individual is thrown out of work by the law, he or she cannot obtain work elsewhere. In the United States, employees who work in small retail, service, and agricultural firms are not covered. Neither are workers in the "underground economy," which includes illegal activities as well as legal transactions that are not reported to evade taxation. Additional insights about the effects of the minimum wage can be gained by thinking about its impacts on two markets simultaneously—the market for labor in the *covered sector*, and the market for labor in the *uncovered sector*. To keep this general equilibrium analysis simple, we assume: (*a*) The *total* amount of labor supplied to the two sectors is fixed; (*b*) workers in both sectors have the same skill levels—for example, a handy person can work as well for a large corporation as work informally for homeowners; and (*c*) people work in whatever sector gives them the higher wage.

This situation is analyzed in Figure 12.2. The horizontal axis represents the total number of workers in the economy. The distance from point *O* measures the number of workers in the covered sector, and the distance from O' measures the number in the uncovered sector. Thus, as we move from left to right, the covered sector increases in size and the uncovered sector decreases.

The schedule MRP_c is the marginal revenue product of labor in the *c*overed sector; its downward slope reflects the diminishing marginal physical product of labor in the covered sector. MRP_u is labor's marginal revenue product in the *u*ncovered sector; as more labor enters the uncovered sector (i.e., as we move to the left), the marginal revenue product decreases there as well.

Now recall that under competition the wage rate equals the marginal revenue product of the last worker employed. Hence, under the three assumptions listed above, prior to the minimum wage each sector must pay the same wage rate. If not, then workers from the low-paying sector would enter the high-paying sector, raising the *MRP* (which equals the wage rate) in the former and lowering it in the latter. In the diagram, the initial wage rate in each sector is w_o; *Oa* workers work in the covered sector and $O'a$ in the uncovered sector.

Suppose now that a minimum wage of $\underline{w}$ is imposed on the covered sector. Because $\underline{w}$ exceeds w_0, every worker would prefer to work in the covered sector. However, at wage $\underline{w}$ firms find it in their interest to reduce employment by *ab* workers. What happens to these *ab* workers who no longer have jobs in the covered sector? Given our assumption that the total supply of labor is fixed, each of these workers seeks employment in the uncovered sector. Therefore, in addition to the $O'a$ workers who were there initially, the uncovered sector must absorb *ab* workers who are thrown out of the covered sector. As a consequence, the wage rate in the uncovered sector falls to w_u.

Figure 12.2 probably overstates the depressing effect of the minimum wage on the wage rate in the uncovered sector because some employees who lose their jobs in the covered sector may find it in their interest to stay unemployed, hoping that they will be lucky enough to find work in the covered sector at $\underline{w}$. With fewer workers going into the uncovered sector, the wage rate there would fall less than indicated in Figure 12.2—but it would still fall.

What lessons does this general equilibrium model provide? Like the partial equilibrium model, it shows that some workers gain and some workers lose under a minimum wage. The winners are still the workers who are lucky enough to get employment in the covered sector. Losers still include workers who used to work in the covered sector and either become unemployed or take jobs with lower wages in the uncovered sector. But the general equilibrium model provides an important new insight. Just because a worker is initially employed in the uncovered sector does not mean that he or she is unaffected by the minimum wage. To the contrary, the losers from the minimum wage include workers in the uncovered sector, whose wages go down because of the influx of workers from the covered sector.

GENERAL EQUILIBRIUM IN A PURE EXCHANGE ECONOMY

The analysis of general equilibrium using supply and demand curves provides valuable insights regarding the linkages between competitive markets. However, with its focus on *market* outcomes, supply and demand analysis tells us little about what is going on at the level of the individual decision maker. Moreover, shifting multiple sets of supply and demand curves is a somewhat unwieldy way

Figure 12.3

Edgeworth Box

Any point in the Edgeworth Box represents an allocation of commodities between two consumers. At point *v*, Cain consumes *Ox* loaves of bread and *Ou* gallons of wine; Abel consumes *O′y* loaves of bread and *O′w* gallons of wine.

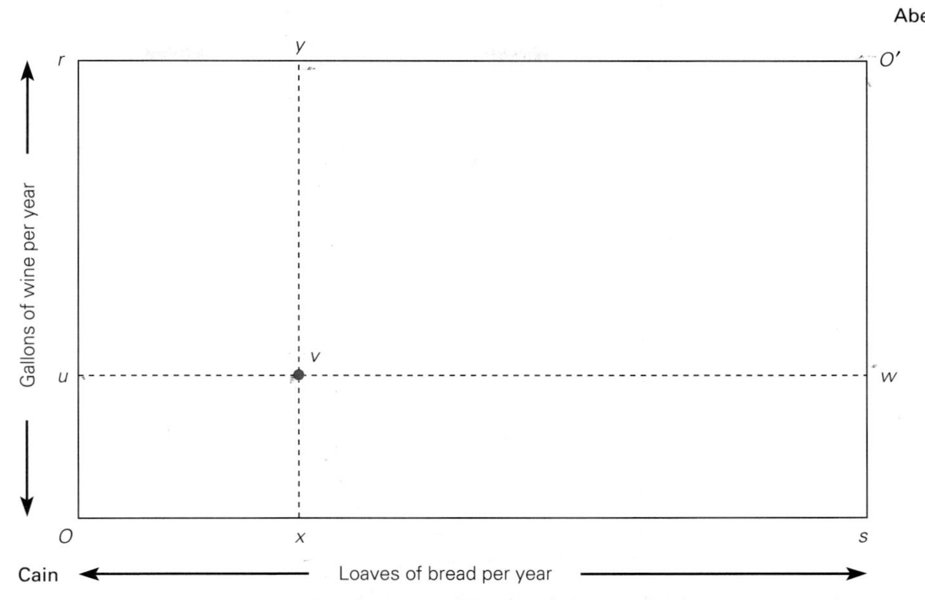

to study how the overall set of prices in the economy is determined. To get around these difficulties, we will employ a more fundamental level of analysis.

We begin by considering a very simple economy. Imagine an island that is inhabited by only two people, Cain and Abel. We assume that Cain and Abel consume two commodities—wine and bread, which are both fixed in total supply. By assuming that the supplies are totally fixed, we can ignore the production side of the economy. (We will return to the production side later.) With production momentarily out of the picture, the only economic problem is to allocate amounts of the two goods between the two people. Such a situation is called a **pure exchange economy**. As simple as this model is, all the important results from the two-good, two-person case hold in economies with many people and commodities.

pure exchange economy An economy in which the quantities supplied of all goods are fixed; the only economic problem is to allocate amounts of the goods among consumers.

Edgeworth Box

An analytical device known as the Edgeworth Box[1] is used to depict the allocation of bread and wine between Cain and Abel. In Figure 12.3 the length of the Edgeworth Box, *Os*, represents the total amount of bread available in the economy; the height, *Or*, is the total quantity of wine. The amounts of the goods consumed by Cain are measured by distances from point *O*; the quantities consumed by Abel are measured by distances from *O′*. For example, at point *v*, Cain consumes *Ou* gallons of wine and *Ox* loaves of bread, while Abel consumes *O′y* loaves of bread and *O′w* gallons of wine. Thus, any point within the Edgeworth Box represents some distribution of bread and wine between Cain and Abel.

Now assume that Cain and Abel each have a set of conventionally shaped indifference curves that depict their preferences for bread and wine. In

[1]Named after the great 19th-century economist F. Y. Edgeworth.

Figure 12.4

Indifference Curves in an Edgeworth Box

For Cain, higher levels of utility are represented by moves to the northeast; for Abel, to the southwest.

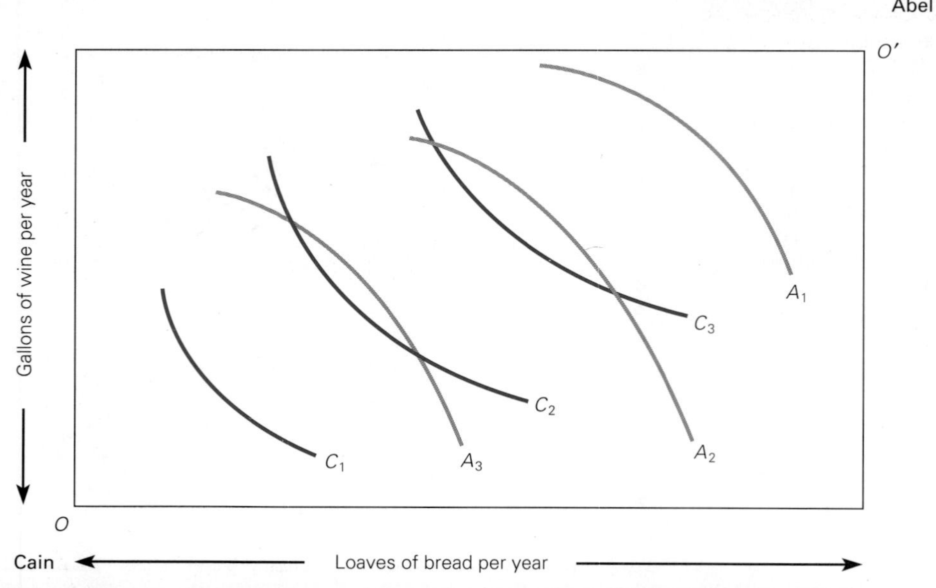

12.2 PROGRESS CHECK

A pure exchange economy is inhabited by two people, Louis and Marie. The economy is endowed with 1,000 apples and 500 oranges. Of these, Louis owns 750 apples and 200 oranges. Sketch an Edgeworth Box to depict this situation.

Figure 12.4, both sets of indifference curves are superimposed onto the Edgeworth Box. Cain's are labeled with a *C*; Abel's are labeled with an *A*. The numbering of indifference curves corresponds to higher levels of utility. Cain is happier on indifference curve C_3 than on C_2 or C_1, and Abel is happier on indifference curve A_3 than on A_2 or A_1. In general, Abel's utility increases as his position moves toward the southwest, while Cain's utility increases as he moves toward the northeast. (PC 12.2)

Suppose that the allocation of bread and wine between Cain and Abel is given initially by point *g* in Figure 12.5. That is, Cain's endowment is *Oc* loaves of bread and *Od* gallons of wine, and Abel's endowment is *O′f* loaves of bread and *O′h* gallons of wine. Given this starting point, our problem is to find a price for wine, and a price for bread, such that:

1. Given this set of prices and their endowments, both Cain and Abel are maximizing utility.
2. Quantity supplied equals quantity demanded in both the wine and bread markets.

By definition, this is the general equilibrium set of prices in a pure exchange economy. To solve this problem, we begin with an arbitrary initial set of prices, see if it "works" and, if it does not, determine how it must be modified. To get things going, suppose that the price of bread, p_b, is \$1 per loaf, and the price of wine, p_v, is \$2 per gallon. With these prices, how much bread and wine will Cain demand? To answer this question, forget Abel for a while and focus on Cain. Recall that his endowment point is *g*, so he starts out with *Oc* loaves of bread and *Od* gallons of wine. Because the price of wine is twice the price of bread, Cain can trade away from his endowment at a rate of one gallon of wine per two loaves of

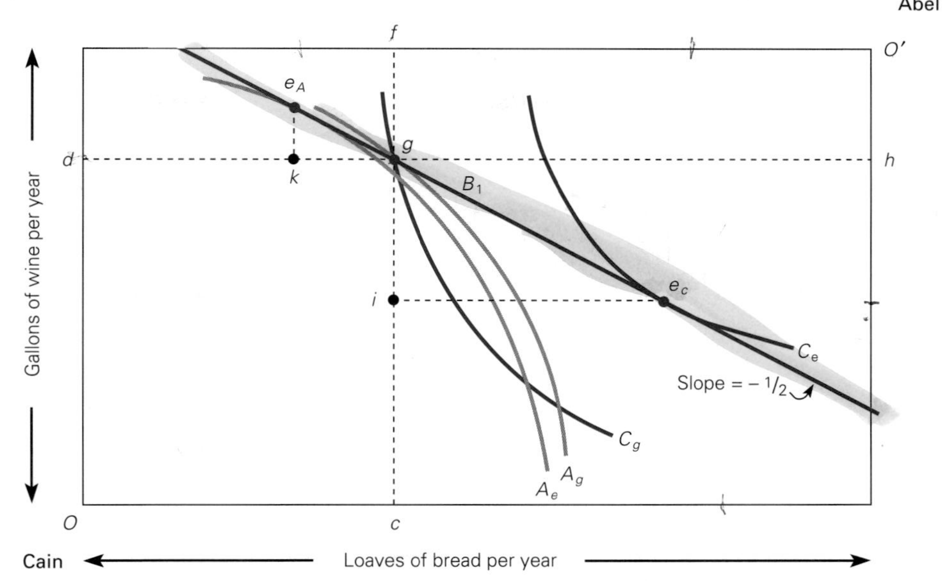

Figure 12.5

Disequilibrium in a Pure Exchange Economy

If the endowment is at g, the price of bread is \$1, and the price of wine is \$2, then each individual's budget constraint is B_1. Given this budget constraint, Cain wants to be at bundle e_C rather than g; Abel wants to be at e_A rather than g. The economy cannot be at two different bundles simultaneously. Hence, this situation cannot be an equilibrium.

bread. Hence, Cain's budget constraint is a straight line through his endowment point with a slope of $-½$. In Figure 12.5, this is line B_1.[2]

It is crucial to realize that given this budget constraint, Cain is not content with consuming bundle g. He would prefer to move from g to e_C, where his utility is higher. (We know this because indifference curve C_e is farther to the northeast than C_g, the indifference curve that runs through the endowment point.) But moving from g to e_C requires selling some wine and buying some bread. Specifically, Cain wants to sell gi gallons of wine and purchase ie_C loaves of bread.

Now let's look at things from Abel's point of view. Point g is also his endowment point; it consists of $O'f$ loaves of bread and $O'h$ gallons of wine. Abel faces the same prices as Cain; hence, his budget line is also B_1, although the consumption bundles available to him are measured from O' rather than O. Given this budget constraint, Abel's most preferred bundle is e_A. (Remember, Abel's utility increases as he moves to indifference curves farther to the southwest.) He would like to sell e_Ak gallons of wine and buy gk loaves of bread.

Is there general equilibrium when $p_b = 1$ and $p_v = 2$? Figure 12.5 tells us that the answer is no. The easiest way to see why is to note that with these prices, Cain and Abel want to be at different points in the Edgeworth Box, but the economy cannot be at two different allocations simultaneously. Alternatively, the situation is not a general equilibrium because the quantity supplied is not equal to the quantity demanded in either market. The wine market has an excess supply because Cain and Abel both want to sell; the bread market has an excess demand because both want to buy.

[2]A straight-line budget constraint implies that the individual is a price-taker, an assumption that is not terribly realistic in a two-person economy. However, price-taking is realistic in a competitive economy with many people, which is what this model is supposed to help us understand.

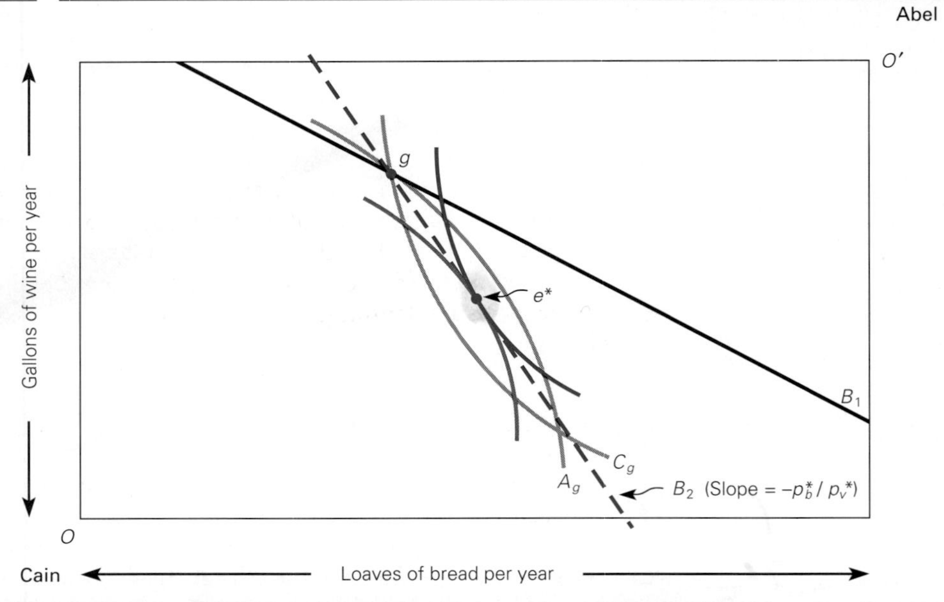

Figure 12.6

General Equilibrium in a Pure Exchange Economy

When the initial allocation is g, e^* is the point consistent with general competitive equilibrium. At e^* both individuals are maximizing utility, given their budget constraints, and the quantity supplied equals the quantity demanded in both markets.

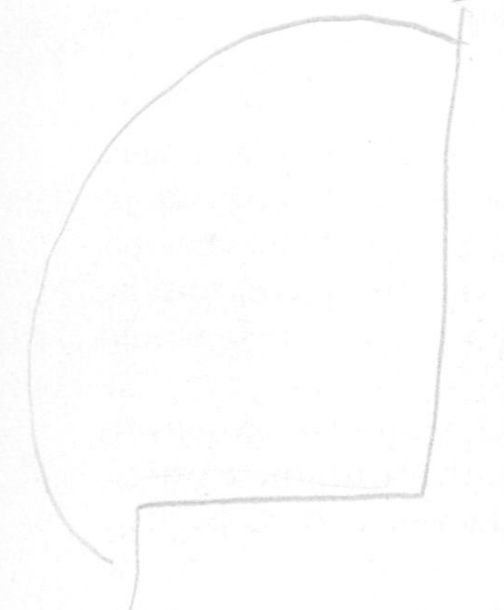

How will markets adjust to this disequilibrium situation? Because there is excess supply of wine and excess demand for bread, p_b will rise relative to p_v. This change in relative prices affects Cain and Abel's mutual budget line. It still passes through the endowment point g, but because of the increase in p_b/p_v it is steeper than B_1. Imagine now that Cain and Abel again maximize utility subject to this new budget constraint. If the quantities supplied and demanded in both markets are not equal, the price ratio changes again and both individuals find new bundles. Only when both people's utility-maximizing decisions are consistent with the equality of supply and demand in both markets do we have general equilibrium. Consider the set of prices p_b^* and p_v^*, which define the slope of line B_2 in Figure 12.6. Given these prices, both Cain and Abel maximize utility at bundle e^*. Moreover, at e^* their choices are compatible because the market quantities supplied and demanded are equal. Hence, p_b^*/p_v^* is the general equilibrium price ratio.

Note that at bundle e^* Cain's and Abel's indifference curves are tangent. This is no accident. As utility maximizers, Cain and Abel each set their marginal rate of substitution (*MRS*) equal to the price ratio. Because they face the same prices, their *MRS*s must be equal. But the *MRS* is just minus the slope of the indifference curve. Two curves through the same point with equal slopes must be tangent.

We have now attained our goal of determining general equilibrium prices in a pure exchange economy. Importantly, this economy is able to "find" the equilibrium in a decentralized fashion. Each individual needs to know only his own tastes, endowment, and the going set of prices. Cain doesn't need to know what Abel is doing, Abel doesn't need to know what Cain is doing, and no central planner is needed to know what either of them is doing. The prices convey all the information required to coordinate the decisions of individuals. This ability to decentralize decision making is one of the chief advantages of a price system.

SECTION RECAP

General equilibrium analysis concerns the determination of prices and outputs in several markets simultaneously. Supply and demand curves provide a useful framework for seeing how a change in one market may affect the entire set of general equilibrium prices. In a pure exchange economy, the focus is on how fixed supplies of various outputs are allocated among individuals. In the pure exchange model, a general equilibrium requires a set of prices such that all individuals are doing as well as they can, and quantity supplied equals quantity demanded in each market. Competition leads to a general equilibrium without the necessity of central planning. Economic activity is coordinated entirely by the price system.

12.2 WELFARE ECONOMICS

In the late 1980s and early 1990s, people in the then communist countries of Eastern Europe concluded that their Stalinist systems of centralized planning were leading to economic stagnation. The response involved experimentation with markets as a mechanism for allocating resources. This extraordinary event provoked a great deal of discussion about the benefits and costs of market systems, both within formerly communist countries and throughout the rest of the world. The fundamental question in this debate was, Do markets provide desirable outcomes?

This debate demonstrates that we want to know not only how a competitive economy works, but whether the results are in some sense "good." This section introduces **welfare economics**, the branch of economic theory concerned with the social desirability of alternative economic states. Welfare economics provides a framework for distinguishing circumstances under which markets can be expected to perform well from those circumstances under which they will produce undesirable results.

welfare economics
The branch of economic theory concerned with the social desirability of alternative economic states.

CONSUMPTION EFFICIENCY

We begin our study of welfare economics with the pure exchange economy discussed in Section 12.1. The Edgeworth Box for this economy is reproduced in Figure 12.7. Suppose that some arbitrary distribution of bread and wine is selected—say point g. C_g is the indifference curve of Cain that runs through point g; A_g is Abel's. Now pose this question: Is it possible to reallocate bread and wine between Cain and Abel in such a way that Cain is made better off, while Abel is made no worse off? We see from the diagram that point h is one such allocation. Cain is better off at this point because indifference curve C_h represents a higher utility level for him than C_g. On the other hand, Abel is no worse off at h because he is on his original indifference curve, A_g.

Can Cain's welfare be further increased without doing any harm to Abel? As long as it is possible to move Cain to indifference curves farther to the northeast while still remaining on A_g, it is possible. This process can be continued until Cain's indifference curve is just touching A_g, which occurs at point d_1 in Figure 12.7. The only way to put Cain on a higher indifference curve than C_{d_1} would be to put Abel on one lower than A_g. An allocation such as point d_1, at which the only way to make one person better off is to make another person worse off,

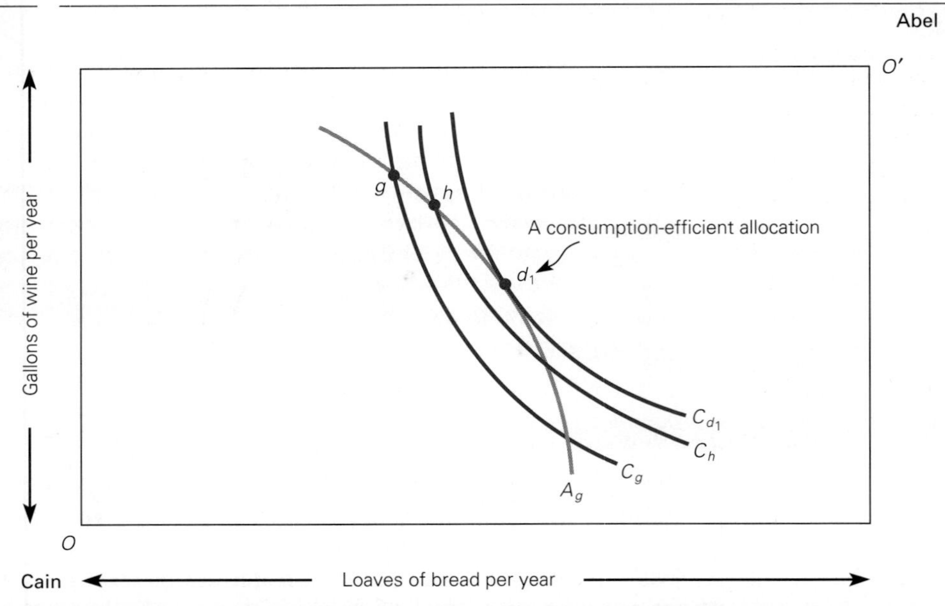

Figure 12.7

Making Cain Better Off without Making Abel Worse Off

Starting at allocation *g*, a move to allocation *h* makes Cain better off without making Abel any worse off. The move from *h* to d_1 accomplishes the same thing. At point d_1, the only way to make one person better off is to make another worse off. Such an allocation is consumption efficient.

consumption efficient
An allocation of commodities such that, given the total supplies of the commodities, the only way to make one person better off is to make another person worse off.

is said to be **consumption efficient**. In a world where supplies of commodities are fixed, consumption efficiency is a useful standard for evaluating the desirability of an allocation of resources. If the allocation is not consumption efficient, then it is "wasteful" in the sense that it is possible to make someone better off without hurting anybody else.

Point d_1 is not the only consumption-efficient allocation that could have been reached by starting at point *g*. In Figure 12.8 we examine whether it is possible to make Abel better off without lowering Cain's utility. Logic similar to that surrounding Figure 12.7 suggests moving Abel to indifference curves farther to the southwest, provided that the allocation remains on C_g. In doing so, point d_2 is isolated. At d_2, the only way to improve Abel's welfare is to move Cain to a lower indifference curve. Then, by definition, d_2 is a consumption-efficient allocation.

So far, we have been looking at moves that make one person better off and leave the other at the same level of utility. It is also possible to make both Cain and Abel better off. At d_3, for example, Cain is better off than at point *g* (C_{d_3} is farther to the northeast than C_g) and so is Abel (A_{d_3} is farther to the southwest than A_g). Point d_3 is consumption efficient because at that point it is impossible to make either individual better off without making the other worse off. It should now be clear that starting at point *g*, a whole set of consumption-efficient points can be found. They differ with respect to how much each of the parties gains from the reallocation of resources.

contract curve
The locus of all the consumption-efficient points in an Edgeworth Box.

Recall that the initial point *g* was selected arbitrarily. The exercise of finding consumption-efficient allocations could be repeated with any starting point. Had point *k* in Figure 12.9 been the original allocation, consumption-efficient bundles such as d_4 and d_5 could have been isolated. The key point is that there is a whole set of consumption-efficient points in the Edgeworth Box. The locus of all the consumption-efficient points is called the **contract curve** and is denoted *MM* in Figure 12.9.

Figure 12.8

Finding Consumption-Efficient Allocations

Starting at point g, the movement to d_2 makes Abel better off and Cain no worse off. Moreover, the only way to make one person better off at d_2 is to make another person worse off. Hence, like d_1, d_2 is consumption efficient. At the consumption-efficient point d_3, both individuals are better off than at the initial allocation, g.

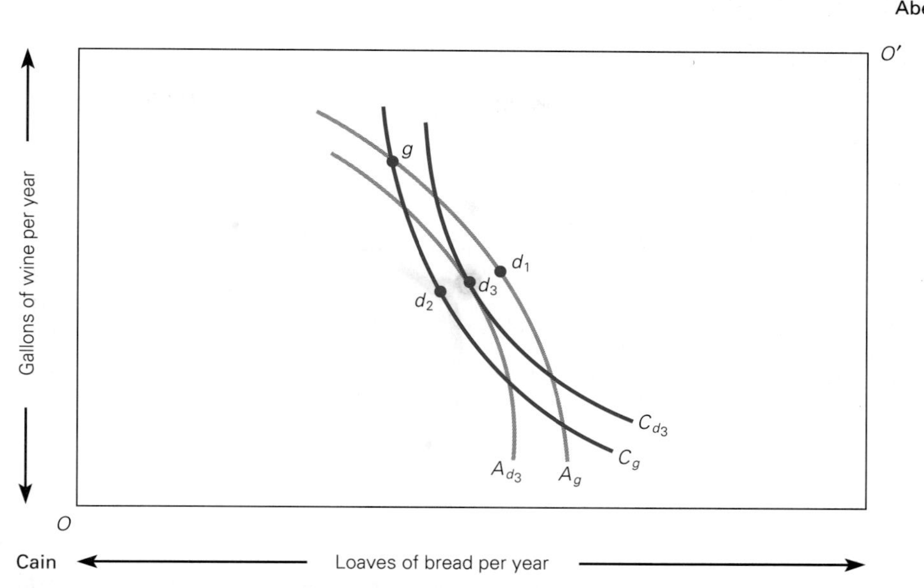

Figure 12.9

The Contract Curve

The choice of a new initial allocation such as k leads to additional consumption-efficient allocations. The contract curve, MM, is the locus of all consumption-efficient points. It is defined by the mutual tangencies between the two consumers' indifference curves.

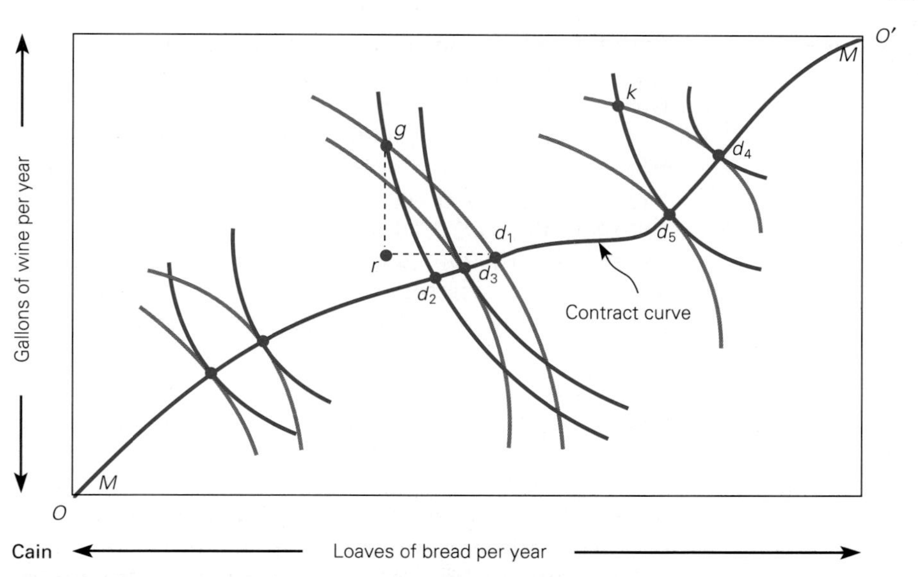

Note that for an allocation to be consumption efficient (to be on MM), it must be a point at which the indifference curves of Cain and Abel are tangent—the slopes of the indifference curves are equal. Now recall that the slope of an indifference curve defines the marginal rate of substitution between the two commodities. Hence, a consumption-efficient allocation of resources requires that marginal rates of substitution be equal for all consumers.[3] Algebraically, a necessary condition for consumption efficiency is

$$MRS_{vb}^{\text{Cain}} = MRS_{vb}^{\text{Abel}} \tag{12.1}$$

where MRS_{vb}^{Cain} is Cain's marginal rate of substitution between bread and wine, and MRS_{vb}^{Abel} is defined similarly.

Although we have been characterizing the movements from some points in the Edgeworth Box to others as "reallocations," we can also think of them as "trades." For example, in Figure 12.9, we can imagine the move from g to d_1 arising as the result of a deal in which Cain trades gr gallons of wine in return for rd_1 loaves of bread from Abel. This observation suggests that *just because one person gains from a trade does not mean that the other person necessarily has to lose.* Indeed, provided that people are fully informed and that there is no coercion, it is hard to imagine why a person would ever agree to a trade if it made him or her worse off. The Roman philosopher Publilius Syrus declared that "to gain without another's loss is impossible." Throughout the centuries, his words have been echoed by other writers. But on the basis of Edgeworth Box analysis, economists emphatically reject this view.

Note that thinking of "reallocations" as "trades" allows us a new interpretation of the contract curve—it shows all the allocations at which the gains from trade are fully exhausted. When people are on the contract curve, there are no further opportunities for mutually beneficial trade. This interpretation also explains the name. *MM* represents the set of contracts for trades that we might expect Cain and Abel to reach through bargaining.

At this point, you might have the following question on your mind: "In Figure 12.6, when Cain and Abel started at point g and traded, we were able to say exactly where they ended up (at point e^*). But in Figure 12.9, when they start at point g, all we can say is that, if they exhaust the gains from trade, they end up somewhere along the contract curve between d_2 and d_1, but we don't know where. Why doesn't 'trade' lead to the same outcome in both diagrams?" The source of the difference is that in Figure 12.6, exchange takes place according to the specific "rule" that everyone is a price taker, and that commodities can only be traded at the rate given by their price ratios. In Figure 12.9, in contrast, Cain and Abel can trade the commodities at any mutually agreeable rate. Because they are not trading at the rate dictated by market-determined prices, we cannot pin down where they end up.

CONSUMPTION EFFICIENCY AND WATER RATIONING

In response to a drought in New Jersey in the mid-1990s, a number of local governments instituted water rationing. Our Edgeworth Box analysis of consumption efficiency can help us analyze this policy.

In Figure 12.10, we examine a community of two people, Bert and Ernie, who consume two commodities, water and a composite of *all other goods.* Ernie's initial consumption of all other goods is Oa, and Bert's is $O'b$. Now suppose that the authorities announce that because of drought conditions, fairness dictates that Bert and Ernie be allotted equal amounts of water. Moreover, to prevent "profiteering" no one is allowed to sell his water to anyone else. Point h, which lies halfway between points a and b, represents the resulting allocation. The key

[3]This assumes no corner solutions, an assumption that will be made throughout.

Figure 12.10

Water Rationing

When each person is allotted an equal share of water, the initial allocation is point *h*. Forbidding the sale of water is inefficient because allocation *h* is off the contract curve.

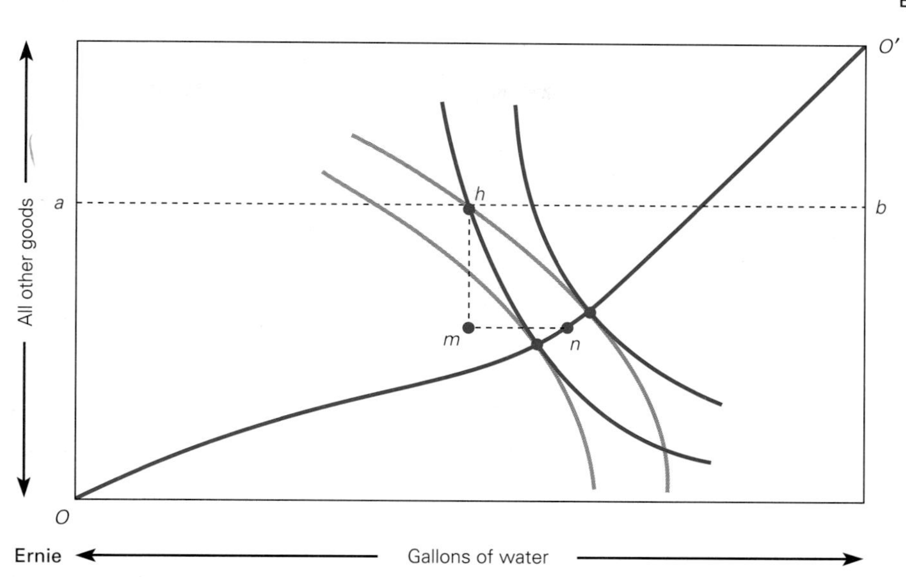

thing to note is that this point is not on the contract curve. Hence, allowing trade would enable one or both of the two individuals to be better off, without anyone being made worse off. For example, if Bert were allowed to sell *mn* gallons of water to Ernie in return for *hm* units of *all other goods*, they would both be happier.

As noted above, in general we cannot tell just how much each person would gain from trade. But we can say that not allowing people to sell their water is inefficient. Intuitively, people like Ernie put a relatively high value on water, perhaps because they like to take a lot of baths. On the other hand, people like Bert may not care much about missing a shower or two, and hence would be happy to trade water for other goods.

This may sound good theoretically, but how could it be implemented? After all, it's hard to imagine the drought victims meeting in the center of town dragging along buckets of water for purposes of trading. A simple solution would be for the local water works to issue *tradeable* ration coupons. Each coupon would entitle the bearer to a gallon of water. Trade in such coupons would achieve the same end as trading the water itself, but it would be much less cumbersome.

Why aren't such schemes employed during droughts? The authorities may believe that it would be "unfair" for some people to end up with less water than others, particularly if the people who sold their water were relatively poor members of the community. Behind this position is the notion that such people cannot be expected to make trades that are in their own interest, and hence must be protected by not allowing them to trade at all.

PRODUCTION EFFICIENCY

The analysis of consumption efficiency assumes that the commodities are fixed in supply. Therefore, the quantities of the inputs devoted to the production of each commodity are also fixed. Clearly, such a setup is inadequate if we wish to have

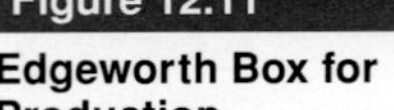

Figure 12.11

Edgeworth Box for Production

In an Edgeworth Box for production, the length and width represent amounts of the respective inputs. Each point in the Edgeworth Box shows the allocation of the inputs between the two outputs.

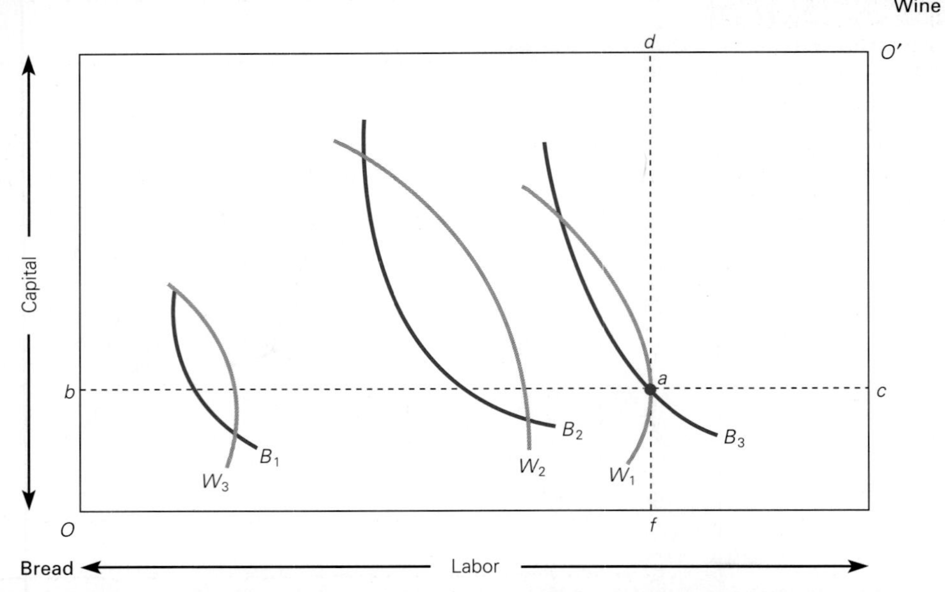

criteria for judging whether productive inputs are allocated efficiently. Hence, we now analyze a model in which the quantities of the various commodities can be altered by reallocating inputs between production of the commodities.

Suppose there are two inputs, labor (L) and capital (K), used to produce bread and wine. The total amount of each input available to the economy is fixed. Figure 12.11 uses an Edgeworth Box to represent this situation. The width of the Edgeworth Box is the total amount of labor, and the height is the total amount of capital. The amounts of the inputs devoted to the production of bread are measured by distances from point O; the amounts devoted to the production of wine from point O'. For example, at point a, Of units of labor and Ob units of capital are devoted to bread production; and $O'd$ units of labor and $O'c$ units of capital are devoted to wine production. Every combination of capital and labor is in turn associated with some quantity of each of the outputs.

Now assume that the production technology for each commodity can be characterized by a set of conventionally shaped isoquants. Figure 12.11 shows both sets of isoquants. Each bread isoquant is labeled with a B, and each wine isoquant with a W. Isoquants farther to the northeast represent greater quantities of bread; those farther to the southwest represent greater quantities of wine.

production efficient
An allocation of inputs such that the only way to increase the output of one commodity is to decrease the output of another commodity.

In an analogy to the notion of consumption efficiency, we characterize an allocation of the inputs as being **production efficient** if the only way to increase the output of one commodity is to decrease the output of another commodity. Using the same sorts of arguments that we employed in Figure 12.9, it is easy to show that production-efficient allocations are defined by mutual tangencies between isoquants. Hence, in Figure 12.12, which reproduces the Edgeworth Box from Figure 12.11, the set of production-efficient allocations is NN.

To obtain an algebraic representation of the condition for production efficiency, recall that the slope of an isoquant is the marginal rate of technical substi-

Figure 12.12

Production-Efficient Allocations

The locus of production-efficient points is defined by the mutual tangencies between the two sets of isoquants. At a production-efficient point, the only way to increase the production of one good is to reduce production of the other.

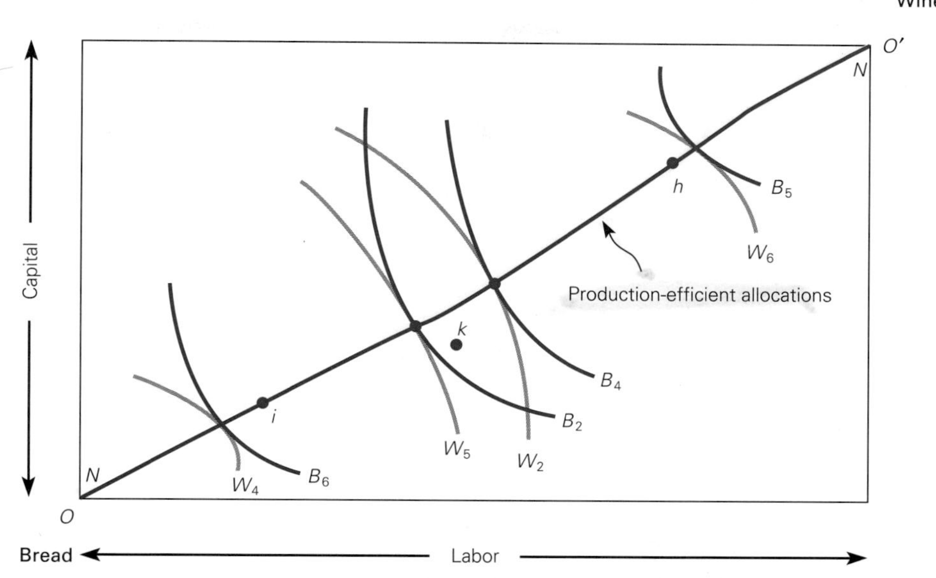

tution between the two inputs ($MRTS_{KL}$). Mutual tangencies are points where the slopes are equal. Hence, the condition for production efficiency is

$$MRTS_{KL}^{\text{bread}} = MRTS_{KL}^{\text{wine}}.\ (\text{PC } 12.3) \qquad (12.2)$$

PRODUCTION POSSIBILITIES CURVE

> **12.3 PROGRESS CHECK**
>
> If the Acme Company gave up two machines in return for one laborer, it could maintain its current level of output. If the Zenith Company gave up two machines, it would require three laborers to maintain its current level of output. Is the allocation of inputs production efficient?

Once the economy is production efficient, the only way to produce more bread is to give up some wine. In Figure 12.13, bread output is plotted on the horizontal axis, and wine on the vertical. Curve *PP* is the **production possibilities curve** derived from the locus of production-efficient allocations. It shows the maximum amount of one output that can be produced, given the amount of the other output. Point *h*′ corresponds to point *h* in Figure 12.12. Here, bread output is relatively high and wine output is relatively low. Point *i*′ in Figure 12.13 corresponds to point *i* in Figure 12.12. Here, bread output is relatively low and wine output is relatively high. Point *k*′ corresponds to point *k* in Figure 12.12. Because *k* is off the locus of production-efficient points, *k*′ must be inside the production possibilities curve. This reflects the fact that, at *k*′, it is possible to increase the production of both commodities.

As shown in Figure 12.13, one option available to the economy is to produce X_1 loaves of bread and Y_1 gallons of wine. The economy can increase bread production from X_1 to X_2. To do this, of course, wine production must fall from Y_1 to Y_2. The ratio of distance ($Y_2 - Y_1$) to distance ($X_2 - X_1$) is called the

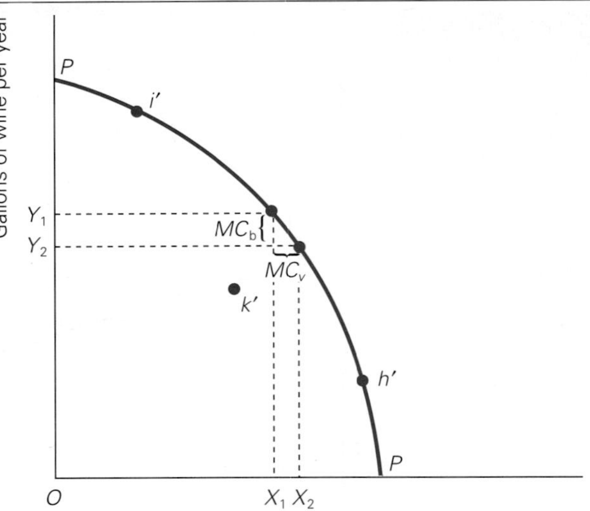

Figure 12.13

Production Possibilities Curve

The production possibilities curve *PP* is the locus of production-efficient points from Figure 12.12. The negative of the slope of the production possibilities curve is the marginal rate of transformation.

marginal rate of transformation
The rate at which the economy can transform one output into another by shifting its resources; the negative of the slope of the production possibilities curve.

marginal rate of transformation of wine and bread (MRT_{vb}) because it shows the rate at which the economy can transform bread into wine. (Of course, bread is not literally "transformed" into wine; resources are released from bread production into wine production.) Just as MRS_{vb} is minus the slope of an indifference curve, MRT_{vb} is minus the slope of the production possibilities curve. That *PP* is bowed outward from the origin reflects the assumption that the *MRT* increases as we move downward along the curve.

It is useful to express the marginal rate of transformation in terms of marginal cost (*MC*)—the incremental production cost of one more unit of output. To do so, recall that bread production can be increased from X_1 to X_2 only at the cost of giving up $(Y_1 - Y_2)$ gallons of wine. In effect, then, the distance $(Y_1 - Y_2)$ represents the incremental cost of producing bread, which we denote MC_b. Similarly, the distance $(X_2 - X_1)$ is the incremental cost of producing wine, MC_v. By definition, the negative of the slope of the production possibilities curve is distance $(Y_2 - Y_1)$ divided by $(X_2 - X_1)$, or MC_b/MC_v. But also by definition, minus the slope of the production possibilities curve is the marginal rate of transformation. Hence, we have shown that

$$MRT_{vb} = \frac{MC_b}{MC_v}. \qquad (12.3)$$

The marginal rate of transformation is the ratio of the marginal costs. This relationship will be important when we discuss whether competitive economies produce efficient outcomes.

PARETO EFFICIENCY

Now is the time to bring our models of exchange and production together. We will *simultaneously* consider how commodities are allocated among individuals, and how inputs are used to produce these commodities. Our goal is to find con-

Pareto efficient
Allocations of commodities and inputs such that the only way to make one individual better off is to make another worse off.

allocation efficient
An allocation of goods such that the marginal rate of transformation between any two goods is equal to consumers' common value of the marginal rate of substitution between the two goods.

ditions for **Pareto efficient**[4] allocations of commodities and inputs—allocations such that the only way to make one individual better off is to make another worse off. When economists use the word *efficient*, they generally have Pareto efficiency in mind.

Clearly, a Pareto-efficient allocation must be consumption efficient (on the contract curve) and production efficient (on the production possibilities curve). Moreover, a Pareto-efficient outcome must be **allocation efficient:**

$$MRT_{vb} = MRS_{vb} \tag{12.4}$$

where MRS_{vb} is the consumers' common marginal rate of substitution. We can demonstrate arithmetically why the equality in Equation (12.4) must hold. Suppose that at a given allocation Cain's MRS_{vb} is 1/3, and the MRT_{vb} is 2/3. By the definition of MRT_{vb}, at this allocation two additional gallons of wine could be produced by giving up three loaves of bread. By the definition of MRS_{vb}, if Cain lost three loaves, he would require only *one* gallon of wine to maintain his original utility level. Therefore, Cain could be made better off by giving up three loaves of bread and having them transformed into two gallons of wine, and no one else would be made worse off in the process. Such a trade is always possible as long as the marginal rate of substitution differs from the marginal rate of transformation. Only when the marginal rate of substitution and marginal rate of transformation are equal is it impossible to make someone better off without making anybody worse off. Hence, $MRT_{vb} = MRS_{vb}$ is a necessary condition for Pareto efficiency. The rate at which bread can be transformed into wine (MRT_{vb}) must equal the rate at which consumers are willing to trade bread for wine (MRS_{vb}).

Figure 12.14 provides a graphical representation of Pareto efficiency. The production possibilities curve *PP* is reproduced from Figure 12.13. At an arbitrarily selected point *f* on curve *PP*, bread output is *Ot* and wine output is *Ou*. By definition, the MRT_{vb} at point *f* is the slope of the PP at that point; this equals the slope of the tangent line B_1.

Given the production levels at point *f*, what points are consumption efficient? To find out, begin by drawing an Edgeworth Box whose width is *Ot* loaves of bread and whose height is *Ou* gallons of wine. We can then isolate the locus of consumption-efficient points by following exactly the same procedure as in Figure 12.9—draw in Cain's and Abel's indifference curves, and find the points of mutual tangency. In Figure 12.14, the locus of consumption-efficient points is denoted *Of*.

utility possibilities frontier
A graph that shows the maximum amount of utility one individual can obtain, given another's level of utility.

Pareto improvement
A reallocation of resources that makes at least one person better off without making anyone else worse off.

Is every point on *Of* Pareto efficient? No. Recall Equation (12.4), which says that both of the marginal rates of substitution have to equal the marginal rate of transformation. Being on the contract curve guarantees that the *MRS*s are equal to each other, but not that they equal the *MRT*. For example, point *v* is on the contract curve, but MRS_{vb} is unequal to the MRT_{vb} at that point. (You can tell because the slope of line B_1 is unequal to the slope of the tangent line B_2 through point *v*.) On the other hand, at point *p* the MRT_{vb} equals the MRS_{vb} because the tangent line B_3 through *p* is parallel to B_1. We conclude that point *p* is a Pareto-efficient allocation.

Is point *p* the only Pareto-efficient allocation? The answer is generally no for two reasons: (1) There may be other points on contract curve *Of* at which the two *MRS*s both equal the *MRT*. (2) Our starting point *f* on the production

[4]Named after the 19th-century economist Vilfredo Pareto.

Figure 12.14

Pareto Efficiency

We can draw an Edgeworth Box for consumption for any point on the *PP* curve. An allocation is Pareto efficient only if (1) the *total* quantities consumed are on the *PP* curve, (2) the allocation is on the contract curve, and (3) the *MRS*s equal the *MRT*. Point *v* satisfies the first two conditions but not the third. Point *p* satisfies all three conditions, and hence is Pareto efficient.

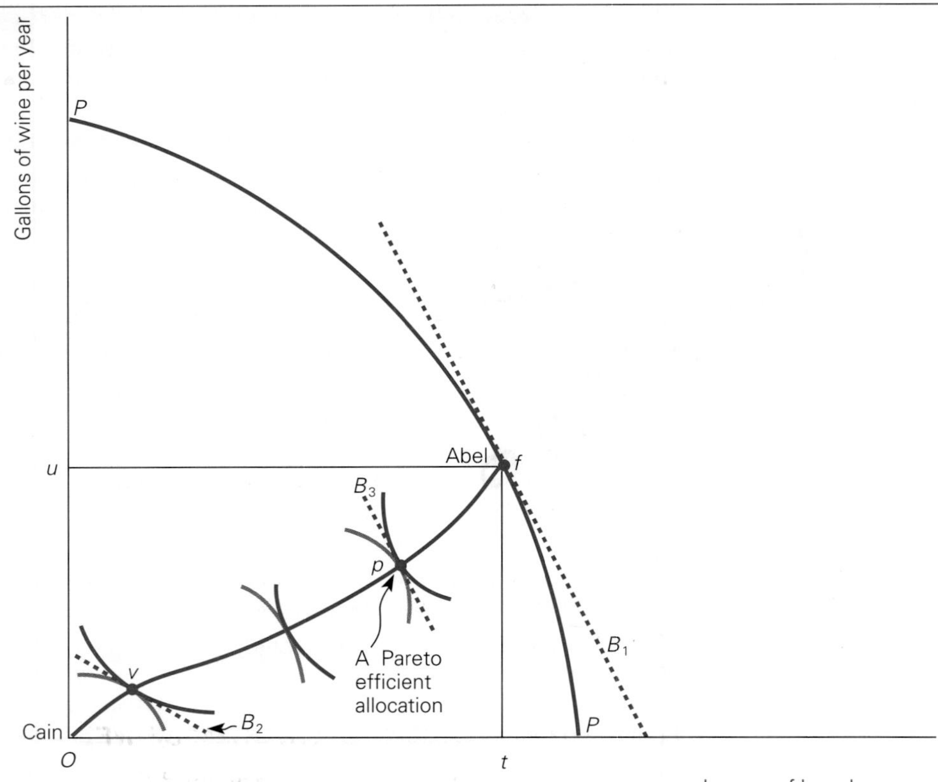

possibilities curve was chosen arbitrarily. We could have chosen any other point, drawn in the associated Edgeworth Box, and found additional Pareto-efficient allocations. In short, there are an infinite number of Pareto-efficient allocations.

This observation is represented in Figure 12.15, which graphs Cain's level of utility (U^C) on the horizontal axis, and Abel's (U^A) on the vertical. The **utility possibilities frontier**, curve *UU*, shows the maximum amount of utility that Cain can obtain, given Abel's level of utility. As one moves along the utility possibilities frontier, the only way to increase Cain's utility is to lower Abel's. Hence, by definition, the points on the utility possibilities frontier are all Pareto efficient. For example, point p' corresponds to the Pareto-efficient allocation *p* from Figure 12.14. On the other hand, point v', which corresponds to allocation *v* in Figure 12.14, is *not* on *UU* because allocation *v* is not Pareto efficient.

A reallocation of resources is said to be a **Pareto improvement** if it makes one person better off without making anyone worse off. In Figure 12.15, the movements from *q* to *r* and from *r* to *z* are both examples of Pareto improvements. A Pareto improvement is possible only at allocations that lie within the utility possibilities frontier. (PC 12.4)

12.4 PROGRESS CHECK

Indicate whether each of the following statements is true or false.

a. Every consumption-efficient allocation of resources is also Pareto efficient.

b. Every Pareto-efficient allocation of resources is also consumption efficient.

c. Every production-efficient allocation of resources is also Pareto efficient.

d. Every Pareto-efficient allocation of resources is also production efficient.

Figure 12.15

Utility Possibilities Frontier

The utility possibilities curve, *UU*, is the locus of Pareto-efficient points. Points inside of *UU* are not Pareto efficient. A movement that improves the utility of one individual without hurting another is a Pareto improvement. Hence, a move from *q* to *r* is a Pareto improvement; so is a move from *r* to *z*.

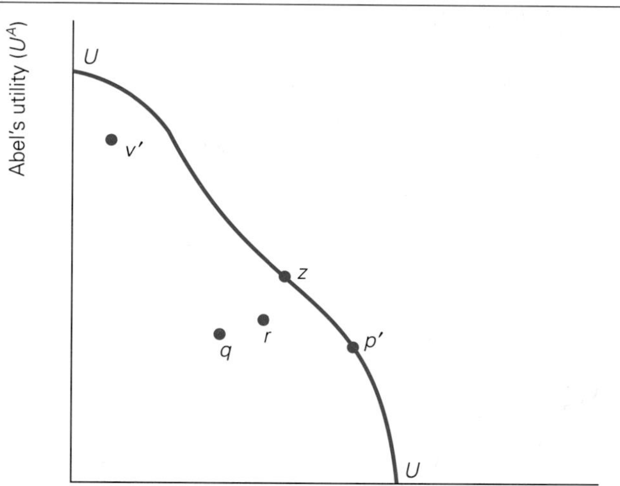

THE FIRST FUNDAMENTAL THEOREM OF WELFARE ECONOMICS

We have now described the necessary conditions for Pareto efficiency, but have not said much about whether a real-world economy will achieve this state. Will a market system "naturally" reach the utility possibilities frontier? The **First Fundamental Theorem of Welfare Economics** (or **First Welfare Theorem**, for short) provides an answer:

> As long as producers and consumers act as price takers and there is a market for every commodity, the equilibrium allocation of resources is Pareto efficient. That is, the economy operates at some point on the utility possibilities frontier.

In other words, an economy composed entirely of price takers—a competitive economy— "automatically" allocates resources efficiently, without any need for centralized direction (shades of Adam Smith's "invisible hand"). In a way, the First Welfare Theorem merely formalizes an old insight: When it comes to providing goods and services, free enterprise systems are amazingly efficient. As Karl Marx and Friedrich Engels observed in the 19th century, "The bourgeoisie, during its rule of scarce 100 years, has created more massive and more colossal productive forces than have all preceding generations together" (Tucker 1978, 477). This sentiment was echoed by the last ruler of the U.S.S.R., Mikhail Gorbachev: "Mankind has not succeeded in creating anything more efficient than a market economy."

Intuition behind the First Welfare Theorem

A rigorous proof of the First Welfare Theorem requires fairly sophisticated mathematics, but we can provide an intuitive justification. We show that with price-taking behavior, the allocation of resources is: (1) consumption efficient, (2) production efficient, and (3) Pareto efficient.

1. *Consumption efficiency.* In terms of our example, the fact that all people face the same prices means that Cain and Abel both pay the same prices per loaf of bread (p_b) and per gallon of wine (p_v). A basic result from the theory of consumer choice is that a necessary condition for Cain to maximize his utility is

$$MRS_{vb}^{\text{Cain}} = p_b/p_v. \tag{12.5}$$

(See Equation 12.2.) Similarly, Abel's utility-maximizing bundle is characterized by

$$MRS_{vb}^{\text{Abel}} = p_b/p_v. \tag{12.6}$$

Equations (12.5) and (12.6) together imply that

$$MRS_{vb}^{\text{Cain}} = MRS_{vb}^{\text{Abel}} \tag{12.7}$$

This condition, though, is precisely the requirement for consumption efficiency, Equation 12.1. Hence, competitive allocations are consumption efficient. This argument is just an algebraic summary of Figure 12.6. Point e^* in that diagram is the competitive equilibrium; because the indifference curves are tangent at that point, it is consumption efficient.

2. *Production efficiency.* Under competition, firms are price takers in factor markets as well as in output markets. Hence, all firms face the same price of labor (w) and price of capital (r). From Chapter 10, we know that to minimize its costs, a bread firm must set its marginal rate of technical substitution equal to the ratio of the prices of labor and capital:

$$MRTS_{KL}^{\text{bread}} = w/r. \tag{12.8}$$

A cost-minimizing wine producer does the same thing:

$$MRTS_{KL}^{\text{wine}} = w/r. \tag{12.9}$$

Equations (12.8) and (12.9) together imply that

$$MRTS_{KL}^{\text{bread}} = MRTS_{KL}^{\text{wine}}, \tag{12.10}$$

which is the necessary condition for production efficiency, Equation 12.2.

3. *Allocation efficiency.* Now that we have shown that competitive economies are both consumption and production efficient, all that remains to demonstrate is that they are allocation efficient; that is, the marginal rate of transformation between two commodities equals the marginal rate of substitution (Equation 12.4). Recall from Chapter 10 that a profit-maximizing competitive firm produces output up to the point at which marginal cost and price are equal. Hence, $p_b = MC_b$ and $p_v = MC_v$ or:

$$\frac{MC_b}{MC_v} = \frac{p_b}{p_v}. \tag{12.11}$$

Now consider Equations (12.5), (12.6), and (12.11) and notice that p_b/p_v appears on the right-hand side of each. Hence, these three equations together imply that $MRS_{vb}^{\text{Cain}} = MRS_{vb}^{\text{Abel}} = MC_b/MC_v$. But from Equation (12.3), $MC_b/MC_v = MRT_{vb}$. Hence, we have $MRS_{vb}^{\text{Cain}} = MRS_{vb}^{\text{Abel}} = MRT_{vb}$, which is just the necessary condition for Pareto efficiency, as was shown in Figure 12.14. Competition, along with maximizing behavior on the part of all individuals, leads to a Pareto-efficient outcome. This concludes the demonstration of the First Welfare Theorem.

Before leaving the First Welfare Theorem, note that Equation (12.11) is another way to express a necessary condition for Pareto efficiency. (This is true because efficiency requires that the *MRT* equal the price ratio, but the *MRT* is the ratio of marginal costs.) A Pareto-efficient allocation of resources requires that prices be in the same ratios as marginal costs, and competition guarantees this condition will be met. The marginal cost of a commodity represents the additional cost to society of providing it. According to Equation (12.11), efficiency requires that the additional cost of each commodity be reflected in its price. Intuitively, if the opportunity cost of a commodity is relatively high, then efficiency requires that its price be relatively high because this provides a signal to consumers to economize on its use.

This discussion raises a very important point: Low prices are not necessarily in the public interest. If the price of a commodity is "too low," in the sense of being less than marginal cost, then consumers receive an incorrect signal of the commodity's opportunity cost to society. They are thus encouraged to squander this commodity. For example, when the international oil cartel, OPEC, drastically raised its prices in the early 1970s, U.S. political leaders bowed to public pressure to restrain domestic oil prices from rising. As a consequence, U.S. consumers faced a price for oil that was below its marginal cost. They wanted to purchase inefficiently large amounts of oil, shortages emerged, and U.S. dependence on foreign oil increased. Most economists agree that the United States would have been better off if the political system had not rejected a market solution to the allocation of oil.

Prices and Decentralization

An important implication of the First Welfare Theorem is that the price system allows Pareto efficiency to be achieved in a totally decentralized setting. No one *directs* people to set their marginal rates of substitution equal to the marginal rate of transformation. Rather, this is the outcome of a process in which each consumer and each producer observes prices and privately makes the decisions that maximize his or her well-being. The coordination that is required to obtain efficiency is done by prices, which provide signals of the relative scarcity of various goods. Because relative prices convey to people all the information they need to allocate resources efficiently, the problem of obtaining an efficient allocation can be solved at the individual level.

Are Competitive Prices Fair?

We have spent a lot of time extolling the efficiency properties of competitively determined prices. In public discussions, however, the focus is often not on the efficiency of prices, but on their fairness. How often have you heard someone say "The price of ______ is outrageous." (Fill in the blank with "housing" or "car insurance," "a college education," or any other commodity of your choice.) Implicit in such statements is the notion that there is some "just" or "fair" price for each commodity, and the existing price is above it. Modern economics categorically rejects the notion that commodities have inherent values that should be reflected in their prices. Rather, prices at a given time reflect the market forces operating at that time. While economists can and do debate whether the existing price of a commodity actually reflects its social marginal cost, there is not much they can say about whether a particular price is "fair."

When it comes to the pricing of consumer goods, this line of argument is fairly uncontroversial. The price of a pound of filet mignon exceeds the price of a pound of chicken livers; if market conditions suddenly changed and this ordering were reversed, your sense of justice probably would not be outraged. However, markets also price the factors of production, including labor, and in this context the notion of "just" prices seems deeply ingrained:

> If there's one rule of economic life, it's that salaries are unfair . . . People who should be paid most are those in human services, those we entrust with the care of our children—teachers, day-care workers—and also people who work in nursing homes. They are on the lowest end of the scale, yet they have the hardest jobs of all (Ver Meulen 1987, 5).

Implicit in this statement is the view that there are inherently "just" relative wages for workers in various occupations. However, it is no more obvious that this is true than that there are inherent just prices for sewing needles and light bulbs.

On the basis of such reasoning, you might reject the notion of inherently just prices, and instead argue that the "fair" set of prices is the set generated by freely operating competitive markets—when market conditions change, the fair set of prices changes. In particular, you might regard it as "just" that each worker be paid the value of his or her marginal product. However, economics says only that competitive prices are Pareto efficient. Given your value judgments, you *might* view efficient prices as fair. But the First Welfare Theorem itself says nothing about fairness.

This line of reasoning does not imply that welfare economics is irrelevant in policy debates that involve matters of equity. If policymakers somehow decide that tinkering with competitive outcomes is required for the sake of justice, then welfare economics can be used to determine how costly (in terms of efficiency) such tinkering is going to be. More generally, if the competitively determined allocation of real income is deemed to be ethically unacceptable, welfare economics provides a framework for evaluating alternative programs for rectifying the injustice.

THE THEORY OF THE SECOND BEST

The First Welfare Theorem seems to have a straightforward policy prescription—if you want efficiency, allow each commodity's price to equal its marginal cost. However, applying the theorem to the real world can be more complicated than this. To see why, imagine a competitive economy with markets for hundreds of commodities. The government is considering imposing a tax on videotapes and asks your opinion about the efficiency consequences. Given that you know the First Welfare Theorem, your answer might well be: "Don't do it. Pareto efficiency requires that price equal marginal cost for every commodity. If you put a tax on videotapes, their price will exceed marginal cost and the allocation of resources will be inefficient."

Now suppose you are given the following information: For various historical reasons, there is already a tax on movie theater tickets. The movie tax cannot be removed; you must take it as a given. How might this information change your advice? Under these conditions, when the videotape tax is imposed, it still creates an efficiency loss in the videotape market. But the story doesn't end there. If videotapes and movies are substitutes, the increase in the consumers' price of videotapes induced by the videotape tax increases the demand for movies. As a consequence, the quantity of movies demanded increases. Now, because movies were taxed under the status quo, the price of movies exceeded their marginal cost and "too few" of them were being consumed. The increase in movie consumption induced by the videotape tax helps push movie consumption back toward its efficient level. There is an efficiency gain in the movie market that helps offset the efficiency loss in the videotape market. In theory, the videotape tax could actually improve overall efficiency.

We have shown that the efficiency consequences of any measure that creates a wedge between price and marginal cost cannot be considered in isolation. If there are other markets in which price is unequal to marginal cost, and the goods in these markets are related, the overall efficiency impact depends on what is going on in all markets. This insight is called the **theory of the second best** because it indicates that if a first best (i.e., Pareto efficient) allocation is impossible to obtain, then a second-best allocation may involve the introduction of additional wedges between price and marginal cost. According to the theory of the second best, two "wrongs" *can* make a "right"!

theory of the second best
If a first-best allocation is impossible to obtain, then a second-best allocation may involve the introduction of additional wedges between price and marginal cost.

The theory of the second best can be quite discomfiting because, strictly speaking, it means that *every* market in the economy must be studied to assess the efficiency implications of a wedge between price and marginal cost in *any* market. In most cases, practitioners simply assume that the amount of interrelatedness between the market of their concern and other markets is sufficiently small that cross-effects can safely be ignored. Although this is clearly a convenient assumption, its reasonableness must be evaluated in each particular case.

THE FIRST WELFARE THEOREM AND TOTAL SURPLUS ANALYSIS

At the end of Chapter 11, we looked at welfare in a partial equilibrium model and argued that welfare was maximized whenever total surplus was maximized. A natural question is: What relationship does surplus analysis have to this chapter's discussion of Pareto efficiency? One might believe that the two have nothing to do with each other, particularly because this chapter concluded that there were an infinite number of Pareto-efficient allocations, but there seemed to be only one such allocation in Chapter 11. Why is there a difference?

It turns out that there really isn't a difference, because surplus maximization is also consistent with a multiplicity of efficient allocations. To see why, recall from Chapter 3 that the market demand curve is found by horizontal summation of individuals' demand curves. Each individual's demand depends in turn on his or her income. Therefore, if the distribution of income changed, so would individuals' demand curves, and the market demand curve as well. But if the market demand curve changes, so does the allocation that maximizes surplus. For example, if income were taken away from teetotalers and given to wine connoisseurs, the market demand curve for wine would shift to the right. There would then be a new Pareto efficient outcome (which would also be the new market equilibrium). In short, there are a large number of Pareto-efficient allocations, each corresponding to a different distribution of real income, just as suggested in Figure 12.15.

THE SECOND FUNDAMENTAL THEOREM OF WELFARE ECONOMICS

The previous section indicated that a competitive economy can end up at several efficient allocations, depending on the initial distribution of income. In light of this observation, one might pose the following question: Can *any and every* Pareto-efficient allocation of resources be attained by some set of competitive prices, assuming there is a suitable assignment of initial endowments? The answer provided by the **Second Fundamental Theorem of Welfare Economics,** or **Second Welfare Theorem,** is yes:

> Provided that all indifference curves and isoquants are convex to the origin, for each Pareto efficient allocation of resources there is a set of prices that can attain that allocation as a general competitive equilibrium.[5]

The Second Welfare Theorem is important because of its implication that, at least in theory, the issues of efficiency and distributional fairness can be separated. If society deems the current distribution of resources to be unfair, it need not interfere with market prices and impair efficiency. Rather, society should transfer resources among people in a way deemed to be fair. Of course, the government needs some way to reallocate resources, and problems may arise if the only mechanisms for doing so (such as taxes) themselves induce inefficiencies. We discuss further the relationship between efficiency and fairness in Section 12.4.

SECTION RECAP

Welfare economics is concerned with the social desirability of alternative allocations of commodities. An important criterion for evaluating an allocation is whether it is Pareto efficient—an allocation such that the only way to make one person better off is to make another person worse off. A Pareto-efficient allocation must be consumption efficient (consumers' indifference curves are tangent) and production efficient (producers' isoquants are tangent). In addition, the marginal rate of substitution between two commodities in consumption must equal the marginal rate of transformation in production. The First Welfare Theorem states that if there is a market for every commodity, and all people and firms are price takers, the allocation of resources will be Pareto efficient. The Second Welfare Theorem says that under certain conditions every Pareto-efficient allocation can be reached by some set of competitive prices.

12.3 THE WELFARE ECONOMICS OF TIME AND UNCERTAINTY

EFFICIENCY AND INTERTEMPORAL RESOURCE ALLOCATION

You might feel perfectly comfortable with the notion that competitive markets lead to an efficient allocation of resources at a given point in time, yet still feel reluctant to accept the idea that competition leads to efficiency across periods of time. Specifically, won't consumers and producers who are interested in high levels of consumption and profits *now* squander society's resources so that there will not be "enough" for the future?

The key to addressing this question is to adopt the approach from Chapter 5—in an intertemporal problem, think of consumption levels during different

[5]For a proof, see Kreps (1990).

time periods as different commodities, the relative prices of which depend on the interest rate. To be more specific, consider Abigail, whose utility depends on *present grain consumption* (g_0) and *future grain consumption* (g_1). Assume that Abigail is a price taker, the price per bushel is \$1 each period, and the interest rate is i. In effect, the price of *present grain consumption* is 1, and the price of *future grain consumption* (in present value terms) is $1/(1 + i)$. As shown in Chapter 5, to maximize her utility Abigail sets

$$MRS_{g_1 g_0} = 1 + i, \tag{12.12}$$

where $MRS_{g_1 g_0}$ is the marginal rate of substitution between future and present grain consumption.

Now let's turn to the producer's side of the problem. Consider John, a price-taking farmer who at present has a certain amount of grain. John can sell to consumers some portion of the grain this year and plant the rest of it to produce more for next year. As shown in Chapter 10, the rules for intertemporal profit maximization are exactly the same as the usual rules; one needs only to make sure that all prices are given in present value terms. Hence, the rule that marginal revenue (here, price) equals marginal cost for each commodity tells us that John produces where $MC_{g_0} = 1$ and $MC_{g_1} = 1/1 + i$. Recalling from Equation (12.3) that the marginal rate of transformation is equal to the ratio of marginal costs gives us

$$MRT_{g_1 g_0} = \frac{MC_{g_0}}{MC_{g_1}} = 1 + i \tag{12.13}$$

Now note that Equations (12.12) and (12.13) both have $(1 + i)$ on the right-hand side, implying that

$$MRT_{g_1 g_0} = MRS_{g_1 g_0}. \tag{12.14}$$

But this is just the condition for allocation efficiency, Equation (12.4)! Hence, competitive markets allocate resources efficiently over time: There is no reallocation between the present and the future that could make someone better off without making someone else worse off. Intuitively, *not* all of the grain is eaten today because producers realize that it is more profitable to invest some of the grain for future production. The relative price of future and present grain conveys to producers information about how much grain to conserve, and to consumers about how much to purchase in each period.

In the current context, the distinctive aspect of the commodity *grain* is that it is renewable—more can be obtained by investing some of the current crop. Similar arguments suggest that markets can efficiently allocate over time nonrenewable resources such as oil and natural gas. As we saw in Chapter 10, the anticipation of higher prices in the future induces owners of these resources not to dump them on the market for a quick profit. Thus, the interests of consumers who may not even be alive today are protected. While there may be circumstances under which government intervention can improve intertemporal efficiency, there is no presumption that this is the case.

EFFICIENCY AND UNCERTAINTY

Doubts can also arise about the efficiency of competition when there is uncertainty. Will markets break down if people don't know precisely what the consequences of their actions are going to be? Not necessarily. Moreover, in some cases

Figure 12.16

Efficient Risk Sharing

The movement from bundle *b* to bundle *d* illustrates efficient risk sharing. If Ernie sells Bert *bh* gallons of water if there is a drought in return for *hd* gallons if it rains, each is better off, because each person's consumption is less drastically affected by the state of the world that occurs.

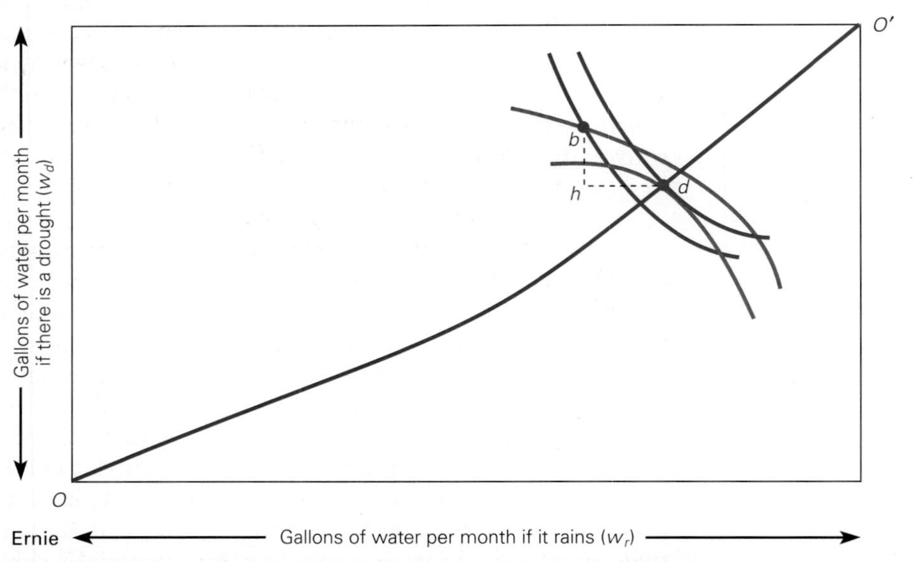

markets provide opportunities for people to reduce or eliminate their exposure to risk altogether. To illustrate this proposition, imagine a situation in which weather forecasters have announced that there may be a drought, but they are not sure. Imagine that Bert and Ernie both own wells, and each well produces more water in the state-of-the-world *rain* than in the state-of-the-world *drought.* Using the framework developed in Chapter 6, there are two contingent commodities, *water if it rains* (w_r) and *water if there is a drought* (w_d). Just like conventional commodities, the allocation of these contingent commodities between two individuals can be analyzed with an Edgeworth Box. In Figure 12.16, the length is w_r and the width is w_d. The initial allocation is at point *b*. Note that at *b*, Ernie has more water than Bert in either state of the world; presumably, his well is deeper than Bert's.

Assume that Ernie and Bert are risk averse, so their indifference curves between w_r and w_d exhibit diminishing *MRS*s. Arguments similar to those surrounding Figure 12.8 tell us that it is in Ernie and Bert's interest to trade to a point on the contract curve, such as *d*. Ernie agrees to give Bert *bh* gallons if there is a drought; in return, Bert agrees to give Ernie *hd* gallons if it rains. This trade allows Bert and Ernie to smooth their water consumption across states of the world; in effect, they are selling insurance to each other, and both are better off. The First Welfare Theorem tells us that as long as a competitive insurance market exists, individuals will bear risk in Pareto-efficient amounts.

Another way in which markets allow people to reduce risk is by providing opportunities for diversification. The stock market plays a crucial role in this context. Consider the case of Gilbert Levin, an engineer who claimed that he had developed a method to synthesize a noncaloric substitute for sugar that looked, cooked, and tasted like the real thing. The problem was that in 1982 it cost \$30,000 to make a pound of the sugar substitute. Levin believed that the cost could be brought down, but that millions of dollars would be required for further research and development. Of course, there was always the possibility that the production cost could not be reduced or that extensive testing would indicate that the substitute was unsafe. No single lender was willing to bear all of this risk. Levin therefore founded the Biospherics Corporation, which sold shares in the venture, and hence spread the risk of the project over a large number of investors. Despite the risks, the existence of the stock market allowed Levin to raise $10 million. The story has a sweet ending. In April 1991, Biospherics stock soared 43.3 percent after it obtained a patent for a method of economically manufacturing D-Tagatose, one of the sugar substitutes.

A related function of the stock market is to allow people to change the riskiness of their portfolios. If you decide that the policies of a particular company are too risky (or not risky enough), you can sell your shares and purchase those of some other corporation. In effect, the stock market allows people to trade risk with one another, allowing a Pareto-efficient allocation of risk.

This discussion has major public policy implications. One often hears claims that because some project is particularly risky, it cannot and will not be done by private firms, and therefore the government must do it. For example, an economics reporter for NBC News asserted that "the Government must go where the private sector fears to tread. It can provide seed capital for risky, big ventures; encourage long-term investing . . ." (Madrick 1993, A21). This argument is unconvincing. One of the things that private markets do *best* is spread risk, so that risky projects can be undertaken (provided that their expected revenues exceed their expected costs). As we will see in the next section, there are definitely circumstances under which markets fail to provide goods in Pareto-efficient amounts. But by itself, the presence of uncertainty does not diminish the ability of competitive markets to allocate resources efficiently.

SECTION RECAP

Earlier chapters examined both consumer and producer decision making when current choices affect the future, and when decisions have to be made in the presence of uncertainty. In terms of our analysis, there was really nothing special about such decisions. Once the notion of a "commodity" was reinterpreted, the conventional approach could be used. The same logic applies to the welfare economics of time and uncertainty. Provided that people are price takers and there is a market for every "commodity," competitive markets lead to efficiency across time periods and to efficiency in risk bearing.

12.4 WELFARE ECONOMICS AND THE REAL WORLD

If properly functioning competitive markets allocate resources efficiently, what more do we have to talk about? In particular, what can economists say about the role the government should play in the economy? Only a very limited government would appear necessary. Its main function would be to establish property rights so that markets can work. Government would provide law and order and a court system. Anything more would be superfluous. However, such reasoning is based on a superficial understanding of welfare economics. Things are really much more complicated for two reasons. First, the First Welfare Theorem need not imply a minimal government if the assumptions behind it are not satisfied by real-world markets. Second, even if all the assumptions are met, the resulting allocation may not be consistent with society's ethical standards. We now discuss each of these points in turn.

MARKET FAILURE

An economy with freely operating markets may fail to generate an efficient allocation of resources for two general reasons. Each type of failure is associated with interesting public policy questions that are discussed in subsequent chapters.

Market Power

The First Welfare Theorem holds only if all consumers and firms are price takers. If some individuals or firms are price makers (they have the power to affect prices), then resources will generally be allocated inefficiently. Why? A firm with market power may be able to raise price above marginal cost by supplying less output than a competitor would. If it does, Equation (12.11), a necessary condition for Pareto efficiency, is violated. An inefficiently small quantity of resources is devoted to the commodity.

Market power can arise in several different contexts. One is monopoly, where there is only a single firm in the market and entry is blocked. Even in the less extreme case of oligopoly (a few sellers), the firms in an industry may be able to increase price above marginal cost. Finally, some industries have many firms, but each firm has some market power because the firms produce differentiated products. For example, a lot of firms produce blue jeans, yet Calvin Klein, Levi's, and Wrangler jeans are regarded by many consumers as distinct commodities. The consequences of market power in various settings are discussed in Chapters 13, 14, and 15.

Nonexistence of Markets

The proof behind the First Welfare Theorem assumes that a market exists for each and every commodity. After all, if a market for a commodity does not exist, we can hardly expect the market to allocate it efficiently. In reality, markets for certain commodities may fail to emerge. Consider, for instance, insurance. As stressed in Chapter 6, in a world of uncertainty insurance is a very important commodity. Despite the existence of firms such as Aetna and Allstate, one simply cannot purchase insurance against certain events. For example, suppose that you wanted to purchase insurance against becoming poor. Would a firm in a competitive market ever find it profitable to supply "poverty insurance"? The likely answer is no, because if you purchased such insurance, you might decide not to work very hard. To discourage such behavior, the insurance firm would have to monitor your behavior to determine whether your low income was due to bad luck or to goofing off. However, performing such monitoring would be very difficult or impossible. Hence, there is no market for poverty insurance.

The problem here is one of *asymmetric information*—one party in a transaction has information that is not available to another. (Only *you* know for sure how hard you are working.) Chapter 17 will show how asymmetric information can destroy a private market, and how this affects resource allocation.

Another type of inefficiency that may arise due to the nonexistence of a market is an *externality*, a situation in which one person's behavior affects the welfare of another in a way that is outside existing markets. Suppose, for example, that Abel begins smoking large cigars, polluting Cain's air, and making him worse off.

Why is this inefficient? Abel uses up a scarce resource, clean air, when he smokes cigars. However, there is no market for clean air that forces Abel to pay for it. Abel in effect pays a price of zero for the clean air, and therefore "overuses" it. The price system is not providing correct signals about the opportunity cost of a commodity.

Externalities have a simple interpretation in the analytics of welfare economics. The derivation of Equation (12.11), implicitly assumed that marginal cost meant *social* marginal cost—it took into account the incremental value of all of society's resources used in production. In our cigar example, however, Abel's *private* marginal cost of smoking is less than the social marginal cost because he does not have to pay for the clean air he uses. The price of a cigar, which reflects its private marginal cost, does not correctly reflect its social marginal cost. Hence, Equation (12.11) is not satisfied and the allocation of resources is inefficient. Incidentally, an externality can be positive—confer a benefit—as well as negative. Think of a molecular biologist who publishes a paper about a novel gene-splicing technique that can be used by a pharmaceutical firm. With a positive externality, the market generates an inefficiently small amount of the beneficial activity. Externality issues are discussed in Chapter 18.

Market Failure and a Role for Government Intervention

The First Welfare Theorem states that a competitive economy with a market for every commodity generates a Pareto-efficient allocation of resources without any government intervention. However, we have just shown that in real-world economies, competition may not hold and not all markets may exist. Hence, the market-determined allocation of resources is not likely to be efficient. There are, then, opportunities for government to intervene and enhance economic efficiency.

It must be emphasized that while efficiency problems provide opportunities for government intervention in the economy, they do not require it. That the market-generated allocation of resources is imperfect does not mean that the government can do better. For example, in certain cases the costs of setting up a government agency to deal with an externality could exceed the cost of the externality itself. Moreover, governments, like people, can make mistakes. Indeed, some argue that the government is inherently incapable of acting efficiently, so that while in theory it can improve upon the status quo, in practice it never will. While extreme, this argument does highlight the fact that the First Welfare Theorem is helpful only in identifying situations in which intervention *may* lead to greater efficiency.

EQUITY

One of the nice things about Pareto efficiency is that it does not depend on measuring and comparing the amounts of utility obtained by individuals. All we need to know is whether making one individual better off would require making another worse off—not how "deserving" each person is. Nevertheless, it is not obvious that every Pareto efficient outcome is desirable. To see why, consult again the utility possibilities function *UU* from Figure 12.15. By definition, all points on *UU* are Pareto efficient, but they represent very different distributions of real income between Cain and Abel. Which point is best? The criterion of Pareto efficiency provides no way to choose among them.

Figure 12.17

Social Indifference Curves

Social indifference curves indicate the rate at which society is willing to trade off one person's level of utility for the other person's.

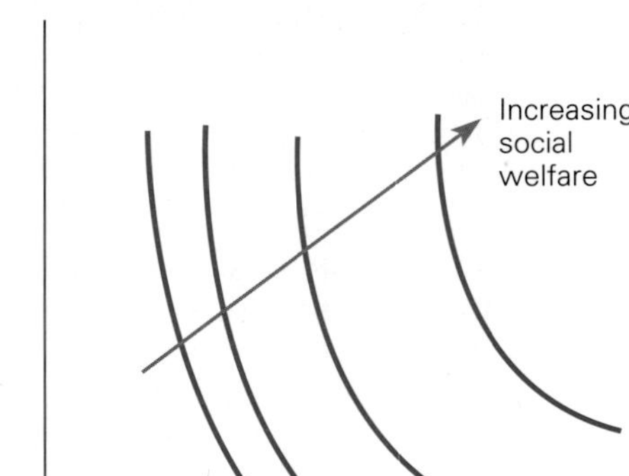

social welfare function A function or schedule that shows how the well-being of society depends upon the utilities of its members.

If we want to choose a point, sooner or later we have to make interpersonal comparisons of utility, which requires that we introduce value judgments. To do so, we postulate a **social welfare function,** which embodies society's views on the relative deservedness of Cain and Abel. Imagine that just as an individual's welfare depends on the quantities of commodities he or she consumes, society's welfare is some function (W) of each individual's utility:

$$\text{Social welfare} = W(U^C, U^A), \tag{12.15}$$

where, as before, U^C is Cain's level of utility, and U^A is Abel's.

We assume that the value of social welfare increases as either U^C or U^A increases.[6] That is, society is better off when any of its members becomes better off. Note that we have said nothing about how society manifests these preferences. Under some conditions, members of society may not be able to agree on how to rank each other's utilities, and the social welfare function will not even exist. For the moment, we simply assume that it does exist.

Just as an individual's utility function for commodities leads to a set of indifference curves for those commodities, so does a social welfare function lead to a set of indifference curves between people's utilities. A typical set of social indifference curves is depicted in Figure 12.17. The downward slope of the curves indicates that if Abel's utility decreases, the only way to maintain a given level of social welfare is to increase Cain's utility, and vice versa. The slopes of the indifference curves represent value judgments about how much society cares about the utilities of the two individuals. Social welfare increases as we move toward the northeast, reflecting the fact that increases in any individual's utility increase social welfare, other things being the same.

[6]Social welfare functions that depend only upon the utilities of individuals are sometimes referred to as "utilitarian" social welfare functions because of their association with the utilitarian social philosophers of the 19th century.

Figure 12.18

Maximizing Social Welfare

A particular Pareto-efficient allocation of resources need not be socially desirable. Point *b* is not Pareto efficient, yet it is preferred to point *a*, which is Pareto efficient.

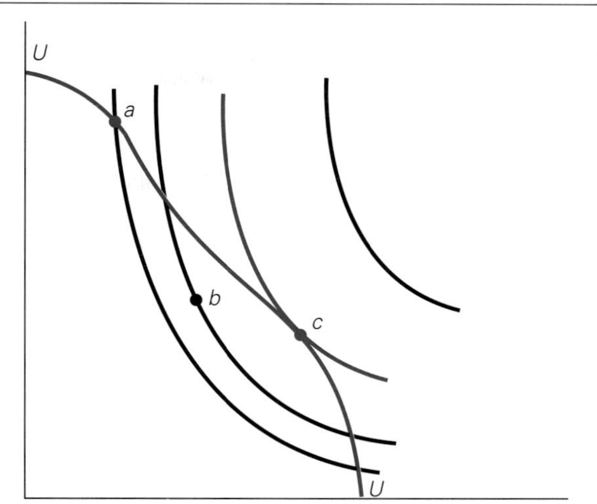

In Figure 12.18, the social indifference curves are superimposed upon the utility possibilities curve from Figure 12.15. Point *a* is not as desirable as point *b* (point *b* is on a higher social indifference curve than point *a*) even though point *a* is Pareto efficient and point *b* is not. Here society's value judgments, embodied in the social welfare function, favor a more equal distribution of real income, inefficient though it may be. Of course, point *c* is preferred to either of these. It is both efficient and "fair."

Now, the First Welfare Theorem indicates that a competitive system with a complete set of markets leads to some allocation on the utility possibilities curve. There is no reason, however, that it will be the particular point that maximizes social welfare. We conclude that, *even if the economy generates a Pareto-efficient allocation of resources, government intervention may be necessary to achieve a "fair" distribution of utility.*

BUYING INTO WELFARE ECONOMICS

Welfare economics provides the basis for the normative work in mainstream economics and it is the framework used to organize the rest of this book. The theory, however, is not uncontroversial.

First, the underlying outlook is highly individualistic, with a focus on people's utilities and how to maximize them. This is brought out starkly in the formulation of the social welfare function, Equation (12.15). The viewpoint expressed in that equation is that the goal of a society is to make its members as happy as possible. However, other societal goals are possible—to maximize the power of that state, to glorify God, and so on. Welfare economics does not have much to say to people with such goals.

Because welfare economics puts people's preferences at center stage, it requires that these preferences be taken seriously; that people know best what gives them satisfaction. A contrary view, deeply ingrained in popular culture, is that big businesses manipulate our tastes—we want what corporations say we should want. If one believes that individuals' preferences are ill-formed or corrupt, a theory that shows how to maximize their utility is ethically irrelevant.

Another possible problem with welfare economics is its concern with results. Situations are evaluated in terms of the allocation of resources, and not of how the allocation was determined. Perhaps a society should be judged by the processes used to arrive at the allocation, not the end results. Are people free to enter contracts? Are public processes democratic? To the extent this view is valid, welfare economics lacks any normative significance.

More generally, people's attitudes toward markets are heavily influenced by factors that have little to do with welfare economics. Roman Catholic tradition has long been hostile to capitalism. Is this because the Church Fathers believe that private markets are unlikely to reach the utility possibilities frontier? Of course not. Their concern is not the allocation of resources, but the effect of the system on people's spiritual well-being. They believe that a selfish spirit pervades market economies, and such selfishness is corrosive to the human soul. As Pope Pius XI wrote, "Free competition, though within its limits, it is productive of good results, cannot be the ruling principle of the economic world. It is necessary that economic affairs be brought . . . into subjection to a true and effective guiding principle."

Indeed, even some defenders of market systems have reluctantly concluded that they lack a moral basis. According to journalist Andy Rooney (1989), the market's "only strength is that it works. . . . It seems sad and a sort of spiritual defeat for us all that an economic system based on doing all for No. 1 is more successful than one based on a noble idea."

However, market enthusiasts are not willing to concede the ethical high ground. Some view the market system as having moral appeal because it is the only method of social organization that views the welfare of the individual as an end in itself, not merely a means to some other end. Moreover, philosophers such as Montesquieu argued that because markets disperse decision making, they help check the power of tyrants, enhance personal liberty, and break the stale cake of custom. A number of observers have stressed the links between economic and political freedom: "You can't tell people to think freely about pig production and nothing else" (Samuelson 1987, 54).

Political and economic freedom do not have to go together. In the mid-1990s, Cuban dictator Fidel Castro began expanding the role of markets in his country. Asked if he thought that this would lead to demands for political change, Castro observed, "I don't exactly understand that free trade and free men have always been associated. I don't think they are twins" (Cordoba 1995, A10). Still, there are some striking examples of the tensions that can be created when dictatorial regimes allow free markets to flourish. In 1992, there was a revolt against a corrupt dictatorship in Thailand. The dictatorial regime had allowed markets to operate, apparently hoping that economic growth without political freedom would produce stability. But, as a journalist noted, "The protests seem to arise from a system that works very well economically and then fosters yearnings for political participation—for freedom of expression as well as freedom from hunger, for votes as well as motorcycles" (Kristof 1992, p. A2).

In short, ideology and politics play crucial roles in conditioning people's attitudes toward markets. Generally, people who put a high weight on personal freedom and whose moral codes emphasize self-responsibility favor free markets, in which individuals make their own decisions and live with the consequences.

Those who view competitive behavior as distressing and favor fraternal and cooperative approaches to problem solving look upon markets with less approval.

We conclude that a great advantage of welfare economics is that it provides a coherent framework for thinking about the desirability of alternative allocations of resources. Because virtually every important public policy problem involves some kind of reallocation of resources, having such a framework is invaluable. Nevertheless, ideological factors that lie outside the realm of welfare economics can and do influence people's views on economic issues.

SECTION RECAP

The assumptions behind the First Welfare Theorem do not hold completely in real world economies. The theorem assumes that all consumers and firms are price takers, but in certain markets, firms or individuals are price makers. The theorem also assumes that a market exists for each and every commodity. However, when asymmetric information or externalities are present, markets may break down. Hence, there is no reason to believe that the real-world allocation of resources is necessarily efficient. Even if it were, government intervention might be appropriate to secure a "fair" distribution of real income. Welfare economics provides an extremely useful framework for evaluating public policy measures whose ostensible purposes are to enhance efficiency and/or increase fairness.

SUMMARY

The circular flow model presented in Chapter 1 illustrated that the various sectors of an economy are inextricably linked together. This chapter reinforced and formalized that insight by discussing general equilibrium analysis, which shows how prices and quantities in all markets are simultaneously determined. A second section introduced welfare economics, providing a framework for determining whether the outcomes generated by an economy are in some sense socially desirable.

- Supply and demand analysis indicates that if markets are linked, then a shift in the supply or demand curve in one market can influence price and output in the others. The markets for commodities are linked if one of them is an input into the production of another, or if the two commodities are substitutes or complements in consumption or production.
- For a set of prices to be consistent with general equilibrium, every firm must be maximizing profits given its technology, every consumer must be maximizing utility subject to his or her budget constraint, and supply must equal demand for each commodity.
- The pure exchange model illustrates the role of the price system as a coordinator of economic activity.
- Welfare economics defines a set of criteria for evaluating economic outcomes. An important criterion is Pareto efficiency, which describes an allocation in which the only way to make one person better off is to make another person worse off.
- For an allocation to be Pareto efficient, every consumer must have the same marginal rate of substitution between any two goods (consumption efficiency), every producer must have the same marginal rate of technical substitution between any two inputs (production efficiency), and the marginal rate of substitution in consumption must equal the marginal rate of transformation in production (allocation efficiency).
- According the First Fundamental Theorem of Welfare Economics, if all households and firms are price takers and there is a market for every commodity, then the allocation of resources will be Pareto efficient. Under these conditions, competitive markets also lead to efficiency in situations involving the allocation of resources over time, and the allocation of resources under uncertainty.
- The Second Fundamental Theorem of Welfare Economics tells us that, provided all individuals'

indifference curves are convex to the origin, any given Pareto-efficient outcome can be realized as a general competitive equilibrium for some set of prices and initial endowments of resources.

- To the extent the assumptions behind the First Welfare Theorem do not hold, real-world economies will produce inefficient outcomes. When firms have market power, for example, prices may exceed marginal costs. Moreover, in the presence of externalities and asymmetric information, markets for certain commodities may not exist.
- A Pareto-efficient allocation of resources may not be socially desirable if the associated distribution of real income is deemed to be unfair. The social welfare function introduces ethical considerations by showing how society is willing to trade off utility among its members.

DISCUSSION QUESTIONS

12.1 Consult Figure 12.2, which models the general equilibrium effects of a minimum wage. Show graphically how much the gainers gain, and how much the losers lose. Are the losses or the gains greater? Explain. Use your answers to evaluate the following claim: "Legislators like the minimum wage because it helps the poor and it does not cost the government anything because the expense is borne by businesses."

12.2 In the 1970s, the United States was contemplating gasoline rationing. Under the proposed plan (which was never implemented), people would be issued ration coupons; each coupon would entitle them to purchase a gallon of gasoline at a price set by the government. An important feature of the plan was that the coupons would be tradeable. Use a pure exchange model to show how the competitive price of the ration coupons would be determined. (For simplicity, you may assume that the gasoline price set by the government was zero. That is, all a person would need for each gallon of gasoline was one coupon.)

12.3 Your airplane crashes in the Pacific Ocean. You land on a desert island with one other passenger. A box containing 100 little bags of peanuts also washes up on the island. The peanuts are the only thing to eat.

In this economy with two people, one commodity, and no production, represent the possible allocations in a diagram, and explain why every allocation is Pareto efficient. Is every allocation fair?

12.4 The government of France levies a tax on foreign-made movies, which it uses to subsidize French films. Is this tax/subsidy system likely to be associated with a Pareto-efficient allocation of resources? Explain.

12.5 Consider an economy which has two inputs, capital and labor, each of which is fixed in total supply. Assume further that the inputs are allocated across two firms, one of which produces guns, and the other butter.

a. State the condition for a production-efficient allocation of capital and labor.

b. Use your answer to part (*a*) to prove that with production efficiency, the ratio of the marginal physical products of capital and labor in gun production must equal the ratio of the marginal physical products of capital and labor in butter production.

c. Former Soviet leader Mikhail Gorbachev stated, "It is particularly important that actual pay of every worker be closely linked to his personal contribution to the end result, and that no limit be set on it." Use the results from part (*b*) to explain why Gorbachev's condition is necessary for production efficiency. (*Hint:* An input's "contribution to the end result" is its marginal revenue product.)

12.6 Anthropologists have noted that in some cultures it is expected that members of a community will help each other out in times of difficulty. For example, if one farmer's crops fail, the neighbors will provide the farmer with extra food. Use a pure exchange model to show how such arrangements can enhance efficiency.

12.7 According to Pope John Paul II, "The social order will be all the more stable, the more . . . it does not place in opposition personal interest and the interests of society as a whole, but rather seeks ways to bring them into fruitful harmony." Do markets constitute a good "social order" according to this criterion? What is the relevance of the First Welfare Theorem to your answer?

12.8 In 1988, *Newsweek* magazine announced that Sam Sebastiani was investing $3 million in a winery in California: "It's an investment that would drive Wall Street crazy: he'll see no return, in the shape of drinkable wine, until around 1993" (Clifton 1988, 48). Why do you think the writer believed that "Wall Street" would view such an investment as "crazy"? What does the First Welfare Theorem have to say about this issue?

12.9 An economy consists of only two people, Eleanor and Franklin.

a. Let the social welfare function be $W = U^E + U^F$, where U^E and U^F are the utilities of Eleanor and Franklin, respectively. Graph the social indifference curves. How would you describe the relative importance assigned to their respective well-beings?

b. Repeat (*a*) when $W = 2U^E + U^F$.

c. Assume that the utility possibility frontier is as given below:

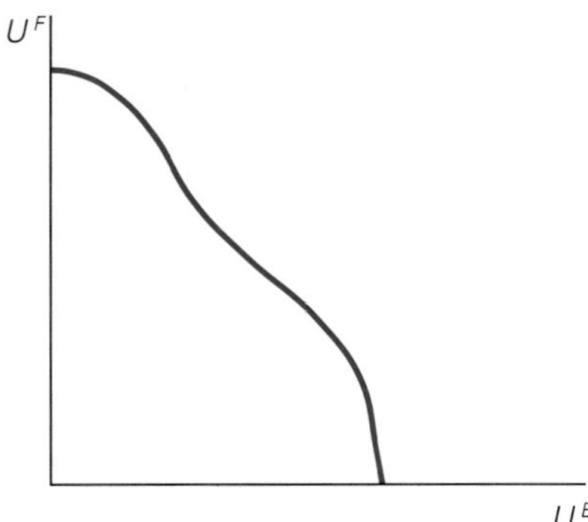

Graphically show how the optimal solution differs between the welfare functions given in parts (*a*) and (*b*).

12.10 Indicate whether or not there is a "market failure" that can justify the existence of each of the following government programs:

a. Under a program of national flood insurance, the government will pay up to \$350,000 to replace your beachhouse if the house is destroyed in a hurricane. The individual must pay a premium, but it is trivial (a few hundred dollars).

b. The federal government subsidizes the purchase of homes of certain first-time buyers with incomes between \$25,000 and \$37,000.

c. The National Energy Policy Act of 1992 requires that all new toilets flush with only 1.6 gallons of water. Toilets manufactured in the 1980s generally consumed 5.5 to 7 gallons per flush.

12.11* Romeo and Juliet inhabit a pure exchange economy with 10 units of X and 20 units of Y. Denote Romeo's consumption of X and Y as x_R and y_R, respectively; denote Juliet's as x_J and y_J. Romeo's utility function is $U^R = x_R^{1/2}y_R^{1/2}$; Juliet's is $U^J = x_J^{3/4}y_J^{1/4}$. Write down an expression for the contract curve in this economy. (*Hint:* Maximize Romeo's utility subject to the constraint that Juliet's utility is some arbitrary level, U_0^J. Note also that $x_R + x_J = 10$ and $y_R + y_J = 20$.)

*This problem is for students who have studied the Appendix to Chapter 3.

PART four
Market Power

The First Welfare Theorem gives us conditions under which markets lead to an efficient equilibrium allocation of goods and services. Unfortunately, some of these conditions often are not met in practice. In the remainder of this book, we will explore what can go wrong in a market economy, and we will see if and how government intervention in markets can improve their efficiency.

One of the assumptions underlying the First Welfare Theorem is that all buyers and sellers take prices as given. Yet many real-world firms can and do influence the prices at which they buy and sell commodities. IBM, Mercedes-Benz, and Sony are just a few of the firms that come to mind. The four chapters in this part of the book consider what happens when economic decision makers recognize their influence over price.

Chapter 13 examines the case of a market with only a single supplier. In such a market, the demand curve faced by the firm is the market demand curve, which is downward sloping. Consequently, the firm recognizes that its output level influences the price at which it can sell its output. As we will see, our two rules for the profit-maximizing choice of output, the marginal output rule and the shut-down rule, remain valid—they hold for *any* profit-maximizing firm. But the application of these rules to a firm with the power to influence price does lead to some new conclusions. In particular, we will see that the market equilibrium no longer entails an efficient level of output.

Non-price-taking behavior also is present in many markets that have multiple sellers. These markets are examined in Chapters 14 and 15. Chapter 14 also examines the consequences of a buyer's recognition that it can influence the price of an input that it purchases. In Chapter 15, we add an extra dimension to these models: Each firm is concerned with the influence of rival firms on the market price and tries to predict the behavior of these rivals in order to choose its own course of action. These strategic interactions can have a significant impact on market behavior and the nature of equilibrium. In Chapter 16 we develop a set of tools that can be used to analyze a wide variety of strategic situations.

CHAPTER

13

Monopoly

> *[M]y view is that everyone who sets eyes on something big and strong and powerful immediately gets the feeling that if the owner knew how to take advantage of its size and scale he would get tremendous results and be a happy man.*
>
> —The Athenian in Plato's *The Laws*

In 1960 the Haloid-Xerox Corporation introduced the model 914, the first modern plain-paper copier. At the time, Xerox faced little competition. There were substitute products—some companies made slow and messy copiers that required the use of specially coated paper, and a person could always copy a book by hand—but consumers did not view these as close substitutes. The management at Haloid-Xerox had to choose the rental prices for its copiers. Had the company been a price taker, the choice would have been easy—simply charge the market price. But there was no market price to take as given. Haloid-Xerox was not a price taker, and the management recognized that fact. Xerox knew that, unlike a price taker, if it wanted to rent more copiers to its customers, it had to lower the price. In other words, Xerox faced a downward-sloping firm-specific demand curve for its output.

Many other firms recognize their influence on the prices of the goods and services that they sell; examples include airlines, restaurants, makers of computer games, and soft drink companies. When the quantity that a firm buys or sells significantly affects the price that the firm faces, the firm is known as a **price maker** because it can influence the price through its choice of quantity. Another way of saying the firm has the ability to influence the market price is to say the firm has **market power.** In this chapter, we will study the positive and normative implications of price-making behavior in a particular market setting called *monopoly.* You may recall that the assumption that all firms and households take prices as given played a central role in last chapter's demonstration that the market economy achieves Pareto efficiency. Given the key role played by price taking in the First Welfare Theorem, it is important to ask how markets perform when economic decision makers are price makers. As we will see, a market with price makers may fail to achieve a Pareto-efficient allocation of resources.

price maker
An economic decision maker that recognizes that its quantity choice has an influence on the price at which it buys or sells a good.

market power
Another name for the firm's ability to influence price.

13.1 THE BASIC MONOPOLY MODEL

THE FUNDAMENTAL ASSUMPTIONS

Our goal is to understand how price-making behavior affects market equilibrium. To construct a full model of market equilibrium, however, we need to make several fundamental assumptions in addition to the one that suppliers are price makers. To find a sensible combination of assumptions, it is helpful to look back at the one model that we have examined in detail so far: perfect competition.

Recall that the perfectly competitive model is based on three key assumptions about the supply side of the market: Suppliers are price takers; suppliers do not behave strategically; and entry into the market by suppliers is perfectly free.

Sometimes these assumptions are inappropriate. The *price-taking assumption*, for example, requires the satisfaction of three conditions: there are many firms in the market, each of which sells only a small part of the market total; consumers consider all of the firms' products to be perfect substitutes; and buyers are perfectly informed about the available suppliers and the prices that they charge. For avocado farmers and nail manufacturers, the price-taking assumption makes sense, but it does not fit many major industries.

The *assumption that suppliers behave nonstrategically* also poorly characterizes some industries. When Ford Motor Company changes the price of its automobiles, it knows full well that General Motors and Toyota will take note and quite possibly change their own prices in response. Similarly, when Heinz, a leading maker of cat food, considers changing the price of its products, it takes the likely responses of Mars and Nestlé into account.

Finally, the *assumption of free entry and exit* is sometimes inappropriate. If you began producing the anti-AIDS drug AZT in the early 1990s, you would have quickly found yourself in court as Wellcome PLC sued you for violating its patent. At the time, no firm had the knowledge needed to produce a competing anti-AIDS drug. Entry into this market was far from free. There are other markets into which entry is limited by the lack of new suppliers who know how to produce the good. In still others, entry is limited by the lack of access to needed inputs. If you wanted to go into the aluminum business, for instance, you would find that the best supplies of bauxite (an ore essential to the production of aluminum) are already controlled by existing producers.

The fact that the perfectly competitive model is based on assumptions that are inappropriate for some markets does not mean that it is a bad model. The role of a model is to distill the essential elements of an economic situation into a simplified form that is amenable to analysis. No single model can serve this role in all possible markets. Instead of seeking one universal model to cover everything, the goal of economics is to develop a useful set of tools that can be used as the situation warrants. Perfect competition is a good model because it helps us understand a large number of important markets.

Our task now is to develop a model for analyzing *monopoly,* a market structure that characterizes an important subset of the markets to which the competitive model does not apply. The first assumption of the monopoly model is that each supplier recognizes that its output choice affects the price.

1. *Sellers are price makers.* A price-making supplier can influence the price at which it sells its output by adjusting its output level. In other words, the de-

Table 13.1
Fundamental Assumptions of the Monopoly Model

	Monopoly	Perfect Competition
1. Seller Influence on Price	Sellers are price makers.	Sellers are price takers.
2. Extent of Strategic Behavior	Sellers do not behave strategically.	Sellers do not behave strategically.
3. Conditions of Entry	Entry into the market is completely blocked.	Entry into the market is free.
4. Buyer Influence on Price	Buyers are price takers.	Buyers are price takers.

mand curve for a price-making firm slopes downward—the price falls as the amount of output sold rises, and vice versa.

Although the first assumption about the supply side of the market is the opposite of the one made in the competitive model, the second assumption of our new model is the same.

2. *Sellers do not behave strategically.* Recall from the Chapter 11 discussion of the assumptions underlying the competitive model that a supplier behaves nonstrategically when it does *not* anticipate any reaction by rival suppliers when it chooses its own actions.

Our third assumption is the opposite of the competitive model. While entry is free under the competitive model, here we assume that:

3. *Entry into the industry is completely blocked.* In other words, no new suppliers can join the industry.

On the demand side, we continue to assume that:

4. *Buyers are price takers.* Table 13.1 summarizes the assumptions and compares them with those of the competitive model.

THE APPROPRIATE MARKET STRUCTURE

To what type of market would we want to apply the model in Table 13.1? To answer this question, we will consider each of our dimensions of market structure in turn.

a. **The size and number of buyers.** Since we want to consider a market in which demanders are price takers, we require many buyers, no one of which is large enough to influence the price. In this respect, our new market structure is the same as perfect competition.

b. **The size and number of sellers.** As we saw in Chapter 11, if there are many sellers in the market and they are producing perfect substitutes, then the suppliers will be price *takers.* If there are only a few suppliers, each of which accounts for a significant percentage of the market supply, then a single supplier may be able to affect the market price. Because our model postulated price-making sellers, we want to consider the small-numbers case. But we also want to examine a market in which a supplier does not behave strategically. Typically, we would expect suppliers in a market with only a handful of firms to take notice of each other and behave strategically. Hence, we will assume here that there is only one firm in the industry. With only one supplier in the market, there is no scope for strategic behavior because there are no rival producers. When there is only one supplier, this market structure is known as a monopoly—*mono* means *one.*

c. The degree of substitutability of different sellers' products. The degree of substitutability among different suppliers' products also influences the extent to which a supplier is a price maker or price taker. In the case of a monopoly, there are no other firms in the market. While this sounds straightforward, it confronts us with a difficult question: What is *the market?* Does your local telephone company have a monopoly in the supply of local telephone services? Most people (and economists too) would say that it does. But the firm does face rivals. The U.S. Postal Service and private overnight and same-day carriers compete with local telephone service to some extent. So does getting people together to talk to one another face to face. None of these substitutes is very close, however, and the local telephone company is best thought of as a monopolist.

More generally, a supplier is said to be a monopolist whenever it produces a good or service for which there is not a close substitute. How close is *close* is a tricky question. The U.S. Department of Justice has suggested looking at whether a sustained 5 percent increase in price by the supplier would cause it to lose economically significant sales to rival producers. Of course, one still must decide what constitutes significant losses. Another way to decide whether two firms produce goods that are close substitutes is to ask whether a change in the price of one product has a substantial effect on the demand for the other one. A cross-price elasticity of .01 is a strong indication that two firms do not produce close substitutes and hence are not product-market rivals. A cross-price elasticity of demand of 7 is a strong indication that the firms do produce substitutes. For elasticities in the middle, the judgment is difficult to make. The ultimate test of a firm's being best modeled as a monopolist is whether: (1) it faces a firm-specific demand curve that slopes downward significantly enough that managers take it into account, and (2) the firm has no rivals whose reactions it has to consider when choosing its profit-maximizing course of action.

13.1 PROGRESS CHECK

In 1992, Airfone was the only company licensed by the Federal Communications Commission to provide telephone service on commercial airliners flying over the United States. Do you think that Airfone was a monopolist?

d. The extent to which buyers are informed about prices and available alternatives. As before, we assume buyers are perfectly informed about the available alternatives. In a monopolized market, this means that all buyers know about the monopolist's price and the characteristics of its product.

e. The conditions of entry. Our model assumes there is only one firm. Hence, this model applies to markets into which entry by new firms is completely blocked by either technological or legal barriers.

The characteristics of a monopolistic market structure are summarized in Table 13.2, where they are compared with those of a perfectly competitive market structure. (PC 13.1)

EQUILIBRIUM

What difference does it make that the firm is a monopolist rather than a perfect competitor? Let's look at the output choice made by California Chemical, the sole producer of Xyzene, a patented product. Recall from our look at firm behavior in Chapter 7 that *any profit-maximizing firm* follows two rules in choosing its output level:

> *The Marginal Output Rule:* If the firm does not shut down, it should produce output at a level where marginal revenue is equal to marginal cost.

Table 13.2

A Monopolistic Market Structure

	Monopoly	Perfect Competition
a. The Size and Number of Buyers	Many buyers, no one of which is large relative to the overall market.	Many buyers, no one of which is large relative to the overall market.
b. The Size and Number of Sellers	One seller.	Many sellers, no one of which is large relative to the overall market.
c. The Degree of Substitutability among Different Sellers' Products	There are no close substitutes.	The outputs of different sellers are homogeneous.
d. The Extent to Which Buyers Are Informed about Prices and Available Alternatives	Buyers are well informed about the offerings of competing suppliers.	Buyers are well informed about the offerings of competing suppliers.
e. The Conditions of Entry	Either technological or legal barriers completely block entry.	Neither technological nor legal barriers to entry exist.

Table 13.3

The Demand and Revenue Curves for Xyzene

When average revenue (price) falls as output rises, marginal revenue must be less than average revenue. This relationship is exemplified by comparing columns (2) and (4).

(1) Quantity (tank cars per month)	(2) Price (per tank car)	(3) Total Revenue	(4) Marginal Revenue (per tank car)
0	—	$ 0	
			$9,000
1	$9,000	9,000	
			7,000
2	8,000	16,000	
			5,000
3	7,000	21,000	
			3,000
4	6,000	24,000	
			1,000
5	5,000	25,000	
			−1,000
6	4,000	24,000	
			−3,000
7	3,000	21,000	

The Shut-Down Rule: If for every choice of output level the firm's average revenue is less than its average economic cost, then the firm should shut down.

A monopolist is no exception to these two rules. To apply them, we need to know the monopolist's cost and revenue functions. A monopolist's cost function is found the same way as any other firm's cost function—follow the process discussed in Chapter 9. The difference between monopoly and competition comes on the revenue side, so we will focus our attention there.

Marginal Revenue for a Monopolist

Columns (1) and (2) of Table 13.3 present data on the market demand curve for Xyzene. Since California Chemical is the only supplier, the market demand curve is also its firm-specific demand curve. The data in Table 13.3 can thus be used to calculate the monopolist's total revenue—the price per unit times the quantity sold—given in column (3). We can also calculate the firm's marginal revenue—the amount by which total revenue increases when the firm produces one more unit of output—given in column (4).

Figure 13.1

The Revenue Effects of an Output Increase

When a monopoly increases its output by one unit, there are two effects on revenue. Revenue rises by the extra amount of output times the price at which it is sold, shaded area *A*. Revenue falls by the decrease in price times the number of units sold, shaded area *B*. Therefore, marginal revenue is area *A* minus area *B*.

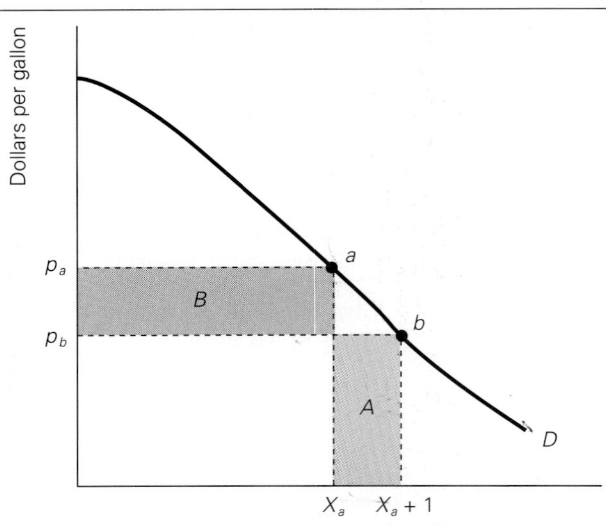

Two points jump out from Table 13.3. First, for some output levels, the marginal revenue is *negative*. Second, California Chemical's marginal revenue is less than its average revenue, which is equal to the price. As we shall see, this relationship holds for any price-making firm and is a fundamental difference from a price-taking firm, whose marginal and average revenue curves coincide (see Chapter 10). The argument made in Chapter 9 about the general relationship between average and marginal curves tells us why the monopolist's average revenue exceeds its marginal revenue. The fact that the average revenue is falling tells us that the marginal revenue is pulling down the average, and the marginal revenue curve must lie below the average revenue curve.

To analyze this phenomenon graphically, consider Figure 13.1, which illustrates the downward sloping average revenue curve for Xyzene. Notice that we use a capital X to denote the firm's output level in the figure because now firm and industry output are the same quantity.

inframarginal units
The units of output that the firm could have sold at the old price, but now must sell at the new, lower price that prevails when it increases its output level.

Suppose that California Chemical is selling X_a gallons of Xyzene, and it decides to sell one more.[1] Figure 13.1 indicates that the quantity rises, but the price must fall as the firm moves along its demand curve from point *a* to point *b*. This has two effects on the firm's revenues. First, California Chemical gets additional revenue from the extra unit sold—the price of the marginal unit, p_b, times the amount of additional output sold, 1 gallon. This additional revenue is given by area A in Figure 13.1. Second, the fall in the price from p_a to p_b has a negative effect on total revenue. There are X_a gallons of Xyzene that the firm could have sold at the old price, but now must sell at the new, lower price. These gallons of Xyzene are known as the **inframarginal units** to distinguish them from the

[1]We are measuring output in terms of gallons per month so that we can draw smooth curves. Even though the management would not literally concern itself with such an exact output choice, the logic behind the firm's choice is the same whether it is choosing how many gallons per month or how many railroad tank cars per month.

Figure 13.2

The Relationship between the Demand Curve and the Marginal Revenue Curve

When the firm is a price maker, the marginal revenue curve lies below the demand curve everywhere except at an output level of zero. At zero output, there are no inframarginal units on which to suffer losses, so the two curves coincide.

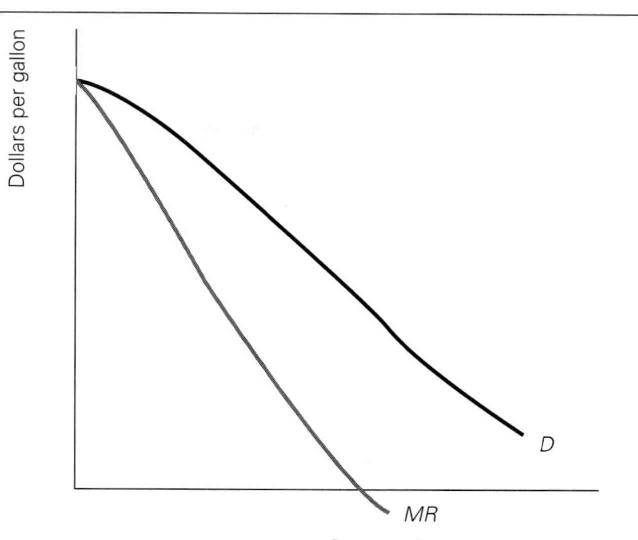

marginal unit under consideration. When the price falls, the firm loses a total of $(p_a - p_b) \times X_a$ on the X_a gallons of Xyzene that it otherwise could have sold at the price of p_a. This loss in total revenue is area B in Figure 13.1. Because of this negative effect on revenue from the sale of the marginal unit, the marginal revenue is less than the price of the marginal unit whenever X_a is greater than 0. In other words, the monopolist's marginal revenue curve lies below the demand curve except at an output level of zero, where the two curves coincide. Figure 13.2 illustrates this relationship between the demand curve (or average revenue curve) and the marginal revenue curve.

We can represent our graphical analysis algebraically to obtain additional insight into the relationship between marginal revenue and the demand curve. The change in total revenue from the sale of the marginal unit of output (area A in Figure 13.1) is equal to the price times the additional quantity. Because the additional quantity is one unit, this part of the change in revenue is simply equal to the price: area $A = p$.

The loss on the inframarginal units (area B in Figure 13.1) is equal to the number of inframarginal units (the original quantity) times the change in price. By using the definition of the slope of the demand curve, s, we can express the loss on inframarginal units in terms of this slope. The slope of the demand curve is equal to the change in the price divided by the change in output. Here, the change in output is equal to 1. Hence, the slope is equal to the price change. Using this fact, the loss on the inframarginal units is the quantity sold times the slope of the demand curve: area $B = X \times s$.

The net effect of an increase in output and the accompanying fall in price is the sum of the two effects identified above. Hence, California Chemical's marginal revenue curve for Xyzene is

$$MR = p + X \times s. \quad (13.1)$$

Figure 13.3

Price Elasticity and the Loss on Inframarginal Units

When demand is highly inelastic, as in Panel A, the loss on the inframarginal units, illustrated by shaded area *C*, is large. When demand is relatively elastic, as in Panel B, the loss on inframarginal units, illustrated by shaded area *F*, is relatively small.

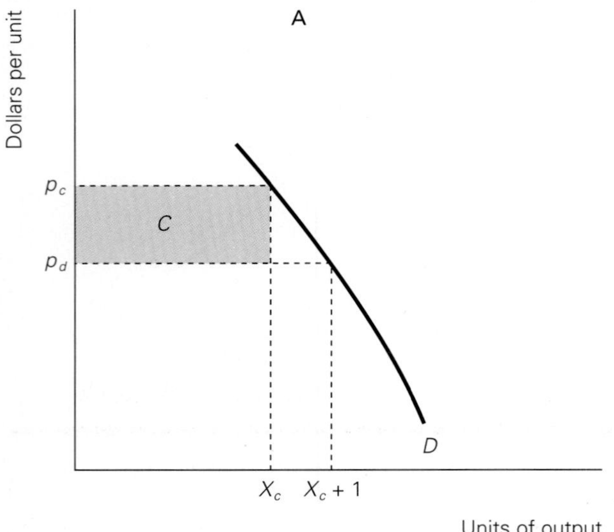

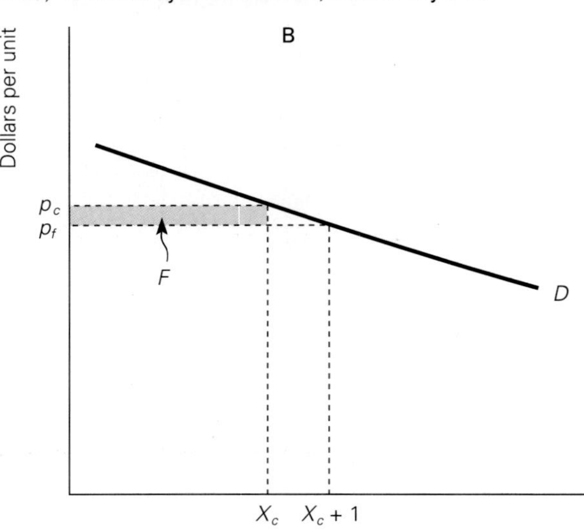

Since a monopolist faces a demand curve that has a negative slope ($s < 0$), Equation (13.1) confirms that, if the monopolist sells any output, the firm's marginal revenue is less than the price at which it sells the output. (PC 13.2)

Our next step is to express the marginal revenue formula in terms of the price elasticity of demand, ϵ. In Chapter 3, Equation (3.4), we showed that the own-price elasticity of market demand is

$$\epsilon = -p/(X \times s). \tag{13.2}$$

Equation (13.2) tells us that $X \times s = -p/\epsilon$. We can use this fact to rewrite Equation (13.1) in terms of the price elasticity of demand:

$$MR = p\{1 - 1/\epsilon\}. \tag{13.3}$$

13.2 PROGRESS CHECK

Suppose that California Chemical spends $20,000 on a new advertising campaign. As a result, the demand for Xyzene shifts upward by exactly $1 per gallon at all output levels. What happens to the firm's marginal revenue curve?

This is a useful expression for marginal revenue. The smaller the price elasticity of demand, the larger is $1/\epsilon$ and the smaller is $1 - 1/\epsilon$. Hence, Equation (13.3) tells us that the less elastic demand is, the lower the monopolist's marginal revenue. This result makes intuitive sense. When demand is highly inelastic, the demand curve is relatively steep, as in Panel A of Figure 13.3. Because a small increase in the quantity leads to a big drop in the price, the loss on the inframarginal units, illustrated by area *C*, is large. On the other hand, when demand is relatively elastic, as in Panel B of Figure 13.3, the loss on inframarginal units, illustrated by area *F*, is relatively small. In the extreme case of infinitely elastic demand, there is no loss on inframarginal units, $1/\epsilon = 0$ and $MR = p$. For the case of infinitely elastic demand, this formula confirms what we already knew: When the firm is a price taker, marginal revenue is equal to price.

Figure 13.4

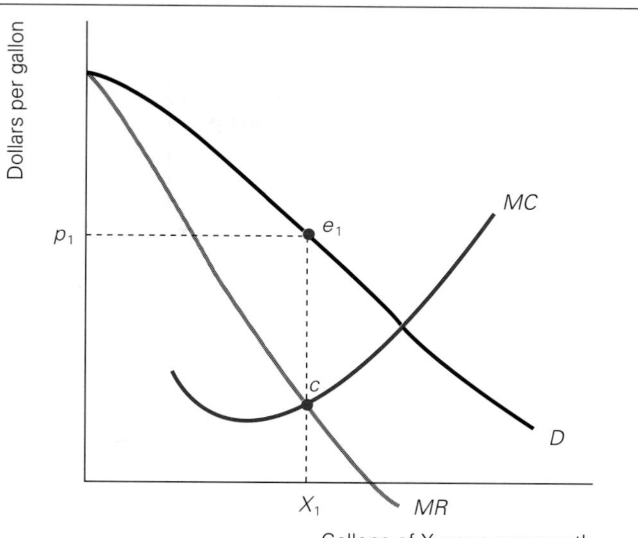

Using the Marginal Output Rule to Find the Monopolist's Equilibrium Price and Output

Like any profit-maximizing firm, the monopolist chooses the output level at which marginal revenue is equal to marginal cost, output level X_1. The equilibrium price is found by going up from X_1 on the horizontal axis until reaching the demand curve at price p_1.

We can gain further intuition behind Equation (13.3) by remembering the results from Chapter 3 relating elasticity and total revenue (Table 3.2). When demand is elastic ($\epsilon > 1$), the firm can raise revenue by lowering the price and selling more output. Hence, when the price elasticity is greater than 1, the firm's marginal revenue is positive. Equation (13.3) confirms this fact: Whenever ϵ is greater than 1, $(1 - 1/\epsilon)$ is positive and so is marginal revenue. On the other hand, if demand is inelastic ($\epsilon < 1$), then $(1 - 1/\epsilon)$ is negative and so is marginal revenue. Finally, when demand is unit elastic, the positive revenue effects of an output increase are exactly offset by the negative effects of the corresponding price decrease. Equation (13.3) confirms that marginal revenue is equal to 0 when $\epsilon = 1$.

Applying the Rules for Profit Maximization

Now that we have the monopolist's marginal revenue curve, we are ready to apply our two rules for the profit-maximizing choice of output level. The first rule tells us that if it remains in business, the monopolist chooses the output level at which marginal revenue is equal to marginal cost, output level X_1 in Figure 13.4. What price does the firm charge for this output? The firm wants to set the highest price at which it can sell X_1 units of output, given the demand for its output. By the definition of the demand curve, the highest price at which the firm can sell X_1 units of output is found by starting at X_1 on the horizontal axis and moving upward until reaching the demand curve at price p_1 in Figure 13.4.

An important implication of this analysis is that, unlike a price-taking firm, the monopolist's profit-maximizing price is *not* simply the common value of *MR* and *MC* at *c* in the figure. *A monopolist charges an equilibrium price that is greater than marginal cost.* The reason for this result is clear from the diagram. For a price-making firm, price is greater than marginal revenue. Any profit-maximizing supplier, a monopolist or otherwise, produces at a point where marginal revenue is equal to marginal cost. It follows that for a price maker, the equilibrium price is greater than the equilibrium level of marginal cost.

Figure 13.5

Using the Shut-Down Rule to Find the Monopolist's Equilibrium Price and Output

Our second general rule for profit maximization says that a monopolist must compare its average revenue with its average economic cost. When output is X_1, average revenue is p_1, which is greater than average cost. Operating at point e_1, the monopolist earns positive economic profit equal to the shaded area.

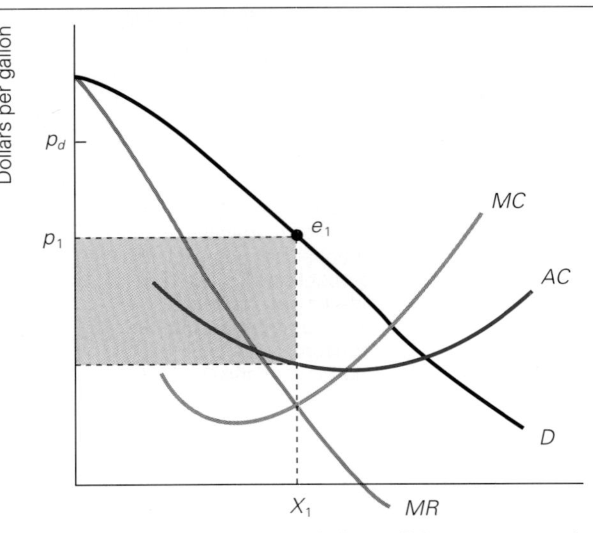

Once we have found the candidate price and output levels, we still have to check whether the monopolist would be better off shutting down. Our second general rule for profit maximization tells us that the firm must compare its average revenue with its average cost. As Figure 13.5 shows, California Chemical's output price is indeed greater than its average cost. Operating at point e_1, the monopolist earns positive economic profit equal to the shaded area, and therefore chooses not to shut down. (PC 13.3)

It is worth comparing our findings about the monopolist's equilibrium with common claim that a monopolist charges "whatever the market will bear"; that is, that the monopolist charges the highest price at which the firm can still make positive sales. As we have just seen in Figure 13.5, this is a poor prediction; a profit-maximizing monopolist will charge less than what the market will bear. California Chemical could continue to make some sales at a price above p_1, such as p_d, but it chooses not to do so. While raising the price from p_1 to p_d would lead to greater profit from the sale of inframarginal units, these gains would be more than offset by the loss in the total number of units sold.

13.3 PROGRESS CHECK

Suppose that California Chemical spends $20,000 on a new advertising campaign that shifts the demand for Xyzene upward by exactly $1 per gallon at all output levels. Graphically illustrate how the monopolist's new equilibrium point compares with point e_1.

Price Elasticity and Profit Maximization

We can employ algebra to obtain further insights into the monopolist's behavior. Using our expression for relating marginal revenue to the price elasticity of demand, Equation (13.3), we can write the $MR = MC$ rule as

$$p\{1 - 1/\epsilon\} = MC. \tag{13.4}$$

When demand is perfectly elastic, $(1 - 1/\epsilon) = 1$, and Equation (13.4) says that the firm should set price equal to marginal cost, our marginal output rule for a price taker. When demand is less than perfectly elastic, $(1 - 1/\epsilon)$ is less than 1 and the equilibrium price is greater than marginal cost. The less price-elastic the demand for a commodity, the greater the gap between the equilibrium price and marginal cost, *ceteris paribus.*

Equation (13.4) also tells us something about the value of the elasticity of demand at the monopolist's profit-maximizing price and quantity levels. Because we know that marginal cost always is positive (the firm never gets something for nothing), it follows that the monopolist's marginal revenue (given by the left-hand side of Equation (13.4)) also must be positive at the profit-maximizing output level. However, Equation (13.4) tells us that the only way that marginal revenue can be positive is for the price elasticity of demand to be greater than 1. We conclude that *demand must be elastic at the monopolist's equilibrium price and output levels.*

There is another way to see why this relationship holds. Suppose that demand were inelastic at the profit-maximizing output level and consider what would happen to the firm's profit if it were to raise its price by a little bit. Since *profit = total revenue − total cost,* the change in profit can be broken down into the change in total revenue and the change in total cost. Moving along the demand curve, the quantity demanded falls as price rises. Therefore, the firm needs to produce less and its total costs fall. Moreover, when demand is inelastic, an increase in price raises the firm's total revenue. Since the price increase raises total revenue and lowers total cost, it raises the monopolist's profit. But this contradicts the fact that the monopolist was supposed to have been producing the profit-maximizing level of output. Therefore, demand cannot be inelastic at the monopolist's equilibrium point.

The Long and the Short of Monopoly

Our discussion of perfect competition in Chapter 11 spent a lot of time distinguishing between short- and long-run decisions. You might be wondering why such distinctions have been absent for monopoly. It is not that this distinction no longer matters, it is just that the analysis is virtually identical for the two cases. If it is making a short-run decision, the monopolist bases its output choice on short-run marginal and average economic costs. If the firm is making a long-run decision, then it bases its output choice on long-run marginal and average economic costs.

The difference in the conditions of entry explains why the distinction between the short and long runs is so much more important under perfect competition than under monopoly. Under perfect competition, new firms can enter the market in the long run. In contrast, further entry into a monopolized market is completely blocked. In the long run, the incumbent merely adjusts its method of production.

In addition to simplifying the analysis of the long run, the lack of free entry has an important implication for profitability. When entry is free—as in a perfectly competitive market—new suppliers are attracted as long as there are positive economic profits to be had. Hence, in the long run, profits are driven to zero. When entry is blocked—as in a monopolized market—the incumbent firm's profit is not dissipated by entry. Although additional suppliers would like to enter the market and earn positive profits, they cannot. Because it does not face the threat of entry, *a monopolist may earn positive economic profit in the long run.*

Monopoly Compared to Perfect Competition

We have now developed two models of product markets: monopoly and perfect competition. How do the equilibria in these two types of market compare? In a way, this is an artificial question; the two models apply to different market

Figure 13.6

The Competitive Equilibrium for Smith and Wesson Oil

When the owner of each well is a price-taker, the supply curve of each individual well coincides with its marginal cost curve, as shown in Panel A. Summing the 10 individual supply curves horizontally, we get the market supply curve shown in Panel B. Taking the intersection of market supply and demand in Panel B yields the competitive equilibrium of $p^{comp} = 6$ and $X^{comp} = 10$.

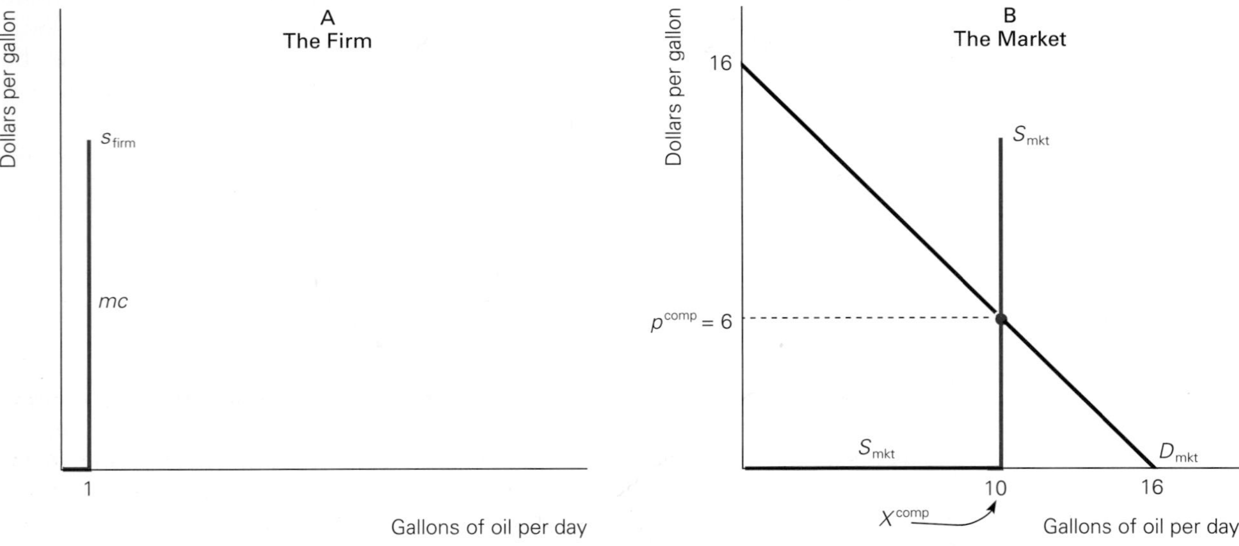

structures. We can, however, obtain an answer by considering a shift from a competitive market structure to a monopolistic one and seeing what happens. Suppose that 10 wells produce Smith and Wesson Oil. Each oil well can produce one gallon per day at no cost, but any single well can produce no more than one gallon per day. The marginal cost curve for an individual well, mc, is shown in Panel A of Figure 13.6. There are no close substitutes for Smith and Wesson Oil—it's the only product you can use to clean your gun *and* fry what you shoot. The market demand for this miracle product is given by $X = 16 - p$.

Suppose that the 10 wells are owned by 10 different owners (one well per owner). If these owners behave competitively as price takers, each firm believes that its firm-specific marginal revenue curve coincides with its firm-specific demand curve and both are flat at the prevailing market price. Hence, each firm maximizes its profit by producing at the point where price is equal to marginal cost. Thus, each firm's supply curve coincides with its marginal cost curve, as indicated in Panel A of Figure 13.6. Summing the 10 individual supply curves horizontally, we get the market supply curve, which is shown in Panel B. Taking the intersection of market supply and demand in Panel B yields the competitive equilibrium of $p^{comp} = \$6$ per gallon and $X^{comp} = 10$ gallons.

Suppose that the 10 well owners all sell out to a robber baron. What are the equilibrium price and quantity once the wells all are owned by a single firm? The single owner is a monopolist and thus a price maker. Figure 13.7 graphs the monopolist's demand and marginal revenue curves.[2] We also need to find the monopolist's marginal cost curve. We do this by looking at how total costs

[2]Algebraically, when the demand function is $X = 16 - p$, the monopolist's total and marginal revenue functions are $R(X) = 16X - X^2$ and $MR(X) = 16 - 2X$, respectively.

Figure 13.7

The Monopolistic Equilibrium for Smith and Wesson Oil

The monopolist chooses the output level at which marginal revenue is equal to marginal cost, 8 gallons per day. Reading up to the demand curve, we see that the firm charges a price of $8 per gallon.

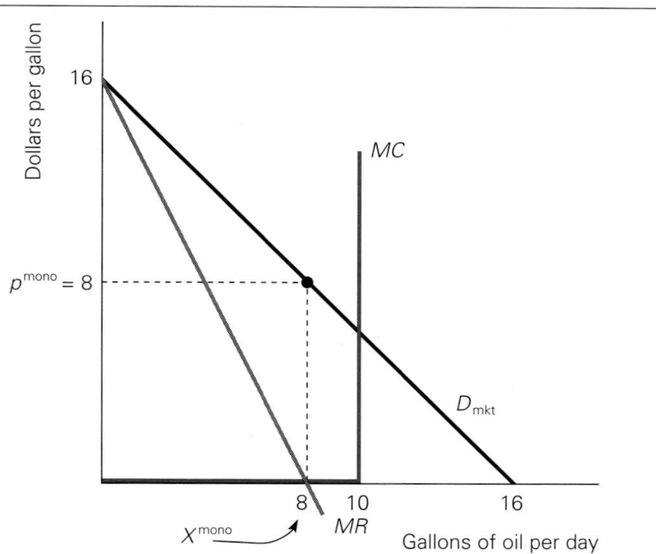

change as the firm increases its output. As long as the firm produces 10 or fewer gallons, its total costs are the same (zero) regardless of the output level, so marginal cost is equal to zero. Producing more than a total of 10 gallons is impossible, so at this point its marginal cost becomes infinite. The resulting marginal cost curve is labeled *MC* in Figure 13.7. Setting marginal revenue equal to marginal cost, we see that, at the monopolistic equilibrium, $X^{\text{mono}} = 8$ gallons of oil are sold at a price of $p^{\text{mono}} = \$8$ per gallon.

Recalling from Figure 13.6 that the competing firms would have sold 10 gallons of oil, we have just illustrated a general point: *A multiplant monopolist produces less output than would perfect competitors facing the same industry demand curve.* Intuitively, this happens because the multiplant monopolist recognizes that when it sells more output, it lowers the price of the gallons of oil it would have sold anyway. In contrast, when the suppliers are perfect competitors, each firm fails to recognize its effect on the market price, and thus the firms expand their output beyond the level at which the monopolist would stop. As we will discuss in the next section, this monopolistic output reduction is one of the reasons that governments often block firms from merging. (PC 13.4)

13.4 PROGRESS CHECK

So far, we have taken the number of Smith and Wesson Oil wells to be fixed. What would happen if entry were free? How many wells would the monopolist set up? What would the competitive and monopolistic output levels be?

TAXING A MONOPOLIST

We considered the effects of taxes in competitive markets. Let's look at what happens when a tax is levied on a monopolist. One sometimes hears the following claim: "Since it can charge any price that it wants to, a monopolist can pass on all of its cost increases to its customers in the form of higher prices. Therefore, a tax does not hurt a monopolist." The monopoly model provides a useful framework for assessing this claim.

Figure 13.8

The Effects of a Unit Tax

D, MR, and *MC* are California Chemical's before-tax demand, marginal revenue, and marginal cost curves, respectively. At the pre-tax equilibrium price (p_1) and quantity (X_1), the monopolist's profit is the sum of shaded areas *A, B,* and *C*. The tax shifts the firm's marginal cost curve upward by \$$t$ per gallon to MC_t. The new equilibrium quantity and price are X_2 and p_2. After-tax profit falls to shaded area *A*.

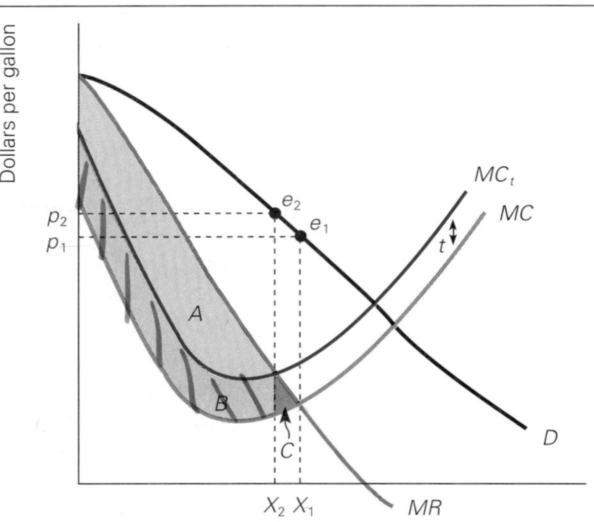

We start by finding the monopolist's equilibrium prior to taxation. *D, MR,* and *MC* in Figure 13.8 illustrate California Chemical's before-tax demand, marginal revenue, and marginal cost curves, respectively. Applying the two rules for profit maximization, the monopolist's equilibrium price and output levels are p_1 and X_1, respectively. To calculate the associated profit (total revenue minus total cost), we need to remember that total cost equals the area under the marginal cost curve up to the quantity produced. Similarly, total revenue is equal to the area under the marginal revenue curve up to the quantity produced. Taking the difference, the figure indicates that California Chemical is earning a positive profit equal to the sum of areas *A, B,* and *C*.

Suppose that the government now levies a unit tax on the monopolist of \$$t$ per gallon of Xyzene sold. As always, the firm produces at the point where marginal revenue is equal to marginal cost, but now the marginal cost of production includes the \$$t$-per-gallon tax. California Chemical's marginal cost curve including the tax, MC_t, is equal to the no-tax marginal cost curve, *MC*, shifted upward by \$$t$ per gallon. The new equilibrium quantity is found where marginal revenue crosses the after-tax marginal cost curve, X_2, in Figure 13.8. Reading off of the demand curve, we see that the new price is p_2. As a result of the tax, the firm produces less output and raises the price. Of course, we also have to check that the firm would not choose to shut down. We will come back to this point shortly. For now, take it as given that the firm continues to produce output.

What happens to the monopolist's profit? While the number of gallons of Xyzene falls, the price per gallon rises, so we need to think carefully to find the answer. We know that the original price maximized the monopolist's profit in the absence of the tax. It follows that raising the price reduces the firm's profit relative to its original level even if we do not subtract the tax out of the firm's profit at the new equilibrium point.[3] Once we subtract the tax, the firm's profit falls by

[3]The monopolist is not being irrational in raising the price in response to the tax because, although the price change lowers *before*-tax profits, it maximizes *after*-tax profits.

even more. We conclude that the claim made above is false: *Even though the firm raises its price in response to a unit tax, a monopolist's profit falls when a unit tax is imposed on it.* And Question 13.4 at the end of this chapter discusses the even greater portion of the burden borne by the monopolist when the tax is a fixed amount, independent of the output level.

We can see the effects of a unit tax graphically by considering that the firm's profit is equal to the area under the marginal revenue curve and over the marginal cost curve up to the quantity sold. Without the tax, California Chemical produces X_1 units of output, and its profit is equal to the sum of shaded areas *A*, *B*, and *C* in Figure 13.8. When the tax is imposed, the firm sells only X_2 gallons of Xyzene, and its profit is equal to shaded area *A*, where we have used the firm's *after-tax* marginal cost curve for the calculation of profit. As a result of the tax, profits fall by the sum of areas *B* and *C*.

We can interpret each of the two shaded areas representing the fall in profits due to the tax. Area *B* is the money actually paid by the firm to the government: The total tax payment is equal to the tax per gallon times the number of gallons sold, or $\$t \times X_2$, and the vertical distance between MC_t and MC is equal to t. Area *C* captures the profits lost when the firm cuts back its output by $X_1 - X_2$ units in response to the tax. Each of these units generates marginal revenue greater than the costs of production. Hence, in the absence of the tax, sales of these units were contributing to the firm's profits. Once the tax is imposed, sales of these units are no longer profitable, and their earlier contribution is lost. (PC 13.5)

13.5 PROGRESS CHECK

Until now, we have not considered the shut-down rule. How can we be sure from Figure 13.8 that California Chemical will not choose to shut down in response to the unit tax?

INCENTIVES TO INNOVATE

While we will generally focus on a monopolist's choice of price and output, there are other decisions a monopolist must make. One of the most important is how much to invest in research and development activities (R&D). Broadly speaking, a firm can undertake two types of R&D. **Process innovation** refers to an idea that lowers the cost of producing existing products, such as a technique that allows a hormone to be synthesized more rapidly. **Product innovation** refers to an idea that gives rise to a new good or service, such as the invention of plain-paper copiers or video cassette recorders. It is worth noting that some R&D has elements of both process and product innovation. The invention of the microprocessor, for example, lowered the cost of producing computing services but it did this so dramatically that it created what most of us think of as a new product, the personal computer.

process innovation
An idea that lowers the cost of producing existing products.

product innovation
An idea that gives rise to a new good or service.

Process Innovation

It is sometimes said that a monopolist does not have an incentive to develop new production processes because doing so makes its existing plant and machinery obsolete. Others have countered with the argument that a monopolist will invest in a new technology whenever doing so lowers its costs. The theory of monopoly can help us understand what the firm's incentives to innovate really are.

Suppose that California Chemical's current marginal cost curve is *MC* in Figure 13.9, but that by undertaking R&D the firm can lower its marginal cost curve

Figure 13.9

The Incentive to Innovate

Without the innovation, the monopolist's marginal cost curve is *MC*, the equilibrium point is e_1, and profit is shaded area *A*. With the innovation, the firm's marginal cost curve falls to *MC*′. The equilibrium point becomes e_3, and the resulting profit is the sum of shaded areas *A* and *B*. Hence, area *B* is the amount that the monopolist is willing to spend to obtain the innovation.

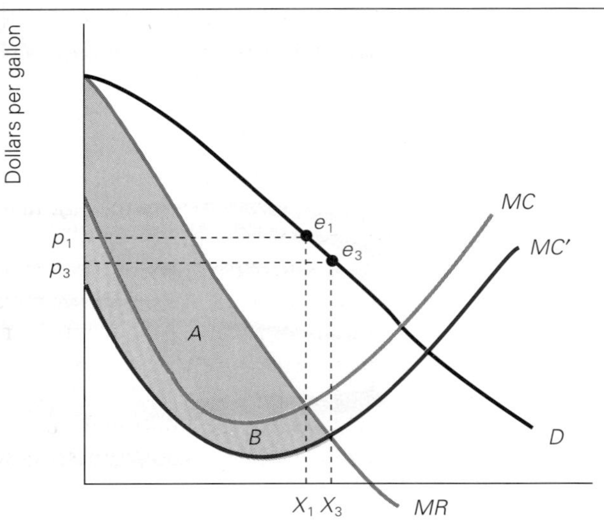

to *MC*′. How much is California Chemical willing to spend to obtain this process innovation? The answer depends on the amount by which the innovation raises the firm's profit. Without the innovation, California Chemical's equilibrium point is e_1. The figure indicates that without the innovation, California Chemical's profit is shaded area *A*. (Here, again, we are using the fact that total revenues and costs are the areas under the corresponding marginal curves.) With the innovation, California Chemical's equilibrium point becomes e_3, and the resulting profit is the sum of areas *A* and *B*. Hence, area *B* represents the amount that the monopolist is willing to spend to obtain the innovation.

Figure 13.9 illustrates that as long as the innovation leads to lower production costs, the monopolist derives benefits from the innovation, even if it means rendering existing plant and machinery obsolete. It is important to keep two points in mind. First, if the existing plant and machinery have no alternative uses (i.e., are sunk expenditures), their economic (opportunity) cost is zero. Consequently, the original marginal cost and thus the value of a process innovation may be low, at least until it is necessary to replace the plant and machinery. The second point is that innovations have costs as well as benefits. The monopolist must compare the benefits of innovation (in the form of lower production costs), with the costs of the R&D needed to develop the innovation. In the present example, if the process innovation costs less than area *B*, then the monopolist will proceed with the project. Otherwise, it will not.

Product Innovation

A firm that successfully innovates a unique product can apply for patent protection that grants the firm a monopoly in the sale of the new product. For such product innovations, the incentive to undertake R&D is the entire amount of monopoly profit that the firm will be able to earn once it obtains the patent. We will have more to say about product innovation when we consider public policy toward monopoly later in the chapter.

SECTION RECAP

We have now seen our second complete model of market equilibrium, monopoly. Like any profit-maximizing firm, a monopolist produces output at a point where marginal revenue is equal to marginal cost. Unlike a price-taking firm, a monopolist's marginal revenue curve and firm-specific demand curve do not coincide. For a monopolist, marginal revenue is less than the price. Since the firm sets marginal revenue equal to marginal cost, it follows that, in equilibrium, price is greater than marginal cost. It also follows that a multiplant monopolist produces less output than perfect competitors facing the same industry demand curve. In addition to the marginal output rule, the monopolist also applies the shut-down rule: average revenue must be no less than average economic cost.

13.2 NORMATIVE ANALYSIS OF MONOPOLY

The positive analysis of monopoly demonstrates that the equilibrium price and output levels in a monopolized market are different from their values in a competitive market with the same cost and demand conditions. We now examine the normative consequences of these differences. We will consider equity and efficiency issues in turn.

EQUITY

We showed earlier how the tools of economics help us determine who gains and who loses from various changes in government policy (such as rent control). Economics also tells us the winners and losers when the market structure shifts from competition to monopoly, as might happen when otherwise competitive firms merge into a monopoly. We know that the change from competition to monopoly leads to higher profit for the suppliers. We also have seen that the equilibrium price rises, which reduces consumer surplus. Therefore, when supply becomes monopolized, the suppliers gain and the consumers lose.

Are these income shifts desirable? The answer depends on our ethical judgments regarding how deserving the suppliers and consumers are. That is, it depends on our social welfare function. Someone whose social welfare function gives equal weight to everyone, for instance, is likely to come up with a different answer than someone whose social welfare function implies that people with relatively low incomes are more deserving than those with high incomes.

Suppose that the social welfare function puts more weight on low-income people than high-income ones. Does this mean that the transfer of income from consumers to suppliers is undesirable? Not necessarily. Monopolization raises the firm's profit and the income of the firm's owners, and it lowers the incomes of consumers. But the consumers may well have higher incomes than many of the owners. While people tend to think of stockholders as wealthy people, over $1.5 trillion of the shares held by Americans are owned by workers' pension funds (U.S. Bureau of the Census 1995, Table 825). The average shareholder in a company that sells cellular telephones could well have a lower income than the average cellular phone buyer. This simple example warns us that we have to be careful when thinking through the equity consequences of a change in the market outcome. Economics provides a useful framework in which to do so.

EFFICIENCY

Turning to questions of efficiency, the First Welfare Theorem tells us that a competitive economy is efficient. When a monopolist behaves noncompetitively, we would suspect that it is not efficient. As we will see, this suspicion is justified. To see why, it is useful to conduct the analysis at two different levels. First, we will analyze the efficiency of monopoly in a partial equilibrium framework. Second, we will use our general equilibrium approach to assess the effects of market power on the efficiency of the market economy as a whole.

A Partial Equilibrium Analysis

The partial equilibrium approach focuses exclusively on the particular market in which the monopolist supplies its output. Along the lines suggested at the end of Chapter 11, we use total surplus, the difference between gross consumption benefits and total cost, as our measure of efficiency. In comparing two outcomes, the one that yields the higher level of total surplus is the more efficient one.

Does the monopolist produce the total-surplus-maximizing level of output? We already know that perfect competition leads to the efficient output level and that monopoly leads to less output than perfect competition. It follows that a monopoly produces less than the total-surplus-maximizing level of output.

We can see the inefficiency of monopoly graphically by looking at the monopolistic Xyzene market one more time. As shown in Figure 13.10, California Chemical sells X_1 units of output at a price of p_1. The resulting level of total surplus is the area under the demand curve and above the marginal cost curve, shaded area A.[4] To see that the monopolist is producing too little output, suppose that it were to sell one additional unit. This $X_1 + 1$st unit of output would generate additional gross consumption benefits equal to the sum of areas B and C in Figure 13.10. The increase in cost is simply the marginal cost of this last unit, shaded area C. Taking the difference between marginal social benefits and marginal cost, we see that total surplus rises by area B. Thus, total surplus is increased by moving beyond X_1.

Indeed, total surplus continues to increase until we reach the output level where the marginal social benefit is equal to the marginal social cost; that is, where the height of the demand curve is equal to the height of the marginal cost curve. This output level is denoted by X_T in Figure 13.11. Taking the difference between total surplus at this output level and total surplus under monopoly, we see that it is lower under monopoly by shaded areas E and F. These areas represent the **deadweight loss of monopoly.** Deadweight loss represents a loss for which there is no offsetting gain. This loss arises under monopoly because there are consumers who would derive benefits from the additional output that are greater than the marginal cost of these units.

deadweight loss of monopoly
The loss in total surplus that arises because a monopolist produces less than the total-surplus-maximizing amount of output.

We can gain further insight into the source of this inefficiency by considering the roles that price plays in this market. A profit-maximizing monopolist uses

[4] Recall from our discussion of consumer surplus in Chapters 4 and 11 that the area under the demand curve represents only an approximation to the compensating variation. As long as income effects on demand are small, this approximation is a good one.

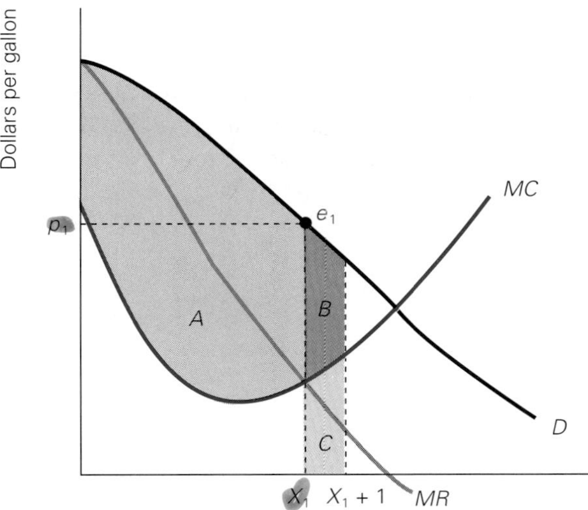

The monopolist sells X_1 units of output at a price of p_1, which results in total surplus of shaded area A. If the monopolist produced one more unit of output, gross consumption benefits would rise by the sum of shaded areas B and C, while the cost increase would be the marginal cost of this last unit, shaded area C. Taking the difference, total surplus would rise by shaded area B.

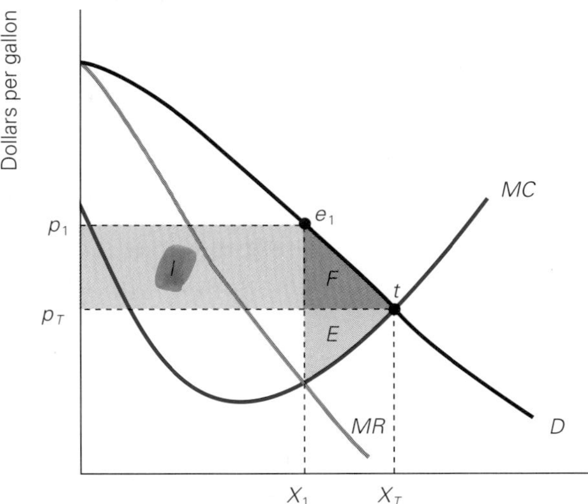

Total surplus is maximized by producing at the output level where the height of the demand curve is equal to the height of the marginal cost curve, X_T. Taking the difference between total surplus at this output level and total surplus under the monopoly outcome, we see that monopoly gives rise to a deadweight loss equal to the sum of shaded areas E and F.

price to serve two roles simultaneously: (1) to provide incentives to consumers making purchase decisions and (2) to transfer income from consumers to itself. When the firm raises the price from the competitive level, p_T in Figure 13.11, to the monopoly level, p_1, the incentive provision is worse. Consumers are induced to buy fewer than the efficient number of units; total consumption falls from X_T to X_1, and total surplus falls by the sum of areas E and F. From the monopolist's perspective, however, the income transfer role is improved. Consumers pay more per unit for those units that they continue to buy, and area I is a pure transfer of income from consumers to the monopolist. For the profit maximizer, the second effect dominates the first, and the monopolist finds price above marginal cost to be desirable. From an efficiency standpoint, only the incentive role of price matters; the pure transfer of surplus from consumers to the monopolist has no effect on the total amount of surplus generated in the market. Since the incentive effect is negative, the monopolist's price is set too high from an efficiency viewpoint.

There is another way to understand the source of deadweight loss. Think about the monopolist's incentive to produce output. When it chooses its output level, the firm is concerned only with its own profit. The monopolist's *private* incentive to increase its output is determined by the change in its profit. Moreover, the change in profit equals the change in producer surplus. (This is due to the assumption that the monopolist is a price-taking buyer in competitive input markets, so that its input decisions have no effect on the producer surplus of the suppliers of its inputs.) Hence, we can write:

Figure 13.12

Consumer Surplus Rises as the Monopolist Increases Its Output Level

When output is at X_g, the associated price is p_g and consumer surplus is shaded area G. In order to increase output to X_h, the firm must lower the price to p_h, which raises consumer surplus to the sum of areas G and H.

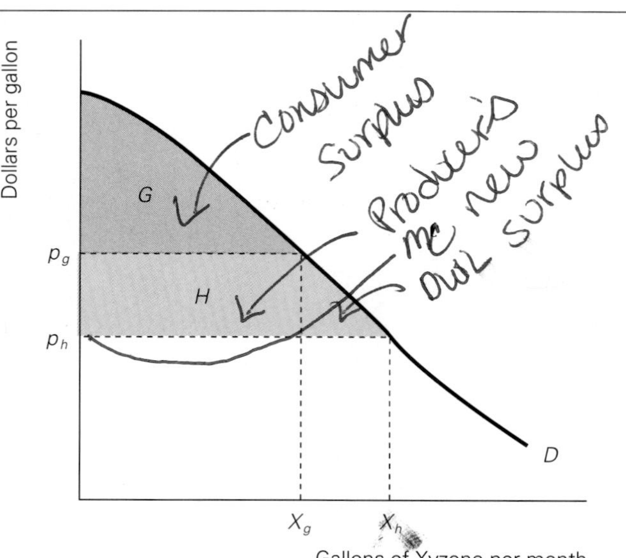

Firm's private incentive = *Change in producer surplus.*

Our measure of efficiency, total surplus, takes consumer surplus and producer surplus into account. Hence, the net benefit to society from additional output, the social incentive to produce more, is equal to the sum of the effects on producer surplus and consumer surplus:

Social incentive = *Change in producer surplus* + *Change in consumer surplus.*

Comparing these expressions for the private and social incentives, the source of the problem is clear—the monopolist fails to take into account the effects of its output choice on consumer surplus.

How does the monopolist's output choice affect consumer surplus? Figure 13.12 tells us that when the output level is X_g, the resulting surplus is equal to shaded area G. How is consumer surplus affected by an increase in output to X_h? To sell more output, the firm must lower the price, which raises consumer surplus by area H. This finding is a general one: Consumer surplus rises with the level of output.

Let's put together what we know. The private incentive to increase output is equal to the change in profit. The social incentive to increase output is equal to the change in profit plus the change in consumer surplus. Since the change in consumer surplus is always positive as output rises, we know that the change in total surplus is always greater than the change in profit. In other words, the monopolist's incentive to increase its output is too small. Consequently, for any given marginal cost curve, the monopolist produces too little output.

A General Equilibrium Analysis

A general equilibrium approach to the normative analysis of monopoly examines its effects within the context of the entire market economy. As we did in

Chapter 12, we can divide the efficiency effects into those concerning production efficiency, consumption efficiency, and allocation efficiency.

Production Efficiency Many people believe that monopolists are wasteful and do not achieve production efficiency. To analyze a monopolist's performance, remember that the higher a firm's cost, the lower its profit, *ceteris paribus*. Hence, a profit-maximizing monopolist acts to minimize its cost. It also is important to remember that a monopolist is a price maker when its comes to selling its output, but a price taker when buying inputs to use in the production of output. Suppose that California Chemical produces Xyzene by using two inputs, labor and capital. As a price taker in the input markets, the monopolist follows the rule for cost minimization: it sets the marginal rate of technical substitution (*MRTS*) between any two inputs (say, capital and labor) equal to their price ratio.

Because we are taking a general equilibrium perspective, we need to know something about the other markets in the economy. If all the other firms in the economy are price takers in their roles as input buyers, the equilibrium values of *MRTS* will be the same across all firms, and our condition for production efficiency (Equation (12.2)) will be satisfied. We conclude that *a profit-maximizing firm that is a price maker in the output market, but a price taker in input markets, makes an efficient input choice.*

We have just seen that a *profit-maximizing* monopolist produces its output efficiently. But when we discussed the theory of the firm in Chapter 7, we noted that managers of a firm that does not face product-market competition may not face pressure to maximize profit. The managers of a monopoly may prefer to enjoy a quiet life rather than to worry constantly about whether the firm is using the best combination of inputs to produce its output. Consequently, if the monopoly is not operated as a profit-maximizing firm, it may indeed suffer from production inefficiency. The important point to note here is that monopolistic greed is not the source of this problem. Rather, the source of the problem is that managers may be free to pursue goals other than profit maximization.

Consumption Efficiency Consumption efficiency requires that every consumer have the same marginal rate of substitution (*MRS*) between the monopolist's good and any other good (Equation (12.1)). Is this condition satisfied in the presence of a monopoly? A nondiscriminating monopolist charges a single price to all of its consumers. If the other firms in the economy also do not engage in price discrimination, then for each commodity there will be a single price charged to all consumers. Because utility-maximizing consumers set their *MRS*s equal to the ratio of product prices (Equation (2.3)), it follows that the equilibrium values of the *MRS* will be the same across all consumers, and our condition for consumption efficiency is satisfied. We conclude that *if other firms in the economy do not engage in price discrimination, then the equilibrium for a nondiscriminating monopolist entails an efficient allocation of output among consumers taking as given the total amount produced.*

Allocation Efficiency Given its output level, a profit-maximizing monopolist chooses an efficient means of production and allocates the output efficiently among consumers. But our partial equilibrium analysis tells us that the firm chooses an inefficient level of output. General equilibrium analysis also suggests that monopoly is inefficient. To see why, recall from the last chapter that a necessary condition for economic efficiency is that the ratio of the prices of any two goods be equal to the ratio of their marginal costs. *If all of the other goods in the economy are sold in perfectly competitive markets at prices equal to their marginal costs, then the monopolist violates the condition for allocation efficiency because it sets the price of its product greater than its marginal costs.* In this case, the economy-wide equilibrium is inefficient because the monopolist produces too little output.

SECTION RECAP

In this section, we have examined the efficiency of monopoly. Provided that it is maximizing profit, a nondiscriminating monopolist chooses an efficient means of producing its output, but produces too little output overall—total surplus would rise if the monopolist produced more output.

13.3 PUBLIC POLICY TOWARD MONOPOLY

Because of the inefficiency of monopoly, a considerable public policy effort is aimed at blocking the creation of monopolies or limiting their ability to exercise market power. Some public policy, however, actually helps create monopolies. In this section, we will examine how these different policies work.

PATENT POLICY

As we noted earlier, a firm that successfully develops a new product, such as a new drug, may be granted patent protection that keeps other firms from entering the market. This public policy might appear inefficient. After all, if the firm were not granted a patent, other producers might copy the idea, resulting in the development of a competitive market. And a competitive market would generate a greater amount of total surplus than would a monopoly.

Why, then, does the government issue patents and block competition? When patent protection is granted, the firm's incentive to innovate is equal to the monopoly profits created by the product. Suppose that the government did not grant patent protection and the firm expected imitators to flood the market as soon as it successfully innovated. In this case, even a successful innovation would generate little or no economic profit. Faced with such a prospect, the firm would have no incentive to undertake the R&D in the first place. Instead of leading to a competitive marketplace, eliminating patent protection could destroy the market altogether!

Of course, it does not follow that a patent has to protect the innovator from competition forever. The current policy of granting most patents for 17 years reflects one judgment about how to make the trade-off between efficient output levels and the stimulation of R&D.

antitrust policy
The set of laws designed to prevent firms from exercising market power by the firms' restricting output and engaging in other anticompetitive behavior.

ANTITRUST POLICY

The monopolist's equilibrium violates our conditions for economic efficiency. This situation sets up a potential role for government intervention to improve efficiency. The set of laws designed to prevent a firm from attaining a monopoly position or to stop a group of firms from collectively acting like a monopolist to restrict output is known as **antitrust policy.** The granddaddy of U.S. antitrust legislation is the Sherman Antitrust Act of 1890. This act proscribes monopolies and attempts to monopolize. This act, and the amendments made to it over the years, form the basis of U.S. antimonopoly policy.

Antitrust authorities can influence firm behavior in two basic ways: *conduct remedies* and *structural remedies.*

conduct remedy
A government-imposed change in firm behavior (conduct) designed to make the market more competitive.

A **conduct remedy** is a government restriction on the firm's behavior. For example, if the government finds that firms have acted together to raise prices (known as *price fixing*), it can punish them and order them to stop. Price fixing firms can be subject to fines, and the managers may be imprisoned. This actually happened when Allis Chalmers, General Electric, and Westinghouse were caught running an illegal cartel to sell turbine generators in the 1950s.

Conduct remedies can limit anticompetitive behavior in two ways. First, they provide a direct means of stopping such conduct. Second, the threat of prosecution may discourage companies from even trying to behave anticompetitively.

While conduct remedies appear to address the problem of monopolies and price fixing head-on, this type of policy has severe difficulties. Antitrust authorities have to monitor the firms continually to see what is going on in the industry and to be sure that the firms are not behaving illegally. Given the complexity of actual firm behavior, this many be a very difficult and expensive task. Moreover, while it may be clear what firms should not be doing, it may be much less clear what they should be doing. In some cases, what appears to be coordinated pricing arises not from explicit collusion by industry members, but as a result of each firm's *individual and independent* recognition that its interests are best served by reducing output below the competitive level in the expectation that other firms will do likewise. It is hard to tell a manager, "Even though you are not colluding with rival producers, you should not make decisions that you think are in your firm's best interest." Even if you could, what would you tell the manager to do instead?

structural remedy
A government-imposed change in the industry structure designed to make the market more competitive.

Because of the problems with conduct remedies, antitrust authorities may choose a **structural remedy,** which alters the industry structure to make it more competitive. The most extreme form of a structural remedy is the forced breakup of an existing firm. In 1911, Standard Oil of New Jersey was broken up into what are today Amoco, Chevron, Exxon, Mobil, and other companies. Starting in 1969, U.S. antitrust authorities spent 15 years arguing that IBM should be broken up because it had monopoly power. Some people have suggested that Microsoft be broken into two separate companies, one responsible for operating systems and the other responsible for applications software and Microsoft's other products. The biggest corporate restructuring in history, the 1984 breakup of the Bell System into AT&T and seven regional telephone companies (such as Nynex, Ameritech, and Pacific Telesis) was in response to concerns about the exercise of market power. A less extreme, and much more common, form of structural remedy is to block mergers before they happen. Of course, blocking a merger is also something of a conduct remedy (it is a limitation on firm behavior).

While the line between structural and conduct remedies is not always sharp, structural remedies do tend to have two general advantages over conduct remedies. First, by creating underlying market conditions that foster competition, a structural remedy obviates the need for continual detailed monitoring of firms' behavior to ensure compliance. (It is much easier to spot a merger than it is to see if firms are setting prices competitively.) Second, once the structural remedy has been imposed, managers can be left free to act in the way that they believe best serves the interests of their firms.

Determinants of Market Structure

Given the problems with conduct remedies, why not always use structural remedies? One answer is that breakups of existing companies are extremely complex to implement (How should employees and capital be divided up? Who is responsible for the pensions of employees who are about to retire? Who gets to keep the half-completed research and development project?). But there is a more important reason. Market structure is not something that we just pull out of the air. It is based on the underlying production technology and consumer tastes. Therefore, before we conclude that it is a good idea to restructure a market, we need to understand the origins of the existing structure. In other words, we must examine the underlying conditions that give rise to an uncompetitive market structure. We will consider three.

Economies of Scale One reason a market may have few firms is that the market is too small to support a large number of firms. This situation arises when economies of scale are strong, so that the average cost curve falls steeply over a broad range of output levels. If many firms attempt to enter such a market, each finds that its sales are so low that is has a very high average cost level—one that exceeds its average revenue.

An extreme case of economies of scale shaping market structure occurs when the full realization of economies of scale necessitates having only one active producer in the industry. An industry is said to be a **natural monopoly** if, over the range of relevant output levels, a single firm can produce the total industry output at less cost than any greater number of firms. If the average cost curve is downward sloping for all levels of output, for example, then any way of dividing a given level of output among producers will give each of them higher average costs than if one firm produced all of the output by itself. Hence, *when average cost declines over the entire range of output levels, the lowest-cost way to produce any given level of output is to have one firm responsible for all of the output; the industry is a natural monopoly.* The distribution of electricity of houses and factories is one example of a natural monopoly. The cheapest way to distribute electricity in a town is to have only one company do it. That way, there is no need to have two sets of wires running from the power plant to the customers.

natural monopoly
An industry in which, over the range of relevant output levels, a single firm can produce the total industry output at less cost than can any greater number of firms.

Suppose that antitrust enforcers split up firms in a market that has only a few suppliers due to the presence of strong economies of scale. This breakup would raise the average costs of producing any given level of market output because the resulting firms would be too small to achieve the benefits of large-scale production. Hence, before concluding that a breakup would be a good thing, we must compare the benefits of increased competition with the increased average cost of production.

Barriers to Entry In addition to the effects of economies of scale, the number of firms in an industry may be limited by barriers to entry. There are two types of barrier: technological and legal. A technological barrier arises when would-be entrants just do not have the necessary knowledge or access to inputs. For example, a tremendous amount of specialized knowledge is needed to operate a semiconductor chip fabrication facility. A potential entrant faces a Catch-22, because the only way to acquire this information is to operate a plant.

A legal barrier arises when there are entry restrictions imposed as a matter of government policy. For instance, governments of most countries severely limit the number of firms allowed to provide long-distance telephone or airline service. Patents are another source of government-imposed barriers to entry. Indeed, patent protection is often one of the reasons that a would-be entrant does not have access to needed technology. In 1996, Genentech used its patents to wage a legal battle against Novo Nordisk AS and other companies to block their entry into the market for genetically engineered human growth hormones. While the government could remove the barriers created by patents by revoking them, it could do so only at the risk of reducing incentives for future innovation.

Product Differentiation When firms' products are differentiated, producers are not price takers even when there are many firms in the market. There are thousands of gasoline stations, for example, and they offer differentiated products. If you live in Butte, Montana, a gas station in Arlington, Texas is not much of a substitute for your corner gas station. This spatial differentiation gives a gas station some market power unless there are other stations close by. Why not put a gas station on every corner? The answer is, of course, that it would be too costly. More precisely, with a large number of small gas stations, suppliers would not be able to realize economies of scale. In a sense, product differentiation amplifies the effects of economies of scale that were discussed earlier. When products are differentiated, competition cannot be achieved just by having many suppliers in the market; there have to be many firms of *each variant* of the good (in our example, many gas stations at each corner). Demand simply may not be large enough to support that many suppliers.

What can be done about product differentiation? When products truly are different (as are gas stations at different locations), it is hard to see what the government can do. Even if the government could eliminate product differentiation, such a policy often would be senseless. Would you recommend that all automobile manufacturers be forced to produce exactly the same car?

There are some markets, however, in which a specific mechanism for supporting product differentiation has come under attack: brand names. Brand names can play a crucial role in maintaining product differentiation. Whether or not you like their products, the names Kodak, American Express, and McDonald's probably mean something to you. When existing firms have well-known and highly regarded brand names, it may be difficult for new firms to enter the market with competing products. Why not force the firms to share their brand names? The Federal Trade Commission actually considered doing just this to Borden in the case of ReaLemon, the dominant brand of concentrated lemon juice for use in cooking.

In the end, Borden was allowed to keep its trademark for itself. Public policy allows brand names because although brand names (like patents) may generate some monopoly power, brand names (again like patents) also provide important incentives. Brand names help give firms incentives to produce high-quality products. When each product is associated with a brand name, consumers form beliefs about which producers supply good products and which ones do not—suppliers develop reputations. When it allows a firm to charge higher prices, a respected brand name is a valuable asset. Hence, suppliers have incentives to invest in their reputations by supplying high-quality goods and services. In contrast, if a firm is not allowed to develop a brand name, it has no way to distinguish itself from rival producers and has much less incentive to produce high-quality products.

Conclusion The following general point emerges from our discussion of the determinants of market structure: *It may be prohibitively costly, or even impossible, to create a competitive market structure in some industries.* Consequently, antitrust authorities may rely on conduct remedies rather than structural ones.

REGULATION OF MONOPOLY

As just discussed, there are situations in which cost conditions or consideration of investment incentives make it impossible or undesirable to restructure a monopolized industry. But the discussion surrounding Figure 13.11 indicates that, if the market has a single producer, it will take advantage of its monopoly position by producing an inefficiently small amount of output.

regulation
The process by which the government engages in pervasive intervention in the operation of a market.

One response to this quandary has been **regulation,** the process by which the government engages in pervasive intervention in the operation of a market. To think about the effects of regulation, consider the provision of local telephone service. This market generally contains too few producers for competition to be viable—most households have only one choice of supplier for local telephone service. As a result, policymakers feel that they cannot rely on market forces alone to determine efficient price and output levels. At the same time, government authorities also believe that it is too inefficient to break existing suppliers into smaller firms. While several companies may offer you their brands of local telephone service, they generally are simply reselling the services of the incumbent monopolist. Policymakers have responded to this dilemma by allowing monopoly provision of local telephone service but maintaining strict government oversight of pricing and input decisions.

Let's examine the regulation of a natural monopoly a little more closely. Figure 13.13 illustrates the cost and demand curves for a local telephone company, Ding-a-Ling Lines. In the absence of government regulation, the firm would provide X_1 households with telephone service at a price of $50 per month. Notice that there would be some consumers who were willing to pay more than the marginal cost of providing them with telephone service, yet who were not consuming the service under the unregulated market equilibrium—there is a range of output levels greater than X_1 for which the D curve is still above the MC curve.

In response to this inefficiency, the government decides to regulate the firm. What should the regulators do? Foremost, they must recognize the following central point: *The regulated firm is a self-interested decision maker.* In other words, the firm that is being regulated will respond to these regulations in the way that best serves *its* interests, not those of the regulator. This point has three important implications.

1. *A regulated firm must be allowed to earn nonnegative profit.* While regulators may be able to tell a firm what to do, given that it is in business, they may not be able to prevent the firm from going bankrupt and ceasing production entirely. Thus, for example, the regulators might want the firm to produce the efficient output level, X_T in Figure 13.14. (We know that X_T is efficient because there the height of the demand curve is equal to marginal cost.) However, the highest price at which the firm can sell this much output is $10, which is less than the corresponding average cost of $23. If the regulators ordered the firm to sup-

Figure 13.13

The Monopoly Equilibrium in the Absence of Regulation

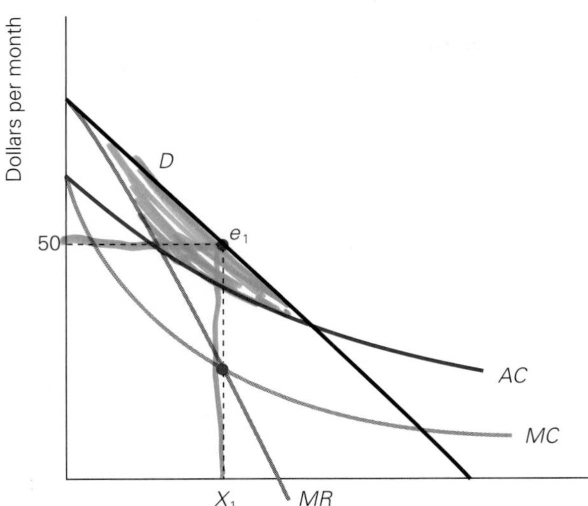

In the absence of government regulation, the firm would provide X_1 households with telephone service at a price of $50 per month.

Figure 13.14

The Regulated Outcome

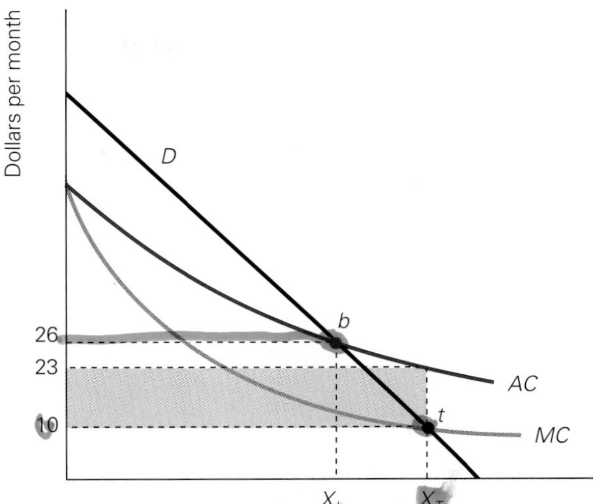

Total surplus is maximized at X_T where marginal social benefit, as measured by the height of the demand curve, is equal to marginal cost. The resulting price is $10. At this price and quantity combination, the firm suffers losses equal to the shaded area. X_b is the highest level of output at which the firm can earn nonnegative profit. The resulting price, $26, is equal to average cost, and Ding-a-Ling earns zero economic profit.

ply X_T units of service, the firm would suffer losses equal to the shaded area in Figure 13.14, and would rather shut down than produce. To keep the firm in business, regulators have to allow it to sell less output. From Figure 13.14, we see that X_b is the highest level of output at which the firm can earn nonnegative profit. At this point, the price of $26 is equal to average cost, and Ding-a-Ling earns zero economic profit.

The regulator's trade-off between total surplus and profit also can be expressed in terms of pricing. To maximize total surplus, the regulators would like the firm to price its output at marginal cost. But to keep the firm in business, they must allow it to price at average cost, which is higher. There is a tension between the income-transfer role of price (generating nonnegative profit for the producer) and the incentive role (inducing consumers to purchase the efficient level of telephone services).

2. *A regulated firm will use its private information to its own advantage.* To implement average-cost pricing, regulators need to know what average cost is. However, regulators typically do not know for certain what the firm's average cost curve looks like. While they may have a general idea, the exact level of the firm's costs is extremely difficult for an outsider to discern, particularly when the underlying technology is changing and the firm can engage in innovation. Even if it is possible for regulators to measure the firm's actual costs, they may have little idea of what the firm's costs could have been if it had engaged in the efficient level of research and development activities.

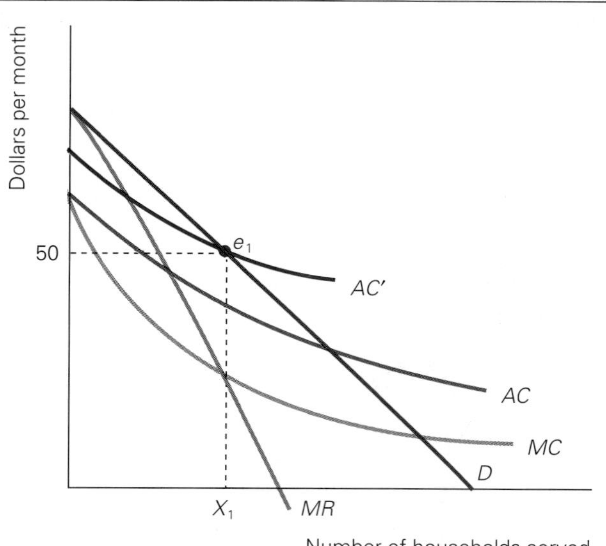

Figure 13.15

The Effects of Misreporting

Knowing that the regulators are going to use cost information to set price, a rationally self-interested firm would claim that it had an average cost curve such as *AC′*. By misreporting its cost curve, the telephone company could induce the regulators to set the monopoly price, $50.

Why not simply ask the firm what its average cost curve is (or should be)? One reason is that the firm may lie to the regulators. Knowing that the regulators are going to use this cost information to set price, a rationally self-interested firm would claim that it had an average cost curve such as *AC′* in Figure 13.15. By misreporting its cost curve, the telephone company could induce the regulators to set the profit-maximizing monopoly price of $50. Of course, the regulators could (and in real life, do) audit Ding-a-Ling's books to limit lying, but the regulators still would not know if these costs were at the level that would result from efficient research and development activities. Moreover, the firm's books might be so complicated that a perfect audit would be nearly impossible, and in any event would be too expensive to conduct regularly. For this reason, regulators are increasingly relying on regulatory mechanisms that do not rely directly on cost data.

3. *Regulatory controls may have unintended consequences*. Ideally, regulators would force Ding-a-Ling to set its price at what would be its average cost level if the firm had undertaken the optimal amount of research and development. Lacking a measure of what costs could have been, regulators might instead force the firm to set its price equal to some measure of its actual average cost. But this policy would have the unintended effect of discouraging socially desirable innovation. Why should a firm spend resources trying to lower its costs if the net effect is going to be a forced reduction in the regulated price that passes all of the benefits of the innovation on to consumers? For this reason, many economists have argued that regulated companies should be allowed to earn increased profits when they engage in cost-reducing innovation.

Following the recommendation of Professor Littlechild, British telecommunications regulators adopted a policy of ***incentive regulation***, under which British Telecom, the principal telecommunications supplier in Britain, is allowed to keep some of the gains from innovation. Many state regulatory commissions adopted a similar policy, as did the U.S. Federal Communications Commission. Under these regulatory schemes, the rates for phone services must fall by a set percent annually, subject to an adjustment for inflation. If the companies can reduce their costs faster than the set rate, they get to pocket the savings. If costs fall more slowly, the firms will find their profits eroded. Either way, telephone companies have strong incentives to work to cut costs.

Conclusion From this brief look at natural monopoly regulation, we have seen that regulators face a difficult task, but economics can provide important insights into the effects of regulation and thus assist in its design and implementation.

SECTION RECAP

While patent policy has the effect of protecting monopoly, most public policy toward monopoly is concerned with limiting its inefficiency. Antitrust policy attempts to block the creation of monopolies or attempts by firms to get together to act like a monopolist. In a situation where it is impossible or undesirable to create a competitive market structure, policy makers may regulate the monopolist to prevent an inefficiently high price and low output.

13.4 PRICE DISCRIMINATION

So far, we have assumed that all consumers are charged the same price for a given good or service. But in many markets, firms charge different prices to different people. For example, Monday through Wednesday nights, the Manhattan bar What Ales You (located around the corner from New York Hospital) charges women less than half as much for drinks as it charges men. Such "ladies' nights" are common. When Mercedes-Benz introduced the 190 sedan to the United States, the same model selling for $26,000 in America was available for roughly $12,000 in West Germany. Pharmaceutical companies frequently charge different prices in different countries for the same drug. Subscriptions to economics journals often are more expensive for libraries than for individuals. Bus companies and movie theaters typically charge lower fares to senior citizens than to other people. A firm that charges different consumers different prices for the same good is said to engage in **price discrimination.**

price discrimination
The practice of charging different consumers different prices for the same good.

Why might a firm find it profitable to engage in price discrimination? The answer comes from the fact that people typically differ in their willingness to pay for a good. The monopolist faces a dilemma. It would like to charge a high price if some people are willing to pay it, but charging a high price induces other consumers not to purchase the good. To illustrate this point, consider the following simple example. Suppose that there are only two potential buyers of a mathematics program called Sum Product—Ms. Rich and Mr. Poor. The marginal cost of producing Sum Product is constant at $10 per copy. Ms. Rich is willing to pay $40 for a copy of Sum Product, while Mr. Poor is willing to pay at most $20 for a copy. Neither consumer is willing to pay anything for additional copies of Sum Product.

We can see the monopolist's dilemma. If it charged $40 in order to extract the most revenue possible from Ms. Rich, then Mr. Poor would not buy the good. The monopolist would earn $30 = $40 − $10. On the other hand, if the monopolist set a price of $20, both consumers would purchase the good, but Ms. Rich would pay less than she is willing to pay. By setting this price, the monopolist sells two copies and earns a profit of $20 = 2 × ($20 − $10). We now see why a firm might like to price discriminate: It would like to charge a high price to consumers with a high willingness to pay, while still selling to consumers with a relatively low willingness to pay. In this example, if the firm can charge $40 per unit to Ms. Rich while charging only $20 per unit to Mr. Poor, then it sells to both and earns a profit of $40 = ($40 − $10) + ($20 − $10). (PC 13.6)

13.6 PROGRESS CHECK

Suppose that Ms. Rich were willing to pay $60 for one copy of the program, and Mr. Poor were willing to pay $40 for one unit. What price would a nondiscriminating monopolist charge? What would a price discriminator do? How does the firm's profit change when it engages in price discrimination?

CONDITIONS NECESSARY FOR PROFITABLE PRICE DISCRIMINATION

In the example just considered, price discrimination significantly raises the firm's profit. Further consideration of this example reveals three conditions that must be satisfied for price discrimination to be profitable.

1. *The firm must be a price maker.*

To see why this condition is necessary, suppose that the supplier were a price taker. In this case, all consumers of the supplier's product would be willing to pay the same price for a unit of the good. The best that the firm could do would be to charge everybody their common willingness to pay for the good, and the ability to charge different customers different prices would be of no value to the firm. In contrast, a price maker faces a downward sloping demand curve so it can profit from charging higher prices to those consumers who are willing to pay more for its output.

But can the firm actually charge different prices to different consumers? A second necessary condition for profitable price discrimination is:

2. *The firm must be able to identify which consumer is which.*

Suppose that you own a restaurant and you are sure that some diners are willing to pay more for the meals than others. If you could, you would like to price discriminate. But you face a difficult problem—it is impossible to tell how much any particular person is willing to pay. If you cannot identify an individual consumer's willingness to pay, then you cannot practice price discrimination. This is one reason that most restaurants charge everyone the same prices. Sometimes, partial identification of consumers' willingness to pay is possible. For instance, even though bar owners cannot tell how much any specific customer is willing to pay for a drink, they know that women typically are willing to pay less than men. While the identification of willingness to pay is not perfect, the monopolist may be able to benefit from being able to divide customers into groups with different demand curves—in this case, men and women.

However, even if the firm has perfect information about consumers' willingness to pay, price discrimination still may not be profitable. The scheme will collapse if those customers who make purchases at low prices can turn around and sell the good to consumers who are being charged high prices. For example, when a bar sells drinks to women for less, some male economists have been known to have women buy drinks for them. When customers whom the firm charges low prices resell their purchases to customers who would otherwise have to pay high prices, customers are said to engage in **arbitrage.** If all customers could practice arbitrage, no one would buy drinks at the higher price, and the attempted price discrimination would be ineffective. Hence, a third condition for profitable price discrimination is:

arbitrage
The process whereby customers whom the firm charges low prices make purchases that they then resell to customers who would otherwise have to pay high prices.

3. *Consumers must not be able to engage in arbitrage.*

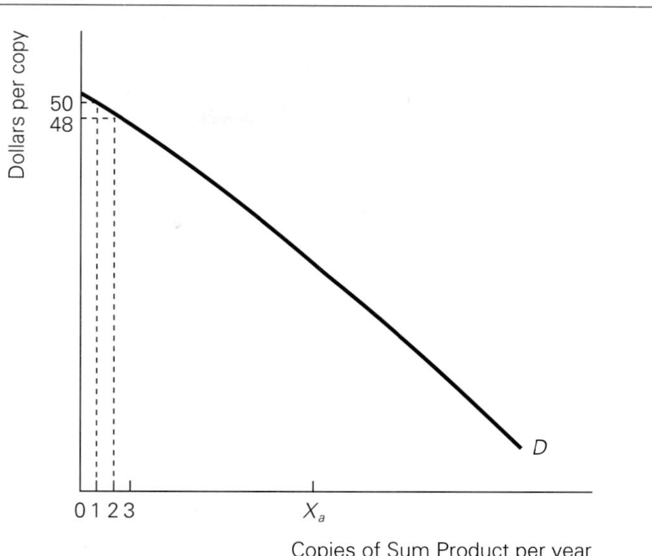

Figure 13.16

A Perfect Price Discriminator Works Its Way Down the Demand Curve

Because it can price discriminate, the firm works its way down the demand curve by selling each unit of the program at a price just equal to the buyer's willingness to pay for that unit (which is given by the height of the demand curve).

Concern with consumer arbitrage explains why the servers in bars on "ladies' nights" are instructed to watch that women do not order drinks for the men sitting with them. It also explains why Mercedes-Benz and other European car manufacturers have sought U.S. Congressional action to stop automobile consumers from going to Europe, buying European models at low prices, and shipping them back for resale in America.

FIRST-DEGREE PRICE DISCRIMINATION

first-degree price discrimination The practice of selling each unit of output at a price just equal to the buyer's maximal willingness to pay for that unit.

perfect price discrimination Another name for first-degree price discrimination.

The story of Ms. Rich and Mr. Poor is an example of a particularly strong form of discrimination known as **first-degree price discrimination.** Under first-degree price discrimination, also known as **perfect price discrimination,** the firm is able to sell each unit of output at a price just equal to the buyer's maximal willingness to pay for that unit. This type of discrimination clearly entails setting prices that differ across consumers. When a single consumer buys more than one unit of good, perfect price discrimination also entails selling different units to the *same consumer* at different prices. If Mary is willing to pay \$2.00 for her first milkshake of the day, but only \$1.00 for the second, then a perfectly price-discriminating soda fountain would charge her \$2.00 for the first shake and \$1.00 for the second.

While real-world firms probably never know enough about the customers to engage in perfect price discrimination, it is an important polar case that helps us understand more realistic kinds. To analyze perfect price discrimination, let's return to the example of Sum Product, but consider what happens when there are many customers, instead of only two. A more plausible demand curve for Sum Product is drawn in Figure 13.16. It is downward sloping for two reasons. First, some people are willing to pay less for a copy of the program than others. Second, some people may be willing to pay for more than one copy—one for the office and one for home—but not be willing to pay as much for the second as for the first.

Figure 13.17

For a Perfect Price Discriminator, the Marginal Revenue Curve and Demand Curve Coincide

As a perfect discriminator, a firm selling $X_b - 1$ units can sell one more unit at a price of p_b without changing the price charged for any of the inframarginal units. Consequently, total revenue rises by shaded area *B*, which is equal to p_b, and the marginal revenue and demand curves coincide. Following the usual $MR = MC$ rule, the monopolist sells a total of X_1 copies of the program.

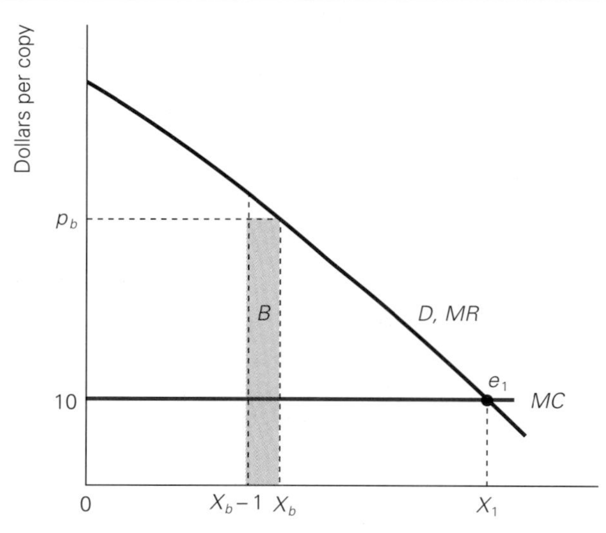

Suppose that the firm were going to sell only one copy of the program. Figure 13.16 tells us that the firm would charge a price of $50. Now, suppose that the firm wants to sell two units. Reading off the demand curve, we see that in order to sell the second unit, the firm has to set the price of *that unit* at $48. Notice, however, that the firm does not have to lower the price of the first unit sold. *Because it can price discriminate,* the firm sets the price of the first unit equal to $50, while at the same time setting the price of the second unit at $48. For higher levels of output, the firm would continue to work its way down the demand curve by selling each unit of the program at a price just equal to the buyer's willingness to pay for that unit (which is given by the height of the demand curve). (PC 13.7)

13.7 PROGRESS CHECK

Suppose that the firm wishes to sell X_a units of Sum Product in Figure 13.16. What price will the firm set for the X_ath unit? Graphically illustrate the total revenue that the firm would earn when selling this amount of output.

How much output does the perfectly discriminating monopolist produce? As always, the firm produces up to the output level at which marginal revenue is equal to marginal cost. The only new thing to worry about is how to calculate marginal revenue for a first-degree price discriminator. Suppose that the firm is selling $X_b - 1$ copies of Sum Product in Figure 13.17 and decides to sell one more. As a perfect price discriminator, the firm can sell the X_bth unit at a price of p_b without changing the price charged for any of the inframarginal units. The sale of the marginal copy of Sum Product raises total revenue by p_b, shaded area *B* in the figure. Unlike a nondiscriminating monopolist, there is no offsetting loss on the inframarginal units. Hence, *for a perfect price discriminator, the marginal revenue curve,* MR, *and the demand curve,* D, *coincide.*

Now that we know Sum Product's marginal revenue curve, we simply find the intersection of this curve with the marginal cost curve, point e_1 in Figure 13.17. The firm sells a total of X_1 copies of Sum Product. Here, we have found a surprising result: *A monopolist practicing first-degree price discrimination produces output up to the point at which the price of the last unit sold is equal to marginal cost.* In other words, the first-degree price discriminating monopolist produces the same amount of output as would a price taker.

Of course, we must also check for shut down. Figure 13.17 shows that Sum Product should stay in business. As always, profit is given by the area under the marginal revenue curve and above the marginal cost curve. This figure clearly indicates that the firm earns positive economic profit.[5]

Welfare Effects of First-Degree Price Discrimination

A firm engaging in perfect price discrimination produces at the level where the demand and marginal cost curves intersect. In Chapter 11, we saw that this is the efficient level of output to produce. In other words, *a perfectly discriminating, profit-maximizing monopolist produces the total-surplus-maximizing amount of output.*

While this result may seem surprising, it has a ready explanation. When the firm can price discriminate perfectly, there is no consumer surplus and the monopolist's profit is equal to total surplus. Since profit and total surplus are equal, when the firm acts to maximize its profit, it also acts to maximize total surplus. This result provides another way of seeing that the distortion in the nondiscriminating monopolist's behavior comes from the consumer surplus wedge between the monopolist's profit and total surplus.

That perfect discrimination leads to efficiency also dramatizes the difference between efficiency and equity considerations. Consumer surplus is lower under first-degree discrimination (it's equal to zero) than under nondiscriminating monopoly. If you believed that consumers were more deserving than the firm, you would favor nondiscriminating monopoly on equity grounds, despite the superiority of perfectly discriminating monopoly on efficiency grounds.

SECOND-DEGREE PRICE DISCRIMINATION

In reality, no firm can observe every individual buyer's willingness to pay for its product. There may, however, be something about the buyer that the seller can observe that reveals information about the consumer's willingness to pay. We will see how a monopolist can use the consumer's own actions as a basis of discrimination. This practice is known as **second-degree price discrimination.**

second-degree price discrimination
Price discrimination in which the same price schedule is offered to all buyers but they sort themselves through self-selection.

We will begin with a simple example in which all consumers are identical. Line D in Figure 13.18 illustrates a single buyer's demand curve for Sum Product (think of the buyer as a business that needs several copies of the program for its corporate computer network). Under nondiscriminatory pricing, the equilibrium price is p_1 in the figure. At this price, consumer surplus is shaded area A. The firm would like to appropriate this surplus but cannot: A higher price would induce consumers to cut back their purchases. The price plays two roles: It generates consumption incentives and it transfers income. In a sense, the two roles are in conflict.

[5]When we apply the shut-down rule, we cannot simply compare the price of the last unit sold with average cost. When the firm is a price discriminator, the firm sells different units of the good at different prices. As the firm works its way down the demand curve, each additional unit of output is sold at a lower price than the earlier units. Hence, the price of the marginal unit is less than the firm's average revenue.

Figure 13.18

A Two-Part Tariff with a Single Type of Consumer

The profit-maximizing two-part tariff has p equal to marginal cost and F equal to the shaded area.

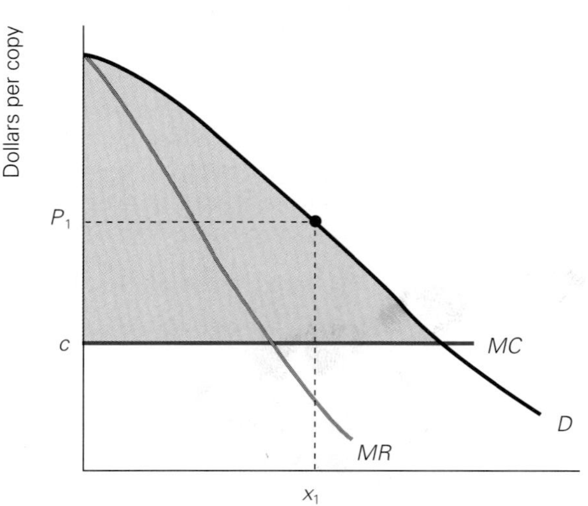

A pricing scheme with two parts can help firm pursue both goals at once. Suppose the firm implements a *two-part tariff*, under which the buyer pays a *fixed fee, F,* for the right to put copies of Sum Product on its network, in addition to a *per unit charge* of p for each desktop computer with a copy of the program.[6] How should the firm set F and p? Given the per unit charge, the firm should set the fixed fee as high as possible without driving away consumers. That is, the fixed fee should equal the consumer surplus. Setting F equal to consumer surplus means that when there is a single type of consumer, the firm is able to appropriate all of the surplus through the fixed fee. In the discussion of first-degree price discrimination, you read that when the firm is able to appropriate all of the surplus, it wants to maximize that surplus. Hence, the profit-maximizing outcome is to set p equal to marginal cost and to set F equal to the shaded area in Figure 13.18.

Now consider the more realistic case where different consumers have different demands. Figure 13.19 illustrates the demand curve of two different consumers. Suppose that the firm were to set the per unit charge equal to marginal cost. Shaded area G is the highest fixed fee it could charge without driving consumer 1 from the market. Notice that two-part pricing does not allow the firm to extract all of the consumer surplus. Consumer 2 enjoys surplus equal to area H. There is an additional role for price: sorting out or discriminating between the two consumers. Three roles is one too many even for a two-part tariff.

The monopolist would like to appropriate some of consumers 2's surplus. Suppose that the firm raises the per-unit price to p_a in Figure 13.19. To keep consumer 1 from dropping out, the firm has to lower the fixed fee by approximately $x_b(p_a - c)$. For consumer 1, the reduction in the fixed fee essentially cancels out the increase in revenues from the higher per-unit charge. Why do it? Because of the effect on revenues from consumer 2. While consumer 2 also

[6]Economists are fond of pointing to Disneyland as the leading example of two-part tariffs because of a well-known (among economists, at least) article noting that Disneyland charges an admission fee and a charge per ride. If they spent less time in the library, more economists would know that Disneyland stopped using two-part tariffs years ago.

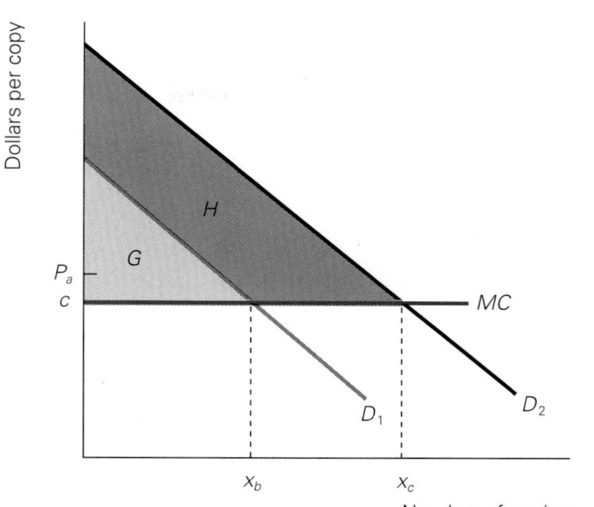

Figure 13.19

A Two-Part Tariff with Two Types of Consumer

If the monopolist sets the per-unit charge equal to marginal cost, then shaded area *G* is the highest fixed fee it can charge without driving consumer 1 from the market. Under this tariff, consumer 2 enjoys surplus equal to area *H*. To extract some of this surplus, the firm will set the per-unit charge above marginal cost.

benefits from the $x_b \times (p_a - c)$ decrease in F, he or she pays approximately $x_c \times (p_a - c)$ more because of the increase in the per-unit charge. Because x_c is greater than x_b, on balance the firm gains from this price increase. While we have not pinned down the exact set of prices, we have demonstrated an important point. In situations such as the one illustrated here, the profit-maximizing two-part tariff generally entails a positive fixed fee and a per-unit price that exceeds marginal cost.

The two-part tariff model helps us understand the pricing of complementary pairs of products. For example, one can view the price of a camera as the fixed charge, and the price of film as the per-unit charge. The classic example of this practice was the pricing of razors and blades (until they started making disposable razors). Finally, it is worth noting that a two-part tariff is an example of the more general phenomenon of quantity discounts, which are granted on everything from food to clothing to commercial aircraft for similar reasons.

Welfare Effects of Second-Degree Price Discrimination

The welfare effects of second-degree price discrimination are complex. However, in the typical case in which demands can be ordered, as in Figure 13.19, the monopolist restricts output below the socially optimal level. We will have more to say about the welfare effects of second-degree price discrimination in Chapter 17.[7]

THIRD-DEGREE PRICE DISCRIMINATION

Let's examine another form of real-world price discrimination, under which the seller can observe some characteristic of the buyer that serves as an indicator of the consumer's willingness to pay. Let's suppose that Sum Product is used by two different types of consumers. One set of users runs the program on mainframe

[7]Surprisingly, a profit-maximizing monopolist may produce *more* total output than the welfare-maximizing amount. This can happen when the firm uses purchase quantities to sort consumers, and different consumers' demand curves cross.

Figure 13.20

Equilibrium without Price Discrimination

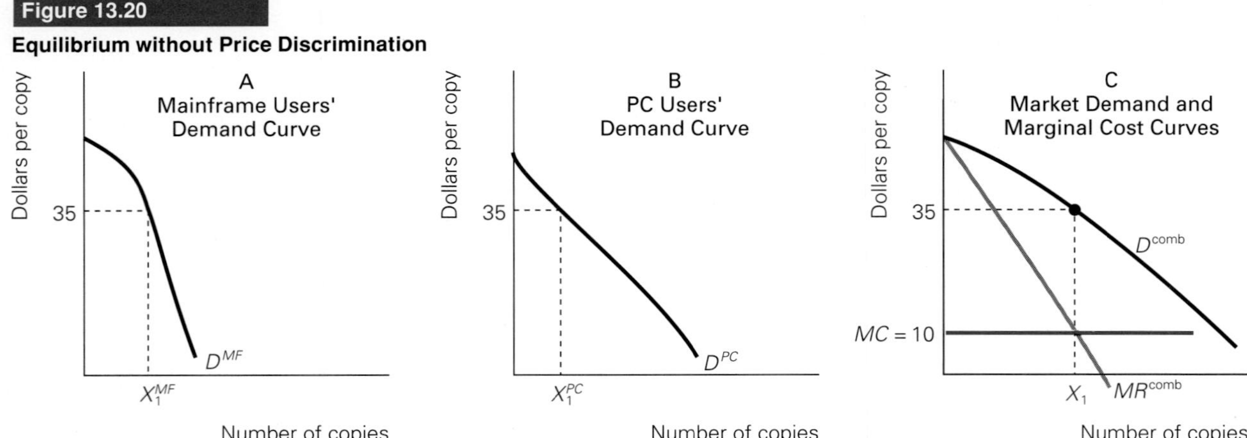

If the firm has to charge the same price to both types of user, the equilibrium price is \$35 for both mainframe and personal computer users. Mainframe users purchase X_1^{MF} copies of Sum Product, while personal computer users purchase X_1^{PC}. Total unit sales are $X_1 = X_1^{MF} + X_1^{PC}$.

computers, and one set runs it on personal computers. The demand curve for Sum Product by mainframe users is given by D^{MF} in Panel A of Figure 13.20; the demand by personal computer users is D^{PC} in Panel B.

If the software monopolist is unable to distinguish between the two groups, or if consumers can engage in arbitrage, the firm then has to charge the same price to both types of user. The total demand for Sum Product is then the horizontal sum of the mainframe and personal computer demand curves, the combined-market demand curve, D^{comb}, illustrated in Panel C of Figure 13.20. The associated marginal revenue schedule is found in the usual manner, and the monopolist's equilibrium output level is where marginal revenue equals marginal cost, quantity X_1 in the figure. The equilibrium price is \$35 for both mainframe and personal computer users. Mainframe users purchase X_1^{MF} copies of Sum Product, while personal computer users purchase X_1^{PC} copies.

Now suppose that the maker of Sum Product can tell whether its customers are going to use the program on a personal computer or on a mainframe, and the firm can prevent arbitrage. Under these circumstances, the monopolist can charge different prices to the two sets of consumers. In effect, the firm can divide what was one overall market into two markets. What prices should the firm set in these markets? In each market, the firm should produce at the point where marginal revenue is equal to marginal cost and set the price accordingly. While stating this general prescription is straightforward, implementing it requires some care.

When marginal costs are constant, it is relatively easy to apply the rules for profit maximization. Continue to suppose that marginal cost is constant at \$10 per copy of program, once the initial copy has been written, as shown in Panels A and B of Figure 13.21. The discriminating monopolist simply applies the marginal output rule to each market, setting marginal revenue *in each market* equal to the constant value of marginal cost. In effect, we find a basic monopoly equilibrium twice. Notice that the firm takes advantage of its ability to price discriminate—it charges \$40 to mainframe users and \$30 to PC users. (PC 13.8)

Figure 13.21

Equilibrium with Third-Degree Price Discrimination

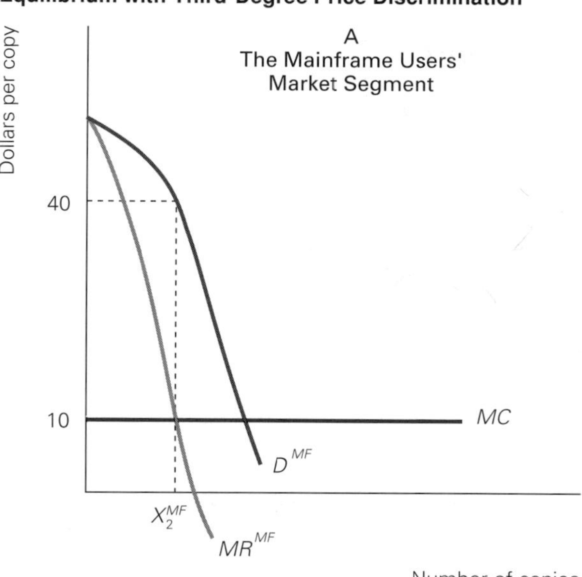

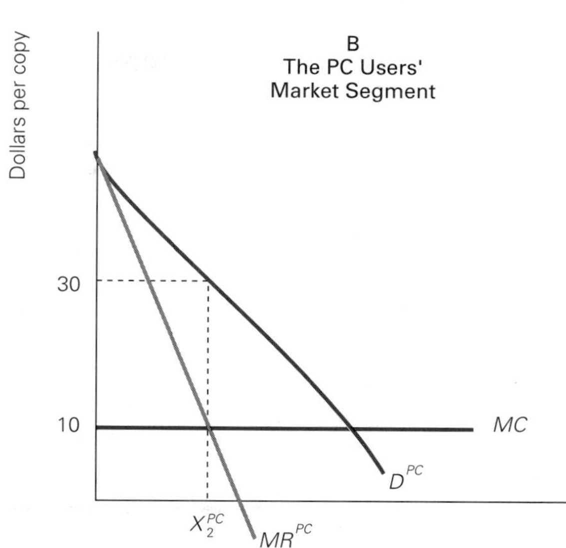

When marginal costs are constant, a discriminating monopolist simply sets marginal revenue *for each market* equal to the constant value of marginal cost. The firm charges a price of $40 to mainframe users and $30 to PC users.

The analysis is not quite so straightforward when marginal cost varies with output. Suppose that the firm has the marginal cost curve shown in Panel C of Figure 13.22. With such a marginal cost curve, the marginal cost of a program in either market depends on *total* output ($X^{MF} + X^{PC}$). Hence, to know the marginal cost of output in one market, the firm needs to know how much output it is selling in the other market. We need to have a way to find the total quantity sold all at once. In other words, to apply the marginal output rule, we need to equate combined marginal revenue with combined marginal cost.

13.8 PROGRESS CHECK

Software companies often offer student discounts on their products. To purchase the software at these reduced rates, a buyer is required to show his or her student ID to the retailer. Why does the retailer insist on being shown the ID card?

Like combined marginal cost, combined marginal revenue depends on total output in the two markets. For a price discriminating monopolist, *we find the combined-market marginal revenue curve by taking the horizontal sum of the individual-market marginal revenue curves.*[8] This is done in Panel C of Figure 13.22. Once we have the combined marginal revenue curve, we can apply the marginal output rule. Taking the intersection of

[8]You might guess that we could find the discriminator's marginal revenue curve by taking the horizontal sum of the PC and mainframe users' demand curves to find the combined-market demand curve and then calculate the combined-market marginal revenue curve from that. We cannot. This approach is invalid because it implicitly assumes that the firm must charge the same price in both markets. In fact, this is the approach that we just used to calculate marginal revenue for the combined markets when the firm could not price discriminate.

Figure 13.22

Finding the Third-Degree Price Discrimination Equilibrium with Nonconstant Marginal Cost

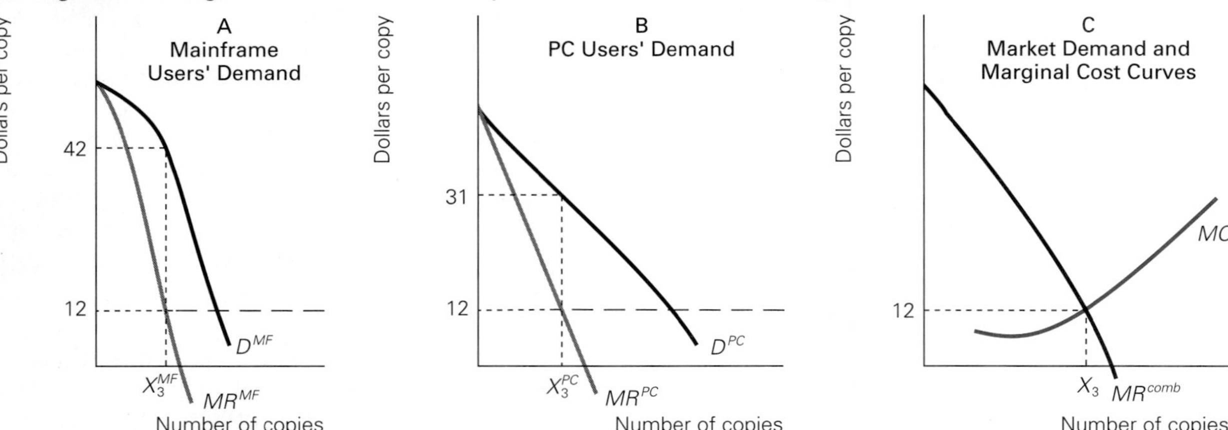

For a price-discriminating monopolist, the combined-market marginal revenue curve is found by taking the horizontal sum of the individual-market *marginal* revenue curves. Taking the intersection of MR^{comb} and MC in Panel C, we see that the firm sells a total of X_3 copies of Sum Product. In the mainframe market, the firm sells X_3^{MF} copies at a price of \$42 per copy. In the PC market, it sells X_3^{PC} copies at a price of \$31 per copy.

the combined-market marginal revenue and marginal cost curves in Panel C, we see that the firm sells a total of X_3 copies of Sum Product. Marginal cost at this output level is \$12 per copy. To find the prices and quantities in the individual markets, we have to go back to the individual-market demand and marginal revenue curves, which are shown in Panels A and B of Figure 13.22. In order for the equilibrium value of marginal revenue to be \$12 in both markets, the individual market quantities must be X_3^{MF} and X_3^{PC} in the mainframe and personal computer markets, respectively.

third-degree price discrimination The practice of identifying separate groups of buyers of a good and charging different prices to these groups.

This type of discrimination, in which the supplier is able to identify separate groups of buyers and charge them different prices, is known as **third-degree price discrimination.** Unlike first-degree price discrimination, third-degree price discrimination is an important real-world phenomenon. While suppliers typically cannot observe an individual buyer's willingness to pay for a good, they often can observe some characteristics of the consumer that give an indication of his or her willingness to pay. "Ladies' nights" are in part an attempt to use one's sex as an indicator of a consumer's willingness to pay for alcoholic beverages. Mercedes-Benz was using geographic location of the buyer as an indication of the buyer's willingness to pay for a model 190. Apparently, Mercedes-Benz believed that Americans were willing to pay more for its automobiles than Germans. Similarly, many movie theaters may believe that senior citizens are less willing to pay for their products than younger people.

Welfare Effects of Third-Degree Price Discrimination

What are the efficiency consequences of the monopolist's dividing its customers into different groups and charging different prices to these groups? Let's begin by looking at how prices are affected. We know that prices to all groups cannot rise. If they did, the monopolist would have been charging a higher price in the absence of discrimination. Similarly, they cannot all fall. If they did, the firm would have charged a lower nondiscriminatory price. We conclude that *if the firm would have sold output to multiple groups in the absence of price discrimination, then some prices rise and some fall when a monopolist practices third-degree price discrimination.* Consider Sum Product again. Suppose that price discrimination leads to a price decrease for PC users and a price increase for mainframe users. Then consumer surplus for PC users rises as a consequence of the price discrimination, while that of mainframe users falls.

This pattern of price changes—under which one set of consumers gains while the other loses—gives us a new perspective on so-called altruistic pricing schemes, such as senior citizen discounts. Our analysis tells us that while third-degree discrimination based on customer age leads to senior citizen discounts, it also leads to surcharges for young people. Rather than a form of altruism, this price scheme may simply be a way to raise the seller's profits.

Clearly, the firm gains profit from the ability to price discriminate—otherwise it would charge a single price. What happens to total surplus? It turns out that we cannot say. On the one hand, we know that price discrimination leads to a violation of a condition necessary for Pareto efficiency, derived in Chapter 12. Under price discrimination, different consumers face different prices. Consequently, consumers do not all have the same marginal rates of substitution in equilibrium. We conclude that third-degree price discrimination has a negative effect on consumption efficiency: Output is inefficiently allocated among consumers. Hence, for a given amount of total output, third-degree price discrimination lowers total surplus. On the other hand, the total amount of output that the monopolist sells in the two markets may rise or fall as a result of price discrimination. We know that an ordinary nondiscriminating monopolist produces less than the efficient amount of total output. When price discrimination leads to a fall in output, this inefficiency is made even worse. But when discrimination leads to an increase in total output, the effect of this output change on total surplus is positive.

What is the net effect of price discrimination on total surplus relative to the monopoly equilibrium without discrimination? Our analysis indicates that *when total output falls under third-degree price discrimination, so does total surplus—the output that is produced is allocated to consumers inefficiently and there is less of it. But when total output rises, the welfare analysis is ambiguous—the output that is produced is allocated inefficiently, but there is more total output.* Consequently, in this case total surplus may rise or fall, depending on the specific details of the market under consideration.

One thing, however, is unambiguous. Whether it rises or falls in comparison with the no-discrimination case, total output under third-degree price discrimination is less than the efficient amount. This must be true because the firm engages in a monopolistic output restriction in each market segment. Since the firm sells too little output to each market segment individually, it clearly sells too little output overall.

SECTION RECAP

A price maker's customers differ in their willingness to pay for the good, and the firm would like to charge each customer exactly what he or she is willing to pay for each unit purchased. Under first-degree price discrimination, the firm does exactly that. Under the more realistic cases of second- and third-degree price discrimination, the best the firm can do is divide its customers up into different classes based on their purchase choices or some observable characteristic, and charge separate prices to different classes.

When the monopolist can engage in first-degree price discrimination, the firm chooses an efficient output level. The welfare effects of second-degree price discrimination are complex and depend on the particular practice under consideration. Under third-degree price discrimination, the firm still produces too little output overall, but may produce more or less output than it would if not allowed to discriminate.

SUMMARY

In this chapter, we studied monopoly, a market structure that is the polar opposite of perfect competition.

- Under monopoly, there is a single producer and entry into the market by additional suppliers is blocked.
- A monopolist recognizes that the amount it sells influences the price it receives for its output. The firm is a price maker.
- For a price-making firm, price is greater than marginal revenue. Hence, when a monopolist produces at a point where marginal revenue is equal to marginal cost, price is greater than marginal cost.
- A price-making firm should shut down if at every output level the price at which it can sell its output is less than the average cost of producing it.
- A monopolist produces less than a competitive industry with the same costs. In fact, a monopolist produces too little output in the sense that total surplus would rise if the firm were to produce more output.
- When consumers differ in their willingness to pay for a firm's output, the firm will find price discrimination profitable if it can identify consumers with different willingness to pay and can keep them from engaging in arbitrage.

DISCUSSION QUESTIONS

13.1 There is a single producer of ZT-1000, a chemical for which there is no close substitute. Entry into this industry by new firms is impossible because ZT-1000 is patented. The industry demand curve for ZT-1000 is downward sloping. ZT-1000 is produced using two inputs, benzene and labor. It takes exactly one gallon of benzene combined with one hour of labor to produce one gallon of ZT-1000. The firm faces perfectly elastic supply curves for its inputs. At present, benzene is available at a price of $2 per gallon and labor is available at $10 per hour. Illustrate the firm's equilibrium price and output choices in a diagram with the demand and relevant cost curves. Be as precise as you can.

13.2 Suppose that the production of ZT-1000 generates fumes within the plant that greatly increase the incidence of cancer among workers. None of the dangerous fumes ever escapes the plant. All of the current employees are aware of the ill effects that the fumes have on their health. The workers would suffer no ill health effects if they were provided with masks containing a filtering system. Masks and filters cost the firm an additional $2 for each hour that an employee works. Suppose that, left alone, the firm would not provide workers with these masks. In response to this health hazard, however, the U.S. government enacts a regulation that requires the industry to provide each worker with a mask that contains a filtering system.

a. How will this regulation affect the firm's choice of output level?

b. What will be the effects of this regulation on the profit of the firm?

c. What will be the effects of this regulation on the workers at the firm? (Be sure to consider employment as well as health effects.) What does the fact that the firm does not find it profitable to provide its workers with masks say about the value that the workers themselves place on the prevention of the ill health effects?

d. What effects will this regulation have on consumers of ZT-1000?

13.3 For U.S. cattle ranchers who want to enter the Japanese beef market, it is crucial to be able to raise the Wagyu breed of cattle, whose meat is very popular in Japan. Unfortunately, it is generally impossible to import the Wagyu breed from Japan. However, a Texan named Don Lively managed to obtain a quantity of Wagyu bull semen. This was the only source of the semen outside Japan, and ranchers from all over the world paid Mr. Lively $250 per vial—enough to get one cow pregnant (Yoder 1990, A1).

a. Assuming that marginal cost of Wagyu semen is zero and that Mr. Lively was maximizing profit, illustrate his price and output decisions.

b. What can you say about the price of elasticity of demand for the semen when the price is $250 per vial?

Now suppose that the government decided to levy a 10 percent tax on the sale of bull semen. That is, Mr. Lively would have to pay 10 percent of his gross revenues to the government.

c. Graphically illustrate Mr. Lively's price and output decisions in the presence of the tax.

d. Who bears the burden of the tax?

e. How would your answer to part *d* change if the buyer had to pay the 10 percent tax?

13.4 In the text, we examined the effects of a unit tax in a monopolized market. Suppose instead that the government levies a lump-sum tax, under which the monopolist has to pay a flat amount of $\$T$, independent of its output level.

a. How does this tax affect the monopolist's equilibrium?

b. How is the burden of this tax split between the firm and its customers?

13.5 Airports limit the number of restaurants that can operate within their facilities. In some instances, all of the food concessions within an airport are granted to a single vendor, who then has to pay rent to the airport. How much should a vendor be willing to pay to the airport to be the sole supplier? What would happen to the rent that the airport could charge if it decided to let a large number of suppliers set up restaurants on its premises?

13.6 Smel's Drive-In is the only place to eat within 50 miles of the Contingent State University campus. As such, Smel's has no competition to speak of. Smel's sells hamburgers to two different types of customer. Economics students drive VWs to Smel's and pay for their burgers with cash. It costs Smel's $1 to provide a burger to these students. Business students drive BMWs and pay for their burgers with American Depress Gold Cards. Because of the charges levied by American Depress, it costs Smel's a total of $1.10 to provide a burger to a charge-card customer. Other than their insistence on using different methods of payment, economics students and business students have *identical* demands (neither perfectly inelastic nor perfectly elastic) for burgers.

a. In the absence of any government restraints, how would Smel's price its burgers? Support your answer graphically and be as precise as you can.

b. From time to time, members of the U.S. Congress become concerned about fairness, and they debate whether legally to mandate that all customers must be charged the same price for a good or service no matter what form of payment they use. How, if at all, would the policy change prices in comparison with part *a*? Who gains from this policy, and who loses? Is this fair?

13.7 In his novel, *The Godfather*, Mario Puzo makes the following observation about the leader of a crime syndicate: "Like many businessmen of genius he learned that free competition was wasteful, monopoly efficient." In what sense is Puzo using the word "efficient"? Contrast it with the economist's use of the term.

13.8 The U.S. Department of Justice has a set of guidelines by which it defines when a firm has market power. Originally, these guidelines said that a firm did not have market power if raising its price by 5 percent would lower the firm's profit. Explain why a monopolist in equilibrium would always pass this test!

13.9 In the text, we examined a monopolist's incentives to undertake R&D that was sure to succeed. Real-life firms are not so lucky. Undertaking R&D is a risky investment. Suppose that Levi's Genes is working on a new bacterium that will eat the toxic wastes produced in the manufacture of memory chips for personal computers. The managers at Levi's Genes estimate that the R&D project will cost $100 million. Their genetic engineers tell them that the project has a one-in-three chance of success. If it fails, Levi's has nothing to sell. If it succeeds, the managers estimate that the firm will earn revenues of $400 million and have production costs of $200 million. Should they undertake the project?

13.10 You read in the text that the threat of shutdown by a natural monopolist can prevent regulators from setting price at its efficient level—marginal cost pricing would lead the firm to suffer economic losses. Our discussion did not distinguish between short- and long-run costs. Suppose that an electric utility has just built a large power plant that has essentially no other use and no salvage value. How do you think that regulators should treat the sunk expenditures on the power plant when setting rates? Be sure to consider the effects on *future* investment by the firm.

13.11 Many public utilities (gas, electricity, and water, for instance) are subject to *rate of return regulation,* under which a firm is allowed to choose its price, subject to its proving that it is not earning too much money. Typically, the firm is allowed to cover all of its expenditures for labor and materials and to earn a *fair* rate of return on its investment. Can you think of any problems with such a regulatory scheme? What does this plan do to the firm's incentives to substitute capital for labor?

More on Price-Making Firms

No pleasure endures unseasoned by variety.
—Publilius Syrus

Consider the following three examples, each of which involves price-making behavior.

- For years, colleges and universities banded together in the National Collegiate Athletic Association (NCAA) to sell the television rights to college football games. Through the NCAA, colleges were able to behave like a monopolist in their dealings with the television networks. When a group of major football colleges defected to form the rival College Football Association (CFA), the resulting legal battle went all the way to the Supreme Court. In 1984, the CFA won the right to break away. In 1990, Notre Dame went one step further. The school decided to depart from the CFA and go it alone. Competition broke out in the sale of television rights.
- There are thousands of rock groups. While your professor may not be able to tell U2 from Pearl Jam, many people can. To their fans, every group produces a distinctive product. A band can therefore raise its concert fee and still continue to play some dates, albeit fewer in number and to smaller crowds than before. In other words, each group faces a downward sloping demand curve for its concerts. In this respect, each group is like a monopolist. But there is a big difference from a monopolized market—there are a great many suppliers, and it is relatively easy for new ones to come into the business.
- Nurses are essential to the operation of a hospital. Any one hospital draws from a fairly narrow pool. In deciding how many nurses to hire, a hospital cannot take the wage paid as a given. Unlike a price taker, a hospital that wants to hire more nurses has to raise the price that it pays (Sullivan 1989). In other words, a hospital faces an upward sloping supply curve

for this input. Because its choice of input level affects how much it has to pay for the input, we say that a hospital is a **price-making buyer**.

price-making buyer
A buyer whose purchase quantity affects the price that it has to pay.

Although price making plays an important role in each situation, no situation exactly fits our model of monopoly. The first two examples concern markets in which there are many suppliers, instead of just one as in monopoly. In the third example, the price making is on the buying side of the market, instead of on the selling side as in monopoly. In this chapter, we will extend our theory of price-making firms to cover these three situations.

We begin by considering markets like that for college football broadcast rights, in which there are multiple producers who attempt to behave jointly like a monopolist rather than as competitors. We will examine the conditions necessary for firms to behave collectively like a monopolist in the way that the colleges and universities did.

The second section of this chapter introduces a new model of equilibrium that applies to markets like the one for live performances by rock groups—each firm is a price maker even though it faces competition from a lot of rival producers who are acting independently and are competing with it. This price making arises from the fact that the firms produce imperfect substitutes. As we will see, many other markets combine the price making of monopoly with the large number of suppliers and free entry conditions of perfect competition.

The final extension beyond the models of Chapter 13 examines price making on the *demand* side of the market rather than the supply side. Hospitals are not the only buyers that recognize that their input or output decisions can influence prices.

14.1 CARTELS

When we compared the monopolistic and competitive equilibria in Chapter 13, we saw that if the firms in an industry behave as price-taking competitors, they earn no profit, but if they can collectively behave like a monopolist, they can each share in the resulting monopoly profit. When suppliers band together to act like a monopolist by restricting output and raising its price, they are said to form a **cartel**. In this section, we will analyze several types of cartel.

cartel
An arrangement under which suppliers band together to restrict output and raise the market price.

CARTELS IN PRODUCT MARKETS

Explicit cartel agreements in product markets are rare in the United States because they are generally illegal. There have been a few notable exceptions. One is the National Collegiate Athletic Association discussed in the introduction. Perhaps the most widespread example of formal cartels in U.S. product markets is the use of *agricultural marketing orders.* Under an agricultural marketing order, the U.S. federal government enforces an agreement among growers to restrict their output of a crop, such as nectarines, raisins, or almonds, to hold the price above its competitive level.

The Full Cartel Outcome

The firms in a cartel earn the greatest joint profit when they collectively behave like a monopolist and maximize industry profits. The price and quantity at which

Figure 14.1

The Full Cartel Outcome

The full cartel industry output, X_c, is determined by the intersection of the industry marginal revenue and industry marginal cost curves. The resulting cartel price is p_c. Industry profit is equal to the shaded area.

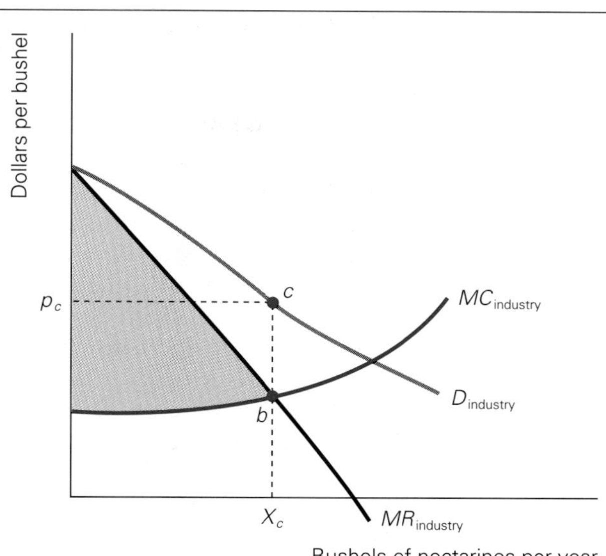

full cartel outcome
The price and quantity at which suppliers' joint profit is maximized.

joint profit is maximized is known as the **full cartel outcome**. To maximize industry profit, the firms should collectively produce the amount of output at which industry marginal revenue is equal to industry marginal cost. Given the industry demand curve, we find the industry marginal revenue curve the same way that we would for a monopolist. The market demand curve for nectarines and the corresponding marginal revenue curve are illustrated in Figure 14.1. To find the industry marginal cost curve, we take the horizontal sum of the firm-specific marginal cost curves. The industry marginal cost curve is also illustrated in Figure 14.1. The industry marginal revenue and industry marginal cost curves intersect at point *b*. The full cartel industry output is X_c, the resulting cartel price is p_c. Industry profit is equal to the shaded area, the area under the marginal revenue curve minus the area under the marginal cost curve up to the quantity produced.

Should we conclude that the cartel will sell X_c units at a price of p_c per unit? Not necessarily. Even if a cartel is legal, there are two important competitive forces that limit the members' ability to achieve the full cartel outcome. First, when a cartel succeeds in holding prices above marginal cost, individual firms have incentives to produce more than their share of the profit-maximizing industry output. Second, new firms are attracted to the industry whenever there are positive economic profits to be made. Thus, to be successful, a cartel must be able (1) to prevent its members from cheating on the agreement by producing too much output and (2) to limit entry by new suppliers. Let's consider these factors in turn.

Cheating on Cartel Agreements

That firms gain *collectively* from adherence to a cartel agreement does not mean that each firm will find adherence to the cartel agreement to be in its *individual* self-interest. A cartel's success may sow the seeds of its own destruction. When a cartel succeeds at raising price above marginal cost, price-taking individual

Figure 14.2

The Incentive to Cheat on a Cartel Agreement

Since marginal revenue is greater than marginal cost from the individual supplier's perspective, the individual supplier has an incentive to cheat on the cartel agreement by increasing output.

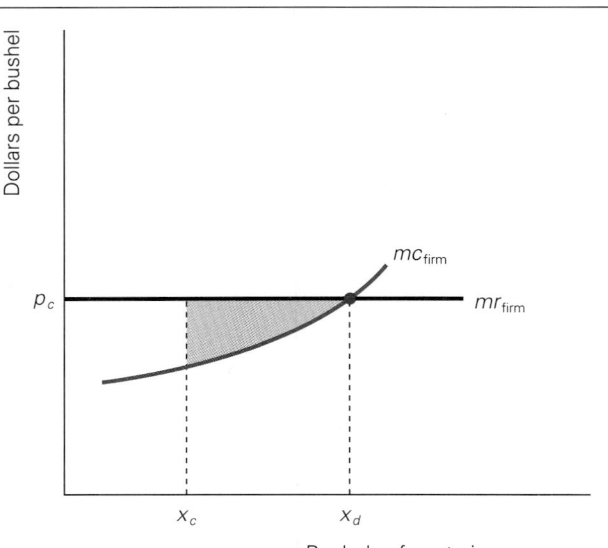

members have incentives to cheat on the agreement by expanding their output levels. Figure 14.2 illustrates such a situation. The price of nectarines is p_c, and each firm is producing its assigned share of the cartel output, x_c bushels. Since the price is greater than the grower's marginal cost of producing nectarines, the grower has an incentive to expand its output to x_d, which increases profit by the shaded area. But if all firms reason this way, market output will rise significantly and the price will fall. Since the firms would be collectively producing more than the cartel output, industry profits would fall.

To achieve the full cartel outcome, the firms need some way to punish cheaters. In the case of the NCAA and the market for television broadcast rights, the following punishment was used: If a team tried to sell the rights to its games on its own, the NCAA would bar its members from playing against the cheater. In the case of agricultural marketing orders, the punishment is meted out by the U.S. government. Farmers who produce too much can be fined. But generally, government assistance is not forthcoming. If the government found evidence of a formal cartel arrangement in a typical industry, instead of enforcing the agreement, it would enforce antitrust policy by prosecuting the firms for an illegal attempt to cartelize the market.

When there is no mechanism for making the cartel agreement binding on cartel members, the scope for profitable cartelization is severely limited. The members require some way to detect and punish suppliers who cheat on the cartel agreement. We will have much more to say about this point in the next chapter where we consider cooperation among firms that cannot rely on legally binding cartel agreements. (PC 14.1)

14.1 PROGRESS CHECK

Japanese government policy is to prop up rice prices. Japanese rice farmers are required by law to produce no more than their quotas and to sell their entire crop to the government at government-set prices. Recently, a number of farmers have flouted the law, producing as much rice as they want and selling it for a lower price. Explain why the farmers are flouting the law.

Entry as a Limit on Cartel Success

The ability to limit cheating by its members is not enough to ensure a cartel's success. The cartel must also be able to limit entry by new firms. Economic theory tells us that if entry into the industry is free, cartel profits will attract new suppliers into the market until profits are driven to zero. Several cartels have tried to ignore these economic forecasts. They limited price competition without fully controlling entry. It is instructive to see how they have failed.

The market for real estate agent *services* is an interesting example of a partial cartel in action. A real estate agent helps someone who is selling a house find a buyer for it.[1] In return for finding a buyer, the agent receives a commission, typically expressed as a percentage of the selling price of the house. For simplicity, we will think of the price of real estate agent services as being a set fee for finding a buyer, but the same sort of analysis could be applied to the percentage rate that the agents charge.

The perfectly competitive model would seem to fit this industry well. Lacking any artificial constraints, the market for real estate brokerage services would have a large number of sellers (agents), and there would be free entry since anyone could set up a real estate office. Moreover, most real estate agents are close substitutes for one another. Finally, real estate agents all have a similar technology, so we would expect them to have similar costs. Under these conditions, price-taking behavior would lead to each firm's setting its price equal to its marginal cost, while free entry would in the long run lead to zero economic profit, or price equal to average cost. Suppose that the cost curves for a single real estate agency look like those pictured in Figure 14.3. Under competition, each firm would produce x_1 units of real estate services at a price of p^{comp} per unit.

Unhappy at the prospect of zero economic profits, suppose that all of the realtors in town get together to raise the price (their commission rate). We would expect this effort to be unsuccessful because of the large number of realtors. Any one realtor might feel that it could cheat on the agreement with little chance of being caught or punished. Such a firm might reason that "the other firms never would lower the prices for the whole market just to punish little old me."

What is a poor realtor to do? What they did do at one time was use the *multiple listing service* (a directory that lists all of the houses for sale) as a means to enforce price fixing. Any realtor who adhered to the price-fixing arrangement was granted multiple listing privileges. Any realtor who was caught violating the price-fixing agreement was banned both from having its houses listed and from buying houses in the listing. A realtor denied these privileges would suffer economic losses, and it was hard to keep cheating a secret because the whole point of cheating was to attract new business by letting people know you charged a low commission. The policy was successful because the realtors had a targeted, and thus credible, punishment for cheating. Any realtor who violated the price-fixing agreement expected to be denied multiple listing privileges and to suffer losses.

What price should the realtors fix to maximize their profits? To find the answer, consider Figure 14.4, which illustrates a typical downward sloping market demand curve for realtor services. Joint profits are maximized at the quantity where industry marginal revenues are equal to industry marginal costs, and the cartel price, p^{cartel}, is then read off of the demand curve. In contrast, the price under competition is p^{comp}, which is associated with output X_1.

In the short run, real estate agencies benefit from the cartel. To see why, note that as price takers, the agencies were earning zero profits and selling more than

[1]Actually, a real estate sale typically involves two realtors, one of whom is said to be the seller's agent and the other the buyer's agent. In most cases, the two realtors both legally represent the interest of the seller. Since the two agents share the same commission, we will simply assume that there is only one agent per transaction.

Figure 14.3

The Competitive Equilibrium for Realtor Services

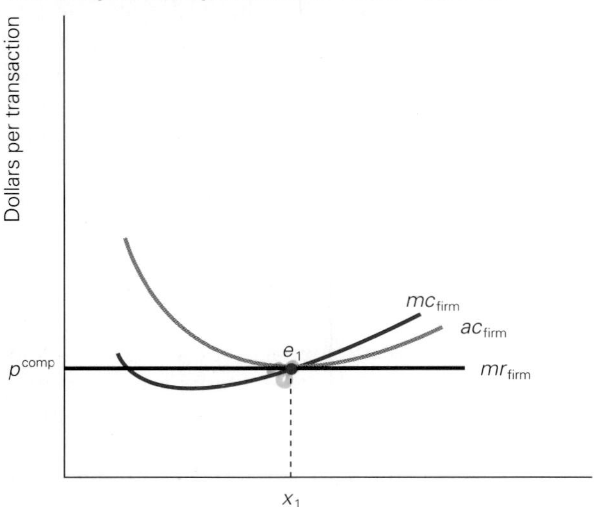

The competitive equilibrium would entail each real estate agency's supplying x_1 units of real estate services at a price of p^{comp} per unit.

Figure 14.4

Comparing the Competitive and Full Cartel Outcomes

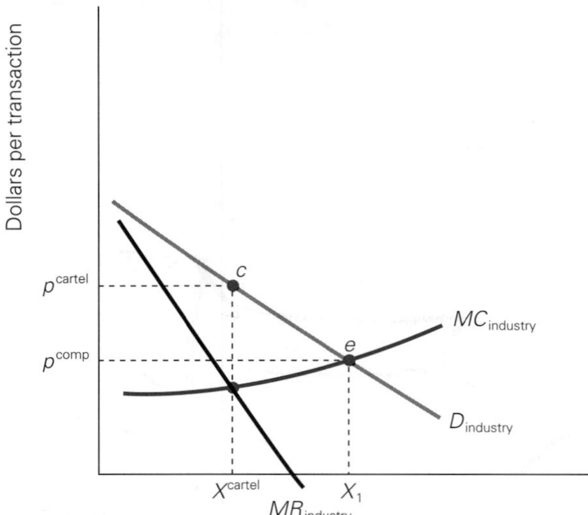

The competitive equilibrium occurs at the intersection of the industry marginal cost and demand curves, point *e*. Joint profits are maximized at the quantity where industry marginal revenue equals industry marginal costs, X^{cartel}. The resulting price is p^{cartel}.

the industry-profit-maximizing level of services. Hence, they were at a point where industry marginal revenue was less than industry marginal cost. Increasing the price to p^{cartel} leads to a fall in industry output and raises the realtors' economic profits.

Unfortunately for the real estate agencies, these profits cannot persist in the long run. As long as profits are positive and entry is free, new realtors are attracted to the market. Normally, we would expect price to fall as industry supply expands. Here, however, the price is held up by the collusive agreement. Hence, the industry quantity demanded by homeowners remains unchanged, as does the total quantity of services supplied by realtors. What changes is the level of sales per realtor. Since there are more realtors chasing the same total amount of business, each one serves fewer clients. Looking at the average cost curve in Figure 14.5, we see that it initially slopes downward, reflecting the economies of scale in providing realtor services. As a result, each realtor finds its average costs rising as its volume falls. Entry continues until the equilibrium average cost is equal to the price set by the cartel. From Figure 14.5, we see that x_2 is the long-run equilibrium level of per-firm output. In equilibrium, there are so many firms, each operating on a small scale with high average costs (each agent spends much of his or her time waiting around for clients), that industry profit is fully dissipated. The realtors hold price up in anticipation of higher profits, but the effect instead is to raise average cost up to the level at which the price is fixed.[2] In short,

[2]In fact, the real estate agents in some areas recognized these effects and tried to limit access to the multiple listing service to restrict entry as well. Such policies did not sit well with the courts.

Figure 14.5

Entry Dissipates the Cartel's Profits

In the long run, entry continues until average cost is equal to the price set by the cartel.

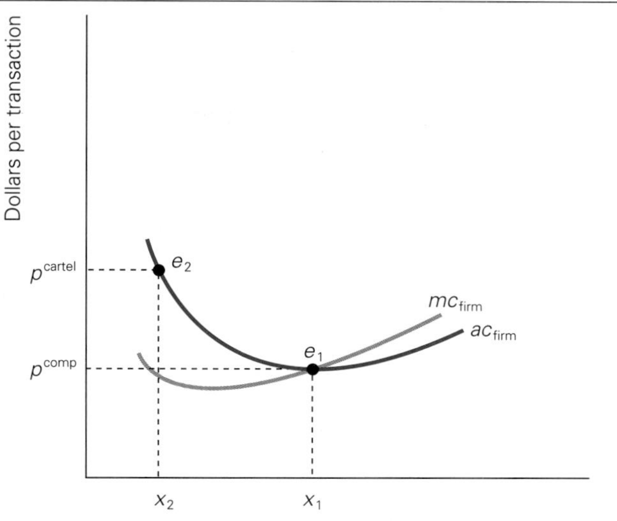

because the realtors cannot keep out new entrants, their cartel fails to generate economic profits in the long run.

Regulation as Cartel Enforcement

Companies in the airline industry relied on a different mechanism to enforce cartel behavior—help from the federal government. Before deregulation in 1978, U.S. government intervention in this market looked more like an attempt to organize a cartel than an attempt to protect consumers. Government rules and regulations restricted both price and entry. While the Civil Aeronautics Board limited air fare increases, it also blocked attempts to lower fares. Moreover, the number of airlines that were allowed to fly between any two cities was strictly limited.

Given the restrictions on both pricing and entry, you might have thought that the cartel would be very effective, but competition found a way to surface. Denied the ability to compete on price, airlines turned to other forms of competition. Given the high ticket prices, each customer was very profitable to the airlines. The desire to attract these customers led to such innovations as putting electric pianos on board Boeing 747s for the passengers to play at their leisure (few did), and having flight attendants wear paper (yes, paper) miniskirts while serving ersatz French cuisine. More significantly, the airlines responded by offering a plethora of flights in order to compete in terms of the convenience of their schedules. Planes flew with a small percentage of their seats occupied, and average costs per passenger rose as a result. Through this "service competition," the airlines competed away many of the potential gains from cartelization. (PC 14.2)

14.2 PROGRESS CHECK

The percentage of seats that are filled on a given flight is known as the *load factor.* What effect do you think airline deregulation had on load factors?

Figure 14.6

Rent Seeking for a Peanut Cartel

With a cartel, output is X_c and rents are area A. Hence, members of the cartel are willing to pay up to A in return for government enforcement of the cartel. If rent-seeking consumes resoures, then the welfare cost of the cartel is $B + A$.

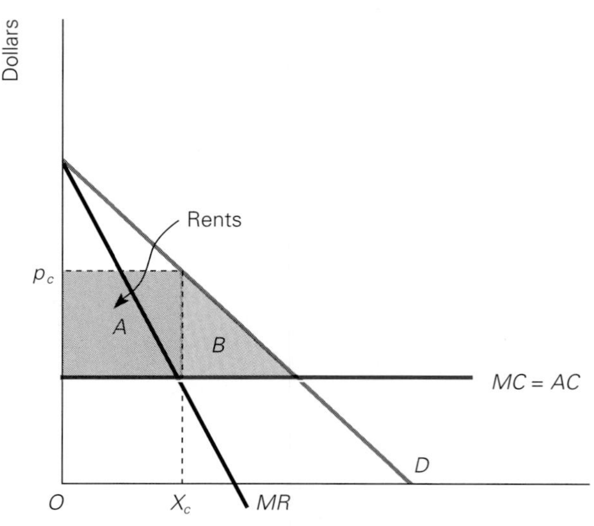

The real estate market and the air travel market both demonstrate that attempts to limit competitive behavior in one dimension may simply redirect, but not eliminate, market forces.

The Welfare Cost of Monopoly Reconsidered

If the firms in an industry can get the government to enforce a cartel (including entry restrictions and limits on non-price competition), then they may be able to enjoy economic profits. It follows that the firms may take actions to convince the government to establish or maintain a cartel for them. This section sketches a model of this process. An implication of the model is that the welfare costs of monopoly may be larger than was suggested in Chapter 13.

Consider the U.S. market for peanuts. In Figure 14.6, the demand for peanuts is *D*, and the associated marginal revenue curve is *MR*. For simplicity, it is assumed the peanut production is characterized by constant average and marginal costs; hence, the marginal cost curve, *MC*, is horizontal and coincides with the average cost curve, *AC*. According to our theory of cartels, it would be in the peanut farmers' interest to coordinate their production and act like a joint monopolist. Acting as a cartel, they would produce a joint output of X_c tons of peanuts (which is determined at the intersection of marginal cost and marginal revenue), charge a price of p_c per ton, and earn economic profits equal to shaded area *A*. However, our theory of cartels also tells us that it may be difficult to maintain a price of p_c. Even if the cartel members are able to set and enforce production quotas, new peanut producers might enter the market to get their share of the economic profits; ultimately, such entry will eliminate the economic profits of the cartel members.

To be successful in the long run, the cartel members need some way to restrict entry. This is where the government comes in. If the cartel members can get the government to use its coercive power to forbid new entrants, then the cartel can be maintained, and the members can continue earning economic profits.

Now, recall that profits are sometimes referred to as "rents." As the peanut example shows, rents can be created for producers in an industry if the government artificially restricts supply. **Rent seeking** refers to activities aimed at obtaining or keeping economic rents. In fact, the peanut industry is a classic example of rent-seeking behavior and its consequences. It is a federal crime to grow peanuts without a license. Further, even if you have a license, the quantity of peanuts you can grow is determined by a government quota. To enforce the quotas, employees of the Department of Agriculture "study aerial photographs to help identify farmers who are planting more than their allotted amount of peanuts. Violators are heavily fined." The rents associated with owning the licenses are huge—according to one estimate, the net rate of return is 51 percent (Bovard 1995, A10). The owners of the licenses make hefty contributions to the political campaigns of elected officials, who keep the quota system in place, despite the fact that the higher peanut prices cost consumers about $513 million per year.

rent seeking
Actions aimed at obtaining or preserving economic profits.

Other examples of rent seeking are easy to find: U.S. auto makers obtain quotas on Japanese auto imports; Japanese rice farmers obtain quotas on U.S. rice imports; tobacco farmers obtain restrictions on the amount of land that can be used for tobacco growing; physicians in Florida obtain rules that make it difficult for physicians from other states to practice medicine there; and the list goes on.

Rent seeking is the driving force behind the demand for political favors, because incumbents in an industry with existing entry restrictions typically are willing to spend money to maintain their favored position. In the same way, firms that see an opportunity to obtain rents if certain government actions are taken will devote resources to convincing politicians and regulators to take those actions. In the caustic words of O'Rourke (1991, 210), "When buying and selling are controlled by legislation, the first things to be bought and sold are legislators."

What is the maximal amount that a group of firms would be willing to pay to obtain or maintain a favored position? Because rents are a payment above that required to stay in an activity, the most that the firms would be willing to pay for their favored position is the total amount of rent. In terms of the peanut cartel example in Figure 14.6, this is shaded area A.

An important implication of the rent-seeking model is that the welfare cost of market power may be higher than we otherwise might have supposed. According to the standard analysis developed in Chapter 13, the welfare cost of monopoly is found (in Figure 14.6) by taking the loss in consumer surplus generated by the monopoly (area $A + B$) and subtracting from it the monopoly's rents (area A). Thus, the welfare cost is area B. This calculation assumes that economic rents represent a lump sum transfer from consumers to producers. That is, while this transfer may have important redistributive implications, it has no impact on efficiency. The theory of rent seeking, however, puts area A in a rather different light. Rent seeking can use up resources—lobbyists spend their time influencing legislators, consultants testify before regulatory panels, advertisers conduct public relations campaigns, and so on. Such resources, which could have been used to produce new goods and services, are instead consumed in a struggle over the distribution of existing goods and services. Hence, area A does not represent a mere lump sum transfer; it is a measure of real resources used up to maintain a position of market power. In short, according to this view, the deadweight loss of monopoly is B *plus* A.

We cannot conclude that area $B + A$ is always the loss, however. In many cases, $B + A$ may overstate the efficiency cost of monopoly, even when rent seeking is present. For example, some rent seeking takes the form of campaign contributions and bribes, and these simply are transfers—they do not "use up" real resources. Nevertheless, an important contribution of the rent-seeking model is that it focuses our attention on the potential size of the waste generated by the government's power to create rents.

LABOR UNIONS

Cartels are not found solely in product markets. Labor unions are an extremely important type of cartel in the U.S. economy. Although unions do many things, in the United States they are largely interested in wages and working conditions. As noted in Chapter 5, both components are important to workers, but our focus here is on union efforts to raise wages.

The United Auto Workers (UAW) has thousands of members. Without a union, their labor would be competitively supplied. Given the demand curve for auto workers shown in Figure 14.7, L_1 workers would be hired at a wage rate of w_1 in equilibrium.

Since the union does exist, the supply of workers is not competitive. The U.A.W. represents these workers in their collective bargaining with the firms in the industry (the automobile manufacturers) over the wage rates. That is, the union puts forth a wage offer, w_a, and no union worker can accept a lower wage. As shown in Figure 14.7, total employment falls from L_1 to L_a. Moreover, because the wage has risen from the competitive level, the number of people willing to work at the prevailing wage rises, from L_1 to L_b. Consequently, the number of workers supplied exceeds the number demanded, and jobs have to be rationed among workers. That's why we see people involuntarily laid off from their jobs. The laid-off workers would like to work at the prevailing wage, but the auto firms do not demand as much labor as workers are willing to supply.

Here again, we see the need for a cartel to have a means of enforcing member discipline. If not for the union contract, those workers who did not get jobs at the union wage would be willing to work for less. Naturally, the firms would be happy to employ them. As a result, the wage would fall, and no firm would hire workers at the union wage. This is one reason why *closed shop agreements* (which forbid nonunion workers from being employed in firms that have unionized workers) are so important to unions.

In summary, we have seen that by acting together, workers may be able collectively to behave like a price-making monopolist. But like any other cartel, to be successful, a union must be able to prevent cheating by its members and to block entry into the market by outsiders.

SECTION RECAP

Suppliers can raise their profits if they successfully band together in a cartel to restrict the quantity supplied below its competitive level and raise price above its competitive level. Any cartel faces two problems. First, when price exceeds marginal cost, individual members find it in their interest to cheat on the cartel agreement. Second, cartel profits may attract new firms into the market, which can both reduce the share of industry profits enjoyed by incumbent suppliers and dissipate overall industry profits, either by increasing the market quantity supplied or by raising the average cost of supplying a given market total.

Figure 14.7

The Effects of a Union

In a competitive labor market, the equilibrium wage would be w_1 and the equilibrium number of workers hired would be L_1. At the union wage of w_a, only L_a workers are demanded and hired. The number of people willing to work at the prevailing wage rises from L_1 to L_b.

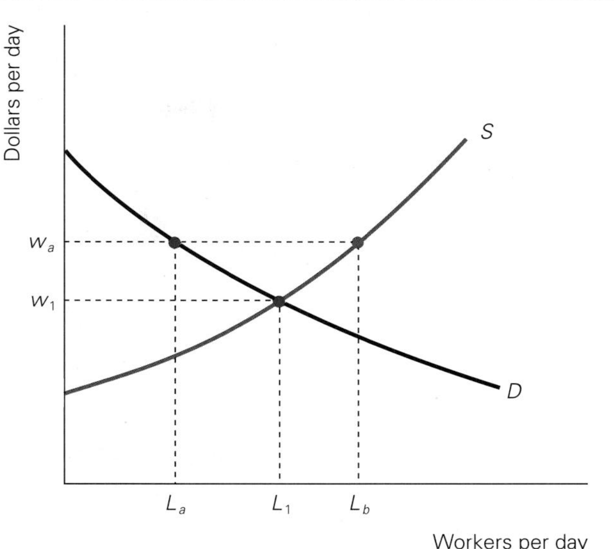

14.2 MONOPOLISTIC COMPETITION

So far, we have considered price making only in markets with either one producer or with several producers who act together to behave as a single decision maker. There are many markets, however, in which producers are price makers even though there are lots of them and they act independently in competition with one another. Price making arises in these situations when the firms produce imperfect substitutes.

As an example, consider ice-cream parlors. No two parlors are the same. Two ice-cream shops may be differentiated both by what they sell (one might sell real ice cream, while the other sells ice milk or frozen yogurt) and by where they are located (they may be miles apart). Because each shop is differentiated from its rivals, each shop faces a downward-sloping firm-specific demand curve. In other words, each ice-cream parlor is a price maker like a monopolist. But this clearly is not a monopolized market. There are many suppliers and new ones can freely enter. The technology needed to operate an ice-cream parlor is widely known, and there are few legal barriers. The number of sellers and the entry conditions resemble those of perfect competition.

Many other markets combine the price making of monopoly with the large number of suppliers and free-entry conditions of perfect competition—clothing stores, record stores, and just about any retail store are examples. Because it combines the features of monopoly and competition, a market with these features is said to be characterized by ***monopolistic competition***. While interesting in its own right, the monopolistic competition model also is an important tool for analyzing issues of product choice and product variety. It is too expensive to produce all conceivable products, and society must make choices about which goods to produce. In most Western economies, these choices are "made by the market." The monopolistically competitive model helps us understand whether the market system leads to the production of the "right" assortment of goods and services.

THE FUNDAMENTAL ASSUMPTIONS

We start by defining the model in terms of our standard set of assumptions about supplier and demander behavior. The first three assumptions of the monopolistically competitive model deal with the supply side of the market.

Like a monopolist, a monopolistic competitor recognizes its influence on price:

1. *Sellers are price makers.* Recall that saying that a firm is a price maker means that it faces a downward-sloping firm-specific demand curve.

A monopolistic competitor recognizes that it affects the price at which it can sell its own output. However, the model assumes that each supplier believes that its actions have no noticeable effect on the prices that other firms can receive for their output, and hence has no effect on the collective actions of other firms. In other words,

2. *Sellers do not behave strategically.* This is an assumption that monopolistic competition shares with both perfect competition and monopoly.

Our last assumption about the suppliers in a monopolistically competitive market concerns the conditions of entry:

3. *Entry into the market is free.* In this regard, monopolistic competition is like perfect competition.

The final assumption concerns the demand side of the market:

4. *Buyers are price takers.* As in competitive and monopolized markets, each buyer believes that it has no influence on the market price.

Table 14.1 summarizes these fundamental assumptions of the monopolistic competition model and compares them with those of perfect competition and monopoly.

THE APPROPRIATE MARKET STRUCTURE

To what type of market does this model apply? To answer this question, we once again consider each dimension of market structure.

a. **The size and number of buyers.** Since demanders are price takers, there must be many buyers, no one of whom is large enough to exert any influence on the price. In this respect, our new market structure is the same as a competitive or monopolistic one.

b. **The size and number of sellers.** As we saw in Chapter 11, the size and number of suppliers affects both the degree of strategic behavior and the extent of price-taking versus price-making behavior by suppliers. When there are many firms in the industry, an action taken by any one of them has little impact on the others, and firms are unlikely to react to one another's actions—suppliers will be nonstrategic. For this reason, monopolistic competition best applies to markets with many suppliers. In this respect, a monopolistically competitive market looks much like a perfectly competitive market.

It might seem like this element of market structure would lead to price-taking behavior, in violation of the first basic assumption of monopolistic competition. However, *by itself,* having a large number of firms in the market does *not* imply that suppliers act as price takers. We must also consider the degree of product differentiation and the extent to which consumers are informed about the available alternatives.

Table 14.1

Fundamental Assumptions of the Monopolistic Competition Model

	Monopolistic Competition	Perfect Competition	Monopoly
1. Seller Influence on Price	Sellers are price makers.	Sellers are price takers.	Seller is a price maker.
2. Extent of Strategic Behavior	Sellers do not behave strategically.	Sellers do not behave strategically.	Seller does not behave strategically.
3. Conditions of Entry	Entry into the market is free.	Entry into the market is free.	Entry into the market is completely blocked.
4. Buyer Influence on Price	Buyers are price takers.	Buyers are price takers.	Buyers are price takers.

c. **The degree of substitutability of different sellers' products.** The first two elements of market structure are like those of a perfectly competitive market. The big difference between monopolistic competition and perfect competition comes in terms of the degree of substitutability among rival suppliers' products, which influences the extent to which a supplier is a price maker or price taker. When the products of different suppliers are not perfect substitutes, a supplier can raise the price of its output without losing all of its sales. Since monopolistic competition is a model of price-making sellers, the most appropriate market structure is one in which consumers consider the products of different firms to be imperfect substitutes. Since consumers view the products as different from one another, the products are said to be **heterogeneous**, or **differentiated**. In contrast, the competitive model applies to markets in which all producers supply goods that are perfect substitutes for one another—what are known as *homogeneous goods*.

heterogeneous products A market is said to have heterogeneous products when consumers view the products of the various producers as being somewhat different from one another.

differentiated products Another name for heterogeneous products.

At this point you might ask, if products are differentiated, why aren't the monopolistic competitors just like a bunch of monopolists? The answer is that while different firms' products are sufficiently differentiated so that each firm is a price maker, the products also are sufficiently close substitutes that the actions of one firm affect the prices and profits of other firms (even though each firm fails to recognize its influence on its rivals).

Monopolistic competitors are best thought of as producing different versions of the same product. Consider magazines. There are many variants, which are differentiated from one another in a number of ways. Some readers enjoy magazines that cover world news and analyze political events. Others like to read about the latest divorces of rich people. Still other readers think there is nothing more interesting than a good article about formatting a hard disk on a personal computer. While many different magazines cater to these different tastes, they compete against one another. The more gossip magazines a consumer purchases, the fewer news magazines he or she is likely to buy.

d. **The extent to which buyers are informed about prices and available alternatives.** Buyers' information about what products and prices different suppliers are offering can strongly affect the market equilibrium. The monopolistic competition model encompasses both well-informed and poorly informed consumers. When each buyer is perfectly informed about the alternatives, he or she purchases from the seller that is offering the best deal in terms of price and product characteristics. If the products are differentiated, each supplier still is a

Table 14.2

A Monopolistically Competitive Market Structure

	Monopolistic Competition	Perfect Competition	Monopoly
a. The Size and Number of Buyers	Many buyers, no one of which is large relative to the overall market.	Many buyers, no one of which is large relative to the overall market.	Many buyers, no one of which is large relative to the overall market.
b. The Size and Number of Sellers	Many sellers, no one of which is large relative to the overall market.	Many sellers, no one of which is large relative to the overall market.	One seller.
c. The Degree of Substitutability among Different Sellers' Products	The outputs of different sellers are heterogeneous.	The outputs of different sellers are homogeneous.	There are no close substitutes.
d. The Extent to Which Buyers Are Informed about Prices and Available Alternatives	Buyers may or may not be well informed about the offerings of competing suppliers.	Buyers are well informed about the offerings of competing suppliers.	Buyers are well informed about the offerings of competing suppliers.
e. The Conditions of Entry	Neither technological nor legal barriers to entry exist.	Neither technological nor legal barriers to entry exist.	Either technological or legal barriers completely block entry.

price maker because some consumers are willing to pay more for its output than are others. This is the interpretation we typically give to monopolistic competition.

However, we could also consider a market in which consumers are imperfectly informed about the available alternatives. Indeed, this lack of information may be the source of the price making. Firm-specific demand may be much less sensitive to price when buyers are imperfectly informed about prices and available alternatives. If you want to sell more output, can you attract new customers with a price cut? Not if no one knows that you have lowered your price. Similarly, when a supplier raises its price, it may retain some of its sales simply because its customers know of no better alternative.

e. **The conditions of entry.** The model assumes that entry is free, so it applies to markets with no technological or legal barriers to new firms.

Table 14.2 summarizes the market conditions for which the monopolistic competition model is most appropriate, and it compares these conditions with those of perfect competition and monopoly.

EQUILIBRIUM

As the name monopolistic competition implies, there is little new in the basic analytics of this model. We simply mix monopolistic pricing with competitive entry. Because this process of entry takes time, it is useful to distinguish between short-run equilibrium with a fixed number of suppliers and long-run equilibrium in which the number of firms is determined as part of the equilibrium process.

Short-Run Equilibrium

Let's begin with the short run, during which the number of firms is fixed. In particular, suppose that the number of firms in the market is fixed at n. Figure 14.8 illustrates the cost and demand curves for a representative firm when

Figure 14.8

The Short-Run Monopolistically Competitive Equilibrium

Like any profit-maximizing firm, when a monopolistic competitor chooses not to shut down, it produces output where marginal revenue is equal to marginal cost, quantity X_1. The resulting economic profit is the shaded area, so the firm will not shut down.

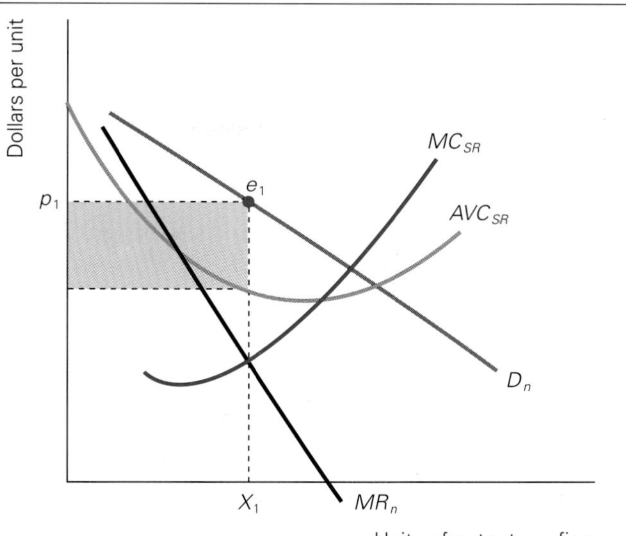

there are n firms in the market. By *representative firm*, we mean that all other firms in the industry are in a similar position in terms of their costs and demand conditions. That is, although each firm produces a different version of the basic good, each firm faces firm-specific demand and cost curves that have the same shape. Clearly, we would expect firms in actual markets to have somewhat different demand and cost curves from one another, but this symmetry assumption allows us to get to the heart of the issues without an unworkably complex model.

The firm-specific demand curve faced by our representative firm is given by D_n in Figure 14.8. As already noted, each firm faces a demand curve or, equivalently, an average revenue curve, that slopes downward. Because the average revenue curve slopes downward, we know that the marginal revenue curve lies below the average revenue curve for all but the first unit of output. The marginal revenue curve for our representative firm is MR_n in Figure 14.8.

This diagram looks much like one for a monopolist. The only visible difference is that we have written n subscripts on the firm-specific demand and marginal revenue curves. These subscripts remind us that the demand faced by any one firm depends on the number of rivals that it has. As we shall see, when there are more firms in the market, the firm-specific demand curve for a representative firm shifts. Unlike the monopoly model, here we have to keep track of the number of firms in the market.

Like any profit-maximizing firm, a monopolistic competitor makes its output choice by applying the two basic output choice rules developed in Chapter 7. First, the firm sets its output level at the point where marginal revenue is equal to marginal cost, quantity X_1 in Figure 14.8. As under monopoly, we find the price the firm charges by reading up to the demand curve. The figure indicates that a firm producing X_1 units of output sells that output at a price of p_1 when there are n firms in the market.

Of course, we must apply the second rule for the profit-maximizing choice of output level as well. We must verify that the firm would rather produce X_1 units of output than shut down entirely. One way to check this condition is to express profit as the quantity produced times the difference between average revenue and average economic (variable) cost, the shaded area in Figure 14.8. We see that the firm is indeed earning positive economic profit and would not want to shut down in the short run.

In summary, the short-run analysis of monopolistic competition is pretty much old hat. Just treat each firm like a little monopolist. The short-run analysis is simple because we do not explicitly deal with the interactions among firms. We merely summarize this interdependence with the subscript n, which indicates that the firm's revenue curves depend on the number of other firms in the industry. In the long run, the number of firms in the market can vary, and our model must deal with this fact.

Long-Run Equilibrium

The difference between the analysis of monopolistic competition and monopoly comes in the long run. Under monopolistic competition, entry into the industry is free and new firms enter as long as there are profits to be made. Would new firms enter, given a situation like the one illustrated in Figure 14.8? You might answer yes because each firm earns positive profit. But this is a trick question. Figure 14.8 shows *short*-run marginal and average costs, while the entry decision is based on *long*-run cost curves. To find the equilibrium number of firms, we need to consider the long-run cost curves faced by our representative firm, as is done in Figure 14.9. The figure indicates that the industry is in a situation in which each supplier earns positive economic profit equal to the shaded area. These profits will attract new firms into the industry. This is precisely what happened in the market for olive oil several years ago. After some highly publicized findings that olive oil can help reduce cholesterol, the demand for olive oil increased. Soon thereafter, a bewildering array of new varieties appeared on the market. One Manhattan grocery store stocked 38 of them.

How does the entry of such new firms affect the market equilibrium? When new firms enter the market, consumers have greater choices and fewer consumers patronize any one firm. Suppose that the number of firms rises from n to n'. As a result, the market is more crowded, so at any given price the firm sells less output: The demand curve faced by our representative firm shifts inward. This shift is illustrated by the new average and marginal revenue curves, $D_{n'}$, and $MR_{n'}$, in Figure 14.10. With these revenue curves, the representative firm sells X_2 units of output at a price of p_2 per unit. As we can see from the diagram, the crowding of the market lowers per-firm profit. As drawn in Figure 14.10, however, profit remains positive even when there are n' firms in the market. Hence, additional firms will find it profitable to enter this market.

When does this process end? As long as a firm can find an output level at which average revenue is greater than average cost, it can earn positive profit. Hence, as long as there is an output level at which the firm-specific demand curve is above the long-run average cost curve, the number of firms in the industry continues to rise. This tells us that, in long-run equilibrium, the average revenue and average cost curves cannot cross one another. If they did, as in Figure 14.10, there would be some output level at which average revenue exceeded average cost and additional entry would be profitable. On the other hand, the industry cannot be in equilibrium if average revenue is everywhere below average cost, as drawn in Figure 14.11. If so, incumbent firms would suffer losses and some of them would leave the market.

Figure 14.9

Positive Economic Profits Will Attract New Entrants in the Long Run

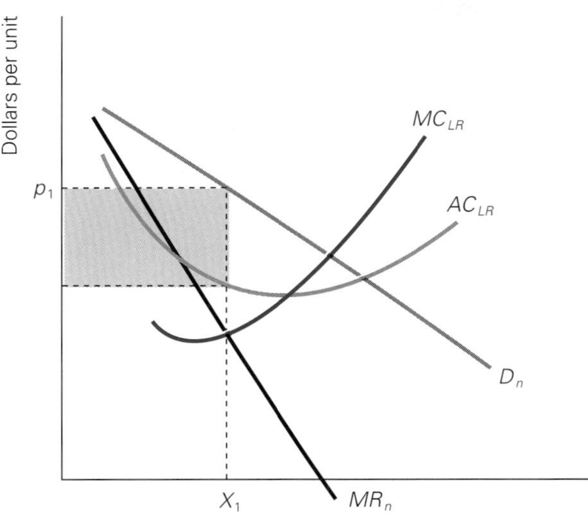

Each supplier in the industry earns positive economic profit equal to the shaded area. These profits will attract new firms into the industry.

Figure 14.10

Entry by New Firms Shifts Inward the Firm-Specific Demand and Marginal Revenue Curves of a Representative Firm

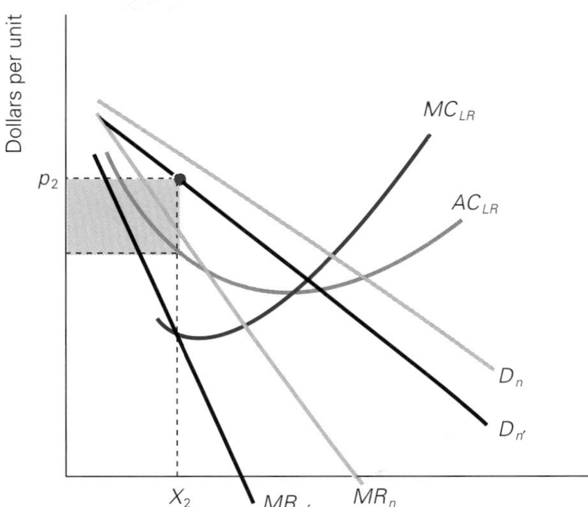

Entry shifts inward the demand curve our representative firm faces. This shift is illustrated by the new firm-specific demand and marginal revenue curves, $D_{n'}$ and $MR_{n'}$.

To determine what the long-run equilibrium looks like, recall that firms in the market must be able to earn zero economic profit. Hence, in long-run equilibrium, each firm in the market must operate at a point where average revenue (price) is equal to average cost. But as we just discussed, there must be no point at which the average revenue curve is above the average cost curve. This can occur only if the demand curve and the average cost curve are tangent at the equilibrium output level. Therefore, in long-run equilibrium, our representative firm must produce at an output level where the demand curve and the average cost curve are tangent, as in Figure 14.12. The price at which the firm can sell X_3 units of output, p_3, is equal to the average cost of producing those units.

Since the firm is a profit maximizer, it must also follow the marginal output choice rule. Hence, at the long-run equilibrium level of output, marginal revenue must be equal to marginal cost. This fact is also illustrated in Figure 14.12. The marginal revenue and marginal cost curves intersect at X_3. You might think that this alignment of the tangency and the intersection is an amazing coincidence. It is not. The average revenue curve (the demand curve) and the marginal revenue curve are two different ways of expressing the same information about revenues. Likewise, the average cost curve and the marginal cost curve are two different ways of expressing the same information about costs. Hence, when the average curves indicate that a certain output level maximizes profit, the marginal curves must also indicate that that output level maximizes profit.

While Figure 14.12 illustrates the long-run equilibrium position of a representative firm, Figure 14.13 gives us another way to determine the long-run number of firms. The $\pi(n)$ curve shows the profits of a single firm when there

Figure 14.11

Economic Losses Will Drive Firms from the Industry in the Long Run

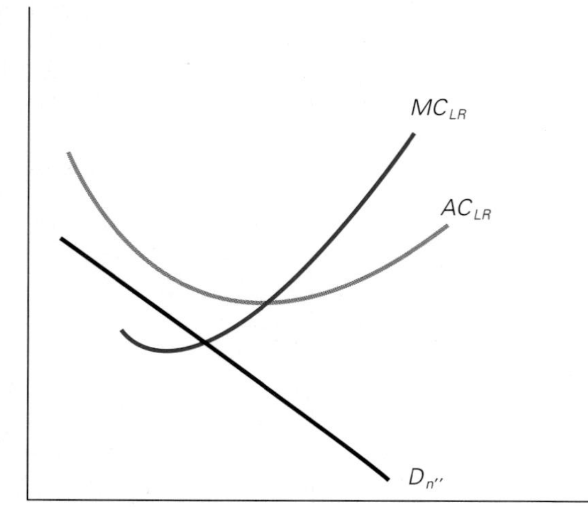

If there are so many firms in the industry that the demand curve is always below the average cost curve, incumbent firms suffer losses if they remain in operation. Some firms will exit the market.

Figure 14.12

The Long-Run Monopolistically Competitive Equilibrium

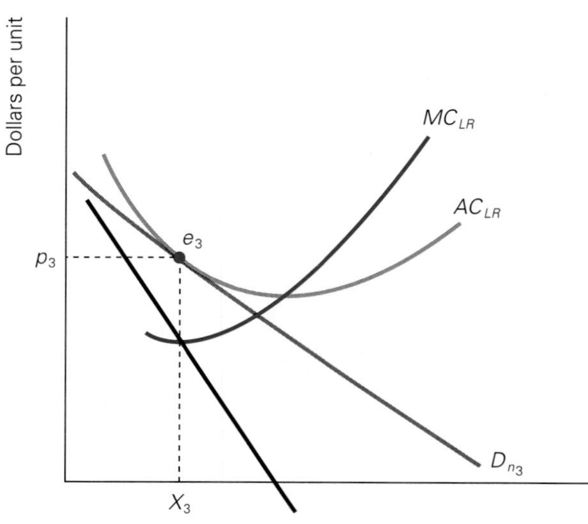

In the long-run equilibrium, a representative firm produces at an output level at which the demand curve and the average cost curve are tangent. The price at which the firm can sell X_3 units of output, p_3, is equal to the average cost of producing those units. The long-run equilibrium output level must also satisfy the marginal output rule: Marginal revenue is equal to marginal cost at X_3.

Figure 14.13

A Single Firm's Profit Falls as More Firms Enter the Industry

The $\pi(n)$ curve shows the profit of a single firm, given that there are n firms in the industry. In the long run, entry or exit will occur until each firm earns zero profit, and the equilibrium number of firms is n_3.

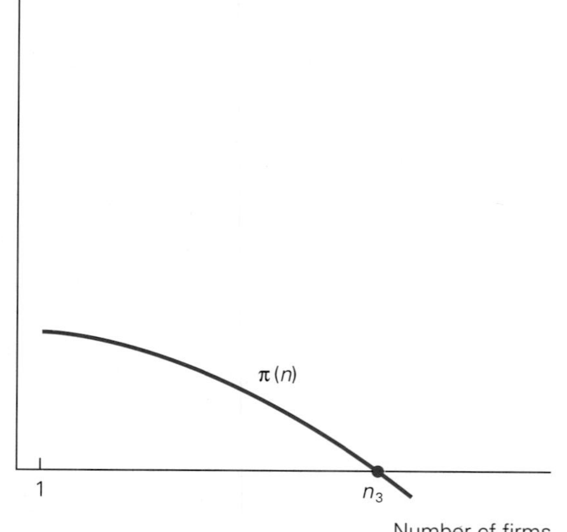

are n firms in the industry and firms are making their profit-maximizing output choices conditional on that number of firms being in the market. In other words, if there are n firms in the market, each one of them earns a profit of $\pi(n)$. As the market becomes more crowded, the profits of any one firm fall, and consequently the $\pi(n)$ curve is downward sloping. When there are fewer than n_3 firms, each one makes positive economic profits, and entry occurs. At any number of firms greater than n_3, firms suffer losses and exit occurs. Hence, in long-run equilibrium there must be exactly n_3 firms. (PC 14.3)

14.3 PROGRESS CHECK

Illustrate the equilibrium position of a representative firm when there are more than n_3 firms in the market.

NORMATIVE ANALYSIS OF MONOPOLISTIC COMPETITION

Why don't we all wear tailor-made clothing? The answer is obvious: For many of us, custom-made clothing is too expensive. The cost of making a single pair of trousers designed to fit one particular person is much greater than the average cost of making thousands of identical pairs to be worn by many different people. In other words, there are economies of scale in producing trousers. *When the production of a good is characterized by economies of scale, variety is costly.* Given that variety is costly in the trouser market, why don't we all wear the same size and style of trousers? Again, the answer is obvious: Some of us would have to wear pants that were very ill-fitting indeed. We are willing to pay higher prices for trousers in order to have a greater selection. In this market and many others, variety is valuable. Hence, a trade-off must be made between the value of increased variety and the associated cost.

Does a monopolistically competitive market make the right trade-off? Do the firms collectively choose the efficient number of products to offer? Since each firm in the model offers only one product, asking whether the right number of products are offered is the same as asking whether the right number of firms are in the market. Before giving the answer to this question, it is useful to consider a false argument that for a long time fooled many economists.

The So-Called Excess Capacity Theorem

A persistent view in the popular culture is that the market produces too many varieties of various products. Consider these lyrics from the song "It's All Too Much":

> I hate this supermarket
> but I have to say it makes me think
> a hundred mineral waters
> it's fun to guess which ones are safe to drink
> two hundred brands of cookies
> 87 kinds of chocolate chip
> They say that choice is freedom
> I'm so free it drives me to the brink.[3]

Do market economies generally have too many kinds of chocolate chip cookies (and other commodities)? To think about this question, recall that under

[3]"It's All Too Much" by Joe Jackson, © 1991 Pokazuka, Ltd. (PRS).

long-run equilibrium, each monopolistic competitor produces output at a level at which its average cost curve is tangent to its average revenue curve. Since the firm's average revenue curve slopes downward, the firm's average cost curve must also be downward sloping at the long-run equilibrium output level, as it is at point e_3 in Figure 14.12. From this fact, some economists incorrectly concluded that there are too many firms in the market under the long-run, monopolistically competitive equilibrium. This incorrect conclusion became known as the *excess capacity theorem* and was based on the following line of argument: Because average costs are decreasing at the equilibrium per-firm output level, industrywide average costs would be lower if the given industry output level were produced by fewer firms, each of which produced more output per firm.

This so-called theorem missed a crucial point—*variety is valuable*. While having fewer firms may lower the average costs of a given amount of total output (somehow measured), it would also reduce the amount of variety. Suppose, for example, that the number of gas stations in the United States were cut in half. The gas stations that remained would indeed have lower average costs as they increased their volumes and took advantage of economies of scale. But consumers would have to drive farther to reach the nearest gas station. Once we consider the added inconvenience, the true cost of obtaining gasoline might well be higher with fewer stations. In short, by itself, a falling average cost curve tells us nothing more than that variety is costly. It does not tell us how these costs compare with the benefits of variety.

At this point, you may have two questions. First, how could economists have mistakenly believed in the excess capacity theorem? Well, it just goes to show the danger of not keeping an open mind when working with a formal model. Second, if the excess capacity theorem is incorrect, then are there or aren't there too many firms in equilibrium?

The Market Equilibrium Compared with the Efficient Outcome

To see whether the market over- or underprovides variety, we must compare the efficient number of firms with the actual number in long-run market equilibrium.

The Efficient Amount of Variety The efficient number of firms balances the increase in average cost against the benefit of variety. Using our partial equilibrium approach, the efficient number of firms is the one that maximizes the level of total surplus, the sum of industry profit and consumer surplus.[4] To see what number of firms maximizes total surplus, it is helpful to look separately at its two components.

Given our convenient assumption that all firms are the same, we find industry profit by simply multiplying the profit per firm, $\pi(n)$, times the number of firms, n. When there are n firms in the market, industry profit is $n \times \pi(n)$. The industry profit curve is graphed in Figure 14.14 along with the per-firm profit curve.

Turning to the demand side of the market, aggregate consumer surplus is graphed as a function of the number of firms in Figure 14.15. The $CS(n)$ curve shows the aggregate surplus enjoyed by consumers when there are n firms in the market. We would expect the $CS(n)$ curve to be upward sloping (as it is in Figure 14.15) for two reasons. First, as more firms enter the market, competition among them becomes more intense and consumers benefit from the lower prices

[4]Here, and throughout this chapter, we assume that the nature of industry equilibrium has no effects on the producer surplus of input suppliers.

Figure 14.14

The Industry Profit Varies as the Number of Firms in the Market Changes

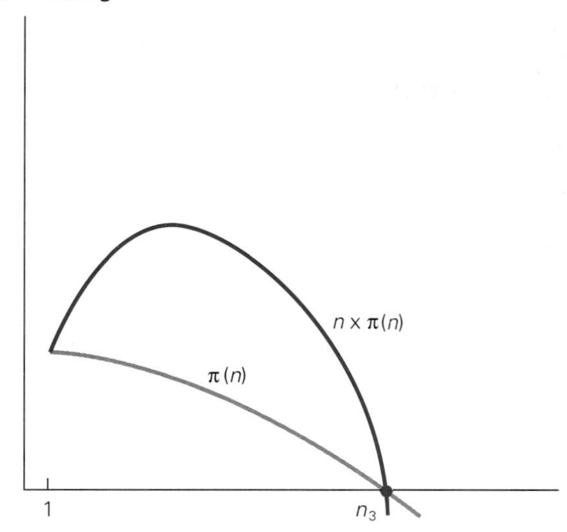

When there are n firms in the market, each firm earns a profit of $\pi(n)$ and industry profit is equal to $n \times \pi(n)$.

Figure 14.15

Market Consumer Surplus Rises as More Firms Enter the Industry

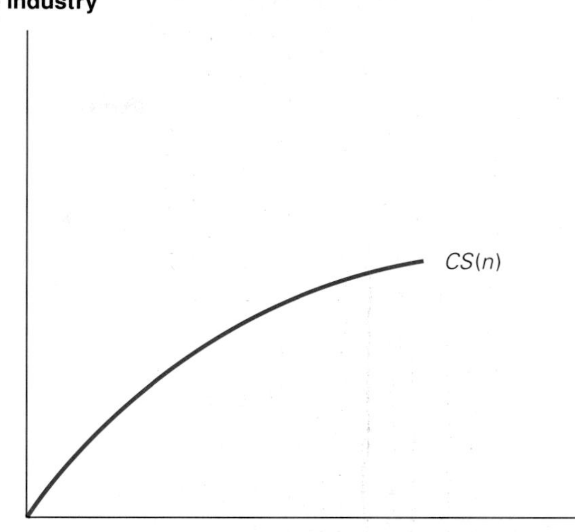

The aggregate surplus enjoyed by consumers when there are n firms (products) in the market is $CS(n)$.

that result. Second, with more firms in the market, consumers have a greater variety of choices and they are more likely to find a product that closely fits their tastes.[5]

We can now express total surplus, $W(n)$, as the sum of its two components:

$$W(n) = n \times \pi(n) + CS(n). \tag{14.1}$$

The total-surplus-maximizing number of firms is found where $W(n)$ reaches its highest value. We can find this point by graphing total surplus as a function of the number of firms in the industry. The total surplus curve is the vertical sum of the $n \times \pi(n)$ and $CS(n)$ curves: the $W(n)$ curve in Figure 14.16. From the figure, we see that the efficient number of firms is n_T. If there are fewer than n_T firms in the industry, the benefits of increased variety outweigh the costs. But further increases in variety above n_T increase the average costs of production by more than they raise gross consumption benefits.

The Comparison How does the market equilibrium number of firms compare to the efficient number? Figure 14.16 illustrates a market in which $n_3 > n_T$—the market equilibrium with free entry leads to too many firms entering the market. There is more product variety than is efficient, which is the same result that many economists alleged was proven by the excess capacity theorem. But this relationship is not the only one possible. In Figure 14.17, for example, $n_3 < n_T$, and the market equilibrium with free entry leads to too few firms entering the market.

[5]It is logically possible for aggregate consumer surplus to fall as the number of firms rises. When there are many firms, each one catering to a very narrow market, the effects of product differentiation may be very strong. As a result, prices may rise faster than consumer benefits, with the net result that consumer surplus falls as the number of firms rises.

Figure 14.16

A Market with Too Many Firms in the Long-Run Monopolistically Competitive Equilibrium

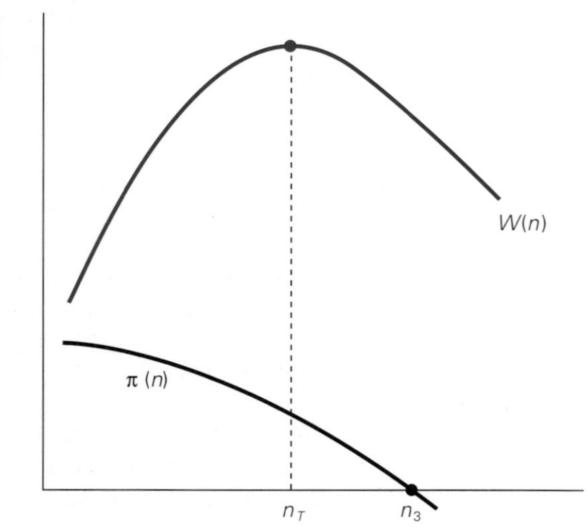

The total surplus curve, $W(n)$, is the vertical sum of the $n \times \pi(n)$ and $CS(n)$ curves from Figures 14.14 and 14.15, respectively. Total surplus is maximized when there are n_T firms in the industry. Comparing n_T with the equilibrium number of firms, n_3, we see that too many firms enter this market.

Figure 14.17

A Market with Too Few Firms in the Long-Run Monopolistically Competitive Equilibrium

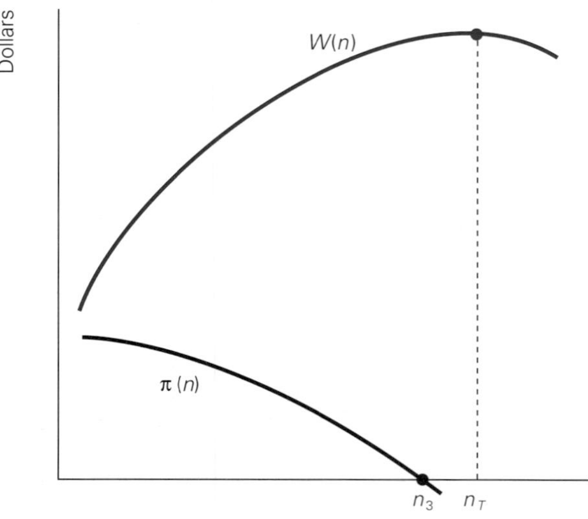

In this example, the market equilibrium with free entry leads to too few firms entering the market; $n_3 < n_T$.

There is less product variety than is socially optimal. We conclude that *the long-run monopolistically competitive equilibrium may have too many or too few firms, depending on the cost and demand conditions.* In some markets, there may be too much variety while in others there is too little. Unfortunately, there is no guarantee that the market provides the right variety of products.

We can gain some insight into the source of this ambiguity by looking at an entry decision in terms of its effect on the profit of the firm entering the market and its effect on the level of total surplus in the market. Suppose that there initially are $n - 1$ firms, and one more firm is contemplating entry. If that firm stays out of the market, it earns zero profit, but if it enters it earns $\pi(n)$. Hence, the net effect on the entrant's profit is simply $\pi(n)$, and this term represents the firm's private incentive to enter the market.

The social incentive for entry is the change in *total* surplus; that is, from society's point of view, a firm should enter when the change in total surplus is positive. The change in total surplus when the nth firm enters the market has three components. First, there is the $\pi(n)$ increase in the entrant's profit. Second, the profit of each of the incumbent firms falls by $\Delta\pi(n) = \pi(n) - \pi(n-1) < 0$. Since there are $n - 1$ incumbents prior to entry by the nth firm, the total effect on the profits of incumbent firms is $(n - 1) \times \Delta\pi(n)$. Third, turning from sellers to buyers, aggregate consumer surplus rises by $\Delta CS(n) = CS(n) - CS(n - 1)$. Taking the sum of these three effects, the change in total surplus is

$$\Delta W(n) = \pi(n) + (n - 1) \times \Delta\pi(n) + \Delta CS(n). \tag{14.2}$$

Recall now that the firm's private incentive to enter is determined solely by $\pi(n)$, the first term in Equation (14.2). Hence, the profit of the entering firm is part of both the firm's own decision and the change in total surplus. The other two terms in Equation (14.2) are part of the change in total surplus, but do not enter into the potential entrant's decision. Hence, these two terms are wedges between the social and private incentives to enter the market.

Let's look at each of these two wedges in turn, beginning with the change in consumer surplus. Entry raises consumer surplus, so $\Delta CS(n)$ is positive. The firm ignores this effect. Therefore, the social incentive to enter the market tends to be greater than the private incentive. Hence, the consumer surplus wedge leads to a bias toward too few firms.

The consumer surplus wedge is familiar from our examination of a monopolist's output decision. Equation (14.2) tells us that in a monopolistically competitive market, there is a second wedge to consider. By entering the market, a firm shifts the demand curves for the products of the $n - 1$ firms already in the industry and lowers their profits. These profits are a part of total surplus, a part that the single firm contemplating entry ignores in making its choice. The term $(n - 1) \times \Delta\pi(n)$ in Equation (14.2) captures this effect on rivals' profits. Since profit per firm falls as the number of firms rises, this term is negative. Because the firm does not take into account these ill effects of its entry, the private incentive to enter is greater than the social incentive.

We now have two wedges working in opposite directions. The consumer-surplus wedge tends to lead to the underprovision of variety, while the rivals' profit wedge tends to lead to excessive entry. The net effect can run in either direction, as we already saw in Figures 14.16 and 14.17.

SECTION RECAP

Many markets combine the price making of monopoly with the large number of suppliers and free-entry conditions of perfect competition. The theory of monopolistic competition provides a model of equilibrium in these markets. Because individual suppliers recognize their influence on price, each supplier restricts output in an attempt to hold up its price and profit. As a result of free entry, however, there are no economic profits in the long-run equilibrium. The monopolistically competitive model allows us to address the question of whether the market provides the right amount of variety. The market may provide too much or too little variety, depending on the circumstances of the particular market under examination.

14.3 MONOPSONY

If you were a coffee grower in East Timor, Indonesia, when it came time to sell your crop, you would find that you had two choices: You could sell your coffee to the P. T. Denok Hernandez International Company, or you could let the coffee rot in the field. Denok is owned by the Indonesian military and they do not allow competition. Consequently, Denok is the sole buyer of coffee grown in East Timor (Bonner 1988, 86). Let's look at the market from Denok's point of view. The supply curve that it faces is the East Timor market supply curve for coffee beans. The company views coffee beans as an input into the production of coffee for export. In buying this input, Denok recognizes that is has a considerable influence on the price of coffee beans in Timor. The more coffee beans it buys, the higher the price that it must pay to buy them. How does this demand-side price making affect its input purchase decision? The answer is provided by a model known as *monopsony*.

THE FUNDAMENTAL ASSUMPTIONS

The monopsony model is built on four fundamental assumptions. On the supply side of the market, the monopsony model is like perfect competition in that

1. *Sellers are price takers.*

2. *Sellers do not behave strategically.* In our example of the Indonesian coffee market, any one coffee supplier perceives itself to be too small a part of the market to influence the price of coffee, either directly through its own output choice or indirectly through its influence on the actions of other suppliers.

Turning to entry, the monopsony model encompasses both free and blocked entry:

3. *The conditions of entry into industry supply may range from completely blocked to perfectly free.* The big difference between monopsony and our earlier models comes on the demand side of the market. Unlike both perfect competition and monopoly, under monopsony the buyers are price makers rather than price takers.

4. *Buyers are price makers.* Table 14.3 summarizes these fundamental assumptions of the monopsony model and compares them with those of perfect competition and monopoly.

THE APPROPRIATE MARKET STRUCTURE

Under what circumstances do these assumptions make sense? Let's consider our dimensions of market structure once again.

a. **The size and number of buyers.** When there are only a few buyers in a market, each one accounts for a substantial portion of the quantity purchased, and changes in one buyer's purchase level may lead to a noticeable change in the market price. The monopsony model is the extreme case in which there is only one buyer. This explains where the name *monopsony* comes from; as before, *mono* indicates that there is only one decision maker, while *sony* indicates that we are concerned with the buyer's side of the market. With only one buyer, the supply curve faced by that buyer is the market supply curve.

b. **The size and number of sellers in the industry.** Like the competitive model, both the supplier price-taking and nonstrategic behavior assumptions are most appropriate when there are many sellers, each of which is a small part of the industry.

c. **The degree of substitutability of different sellers' products.** Again like the competitive model, price taking by suppliers is most likely when the firms produce products that are close substitutes for one another.

d. **The extent to which buyers are informed about prices and available alternatives.** Price taking among sellers is more likely when the buyer is well informed about the available alternatives than when it is not.

Table 14.3

Fundamental Assumptions of the Monopsony Model

	Monopsony	Perfect Competition	Monopoly
1. Seller Influence on Price	Sellers are price takers.	Sellers are price takers.	Seller is a price maker.
2. Extent of Strategic Behavior	Sellers do not behave strategically.	Sellers do not behave strategically.	Seller does not behave strategically.
3. Conditions of Entry	Entry into the market may be blocked or free.	Entry into the market is free.	Entry into the market is completely blocked.
4. Buyer Influence on Price	Buyers are price makers.	Buyers are price takers.	Buyers are price takers.

Table 14.4

A Monopsonistic Market Structure

	Monopsony	Perfect Competition	Monopoly
a. The Size and Number of Buyers	One buyer.	Many buyers, no one of which is large relative to the overall market.	Many buyers, no one of which is large relative to the overall market.
b. The Size and Number of Sellers	Many sellers, no one of which is large relative to the overall market.	Many sellers, no one of which is large relative to the overall market.	One seller.
c. The Degree of Substitutability among Different Sellers' Products	The outputs of different sellers are homogeneous.	The outputs of different sellers are homogeneous.	There are no close substitutes.
d. The Extent to Which Buyers Are Informed about Prices and Available Alternatives	Buyer is well informed about the offerings of competing suppliers.	Buyers are well informed about the offerings of competing suppliers.	Buyers are well informed about the offerings of competing suppliers.
e. The Conditions of Entry	Technological and legal barriers to entry may or may not exist.	Neither technological nor legal barriers to entry exist.	Either technological or legal barriers completely block entry.

e. **The conditions of entry.** As long as there are enough sellers in the market that they behave as nonstrategic price takers, the monopsony model applies equally well to markets into which entry is free and to markets into which entry is completely blocked.

Table 14.4 summarizes the market conditions for which the monopsony model is appropriate and provides comparisons with perfect competition and monopoly.

THE MONOPSONISTIC EQUILIBRIUM

Because coffee beans are an input for the Denok coffee exporting company, its demand for beans is a derived demand and is determined by their marginal revenue product. When we studied the input choices of a price-taking buyer in Chapter 10, we derived a general factor hiring rule that applies to *any* profit-maximizing firm, including a monopsonist:

Factor Hiring Rule: A profit-maximizing firm should hire a factor up to the point at which its marginal revenue product is equal to its marginal factor cost ($MRP = MFC$).

From our earlier analysis of derived demand, we know that the marginal revenue product of a factor is equal to the factor's marginal physical product times the firm's marginal revenue of output. We know from Chapter 10 that if the monopsonist is a price taker *in its role as a producer of output*, then its marginal revenue of output is equal to the price of output that it takes as given. If the monopsonist is a price maker, then it simply finds its marginal revenue curve as we did when we examined monopoly in Chapter 13. There is nothing special or new about monopsony here. The difference between a monopsonist and an input price taker comes in terms of the marginal factor cost.

Marginal Factor Cost for a Monopsonist

The process for finding a monopsonist's marginal factor cost curve is much like the one we used to find a monopolist's marginal revenue curve. There, we started with an average revenue curve (that is, a demand curve), and we derived the corresponding marginal revenue curve. For a monopsonist, we start with an average factor cost curve, and we derive the corresponding marginal factor cost curve.

Columns (1) and (2) of Table 14.5 present hypothetical data on the market supply schedule for coffee beans. It is important to note two things about this schedule: (1) it is also the supply schedule faced by the firm (because the firm is the only demander of coffee beans); and (2) the supply schedule is also the firm's average factor cost schedule. Point (2) follows from the fact that the supply schedule tells us how much *per unit* the firm must pay to buy any given amount of the input.

Marginal factor cost is defined as the increase in the firm's total expenditures on inputs when it hires one more unit of a factor. Looking at the change in total factor cost as the firm increases its input use by one unit, we can calculate the firm's marginal factor cost, which is given in column (4) of Table 14.5. Notice that for all but the first unit of output, the price-making buyer's marginal factor cost exceeds its average factor cost. This phenomenon makes perfect sense, given the argument made in Chapter 9 about the general relationship between average and marginal curves. That the average factor cost curve (the supply curve) is rising implies that the marginal factor cost is pulling up the average. To do so, the marginal factor cost curve must be above the average factor cost curve. The curves are graphed in Figure 14.18.

Just as we did when looking at a monopolist's marginal revenue curve, we can gain further insight into a monopsonist's marginal factor cost by expressing it in terms of price elasticity. Recall from Chapter 11 that the price elasticity of supply, ϵ_S, is the percentage change in the quantity supplied divided by the percentage change in price that induced it. Following a procedure similar to the one used in Chapter 13 to express the monopolist's marginal revenue in terms of the price elasticity of demand for the output that the firm sells (Chapter 13, page 416), we can express the monopsonist's marginal factor cost in terms of the price elasticity of supply for the input that the firm buys:

$$MFC = p\{1 + 1/\epsilon_S\}. \qquad (14.3)$$

Table 14.5

A Monopsonist's Total and Marginal Factor Cost Functions

When the price rises as the quantity purchased rises, marginal factor cost must be greater than the price of the marginal unit. Comparing columns (2) and (4), we see that this relationship holds.

(1) Quantity (tons of coffee beans per year)	(2) Price ($000 per ton)	(3) Total Factor Cost ($000 per year)	(4) Marginal Factor Cost ($000 per ton per year)
0	*	0	
1	1.00	1.00	1.00
2	1.05	2.10	1.10
3	1.06	3.18	1.08
4	1.07	4.28	1.10
5	1.09	5.45	1.17
6	1.12	6.72	1.27
7	1.16	8.12	1.40

The smaller the price elasticity of supply, the larger are $1/\epsilon_S$ and $\{1 + 1/\epsilon_S\}$. Hence, Equation (14.3) tells us that the less elastic is supply, the larger the gap between marginal factor cost and the price of the factor. When supply is highly inelastic, it takes a large price increase to induce producers to supply a little bit more output, and the monopsonist counts this large price increase as a cost. On the other hand, when supply is relatively elastic, there is little rise in the price of the inframarginal units. In the extreme case of infinitely elastic supply, there is no loss on inframarginal units: The firm is a price taker, and marginal factor cost is equal to the price of the factor.

Equilibrium

Now that we know buyer's marginal factor cost curve, we are ready to find the equilibrium price and quantity levels. Figure 14.19 reproduces the upward-sloping supply schedule for coffee beans and the corresponding marginal factor cost curve. A downward-sloping marginal revenue product curve also is graphed. Applying the factor hiring rule, the coffee firm purchases beans up to the quantity at which the marginal factor cost is equal to the marginal revenue product, B_1 in Figure 14.19. What price does the firm pay for the input? The monopsonist wants to pay the lowest price at which suppliers are willing to provide B_1 units of the input. By the definition of the supply curve, the lowest price at which the firm can purchase B_1 units of the input is the height of the supply curve at this quantity. The equilibrium price is found by going up from B_1 on the horizontal axis until reaching the supply curve at the price p_1 in Figure 14.19. Notice that the monopsonist does *not* set price equal to the common value of marginal revenue product and marginal factor cost. This is a consequence of buyer price making. A buyer that perceived itself to be a price taker would have a marginal factor cost curve that coincided with the average factor cost, or supply, curve. Hence, a price-taking buyer's equilibrium would be at point *t*. We conclude

14.4 PROGRESS CHECK

Suppose that the Denok coffee company is a price taker in its role as a seller in the world coffee market. Show graphically what happens to the company's marginal revenue product curve when the world price of coffee rises by 10 percent. Show graphically what happens to the equilibrium price that the company pays for beans and the quantity that it purchases.

Figure 14.18

For a Price-Making Buyer, the Marginal Factor Cost Curve Lies above the Supply Curve

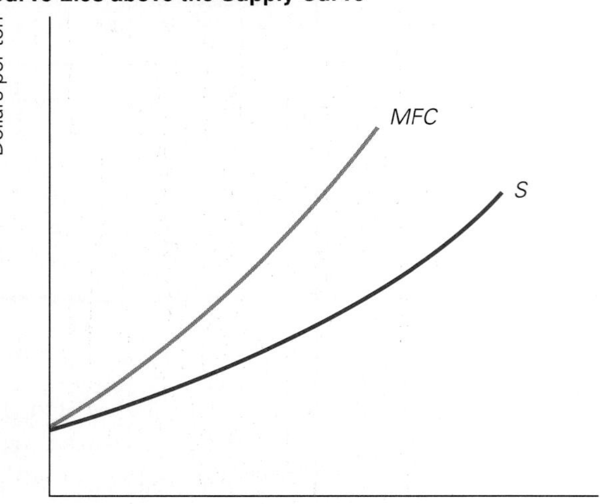

Because the factor supply curve facing a monopsonist slopes upward, the marginal factor cost curve lies above the supply curve.

Figure 14.19

The Monopsonistic Equilibrium

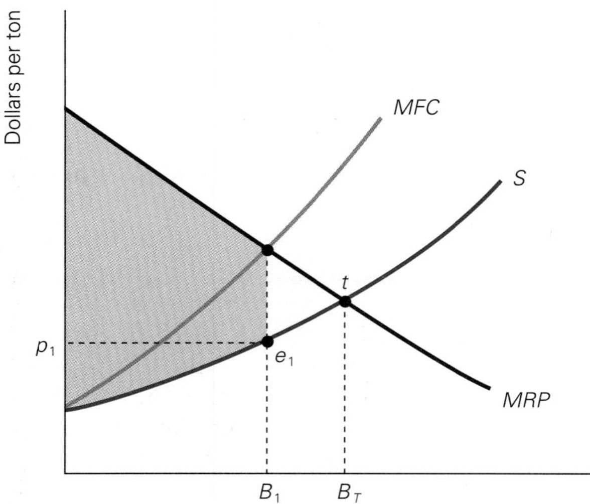

Applying the factor hiring rule, a profit-maximizing firm purchases beans up to the quantity at which the marginal factor cost is equal to the marginal revenue product, B_1. The equilibrium price is found by going up from B_1 on the horizontal axis until reaching the supply curve at price p_1.

that *a price-making buyer purchases less than would a price-taking buyer facing the same supply curve and having the same marginal revenue product curve.* (PC 14.4)

NORMATIVE ANALYSIS OF MONOPSONY

A monopsonist purchases less of an input than a price-taking buyer would. This fact has implications for both equity and efficiency.

Equity

Who gains and who loses when a market structure shifts from price taking to monopsony? We have just shown that the change from price taking to monopsony leads to a lower equilibrium factor price. This reduces the surplus of suppliers in the market. We also know that the buyer benefits from its ability to influence the price of the input. In our particular example, coffee farmers' real incomes are lowered by the monopsony while Denok's owners' incomes are increased. There is one other group that may be affected—consumers of the output produced by the monopsonist. The effect of Denok's monopsony on coffee drinkers depends on whether the firm has market power in its role *as a seller*. As a monopsonist, the firm produces less final output (coffee beans for export). If the firm is a price taker as a seller in the coffee bean export market, then the price of coffee to consumers is unaffected. If, however, the firm is a price maker as a coffee seller, then the price of coffee to consumers rises, and coffee consumers are worse off. Since East Timorese coffee is a high-quality coffee with particular flavor characteristics, the firm probably does not face a perfectly elastic demand curve for its exports. Hence, consumers probably do suffer from a price increase.

Efficiency

Turning to the examination of efficiency, it is useful to look from both the partial equilibrium and general equilibrium viewpoints.

Partial Equilibrium Analysis The partial equilibrium approach dictates that we examine the level of total surplus in the monopsonized input market. We find the level of total surplus by looking at the area under the social marginal benefit curve and above the social marginal cost curve up to the equilibrium quantity. When the monopsonist is a *price-taking seller* of output, its marginal revenue product curve is equal to the price paid for the output times the marginal physical product of the input. Since it reflects the price paid for the monopsonist's output, the marginal revenue product captures the marginal social benefit from the additional consumption. Similarly, if the input is supplied under competitive conditions, the height of the supply curve represents the input's social marginal cost. Therefore, under these conditions, total surplus is the shaded area under the marginal revenue product curve and above the supply curve in Figure 14.19.

The figure indicates that *from an efficiency perspective, the monopsonist purchases too little of the input.* The marginal revenue product curve lies above the supply curve for the quantities between B_1 and B_T, which tells us there are farmers who are willing to supply coffee beans at a price that is less than their marginal revenue product. To see the full extent of the surplus loss due to monopsony, we can compare the monopsonistic equilibrium with the outcome under which total surplus is maximized. A total-surplus-maximizing supplier would purchase coffee beans up to the quantity where the marginal social benefit (given by the height of the *MRP* curve) is equal to the marginal social cost (given the height of the supply curve)—B_T in Figure 14.19 and reproduced in Figure 14.20. When the input level is B_T total surplus is equal to the area under the marginal revenue product curve and above the supply curve from 0 up to B_T tons. Taking the difference between total surplus when the input level is B_T and when it is B_1, we see that total surplus is lower under monopsony by the sum of shaded areas *H* and *I* in Figure 14.20. This area represents the **deadweight loss of monopsony**.

deadweight loss of monopsony
The loss in total surplus that arises because a monopsonist purchases less than the total-surplus-maximizing amount of an input.

Why does the monopsonist purchase too little? We can answer this question by looking at what happens to the surplus enjoyed by the buyer and sellers when the quantity rises from the monopsonistic level to the total-surplus-maximizing one. To increase its purchase from B_1 to B_T, the coffee company would have to raise the price that it pays for coffee beans from p_1 to p_T. The producers' surplus in the coffee bean market would rise by the sum of shaded areas *I* and *J*. The buyer's surplus, Denok's profit, would rise by area *H minus* area *J*. Areas *H* and *I* represent the net social gain in going from B_1 to B_T (hence, they are equal to the deadweight loss of monopsony). Area *J*, on the other hand, represents neither a loss nor gain in total surplus. It is simply a transfer from the monopsonist to the input suppliers. Although it is not a loss in total surplus, area *J* is a private loss to the monopsonist from increasing its purchase level. Because it treats the increase in the amount paid for inframarginal units as a loss, while socially this amount is a pure transfer, Denok purchases too little of the input. Any other profit-maximizing monopsonist behaves in the same way.

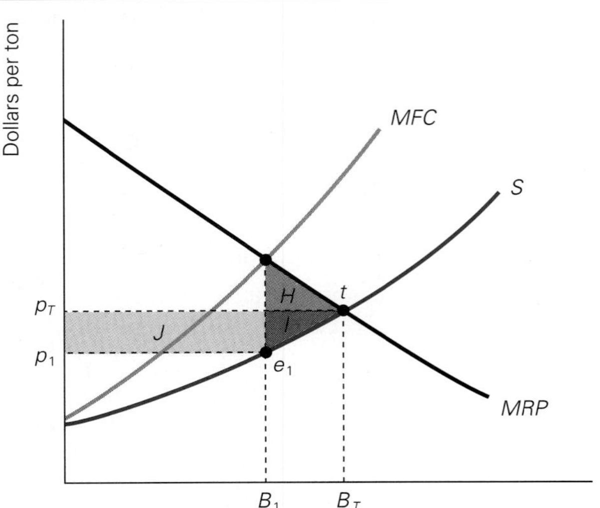

Figure 14.20

The Deadweight Loss of Monopsony

A total surplus maximizing buyer would purchase coffee beans up to the point where the marginal social benefit (given by the height of the marginal revenue product curve) is equal to the marginal social cost (given by the height of the supply curve). This input level is denoted by B_T. In comparison with the monopsonistic equilibrium, total surplus rises by the sum of areas *H* and *I*, the deadweight loss of monopsony.

General Equilibrium Analysis A general equilibrium approach to the normative analysis of monopsony requires that we examine its effects within the context of the entire market economy. We will consider the efficiency effects of monopsony under the assumption that all other markets in the economy are perfectly competitive.

We begin by considering production efficiency. Like any cost-minimizing firm, a monopsonist using two inputs, labor and beans, follows the rule

$$MRTS = MFC_L/MFC_B.^6 \qquad (14.4)$$

Suppose that the coffee company is a price taker in the labor market. Then MFC_L is equal to the prevailing wage rate. Since the firm is a price maker in the coffee bean market, MFC_B exceeds the price of coffee beans. Hence, unlike other firms, the monopsonist does not set the marginal rate of technical substitution equal to the ratio of the price of labor to the price of coffee beans. Thus, the firm's equilibrium fails to meet our condition for the socially efficient use of inputs (Equation (12.2)). We conclude that, *given the level of output that it chooses, a profit-maximizing monopsonist chooses a socially inefficient means of production.*

We next examine the effects of monopsony on allocation efficiency in the monopsonist's output market. In Chapter 12, we saw that a necessary condition for economic efficiency is that the ratio of the prices of any two goods be equal to the ratio of their social marginal costs. If all of the other goods in the economy are being sold at prices equal to their social marginal costs, then the monopsonist violates this condition even if it sets its output price equal to its marginal cost. Why? Because its private marginal cost (given by the marginal factor cost curve) is not equal to social marginal cost (given by the height of the factor supply curve).

[6]For a discussion of cost minimization, see Chapter 9.

BUYER CARTELS: AMATEUR AND PROFESSIONAL ATHLETICS

Just as sellers may collude to exercise collective monopoly power, buyers may collude to exercise collective monopsony power. Some of the best-known buyer cartels are the professional sports leagues. Prior to 1976, the *reserve clause* forced each professional baseball player to deal with a single team. In effect, each team hired players from a set pool of people who were tied to that team. Thus, a team had monopsony power. The drafts in the professional baseball, basketball, and football leagues all have similar effects. Under a draft system, a player entering the league (say, a player coming out of college) can either sign with the team that has drafted him or forget about playing in that league.

Numerous studies of professional sports have found that these buyers' cartels have significant effects. For instance, Scully (1974) found that baseball players were paid salaries far below their marginal revenue products. Sommers and Quinton (1982) looked at how baseball salaries changed after the reserve clause was weakened and certain players were allowed to go to whichever team they chose. Sommers and Quinton found that competition for these so-called *free agents* drove their salaries up to approximately their marginal revenue products. Indeed, as the result of the continued relaxation of earlier restrictions on free agency, the salaries of professional basketball players exploded in 1996. Several players received multiyear contracts valued at over $100 million, whereas only a few years earlier contracts in the range of $60 million were rare. (PC 14.5)

While professional sports teams have managed to exercise significant monopsony power, perhaps the most effective buyer cartel has been the one run by universities. Universities generally pay players on their basketball and football teams only a tiny fraction of the revenues that these players generate for their schools. The National Collegiate Athletic Association conducts investigations to make sure that no school cheats on this cartel agreement by paying high wages to players. (Such wages might take the form of direct cash payments or in-kind transfers such as sports cars and apartments.) For football, the university cartel also gets help from the National Football League (NFL). For years, the NFL refused to hire players who had remaining college eligibility and whose classes had not yet graduated. Finally, in 1990, under the threat of lawsuits brought by athletes hoping to enter the NFL before their classes graduated, the NFL agreed to take underclassmen, but only under restrictive conditions. The NFL and universities continued to do what they could to ensure that college athletes were paid far below their marginal revenue products.

14.5 PROGRESS CHECK

From time to time, a new professional sports league (usually with the word *World* in its name) is created to rival an existing league. What effect do you think that the creation of a new league has on the salaries of players in the sport for which the new league is formed?

SECTION RECAP

A monopsony is a market in which there is price making on the buyer side. Like any profit-maximizing firm, a monopsonist purchases an input up to the point where marginal revenue product is equal to marginal factor cost. Unlike a price-taking buyer, a monopsonist's marginal factor cost curve and factor supply curve do not coincide. For a monopsonist facing an upward sloping supply curve, marginal factor cost is greater than the factor price. Since the firm sets marginal revenue product equal to marginal factor cost, it follows that, in equilibrium, marginal revenue product is greater than the price of the factor. A profit-maximizing monopsonist purchases an inefficiently low quantity of the input; total surplus would rise if the monopsonist purchased more.

SUMMARY

In this chapter, we studied several extensions of the theory of price-making firms presented in Chapter 13. We examined the output choices of firms in markets with multiple price-making sellers, and we considered the behavior of price-making input buyers.

- Suppliers will raise their profits if they can successfully band together as a cartel to restrict the quantity supplied and raise price above its competitive level.
- In the absence of some enforcement mechanism, a cartel's success is limited by the fact that prices above marginal cost tempt individual members to cheat on the cartel agreement.
- A cartel's success also may be limited by the fact that economic profits can attract new firms into the market, both reducing the share of industry profits enjoyed by incumbent suppliers and dissipating overall industry profits by driving down the market price or by raising the average costs of production.
- Many markets have a large number of sellers and free entry, but each firm is still a price maker because it offers a differentiated product. Such an industry structure is called monopolistic competition.
- Like a monopolist, each monopolistic competitor operates at a point where price is greater than marginal cost. Due to free entry, however, a monopolistic competitor earns zero economic profit in the long-run market equilibrium.
- The monopolistically competitive equilibrium may entail too much or too little variety, depending on the relative strengths of the consumer-surplus wedge and the rivals' profit wedge between the private and social incentives.
- A monopsony is a market with a single buyer. A monopsonist recognizes that the amount it buys influences the price that it pays for its inputs. The firm is a price maker in its role as a buyer.
- A monopsonist follows the usual factor hiring rule: Hire an input up to the point at which its marginal revenue product is equal to its marginal factor cost. For a monopsonist, the marginal factor cost of an input exceeds its price. Hence, under monopsony, the marginal revenue product of an output is greater than its price.
- A monopsonist purchases an inefficiently low quantity of the input for which it is a price maker.

DISCUSSION QUESTIONS

14.1 Cartel members often differ in terms of their production costs, product qualities, or reputations with consumers. How would such differences affect the full cartel outcome? Do you think these differences make it easier or harder for suppliers to reach and sustain a cartel agreement?

14.2 Suppose that a union successfully raises the wage in an industry above the competitive level. How does this wage increase affect workers, the firms that employ them, and the consumers who buy the products made by these firms? Does total surplus rise or fall as a result of the wage increase?

14.3 Indonesia is the world's largest exporter of plywood made from hardwood. Mohomad Hussan "is the chairman of Apkindt, Indonesia's association of plywood makers. This position enables him to tell the country's 130-odd producers how much they will sell, to whom, and at what price. Asked how he manages to enforce this discipline, Mr. Hussan replies simply, 'I sign the approval for revoking a company's export license.'" (*The Economist*, April 18, 1992, 62).

In answering this question, assume for simplicity that Indonesia is essentially the only supplier of plywood made from hardwood.

a. How would you characterize the market structure in this market?

b. Explain carefully why Hussan needs to be able to threaten the various plywood producers with revocation of their export licenses.

c. Suppose that Apkindt dissolved so that each producer was able to set its own price and quantity. What would happen to: (i) the price of plywood, (ii) the quantity sold, (iii) industry profits, and (iv) total surplus?

14.4 You have been asked by the Airline Pilots' Association to advise them on the consequences for their members of a proposed wage increase. The union gets to set the wage, but the airlines get to choose how many workers to hire. The union is concerned that holding out for a higher wage will lower the number of their members who are employed. What effects do you think that the wage increase will have on employment? On the total income that the workers receive? (*Hint:* Think about what conditions affect derived demand in general.)

14.5 Is the following claim true or false? Explain your answer:

> If consumers all have different tastes for a certain good, then the efficient outcome is to produce a different variety of that good for each consumer.

14.6 The women's fashion industry has the following characteristics: Individual products are highly differentiated by style to suit a wide variety of tastes; entry is easy (get a sewing machine), with many firms coming into and exiting the industry; and there are many firms, which behave independently of one another.

a. What type of industry is this: perfectly competitive, monopolistic, or monopolistically competitive? Explain your answer.

b. Illustrate the short-run equilibrium position for a representative firm that is earning short-run economic profit but suffering long-run economic losses.

c. What will happen to the number of firms in the industry in the long run? Illustrate the long-run equilibrium position of a representative firm.

14.7 Suppose that a city passes a new ordinance placing a licensing fee of $1,000 a month on pizza parlors. Describe the effects that you would expect this tax to have on pizza consumers and suppliers. Be sure to consider both the short-run and long-run effects.

14.8 Some people in large cities complain that there are too many coffee shops in their communities. Use the model of monopolistic competition to explain why, theoretically, there may be either more or fewer than the total-surplus-maximizing number of coffee houses.

14.9 Boeing hires thousands of aerospace engineers in the Seattle area. When it develops a new airplane, the increase in the number of engineers hired by Boeing tightens the labor market and drives up engineers' wages. Suppose that Boeing is contemplating ramping up employment to launch a new airframe.

a. Assume that all engineers are paid the same amount. Draw a diagram to illustrate the change in expenditures on inframarginal workers when Boeing hires additional engineers. Use this diagram to explain why the resulting marginal factor cost curve lies above the supply curve.

b. How would your answer to part *a* change if Boeing can hire new engineers at a higher wage without having to give raises to those engineers already working for the company?

14.10 Consider an oil refinery located in a remote town in Arizona. Suppose that the refinery has a downward-sloping marginal revenue product curve and faces an upward-sloping labor supply schedule.

a. Assuming that the refinery must pay all of its workers the same wage, show graphically how many workers the firm will hire. Explain your solution and compare it with the competitive outcome.

Suppose that a union is organized by the refinery workers. The union announces that its members will provide as many hours of labor as the firm wants to hire at a wage of w_0 dollars per hour. If the firm pays less than w_0 dollars per hour, no union member will work in the refinery. There are no nonunion members who have the skill to work in the refinery.

b. Show that the employment level when the union sets the wage may be higher than the employment level in part *a* even if w_0 is higher than the equilibrium wage that you calculated in part *a*.

14.11 Consider a monopsonist that can engage in first-degree price discrimination. That is, the firm can pay for each unit of the input just what the supplier of that unit requires to produce it. What is the relationship between the marginal factor cost curve and the factor supply curve? How much of the input will the monopsonist purchase? Will total surplus rise or fall in comparison with a monopsonist that cannot discriminate?

CHAPTER 15

Oligopoly and Strategic Behavior

> ***Putnam:***
> *Do you have a suggestion for me?*
>
> ***Crandall:***
> *Yes, I have a suggestion for you. Raise your [expletive deleted] fares 20 percent. I'll raise mine the next morning.*
>
> ***Putnam:***
> *Robert, we . . .*
>
> ***Crandall:***
> *You'll make more money, and I will too.*
>
> ***Putnam:***
> *We can't talk about pricing.*
>
> ***Crandall:***
> *Oh [expletive deleted], Howard. We can talk about any [expletive deleted] thing we want to talk about.*

The telephone conversation detailed on the left took place between Robert Crandall, the Chief Executive Officer of American Airlines, and Howard Putnam, then chairman of the now-bankrupt Braniff Airlines. Airline presidents typically do not talk to each other about their pricing (it generally is illegal to do so), but they do spend a lot of time thinking about each other's pricing.

An airline is interested in its rivals' prices because they affect its own demand and profits. Moreover, an airline is interested in how its rivals will react to changes in its prices. These responses are of interest because they affect the profitability of the airline's own pricing decisions. Indeed, the failure to predict these responses correctly can be costly. On May 26, 1992, Northwest Airlines introduced a fare that allowed a child to fly free with an adult. The airline's executives had hoped to stimulate vacation travel on Northwest. But the next day, American Airlines responded by offering half-price fares for everyone, and other airlines quickly followed suit (McDowell 1992, 1). The ensuing fare war led to millions of dollars in losses for the airlines.

Firms take each others' actions into account when they collectively realize that the actions of any one firm affect the firm-specific demand curves faced by all members of the industry. When Northwest lowered the price of its flights, the demand for American flights (a substitute) shifted inward. Similarly, a change in

American Airlines' fares shifted the demand for Northwest flights. Both Northwest and American knew about these effects. When firms are aware that the price or output choices made by any one of them affects the profits of all, they are said to recognize their **mutual interdependence**.

mutual interdependence The price or output choices made by any one firm affects the profits of all.

The recognition of mutual interdependence has two important consequences. First, each firm is concerned with what its rivals are up to. Consequently, each firm must either observe or predict what actions the other producers are taking. Second, each firm knows that the other producers are watching it and will respond to its actions. Thus, the firm must take its rivals' reactions into account when deciding what to do. Randall Malin, then executive vice president for marketing at USAir, put it succinctly: "If I know that if I cut my fare $20 today, you're going to cut yours $20 tomorrow, then it's stupid for me to do it" (Eichel 1989, D4). Recall that whenever a firm takes the potential reactions of other firms into account in choosing its best course of action, that firm is said to behave *strategically*.

Airlines recognize their mutual interdependence. So do many other real-world firms. Throughout the 1980s, whenever one of the "big three" U.S. automobile manufacturers (General Motors, Ford, and Chrysler) announced a rebate program that lowered the price of a car (often by $1,000), the other two firms quickly followed suit. Throughout the early 1990s, the personal computer industry went through a series of dramatic price cuts, where one firm would lower its prices by as much as 30 percent only to see its rivals do the same in response.

In the models we have examined so far, the suppliers do not recognize their mutual interdependence. Although in many ways polar opposites, perfect competition and monopoly are similar in that both models assume that there is no strategic interaction among firms. Under monopoly there are no other firms to worry about. Under perfect competition, each firm believes that it is too small a part of the market for its actions to have noticeable effects on other producers—when deciding how many acres of wheat to plant, farmer Jones does not have to worry about how much the neighbors are planting, because none of their actions has any discernable impact on the price of wheat. Similarly, each firm in a monopolistically competitive market takes the behavior of other producers to be independent of its behavior. We therefore need to develop a new type of model in order to understand markets in which the recognition of mutual interdependence is important.

The goal of this chapter is to develop a set of models that help us understand strategic behavior. As usual, we will begin by laying out the fundamental assumptions underlying these models. The next task is to identify the sort of market structure for which these assumptions are appropriate. We then analyze behavior in these markets. As we will see, there is no single model of how strategic sellers behave. Rather, we will develop several different models that are variations on a common theme. Each model attempts to show how rational, profit-maximizing firms respond to the recognition of their mutual interdependence.

THE FUNDAMENTAL ASSUMPTIONS

Suppliers' recognition of their mutual interdependence is the key feature that distinguishes our new model from those considered earlier. However, we must also define it in terms of our full set of standard assumptions about supplier and demander behavior.

The first three assumptions concern decision makers on the supply side of the market. The essence of strategic behavior is that suppliers recognize that they affect one another. This makes sense only if each firm's choice affects the price at which it and other firms can sell output:

1. *Sellers are price makers.* Not only does each firm recognize that it is a price maker, but each firm recognizes that its actions have a noticeable effect on the prices that other firms can receive for their output. Hence, each firm recognizes that it has an effect on the actions of these other firms:

2. *Sellers behave strategically.* With respect to the conditions of entry, the model is broad enough to encompass both completely blocked and perfectly free entry:

3. *The conditions of entry may range from completely blocked to perfectly free.* This chapter focuses on markets into which further entry is blocked completely.[1]

The remaining assumption of the model deals with the demand side of the market:

4. *Buyers are price takers.* As in competitive, monopolistic, and monopolistically competitive markets, each buyer believes that it has no influence on the market price.

Table 15.1 summarizes these fundamental assumptions of our new model and compares them with the assumptions of perfect competition and monopoly.

THE APPROPRIATE MARKET STRUCTURE

We next identify the set of circumstances (market structures) under which the four basic assumptions are sensible. In particular, we are interested in conditions under which the recognition of mutual interdependence and the resulting strategic interactions are likely to be important.

a. **The size and number of buyers.** Since we assume that demanders are price takers, we are interested in markets with many buyers, no one of whom is large enough to exert any influence on the price. In this respect, our new market structure is no different than competition or monopoly.

b. **The size and number of sellers.** The number of firms in the industry affects both the degree of strategic behavior and the extent of price-taking versus price-making behavior by suppliers. When there are many firms, an action taken by any one of them has little impact on the others, and producers are unlikely to react to one another's actions. In contrast, when there are relatively few (but more than one) firms in an industry, each firm is a significant part of the market and the firms are likely to recognize their mutual interdependence. This small numbers case is known as *oligopoly.* Just as monopoly refers to a market with one ("mono") producer, oligopoly refers to a market with a few ("olig") producers. Oligopoly is an extremely important market structure. In many major markets, a relatively small number of firms account for a large percentage of the industry

[1] Chapter 16 examines markets into which entry is possible.

Table 15.1

Fundamental Assumptions of the Oligopoly Model

	Oligopoly	Perfect Competition	Monopoly
1. Seller Influence on Price	Sellers are price makers.	Sellers are price takers.	Seller is a price maker.
2. Extent of Strategic Behavior	Sellers behave strategically.	Sellers do not behave strategically.	Seller does not behave strategically.
3. Conditions of Entry	Entry into the market may be blocked or free.	Entry into the market is free.	Entry into the market is completely blocked.
4. Buyer Influence on Price	Buyers are price takers.	Buyers are price takers.	Buyers are price takers.

Table 15.2

Some Oligopolistic Industries

Industry	Leading Producers[1]	Combined Market Share
Cold cereals sold in the United States	Kellogg's, General Mills, Post	75 percent[2]
Commercial airliners worldwide	Boeing, Airbus, McDonnell Douglas	94 percent[3]
Heavy trucks sold in the United States	Freightliner, Paccar, Navistar, Volvo GM, Mack Trucks	90 percent[4]
Pasta sold in the United States	Borden, Hershey, CPC International	60 percent[5]
PC servers worldwide	Compaq, IBM, Hewlett-Packard	60 percent[6]
Sports drinks sold in the United States	Quaker, PepsiCo, Coca-Cola	96 percent[2]

[1]Listed in order of market share.
[2]Source: Quaker Oats Company as reported by *The New York Times*, Aug. 7, 1996, C1, C4.
[3]Source: Boeing as reported by *The Wall Street Journal*, Jan. 5, 1996, B4.
[4]Source: American Trucking Association and industry sources as reported by *The Wall Street Journal*, Jan. 18, 1996, B4.
[5]Source: Information Resources Inc. as reported by *The Wall Street Journal*, Nov. 16, 1993, B16.
[6]Source: International Data Corp. as reported by *The Wall Street Journal*, May 29, 1996, B4.

output. Until 1996, for example, only two cellular telephone companies offered service in any particular city. A similarly small number of cellular providers operate in most other countries today. Table 15.2 presents a sample of other markets where a few firms supply most of the industry output.

c. **The degree of substitutability of different sellers' products.** Oligopoly allows for products that range from perfect substitutes to products that are highly differentiated. The only requirement is that products be close enough substitutes that producers recognize their influence on one another.

d. **The extent to which buyers are informed about prices and available alternatives.** Since individual suppliers face downward-sloping demand curves, oligopoly is a broad enough model to encompass both well-informed and poorly informed consumers.

e. **The conditions of entry.** Oligopoly allows for conditions of entry ranging from completely blocked to perfectly free.

Table 15.3 summarizes the characteristics of an oligopolistic market structure and compares them with the characteristics of perfectly competitive and monopolistic market structures.

Table 15.3
An Oligopolistic Market Structure

	Oligopoly	Perfect Competition	Monopoly
a. The Size and Number of Buyers	Many buyers, no one of which is large relative to the overall market.	Many buyers, no one of which is large relative to the overall market.	Many buyers, no one of which is large relative to the overall market.
b. The Size and Number of Sellers	Few sellers, each of which is large relative to the overall market.	Many sellers, no one of which is large relative to the overall market.	One seller.
c. The Degree of Substitutability among Different Sellers' Products	The outputs of different sellers may or may not be differentiated.	The outputs of different sellers are homogeneous.	There are no close substitutes.
d. The Extent to Which Buyers Are Informed about Prices and Available Alternatives	Buyers may or may not be well informed about the offerings of competing suppliers.	Buyers are well informed about the offerings of competing suppliers.	Buyers are well informed about the offerings of the sole supplier.
e. The Conditions of Entry	Technological and legal barriers to entry may or may not exist.	Neither technological nor legal barriers to entry exist.	Either technological or legal barriers completely block entry.

15.1 QUANTITY-SETTING OLIGOPOLISTS

Oligopoly models come in several different forms, some of which are quite complicated. We will begin by considering a relatively simple model, based on the following additional assumptions:

duopoly
A market in which there are only two suppliers.

1. *There are two firms in the industry.* A market with just two firms is called a **duopoly** ("duo" for two).
2. *Further entry into the market is completely blocked.* Therefore, we have to consider the behavior of only the two firms that already are in the market.
3. *The firms produce homogeneous products.* While oligopoly encompasses both homogeneous and differentiated product industries, markets with homogeneous products are easier to analyze.
4. *The firms have identical, constant marginal costs equal to* c. This assumption implies that, if a firm's output level is x, then its total cost is $c \times x$.

Although these assumptions are restrictive (for instance, few firms have marginal costs that are the same for all levels of output), this model brings out many important features of oligopolistic behavior that are present more generally. For concreteness, we will use the model to analyze the behavior of two airlines, Air Lion and Beta Airlines, which serve the route between two cities. Suppose that the two airports are so congested that no additional gate space or landing slots are available. Hence, entry by new carriers onto this route is impossible. Finally, assume that the two airlines offer equally bad food and have the same flight schedules, so that consumers view them as offering identical services.[2] Our goal is to determine each firm's output level and the associated price of a ticket.

[2]USAir and Delta Airlines face a similar set of conditions in their competition to provide shuttle service between New York's La Guardia Airport and Washington, D.C.'s National Airport.

MARKET EQUILIBRIUM

Our two firms are in a funny position when they choose their output levels. They are competitors in the everyday sense of the word. Each firm cares only about its own profit, and if it can raise that profit by increasing its output at the expense of its rival, it will do so. Yet the relationship between the two airlines is not completely antagonistic. As we know from the theory of cartels in Chapter 14, if Air Lion and Beta Airlines can cooperate to hold down the total number of tickets sold, they may be able to increase the profits of both firms.

Chapter 14 also taught us that two important factors influence the likelihood of successful cartelization. First, the easier is entry, the harder it is to form a cartel. For now, we are assuming that entry is completely blocked, so it is not an obstacle to joint profit maximization. The second factor is the sort of agreements or contracts that are available to the firms. If entry by new firms is blocked and the incumbent firms can sign a binding agreement that the government will enforce, it is possible to achieve the cartel outcome.

In most industries in the United States, collusive agreements among producers are illegal. For example, a few years ago the milk firm, Pet, Inc., was fined $3.5 million after it was found guilty of conspiring with other companies to submit artificially high bids to supply milk to various school districts.[3] Where collusion is illegal, firms are not about to go into court seeking to have their agreement enforced. Moreover, when the cartel members are different countries (e.g., the oil-producing nations of the OPEC cartel), there is generally no effective judicial enforcement mechanism. How would Saudi Arabia take Iran to court for producing too much oil?

When producers cannot rely on the courts or some other third party to enforce their collusive agreement, the producers must instead rely on agreements that enforce themselves. A **self-enforcing agreement** is one in which each firm finds that abiding by the agreement is in its self-interest, given that the other firms also do so. In other words, *not cheating* is each firm's profit-maximizing course of action. Since no firm has an incentive to cheat on a self-enforcing agreement, an external enforcement mechanism is not needed. On the other hand, if an agreement is not self-enforcing, it cannot be effective without a third party to enforce it because, by definition, some firm will have incentives to violate the agreement and there is no one to stop it.

self-enforcing agreement
An agreement among firms is self-enforcing when it is in each firm's self-interest to abide by the agreement, given that the other firms also are abiding by it.

Before examining the effects of having to rely on self-enforcing agreements, we should note another consequence of the illegality of collusive agreements. Firms in an industry typically do not reach an explicit agreement regarding their prices or quantities. Rather, the firms reach a **tacit agreement**, whereby each firm deduces what the implicit agreement among them is without actually discussing it with the other firms. Thus, when we speak of an *agreement* among firms, you should not think of it as a piece of paper that literally spells out what each firm will do. The agreement is more of a common understanding about how suppliers will behave.

tacit agreement
A situation in which firms come to a common understanding about how they should behave in a market without actually discussing it among themselves.

[3]You might be wondering about the conversation in the introduction between Robert Crandall and Howard Putnam. Had they been discovered by a third party, the two might well have been prosecuted for attempted price fixing. But Putnam turned Crandall in to antitrust authorities, who concluded that they could not prosecute Crandall—since Putnam had turned him in, there was no collusion!

Equilibrium Defined

Our earlier notions of equilibrium all characterize a situation in which no economic decision maker wants to change his or her action given the market outcome, and hence there is a tendency for the market to stay put at that outcome. The notion of a self-enforcing agreement is in the same spirit.

The notions of equilibrium and self-enforcing agreements rely heavily on the idea that a firm acts in its own self-interest. Given the interdependence of firms, however, it is not immediately clear what is, in fact, in a firm's self-interest. To see why, consider what price the firms receive for their output. This price depends on the amount of output that they sell. Figure 15.1 graphs the market demand curve for seats on the airline route, $D(p)$. This notation allows us to represent explicitly and compactly how the quantity demanded depends on the price. For example, $D(200)$ is the quantity demanded when the price is $200 per seat. Of course, this relationship has been implicit in every demand curve that appeared in earlier chapters. In this chapter, it will be useful to employ notation that is more explicit.

As always, we also can use the demand curve to see how the price depends on the total quantity sold in the market. Note that the horizontal axis in Figure 15.1 is the total number of passengers flown, the *market* quantity. The market quantity is in turn equal to the sum of the firm-specific output levels chosen by the two airlines. If Air Lion sells 450 seats per day and Beta sells 200, the market quantity is 650 seats per day. Figure 15.1 indicates that $150 is the highest price at which Air Lion can sell 450 tickets and Beta can sell 200 tickets simultaneously.

That the price received by either firm depends on the quantities produced by both of them brings out the firms' mutual interdependence. Suppose that Beta increases the number of tickets sold from 200 to 400. If Air Lion holds its output constant at 450, the market quantity rises to 850 seats per day and the ticket price falls to $115 in Figure 15.1. As a result of this price decline, Air Lion's profit falls—it receives less money for its output. Similarly, an increase in Air Lion's output lowers Beta's profit, *ceteris paribus.* Thus, each firm's profit depends not only on its own output level, but also on its rival's output level. The firms are mutually dependent on one another.

Because the firms' profits and the market price of a flight between the two cities depend on the output of both firms, Air Lion's profit-maximizing output choice is different when Beta Airlines sells 200 tickets per day than when Beta sells 400. Air Lion must make its choice of action based on what it *believes* Beta is doing. When a firm (or any economic actor) chooses the best course of action, *given what the other firms are doing*, we say that the firm chooses a **best response**. This term is somewhat misleading, because Air Lion does not literally respond to Beta's choice—the two firms choose their output levels simultaneously. This quantity is better thought of as Air Lion's best output choice, given that it believes that Beta is going to sell a certain number of seats. A firm that chooses a best response is acting in its self-interest, given its beliefs about its rivals.

best response
A decision maker's best course of action, given what the other decision makers are doing.

Nash equilibrium
A market is at a Nash equilibrium when each firm is choosing the strategy that maximizes its profit, given the strategies of the other firms in the market.

Having defined what is in an oligopolist's self-interest, we can now apply our general notion of equilibrium to the specific case of oligopoly: A market is in equilibrium when every firm pursues a strategy that is a best response to the strategies of the other firms in the market. In other words, a market is in equilibrium when no firm wants to change its behavior unilaterally. This type of equilibrium is called a **Nash equilibrium** after the Nobel Prize-winning mathematician and

Figure 15.1

The Market Demand for Seats

When Air Lion sells 450 seats per day and Beta Airlines sells 200, the market quantity is 650 and the price is $150 per seat. If Beta increased its output from 200 to 400 tickets per day while Air Lion held its output constant at 450, the market quantity would rise to 850 seats per day and the price would fall to $115 per seat.

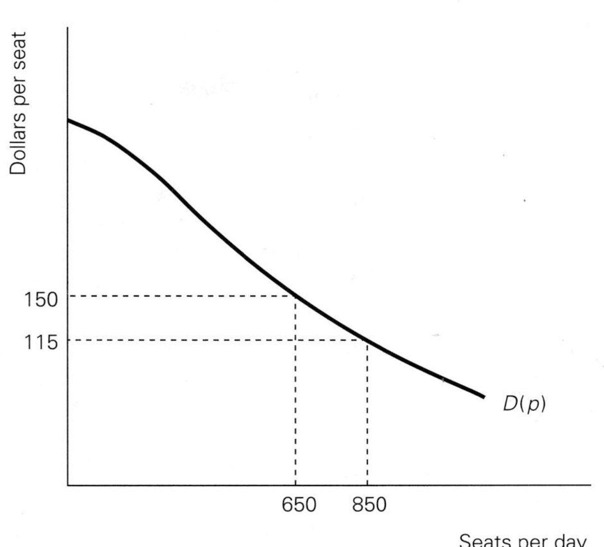

economist, John Nash. In the example, a firm's strategy consists of its choice of output level: y for Air Lion, and z for Beta. A Nash equilibrium in quantities consists of two output levels, y_1 and z_1, such that:

1. Given that Beta Airlines sells z_1 tickets, Air Lion's profit is maximized by selling y_1 tickets.

and

2. Given that Air Lion sells y_1 tickets, Beta Airlines' profit is maximized by selling z_1 tickets.

Because this type of market was first studied by Augustin Cournot in 1838, a Nash equilibrium in a market in which each firm chooses a single level of output is also known as a **Cournot equilibrium**, or **Cournot-Nash equilibrium**.

Cournot equilibrium
A Nash equilibrium in a market in which each firm's strategy consists of its choice of output level.

The notion of Nash equilibrium captures the idea that an agreement must be self-enforcing to be viable. If the firms agree that each will produce its Nash equilibrium output level, then it will be in each firm's self-interest to abide by the agreement, *given that it believes the other firm is doing so as well.* Conversely, if the firms try to agree on a set of output levels that do not constitute a Nash equilibrium, at least one of the firms can raise its profit by cheating on the agreement. Such an agreement is thus not self-enforcing; therefore, it is unlikely to be successfully implemented.

FINDING A COURNOT EQUILIBRIUM

With the notion of Nash equilibrium in hand, let's find what agreement is reached by Air Lion and Beta Airlines.

Figure 15.2

The Market Demand Curve and Air Lion's Residual Demand Curve

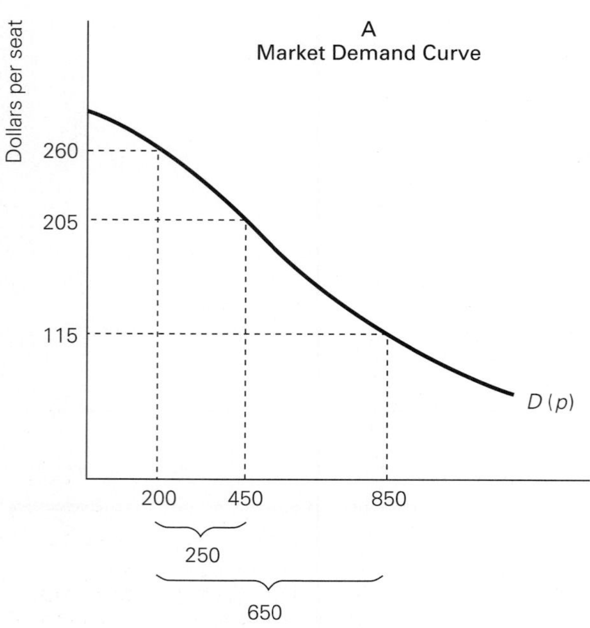

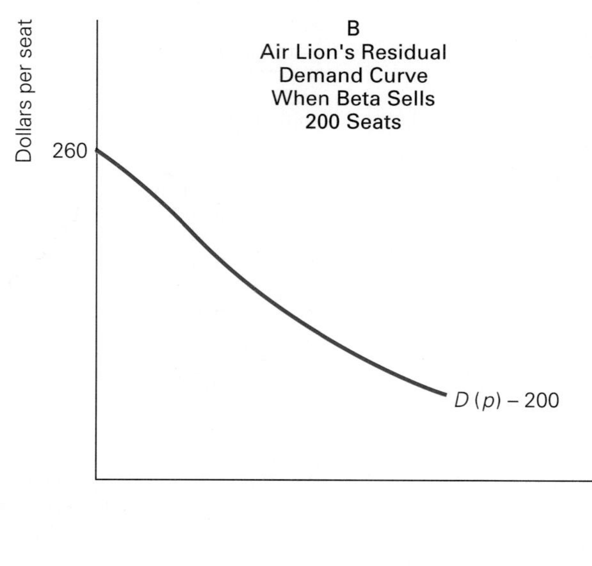

When Beta sells 200 tickets per day, $650 = D(115) - 200$ is the largest number of tickets that Air Lion can sell at a price of \$115. Similarly, $250 = D(205) - 200$ is the largest number of tickets that Air Lion can sell at a price of \$205. Panel B illustrates Air Lion's residual demand curve, given that Beta is selling 200 seats per day.

Deriving the Best-Response Functions

Like any profit-maximizing firm, a Cournot duopolist produces at the output level at which marginal revenue is equal to marginal cost. In order to apply the marginal output rule to an oligopolist, we need to know what an oligopolist's marginal revenue curve looks like. We start by finding the supplier's *firm-specific* demand curve. The *market* demand curve for flights between the two cities, $D(p)$, is drawn in Panel A of Figure 15.2. Suppose that the price is \$115 and Beta sells 200 seats per day. Then $650 = D(115) - 200$ is the greatest number of tickets that Air Lion can sell without driving the price of a ticket lower than \$115. Similarly, if Beta sells 200 seats per day, then 250 seats per day is the most output that Air Lion can sell without driving the price lower than \$205. We have now found two points on Air Lion's firm-specific demand curve, *given that Beta's output is 200 seats per day*: Air Lion can sell 250 seats at a price of \$205, and it can sell 650 seats at a price of \$115.

residual demand curve The firm-specific demand curve faced by a supplier, given the price or output strategies chosen by its rivals.

To find each of these points, we have taken the market quantity at a particular price and subtracted the 200 seats per day sold by Beta. We could follow this procedure to find the quantity of Air Lion's output demanded at any other price. The resulting firm-specific demand schedule is $D(p) - 200$, graphed in Panel B of Figure 15.2. Because this curve shows how much of the market demand is "left over" for Air Lion after Beta sells its output, this curve is known as Air Lion's **residual demand curve**.

Figure 15.3

An Increase in Beta's Output Shifts Air Lion's Residual Demand Curve Inward

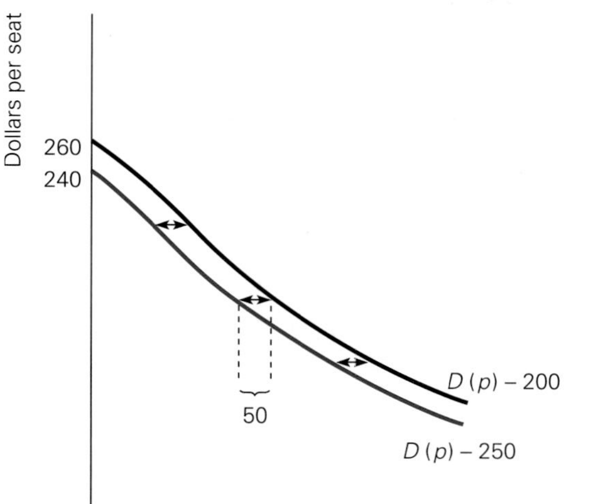

If Beta sells 250 seats per day rather than 200, Air Lion's residual demand curve shifts from $D(p) - 200$ to $D(p) - 250$.

Figure 15.4

Using Air Lion's Residual Demand Curve to Find Its Total Revenue

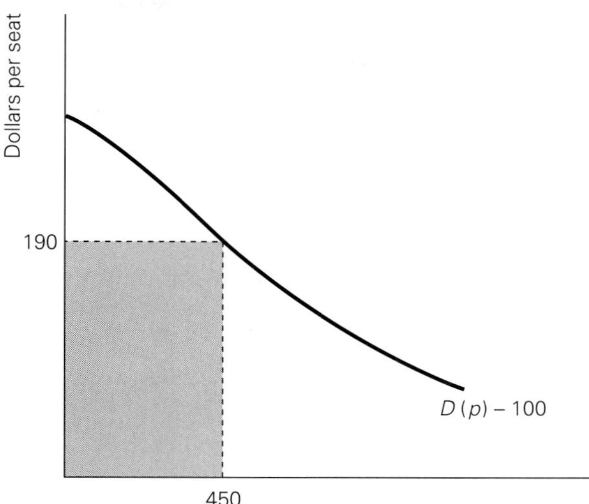

Air Lion's residual demand curve when Beta is selling 100 tickets is $D(p) - 100$. If Air Lion sells 450 tickets it can charge a price of $190 per ticket and earn total revenue of $190 × 450, the shaded area.

15.1 PROGRESS CHECK

Suppose that Beta sells 100 tickets per day. Sketch Air Lion's residual demand curve in Figure 15.3.

It is important to recognize that Air Lion has a different residual demand curve for each value of Beta's output level. If Beta sells more seats, say 250 per day, then Air Lion's residual demand curve shifts inward to $D(p) - 250$, as shown in Figure 15.3. Intuitively, this makes sense—the more that Beta produces, the smaller the residual left for Air Lion to sell at any given market price. (PC 15.1)

Air Lion's residual demand curve shows the price per ticket that Air Lion can charge at any output level, given that Beta is selling some set number of tickets. Figure 15.4 shows Air Lion's residual demand curve when Beta is selling 100 tickets. If Air Lion sells 450 tickets, it can charge a price of $190 per ticket and have a total revenue of $85,500 (= 190 × 450), the shaded area in the diagram. Similarly, we can calculate Air Lion's marginal revenue by calculating the change in total revenue when it sells one more seat. Air Lion's entire marginal revenue curve when Beta sells 100 seats is illustrated in Figure 15.5, where it is labeled mr^A. Like its residual demand curve, Air Lion's firm-specific marginal revenue curve depends on Beta's output level. Of course, we could follow the same process to find Beta's marginal revenue curve for any level of Air Lion's output.

With the firm's marginal revenue curve in hand, we can equate marginal revenue to marginal cost to find the profit-maximizing output level, given the other firm's output choice. Figure 15.5 graphs Air Lion's horizontal marginal cost

Figure 15.5

Air Lion's Profit-Maximizing Output Level When Beta Airlines Sells 100 Tickets

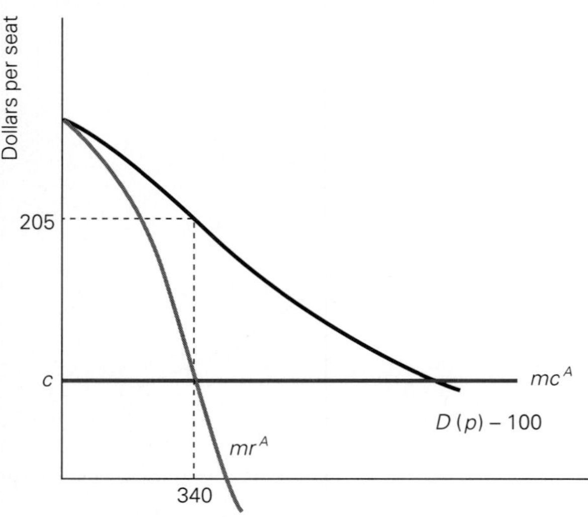

When Beta sells 100 seats, Air Lion's marginal revenue curve is mr^A and its profit-maximizing output level is 340 seats. This output is associated with a price of $205.

Figure 15.6

When Output Level Changes, So Does Air Lion's Profit-Maximizing Output Level

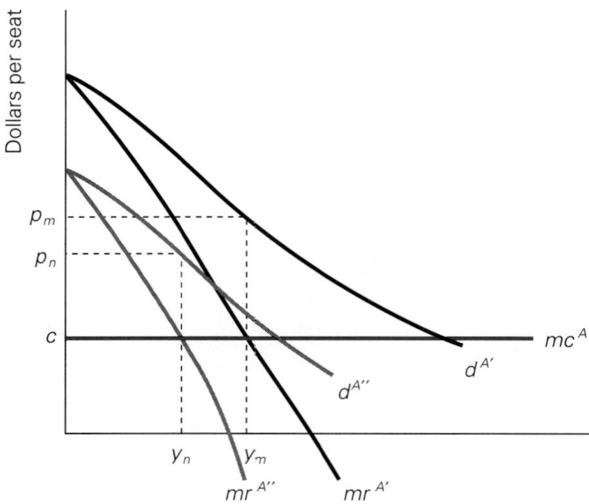

Air Lion's residual demand curve is $d^{A'}$ when Beta's output is relatively low, $mr^{A'}$ is the associated marginal revenue curve, and y_m is the associated profit-maximizing output level. Air Lion's residual demand curve is $d^{A''}$ when Beta's output is relatively high; in this case, Air Lion's profit-maximizing output level is y_n tickets.

curve as well as its marginal revenue curve. Applying the marginal output rule, Air Lion's profit-maximizing output level is 340 tickets, given that Beta sells 100 tickets. This output is associated with a price of $205.

We have stressed that Air Lion's residual demand and marginal revenue curves depend on Beta's output level. Hence, so too does Air Lion's profit-maximizing output choice. This fact is illustrated in Figure 15.6. There, $d^{A'}$ is Air Lion's residual demand curve when Beta's output is relatively low; $mr^{A'}$ is the associated marginal revenue curve and y_m tickets the associated profit-maximizing output level. On the other hand, $d^{A''}$ and $mr^{A''}$ are Air Lion's residual demand and marginal revenue curves when Beta's output is relatively high; in this case, Air Lion's profit-maximizing output level is y_n tickets. In the same way, we can calculate Air Lion's profit-maximizing output level whatever Beta's output level. In other words, for whatever decision taken by Beta, we can find Air Lion's best response.

best-response curve A schedule showing a decision maker's best course of action for each set of choices made by other decision makers.

reaction curve Another name for a best-response curve.

The entire schedule showing Air Lion's best response to each output level that Beta might choose is illustrated in Figure 15.7, where it is labeled $y^*(z)$. This notation reminds us that Air Lion's profit-maximizing output level, y^*, depends on Beta's output level, z. This curve is known as Air Lion's **best-response curve**, or **reaction curve**. We can find Air Lion's best response to a particular level of Beta's output as follows: Locate Beta's output level, say 240 seats per day, on the vertical axis. Then read across to Air Lion's reaction curve, point *a* in the figure.

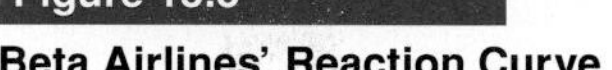

Figure 15.7

Air Lion's Reaction Curve

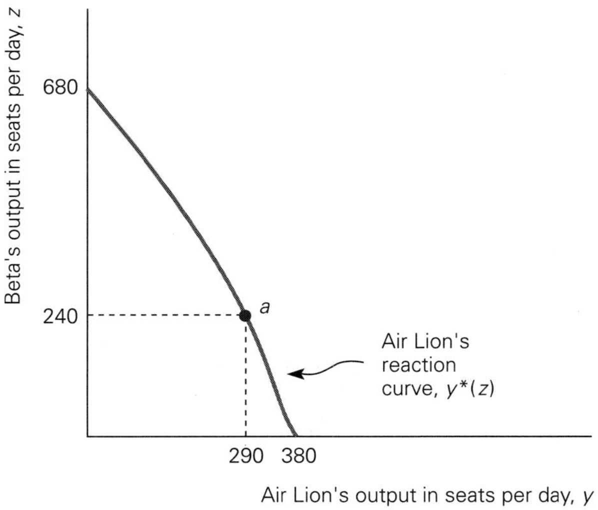

Air Lion's reaction curve tells us Air Lion's profit-maximizing output choice, given what it believes about Beta's output level. When Beta is selling 240 seats per day, Air Lion's best response is to sell 290 seats per day.

Figure 15.8

Beta Airlines' Reaction Curve

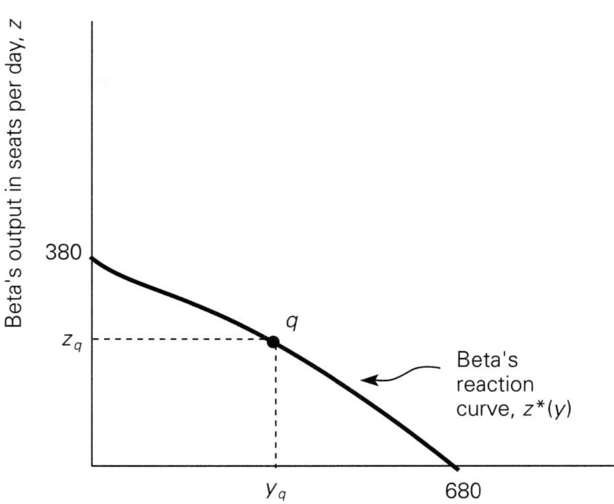

Beta's reaction curve tells us Beta's profit-maximizing output choice, given what it believes about Air Lion's output level. When Air Lion is selling y_q seats per day, Beta's profit-maximizing output choice is z_q.

From there, we read down to the horizontal axis, which measures Air Lion's output level, to find that 290 seats per day is Air Lion's best response.

A similar procedure can be used to find Beta's best response to any output level chosen by Air Lion. Beta's reaction curve is labeled $z^*(y)$ in Figure 15.8. Because this is Beta's reaction curve, we start at Air Lion's output level on the horizontal axis, read up to Beta's reaction curve, and then read across to find Beta's output level. The figure indicates that if Air Lion sells y_q seats per day, then Beta's best response is to sell z_q.

Using Reaction Curves to Find the Cournot Equilibrium

Now that we know what each firm will do, given the other firm's output, we are ready to put the two reaction curves together to find a Cournot-Nash equilibrium. Figure 15.9 graphs the reaction curves of both Air Lion and Beta. By definition, in equilibrium each firm must choose a best response to the other, so that once at the equilibrium point, neither firm wants to make a unilateral move away from it. Graphically, this means that each firm must be on its reaction curve.

To see why the equilibrium point must lie on both reaction curves simultaneously, consider point *f*, which lies on neither curve in Figure 15.9. Suppose that the firms had agreed to have Air Lion sell 200 seats per day and Beta 340. Beta's reaction curve tells us that, if Air Lion is selling 200 seats per day, then Beta's profit is maximized by selling 300 seats per day, point *g* on Beta's reaction curve. Hence, if Beta Airlines believes that Air Lion is going to stick to the agreement, Beta wants to cheat. Similarly, if Air Lion believes that Beta is going to

Figure 15.9

Testing Whether an Outcome Is an Equilibrium

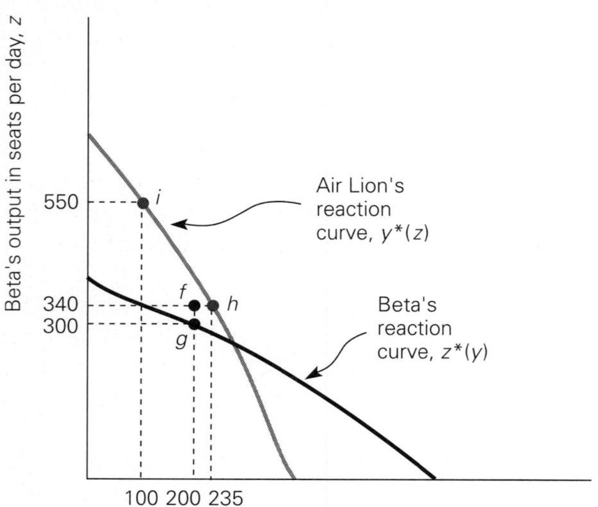

Point *f* cannot be an equilibrium. If Air Lion is selling 200 seats per day, then Beta's profit is maximized by selling 300 seats per day, point *g* on Beta's reaction curve. Similarly, if Beta is selling 340 tickets per day, then Air Lion's profit is maximized by selling 235 tickets per day, point *h* on Air Lion's reaction curve. $y = 200$ and $z = 340$ are not mutual best responses, and hence do not constitute a Cournot equilibrium.

Figure 15.10

Finding the Cournot Equilibrium

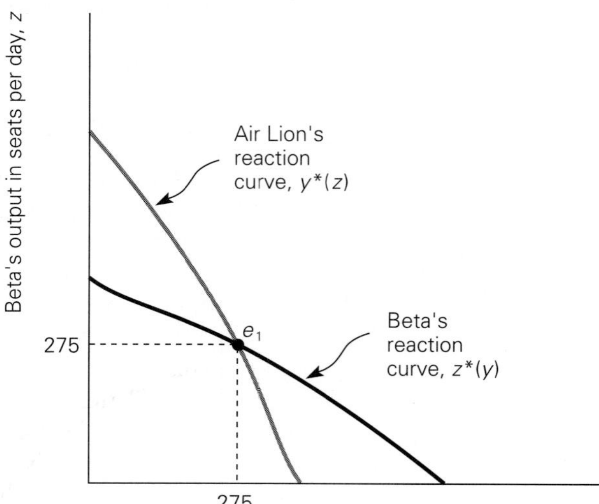

To be in equilibrium, each firm must be at a point on its reaction curve. Point e_1 is the only one that is on both reaction curves. Therefore, e_1 is the unique Cournot-Nash equilibrium.

15.2 PROGRESS CHECK

Suppose that the two airlines tried to reach an agreement to have Beta sell 550 tickets per day and Air Lion 100, point *i* in Figure 15.9. Would each firm want to stick to this agreement if the other one did? In other words, is this pair of output levels a Cournot equilibrium?

stick to the agreement by selling 340 tickets per day, Air Lion will want to sell 235 tickets per day, point *h* on Air Lion's reaction curve. Air Lion does not want to abide by the agreement either. Since each firm wants to cheat on the agreement if it believes that the other firm is abiding by it, this agreement clearly is not self-enforcing. We conclude that $y = 200$ and $z = 340$ is not a Cournot equilibrium. (PC 15.2)

We have to find a pair of output levels that is on both reaction curves at once. Such a pair is represented by point e_1 in Figure 15.10. Suppose that two airlines agree to sell 275 seats per day each. Reading off of Beta's reaction curve, we see that if Air Lion is selling 275 seats per day, Beta's profit is maximized by selling 275 seats per day. Hence, if Beta believes that Air Lion is going to stick to the agreement, then Beta wants to do so as well. Similarly, if Air Lion believes that Beta is going to sell 275 tickets per day, Air Lion's profit is maximized by upholding its end of the agreement and selling 275 tickets per day. Point e_1 represents a pair of output levels that can be supported by a self-enforcing agreement. We conclude that *the Cournot-Nash equilibrium is found at the intersection of the two reaction curves.*

COMPARISON OF COURNOT, MONOPOLY, AND PERFECT COMPETITION

Because a duopoly has fewer firms than a perfectly competitive market, but more firms than a monopoly, you might suspect that the Cournot duopoly equilibrium lies between the competitive and monopolistic equilibria. In this section, we investigate whether this conjecture is correct.

Viability of the Full Cartel Agreement

We know that the two airlines would like to attain the full cartel outcome if they could. Can the full cartel outcome be supported by a self-enforcing agreement? To answer this question, we must investigate the firm's incentives to cheat on an agreement to restrict output to the joint-profit-maximizing level. Let X^{mono} denote the monopoly level of *industry* output. Under the full cartel agreement, the two firms would promise to sell a total of X^{mono} tickets. Suppose the firms agree to split this output equally between them. If Air Lion believes that Beta is going to sell $X^{mono}/2$ tickets, is it in Air Lion's self-interest to honor the agreement by selling $X^{mono}/2$ tickets as well?

Air Lion's incentive to raise its output above $X^{mono}/2$ is the change in Air Lion's profit when it sells one more ticket—Air Lion's marginal revenue minus its marginal cost. Recall that Air Lion's marginal cost is c at this (and every) output level. The trick is to characterize Air Lion's marginal revenue.

To begin, consider *industry* marginal revenue. Then we will relate it to Air Lion's *firm-specific* marginal revenue. Industry marginal revenue has three components: (a) a revenue gain from the additional unit that is sold; (b) a revenue loss because the increase in industry output lowers the price received by Air Lion for the tickets that it was selling before the output change; and (c) a revenue loss because the increase in industry output lowers the price received by Beta for the seats that it was selling before the output change. These components are illustrated in Figure 15.11, as areas A, B, and C, respectively.

With this discussion of industry marginal revenue as background, let's calculate an individual firm's marginal revenue. When Air Lion sells one more ticket, there is a revenue gain from selling the additional ticket (area A), but there is a revenue loss because the price is driven down on the units that Air Lion already was selling (area B). Comparing the industry and firm-specific marginal revenues, we see that Air Lion ignores the adverse effect that its output expansion has on Beta (area C) when calculating its marginal revenue. Similarly, Beta ignores the negative effect that its expansion has on Air Lion (area B). Thus, in each case, the marginal revenue to a firm exceeds the marginal revenue to the industry.

To complete the argument, we need to recall that at the cartel output, X^{mono}, marginal revenue for the industry as a whole is equal to marginal cost because X^{mono} maximizes industry profit. But in Figure 15.11 we showed that the marginal revenue of an individual firm exceeds the marginal revenue for the industry as a whole. It follows that the marginal revenue of an individual firm exceeds marginal cost at the cartel outcome. Because each firm's marginal revenue exceeds its marginal cost, each airline has an incentive to expand its output beyond $X^{mono}/2$ tickets if it believes its rival is trying to achieve the cartel outcome. We conclude that it would be in the self-interest of each of the two firms to cheat on a cartel agreement. Thus, the full cartel outcome is not a Cournot-Nash equilibrium. Any attempt to restrict output to a lower level would give rise to even

Figure 15.11

The Components of Industry Marginal Revenue

Industry marginal revenue has three components: area *A*, a revenue gain from the additional unit that is sold; area *B*, a revenue loss from the fall in the price received by Air Lion for the tickets that it was selling before the output change; and area *C*, a revenue loss from the fall in the price received by Beta for the seats that it was selling before the output change.

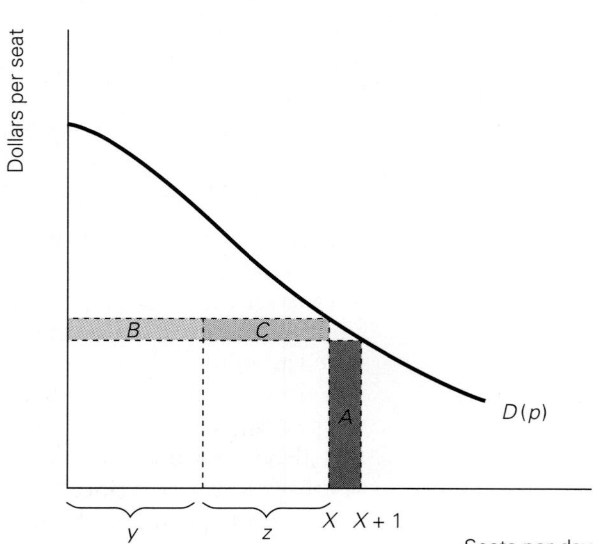

greater incentives to cheat. Therefore, *Cournot duopolists collectively produce more output than would a monopolist.*

This model goes a long way in explaining why, in the absence of binding agreements, cartels so often fail. At various times in the past two decades, suppliers of tin, nickel, coffee, cocoa, natural rubber, cotton, and potash all have attempted to restrict supplies and raise prices. None of these attempts succeeded for any significant length of time.

Are We Back to Perfect Competition?

We have seen that the two firms would have incentives to cheat on a full cartel agreement by producing too much output. Would this cheating lead all the way to the competitive outcome? The answer is no. Each firm recognizes that it can influence the price, and thus each firm's marginal revenue curve is below its average revenue curve. (See, for example, Figure 15.5.) Hence, when Air Lion or Beta sets its marginal revenue equal to marginal cost, the resulting price is greater than marginal cost. Since each firm recognizes that it has some market power, each firm produces at least somewhat below the perfectly competitive level.

We can also see this fact algebraically. To do so, recall from Chapter 13 (Equation (13.3)) that a firm's marginal revenue can be expressed in terms of the price elasticity of the firm-specific demand curve, $mr = p\{1 - 1/\epsilon_{firm}\}$. This expression is more useful if we rewrite it in terms of the market price elasticity of demand. In Chapter 11 (page 330), we saw that $\epsilon_{firm} = \epsilon_{mkt}/m$, where m is the firm's market share. By substituting this expression for ϵ_{firm} into our formula for marginal revenue, we find that $mr = p\{1 - m/\epsilon_{mkt}\}$.

With this expression for marginal revenue, the oligopolist's equilibrium condition that marginal revenue equal marginal cost can be expressed as

$$p\{1 - m/\epsilon_{mkt}\} = c. \tag{15.1}$$

The neat thing about this formula is the way it relates the firm's market share to the firm's power to influence price. If Beta were a monopolist, then m would be equal to one, and this formula would reduce to our earlier monopoly formula, Equation (13.3). On the other hand, if there were many firms in the market, m would be near zero, and Beta would produce at a point where price is almost equal to marginal cost. Equation (15.1) tells us that the smaller is a firm's market share, the more the firm behaves like a competitive price taker and the less like a monopolistic price maker. (PC 15.3)

> **15.3 PROGRESS CHECK**
>
> Use the formula in Equation (15.1) to determine the relationship between price and marginal cost when there are two firms who split the market equally, and the price elasticity of demand is unity. How would your answer change if there were four firms in the industry, all of whom had equal sales?

To summarize: *Under the Nash-Cournot equilibrium, the level of industry output is greater than the joint-profit-maximizing level and less than the competitive level.* Notice too, that since entry is blocked, Cournot oligopolists may earn positive economic profits in the long run even though they are unable to cooperate fully enough to attain the joint-profit-maximizing outcome.

We can also say something about the levels of consumer and total surplus under different market structures. As we saw in our normative analysis of monopoly, as market output rises, price falls, and consumer surplus increases. Given the relationship between industry outputs under different market structures, consumer surplus under Cournot duopoly is greater than under monopoly, but lower than under perfect competition. We also know that the monopoly output level is less than the total-surplus-maximizing amount, while the competitive output level is equal to it. Hence, total surplus under Cournot duopoly also falls between that of monopoly and perfect competition.

AN ALGEBRAIC EXAMPLE OF COURNOT EQUILIBRIUM

In this subsection, we algebraically calculate explicit values for the Cournot equilibrium levels of price, outputs, and profits. Doing so strengthens our understanding of the Nash equilibrium concept and provides a means to verify the general properties of Cournot equilibrium that we have identified above. Moreover, this example allows us to explore what happens when the two firms' marginal costs of production are unequal.

Assumptions of the Example

For purposes of this example, we make two additional assumptions about the demand and cost functions:

1. *Market demand is linear,* $D(p) = \alpha - p$, where α is a positive constant. Figure 15.12 graphs this market demand curve. α represents the price at which demand is cut off entirely (the so-called *choke price*). Notice that the slope of this demand curve is -1.
2. *The two firms' marginal costs may differ from one another.* Let c_a denote Air Lion's (constant) marginal cost level, and let c_b denote Beta's.

Calculating the Reaction Curves

Given that it believes Beta is selling z tickets, Air Lion's residual demand curve is

$$d^A(p) = \alpha - z - p. \tag{15.2}$$

As we showed in Equation (13.1) of Chapter 13, Air Lion's marginal revenue is

$$mr^A = price + (Air\ Lion\text{'s}\ quantity) \times (slope\ of\ demand\ curve) \tag{15.3}$$

Equation (15.2) tells us that the slope of Air Lion's firm-specific demand curve is -1. Hence, when the price is p and Air Lion's output is y, Air Lion's marginal revenue is $mr^A = p - y$. This formula is not quite in a usable form because it depends on price, but price itself is determined by the quantities chosen. We need to rewrite the formula so that it depends entirely on quantities. We can do this by using our formula for the market demand curve. Since $y + z = \alpha - p$, it follows that $p = \alpha - z - y$. We can substitute this expression for p into our expression for Air Lion's marginal revenue: $mr^A = (\alpha - z - y) - y$, or

$$mr^A = \alpha - z - 2y \tag{15.4}$$

We can now apply the marginal output rule, which tells us that the firm equates its marginal revenue with marginal cost, or

$$\alpha - z - 2y = c_a. \tag{15.5}$$

Rearranging terms, we can express Air Lion's profit-maximizing output level as a function of Beta's output level:

$$y^*(z) = (\alpha - c_a - z)/2. \tag{15.6}$$

Equation (15.6) is Air Lion's reaction curve for this example. It is graphed in Figure 15.13. Using the same procedure, it is easy to express Beta's profit-maximizing output level as a function of Air Lion's output. These calculations show that Beta's reaction curve is

$$z^*(y) = (\alpha - c_b - y)/2 \tag{15.7}$$

Calculating the Cournot Equilibrium

To find the Cournot equilibrium, we need to find a pair of output levels that is on both reaction functions. Figure 15.14 does this graphically. Point e_1 is the Nash-Cournot equilibrium, and it has coordinates[4]

$$y_1 = (\alpha - 2c_a + c_b)/3 \tag{15.8}$$

and

$$z_1 = (\alpha - 2c_b + c_a)/3. \tag{15.9}$$

[4]Algebraically, an agreement is self-enforcing if and only if it is on both reaction curves: $y_1 = (\alpha - c_a - z_1)/2$ and $z_1 = (\alpha - c_b - y_1)/2$. We have two linear equations and two unknowns. Substituting the expression for z_1 into the expression for y_1, we obtain

$$y_1 = \{\alpha - c_a - \tfrac{1}{2}(\alpha - c_b - y_1)\}/2.$$

This is a single equation with one unknown which can be solved to obtain the answer given in the text.

Figure 15.12

The Market Demand Curve

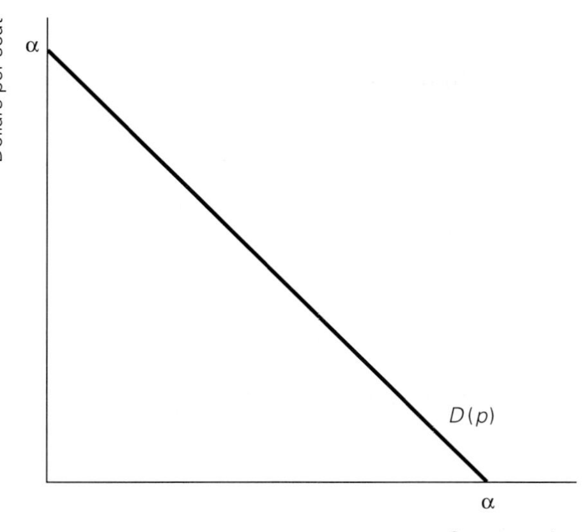

When the market demand curve is $D(p) = \alpha - p$, it is impossible to sell any units at a price greater than α, and the slope of the demand curve is -1.

Figure 15.13

Air Lion's Reaction Curve

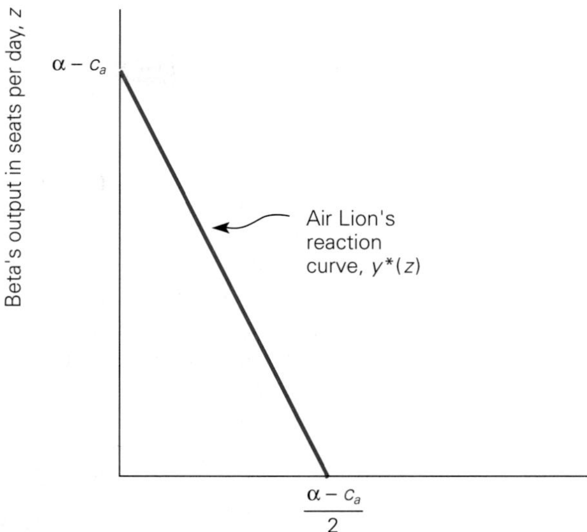

When demand is linear and marginal cost is constant, the equation representing Air Lion's reaction curve is $y^*(z) = (\alpha - c_a - z)/2$.

Figure 15.14

The Cournot Equilibrium

Point e_1 represents a pair of output levels that is on both reaction curves. Hence, point e_1 is the Nash-Cournot equilibrium in this example.

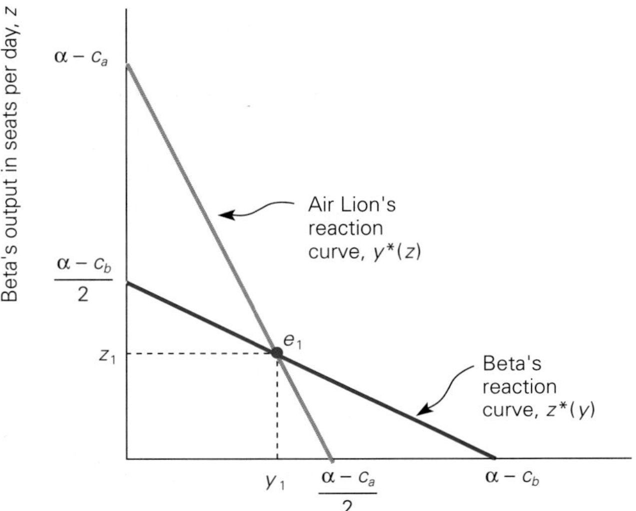

We now know the Cournot equilibrium levels of output when demand is linear and firms have constant marginal costs; an agreement is self-enforcing if and only if it entails the quantities given in Equation (15.8) and (15.9).

A Numerical Example Some specific numerical values may help in interpreting these algebraic results. Suppose that market demand is $D(P) = 900 - p$, Air Lion has a marginal cost of \$200, and Beta Airlines has a marginal cost of \$100.

Given these assumptions, Air Lion faces a residual demand curve of $d^A(p) = 900 - z - p$, and its marginal revenue is equal to $900 - z - 2y$. (Just substitute $\alpha = 900$ into the expression for marginal revenue in the right-hand side of Equation (15.4).) Applying the marginal output rule and setting marginal revenue equal to marginal cost, Air Lion chooses the output, y, to satisfy $900 - z - 2y = 200$. Rearranging terms, Air Lion's best response to Beta's output choice is $y^*(z) = 350 - z/2$. This is, of course, the same answer that we would have gotten by plugging the specific values of α, c_a, and c_b into Equation (15.6). (PC 15.4)

15.4 PROGRESS CHECK

What output level maximizes Beta's profit when Air Lion is selling 200 seats per day? Derive a general expression for Beta's best response to Air Lion's output level.

Now that we have both of the best-response functions, we can solve for the Cournot equilibrium output levels. We require values of y and z such that $y = 350 - z/2$ and $z = 400 - y/2$. Solving these two equations simultaneously, we find that $y_1 = 200$ seats per day and $z_1 = 300$. Notice that, as we might expect, the lower-cost firm ends up with a bigger market share. Notice too, that these are the same output levels that we would have found by substituting the specific values of α, c_a, and c_b into Equations (15.8) and (15.9).

Comparative Statics

Let's go back to general values of α, c_a and c_b, and consider Equations (15.8) and (15.9) further. These equations tell us that a reduction in a firm's own marginal cost leads it to produce more output. This result makes intuitive sense; the lower the firm's marginal cost, the greater the firm's incentive to produce output. Moreover, the equations tell us that a change in either firm's marginal cost affects the *other* firm's output. For example, if Air Lion's marginal cost, c_a, falls, then Beta's output, z, falls as well. Intuitively, Beta knows that the fall in Air Lion's marginal cost raises Air Lion's output level, and Beta reduces its output in response to Air Lion's increase.

To pursue the analysis further, we can derive an explicit expression for each firm's equilibrium profits. Air Lion's profit is equal to (*price* − *average cost*) × *quantity*. Air Lion's average cost is c_a, while the price is $p_1 = \alpha - z_1 - y_1$. Hence, Air Lion's equilibrium profit level is $(\alpha - z_1 - y_1 - c_a) \times y_1$. We can use the equilibrium output levels given by Equations (15.8) and (15.9) to express Air Lion's equilibrium profit solely in terms of the underlying demand and cost conditions:

$$\pi_1^A = \left(\frac{\alpha + c_a + c_b}{3} - c_a\right) \times \left(\frac{\alpha - 2c_a + c_b}{3}\right). \tag{15.10}$$

Combining terms, this expression for equilibrium profit simplifies to

$$\pi_1^A = \frac{(\alpha - 2c_a + c_b)^2}{9}. \tag{15.11}$$

Equation (15.11) embodies two important results:

1. *A firm's profit falls when its own cost rises.* As one expects, increase in Air Lion's cost, c_a, lowers its profit, *ceteris paribus.*

2. *A firm's profit rises when its rival's cost rises.* An increase in Beta's marginal cost, c_b, raises Air Lion's profit. Why? The key to the answer is found in the expression for Beta's equilibrium output level, Equation (15.9), which indicates that an increase in Beta's cost leads to a decline in Beta's equilibrium level of output. This decline shifts Air Lion's residual demand curve outward, increases the equilibrium price, and thus raises Air Lion's equilibrium profit. (PC 15.5)

15.5 PROGRESS CHECK

What happens to Beta's equilibrium profit when Beta's marginal cost rises? When Air Lion's marginal cost rises? Explain why Beta's profit is affected this way.

An analogous argument can be used to show that Beta's equilibrium profit is

$$\pi_1^B = \frac{(\alpha - 2c_b + c_a)^2}{9}. \tag{15.12}$$

Comparison of Cournot Duopoly, Competition, and Monopoly

It is instructive to compare the Cournot outcome with the competitive and monopolistic solutions when both firms have marginal costs of c.

> *Cournot Duopoly.* Substituting $c_a = c = c_b$ in Equations (15.8) and (15.9), we know that each firm sells $\frac{1}{3}(\alpha - c)$ seats per day when marginal costs are equal. The market output with Cournot firms, X^{cour}, is just double the per-firm level, or $\frac{2}{3}(\alpha - c)$. The resulting price is $p^{cour} = \frac{1}{3}(\alpha + 2c)$.
>
> *Competition.* Under the competitive solution, each firm produces at a point where the price, p^{comp}, is equal to marginal cost, c. Plugging this price into the market demand curve, the competitive market output level is $X^{comp} = (\alpha - c)$.
>
> *Monopoly.* Under monopoly, the sole supplier produces where *industry* marginal revenue is equal to marginal cost, c. Since industry marginal revenue is $\alpha - 2X$, the monopoly solution is $X^{mono} = \frac{1}{2}(\alpha - c)$, which results in a price of $p^{mono} = \frac{1}{2}(\alpha + c)$.

These results are summarized in Table 15.4, which also uses the equilibrium values of prices and output levels to calculate industry profits, consumer surplus, and total surplus. Just as our general analysis in the previous subsection indicated, the Cournot duopoly falls in between the monopolistic and competitive equilibria: $X^{mono} < X^{cour} < X^{comp}$, and $p^{mono} > p^{cour} > p^{comp}$. Consumer and total surplus exhibit the same pattern as output; each is smallest under monopoly and largest under perfect competition, with Cournot duopoly falling in between. Profits follow the same pattern as prices; they are highest under monopoly and lowest under perfect competition, with Cournot duopoly again falling in between.

Table 15.4

A Comparison of Cournot Duopoly with Perfect Competition and Monopoly for the Linear Demand, Constant Cost Example

	Perfect Competition	Cournot Duopoly	Monopoly
Market quantity	$(\alpha - c)$	$\frac{2}{3}(\alpha - c)$	$\frac{1}{2}(\alpha - c)$
Price	c	$\frac{1}{3}(\alpha + 2c)$	$\frac{1}{2}(\alpha + c)$
Industry profit	0	$\frac{2}{9}(\alpha - c)^2$	$\frac{1}{4}(\alpha - c)^2$
Consumer surplus	$\frac{1}{2}(\alpha - c)^2$	$\frac{2}{9}(\alpha - c)^2$	$\frac{1}{8}(\alpha - c)^2$
Total surplus	$\frac{1}{2}(\alpha - c)^2$	$\frac{4}{9}(\alpha - c)^2$	$\frac{3}{8}(\alpha - c)^2$

The market demand curve is $D(p) = \alpha - p$. Each firm has a constant marginal cost of c. The results are shown for $\alpha > c$.

SECTION RECAP

When each firm makes a once-and-for-all choice of output level by taking into account the output levels that it believes other firms are choosing, the market is said to be a Cournot oligopoly. Like any profit-maximizing firm, a Cournot oligopolist produces where marginal revenue is equal to marginal cost. The new feature of this model is that every supplier explicitly recognizes that its marginal revenue depends on what rival firms are doing. When the market has two suppliers, the Cournot levels of market output, price, or profits fall between those of competition and monopoly.

15.2 PRICE-SETTING OLIGOPOLISTS

You might object to the Cournot model on the grounds that "real firms" choose prices rather than quantities. Monsieur Joseph Bertrand had this same reaction to the Cournot model in 1883. In many instances, it is indeed more appropriate to model firms as choosing prices rather than quantities. In this section, we examine the behavior of such markets. After seeing the different implications of price setting and quantity setting, we will discuss how to determine which model is more appropriate to apply in any particular market.

BERTRAND COMPETITION

Bertrand equilibrium A Nash equilibrium in a market in which each firm's strategy consists of its choice of the price at which to sell its output.

A Nash equilibrium among firms that choose prices is known as a **Bertrand equilibrium** (or a **Bertrand-Nash equilibrium**). The firms that choose prices are known as Bertrand rivals. Suppose that our two firms, Air Lion and Beta Airlines, simultaneously have to set the prices that they will charge during the time under consideration. Now, a firm's strategy consists of its choice of price: p^A for Air Lion, and p^B for Beta Airlines. A "Nash equilibrium in prices" consists of two prices, p_1^A and p_1^B, such that:

1. Given that Beta Airlines charges p_1^B per ticket, Air Lion's profit is maximized by charging p_1^A per ticket.

and

2. Given that Air Lion charges p_1^A per ticket, Beta Airlines' profit is maximized by charging p_1^B per ticket.

In short, under a Bertrand equilibrium, neither firm wants to change its ticket price, given the price that its rival is charging.

Figure 15.15

Beta's Firm-Specific Demand Curve When Air Lion Charges $130 per Ticket

When Air Lion's price is $130, Beta's firm-specific demand curve shows that Beta makes no sales if its price is above $130, makes all of the industry sales if its price is below $130, and gets one-half of the market if its price is equal to $130.

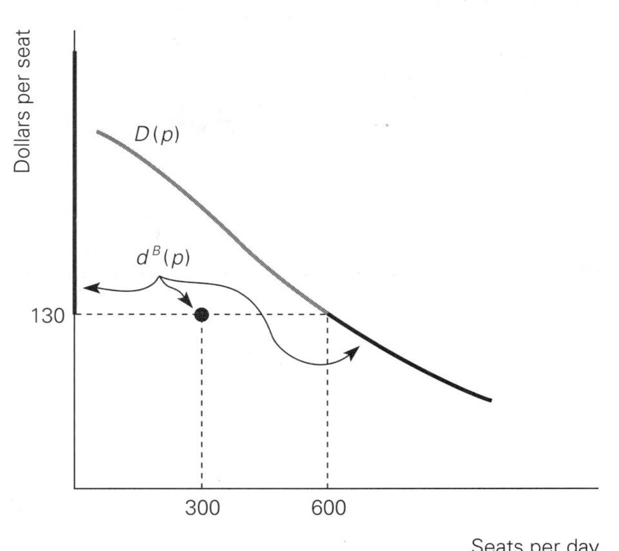

Let's find the Bertrand equilibrium for this market. As before, the market demand curve is given by $D(p)$. Of course, to determine what the firms do, we need to know their firm-specific demand curves. This being an oligopoly, our two airlines are mutually dependent on one another—the demand for one firm's output depends on the other firm's behavior. There are three cases to consider:

1. *Air Lion charges a higher price than Beta.* In this case, all passengers fly on Beta—since the services are identical, all consumers buy from the cheaper supplier. Air Lion sells no seats, and Beta sells $D(p)$, where p is the price charged by Beta.
2. *Air Lion charges a lower price than Beta.* When Air Lion charges the lower price, everything from the previous case is reversed. Now all travelers fly on Air Lion. Beta sells no seats, and Air Lion sells $D(p)$, where p is now the price charged by Air Lion.
3. *Air Lion and Beta charge the same price.* When the two firms set equal prices, consumers are indifferent between the two airlines. For simplicity, we assume that customers evenly divide themselves between the two firms. Each firm sells half of the market quantity, or $D(p)/2$, where p is the common price charged by the two firms.

Consider some arbitrarily selected price that Air Lion might charge, say $130 per seat. The resulting firm-specific demand curve that Beta faces is drawn in *black* in Figure 15.15. The horizontal axis measures the number of seats per day that Beta sells when its price is the value indicated on the vertical axis. This firm-specific demand curve shows that Beta makes no sales if its ticket price is greater than $130, makes all of the industry sales if its ticket price is less than $130, and gets one half of the market if its ticket price is equal to $130. Of course, if Air Lion's price changes, so does Beta's firm-specific demand curve. (PC 15.6)

15.6 PROGRESS CHECK

Draw Beta's firm-specific demand curve when Air Lion's price is $100.

Figure 15.16

Beta's Profit When It Matches Air Lion's Price

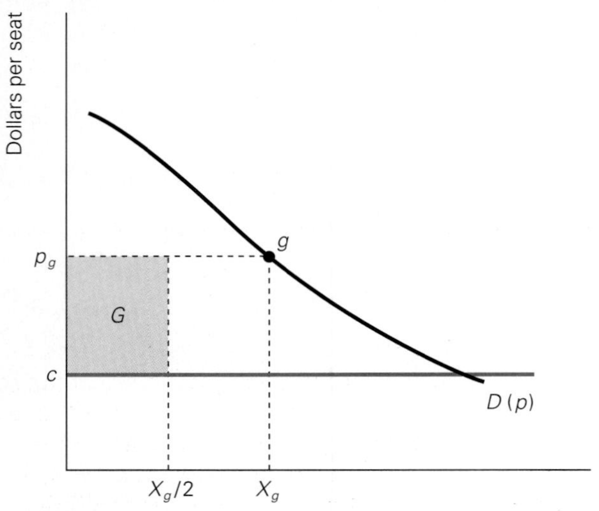

If Air Lion sets its ticket price equal to p_g, and Beta sets its price equal to p_g as well, the two firms split the market equally. Beta would sell $X_g/2$ flights at a price of p_g. The resulting profit would be shaded area *G*.

Figure 15.17

Beta's Profit When It Undercuts Air Lion's Price

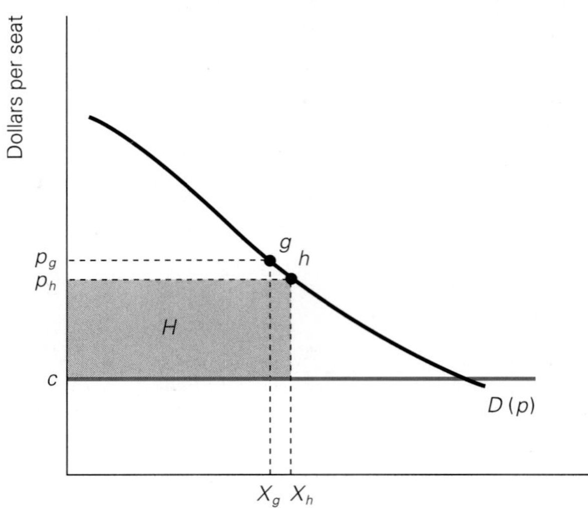

If Beta undercuts Air Lion's price of p_g by setting a price of p_h, Beta makes all of the industry sales. Beta would sell X_h seats at a price of p_h and earn a profit equal to shaded area *H*.

To complete the basic setup, we go back to the assumption that the two firms both have constant marginal costs equal to c.

Finding the Bertrand Equilibrium

Figure 15.16 illustrates the market demand curve and the common level of marginal cost. Our problem is to find a pair of prices that can be supported as a self-enforcing agreement. Clearly, neither firm's price will be less than c, because the shut-down rule tells us that at such a price the firm would prefer to shut down rather than produce.

Can there be an equilibrium at a price greater than marginal cost? Consider price p_g in Figure 15.16. Both firms' charging p_g is a Bertrand-Nash equilibrium only if each firm finds p_g to be its profit-maximizing price, given that the other firm is charging p_g. What would Beta's profit-maximizing price be if Air Lion were charging p_g? Any price greater than p_g would result in zero sales and zero profit. If Beta set its price equal to p_g, the two firms would split the market equally, each selling $X_g/2$. Beta's profit would be $(p_g - c) \times X_g/2$, which is shaded area *G* in Figure 15.16. Since Beta earns positive profit at this price, it clearly is better than setting any price greater than p_g. But what about a lower price? If Beta sets its price lower than Air Lion's, say p_h in Figure 15.17, then Beta makes all of the industry sales. Beta sells X_h seats at a price of p_h and earns a profit of $(p_h - c) \times X_h$, shaded area *H* in Figure 15.17.

Table 15.5

A Comparison of Bertrand Duopoly with Perfect Competition, Cournot Duopoly, and Monopoly for the Linear Demand, Constant Cost Example

	Bertrand Duopoly	Perfect Competition	Cournot Duopoly	Monopoly
Market quantity	$(\alpha - c)$	$(\alpha - c)$	$\frac{2}{3}(\alpha - c)$	$\frac{1}{2}(\alpha - c)$
Price	c	c	$\frac{1}{3}(\alpha + 2c)$	$\frac{1}{2}(\alpha + c)$
Industry profit	0	0	$\frac{2}{9}(\alpha - c)^2$	$\frac{1}{4}(\alpha - c)^2$
Consumer surplus	$\frac{1}{2}(\alpha - c)^2$	$\frac{1}{2}(\alpha - c)^2$	$\frac{2}{9}(\alpha - c)^2$	$\frac{1}{8}(\alpha - c)^2$
Total surplus	$\frac{1}{2}(\alpha - c)^2$	$\frac{1}{2}(\alpha - c)^2$	$\frac{4}{9}(\alpha - c)^2$	$\frac{3}{8}(\alpha - c)^2$

The market demand curve is $D(p) = \alpha - p$. Each firm has a constant marginal cost of c. The results are shown for $\alpha > c$.

Is Beta's profit higher at price p_b or p_g? If Beta chooses p_b sufficiently close to p_g, Beta earns greater profit by undercutting Air Lion's price than by matching it. To see why, suppose that Beta just barely undercuts Air Lion's price. How does area H in Figure 15.17 compare with area G in Figure 15.16? The heights of the two areas, the respective price-cost margins, are roughly the same: $(p_b - c)$ is approximately equal to $(p_g - c)$. But the widths of the two areas are much different. By undercutting Air Lion's price, Beta roughly doubles its output; X_b is just slightly more than double $X_g/2$. Hence, in Figure 15.17, where Beta undercuts Air Lion's price, the area representing Beta's profit is roughly double the area representing its profit in Figure 15.16, where Beta matches Air Lion's price. If Air Lion sets its price greater than marginal cost, then Beta maximizes its profit by undercutting Air Lion's price.

Now, since Beta would undercut Air Lion's price, Air Lion would make no sales and earn no profit. But this cannot be an equilibrium because, *given the price charged by Beta*, Air Lion could earn positive profit by slightly undercutting Beta's price. But then Beta would want to undercut Air Lion's new price, and so on. We conclude that there can be no equilibrium in which the two firms set their prices greater than marginal cost.

The last candidate for an equilibrium is for both firms to set their prices equal to marginal cost. At this level, there clearly is no incentive for either firm to cut its price—the price-cutting firm would end up selling tickets below cost. There also is no incentive for a firm to increase its price since it would be unable to make any sales at the higher price. Therefore, each firm's setting its price equal to c is a self-enforcing agreement. Under this Bertrand equilibrium, each firm sells $D(c)/2$ flights and earns zero profit.

While we have looked at the Bertrand model with two suppliers, a similar equilibrium arises with any larger number of suppliers as well. (PC 15.7)

We conclude that *when all firms have marginal costs that are constant at* c, *the Bertrand equilibrium entails all firms setting their prices equal to* c. Table 15.5 compares the Bertrand equilibrium with the others that we have found. From the table, we see that the Bertrand-Nash equilibrium has the same output, price, profit, and surplus profit levels as the competitive outcome. Hence, industry output, consumer

15.7 PROGRESS CHECK

Suppose there are three firms, each with a constant marginal cost of \$10, in an industry with a market demand curve of $D(p) = 310 - p^2$. Explain why the equilibrium price cannot be \$13. What are the equilibrium price and industry output levels in this market?

Figure 15.18

The Effects That Beta's Cheating Has on Air Lion's Price When the Firms Are Cournot Duopolists

If the two airlines agreed to have Air Lion sell 450 seats per day and Beta 450, the resulting price would be 100. If Beta cheated on the agreement and actually sold 600 seats, the price at which Beta sold its output would fall to 77. More important, the price at which Air Lion sold its output also would fall to 77—since Air Lion had decided to sell 450 seats, the airline would make whatever price adjustment was necessary to do so.

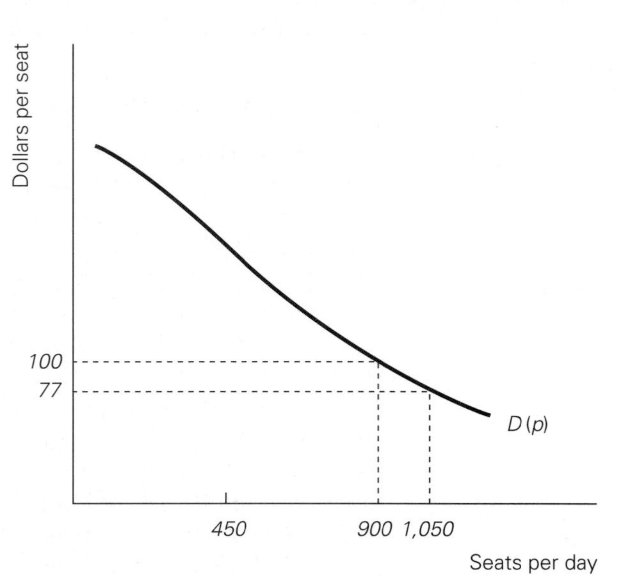

surplus, and total surplus are greater under Bertrand duopoly than under Cournot duopoly or monopoly, and price and industry profit are lower.

COURNOT OR BERTRAND?

We have looked at two oligopoly models: Cournot, in which firms set quantities, and Bertrand, in which they set prices. These two models yield strikingly different predictions about firm behavior, giving rise to two important and closely related questions: (1) Why do the models generate such different results? and (2) Given that the answers are so different, which model should we believe?

Why Are Bertrand and Cournot Duopolies So Different?

We will start with the question of why Cournot oligopolists are able to restrict output and keep the price above marginal cost while Bertrand firms are not. Think about the *pricing* strategy implicitly used by the quantity-setting Cournot firms. Suppose that the two airlines have agreed that Air Lion and Beta each will sell 450 tickets per day. As shown in Figure 15.18, under this agreement each firm sells its output at a price of 100. Now let's consider what happens if Beta cheats on the agreement and actually sells 600 tickets. The price at which Beta sells its output falls to 77. More important, the price at which Air Lion sells its output also falls to 77— since Air Lion has decided to sell 450 seats, the airline makes whatever price adjustment is necessary to do so. The fact that Air Lion's price falls in response to Beta's cheating means that Beta does not get the whole market just by lowering its price a little.

Cheating among Bertrand firms is a different story. Again suppose that Air Lion and Beta have reached an agreement under which the price is 100 and each firm sells 450 tickets. Now, if Beta cheats by lowering its price slightly, Air Lion does not lower its price to match—a Bertrand firm sticks with the price that it has set. Consequently, Beta could get the whole market at almost the same price, and the incentive to cheat is much larger than it was under Cournot rivalry.

Which Model Should We Use?

The answer to our second question is: sometimes Cournot, sometimes Bertrand, and sometimes neither. Unfortunately, there is no all-purpose theory of oligopolistic behavior that applies to every market. The important question therefore becomes: How do we know which model is appropriate for a given market? Fortunately, the explanation of why the two models give such different predictions provides a basis for choosing which model to apply in any particular case.

The key consideration is whether it takes longer for a firm to adjust its price or its quantity. The quantity-setting Cournot model is appropriate when firms make fixed production plans, so that it is hard to adjust their output levels once they have been planned. Cournot is thus a good model of markets in which there are long production lead times, or where firms need to invest in specialized capacity to produce the good. Think about building a supermarket, for instance. The owner needs to decide how large the store will be and how many checkout counters to have. After that, the level of output is largely fixed: only so many customers can be checked out in a day. Similar effects arise with gas stations and the number of pumps. Las Vegas hotels are another example. It takes a long time to build additional hotel rooms, and once the rooms are built the expenditures are sunk so that it does not make sense to reduce capacity. Given the relatively low marginal cost of utilizing a room that already has been constructed, choosing the number of rooms to build is like choosing the hotel's output level. In a similar vein, alumina refining plants have to be operated near capacity or shut down entirely—again the capacity choice is like an output choice (Wells 1985, 10). In all of these markets, once a firm has chosen a capacity (output) level, it can be expected to stick with it for a while, as in the Cournot model.

There are other markets, however, in which firms commit to prices rather than to quantities. In these markets, the price-setting Bertrand model is appropriate. Once a mail-order catalog is printed, for example, it is too late to change prices. This type of situation also arises in markets where firms compete by "bidding" for business. Consider the market to provide telephone service to the U.S. government. The firms seeking this business have to submit fixed prices to the government so that it can decide from whom to purchase services. Suppose that two firms agree to collude and submit high bids, but that one of them cheats by submitting a low bid. The firm sticking to the agreement does not have a chance to lower its bid in response. Instead, the cheater gets all of the business, just as in the Bertrand model. The Bertrand model applies to many other markets as well. Large industrial buyers often ask potential suppliers to submit written bids stating what price they would charge to supply a specified quantity of an input. If you want to sell motherboards to a company manufacturing clones of IBM personal computers, for example, you may be asked to submit a bid stating the price at which you are willing to supply 20,000 motherboards. In choosing your bid, you need to consider your costs as well as the bids you believe your rivals are likely to submit. If you expect a rival to set a price above your marginal cost, then you will set a price below your rival's in order to win the sales. But knowing this fact, your rival will want to set a lower bid to avoid being undercut. Such pressures push the firms' bids down toward marginal cost, which is of course why buyers use this bidding process. This form of behavior is nicely captured by the Bertrand model.

In looking at these examples, you may have noticed something odd about how we decide which model is appropriate—the variable that the firm chooses often or can adjust quickly is *not* the right one on which to concentrate. We want to focus on the choices to which the firm has to stick. In most markets, prices can be adjusted more quickly than quantities. Changing price is just a matter of printing new price lists, while changing quantities means the firm actually has to alter its production operations. Although your intuition may tell you that the price-setting Bertrand model is the right way to think about most markets, the quantity-setting Cournot model often is more appropriate.

Before getting too worried about which model is the correct one, you should note two important points. First, the Cournot and Bertrand models are not as far apart as one might suppose. Both models illustrate the difficulty of collusion and the importance of oligopolistic interaction. Moreover, the predictions of these two models are much closer to one another when the firms produce differentiated products rather than homogeneous ones. When rival firms' products are imperfect substitutes for one another, a small price difference does *not* induce everyone to buy from the lower-price firm; some consumers purchase the higher-price good because they believe that it is better. Consequently, the gains from cheating under Bertrand are not so dramatic when products are differentiated; as in Cournot, a firm's sales do not take a huge jump upward. Therefore, when products are differentiated, Bertrand oligopolists, like Cournot oligopolists, are able to set price above marginal cost but below the full cartel price.

The second point is that neither model is the last word in the theory of oligopoly. Rather, each one is an important building block in the development of this theory. Each model shows us how mutual interdependence influences the nature of firms' decision making, and helps us understand the difficulties that firms may have in sustaining a tacit agreement to hold output at the cartel level. Both models, however, fail to take into account an important real-world feature: Firms often interact with each other repeatedly, whether they are choosing prices or quantities. Once we incorporate this feature, the quantity-setting and price-setting models generate much closer predictions about firm behavior than when firms interact on a once-and-for-all basis.

SECTION RECAP

When oligopolistic firms choose prices on a once-and-for-all basis, the market is said to be a Bertrand oligopoly. When all firms have the same, constant level of marginal cost, they all set their prices equal to marginal cost in equilibrium. They are driven to this point because each firm has a strong incentive to undercut the price of its rivals whenever that price is greater than marginal cost. Hence, even when there are only two firms in the market, Bertrand rivals behave like perfect competitors. However, to the extent that their products are differentiated, Bertrand rivals may be able to keep price above the competitive level, although below the cartel level.

15.3 COOPERATION AND PUNISHMENT

As noted at the beginning of this chapter, to choose a profit-maximizing course of action, an oligopolist must: (1) form beliefs about what rival firms are up to, and (2) take into account how the rival firms will react to its actions. The

Cournot and Bertrand models of duopoly do a good job of capturing the first item—a firm's profit-maximizing action explicitly depends on its beliefs regarding the other firm's behavior. But these models fail to capture the need to consider rivals' reactions. Since the firms each make a *single choice*, and they do so *simultaneously*, there is no chance for either firm to react to the other.

A more realistic model must take into account the fact that firms make choices *repeatedly*. With repeated decision making, firms can base their decisions at a given time on actions that have been taken in the past—firms can react to their rivals' behavior. In particular, if one firm cheats on the agreement today, another firm may be able to punish it in the future. For example, Air Lion might say to Beta: "Let's set the cartel price for tickets by restricting our flights. I know that you will have an incentive to sell more than your share of tickets. But if you cheat on this agreement and I catch you, I will flood the market with output so that the price will fall and you will never earn a profit again." Robert Crandall notwithstanding, actual airlines typically do not make explicit speeches like this to one another (they are illegal), but managers do go through a similar thought process. The Trump Shuttle and Pan Am used to compete on New York-Washington shuttle. The president of the Trump Shuttle once stated: "There are only two of us in the market—what do you think Pan Am is going to do if I cut prices?" (Bradsher 1989, D1).

Airlines are not the only ones to worry about future punishment for current cheating on an agreement to hold down industry output. Several years ago, Tanzania decided to quit the world diamond cartel, whose members included South Africa, the (then) Soviet Union, Namibia, Tanzania, and most other diamond-producing nations. The cartel "reacted by depressing prices for the quality of stones sold by Tanzania. Soon afterward, a duly chastened Tanzania returned to the syndicate" (Farnsworth 1988, E3).

In this section, we will develop a model that captures this type of behavior. Unlike the Cournot and Bertrand models, this one takes into account *both* (1) firms' needs to form beliefs about what rival firms are up to, and (2) firms' needs to take their rivals' reactions into account.

A MODEL OF REPEATED INTERACTION

Suppose that Air Lion and Beta Airlines are trying to reach a self-enforcing agreement to hold the number of flights down and the price up. Unlike our earlier models, let's suppose that Air Lion and Beta make new choices each day. How should Air Lion decide whether to cheat on an implicit agreement with Beta? Being a rational profit maximizer, Air Lion has to consider the costs and benefits of cheating.

The benefits from cheating are clear. If the other firm is restricting output to keep the price up, it is profitable for the cheater to expand its sales, and the cheater earns greater per period profits, at least until it is caught. Let π^s denote Air Lion's profit per day if it "sticks" to the agreement, and π^c its profit per day if it "cheats" on the agreement (since all of the calculations are the same for the two firms, we will leave off the subscript labeling which firm is which). The difference between these two profit levels, $\pi^c - \pi^s$, is the per-day gains to cheating and getting away with it. It may take Beta a while to detect Air Lion's cheating. If it takes Beta T days to detect Air Lion's duplicity, then cheating allows Air Lion to earn an additional $\pi^c - \pi^s$ per day for T days. These gains from cheating are shaded area A in Figure 15.19.

Figure 15.19

The Costs and Benefits of Cheating

If it takes Beta T days to detect Air Lion's duplicity, then cheating allows Air Lion to earn an additional $\pi^c - \pi^s$ per day for T days, shaded area A. Once Air Lion has been caught cheating, it suffers a net punishment of $\pi^s - \pi^p$ per day. This punishment takes place from the T + 1st day onward, and the cost of cheating is shaded area B.

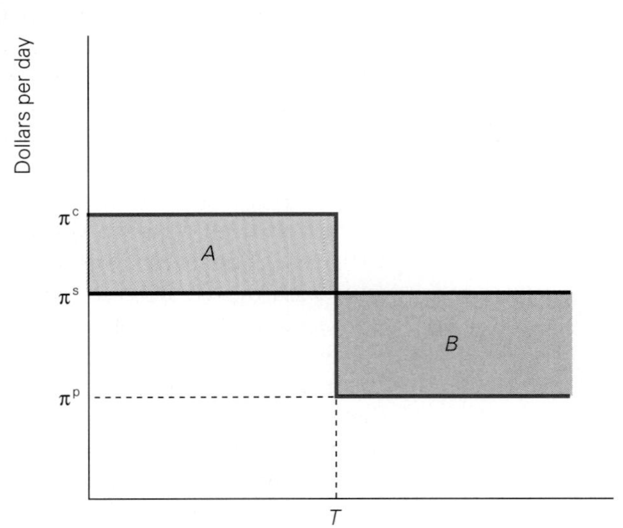

15.8 PROGRESS CHECK

Suppose that the amount of profit enjoyed by a firm when no one cheats rises from π^s to a higher value $\pi^{s'}$, while the cheating profit, π^c, and the punishment profit, π^p, stay the same. What happens to the incentive to cheat?

Cheating has costs as well. Once Beta has caught Air Lion cheating, Beta may take actions to lower Air Lion's later profit. Let π^p denote Air Lion's per-day flow of profit while being "punished" for cheating. Relative to abiding by the agreement and not being punished, this punishment costs Air Lion $\pi^s - \pi^p$ per day. When cheating takes T days to detect, the punishment takes place from the T + 1st day onward. This cost is shaded area B in Figure 15.19.

Of course, a firm cannot make its cheating decision solely by comparing areas A and B. The various flows of benefits and costs are received at different points in time, so that we must compare the *present values* of the benefits and costs (see Chapter 5). The firm cheats if and only if the present value of the gains from cheating exceeds the present value of the losses from being punished. (PC 15.8)

GENERAL PREDICTIONS

The setup in Figure 15.19 allows us to identify several factors that influence whether firms are likely to collude successfully.

1. *The longer it takes to catch a cheater, the greater the incentive to cheat.* There are two reasons for this relationship. First, the longer the detection lag, the longer the cheater can reap the gains from cheating, and the greater the present value of the gains from cheating. Second, the longer the detection lag, the longer the punishment is put off, and the smaller the present value of the punishment. (Remember, the farther into the future some given amount of money is paid or received, the smaller its present value.) Since an increase in the detection lag raises the benefits of cheating and lowers the costs, it raises the incentive to cheat and makes collusion more difficult.

2. *The less likely it is that a cheater will be caught, the greater the incentive to cheat.* We could make our model of cheating and punishment more realistic by

allowing for uncertainty with respect to when and if cheating will be detected. When the detection lag is uncertain, a firm has to look at the *expected* benefits and costs of cheating. Although taking expectations into consideration makes the calculations of benefits and costs more complicated, it is clear that if the firm is unlikely to get caught, then the expected benefits of cheating are high relative to the expected costs. Collusion is thus harder to sustain.

3. *The harsher the punishment that a cheater faces, the lower the incentive to cheat on an agreement.* The lower is π^p, the greater the cost of cheating (area B in Figure 15.19), and the easier it is to sustain a collusive agreement.

Condition (3) tells us that the firms want π^p to be as low as possible to deter cheating and sustain collusion. But how low is possible? As noted earlier, a firm or firms may threaten to punish any cheater very harshly by flooding the market with output and driving down the market price. The problem with such threats, however, is that carrying them out lowers the profits of both the punished and the punisher. Will a firm carry out such a costly punishment if it detects cheating? The potential cheater may believe not. And if the firm doubts it will be punished, then it will go ahead and cheat.

Consider, for instance, two owners of ice-cream trucks, each of whom sells popsicles and ice-cream cones to children on the street. Moreover, suppose that the driver-owners have reached an agreement to keep popsicle prices high. To enforce this agreement, one driver says to the other: "If you charge $1.95 for a Fruit Freezie instead of $2.00, I will drive my truck head on into yours and kill us both." Unless there is good reason to suspect that this driver is crazy, such a threat is not likely to have much influence on the other driver's pricing decision. It clearly would not be in the driver's self-interest to carry out the threatened punishment in response to cheating by the other driver. In deciding whether to cheat, a firm takes into account only those threats that it believes actually would be executed. In other words, to have a deterrent effect, a threat must be believable, or **credible**. In situations where firms can react to one another's earlier actions, we now have a second condition that an agreement must satisfy in order to be self-enforcing. In addition to satisfying the Nash condition, an agreement must also satisfy the

credible
A threat or promise by a firm is credible only if it would be in the firm's self-interest to carry out the threat or promise if called upon to do so.

> **Credibility Condition:** Any threats (or promises) contained in a self-enforcing agreement must be credible. That is, if a firm makes a threat, it must be in the firm's self-interest to carry out the threat if called upon to do so.[5]

If an agreement calls for a particular punishment against a cheater, the firm that is responsible for meting out the punishment must not have an incentive to cheat on *the agreement to punish the cheater*. Each firm's profit-maximizing course of action must be to carry out all of its part of the agreement.

The first three general conclusions about the likely success of collusion all follow from the balancing of the costs and benefits of cheating on a collusive agreement. A fourth general conclusion follows from the fact that most firms' ability to communicate is limited and they must use tacit agreements to collude. While members of cartels among nations (e.g., OPEC) can talk to one another, members of a group of American, or German, or British firms trying to collude cannot legally get together to discuss their plans.[6] The firms must reach an implicit agreement without actually discussing it among themselves. The need to

[5]We will examine an explicit, formal model of repeated interaction in the next chapter.

[6]As noted in Chapter 14, there are a few exceptions, such as agricultural marketing orders.

reach an agreement in this way makes collusion more difficult, and it leads to our final general conclusion.

4. *The more complex the collusive agreement has to be, the less likely it is to succeed.* When firms must tacitly collude rather than reach a formal agreement, increased complexity gives rise to more chances for mistakes and makes it difficult for firms to be sure that their tacit understandings are correct.

MARKET STRUCTURE AND COLLUSION

Our theory of repeated oligopoly led to four general predictions about the circumstances under which collusion is likely to succeed. We now use these predictions to examine the effects of specific elements of market structure on the likelihood of successful collusion.

a. **The more that the firms' costs differ, the less likely is cooperation, *ceteris paribus.*** To see why, note that when the firms' marginal costs are identical and constant, total profits are independent of the way in which the output is divided among the firms; industry total cost is simply the common value of marginal cost times the quantity produced. Things are different when costs differ across firms. When Beta has lower marginal costs than Air Lion, for example, industry total cost is always lowest—and industry profit always highest—when Beta carries all of the passengers. But, while having Beta sell all of the tickets maximizes industry profit, it also leads to Air Lion's earning no profit. Since Air Lion gets zero profit under this agreement, Air Lion has no incentive to abide by it.

This situation leaves our firms with two choices. One option is for Beta to make all of the sales and then pass some money on to Air Lion. Such cash transfers are called *side payments* because they are made on the side to support an agreement. In the United States, however, side payments generally are illegal. The other option is to split production between the two firms. For example, they could each carry half of the passengers. The problem with this approach is that having Air Lion produce output results in higher average costs and lower industry profits.

Production by the higher-cost firm leads to another problem. Firms with differing costs tend to disagree on how the commodity should be priced. Typically, a firm with a high marginal cost wants the colluding firms to set a higher price and lower industry output than does a low-cost firm. (This conclusion follows from the application of our marginal output choice rule.) This disagreement makes it difficult to collude. Cost differences also increase the complexity of the agreement that the firms have to reach, and thus make it harder for firms to reach a set of prices and output levels that are acceptable to all. For producers who cannot explicitly communicate with one another due to antitrust restraints, the problem is especially difficult.

Before closing this discussion, we should note that under one set of circumstances, cost differences may actually ease the difficulty of reaching a tacit agreement. When there is one firm that clearly has the lowest costs in the industry, that firm may be seen by other producers as a natural "industry leader." Other producers may look to this firm to take the lead in setting price or output levels. By providing a focal point around which to coordinate their actions, the presence of a leader may make collusion easier to achieve.

b. **The more that demand varies from period to period, the less likely is cooperation, *ceteris paribus.*** Suppose that for some reason unknown to Beta and Air Lion, some days travelers just do not fly very much between the two cities the airlines serve. Consequently, the market demand curve for flights on this route varies a lot from day to day. Suppose further that one day Air Lion notices that its sales are particularly low. This may be because it is an off day for air travel. Or it may be due to Beta's cheating on their price agreement. In such a situation, Air Lion may incorrectly assume that Beta is cheating and take retaliatory action, triggering a price war. To prevent such wars from occurring frequently, sometimes the two firms will just have to shrug off seeing their demand fall. But if they do this, then a firm may reason that it can cheat without getting caught. The net result is that collusion is hard to sustain. In contrast, stable demand makes cheating easier to detect, and the threat of being caught sustains collusion.

c. **The easier it is for firms to monitor their rival's output levels, the more likely is cooperation, *ceteris paribus.*** If the firms can monitor one another, then no one can cheat for long without getting caught. Industry trade associations sometimes collect information that is used to detect and, thus, to deter cheating. Until the U.S. Department of Justice prosecuted them, the American Hardwood Manufacturers' Association collected data on the prices charged by each of its members and reported these prices to all of the other firms in the association weekly. A few years ago, Lloyd's of London (the famous insurance market) was hired by OPEC to monitor oil output levels of the member countries because cheating had become so widespread.

d. **Product differentiation may increase or decrease the likelihood of cooperation, *ceteris paribus.*** Recall that so far we have assumed that the two firms' outputs are regarded as identical by consumers. Now suppose that Air Lion and Beta Airlines are viewed as providing distinct services (say because they offer flights at different times). Product differentiation has several effects. First, when a firm lowers its price, it will attract additional sales, but not as many as when its product is regarded as identical to that of the other firm. (Some people will stick with the higher-priced carrier because its schedule better fits theirs.) This lowers the gains to cheating. A second effect runs in the opposite direction, however. Product differentiation makes punishment more difficult because it becomes harder to shift inward a rival's firm-specific demand curve when your product and your rival's product are imperfect substitutes. Even if you set your price below marginal cost, your rival still could earn economic profit if the differentiation were strong enough. This makes it more difficult for you to pose a strong credible threat.

Product differentiation also affects the complexity of the agreement that the firms have to reach, making it harder for firms to reach a set of prices and output levels that are acceptable to all. OPEC runs into this problem when members try to set the price of oil. In reality, there is no one commodity called "oil," but many different qualities of oil, and some supplies are located closer to consumers than others. Since the member nations have different types of oil, they have different preferences concerning the appropriate prices. For other groups of producers who (unlike OPEC) cannot explicitly communicate with one another due to antitrust restraints, the problem is even more severe.

e. **When prices are negotiated with each customer separately, collusion is less likely to be successful, *ceteris paribus.*** Up to this point, our oligopoly models have assumed many buyers, each of whom is a price taker and buys at publicly announced prices. There are, however, oligopolistic markets in which the buyers are not simply part of a faceless horde. Our theory of repeated oligopolistic interaction has something to say about these markets as well. When there are a few large buyers with whom the sellers communicate directly, a seller can make price cuts secretly. In such a market, detection lags may be very long. And we have seen that the longer the detection lags, the less likely there is cooperation, *ceteris paribus.* This type of effect suggests collusion will tend to be difficult in intermediate goods markets where the buyers are businesses placing huge orders and bargaining over the prices for each deal separately. In the 1960s, the market for large turbine power generators was an oligopoly dominated by two firms, General Electric and Westinghouse. Privately owned power companies who purchased the generators typically engaged in confidential bargaining with the two suppliers. Customers were able to capitalize on the rivalry between the two companies to get discounts off the list prices. General Electric "solved" this problem by hiring an accounting firm to guarantee that no customer got a lower price than any other—in effect, getting rid of secret price cuts. Westinghouse followed suit, and the price cutting ceased (Porter 1980).

f. **When individual orders are large relative to the overall market, collusion is less likely to be successful, *ceteris paribus.*** If a single order is large enough, a firm may gain so much by cheating to get that order that the threat of later punishment is not an effective deterrent. Some state governments use this fact to encourage more competitive bidding by their suppliers. For example, a state will pool all of its annual demand for concrete into a single, very large order that is then put out for a single bid. With a large enough single order, firms may tend to ignore the future and behave as if they are making a single once-and-for-all sale. And we saw that Bertrand competitors tend to drive prices down to marginal cost in such a situation.

g. **The more firms in a market, the less likely is cooperation, *ceteris paribus.*** This is perhaps the most important of the theory's predictions, and it comes last on our list because it relates to many of the points already made. An increase in the number of firms makes collusion more difficult for several reasons. First, when there are many firms, the per-period gain from cheating may be quite large. If there are many producers, each one restricting its output to keep price up, any one of them will find that its firm-specific marginal revenue is much greater than its marginal cost. This relationship follows from the fact that any one producer's inframarginal units are only a small fraction of the total inframarginal units and it ignores the effects of its output change on rival producers.

Second, the increased complexity that arises when there are many parties to the agreement makes successful collusion less likely. There are more chances for misunderstandings under tacit agreements, and it is more likely that the firms will differ in terms of either costs or product characteristics.

It also may be harder to detect cheating when there are many producers rather than a few. Cheating by a single producer among many may not affect price dramatically. Even if the price is noticeably affected, it may be difficult to tell which producer is at fault. Knowing this, a firm is more likely to cheat. Moreover, if a cheater is detected, the other firms in the industry may find it too costly to have a price war just to punish one small member of the industry. As long as the firm takes only a small percentage of the business away from each of its rivals, cheating may be less damaging to the rivals' profits than would an extensive price war. If so, the price war is not a credible threat. And cheating is not deterred if the threat of punishment is not credible.

In summary, with many firms, a collusive agreement is likely to fail. When there are few producers, attempts to collude are less likely to run into trouble. For example, in the nutmeg industry, Indonesia and Grenada produce 98 percent of the world's output. In 1988, the Indonesian Nutmeg Association and the Grenada Cooperative Nutmeg Association entered into a cartel agreement. Our theory predicts that this cartel should be successful, and so far it appears to be working quite well. (PC 15.9)

15.9 PROGRESS CHECK

When the U.S. automobile market became more open to international trade, what do you think happened to the ability of the U.S. auto makers to hold prices up?

SECTION RECAP

In many markets, firms make price or output decisions repeatedly. In such situations, firms can set up collusive agreements that rely on the threat of punishment to deter cheating. A key issue is whether the threatened punishment is credible. If it is not, then it will not deter firms from cheating, and the collusive agreement will break down. As we stressed at the outset of this chapter, there is no single model of oligopoly that applies in all cases. Nevertheless, our general approach—searching for equilibria that are self-enforcing agreements—generates a number of predictions with respect to the general determinants of the likelihood of successful collusion, as well as about the specific effects of market structure.

SUMMARY

In this chapter we have examined oligopoly. Unlike the suppliers in all of our earlier models, oligopolists behave strategically.

- The distinguishing feature of oligopoly is that firms explicitly worry about one another's actions—the producers recognize their mutual interdependence.
- Firms would like to collude, but their ability to do so is typically limited by the need to rely on self-enforcing agreements.
- When firms compete by choosing output levels on a once-and-for-all basis, they are said to be Cournot firms. The Cournot equilibrium falls between the monopolistic and competitive outcomes in terms of market quantity, price, profits, and total surplus.
- When firms compete by choosing prices on a once-and-for-all basis, they are said to be Bertrand competitors. For homogeneous goods that are produced at a constant cost, the equilibrium price is equal to marginal cost, as in the perfectly competitive equilibrium.
- By assuming that firms make once-and-for-all decisions, the Cournot and Bertrand models fail to capture an important element of many real-world markets—firms may take actions repeatedly. With repeated interaction, firms may be able to sustain collusion by threatening to punish any firm that violates the collusive agreement.
- A critical issue is whether threats of punishment are credible. Because firms do not expect them to be carried out, incredible threats do not deter cheating on collusive agreements.
- Our theory of oligopoly generates a number of general predictions about the determinants of successful collusion. When it takes a long time to detect cheating, or a cheater is unlikely to get caught, collusion is less likely to be successful. The harsher the punishments that firms can credibly threaten, the more likely collusion will succeed. The need to collude tacitly, rather than explicitly, makes collusion more difficult.
- Our theory of oligopoly generates several specific predictions about the effects of market structure on the likely success of collusion. Cost differences, demand fluctuations, individual negotiations with customers, large individual orders, and a large number of suppliers all make collusion more difficult. Trade groups that can monitor supplier behavior make collusion easier, while product differentiation has an ambiguous effect.

DISCUSSION QUESTIONS

15.1 According to the economist John Kenneth Galbraith, "So long as there are only a few massive firms in an industry, each must act with a view of the welfare of all." Do you agree?

15.2 In 1991, two large health food stores opened across the street from each other in the Washington, D.C. suburb of Rockville, Maryland. They were the only two major health food stores in the Washington area. Discuss the information that you would need to determine whether the duopolists could successfully collude to hold their prices above marginal cost.

15.3 In the text, we considered Bertrand duopolists with identical marginal costs. Now, suppose that Air Lion's marginal cost, c_a, is lower than Beta's marginal cost, c_b.

a. Use the argument made in Section 15.2 to show that there is no equilibrium at a price greater than c_b.

b. Show that if the price were just equal to c_b, Air Lion would have an incentive to undercut Beta's price. Would Beta have an incentive to match or beat the price cut?

c. Explain why Air Lion is the only one that makes sales in equilibrium. Derive an expression for Air Lion's equilibrium profit in terms of the demand curve and the two firms' marginal cost levels.

15.4 Many government agencies, such as publicly owned power companies that purchase generating equipment, make purchases based on the following bidding procedures. The government agency describes what it would like to purchase and asks firms to submit secret (what are known as "sealed") bids. After the firms have submitted their bids, the government announces what all of the bids were and then makes its purchase from the lowest bidder. Some economists have criticized this procedure on the grounds that revealing all of the bids makes it easier for the firms to collude. Do you agree? In answering this question, be sure to think about the fact that, over time, the same set of firms compete with each other on many bids.

15.5 In the text, we examined Cournot duopoly. Cournot markets can have more firms. Suppose that the market demand curve for some airline market is $D(p) = 1{,}000 - p$ and each airline has constant marginal costs of \$100.

a. What are the equilibrium price and output levels when there are two airlines in the market?

b. What are the equilibrium price and output levels when there are three airlines in the market? (*Hint:* Express the profit-maximizing output level for one firm [its best response] in terms of the *total* output of the *other two* airlines. Then use the fact that the firms all have the same output levels in equilibrium.)

c. How do the equilibrium market price and market output levels when there are three airlines compare with the equilibrium levels when there are only two airlines? Give an intuitive explanation for this pattern.

d. What do you think would happen if there were still more firms in the market? Can you find a general algebraic formula that expresses the equilibrium price and market output levels in terms of the number of firms, n? What happens as n gets very large?

15.6 Consider a firm that is the sole producer of Soybean Helper (entry is blocked by the fact that no other producer realizes that this product is merely hamburger). The manufacturer's cost of producing soybean helper is \$3 per patty.

Soybean Helper is used to make soy burgers. There are two outlets for soy burgers, and these outlets are Bertrand duopolists. Consumers view the two outlets as providing perfect substitutes. The market demand curve for soy burgers is $D(p) = 100 - p$. There is only a single period of sales.

To produce one soy burger, an outlet must use 10 minutes of labor and 1 patty of soybean helper. The outlets take the price of labor as given at \$6 per hour. The manufacturer sells soybean helper to the outlets at a wholesale price of q per patty.

a. Derive the cost function faced by an outlet. How is this cost function affected by changes in the wholesale price?

b. What wholesale price should the manufacturer set to maximize its profits? (*Hint:* Solve for the equilibrium quantities in the retail market in terms of the wholesale price. The manufacturer's revenue is then equal to the sum of these quantities multiplied by the wholesale price.)

15.7 Again, consider the problem faced by the producer of Soybean Helper. But now suppose that the two outlets are Cournot rivals. What wholesale price should the manufacturer set?

15.8 Using our theory of oligopoly, discuss whether you think it would be easier to collude with respect to the level of advertising or the quantity of output.

15.9 We can also apply our theory of oligopoly to situations involving uncertainty. In this problem, we will examine the effects of cooperation on oligopolists' incentives to conduct risky R&D. Suppose that there are two firms in the industry. These firms are Bertrand rivals, and there is only one period of production. Market demand is $D(p) = 200 - p$. If neither firm conducts R&D, then each firm has total costs of $\$50 \times x$ (i.e., marginal cost is constant at \$50).

Each firm has a single R&D project available to it (there is a different project for each firm). The cost of running a project is \$1,000. If the project is successful, then the firm's (constant) marginal costs drop from \$50 to \$10. If the project is unsuccessful, then the firm's marginal costs remain at \$50. Each firm believes that the probability of success for any given project is equal to ½. The success of one firm's project is independent of the success of the other firm's project.

a. Should firm 1 undertake its project if it believes that firm 2 is not going to undertake its project? (*Hint:* Throughout the problem, you have to solve for *expected* profits, since the outcomes of the projects are uncertain.)

b. Should firm 1 undertake its project if it believes that firm 2 is going to undertake its project?

c. In equilibrium, will the two firms undertake their projects or not?

Pointing to the apparent success of cooperative research in Japan, many people in the United States are calling for a more permissive antitrust treatment of research joint ventures between product-market competitors. Suppose that the firms are allowed to form a research joint venture. Under this arrangement, the firms agree to share the results of any successful project that they conduct. Thus, if the joint venture conducts a successful project, both firms' marginal costs fall to \$10. If the venture does not conduct a successful project, both firms' marginal costs remain equal to \$50.

d. To make your life easier, suppose that the joint venture cannot conduct more than one project. Will the firms choose to conduct one project or none?

e. Explain why you (should have) obtained different answers to parts *c* and *d*. Do you see any implications for public policy toward research joint ventures?

15.10 Just as monopoly on the buyer side of the market is known as monopsony, oligopoly on the buyer side of the market is known as *oligopsony.* The market for major league baseball players provides a good example of oligopsony in action. In 1989, the owners of the baseball teams that hire the players were found to have colluded to hold down free agents' salaries by refusing to bid for them (a free agent is a player who can choose for which team he plays). Shortly after this ruling, the annual league winter meetings (at which free agents negotiate contracts with teams) were held. At those meetings, free agent salaries rocketed upward in comparison with previous years. Is this pattern of behavior what we would expect, based on economic theory? Does the fact that players' salaries generally are well known help or hurt the team owners' attempts to collude to hold down salaries?

15.11* Bill and Hillary run competing golf schools. The daily demand for lessons at Bill's golf school is given by $D_B(p_B, p_H) = 100 - 2p_B + p_H$, where p_B is the price charged by Bill's school for a lesson, and p_H is the price charged by Hillary's school. The daily demand curve faced by Hillary's golf school is given by $D_H(p_B, p_H) = 100 - 2p_H + p_B$. Each school can serve customers at a constant cost of \$10 per lesson.

Find the Bertrand-Nash equilibrium when the two golf schools have to set their rates once and then stick with them forever.

*This problem requires the use of calculus.

CHAPTER

16

Game Theory

> *When the One Great Scorer comes to write against your name—*
> *He marks—not that you won or lost—but how you played the game.*
>
> —Grantland Rice

Brazil and Italy had played through two overtimes to a 0-to-0 tie in the final game of the 1994 World Cup. For the first time, the world championship of soccer ("football" to everyone in the world except Americans) was being decided by a penalty kick shoot-out. One by one, each team sent five players to take shots at the goal from a few yards in front of the net. The score was Brazil 3 and Italy 2 as Baggio, the European player of the year, stepped up to take the fifth, and possibly final, kick for Italy. Taffarel, Brazil's goalie, knew that once the ball left Baggio's foot, it would be too late to react. He had to make up his mind to throw his body one way or the other just as Baggio kicked the ball. Which way should Taffarel go? It all depended on what he thought Baggio was going to do. Which way should Baggio kick the ball? It all depended on what he thought Taffarel was going to do.

The situation just described is a "game" in two senses of the word. One, it is a sport. Two, it is a strategic situation: Each decision maker has to take into account what he or she thinks the other is going to do. Economists call any strategic situation—including, for example, oligopoly—a **game**. The notion of Nash equilibrium that we used in Chapter 15 to analyze oligopoly is part of a larger set of tools for analyzing strategic behavior—in economics, politics, card games, and other arenas of conflict—known as **noncooperative game theory**. This theory is labeled "noncooperative" because each decision maker acts solely in his or her own self-interest. Despite the label, the theory is relevant to the analysis of cooperation. Even "selfish" economic agents will cooperate if doing so is in their self-interest. For example, a self-enforcing agreement among firms to cooperate in restricting industry output is noncooperative in the technical sense of the word—each firm adheres to the agreement solely because it is in the firm's self-interest to do so.

game
A situation in which strategic behavior is an important part of decision making.

noncooperative game theory
A set of tools for analyzing decision making in situations where strategic behavior is important.

In this chapter, we develop a useful way to represent strategic situations graphically, and we use this representation to analyze oligopoly further. In particular, we use game theory to investigate the behavior of oligopoly when there is a threat of entry. We will also see how game theory provides important insights into behavior in a variety of other strategic situations.

16.1 SOME FUNDAMENTALS OF GAME THEORY

players
The decision makers in a game.

strategy
A player's plan of action in a game.

actions
The particular things that are done according to a player's strategy for a game.

payoffs
The rewards enjoyed by a player at the end of a game.

In any game there are decision makers; they are called **players**. In blackjack, the players are the dealer and the bettors. In oligopoly, the players are the firms in the industry. The choices that a player makes are called a **strategy**, and the particular things done according to a strategy are called **actions**. A blackjack player's strategy must indicate whether to stand or take another card when he or she already has 16 points. The action taken is then either "stand" or "take a card." An oligopolist's strategy may specify how it will respond to cheating by another firm. The action taken in a given period might then consist of setting a particular price. At the end of the game, players get **payoffs**, depending on what has happened. The bettors have winnings or losses; the oligopolists, profits. Of course, the game must be played according to some set of rules. In blackjack, the rules are explicitly spelled out. The rules in an oligopoly game are somewhat more difficult to discern, and we will have more to say about them below.

GAME TREES: DECISION TREES FOR STRATEGIC SITUATIONS

game tree
An extension of a decision tree that provides a graphical representation of a strategic situation.

We need a convenient way to represent the rules of the game, such as who moves when and what each player knows when it is his or her turn to move. If we simply were to list the rules, they might be very complicated, and it could be difficult to find an equilibrium. In Chapter 6, we saw how a decision tree could be used to break down a problem and simplify finding a solution. Here, we will develop a very similar tool known as a **game tree**. The main difference between a game tree and a decision tree is that several different players make moves in a game tree, but only one player makes moves in a decision tree.

To illustrate the use of a game tree, let's again consider the situation of Air Lion and Beta Airlines. In the last chapter, we assumed that Air Lion and Beta made their decisions in any given period simultaneously. Here, however, we initially assume that Air Lion chooses its output level first, and then Beta responds. To keep things simple, assume that each firm has only two possible output levels: "high" and "low." Air Lion's decision is depicted in Figure 16.1. A little square called a *decision node* is used to represent a point at which a decision has to be made. Because there are two players, we have to provide a label that indicates whose decision node it is. If it were simply a decision tree for Air Lion, we would put payoffs at the end of each of the two branches. But the situation we are modeling is a game, and we need to take Beta's actions into account before we can calculate Air Lion's payoffs.

Beta has the same possible actions, "high" and "low," as Air Lion. But there is an important difference between the two firms. Before choosing its output level, Beta gets to see what choice Air Lion has made. As a result, Beta has two different decision nodes in Figure 16.2, one for the contingency that Air Lion chooses "high" and one for the contingency that Air Lion chooses "low."

The payoffs for each possible outcome (combination of actions) are represented at the end of each final branch. Since there are two players, we have to list two payoffs at the end of each branch, one for each player. The first number in

Figure 16.1

Air Lion's Decision

When Air Lion makes its output choice first and has only two possible output levels, "high" and "low," Air Lion's choice problem is represented by a single decision node with two branches.

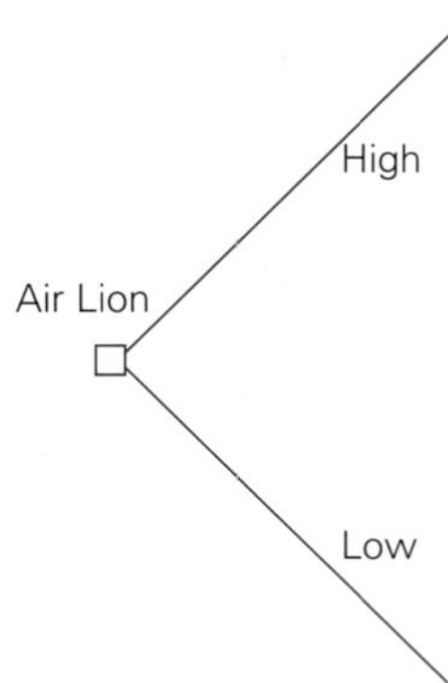

each pair is Air Lion's payoff for that outcome; the second is Beta's. For example, if Air Lion's output is "high" and Beta's output is "low," then Air Lion earns a profit of $6,000 and Beta earns $1,000.

Although we have looked at the *actions* that the two firms can take, we have not yet looked at their *strategies.* A firm's strategy specifies the actions the firm will take in any situation that it might face in the game. In other words, a strategy specifies what action the firm will take at each of its decision nodes. Air Lion chooses its output level first and has only one decision node. For Air Lion, the strategy is simply: *Produce "high" or produce "low."* (We will use italics to distinguish strategies from actions.) Beta's strategy is more complicated than Air Lion's. As we just saw, Beta has two decision nodes in the game tree because Beta gets to see what choice Air Lion has made before making its own choice. Beta's strategy has to specify what the firm will do at each of its decision nodes. Rather than choosing a simple action ("high" or "low"), Beta chooses a **decision rule** that specifies what action it will take conditional on what Air Lion has done. That is, it specifies which action is to be taken at each of Beta's two decision nodes. One possible strategy for Beta is the following: *If Air Lion produces "high," then I will produce "low," and if Air Lion produces "low," then I will produce "high."* (PC 16.1)

decision rule
A strategy that specifies what action will be taken conditional on what happens earlier in the game.

16.1 PROGRESS CHECK

There are three other decision rules that Beta could choose if it wanted to do so. Identify these three strategies.

DOMINANT STRATEGY EQUILIBRIUM

Now that we have a way to represent the rules of the game and its outcome, we can find the equilibrium. What would we expect Air Lion and Beta to do in the game illustrated by Figure 16.2? Consider Beta's strategy first. Suppose that Air Lion has chosen "low." Then Beta would earn $6,000 by choosing "high" and $3,000 by choosing "low." Thus, conditional on Air Lion's choosing "low," Beta's payoff is maximized by choosing "high." If Air Lion had chosen "high," then Beta would choose "high" for a payoff of $4,000 rather than "low" for a payoff of $1,000. Hence, no matter what Air Lion's strategy is, one best strategic response for Beta is to *produce "high" no matter what Air Lion does.* A strategy that works at least as well as any other one, no matter what the other player does, is known as a **dominant strategy**. There is no reason for players to use anything other than their dominant strategy, *if* they have one (this is a big "if," because in

dominant strategy
A strategy that works at least as well as any other one, no matter what any other player does.

Figure 16.2

A Game in Which Both Firms Have Dominant Strategies

When Beta gets to see what choice Air Lion has made, Beta has two different decision nodes, one for the contingency that Air Lion chooses "high," and one for the contingency that Air Lion chooses "low." Since Air Lion's strategy (*produce "high"*) and Beta's strategy (*produce "high" no matter what Air Lion does*) are dominant strategies, there is a dominant strategy equilibrium in which the two firms play these strategies.

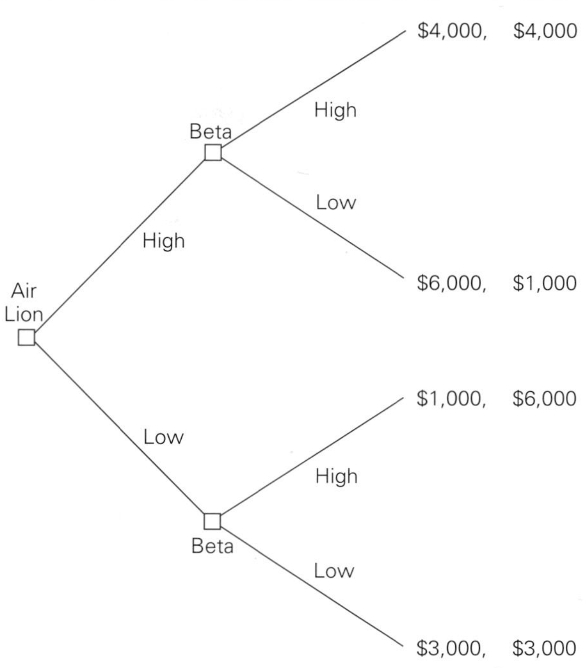

many situations there is no dominant strategy). Hence, in equilibrium, we would expect Beta to choose the strategy *produce "high" no matter what Air Lion does.*

What about Air Lion's strategy? If Air Lion chooses "low," its payoff is $3,000 if Beta responds by producing "low," or $1,000 if Beta responds by producing "high." Similarly, if Air Lion chooses "high," then its payoff is either $6,000 or $4,000, depending on how Beta responds. Notice that Air Lion does better by choosing "high," no matter how Beta responds. Hence, *produce "high"* is a dominant strategy for Air Lion to follow, and this is what we would expect Air Lion to do in equilibrium.

In this situation, each firm has a dominant strategy and would have to be crazy to play anything else. We conclude that *when each player has a dominant strategy, the only reasonable equilibrium outcome is for each player to use its dominant strategy.* The set of dominant strategies and the resulting outcome are known as a **dominant strategy equilibrium**. In the game played by our two airlines, the pair of strategies *produce "high"* for Air Lion and *produce "high" no matter what Air Lion does* for Beta constitute a dominant strategy equilibrium.

dominant strategy equilibrium
An outcome in a game in which each player follows a dominant strategy.

At this point, you may be wondering how this notion of equilibrium corresponds to that used in Chapter 15. There, we required an equilibrium to satisfy two conditions: the Nash condition and the credibility condition. Recall that the Nash condition requires that no firm be able to gain by *unilaterally* changing what it is doing—each firm must play a best response to what the other firm is doing. In the language of game theory, each player's equilibrium strategy must be a best response to the equilibrium strategy chosen by the other player. Since a dominant strategy is a best response to anything, a dominant strategy equilibrium clearly satisfies the Nash condition.

What about the credibility condition? It requires that each time a firm is called upon to make a move (i.e., at each of the firm's decision nodes), it is in the firm's self-interest to carry out the action called for by its strategy. This property clearly is satisfied by Air Lion's strategy; since there is only one part to Air Lion's strategy, the Nash condition alone guarantees that Air Lion would want to carry out that strategy. The credibility condition is more complicated for Beta, because its strategy has two parts that must be checked. First, the credibility condition is satisfied by Beta's decision to produce "high" in response to a high output level by Air Lion. Since this is the action the firm actually takes in equilibrium, it too is taken care of by the Nash condition. The real issue is whether Beta's *threatened* response of high output to low output by Air Lion is credible. Looking at the game tree in Figure 16.2, we see that it is; if Air Lion chose "low," then Beta would earn \$6,000 by producing "high" and only \$3,000 by producing "low." It is no coincidence that Beta's strategy is credible. Since Beta is playing a dominant strategy, we know that no matter what Air Lion does, Beta's equilibrium strategy does at least as well as any other. It would be in Beta's self-interest to carry out any part of its strategy if called upon to do so. In summary, the dominant strategy equilibrium that we found satisfies both the Nash condition and the credibility condition.

PERFECT EQUILIBRIUM

The oligopoly game just examined in Figure 16.2 works out simply because there is a dominant strategy equilibrium. Unfortunately, in most games there is no dominant strategy equilibrium. Figure 16.3 illustrates one such game. In this new game, *if Air Lion produces "high," I will produce "low," and if Air Lion produces "low," I will produce "high"* is a dominant strategy for Beta. Air Lion, however, does not have a dominant strategy. Suppose Beta's strategy is *if Air Lion produces "high," I will produce "low," and if Air Lion produces "low," I will produce "high."* Given Beta's strategy, Air Lion would earn \$6,000 by producing "high" and \$2,000 by producing "low." Air Lion's best response is *produce "high."* But now suppose that Beta's strategy is to *produce "high" no matter what Air Lion does.* In this case, Air Lion would earn \$1,000 by producing "high" and \$2,000 by producing "low." Air Lion's best response is *produce "low."* Air Lion's best response depends on the strategy chosen by Beta.

The problem faced by Air Lion's managers is that they have to make their decision first. What should they expect Beta to do? We just argued that the most reasonable expectation is that a firm will play a dominant strategy if it has one. Although Air Lion does not have a dominant strategy, Beta does: *If Air Lion produces "high," I will produce "low," and if Air Lion produces "low," I will produce "high."* Game theory is based on the assumption that each player believes that the other players are rational. Hence, Air Lion should expect Beta to play its dominant strategy because Beta would have to be irrational to play anything else. Since Air Lion expects Beta to play the strategy *if Air Lion produces "high," I will produce "low," and if Air Lion produces "low," I will produce "high,"* Air Lion chooses the strategy *produce "high."*

Let's step back for a moment and consider how we have found the equilibrium for this game. We noted that Air Lion Airlines has to form a prediction about what Beta is going to do. We concluded that the only rational thing to expect is that Beta will respond to Air Lion's move by taking the action that maximizes Beta's profit, *taking as given what Air Lion has done.* In terms of the

Figure 16.3

A Game in Which Only Beta Has a Dominant Strategy

Two outcomes can arise when the firms use strategies satisfying the Nash condition. In one, Air Lion plays *produce "high"* and Beta plays *if Air Lion produces "high," I will produce "low," and if Air Lion produces "low," I will produce "high."* In the other, Air Lion chooses *produce "low"* and Beta chooses *produce "high" no matter what Air Lion does*. The first pair of strategies also satisfies the credibility condition. The second does not—Beta's threat to produce "high" in response to "high" is not credible. Hence, only the first pair of strategies constitutes a perfect equilibrium for this game.

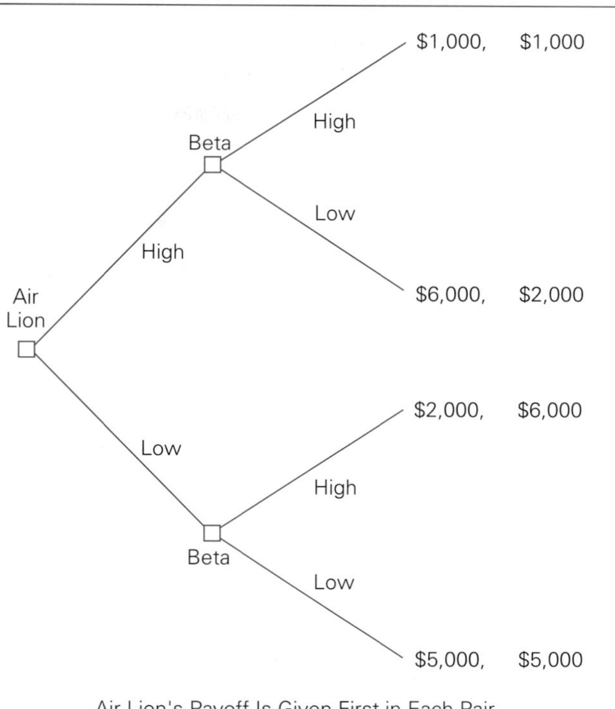

game tree, the procedure is the following one: Find the last decision that a player makes before receiving the payoffs. For each of these decision nodes, find the action that maximizes that decision maker's profit. Construct a strategy by saying that the firm chooses its profit-maximizing action at each of its decision nodes. Now, use the resulting strategy to calculate what the player moving earlier should do. Because we start at the end of the tree rather than at the beginning, this process is known as *backward induction*. You may recall that this is the same procedure used back in Chapter 6 (page 190) to solve decision problems that entailed sequential choices.

If you think about this procedure, you will recognize that it implicitly forces Air Lion to ignore any incredible threats or promises by Beta; when it is Beta's turn to move, the airline is going to do what is in its self-interest at that time. Indeed, this example shows why we need the credibility condition in addition to the Nash condition. If all we did was apply the Nash condition, there would be two candidates for the equilibrium outcome. One outcome is where Air Lion's output is high and Beta's is low. This outcome arises when Air Lion's strategy is *produce "high"* and Beta's strategy is *if Air Lion produces "high," I will produce "low," and if Air Lion produces "low," I will produce "high."*[1] The other outcome is where Air Lion's output is low and Beta's is high. This outcome arises when Air Lion's strategy is *produce "low,"* and Beta's strategy is *produce "high" no matter what Air Lion does.*

[1]This outcome also arises when Air Lion's strategy is *produce "high"* and Beta's strategy is *produce "low" no matter what.* Since these strategies gives rise to exactly the same outcome as the strategies in the text, they will not be discussed further.

The story behind the second candidate for equilibrium is unconvincing. Air Lion chooses a low level of output to keep Beta from later hurting *both* firms by playing "high" in response to "high." It does not seem sensible for Air Lion to take Beta's threat seriously. Recall that our notion of credibility is the following: A threat is credible only if it would be in the firm's self-interest to carry the threat out. Interpreted within the context of a game, this condition requires that, whenever it is a particular player's turn to move, the action called for by that player's equilibrium strategy must be one that is in the player's self-interest to take *at the time that the move is made.* Beta has threatened to choose "high" if Air Lion chooses "high." But suppose that Air Lion called Beta's bluff by choosing "high." What should Air Lion predict that Beta would do in response? If Air Lion has chosen "high," the threat has not worked. *At the time that Beta makes its move,* its self-interest dictates that it choose "low" rather than the threatened "high." Hence, Beta's threat to produce "high" is not credible. Knowing this, Air Lion should expect Beta to choose "low" in response to Air Lion's choice of "high." Air Lion should therefore choose "high" because this will lead to Beta's choosing "low" and Air Lion's earning \$6,000 rather than \$2,000. As in our earlier discussion of cooperation and punishment in Chapter 15, incredible threats should be ignored, and we can reject this equilibrium as unreasonable.

We conclude that the equilibrium outcome is for Air Lion to produce the high output level and earn a profit of \$6,000, while Beta produces a low output level and earns \$2,000. As we have seen, *produce "high"* is Air Lion's best response to Beta's dominant strategy. And, by definition, Beta's dominant strategy is a best response to Air Lion's strategy. We have shown that this pair of strategies satisfies both (1) the Nash condition, and (2) the credibility condition. An equilibrium outcome that satisfies these two conditions is known as a **perfect equilibrium**.[2]

perfect equilibrium
A set of strategies that satisfies both the Nash condition and the credibility condition.

SECTION RECAP

Game theory provides an important set of tools for analyzing strategic situations. Game trees are a graphical means of representing the rules of the game, such as the set of choices open to each player and when each player is able to take actions. The notion of perfect equilibrium embodies both the Nash best-response condition and the credibility condition that we established were desirable properties of equilibria when we examined oligopoly in the previous chapter. Perfect equilibrium extends these concepts to a wide variety of other strategic situations.

16.2 APPLYING GAME THEORY: OLIGOPOLY WITH ENTRY

In many oligopolistic markets, the incumbent firms face the threat of entry. When it started making plain-paper copiers, Xerox was alone in the industry. Today, Canon, Mita, Sharp, and others are active participants in this market. In 1965, four domestic automobile producers dominated the American automobile market. As everyone knows, since then there has been dramatic entry by a variety of foreign firms. In this section, we apply the tools of game theory to analyze oligopoly when entry is possible.

[2]A perfect equilibrium is also sometimes called a *subgame perfect equilibrium.* Notice that any dominant strategy equilibrium is a perfect equilibrium, but (as this example shows), a perfect equilibrium may not be a dominant strategy equilibrium.

We analyze the case of a single incumbent producer who faces the threat o. entry by a single potential entrant. Suppose that the incumbent firm, Jersey Pharmaceutical, is the sole producer of a drug on which the patent has just expired. General Generic is considering whether to enter this market now that anyone is free to manufacture and sell the drug. It might seem like we are back to looking at a simple monopolized industry since there initially is only one firm in the market. But the situation is, in reality, much closer to oligopoly without entry than it is to monopoly without entry. The similarity between this case and oligopoly without entry arises because both are instances in which strategic behavior is important. A monopolist who does not face the threat of entry is not engaged in a strategic situation. A single incumbent facing a potential entrant is.

In deciding whether to come into the market, General Generic has to form beliefs about the post-entry equilibrium. As a manager at General, you would have to ask: "What will happen after we come into the market?" If the expected post-entry equilibrium would yield positive economic profit, then General Generic should enter the market. If not, the firm should stay out. Now, if the market under consideration were a perfectly competitive one, you could figure out General's potential profit simply by taking the market price of output as given. You could do this because, as an entrant into a perfectly competitive industry, General Generic would be so small relative to the rest of the market that the entry would make essentially no difference to the market equilibrium. The equilibrium price before entry would thus be a good predictor of the price after entry. Things are not so simple for a firm such as General Generic that is considering entry into an industry with only one or a few incumbents. The entrant must form more sophisticated expectations of how the incumbent or incumbents will react to the entrant's coming into the market.

For its part, an incumbent would like to scare off the entrant by threatening an unpleasant welcome to the industry. The incumbent could threaten to shoot the kneecaps of the entrant's managers or to blow up their offices. While firms have, at times, been accused of using such tactics, the typical threats used by incumbents are considerably less harsh. For example, Jersey Pharmaceutical might threaten to produce a large amount of the drug and drive down the market price. As usual, we must ask whether this threat is credible. Will the entrant be scared off or will General Generic call the incumbent's bluff by coming in? If the threat is found to be incredible, is there some way for the incumbent to make its threat credible? The tools of game theory can help us answer these questions.

Figure 16.4 illustrates the game tree representing the entrant's decision whether to come in and the incumbent's output response. As the tree shows, General Generic moves first, and Jersey Pharmaceutical makes its output decision after seeing whether General Generic has decided to enter. The strategy for the potential entrant is either to *"enter"* or *"stay out."* Since it makes its decision second, the incumbent's strategy specifies what it will do contingent on the action taken by the potential entrant. The following is an example of a strategy available to the management of Jersey Pharmaceutical: *if General Generic chooses "enter," then we will choose "high output," and if General Generic chooses "stay out," then we will choose "low output."*

There are two pairs of strategies that satisfy the Nash condition for this game. In one, General Generic plays the strategy *"keep out"* and Jersey Pharmaceutical plays *produce "high output" no matter what General Generic does.* To verify that this is a Nash equilibrium, we need to check that each firm is choosing a best response to what the other firm is doing. Could either firm increase its profit by

Figure 16.4

An Entry Game

Two outcomes in this game satisfy the Nash condition. In one General Generic plays the strategy *"stay out"* and Jersey Pharmaceutical plays *produce "high output" no matter what General Generic does*. In the other, General Generic plays *"enter"* and Jersey Pharmaceutical plays *if General Generic chooses "enter," then we will choose "low output," and if General Generic chooses "stay out," then we will choose "high output."* Only the second outcome satisfies our credibility condition. The threat to produce "high output" in response to "enter" in the first Nash outcome is not credible.

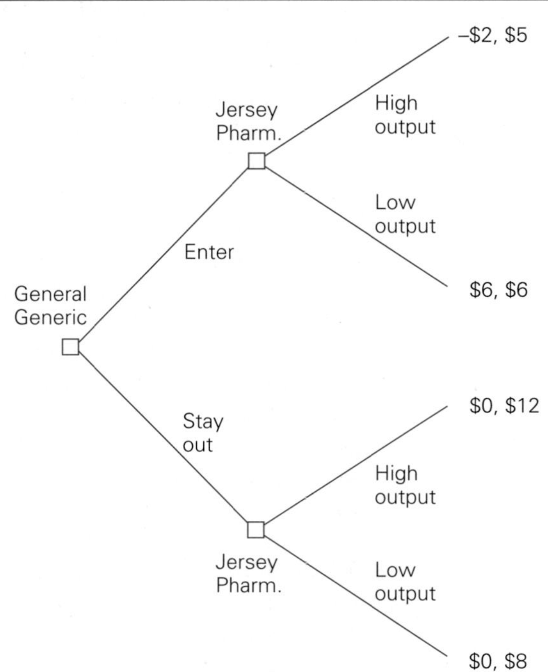

General Generic's Payoff Is Given First in Each Pair (all figures in millions)

changing its strategy while the other firm's strategy remains the same? In the outcome being considered, General Generic earns a payoff of $0, while Jersey Pharmaceutical earns $12 million. If General Generic were to enter, then its profit would be −$2 million since Jersey's strategy entails producing a high output level in response to entry. Hence, General Generic has no incentive to change its strategy. What about Jersey Pharmaceutical? Given that the potential entrant is staying out of the market, the incumbent's profit is maximized by producing "high output" rather than "low output" ($12 million is more than $8 million). Jersey Pharmaceutical has no incentive to change its strategy. Since each firm is choosing a best response to the strategy of the other, this pair of strategies satisfies the Nash condition.

In the other outcome, General Generic chooses *"enter"* and Jersey Pharmaceutical plays the strategy *if General Generic chooses "enter," we will choose "low output," and if General chooses "stay out," we will choose "high output."*[3] When the two firms play these strategies, General Generic and Jersey Pharmaceutical each earn a profit of $6 million. (PC 16.2)

16.2 PROGRESS CHECK

Verify that this second pair of strategies also satisfies the Nash condition that each strategy be a best response to the other.

Clearly, Jersey Pharmaceutical prefers the outcome under which General Generic stays out of the market while General Generic pre-

[3]The strategies *"enter"* and *choose "low" no matter what the entrant does* also satisfy the Nash condition. These strategies give rise to exactly the same outcome (the potential entrant comes in and the incumbent chooses the low level of output) as do the strategies in the text and so will not be discussed further.

fers the outcome under which it comes into the market. Is there some way to choose between the two outcomes? There is; only the second one, in which entry occurs, satisfies our credibility condition. In the first outcome, the potential entrant chooses to stay out because the incumbent has threatened to choose the high level of output in response to entry. But suppose that General Generic tested this threat by entering. Once General has actually entered the market, it is not in Jersey's self-interest to carry out the threat—Jersey can earn $6 million by producing the low output level, but only $5 million by producing the high output level. Therefore, the threat to produce a high level of output if entry occurs is not credible. Knowing that this threat will not be carried out, General will expect to earn $6 million by entering and will choose to do so. The only perfect equilibrium (that is, the only strategy pair that satisfies both our Nash condition and our credibility condition) is for General Generic to choose *"enter"* and Jersey Pharmaceutical to choose *if General Generic chooses "enter," we will choose "low output," and if General Generic chooses "stay out," we will choose "high output."* In the unique perfect equilibrium, General Generic enters the market and Jersey Pharmaceutical produces the low output level.

Note the irony in this situation. When an incumbent has the ability to collude with the entrant in setting post-entry output levels, that ability may make the incumbent worse off. The reason is that the potential entrant will take the possibility (and profitability) of collusion into account when deciding whether to come into the market. Knowing that the post-entry equilibrium will be a collusive one makes entry attractive. Even under the fully collusive duopoly outcome, however, the incumbent earns less than it would if it had retained its monopoly position.

CREDIBLE THREATS AND COMMITMENT

In the example above, the incumbent would like to scare off the entrant by threatening to produce "high output" in response to a choice of "enter." This threat is not credible, however, and we would expect the entrant to come into the market. This is an example of a phenomenon that was present in our earlier discussions of cartels and oligopolistic behavior: In many instances, one firm would like to threaten another, but incredible threats will be ignored. In this section, we will see how a firm can take actions to make otherwise incredible threats credible. Taking such actions is known as engaging in commitment. **Commitment** is the process whereby a firm irreversibly alters its payoffs in advance so that it will be in the firm's self-interest to carry out the threatened (or promised) action when the time comes. In this example, the incumbent would like to commit itself to responding to entry by producing "high output."

commitment
The process whereby a player irreversibly alters its payoffs in advance so that it will be in the player's self-interest to carry out a threatened (or promised) action when the time comes.

What sort of actions could Jersey Pharmaceutical take to make this threat credible? One possibility is for the incumbent to incur sunk expenditures to construct a large plant with low marginal costs, so that producing the high level of output is the profit-maximizing response to entry. Suppose with the large plant, the payoffs look like those in Figure 16.5. Once this plant has been constructed, the incumbent's threat to produce "high output" in response to "enter" is credible. If entry occurs, it is in Jersey Pharmaceutical's self-interest to choose "high output," which yields a payoff of $4 million, instead of choosing "low output," which results in a profit of only $3 million. Thus, in the unique perfect equilibrium, the potential entrant decides to "stay out" and the incumbent chooses "high output." The equilibrium strategies are *"stay out"* for General Generic

Figure 16.5

An Entry Game in Which the Incumbent Has a Large Plant

Once the large plant has been constructed, the incumbent's threat to produce "high output" in response to "enter" is credible—it yields Jersey Pharmaceutical $4 million, while "low output" yields $3 million. The equilibrium strategies are *"stay out"* for General Generic and *produce "high output" no matter what General Generic does* for Jersey Pharmaceutical.

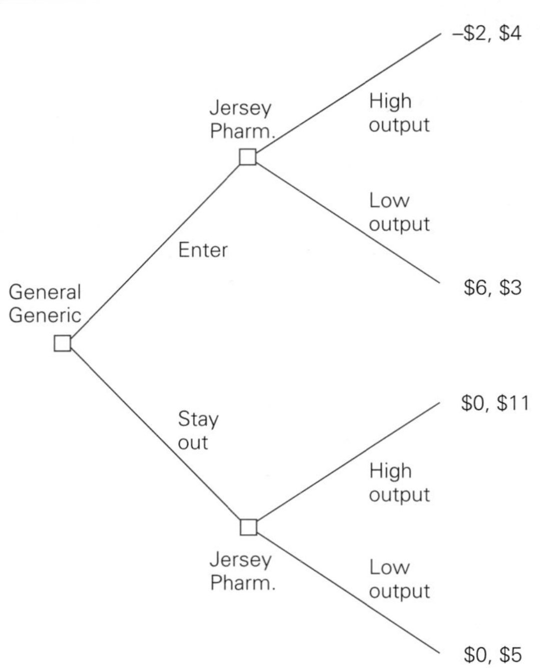

and *produce "high output" no matter what General Generic does* for Jersey Pharmaceutical.

We have seen what would happen if the incumbent had a small plant (Figure 16.4) and what would happen if it had a large plant (Figure 16.5). Now suppose that, before entry can occur, the incumbent gets to choose which size plant to construct. Figure 16.6 illustrates the resulting game tree. The figure is formed by joining the trees from the two figures for the small and large plants. How should Jersey Pharmaceutical expect General Generic to react to Jersey's plant choice? And when General Generic chooses whether to enter the market, what reaction should it expect from Jersey Pharmaceutical? We can answer these questions by extending our earlier procedure for finding a perfect equilibrium—we work backwards through the tree.

We start by finding the last decisions in the game. Fortunately, we have already done most of the work. From our analysis of the two games in which the plant size was fixed, we know that General Generic will "enter" and Jersey Pharmaceutical will produce "low output" if the incumbent constructs the small plant. We also know that General Generic will "stay out" and Jersey Pharmaceutical will produce "high output" if the incumbent constructs the large plant. Because it earns $11 million from choosing "large plant" and only $6 million from choosing "small plant," Jersey Pharmaceutical chooses "large plant." In equilibrium, Jersey Pharmaceutical chooses "large plant," General Generic chooses "stay out," and Jersey produces "high output."

Note that, *given that entry does not occur*, the incumbent would rather have the smaller plant. The $12 million payoff at the end of the branch (small plant, stay out, and high output) in Figure 16.6 is larger than the $11 million payoff at

Figure 16.6

Commitment in an Entry Game

When the incumbent can choose its plant size, Jersey Pharmaceutical can use a large plant as a form of commitment to deter entry. In equilibrium, Jersey Pharmaceutical constructs the "large plant," General Generic chooses "stay out," and Jersey produces "high output."

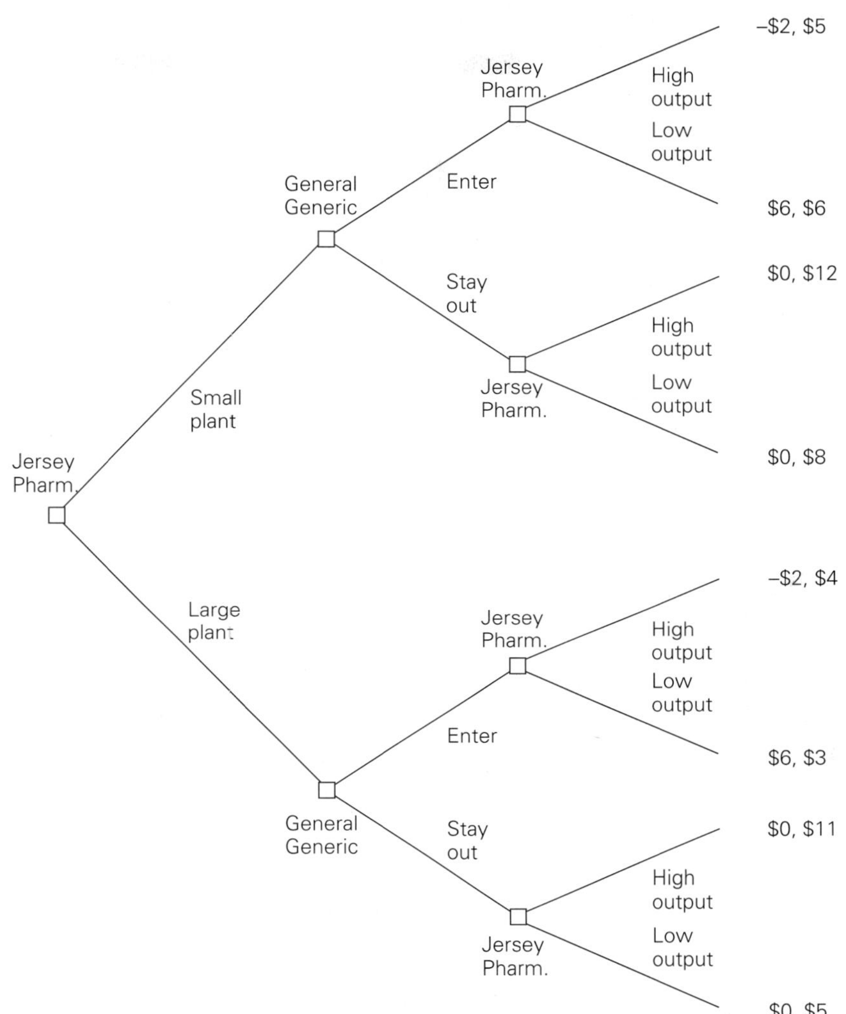

the end of the branch (large plant, stay out, and high output). The incumbent is not being irrational, however—the plant had to be built to keep the potential entrant out. The incumbent does better with the large plant and no entry than it would do with the small plant and entry ($11 million is greater than $6 million). The extra cost associated with the large plant can be thought of as an investment in entry deterrence.

Building a large plant is not the only way for the incumbent to deter entry by committing itself to an aggressive response. The incumbent might instead invest in cost-reducing research and development (R&D), and in that way make producing the high output level a rational response to entry. Or the firm might sign contracts with existing customers that legally bind the firm to match any future offer made by an entrant, thus committing the incumbent to fight any attempt by an entrant to take customers away.

MORE ON STRATEGIC INVESTMENT IN OLIGOPOLY

We have discussed the use of a strategic investment as a form of commitment in the context of a single incumbent facing the threat of entry. Strategic investment effects are present in markets where there are multiple incumbents as well, even if no additional entry is anticipated. When a firm engages in cost-reducing R&D, the firm will enjoy lower production costs in the future. A fall in production costs will increase profit for several reasons. First, the firm will have lower costs for any given level of production. Thus, at its old output level, the firm's profits would rise. Second, the firm may adjust its output level to reflect its new cost structure. When marginal costs fall as a result of R&D, the firm will expand its output until it is at the point where the marginal revenue curve crosses the new, lower marginal cost curve. Because, over the range of expansion, marginal revenue is greater than marginal cost, profit increases as the firm expands. These first two effects arise whether the firm is a perfect competitor, a monopolist, or an oligopolist.

When the firm is an oligopolist in a strategic market situation, the reduction in marginal cost has a third effect. The firm whose marginal costs have fallen has an increased incentive to produce output. The other firms in the industry must take this fact into account when they choose their output levels. Consequently, the other firms may cut back their output levels in the face of a more aggressive (i.e., lower-cost) rival.[4] The reduction in its rivals' output drives up the price that the firm conducting the R&D receives for its output. Thus, the firm counts this "strategic effect" as one of the benefits of R&D. In both an oligopolistic market and a market with a single firm facing the threat of entry, strategic investment can commit a firm to behave more aggressively, which then makes its rivals (the other oligopolists or the potential entrant) retreat. (PC 16.3)

16.3 PROGRESS CHECK

Do strategic investment effects arise under perfect competition? Under monopolistic competition? How about monopoly with blocked entry?

SECTON RECAP

The tools of game theory generate new insights into the theory of oligopoly. In particular, they allow us to understand the interaction between an incumbent firm and a potential entrant. The incumbent would like to threaten the entrant to deter the latter from coming into the market. Such threats may not be credible, however, unless the firm makes visible commitments such as increased capacity.

16.3 GAMES OF IMPERFECT AND INCOMPLETE INFORMATION

Thus far, we have examined game trees in which the firms move one after the other, and each firm can observe all of the earlier actions (if any) taken by its rival. Real life need not be so neat. When it is a firm's turn to choose a price or output level, it may not be able to tell what its rival has done or is doing. One reason that a firm may not know about its rival's move is that the two firms make their choices simultaneously. A second reason is that even though the other firm has already chosen its action, the firm choosing second is unable to observe the first firm's decision before having to make its own choice. A game in which some player must make a move but is unable to observe the earlier or simultaneous move of some other player is said to be a **game of imperfect information**.

game of imperfect information
A game in which some player must make a move but is unable to observe the earlier or simultaneous move of some other player.

[4]This effect arises in Equation (15.8), for example.

The games we considered so far also assumed that each player knew everything there was to know about the other one. In our duopoly game, Air Lion predicted what Beta Airlines would do by thinking about which actions would be in Beta's self-interest. But it could be the case that Air Lion has only an imprecise idea of what Beta's payoffs look like. For instance, Air Lion might be unsure of Beta's cost level. Whenever one or more of the players is unsure about some part of the tree (such as the other player's payoffs), the situation is said to be a **game of incomplete information**.

game of incomplete information
A game in which some player is unsure about some of the underlying characteristics of the game, such as another player's payoffs.

You can think about the difference between these two new types of games as follows. In a game of imperfect information, a player is unsure about an earlier move made by someone else—the player, when it is his or her turn to move, is not sure exactly where he or she is in the tree. In contrast, in a game of incomplete information, the player is not sure exactly what the tree looks like. In this section, we will see how to extend game theory to deal with games of imperfect information and with games of incomplete information. In doing so, we will greatly increase the set of real world situations into which game theory can provide valuable insights.

THE PRISONERS' DILEMMA: A GAME OF IMPERFECT INFORMATION

Consider this: Two investment bankers, Mike and Ivan, decide to make a couple of hundred million dollars with an inside trading scheme and a few other stock swindles. Thereafter, they are caught by the police and put in separate interrogation rooms. The district attorney has enough evidence to convict both Mike and Ivan for a lesser charge, but she wants to convict them of a more serious charge, for which she needs additional evidence. The district attorney goes to Ivan and offers him a plea bargain—a reduced prison term in return for testifying against Mike (which will increase his prison term). *Simultaneously*, the district attorney's assistant goes to Mike and offers the same deal if he will turn in Ivan. Each inside trader must choose between "confess" and "keep quiet." Figure 16.7 illustrates the tree for this game of imperfect information. The dashed oval around the two decision nodes for Ivan is used to represent the fact that Ivan cannot distinguish between these two points at the time he makes his decision. In other words, he cannot see whether Mike has chosen to "confess" or "keep quiet." Since he cannot see what Mike has done, Ivan cannot make his choice contingent on Mike's. Thus, Ivan must choose between the strategies, *"keep quiet"* and *"confess."*

Once we have a way to represent Ivan's lack of information about Mike's action, finding the equilibrium is straightforward. Notice that the payoffs are measured in utils, so a longer prison term means a lower utility level, *ceteris paribus*. For each player (inside trader), *"confess"* is a dominant strategy. The unique equilibrium outcome is for both to confess, even though both bankers are better off when they keep quiet than when they confess. (PC 16.4)

16.4 PROGRESS CHECK

Suppose that instead of sending her assistant, the district attorney goes to see Mike herself, and *afterward* she offers a plea bargain to Ivan. Moreover, suppose that the district attorney refuses to tell Ivan what Mike has done (Ivan would not believe the district attorney anyway). How would the game tree for Ivan and Mike change?

Based on this sort of story, such a situation—in which the two players each have a dominant strategy, but playing these strategies leads to an outcome in which both sides are worse off than if they

Figure 16.7

The Prisoners' Dilemma

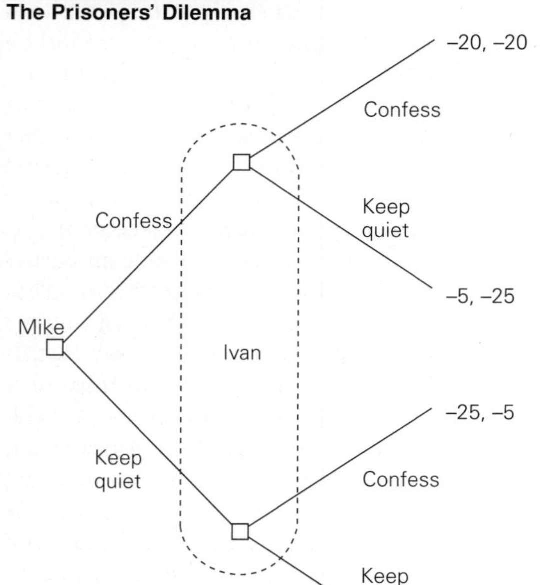

When Mike and Ivan make their decisions simultaneously, the dashed oval around Ivan's two decision nodes represents the fact that Ivan cannot distinguish between these two points at the time he makes his decision. For each inside trader, *"confess"* is a dominant strategy. The unique equilibrium outcome is for both to confess, even though both would be better off if they both kept quiet.

Figure 16.8

The Duopolists' Dilemma

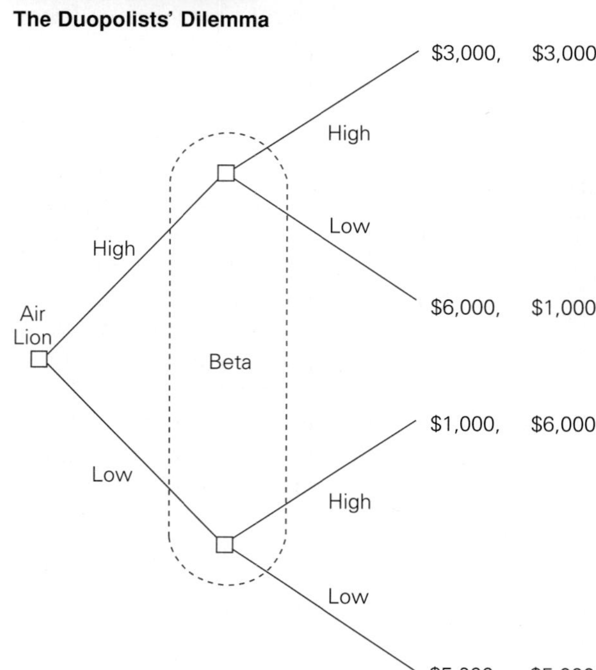

When Air Lion and Beta make their output choices simultaneously, the dashed oval around Beta's two decision nodes represents the fact that Beta cannot distinguish between these two points at the time that it makes its decision. Since *produce "high"* is the dominant strategy for each firm, the unique equilibrium in this game is for Air Lion and Beta each to choose *produce "high."*

prisoners' dilemma
A strategic situation in which the two players each have a dominant strategy, but playing this pair of strategies leads to an outcome in which both sides are worse off than they would be if they cooperated by playing alternative strategies.

collectively chose other strategies—has become known as the **prisoners' dilemma**, even if the players are not literally prisoners. The prisoners' dilemma structure applies to many important situations. Let's go back to our two airlines. Suppose that Air Lion and Beta Airlines have to make their output choices simultaneously. Figure 16.8 illustrates the game tree for this game of *imperfect* information. Again, the dashed oval around the two decision nodes for Beta is used to represent Beta's inability to distinguish between these two points at the time that it makes its decision. That is, when choosing its output level, Beta does not know if Air Lion has chosen "high" or "low." Therefore, Beta *cannot* adopt a strategy such as *produce "low" if Air Lion produces "high" and produce "high" if Air Lion produces "low,"* in which Beta's choice of action is contingent on what Air Lion has chosen. Rather, Beta's strategy is simply either *produce "high"* or *produce "low."*

For each firm, the better strategy, no matter what the other firm does, is to choose the high level of output. In other words, *produce "high"* is a dominant strategy for each firm. In the resulting dominant strategy equilibrium, each firm chooses "high" and earns a profit of $3,000. Notice how the structure of the payoffs in this game gives rise to a tension between the gains from cooperation and the incentives to compete. In equilibrium, each firm produces "high" even though each firm would be better off if both produced "low"—each firm would earn a profit of $5,000 instead of $3,000.

If the firms could sign a binding agreement enforced by a third party, we would expect them to choose the outcome under which each firm chose "low." But the firms cannot rely on the courts to enforce their agreement. Instead, they have to rely on self-enforcing agreements. The problem is that an agreement to produce "low" is not self-enforcing. To see why, suppose the two airlines agreed to have each produce "low." If Beta expected Air Lion to choose "low," Beta would have an incentive to cheat by producing "high"—Beta would earn $6,000 rather than $5,000. But Air Lion would never stick to the agreement to produce "low" in the first place; producing "high" is more profitable. The only self-enforcing agreement leads to both firms' producing "high." This game and the associated equilibrium constitute yet another demonstration that cooperation among self-interested parties may be difficult to achieve; the incentives to cheat may prevent the firms from enjoying the potential gains from cooperation. As you can see, the oligopolists' problem has the same structure as the inside traders' problem. Consequently, oligopolists often are described as facing a prisoners' dilemma.

MIXED STRATEGIES

When we left them, Baggio and Taffarel were trying to figure out which way Baggio was going to kick the ball in the World Cup final. Because the goalie cannot wait to see which way the kick is going, this is a game of imperfect information. Figure 16.9 illustrates a game tree for this situation. The numbers are in utils and are chosen solely to capture the fact that Baggio wants to score and Taffarel wants to stop him.

Now, let's look for an equilibrium. Suppose Baggio kicks to the left. Then the goalie should go left. But if the goalie goes left, then Baggio should kick to the right. So, it cannot be an equilibrium for Baggio to go left. But the same logic says that Baggio cannot go right. Baggio always wants to go the opposite direction of the goalie, but the goalie always wants to go the same direction as Baggio. They cannot both be satisfied at once. We have just shown that when both players' strategies are simply *always go "right"* or *always go "left,"* there is no equilibrium.

Always go "right" and *always go "left"* are each an example of what is known as a **pure strategy**. When you play a pure strategy, you have a definite action that you will take each time it is your time to move. Another possibility is to randomize among the actions you will take at a particular decision node. For instance, Baggio can pursue a strategy of going right 30 percent of the time and left 70 percent of the time. When a player in a game randomizes across actions like this, he is said to be pursuing a **mixed strategy**.

pure strategy
A strategy that specifies a specific action at each decision point.

mixed strategy
A strategy that allows for randomization among actions at some or all decision points.

Although the soccer shoot-out has no equilibrium in pure strategies, there is an equilibrium in which the players choose mixed strategies. Let's find it. Suppose Baggio kicks right 70 percent of the time. Then the goalie should go left all of the time, because that gives him the greatest chance of stopping the ball. But then Baggio should always kick right. So kicking right 70 percent of the time cannot be part of an equilibrium. Indeed, you should convince yourself that any

Figure 16.9

Equilibrium in a Soccer Shoot-Out Entails Mixed Strategies

The goalie always want to go the same way as the kicker, but the kicker always wants to go the opposite direction from the goalie. Hence, there is no equilibrium in pure strategies. There is, however, an equilibrium in mixed strategies: Each player randomly goes "left" half of the time and "right" the other half. Neither player can make himself better off by switching his strategy, given the strategy being played by his opponent.

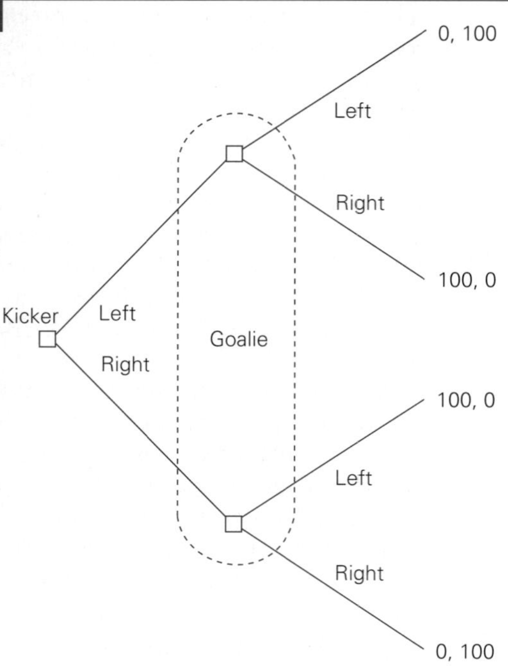

Kicker's Payoff Is Given First in Each Pair (payoffs in utils)

percentage other than 50-50 is subject to the same problem: The goalie should always go the way the ball is kicked more often, but then the kicker should aim the other way.

Now suppose that Baggio kicks right half the time and left the other half. It doesn't matter which way the goalie goes, he will be correct half of the time no matter what. Now, if the goalie tends to go one way more than the other, the kicker will want to go the other direction all of the time. But then we are back to the problem above. Thus, the only candidate equilibrium strategy for the goalie is to *go "right" half of the time and go "left" half of the time.* When this is the goalie's strategy, it doesn't matter which way Baggio chooses to kick.

What we have just shown is this. If one player randomizes 50-50 between "right" and "left," then it is a best response for the other player to randomize 50-50 between "right" and "left." In other words, each player's choosing to randomize equally between right and left is a Nash equilibrium. (PC 16.5)

16.5 PROGRESS CHECK

There actually are three choices: right, left, or middle. Draw a tree for this game when the kicker and the goalie each have three choices. Describe the sets of possible strategies for each player. Explain why the equilibrium must be ⅓ each way.[5]

So what did Baggio do? He miss-hit the ball and kicked it over the goal, giving Brazil its record fourth World Cup. Game theory is good stuff, but you still have to execute.

Mixed strategies are important in many other sports. For instance, in choosing between running and passing in American football, a "balanced attack" is an important part of "keeping the

[5]The choice of three actions led to the following bizarre scene: As one of the players in the shoot-out kicked a booming shot, the goalie dove to the right—just in time to get out of the way and let the ball go into the goal exactly where the goalie had been standing.

defense guessing." The choice of when to serve wide or down the middle is an important part of the tennis strategy. And in business rivalry it often is advantageous to keep your rivals guessing about what you are planning to do.

These examples notwithstanding, mixed strategies strike many people as odd. If the other players all *believe* you are randomizing according to the theory, there is no need for you actually to go to the trouble. From your perspective, any one action you are supposed to randomize over is as good as any other (otherwise you would not be willing to randomize among them). So, why would anyone ever both tossing a coin, rolling a die, or in some other way generate the randomness that game theory calls for?

In the light of this troubling question, how should we think about mixed strategies? It probably makes the most sense to think of them not as actual random strategies, but more as a representation of other players' *beliefs*.[6] The model does not require that you literally toss a coin when choosing whether to serve wide or down the middle in tennis. Rather, you try to avoid falling into a predictable pattern, with the net result that the other player's *beliefs* are the same as they would be if you truly were randomizing. While mixed strategies may seem a bit strange to you, they capture the intuitive notion that it can be to one's strategic advantage to keep rival players unsure about what your future moves will be.

A BARGAINING GAME OF INCOMPLETE INFORMATION

Now, let's consider a game of incomplete information. Suppose there is a single seller bargaining with a single buyer. The seller, Gepetto, can produce one custom cuckoo clock for $1,000. The way the bargaining works is that Gepetto makes a take-it-or-leave-it offer to the buyer. The buyer then "accepts" or "rejects" the offer. If Gepetto knew the buyer's willingness to pay for the clock, he would set his price at that level, as long as it was at least $1,000. But what happens when the seller is unsure about the buyer's willingness to pay? In particular, he knows the buyer values the item at either $1,500 or $2,000, but he is unsure which. Thus, he does not know whether to set the price at $1,499 or $1,999.[7]

At first glance, it is not obvious that a single game tree can be drawn to represent this situation. There is one set of payoffs (and associated game tree) for a low-value buyer and another for a high-value buyer. Gepetto would not know which tree to use. Fortunately, we can model this situation as a single tree if we simply combine two earlier tricks. Figure 16.10 presents a game tree for this situation. As in decision trees, we can use a move by Nature to represent a player's uncertainty about some or all of the parameters of the game. Here, the seller's uncertainty about the buyer's valuation of the good is captured by having Nature make an unobservable move to pick the buyer's valuation. Of course, Gepetto cannot see what move Nature has made. Viewing Nature as a special player, we have a game of imperfect information and we draw a dashed oval around Gepetto's two decision nodes to represent the fact he cannot distinguish between them at the time he makes his decision.

To decide what price to charge, Gepetto has to form a prediction about how the buyer will react to his offer. When he sets the higher price, Gepetto's

[6]You may recall from the last chapter that we interpreted Cournot reaction functions in terms of reacting to beliefs, rather than the actual quantity chosen by the other firm.

[7]By pricing just below the buyer's value, the seller is giving the buyer an incentive to accept the offer. You should convince yourself that it never makes sense to set a price that is greater than $1,500 but less than $1,999.

Figure 16.10

Bargaining under Incomplete Information

The seller's uncertainty about the buyers' valuation of the good is captured by having Nature make an unobservable move to pick the buyer's valuation of the good. Nature chooses "high value" with probability β. Since the seller cannot see the move that Nature has made, we draw a dashed oval around his two decision nodes to represent the fact that he cannot distinguish between them. The expected profits from setting the high price are $\beta \times (\$1{,}999 - \$1{,}000) + (1 - \beta) \times \$0 = \beta \times \$999$. Setting the low price yields profits of \$499. Hence, the seller will set the high price if $\beta \geq 499/999$, and will set the low price otherwise.

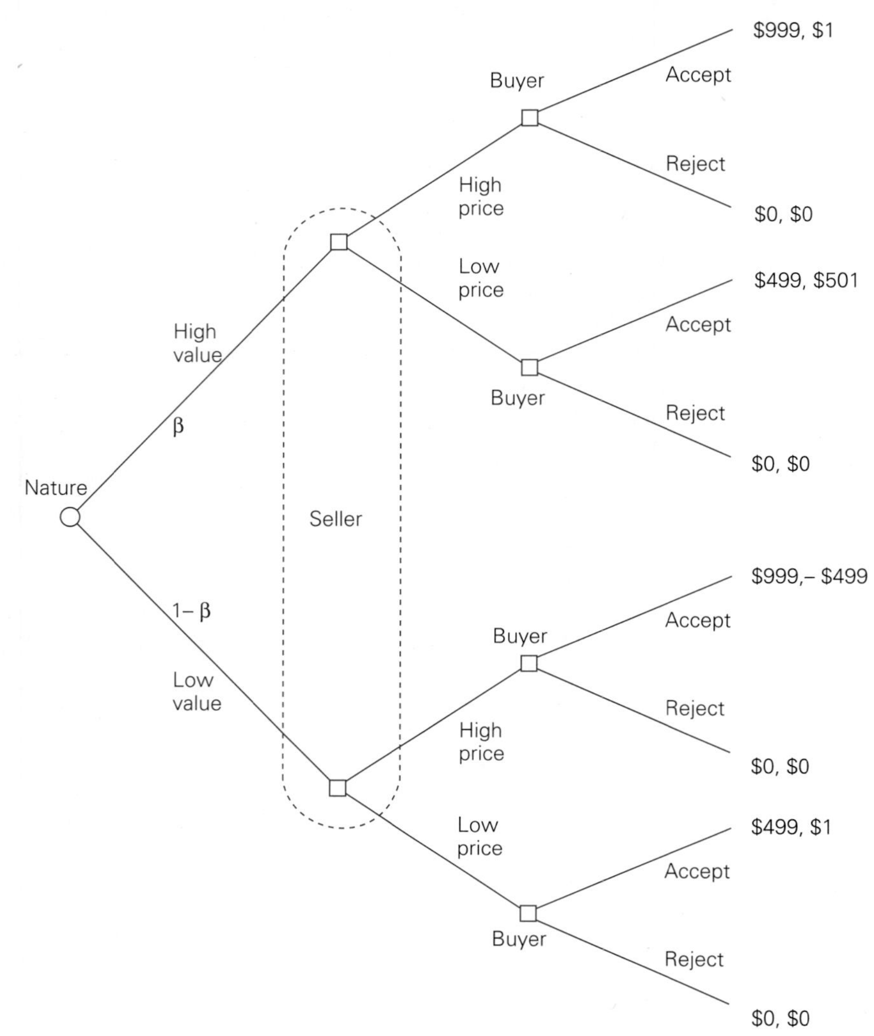

prediction will depend on whether he believes the buyer places a low or high value on the clock. If the buyer places the low value on the item, then the buyer will "reject" an offer of \$1,999. But if the buyer places a high value on the clock, she will "accept." We reach this conclusion by working backward through the tree. Faced with a price of \$1,999, a high-value buyer will act in her self-interest by choosing to "accept." And if the buyer places a low value on the good, she will respond to a price of \$1,999 by choosing "reject." Similar reasoning establishes that both types of buyer will "accept" an offer of \$1,499.

The seller has to decide whether to set a low price and make a sure sale or set a high price and make a sale only if the buyer turns out to place a high value on the clock. Setting the low price yields profits of \$499 = (\$1,499 − \$1,000). To calculate the profitability of setting a high price, the seller has to form beliefs about Nature's move (i.e., about the relative likelihood of the low and high valuations). Let β denote Gepetto's belief about the probability that the buyer has a high value for the clock, and let $(1 - \beta)$ denote his belief about the probability that the buyer places a low value on it. The expected profits from the high price are

$$\beta \times (\$1{,}999 - \$1{,}000) + (1 - \beta) \times \$0 = \beta \times \$999. \qquad (16.1)$$

Hence, Gepetto will set the high price if $\beta \times \$999$ is greater than \$499, and will charge the low price otherwise. In other words, Gepetto sets the high price only if he is sufficiently optimistic that the buyer places a high value on the clock. Specifically, he sets the high price only if he believes $\beta \geq 499/999$.

LIMIT PRICING: A GAME OF INCOMPLETE INFORMATION

Let's consider another game of incomplete information. Once again, suppose that a firm is considering entry into what is at present a monopolized industry. But now suppose that the potential entrant is unsure of whether the incumbent's marginal costs are low or high. The potential entrant is interested in the incumbent's costs because they affect the incumbent's payoffs and thus influence the incumbent's optimal reaction to entry.

Figure 16.11 presents a game tree for this situation. The entrant's uncertainty about the incumbent is captured by having Nature make an unobservable move to pick the incumbent's marginal cost function. Because the potential entrant cannot see what move Nature has made, we have a game of imperfect information and we draw a dashed oval around the potential entrant's two decision nodes to represent the fact that the firm cannot distinguish between them at the time it makes its decision.

You may have noticed that the structure of the tree in Figure 16.11 looks much like that of the tree in Figure 16.6, where the incumbent chose its plant size. The key difference is that here Nature, not the incumbent, is making the initial choice. Unlike the incumbent, Nature does not optimize its strategy. Rather, Nature's strategy simply represents the players' beliefs about the likely state of the world.

To decide whether to come into the market, the entrant has to form a prediction about the post-entry equilibrium. This prediction will depend on whether the entrant believes the incumbent has high or low marginal costs. If the incumbent has low costs and the entrant comes in, then the incumbent will choose "high output" and the entrant will suffer losses of −\$3 million. Again, we reach this conclusion by working backward through the tree—faced with entry, a low-cost incumbent will act in its self-interest by producing "high output." Similarly, if the incumbent has high costs, then it will respond to entry by choosing "low output," and the entrant will earn \$4 million.

To assess the desirability of its entering, the entrant has to form beliefs about the relative likelihood of the high and low cost levels. Let ρ denote the entrant's belief about the probability that the incumbent has high costs, and let $(1 - \rho)$ denote the entrant's belief about the probability that the incumbent has low costs. The expected profits from entry are

$$\rho \times (\$4 \text{ million}) + (1 - \rho) \times (-\$3 \text{ million}) = \$(7\rho - 3) \text{ million} \qquad (16.2)$$

The expected profits from staying out of the market are \$0. Hence, the potential entrant will come into the market if $\rho \geq 3/7$ and will stay out otherwise. Intuitively, the potential entrant will come in if it is sufficiently optimistic that the incumbent has high costs and will be a weak rival.

Figure 16.11

An Entry Game of Incomplete Information

The entrant's uncertainty about the incumbent's payoffs is captured by having Nature make an unobservable move to pick the incumbent's marginal cost level. Nature chooses "high cost" with probability ρ. Since the potential entrant cannot see what move Nature has made, we draw a dashed oval around the potential entrant's two decision nodes. The expected profits from entry are $\rho \times$ (\$4 million) + $(1 - \rho) \times$ (−\$3 million) = \$$(7\rho - 3)$ million. Staying out of the market yields \$0. Hence, the potential entrant comes into the market if $\rho > 3/7$, and stays out otherwise.

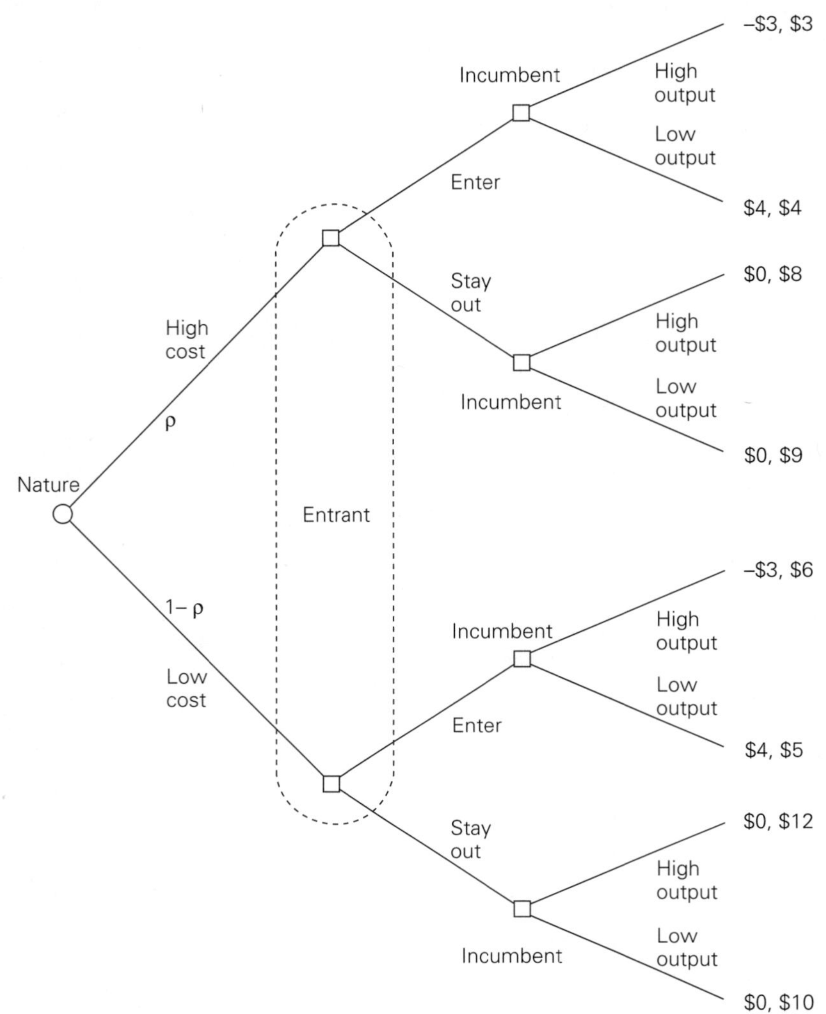

The potential entrant would like to figure out what the incumbent's true costs are. If the potential entrant can observe some action by the incumbent prior to making the entry decision, the potential entrant may be able to draw inferences about the incumbent's underlying costs. Figure 16.12 illustrates an extended version of the game in Figure 16.11. Here, the incumbent chooses output in two periods. The key feature is that, before deciding whether to enter the market, the potential entrant gets to see the incumbent's initial output choice.

Suppose that the entrant ignored the incumbent's first-period output choice. Further, suppose that $\rho = 2/7$. In this case, the potential entrant would stay out. Knowing this fact, a low-cost incumbent would maximize its profit by choosing "high output" in each period, while a high-cost incumbent would choose "low output" in each period. The potential entrant would be foolish to ignore the incumbent's first-period output choice. By looking at the incumbent's initial choice, the potential entrant could infer the incumbent's cost level. If the

Figure 16.12

A Limit Pricing Game

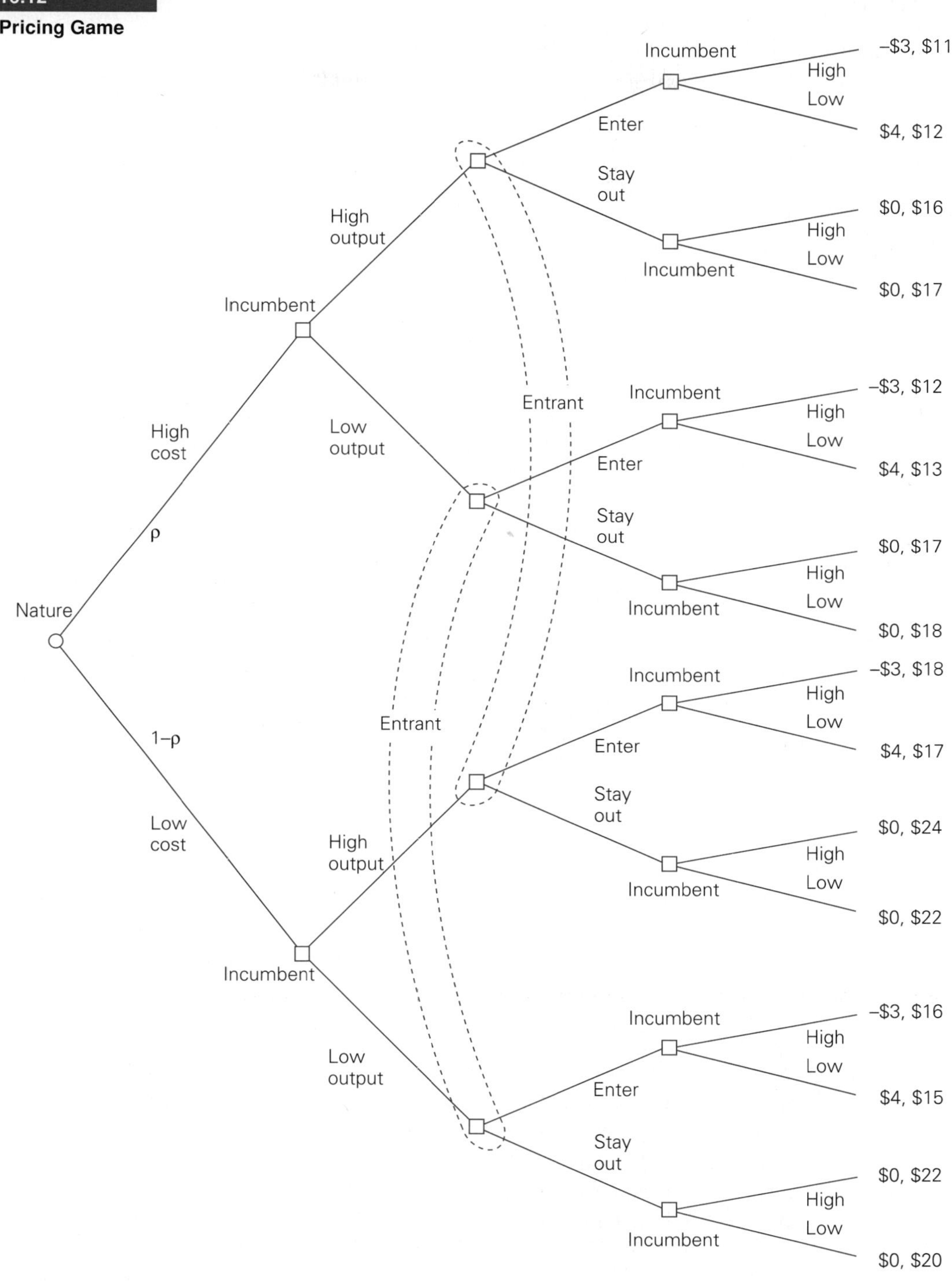

The equilibrium strategies are as follows. The incumbent's equilibrium strategy is *produce "high output" in the first period; in the second period, produce "high output" if costs are low, and "low output" if costs are high.* The entrant's equilibrium strategy is *"enter" if and only if the incumbent produces "low output" in the first period.* Hence, the entrant stays out of the market.

potential entrant believed that the incumbent was following the strategy just outlined, then the potential entrant should adopt the strategy *"enter" if and only if the incumbent chooses "low output" in the first period.*

We are not done yet, however. The incumbent should account for the fact that the entrant is making such inferences. Suppose that both the high-cost and low-cost incumbent choose "high output" in the first period. Then the entrant would be able to draw no inference from the first-period output level. Given the low value of ρ, the potential entrant would stay out of the market. Thus, in making its first-period output choice, a high-cost incumbent compares the payoff at the end of the branch (low output, enter, low output) with the payoff at the end of the branch (high output, stay out, low output). Since \$17 million is more than \$13 million, it is more profitable to choose "high output" in the first period than to choose "low output."

The net result of all this is that the equilibrium strategies are as follows. The incumbent's equilibrium strategy is *produce "high output" in the first period; in the second period, (whether or not entry occurs) produce "high output" if costs are low, and "low output" if costs are high.* The entrant's equilibrium strategy is *"enter" if and only if the incumbent produces "low output" in the first period.*

Notice how the high-cost incumbent distorts its behavior to conceal its true cost level from the potential entrant. You might think that the incumbent is trying to trick the potential entrant into thinking that the incumbent is a low-cost firm. But a rational entrant anticipates that a high-cost incumbent will do this. The value to the incumbent is not that the entrant is fooled into thinking that the incumbent has low costs. Rather, the advantage is that the entrant is prevented from obtaining the information about costs that he or she would like and, given the lack of information, chooses to stay out of the market. The practice of setting a high output level or a low price to deter entry is known as **limit pricing**.

limit pricing
The practice of setting a high output level, or a low price, to deter entry.

This example is just one of many situations in which a potential entrant looks at the incumbent's actions to make inferences about some underlying characteristic of the incumbent or its market. In the example, the entrant looks at the incumbent's price and output in order to infer the incumbent's cost level. In other cases, a potential entrant might want to forecast market growth. Since the incumbent has experience in the industry, its prediction of market growth might be particularly valuable to the entrant. One way for the potential entrant to obtain this information may be to look at what investment in new capacity the incumbent is making.[8]

SECTION RECAP

Game theory can readily be extended to situations in which players are unable to see one another's earlier moves—games of imperfect information—as well as situations in which players are unsure about some aspects of the game itself—games of incomplete information. In each case, the key graphical tool show that a player may not be able to distinguish between two or more of his or her decision nodes in the game tree. The prisoner's dilemma is an important game of imperfect information. It demonstrates how the need to rely on self-enforcing agreements (as embodied by the Nash condition) may limit parties' ability to cooperate even when it would be in their collective self-interest to do so. Some games do not

[8]In the next chapter, we will consider many more situations in which one economic decision maker tries to figure out what another one knows by looking at his or her actions.

have equilibria when the players are restricted to pure strategies. Mixed strategies capture the notion that it may be in a player's self-interest to keep the other players guessing about his or her future actions.

16.4 REPEATED GAMES

While decisions such as whether to enter a market involve one-time actions, there are many situations in which players find themselves repeatedly making the same decisions. For example, in the last chapter we informally discussed the interaction of oligopolists who chose new output levels or prices each day. In this section, we look in detail at one model of repeated price setting to examine carefully the costs and benefits of cheating. This model also demonstrates the dramatic way in which repeated oligopolistic interaction can affect the equilibrium outcome relative to situations in which firms make once-and-for-all choices. Let's reconsider the attempt of Air Lion and Beta Airlines to reach a self-enforcing agreement to hold up the price of a ticket. Now, however, let's allow for the firms' getting to choose new prices daily; specifically, at the start of each day the two firms simultaneously choose their prices for that day. The per-day demand curve is $D(p)$. Each day's choice of prices constitutes a Bertrand game within the overall game. The overall game is made up of the repeated play of this component game, also known as a *stage game*.

Given this setup, what equilibrium do we expect to emerge? One possible equilibrium is that each day the firms choose the same price that they would if they were each making only a single, once-and-for-all choice. That is, each day both airlines set their prices equal to the common value of marginal cost, c. To see that this is an equilibrium outcome, note that if each firm expects the other to set price equal to the common value of marginal cost, then it might as well do the same. Thus, there is no incentive to cheat on the agreement to set the price equal to marginal cost each day, and this agreement is self-enforcing (i.e., it is a Nash equilibrium). Unfortunately, from the firms' point of view, the agreement is not worth much—the firms earn zero economic profits.

Under the agreement just outlined, the firms do not take advantage of their repeated dealings with one another. One type of implicit agreement that does make use of the repeated interaction is known as a *grim-trigger* strategy. Suppose that the firms agree that each firm will charge price p_s daily as long as no one has cheated in the past (i.e., p_s has always been charged in the past). If anyone does cheat, then the firms (including the cheater) "agree" to punish the cheater by setting all future prices equal to marginal cost. This type of strategy gets its name from the fact that the detection of cheating "triggers" an infinitely long punishment (a "grim" prospect indeed).

Let's analyze whether a grim-trigger strategy is self-enforcing and credible. To determine whether an agreement is self-enforcing, we need to know whether the benefits from cheating are less than the costs. As we saw in Chapter 15, the costs and benefits of cheating depend on the per day profits associated with sticking to the agreement, π^s, getting away with cheating, π^c, and getting punished, π^p.

If the firms have agreed to charge a price of p_s and neither firm cheats, then the two firms split the market sales of $D(p_s)$. Hence, the per day profit from sticking to the agreement is

$$\pi^s = ½D(p_s) \times \{p_s - c\}. \tag{16.3}$$

Now consider what a cheater earns each day that it escapes detection. Suppose that Beta abides by the agreement and sets its price equal to p_s. As we saw when analyzing Bertrand duopoly, by just barely undercutting Beta's price, Air Lion can earn a per day profit of approximately[9]

$$\pi^c = D(p_s) \times \{p_s - c\}. \tag{16.4}$$

We will simplify the calculations below by making use of the fact that this value of π^c is exactly twice the value of π^s given by Equation (16.3).

Under the threatened punishment, a cheater earns no profit once it has been caught: $\pi^p = 0$. Before comparing the costs and benefits of cheating, we need to make sure that the threatened punishment is credible: Is the agreement to punish a cheater this way itself a self-enforcing agreement? Our earlier discussion showed that it is. Given that one firm prices at marginal cost in every period, it is in the other firm's interest also to price at marginal cost. Hence, if each firm expects the other to respond to cheating by setting price equal to marginal cost, it is in the firm's self-interest to do so as well. In short, the punishment is credible.

We are now ready to calculate the costs and benefits of cheating. Since the benefits accrue over time, we need to discount them. Let i denote the per-day interest rate. A key determinant of these costs and benefits is how long it takes to detect cheating. Let's begin by analyzing what happens when a firm can get away with cheating for only one day before being caught. The benefit of cheating is the present value of the extra profit that Air Lion earns during the time that it gets away with it. Since Air Lion goes undetected for just one day, the benefit is $\pi^c - \pi^s = \pi^s$ (recall π^c is twice π^s). The cost of cheating is the present value of the profits that are forgone when the firm is punished. Since the firm could have earned π^s each day but instead earns 0, the cost of the punishment in terms of forgone profit is

$$\pi^s/(1 + i) + \pi^s/(1 + i)^2 + \pi^s/(1 + i)^3 + \cdots \tag{16.5}$$

Applying our standard discounting formula for a perpetuity (see Chapter 5, page 151), the cost of cheating is equal to π^s/i.

Comparing the benefit of cheating, π^s, with the cost, π^s/i, we see that unless Air Lion has an interest rate of at least 100 percent per day, it will not cheat! When $i < 100$ percent, these grim-trigger strategies constitute a perfect equilibrium that supports pricing at p_s. Remarkably, this result is *independent of the particular value of p_s* (as long as p_s is greater than c so firms do not suffer losses). This fact tells us that, if the firms can sustain a price 2 cents greater than marginal cost with a self-enforcing agreement, then they can sustain the full cartel price as well. What a difference repeat play can make! Bertrand firms, who make once-and-for-all price choices, set price equal to marginal cost and earn no profit. Firms that set prices repeatedly, however, can end up charging the monopoly price and splitting the monopoly profits. The difference arises entirely because Bertrand firms cannot punish one another for cheating, but firms that interact repeatedly can.

This example suggests collusion should be easy. But the example misses some important features of actual markets that we discussed in the last chapter. One of the most important is that a firm may be able to escape detection from cheating

[9]Equation (16.4) is an approximation because Air Lion would have to undercut p_s slightly. It is sufficiently close that we will not worry about the difference.

for more than one day before being punished. To see the effects of such a punishment lag, suppose that a firm could get away with cheating for two days before being punished. In this case, a cheater gains $\pi^c - \pi^s$ for two days before being punished. Since $\pi^c - \pi^s = \pi^s$, getting away with cheating for a second day is worth $\pi^s/(1 + i)$ in present-value terms. Hence, the present value of the total benefit of cheating rises to

$$\pi^s + \pi^s/(1 + i) = \pi^s \times (2 + i)/(1 + i). \tag{16.6}$$

What about the cost of cheating? Once punished, the per-day decline in the firm's profit is again $\pi^s - \pi^p = \pi^s$. Now, however, the punishment does not begin for two days, so its present value is

$$\pi^s/(1 + i)^2 + \pi^s/(1 + i)^3 + \pi^s/(1 + i)^4 \cdots \tag{16.7}$$

Comparing expression (16.7) with expression (16.5), we see that the cost of cheating when there is a two-period lag is equal to the cost when there is a one-period lag divided by $(1 + i)$ to account for the fact that the punishment starts one period later. Dividing π^s/i by $(1 + i)$, the cost of cheating is now $\pi^s/\{i(1 + i)\}$, which is lower than when detection takes only one day.

Since the benefits of cheating have risen, and the costs of cheating have fallen, it is harder to deter cheating. The comparison of the benefits of cheating, $\pi^s(2 + i)/(1 + i)$, with the cost, $\pi^s/\{i(1 + i)\}$, depends on whether $(2 + i)$ is greater than $1/i$. Now, the critical value of the per day interest rate i is $\sqrt{2} - 1$, which is approximately 0.41. When a firm can get away with cheating for two days, collusion will be successful if and only if the per day interest rate is less than 41 percent. This still is an extremely high interest rate, but it is much lower than the earlier critical value of 100 percent per day. If the lag between cheating and punishment were longer, then the incentive to cheat would be larger still, and collusion would fail at even lower interest rates.

Other Strategies Grim-trigger strategies are not the only strategies available to firms. For instance, the punishment might vary over time in some complicated way. It is worth considering whether the firms could increase their profits by adopting more complicated strategies. As we already discussed, the harsher the penalty, the greater the degree of collusion that can be supported. A first question thus is: Can the firms find a more severe credible punishment? In our example, the answer is no. Under the proposed strategies, cheating is met with marginal cost pricing forever afterward, and the cheater's profit following detection is zero. No stronger punishment is available to the firms because any attempt to drive the cheater's profit below zero would simply lead to the cheater's shutting down. Moreover, no one would believe that the firm carrying out the punishment would set its price below marginal cost anyway. For the market setting that we have examined here, grim-trigger strategies provide the harshest possible credible punishment, and thus support the greatest degree of collusion possible.

More complicated strategies may yield harsher penalties in other circumstances, however, as when firms set their quantities repeatedly or when products are differentiated. Moreover, in a world where mistakes are possible, firms do not always want to impose the harshest possible punishment. It often is difficult for firms to verify whether their rivals are abiding by an agreement. Since agreements to collude often are tacit, misunderstandings can occur. Further, it may take the firms in an industry a while to figure out their optimal collusive arrangement.

There will be no benefits from colluding if simple mistakes or the learning process itself trigger punishments that last forever. To err may be human, but to forgive can be profitable.

FINITELY REPEATED GAMES

In the repeated pricing game we just examined, the firms set new prices each day forever. Equivalently, the players know that the game will end some day, but they don't know in advance when that will be. Because there is no set end point, such situations are sometimes called *infinitely repeated games.* It turns out that the situation is much different when both players know that the game will end on a certain date.

Recall that to find a perfect equilibrium, we worked back from the end of the game tree through a process known as *backward induction.* We can use the logic of backward induction to derive a powerful result for situations with repeated price setting for a *fixed* number of periods, an example of a so-called *finitely repeated game.* Suppose that Air Lion and Beta both know that Beta is going to shut down exactly two years from now. How should they behave in the meantime? To answer this question, we start by thinking through what will happen on the last day Beta is in business. At that point, the firms will be facing a standard, one-time Bertrand pricing game. We know from the last chapter that each firm will price at marginal cost and neither firm will earn economic profits. What about the day before that? No matter what a firm does on that day, it knows that the next day will have pricing at marginal cost. So, there is no scope for threats or promises or any sort of punishment for failing to hold price above cost on the penultimate day. Because the future price is essentially set, a firm should choose its price on the next-to-last day as if there were no other day. But then we get the standard Bertrand outcome for this day, too.

This same logic applies to the third day from the end. Indeed, as we keep working backward we find that the outcome in every period is equivalent to the one-time Bertrand outcome. Not only that, but this logic applies equally well to any other repeated game for which there is only one Nash equilibrium for the stage game played once in isolation. We have just shown that *when there is a unique Nash equilibrium of the stage game, the unique perfect equilibrium of the finitely repeated game is simply the one-shot equilibrium repeated in every period.*[10]

SECTION RECAP

Players sometimes play multi-round games that consist of a stage game played over and over. When the game has no definite ending point—an infinitely repeated game—the perfect equilibrium of the repeated game can be very different from the equilibrium that arises when the component stage game is played just once. When there is a known end point—a finitely repeated game—and there is a unique Nash equilibrium for the stage game, the unique perfect equilibrium of the repeated game has the same outcome in each period as when the stage game is played just once.

[10]This result does not hold when there are two or more equilibria in the stage game itself. In such situations firms can, in effect, make threats and promises about which stage-game equilibrium they will choose in the last period and then work backward from there.

SUMMARY

Noncooperative game theory provides a set of tools for analyzing oligopoly as well as strategic behavior in many other areas of economics and politics.

- Game trees provide a convenient way to represent strategic situations.
- The notion of a perfect equilibrium captures the two features of equilibrium that we required for oligopoly: the Nash condition and the credibility condition.
- Perfect equilibrium embodies the Nash condition by imposing the requirement that each player choose an optimal strategy, given the strategies chosen by the other players in the game.
- Perfect equilibrium embodies the credibility condition by requiring that each player would find it to be in her self-interest to carry out any part of her chosen strategy if called upon to do so.
- A game of imperfect information is a situation in which some player must make a move but is unable to observe an earlier or simultaneous *move* of another player.
- A game of incomplete information is a situation in which a player is not sure about some characteristic of the *structure* of the game being played.
- The tools of noncooperative game theory help us understand the process of entry into oligopolistic markets. Incredible threats by an incumbent firm will not serve as entry deterrents. An incumbent firm may be able to make investments that make its threats credible. A high-capacity plant, for example, may commit an incumbent to responding aggressively to entry. Thus, building such a plant may be an investment in entry deterrence. An incumbent firm may also invest in entry deterrence by setting a low price to make potential entrants worry that the incumbent may be a low-cost firm.
- When a player randomizes over his or her choice of action to keep rivals guessing, the player is said to follow a mixed strategy.
- When players play the same game within a game again and again, the overall game is called a repeated game. In comparison with the Bertrand model, the infinitely repeated pricing game illustrates the tremendous difference that the ability for players to respond to one another can make.

DISCUSSION QUESTIONS

16.1 There is a theorem proving that there is a "solution" to chess. That is, there is a perfect equilibrium in which one of the players can guarantee itself at least a tie. While one can prove that such an equilibrium exists, no one knows what it is. Hence, international grand masters are able to make a great deal of money playing chess. What does this tell us about applying game theory to real-world situations?

16.2 It is often suggested that competing firms are engaged in a prisoners' dilemma when it comes to choosing their advertising expenditures.

a. Draw a game tree to illustrate a duopoly market in which the suppliers must simultaneously choose their advertising levels. Put in payoffs that give this game a prisoners' dilemma structure. Does this pattern of payoffs seem to fit the real world situation?

The U.S. government now forbids cigarette advertising on television, but at one time it did not. Some observers have claimed that the government ban on television advertising may actually have raised cigarette industry profits by limiting costly advertising campaigns that largely cancel one another out.

b. Is this story consistent with the model of industry behavior that you developed in part *a*?

16.3 Up through 1996, most cities in the United States had one local telephone company and one cable television company. Moreover, regulation typically prevented additional firms from entering either business. The Telecommunications Act of 1996 made it much easier for telephone companies to enter the cable television business and cable companies to enter the telephone business. Many management consultants concluded that—compared to each staying out of the other's market—cable and telephone companies would end up losing money if each went into the other's business. Yet, these consultants also concluded that each firm would find entering the other's market too attractive to resist.

a. Use the insights of the prisoners' dilemma to explain these apparently contradictory predictions.

b. What difference does it make, if any, that each firm can monitor the other's entry decisions and thus make its own decision contingent on that of the other firm in its local market?

16.4 Consider again the entry game examined in Section 16.2. Contrary to the situation depicted in Figure 16.6, suppose that General Generic makes its entry decision (i.e., constructs its own plant) *before* Jersey Pharmaceutical makes its plant investment decision.

a. Draw a game tree for this new situation.

b. Describe the equilibrium. Will General Generic choose to enter? Which size plant will Jersey Pharmaceutical choose to construct?

16.5 Go back to the situation depicted in Figure 16.6, but make one change. Suppose that prior to Jersey Pharmaceutical's making its plant choice, General Generic can announce whether it intends to enter this market. The announcement is nonbinding and is costless to make.

a. Draw a game tree for this new situation.

b. Describe the equilibrium. Will General Generic announce that it intends to enter? Which size plant will Jersey Pharmaceutical choose to construct? Will General Generic enter? In answering this question, be sure to state carefully what constitutes each firm's equilibrium *strategy.*

16.6 Auctions are used to sell a wide variety of goods, ranging from paintings to licenses for offering wireless telephone service. Under a so-called *Dutch auction* (in the Netherlands, they use it to sell fresh flowers at wholesale to florists), there is an auctioneer who announces a very high price and then calls out successively lower prices. The first bidder to accept the auctioneer's price is declared the winner and receives the item for the price the auctioneer had last called out. Under a sealed-bid auction, each buyer submits a secret bid stating how much he or she is willing to pay. The bids are then opened and the item is sold to the highest bidder at the price submitted. Show that in terms of the strategies available to the players, what each player knows about the others, and thus what the equilibrium outcome will be, a Dutch auction is equivalent to a sealed-bid auction.

16.7 Consider the following market. There is a single incumbent and a single potential entrant. Each firm has constant marginal costs of c per unit, and the product is undifferentiated. To enter the market, the new firm would have to incur a one-time cost of $1,000. Resolve the following apparent paradox: If the post-entry game is a Bertrand duopoly, then neither firm will make any profits, while under a Cournot duopoly they would. The incumbent, however, would rather be in a situation where the post-entry interaction is Bertrand rather than Cournot.

16.8 The United States stations thousands of troops in South Korea. Ostensibly, these troops are there to help the South Korean military repulse any attempted invasion by North Korea. There are, however, far too few troops to do the job. Some say the real role of these troops is to serve as a commitment by the United States to come to South Korea's aid in the event of an invasion. Draw a game tree that captures the notion of the American troops' serving as a form of commitment.

16.9 Consider the game in Figure 16.12 one more time. Now suppose that the entrant believes there is a 6/7 chance that the incumbent has high costs (that is, $\rho = 6/7$). Show that, in equilibrium, the incumbent will not try to confuse the potential entrant by producing "high output" in the first period when it has high costs.

16.10 Consider the model of repeated price setting on page 543). Suppose that a cheater could get away with three periods of cheating before being found out. Assume that even if the firm cheated for only one period, it would be discovered two periods later.

a. Is there a zero-profit equilibrium in this market?

b. Can the full cartel outcome be supported by a self-enforcing agreement if $i = .2$? What if $i = 2.0$? What if $i = 20$? Find a critical value for the interest rate that determines whether or not the cartel outcome can be supported.

16.11 In Problem 15.11, we looked at the rivalry between Bill's and Hillary's golf schools. Recall that the daily demand for golf lessons at Bill's and Hillary's were $D_B(p_B, p_H) = 100 - 2\,p_B + p_H$ and $D_H(p_B, p_H) = 100 - 2\,p_H + p_B$, respectively, where p_B is Bill's price and p_H is Hillary's price. In the last chapter, we found the Bertrand equilibrium when the schools set price once and for all.

Now suppose that Bill and Hillary choose prices repeatedly; that is, every day they set new prices based on what happened the day before.

a. Is there an equilibrium in which the schools simply charge the prices found last chapter, where each school chooses a single price once and for all?

b. Would you expect the schools to achieve a more profitable equilibrium than the one described in part *a*? How does your answer depend on whether the firms are unsure when they will go out of business or whether they know that there is a definite date on which one of them is going to go out of business?

5

PART five

Missing Markets

The circular flow model of the economy indicates that firms and households "meet" in markets. As we saw in Parts Three and Four, markets can have various structures. But whatever the particular structure, the market puts a price on each commodity and each input, and determines how much of it will be exchanged. An implicit assumption behind this analysis is that a market exists for each and every item. In contrast, in the real world markets for some commodities fail to emerge. This part of the book is devoted to exploring why markets for some commodities are missing, what the consequences are, and how public policies might cope with these consequences.

Chapter 17 deals with one important reason for missing markets, asymmetric information. Asymmetric information refers to a situation in which one party to a transaction has more information than another. For example, when you purchase life insurance, you have better information about your medical status and your health habits than the insurance company does. Previous chapters stressed that imperfect information and uncertainty per se preclude neither rational decision making nor efficient allocation of resources by competitive markets. However, Chapter 17 shows that when the lack of information is asymmetric, a market can be destroyed, leading to inefficiencies. Indeed, asymmetric information can have important effects on behavior even when the market is not completely destroyed.

Chapter 18 deals with externalities, situations in which the behavior of a person or firm *directly* affects the welfare of *another* person or firm. An important example of an externality is air pollution. The basic reason that pollution is a problem is that there is no market for the commodity "clean air." The chapter shows that some of the most creative governmental responses to externalities involve creation of artificial markets, which can mimic the efficient results of conventional competitive markets. These proposals demonstrate the usefulness of microeconomic theory as a tool for dealing with social problems.

CHAPTER 17

Asymmetric Information

> *How little one is permitted to know about another person. Even if one is very attentive.*
>
> —Amos Oz

While seeing the world as a college student, one of the authors of this text took a long train trip through what was then Yugoslavia. The train made periodic stops, and at one village, a local merchant boarded the train, offering gold jewelry for sale. He offered to sell a single bracelet for $50. Ever wary, your author voiced some doubt about the gold content of the bracelet. The merchant bit into the bracelet and held a match to it to prove that it was pure gold. Not seeing the point of either of these gestures, the author again expressed his skepticism. The seller responded by offering *two* bracelets for a *total* of $50. "Too much," he was told. So he threw in a gold ring and offered the package for $40. "But are they really gold?" he was asked. "Yes, pure gold," the merchant replied, and to prove his sincerity he offered the two bracelets and two rings for a total of $5. "No, thank you," said your wily author, "at that price they couldn't possibly be real gold."

Other than showing that even the authors were young once, this story illustrates an important point. In many transactions, the people involved have different amounts of information. In this example, the potential buyer did not know whether the jewelry was made of gold, although the seller certainly knew it was not. There are many other situations in which one side of a deal knows something that the other does not. When you buy a used car, the person selling it knows a lot more about whether it is a "lemon" than you do. When a firm hires a new employee, that worker may have a much better idea about his or her ability than the firm. Whenever one side of the market has better information than the other, the situation is one of **asymmetric information**.

asymmetric information A situation in which one side of an economic relationship has better information than the other.

In many instances of asymmetric information, the less-informed side knows that the other side has more information. Given this awareness, the less-informed side of the deal may be able to make inferences from the informed side's actions. In the example above, the seller's final offer of two bracelets and two rings for only $5 was an excellent indicator that there was no gold in them—if there were, he never would have offered to sell them at such a low price. This sort of inference often is made in markets with asymmetric information, and we will see that it can fundamentally alter how markets perform.

This chapter explores the problems asymmetric information poses for market performance by examining several situations in which this phenomenon arises. In addition to considering the problems raised, we will examine some of the many institutions that help solve them, including McDonald's, discount airfares, deductibles on automobile insurance, and universities.

Broadly speaking, there are two types of information that an economic decision maker might lack but desire, and we will divide our discussion along these lines. In the first case, one side knows some *characteristic* of itself that the other does not. In the Yugoslav jewelry example, the seller knew whether his bracelets were made of gold. Similarly, when you buy a used car, the previous owner probably has a much better idea about its quality than you do. In most markets, we expect the seller to know more about the good than the buyer. There are, however, markets in which the buyer is the better-informed party. When you buy life insurance, for example, you probably know more about your health and family history of heart disease than does the insurance company selling you a policy. Indeed, according to a recent study, "People's answer to the simple question, 'Is your health excellent, good, fair, or poor' is a better predictor of who will live or die over the next decade than even a rigorous physical examination" (Goleman 1991, B13). Whenever one side of a transaction knows something about itself (how good the product is or the likelihood of death) that the other one does not, we say it is a situation of **hidden characteristics**.

hidden characteristics
Things that one side of a transaction knows about itself that the other side would like to know but does not.

hidden actions
Actions taken by one side of an economic relationship that the other side of the relationship cannot observe.

The second type of asymmetric information arises when one side of a transaction can take an *action* that affects the other side but which the other side cannot directly observe. When a firm hires an employee, for example, the firm wants her to work hard. But it may be difficult to observe whether she sometimes goofs off. Similarly, a company selling you home insurance cares about whether you smoke in bed, but may not be able to tell if you do. Whenever one side of an economic relationship takes actions that the other side cannot observe, it is a situation of **hidden action**.

17.1 SIGNALING AND SCREENING

In this and the following section, we will examine the effects of hidden characteristics on the operation and performance of markets. What makes markets with hidden characteristics interesting is that there may be indirect ways for the uninformed party to infer what is going on. We will start by considering a monopolist who would like to know how much each of its customers is willing to pay for its product.

ANOTHER LOOK AT PRICE DISCRIMINATION

Typically, consumers know how much they are willing to pay for a good, but the firm selling to them does not. Consider the problem faced by Fair Chance Airlines. Fair Chance flies a direct route from Paris, France, to Paradise, New Jersey, to deliver air freight. The firm has calculated that the marginal cost of adding passengers to the flight is $120 per passenger. There are only two potential passengers for this flight—a businessman and a beach bum. The businessman is willing to pay \$500 for the flight, but wants to stay for one day only. If he has to stay for more than one day, he is willing to pay only \$250. The beach bum is willing to pay at most \$200 for a flight. Being a bum, he does not much care about the trip's length, although left to his own devices he would go for two weeks. Neither consumer is willing to pay anything for additional flights to Paradise.

Fair Chance faces a dilemma—it would like to charge \$500 per ticket in order to extract the surplus from the business traveler, but charging a high price will discourage the beach bum from purchasing a ticket. Following this policy, Fair Chance would earn \$380 = \$500 − \$120. On the other hand, if Fair Chance charged \$200 per ticket to attract the beach bum, both types of consumers would take the flight, Fair Chance would sell twice as many tickets but earn a smaller profit of \$160 = 2 × (\$200 − \$120). Hence, if the airline has to charge the same price to both consumers, it will sell tickets for \$500 each, and only the businessman will choose to fly.

Our look at monopoly in Chapter 13 indicated that when consumers differ in their willingness to pay for a good, the seller of that good can increase its profit if it can charge different prices to different people based on their willingness to pay—that is, if it can practice price discrimination. If Fair Chance could charge \$500 per flight to the businessman while charging only \$200 per flight to the beach bum, it could sell to both and earn a profit of \$460 = (\$500 − \$120) + (\$200 − \$120).

As shown in Chapter 13, three conditions must be satisfied for price discrimination to be profitable:

1. *The firm must be a price maker.*
2. *The firm must be able to identify consumers with different demands for its product.*
3. *The consumers must not be able to engage in arbitrage.*

That the two consumers differ in their willingness to pay for the firm's product (and both are willing to pay more than the marginal cost of production) tells us that Fair Chance satisfies condition 1. As long as the tickets are not transferable, condition 3 is satisfied as well. But what about condition 2? Fair Chance needs some basis for the two different fares that it would like to charge. Fair Chance would like to base its fares on the passengers' willingness to pay. But willingness to pay is a hidden characteristic.

One approach would be to ask the customers how much they were willing to pay. Alternatively, the airline might ask passengers whether they were traveling for business or pleasure, and then charge accordingly. We would not expect either of these approaches to be very effective. If an airline grants lower fares to anyone who claims to be on vacation, everyone will make that claim. When price is the only difference between the two types of tickets, everyone wants the low-price ticket, and offering two fares does not help sort the consumers.

signal
An observable indicator of a hidden characteristic.

Fair Chance needs to find some indicator, or **signal**, of a person's willingness to pay. What signal is available? The firm could try looking at people's clothes (are their shirts made of blue oxford cloth or Hawaiian floral prints?). But if the airline tried this tactic, business travelers might well start wearing Bermuda shorts. A potentially more effective signal is a consumer's willingness to take a long trip. Recall that, in addition to being willing to pay more overall than the beach bum, the businessman does not want to stay on his trip as long.

The management of Fair Chance can sort consumers by offering fares that differ both in terms of the price and the restrictions that are placed on the traveler. Suppose that Fair Chance offers (1) a coach fare of $449 that has no restrictions on when it can be used, and (2) a special "vacation fare" of $200 that can be used only if the traveler goes on a trip of at least two weeks. Given this choice, the beach bum selects the second option; it's cheaper, and he was going for two weeks anyway. What about the business traveler? A flight with a two-week minimum length of stay is worth $250 to him and has a cost of $200. Hence, this option would yield consumer surplus of $50. Alternatively, he can pay $449 for a restriction-free flight that is worth $500. This option yields consumer surplus of $51. Hence, the businessman chooses the full-fare, coach ticket; in effect, he is willing to pay $249 not to have to stay for two weeks.

Notice that although the monopolist does not know whether any particular person is a business traveler or a beach bum, in equilibrium each person reveals his type to the airline. The airline uses the two different fares as a **self-selection device**. That is, the airline offers a set of choices, and it lets the consumers select from among them. A consumer's choice tells the firm what type of person that customer is. Whenever the uninformed party (here, the airline) sets up a mechanism for sorting the informed parties (here, the potential passengers) based on the signals that they transmit (here, their willingness to stay for two weeks), the uninformed party is said to be engaging in **screening**.

self-selection device
A mechanism in which an informed party in an economic relationship is offered a set of options, and the choice made by the informed party reveals his or her hidden characteristic.

screening
An uninformed party's attempt to sort the informed parties.

Does the firm's knowledge about which type of customer is which once they have bought their tickets mean that the firm can perfectly price discriminate? No, it does not. Even though the firm knows everyone's willingness to pay *after the fact*, this is not the same as a situation in which the firm can tell how much people are willing to pay just by looking at them. If the firm could directly identify each customer's willingness to pay, and prevent arbitrage, it would charge $500 to the business traveler and $200 to the beach bum. But Fair Chance cannot directly observe willingness to pay. At prices of $500 and $200, the business traveler would purchase the vacation fare—at these prices, the vacation fare yields consumer surplus of $50, while the coach fare yields $0 consumer surplus. In effect, the businessman would "pretend" to be a beach bum by staying for two weeks to save $300. To keep him from pretending to be a beach bum, the airline has to allow the businessman to enjoy at least $50 of consumer surplus even at the higher fare. Consequently, $450 is the most that the airline can charge to the business traveler (while still selling to the beach bum at a price of $200). The airline's lack of information costs it $50 in revenue it cannot collect from the businessman.

In Chapter 13, we saw that this type of price discrimination, in which the same price schedule is offered to all buyers but they sort themselves through self-selection, is known as *second-degree price discrimination.* It is worth taking a minute to think more about the relationship between second- and third-degree price discrimination. Both are concerned with a hidden-characteristic problem—the firm wants to know each consumer's willingness to pay, but does not. There is, however, an important difference. In our earlier examination of third-degree price discrimination (see Chapter 13), we considered examples in which the firm could simply observe some fixed characteristic of the consumer that gave an indication of the consumer's willingness to pay. For example, a firm might use the fact that a person's sex is correlated with that person's willingness to pay to enter a singles bar. When a bar offers lower prices to women, it is not worried that some men will have sex change operations solely to get cheaper drinks. Under second-degree price discrimination, however, the firm offers the same set of prices to everyone and bases those prices on some action that the consumer himself chooses (e.g., whether to go away on a trip for two weeks). The action taken by the consumer serves as a signal of the underlying characteristic on which the firm really would like to base its price. Since the signal on which the firm bases its price is the subject of consumer choice, the pricing problem can be complicated—the firm has to take into account the way in which consumers respond to changes in its set of prices. In the case of Fair Chance, it has to set the price differential at no more than $250 in order to induce the business traveler to reveal himself as such. In contrast, consumer self-selection is not an issue under third-degree price discrimination. (PC 17.1)

17.1 PROGRESS CHECK

Suppose that All American Airlines also faces only two types of passengers. One is a businessman who is willing to pay $500 to go for one day but only $250 if he has to stay for two weeks. The other type is a beach bum who also prefers to go for one day; he is willing to pay $400 to go for one day, but only $350 if he has to stay for two weeks. All American Airlines' marginal cost is $120 per passenger. How many types of tickets will All American Airlines offer? What are the profit-maximizing prices for these tickets?

Normative Analysis of Second-Degree Price Discrimination

When feasible, second-degree price discrimination can raise the seller's profit. Let's take another look at what happens to total surplus, which includes consumer surplus in addition to profit. We must consider two types of effects. First, there are allocative efficiency effects—different amounts of the good may be produced and consumed when second-degree discrimination is used than when it is not. In the case of Fair Chance, these allocative efficiency effects are positive. Recall that Fair Chance would sell a ticket solely to the businessman if discrimination were impossible—selling one type of ticket for $500 yields greater profit than does selling a single type of ticket for $200. As we just saw, however, when it can use price discrimination, Fair Chance sells to both types of passengers. Since the beach bum is willing to pay more than the marginal cost of the service, this increase in consumption raises the level of total surplus by $80 = $200 − $120.

There is another set of welfare effects to consider. To sort the consumers, the firm has to offer two different types of tickets. One of the tickets (the vacation fare) places what may be a surplus-reducing restriction on the consumer—a person may have to stay longer than he or she otherwise would want. In our example, this effect does not arise because the beach bum was going to travel for two weeks anyway. Hence, second-degree price discrimination unambiguously raises total surplus. This need not always be the case, however, as Progress Check 17.2 demonstrates. (PC 17.2)

17.2 PROGRESS CHECK

Consider again All American Airlines from Progress Check 17.1. Show that second-degree price discrimination by All American lowers total surplus in comparison with a situation in which the firm must offer only one fare to everyone.

Lastly, offering two fares is more costly than offering just one, and these costs reduce total surplus, *ceteris paribus*.

Real-World Screening

The examples we have worked through are artificially simple. Nevertheless, anyone who has flown on a commercial airline knows that these examples capture a real-world phenomenon. In 1996, a passenger flying from San Francisco to Washington, D.C. could get a round-trip ticket for $400 if he or she were willing to stay in Washington over Saturday night. If the passenger were unwilling to do so, the fare was over $1,400! What appears to be a very puzzling form of pricing makes perfect sense once we recognize the use of screening. The airlines were sorting business travelers, who did not want to spend their weekends away from home in Washington, D.C., from people who were traveling on vacation, and were planning to stay over the weekend anyway. The airlines engaged in this sorting in order to charge high prices to business people while charging low prices to other travelers with lower willingness to pay.[1]

Screening customers is not a new practice. Back in the 1850s, the French national railway refused to make third class more pleasant. In violation of regulations, they did not install windows in the third-class coaches. Consequently, soot from the engine's smokestack would cover the passengers' clothing (Walras 1980). The railway was not acting out of malice. It was simply trying to maximize profit. The railway faced the following problem. It wanted to serve low-income passengers, who were willing to pay only low fares. But by offering cheap third-class tickets, the railroad risked taking profit away from itself—passengers might opt for the cheaper third-class tickets instead of expensive first-class tickets. Apparently, the management believed that rich passengers cared more about soiling their clothing than did lower-income passengers. By making third class less desirable to rich people, the railroad attempted to encourage rich people to ride in first class while still serving low-income passengers in third class. In short, the railway was engaging in screening through self-selection.

COMPETITIVE MARKET SIGNALING

Under second-degree price discrimination, a firm with market power uses a signal to sort consumers and discriminate among them. The use of signals also can be an important phenomenon in competitive markets. Let's consider a competitive labor market in which half the workers are of low ability and have marginal revenue products of $200 per week. The other half of the workers are of high ability and have marginal revenue products of $400 per week.

To study the effects of asymmetric information, it is useful first to note what happens when information is symmetric. This outcome gives us a baseline for comparison. Suppose that ability is observable to everyone. That is, both a worker and all of the firms who might hire her know her ability. Since the labor market is perfectly competitive, each worker is paid her marginal revenue product in equilibrium—low-ability workers are paid $200 per week, and high-ability workers receive $400 per week.

Now suppose one cannot determine an individual's ability just by looking at the person. In particular, suppose that, although a worker knows his or her own ability, there is no way for a firm to tell if a particular worker is of low or high

[1]Given the size of the fare differences, you might wonder why people didn't buy two of the discount tickets and thus pretend to stay over a Saturday night. Some, like your authors, did, but not enough engaged in this arbitrage to make the pricing unprofitable for the airlines.

ability at the time of hiring. When hiring a worker, the firm knows only that there is a 1/2 chance that the individual is a low-ability worker and a 1/2 chance that he or she is a high-ability worker. Because the firm cannot be sure of the worker's ability, the firm must compare the wage with the worker's *expected* marginal revenue product, which is $300 = 1/2 × $200 + 1/2 × $400. In equilibrium, firms pay workers a weekly wage of $300.

Let's compare this outcome with the one that arises when ability is observable to everyone. Low-ability workers are better off—they receive $300 per week instead of $200. But high-ability workers are worse off—they receive only $300 per week instead of $400. Firms are indifferent between the two outcomes because in either case a worker is paid his or her marginal revenue product on average.

High-ability workers are hurt by the lack of information. Naturally, they would like to reveal themselves as high-ability workers so that their wage would be bid up to $400 per week. But how can they do this? It is not enough simply to claim to be a high-ability worker; anyone could do that. Just as Fair Chance had to find some means to get the beach bum to signal his low willingness to pay in a way that the business traveler would be unwilling to mimic, high-ability workers need to be able to send a signal that low-ability people would be unwilling to send. In the airline example, staying for two weeks provided a signal of having a low willingness to pay. In labor markets, going to school may be the signal (Spence 1974).

Think about going to college. Going to college is not cheap. In addition to the direct monetary costs such as tuition and the cost of textbooks, there also are significant nonmonetary costs. Writing term papers and studying subjects other than economics are no fun—these activities are costly. Most important for the current analysis, these costs may vary with ability. In particular, if ability at work and ability in school are closely related, going to school may be costlier for low-ability workers than for high-ability ones. The reason for this relationship is that people of low ability are likely to find school to be more of a struggle and have to work harder to keep up with its demands.

If college is so costly, why would anyone, of high or low ability, go? There must be some offsetting benefits. To keep the example simple, assume for the moment that there is only one reason to go to college: to earn more money when you graduate. Suppose that people considering college observe the following fact: A person with a college degree earns $200 per week more than a nongraduate. The curve relating a person's income (units of *all other goods*) to his or her level of schooling (years of *education*) is drawn in Figure 17.1. This curve is a budget constraint for a worker—it tells us which combinations of income levels and education levels are available.

Choosing a point on this budget constraint amounts to choosing how much education to obtain. To see how an individual makes this decision, we need to draw his or her indifference map, which shows the individual's preferences over two commodities: *education* and *all other goods.* As we have been assuming all along, *all other goods* is an economic good. But we have made the (possibly unrealistic) assumption that going to college is no fun. Hence, *education* is an economic bad. Recall from Chapter 2 that when we graph preferences for one economic good and one economic bad, the resulting indifference curves slope upward. A person will not attend more school unless he or she is compensated with more of *all other goods.* Figure 17.2 illustrates the indifference map for a

Figure 17.1

The Income-Schooling Budget Curve

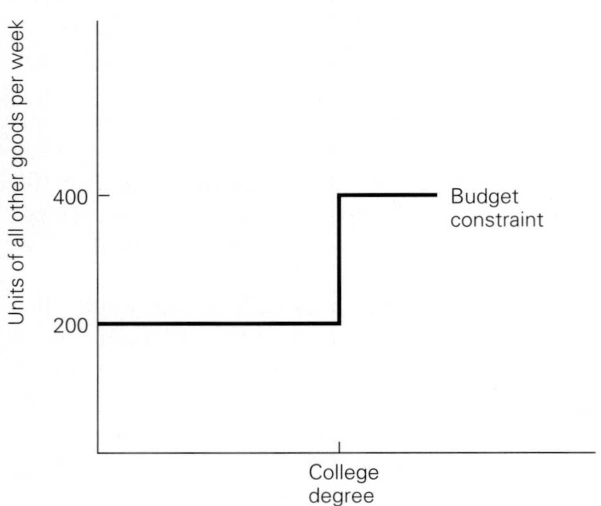

The curve relating income to the level of education is the budget constraint—it tells us which combinations of income levels and education levels are available.

Figure 17.2

Equilibrium Education Choice for a High-Ability Worker

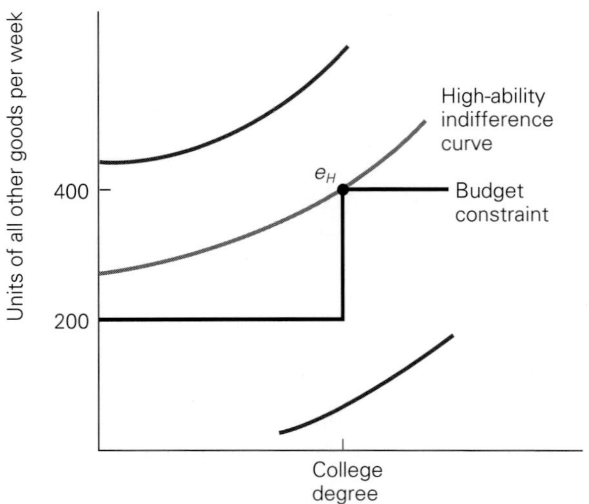

This indifference map represents a high-ability worker's tastes. Given the worker's budget constraint, a high-ability worker chooses to graduate from college in order to earn an additional $200 per week, point e_H.

high-ability worker along with the corresponding budget constraint. The figure indicates that a high-ability worker chooses to get a college degree in order to earn an additional $200 per week.

What about low-ability workers? By assumption, the disutility of going to college is higher for these workers. Therefore, the low-ability person needs greater compensation for getting through an additional year of school than does the high-ability person, *ceteris paribus.* Hence, as shown in Figure 17.3, low-ability people have steeper indifference curves than high-ability workers. Figure 17.4 finds a low-ability worker's equilibrium by superimposing the indifference map on the worker's budget constraint (reproduced from Figure 17.1). Figure 17.4 indicates that a low-ability worker chooses not to go to college, and consequently earns $200 per week.

In equilibrium, everybody who completes college is paid $400 per week while a worker who does not complete college is paid $200 per week. If, as we are assuming here, college has no effect on a person's marginal revenue product, why would firms pay higher wages to people who graduate from college? The answer lies in the different amounts of education chosen by high- and low-ability workers. In equilibrium, only high-ability people go to college, so a firm knows that a college graduate has a marginal revenue product of $400. Similarly, the firm knows that people who graduate only from high school are low-ability workers and have marginal revenue products of $200. Hence, in this model, while

Figure 17.3

Indifference Maps for Low- and High-Ability Workers

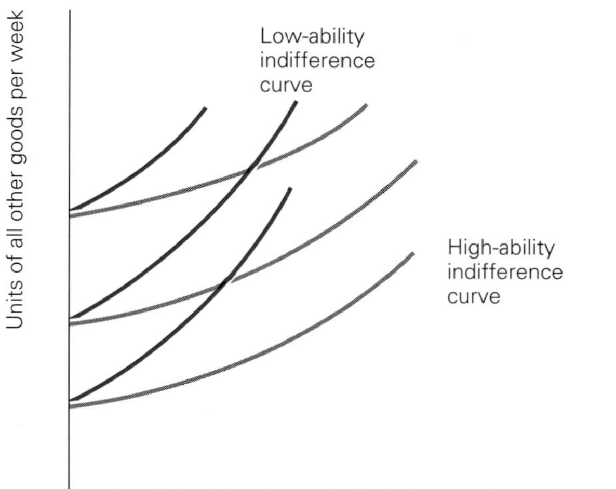

When a low-ability person finds school to be more of a struggle than a high-ability person, a low-ability person has steeper indifference curves (the blue curves) than a high-ability person (the gray lines), *ceteris paribus*.

Figure 17.4

Equilibrium Education Choice for a Low-Ability Worker

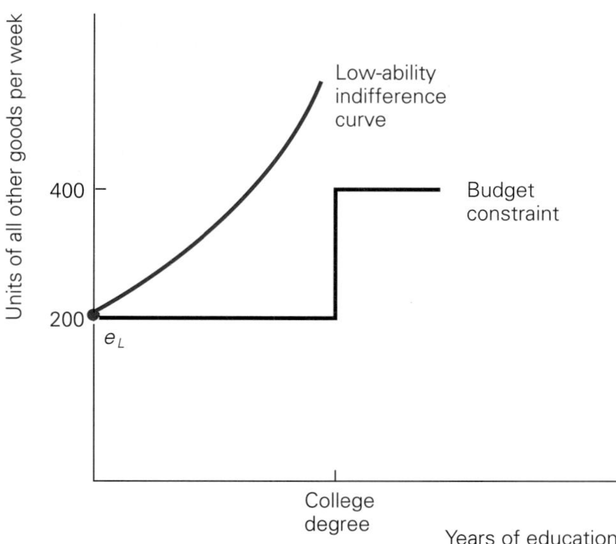

A low-ability worker maximizes utility at point e_L—this worker does not to go to college and consequently earns $200 per week.

education does not *enhance* ability, it does *signal* ability. Figure 17.5 emphasizes this point by showing the two equilibrium points on the same graph.

In contrast, if all workers had the same taste for education, or if workers differed in their taste for education in a way that was not systematically related to ability, then education could not serve as a signal, because it would not be systematically related to ability.

Normative Analysis of Education as a Signal

How does the use of education as a signal affect the surplus of different types of workers? Low-ability workers clearly are worse off; their wages fall from $300 to $200 per week. What about high-ability workers? Their wages rise—from $300 to $400—but they have to spend more years in school. Figure 17.5 is drawn so that the extra costs of schooling are greater than the $100 gain in wages. (We know this because the high-ability indifference curve intersects the vertical axis at a point that is below 300.) Consequently, a high-ability worker would rather be at point *a* than at point e_H.[2] Therefore, both types of worker are worse off.

[2]Why does a high-ability worker go to school? Because point *a* is not available to the worker. If she did not go to college, she would be paid $200 per week, not $300. When all other high-ability people are going to school to signal their ability and she does not, employers will think she is a low-ability person. To avoid being thought of as a low-ability worker, she needs to signal as much as all of the other high-ability workers. She is caught up in a rat race.

Figure 17.5

Equilibrium Education Levels

Because of the differences in their preferences, high-ability workers choose to go to college, point e_H, while low-ability workers choose not to, point e_L. Both types of worker would be better off if they could all be at point a, where they would be paid the marginal revenue product for the average worker and no one would obtain education.

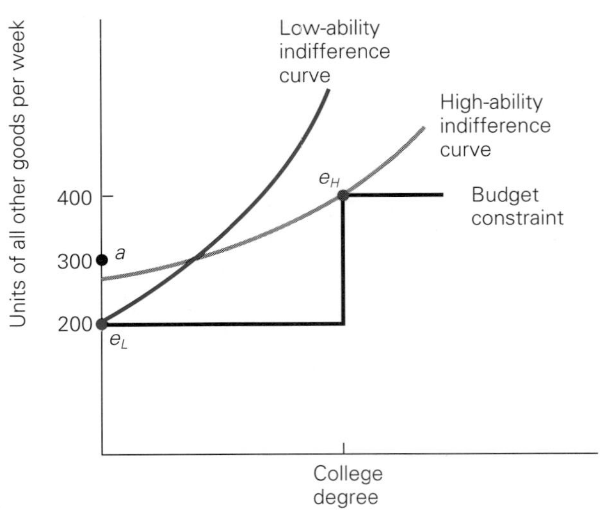

Because the employers are competitive firms, their profits are zero in any case. All of the workers are worse off and the employers are unaffected, so it follows that total surplus in this market falls as a result of signaling.

In fact, the fall in total surplus is just equal to the cost of the additional education. Since profit does not change, the change in total surplus is just the change in worker surplus. But the workers receive wages of $300 per week on average *whether or not there is signaling*. The only effect of signaling is to change the distribution of income across workers of different types. When a person obtains additional education to signal that he or she has a high ability level, that action also makes it clearer that the people not attaining high education levels are low-ability workers. A person's signaling thus has a positive effect on his or her income, but a negative effect on other workers' income. Workers spend money on education, but collectively they earn the same amount when no one obtains education as when only high-ability workers do. Hence, workers collectively are worse off by the full cost of education. Indeed, since education in this model is assumed to generate no social benefits, all of its costs constitute a net loss to society, regardless of the particular numerical values used. (PC 17.3)

17.3 PROGRESS CHECK

In the example above, a high-ability worker prefers a wage of $300 at the low education level to a wage of $400 coupled with the high education level. Suppose instead that a high-ability worker prefers to have the higher income and education level (although years of schooling still is an economic bad). What would be the effects of signaling on total surplus?

Is Education Really Just a Signal?

There is considerable anecdotal evidence that the screening model of education has some validity. For instance, one journalist noted that "corporate America has come to rely on the college degree as the safest guarantee that an applicant has the skills, discipline and maturity to tackle a job" (Uchitelle 1990, A1). Nevertheless, the conclusions of the simple model of education as a signal are very disturbing to many people, and it is important to consider possible shortcomings of the model. Before discussing some qualifications to the education-as-a-signal model, it is instructive to consider two objections that are not valid. First, you might dismiss the signaling argument on the grounds that no high school senior will say, "I'm going to get a college education to signal my ability." While this may be true, it also is irrelevant. From the point of view of workers in the model, all that is important is that they recognize that wages rise with the level of educational attainment. Workers need not know why firms will pay them higher wages for going to college, only that they do. Similarly, employers do not have to be aware of the mechanism by which education works as a signal. Rather, they simply rely on the fact that, in equilibrium, workers with more education are more productive workers.

The second invalid objection is that the example above is too special to lead to any believable conclusions. For instance, introspection suggests that students learn *something* in college, although it may not directly raise their marginal revenue products. While this example *is* a very special one, it is possible to generalize the analysis without overturning the basic results. We could, for instance, allow education to have some direct effect on marginal revenue products and still show that people obtain inefficiently large amounts of education. Similarly, the model could be extended so that there was not a single large jump in wages for graduating from college. Instead, wages might rise with each additional year of schooling. Again, the basic result of overinvesting in education would remain intact.

There are legitimate reasons to doubt that education is *just* a signal. In reality, education almost certainly has several types of social benefits that are left out of the simple signaling model. First, worker productivity may depend on both innate ability and on skills learned in college. This is the view embodied in the human capital model of Chapter 5. Second, for many people, attending college is a form of consumption—the marginal utility of education is positive, not negative as in Figure 17.5.

That self-employed workers choose to go to school provides a piece of evidence against the pure-signaling hypothesis. If education were *solely* a signal, people planning to be self-employed would have no reason to attend college. When you are the boss, you do not need to "signal" to discern your own ability. For these people, education is either a form of consumption or an investment that increases productivity. Either way, education must be providing some benefit.

Education can provide social benefits even if it does not directly raise productivity or generate consumption benefits. This final type of benefit arises when education serves as a basis for sorting workers into different kinds of jobs. Suppose that there were two types of job—one kind that anyone can perform, and another that only high-ability workers can do. Through its role as a signal, education can help employers avoid placing low-ability workers in the job at which they ultimately would fail. By preventing the mismatching of workers with jobs, signaling can raise productivity on average. Even if medical schools merely served to signal which people were innately competent to perform brain surgery, they would be providing a valuable service.

In light of all these qualifications, it would be silly to conclude that educational costs are solely a deadweight loss. The human capital model of education cannot be dismissed. The signaling model does offer an important insight, however—because of the asymmetry of information, people tend to obtain too much education.

SECTION RECAP

The informed side of a market often is able to transmit its information to the uninformed side of the market by sending a signal. The key feature of a signal is that people with different characteristics choose to transmit different values of the signal. The process by which the uninformed side of the market uses signals to sort the informed side of the market is known as screening. Second-degree price discrimination, such as the use of special air fares with travel restrictions, is one example of screening. Signals can also play an important role in competitive markets. In labor markets, for example, education may be a signal for an individual's ability.

17.2 ADVERSE SELECTION

In the models of second-degree price discrimination and competitive signaling just explored, the uninformed side of the market makes inferences about the informed side by looking at a signal. In some markets, the very fact that the informed party wants to deal with the uninformed party can serve as a signal. The story in the introduction to this chapter is one example. The fact that the merchant was so eager to sell the "gold" jewelry at such a low price was a good indicator that the merchant knew that the jewelry was fake. Consequently, the author did not want to buy from him. In a similar vein, the comedian Groucho Marx once said that he would never join a club that would be willing to let him in.

This phenomenon—the uninformed party does not want to deal with anyone who wants to deal with him—arises in many important markets with hidden characteristics. For instance, suppose that you are in the market for a used car. You know that even for a given make and model, some automobiles are well made while others have constant problems ("lemons"). It may be impossible to determine whether a car is a lemon without first owning it for a while. Which type of car should you expect to get when you buy a used car? To answer this question, ask yourself: Who has a greater incentive to sell his or her car, a person with a good car or a person with a lemon? Clearly, the person with a lemon. Knowing this, you should expect the average quality of a used car to be low, and your willingness to pay for a used car should thus be low as well. But if used cars sell for low prices, then why would anyone with a good car sell one? There is a feedback effect that leads to an even lower average quality of used cars—the lower the average quality, the lower the price that buyers are willing to pay, and hence the lower the average quality of the cars people are willing to sell. This downward spiral may continue until the market is wiped out or until the average price and quality both are at low levels. This model thus predicts that used cars will tend to be of low quality and that a seller usually will take a beating when he tries to sell a good car—no one will believe him.

adverse selection
The phenomenon under which the uninformed side of a deal gets exactly the wrong people trading with it (i.e., it gets an adverse selection of the informed parties).

The key feature of the used-car market just described is that the uninformed side of a deal gets exactly the wrong people trading with it. In such situations, the uninformed party is said to get an **adverse selection** of the informed parties. In the used-car market, the buyer gets an adverse selection of sellers. There are many other examples of adverse selection. Consider a life insurance company. Here, the buyer characteristic about which the insurance company cares is the buyer's life expectancy. From the company's point of view, the ideal customer would never die. Since potential insurance buyers likely know more about their health than does the company, this is a situation of hidden characteristics. When the firm cannot observe the life expectancy of different people, it must offer the same policy to everyone. Who will find this insurance to be the most valuable? Those people who are most likely to collect benefits because they are in poor health. But these are the very people that the insurance company does not want as customers! Thus, the insurance company gets an adverse selection of buyers. And, as in our earlier used car example, adjusting the price (here, upward) to reflect this adverse selection may further drive out the good customers, making the problem worse. (Note the difference from the used car market, where there was an adverse selection of *sellers* and prices fell as a result of the adverse selection problem.)

Adverse selection arises whenever there is a hidden characteristics problem and people on the informed side of the market self-select in a way that is harmful to the uninformed side of the market. In this section, we will study how adverse selection affects market performance and how private and public decision makers can react to it.

MORE ON INSURANCE MARKETS

We can apply indifference curve analysis to deepen our understanding of adverse selection. Recall that in Chapter 6 we examined the decision of an obstetrician named Scarlet to purchase insurance to cover malpractice suits. Scarlet faces an uncertain decision—she has a .4 chance of being sued each year, and she has to choose how much to insure against this possibility. For simplicity, we assume Scarlet always loses the case if she is sued. Scarlet's decision is analyzed in Figure 17.6. Scarlet's consumption if she is sued is measured on the horizontal axis while her consumption if there is no suit is measured on the vertical axis. By buying insurance, Scarlet trades off *consumption if not sued* (which goes down because of the insurance premium) against *consumption if sued* (which rises because of the insurance coverage). Scarlet's indifference curves are illustrated in Figure 17.6. In Chapter 6 we saw that the slope of her indifference curves where they intersect the 45° line is -1 times the odds of being sued. Recall that the odds of being sued are equal to the probability of being sued divided by the probability of not being sued. Hence, Scarlet's odds of being sued are $.4/(1 - .4) = 2/3$, and her indifference curves all have a slope of $-2/3$ along the 45° line.

Now, consider Priscilla's demand for malpractice insurance. Priscilla is a better obstetrician than Scarlet and has only a .2 chance of being sued each year. In all other respects, Priscilla and Scarlet have the same preferences. As we saw in Chapter 6, Priscilla's indifference curves are flatter than

17.4 PROGRESS CHECK

Suppose that Dr. Canard is a really bad obstetrician, with a .6 chance of being sued. Graphically illustrate his indifference curves in comparison with Scarlet's and Priscilla's.

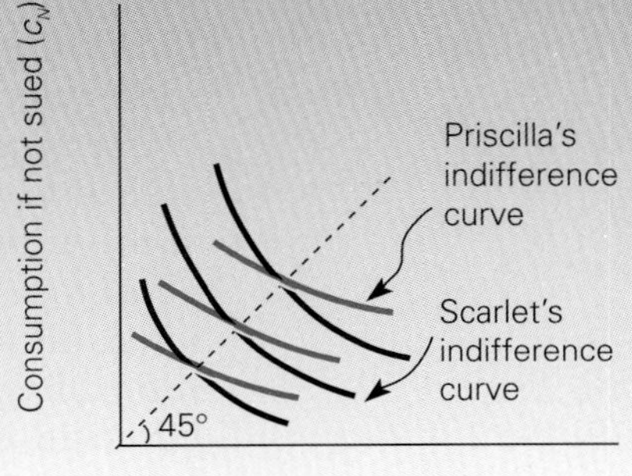

Figure 17.6

Scarlet's Indifference Map

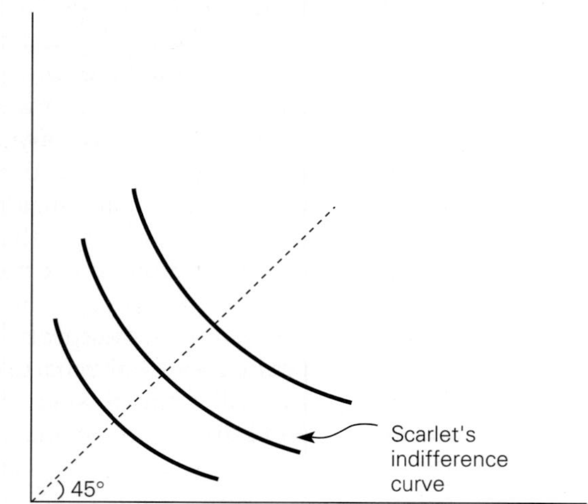

Where they cross the 45° line, Scarlet's indifference curves all have a slope of −2⁄3, which is −1 times the odds of her being sued.

Figure 17.7

Priscilla's Indifference Map Compared to Scarlet's

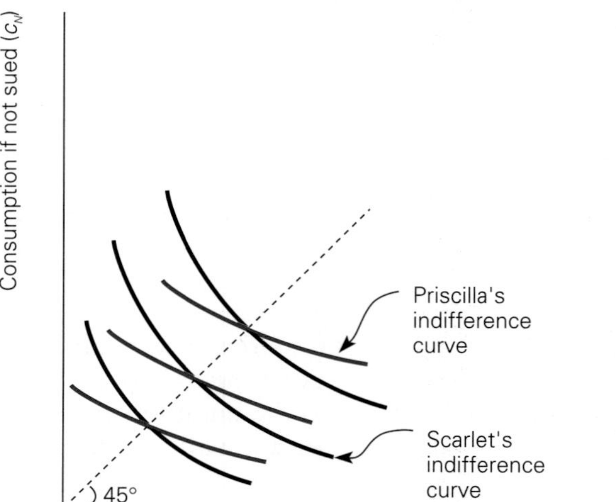

Priscilla's probability of being sued is lower than Scarlet's, but in all other respects Priscilla and Scarlet have the same preferences. Therefore, Priscilla's indifference curves are flatter than Scarlet's. Where they cross the 45° line, Priscilla's indifference curves have a slope of −1⁄4, while Scarlet's have a slope of −2⁄3.

Scarlet's. Since Priscilla's odds of being sued are .2/(1 − .2) = 1/4, the slope of her indifference curves where they intersect the 45° line is −1/4. Intuitively, because Priscilla is less likely to be sued, she is less willing to give up *consumption if not sued* in return for another unit of *consumption if sued*. Figure 17.7 graphs the two doctors' indifference maps together. (PC 17.4)

The Full-Information Equilibrium

Our ultimate goal is to understand what happens when doctors know more about their abilities than the insurance companies. As a benchmark, first consider the market equilibrium when everyone is fully and symmetrically informed; that is, each doctor and her insurance company know her particular chance of being sued. A competitive insurance company is willing to provide a policy at a price equal to marginal cost, so that the policy just breaks even. As we showed in Chapter 6, this means that the premium per dollar of coverage is $1.00 times the probability of the "bad" outcome. Hence, Scarlet pays $.40 to buy $1.00 of coverage. Since Scarlet has to pay the premium whether or not she is sued, her level of *consumption if not sued* falls by $.40, and her level of *consumption if sued* rises by $.60 (= $1.00 − $.40). Scarlet must take a decrease in *consumption if not sued* to get an increase in *consumption if sued* at a rate of .40/.60 = 2/3, which is simply her odds of being sued. If she buys no insurance, Scarlet remains at her endowment point, point *a* in Figure 17.8. Hence, Scarlet's budget line runs through point *a* and has a slope of −2/3, as illustrated in Figure 17.8.

The slope of Scarlet's indifference curves where they cross the 45° line is −2/3, her odds of being sued. This is the same as the slope of her budget line when she is offered insurance at fair odds. As Figure 17.8 shows, Scarlet's equilibrium is at point e_1, where her indifference curve is tangent to her budget line. Since point e_1 lies on the 45° line, Scarlet's consumption level is independent of whether she is sued. This result confirms our earlier finding that a risk-averse person insures herself fully when offered a policy at an actuarially fair price (see Chapter 6).

Since Priscilla has a lower likelihood of collecting on her insurance, the company is willing to sell her a policy with a lower premium and, as shown in Figure 17.8, her budget line is flatter. Like Scarlet, Priscilla purchases insurance until she is on the 45° line, point e_2 in the figure. Notice that because she is offered insurance at a lower price, Priscilla's equilibrium consumption is higher than Scarlet's even though both doctors have endowment point *a*. In summary, under the full-information equilibrium, each doctor purchases complete insurance, but Scarlet pays a higher premium because she is more likely to be sued.

The Asymmetric-Information Equilibrium

A doctor is likely to know much more about his or her ability than an insurance company. Suppose that each doctor knows how likely he or she is to be sued, but the insurance company has some sense only of the average across all doctors. A key feature of the *full* information equilibrium was that the two types of doctors paid different prices for insurance. When the insurance company does not know any particular doctor's probability of being sued, it is impossible to make a high-risk physician pay more than a low-risk physician for the same policy.

What happens when the insurance firm offers the same policy to all doctors, and what price should it set? Suppose that the firm tries to offer a policy that will break even *on average*. Since half of the doctors are low risk and the other half are high risk, the average chance of being sued is $1/2 \times .2 + 1/2 \times .4 = .3$. When the average chance of being sued is .3, the actuarially fair premium is $.30 per dollar of coverage. The resulting fair odds line is shown in Figure 17.9.

Will this policy allow the insurance company to break even? You might think that the answer is yes, since the premium reflects the average chance of a doctor's being sued. But this answer assumes that the two doctors buy the same amount of insurance. To answer this question correctly, consult Figure 17.10, which illustrates the levels of insurance coverage that the two doctors would purchase. Two points jump out. One, Priscilla buys less than full insurance—point e_3 lies above the 45° line. The reason for this outcome is that, at the average rate, the insurance is actuarially unfair against her. Rather than buy full insurance at an unfair rate, Priscilla bears some of the risk herself.

At the same time, if she could, Scarlet would choose point *b*, where she would be better off being sued than not! This seemingly peculiar outcome arises because the insurance is actuarially unfair in Scarlet's favor. Not surprisingly, insurance companies typically do not let people bet against themselves. You will have a hard time buying an insurance policy that pays you *more* than a dollar for every dollar that you lose. Consequently, only the segment of the fair odds line going from point *a* to the 45° line is available to Scarlet. Faced with this set of options, Scarlet chooses to insure herself fully at point e_4.

Figure 17.8

The Full-Information Equilibrium

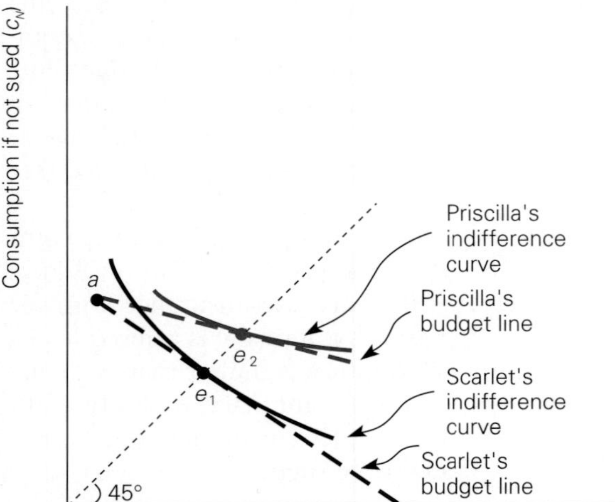

When each doctor is offered insurance at what are fair odds for her, each one purchases full insurance. Since Scarlet has a greater chance of being sued, her fair odds line is steeper than Priscilla's. The fact that endowment point *a* is not on the vertical axis reflects the assumption that a doctor with no insurance will enjoy some consumption even if sued.

Figure 17.9

The Budget Line When the Insurance Premium Is Based on the Average Probability of Being Sued

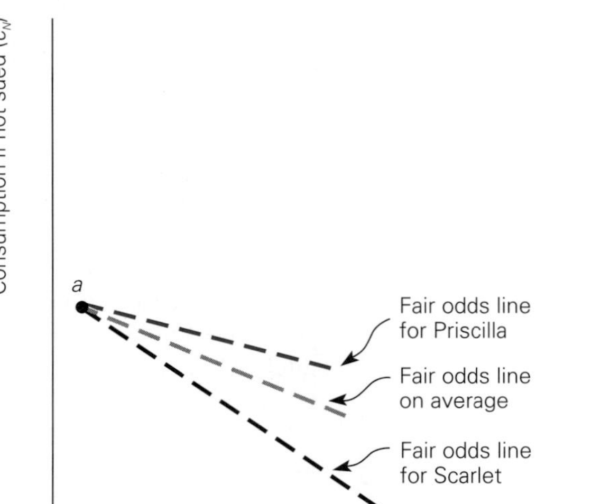

When half of the doctors buying insurance are low risk and the other half are high risk, the average chance of being sued is $\frac{1}{2} \times .2 + \frac{1}{2} \times .4 = .3$. Hence, the actuarially fair premium is \$.30 per dollar of coverage, and the resulting budget line has a slope of $-3/7$.

Notice that even with this restriction, Scarlet purchases more than half of the coverage sold in the market. Because Scarlet has a higher probability of being sued, the insurance company finds itself paying out more than it had calculated. At a premium of \$.30, the firm loses money. To break even, the company has to set a higher premium. But the increase in the premium induces Priscilla to buy even less insurance, while Scarlet continues to buy full insurance as long as the rate is less than the one that would be actuarially fair (given *her* probability of being sued). As Priscilla reduces her coverage, the company has to raise its premium even further to cover the payments made to Scarlet. Depending on the particular shapes of the doctors' indifference curves, this process continues until one of two things happens.

One, Priscilla may drop out of the insurance market altogether. This happens when Priscilla's tastes are such that she buys no insurance at all when she is offered a policy at a price of \$.40 per dollar of coverage, the price that is actuarially fair for Scarlet. Since Scarlet would be the only one purchasing insurance, the company would just break even by charging \$.40 per dollar of coverage. This outcome is an equilibrium, as illustrated in Figure 17.11.[3]

Alternatively, with a different set of tastes, Priscilla remains in the market along with Scarlet. That is, there is a premium such that Priscilla will choose to

[3]For technical reasons, we have to assume that an insurance company cannot charge premiums where the cost per dollar of coverage varies with the amount of coverage.

Figure 17.10

Priscilla and Scarlet's Equilibrium Choices When Offered Insurance at a Premium Based on the Average Probability of Being Sued

When offered insurance at a premium of $.30 per dollar of coverage, Priscilla buys less than full insurance, point e_3, since the insurance is actuarially unfair against her. If she could, Scarlet would choose point b, but the insurance company will not allow her to over-insure. When only the segment of the fair odds line going from point a to the 45° line is available to Scarlet, she insures herself fully at point e_4.

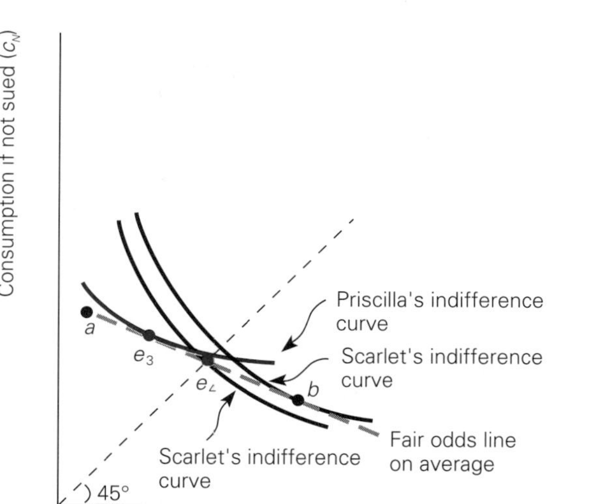

buy some insurance, and the insurance company breaks even on average, given the amounts of insurance the two doctors purchase. Figure 17.12 illustrates this outcome. Since the equilibrium price is actuarially unfair in Scarlet's favor, she still buys as much insurance as she can—the insurance company limits her to buying no more than complete insurance. The equilibrium price is actuarially unfair to Priscilla (the premium partially reflects Scarlet's high risk of being sued), so she buys less than full insurance—but she is sufficiently risk averse that she is willing to buy some insurance anyway. (PC 17.5)

17.5 PROGRESS CHECK

Show that if Priscilla were risk neutral instead of risk averse, she would buy no insurance in equilibrium. What would be the equilibrium price of insurance? How much insurance would Scarlet buy?

The Efficiency Effects of Adverse Selection

Comparing the full-information and asymmetric-information equilibria allows us to see how asymmetric information affects Priscilla, Scarlet, and the insurance company. Under full information, each doctor purchases full insurance at a price that is actuarially fair for her, and their insurance company breaks even.

We saw that there are two possibilities to consider under asymmetric information. If Priscilla drops out of the insurance market entirely, then Scarlet and the insurance company are unaffected because Scarlet obtains actuarially fair insurance and the insurance company breaks even. But Priscilla is worse off since she is risk averse and ends up bearing all of the risk associated with her being sued.

The analysis is a little more complicated when Priscilla remains in the market (Figure 17.12). In this case, Scarlet gains from the asymmetric information, since her rate is lower than the one that is actuarially fair for her. Also notice that Scarlet purchases complete insurance, just as she did in the full-information case. Priscilla is worse off under the asymmetric-information case because she pays a higher

Figure 17.11

The Asymmetric-Information Equilibrium When Priscilla Drops Out of the Market

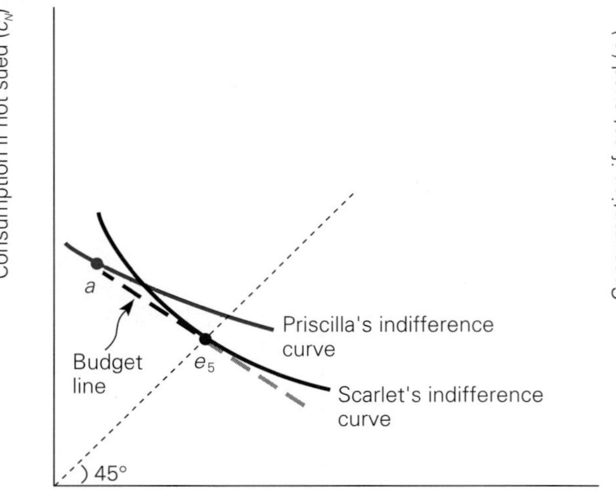

If Priscilla chooses to buy no insurance at all when it is offered at odds that are actuarially fair for Scarlet, it is an equilibrium for the firm to offer insurance at that price. Scarlet is the only one purchasing insurance, and the company breaks even by charging a premium of $.40 per dollar of coverage.

Figure 17.12

The Asymmetric-Information Equilibrium When Priscilla Remains in the Market

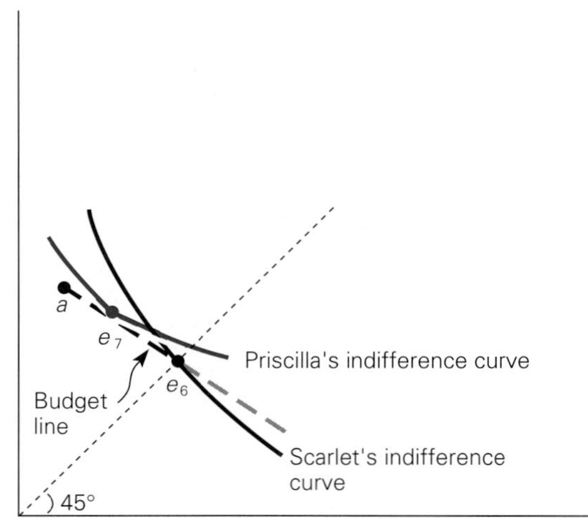

When Priscilla is not driven from the market entirely, the insurance company sets a premium that falls in between the two premiums that it would charge in the full-information outcome. Since the equilibrium price is actuarially unfair in Scarlet's favor, she buys as much insurance as she can, point e_6. Since the equilibrium price is actuarially unfair against Priscilla, she buys less than full insurance, point e_7.

than actuarially fair rate and she is not fully insured in equilibrium. The insurance company breaks even whether there is full information or not. It follows that the monetary gain to Scarlet from lower rates is just equal to the monetary loss to Priscilla from higher rates on the insurance she actually buys in equilibrium. So far, it looks like there is no overall effect on total surplus, but there is. Total surplus falls because Priscilla suffers an additional loss for which there is no offsetting gain—under asymmetric information she ends up with incomplete insurance and bears some of the risk.

So far, we have shown that the market does not perform as well when doctors and the insurance companies are asymmetrically informed as when they are fully informed. But we have not shown that the *asymmetry* of information leads to any efficiency losses. To see if efficiency losses arise from the asymmetry of information, we have to be careful about the standard that we set. We do not want to say that the insurance market is inefficient just because the companies do not know each person's probability of being sued. After all, information is a commodity and, like other commodities, it is scarce. By itself, the fact that something is scarce tells us nothing about efficiency. Therefore, we want to reserve the term *inefficient* for situations in which the market does not perform as well as it could, *given the information available.*

To examine the efficiency consequences of asymmetric information, we will compare the asymmetric information outcome with one in which *no one* knows any individual doctor's risk of being sued. What happens when the doctors and

Figure 17.13

Equilibrium When All Parties Are Symmetrically Uninformed

When Scarlet and Priscilla each know only the average probability of being sued for all doctors, rather than their individual probabilities, each doctor's indifference map is based on the average probability, .3. Specifically, each indifference curve has a slope of $-3/7 = -.3/(1 - .3)$ at the point where it intersects the 45° line. This is just the slope of the budget line. Both doctors purchase full insurance at point e_8.

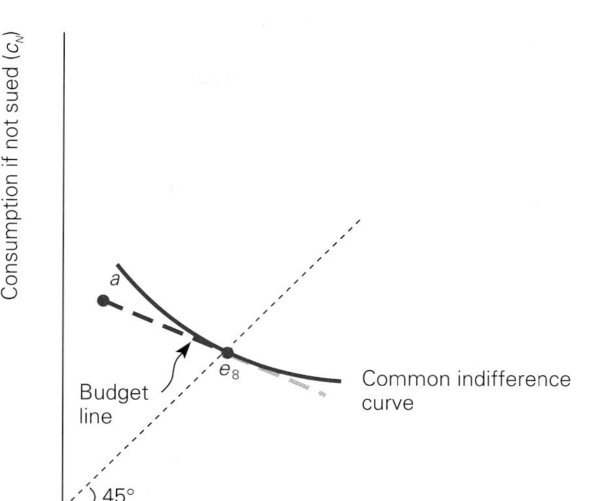

insurance company are equally uninformed? Suppose that Scarlet and Priscilla each know only the average likelihood of being sued for all doctors, rather than their individual chances of being sued. In this case, the insurance company knows as much as the doctors, and there is no asymmetry of information. Each person's indifference map (between consumption if sued and consumption of not sued) is based on the average chance of being sued, .3. Specifically, each indifference curve has a slope of $-3/7 = .3/(1 - .3)$ at the point where it intersects the 45° line. Such an indifference map is drawn in Figure 17.13. The associated fair-odds (budget) line also is drawn in the figure. From the diagram, we can see what happens when a firm offers insurance at an actuarially fair price based on the average risk of a claim. At a price of \$.30 per dollar of coverage, everyone buys full insurance and the firm breaks even on average. Since everyone purchases full insurance, the equilibrium entails an efficient allocation of risk bearing—the risk-averse doctors bear none of the risk while the risk-neutral insurance company bears all of it.

We have just shown that when the two sides of the market are symmetrically uninformed, there is no problem. Similarly, we showed above that if the two sides of the market both know the risks faced by any given individual, there is no problem—the firm simply offers one kind of policy to high-risk people and a different kind to low-risk people. The only situation in which risk-averse people are forced to bear risk is the one in which there is asymmetric information. We conclude that the *asymmetry of information, not just the lack of information, is the key to the problem.*

Market Responses to Adverse Selection

Our theory indicates that asymmetric information can have adverse consequences for efficiency. If this theory is correct, we should see institutions develop that deal with these problems. Indeed, in a variety of actual insurance markets, firms do respond to asymmetric information.

Insurance and Testing for AIDS The problem of adverse selection is one reason why most insurance companies require a medical exam before you can purchase life insurance from them. They know that you can go to a doctor before you decide whether to buy insurance, and the company wants to avoid insuring people who are planning to collect soon. This phenomenon is one of the factors behind the controversy over insurance companies to test potential customers for AIDS before issuing policies.

You might think that (from an efficiency viewpoint, at least) testing by insurance companies completely solves the adverse-selection problem. It does and it doesn't. Testing does tell the insurance company who is a high-risk customer. But the test has no social value—the test does not lead to anyone's taking actions that increase the level of total surplus. Rather, it simply allows the insurance company to avoid making payments to the estates of high-risk people. From a social point of view, the cost of testing is a waste. Moreover, for one set of people, the ability to reduce risk by purchasing insurance is lost—people who have AIDS (even those who do not yet know it) are prevented from purchasing insurance.

Should the government ban such testing? You may think that a ban on testing would solve the problem. But then we are back to the original adverse-selection problem. If they are unable to test for AIDS and face a large number of policyholders with the disease, companies may refuse to sell any policies at all. Or they may close their offices in large urban areas, which generally have a higher incidence of AIDS in their populations than rural areas. Or insurance companies may charge extremely high premiums. A flat ban on testing may not have the effects that policymakers would like. There is no easy solution to the problems posed by asymmetric information in this market.

Group Health Plans Many workers receive health insurance benefits from their employers. These benefits typically take the form of automatic enrollment in a particular health insurance program. Since everyone in the firm is enrolled, these programs are known as *group plans.* A typical insurance company offers group rates that are significantly below the rates charged to individuals. There are several reasons for this. One, some of the administrative costs are borne by the employer rather than the insurance company. Two, the employer may shop around more than a single worker, resulting in greater competition among insurance companies and better deals for the buyers. But neither of these reasons is sufficient to explain the size of the difference. A third reason comes into play—since group insurance is mandatory for all employees, there is no adverse-selection problem. Under automatic enrollment, there is no chance for employees who are likely to collect insurance benefits to purchase more insurance than people who are not. Since everyone has to receive insurance coverage, the insurance firm faces the average risk of having to pay benefits on a policy. If enrollment were not automatic, people who knew that they were likely to have low health-care expenses would choose not to purchase insurance, while those likely to have high expenses would join. As in our malpractice example, the insurance company would face an adverse selection of policyholders.

Targeted Insurance Rates In the absence of direct observation of risk, an insurance company may base its premiums on indirect measures. Since, on average, women live longer than men, a company's cost of providing life insurance to a

45-year-old woman is only 84 percent of the cost of providing life insurance to a 45-year-old man (Seligman 1983, 85). Competitive insurance companies would offer lower life insurance rates to women than to men. A similar effect rises with automobile insurance. Despite the negative stereotype of "women drivers," women under age 25 are, on average, noticeably better drivers than men under 25. Consequently, insurance companies have been willing to sell auto insurance to young women for only 60 percent of what they charge young men.

Sex-based rates are extremely controversial. Many people argue that sex-based rates constitute unfair discrimination. After all, some men clearly live longer than some women. And there are some young men who are better drivers than some young women. In response to these arguments, Hawaii, Michigan, Montana, North Carolina, and Pennsylvania have laws mandating "unisex" insurance ratings (Nordheimer 1996, 21).

Other people have argued that banning sex-based auto and life insurance rates would discriminate against women by ignoring actuarial facts. One can even argue that, if anything, insurance companies have been charging auto insurance rates that discriminate against women. While women paid only 60 percent of the price paid by men for auto insurance, the cost of providing auto insurance to women was only 50 percent of the cost of insuring male drivers (Seligman 1983, 85). Although women are unfortunately catching up with men in terms of bad driving, the National Association of Independent Insurers estimated that unisex-rating laws still force a young woman to pay about $400 per year more than she would if rates were based on actuarial differences in accident rates across sexes (Nordheimer 1996, 21).

Should the government allow insurance companies to base life insurance rates on sex? Should they be allowed to base automobile insurance rates on sex, age, and marital status? Economics per se does not answer these questions. But it does provide important insights into these issues, and it helps us think through the likely effects of alternative policies. Economics tells us that market forces will push firms toward using such indicators of risk when they can. And it tells us that firms will try to get around government attempts to limit this sort of behavior. If the government insists that all drivers be charged the same rate, for example, then companies may attempt to find excuses to deny male drivers' applications for insurance.

OTHER MARKETS IN WHICH ADVERSE SELECTION IS IMPORTANT

Adverse selection is not confined to insurance markets. We already saw one example when we discussed the used-car market. This section briefly discusses two other markets in which adverse selection effects can be important.

Labor Markets

Adverse selection may arise in factor markets as well as in product markets. Suppose that, as in our earlier job market signaling example, there is a competitive labor market in which half the workers are of low ability with a marginal revenue product of $200 per week, and the other half of the workers are of high ability with a marginal revenue product of $400 per week. We will make two important changes from our earlier example. One, let's suppose that education is not available as a signal of ability in this market. Two, suppose that the workers have employment opportunities in other industries. In particular, suppose that these opportunities depend on people's abilities. Low-ability workers can earn $100 per week in their best alternative while high-ability workers can earn $250 per week in theirs.

Now consider what happens when firms in this industry try to hire workers. Because even the low-ability workers have marginal revenue products of $200 per week, firms in this industry will compete to hire workers until the wage is driven up to at least $200 per week. Could the equilibrium wage be higher than $200 per week? Suppose that a firm offers to pay $225 per week. Since this wage is lower than the $250 opportunity wage of high-ability workers, only low-ability people accept a job. But then the firm is paying its workers more than their marginal revenue product. Such an outcome cannot be a competitive equilibrium. The same conclusion holds for any wage greater than $200 but less than $250 per week. But look what happens if the firm offers more than $250 per week, say $275 per week. At this wage, both high- and low-ability workers seek employment in the industry. Since both types of workers are attracted, the firm finds that on average its workers have marginal revenue products equal to $300 per week, $1/2 \times$ $200 + $1/2 \times$ $400, and the firm finds it profitable to raise its wage offer. But so do other firms. In fact, this process continues until the market wage is bid up to $300 per week.

17.6 PROGRESS CHECK

Suppose that all of the firms could observe any particular worker's ability level. How much would a low-ability worker be paid? A high-ability worker?

This example illustrates an important and surprising point. In a market with a hidden characteristic, a buyer may be better off by paying a higher price. In the present example, by paying a higher wage, a firm gets workers who on average are more productive, which makes the wage increase profitable to the firm. Raising wages to improve the productivity of the workforce is known as paying **efficiency wages**, and adverse-selection problems provide an important motivation for this practice. (PC 17.6)

efficiency wages
The practice of raising wages to improve the productivity of the workforce.

The Market for Human Blood

Over the years, there has been much concern about the quality of the supply of human blood available for transfusions. The most recent occasion has been the major public worry over contamination by the virus that causes AIDS. For decades, however, there has been significant concern with post-transfusion hepatitis, an inflammatory liver disease that turns the victim's skin yellow and in a small percentage of cases is fatal. Although procedures are available to test donated blood, between 3 and 10 percent of transfusion recipients develop hepatitis (Drake et al. 1982, 30). An important problem confronting blood banks and public policymakers is whether there are ways to reduce the incidence of hepatitis by screening potential donors.

In 1981 alone, roughly 8 million Americans supplied blood. About 70 percent of these people received no financial reward for their donations. Roughly a quarter of the suppliers were either paying off debts (measured in blood) that were run up by friends or relatives receiving transfusions, or received a reward in the form of preferential future access to the blood supply for themselves and their families. The remaining 3 or 4 percent were paid cash for their donations, so-called *commercial blood* (Drake et al. 1982, 5–6).

Commercial blood is controversial. People worry about its quality, arguing that people who are driven by the profit motive to provide blood are more likely to be alcoholics, drug addicts, and others who might have serious infectious diseases than are voluntary donors. In other words, there is an adverse-selection problem among commercial donors. Numerous studies have indeed found a much higher incidence of hepatitis in commercially collected blood. In many ways, this market behaves like an efficiency wage market turned upside down—paying for blood has the effect of *lowering* its average quality. In part out of concern for its quality, the percentage of blood obtained commercially in the United States has fallen over the years. And back in the 1960s, Japan switched from a system relying largely on commercial blood to one relying primarily on voluntary blood after the American ambassador to Japan contracted hepatitis from a transfusion of commercial blood (Drake et al. 1982, 119).

GOVERNMENT RESPONSES TO HIDDEN CHARACTERISTICS

We have shown that the market responses to the problems raised by hidden characteristics may fall short of achieving what would be the efficient outcome if everyone were fully informed. This situation opens the possibility that government intervention could improve matters, but we must recognize that the government itself may be imperfectly informed. Still, there may be ways in which government intervention can help.

Private group insurance programs can help overcome adverse-selection problems by preventing people from self-selecting. Some government programs also rely on this principle. Virtually all of the Western industrialized nations have compulsory public pension programs, such as the Social Security system in the United States. A key attribute of these programs is that workers have no choice; they must join the pension plan. In this way, adverse selection is avoided.

Another type of government intervention falls under the heading of *information policies*. In response to a lack of consumer information in a market, the government may do several things to improve the information flow and move the market toward the full-information equilibrium. Through the Federal Trade Commission, for example, the U.S. government prohibits false and deceptive advertising. While this policy hurts firms with bad products (they cannot try to fool consumers), it actually helps firms with good products because they can tell consumers the truth without being suspected of lying.

In some markets, the firms would not be sure what to say even if they wanted to tell the truth about their products. There might be no recognized measure of quality. In such instances, the government can serve a useful role by establishing a standardized scoring system. For example, the Federal Trade Commission adopted a standard for measuring the amount of tar in cigarettes. Establishment of this standard allowed manufacturers of low-tar cigarettes to advertise this fact. Definition of words like "natural" and "light" for food also are subject to government regulations.

In addition to controlling what firms are allowed to say if they want to, the government sometimes intervenes to make disclosure of certain facts mandatory. Home appliances such as dishwashers and refrigerators must be labeled with their federal energy-efficiency ratings. There also are many mandatory disclosure requirements in financial and real estate markets. In California, for example, the seller of a house is legally obligated to disclose any known defects with the house. In some instances, used-car dealers are also supposed to disclose known defects.

Interestingly, the logic of adverse selection suggests that *mandatory* disclosure may be unnecessary. What do you think consumers would make of a company that refused to release certain information about its product that would be valuable in helping consumers assess its quality? They probably would conclude that the company had something to hide. Hence, market forces may push firms to reveal such information. The market may not work, however, in cases in which the information hurts all firms and consumers are not aware that the information even exists. In such markets, competition alone provides no incentive for voluntary information disclosure. There is no reason to believe that cigarette companies would have voluntarily warned consumers of the health risks associated with smoking, for instance.

In closing our discussion of government information policies, we should recognize that they may not be able to push the market all the way to the full-information equilibrium. With or without government intervention, information still may be costly to collect and disseminate. And the government policies themselves have costs.

SECTION RECAP

In many markets with asymmetric information, the uninformed party finds itself dealing with exactly the type of informed party with which it would least like to deal. The uninformed party is confronted with an adverse selection of partners. Adverse selection is an important phenomenon in insurance, labor, and other markets. Problems of adverse selection may give rise to efficiency losses, but there are a variety of ways in which private parties and the government can respond.

17.3 HIDDEN ACTIONS

In situations of hidden characteristics discussed above, a person's type is beyond his or her control. In the labor market example, a worker's ability was not something that the worker consciously chose. In many other situations, an economic agent controls some feature that is important to the other side of the market. Suppose that you own your own shoe store, and you want to hire a salesperson. You want your employee to do a good job serving your customers. But when you are out of the store, you cannot be sure that he is working hard; he may simply tell the customers to go away so that he can rest. Similarly, when you hire someone to fix your car, you want her to charge you only for what's broken. But that may be very hard for you to determine, as evidenced in 1992 when authorities in California revealed that Sears had fraudulently overcharged thousands of customers on their auto repair bills.

These situations exemplify what we defined earlier as a *principal-agent relationship*. In Chapter 7 we said that a principal-agent relationship exists whenever one party, *the principal*, hires a second party, *the agent*, to perform some task on the first party's behalf. What makes a principal-agent relationship interesting is that the principal and the agent may have different objectives, and the principal cannot directly monitor the agent's behavior. Hence, the principal has to worry about what the agent will do. That's why you have to be on your toes when you take your car to be fixed.

There are many other situations that have these three important features:

1. One side of an economic relationship, the agent, takes an action that affects the other side, the principal (e.g., the shoe salesman chooses how hard to work).

2. The principal cannot observe the action taken by the agent (e.g., the store owner sometimes has to leave the store and cannot keep an eye on the salesman).
3. The principal and the agent disagree on which action is the best one for the agent to take (e.g., the store owner would like the salesman to work hard, but the salesman would like to take it easy, *ceteris paribus*).

To emphasize the element of choice, we refer to these situations as ones of *hidden actions* rather than hidden characteristics.

Before studying hidden actions in detail, let's think carefully about the difference between hidden actions and hidden characteristics. In a hidden-characteristic situation, economic relationships (such as the terms under which workers are compensated) have to be designed to transfer information from the informed party to the uninformed party. Information transmission is what signaling is all about. In situations of hidden action, however, incentives are the problem. The uninformed party wants to make sure that the informed party has the right incentives to take an action. But, because the action is inherently unobservable, it is impossible to write a contract directly giving the informed party the proper incentives.

The following example may help clarify the distinction. Suppose that you would like a part-time job tutoring people in how to use word processors. The company hiring you is clearly concerned with how well you do your job. To some extent your performance will depend on what *actions* you choose to take (Will you be rude to your students?) *after* you have been hired. And to some extent your performance will depend on *characteristics* (Are you good at explaining things clearly?) that you possessed *before* you were hired. To get you to take the right action, the contract has to give you the right incentives. With respect to characteristics, there may be nothing that can be done to change yours. Rather, the firm's interest is in finding out your characteristics and not hiring you if they are bad.

MORAL HAZARD IN INSURANCE MARKETS

The problem of hidden actions, like the problem of adverse selection, was first studied in the insurance industry. Hidden action problems arise in this industry when a policyholder may take unobservable actions that affect the probability that he or she will suffer a loss and file an insurance claim. Because the informed side may take the "wrong" action (i.e., not do enough to prevent an accident), situations of hidden action have been given the name **moral hazard**.

moral hazard
Another name given to situations of hidden action because, in such cases, the informed side may take the "wrong" action.

Fire Prevention in the Absence of Insurance

A homeowner can reduce the chance of a serious fire by purchasing extremely sensitive smoke and heat detectors, constantly buying new appliances, replacing the wiring in the house, and never ever using a hot plate. We can lump all of these activities under the heading of *care*. We will measure care in terms of the amount of money spent on prevention—one unit of *care* costs $1.

The reason for taking care is that it reduces the risk of fire, thus reducing the expected damage from fire. The *TD* curve in Panel A of Figure 17.14 shows the expected total damages associated with each level of care. The downward slope

Figure 17.14

Expected Total Damages and the Marginal Benefits of Care

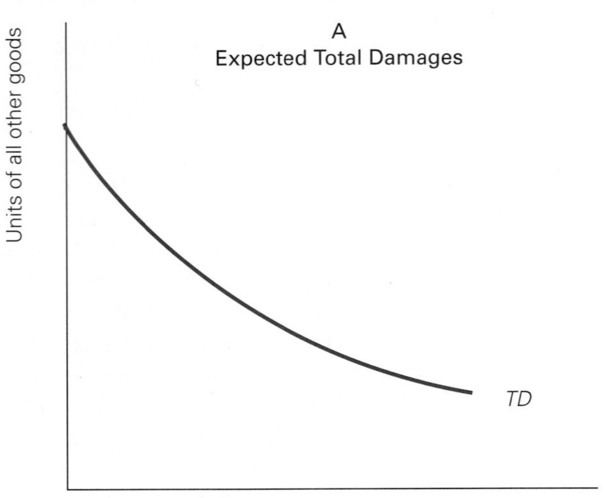

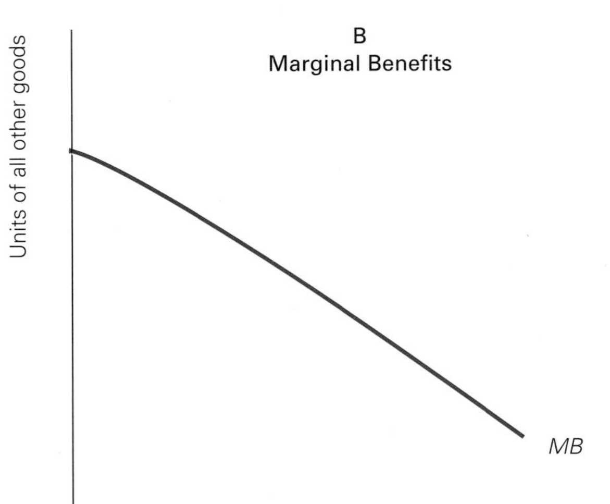

The *TD* curve in Panel A shows the expected total damages associated with each level of *care*. It slopes downward because an increase in care leads to a decrease in the chance of a fire. The *MB* curve in Panel B shows the marginal benefits (reduction in expected damages) for each care level. The height of the *MB* curve is equal to −1 times the slope of the *TD* curve. Its downward slope reflects the fact that as additional care is taken, the last increment of care has less of an effect on the risk of fire than the earlier units of care.

of the total damages curve reflects the fact that an increase in care leads to a decrease in the chance of a fire.

The marginal benefit of increased care is the marginal reduction in expected damages and is represented by the *MB* curve in Panel B of Figure 17.14. Since it measures the marginal reduction in expected total damages, the height of the *MB* curve is equal to −1 times the slope of the *TD* curve. The downward slope of *MB* curve reflects the fact that, as additional care is taken, the incremental reduction in the risk of fire decreases.

How much care does our homeowner undertake? As a rational decision maker, the homeowner purchases care just up to the point where its marginal benefit and marginal cost are equal. Figure 17.15 graphs both the marginal benefit curve, *MB*, and the marginal cost curve, *MC*. Notice that since each additional unit of care costs $1, the marginal cost curve is flat at a height of 1. Applying the marginal choice rule for the homeowner, the equilibrium is point e_1 in Figure 17.15.

Moral Hazard and the Effects of Insurance

Now suppose that the homeowner buys fire insurance that covers the complete cost of rebuilding her home and replacing all of its contents. How does this insurance policy affect the situation illustrated in Figure 17.15? First, note that the insurance has no effect on the marginal cost of care. But the insurance dramatically affects the marginal benefit of care as seen *from the homeowners' perspective.*

Figure 17.15

The Equilibrium Care Level with No Insurance

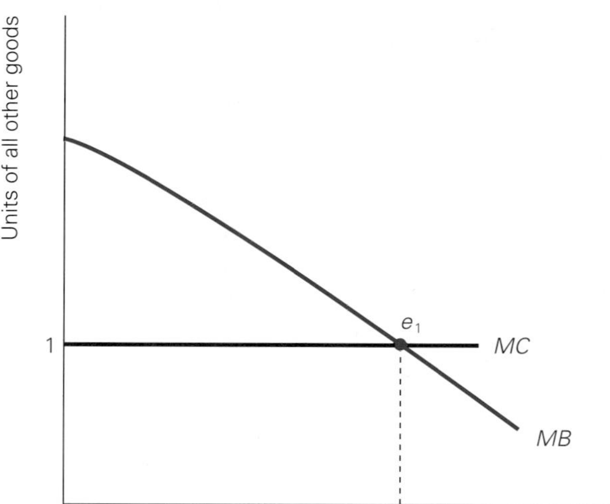

Since each additional unit of care costs $1, the marginal cost curve is flat at a level of 1. In equilibrium, the homeowner chooses the care level at which the marginal benefit is equal to marginal cost, point e_1.

Figure 17.16

The Equilibrium Care Level with Insurance

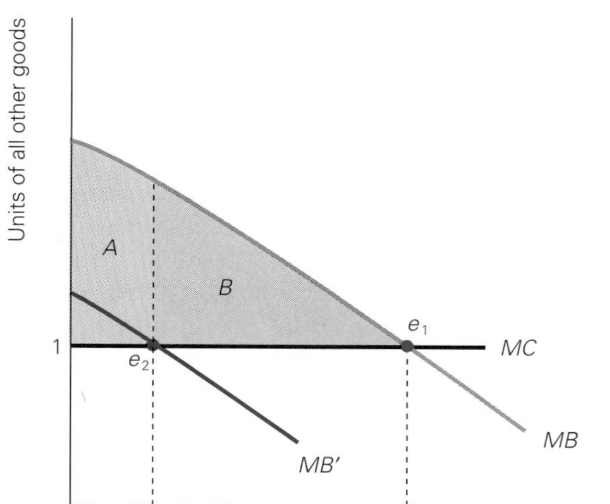

When the homeowner purchases insurance, the marginal benefit of care shifts downward from *MB* to *MB′*. With insurance, the homeowner's marginal benefit of care is equal to the marginal cost of care at point e_2. Comparing points e_1 and e_2, we see that the homeowner undertakes less care when insured.

Since the costs of replacing the house are covered by the insurance, the homeowner does not count the reduction in the chance of a fire as much of a benefit—he or she does not have to pick up the bill if there is a fire. Of course, even with 100 percent insurance coverage, the homeowner still derives some benefits from fire prevention. If nothing else, reducing the risk of fire lessens the chance of being killed in a blaze. Hence, the marginal benefit of care still is positive, but it is less than it was without the insurance. Figure 17.16 shows the homeowner's lower marginal benefit curve with insurance, *MB′*. For comparison, the uninsured marginal benefit curve also is drawn. With insurance, the homeowner's marginal benefit and cost of care are equal at point e_2. Comparing points e_1 and e_2, we see that the homeowner undertakes less care when insured. This result is completely intuitive—since the homeowner bears less of the cost of a fire when insured, he or she does less to prevent one. Of course, the less care the homeowner takes, the greater the chance of a fire, and the greater the chance that the insurance company will have to pay a claim. That is why there is a moral hazard problem from the firm's perspective.

The effect of moral hazard is most dramatic when the homeowner overinsures to get more money for the property when it burns down than he or she could get by selling it on the open market. When a house is worth more burned down than standing, the owner has an incentive to see to it that an "accident" occurs. This is one case in which moral hazard clearly deserves its name. While you might think that it is unlikely that people would burn down their own house to collect the insurance money, landlords have burned down apartment buildings for just such reasons. And when a commercial building burns down, one of the first things the fire marshal investigates is whether any of the businesses in it were failing and worth more burned out than operating.

Such extreme moral hazard behavior is not confined to the market for fire insurance. In recent years, a severe form of the problem also surfaced in the auto insurance market: Some mornings cars would stick out of the Merrimack River because "so many people dumped their cars into the river, to file stolen-car claims, that the last car in the night before had fallen onto a stack of others and would not sink" (Kerr 1992, A3). Auto insurers are not the only ones with this problem. In 1995, multimillionaire George Lindemann, Jr., was convicted of hiring "a small-time hood" to kill a horse so Lindemann could collect the $250,000 for which it was insured (*Sports Illustrated*, October 2, 1995, 13).

Efficiency Effects of Moral Hazard

Burning down an otherwise sound building simply to collect on the insurance clearly is wasteful and inefficient. But things appear not to be so clear in the less extreme case in which the homeowner merely reduces the care level. In terms of Figure 17.16, although point e_2 involves a higher chance of fire, it also involves lower expenditures on fire-prevention resources. So, why does moral hazard reduce efficiency? The reason is that the insurance does nothing to reduce the total cost of a fire to society as a whole. While the homeowner does not have to pay for the rebuilding when he or she has insurance, the company does have to pay. Thus, the original marginal benefit curve (the homeowner's benefit curve when he or she buys no insurance) represents the true *social* marginal benefit curve. In the absence of insurance, the homeowner's *private* benefit curve is the same as the social one, and the homeowner chooses the care level that maximizes the difference between benefits and costs. At point e_1 in Figure 17.16, total surplus is the sum of shaded areas A and B. In contrast, when he or she has insurance, the homeowner's private marginal benefit curve lies below the social marginal benefit curve. At the homeowner's equilibrium point, e_2, total surplus is shaded area A alone. Total surplus falls by area B because the homeowner takes too little care to prevent a fire.

Another way to see the inefficiency of the market equilibrium with moral hazard is to note that the policyholder would be better off if the insurance company could observe his or her care level and order the policyholder to undertake level e_1. Why would the homeowner benefit? The answer follows from the fact that a competitive insurance company sets a premium that breaks even. When all policyholders choose low levels of care, insurance rates must rise to cover the increase in expected claims. This increase is equal to the change in total benefits.[4] But we already saw that the benefits of care exceed the costs over the range from e_2 to e_1, so the premium rises by more than the cost of care falls. Why then, does the homeowner choose the low level of care? Because even if the high level were chosen, the insurance company would not believe the homeowner. Remember, the essence of the moral hazard problem is that one side of the market cannot see what the other side is up to. Here, the insurance company cannot see what

[4]To be precise, the private, no-insurance marginal benefit curve reflects the homeowner's attitudes toward risk. When she is risk averse, the homeowner's benefit from avoiding the chance of a loss is greater than the insurance company's expected cost of paying for the fire damage.

Figure 17.17

The Effects of Co-Insurance

In the absence of insurance (a co-payment rate of 100 percent), the benefits of care are given by the top marginal benefit curve, *MB*, and the equilibrium is at point e_1. Under full insurance (a co-payment rate of 0 percent), the homeowner's benefits from care are given by the bottom marginal benefit curve, *MB′*, and the equilibrium is at a low level of care, point e_2. With a co-payment rate of 50 percent, the marginal benefit curve, *MB″*, falls between the no-insurance and full-insurance curves, and the equilibrium care level is at e_3.

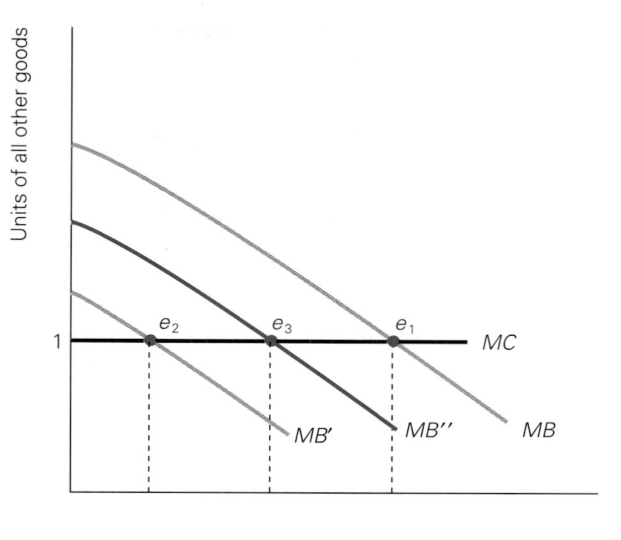

care level has been taken, so it cannot base its rates on the care level. And given that the homeowner is going to be charged the same premium no matter what he or she does, the homeowner rationally chooses the care level at point e_2.

Co-Insurance and Deductibles

co-insurance
A provision in an insurance policy under which the policyholder picks up some percentage of the bill for damages when there is a claim.

The problem of moral hazard arises because insurance reduces the incentives for care. One way to mitigate this problem is to reduce the level of insurance and require the policyholder to bear some of the costs of a claim. This cost sharing generally takes one of two forms. First, many insurance policies have what is known as **co-insurance**: The insurance company pays for less than 100 percent of the bill, and the policyholder picks up the rest. Many health insurance policies, for example, have a 20 percent co-insurance rate. That means that someone who gets sick and runs up a \$1,000 medical bill gets reimbursed \$800 (= .80 × \$1,000) by the insurance company, and pays \$200 (= .20 × \$1,000) as a co-payment. The reason that insurance companies use co-payment schemes is a simple one—the higher the co-payment rate, the more the policyholder avoids "frivolous" trips to the doctor, and the greater the incentives to take preventative care.

Returning to the case of the homeowner purchasing fire insurance, Figure 17.17 illustrates why a co-payment rate increases our homeowner's incentives to take care to prevent a fire. In the absence of insurance (a co-payment rate of 100 percent), the homeowner bears all of the costs of damage and has strong incentives to avoid a fire; the benefits of care are given by schedule *MB* and the equilibrium is at point e_1. Under full insurance (a co-payment rate of 0 percent), the homeowner bears none of the direct financial damages, and the equilibrium is at a low level of care, point e_2. With a co-payment rate of 50 percent, the homeowner bears half of the financial costs of a fire. The marginal benefit curve, *MB″*, then falls between the no-insurance and full-insurance curves. So does the equilibrium care level, e_3. With a 50 percent co-payment rate, the homeowner gets some benefits from insurance but still has a relatively strong incentive to take care.

deductible
A provision in an insurance policy under which the person buying the insurance has to pay the initial damages up to some set limit.

Another means of making the insurance holder bear some of the risk is to have a **deductible** in the insurance policy. Under a deductible, the person buying the insurance has to pay the initial damages up to some set limit. A homeowner's fire insurance policy might not cover the first $1,000 of damage. An earthquake policy on an expensive house might have a $50,000 deductible. This means that if an earthquake does $40,000 worth of damage, the homeowner pays the entire bill. But if the earthquake is really big and does $150,000 worth of damage, the homeowner pays the first $50,000, and the insurance company pays the remaining $100,000. A deductible this size gives the homeowner incentives to keep the house well maintained and to invest in measures such as reinforced foundations that minimize the likely damage from a quake. At the same time, the homeowner is covered in the event of a truly catastrophic loss.

Do co-insurance and deductibles solve all of the moral hazard problem? No. First, some moral hazard remains as long as the co-insurance rate is not 100 percent or the deductible is not infinite (i.e., as long as the person buys some insurance). Second, to the extent that the co-insurance rate or the deductible are positive, the consumer purchases less than full insurance. But in the absence of moral hazard, the efficient outcome would entail risk-averse households' purchasing full insurance.

EMPLOYER-EMPLOYEE RELATIONSHIPS

The problem of hidden actions goes well beyond worrying about accident prevention. Another important area in which moral hazard arises is employer-employee relationships. We looked at one example of moral hazard in an employment relationship in Chapter 7 when we examined whether it is reasonable to assume that firms act to maximize profits. That discussion centered on the fact that most large companies are not managed by their owners, and that owners and managers may have differing goals. Since the managers' actions may affect the value of the owners' firm, owners care about their managers' actions. But managers' effort may be difficult to monitor, particularly in the case of a manager who has to spend time thinking rather than physically making something.

Problems of moral hazard are important in many other employer-employee relationships. The manager of a large department store may not be able to see how hard all of the clerks are working—there are too many of them to watch all at once. And it is very difficult for a company to observe directly its employees' effort levels when they are traveling salespeople or repair personnel who make on-site visits to customers' locations.

We can extend our earlier analysis of labor supply to see how employers can deal with worker moral hazard. In the model analyzed in Chapter 5, we assumed that labor was measured simply in terms of hours on the job and that firms could observe it. When the worker was paid by the hour, the level of pay was thus perfectly tied to the amount of labor. But as our examples above illustrate, a person often can vary the degree of effort that he or she puts into the work while on the job. Hence, it is important to extend our analysis of labor supply to cases in which the employer cannot perfectly observe the amount of effort expended by the employee and thus cannot directly tie pay to effort.

Figure 17.18

The Manager's Indifference Map

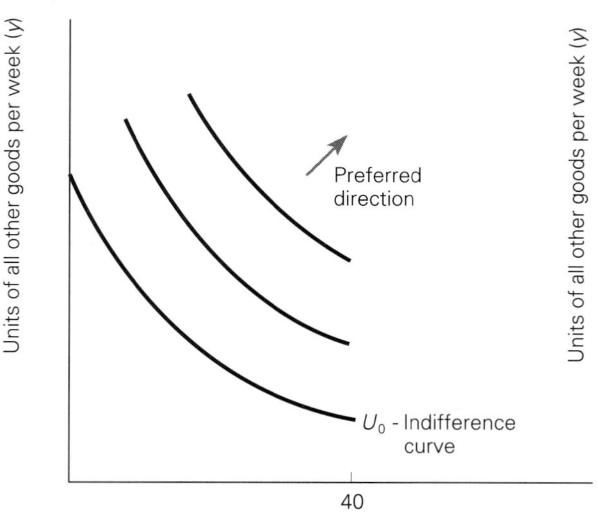

Alex's indifference map represents his tastes for shirking and *all other goods*. Since the more he shirks, the more on-the-job leisure Alex consumes; shirking is an economic good.

Figure 17.19

The Effects of Shirking on Profit

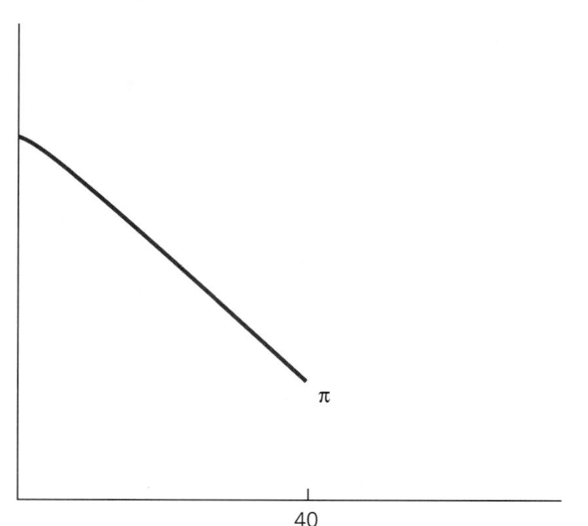

The height of the π curve shows the firm's profit (measured in terms of the amount of *all other goods* that it can buy) for each level of shirking by Alex. The π curve slopes downward because, as Alex's consumption of shirking rises, he devotes less effort to the firm, and the firm's profit falls, *ceteris paribus*.

Consider the case of Alex, a manager who consumes leisure and our composite commodity, *all other goods*. Leisure includes both leisure away from the workplace and "on-the-job leisure," such as not working as hard as possible while in the office, and taking lots of coffee breaks. Suppose that Alex has no choice but to be in the office 40 hours per week if he wants to keep his job (whether he is physically in the office can be monitored). He still can choose the amount of leisure consumed by adjusting the extent to which he shirks at his job. Let s denote the amount of *shirking* in which Alex engages per week, and let y denote the amount of *all other goods* consumed per week. Alex's utility depends on the amounts of *shirking* and *all other goods* that he consumes. Since the more he shirks, the more on-the-job leisure Alex consumes; shirking is an economic good. As usual, we measure *all other goods* in units such that the price is $1 per unit. In Figure 17.18 we characterize Alex's tastes for shirking and *all other goods* in an indifference curve diagram with hours of shirking on the horizontal axis and units of *all other goods* on the vertical axis.

Alex's welfare rises as he shirks more, *ceteris paribus*. But his employer's profit falls—the more that Alex shirks, the less effort he devotes to running the firm and maximizing its profit. Figure 17.19 illustrates this relationship by graphing hours of shirking on the horizontal axis and profit (measured in terms of the amount of *all other goods* that it can buy) on the vertical. The downward slope of the π curve reflects the fact that as Alex's consumption of shirking rises, the profit of the firm falls, *ceteris paribus*.

Figure 17.20

The Equilibrium Outcome When Effort is Observable

The owners' income is equal to the vertical distance between the π curve and Alex's U_0-indifference curve. When the amount of shirking is observable, the owners choose the level of shirking at which this distance is greatest, s_1 in the figure. At this level of shirking, the owners must pay Alex y_1 to keep him from quitting his job.

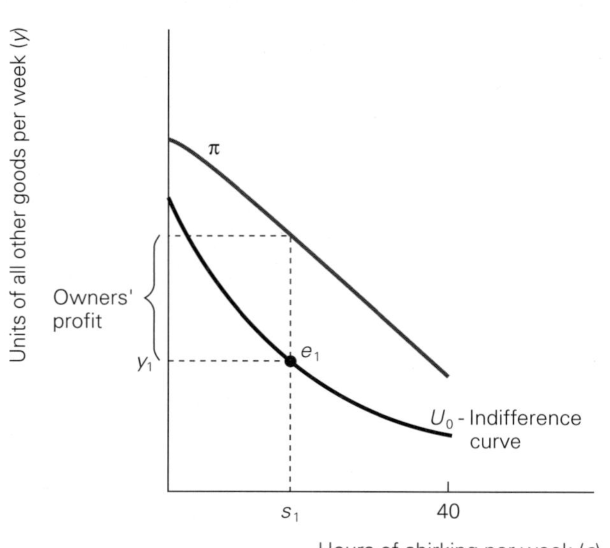

Observable Shirking

Now that we have a graphical representation of Alex's tastes and the trade-off between leisure and profit, we are ready to examine his effort decision. To begin, assume that Alex's level of effort is observable, so that the owners of the firm can see how much he is shirking. This case provides a basis for comparison with what happens when shirking is a hidden action. When shirking is observable, the owners can tell Alex how hard to work, and they can then check whether he is following their instructions. If he is not, they can fire him. However, the owners do face a constraint—to retain Alex, he must be paid enough so that he does not quit. Suppose that Alex could attain a utility level of U_0 utils by working elsewhere. The owners must offer him a combination of shirking and *all other goods* that lies on or above the U_0-indifference curve in Figure 17.18. Because the more that Alex is paid, the less income is left for them, the owners will pay Alex just enough to keep him on his U_0-indifference curve and no more.

The owners' income is equal to the profit of the firm minus what they pay to Alex. To find this amount graphically, we need to draw the firm's profit curve and Alex's U_0-indifference curve on the same graph. This is done in Figure 17.20. The owners' income is equal to the vertical distance between the π curve and Alex's U_0-indifference curve. To maximize their profits, the owners choose the level of shirking at which this distance is greatest, s_1 in the figure. At this level of shirking, the owners must pay Alex y_1 to keep him from quitting his job. Even though the owners can see how much Alex shirks, he still shirks s_1 hours per week in equilibrium. This important finding does not mean that either Alex or the owners are being wasteful or irrational. Leisure is a valuable economic good, so there is nothing wrong with Alex's sacrificing some income in return for some leisure. Similarly, it is perfectly rational for the owners to allow Alex to enjoy some shirking, because this allows them to pay a lower wage and enjoy higher profits. Indeed, this model partially explains why many firms provide pleasant cafeterias and recreational facilities for their employees.

Unobservable Shirking

Suppose that the owners of the firm cannot observe how hard Alex works. Now, the owners cannot base Alex's compensation directly on the amount he shirks, and they cannot threaten to fire him for failing to work hard enough. What can the owners do?

A Flat Salary Suppose that Alex is paid a flat salary of $5,000 per week for his services. Alex can then consume 5,000 units of *all other goods* no matter how much he shirks. More formally, when Alex is paid a flat salary, the opportunity cost of shirking in terms of forgone consumption of *all other goods* is zero. The only limit on the level of shirking is the amount of time spent at work. The resulting budget constraint is shown in Figure 17.21, which also illustrates Alex's indifference map.

From this figure, we see that Alex chooses point e_2 on his budget constraint, and he shirks as much as he can get away with, 40 hours per week. This result makes perfect sense. Why should he put in any more than the minimal effort into the job when he is going to get paid $5,000 per week no matter what? Of course, we still have to check if Alex would rather work here or elsewhere. Recall that to keep Alex from quitting, the owners have to make sure that his consumption bundle is on or above his U_0-indifference curve. Figure 17.21 indicates that when the owners pay Alex $5,000 per week, his consumption bundle is well above his U_0-indifference curve. The owners can therefore raise their income by paying Alex less. Since Alex will consume 40 hours of shirking per week no matter what his salary, we can find how much the owners will pay him by looking at the height of his U_0-indifference curve where the level of shirking is 40. From Figure 17.22, we see that when Alex is paid a flat salary of $\$F_3$ per week, he consumes 40 hours of shirking per week and is at point e_3 on his U_0-indifference curve. At any flat salary less than $\$F_3$, Alex will quit.

Let's compare the outcomes when shirking is observable to the owners (Figure 17.20) and when it is not (Figure 17.22). These figures show that profit is higher and shirking is lower when the owners can see the amount of shirking. Why? When paid a flat salary, Alex bears none of the cost (the forgone profit) of his shirking but does reap the benefit. Alex has no incentive to limit the amount of leisure consumed, and he shirks as much as possible. The owners, however, do bear the cost. When the owners can observe the amount of shirking, they make a trade-off between the amount that they pay Alex in terms of shirking and *all other goods.*

Performance-Based Compensation An owner who implemented a flat salary scheme would not be happy with the result: a manager who put no effort into managing. From this fact, we would expect to see schemes that provide incentives for effort to emerge. That is, we would expect to see firms use *performance-based compensation schemes.* The owners of a firm might, for example, tie the manager's pay to the profitability of the firm. Suppose that Alex were paid the profit of the firm less some base amount. Algebraically, Alex would receive $\pi - G$, where G is some fixed amount of money. For example, if G were $5,000 per week and the firm's profit $9,000, Alex would earn $4,000 per week. If profit were $6,000 instead, Alex would earn only $1,000. Since the manager gets all of the leftover, or "residual," profit, the manager is said to be a **residual claimant** under this scheme. Although this contract may seem a little strange to you, such

residual claimant
A party to a contract who gets all of the leftover, or "residual," profit.

Figure 17.21

The Manager's Equilibrium When Pay Is a Flat Salary

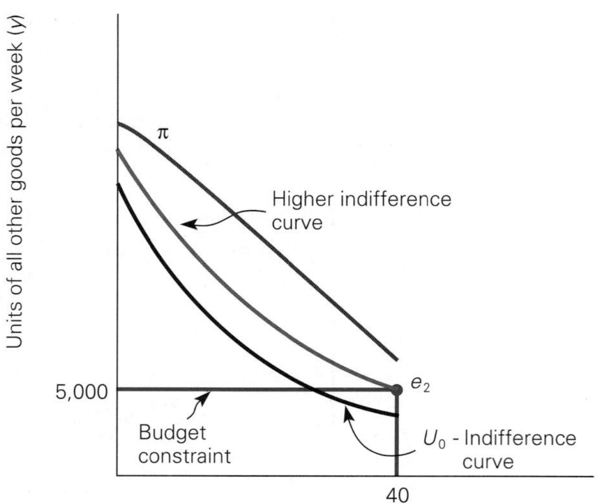

When paid a flat salary, Alex chooses to shirk as much as possible. If paid $5,000 per week, for instance, he chooses point e_2 on his budget constraint and shirks 40 hours per week.

Figure 17.22

The Equilibrium Outcome When Effort Is Unobservable and the Manager Is Paid a Flat Salary

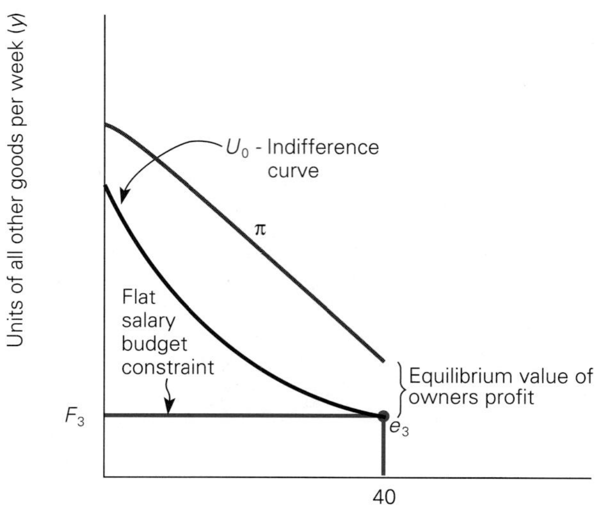

To keep Alex from quitting, the owners have to make sure that he is on or above his U_0-indifference curve. Since Alex will consume 40 hours of shirking no matter what his salary is, the owners will pay him a flat salary of $\$F_3$, and he will consume 40 hours of shirking at point e_3 on his U_0-indifference curve.

contracts do exist. In Venice, waiters pay a fixed fee for the right to work in a restaurant. The waiter then gets to keep all of the tips that he or she can collect. In the United States, hair cutters sometimes pay for the right to work in a beauty salon; the hair cutters get to keep the fees and tips they earn. Similarly, entrepreneurs who operate fast-food franchises often agree to pay an up-front fixed fee for that right and then get the residual profit.

There is another way to make an employee a residual claimant— sell the employee the company. In the late 1980s, the managers at several companies got huge bank loans to purchase all of the shares of the companies that they managed, so-called *management buyouts.* Under a management buyout, the previous owners are paid a fixed fee for their shares, and the banks making the loans to the managers are repaid according to a fixed-interest schedule. Any profit earned by the firm above these amounts is kept by the managers who have engineered the buyout. The managers become residual claimants.

Suppose that the current owners decide to make Alex a residual claimant. How will he respond to this scheme? To find his budget constraint under this compensation scheme, we start by drawing the π curve again in Figure 17.23. Suppose that the value of G is $1,000. We shift the π curve downward by 1,000 to reflect the fact that Alex does not get to keep all of the profit—he must pay $1,000 to the owners of the firm. The resulting budget constraint is labeled $\pi - 1,000$ in Figure 17.23. Drawing Alex's indifference map in the same diagram, we

Figure 17.23

The Manager's Equilibrium When Paid as a Residual Claimant

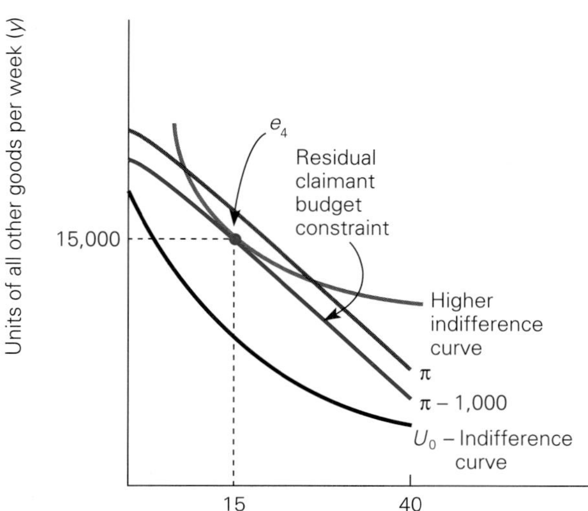

To find the manager's budget constraint when Alex is a residual claimant and has to pay $1,000 to the owners of the firm, we shift the π curve downward by 1,000. The resulting budget constraint is labeled π − 1,000. Drawing in Alex's indifference map in the same diagram, we see that he consumes 15 hours of shirking. We also see that Alex's equilibrium point lies above the U_0-indifference curve, so his utility is greater than necessary to keep him on the job.

Figure 17.24

The Equilibrium Outcome When Effort Is Unobservable and the Manager Is Paid as a Residual Claimant

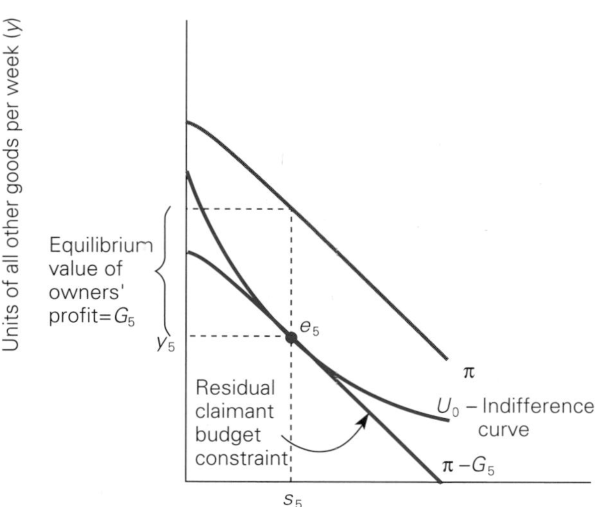

The owners choose the value of *G* so that Alex's resulting equilibrium bundle (point e_5) lies on his U_0-indifference curve.

see that he maximizes utility at point e_4, where he consumes 15 hours of shirking per week. We also see that Alex's equilibrium point lies above the U_0-indifference curve, so he does not quit his job when paid according to this scheme.

How should the owners choose *G*? The higher the value of *G*, the higher the owners' profit, because *G* is what the owners get to keep. But if *G* is set too high, Alex refuses to work for the firm. Once again, the owners have to choose a value of *G* such that Alex's resulting equilibrium point lies on or above his U_0-indifference curve. In this case, the equilibrium value of the fixed charge is G_5, and the equilibrium is at point e_5 in Figure 17.24.

Does Alex still devote his entire time to the consumption of shirking? The figure indicates that he does not. Moreover, even though Alex works harder when he is a residual claimant than when he is paid a flat salary, he is not worse off: e_2 and e_5 are on the same indifference curve (U_0). How can this be? The answer is that although Alex works harder when he is a residual claimant, he also consumes more units of *all other goods.*

Which regime do the owners prefer, the flat salary or the residual claimant? We can answer this question by making use of the following important fact: The residual claimant outcome is the same one that arises when effort is observable. We know this because Alex, as a residual claimant, makes his shirking decision to maximize the vertical distance between the $\pi - G$ curve and his U_0-indifference curve. But this leads to the same choice of shirking as does maximizing the vertical distance between the π curve and his U_0-indifference curve, which is what the owners do when effort is observable. In other words, $s_1 = s_5$. Moreover, $y_1 = y_5$.

Why is the equivalence of these two outcomes useful in comparing the residual claimant scheme with a flat salary? It is helpful because when the owners are able to observe the amount of shirking, they choose the equilibrium level of shirking to maximize their profit subject to the requirement that Alex's utility be at least U_0. This means that the residual claimant scheme also maximizes the owners' profit subject to the requirement that Alex's utility be at least U_0. When Alex is paid a flat salary, the equilibrium entails more shirking than either of the other two outcomes. It follows that the use of a residual claimant contract, in comparison with paying Alex a flat salary, raises the owners' income.

17.7 PROGRESS CHECK

Suppose that Alex's outside opportunity improved so that it yielded him a higher utility level. Show graphically what would happen to the equilibria in each of the three cases analyzed above.

Remember that Alex's utility is unaffected by the choice of contract type. In all three cases, his equilibrium utility level is U_0. We have just shown that by switching from a flat salary to a residual claimant scheme, the owners can increase their income without making the manager any worse off—the residual claimant contract leads to a Pareto improvement over the flat salary. (PC 17.7)

Two Puzzles

Our theory suggests that performance-based compensation schemes such as residual claimant contracts are superior to flat salaries. Yet many managers are paid flat salaries, and very few are paid as pure residual claimants. These facts raise two related puzzles: (1) Why do people paid on salary do any work? and (2) If residual claimant contracts have such good incentive properties, why aren't all contracts of this form?

There are several reasons why someone on a flat salary would continue to work. One is that not everyone considers shirking to be an economic good. At some point, people may take pride in doing their jobs well, or they may feel guilty about taking advantage of their employers. Another reason is that even someone on a straight salary is subject to a performance scheme of sorts. Firms typically monitor their employees, and if one shirks he or she may get caught and possibly fired or might later be denied a promotion. In either case, the worker's pay is tied to performance.

Turning to the second question, we saw in Chapter 7 that the presence of managerial risk aversion provides one answer. A residual claimant bears all of the risk associated with the business. There is no sharing of risk with the firm's owners. However, the owners are likely to be diversified, and we would expect them to be risk neutral or at least less risk averse than the manager. Risk-neutral owners should bear all of the risk since it does not reduce their utility—just the opposite of the residual claimant result. If the owners are risk averse as well, the economically efficient arrangement is to share the risk. Thus, the relative rarity of residual claimant contracts is really not surprising.

If risk bearing lowers the manager's utility, why not offer the manager the equivalent of full insurance? Because we saw that if the owners fully insure the manager against risk by offering a flat salary, the manager has strong incentives to shirk. In short, tying a manager's compensation to the firm's profit strengthens his or her incentives to work hard, but at the same time it can expose the manager to a great deal of risk. Selecting a compensation scheme involves a trade-off between providing incentives and sharing risk. These considerations help explain why Chick-fil-a, the third largest chain of chicken restaurants in America, splits the profits of each restaurant 50-50 with its manager and guarantees that the manager will earn at least $30,000 annually (Dobrzynski 1996, C3). Note the similarity to the problem of moral hazard in an insurance market. With full insurance, a policyholder has little incentive to be careful. Limiting the amount of coverage partially restores incentives, but it also exposes the policyholder to risk.

Concern about employee effort and the design of compensation schemes also arises for jobs farther down the corporate ladder. Some manufacturing companies rely on performance-based compensation schemes for their production workers. The Lincoln Electric Corporation (a maker of welding equipment) pays its employees on a **piece rate** basis: An employee gets paid a fixed amount for each unit of output that he or she produces. Such contracts provide strong work incentives, but if something goes wrong with the machines needed to produce output, the workers may be out of luck. Workers who recognize this risk will want higher piece rates to compensate them for bearing such risk. That is one reason why most companies pay flat hourly wages and rely on direct monitoring by foremen to make sure that the workers are indeed working. From a firm's point of view, one of the advantages of an assembly line is that it helps the firm monitor its employees. When cars start coming off the assembly line without windshield wipers, it is clear to the management which employee was not working "hard enough."

piece rate
A pay scheme under which an employee gets paid a fixed amount for each unit of output ("piece") that he or she produces.

MORAL HAZARD IN PRODUCT MARKETS

Up to this point, we have largely been concerned with moral hazard problems involving hidden actions taken by households. Considerations of moral hazard by firms also arise. As anyone who has ever gone to a bad movie can testify, sometimes you pay for something without knowing exactly what you are getting for your money. When manufacturers know the quality of their products but consumers do not (at least prior to making purchases), we have a situation of asymmetric information about an action, the firm's choice of product quality. There is a potential moral hazard problem because a firm can reduce its costs by lowering its product's quality, which lowers consumer welfare, *ceteris paribus.*

Interestingly, a firm may actually suffer from having the ability to cheat consumers. Rational consumers will expect the firm to produce a low-quality product, which the firm will in fact produce. No one is fooled in equilibrium, but the market for the high-quality product is destroyed. Both the firm and the consumers may want a way out of this problem.

Reputation as a Hostage

One of the most important market responses to problems of moral hazard in product markets is the development of firm reputations or brand names. Reputations can arise when consumers make repeated purchases in the market and they can learn from experience whether the product they have bought is a good one. If a firm can never change the quality of its product, the process by which consumers learn about product quality is a simple one—they buy something once and see how good it is. This information then guides all future purchases.

In most industries, however, a firm can vary the quality of its product over time. In these industries, it is less obvious that past quality is a good indicator of future quality. But it can be, as the following example shows. Suppose that Chez Maison is a self-styled bistro in Los Angeles. On any given day, the owners of the restaurant could choose to lower the quality of the food by using cheaper ingredients. Since people decide to dine at the restaurant before seeing their food, the decision to serve crummier food one night would have no effect on the demand for the restaurant's food on that night. Since revenues would be unaffected, but costs would fall, it looks like Chez Maison should switch to cheaper ingredients.

This switch would indeed raise profits for one night. But what would be the long-run effects? At least some people would recognize that they had been served poor food, and they might well conclude that the restaurant would serve bad food in the future. Hence, serving bad food on one night damages the restaurant's reputation and thus lowers future demand. Once this effect on future revenues is taken into account, Chez Maison may find that it is not profitable to cut the quality of its food. A firm's incentive to maintain a reputation is much like an oligopolist's incentive not to cheat on a collusive agreement with other firms. While cheating today leads to gains, punishment in the future (lost patronage for the restaurant, or aggressive behavior by rivals in the case of collusive oligopoly) may wipe out those gains.

Does the presence of reputations restore the market equilibrium to the full-information perfectly competitive outcome? Not quite. Think about how reputation works as an incentive to keep quality high. While cheating leads to gains today, it leads to the loss of sales in the future. For this loss of future sales to be a punishment, these sales must be made at a price that exceeds marginal cost. If the firm were simply making these sales at a price equal to marginal cost, it would not mind losing them to make additional profits today by cheating. In short, *for the threatened loss of reputation to be an effective deterrent to cheating, having a good reputation must allow the firm to earn positive economic profits on future sales.*[5] But as we showed in Chapters 12 and 13, when price exceeds marginal cost, the allocation of resources is inefficient. Thus, while the establishment of reputations can help overcome problems of asymmetric information, it will not restore the market to a fully efficient competitive equilibrium.

Our analysis of reputations helps explain why there are brand names and why companies that make many different products, like General Electric, often use the same brand name for all of them. Every time it sells one of its products, the entire firm's reputation is on the line. A consumer who is unhappy with his GE refrigerator is less likely to buy a GE washing machine. In effect, the firm's reputation is a hostage that it offers the consumer in order to ensure that it is providing a good product. Consumers can therefore be confident that a multiproduct firm has incentives to manufacture good products. As with our earlier discussion of signaling, it is not essential that consumers recognize how the reputation mechanism actually works. When a consumer goes into a supermarket and sees GE light bulbs on the shelf, all that matters is that he or she expects them to be of high quality, given GE's generally good reputation.[6]

[5]Note that, if *establishing* a reputation is costly, the present value of the stream of profits earned over the firm's lifetime might still be zero.

[6]There are limits to these effects. It is unlikely that any airline executive has chosen to buy GE jet engines for the company's aircraft because of a good experience with a GE refrigerator.

The theory of reputation also provides one explanation of the success of McDonald's and other large fast-food franchises. McDonald's allows thousands of different fast-food outlets to establish a common reputation. This reputation can be important for people who are traveling and are unfamiliar with the quality of local restaurants. It's not that the food is good, it's that it is dependable anywhere you go. There is a Big Mac waiting for you in Kyoto, and you already know what it will taste like.

SECTION RECAP

One side of an economic relationship often takes an action that affects the other side, and the action taken is unobservable to the party not making the choice—it is a hidden action. When the two sides of the relationship disagree on which action is the best to take, the informed side may take the "wrong" action from the perspective of the uninformed side—there is a problem of moral hazard. People who purchase insurance, for example, may not do enough to prevent accidents. Employees may not work hard enough. There are several market responses to problems of moral hazard that attempt to restore incentives. Insurance companies, for example, may use co-insurance and deductibles to make their customers bear some of the costs of an accident. Employers may use performance-based compensation schemes. None of these solutions, however, completely overcomes the effects of asymmetric information.

SUMMARY

Asymmetric information describes a situation in which one side of the market has better information than the other. In this chapter, we have seen that asymmetric information can have dramatic effects on the workings of markets.

- Whenever one side of a transaction knows something about itself that the other one does not, we are dealing with a situation of hidden characteristics.
- In a market with a hidden characteristic, the informed side of the market may take some action to signal what it knows about itself. For instance, your going to college may signal to employers that you know you are a high-ability worker.
- The uninformed side in a market with hidden characteristics may set up a self-selection device to learn what the informed side knows about itself. For example, an airline may screen (sort) its customers by offering a set of fares and then using each consumer's choice as a signal of that person's willingness to pay.
- In some situations with hidden characteristics, the uninformed party may get an adverse selection of the informed parties. An insurance company, for example, may find that the people who most want to buy insurance from it are the ones who are most likely to collect.
- Whenever one side of an economic relationship takes actions that the other side cannot observe, we are dealing with a situation of hidden action.
- In situations with hidden actions, the informed side may take the "wrong" action and engage in what is known as moral hazard. An insurance policyholder may fail to take enough care to prevent an accident, or a worker may shirk on the job.
- In situations of moral hazard, the parties may design the contracts that govern the relationship between them in such a way as to provide incentives to the informed party. For example, by tying its workers' wages to the firm's performance, an employer gives its employees an incentive to work hard.

DISCUSSION QUESTIONS

17.1 A company selling you life insurance would like to know if you have a healthy diet, whether you smoke, and whether your family has a history of heart disease. For each of these pieces of information, is the firm concerned with a hidden action or a hidden characteristic?

17.2 A restaurant in New York City sells a single lobster for \$15 and two lobsters for \$23 total, with the implicit requirement that the same diner eat both lobsters (if a couple tries to share a double lobster dinner, the waiters make unpleasant faces at the two diners).
a. Explain why the restaurant charges different prices for the first and second lobsters.[7]
b. Why does the management order the waiters to make the aforementioned unpleasant faces?

17.3 "In an effort to woo buyers of high-priced European cars, the Ford Motor Company [introduced] a new marketing tactic with the debut of its Merkur Scorpio model: a guarantee on resale value" (Holusha 1987, D1). Explain why an automaker's willingness to offer a resale guarantee for its cars may serve as a signal of their quality.

17.4 If you want to fly between San Francisco and Los Angeles, you may find that the amount that you have to pay depends on what time of day you want to fly. Compare the motivation for this practice with the practice of charging less if you are willing to make your reservations over a month in advance.

17.5 Insurance companies increasingly have the ability to test people for their genetic likelihood of suffering from certain diseases. Do you think that this sort of testing is a good idea? Is it efficient? Who gains, and who loses?

17.6 Suppose that 10 employees work together as a team to produce output. It is impossible for the management of their firm to tell how hard any one employee is working. The management can, however, observe the team's output and thus can tell how hard the employees are working on average. Can you think of a performance-based compensation scheme that will give the employees the incentive to make efficient shirking decisions? Do you see any problems with your scheme?

17.7 At least implicitly, many managers are paid according to *relative performance schemes* under which the manager's pay is tied to the performance of similar firms. When her firm does badly, a manager is not penalized with low pay if it turns out that all of the firms in the same industry did badly. But she does suffer a loss in pay if the firm under her control does poorly in comparison with other firms in the industry. What is the advantage of paying a manager based on her firm's performance relative to other firms, rather than simply on an absolute scale (as with a residual claimant contract)?

17.8 Companies selling home fire insurance often will provide a discount to policyholders who have smoke alarms (ownership of smoke detectors is something that the company can check in the event that a major fire occurs). Suppose that it costs a homeowner \$20 to purchase and install a smoke detector. Moreover, suppose that expected losses fall by \$200 as the result of having a smoke detector in operation.
a. How much of a discount will perfectly competitive insurance companies give to someone who has installed a smoke detector? Why do they give this discount?
b. Suppose that there is a monopoly provider of fire insurance. How much of a discount will it offer policyholders who install smoke detectors? Why will the monopolist grant this discount?

17.9 In Section 17.3 we examined an agency relationship between a firm's owner and manager. In the example we considered, the firm's profit, π, had a deterministic relationship to the amount of shirking, s. In effect, the owners could see how hard the manager had worked by looking at the firm's profit level. In actual markets, things are never so straightforward. Typically, for any given level of managerial effort, a variety of different outcomes are possible. For instance, even when the manager works hard, the firm may do poorly for other reasons. One still would expect, however, that the less a manager shirks, the higher the firm's profits are *on average*.

Suppose that Alexandra is a manager who must choose one of two shirking levels. If she chooses to *goof off*, then the firm earns low

[7]As a result of using an earlier version of this book, two students eating in this restaurant were able to impress the owner with their knowledge of the theory of food pricing. In response, the owner promised them a 20 percent lifetime discount at his restaurant.

profits, π_L, with probability .8 and high profits, π_H, with probability .2. On the other hand, if she chooses to *work hard*, then the firm earns low profits with probability .3 and high profits with probability .7.

Do you think that a residual claimant contract can be effective in this setting when the manager is risk neutral? Do you see any problems with a residual claimant contract when the manager is risk averse?

17.10 The 19th-century explosive business was profitable but dangerous. Explosions frequently destroyed factories and killed employees. When the Du Pont family came to the United States from France to manufacture black powder, they continued a French tradition. The member of the Du Pont family who owned and managed the gunpowder mill (and was responsible for overseeing the workers' safety) lived right next to the mill with his wife and children. Use the theory of moral hazard to explain why such a rich family would choose to live in such a dangerous place.

17.11 The use of reputation to ensure product quality is much like our theory of repeated oligopoly in which the threat of future punishment deters cheating on a collusive agreement. In our theory of oligopoly, we saw that the frequency of interaction was an important determinant of the success of a collusive agreement. Drawing the analogy from oligopoly theory, explain why reputation may be more effective when a firm uses a single brand name for many of its products. In answering this question, keep in mind the example of General Electric's sale of major appliances.

17.12 In the text, we studied the effects of reputation in markets with hidden actions. Reputation also can be important in markets with hidden characteristics. Suppose that a used-car dealer can observe the quality of the cars that it sells, but a typical buyer cannot, at least not until he or she gets it home and drives it for a few months. Discuss how the existence of used-car dealers may be a response to the hidden characteristics problem in the used-car market. Be sure to explain why a used-car dealer can more effectively develop a reputation than the owner of a single car wishing to sell that vehicle.

17.13 An entrepreneur has hired an employee to undertake an independent project. If the project "fails," it will lose \$20,000. If it "succeeds," the project will earn \$100,000. The employee can choose to "work" or "shirk." If she shirks, the project will fail for sure. If she works, the project will succeed half of the time, but will still fail half of the time. *Ceteris paribus*, the employee's utility is the equivalent of \$10,000 lower if she works than if she shirks. In addition, the employee could earn \$10,000 in another job (where she would shirk). The entrepreneur is choosing whether to pay the employee a "flat salary" of \$20,000 (which she gets no matter how the project turns out) or a "performance plan" (under which the employee earns \$0 if the project fails and \$40,000 if it succeeds). Both parties are risk neutral. Use a game tree to figure out which compensation scheme the entrepreneur should use.

CHAPTER

18

Externalities and Public Goods

I must go down to the seas again,
if only to lament
The prevalence of salty spume
imbued with offal scent
And pray that we can find a way
to clear the mass of muck in it
Before Poseidon's trident ends up
permanently stuck in it.

—Felicia Lamport*

Many factories in the midwestern United States emit sulfur oxides and nitrogen oxides into the air. Once in the air, these chemicals react with water vapor to create acids, which fall to earth in the rain and snow in areas as far away as New England and Canada. The consequent increase in the general level of acidity has harmful effects on plant and animal life. Victims of acid rain such as fishery owners complain bitterly. Responding to political pressures, the governments of the United States and Canada are trying to negotiate means of reducing acid rain.

The First Welfare Theorem suggests that markets allocate resources efficiently. Acid rain is the outcome of the operation of markets. Does this mean that acid rain is efficient? And if not, what role is there for government intervention? To answer these questions, we must distinguish different ways in which people can affect each other's welfare.

Suppose that large numbers of people become concerned about their cholesterol levels and decide to consume less beef and more oat bran. As demand for oat bran increases, the price increases, making oat bran producers better off, but decreasing the welfare of people who were already consuming oat bran. As the demand for beef falls, its price falls, affecting the welfare of those who continue to consume beef, beef producers, owners of feed grain firms, and so forth. By the time the economy settles into a new general equilibrium, the distribution of real income has changed substantially.

*"Sea Griever (with the Connivance of John Masefield)," by Felicia Lamport, August 10, 1988 (Op-Ed).

The distinctive aspect of this example is that although people are influencing each other's welfare, all of the effects are transmitted by means of changes in market prices. Suppose that prior to the change in tastes, the allocation of resources was Pareto efficient—all marginal rates of substitution equaled the corresponding marginal rates of transformation. The shifts in supply and demand curves change relative prices. However, the First Welfare Theorem tells us that as long as consumers maximize utility, producers maximize profits and all individuals and firms are price takers, then the new equilibrium is also Pareto efficient. Thus, although the behavior of some people affects the welfare of others, it does not automatically imply inefficiency. As long as the effects are transmitted through prices, the new allocation is just as efficient as the original one.[1] Of course, the new pattern of prices may be more or less desirable from a distributional point of view, depending upon one's ethical judgments. For the moment, however, our focus is on the efficiency of the allocation, not its fairness.

The acid rain and cholesterol examples embody different types of interaction. The decrease in welfare of the fishery owners is not a result of price changes. Rather, the output choices of the steel factories directly affect the fisheries' production functions. For any given quantities of their inputs, the fisheries produce less output in the presence of acid rain. When the activity of one entity (a person or a firm) directly affects the welfare of another in a way that is not transmitted by market prices, that effect is called an **externality** (because one entity directly affects the welfare of another entity that is "external" to it). Unlike effects that are transmitted through market prices, externalities can adversely affect economic efficiency. This chapter analyzes externalities, why they can lead to inefficiencies, and how society can deal with them. We also discuss a special kind of commodity called a "public good." Public goods are closely related to externalities and, like externalities, are often associated with efficiency problems.

externality
A direct effect of the actions of one person or firm on the welfare of another person or firm, in a way that is not transmitted by market prices.

18.1 EXTERNALITIES AND EFFICIENCY

In this section we analyze the efficiency consequences of externalities from several viewpoints.

MISSING MARKETS

To think about the efficiency implications of an externality, we must specify carefully its costs and benefits. Returning to the acid rain example, assume for simplicity that its only cause is the emission of sulfur oxides, that steel factories are the only source of sulfur oxides, and that fisheries are the only victims of the associated acid rain. The marginal cost of each unit of sulfur oxide discharged is equal to the incremental damage done to the fishery by that unit. We assume that as the amount of discharge increases, the damage worsens at an increasing rate—the first few emissions of sulfur oxides do little harm, but as the pollution accumulates, the incremental number of fish killed goes up ever faster. In Figure 18.1, the quantity of discharge (Z) is measured on the horizontal axis and dollars on the vertical. The upward slope of the MC schedule reflects the assumption that the marginal cost of the damage increases.

[1]Effects on welfare that are transmitted through prices are sometimes referred to as "pecuniary externalities." Mishan (1971) argues convincingly that because such effects are part of the normal functioning of a market, this is a confusing appellation. It is mentioned here only for the sake of completeness, and is ignored henceforth.

Figure 18.1

Actual versus Efficient Levels of Pollution

In the absence of corrective action, polluters produce emissions as long as their marginal benefit is positive, just up to level Z_1. The efficient quantity of pollution is Z^*.

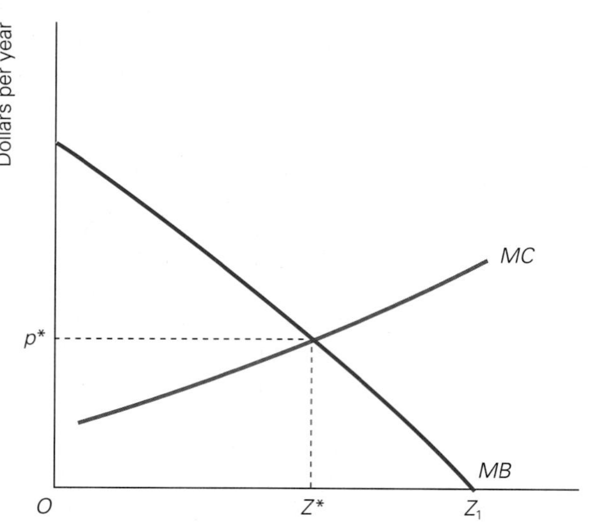

Strange as it may seem, sulfur oxide emissions have benefits as well as costs. Imagine that emissions are at some particular level, say eight parts per 100 million, and that the steel factories are required to cut back by one part per 100 million. This can be done in two ways:

1. The factories can reduce their output. Society therefore loses the surplus on the sale of this output.
2. The factories can produce the same amount of output, but they can use more expensive inputs. For example, they can use "cleaner" types of coal that produce fewer sulfur oxides. Or they can install scrubbers on their smokestacks. The use of more expensive inputs also is a cost to society.

In effect, then, the marginal benefit of an extra unit of sulfur oxides is the extra output associated with that pollution and/or the cost savings that the production of the pollution allows. We assume that these marginal benefits to emissions decline with the quantity of the emissions; this might be due to the fall in the consumers' marginal valuation of the factory output as the quantity increases. The assumption of a decreasing marginal benefit is reflected in the downward slope of the *MB* schedule in Figure 18.1.

Our usual marginalist logic indicates that from society's point of view the efficient amount of pollution is Z^*, where the marginal cost just equals the marginal benefit. The big question is whether the *actual* amount of pollution will be Z^*. The answer is quite likely to be no. To see why, consider the decision about how much to pollute from a typical factory's standpoint. The factory incurs no costs for the damage it does to the fisheries. Therefore, the factory continues to pollute as long as there is *any* incremental benefit to itself, regardless of the cost of the pollution to other parties. That is, it pollutes just up to the point where the marginal benefit of emissions is zero, level Z_1 in the figure. Since Z_1 is greater than Z^*, the equilibrium amount of pollution is inefficiently high.

What is the source of this inefficiency? By producing sulfur oxides, the factories are in effect using up the commodity "clean air." If clean air were a "typical" competitive commodity, its price would be determined by supply and demand (at p^* in Figure 18.1). At the same time, the theory of welfare economics tells us that it would be used efficiently. However, there is no market for clean air, and people treat its price as if it were zero. Clearly, *if the market for a commodity is missing, we cannot rely on market forces to provide it efficiently.* Strictly speaking, then, the adverse efficiency consequences of externalities are not due to a "market failure"; they are due to the failure of a market to emerge.

The "missing market" interpretation of an externality is important because it allows us to focus on the reason why externalities can lead to inefficiencies. No one owns the air, and therefore people can use it for free. The externality's detrimental impact on efficiency is a consequence of the failure or inability to establish ownership rights. If someone owned the clean air and could charge a price for its use, then a market for it would emerge and there would be no efficiency problem.

Suppose, for example, that the fisheries owned the clean air. They could charge the factories a fee for polluting that reflected the damage done to their catch. The factory owners would take these charges into account when making production decisions and would no longer use the clean air inefficiently. On the other hand, if the steel manufacturers owned the clean air, they could make money by charging the fishery owners for the privilege of having clean air. This would give the factory owners an incentive not to pollute "too much." Otherwise, they could not make much money from the fishery owners. In short, once the steel producers owned the rights to the clean air, they would no longer treat it as free. If they could sell clean air to others, then the clean air would have an opportunity cost.

The point is that as long as *someone* owns a resource, its price reflects the value for alternative uses, and the resource is therefore used efficiently. In contrast, resources that are owned in common are abused because no one has an incentive to economize in their use.

To expand on the subject, note the following four characteristics of externalities:

- *They can be produced by individuals as well as firms.* At Mount Holyoke College, a group of students founded the Lunar Howling Club to help them let off steam. Each night at 10 P.M., members assemble to howl and whimper at the moon for 10 to 15 minutes. However, nonhowlers who live in dormitories near the howling site complain about the noise. The Howling Club lowers the welfare of others by using up the common resource, a quiet environment.
- *There is an important reciprocal aspect to externalities.* In our Howling Club example, it seems natural to characterize the howlers as the "polluters." But the howlers are just as likely to regard the students who insist on quiet as "polluting" their howling environment. In other words, it is not obvious who "ought" to have property rights. In 1905, the governor of Pennsylvania vetoed a law that put restrictions on public spitting on the grounds that "It is a gentleman's right to expectorate." These days, of course, it is uncontroversial that nonspitters have the right to spit-free public areas. On the other hand, whether smokers or nonsmokers have property rights in public spaces is still very much a disputed issue. Later,

we will explore how the distribution of property rights affects the allocation of resources in externality situations.

- *Externalities can be positive or negative.* If you plant a beautiful flower garden in front of your house, your neighbors benefit directly by your actions. This is an example of a *positive externality*—the behavior of one entity has a direct positive effect on the welfare of another. If your neighbors do not pay you for these benefits, you may not consider them when deciding how many flowers to plant. The same kind of logic used in Figure 18.1 suggests that in the case of a positive externality, an inefficiently low level of the activity may be undertaken. (See Discussion Question 18.4.)
- *Zero pollution is not, as a general rule, socially desirable.* Figure 18.1 indicates that finding the "right" amount of pollution requires finding the best trade-off between its benefits and costs, and this generally occurs at some positive level of pollution. Because virtually all productive activity involves some pollution, the requirement that pollution be set at zero would be equivalent to no production whatsoever, clearly an inefficient solution. If all this seems only like common sense, it is. But note that the U.S. Congress once set as a national goal that "the discharge of pollutants into the navigable waters be eliminated by 1985" (Baumol and Oates 1979, 211). (PC 18.1)

18.1 PROGRESS CHECK

Route 101 between San José and San Francisco is one of the busiest highways in the country. Whenever a person takes his or her car onto the highway during rush hour, the congestion increases. Explain why an externality is present. What market is missing?

PRIVATE COST VERSUS SOCIAL COST

So far our analysis has focused on the missing market for the externality. We now take a look at the market for the commodity whose production creates the externality.

In the acid rain example, clean air is essentially an input to the factories' production process. Clean air gets "used up" just like other inputs, such as labor and capital. And, like its other inputs, clean air has a cost. However, there is a crucial difference between clean air and the steel firm's other inputs—the firm incurs no cost for using the clean air. We showed in Chapter 11 that if the steel market is competitive, in equilibrium the price will equal the producers' *private* marginal cost, which is based on the costs that they must pay for the factors of production they employ. However, the First Welfare Theorem suggests that to obtain efficiency, price should equal **social marginal cost**, which includes *all* the costs of production, including the external damage to other people and firms. In the presence of an externality, the price of steel conveys an incorrect signal of steel's opportunity cost to society. Steel is priced too cheaply, and an inefficiently large quantity is exchanged.

social marginal cost Incremental cost of production which includes the opportunity cost of all scarce resources, whether priced or not.

To analyze this phenomenon graphically, assume that the relationship between the quantity of steel produced and the resulting quantity of pollution is fixed (i.e., there are no possibilities for reducing pollution by means of input substitution). In Figure 18.2, the horizontal axis measures steel output and the vertical measures dollars. The schedules D and S are the demand and supply for steel, respectively. The marginal damage done to fisheries at each level of output is represented by schedule MD in Figure 18.2. MD is drawn sloping upward,

Figure 18.2

An Externality Problem

In the absence of any intervention, output is X_1, at the intersection of the demand (D) and supply (S) curves. However, because steel production leads to marginal damages of MD, social marginal cost (SMC) is greater than private marginal cost (PMC), which is embodied in the supply curve. Efficiency requires that only output X^* be produced. The associated price, p^*, embodies the entire social marginal cost.

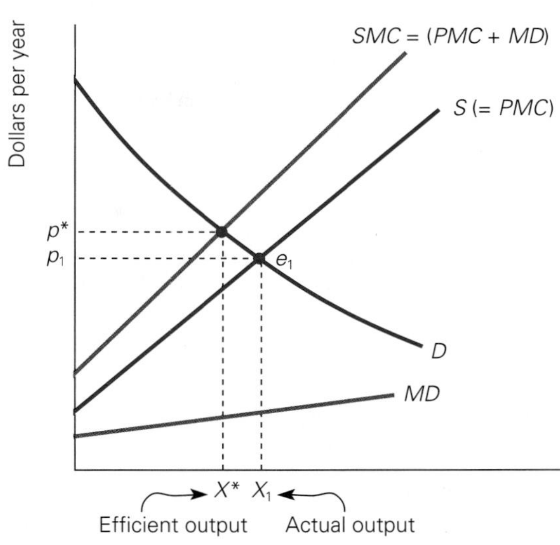

reflecting the assumption that as the fisheries are exposed to acid rain, they become worse off at an increasing rate.[2]

The equilibrium is at point e_1, where the demand and supply curves intersect. Is this equilibrium efficient? Our earlier discussion suggests that it is not. To see why, recall from Chapter 11 that the supply curve S shows the marginal cost to producers of producing each level of output. Hence, the equilibrium e_1 reflects a situation in which the marginal benefit of another unit to society (as measured by the demand curve) equals the *private* marginal cost (PMC).

From society's viewpoint, however, production should be expanded up to the point at which the marginal benefit to society is equal to the *social* marginal cost (SMC). The social marginal cost has two components. The first comprises the private marginal costs, which are embodied in the supply curve. The second component is the marginal damage done to fisheries as reflected in MD. Hence, the social marginal cost is PMC plus MD. Graphically, the social marginal cost schedule, SMC in Figure 18.2, is found by adding together the heights of S and MD at each level of output. Note that, by construction, the vertical distance between SMC and S is MD. (Because $SMC = PMC + MD$, it follows that $SMC - PMC = MD$.)

Efficiency from a social standpoint requires production of only those units of output for which SMC exceeds the marginal value of the unit. Thus, output should be produced just up to the point at which SMC and D intersect, at X^*. The demand curve tells us that this is the quantity of output demanded only if the price increases to p^*.

Figure 18.2 indicates that when externalities are present, there is no reason to expect a competitive market to produce the socially efficient level of output.

[2]You may wonder about the relationship between the MD curve in Figure 18.2 and the MC curve in Figure 18.1. The MC curve shows the damages per unit of pollution, while the MD curve shows the damages done by the pollution generated by production of a unit of steel.

Figure 18.3

Net Gain from Moving to an Efficient Output Level

When output falls from X_1 to X^*, consumption benefits fall by the associated area under the demand curve, area ($B + C$). Simultaneously, private resource costs fall by the area under the supply curve (C) and external costs fall by area ($A + B$). Hence, on balance, society comes out ahead by area A.

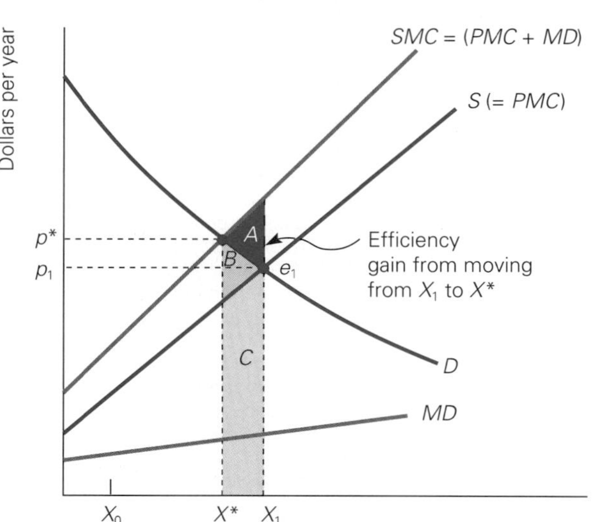

In particular, when a good is associated with a negative externality, "too much" of it is produced relative to the efficient output ($X_1 > X^*$). This corresponds to the result in Figure 18.1 that the actual amount of pollution exceeds the efficient amount.

The model not only shows that efficiency would be enhanced by a move from X_1 to X^*, but also provides a way to measure the benefits from doing so. Figure 18.3 replicates from Figure 18.2 the demand (D), private marginal cost (S), marginal damage (MD), and social marginal cost (SMC) schedules. When output is cut from X_1 to X^*, there are both costs and benefits. The cost is the reduction in consumption benefits generated by the loss of $X_1 - X^*$ tons of steel. As shown in Chapter 4, this reduction in gross consumption benefits is approximated by the area under the demand curve D between X^* and X_1, area ($B + C$).

The benefit in moving from X_1 to X^* is the associated saving in production costs. This has two components. First is the value of resources paid for by the steel producers, which is measured by the area under the private supply curve between X^* and X_1, area C. Second is the reduction of external costs imposed upon fishery owners. For each unit that steel output is reduced, fishery owners gain an amount equal to that unit's marginal damage, which is measured by the vertical distance between SMC and the supply curve, S. Thus, the reduction of steel output from X_1 to X^* reduces these external costs by area ($A + B$). In summary, the total saving in resources by moving from X_1 to X^* is the sum of areas A, B, and C.

18.2 PROGRESS CHECK

Explain carefully why in Figure 18.3 there would be "too little" pollution if X_0 tons of steel were produced each year.

Putting this all together, the benefit of moving from X_1 to X^* is area ($A + B + C$) and the cost is area ($B + C$). If society values a dollar to each person equally, then moving from X_1 to X^* yields a net gain to society equal to the difference, which is area A. Thus, not only can we make the qualitative statement that society would be better off at the efficient output level, we can measure the size of the benefit—area A. Using the jargon developed in Chapter 11, moving from X_1 to X^* increases total surplus by area A. Indeed, total surplus is maximized at X^*. (PC 18.2)

SECTION RECAP

An externality occurs when the behavior of one entity directly affects the welfare of another in a way that is not transmitted by market prices. Externalities arise because of the failure or inability to assign property rights to some resource. As a consequence, no market for that resource emerges, and there is no mechanism for assuring that the resource is used efficiently. In terms of welfare economics, the private and social marginal costs of a commodity differ, so there is no guarantee that a necessary condition for Pareto efficiency (price equals social marginal cost) will be satisfied.

18.2 RESPONSES TO EXTERNALITIES

In the presence of an externality, the market allocation of resources is inefficient if nothing is done about it. This section discusses how both the private and public sectors can respond to externalities.

PRIVATE RESPONSES

Under some circumstances, private individuals can avoid the inefficiencies of externalities without any governmental action. Several mechanisms can be employed.

Mergers

One way to solve the problems posed by an externality is to "internalize" it by combining the involved parties. For simplicity, imagine that there is only one steel firm and one fishery involved in the acid rain scenario. As stressed above, if the steel firm took into account the damages it imposed on the fishery, then a net gain would be possible. (Refer back to the discussion surrounding Figure 18.3.) Thus, if the steel firm and the fishery coordinated their activities, the profit of the joint enterprise would be higher than the sum of the profits of the two individual enterprises when they don't coordinate. In effect, by failing to act together, the two firms are throwing away money! The market, then, provides a very strong incentive for the two firms to merge—the fishery can buy the steel mill, the steel mill can buy the fishery, or some third party can buy them both. Once the two firms merge, the externality is internalized—it is taken into account by the party that generates the externality. For instance, if the steel manufacturer purchased the fishery, it would willingly produce less steel than before, because at the margin, doing so would increase the profits of its fishery subsidiary more than it decreased the profits from the steel subsidiary. Consequently, the existence of external effects would not lead to inefficiency. Indeed, an outside observer would not even characterize the situation as an externality, because all decisions would be made within a single firm.

An important example of a merger-like response relates to research and development (R&D), which creates positive externalities because the research done by one firm can be utilized by another firm even though the latter does not purchase a license to use the inventive output. When the innovating firm receives no payment from the other companies that benefit from its R&D through spillovers, the firm making the investment decision does not count these spillovers as benefits and may have inefficiently low research incentives. For example, Bernstein and Yan (1995) estimated that the social rates of return to R&D investment in 10 Canadian and Japanese manufacturing industries are 1.5 to 12.0 times the private returns.

A joint research venture can serve as a mechanism that internalizes the externalities. This internalization is accomplished by having firms commit to payments before the R&D is conducted and, hence, before any spillovers can occur. With this method of organization, the incentives to undertake the research jointly are based on the collective benefits enjoyed by all of the participating firms. In effect, it is as if the firms had merged for the purpose of conducting R&D. Examples of research consortia include Sematech, a collection of American firms funding the development of better production processes for producing microchips, and a collection of the world's leading aircraft manufacturers working to solve some of the technological and environmental problems associated with a large supersonic commercial passenger plane.

Social Conventions

Unlike firms, individuals cannot merge in order to internalize externalities. However, certain social conventions can be viewed as attempts to force people to take into account the externalities they generate. School children are taught that littering is not "nice." If this teaching is effective, children learn that even though they bear a small cost by holding on to a candy wrapper until they find a garbage can, they should incur this cost because it is less than the cost imposed on other people by having to view their unsightly garbage. Think about the golden rule, "Do unto others as you would have others do unto you." A (much) less elegant way of expressing this sentiment is "Before you undertake some activity, take into account its external marginal benefits and costs." Some moral precepts, then, induce people to empathize with others, and hence internalize the externalities that their behavior may create. In effect, these precepts correct for missing markets.

Bargaining and the Coase Theorem

We suggested earlier that externalities can lead to efficiency problems if no one owns a resource and no one can force people to pay for its use. If the main reason that externalities lead to inefficiencies is the absence of ownership rights, perhaps the most straightforward way to "cure" the problem is to put the resource in question into private hands. Again, assume for simplicity that there is one steel firm and one fishery involved in the externality. Suppose that ownership of clean air is assigned to the steel firm. Assume further that it is costless for the fishery and the steel firm to bargain with each other. Is it possible for the two parties to strike a bargain that will result in an efficient outcome?

This situation is depicted in Figure 18.4. The setup is basically the same as that in Figure 18.2, except that because only a single steel firm is involved, the demand schedule is the horizontal line *MR*, reflecting the assumption that the firm is a price taker. Like any profit-maximizing concern, the steel firm takes no action unless the marginal benefit of that action is at least as big as the marginal cost. Hence, the steel firm's owner is willing *not* to produce a given unit of output as long as he receives a payment that exceeds his net incremental gain from

Figure 18.4

The Coase Theorem

At every point to the right of x^* the marginal damage to the fishery exceeds the net marginal benefit to the steel mill. Hence, regardless of who has property rights, there is an incentive for a bargain that would reduce output to x^*. Similarly, if the starting point is an output to the left of x^*, there is an incentive to increase output to x^*.

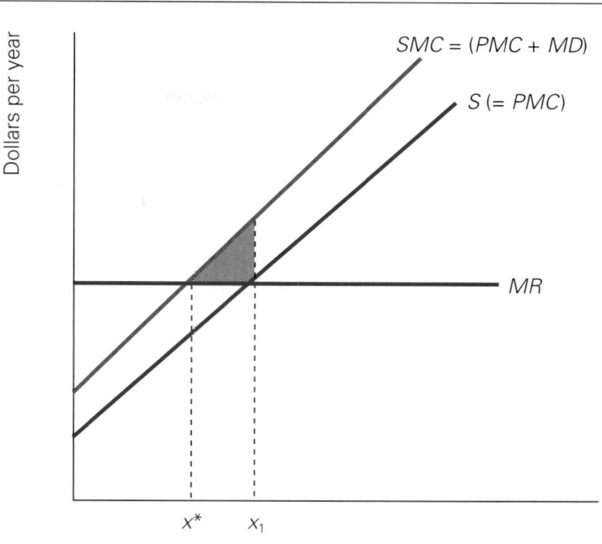

producing that unit. His net incremental gain is the marginal revenue minus the private marginal cost, or $MR - PMC$. On the other hand, the fishery is willing to pay the steel firm not to produce a given unit as long as the payment is less than the marginal damage done to it, MD. *As long as the amount that the fishery is willing to pay the steel firm (MD) exceeds the cost to the steel firm of not producing (MR − PMC), then the opportunity for a bargain exists.*

In Figure 18.4, the vertical distance between MR and S reflects the minimum bribe that the steel firm requires to forgo the production of each unit of output. The vertical distance between SMC and S reflects the maximum size of the bribe that the fishery would be willing to pay to stop the steel firm from producing each unit of output. According to the graph, at all levels of steel output to the left of x^*, the incremental bribe that the fishery is willing to pay is less than the amount required by the steel factory. Hence, production will take place at least until x^*. However, at any output level to the right of x^*, the incremental bribe exceeds the amount required by the steel firm. The two parties can therefore make a bargain in which the steel firm agrees not to produce beyond x^* in return for some amount of money. In short, private bargaining leads to a situation in which output is at precisely the optimal value, x^*. We cannot tell without more information exactly how much the fishery will end up paying the steel firm. This depends on the relative bargaining strengths of the two parties. Regardless of how the gains from the bargain are divided, however, production ends up at x^*.

Now suppose that the shoe is put on the other foot, and the fishery is assigned the ownership rights. The bargaining now is over how much the steel firm pays the fishery for permission to pollute. The fishery is willing to accept additional pollution as long as the payment is greater than the marginal damage (MD) to the fishing enterprise. The steel firm finds it worthwhile to pay for the privilege of producing one more ton of steel as long as the amount it pays is less than the value of ($MR - PMC$) for that ton of output. Reasoning similar to that above suggests that the two firms have every incentive to reach an agreement whereby the fishery sells the steel firm the right to produce at x^*.

The conclusion is that *the efficient solution will be achieved independently of who is assigned the ownership rights, as long as someone is assigned those rights.*[3] This result, known as the **Coase Theorem** (after the Nobel laureate economist Ronald Coase) implies that once ownership rights to a resource are established, externalities create no inefficiency problems, because individuals will bargain their way to an efficient solution. The reason is that, by definition, the presence of an inefficiency means that it is possible for the parties involved to gain by getting together and eliminating it. Suppose, for example, that the efficiency gain involved in moving from x_1 to x^* (the shaded area in Figure 18.4) is \$1 million a year. The Coase Theorem asserts that the parties involved do not throw away money; by bargaining together, they can each get their hands on some of it. The Coase Theorem does not tell us how the parties split the money, only that they do not leave it sitting on the table.

Coase Theorem
Assuming there are no bargaining costs, once ownership rights to a resource are established, individuals will bargain their way to an efficient use of the resource.

It is important to note that even if the particular pattern of ownership of the resource is irrelevant from the point of view of efficiency, it is quite relevant from the point of view of income distribution. Ownership rights are valuable; if the fishery owns the clean air it will increase the fishery owners' income relative to the steel owners', and vice versa.

One neat example of the Coase Theorem in action relates to apple growers and beekeepers. Bees pollinate the trees in an apple orchard, and the orchard provides the nectar that the bees use to produce honey. Two positive externalities are present. First, when the orchard owner plants more apple trees, he increases the welfare of the beekeeper. Second, when the beekeeper purchases more bees, she makes the apple grower better off. One might guess that this situation would lead to inefficiently low quantities of both bees and apple trees. Not necessarily. Cheung (1973) documented how orchard owners and beekeepers in the state of Washington actually pay each other for their services. The agreements are enforced in very carefully written contracts. As the Coase Theorem predicts, because both parties can benefit by cooperating, they do cooperate and the externality does not create an efficiency problem. (PC 18.3)

18.3 PROGRESS CHECK

Suppose the property rights in the situation depicted in Figure 18.4 belong to the fishery. Show on the diagram the size of the largest bribe that the steel firm would be willing to pay for permission to produce x^* units. Show that the incremental bribe that the steel firm is willing to pay for producing more than x^* units is not enough to induce the fishery to give permission.

Assigning property rights along Coasian lines could help solve some significant environmental problems. One commentator, for example, urged that property rights be assigned to rivers in the United States, pointing out that "in England and Scotland, private ownership of the rivers and waterways has successfully prevented overfishing and controlled water pollution for 800 years. The owners simply charge others for the right to fish in their section of the river. Consequently, the owners have an economic incentive to maintain the fish population and keep the waterway clean" (Conda 1995, A18).

Can we assume that the Coase Theorem can always be relied upon to "solve" society's externality problems? Unfortunately, no. There are several reasons why private negotiation may fail to remedy externality problems.

[3]More precisely, the outcome is x^* regardless of who owns the resource, as long as no one's demand curve depends on his or her level of income. Under this assumption, monetary transfers between the parties do not change the positions of the demand curves, and hence do not change x^*.

Reasons for Failure of Negotiations

Costs of Bargaining The Coase Theorem assumes that the costs of bargaining do not deter the parties from finding their way to the efficient solution. However, externalities such as air pollution involve literally millions of people (both polluters and pollutees). It is difficult to imagine them getting together for negotiations at a sufficiently low cost to make it worthwhile.

Related to this phenomenon is the fact that no single victim of pollution may believe that it is in his or her interest to enter negotiations. Getting involved in bargaining has costs—one has to learn the facts of the case, attend negotiation meetings, perhaps hire an attorney, and so forth. Any given individual may think, "Why should I endure all this hassle and expense? Let someone else do it, and I'll still benefit from the reduction in pollution." Of course, everyone else has the same incentive. Hence, no one takes the trouble to get involved, and no bargaining takes place. This is an example of the *free-rider problem* discussed in Chapter 7: Each individual has the incentive to let other people incur the costs while he enjoys the benefits.

We can use the tools of game theory to explore this phenomenon further. Imagine that there are two pollution victims, Harry and Bess, each of whom currently has a utility level of 35 utils. Each person is contemplating getting involved in negotiations with the polluter, and they make their choices simultaneously. There are four possibilities:

1. *Neither of them participates in negotiations with the polluters.* Harry and Bess continue to get dumped on, and each still has a utility level of 35 utils.
2. *Both participate in negotiations.* Getting involved costs each of them the equivalent of 60 utils. However, with both of them at the bargaining table, it is certain that they will win major concessions from the polluters worth 80 utils to each of them. Hence, both Harry and Bess come out ahead by 20 utils, leaving each with a total of 55 utils.
3. *Bess participates in negotiations while Harry free rides.* Without both parties at the bargaining table, there is some probability that the negotiations will not go well for the pollution victims. The *expected* gain from the negotiations is 40 utils. For Bess, the expected utility of negotiations is 40 utils minus the cost of 60 utils, leaving her with 15 utils ($= 35 + 40 - 60$). For Harry, on the other hand, there is an expected gain of 40 utils, with no associated costs, because he is free riding. Hence, if Bess participates and Harry stays home, his expected utility rises to 75.
4. *Harry participates and Bess free rides.* This is symmetric to the third case. Now Bess's expected utility is 75 and Harry's is 15.

All of this information is summarized in the game tree in Figure 18.5.[4] Note that the structure of this game is identical to the *prisoners' dilemma* game introduced in Chapter 16. Just as it was a dominant strategy for both of the prisoners to *confess*, it is a dominant strategy for both pollution victims to *free ride.* The incentive to let the other person bear the costs leads to neither person entering negotiations, and they are both worse off as a result. Incidentally, this example

[4]Note that we have condensed the tree by putting *expected* payoffs at the terminal nodes. To construct a full tree, we would need to know the probabilities of success and failure at the bargaining table (and how these probabilities depend on Harry and Bess's participation). We would then use chance nodes to represent uncertainty about the final outcome. The condensed tree, however, contains all of the information we need for the present discussion.

Figure 18.5

A Prisoners' Dilemma for Pollution Victims

The structure of the free-rider problem is identical to the prisoners' dilemma. The dominant strategy for each individual is to free ride—to choose not to participate in negotiations in the hope that the other party will participate.

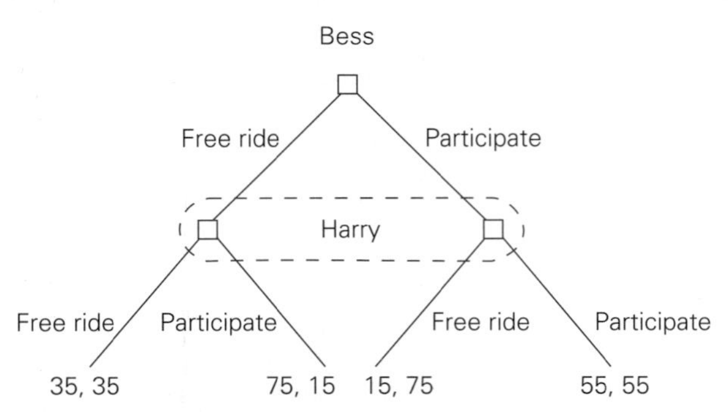

shows how game theory can give insights into phenomena way beyond the scope of oligopoly behavior.

Difficulty in Identifying Source of Damages Another practical problem with the Coase Theorem is that it assumes that resource owners can identify the source of damages to their property and legally prevent damages. Consider again the important case of air pollution. Even if ownership rights to air were established, it is not clear how the owners would be able to identify which of thousands of potential polluters was responsible for dirtying their air space and for what proportion of the damage each was liable. The acid rain case discussed earlier is a good example of this problem.

Asymmetric Information Even if ownership rights are established and the number of parties is small, it does not necessarily follow that efficient bargaining will take place. Consider the situation of two roommates, Esau and Jacob. Esau smokes, Jacob does not, and Esau "owns" the air in the sense that smoking is allowed by law. The pleasure of smoking is worth \$10 to Esau; the benefit of clean air is worth \$15 to Jacob. According to the Coase Theorem, they should be able to reach an agreement by which Jacob pays Esau some amount greater than \$10 but less than \$15 to get Esau to stop. However, the fact that smoking is worth \$10 to Esau is probably information that Esau has but which Jacob does not. Jacob may think that smoking is only worth \$8 to Esau, and therefore offer a payment of only \$8.50. When Esau rejects the offer out of hand, Jacob might believe that Esau is simply bluffing, and break off negotiations.

In short, when everybody's preferences and opportunities are common knowledge, negotiations can lead to an efficient solution. But if this is not the case, bargaining may be expensive, take a long time, and ultimately be unsuccessful. This is another example of the phenomenon discussed in the last chapter—asymmetric information can create inefficiencies. (PC 18.4)

18.4 PROGRESS CHECK

From time to time, used hypodermic needles from unknown hospitals wash up on beach shores in New York, New Jersey, and California. Identify the externality in this situation, and explain whether or not the Coase Theorem would lead to its "correction."

GOVERNMENT RESPONSES TO EXTERNALITIES

There are several ways in which the government can intervene when externalities are present.

Figure 18.6

Regulation of Two Polluting Gardeners

Suppose that the marginal damage due to pesticide use is *d*. Efficiency requires that each person purchase pesticides up to the point that private marginal cost (*PMC*) plus *d* equals his or her marginal benefit. Hence, if individuals' marginal benefit schedules differ, then a regulation requiring that everyone cut back by the same amount is inefficient.

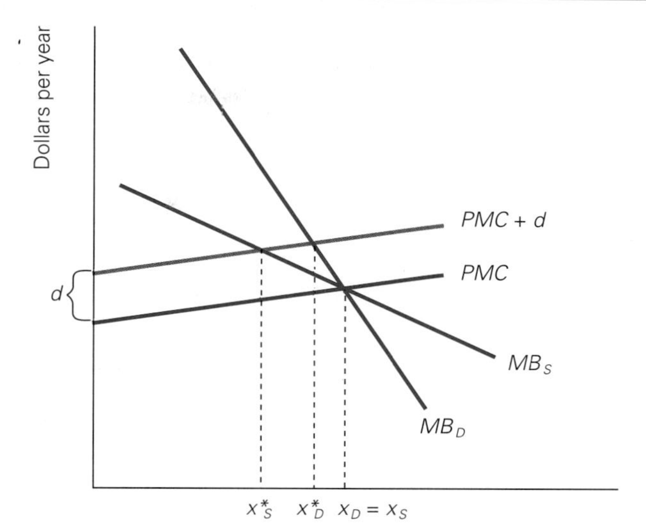

Regulation

In most countries, the main approach for dealing with environmental problems is regulation. Under regulation, each polluter is told to reduce pollution by a certain amount or else face legal sanctions. Let's think about the efficiency consequences of regulation in the context of an important problem, the damage caused by some chemical pesticides in agriculture. Consider two gardeners, Saul and David, whose use of chemical pesticides creates health hazards for neighboring pets. In Figure 18.6, pounds of pesticide are measured on the horizontal axis and dollars on the vertical. MB_S is Saul's marginal benefit schedule while MB_D is David's. Although both curves are drawn sloping downward to reflect a diminishing marginal physical product of pesticides, they have different slopes, perhaps because the two gardeners raise different crops. For expositional ease only, David and Saul are assumed to have identical private marginal cost (*PMC*) schedules and to use equal amounts of pesticides: $x_D = x_S$.

Suppose that each pound of pesticide produces $\$d$ worth of harm to the neighboring pets. Then efficiency requires that each person's pesticide use be determined by the intersection of his marginal benefit curve with the sum of his private marginal cost curve and *d*. The efficient quantities are denoted $x_D{}^*$ and $x_S{}^*$ in Figure 18.6. The crucial thing to observe is that efficiency does not require the men to reduce their pollution equally. The marginal benefit of pesticides is greater in David's garden than in Saul's, so efficiency requires a smaller reduction for David. More generally, each individual's (or firm's) appropriate reduction of pesticides depends on the shapes of that individual's marginal benefit and private marginal cost curves. Hence, a regulation that mandates all people to cut back by equal amounts (either in absolute or proportional terms) may lead to one person's using too much pesticide and another too little. In general, when the marginal benefits and costs of polluting are different for various activities, the efficient quantities of pollution for each activity also differ.

A good example of this phenomenon is automotive pollution. A car that operates in a relatively uninhabited area creates less damage than one that operates in a heavily populated area. What sense does it make for both cars to have exactly the same emissions standard? Under U.S. policy, all cars must meet standards that were set to improve the air quality in just a half dozen heavily polluted cities. Clearly, this policy is inefficient. Of course, the regulatory body could assign each polluter its specially designed production quota. But in the presence of a large number of polluters, this is administratively infeasible.

Corrective Taxes

Consider again the case of acid rain that was analyzed in Figure 18.2. Steel is produced in inefficiently large quantities because input prices incorrectly signal social costs. Specifically, because steelmakers' input prices are "too low," the price of steel is "too low." A natural solution, suggested by the British economist A. C. Pigou, is to levy a tax on the polluter that makes up for the low input prices. A **Pigouvian tax** is a tax levied upon each unit of a polluter's output in an amount just equal to the marginal damage it inflicts at the efficient level of output. Figure 18.7 reproduces the setup of Figure 18.2. In this case, the marginal damage done at the efficient output X^* is distance t. (Remember that the vertical distance between *SMC* and the supply curve is *MD*.) Thus, t is the size of the Pigouvian tax.

Pigouvian tax
A tax levied upon each unit of pollution in an amount just equal to the marginal damage it inflicts upon society at the efficient level of output.

How do producers react when a tax of t dollars per ton of steel is imposed? The tax raises their effective marginal cost. For each ton they produce, steel firms have to make payments both to the suppliers of their inputs (measured by the distance up to S) and to the tax collector (measured by t). Geometrically, their new marginal cost schedule is found by adding t to S at each level of output. This is done by shifting S up by a vertical distance equal to t.

The analysis of tax incidence in a competitive market (Chapter 11) tells us that the new equilibrium is at point e_2, the intersection of the *effective* supply curve ($S + t$) and the demand curve (D). The resulting output level is the efficient one, X^*. In effect, *the Pigouvian tax forces the steelmakers to take into account the costs of the externality that they generate, and hence induces them to produce efficiently.* The tax brings in revenue of t dollars for each of the X^* units produced. Hence, tax revenue is $t \times X^*$, the shaded area in Figure 18.7. Out of a sense of fairness, it would be tempting to use the tax revenues to compensate the fisheries, who still are being hurt by acid rain, although to a lesser extent than before the tax. However, caution must be exercised. If it becomes known that anyone who fishes along the river receives government compensation, then some people may choose to fish there who otherwise would not have done so. The result is an inefficiently large amount of fishing. (PC 18.5)

18.5 PROGRESS CHECK

According to Becker and Grossman (1994, A12), each pack of cigarettes smoked creates about 68 cents of externalities borne by other members of society. (The externalities include the costs of cigarette smokers' excess use of health services, costs of fetal death, secondhand smoke, etc.). Explain how a Pigouvian tax could be used to correct the externality.

There are practical problems in implementing a Pigouvian tax scheme. To start, the government must determine the marginal damage function. This requires the answers to several potentially difficult questions:

Which Activities Produce Pollutants? The types and quantities of pollution associated with various production processes must be identified. The acid rain example is quite informative in this context, because scientists do not know just

Figure 18.7

Pigouvian Tax

A Pigouvian tax is a tax per unit in an amount equal to the marginal damage at the efficient output level. In this case, the Pigouvian tax of t shifts the effective supply curve from S to the dashed line $S + t$, so that output is X^*. The Pigouvian tax produces revenues equal to the shaded area.

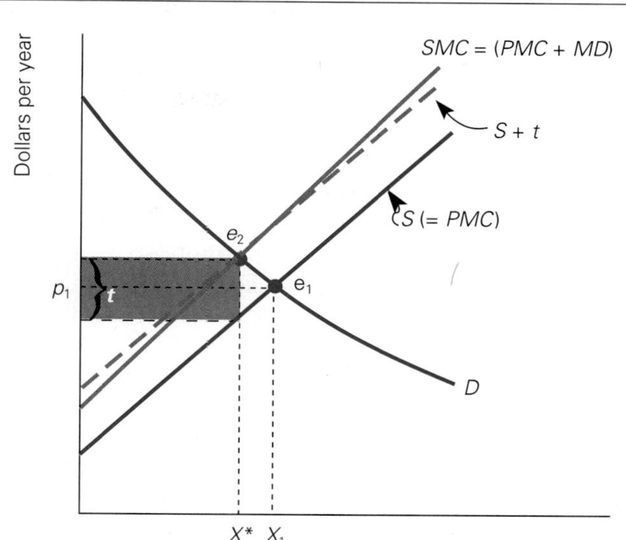

how much of acid rain is associated with production activities and how much with natural activities such as plant decay and volcanic eruptions. Moreover, it is hard to determine what amounts of nitrogen and sulfur emissions generated in a given region eventually become acid rain. It depends in part on local weather conditions and in part on the extent to which other pollutants such as nonmethane hydrocarbons are present. On the other hand, in some cases it is not too hard to measure pollution fairly cheaply and accurately. For example, lead emissions can be determined straightforwardly from a knowledge of the lead content of a particular fuel and the amount of the fuel burned.

Which Pollutants Do Harm? The ability of scientists to conduct large-scale controlled experiments on the effects of pollution is severely limited. Hence, it is often difficult to pinpoint the effect of a given pollutant. Acid rain may be a case in point: Preliminary results from the federal government's 10-year, $500 million National Acid Precipitation Assessment Program "suggests that acid rain is having virtually no effect on agricultural output, and that its effects on forests are limited to mountain tops in the northeastern United States" (Portney 1990, p. 175). This finding has led some scientists to disagree with the consensus that acid rain causes great damage in the United States. Similarly, there is major controversy about the health effects of secondhand smoke on those who share space with cigarette smokers. In principle, one can deal with such uncertainty problems by the usual method of computing *expected* damages. (See Chapter 6.) But great disagreement about the probabilities of the various possible outcomes could make it difficult to produce an expected marginal damage function that everyone would find convincing.

What Is the Value of the Damage Done? Even if the physical damage a pollutant creates is determined, the value of getting rid of it must be calculated. When economists think about measuring the "value" of something, typically they think in terms of people's willingness to pay for it. If you are willing to pay $221 for a 10-speed bicycle, then that is its value to you.

Unlike 10-speed bicycles, there is no explicit market in which pollution is bought and sold. (That's the reason for the problem in the first place.) How then can people's marginal willingness to pay for pollution removal be measured? Some attempts have been made to infer it by studying housing prices. When people shop for houses, they consider both the quality of the house itself and the characteristics of the neighborhood, such as cleanliness of the streets and quality of schools. Suppose in addition that families care about the level of air pollution in the neighborhood. Consider two identical houses situated in two identical neighborhoods, except that the first is in an unpolluted area, and the second is in a polluted area. We expect the house in the unpolluted area to have a higher price. This price differential measures people's willingness to pay for clean air.

Statistical analyses of the relationship between housing prices and environmental quality have tried to estimate this differential. Such studies are complicated by researchers' inability to find absolutely identical houses, so they must therefore try to control for price differences due to number of rooms, quality of plumbing, and so on. The results of one careful analysis by Smith and Huang (1995) imply that people would be willing to pay roughly $162 (in 1995 dollars) to obtain a one-unit reduction in the concentration of particulates (in micrograms per cubic meter).

In light of the difficulties in estimating the marginal damage function, it is bound to be hard to find the "correct" Pigouvian tax rate. Still, sensible compromises can be made. Suppose that a certain type of automobile produces noxious fumes. In theory, a tax based on the number of miles driven will enhance efficiency. But a tax based on miles driven might be so cumbersome to administer as to be infeasible. The government might instead consider levying a special sales tax upon the car, even though it is not ownership of the car per se that determines the size of the externality, but the amount it is driven. The sales tax would not lead to the most efficient possible result, but it still might lead to a substantial improvement over the status quo. Remember, the relevant issue is not whether Pigouvian taxes are a perfect method of dealing with externalities, but whether they are likely to be better than the alternatives.

In this context, it is useful to note that taxes on various types of pollution have been imposed in Europe. In 1990, France became the first country in the world to enact a tax on air pollution. Under the law, emissions of sulfur dioxide are taxed at a rate of 150 francs (about $30) per ton. In the Netherlands, where taxes on other types of pollutants have been in effect for several years, there is some evidence that the taxes have substantially lowered pollution (Hahn 1989).

Although we have been discussing Pigouvian taxation in the context of environmental damage, it is equally relevant for dealing with other kinds of externalities. Heavy trucks, for example, create externalities by damaging highways, which increases the wear and tear on other vehicles using the roads and raises highway maintenance costs. The marginal damage depends on the weight of the truck and the number of axles. (Interestingly, automobiles have virtually no effect on the physical condition of highways.) Small and Winston (1986) estimate that if trucking firms in the United States were forced to pay a tax equal to the marginal damage caused by their vehicles, the welfare gain to society—the equivalent of area A in Figure 18.3—would be $1.2 billion per year.

Figure 18.8

Market for Pollution Rights

When the government auctions off pollution rights, the supply curve is perfectly inelastic. The equilibrium effluent fee is p_1. Firms that are not willing to buy permission to pollute at this price must either cut output or change their technology.

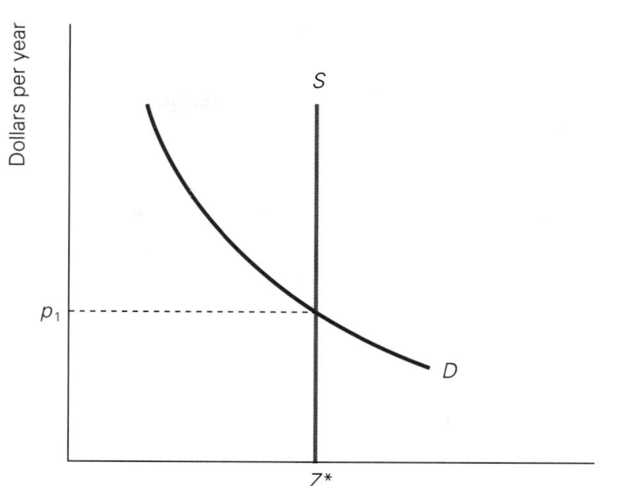

Creating a Market

As we emphasized above, the inefficiencies associated with externalities can be linked to the absence of a market for the relevant resource. This suggests another way in which governmental action could enhance efficiency—sell producers permits to pollute. By doing so, the government in effect creates a market for clean air that otherwise would not have emerged. Under this scheme, the government announces that it will sell permits to spew Z^* of pollutants into the air (the quantity of pollutants associated with output X^*). Firms bid for the right to own these permissions to pollute, and the permissions go to the firms with the highest bids. The fee charged is that which clears the market, so the amount of pollution equals the level set by the government. The price paid for permission to pollute is called an **effluent fee**. Like a Pigouvian tax—and unlike mandatory across-the-board cutbacks—an effluent fee provides incentives to reduce pollution efficiently.

effluent fee
The price paid for permission to pollute.

The effluent fee approach is illustrated in Figure 18.8. The horizontal axis measures the number of *rights to produce sulfur oxides*, and the vertical measures the price of these rights in dollars per year. The government announces that it will auction off Z^* pollution rights, so the supply of pollution rights is perfectly inelastic at Z^*. The demand for pollution rights, D, is downward sloping. The equilibrium price per unit is p_1. Those firms that are not willing to pay p_1 for each unit of pollution they produce must either reduce their output, or adopt a cleaner technology.

The scheme also works if, instead of auctioning off the pollution rights, the government assigns them to various firms who are then free to sell them to other firms. The market supply is still perfectly inelastic at Z^*, and the price of p_1 still emerges. The reason that nothing changes is that a given firm is willing to sell its pollution rights provided that the firm values these rights at less than p_1. Importantly, even though the efficiency effects are the same as those of the auction, the distributional consequences are radically different. With the auction, the money goes to the government; with the other scheme, the money goes to the firms that were lucky enough to be assigned the pollution rights.

In any case, in this simple model the effluent fee and the Pigouvian tax both achieve the efficient level of pollution. Implementing both requires knowledge of who is polluting and in what quantities. How is one to choose between them? Cropper and Oates (1992) argue that the auction scheme has some practical advantages over the tax. One of the most important is that the auction scheme reduces uncertainty about the ultimate level of pollution. If the government is certain about the shapes of the private marginal cost and marginal benefit schedules of Figure 18.7, then it can safely predict how a Pigouvian tax will affect behavior. But if there is poor information about these schedules, it is hard to know how much a particular tax will reduce pollution. If lack of information forces policymakers to choose the pollution standard arbitrarily, with a system of pollution permits, there is more certainty that this level will be obtained. In addition, under the assumption that firms are profit maximizers, they will find the cost-minimizing technology to attain the standard.

Moreover, when the economy is experiencing inflation, the market price of pollution rights would be expected to keep pace automatically while changing the tax rate could require a lengthy administrative procedure. On the other hand, one possible problem with the auctioning scheme is that incumbent firms might be able to buy up pollution licenses in excess of the firms' cost-minimizing requirements to deter other firms from entering the market. Whether such strategic behavior is likely to occur is hard to predict.

Although regulation has been the chosen method for dealing with pollution, the market approach is beginning to make some inroads. In 1990, new amendments to the U.S. Clean Air Act instituted the first large-scale program for trading emissions. Under this program, the government sets a maximum annual national level for sulfur dioxide emissions from coal-fired power plants. For each unit of sulfur dioxide a firm produces, it must possess an emission permit or face a heavy fine. Firms are allowed to buy and sell the permits, and they do. In 1992, for example, Wisconsin Power and Light, one of the cleanest utilities, sold pollution rights for about 10,000 tons of sulfur dioxide to the Tennessee Valley Authority. In effect, there is a market for entitlements to pollute, much along the lines described in Figure 18.8. Businesses have not been the only ones to participate in this market. In 1995, a group of law students pooled $3,256 to buy permits to emit 18 tons of sulphur dioxide. "Instead of selling the allowances for a profit at a future auction, the students said they would let them expire unused—yielding a reduction, albeit a small one, in pollution" (*New York Times* 1995, A28).

A number of empirical studies have sought to compare the costs of obtaining a given reduction in pollution by using regulations and by using economic incentives such as auctioning pollution rights. The particular results depend on the type of pollution being considered and the site of the pollution. In every case, though, economic incentives have been found to provide a much cheaper solution; in some instances, the incentive approach is only one-tenth the cost of regulation (Cropper and Oates 1992, 686). Hence, the expansion of the use of emissions trading in the Clean Air Act Amendments of 1990 is a positive development.

SECTION RECAP

Both private and public responses to externalities can reduce or eliminate their adverse efficiency consequences. Two firms involved in an externality situation may have an incentive to merge in order to "internalize" the externality. If one party imposes an externality on another, then they have an incentive to bargain their way to an efficient solution as long as ownership rights are established and transactions costs are low. In cases where transactions costs are not negligible, however, such bargaining may not take place. In these situations, public remedies such as Pigouvian taxation or creating a market for trading emissions may be appropriate. The basic idea behind these policies is to force people who create externalities to take their costs (or benefits) into account.

18.3 PUBLIC GOODS

public good
A commodity that is nonrival in consumption.

We have seen that in the case of externalities, markets for certain commodities may fail to emerge, and efficiency suffers as a consequence. In this section we discuss another situation where nonexistence of a market is a problem. This is when a commodity is a **public good**, defined as a commodity that is nonrival in consumption. "Nonrival" means that when one household partakes of the commodity's benefits, it does not diminish the benefits received by all other consumers of the commodity. In more technical terms, once a public good is provided, the marginal cost of another person's consuming it is zero. In contrast, consumption of a *private good* is rival. For example, national defense is a public good because my consumption of the services provided by the armed forces does not at all diminish your ability to consume the same services. Bread, on the other hand, is a private good, because if I eat a loaf, you cannot eat it too. This section discusses the efficiency problems associated with public goods.

EFFICIENT PROVISION OF PUBLIC GOODS

In Chapter 12, we derived conditions for the Pareto-efficient allocation of *private* goods and argued that under certain circumstances, these conditions would be met by private markets. Specifically, we showed that if there are two *private* goods, bread (b) and wine (v), and two people, Cain and Abel, then a necessary condition for Pareto efficiency is

$$MRS_{vb}^{Cain} = MRS_{vb}^{Abel} = MRT_{vb}, \tag{18.1}$$

where MRS_{vb}^{Cain} is Cain's marginal rate of substitution between bread and wine, MRS_{vb}^{Abel} is Abel's, and MRT_{vb} is the marginal rate of transformation between bread and wine. We now discuss the condition for efficient provision of a *public* good.

Before turning to a formal derivation, let's develop the condition intuitively. Suppose that Cain and Abel both enjoy flower gardens. Abel's enjoyment of a garden does not diminish Cain's, and vice versa. Hence, a garden is a public good. The size of the garden can be varied, and both individuals prefer bigger to smaller gardens, *ceteris paribus.* Suppose that the garden is currently 100 square feet, and can be expanded at a cost of $7 per square foot. Cain would be willing to pay $6 to expand the garden by another square foot, and Abel would be willing to pay $5.50. Is it efficient to increase the size of the garden by a square foot?

As usual, we must compare the marginal benefit to the marginal cost. To compute the marginal benefit, note that because consumption of the garden is nonrival, the 101st square foot can be consumed by *both* Cain and Abel. Hence, the marginal benefit of the 101st square foot is the *sum* of what they are willing to pay, which is $11.50. Because the marginal cost is only $7, it pays to acquire the 101st square foot. More generally, if the sum of individuals' willingness to pay for an additional unit of a public good exceeds its marginal cost, efficiency requires that the unit be purchased; otherwise, it should not. Hence, efficient provision of a public good requires that the sum of each person's marginal valuation on the last unit just equal the marginal cost.

To derive this result graphically, consider Panel A of Figure 18.9, which measures the size of a garden in square feet (G) on the horizontal axis, and the price per square foot (p) on the vertical. Cain's demand curve for gardens is d^C. Abel's demand curve for gardens is d^A in Panel B. How do we derive the group willingness to pay for gardens? To find the group demand curve for a *private* good, we *horizontally* sum the individual demand curves. (See Chapter 3.) That procedure allows different people to consume different quantities of the good at the same price. For a private good, this is fine. As already noted, however, the services produced by the garden are consumed in equal amounts by both people. (We use a capital G for quantity to remind ourselves that each individual consumes the market quantity.) If Cain consumes a 100 square-foot garden, then Abel also consumes a 100 square-foot garden. It literally makes no sense to try to sum the *quantities* of a public good that the individuals would consume at a given price.

Instead, we find the group willingness to pay for gardens by adding the prices that each would be willing to pay for a given quantity. It is important to note that even though everyone can consume the same quantity of a public good, there is no requirement that this consumption be valued equally by all. For example, the demand curve in Panel A tells us that Cain is willing to pay $7 per square foot when he consumes G_a square feet, while Panel B indicates that Abel is willing to pay $8 when he consumes G_a square feet. Their group willingness to pay for G_a square feet is the sum of what each is willing to pay, or $15. Thus, if we define D^{C+A} in Panel C to be the group willingness-to-pay schedule, then the height of the D^{C+A} curve at quantity G_a must be $15.[5] Other points on D^{C+A} are determined by repeating this procedure for each level of public good production. For a public good, the group willingness to pay is found by *vertical summation* of the individual demand curves.

Note the symmetry between private and public goods. With a private good, everyone puts the same value on the good (at the margin), but people can consume different quantities. Therefore, demands are summed horizontally over the differing quantities. For public goods, everyone consumes the same quantity, but people can value the good differently (at the margin). Vertical summation is required to find the group willingness to pay.

The efficient garden size is found at the point where group willingness to pay for an additional unit just equals the marginal cost of producing a unit. In Panel C, the marginal cost schedule, S, is superimposed on the group willingness-to-pay curve D^{C+A}. The intersection occurs at output G^*, where the total willingness to pay is equal to $8 (= $5 + $3).

[5] D^{C+A} is not a conventionally defined demand schedule, because it does not show the quantity that would be demanded at each price. However, we use this notation to highlight the similarities to the private good case, where the demand curve can also be interpreted as a willingness-to-pay schedule.

Figure 18.9

Efficient Provision of a Public Good

Group willingness to pay for a public good is found by vertical summation of demand curves. At the efficient level of the public good, G^*, the sum of the marginal rates of substitution equals the marginal rate of transformation.

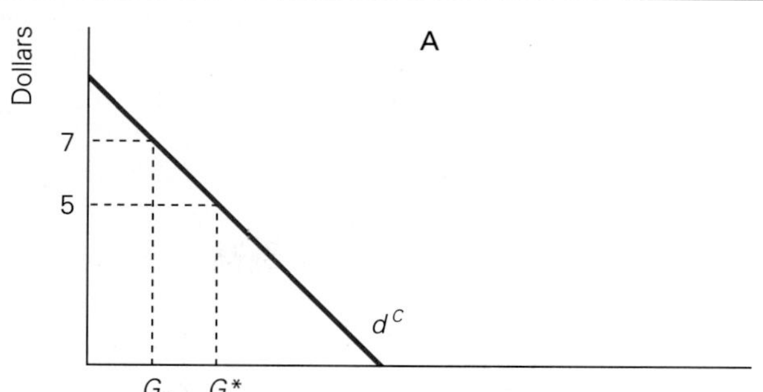

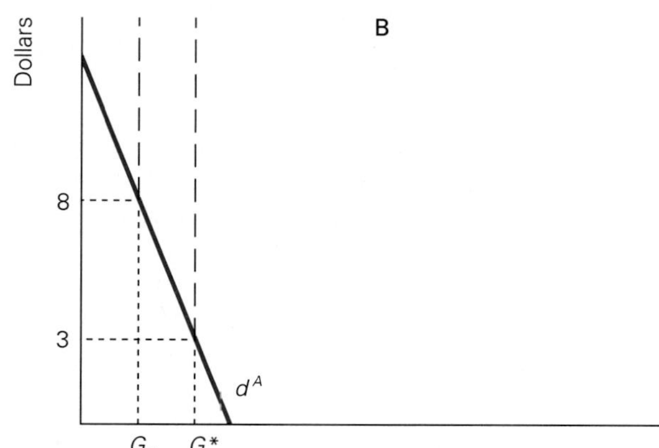

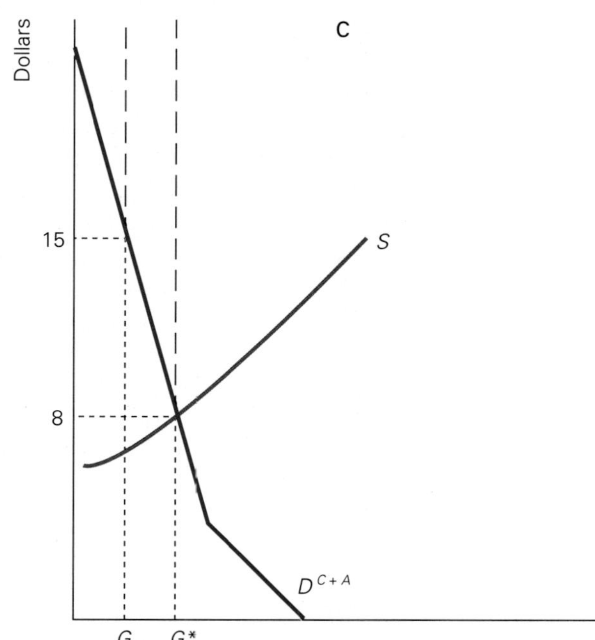

Recall from Chapter 4 that every point on an individual demand curve for a commodity approximately represents the marginal rate of substitution between it and some other commodity. For convenience, suppose that the other commodity is wine, and wine is measured in units such that the price per unit is \$1. Then at any point on Cain's demand curve, the distance down to the *X*-axis is MRS_{gv}^{Cain}, where MRS_{gv}^{Cain} is Cain's marginal rate of substitution between gardens (g) and wine (v). Similarly, at any point on Abel's demand curve, the distance to the *X*-axis is MRS_{gv}^{Abel}. Finally, the marginal cost of a commodity can be viewed as the marginal rate of transformation between it and some other commodity. Again letting wine be the "other" commodity, this means that any point on the *S* curve gives the marginal rate of transformation between garden size and wine, MRT_{gv}.

Now let us use this information to reinterpret what's happening in Figure 18.9. At the efficient output, G^*, the marginal cost is equal to the sum of what Cain is willing to pay (\$5) and what Abel is willing to pay (\$3). However, the sum of Cain's willingness to pay and Abel's willingness to pay is $MRS_{gv}^{Cain} + MRS_{gv}^{Abel}$, and the marginal cost of G^* is MRT_{gv}. Hence, the situation at G^* in Panel C can be represented algebraically as:

$$MRS_{gv}^{Cain} + MRS_{gv}^{Abel} = MRT_{gv}. \qquad (18.2)$$

Contrast this with the conditions for efficient provision of a private good described in Equation (18.1). For a *private* good, efficiency requires that each individual have the same marginal rate of substitution, and that this equal the marginal rate of transformation. Equation (18.2) is just the intuitive result from the beginning of this subsection: *Because everybody must consume the same amount of the public good, its efficient provision requires that the total valuation they place on the last unit provided—the sum of the MRSs—equal the incremental cost to society of providing it—the MRT.* (PC 18.6)

18.6 PROGRESS CHECK

Every year a community of three people (Woodrow, Teddy, and William) has a fireworks display. The marginal cost of each rocket is constant at \$130. Currently, the display consists of 75 rockets. The marginal value of the 75th rocket for Woodrow is \$9; for Teddy it is \$77; and for William it is \$12. From an efficiency point of view, is the rocket display too big, too small, or the correct size? Relate your answer to Equation (18.2).

Impure Public Goods

In our garden example, it was perfectly clear which goods were private and which public. However, *classification as a public good is not an absolute. It depends on market conditions and the state of technology.* The reading room of a large library can be considered a public good when there are few people present. But as the number of users increases, crowding and traffic problems occur that are inimical to serious scholarly research. The same "quantity" of library is being "consumed" by each person, but because of congestion, its quality can decrease with the number of people. Hence, the nonrivalness criterion is no longer strictly satisfied. (The Library of Congress deals with this problem by severely limiting access to high school students.) In many cases, it is useful to think of "publicness" as a matter of degree. A pure public good satisfies the definition exactly. Consumption of an **impure public good** is to some extent rival. It is difficult to think of many examples of really pure public goods. However, just as analysis of pure competition yields important insights into the operation of actual markets, so the analysis of pure public goods helps us to understand actual public goods, which may be impure.

impure public good
A commodity that is somewhat nonrival in consumption.

MARKET PROVISION OF PUBLIC GOODS

nonexcludable
A good for which preventing consumption is prohibitively expensive.

Now that we have the condition for Pareto-efficient provision of a public good, the key question is whether it will be met by private markets. To answer this question, we must introduce the notion of nonexcludability. The consumption of a good is **nonexcludable** when it is either very expensive or impossible to prevent anyone from consuming the good even if he or she refuses to pay for it. Many nonrival goods are also nonexcludable. For example, national defense services are nonexcludable, because no particular individual can be prevented from taking advantage of the protection they provide. By definition, when one person provides a nonexcludable public good, it affects the welfare of every person in the society. Hence, *a nonexcludable public good is simply a kind of positive externality.*

Nonexcludability and nonrivalness do not have to go together. Consider the streets of a downtown urban area during rush hour. Nonexcludability generally holds, because it is infeasible to set up enough toll booths to monitor traffic. But consumption is certainly rival, as anyone who has ever been caught in a traffic jam can testify. On the other hand, many people can enjoy a huge seashore area without diminishing the pleasure of others. Despite the fact that individuals do not rival each other in consumption, exclusion is quite possible if there are few access roads. This example also suggests that nonexcludability, like nonrivalness, is not an absolute. It depends on the state of technology and on legal arrangements. (PC 18.7)

18.7 PROGRESS CHECK

In many supermarkets, commodities are labeled with bar codes that allow scanning machines to identify the product. It is also possible to put bar codes on automobiles, so that scanners can automatically identify drivers on city streets. How would the use of such scanners affect the "excludability" of city streets?

If a public good is excludable, will private markets provide it in efficient quantities? Assume that the garden from our example above is excludable—it is possible to fence the garden off from public view. Suppose that a profit-maximizing entrepreneur sells tickets to gain entrance. Recall from Chapter 12 that Pareto efficiency requires that price equal marginal cost. Because a public good is nonrival in consumption, by definition the marginal cost of providing it to another person is zero. Hence, the efficient price is zero. But if the entrepreneur charges everyone a price of zero, then he cannot stay in business.

Is there a way out? Suppose: (*a*) that the entrepreneur knows each person's demand curve for the public good and (*b*) that it is difficult or impossible to transfer the good from one person to another. (In this case, you can't sell your admission ticket to anybody else.)

Under these conditions, the entrepreneur could charge each person an individual price based on that person's willingness to pay; that is, practice perfect price discrimination as discussed in Chapter 13. People who valued the garden at only a penny would pay exactly that amount; even they would not be excluded from attending. Thus, everyone who put any positive value on the garden would view it, which is an efficient outcome. However, because those who valued the garden a lot would pay a very high price, the enterprise would still be profitable.

Perfect price discrimination may seem to be the solution until we recall that condition (*a*) requires knowledge of everybody's preferences. But of course, if individuals' demand curves were known, there would be no problem in determining the optimal provision in the first place. Without this information, the entrepreneur cannot price discriminate. When the entrepreneur has to charge the same price to everyone, he sets that price greater than zero in order to raise revenues. But then some people who place relatively low, but positive, values on the garden are inefficiently excluded. Thus, we conclude that *even if a public good is excludable, private provision is likely to lead to efficiency problems.*

When the public good is nonexcludable, things become even more problematic. To see why, note that when a *private* good is exchanged in a competitive market, an individual has no incentive to lie about how much he or she values it. If Abel is willing to pay the going price for a gallon of wine, then he has nothing to gain by failing to make the purchase. This kind of behavior is implied by the assumption that people are price takers.

In the case of a nonexcludable public good, people may have incentives to hide their true preferences. Suppose that fencing off the garden is infeasible. Cain may falsely claim that flowers mean nothing to him. If he can get Abel to foot the entire bill, Cain can still enjoy the garden and yet have more money to spend on bread and wine. This incentive to let other people pay while you enjoy the benefits is another example of the free-rider problem that we saw in Chapter 7 and earlier in this chapter. Of course, Abel also would like to be a free rider. But if everyone chooses to free ride, they all will end up looking at weeds instead of flowers. Hence, *there is a good chance that the market will fall short of providing the efficient amount of the public good.* No "automatic" tendency exists for markets to reach allocation G^* in Figure 18.9.

RESPONSES TO THE PUBLIC-GOOD PROBLEM

Given that a nonexcludable public good is just a special kind of positive externality and that externalities are associated with potential efficiency problems, it is not surprising that public goods also present efficiency problems. We showed earlier in this chapter that when ownership rights can be established and bargaining costs are low, individuals can bargain their way to an efficient allocation. However, this result is unlikely to be of much relevance for public goods. Some, like national defense, affect everyone in the society; the costs of getting the whole country together for bargaining would be prohibitive. Moreover, in light of the free-rider problem, bargaining might not be efficient anyway.

It must be emphasized that free ridership is not a *fact*; it is an implication of the *hypothesis* that people maximize a utility function that depends only on their own consumption of goods. To be sure, one can find examples in which public goods are not provided because people free ride. Attempts to set up communal coffee pots in the faculty lounges of economics departments often fail for this reason—while everyone is happy to drink the coffee, no one is willing to refill the pot when it runs out. On the other hand, much evidence suggests that individuals can and do act collectively without government coercion. Some coffee clubs succeed. And people often donate money to support churches, libraries, art museums, theaters, and other facilities that add to a community's quality of life. One prominent economist has even argued, "I do not know of many historical records or other empirical evidence which show convincingly that the problem of correct revelation of preferences has been of any practical significance" (Johansen 1977, 147).

These observations do not prove that free ridership is irrelevant. Although some goods that appear to have "public" characteristics are privately provided, others that "ought" to be provided (on grounds of efficiency) may not be. Moreover, the quantity of those public goods that are privately provided may be insufficient. The key point is that the importance of the free-rider problem can vary across situations. Just as in the case of externalities, both public and private responses may remedy the inefficiencies that arise due to the nonexistence of competitive markets for public goods.

publicly provided private goods Rival commodities that are provided by governments.

In this context, note that simply because a commodity is provided by the public sector does not necessarily mean that it is a "public good" according to our definition. There are many cases of **publicly provided private goods**—rival commodities that are provided by governments. Medical services and housing are two examples of private goods that are sometimes provided publicly. Similarly, as we have already noted, public goods can be provided privately. Think of an individual who tidies up the communal bathroom in a dormitory.

SECTION RECAP

A public good is nonrival in consumption—one person's consumption of the good does not interfere with anyone else's. Efficient provision of a public good requires that the *sum* of the marginal rates of substitution between the public and private goods equals the marginal rate of transformation. Whether the public good is excludable or nonexcludable, there is no "automatic" tendency for this condition to be fulfilled. Government intervention may be required to obtain efficient provision of public goods.

SUMMARY

The First Welfare Theorem says that if everyone is a price taker and there is a market for every commodity, then the allocation of resources is Pareto-efficient. This chapter discusses externality situations, in which a market may not exist, and the allocation of resources may therefore be inefficient.

- An externality occurs when the activity of one person or firm affects the welfare of another person or firm in a way that is not transmitted by market prices. An externality may be negative (it imposes a cost on the other party) or positive (it benefits the other party).
- An externality may lead to inefficiencies because the individual performing the activity does not take into account the marginal damages or marginal benefits that accrue to other people.
- An externality does not necessarily lead to inefficiencies. Mergers and certain social conventions are two ways in which people are induced to account for externalities.
- According to the Coase Theorem, as long as property rights are assigned and transaction costs are negligible, people will bargain their way to an efficient solution.
- When private parties cannot solve an externality problem, then in principle, government intervention can enhance efficiency. Levying Pigouvian taxes and creating markets in pollution rights are two possible policies. Economists generally prefer these policies to the more common approach of regulation.
- A pure public good is nonrival in consumption. Efficient provision of a pure public good requires that the sum of everybody's marginal rates of substitution equal the marginal rate of transformation.
- A public good is nonexcludable when it is difficult or impossible to prevent someone from consuming it. A nonexcludable public good is a kind of positive externality.

DISCUSSION QUESTIONS

18.1 Several years ago in North Carolina "25 million gallons of watery waste from 10,000 hogs spilled out of a holding lagoon at the Oceanview Hog Farm and poured over soybean plants, tobacco fields and into creeks and rivers. The spill killed more than 3,000 fish." The spill destroyed part of the tobacco crop, but the soybeans were "probably helped by the spill, since they can stand a lot more nitrogen" (Smothers 1995, A10).

Identify the externalities in this situation.

18.2 "In Los Angeles and other California areas popular for filming, residents are sometimes making thousands of dollars from movie crews by promising to vacate outdoor sets, tone down noise or otherwise stop harassing them . . . People blow horns, walk through shots, make their dogs bark or crank their stereos. And they all demand money to stop . . . Sometimes, hecklers wind up in jail when film production people decide to take the time to press charges under public nuisance laws. But enlisting law enforcement does not always stop the harassment." (Roane 1995, A14).

Explain the externality in this situation, and relate it to the inability to establish property rights.

18.3 The 1990 amendments to the U.S. Clean Air Act mandate that "starting with 1998 models, fleets of 10 or more cars in the two dozen smoggiest cities must run 80 percent more cleanly than today's autos. Trucks must be 50 percent cleaner" (*Wall Street Journal*, October 29, 1990, p. A7). Is this likely to be an efficient way to reduce pollution?

18.4 In the diagram below, schedule MB^L indicates the marginal benefit to Laurel from painting his house, and MC represents the marginal cost. Laurel's neighbor, Hardy, likes seeing a nicely painted house when looking out his window.

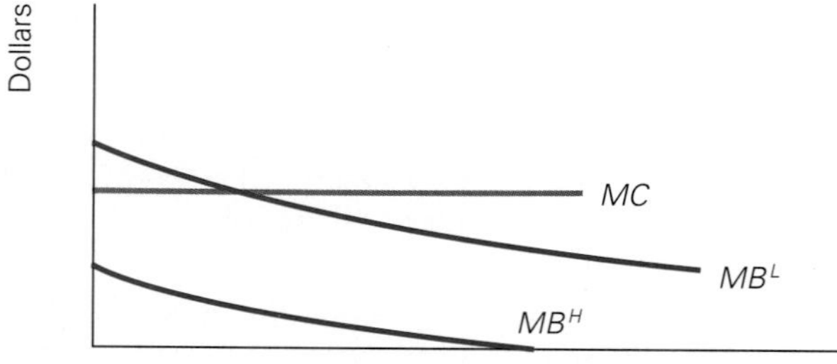

The marginal benefit to Hardy from painting done by Laurel is shown by schedule MB^H.

a. What is the socially efficient amount of painting?

b. In the absence of any bargaining between Laurel and Hardy, how much painting is done?

c. What is the joint gain if Laurel and Hardy bargain their way to an efficient solution?

d. Suppose that bargaining is impossible. Suggest a Pigouvian ***subsidy*** that will lead to an efficient outcome.

18.5 Consider again the regulatory example in Figure 18.6.

a. Suppose that in the name of "fairness," David and Saul are ordered to cut their use of pesticides by the same amount—from x_S to x_S^*. How much more costly is this solution than the fully efficient policy?

b. Suppose that David and Saul are both ordered to cut their use of pesticides to $(x_S^* + x_D^*)/2$. What are the efficiency costs of this regulation in comparison with the optimal policy?

18.6 The U.S. government's corporate average fuel economy (CAFE) standards dictate the gasoline mileage that cars must obtain. An alternative approach to reducing gasoline consumption and its attendant pollution would be to levy a tax on gasoline. Compare the CAFE approach and the taxation approach.

18.7 In each of the following situations, explain whether or not the Coase Theorem would be likely to provide a basis for dealing with the externality.

a. The Ganges River in India receives industrial effluents, including toxic heavy metals, from hundreds of tanneries that operate along its banks. Further, millions of gallons of raw sewage are spilled into the river from hundreds of cities, towns, and villages.

b. Many scientists believe that global warming is caused by carbon dioxide that is released when coal, oil, and wood are burned.

c. My neighbor owns a "bug zapper," an electrical device that kills insects. The longer that she keeps the zapper on, the fewer the number of mosquitoes that appear in my backyard.

18.8 Which of the following are public goods?

a. Public television.
b. Commercial broadcast television.
c. A community swimming pool.
d. Honesty.
e. AIDS research.

18.9 The public good Z can be provided at a constant marginal cost of \$12. Cagney's demand for Z is $Z = 20 - p_z$, and Lacey's is $Z = 16 - 2p_z$, where Z is the quantity demanded and p_z is the price per unit. What is the Pareto-efficient level of Z?

18.10 "Just because a public good is *provided* by the public sector does not mean that it has to be *produced* by the public sector." Do you agree? Why or why not?

18.11 Explain how the free-ridership problem in the provision of public goods can be modeled as a prisoners' dilemma game.

18.12 Suppose that it costs \$25,000 per day to build and maintain a bridge potentially serving 20,000 people. 10,000 of these people are willing to pay \$2 per day to cross the bridge, while the other 10,000 value the bridge at \$1 per day.

a. Assuming that there is no congestion, is it efficient to build the bridge? Find an efficient toll to charge people for crossing. Will this toll cover the costs of building and operating the bridge? Can you find a toll that will raise revenues sufficient to cover these costs?

b. Is the bridge a public good? Is it excludable? What does your answer to part *a* indicate about a possible role for government intervention?

Now suppose that the bridge becomes congested when more than 10,000 per day use it. For simplicity, make the extreme assumption that when any number of people greater than 10,000 per day use the bridge, the benefits to each person crossing the bridge fall by \$.60 per day.

c. Assuming that the bridge is built, find an efficient toll to charge people for crossing the bridge under these conditions.

d. Is it efficient to build the bridge under these conditions?

***18.13** Firm 1 produces output Q_1, which it sells in a competitive market at a price of 800. Firm 2 produces output Q_2, which it sells in a competitive market at price 1,600. Firm 1's cost function is $C_1 = 100\ Q_1^2$; firm 2's cost function is $C_2 = 50\ Q_2^2 + 50\ Q_1$.

a. Explain why an externality is present in this situation.

b. What are the socially efficient outputs for each firm? (*Hint:* Find the values of Q_1 and Q_2 that maximize *joint* profits.)

c. What outputs would you expect if the firms merged? If the firms did not merge?

d. Suggest a tax policy that could be used to attain the socially efficient output.

*This problem is for students who have studied the material in the Appendix to Chapter 9.

Progress Check Solutions

If you are unable to answer the Progress Check correctly, go back and reread the preceding pages in the text before moving forward.

Chapter 1

1–1. Oil consumption has an opportunity cost for Saudi Arabia. It is the goods and services Saudi Arabia could have received by selling, rather than consuming, the oil.

1–2. As shown below, the downward shift of the marginal benefit curve causes Bert to choose fewer years of education.

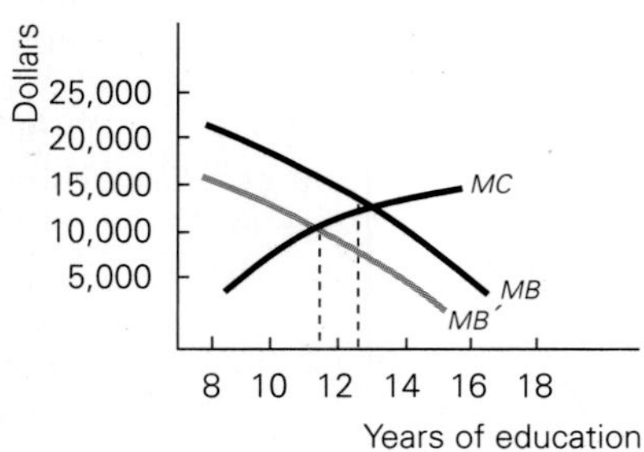

1–3.

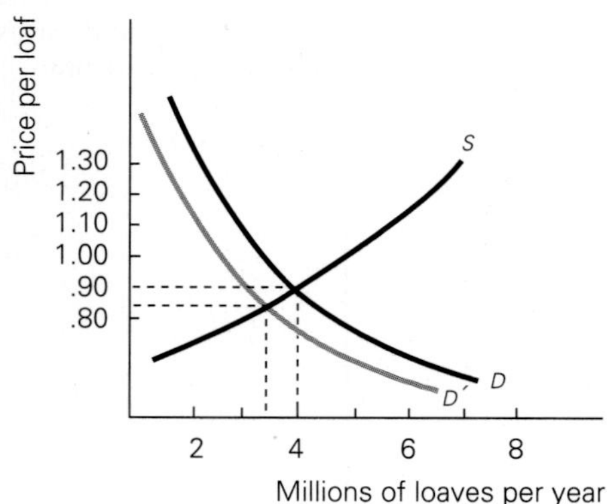

As shown in the preceding figure, the increase in the price of butter (a complement) induces a downward shift in the demand for bread. The price and quantity both fall, as determined by the intersection of D' and S.

Chapter 2

2–1. No, we cannot predict which bundle our "hacker" will choose. The assumption of completeness requires only that she have a preference (or express indifference). Nonsatiation is not violated by the selection of either bundle in this example.

2–2. Louise's marginal rate of substitution of Russian novels for comic books is 1.5 (= 3⁄2).

2–3. U_0 represents the utility associated with having 50 cents. Our consumer is indifferent between holding 10 nickels or 5 dimes, or any possible combination in between.

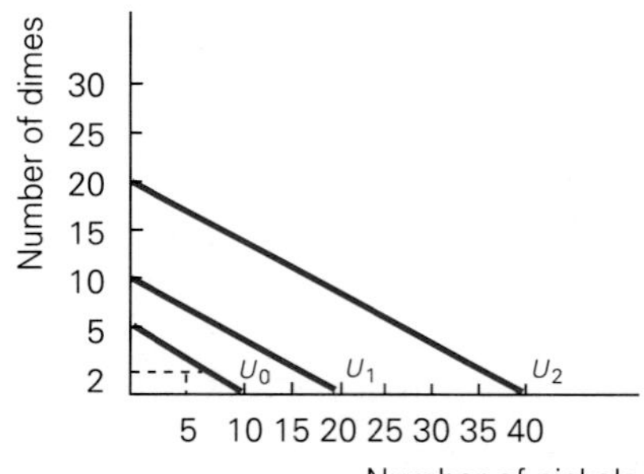

2–4. *a.* The President's budget constraint is $500{,}000 = 50{,}000 \times f + 10{,}000 \times s$, where f is the number of faculty positions and s is the number of scholarships offered.

b. The opportunity cost of a faculty position is five scholarships.

c. See line B_0 in the following figure.

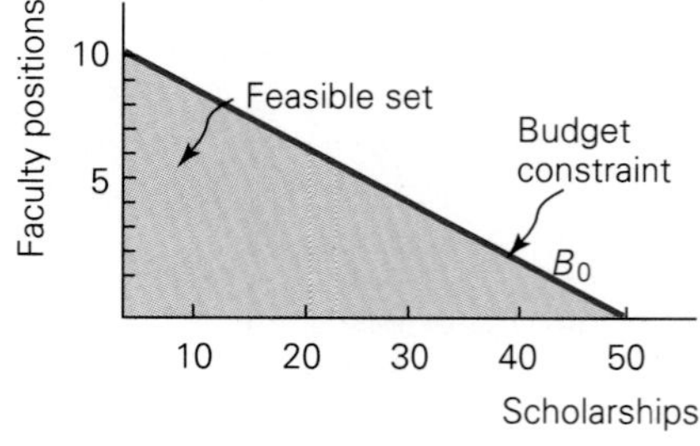

d. The budget constraint shifts in from B_0 to B_1 as the budget is reduced to \$300,000.

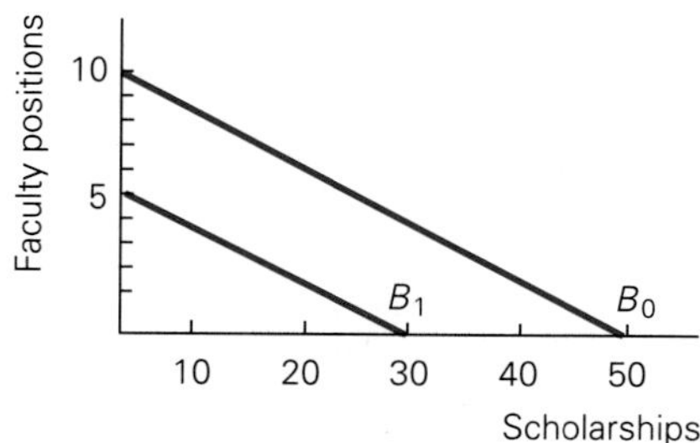

e. With a constant budget of \$500,000, the constraint pivots as the cost of faculty positions drops to \$25,000. B_2 marks off a larger feasible set than B_0.

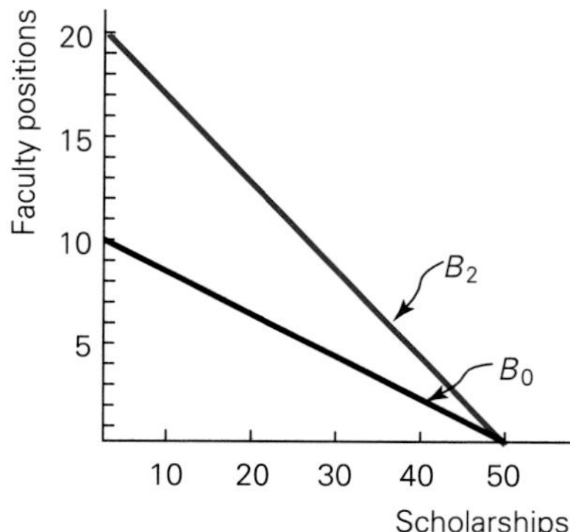

2–5. See the following figure.

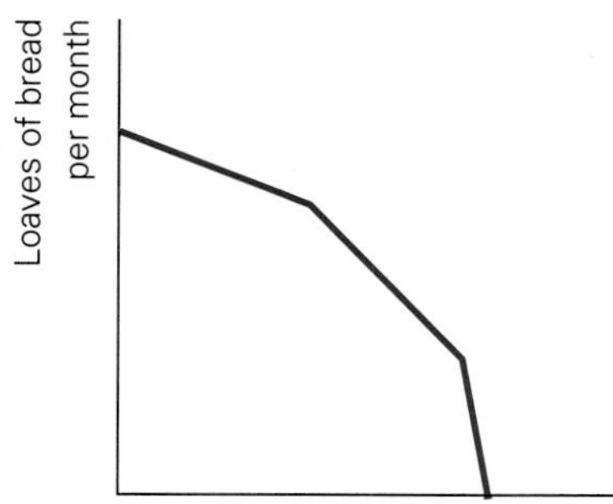

2–6. The budget constraints show that tapes can be traded for records at a rate of five to one (records are five times as expensive as tapes). Victoria's *MRS* is ⅕. Albert, who is at a corner, has an *MRS* that is greater than ⅕.

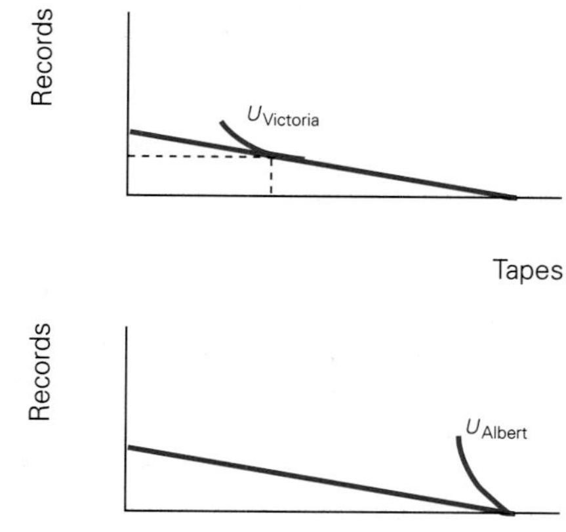

2–7. Willy is not maximizing his utility. He is getting greater marginal utility from his last dollar spent on car transportation than from his last dollar spent on bus transportation: $80/.3 > 150/.6$. Therefore, Willy should increase his consumption of car transportation until the equilibrium condition $\frac{MU_x}{p_x} = \frac{MU_y}{p_y}$ is satisfied.

Chapter 3

3–1. When the price of hamburgers falls, the budget constraint moves from B_1 to B_2. At the new equilibrium, hamburger consumption is greater, but taco consumption is the same.

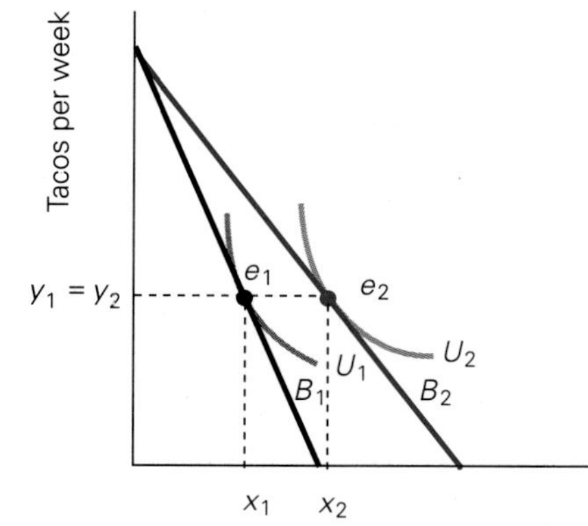

3–2. An increase in the price of polyester shirts induces an outward shift in the demand curve for cotton shirts (to d'), as the two goods are substitutes. Since the whole demand schedule shifts, this represents a change in demand.

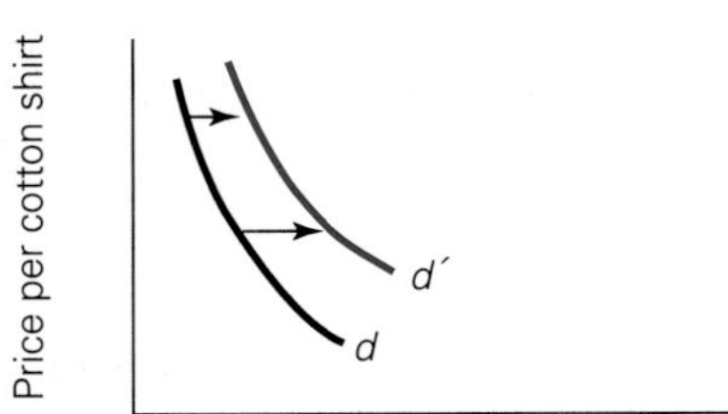

3–3.

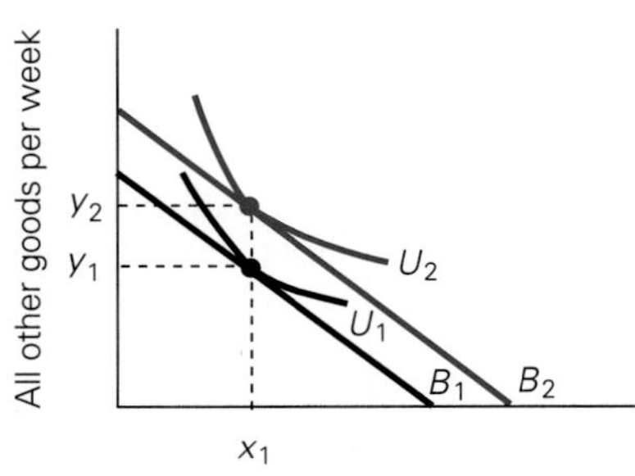

At income levels represented by B_1 and B_2 in the preceding diagram, the individual chooses the same number of bottles of wine, x_1. Therefore the individual spends the entire increase in his or her income on *all other goods*. [$(y_2 - y_1)$ is the amount the income increased.]

3–4. The vouchers free up money that people would have spent on food. They can spend this money on alcohol or drugs. Because money is fungible, a voucher and cash have the same impact on spending.

3–5. The quantity demanded for beef will fall 19.1 percent. Since we know from the elasticity formula that a 1 percent increase in price leads to a 1.91 percent fall in quantity demanded, no units of measurement are required for this calculation.

3–6. Arc elasticity of demand $= \dfrac{-\Delta X}{\overline{X}} \div \dfrac{\Delta p}{\overline{p}}$.

Therefore, $\epsilon = \dfrac{1 \text{ million}}{4.5 \text{ million}} \div \dfrac{\$500}{\$2{,}750}$, or $\epsilon = 1.2$.

3–7. Coffee and cigarettes appear to be complements, so the cross-elasticity of demand is negative.

Chapter 4

4–1.

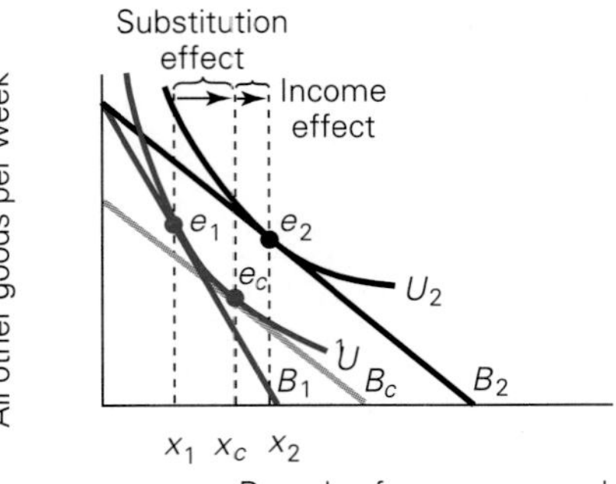

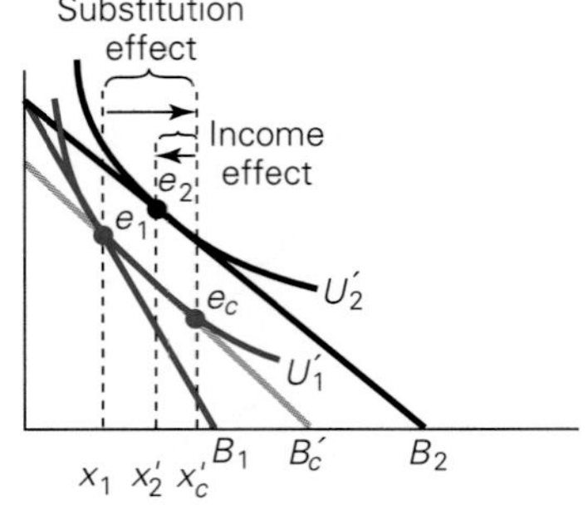

In the first diagram, sugar is a normal good: When the price falls, both the substitution and the income effects cause the consumer to purchase more sugar. In the second diagram, the income effect (x_c' to x_2') causes the consumer to purchase less sugar, thus sugar is inferior. However, as is usually the case, the substitution effect dominates the income effect and the amount of sugar consumed is higher due to the price decrease ($x_2' > x_1$).

4–2. The compensating variation is based on the new prices faced by the subway rider, and is represented by C in the diagram below. The equivalent variation (E) is based on the old prices, and answers the question: How much money would you have to take away from the subway rider to lower his or her welfare as much as the increase in the price of a subway ride.

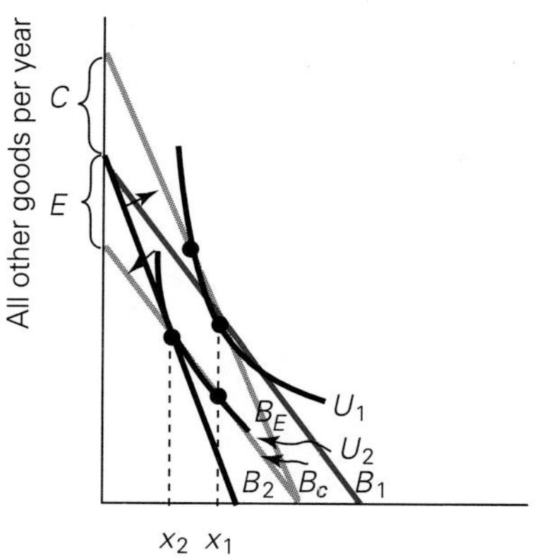

4–3. Calculating the change in welfare involves finding the sum of the areas of rectangle A and triangle B:

A = (\$8 − \$6) × (6 − 0) = \$12
B = .5 × (\$8 − \$6) × (10 − 6) = \$4
A + B = \$16.

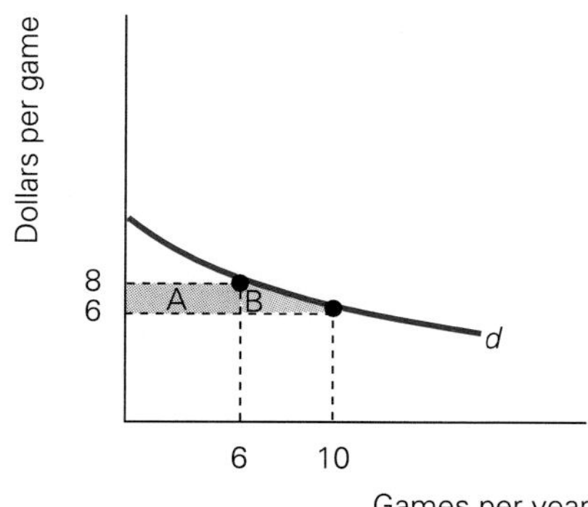

4–4. *a.* False. The "Law" of Demand is not a theoretical necessity. A rational individual may demand more of an inferior good as its price increases if the income effect dominates the substitution effect. However, economists have found no examples of such a good.

b. True. The compensated demand curve measures the substitution effect, holding utility constant. Since the substitution effect always works to reduce quantity demanded when price increases, the compensated demand curve must slope downward.

c. False. The relationship between the slopes of the compensated and ordinary demand curves depends on whether the commodity in question is normal or inferior. For a normal good, the compensated demand curve is steeper than the ordinary demand curve. For an inferior good, the opposite is true.

Chapter 5

5–1. The financial planner is suggesting that, when the tax goes up, individuals "should" work less. This is not necessarily the case. In the diagrams below, both A and B begin with the same bundle of leisure and consumption, e_1. The tax imposed on wage income pivots the budget constraint to B_2, reducing the opportunity cost of leisure. For A, it makes sense to supply more labor after the tax goes up, because the income effect dominates the substitution effect. For B, it makes sense to work less after the tax increase (as suggested by the financial planner). For B, the substitution effect dominates the income effect.

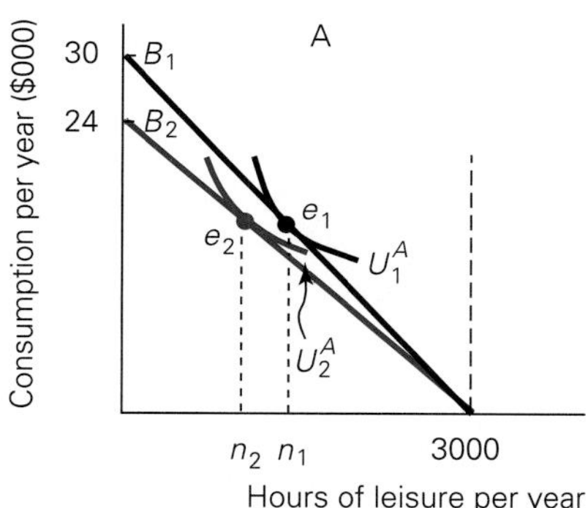

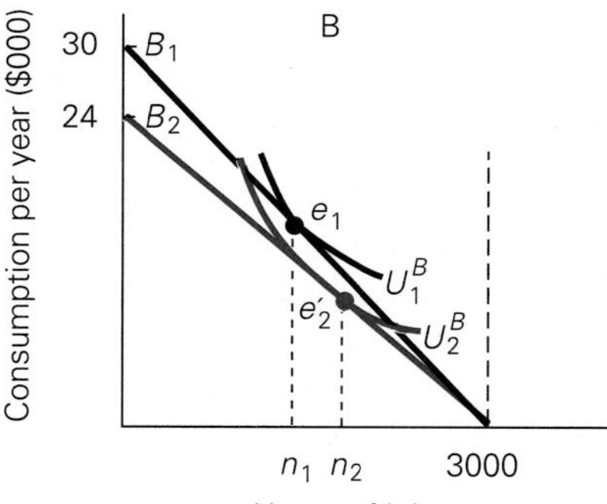

5–2. Assume for simplicity that, like AFDC, Supplemental Security Income is reduced a dollar for each dollar earned. (In reality, this is not quite the case.) In the figure below, the individual confronted with the kinked budget constraint maximizes utility by not working at all.

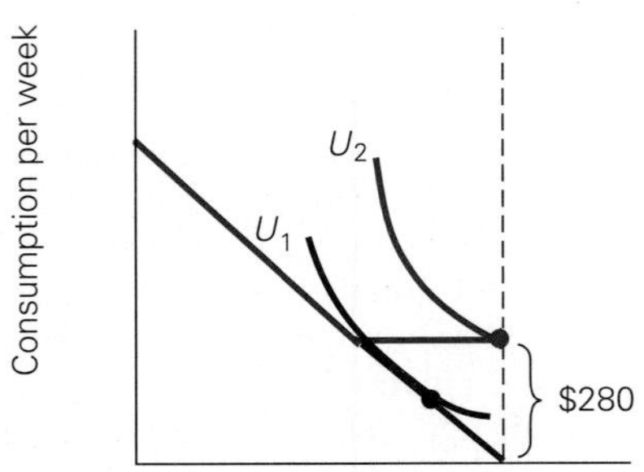

5–3. See the figure below.

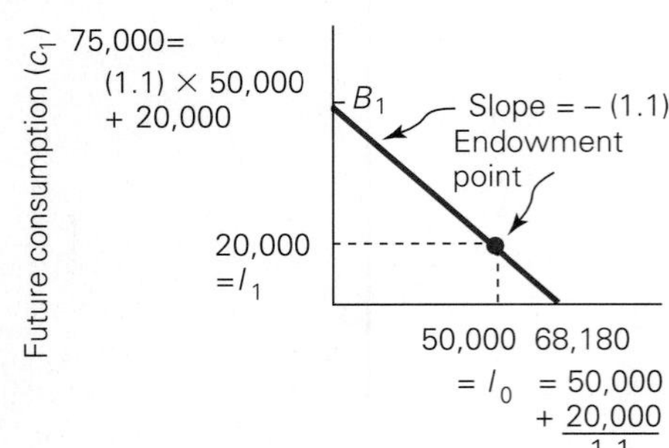

5–4. The increase in interest rates causes a borrower, through the substitution effect, to reduce current consumption. The income effect works in the same direction: The increase in the interest rate makes the individual relatively poorer. Thus, the described reduction in current consumption is consistent with our analysis.

5–5. In the following figure, the tax cut pivots the intertemporal budget constraint through the endowment point *a*. As drawn, current consumption increases ($c_0' > c_0$) as a result of the policy, that is, saving decreases. It is possible to represent the preferences of an individual who would decrease current consumption following such a tax cut if his or her income effect dominates the substitution effect.

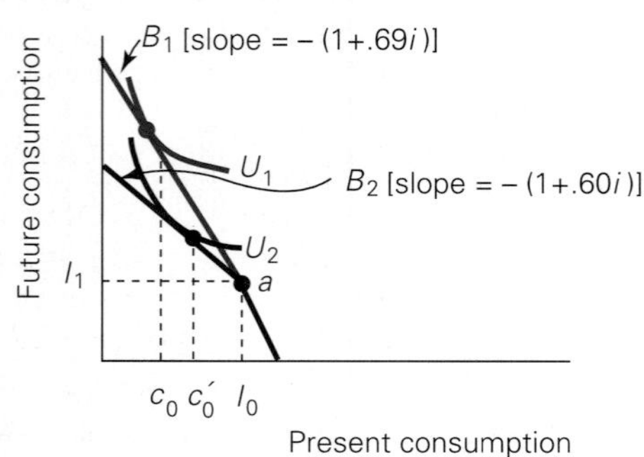

5–6. *a*. $PV_a = \dfrac{\$1{,}000{,}000}{(1 + .05)^{20}} = \$376{,}889.$

b. $PV_b = \$25 + \dfrac{\$50}{1.05} = \$72.62.$

c. $PV_c = \dfrac{\$625}{.05} = \$12{,}500.$

Chapter 6

6–1. The states of the world are "injured" and "not injured." The contingent commodities are *consumption if she enters the tournament* and *consumption if she has to sit it out.*

6–2. Expected income for a meatpacker is:

$$E(I) = .33 \times \$12{,}000 + .67 \times \$42{,}000 = \$32{,}100.$$

6–3. The odds of winning are 1 to 5 (= ⅙ ÷ ⅚). The slope of the fair odds line is minus the probability of the contingency on the horizontal axis divided by the probability of the contingency on the vertical axis, or – ⅕, as depicted in the figure below. The line passes through the endowment point *a* because the individual has the option of not taking the bet.

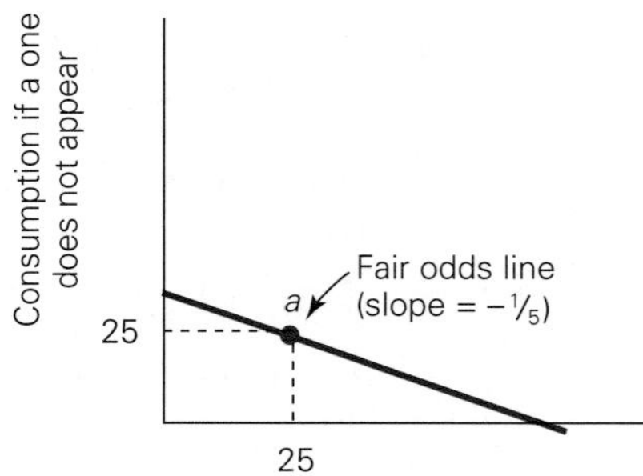

6–4. The expected value of a one dollar bet under this scheme is:

$$E(B) = .5 \times \$1 - .5 \times \$1.20 = -\$.10.$$

Since the expected value of the bet is negative, it is not a fair bet. To calculate the fair odds for a bet with these payoffs, set the expected value of the bet equal to zero.

$$0 = \rho \times \$1 - (1 - \rho) \times \$1.20.$$

Thus, $\rho = .545$. Minus one times the ratio of the probabilities, $-.545/.455 = -1.2$, is the slope of the fair odds line. It is graphed in the following diagram.

In order to make the bet fair, the expected value must be zero. Thus, from the calculation above, the probability of a head must be 0.545 if the bet is to be fair; the odds for a head must be 1.2 to 1.

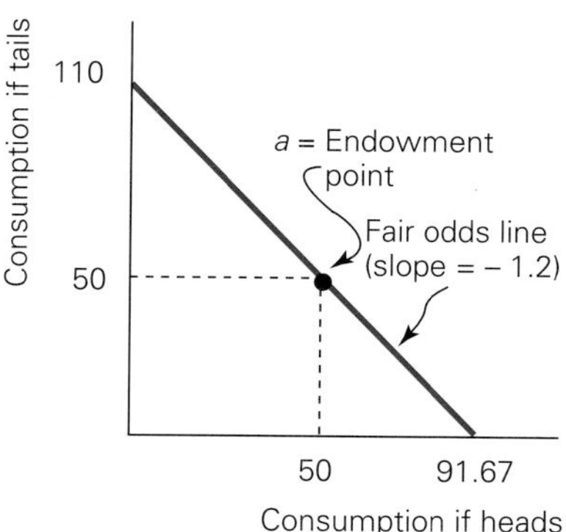

6–5. $E(A) = \$1{,}000$, as it is certain.
$E(B) = .5 \times 500 + .5 \times 2{,}000$
$= \$1{,}250$.

Both the risk-neutral person and the risk lover will accept option *B*, as it has a higher expected value. We need more information to predict what the risk averter will do: It depends on *how* risk averse he is. The expected value of *B* may be enough higher to induce him to take the gamble.

6–6. If the insurance were actuarially fair, it would cost only $0.10 per dollar of coverage. Since the insurance is actuarially unfair, Mike will not fully insure. A risk-averse individual ends up at a point like *b* in the diagram below, spending ($50,000 – $$c_N$) on insurance. In contrast, full insurance is represented by point *d*.

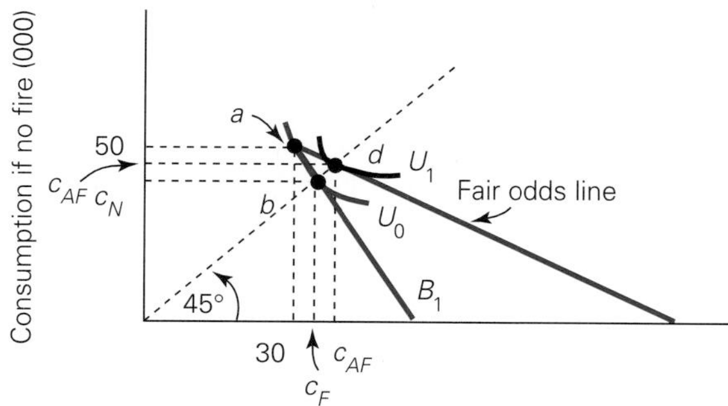

6–7. $U_{LAW} = 0.4 \times 7936 + 0.6 \times 4479.75 = 5861.85$. $U_{BUS} = 0.2 \times 11{,}856 + 0.8 \times 4479.75 = 5955$. Because $U_{BUS} > U_{LAW}$, he chooses business school.

6–8. If there is no radon, the house brings in $1,990 (U = 57.9) and the savings account yields $390 (U = 49.7). If there is radon, the house brings in $440 (U = 50.9) and the savings account again brings in $390 (U = 49.7). Regardless of the state of the world, the house is a better investment than the savings account. Hence, there is no reason to pay any money for the radon test.

Chapter 7

7–1. If he could not sublet the blending machine, it would have no alternative use. In this case, the opportunity cost of using the machine to produce ice cream would be $0 and the entire $1,000 on the remaining lease would be a sunk expenditure. If Jim could lease the machine for $1,200, then the machine's opportunity cost—its value in its best alternative use—would be $1,200.

7–2. When the machine is worthless to anyone but Jim, the machine's opportunity cost is $0 since that is the most Jim can get from selling it. This answer depends crucially on the fact that Jim already has purchased the machine. If he had not yet bought it, then the entire $8,000 purchase price of the machine would be an economic cost since he would have kept the $8,000 if he had not purchased the machine. In other words, before Jim purchases the machine, $8,000 is not a sunk expenditure, and after he has purchased the machine, it is.

Now suppose that Jim is considering whether to buy the machine and then sell it at the end of the year for $8,000. In this case, the economic cost of buying the machine and using it for one year would not be $0. Jim still would incur the opportunity cost of the forgone interest, $i \times$ $8,000, where i is the annual interest rate that Jim could have earned.

7–3. Starting at 7 thousand gallons per month on the horizontal axis of Figure 7.2, we go up to the demand curve, and then read across to the vertical axis to find that the price is $4 per gallon. We then multiply the price times the quantity to find that the firm earns a total revenue of $28,000 per month (= 7 thousand gallons per month × $4 per gallon).

7–4. Marginal cost is the change in total cost due to the production of one more unit of output. From Table 7.6, we see that total cost rises from $12,500 to $14,500 when output is increased from 5 thousand to 6 thousand gallons per month. Hence, the marginal cost is $2,000 per thousand gallons per month.

7–5. At an output level of x_b, average revenue is less than average cost. Hence, the firm would suffer losses equal to the shaded area in the diagram:

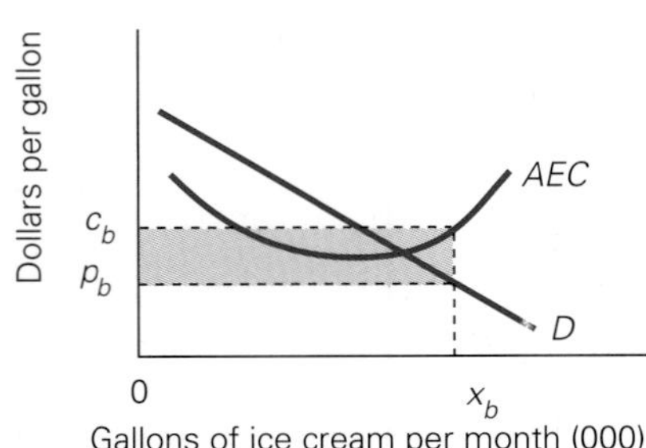

Chapter 8

8–1. We need to use the x_{200}-isoquant to answer this question. The figure below reproduces this isoquant from Figure 8.2. If National Motors has 200 robots in its plant, then reading across from 200 on the vertical axis in the figure over to the x_{200}-isoquant and down to the horizontal axis, we see that the firm must hire 1,500 workers per day in order to produce 200 cars per day. Similarly, if National Motors has 300 robots in its plant, then the firm must hire 750 workers per day in order to produce 200 cars per day.

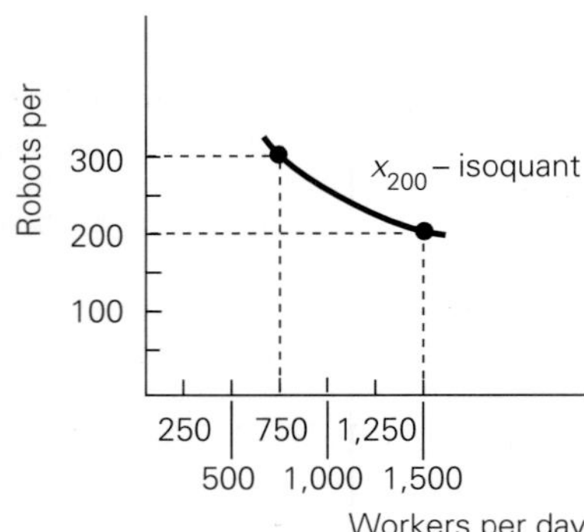

8–2. The marginal physical product of capital represents the additional output that the firm can produce when it hires one more unit of capital, holding the amount of labor constant. If using an additional ΔK units of capital raises output by ΔX, then the marginal physical product of capital is $MPP_K = \Delta X \div \Delta K$.

8–3. The marginal physical product of labor, given that the firm has hired four workers, is equal to the increase in total output when the firm goes from employing four workers to employing five. Looking at Table 8.2, we see that by hiring a fifth worker, the firm can increase its production from 70 units of output to 147. Taking the difference, we find that $MPP_L = 77$.

8–4. Since the marginal physical product is constant, we know that the *slope* of the total product curve is constant as well. Thus, the total physical product curve is a straight line, as shown in the figure below.

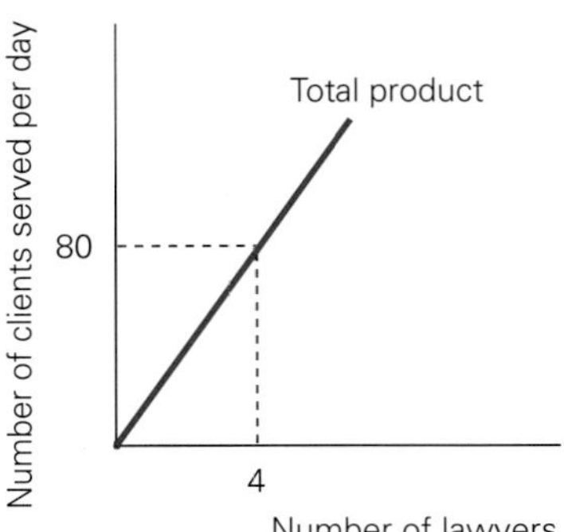

8–5. The output of the production function can be thought of as damage inflicted on the enemy's ability to wage war. The variable input here is air strikes. Other inputs include infantry, tanks, and naval ships.

8–6. The production function $F(L, K) = L \times K$ is an example of a technology exhibiting constant marginal returns for both labor and capital. Increasing labor by ΔL raises output by $\Delta X = (L + \Delta L) \times K - L \times K = \Delta L \times K$. Hence, $MPP_L = \Delta X \div \Delta L = K$. Similar calculations show $MPP_K = L$. The marginal rate of technical substitution is equal to the ratio of the marginal physical products of labor and capital, $MRTS = MPP_L/MPP_K = K/L$. When the firm uses 10 units of labor and 5 units of capital, $MPP_L = 5$, $MPP_K = 10$, and $MRTS = \frac{1}{2}$. When the firm uses 10 units of labor and 20 units of capital, MPP_L rises to 20, while MPP_K remains at 10. Consequently, $MRTS$ rises to $^{20}/_{10} = 2$.

8–7. *MRTS* is equal to -1 times the slope of the isoquants. The figure below presents an isoquant map that illustrates an increasing *MRTS*.

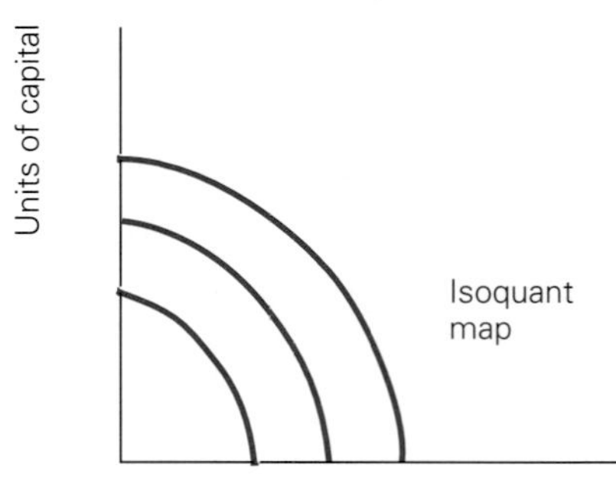

8–8. The figure below illustrates one such isoquant map. When production exhibits decreasing returns to scale, the firm has to more than double its input levels in order to double its output level. The $2x_a$-isoquant is sufficiently far above the x_a-isoquant that the firm has to more than double its inputs to go from the lower isoquant to the higher one.

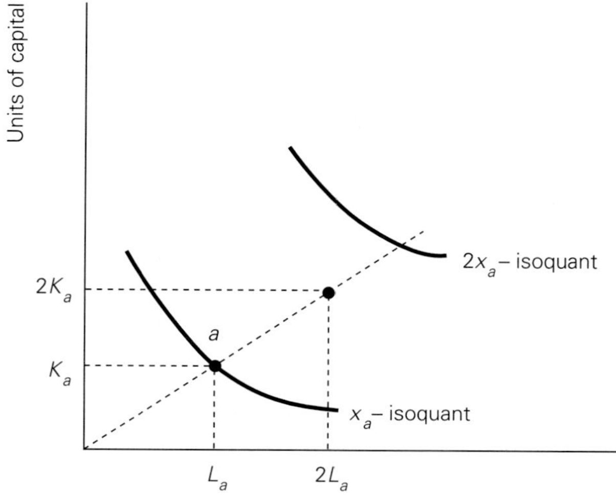

8–9. This technology exhibits increasing returns to scale. When a firm with this technology doubles its input levels, its output more than doubles; in fact, it quadruples. For example, $F(3, 4) = 10 \times 3 \times 4 = 120$, while $F(6, 8) = 10 \times 6 \times 8 = 480$.

Chapter 9

9–1. As shown in Panel A below, when there are increasing marginal returns to labor, the MPP_L curve slopes upward. Because $MC = w/MPP_L$, MC falls as the quantity of labor is increased to produce more output. The resulting short-run marginal cost curve is downward sloping, as shown in Panel B.

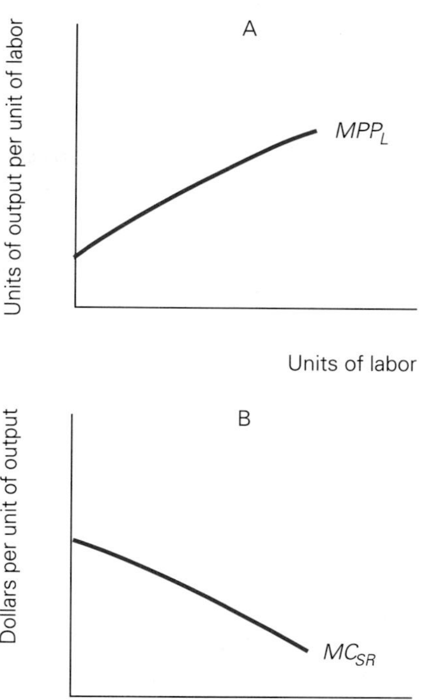

9–2. As shown in the figure below, when there are constant marginal returns to labor, w/MPP_L is constant and the short-run average variable cost curve is flat.

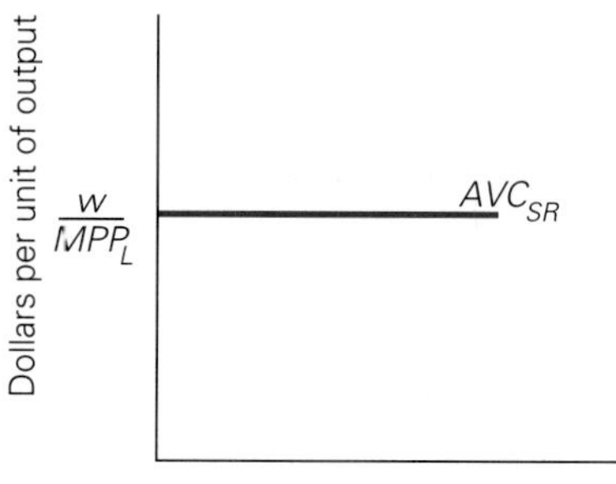

9–3. Whenever the short-run marginal cost curve is below the short-run average total cost curve, the average total cost curve must be falling because the last unit is pulling down the average. Whenever the short-run marginal cost curve is above the short-run average total cost curve, the average cost curve must be rising because the last unit is pulling up the average. Hence, the two curves must intersect at the low point on the short-run average total cost curve.

9–4. The equation for this isocost line is $\$100 \times L + \$200 \times K = \$400{,}000$, which is graphed in the figure below as $IC_{400,000}$. Since the factor price ratio is the same as for the other isocost lines, this one also has a slope of $-\frac{1}{2}$.

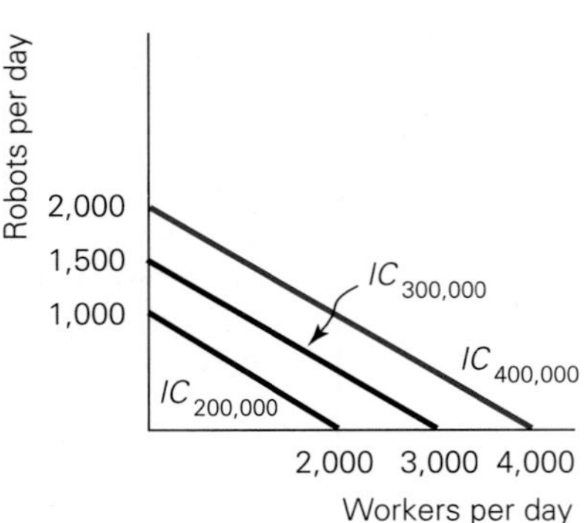

9–5. Each isocost line in the new map would pivot downward from an old one—the number of workers that can be hired alone with a given amount of money remains unchanged and the number of robots that can be purchased alone falls. This is illustrated for the isocost line corresponding to an input expenditure of \$300,000 in the following figure.

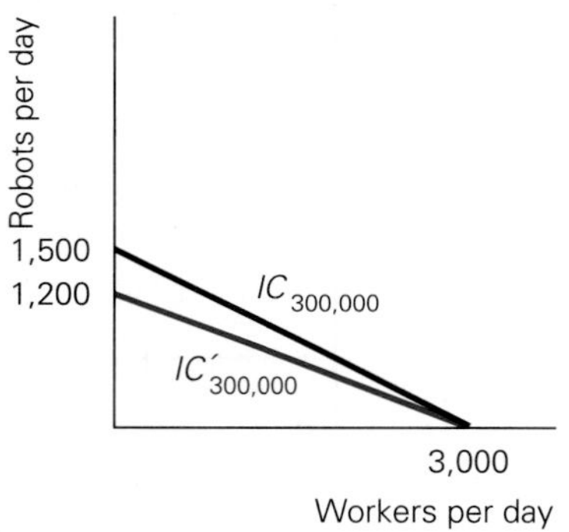

9–6. We can answer this question by applying our condition for cost minimization, Equation (9.7). For this firm, $MPP_K/r = .3/200 = .0015$, while $MPP_L/w = .1/100 = .0010$. The condition for cost minimization is not satisfied. Since MPP_K/r is greater than MPP_L/w, the firm could produce the same output at lower cost by hiring more robots and fewer workers. This result makes sense—at the margin, robots are three times as productive as workers, but they cost only twice as much.

9–7. The increasing returns to scale of the Union Pacific Railway's technology corresponds to Panel B in Figure 9.17. Panel C represents the decreasing returns to scale technology of General Motors.

Appendix 9A

9A–1. $MPP_K = \partial F/\partial K = \frac{1}{2}L^{1/2}K^{-1/2}$. Differentiation of the marginal physical product for capital shows that it exhibits diminishing marginal returns: $\partial MPP_K/\partial K = -\frac{1}{4}L^{1/2}K^{-3/2} < 0$.

Chapter 10

10–1. Since the firm can always sell an additional ton of cherries for \$200 without having to change the price of any other tons sold, its marginal revenue curve in the figure below is flat at \$200. This curve is also the demand and average revenue curve.

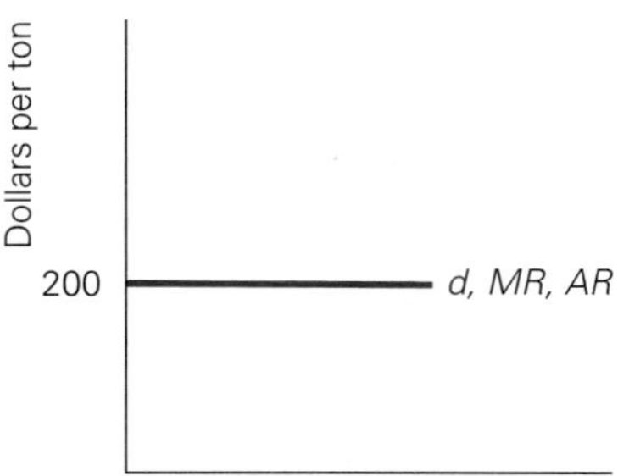

10–2. The shaded area in the figure below represents the loss in profit that the firm suffers by producing an additional 10 tons of cherries for which the marginal cost is greater than the marginal revenue.

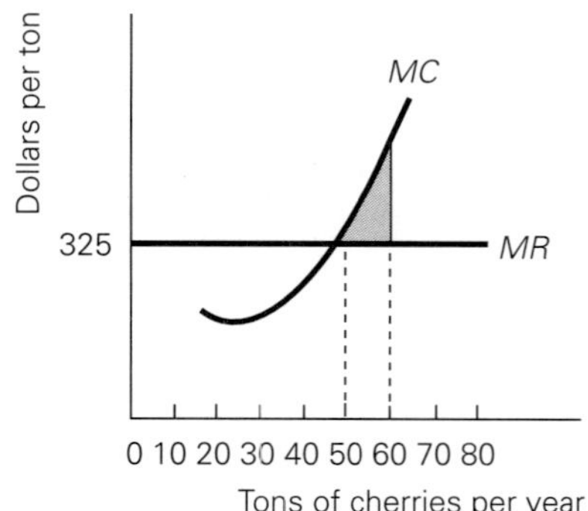

10–3. This firm should not shut down when it can sell output at a price of \$460 per ton. Since the minimal level of average economic cost is \$350, there is a whole range of output levels at which average revenue exceeds average economic cost. Hence, there is a range of output levels at which the firm can earn positive profit by staying in business. For instance, as shown by the shaded area in the figure below, if the firm produced and sold 100 tons of cherries, it would earn a profit of (\$460 − \$350) × 100 = \$11,000. While we need the marginal cost curve to find the profit-maximizing output level, we do not need it to identify whether there is some output level at which the firm can earn positive profit.

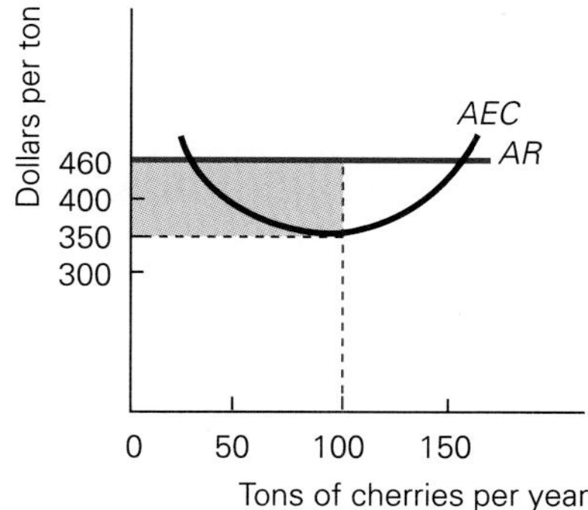

10–4. The "cost" of raising a turkey referred to in the quotation may well be an accounting cost that includes expenditures on fixed inputs. A profit-maximizing turkey farmer will continue to stay in business as long as the average economic, or opportunity, cost is lower than the price. In the short run, economic costs do not include expenditures on fixed inputs.

10–5. A share of the demand for tractors is due to wheat farmers. The factor hiring rule for a price taker tells us that a wheat farmer who is a price taker in both the tractor market and the wheat market maximizes profit by purchasing tractors up to the point at which the marginal revenue product of tractors (the marginal physical product of a tractor times the price of wheat) is equal to the price of a tractor. When the price of wheat rose, the marginal revenue product curve for tractors used in wheat farming shifted upward. Hence, wheat farmers' demand for tractors increased.

10–6. The following figure illustrates the isoquant diagram. The isoquant labeled in the figure is the one on which the firm must choose its input combination to hold output constant. The original isocost map is shown with solid lines. The increase in the price of capital results in a new family of isocost curves, each member of which is an old one pivoted downward around its intercept with the horizontal axis. The new isocost map is given by the dashed lines in the figure. From the figure, we see that the equilibrium input combination shifts from e_1 to e_2—the rise in the price of capital leads the firm to substitute labor for capital.

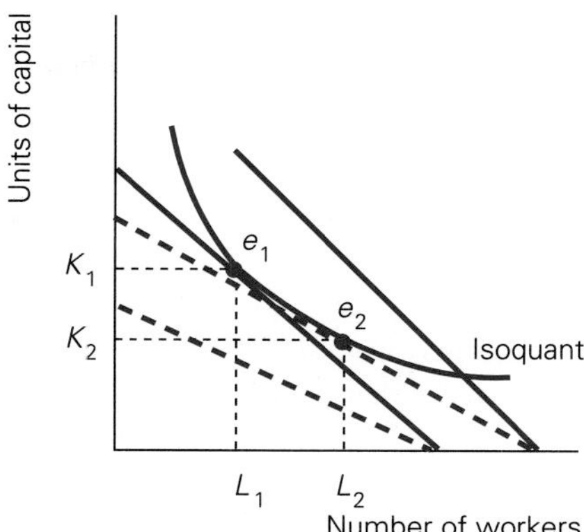

10–7. By the factor hiring rule, the firm will purchase machines up to the point at which the marginal revenue product of machines is equal to \$30,000. The figure below reproduces Figure 10–21. From this figure, we see that the firm will purchase 4 machines when p_M = \$30,000.

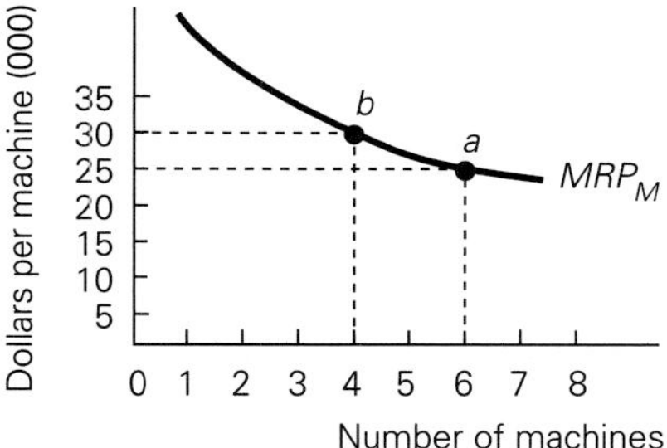

Chapter 11

11–1. The automobile industry does not fit several important structural conditions of the perfectly competitive model. A few sellers, the major American and Japanese producers, account for a large percentage of all automobiles sold. These firms are not price-taking sellers, and they are unlikely to behave nonstrategically. Moreover, products are differentiated, making it more likely that suppliers are not price takers. Buyers, on the other hand, are numerous and small relative to the market. Hence, most of them are price takers, as in the competitive model.

11–2. From Figure 11.1, we see that Bowles Cherries would supply 40 tons of sour cherries at this price, while Redding Farm would supply 75. The market quantity thus would be 115 tons. The following figure illustrates how we find the market quantity supplied by taking the horizontal sum of the individual quantities supplied.

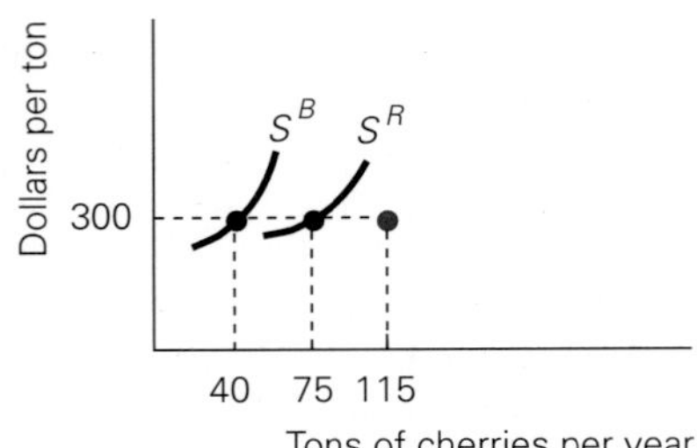

11–3. Output level x_1 does indeed satisfy the two rules for profit maximization. From Figure 11.2, Panel A, we can see that price is equal to marginal cost, so the marginal output rule for a price taker is satisfied. Moreover, price is greater than average cost, so the shut-down rule is satisfied.

11–4. At a price of p_c, the firm would produce x_c tons of cherries per year (see figure below). At this output level, price is equal to marginal cost and is greater than average cost. Since the firm would be earning positive economic profit (the shaded area in the figure), an unlimited number of firms would enter the market, and the market quantity supplied would be unlimited as well.

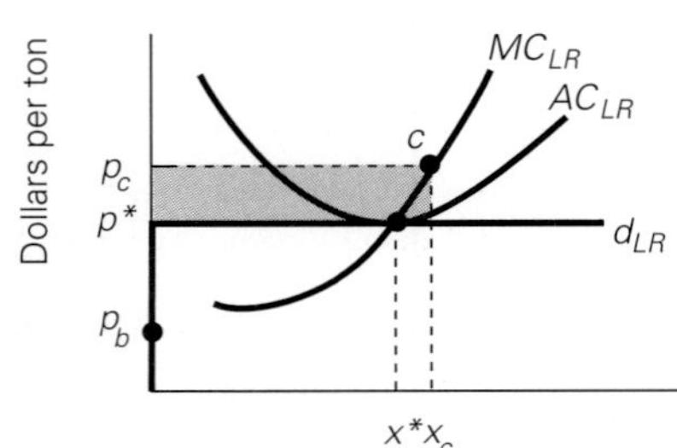

11–5. As shown in the figure below, when supply is perfectly inelastic and demand is less than perfectly inelastic, suppliers bear the full burden of the tax. The price paid by land buyers net of the tax remains unchanged.

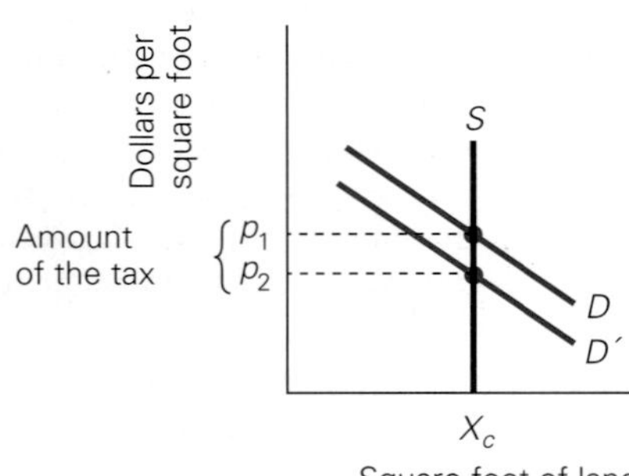

11–6. As shown in the figure here, total surplus falls by the shaded area when the level of total output is X_b rather than X_1.

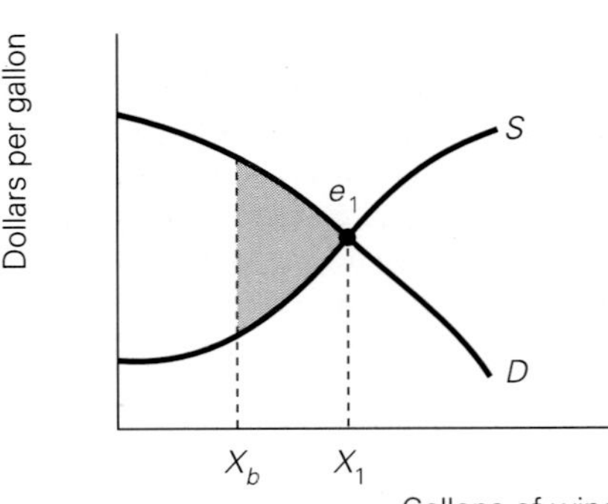

11–7. As shown in Panel A below, consumer surplus falls by shaded area *G*. Looking at Panel B, we see that producer surplus in the absence of the tax is equal to the sum of areas *H* and *I*. After the tax, producer surplus is equal to the sum of areas *I* and *J*. Hence, producer surplus changes by area *J* minus area *H*. We know that the net effect is a fall in producer surplus because area *H* is both higher and wider than area *J*.

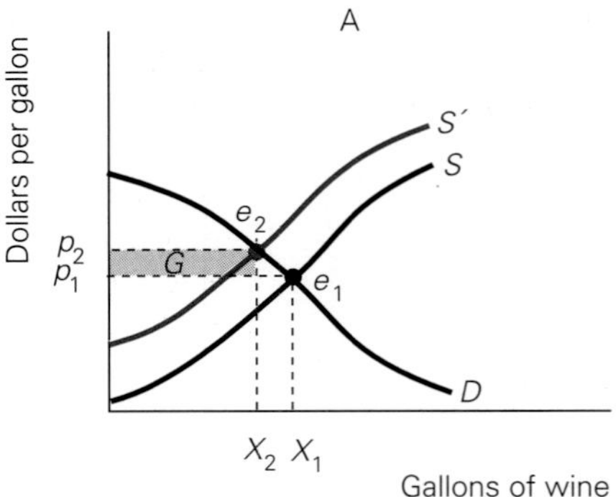

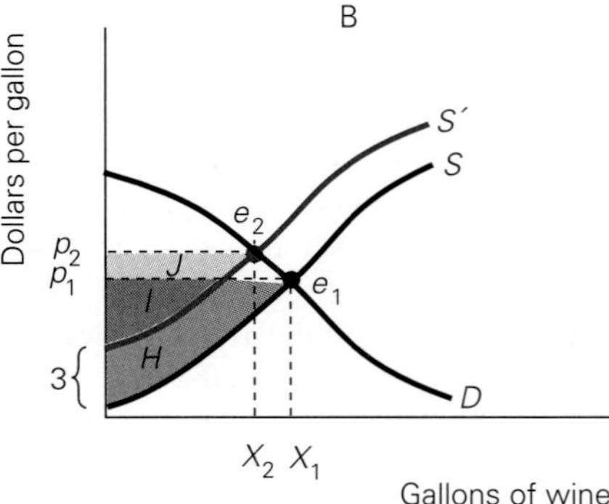

Chapter 12

12–1. Increases in the price of cotton might lead to greater demand for cotton-growing land, increasing the incomes of some landlords. Demand for machine tools used in cotton production also could grow, leading to an increase in their prices and increases in the incomes of the factors used to produce them. Increases in cotton prices would raise the price of cotton apparel, reducing the welfare of consumers who buy cotton clothes, but improving the welfare of polyester producers as consumers seek substitutes.

12–2. The figure below illustrates the resulting Edgeworth Box.

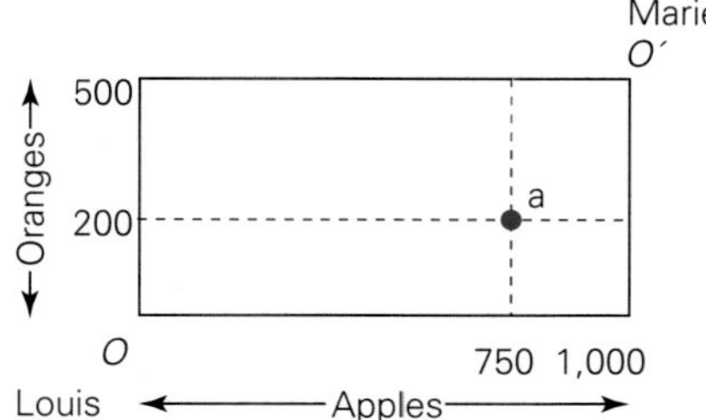

12–3. This is not a production-efficient allocation of resources, as the marginal rates of technical substitution are not equal ($MRTS^A = 2$ and $MRTS^Z = 2/3$). Acme could trade machines to Zenith in exchange for laborers, allowing total output to increase.

12–4. Parts (*b*) and (*d*) are true, by definition. Parts (*a*) and (*c*) are false: Pareto efficiency requires that an allocation be consumption efficient *and* production efficient *and* that the *MRT* equal the *MRS* for each individual.

Chapter 13

13–1. Airfone was best thought of as a monopolist. It faced competition (people could wait and make calls after landing) but the substitutes were imperfect—Airfone faced a downward sloping demand curve for its product. Airfone almost certainly did not worry that long-distance telephone carriers would change their rates in response to changes in its prices. Its customers simply represented a too-small portion of overall long-distance telephone traffic to be worth worrying about. While the technology was available for other firms to provide airborne telephone service, entry was blocked by the government licensing requirement.

13–2. Our expression for marginal revenue, Equation (13.1), tells us that marginal revenue is equal to *price* + *quantity* × (*slope of the demand curve*). Since the demand curve is shifted upward everywhere by exactly the same amount, the slope of the demand curve at any given quantity is unaffected by this change. The price associated with any quantity, however, is $1 higher. Hence, the marginal revenue curve shifts upward by $1.

13–3. The figure below illustrates the shift in the demand curve for Xyzene. The new demand curve is labeled D'. We find the new equilibrium using the new marginal revenue curve, which we found in Progress Check 13–2 to be equal to the old one shifted upward by $1. Since the advertising already has been purchased, it is a sunk expenditure and does not affect the cost curves. Finding the output level at which marginal revenue is equal to marginal cost, the new equilibrium quantity is X_2. Reading off the new demand curve to find the highest price at which the firm can sell this amount of output, we see that the new equilibrium price is p_2.

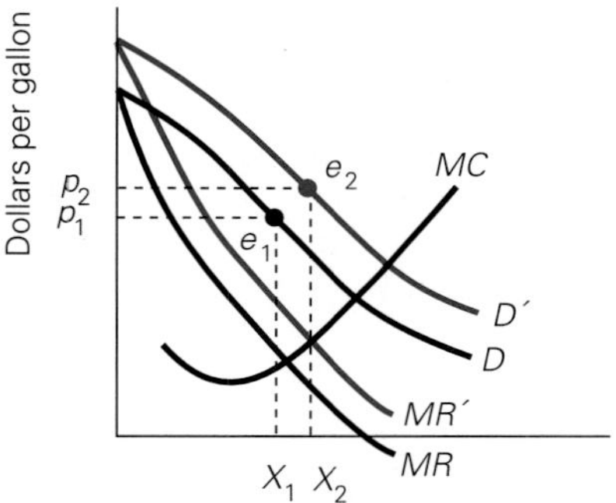

13–4. With free entry and a competitive market, entry will continue as long as profit can be made. In the long run, price will be driven to the minimum of long-run average cost. For this particular example, this value is $0. Hence, entry will continue until there are 16 firms in the market and the price is $0 per gallon. The monopolist would continue to sell 8 gallons because that output maximizes its profit. With long-run entry, the gap between the monopolistic and competitive output levels is even greater. (You might want to try answering this question for the more realistic case in which there is a $1 cost of setting up a well.)

13–5. After the tax is imposed, the firm can earn profit equal to shaded area *A* in Figure 13.8 by producing X_3 units of output. The firm earns a greater economic profit by remaining in operation than by shutting down.

13–6. A nondiscriminating firm would have to choose between selling solely to Ms. Rich at a price of $60, and selling to both Ms. Rich and Mr. Poor at a price of $40. Selling to both would yield a profit of $60 = 2 × ($40 − $10), which is greater than the profit from selling just to Ms. Rich, $50 = $60 − $10. A discriminating firm would charge \$60 to Ms. Rich and \$40 to Mr. Poor, for a total profit of \$80 = (\$60 − \$10) + (\$40 − \$10). Price discrimination raises profit by \$20.

13–7. As shown in the figure below, the firm would find the price of the X_ath unit by reading up from X_a on the horizontal axis to the demand curve and then over to p_a on the vertical axis. Since the revenue earned from each unit is equal to the height of the demand curve at that output level, total revenue would be given by the area under the demand curve from an output of 0 up to X_a, the shaded area in the figure.

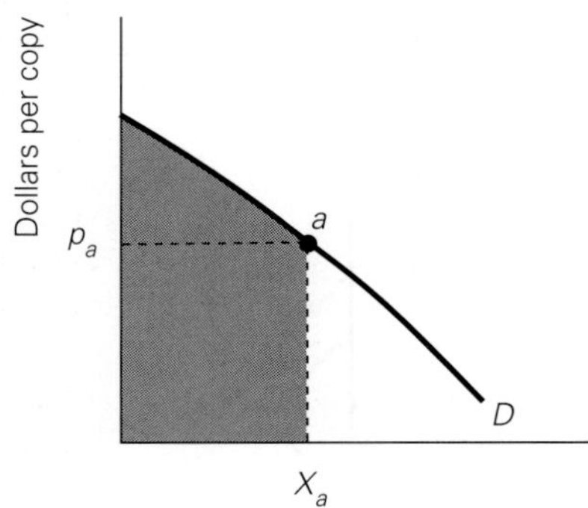

13–8. The companies apparently believe that students generally have a lower willingness to pay for software than do business users. Thus, they charge lower prices to students. To prevent business users from taking advantage of these lower prices, the retailers demand to see student IDs. While an enterprising student could try to engage in arbitrage by selling the software to business users after obtaining it at a discount, the transactions costs of doing this are sufficiently high that it does not seem to be a problem.

Chapter 14

14–1. Given the propped-up prices and the restricted quantities being produced, the rice market is at a point where an individual farmer's marginal revenue from rice production is greater than marginal cost. Indeed, even at a price below the government-set price, marginal revenue exceeds marginal cost, so that an individual farmer increases profits by growing additional rice in excess of the quota and selling it below the official price. Of course, if all farmers act this way, they may significantly drive down the price of rice and reduce industry profits.

14–2. As a result of airline deregulation, firms could engage in price competition to attract passengers instead of offering excessive numbers of flights. We would expect load factors to rise and average costs to fall. This is, in fact, what happened.

14–3. When there are more than n_3 firms in the market, the market is too crowded for a representative firm to avoid suffering economic losses. The figure below illustrates this situation—the firm-specific demand curve faced by a representative supplier lies completely below the firm's average cost curve, and the firm is better off shutting down. Some firms will choose to exit the market.

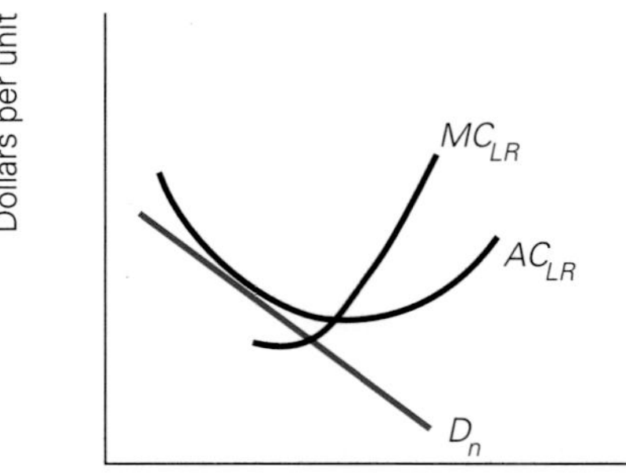

14–4. When the monopsonist is a price taker in the output market, the firm's marginal revenue product curve rises in proportion to the price change, here 10 percent. This upward shift is illustrated in the following figure, where the equilibrium quantity rises to B_2, and the equilibrium price rises to p_2.

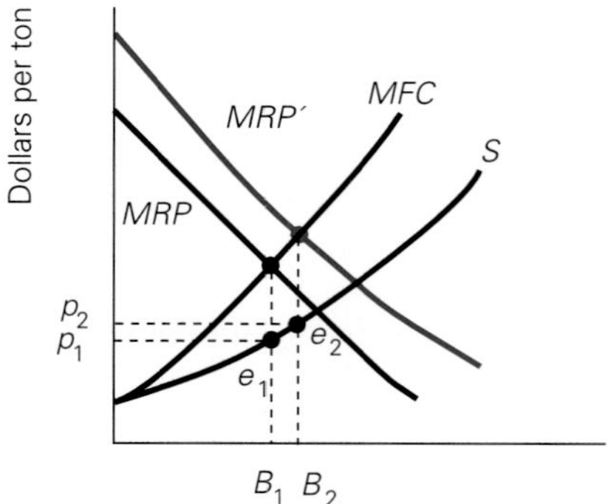

14–5. We would expect the competition between the new and the established leagues to drive up players' salaries. That is just what happened when the World Hockey Association and the World Football League began their brief existences.

Chapter 15

15–1. Air Lion's residual demand is what's left after subtracting the output produced by Beta Airlines from the market total. Hence, $d^A(p) = D(p) - 100$ when Beta sells 100 tickets per day. This residual demand curve is graphed in the figure below.

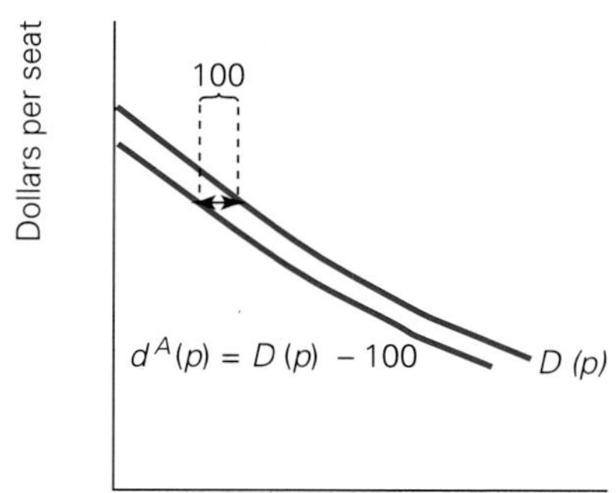

15–2. This pair of output levels is not a Cournot equilibrium. From the following figure, we see that if Beta were selling 550 seats per day, then Air Lion would indeed want to sell 100 seats per day (point *i* is on Air Lion's reaction curve). The problem is that Beta would not want to stick to its part of the deal. From Beta's reaction curve, we see that Beta would want to sell 340 tickets per day if it believed that Air Lion were selling 100, point *j*.

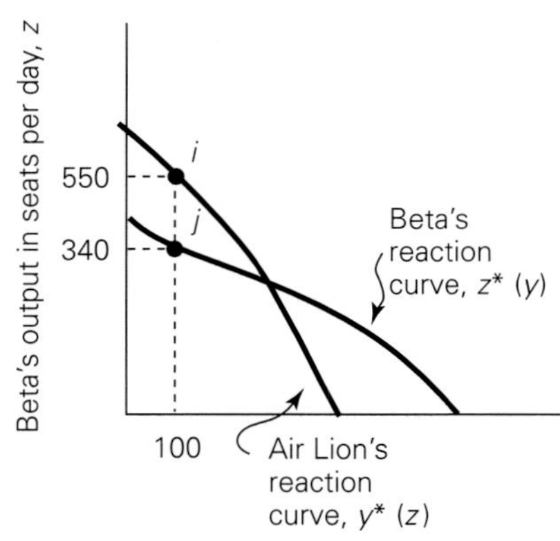

15–3. Substituting the values $m = .5$ and $\epsilon_{mkt} = 1$ into Equation (15.1), we get $p \times (1 - .5/1) = c$. In words, price times .5 is equal to marginal cost, so price is double marginal cost. With four firms, $m = .25$, and the formula is $p \times (1 - .25/1) = c$. In this case, price times .75 is equal to marginal cost, so price is 4/3 marginal cost. With more firms, the market is more competitive, and price is closer to marginal cost.

15–4. When Air Lion is selling 200 seats per day, Beta's residual demand curve is $900 - 200 - p = 700 - p$. The associated marginal revenue curve is $700 - 2z$. Setting marginal revenue equal to marginal cost, we have $700 - 2z = 100$. Solving this equation, we find that Beta's best response is to sell 300 seats per day. For an arbitrary value of y, Beta's marginal revenue curve is $900 - y - 2z$. Solving $900 - y - 2z = 100$ for y, we find that Beta's best response to y is $z^*(y) = 400 - y/2$.

15–5. From the formula for Beta's equilibrium profit, Equation (15.12), we see that an increase in Beta's marginal cost, c_b, lowers its profit, *ceteris paribus*. However, an increase in Air Lion's marginal cost, c_a, raises Beta's profit, *ceteris paribus*. An increase in Air Lion's cost leads to a decline in Air Lion's equilibrium level of output, which shifts Beta Airlines' residual demand curve outward. This outward shift in residual demand raises Beta's equilibrium profit.

15–6. As shown in the figure below, when Air Lion sets a price of \$100, Beta makes no sales if its price is greater than \$100, makes all of the industry sales if its price is less than \$100, and gets one-half of the market if its price is equal to \$100.

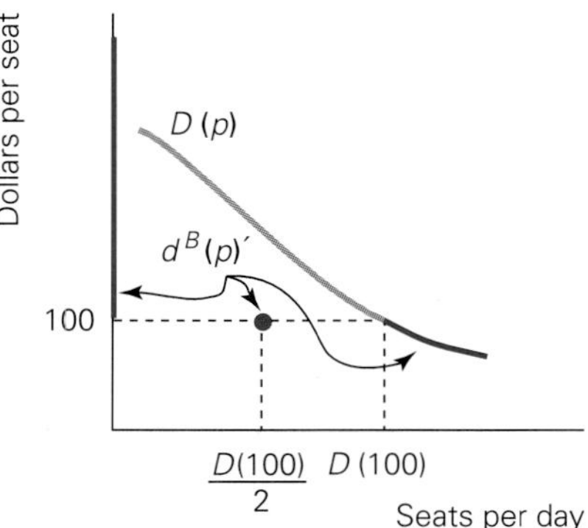

15–7. At a price of \$13, the market quantity demanded would be $141 = 310 - 13^2$ and each firm would sell 47 units of output for a profit of $\$141 = 47 \times (\$13 - \$10)$. By lowering its price just slightly, however, a firm could raise its profit to almost $\$423 = 141 \times (\$13 - \$10)$. By the same argument made in the text for the case of two producers, each firm will keep undercutting the others until price is driven down to marginal cost. Once price is equal to \$10, there is no incentive for any firm to lower its price further to attract business. Hence, the equilibrium price is \$10. At this price, the market quantity demanded is $210 = 310 - 10^2$.

15–8. As shown in the following figure, the incentive to cheat falls. The increase in profit from sticking to the agreement reduces the gains to cheating from the sum of areas *C* and *D* to area *D* alone, while it increases the cost of being punished from area *E* alone to the sum of areas *E* and *F*. The benefits of cheating fall while the costs rise. Of course, to be precise, all of the areas have to be adjusted to be in present-value terms.

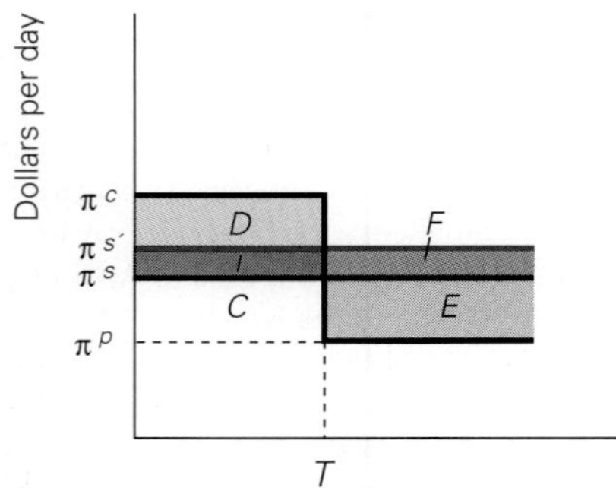

15–9. When the market became more open to international trade, the ability of domestic producers to hold prices up fell, as our theory would predict. There were more producers leading to a greater divergence between firm-specific and industry marginal revenue. Tacit communication was more difficult with an increased number of players, many of whom were foreign. Moreover, there was greater variation in the cost structures of the different producers as well as greater variation in the types of cars sold. All of this made tacit cooperation more difficult.

Chapter 16

16–1. Each of Beta's strategies is a decision rule specifying what action it will take conditional on what it sees that Air Lion has done. The other three possible decision rules for Beta to follow are: (1) *if Air Lion produces "high," then I will produce "high," and if Air Lion produces "low," then I will produce "low"*; (2) *produce "low" no matter what Air Lion does*; and (3) *produce "high" no matter what Air Lion does.*

16–2. We need to verify that each firm's strategy is a best response to the strategy chosen by the other firm. When General Generic chooses the strategy "*enter*," Jersey Pharmaceutical earns $6 million if it chooses a decision rule that leads it to produce "low output" when General Generic chooses "enter," and $5 million if it adopts a decision rule that leads to its producing "high output" when General chooses "enter." The choice Jersey would make if General chose "stay out" does not matter for Jersey's profits, since General is coming in. Thus, the strategy *if General Generic chooses "enter," then we will choose "low output," and if General Generic chooses "stay out," then we will choose "high output"* is one best response for Jersey Pharmaceutical to General Generic's strategy of "*enter*."

When Jersey Pharmaceutical chooses the strategy *if General Generic chooses "enter," then we will choose "low output," and if General Generic chooses "stay out," then we will choose "high output,"* General Generic earns $6 million by choosing "*enter*" and $0 by choosing "*stay out*." "*Enter*" is General Generic's best response.

Each firm's strategy is a best response to the other's. This pair of strategies is a Nash equilibrium.

16–3. Strategic investment effects do not arise under perfect competition, monopolistic competition, or monopoly without entry. Each firm in a perfectly competitive or monopolistically competitive industry believes that it is too small to influence rival firms' behavior. A monopolist who faces no threat of entry has no rivals against whom to be strategic.

16–4. The game tree for Mike and Ivan would not change at all. Even though Mike moves first, Ivan cannot see what Mike has done. Therefore, Ivan cannot make his action contingent on what Mike has done—Ivan's two decision nodes still would be in the same information set as drawn in Figure 16.7. It is just as if the two inside traders had to make their choices simultaneously.

16–5. The figure below illustrates the game tree with three choices. In equilibrium each player must go each direction one-third of the time as follows. *If* the kicker went one direction more than the others, then the goalie always should go that direction. But if the goalie always goes one direction, then the kicker should go a different way for sure. Thus, in any equilibrium the kicker must go each way equally. Similarly, *if* the goalie went one direction less than the others, then the kicker should always go that way. But then the goalie should go that way all of the time. Therefore, the goalie must go each direction equally. Given that each player goes each direction one-third of the time, there is nothing that either one can do to improve his payoff: The strategies form a Nash equilibrium.

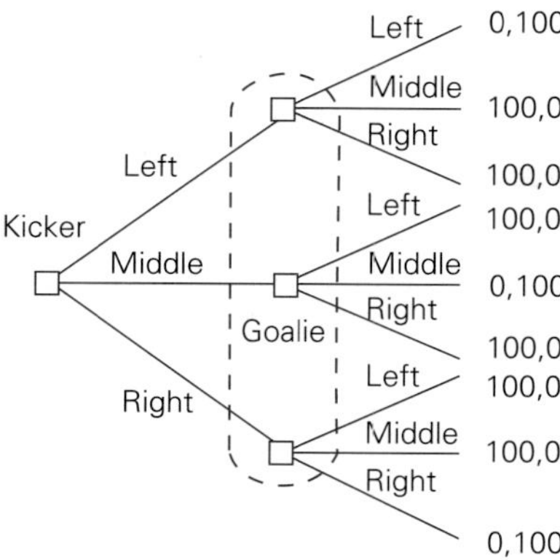

Kicker's payoff given first in each pair.

Chapter 17

17–1. Although the beach bum does not like staying for two weeks, it does not bother him as much as it bothers the businessman. All American can sort its customers by offering a vacation fare of S350 and a coach fare of $500. The firm earns a profit of $610. If the firm were to offer a single fare to everyone, its profit would be greatest by selling an unrestricted ticket at a price of $400. Both types of consumer would buy the ticket, and the firm's profit would be S560.

17–2. As shown in Progress Check 17–1, when it can offer more than one fare, All American sorts its customers by offering a vacation fare for $350 and a coach fare of $500. The firm earns a profit of $610 while neither customer earns any consumer surplus, so total surplus is $610. If the firm were to offer a single fare to everyone, it would sell unrestricted tickets to both types of passenger at a price of $400. The firm's profit would be $560, the beach bum's comsumer surplus would be $0, and the business traveler's consumer surplus would be $100, for a total of $660. Comparing the two outcomes, we see that total surplus is greater without discrimination than with.

17–3. As before, low-ability workers are hurt by the signaling—their weekly wage falls from $300 to $200, and point e_L is less desirable than point a. High-ability workers are helped by the signaling—they value the $100 wage increase more than they dislike the extra schooling. The figure below illustrates this situation; a high-ability worker prefers e_H to point a. The important point to note, however, is that total surplus still falls by the full cost of education. The wage gain to high-ability workers still comes entirely at the expense of low-ability workers. In this simple model of education as a signal, education generates no social benefits and its entire cost is a deadweight loss to society.

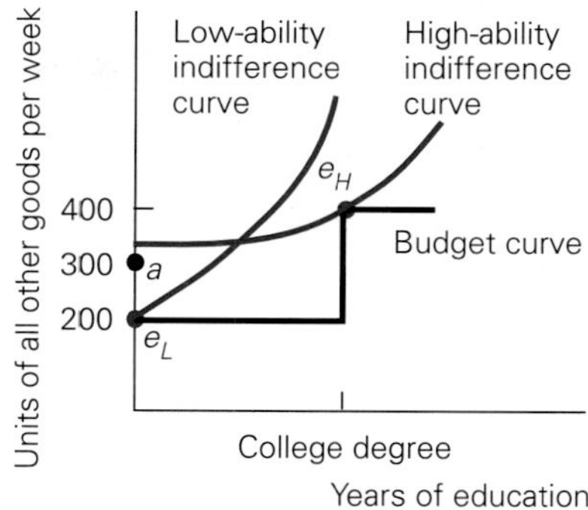

17–4. Because he has the highest probability of being sued of any of the three doctors, Dr. Canard has the steepest indifference curves. The following figure illustrates Dr. Canard's indifference curves for *consumption if sued* and *consumption if not sued.* Notice that where they cross the 45° line the indifference curve all have a slope of −3/2, Dr. Canard's odds of being sued.

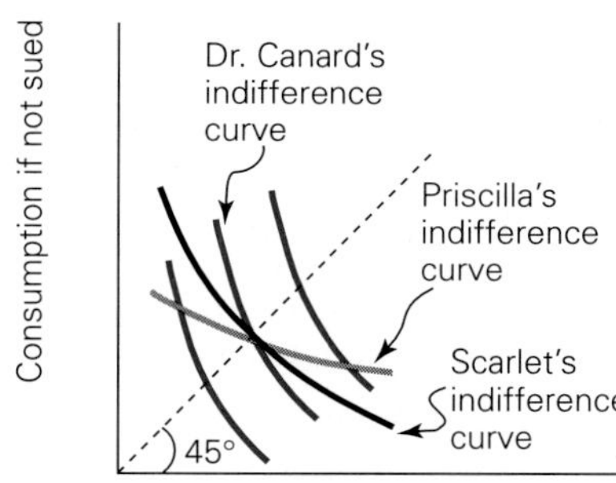

17–5. As long as Scarlet is in the market, the insurance company charges a rate that is actuarially unfair for Priscilla. If Priscilla were risk neutral, then she would purchase no insurance at such a rate. When Priscilla drops out of the market, Scarlet is offered insurance at the rate that is actuarially fair for her. Since she is risk averse, Scarlet purchases full insurance when it is offered at an actuarially fair price.

17–6. In this case, the firms would bid each worker's wage up to her individual marginal revenue product. Thus, low-ability workers each would be paid $200 per week while high-ability workers each would be paid $400 per week.

17–7. Call Alex's new opportunity utility level U_0'. Graphically, the owners of the firm now have to ensure that his equilibrium point is on or above the U_0'-indifference curve in the figure below.

The analysis in the text would be unaffected except that the equilibrium points now would all fall on this higher opportunity-utility indifference curve. The flat-salary equilibrium is at point e_6, while the observable-effort and residual-claimant equilibria are both at point e_7.

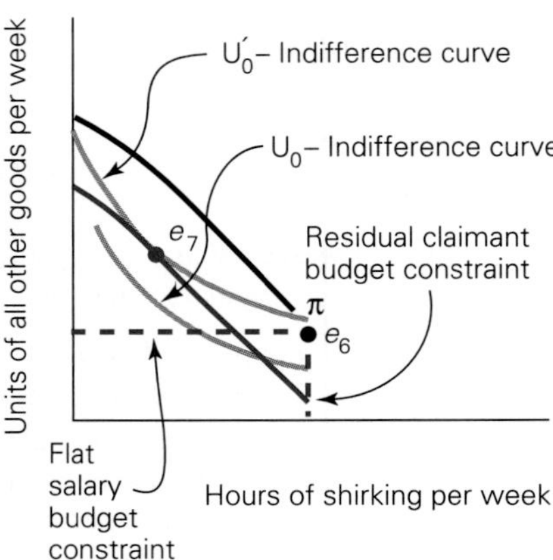

Chapter 18

18–1. An externality occurs when you enter a crowded highway because you do not consider the effect you have on other drivers by increasing congestion. Your driving slows down others. These other drivers would be willing to pay you to stay home, if such a market existed. The market for "clear roads" is missing.

18–2. At X_0, social marginal benefit (measured by the height of the demand curve) exceeds social marginal cost (the height of the *SMC* curve). Therefore, society would realize a net gain by producing another unit of steel. This argument holds as we increase steel production up to the point X^*—the efficient output level.

18–3. The maximum bribe the steelmaker is willing to pay for each unit is the difference between *MR* and *PMC*. Therefore, the total bribe for x^* units is the shaded area in the diagram below. At any point beyond x^*, the maximum bribe ($MR - PMC$) is less than the marginal damage to the fishery ($SMC - PMC$), so there is no deal. For example, distance *no* is less than distance *mo*.

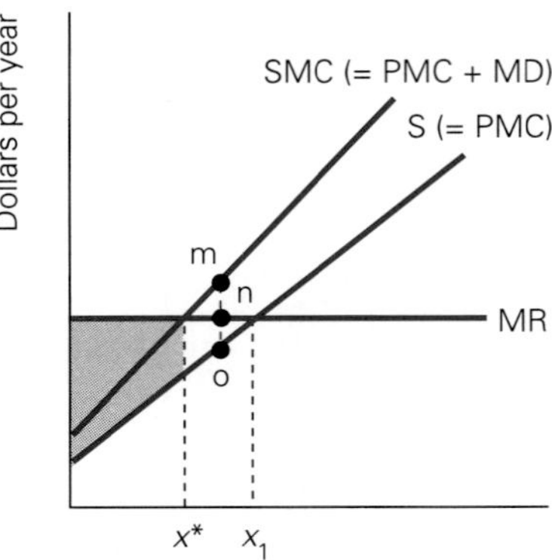

18–4. The externality here is "dirty water and unsafe beaches" imposed on the public by the hospitals. Applying the Coase Theorem would not correct this situation because we cannot identify the negligent agents (e.g., the hospitals, waste collection companies). Without enforcement capability, it doesn't matter whether there is an agreement regarding pollution such as Coase proposed. In addition, the number of agents involved (polluters, and particularly beachgoers) is large, making bargaining difficult.

18–5. If the calculation is correct, then a tax of 68 cents per pack would make the social marginal cost of cigarettes equal to the private marginal cost. The full social cost of smoking would then be reflected in its price, and an efficient quantity of cigarettes would be consumed.

18–6. The marginal value of the public good, fireworks, is the sum of the individual valuations:

$$\text{Social Marginal Value} = 9 + 77 + 12 = 98.$$

Since marginal value is less than marginal cost, the community's fireworks display is too large. The sum of the individual *MRS*s is less than the *MRT*. Efficiency requires that these two quantities be equal.

18–7. Excludability of city streets requires the ability to enforce the rules of access. If drivers were identifiable, penalties could be constructed so that a form of excludability could be achieved.

References

Akerlof, George; Andrew K. Rose; and Janet L. Yellen. "East Germany in from the Cold: The Economic Aftermath of Currency Union." Brookings Papers in Economic Activity, 1991.

Ambrose, Stephen E. *Eisenhower, The President.* Vol. 2. New York: Simon & Schuster, 1984.

Barringer, Felicity. "In the Worst of Times, America Keeps Giving." *The New York Times,* Mar. 15, 1992: E6.

———. "When G-Notes Are Small Change." *The New York Times,* Oct. 16, 1994, p. E5.

Baumol, William J. *Business Behavior, Value and Growth.* 1st ed. rev. New York: Harcourt Brace Jovanovich, 1967.

Baumol, William J., and Hilda Baumol. "The Economics of Musical Composition in Mozart's Vienna." Princeton University, Working Paper, October 1991.

Beazley, Ernest J. "Steel Companies Get Price Boosts Out of Detroit." *The Wall Street Journal,* July 5, 1988, p. 2.

Becker, Gary S., and Michael Grossman. ". . . And Cigarette Revenues Up in Smoke." *The Wall Street Journal,* Aug. 9, 1994, p. A12.

Benjamin, Daniel. "The Baby Dearth In a German Village Inspires a Bounty." *The Wall Street Journal,* July 20, 1994, pp. A1, A6.

Berndt, Ernst R.; Ann F. Friedlaender; and Judy Chiang. "Interdependent Pricing and Markup Behavior: An Empirical Analysis of GM, Ford and Chrysler." Working Paper No. 3396. National Bureau of Economic Research, Cambridge, MA, June 1990.

Bernstein, Jeffrey I., and Xiaoyi Yan. "International R&D Spillovers between Canadian and Japanese Industries." Working Paper No. 5401. National Bureau of Economic Research, Cambridge, MA, Dec. 1995.

Bingham, Bradford. "Letters." *The New York Times,* May 4, 1988, p. A26.

Blackburn, McKinley L.; David E. Bloom; and Richard B. Freeman. "Changes in Earnings Differentials in the 1980s: Concordance, Convergence, Causes and Consequences." Working Paper No. 3901. National Bureau of Economic Research, Cambridge, MA, Nov. 1991.

Blank, Rebecca M. "Women's Paid Work, Household Income, and Household Well-Being." In *The American Woman, 1988–89.* Sara E. Rix, ed. New York: W. W. Norton, 1988.

"Blood Money Conviction." *Sports Illustrated* 83, no. 14 (Oct. 2, 1995), p. 13.

Bonner, Raymond. "A Reporter at Large (Indonesia)." *The New Yorker,* June 13, 1988, pp. 72–91.

Bovard, James. "This Farm Program Is Just Plain Nuts." *The Wall Street Journal,* Aug. 30, 1995, p. A10.

Bradsher, Keith. "A White-Gloved Duel For the Shuttle's Skies." *The New York Times,* Aug. 31, 1989, pp. D1, D4.

Brockway, George P. "How Good Is Greed?" *The New Leader,* May 2, 1988, pp. 15–16.

———. "Serving Two Maximizers." *The New Leader,* Mar. 7, 1988, pp. 13–64.

Burros, Marion. "Dumplings and a Smile." *The New York Times,* June 15, 1988, p. C1.

Butler, Steven, and Louise Keyhoe. "Partners Thank Each Other for the Memory." *Financial Times,* July 14, 1992, p. 17.

Campbell, John Y., and N. Gregory Mankiw. "The Response of Consumption to Income: A Cross-Country Investigation." *European Economic Review* 35 (May 1991), pp. 723–56.

"The Changing Clean-Air Law." *The Wall Street Journal,* Oct. 29, 1990, p. A7.

Cheung, Steven N. S. "The Fable of the Bees: An Economic Investigation." *Journal of Law and Economics* 16, no. 1 (Apr. 1973), pp. 11–34.

Christian, Nicole M. "Sales Boom Is Going Bust for Makers of 18-Wheelers." *The Wall Street Journal,* Jan. 18, 1994, p. B4.

Clifton, Tony. "A Rush for Liquid 'Gold.'" *Newsweek,* July 11, 1988, p. 48.

Clinton, Bill, and Al Gore. *Putting People First: How We Can All Change America.* New York Times Books, 1992.

Clotfelter, Charles. *Federal Tax Policy and Charitable Giving.* Chicago: University of Chicago Press, 1985.

Coase, Ronald M. "The Nature of the Firm." *Economica* 4 (1937), pp. 386–405.

Cole, Jeff. "Boeing Says It Won a 68% Share of Orders for New Jets Last Year." *The Wall Street Journal*, Jan. 5, 1996, p. B4.

Conda, Cesar V. "An Environment for Reform." *The Wall Street Journal*, Jan. 23, 1995, p. A18.

Cowans, Kenneth W. "The Munificent Ebenezer Scrooge." *The Wall Street Journal*, Dec. 24, 1991, p. A.6.

Cropper, Maureen L., and Wallace E. Oates. "Environmental Economics: A Survey." *Journal of Economic Literature* 30, no. 2 (June 1992), pp. 675–740.

Daily Tax Reporter, Feb. 7, 1991, p. G-6.

de Córdoba, José; Carla Anne Robbins; and Thomas T. Vogel Jr. "Castro Praises U.S. Corporate Style, Clings to Hard Line on Political Issues." *The Wall Street Journal*, Oct. 25, 1995, p. A10.

Deaton, Angus. "Quality, Quantity, and Spatial Variation of Price." *American Economic Review* 78, no. 3 (June 1988), pp. 418–30.

DePalma, Anthony. "In Suriname's Rain Forests, A Fight Over Trees vs. Jobs." *The New York Times*, Sept. 4, 1995, p. L1.

Dickson, Martin. "Painful Adjustments in U.S." *Financial Times*, June 28, 1993, p. III.

Disney Company, Walt. Form 10-K, 1995.

"Disney Omits Eisner Bonus: He'll Get By with $750,000." *The New York Times*, Jan. 4, 1994, p. D6.

Dobrzynski, Judith. "Chicken Done to a Golden Rule." *The New York Times*, Apr. 3, 1996, pp. C1, C3.

Drake, Alvin W., Stan N. Finkelstein, and Harvey M. Sapolsky. *The American Blood Supply*. Cambridge: MIT Press, 1982.

Driscoll, James. "Consumer Protection Could Kill AIDS Patients." *The Wall Street Journal*, Mar. 6, 1991, A8.

Dunn, Ashley. "For Elderly Immigrants, a Retirement Plan in U.S." *The New York Times*, Apr. 16, 1995, p. 1.

Economic Report of the President 1987. Washington, DC: Government Printing Office, 1987.

Economic Report of the President 1988. Washington, DC: Government Printing Office, 1988.

Economic Report of the President 1990. Washington, DC: Government Printing Office, 1990.

Economic Report of the President 1994. Washington, DC: Government Printing Office, 1994.

Eichel, Larry. "Looking for Place to Land in Era of Deregulation." *Sunday Times Union*, Dec. 10, 1989, pp. D1, D4.

Faber, Harold. "Cherry Farmers Worry As Prices Fall." *The New York Times*, July 5, 1987, p. 16.

Fabricant, Florence. "Improved Airline Food Is Earning Its Wings." *The New York Times*, May 19, 1993, pp. B1, B6.

Fanning, Deirdre. "The Executive Life." *The New York Times*, Feb. 4, 1990, sec. 3, p. 29.

Farnsworth, Clyde H. "OPEC Isn't the Only Cartel That Couldn't." *The New York Times*, Apr. 24, 1988, p. E3.

Feder, Barnaby. "Quaker Oats and Iced Tea Just Won't Mix." *The New York Times*, Aug. 7, 1996, pp. C1, C4.

Friedlaender, Ann F., et al. "Rail Costs and Capital Adjustments in a Quasi-Regulated Environment." Working Paper No. 3841. National Bureau of Economic Research, Cambridge, MA, Sept. 1991.

Friedman, Milton, and Leonard J. Savage. "The Utility Analysis of Choices Involving Risk." *Journal of Political Economy* 56 (Aug. 1948), pp. 279–304.

Galbraith, John Kenneth. *American Capitalism*. Cambridge, MA: Riverside Press, 1956.

Garen, John. "Compensating Wage Differentials and the Endogeneity of Job Riskiness." *Review of Economics and Statistics* 70, no. 1 (Feb. 1988), pp. 9–16.

Gish, John J. "Curb Congress by Line-Item Veto." *The New York Times*, Mar. 1, 1988, p. A22.

Glaberson, William. "Misery on the Meatpacking Line." *The New York Times*, June 14, 1987, p. F1.

Goleman, Daniel. "Mortality Study Lends Weight to Patient's Opinion." *The New York Times*, Mar. 21, 1991, p. B13.

Gomes, Lee. "H-P Aims at High End of the Business Computing Market." *The Wall Street Journal*, May 29, 1996, p. B4.

Gould, Lois. "Ticket to Trouble." *New York Times Magazine*, Apr. 23, 1995, p. 40.

Graham, Ellen. "Study Now, Pay Later: Students Pile On Debt." *The Wall Street Journal*, Aug. 11, 1995, p. B1.

Greenhouse, Steven. "New French Cause Célèbre: A Book Calling Nation Lazy." *The New York Times*, June 20, 1987, p. A1.

Griliches, Zvi. "Productivity, R&D, and Basic Research at the Firm Level in the 1970s." *American Economic Review* 76, no. 1 (March 1986), pp. 141–54.

Grossman, Michael, et al. "Policy Watch: Alcohol and Cigarette Taxes." *Journal of Economic Perspectives* 7, no. 4 (Fall 1993), pp. 211–22.

Hahn, Robert W. "Economic Prescriptions for Environmental Problems: How the Patient Followed the Doctor's Orders." *Journal of Economic Perspectives* 3, no. 2 (Spring 1989), pp. 95–114.

Hamermesh, Daniel S. "The Demand for Labor in the Long Run." In *The Handbook of Labor Economics*. Vol. 1. Orley Ashenfelter and Richard Layard, eds. New York: North Holland, 1986.

Hansson, Ingemar, and Charles Stuart. "Tax Revenue and the Marginal Cost of Public Funds in Sweden." *Journal of Public Economics* 27 (Aug. 1985), pp. 331–54.

Hargreaves, Deborah, and Maggie Urry. "Pretty Penny on the Price of a Pinta." *Financial Times,* July 27, 1993, p. 19.

Hausman, Jerry A., and James M. Poterba. "Household Behavior and the Tax Reform Act of 1986." *Journal of Economic Perspectives* 1, no. 1 (Summer 1987), pp. 101–19.

Hawking, Stephen W. *A Brief History of Time.* New York: Bantam Books, 1988.

Hicks, John R. *Value and Capital.* 2nd ed. Oxford: Clarendon Press, 1946.

Holinger, Peggy, and Alice Rawsthorn. "Tapie Hands on Baton to Pentland." *Financial Times,* July 8, 1992, p. 19.

Holusha, John. "At Ford, a Resale Guarantee." *The New York Times,* May 20, 1987, p. D1.

"Hong Kong Program: Addicts without AIDS." *The New York Times,* June 17, 1987, p. 1.

Houthakker, H. F., and Lester B. Taylor. *Consumer Demand in the United States: Analyses and Projections.* 2nd ed. Cambridge: Harvard University Press, 1970.

Huber, Charles S. "If I Were President . . ." *Princeton Alumni Weekly,* June 10, 1987, p. 50.

Hufbauer, Gary C., and Kimberly Ann Elliott. *Measuring the Costs of Protection in the United States.* Washington, DC: Institute for International Economics, 1994.

Hurd, Michael D. "Savings and Bequests." Working Paper No. 1826. National Bureau of Economic Research, Cambridge, MA, Jan. 1986.

Hwang, Suein L. "Marketscan: Pasta Becomes a Soft Spot for Borden Inc." *The Wall Street Journal,* Nov. 16, 1993, p. B16.

"I.B.M. Officer Will Retire; Pay Cuts Due." *The New York Times,* Feb. 25, 1992, p. C1.

"Increasingly, a Call to 411 Rings a Computer." *The New York Times,* May 7, 1995, p. L30.

"Is There a Whopper in the Future for Turkey?" *The New York Times,* Nov. 11, 1992, p. D2.

Johansen, Leif. "The Theory of Public Goods: Misplaced Emphasis?" *Journal of Public Economics* 7, no. 1 (Feb. 1977), pp. 147–52.

Joint Committee on Taxation, U.S. Congress. "Selected Materials Relating to the Federal Tax System Under Recent Law and Various Alternative Tax Systems." Washington, DC: U.S. Government Printing Office, Mar. 14, 1996.

Keller, Bill. "For Russians, Food Buying Is No Bargain." *The New York Times,* Sept. 16, 1988, p. A8.

———. "Soviet Legislators Back Market Economy, but Balk at Bread Price Increase." *The New York Times,* June 14, 1990, p. A18.

Keppel, Bruce. "Plan to Reward Efficient Phone Firms OKd by PUC." *Los Angeles Times,* Oct. 13, 1989, pp. D1, D5.

Kerr, Peter. "Blatant Fraud Pushing Up the Cost of Car Insurance." *The New York Times,* Feb. 6, 1992, p. A3.

Killingsworth, Mark R., and James J. Heckman. "Female Labor Supply: A Survey." In *The Handbook of Labor Economics.* Vol. 1. Orley Ashenfelter and Richard Layard, eds. New York: North Holland, 1986.

Kotlikoff, Laurence J., and Lawrence H. Summers. "Tax Incidence." In *The Handbook of Public Economics.* Vol. 2. Alan J. Auerbach and Martin Feldstein, eds. Amsterdam: North Holland, 1987.

Kramon, Glenn. "Why Kaiser Is Still the King." *The New York Times,* July 2, 1989, sec. 3, pp. 1, 9.

Kreps, David M. *A Course in Microeconomic Theory.* Princeton, NJ: Princeton University Press, 1990.

Kristof, Nicholas D. "A Changing Asia." *The New York Times,* May 22, 1992, p. A2.

———. "Rural China Reaps Fruits of Capitalism." *The New York Times,* Dec. 1, 1991, p. A15.

Kroch, E., and K. Sjoblom. "Education and the National Wealth of the United States." *Review of Income and Wealth,* Mar. 1986, pp. 87–106.

Krueger, Alan B. "How Computers Have Changed the Wage Structure: Evidence from Microdata, 1984–1989." *Quarterly Journal of Economics,* Feb. 1993, pp. 33–60.

Labaton, Stephen. "S.E.C. Proposal on Executive Pay Expected." *The New York Times,* Feb. 13, 1992, p. C1.

Lewin, Tamar. "Sudden Nurse Shortage Threatens Hospital Care." *The New York Times,* July 7, 1987, pp. A1, A19.

Lipton, James. *An Exaltation of Larks.* New York: Penguin Books, 1977.

Madrick, Jeff. "Why Knock Public Investment." *The New York Times,* Jan. 19, 1993, p. A21.

McDowell, Edwin. "Airlines Tally the Damage from Summer's Fare War." *The New York Times,* Sept. 12, 1992, pp. 1, 21.

Miller, Mark. "Taking On 'Death Futures.' " *Newsweek,* Mar. 21, 1994, p. 54.

Minford, Patrick; Michael Peel; and Paul Ashton. *The Housing Morass.* West Sussex, Eng.: Gordon Pro-Print, 1987.

Mishan, E. J. "The Postwar Literature on Externalities: An Interpretive Essay." *Journal of Economic Literature* 9, no. 1 (Mar. 1971), pp. 1–28.

Modigliani, Franco. "Life Cycle, Individual Thrift, and the Wealth of Nations." *American Economic Review* 76, no. 3 (June 1986), pp. 297–313.

Moffitt, Robert. "Incentive Effects of the U.S. Welfare System: A Review." *Journal of Economic Literature* 30 (Mar. 1992), pp. 1–61.

Moriarty, Rowland T., and Benson P. Shapiro. "The Airframe Industry (A)." Revised. Boston: Harvard Business School, 1981.

Neumark, David, and William Wascher. "Evidence on Employment Effects of Minimum Wages and Subminimum Wage Provisions from Panel Data on State Minimum Wage Laws." Working Paper No. 3859. National Bureau of Economic Research, Cambridge, MA, 1991.

Newman, Barry. "Poles Find the Freeing of the Economy Lifts Supplies—and Prices." *The Wall Street Journal*, Feb. 21, 1990, pp. A1, A10.

"New Wind for the Panting Giant." *The New York Times*, Sept. 10, 1989, p. A22.

Nomani, Asra Q. "Airlines Draw Fire for Fares Linked to Fuel." *The Wall Street Journal*, Jan. 17, 1990, p. B1.

Nordheimer, Jon. "Gender Gap Not Worth Closing." *The New York Times*, Aug. 10, 1996, pp. 19, 21.

Norris, Floyd. "Refined Risk: A Bond Deal Offers 18.5%." *The New York Times*, Feb. 19, 1995, p. F1.

O'Rourke, P. J. *Parliament of Whores.* New York: Atlantic Monthly Press, 1991.

Oates, Wallace E. "The Environment and the Economy: Environmental Policy at the Crossroads." In *American Domestic Priority—An Economic Appraisal.* John M. Quigley and Daniel L. Rubinfeld, eds. Berkeley: University of California Press, 1985.

Ono, Yumiko. "If Cigarette Industry Coughs, Remote Areas Expect to Catch Cold." *The Wall Street Journal*, Oct. 26, 1995, p. A1.

Passell, Peter. "Hiring Russian Scientists: Exploitation of the Workers?" *The New York Times*, June 4, 1992, p. D1.

Pasztor, Andy, and Walter S. Mossberg. "Bush Is Likely to Be Urged to Shift to Ground Attacks." *The Wall Street Journal*, Feb. 11, 1991, p. 13.

Pawlowsky, Mark. "T-Shirt Owner's Lament: Too Many T-Shirt Shops." *The Wall Street Journal*, July 31, 1995, p. B1.

Pechman, Joseph A., ed. *World Tax Reform.* Washington, DC: The Brookings Institution, 1988.

Pencavel, John. "Labor Supply of Men: A Survey." In *Handbook of Labor Economics.* Vol. 1. Orley Ashenfelter and Richard Layard, eds. New York: North Holland, 1986.

Pennar, Karen. "Is the Financial System Shortsighted?" *Business Week*, Mar. 3, 1986, pp. 82–83.

Petrosky, Henry. "The Boeing 777." *American Scientist* 83, no. 6 (Nov.–Dec. 1995), p. 519.

Polinsky, A. Mitchell, and David T. Ellwood. "An Empirical Reconciliation of Micro and Grouped Estimates of the Demand for Housing." *Review of Economics and Statistics* 61, no. 2 (May 1979), pp. 199–205.

Pommerehne, Werner W., and Gebhard Kirchgassner. "The Decline of Conventional Culture: The Impact of Television on the Demand for Cinema and Theatre Performances." In *Economic Efficiency and the Performing Arts.* Nancy K. Grant, William S. Henden, and Virginia L. Owen, eds. Akron, OH: Association for Cultural Economics, 1987.

Porter, Michael E., and Pankaj Ghemawat. "General Electric vs. Westinghouse in Large Turbine Generators (A) (B) (C)." Boston: Harvard Business School, 1980.

Portney, Paul R. "Policy Watch: Economics and the Clean Air Act." *Journal of Economic Perspectives*, Fall 1990, pp. 178–82.

Poterba, James M. "Tax Policy to Combat Global Warming: On Designing a Carbon Tax." Working Paper No. 3649. National Bureau of Economic Research, Cambridge, MA, 1991.

———. "Tax Subsidies to Owner Occupied Housing: An Asset Market Approach." *Quarterly Journal of Economics* 99, no. 4 (Nov. 1984), pp. 729–52.

Ramirez, Anthony. "All About/Toothpaste." *The New York Times*, May 13, 1990, p. 11.

———. "Borden Thinks the U.S. Wants a National Pasta." *The New York Times*, June 21, 1990, pp. D1, D5.

Rappaport, Peter. "Reply to Professor Itennipman." *Journal of Economic Literature* 26, no. 1 (Mar. 1988), pp. 86–91.

Rauber, Paul. "Sticks & Stones (Landlord of the Month)." *Express* 12, no. 18 (Feb. 9, 1990), pp. 2, 30.

Reinhold, Robert. "Hard Times Dilute Enthusiasm for Clean-Air Laws." *The New York Times*, Nov. 16, 1993, p. A1.

———. "Las Vegas Transformation: From Sin City to Family City." *The New York Times*, May 30, 1989, p. A1.

Reisner, Marc. "No Country on Earth Has Misused Water As Extravagantly As We Have." *The New York Times*, Oct. 30, 1988, p. E4.

Roane, Kit R. "Cost of 'Quiet on Set' is Escalating." *The New York Times*, July 27, 1995, p. A14.

Rooney, Andy. "No Reds To Kick Around Anymore?" *The New York Times*, June 26, 1989, p. A19.

Rose, Frank. "If It Feels Good, It Must Be Bad." *Fortune*, Oct. 21, 1991, p. 100.

Rosen, Sherwin. "Contracts and the Market for Executives." Working Paper No. 3542. National Bureau of Economic Research, Cambridge, MA, Dec. 1990.

Rosenbaum, David E. "High Credit Card Rates: A Luxurious Necessity." *The New York Times*, Nov. 24, 1991, p. E2.

Rosenberg, Nathan, and L. E. Birdzell, Jr. *How the West Grew Rich.* New York: Basic Books, 1986.

Ruhm, Christopher. "Economic Conditions and Alcohol Problems." Working Paper No. 4914. National Bureau of Economic Research, Cambridge, MA, 1994.

Samuelson, Paul A. "The Pure Theory of Public Expenditure." *Review of Economics and Statistics* 36, no. 4 (Nov. 1954), pp. 387–89.

Samuelson, Robert J. "The Ghost of Adam Smith." *Newsweek*, Feb. 9, 1987, p. 54.

———. "The Squeeze on Services." *Newsweek*, Jan. 25, 1988, p. 50.

Sandmo, Agnar. "Income Tax Evasion, Labour Supply, and the Equity-Efficiency Trade-off." *Journal of Public Economics* 16, no. 3 (Dec. 1981), pp. 265–88.

Savage, Peter. "Magnesium Production: More Efficient, Less Costly." *Chemical Week* 140, no. 19 (May 20, 1987), pp. 34, 37.

Schlender, Brenton. "Apple Slips as Result of Hoarding Chips." *The Wall Street Journal*, Jan. 30, 1989, p. A6.

Schmemann, Serge. "Yeltsin, Risking Unrest, Ends Russia's Fixed-Price System." *The New York Times*, Jan. 2, 1992, p. A1.

Schneider, Keith. "Big Farm Companies Try Hand at Organic Methods." *The New York Times*, May 28, 1989, p. L1.

Schwadel, Francine, and Robert Johnson. "More Consumers Find Variable-Rate Loans a Burden As Rates Rise." *The Wall Street Journal*, June 3, 1988, p. 1.

Scully, Gerald W. "Pay and Performance in Major League Baseball." *American Economic Review* 64, no. 6 (Dec. 1974), pp. 915–30.

Seabrook, John. "A Reporter at Large (Gold Mining)." *The New Yorker*, Apr. 24, 1989, pp. 45–81.

Sebastian, Pamela. "A Wheat Planting Boom Is Building across the Northern Plains." *The Wall Street Journal*, Feb. 20, 1992, p. A1.

Seligman, Daniel. "Insurance and the Price of Sex." *Fortune*, Feb. 21, 1983, pp. 84–85.

"Shades of Green." *The Economist*, Apr. 18, 1992, pp. 62–63.

Simon, Paul. "The Explosive Growth of Gambling in the United States." *The Congressional Record for the 104th Congress,* July 31, 1995.

Small, Kenneth A., and Clifford M. Winston. "Welfare Effects of Marginal-Cost Taxation of Motor Freight Transportation: A Study of Infrastructure Pricing." In *Studies in State and Local Public Finance.* Harvey S. Rosen, ed. Chicago: University of Chicago Press, 1986.

Smeeding, Timothy M. "Alternative Methods for Evaluating Selected In-Kind Transfer Benefits and Measuring Their Effect on Poverty." U.S. Bureau of the Census, Technical Paper No. 50. Washington, DC: Government Printing Office, 1982.

Smith, V. Kerry, and Ju-Chin Huang. "Can Markets Value Air Quality? A Meta-Analysis of Hedonic Property Value Models." *Journal of Political Economy* 103, no. 1 (Feb. 1995), pp. 209–27.

Smothers, Ronald. "Spill Puts a Spotlight On a Powerful Industry." *The New York Times*, June 30, 1995, p. A10.

Sommers, Paul M., and Noel Quinton. "Pay and Performance in Major League Baseball: The Case of the First Family of Free Agents." *Journal of Human Resources* 17, no. 3 (Summer 1982), pp. 426–35.

Spence, A. Michael. *Market Signaling.* Cambridge: Harvard University Press, 1974.

Sterngold, James. "Debacle on the High Seas." *The New York Times*, sec. 2, pp. 1, 22–23.

———. "Why Japanese Adore Vending Machines." *The New York Times*, Jan. 5, 1992, pp. A1, A12.

Steuerle, C. Eugene. *The Tax Decade.* Washington, DC: Urban Institute Press, 1992.

Stevenson, Richard W. "Airbus's Latest Entry Flies into the Storm." *The New York Times*, Mar. 4, 1993, pp. C1, C2.

———. "Big Crop Tests Almond Sellers." *The New York Times*, Sept. 8, 1987, p. D1.

"Sticker Shock: Increased Taxes Prompt Wealthy to Cut Spending." *The Wall Street Journal*, Jan. 11, 1994, p. A5.

Stigler, George. *The Theory of Price.* 3rd ed. New York: Macmillan, 1966.

Stuart, Toby, and David Collis. "Cat Fight in the Pet Food Industry (A) and (C)." Boston: Harvard Business School, 1991.

Sudetic, Chuck. "Cigarettes a Thriving Industry in Bleak Sarajevo." *The New York Times*, Sept. 5, 1993, p. L3.

Sullivan, Daniel. "Monopsony Power in the Market for Nurses." Working Paper No. 3031. National Bureau of Economic Research, Cambridge, MA, July 1989.

Tagliabue, John. "Poland Announces Big Economic Shift with Rise in Prices." *The New York Times*, Oct. 11, 1987, p. L1.

Tarr, David D., and Morris E. Morkre. *Aggregate Costs to the United States of Tariffs and Quotas on Imports: General Tariff Cuts and Removal of Quotas on Automobiles, Steel, Sugar, and Textiles.* Bureau of Economics Staff Report to the Federal Trade Commission, Dec. 1984.

Treaster, Joseph B. "Costly and Scarce, Marijuana Is a High More Are Rejecting." *The New York Times*, Oct. 29, 1991, p. A1.

Tregarthen, Suzanne. "Kenneth Arrow." *The Margin*, Spring 1992, p. 82.

Tucker, Robert C., ed. *The Marx-Engels Reader.* 2nd ed. New York: W.W. Norton, 1978.

Turner, Richard, and John R. Emshwiller. "Movie-Research Czar Is Said by Some to Sell Manipulated Findings." *The Wall Street Journal*, Dec. 17, 1993, p. A1.

U.S. Bureau of the Census. *Statistical Abstract of the United States: 1991.* 111th ed. Washington, DC: Government Printing Office, 1991.

———. *Statistical Abstract of the United States: 1994.* 114th ed. Washington, DC: Government Printing Office, 1994.

———. *Statistical Abstract of the United States: 1995.* 115th ed. on CD-ROM. Washington, DC: Government Printing Office, 1995.

U.S. Congress. Congressional Budget Office. *Financing Municipal Water Supply Systems.* Washington, DC: U.S. Government Printing Office, May 1987.

———. *Student Aid and the Cost of Postsecondary Education.* Washington, DC: Government Printing Office, 1991.

U.S. Reports. *Cases Adjudged in the Supreme Court.* Vol. 351. Washington, D.C., 1956.

Uchitelle, Louis. "Surplus of College Graduates Dims Job Outlook for Others." *The New York Times*, June 18, 1990, p. A1.

van Ours, Jan C. "The Price Elasticity of Hard Drugs: The Case of Opium in the Dutch East Indies, 1923–1938." *Journal of Political Economy* 103, no. 2 (Apr. 1995), pp. 261–79.

Vecsey, George. "Notre Dame and Others Are Now Picking on Their Own Size." *The New York Times*, Feb. 8, 1990, p. B12.

Ver Muelen, Michael. "What People Earn." *Parade Magazine*, June 14, 1987, p. 5.

Voith, Richard. "The Long-Run Elasticity of Demand for Commuter Rail Transportation." *Journal of Urban Economics* 30 (Nov. 1991), pp. 360–72.

Walras, Léon. "The State and the Railways." P. Holmes, trans. *Journal of Public Economics* 13, no. 1 (Feb. 1980), pp. 81–100.

Wells, John R. "Note on the Aluminum Industry in 1983 (A)" Revised. Boston: Harvard Business School, 1987.

"A Wheat Planting Boom." *The Wall Street Journal*, Feb. 20, 1992, p. A1.

"Where Does All the Money Go?" *Consumer Reports*, Sept. 1986, pp. 581–92.

Whitney, Craig R. "In Europe, Touches of Leanness and Meanness." *The New York Times*, Jan. 1, 1995, p. E5.

Wilkerson, Isabel. "Shift in Feelings on the Homeless." *The New York Times*, Sept. 2, 1991, p. A1.

Williams, Leonard W. "Letter to the Editor." *The Wall Street Journal*, Nov. 24, 1993, p. A17.

Williamson, Oliver E. *The Economic Institutions of Capitalism.* New York: Free Press, 1985.

———. *The Economics of Discretionary Behavior: Managerial Objectives in a Theory of the Firm.* Englewood Cliffs, NJ: Prentice Hall, 1964.

Willig, Robert D. "Consumer Surplus without Apology." *American Economic Review* 66, no. 4 (Sept. 1976), pp. 589–97.

"Woman's Longevity Sours Real Estate Deal." *Trenton Times*, Dec. 29, 1995, p. B2.

Wong, Yue-Chim, and Pals-Wai Liu. "The Distribution of Benefits among Public Housing Tenants in Hong Kong and Related Policy Issues." *Journal of Urban Economics* 23, no. 1 (Jan. 1988), pp. 1–20.

Wren, Christopher S. "Breaking Out." *The New York Times Magazine*, Aug. 14, 1988, p. 22.

WuDunn, Sheryl. "To Pinch Yen: Freeze Rice and Save Bath Water." *The New York Times*, Sept. 15, 1995, p. A4.

Yoder, Stephen K. "In This Bully Battle with Japan, the Cry Is 'Toro, Toro, Toro.' " *The Wall Street Journal*, Sept. 28, 1990, p. A21.

Young, Peter S. "Moving to Compensate Families in Human-Organ Market." *The New York Times*, July 8, 1994, p. B7.

Zachary, G. Pascal. "Nursing Homes Are Often Hotbeds of Injury for Aides." *The Wall Street Journal*, Mar. 20, 1995, p. B1.

Zimmerman, Kim. "Automation Helps Struggling Branch Double Deposits." *Bank Systems & Equipment* 25, no. 9 (Sept. 1988), pp. 90–91.

Index